# Operas in English

# Operas in English

## A Dictionary

**Revised Edition**

## Margaret Ross Griffel

Volume 2

THE SCARECROW PRESS, INC.
*Lanham • Toronto • Plymouth, UK*
2013

Published by Scarecrow Press, Inc.
A wholly owned subsidiary of The Rowman & Littlefield Publishing Group, Inc.
4501 Forbes Boulevard, Suite 200, Lanham, Maryland 20706
www.rowman.com

10 Thornbury Road, Plymouth PL6 7PP, United Kingdom

British Library Cataloguing in Publication Information Available

**Library of Congress Cataloging-in-Publication Data**
Griffel, Margaret Ross.
  Operas in English : a dictionary / Margaret Griffel. — Rev. ed.
    v. cm.
  Includes bibliographical references and index.
  ISBN 978-0-8108-8272-0 (cloth : alk. paper) — ISBN 978-0-8108-8325-3 (ebook)  1. Opera—Dictionaries.  I. Title.
  ML102.O6G74 2013
  782.103—dc23
                          2012031874

# Contents

# Appendix 1: Composers

Dates and places of birth and death are given where known. Each entry includes short title and year and city of premiere. *Year of composition (no performance information available). +Libretto by composer. See pp. 638–40 for adaptations and arrangements; Index of Names, pp. 897–984, which includes composers of other English and non-English settings.

**A' BECKETT, MARY**
b. London, 1817; d. there, Dec. 11, 1863

| | | |
|---|---|---|
| *Agnes Sorel* | 1835 | London |
| +*Little Red Riding Hood* | 1842 | London |

**ABELS, MICHAEL**
b. Phoenix, AR, 1962

| | | |
|---|---|---|
| *Hit and Run* | 2001 | New York |
| *Homies & Popz* | 2000 | Los Angeles |

**ADAMO, MARK**
b. Philadelphia, 1962

| | | |
|---|---|---|
| +*Avow* | 1999 | New York |
| +*Little Women* | 1998 | Houston |
| +*Lysistrata* | 2005 | Houston |

**ADAMS, H. LESLIE**
b. Cleveland, Dec, 30, 1932

| | | |
|---|---|---|
| *Blake* | 1985 | Oberlin, OH |

**ADAMS, JOHN**
b. Worcester, MA, Feb. 15, 1947

| | | |
|---|---|---|
| *Death of Klinghoffer* | 1991 | Brussels |
| *Dr. Atomic* | 2005 | San Francisco |
| *I Was Looking at the Ceiling* | 1995 | Berkeley, CA |
| *Nixon in China* | 1987 | Houston |

**ADASKIN, MURRAY**
b. Toronto, Mar. 28, 1906; d. Victoria, BC, May 6, 2002

| | | |
|---|---|---|
| +*Grant, Warden of the Plains* (lib. with Bayer) | 1967 | Winnipeg, MB |

**ADDISON, JOHN**
b. London, ca. 1766; d. there, Jan. 30, 1844

| | | |
|---|---|---|
| *False Alarms* (with Braham, King) | 1807 | London |
| *Free and Easy* | 1816 | London |
| *My Aunt* | 1815 | London |
| *My Uncle* | 1817 | London |
| *Russian Imposter* | 1809 | London |

**ADÈS, THOMAS**
b. London, Mar. 1, 1971

| | | |
|---|---|---|
| *Powder Her Face* | 1995 | London |
| *Tempest, The* | 2004 | London |

**ADLER, SAMUEL**
b. Mannheim, Ger., Mar. 4, 1928

| | | |
|---|---|---|
| *Lodge of Shadows* | 1988 | Fort Worth, TX |
| *Outcasts of Poker Flat* | 1962 | Denton, TX |
| *Wrestler, The* | 1972 | Dallas |

**ADOLPHE, BRUCE**
b. New York, May 31, 1955

| | | |
|---|---|---|
| *Amazing Adventure of Alvin Allegretto* | 1995 | New York |
| *False Messiah* | 1983 | New York |

| | | |
|---|---|---|
| +*Let Freedom Sing* | 2009 | Washington, D.C. |
| *Marita and Her Heart's Desire* | 1995 | New York |
| *Mikhoels the Wise* | 1982 | New York |
| +*Tell-Tale Heart* | 1982 | Boston |

**AHLSTROM, DAVID**
b. Lancaster, NY, Feb. 22, 1927; d. San Francisco, Aug. 23, 1992

| | | |
|---|---|---|
| +*Aesop's Fables* | 1986 | San Francisco |
| *America, I Love You* | 1981 | New Orleans |
| *Birds, The* | 1990 | San Francisco |
| *Bishop's Horse* | 1984 | San Francisco |
| *Charlie's Uncle* | 1954 | Columbus, OH |
| +*Doctor Faustus* | 1982 | San Francisco |
| +*Fourth Day* | 1961* | |
| +*My Heart's in the Highlands* | 1955* | |
| +*Open Window* | 1953 | Cincinnati, OH |
| *Three Sisters Who Are Not Sisters* | 1953 | Cincinnati, OH |

**AIN, NOA**
b. Brooklyn, NY, 1941

| | | |
|---|---|---|
| *Angels' Voices* | 1996 | Washington |
| +*Outcast, The* | 1994 | Houston |
| +*Trio* | 1984 | Philadelphia |

**AITKEN, HUGH**
b. New York, Sept. 7, 1924

| | | |
|---|---|---|
| +*Fables* | 1975 | Washington |
| +*Felipe* | 1981* | |

**ALBÉNIZ, ISAAC**
b. Camprodín, Spain, May 29, 1860; d. Cambô-les-Bains (Pyrénées), May 18, 1909

| | | |
|---|---|---|
| *Magic Opal* | 1893 | London |

**ALBRIGHT BILLINGSLEY, LOIS**
b. Billingsley, IN, May 17, 1904

| | | |
|---|---|---|
| *Hopitu* | 1955 | New York |

**ALDRIDGE, ROBERT**
b. Richmond, VA, Sept. 7, 1954

| | | |
|---|---|---|
| *Elmer Gantry* | 1992 | Boston |

**ALEXANDER, WILLIAM P.**
b. Lompoc, CA, Nov. 8, 1927

| | | |
|---|---|---|
| +*Monkey's Paw* | 1972 | Edinboro, PA |

**ALLANBROOK, DOUGLAS**
b. Melrose, MA, Apr. 1, 1921; d. Annapolis, MD, Jan. 29, 2003

| | | |
|---|---|---|
| *Ethan Frome* | 1952* | |
| | 1981 | Baltimore |
| *Nightmare Abbey* | 1960* | |

**ALLEN, GEORGE BENJAMIN**
b. London, Apr. 21, 1822; d. Queensland, Austral., Nov. 30, 1897

| | | |
|---|---|---|
| *Castle Grim* | 1865 | London |

| | | |
|---|---|---|
| *Fayette* | 1892 | Brisbane? |
| *Wicklow Rose* | 1882 | Manchester |

**ALLEN, JUDITH.** *See* **SHATIN, JUDITH.**

**ÁLVAREZ, GEOFFREY**
b. London, 1961

| | | |
|---|---|---|
| *European Story* | 1993 | London |
| *Tell-Tale Heart* | 1984 | London |

**ALWYN, WILLIAM**
b. Northampton, Eng., Nov. 7, 1905; d. Southwold, Sept. 11, 1985

| | | |
|---|---|---|
| +*Juan (The Libertine)* | 1971* | |
| +*Miss Julie* | 1979 | London |

**AMES, ROGER**
b. Cooperstown, NY, Dec. 2, 1944

| | | |
|---|---|---|
| +*Amarantha* (lib. with T. Nolen) | 1980 | New London |
| +*Amistad* | 1980* | |
| *Angel Face* | 1987 | Brooklyn, NY |
| *Hearts on Fire* | 1995 | Minneapolis, MN |

**AMRAM, DAVID**
b. Philadelphia, Nov. 17, 1930

| | | |
|---|---|---|
| *Final Ingredient* | 1965 | New York |
| *Twelfth Night* | 1968 | Glens Falls, NY |

**ANDERSON, BETH**
b. Lexington, KY, Jan. 3, 1950

| | | |
|---|---|---|
| +*Queen Christina* | 1973 | Oakland, CA |

**ANDERSON, DOUGLAS**

| | | |
|---|---|---|
| *Faust Triumphant* | 1995 | New York |

**ANDERSON, GARLAND**
b. Union City, IA, June 10, 1933; d. 2001

| | | |
|---|---|---|
| *Soyazhe* | 1979 | Central City, CO |

**ANDERSON, LAURIE**
b. Chicago, June 5, 1947

| | | |
|---|---|---|
| *Empty Places* | 1989 | Charleston, SC |
| *United States* | 1982 | Brooklyn, NY |

**ANDERSON, T[HOMAS] J[EFFERSON], Jr.**
b. Coatesville, PA, Aug. 17, 1928

| | | |
|---|---|---|
| *Slip Knot* | 2003 | Evanston, IL |
| *Soldier Boy, Soldier* | 1982 | Bloomington, IN |
| *Walker* | 1993 | Boston |

**ANDRIESSEN, LOUIS**
b. Utrecht, Holl., June 6, 1939

| | | |
|---|---|---|
| *Rosa, a Horse Opera* | 1994 | Amsterdam |
| *Writing to Vermeer* | 1999 | Amsterdam |

**ANTHEIL, GEORGE**
b. Trenton, NJ, July 8, 1900; d. New York, Feb. 12, 1959

| | | |
|---|---|---|
| +*Brothers, The* | 1954 | Denver |
| +*Flight* (lib. with B. Antheil) | 1930* | |
| *Helen Retires* | 1934 | New York |
| +*Transatlantic* | 1930 | Frankfurt |
| *Venus in Africa* | 1957 | Denver |
| *Volpone* | 1953 | Los Angeles |
| *Wish, The* | 1955 | Louisville, KY |

**ANTILL, JOHN HENRY**
b. Sydney, Apr. 8, 1904; d. there, Dec. 29, 1986

| | | |
|---|---|---|
| +*Endymion* | 1924* | |
| | 1953 | Sydney |
| *First Christmas* | 1969 | Sydney |
| +*Music Critic* | 1953 | Sydney |

**ANTONIOU, THEODORE**
b. Athens, Greece, Feb. 10, 1935

| | | |
|---|---|---|
| *Bacchae* | 1992 | Boston |

**APIVOR, DENIS**
b. Collinstown, West Meath, Ire:; Apr. 14, 1916; d. Robertsbridge, East Sussex, Eng., May 27, 2004

| | | |
|---|---|---|
| +*Bouvard and Pécuchet* | 1971–74* | |
| +*She Stoops to Conquer* | 1943–47* | |
| +*Ubu Roi* | 1966–67* | |
| *Yerma* | 1961 | BBC |

**APPLEBAUM, EDWARD**
b. Los Angeles, Sept. 28, 1937

| | | |
|---|---|---|
| *Frieze of Life* | 1983 | Newport Beach, CA |

**APPLEBAUM, LOUIS**
b. Toronto, Apr. 3, 1918; d. there, Apr. 20, 2000

| | | |
|---|---|---|
| *Erewhon* | 2000 | Ottawa, ON |

**APPLETON, ADELINE**
b. Waverly, IA, Nov. 29, 1886; d. Milwaukee, 19??

| | | |
|---|---|---|
| +*Witches' Well* (lib. with P. Davis) | 1928 | Tacoma, WA |

**APPLETON, JON**
b. Los Angeles, Jan. 4, 1939

| | | |
|---|---|---|
| +*Lament of Kamuela* | 1983 | Hanover, NH |

**ARCHER, VIOLET**
b. Montreal, Apr. 24, 1913; d. Ottawa, Feb. 21, 2000

| | | |
|---|---|---|
| *Meal, The* | 1985 | Edmonton, AB |
| *S anarelle* | 1974 | Edmonton, AB |

**ARGENTO, DOMINICK**
b. York, PA, Oct. 27, 1927

| | | |
|---|---|---|
| +*Aspern Papers* | 1988 | Dallas |
| *Boor, The* | 1957 | Rochester, NY |
| +*Casanova's Homecoming* | 1985 | St. Paul |
| *Christopher Sly* | 1963 | Minneapolis |
| *Colonel Jonathan the Saint* | 1961* | |
| | 1971 | Denver |
| *Dream of Valentino* | 1994 | Washington |
| *Masque of Angels* | 1964 | Minneapolis |
| *Miss Havisham's Fire* | 1979 | New York |
| *Miss Havisham's Wedding Night* | 1981 | Minneapolis |
| *Postcard from Morocco* | 1971 | Minneapolis |
| *Shoemaker's Holiday* | 1967 | Minneapolis |
| *Sicilian Limes* | 1954 | Baltimore |
| *Voyage of Edgar Allan Poe* | 1976 | St. Paul, MN |
| *Water Bird Talk* | 1977 | Brooklyn, NY |

**ARIA, PIETRO**
b. Italy, ca. 1897

| | | |
|---|---|---|
| *Jericho Road* | 1969 | Philadelphia |

## ARLAN, DENNIS [DENNIS ARLAN HIRSCHBEIN]

b. Detroit, 1945; d. New York, Apr. 2, 1979

| | | |
|---|---|---|
| *Ballad of the Bremen Band* | 1977 | Katonah, NY |
| *Daughter of the Double* | 1978 | Katonah, NY |
| *Duke of Dingle* | | |
| *Meanwhile, Back at Cinderella's* | 1976 | New York |

## ARMOUR, EUGENE

b. 1929

| | | |
|---|---|---|
| *We're Back* | 1981 | New York |

## ARNE, MICHAEL

b. London, ca. 1740; d. there, Jan. 14, 1786

| | | |
|---|---|---|
| *Almena* (with Battishill) | 1764 | London |
| *Artifice, The* | 1780 | London |
| *Cymon* | 1767 | London |
| *Edgar and Emmeline* | 1761 | London |
| *Elfrida* | 1772 | London |
| *Emperor of the Moon* | 1777 | London |
| *Fairy Tale* | 1777 | London |
| *Hymen* | 1764 | London |
| *Linco's Travels* (with J. Vernon) | 1767 | London |
| *Maid of the Vale* | 1775 | London |
| *Positive Man* (with S. Arnold) | 1782 | London |
| *Tom Jones* | 1769 | London |
| *Tristram Shandy* | 1783 | London |
| *Vertumnus and Pomona* | 1782 | London |

## ARNE, THOMAS AUGUSTINE

b. London, Mar. 12, 1710; d. there, Mar. 5, 1778

| | | |
|---|---|---|
| *Achilles in Petticoats* | 1773 | London |
| *Alfred* | 1740 | London |
| *Arcadian Nuptials* | 1764 | London |
| +*Artaxerxes* | 1762 | London |
| *Birth of Hercules* | 1763* | |
| *Blind Beggar* | 1741 | London |
| *Britannia (Love and Glory)* | 1734 | London |
| *Britannia* | 1755 | London |
| *Caractacus* | 1776 | London |
| *Comus* | 1738 | London |
| +*Cooper, The* (lib. prob. by comp.) | 1772 | Katonah |
| *Dido and Aeneas* | 1734 | Katonah |
| +*Don Saverio* (lib. prob. by comp.) | 1750 | London |
| *Eliza* | 1754 | London |
| *Fairy Prince* | 1771 | London |
| +*Guardian Outwitted* | 1764 | London |
| (lib prob. by comp.) | | |
| *Henry and Emma* | 1749 | London |
| *Hospital for Fools* | 1739 | London |
| *Judgment of Paris* | 1742 | London |
| *King Pepin's Campaign* | 1745 | London |
| *Lethe* | 1749 | London |
| *Love Finds the Way* | 1777 | London |
| (with Sacchini, Fisher) | | |
| *Love in a Village* | 1762 | London |

| | | |
|---|---|---|
| *May Day* | 1775 | London |
| *Miss Lucy in Town* | 1742 | London |
| *Opera of Operas* | 1733 | London |
| +*Phoebe at Court* (lib prob. by comp.) | 1776 | London |
| *Picture, The* | 1745 | London |
| *Pincushion, The* | 1756 | Dublin |
| *Rosamond* | 1733 | London |
| *Rose, The* (lib. prob. by comp.) | 1772 | London |
| *Sheep Shearing* | 1754 | London |
| +*Sot, The* | 1775 | London |
| +*Squire Badger* | 1772 | London |
| *Tempest, The* | 1746 | London |
| *Temple of Dullness* | 1745 | London |
| *Thomas and Sally* | 1760 | London |
| *Triumph of Peace* | 1748 | London |

## ARNELL, RICHARD

b. London, Sept. 15, 1917; d. Bromley, Kent, Eng., Apr. 10, 2009

| | | |
|---|---|---|
| *Combat Zone* | 1969 | Hempstead, NY |
| *Love in Transit* | 1958 | London |
| +*Moon Flowers* | 1959 | Kent, Eng. |
| *Petrified Princess* | 1959 | London |

## ARNOLD, MALCOLM

b. Northampton, Eng., Oct. 21, 1921; d. Norwich, Eng., Sept. 23, 2006

| | | |
|---|---|---|
| *Dancing Master* | 1962 | London |
| *Open Window* | 1956 | BBC |

## ARNOLD, MAURICE (MAURICE ARNOLD STROTHOTTE)

b. St. Louis, Jan. 19, 1865; d. New York, Oct. 23, 1937

| | | |
|---|---|---|
| *Merry Benedicts* | 1896 | Brooklyn, NY |

## ARNOLD, SAMUEL

b. London, Aug. 10, 1740; d. there, Oct. 22, 1802

| | | |
|---|---|---|
| *Agreeable Surprise* | 1781 | London |
| *Amintas* (with Guglielmi et al.) | 1769 | London |
| *April Day* | 1777 | London |
| *Auld Robin Gray* | 1794 | London |
| *Banditti, The* | 1781 | London |
| *Bannian Day* | 1796 | London |
| *Baron Kinkverkankots…* | 1781 | London |
| *Basket Maker* | 1790 | London |
| *Battle of Hexham* | 1789 | London |
| *Birth-Day, The* | 1783 | London |
| *Britain's Glory* | 1794 | London |
| *Cambro-Britons* | 1798 | London |
| *Castle of Andalusia* | 1782 | London |
| *Children in the Wood* | 1793 | London |
| *Daphne and Amintor* | 1765 | London |
| *Dead Alive* | 1781 | London |
| *Death of Captain Faulknor* | 1795 | London |
| *Don Quixote* | 1774 | London |
| *Enchanted Wood* | 1792 | London |
| *Fairies' Revels* | 1802 | London |
| *False and True* | 1798 | London |
| *Fire and Water!* | 1780 | London |

| | | |
|---|---|---|
| Gipsies, The | 1778 | London |
| Gretna Green | 1783 | London |
| Hovel, The | 1797 | London |
| How to Be Happy | 1794 | London |
| Hunt for the Slipper | 1784 | London |
| Inkle and Yarico | 1787 | London |
| Irish Legacy | 1797 | London |
| Lilliput | 1777 | London |
| Love and Madness! | 1795 | London |
| Love and Money | 1795 | London |
| Madman, The | 1770 | London |
| Magnet, The | 1771 | London |
| Maid of the Mill | 1765 | London |
| Mountaineers, The | 1793 | London |
| New Spain | 1790 | London |
| None So Blind | 1782 | London |
| Peeping Tom | 1784 | London |
| Portrait, The | 1770 | London |
| Positive Man (with M. Arne) | 1782 | London |
| Revenge, The | 1770 | London |
| Review, The | 1800 | London |
| Rosamond | 1767 | London |
| Royal Garland | 1768 | London |
| Rule Britannia | 1794 | London |
| Servant Mistress | 1770 | London |
| Sheep Shearing | 1777 | London |
| Shipwreck, The | 1796 | London |
| Siege of Curzola | 1786 | London |
| Silver Tankard | 1781 | London |
| Sixty-Third Letter | 1802 | London |
| Son-in-Law | 1779 | London |
| Spanish Barber | 1777 | London |
| Summer Amusement | 1779 | London |
| Summer's Tale | 1765 | London |
| Surrender of Calais | 1791 | London |
| Throw Physic to the Dogs! | 1798 | London |
| Tom Jones | 1769 | London |
| Turk and No Turk | 1785 | London |
| Two to One | 1784 | London |
| Ut Pictora Poesis! | 1789 | London |
| Veteran Tar | 1801 | London |
| Virginia | 1800 | London |
| Weathercock, The | 1775 | London |
| Wedding Night | 1780 | London |
| Who Pays the Reckoning? | 1795 | London |
| Zorinski | 1795 | London |

ARNSTEIN, IRA B.
b. Ger, 1879? d New York, 19??

| | | |
|---|---|---|
| Song of David | 1925 | New York |

ARTEAGA, EDWARD
b. Vancouver? July 15, 1950

| | | |
|---|---|---|
| Maria Concepcion | 2004* | |

ASCHAFFENBURG, WALTER
b. Essen, Ger., May 20, 1927; d. 2005

| | | |
|---|---|---|
| Bartleby | 1964 | Oberlin, OH |

ASH, PETER
b. IA, 1961

| | | |
|---|---|---|
| Golden Ticket | 2010 | St. Louis |

ASHLEY, ROBERT
b. Ann Arbor, Mich., Mar. 28, 1930

| | | |
|---|---|---|
| +Atalanta | 1982 | Paris |
| +Atalanta Strategy | 1985 | Montreal |
| Balseros | 1997 | Miami Beach, FL |
| +Celestial Excursions | 2003 | Berlin |
| +Concrete | 2007 | New York |
| +Dust | 1999 | New York |
| +In Memoriam | 1964 | Ann Arbor, MI |
| Lessons, The | 1981 | New York |
| Music with Roots | 1976 | Paris |
| +My Brother Called | 1988 | Chicago |
| +Now Eleanor's Idea, tetralogy: | | |
| +eL/Aficionado | 1988 | Marseilles |
| Foreign Experiences | 1987* | |
| | 1991 | New York |
| Improvement | 1986* | |
| | 1991 | New York |
| Now Eleanor's Idea | 1988* | |
| | 1991 | New York |
| +Perfect Lives | 1978 | Minneapolis |
| +That Morning Thing | 1968 | Ann Arbor, MI |
| +When Opportunity Knocks | 1984–85* | |

ASHMAN, MIKE [VINCENT CROCKER]
b. Hertford, Eng., Apr. 16, 1950

| | | |
|---|---|---|
| José's Carmen | 1984 | London |

ASTON, PETER
b. Birmingham, Eng., Oct. 5, 1938

| | | |
|---|---|---|
| +Sacrapant | 1967* | |

ATTWOOD, THOMAS
b. London, Nov. 23, 1765; d. there, Mar. 24, 1838

| | | |
|---|---|---|
| Adopted Child | 1795 | London |
| Albert and Adelaide (with D Steibelt) | 1798 | London |
| Bondocani, Il (with J. Moorehead) | 1800 | London |
| Britain's Brave Tars!! | 1797 | London |
| Caernarvon Castle | 1793 | London |
| Castle of Sorrento | 1799 | London |
| David Rizzio (with Braham et al.) | 1820 | London |
| Day at Rome | 1798 | London |
| Devil of a Lover | 1798 | London |
| Elphi Bey (with Horn, Smart) | 1817 | London |
| Escapes, The | 1801 | London |
| Fairy Festival | 1797 | London |
| Fast Asleep | 1797 | London |
| Guy Mannering (with H. R. Bishop) | 1816 | London |
| Hermione | 1800 | London |
| Irish Tar | 1797 | London |

| | | |
|---|---|---|
| *Mouth of the Nile* | 1798 | London |
| *Old Cloathsman* | 1799 | London |
| *Ozmyn and Daraxa* | 1793 | London |
| *Packet Boat* | 1794 | London |
| *Poor Sailor* | 1795 | London |
| *Prisoner, The* | 1792 | London |
| *Red-Cross Knights* | 1799 | London |
| *Reform'd in Time* | 1798 | London |
| *Sea-Side Story* | 1801 | London |
| *Smugglers, The* | 1796 | London |
| *St. David's Day* | 1800 | London |
| *True Friends* | 1800 | London |

**ATWELL, SHIRL JAE**
b. KY, 1949

| | | |
|---|---|---|
| *Sagegrass* | 1986 | New York |

**AUSTIN, JOHN**
b. Mt. Vernon, NY, June 8, 1954

| | | |
|---|---|---|
| +*Orpheus* | 1967 | Chicago |

**AUSTIN, LARRY**
b. Duncan, OK, Sept. 12, 1930

| | | |
|---|---|---|
| *Euphonia 2344* | 1998 | Bloomington, IN |

**AXELROD, LAWRENCE**
b. 1960

| | | |
|---|---|---|
| +*Aria da capo* | 1997* | |

**BABER, JOSEPH**
b. Richmond, VA, 1957

| | | |
|---|---|---|
| *Frankenstein* | 1976 | Lexington, KY |
| *River of Time* | 2009 | Lexington, KY |
| *Rumpelstiltskin* | 1977 | Lexington, KY |
| *Samson and the Witch* | 1995 | Lexington, KY |

**BACH, JAN**
b. Forrest, IL, Dec. 11, 1937

| | | |
|---|---|---|
| +*Student from Salamanca* | 1980 | New York |
| +*System, The* | 1974 | New York |

**BACH, JOHANN CHRISTIAN**
b. Leipzig, Sept. 5, 1735; d. London, Jan. 1, 1782

| | | |
|---|---|---|
| *Fairy Favour* | 1767 | London |
| *Menalcas* | 1764 | Salisbury, Eng. |

**BACH, LEONHARD EMIL**
b. Posen [Poznán], Mar. 11, 1849; d. London, Feb. 15, 1902

| | | |
|---|---|---|
| *Irmengarda* | 1892 | London |
| *Lady of Longford* | 1896 | London |

**BACHLUND, GARY**
b. Los Angeles? 1947

| | | |
|---|---|---|
| *Alice* | 2004* | |
| *Four Fables:* | | |
| +*Prelude to a Fable* | 1994* | |
| | 2001 | Pasadena, CA |
| +*Emperor's New Clothes* | 1994* | |
| (lib. with Shulman) | 2001 | Pasadena, CA |
| +*Little Match Girl* | 1994* | |
| | 2001 | Pasadena, CA |

| | | |
|---|---|---|
| *Love Charm* | 1994* | |
| | 2001 | Pasadena, CA |

**BACON, ERNST**
b. Chicago, May 26, 1898; d. Orinda, CA, Mar. 16, 1990

| | | |
|---|---|---|
| *Drumlin Legend* | 1949 | New York |
| *Tree on the Plains* | 1942 | Spartanburg, SC |

**BAILEY, CARROL**

| | | |
|---|---|---|
| +*De Soto* | 1998* | |
| | 2008 | Gainesville, FL |

**BAINTON, EDGAR LESLIE**
b. London, Feb. 14, 1880; d. Sydney, Dec. 8, 1956

| | | |
|---|---|---|
| *Crier by Night* | 1919* | |
| | 1942 | ABC |
| +*Oithona* | 1915 | Glastonbury, Eng. |
| *Pearl Tree* | 1927* | |
| | 1944 | Sydney |

**BAKER, LARRY**
b. Ft. Smith, AR, Sept. 7, 1948

| | | |
|---|---|---|
| *Haydn's Head* | 1987 | Cleveland |

**BAKSA, ROBERT**
b. New York, Feb. 7, 1938

| | | |
|---|---|---|
| +*Aria da capo* | 1968 | New York |
| +*Red Carnations* | 1974 | New York |

**BALADA, LEONARDO**
b. Barcelona, Sept. 22, 1933

| | | |
|---|---|---|
| +*Hangman, Hangman!* | 1982 | Barcelona |
| +*Town of Greed* (lib. with A. Midani) | 2001 | Pittsburgh |
| *Zapata!* | 1985 | Pittsburgh |

**BALFE, MICHAEL**
b. Dublin, May 15, 1808; d. Rowney Abbey, Hertfordshire, Eng., Oct. 20, 1870

| | | |
|---|---|---|
| *Armourer of Nantes* | 1863 | London |
| *Bianca* | 1860 | London |
| *Blanche de Nevers* | 1863 | London |
| *Bohemian Girl* | 1843 | London |
| *Bondman, The* | 1846 | London |
| *Castle of Aymon* | 1844 | London |
| *Catherine Grey* | 1837 | London |
| *Daughter of St. Mark* | 1844 | London |
| *Devil's in It* | 1852 | London |
| *Diadesté* | 1838 | London |
| *Enchantress, The* | 1845 | London |
| *Geraldine* | 1843 | Dublin |
| *Joan of Arc* | 1837 | London |
| *Keolanthe* | 1841 | London |
| *Knight of the Leopard* | 1891 | Liverpool |
| *Letty* | 1871 | London |
| *Maid of Artois* | 1836 | London |
| *Maid of Honour* | 1847 | London |
| *Moro* | 1882 | London |
| *Puritan's Daughter* | 1861 | London |
| *Rose of Castille* | 1857 | London |

| | | |
|---|---|---|
| *Satanella* | 1860 | London |
| *Sicilian Bride* | 1852 | London |
| *Siege of Rochelle* | 1835 | London |
| *Sleeping Queen* | 1864 | London |

BALIN, MARTY [MARTYN JEREL BUCHWALD]
   b. Cincinnati, Jan. 30, 1942

| | | |
|---|---|---|
| *Rock Justice* | 1979 | San Francisco |

BALK, H. WESLEY
   b. St. Paul, MI, 1933; d. Minneapolis, Mar. 21, 2003

| | | |
|---|---|---|
| *Newest Opera in the World* | 1974 | Minneapolis |

BALKIN, ALFRED [ALAN BLAKE]
   b. Boston, Aug. 12, 1931

| | | |
|---|---|---|
| +*Musicians of Bremen* | 1982 | New York |

BALL, MICHAEL
   b. Manchester, Eng., Nov. 10, 1946

| | | |
|---|---|---|
| *Belly Bag* | 1992* | |

BANFIELD, RAFFAELLO DE [RAPHAEL DOUGLAS]
   b. Newcastle upon Tyne, Nov. 17, 1922; d. Rive d'Arcano, Italy, Jan. 7, 2008

| | | |
|---|---|---|
| *Alissa* | 1965 | Geneva |
| *Lord Byron's Love Letter* | 1955 | New Orleans |

BANFIELD, WILLIAM
   b. Detroit, 1961

| | | |
|---|---|---|
| *Fisherman's Dock* | 1998 | St. Paul, MN |
| *Gertrude Stein* | 2005 | New York |
| *Luyala* | 2000 | Durham, NC |
| +*Soul Gone Home* | 2001 | Durham, NC |

BANISTER, JOHN
   b. ca. 1630, London; d. there, Oct. 3, 1679

| | | |
|---|---|---|
| *Circe* | 1677 | London |
| *Tempest, The* (with Locke et al.) | 1674 | London |

BANTOCK, GRANVILLE
   b. London, Aug. 7, 1868; d. there, Oct. 16, 1946

| | | |
|---|---|---|
| *Caedmar* | 1892 | London |
| *Eugene Aram* | 1892* | |
| +*Pearl of Iran* | 1894 | Leipzig |
| *Seal-Woman* | 1924 | Birmingham |

BARAB, SEYMOUR
   b. Chicago, Jan. 9, 1921

| | | |
|---|---|---|
| +*American Punchlines* | 1994 | New York |
| +*At Last I've Found You* | 1984 | Charlotte, SC |
| *Chanticleer* | 1956 | Aspen, CO |
| +*Duel, The* | 2007 | New York |
| +*Fair Means or Foul* | 1985 | New York |
| +*Father of the Child* | 1985 | Bayside, NY |
| +*Fortune's Favorites* | 1982 | New York |
| *Game of Chance* | 1957 | Rock Island, IL |
| +*I Can't Stand Wagner* | 1986 | New York |
| +*License to Marry* | 2005 | Erie, PA |
| +*Little Red Riding Hood* | 1958 | San Francisco |
| +*Little Stories* | 1979 | New York |
| *Maletroit Door* | 1960 | New York |

| | | |
|---|---|---|
| +*Not a Spanish Kiss* | 1977 | New York |
| +*Ondine* | 1995 | New York |
| +*Only a Miracle* | 1985 | New York |
| +*Out the Window* | 1985 | New York |
| +*Perfect Plan* | 2004 | New York |
| +*Philip Marshall* | 1974 | Chautauqua, NY |
| +*Piece of String* | 1985 | Greeley, CO |
| +*Pied Piper of Hamelin* | 1998 | Norfolk, VA |
| +*Pizza con funghi* | 1989 | New York |
| +*Predators* | 1985 | New York |
| +*Rajah's Ruby* | 1958 | New York |
| +*Ruined Maid* | 1981 | New York |
| +*Say Cheese* | 1995 | Queens, NY |
| +*Scenes in Wonderland* | 2000 | New York |
| +*Snow White* | 1988 | Oklahoma City |
| +*Toy Shop* | 1978 | New York |
| +*Who Am I?* | 1988 | New York |

BARATI, GEORGE
   b. Györ, Hung, Apr. 3, 1913; d. Los Gatos, CA, June 22, 1996

| | | |
|---|---|---|
| *Noelani* | 1971 | Aptos, CA? |

BARBER, SAMUEL
   b. West Chester, PA, Mar. 9, 1910; d. New York, Jan. 23, 1981

| | | |
|---|---|---|
| *Antony and Cleopatra* | 1966 | New York |
| *Hand of Bridge* | 1959 | New York |
| *Vanessa* | 1958 | New York |

BARKER, PAUL ALAN
   b. 1956

| | | |
|---|---|---|
| *Albergo Empedocle* | 1990 | London |
| +*Malinche, La* | 1989 | London |
| +*Marriages between Zones 3, 4, and 5* | 1985 | London |
| +*Pillow-Song* | 1985 | London |

BARKIN, ELAINE R.
   b. Bronx, New York, Dec. 15, 1932

| | | |
|---|---|---|
| +*De Amore* | 1982 | Oberlin, OH |

BARKWORTH, JOHN EDMOND
   b. Beverley, Eng., May 20, 1858; d. Geneva, Nov. 18, 1929

| | | |
|---|---|---|
| +*Romeo and Juliet* | 1916 | Middlesbrough |

BARLOW, DAVID
   b. Rothwell, Northamptonshire, Eng., May 20, 1927; d. Newcastle upon Tyne, June 9, 1975

| | | |
|---|---|---|
| *David and Bathsheba* | 1969 | Newcastle u: Tyne |
| +*Judas Iscariot* | 1974* | |
| +*Selfish Giant* | 1974* | |

BARNARD, FRANCIS

| | | |
|---|---|---|
| +*Glory Coach* | 1982 | New York |
| +*Nativity in Threes* | 1975* | |

BARNES, EDWARD
   b. Gettysburg, PA, Dec. 16, 1957

| | | |
|---|---|---|
| *Feathertop* | 1980 | New York |
| +*Muskrat Lullaby* | 1989 | Los Angeles |
| *Place to Call Home* | 1992 | Los Angeles |
| +*Vagabond Queen* | 1989 | Los Angeles |

**BARNETT, DAVID**
b. New York, Dec. 1, 1907; d. Weston, CT, Dec. 7, 1985

| | | |
|---|---|---|
| *Inner Voices* | 1972 | New York |

**BARNETT, JOHN**
b. Bedford, Eng., July 15, 1802; d. Leckhampton, Eng., Apr. 17, 1890

| | | |
|---|---|---|
| *Before Breakfast* | 1826 | London |
| *Fair Rosamond* | 1837 | London |
| *Farinelli* | 1839 | London |
| *Mountain Sylph* | 1834 | London |
| *Robert the Devil* | 1830 | London |
| *Soldier's Widow* | 1833 | London |
| *Win Her* | 1832 | London |

**BARON, MAURICE**
b. Lille, France, Jan. 1, 1889; d. Oyster Bay, NY, Sept. 5, 1964

| | | |
|---|---|---|
| *François Villon* | 1940 | New York radio |
| *Gay Musketeers* | 1925* | |

**BARRY, GERALD**
b. County Clare, Ire., Apr. 28, 1952

| | | |
|---|---|---|
| *Bitter Tears of Petra von Kant* | 2005 | Dublin |
| *Intelligence Park* | 1990 | London |
| *Things That Gain* | 1980 | London |
| *Triumph of Beauty and Deceit* | 1995 | London |

**BARTHELEMON [BARTHÉLEMON], FRANÇOIS-HIPPOLYTE**
b. Bordeaux, France, July 27, 1741; d. Christ Church, Surrey, July 20, 1808

| | | |
|---|---|---|
| *Belphegor* | 1778 | London |
| *Election, The* | 1774 | London |
| *Magic Girdle* | 1770 | London |
| *Maid of the Oaks* | 1774 | London |
| *Noble Pedlar* | 1770 | London |
| *Oithona* | 1768 | London |
| *Orpheus* | 1767 | London |
| *Portrait, The* | ca. 1771 | Dublin |
| *Zingara, La* | 1773 | London |

**BARTHELSON, JOYCE [HELEN JOYCE HOLLOWAY]**
b. Yakima, WA, May 18, 1900; d. 1986

| | | |
|---|---|---|
| +*Chanticleer* | 1967 | New York |
| +*Devil's Disciple* | 1977 | White Plains |
| +*Feathertop* | 1968 | New York |
| *King's Breakfast* | 1973 | Atlantic City |
| *Lysistrata* | 1981 | New York |

**BASKIN-WATSON, PAMELA**
b. Kansas City, KS, 1953

| | | |
|---|---|---|
| *Meetin', The* | 1997 | New York |

**BATES, MASON**
b. VA, 1977

| | | |
|---|---|---|
| +*California Fictions* | 2006 | New York |

**BATES, WILLIAM**
fl London, ca. 1750–1780

| | | |
|---|---|---|
| *Device, The* | 1777 | London |
| *Flora* | 1770 | London |

| | | |
|---|---|---|
| *Jovial Crew* | 1760 | London |
| *Ladies' Frolick* | 1770 | London |
| *Pharnaces* | 1765 | London |
| *Second Thought Is Best* | 1778 | London |
| *Theatrical Candidates* | 1775 | London |

**BATH, HUBERT**
b. Barnstaple, Eng., Nov. 6, 1883; d. Harefield, Eng., Apr. 24, 1945

| | | |
|---|---|---|
| *Bubbles* | 1923 | Belfast |
| +*Spanish Student* | 1904 | London |

**BATTISHILL, JONATHAN**
b. London, May 1738; d. Islington, London, Dec. 10, 1801

| | | |
|---|---|---|
| *Almena* (with M. Arne) | 1764 | London |

**BAULD, ALISON**
b. Sydney, May 7, 1944

| | | |
|---|---|---|
| +*Nell* | 1988 | London |

**BAUMAN, JON WARD**
b. Big Rapids, MI, June 7, 1939; d. 2009

| | | |
|---|---|---|
| *Dialogues* | 1987 | Frostburg, MD |

**BAUMGARTEN, KARL**
b. Lübeck, Ger., ca. 1740; d. London, 1824

| | | |
|---|---|---|
| *William and Nanny* | 1779 | London |

**BAYLOR, (HUGH) MURRAY**
b. What Cheer, IA, Apr. 8, 1913; d. June 3, 1992

| | | |
|---|---|---|
| *By Gemini* | 1949 | Galesburg, IL |

**BEACH, AMY**
b. Henniker, NH, Sept. 5, 1867; d. New York, Dec. 27, 1944

| | | |
|---|---|---|
| *Cabildo* | 1932* | |
| | 1945 | Athens, GA |

**BEACH, JOHN PARSONS**
b. Gloversville, NY, Oct. 11, 1877; d. Pasadena, CA, Nov. 6, 1953

| | | |
|---|---|---|
| *Pippa's Holiday* | 1915 | Paris |

**BEADELL, ROBERT**
b. Chicago, June 18, 1925

| | | |
|---|---|---|
| *Sweetwater Affair* | 1961 | Lincoln, NE |

**BEALL, JOHN**
b. Belton, TX, 1942

| | | |
|---|---|---|
| *Ethan Frome* | 1997 | Morgantown, WVA |

**BEALL, MARK**
b. Nashville, TN?

| | | |
|---|---|---|
| *Going, The* | 1987 | Cincinnati |

**BEAMISH, SALLY**
b. London, Aug. 26, 1956

| | | |
|---|---|---|
| *Ease* | 1993 | London |
| *Monster* | 2002 | Glasgow |

**BEASER, ROBERT**
b. Boston, MA, May 29, 1954

| | | |
|---|---|---|
| *Food of Love* | 1999 | Cooperstown, NY |

**BEATH, BETTY**
b. nr. Bundaberg, Queensland, Austral., Nov. 19, 1932

| | | |
|---|---|---|
| *Abigail and the Bushranger* | 1974 | Brisbane |
| *Francis* | 1974 | Brisbane |

BECK, JEREMY
  b. Painesville, OH, Jan. 15, 1960

| | | |
|---|---|---|
| +*Anne Boleyn* | 1984 | New York |
| +*Biddle Boys* | 2001 | Pittsburgh |
| *Highway, The* | 2000 | New York |
| *Laughter in Jericho* | 1997 | New York |
| *Review* | 2009 | Houston |

BECKER, JOHN J.
  b. Henderson, KY, Jan. 22, 1886; d. Wilmette, IL, Jan. 21, 1961

| | | |
|---|---|---|
| *Deirdre of the Sorrows* | 1945* | |
| | 1956 | Chicago |
| *Faust* | 1951* | |
| | 1965 | Los Angeles |
| *Privilege and Privation* | 1939* | |
| | 1982 | Amsterdam |

BECKFORD, WILLIAM
  b. Fonthill, Eng., Sept. 29, 1760; d. Bath, May 2, 1844

| | | |
|---|---|---|
| *Arcadian Pastoral* | 1782 | London |

BECKLER, STANWORTH R.
  b. Escondido, CA, Dec. 26, 1923; d. Mar. 2010

| | | |
|---|---|---|
| *Outcasts of Poker Flat* | 1960 | Stockton, CA |

BECKLEY, CONNIE
  b. PA, 1951

| | | |
|---|---|---|
| *Funeral of Jan Palach* | 1990 | New York |

BECKWITH, JOHN
  b. Victoria, BC, Mar. 9, 1927

| | | |
|---|---|---|
| *Crazy to Kill* | 1989 | Guelph, ON |
| *Night Blooming Cereus* | 1959 | Toronto |
| *Shivaree, The* | 1982 | Toronto |
| *Taptoo!* | 1999 | Montreal |

BEDFORD, DAVID
  b. London, Aug. 4, 1937; d. Oct. 1, 2011

| | | |
|---|---|---|
| *Death of Baldur* | 1980 | Elgin, Scot |
| *Fridiof's Saga* | 1981 | Elgin, Scot |
| *Ragnarok* | 1982 | Elgin, Scot |
| +*Return of Odysseus* | 1988 | London |
| +*Rime of the Ancient Mariner* | 1979 | London |

BEECHAM, ADRIAN WELLES
  b. London? Sept. 3, 1904; d. 1982

| | | |
|---|---|---|
| +*Merchant of Venice* | 1922 | Brighton, Eng. |

BEECROFT, NORMA
  b. Oshawa, ON, Apr. 11, 1934

| | | |
|---|---|---|
| *Dissipation of Purely Sound* | 1988 | Toronto |

BEEFERMAN, GORDON
  b. Cambridge, MA, 1976

| | | |
|---|---|---|
| +*Greek Gaze* (lib. with Kenny) | 1998 | Ann Arbor, MI |
| *Rat Land* | 2007 | New York |

BEESON, JACK HAMILTON
  b. Muncie, IN, July 15, 1921; d. New York, June 6, 2010

| | | |
|---|---|---|
| *Captain Jinks* | 1975 | Kansas City, MO |
| *Cyrano* | 1994 | Hagen, Ger |
| *Dr. Heidegger's Fountain of Youth* | 1978 | New York |

| | | |
|---|---|---|
| +*Hello Out There* | 1954 | New York |
| +*Jonah* | 1950* | |
| *Lizzie Borden* | 1965 | New York |
| +*My Heart's in the Highlands* | 1970 | New York, NET |
| + *Practice in the Art of Elocution* | 1999 | New York |
| +*Sorry, Wrong Number* | 1999 | New York |
| *Practice in the Art of Elocution* | 1999 | New York |
| *Sweet Bye and Bye* | 1957 | New York |

BELL, ALLAN GORDON
  b. Calgary, May 23, 1953

| | | |
|---|---|---|
| *Turtle Wakes* | 2001 | Calgary |

BELL, W[ILLIAM] H[ENRY]
  b. St. Albans, Eng., Aug. 20, 1873; d. Gordon's Bay, Cape Province,
    Apr. 13, 1946

| | | |
|---|---|---|
| +*Dr. Love* | 1930* | |
| +*Mouse Trap* | 1928* | |

BENDER, ELLEN
  b. Boston? 1949

| | | |
|---|---|---|
| *Marble Faun* | 1996* | |
| *Rappaccini's Daughter* | 1992 | Boston |

BENEDICT, JULIUS
  b. Stuttgart, Nov. 27, 1804; d. London, June 5, 1885

| | | |
|---|---|---|
| *Bride of Song* | 1864 | London |
| *Brides of Venice* | 1844 | London |
| *Crusaders, The* | 1846 | London |
| *Gipsy's Warning* | 1838 | London |
| *Lily of Killarney* | 1862 | London |

BENJAMIN, ARTHUR
  b. Sydney, Sept. 18, 1893; d. London, Apr. 9, 1960

| | | |
|---|---|---|
| *Devil Take Her* | 1931 | London |
| *Mañana* | 1956 | BBC |
| *Prima Donna* | 1949 | London |
| *Tale of Two Cities* | 1953 | BBC |
| *Tartuffe* (posth.) | 1964 | London |

BENJAMIN, GEORGE
  b. London, Jan. 31, 1960

| | | |
|---|---|---|
| *Into the Little Hill* | 2006 | Paris |

BENJAMIN, THOMAS
  b. Bennington, VT, Feb. 17, 1940

| | | |
|---|---|---|
| *Alien Corn* | 2005 | Baltimore |
| *Chicken Little* | 1985 | Houston |
| *Rehearsal, The* | 1981 | New York |

BENNETT, RICHARD RODNEY
  b. Broadstairs, Kent, Eng., Mar. 29, 1936

| | | |
|---|---|---|
| *Ali the King's Men* | 1969 | Coventry |
| *Ledge, The* | 1961 | London |
| *Mines of Sulphur* | 1965 | London |
| *Penny for a Song* | 1967 | London |
| *Victory* | 1970 | London |

BENNETT, ROBERT RUSSELL
  b. Kansas City, MO, June 15, 1894; d. New York, Aug. 17, 1981

| | | |
|---|---|---|
| *Carmen Jones* | 1943 | New York |

| | | |
|---|---|---|
| *Enchanted Kiss* | 1945 | New York |
| *Endymion* | 1927* | |
| | 1935 | Rochester, NY |
| *Maria Malibran* | 1935 | New York |

**BEREZOWSKY, NICOLAI**
b. St. Petersburg, May 17, 1900; d. New York, Aug. 27, 1953

| | | |
|---|---|---|
| *Babar the Elephant* | 1953 | New York |

**BERGERSEN, [LOUIS] BALDWIN**
b. Vienna, Feb. 20, 1914; d. New York, Apr. 17, 2000

| | | |
|---|---|---|
| *Far Harbour* | 1948 | New York |

**BERGSMA, WILLIAM**
b. Oakland, CA, Apr. 1, 1921; d. Seattle, WA, Mar. 18, 1994

| | | |
|---|---|---|
| +*Murder of Comrade Sharik* | 1973* | |
| | 1986 | Brooklyn, NY |
| *Wife of Martin Guerre* | 1956 | New York |

**BERKELEY, LENNOX**
b. Boar's Hill, nr. Oxford, May 12, 1903; d. London, Dec. 26, 1989

| | | |
|---|---|---|
| *Castaway* | 1967 | Aldeburgh |
| *Dinner Engagement* | 1954 | Aldeburgh |
| *Nelson* | 1954 | London |
| *Ruth* | 1956 | London |

**BERKELEY, MICHAEL**
b. London, May 29, 1948

| | | |
|---|---|---|
| *Baa Baa Black Sheep* | 1993 | Cheltenham, Eng. |
| *Jane Eyre* | 2000 | Cheltenham, Eng. |

**BERKOWITZ, SOL**
b. Warren, OH, Apr. 27, 1922

| | | |
|---|---|---|
| *Fat Tuesday* | 1956 | Tamiment, PA |

**BERNARDO, JOSÉ RAOUL**
b. Havana, Oct. 3, 1938

| | | |
|---|---|---|
| *Child, The* | 1974 | Albany, NY |

**BERNSTEIN, DAVID S.**
b. Boston, 1942

| | | |
|---|---|---|
| *Ilbrahim* | 1994 | Akron, OH |
| *Method for Madness* | 1999 | Akron, OH |
| *Tell-Tale Heart* | 1999 | Akron, OH |

**BERNSTEIN, LEONARD**
b. Lawrence, MA, Aug. 25, 1918; d. New York, Oct. 14, 1990

| | | |
|---|---|---|
| *Candide* | 1956 | Boston |
| *Quiet Place* | 1983 | Houston |
| +*Trouble in Tahiti* | 1952 | Waltham, MA |
| *West Side Story* | 1957 | New York |

**BERRY, WALLACE**
b. La Crosse, WI, Jan. 10, 1928; d. Vancouver, Nov. 16, 1991

| | | |
|---|---|---|
| +*Admirable Bashville* | 1954* | |

**BETTS, LORNE**
b. Winnipeg, MB, Aug. 2, 1918; d. Hamilton, ON, Aug. 5, 1985

| | | |
|---|---|---|
| *Riders to the Sea* | 1955* | |
| *Woodcarver's Wife* | 1960* | |

**BEVERIDGE, THOMAS**
b. New York, Apr. 6, 1938

| | | |
|---|---|---|
| *Dido and Aeneas* | 1958 | Boston |

**BEVERSDORF, THOMAS**
b. Yoakum, TX, Aug. 8, 1924; d. Bloomington, IN, Feb. 15, 1981

| | | |
|---|---|---|
| *Hooligan, The* | 1969* | |
| *Metamorphosis* | 1968* | |

**BEZANSON, PHILIP**
b. Athol, MA, Jan. 6, 1916; d. Hadley, MA, Mar. 11, 1975

| | | |
|---|---|---|
| *Golden Child* | 1959 | Iowa City |
| *Stranger in Eden* | 1963* | |

**BIALES, ALBERT**
b. Cleveland, OH, 1929

| | | |
|---|---|---|
| *Belisa* | 1989 | St. Paul, MN |
| +*Dragon, The* | 1996 | St. Paul, MN |
| *Mozart in Manhattan* | 2005 | St. Paul, MN |

**BIELAWA, HERBERT**
b. Chicago, Feb. 3, 1930

| | | |
|---|---|---|
| *Bird in the Bush* | 1962 | Los Angeles |

**BIELAWA, LISA**
b. San Francisco, 1968

| | | |
|---|---|---|
| *Phrenic Crush* | 1997 | San Francisco |
| *Vireo* | 1995* | |

**BILOTTA, JOHN G.**
b. Waterbury, CT

| | | |
|---|---|---|
| *Quantum Mechanic* | 2007 | American Fork, UT |
| *Trifles* | 2010 | Berkeley, CA |

**BIMBONI, ALBERTO**
b. Florence, Italy, Aug. 24, 1882; d. New York, June 18, 1960

| | | |
|---|---|---|
| *In the Name of Culture* | 1949 | Rochester, NY |
| *Winona* | 1926 | Portland, OR |

**BINDER, ABRAHAM WOLFE**
b. New York, Jan. 13, 1895; d. there, Oct. 10, 1966

| | | |
|---|---|---|
| *Goat in Chelm* | 1960 | New York |

**BINDER, JOHN A.**
b. 1946

| | | |
|---|---|---|
| *Buxtehude's Daughter* | 1989* | |
| +*Council on the Arts* | 1997* | |
| +*Gift, The* (lib. with Grolnic) | 1997* | |

**BINGHAM, SUSAN ADAMS HULSMAN**
b. Waltham, MA, May 31, 1944

| | | |
|---|---|---|
| *Alice Meets the Mock Turtle* | 1988 | New York |
| +*Anniversary Tales* | 2000 | New Haven |
| +*Eli W.* | 1984 | New Haven |
| *Emperor and the Nightingale* | 1982 | New Haven |
| +*Folktale Operas* | 1992 | New Haven |
| +*Fisherman and His Wife* | 1987* | |
| +*Gift of the Magi* | 1984 | New Haven |
| +*Last Leaf* | 1984 | New Haven |
| +*Rabbi Nachman's Chair* | 1995 | New Haven |
| +*Sacrifice of Isaac* | 1980 | New Haven |
| *Wild Swans* | 1988 | New Haven |

**BIRD, ARTHUR**
b. Belmont, MA, July 23, 1856; d. Berlin, Dec. 22, 1923

| | | |
|---|---|---|
| *Daphne* | 1895 | New York |

## BIRD, HUBERT
b. Joplin, MO, 1939

| | | |
|---|---|---|
| *Powerful Potion of Dr. D* | 2003 | Springfield, MO |

## BIRTWISTLE, HARRISON
b. Accrington, Lancashire, Eng., July 15, 1934

| | | |
|---|---|---|
| *Bow Down* | 1977 | London |
| *Down by the Greenwood Side* | 1969 | Brighton, Eng. |
| *Gawain* | 1991 | London |
| *Io Passion* | 2004 | Aldeburgh |
| *Last Supper* | 2000 | Berlin |
| *Mask of Orpheus* | 1986 | London |
| *Minotaur, The* | 2008 | London |
| *Passion of Io* | 2004 | Aldeburgh |
| *Punch and Judy* | 1968 | Aldeburgh |
| *Second Mrs. Kong* | 1994 | Glyndebourne |
| *Yan Tan Tethera* | 1986 | London |

## BISCARDI, CHESTER
b. Kenosha, WI, Oct. 19, 1948

| | | |
|---|---|---|
| *Tight-Rope* | 1986 | Madison, WI |

## BISHOP, HENRY ROWLEY
b. London, Nov. 18, 1786; d. there, Apr. 30, 1855

| | | |
|---|---|---|
| *Adelaide* | 1830 | London |
| *Aethiop, The* | 1812 | London |
| *Aladdin* | 1826 | London |
| *Alchymist, The* | 1832 | London |
| *Angelina* (with L. Gesualdo?) | 1804 | London |
| *Antiquary* | 1820 | London |
| *Barber of Seville* | 1818 | London |
| *Battle of Bothwell Brigg* | 1820 | London |
| *Bottle of Champagne* | 1832 | London |
| *Brazen Bust* | 1813 | London |
| *Burgomaster of Saardam* | 1818 | London |
| *Circassian Bride* | 1809 | London |
| *Clari* | 1823 | London |
| *Comedy of Errors* | 1819 | London |
| *Comus* | 1815 | London |
| *Cortez* | 1823 | London |
| *Cymon* (with M. Arne) | 1815 | London |
| *December and May* | 1818 | London |
| *Demon, The* | 1832 | London |
| *Don John* | 1821 | London |
| *Doom-Kiss* | 1832 | London |
| *Duke of Savoy* | 1817 | London |
| *Englishmen in India* | 1827 | London |
| *Fall of Algiers* | 1825 | London |
| *Farmer's Wife* (with Davy et al.) | 1814 | London |
| *Faustus* | 1825 | London |
| *For England, Ho!* | 1813 | London |
| *Fortunate Isles* | 1840 | London |
| *Freischütz, Der* | 1824 | London |
| *Guillaume Tell* | 1838 | London |
| *Guy Mannering* | 1816 | London |

| | | |
|---|---|---|
| *Haroun Alraschid* | 1813 | London |
| *Harry le Roi* | 1813 | London |
| *Heart of Midlothian* | 1849 | London |
| *Heir of Vironi* | 1817 | London |
| *Henri Quatre* | 1820 | London |
| *Hofer* | 1830 | London |
| *Home Sweet Home* | 1829 | London |
| *Humorous Lieutenant* | 1817 | London |
| *John of Paris* | 1814 | London |
| *Knight of Snowdoun* | 1811 | London |
| *Knights of the Cross* | 1826 | London |
| *Law of Java* | 1822 | London |
| *Libertine, The* | 1817 | London |
| *Love Charm* | 1831 | London |
| *Magic Fan* | 1832 | London |
| *Magpie or the Maid?* | 1815 | London |
| *Maid Marian* | 1822 | London |
| *Maid of the Mill* | 1814 | London |
| *Maniac, The* | 1810 | London |
| *Marriage of Figaro* | 1819 | London |
| *Masaniello* | 1829 | London |
| *Midsummer Night's Dream* | 1816 | London |
| *Miller and His Men* | 1813 | London |
| *Montrose* | 1822 | London |
| *Native Land* | 1824 | London |
| *Night before the Wedding* | 1829 | London |
| *Ninetta* | 1830 | London |
| *Noble Outlaw* | 1815 | London |
| *Poor Vulcan* | 1813 | London |
| *Rencontre, The* | 1827 | London |
| *Roland for an Oliver* | 1819 | London |
| *Romance of a Day* | 1831 | London |
| *Rural Felicity* | 1834 | London |
| *Secret Mine* | 1813 | Dublin |
| *Sedan Chair* | 1832 | London |
| *Slave, The* | 1816 | London |
| *Sonnambula, La* | 1833 | London |
| *Talisman, The* | 1825 | London |
| *Telemachus* | 1815 | London |
| *Tyrolese Peasant* | 1832 | London |
| *Under the Oak* | 1830 | London |
| *Vintagers, The* | 1809 | London |
| *Virgin of the Sun* | 1812 | London |
| *Wandering Boys* | 1814 | London |
| *Who Wants a Wife?* | 1816 | London |
| *Yelva* | 1829 | London |
| *Zuma* (with Braham) | 1818 | London |

## BISSELL, KEITH
b. Meaford, ON, Feb. 12, 1912; d. Newmarket, nr. Toronto, May 9, 1992

| | | |
|---|---|---|
| +*Miraculous Turnip* | 1983 | Toronto |

## BLACKFORD, RICHARD
b. London, January 13, 1954

| | | |
|---|---|---|
| *Gawain and Ragnall* | 1983 | Birmingham |
| +*Metamorphoses* | 1983 | London |
| *Sir Gawain and the Green Knight* | 1978 | Blewbury, Oxfordshire, Eng. |

**BLAKE, DAVID**
b. London, Sept. 2, 1936

| | | |
|---|---|---|
| *Plumber's Gift* | 1989 | London |
| *Scoring a Century* | 2010 | Birmingham |
| *Toussaint* | 1977 | London |

**BLAKE, HOWARD**
b. London, Oct. 28, 1938

| | | |
|---|---|---|
| +*Station, The* | 1992 | Haywards Heath, W. Sussex |

**BLAKESLEE, S. EARLE**
b. Oberlin, OH, Nov. 2, 1883; d. San Luis Obispo, CA, Mar. 9, 1972

| | | |
|---|---|---|
| *Legend of Wiwaste* (lib. with F. Blakeslee) | 1926 | Ontario, CA |

**BLANK, ALLAN**
b. New York, Dec. 27, 1925

| | | |
|---|---|---|
| *Aria da capo* | 1958–60* | |
| *Excitement at the Circus* | 1969 | Paterson, NJ |
| +*Magic Bonbons* | 1983* | |
| *Noise, The* | 1986 | Richmond, VA |

**BLEWITT, JONATHAN**
b. London, July 19, 1782; d. there, Sept. 4, 1853

| | | |
|---|---|---|
| *Actors al fresco* (with Cooke, Horn) | 1823 | London |
| *Auld Robin Gray* | 1828 | Surrey |
| *Boy of Santillane* (with Cooke) | 1827 | London |
| *My Old Woman* | 1829 | London |
| *Paul Clifford* (with G. Rodwell) | 1835 | London |
| *Talisman, The* | 1828 | Surrey |

**BLISS, ARTHUR**
b. London, Aug. 2, 1891; d. there, Mar. 27, 1975

| | | |
|---|---|---|
| *Olympians, The* | 1949 | London |
| *Tobias and the Angel* | 1960 | London, BBC |

**BLITZSTEIN, MARC**
b. Philadelphia, Mar. 2, 1905; d. Fort-de-France, Martinique, Jan. 22, 1964

| | | |
|---|---|---|
| +*Condemned, The* | 1932* | |
| +*Cradle Will Rock* | 1937 | New York |
| +*Harpies, The* | 1931* | |
| | 1953 | New York |
| +*Idiots First* | 1962–64* | |
| (compl. L. Lehrman) | 1974 | Ithaca, NY |
| +*Magic Barrel* | 1962–64* | |
| +*No for an Answer* | 1941 | New York |
| *Parabola and Circula* | 1929* | |
| *Regina* | 1949 | New Haven |
| *Sacco and Vanzetti* | 1959–64* | |
| (compl. L. Lehrman) | 2001 | Westport, CT |
| *Triple Sec* | 1929 | Philadelphia |

**BLOW, JOHN**
b. Newark-on-Trent, bapt. Feb. 23, 1649; d. Westminster, London, Oct. 1, 1708

| | | |
|---|---|---|
| *Venus and Adonis* | ca. 1683 | London/Windsor |

**BLUMENFELD, HAROLD**
b. Seattle, Oct. 15, 1923

| | | |
|---|---|---|
| +*Amphitryon 4* | 1962* | |
| *Borgia Infami* | 2003 | New York |
| *Breakfast Waltzes* | 1991* | |
| | 1997 | Des Moines, IA |
| *Fourscore* | 1984* | |
| | 1989 | Cincinnati, OH |
| *Fritzi* | 1979* | |
| | 1988 | Chicago |
| *Seasons in Hell* | 1996 | Cincinnati, OH |

**BLYTON, CAREY**
b. Beckenham, Kent, Mar. 14, 1932; d. Woodbridge, Suffolk, July 13, 2002

| | | |
|---|---|---|
| +*Dracula* | 1984 | London |
| +*Frankenstein* | 1987* | |
| *Girl from Nogami* | 1978 | London |
| +*Sweeney Todd* | 1980* | |

**BO, THOMAS CARLO**

| | | |
|---|---|---|
| +*Shadows of the City* (lib. with L. Rodgers, A. Samtur) | 2010 | New York |

**BODY, JACK**
b. Te Aroha, NZ, Oct. 7, 1944

| | | |
|---|---|---|
| *Alley* | 1998 | Wellington |

**BOESING, PAUL**
b. Madison, WI, 19??

| | | |
|---|---|---|
| *Wanderer, The* | 1970 | Minneapolis, MN |

**BOHMLER, CRAIG**
b. Los Gatos, CA, 1956

| | | |
|---|---|---|
| *Achilles Heel* | 1993 | Houston, TX |
| *Harlot and the Monk* | 1985 | Banff, AB |
| *Tale of the Nutcracker* | 1999 | San Jose, CA |

**BOHRNSTEDT, WAYNE**
b. Onalaska, WI, Jan. 19, 1923

| | | |
|---|---|---|
| *Necklace, The* | 1956 | Redlands, CA |

**BOKSER, ZELMAN**
b. 1951

| | | |
|---|---|---|
| *Woman Who Dared* | 1984 | Rochester, NY |

**BOLCOM, WILLIAM**
b. Seattle, May 26, 1938

| | | |
|---|---|---|
| *Casino Paradise* | 1989 | Philadelphia |
| *Dynamite Tonite* | 1963 | New York |
| *Greatshot* | 1969 | New Haven, CT |
| *Lucrezia* | 2008 | New York |
| *McTeague* | 1992 | Chicago |
| *View from the Bridge* | 1999 | Chicago |
| *Wedding, A* | 2004 | Chicago |

BOND, VICTORIA
  b. Los Angeles, May 6, 1945

| | | |
|---|---|---|
| *Clara* | 2010 | New York |
| *Gulliver* | 1988 | Louisville, KY |
| *Molly ManyBloom* | 1991 | Albany, NY |
| *More Perfect Union* | 2004 | New York |
| *Mrs. President* | 2000 | New York |
| *Travels* | 1995 | Roanoke, VA |

BOOTH, THOMAS LYKES
  b. U.S., 19??

| | | |
|---|---|---|
| +*Gentlemen in Waiting* | 1967 | New York? |

BOOTHAM, IVAN
  b. Eng, 1939

| | | |
|---|---|---|
| +*Death of Venus* | 2002 | Wellington, NZ |
| +*Pictures* (lib. with J. Commons) | 2002* | |

BOREN, MURRAY
  b. UT? 1950

| | | |
|---|---|---|
| *Book of Gold* | 2005 | Provo, UT |
| *Dead, The* | 1993 | New York |
| *Emma* | 1984 | Provo, UT |

BORROFF, EDITH
  b. New York, Aug. 2, 1925

| | | |
|---|---|---|
| +*Sun and the Wind* | 1977 | Binghamton, NY |

BORTZ, YURI
  b. 1970

| | | |
|---|---|---|
| +*Maker of Dreams* | 2001 | New York |

BOSWELL, WILLIAM
  b. Cynthiana, KY, June 18, 1948

| | | |
|---|---|---|
| *Frog-Hopping* | 1982 | Brooklyn, NY |
| *Scene Changes* | 1984 | Brooklyn, NY |

BOTTI, SUSAN
  b. Cleveland, 1962

| | | |
|---|---|---|
| +*Telaio: Desdemona* | 1995 | Brookfield Hills, MI |
| +*Wonderglass* | 1993 | Brookfield Hills, MI |

BOUCHARD, LINDA
  b. Val d'Or, QC Province, May 21, 1957

| | | |
|---|---|---|
| +*House of Words* (with R. Armstrong) | 2003 | New York |
| *Triskelion* | 1982 | New York |

BOUCK, MARJORIE L.
  b. 1919; d. Richmond, VA, Sept. 12, 2006

| | | |
|---|---|---|
| +*Aria da capo* | 1974* | |

BOUGHTON, RUTLAND
  b. Aylesbury, Eng., Jan. 23, 1878; d. London, Jan. 24, 1960

| | | |
|---|---|---|
| +*Agincourt* | 1924 | Glastonbury, Eng. |
| *Alkestis* | 1922 | Glastonbury, Eng. |
| +*Avalon* | 1944–45* | |
| +*Bethlehem* | 1915 | Street, Eng. |
| *Birth of Arthur* | 1909* | |
| | 1920 | Glastonbury, Eng. |
| +*Chapel in Lyonesse* | 1914 | Glastonbury, Eng. |

| | | |
|---|---|---|
| +*Ever Young* | 1929* | |
| | 1935 | Bath, Eng. |
| +*Galahad* | 1943–44* | |
| *Immortal Hour* | 1914 | Glastonbury, Eng. |
| +*Lily Maid* | 1934 | Stroud, Eng. |
| *Moon Maiden* | 1918 | Glastonbury, Eng. |
| +*Queen of Cornwall* | 1924 | Glastonbury, Eng. |
| *Round Table* | 1916 | Glastonbury, Eng. |
| *Seraphic Vision* | 1924 | Glastonbury, Eng. |

BOURGEOIS, DEREK
  b. Kingston upon Thames, Eng., Oct. 16, 1941

| | | |
|---|---|---|
| *Christmas on the Underground* | 1996* | |
| *Rumpelstiltskin* | 1974* | |

BOURY, ROBERT
  b. Wheeling, WVA, 1946

| | | |
|---|---|---|
| *Bowl, Cat, and Broomstick* | 1989 | Little Rock, AR |
| *Juniper Tree* | 1990 | Atlanta, GA |

BOWDEN, MARK
  b. 1979

| | | |
|---|---|---|
| *Song of Rhiannon* | 2008 | London |

BOWERS-BROADBENT, CHRISTOPHER
  b. 1945

| | | |
|---|---|---|
| *Pied Piper of Hamelin* | 1972 | London |

BOWLES, ANTHONY
  b. ca. 1931; d. London, Mar. 15, 1993

| | | |
|---|---|---|
| *Grub Street Opera* | 1986 | New York |

BOWLES, PAUL
  b. Jamaica, NY, Dec. 30, 1910; d. Tangier, Morocco, Nov. 18, 1999

| | | |
|---|---|---|
| *Denmark Vesey* | 1937 | New York |
| +*Wind Remains* | 1943 | New York |
| +*Yerma* | 1958 | Denver |

BOYACK, JEANETTE

| | | |
|---|---|---|
| *Birthday of the Infanta* | 1957* | |

BOYCE, WILLIAM
  b. London, bapt Sept. 11, 1711; d. Kensington, Feb. 7, 1779

| | | |
|---|---|---|
| *Chaplet, The* | 1749 | London |
| *Florizel and Perdita* | 1756 | London |
| *Peleus and Thetis* | ca. 1740 | London |
| *Rehearsal, The* | 1750 | London |
| *Secular Masque* | ca. 1746 | London |
| *Shepherd's Lottery* | 1751 | London |
| *Tempest, The* | 1757 | London |

BOYD, ANNE
  b. Sydney, Apr. 10, 1946

| | | |
|---|---|---|
| *Beginning of the Day* | 1980* | |
| *Little Mermaid* | 1978* | |
| | 1986 | Sydney |
| *Rose Garden* | 1972 | York, Eng. |

BOYTON, WILLIAM
  b. ca. 1750; d. ca. 1818

| | | |
|---|---|---|
| *British Sailor* | 1789 | London |

**BRAHAM, DAVID**
b. London, 1834; d. New York, Apr. 11, 1905

| | | |
|---|---|---|
| *Mulligan Guard Ball* | 1879 | New York |
| *Reilly and the 400* | 1891 | New York |

**BRAHAM, JOHN**
b. London, Mar. 20, 1774; d. there, Feb. 17, 1856

| | | |
|---|---|---|
| *Americans, The* (with King) | 1811 | London |
| *David Rizzio* (with Attwood et al.) | 1820 | London |
| *English Fleet* | 1803 | London |
| *False Alarms* (with King et al.) | 1807 | London |
| *Family Quarrels* | 1802 | London |
| *Isidore de Merida* | 1827 | London |
| *Narensky* (with Horn, Reeve) | 1814 | London |
| *Paragraph, The* | 1804 | London |
| *Taming of the Shrew* (with Cooke) | 1828 | London |
| *Zuma* (with Bishop) | 1818 | London |

**BRAND, MAX**
b. Lemberg (Lwów), Apr. 26, 1896; d. Langenzersdorf, nr. Vienna, Apr. 5, 1980

| | | |
|---|---|---|
| +*Gate, The* | 1944 | New York |
| +*Stormy Interlude* | 1955* | |
| | 1996 | Vienna |

**BRANDT, WILLIAM EDWARD**
b. Butte, MT, Jan. 14, 1920

| | | |
|---|---|---|
| +*No Neutral Ground* | 1961 | Pullman, WA |

**BRAXTON, ANTHONY**
b. Chicago, June 4, 1945

| | | |
|---|---|---|
| +*Shala Fears for the Poor* | 1996 | New York |

**BRAY, JOHN**
b. Eng, June 19, 1782; d. Leeds, June 19, 1822

| | | |
|---|---|---|
| *Alberto Albertini* | 1811 | New York |
| *Hamlet Travestie* | 1811 | London |
| *Indian Princess* | 1808 | Philadelphia |

**BRÉGENT, MICHEL-GEORGES**
b. Montreal, Jan. 29, 1948; d. there, Sept. 4, 1993

| | | |
|---|---|---|
| +*Realitillusion* | 1988 | Toronto |

**BREIL, JOSEPH**
b. Pittsburgh, June 29, 1870; d. Los Angeles, Jan. 23, 1926

| | | |
|---|---|---|
| *Legend, The* | 1919 | New York |
| +*Love Laughs at Locksmiths* | 1910 | Portsmouth, ME |
| +*Professor Tattle* | 1913 | New York |

**BRENT-SMITH, ALEXANDER**
b. Gloucester, Eng., Oct. 8, 1889; d. there, July 3, 1950

| | | |
|---|---|---|
| +*Age of Chivalry* | 1950 | Gloucester, Eng. |
| +*Captain's Parrot* | 1949 | Stroud, Eng. |

**BRETTINGHAM SMITH, JOLYON**
b. Southampton, Eng., Sept. 9, 1949

| | | |
|---|---|---|
| *Death of Cuchulain* | 1973* | |
| | 1975 | Bielefeld, Ger. |

**BRIAN, HAVERGAL**
b. Dresden, Staffordshire, Jan. 29, 1876; d. Shoreham, Sussex, Nov. 28, 1972

| | | |
|---|---|---|
| +*Agamemnon* | 1957* | |
| | 1971 | London |
| *Cenci, The* | 1952* | |
| | 1997 | London |
| +*Tigers, The* | 1919* | |
| | 1976 | London |

**BRIDGE, FRANK**
b. Brighton, Eng., Feb. 26, 1879; d. Eastbourne, Jan. 10, 1941

| | | |
|---|---|---|
| *Christmas Rose* | 1929* | |
| | 1931 | London |

**BRISMAN, HESKEL**
b. New York, Mar. 12, 1923; d. Ocean County, NJ, May 11, 2001

| | | |
|---|---|---|
| *Three Strangers* | 1962* | |
| *Whirligig* | 1977 | Muncie, IN |

**BRISTOW, GEORGE F.**
b. Brooklyn, NY, Dec. 19, 1825; d. New York, Dec. 13, 1898

| | | |
|---|---|---|
| *Rip Van Winkle* | 1855 | New York |

**BRITTEN, BENJAMIN**
b. Lowestoft, Suffolk, Nov. 22, 1913; d. Aldeburgh, Dec. 4, 1976

| | | |
|---|---|---|
| *Albert Herring* | 1947 | Glyndebourne |
| *Billy Budd* | 1951 | London |
| *Burning Fiery Furnace* | 1966 | Aldeburgh |
| *Curlew River* | 1964 | Aldeburgh |
| *Death in Venice* | 1973 | Aldeburgh |
| *Gloriana* | 1953 | London |
| *Golden Vanity* | 1967 | Aldeburgh |
| *Let's Make an Opera!/Little Sweep* | 1949 | St. Louis |
| +*Midsummer Night's Dream* | 1960 | Aldeburgh |
| *Noyes Fludde* | 1958 | Aldeburgh |
| *Owen Wingrave* | 1971 | London, BBC |
| *Paul Bunyan* | 1941 | New York |
| *Peter Grimes* | 1945 | London |
| *Prodigal Son* | 1968 | Aldeburgh |
| *Rape of Lucretia* | 1946 | Glyndebourne |
| *Turn of the Screw* | 1954 | Venice |

**BROADSTOCK, BRENTON**
b. Melbourne, Dec. 12, 1952

| | | |
|---|---|---|
| +*Fahrenheit 451* | 1992 | Sydney |

**BROEKMAN, DAVID**
b. Leiden, Neth., May 13, 1899; d. New York, Apr. 1, 1958

| | | |
|---|---|---|
| *Barbara Allen* | 1954 | New York |

**BROMHEAD, JEROME DE**
b. Waterford, Ire, Dec. 2, 1945

| | | |
|---|---|---|
| *New Lands* | 1993 | Dublin |

**BROOKS, RICHARD**
b. Syracuse, NY, Dec. 26, 1942

| | | |
|---|---|---|
| +*Moby Dick* | 1987* | |
| *Rapunzel* | 1971 | Binghamton, NY |
| *Robert and Hal* | 2004 | New York |

**BROTONS, SALVADOR**
b. Barcelona, July 17, 1959

| | | |
|---|---|---|
| *Reverend Everyman* | 1990 | Tallahassee, FL |

BROWN, ALLYSON
+*Miranda*                                    1985      Houston
BROWN, RICHARD
b. Gloversville, NY, Feb. 21, 1947
*Gift of the Magi*                            1985*
BRUCE, DAVID
b. Eng., 1970
*Bird in Your Ear*                            2008      Annandale-on-Hudson, NY
*Has It Happened Yet?*                        2002      London
*Out of the Ordinary*                         2007      London
*Push!*                                       2006      London
*Seven Tons of Dung (Shorts)*                 1999      Battersea, London
BRUCE, (FRANK) NEELY
b. Memphis, TN., Jan. 21, 1944
*Americana*                                   1980      Middletown, CT
+*Hansel and Gretel*                          1997      W. Hartford
+*Pyramus and Thisbe*                         1965      Tuscaloosa, AL
*Trials of Psyche*                            1971      Urbana-Champaign, IL
BRUMBY, COLIN JAMES
b. Melbourne, June 18, 1933
*Donna, La*                                   1988      Sydney
+*Fire on the Wind*                           1991      Brisbane
*Heretic, The*                                1999*
+*Lorenzaccio*                                1986      Sydney
+*Marriage Machine*                           1972      Sydney
*Seven Deadly Sins*                           1970      Brisbane
*Summer Carol*                                1991      Canberra
BRYAN, CHARLES F.
b. McMinnville, TN, July 26, 1911; d. Pinson, AL, Aug. 7, 1955
*Singin' Billy*                               1952      Nashville, TN
BRYANT, CURTIS
b. 1949
*Zabette*                                     1999      Atlanta
BRYARS, GAVIN
b. Yorkshire, Eng., Jan. 16, 1943
*Doctor Ox's Experiment*                      1997      London
*Medea*                                       1982      New York
BRYSON, ERNEST ROBERT
b. Liverpool, 1867; d. St Briavels, Gloucestershire, 1942
*Leper's Flute*                               1926      Glasgow
BUCCI, MARK
b. New York, Feb. 26, 1924; d. Camp Verde, AZ, Aug. 22, 2002
*Boor, The*                                   1949      New York
+*Dress, The*                                 1953      New York
+*Hero, The*                                  1965      New York
+*Sweet Betsy from Pike*                      1953      New York
+*Tale for a Deaf Ear*                        1957      Lenox, MA
BUCHANAN, DOROTHY QUITA
b. Christchurch, NZ, Sept. 28, 1945
*Greenleaf*                                   1985*
*It Began with a Pony*                        2003      Wellington

*Mansfield Stories:*
  *Daughters of the Late Colonel*             1999      Wellington
  *Miss Brill*                                1998      Wellington
  *Woman at the Store*                        1998      Wellington
BUCHAROFF [BUCHHALTER], SIMON
b. Berdichev, Russia, Apr. 20, 1881; d. Chicago, Nov. 24, 1955
*Lover's Knot*                                1916      Chicago
BUCK, DUDLEY
b. Hartford, CT, Mar. 10, 1839; d. West Orange, NJ, Oct. 6, 1909
*Deseret*                                     1880      New York
+*Serâpis*                                    1889*
BUCKLEY, JOHN
b. Templeglantine, Co. Limerick (Ire.), Dec. 19, 1951
*Words upon the Window Pane*                  1991      Dublin
BUGG, G. WILLIAM
b. Memphis, TN, Oct. 27, 1943
*Bartolo*                                     1986      Birmingham, AL.
BUHR, GLENN
b. Winnipeg, ON, Dec. 18, 1954
*Heavenfields*                                1995      Victoria, BC
BULLER, JOHN
b. London, Feb. 7, 1927; d. Sherbourne, Warwickshire, Sept. 12, 2004
+*Bacchae, The*                               1992      London
BURGESS, HENRY
fl ca. 1738 to 1781
*Coffee House* (with H. Carey)                1738      London
BURGHERSH, LORD JOHN FANE
b. London, Feb. 3, 1784; d. Wansford, Northamptonshire, Oct. 16, 1859
*Catherine*                                   1830      London
BURGON, GEOFFREY
b. Hambleton, Hampshire, Eng., July 16, 1941; d. Gloucester, Sept. 21, 2010
+*Hard Times*                                 1991*
*Joan of Arc*                                 1970*
*Orpheus*                                     1982      Wells, Somerset
BURKE, RICHARD
b. New York, Oct. 12, 1947
+*Game of Poker*                              2009      New York
BURNEY, CHARLES
b. Shrewsbury, Eng., Apr. 7, 1762; d. Chelsea, Apr. 12, 1814
+*Cunning Man*                                1766      London
*Midsummer Night's Dream*                     1763      London
*Robin Hood*                                  1750      London
BURNHAM, CARDON
b. Kewanee, IL, Feb. 25, 1927
*Aria da capo*                                1955      New Orleans
+*Nitecap*                                    1956      New Orleans
BURRELL, DIANA
b. Norwich, Eng., Oct. 28, 1948
+*Albatross, The*                             1997      London

**BURRITT, LLOYD**
b. Vancouver, June 7, 1940

| | | |
|---|---|---|
| *Dream Healer* | 2008 | Vancouver |

**BURRS, LESLIE SAVOY**
b. Philadelphia

| | | |
|---|---|---|
| +*Egypt's Nights* | 2008 | Philadelphia |
| *Vanqui* | 1999 | Columbus, OH |

**BURT, FRANCIS**
b. London, Apr. 28, 1926

| | | |
|---|---|---|
| *Barnstable* | 1969 | Kassel, Ger. |
| +*Volpone* | 1960 | Stuttgart, Ger. |

**BURTCH, MERVYN**
b. Wales, 1929

| | | |
|---|---|---|
| *Child, Book, and Broomstick* | 2000 | Vancouver |
| *Selfish Giant* | 1969 | BBC, Wales |

**BURTON, STEPHEN DOUGLAS**
b. Whittier, CA, Feb. 24, 1943

| | | |
|---|---|---|
| +*American Triptych:* | 1975* | |
|    *Benito Cereno* | | |
|    *Dr. Heidegger's Experiment* | | |
|    *Maggie* | 1989 | Alexandria, VA |
| *Duchess of Malfi* | 1978 | Vienna, VA |
| +*No Trifling with Love* | 1970* | |

**BUSBY, GERALD**
b. Tyler, TX, 1935

| | | |
|---|---|---|
| *Cousin Lillie* | 1985* | |
| *Orpheus in Love* | 1992 | New York |
| *Sleepsong* | 1985 | Houston |
| *Viola* | 1985 | Houston |

**BUSCH, DENNIS**
b. ?, Mar. 28, 1947

| | | |
|---|---|---|
| +*Alchemist of Trenton* | 1982* | |
| +*Idle Rumor* | 1986* | |
| +*Secret of the Mirror* | 1983* | |
| +*Simple Decision* | 1982* | |

**BUSH, ALAN**
b. Dulwich, Eng., Dec. 22, 1900; d. Watford, Eng., Oct. 31, 1995

| | | |
|---|---|---|
| *Ferryman's Daughter* | 1964 | Letchworth, Eng. |
| *Joe Hill* | 1970 | Berlin (East) |
| *Men of Blackmoor* | 1956 | Weimar |
| *Press Gang* | 1947 | Letchworth, Eng. |
| *Sugar Reapers* | 1966 | Leipzig |
| *Wat Tyler* | 1953 | Leipzig |

**BUSH, GEOFFREY**
b. London, Mar. 23, 1920; d. there, Feb. 24, 1998

| | | |
|---|---|---|
| *Blind Beggar's Daughter* | 1954 | Farnham, Eng. |
| *Cat Who Went to Heaven* | 1976 | Croydon, London |
| +*Equation, The* | 1968 | London |
| +*If the Cap Fits* | 1956 | Cheltenham, Eng. |
| +*Lord Arthur Savile's Crime* | 1972 | London |
| +*Love's Labour's Lost* | 1988* | |

**BUSKIRK, CARL VAN**
b. 1907; d. ca. 1993

| | | |
|---|---|---|
| *Land between the Rivers* | 1956 | Bloomington, IN |

**BUTLER, MARTIN (CLAINES)**
b. Romsey, Eng., Mar. 1, 1960

| | | |
|---|---|---|
| *Better Place* | 2001 | London |
| *Craig's Progress* | 1994 | London |
| *Siren's Song* | 1986 | Heraklion, Crete |

**BUTLER, O'BRIEN (WHITWELL)**
b. Cahersiveen, Ire., ca. 1870; d. May 7, 1915 (on *Lusitania*)

| | | |
|---|---|---|
| *Muirgheis* | 1903 | Dublin |

**BUTLER, THOMAS HAMLY**
b. London, ca. 1755; d. Edinburgh, 1823

| | | |
|---|---|---|
| *Calypso* | 1779 | Dublin |
| *Widow of Delphi* | 1780 | London |

**BUTTS, ROBERT W.**

| | | |
|---|---|---|
| +*Tell-Tale Heart* | 2010 | Rockaway, NJ |

**BYRD, WILLIAM CLIFTON**
d 1974

| | | |
|---|---|---|
| *Lyneia* | 1949 | Cincinnati, OH |
| *Scandal at Mulford Inn* | 1954 | Cincinnati, OH |

**BYRNE, DAVID**
b. Dumbarton, Scot, May 14, 1952

| | | |
|---|---|---|
| *Forest, The* | 1988 | Berlin (West) |
| *Knee Plays* | 1984 | Minneapolis, MN |

**CABANISS, THOMAS**

| | | |
|---|---|---|
| +*Denmark Vesey* | 1987 | Waterford, CT |
| +*German Refugee* | 2008 | New York |
| *Sandman, The* | 2002 | Brooklyn, NY |

**CADMAN, CHARLES WAKEFIELD**
b. Johnstown, PA, Dec. 24, 1881; d. Los Angeles Dec. 30, 1946

| | | |
|---|---|---|
| *Garden of Mystery* | 1925 | New York |
| *Land of the Misty Water* | 1909–12* | |
| *Shanewis* | 1918 | New York |
| *Sunset Trail* | 1922 | Denver, CO |
| *Willow Tree* | 1932 | NBC radio |
| *Witch of Salem* | 1926 | Chicago |

**CAGE, JOHN**
b. Los Angeles, Sept. 5, 1912; d. New York, Aug. 12, 1992

| | | |
|---|---|---|
| *Europeras 1 & 2* | 1987 | Frankfurt |
| *Europeras 3 & 4* | 1990 | London |
| *Europera 5* | 1991 | Buffalo |

**CAIN, THOMAS LEWIS**
b. 1951

| | | |
|---|---|---|
| +*Jack and Roberta* | 1981 | Riverdale, MD |
| +*Lesson, The* | 1979 | Riverdale, MD |
| +*Price of Eggs* | 1982 | Riverdale, MD |

**CALDWELL, MARY ELIZABETH**
b. Tacoma, WA, Aug. 1, 1909; d. Pasadena, CA, Nov. 15, 2003

| | | |
|---|---|---|
| +*Gift of Song* | 1961 | Pasadena, CA |
| *Pepito's Golden Flower* | 1955 | Pasadena, CA |

**CALLAHAN, JAMES P.**
b. US

| | | |
|---|---|---|
| *Processions* | 1996 | St. Paul, MN |
| *Sanctuary* | 2003 | St. Paul, MN |

**CALLCOTT, JOHN W.**
b. London, Nov. 20, 1766; d. Bristol, May 15, 1821

| | | |
|---|---|---|
| *Mistakes of a Day* | 1787 | Norwich, Eng. |

**CALTABIANO, RONALD**
b. New York, Dec. 7, 1959

| | | |
|---|---|---|
| +*Marrying the Hangman* (lib. with B. Twist) | 2000 | New York |

**CAMERON, KATRINA**

| | | |
|---|---|---|
| *First Word* | 1996 | New York |

**CAMILLERI, CHARLES**
b. Hamrun, Malta, Sept. 7, 1931; d. Jan. 3, 2009, Naxxar, Malta

| | | |
|---|---|---|
| *Melita* | 1968 | Belfast |

**CAMPBELL, COLIN MacLEOD**
b. London, Mar. 12, 1890; d. Surrey, June 24, 1953

| | | |
|---|---|---|
| *Thais and Talmane* | 1921 | Manchester |

**CANNING, THOMAS**
b. 1911; d. 1989

| | | |
|---|---|---|
| *Beyond Belief* | 1956 | Rochester, NY |

**CANNON, PHILIP**
b. Paris, Dec. 21, 1929

| | | |
|---|---|---|
| *Dr Jekyll and Mr. Hyde* | 1973 | New York |
| *Man from Venus* | 1967 | Waltham Abbey, Essex, Eng. |
| *Morvoren* | 1964 | London |

**CANTRICK, ROBERT B.**
b. Adrian, MI, Dec. 8, 1917; d. Amherst, NY, Apr. 7, 2006

| | | |
|---|---|---|
| *Three Mimes* | 1969* | |
| | 1994 | New York |

**CAPERS, VALERIE**
b. Bronx, NY, May 24, 1935

| | | |
|---|---|---|
| *Paul Laurence Dunbar* | 1988 | New York |
| *Sojourner* | 1995 | New York |

**CARBON, JOHN**
b. Chicago, 1951

| | | |
|---|---|---|
| *Benjamin* | 1987 | Lancaster, PA |
| *Disappearing Act* | 2008* | |
| +*Marie Laveau* | 1983* | |

**CAREY, CLIVE**
b. Sible Hedingham, Eng., May 30, 1883; d. London, Apr. 30, 1968

| | | |
|---|---|---|
| *All Fools' Day* | 1921 | Glastonbury, Eng. |

**CAREY, HENRY**
b. Yorkshire?, 1687; d. London, Oct. 4, 1743

| | | |
|---|---|---|
| *Betty* (arr. songs) | 1732 | London |
| *Britannia* | 1734 | London |
| *Chrononhotonthologos* | 1734 | London |
| *Coffee House* (with Burgess) | 1738 | London |
| +*Contrivances, The* | 1729 | London |
| *Damon and Phillida* (arr. songs) | 1729 | London |
| *Generous Freemason* (arr. songs?) | 1730 | London |
| +*Happy Nuptials* | 1733 | London |
| +*Honest Yorkshireman* | 1735 | London |
| *Love in a Riddle* (arr. songs) | 1729 | London |
| *Mock Doctor* (with Jones, Seedo) | 1732 | London |
| +*Nancy* | 1739 | London |
| *Quaker's Opera* (arr. songs) | 1728 | London |

**CARL, ROBERT**
b. 1954

| | | |
|---|---|---|
| *Harmony* | 2006 | New York |

**CARLOS, WENDY [WALTER]**
b. Pawtucket, RI, Nov. 14, 1939

| | | |
|---|---|---|
| *Noah* | 1965* | |

**CARLSEN, PHILIP**
b. Coulee Dam, WA, 1951

| | | |
|---|---|---|
| +*Implications of Melissa* | 1982 | Brooklyn, NY |

**CARLSON, DAVID**
b. Ventura, CA, Mar. 13, 1952

| | | |
|---|---|---|
| *Anna Karenina* | 2007 | Miami |
| *Constellations* | 2000 | Cooperstown, NY |
| *Dreamkeepers* | 1996 | Salt Lake City, UT |
| *Midnight Angel* | 1993 | St. Louis, MO |

**CARMINES, AL (ALVIN)**
b. Hampton, VA, July 5, 1936; d. New York, Aug. 9, 2005

| | | |
|---|---|---|
| +*Duel, The* | 1974 | Brooklyn, NY |
| +*Joan* | 1971 | New York |
| +*Journey of Snow White* | 1971 | New York |

**CARPENTER, GARY**
b. 1951

| | | |
|---|---|---|
| *Doggone (Shorts)* | 2000 | Battersea, London |
| *Lost Domain* | 1984 | Bracknell, Berk., Eng. |

**CARR, BENJAMIN**
b. London, Sept. 12, 1768; d. Philadelphia, May 24, 1831

| | | |
|---|---|---|
| *American in London* | 1798 | Philadelphia |
| *Archers, The* | 1796 | New York |
| *Bourneville Castle* | 1797 | New York |
| *Philander and Silvia* | 1792 | London |

**CARR, F[RANK] OSMOND**
b. 1858; d. 1916

| | | |
|---|---|---|
| *His Excellency* | 1894 | London |

**CARROLL, BRAD**
b. US, 19??

| | | |
|---|---|---|
| *Cio Cio San* | 2005 | Hot Springs, AZ |

**CARTER, CHANDLER**
b. Four Oaks, NC

| | | |
|---|---|---|
| *No Easy Walk to Freedom* | 1994* | |
| | 2000 | Hempstead, NY |
| *Strange Fruit* | 2007 | Chapel Hill, NC |

**CARTER, ELLIOTT**
b. New York, Dec. 11, 1908; d. there, Nov. 5, 2012

| | | |
|---|---|---|
| *Tom and Lily* | 1934* | |
| *What Next?* | 1999 | Berlin |

CARTER, ERNEST
b. Orange, NJ, Sept. 3, 1866; d. Stamford, CT, June 21, 1953

| | | |
|---|---|---|
| +*Blonde, Donna* | 1931 | Brooklyn, NY |
| *White Bird* | 1922 | New York |

CARTER, THOMAS
b. Dublin, ca. 1735; d. London, Oct. 12, 1804

| | | |
|---|---|---|
| *Birth Day, The* | 1787 | London |
| *Constant Maid* | 1788 | London |
| *Fair Americans* | 1782 | London |
| *Just in Time* | 1792 | London |
| *Milesian, The* | 1777 | London |
| *Rival Candidates* | 1775 | London |

CARYLL, IVAN [FÉLIX TILKINS]
b. Liège, May 12, 1861; d. New York, Nov. 29, 1921

| | | |
|---|---|---|
| *Duchess of Dantzic* | 1903 | London |
| *Lucky Star* | 1899 | London |
| *Pink Lady* | 1911 | New York |

CASCARINO, ROMEO
b. Philadelphia, Sept. 28, 1922; d. 2002

| | | |
|---|---|---|
| *William Penn* | 1982 | Philadelphia |

CASEY, PETER J.
b. Austral

| | | |
|---|---|---|
| +*Devil Builds a Chapel* | 2010 | Melbourne |

CASKEN, JOHN
b. Barnsley, Eng., July 15, 1949

| | | |
|---|---|---|
| +*God's Liar* (lib. with Warner) | 2001 | London |
| +*Golem* (lib. with Audi) | 1989 | London |

CASSELS-BROWN, ALASTAIR
b. London, 1927; d. Concord, NH, Nov. 30, 2001

| | | |
|---|---|---|
| *Sredni Vashtar* | 1983* | |

CAVE, MICHAEL
b. Springfield, MO, May 17, 1944

| | | |
|---|---|---|
| +*Pandora's Box* | 1971 | Los Angeles |

CECCONI-BATES, AUGUSTA
b. Syracuse, New York, Aug. 9, 1933

| | | |
|---|---|---|
| +*Molly Brant* | 2003 | Kingston, ON |

CEELY, ROBERT
b. Torrington, CT, Jan. 17, 1930

| | | |
|---|---|---|
| *Automobile Graveyard* | 1995 | Boston |

CELLIER, ALFRED
b. London, Dec. 1, 1844; d. there, Dec. 28, 1891

| | | |
|---|---|---|
| *Charity Begins at Home* | 1872 | London |
| *Doris* | 1889 | London |
| *Dorothy* | 1886 | London |
| *Masque of Pandora* | 1881 | Boston |
| *Mountebanks* | 1892 | London |
| *Nell Gwynne* | 1878 | Manchester |
| *Sultan of Mocha* | 1874 | Manchester |
| *Tower of London* | 1875 | Manchester |

CERRONE, CHRISTOPHER
b. Huntington, NY, 1984

| | | |
|---|---|---|
| +*Invisible Cities* | 2009 | New York |

CERVETTI, SERGIO
b. Dolores, Uruguay, Nov. 9, 1941

| | | |
|---|---|---|
| *Elegy for a Prince* | 2007 | New York |

CESARINI, CARLO FRANCESCO
b. San Martino, Italy, 1666; d. after Sept. 2, 1741

| | | |
|---|---|---|
| *Love's Triumph* (with Violone, Gasparini) | 1708 | London |

CHADWICK, GEORGE W.
b. Lowell, MA, Nov. 13, 1854; d. Boston, Apr. 4, 1931

| | | |
|---|---|---|
| *Judith* | 1901 | Worcester, MA |
| *Love's Sacrifice* | 1923 | Chicago |
| *Padrone, The* | 1912* | |
| | 1995 | Waterbury, CT |
| *Tabasco* | 1894 | Boston |

CHAN, KA NIN
b. Hong Kong, Dec. 3, 1949

| | | |
|---|---|---|
| *Ice Time* | 2004 | Toronto |
| *Iron Road* | 2001 | Toronto |
| *Weaving Maiden* | 2006 | Toronto |

CHANCE, FRED
b. 1960; d. Cleveland, Dec. 5, 1993

| | | |
|---|---|---|
| +*Stiff* | 1985 | Houston |

CHANLER, THEODORE WARD
b. Newport, RI, Apr. 29, 1902; d. Boston, July 27, 1961

| | | |
|---|---|---|
| *Pot of Fat* | 1955 | Cambridge, MA |

CHAPIN, TOM
b. New York, 1945

| | | |
|---|---|---|
| *Magic Fishbone* | 1988 | New York |

CHARPENTIER, GABRIEL
b. Richmond, QC, Sept. 13, 1925

| | | |
|---|---|---|
| +*English Lesson* | 1968 | Stratford, ON |
| +*Orpheus II* | 1972 | Stratford, ON |
| +*Tea Symphony* | 1972 | Banff, AB |

CHAULS, ROBERT
b. Port Chester, NY, July 18, 1942

| | | |
|---|---|---|
| +*Alice in Wonderland* | 1976 | Van Nuys, CA |
| *Thirteen Clocks* | 1983 | Waterford, CT |

CHÁVEZ, CARLOS
b. Calzada de Tacube (nr. Mexico City), June 13, 1899; d. Mexico City, Aug. 2, 1978

| | | |
|---|---|---|
| *Visitors, The* | 1957 | New York |

CHEN, EVAN H.
b. Beijing, 1972

| | | |
|---|---|---|
| *Bok Choy Variations* | 1995 | St. Paul, MN |

CHEN, JUSTINE FANG
b. Brooklyn, NY, Feb. 18, 1975

| | | |
|---|---|---|
| *Chicken or Beef?* | 2008 | Toronto |
| *Decoherence* | 2008 | Toronto |
| +*Dragon, The* | 2010* | |
| +*Jeanne* | 2008 | New York |
| +*Maiden Tower* | 2005 | New York |
| *River by the Residential Schoolhouse* | 2008 | Toronto |
| +*Three, Two, One, Bang!* | 2008 | Carrboro, NC |
| *Voice for a Future Nightingale* | 2008 | Toronto |

CHESLOCK, LOUIS
b. London, Sept. 25, 1899; d. Baltimore, July 19, 1981

| | | |
|---|---|---|
| *Jewel Merchants* | 1940 | Baltimore |

CHESWORTH, DAVID
b. Stoke, Eng., Mar. 31, 1958

| | | |
|---|---|---|
| *Two Executioners* | 1994 | Melbourne |

CHILD, FRANCIS JAMES
b. Boston, Feb. 1, 1825; d. there, Sept. 11, 1896

| | | |
|---|---|---|
| *Pesceballo, Il* | 1862 | Boston |

CHIN, UNSUK
b. Seoul, July 14, 1961

| | | |
|---|---|---|
| *Alice in Wonderland* | 2007 | Munich |

CHING, (J.) MICHAEL
b. Honolulu, 1958

| | | |
|---|---|---|
| *Buoso's Ghost* | 1997 | Memphis, TN |
| *Corps of Discovery* | 2003 | Columbia, MO |
| *Cue 67* | 1992 | Norfolk, VA |
| +*Faith: DWF, 235* | 1999 | New York |
| *King of the Clouds* | 1993 | Dayton, OH |
| *Leo* | 1985 | Houston |
| *Out of the Rain* | 1999 | Wilmington, DE |
| *Reunion* | 1998 | Wilmington, DE |

CHISHOLM, ERIK
b. Glasgow, Jan. 4, 1904; d. Cape Town, June 8, 1965

| | | |
|---|---|---|
| +*Canterbury Tales*, trilogy, 1961–62* | | |
|    *Nonnes Preestes Tale* | 1961* | |
|    *Pardoner's Tale* | 1961 | Cape Town |
|    *Wyf of Bathes Tale* | 1962* | |
| +*Caucasian Chalk Circle* | 1963* | |
| +*Dark Sonnet* | 1952 | Cape Town |
| +*Feast of Samhain* | 1941* | |
| +*Importance of Being Earnest* | 1963* | |
| +*Inland Woman* | 1953 | Cape Town |
| +*Life and Loves of Robert Burns* | 1963* | |
| +*Midnight Court* | 1954–61* | |
| +*Murder in Three Keys*, trilogy: | 1954 | New York |
|    *Black Roses* | 1954 | New York |
|    *Dark Sonnet* | 1952 | Cape Town |
|    *Simoon* | 1954 | New York |

CHLARSON, LINDER
b. 1936; d. New York, Oct. 27, 1998

| | | |
|---|---|---|
| *Binding of Isaac* | 1998 | Norwalk, CT |
| *Love and Psyche* | 1978* | |
| +*Montezuma's Death* | 1980* | |
| +*Mr. Lion* | 1982 | New York |
| +*Mountain Windsong* | 1995 | Tallequah, OK |
| +*Trio Sonata* | 1985 | New York |

CHUDACOFF, EDWARD
b. 1925

| | | |
|---|---|---|
| *Circus, The* | 1953 | Interlochen, MI |

CIONEK, EDMUND FRANCIS

| | | |
|---|---|---|
| *Henry David Thoreau* | 2003 | Nw York |
| *SPACE* | 1991 | New York |

CIPULLO, TOM
b. 1959

| | | |
|---|---|---|
| +*Glory Denied* | 2006 | New York |

CLAFLIN, AVERY
b. Keene, NH, June 21, 1898; d. Greenwich, CT, Jan. 9, 1979

| | | |
|---|---|---|
| +*Fall of the House of Usher* | 1923* | |
| *Grand Bretèche* | 1957 | New York |
| *Hester Prynne* | 1934 | Hartford |
| *Uncle Tom's Cabin* | 1964 | New York |

CLAPP, PHILIP GREELEY
b. 1888; d. 1954

| | | |
|---|---|---|
| *Taming of the Shrew* | 1948* | |

CLARK, SONDRA
b. 1941

| | | |
|---|---|---|
| *Dalmatia and Dalmatio* | 2002 | San Francisco |

CLARKE, HENRY LELAND
b. Dover, NH, Mar. 9, 1907; d. Mar. 30, 1992

| | | |
|---|---|---|
| *Loafer and the Loaf* | 1956 | Los Angeles |
| *Lysistrata* | 1972* | |
| | 1984 | Marlboro, VT |

CLAY, FREDERIC
b. Paris, Aug. 3, 1838; d. Great Marlow, Eng., Nov. 29, 1889

| | | |
|---|---|---|
| *Ages Ago* | 1869 | London |
| *Black Crook* (with Jacob) | 1872 | London |
| *Cattarina* | 1874 | Manchester |
| *Constance* | 1865 | London |
| *Court and Cottage* | 1862 | London |
| *Don Quixote* | 1876 | London |
| *Gentleman in Black* | 1870 | London |
| *Golden Ring* | 1883 | London |
| *Happy Arcadia* | 1872 | London |
| *In Possession* | 1871 | London |
| *Merry Duchess* | 1883 | London |
| *On the March* (arr. Solomon, Crook) | 1896 | Sheffield, Eng. |
| *Oriana* | 1873 | London |
| *Out of Sight* | 1860 | London |
| *Princess Toto* | 1876 | Nottingham, Eng. |

CLAYTON, THOMAS
b. London, bapt Oct. 28, 1673; d. there, buried Sept. 23, 1725

| | | |
|---|---|---|
| *Arsinoe* (with G. Bononcini) | 1705 | London |
| *Prunella* | 1708 | London |
| *Rosamond* | 1707 | London |

CLEVE, V. de

| | | |
|---|---|---|
| *Bird Catcher* | 1799 | London |

CLIFTON, ARTHUR [PHILIP ANTONY CORRI]
b. Edinburgh, ca. 1784; d. Baltimore, Feb. 19, 1832

| | | |
|---|---|---|
| *Enterprise, The* | 1822 | Baltimore, MD |

CLOKEY, JOSEPH WADDEL
b. New Albany, IN, Aug. 28, 1890; d. Covina, CA, Sept. 14, 1960

| | | |
|---|---|---|
| *Nightingale, The* | 1925 | Miami |
| *Pied Piper of Hamelin* | 1920 | Miami |

CLUTSAM, GEORGE H.
b. Sydney, Sept. 26, 1866; d. London, Nov. 17, 1951

| | | |
|---|---|---|
| +*Summer's Night* | 1910 | London |

COATES, ALBERT
b. St. Petersburg, Apr. 1882; d. Milnerton, nr. Cape Town, Dec. 11, 1953

| | | |
|---|---|---|
| *Gainsborough* | 1941 | Los Angeles |
| *Myth Beautiful* | 1920 | London |
| *Pickwick* | 1936 | London |
| *Samuel Pepys* | 1929 | Munich |
| +*Van Hunks and the Devil* | 1952 | Cape Town |

COCKSHOTT, GERALD WILFRED
b. Bristol, Eng., Nov. 15, 1915; d. London, Feb. 3, 1979

| | | |
|---|---|---|
| +*Apollo and Persephone* | 1954 | Kirkwall, Scot |
| +*Faun in the Forest* | 1959 | Westport, CT |

COE, KENTON
b. TN, Nov. 12, 1932

| | | |
|---|---|---|
| *Rachel* | 1989 | Knoxville, TN |

COGAN, PHILIP
b. Cork? Ire., 1748; d. Dublin, Feb. 3, 1833

| | | |
|---|---|---|
| *Contract, The* | 1782 | Dublin |
| *Love in a Blaze* | 1799 | Dublin |
| *Ruling Passion* | 1778 | Dublin |

COHEN, JOEL
b. Providence, RI, May 23, 1942

| | | |
|---|---|---|
| +*Tristan and Iseult* | 1988 | New York |

COHEN, STEVE
b. New York, Sept. 3, 1954

| | | |
|---|---|---|
| *Cop and the Anthem* | 1982 | New York |
| *Pizza del destino* | 1980 | Lake George, NY |

COHN, JAMES
b. Newark, NJ, Feb. 12, 1928

| | | |
|---|---|---|
| *Fall of the City* | 1955 | Athens, OH |

COID, MARSHALL
b. 195?

| | | |
|---|---|---|
| *Bundle Man* | 1993 | New York |

COKE, ROGER SACHEVERELL
b. Derbyshire, Eng., Oct. 20, 1912; d. there 1972

| | | |
|---|---|---|
| +*Cenci, The* | 1959 | London |

COLE, HUGO
b. London, July 6, 1917; d. there, Mar. 2, 1995

| | | |
|---|---|---|
| +*Asses' Ears* | 1950 | Los Angeles |
| +*Fair Traders* | 1971 | Wokingham, Eng. |
| *Falcon, The* | 1968 | Bath |
| *Flax into Gold* | 1966 | Oxford |
| +*Jonah* | 1967* | |
| +*Persephone* | 1955 | London |
| +*Statue for the Mayor* | 1952 | London |
| +*Tunnel, The* | 1960 | London |

COLEMAN, EDWIN
b. Eng, 19??

| | | |
|---|---|---|
| *Christmas Carol* | 1962 | London, BBC |

COLGRASS, MICHAEL
b. Chicago, Apr. 22, 1932

| | | |
|---|---|---|
| +*Nightingale, Inc.* | 1975 | Urbana, IL |
| +*Something's Gonna Happen* | 1978 | Toronto |
| +*Virgil's Dream* | 1967 | Brighton, Eng. |

COLILLA, ROBERT A.
b. 1934

| | | |
|---|---|---|
| *Hello Out There* | 1990* | |

COLLINGWOOD, LAWRANCE ARTHUR
b. London, Mar. 14, 1887; d. Killin, Perthshire, Eng., Dec. 19, 1982

| | | |
|---|---|---|
| *Death of Tintagiles* | 1950 | London |
| +*Macbeth* | 1934 | London |

COLLINS, ANTHONY [VINCENT BENEDICTUS]
b. Hastings, Eng., Sept. 3, 1893; d. Los Angeles, Dec. 11, 1963

| | | |
|---|---|---|
| *Catherine Parr* | 1949 | New York |

COLLINS, JOSEPH EDWARD
b. Joliet, IL, Nov. 10, 1866; d. Chicago, Dec. 1, 1951

| | | |
|---|---|---|
| +*Daughter of the South* | 1938 | Chicago |

CONDELL, HENRY
b. London, 1757; d. there, June 24, 1824

| | | |
|---|---|---|
| *Aladdin* (with W. Ware) | 1813 | London |
| *Bridal Ring* (with Pelissier) | 1810 | London |
| *Transformation* | 1810 | London |
| *Up to Town* (with Reeve et al.) | 1811 | London |
| *Who Wins?* | 1810 | New York |

CONSTANTINIDES, DINOS
b. Greece, 1929

| | | |
|---|---|---|
| *Antigone* | 1993 | Baton Rouge |
| *Intimations* | 1982 | Brooklyn, NY |

CONTE, DAVID
b. Denver, CO, Dec. 20, 1955

| | | |
|---|---|---|
| *America Tropical* | 2007 | San Francisco |
| *Dreamers, The* | 1996 | Sonoma, CA |
| *Famous* | 2007 | San Francisco |
| *Firebird Motel* | 2003 | San Francisco |
| *Gift of the Magi* | 1998 | San Francisco |

CONVERSE, FREDERICK
b. Newton, MA, Jan. 5, 1871; d. Westwood, MA June 8, 1940

| | | |
|---|---|---|
| *Immigrants, The* | 1912* | |
| *Pipe of Desire* | 1906 | Boston |
| +*Sacrifice, The* | 1911 | Boston |

CONVERY, ROBERT
b. Wichita, KA, Oct. 4, 1954

| | | |
|---|---|---|
| +*Pyramus and Thisbe* | 1982 | Waterford, CT |

CONYNGHAM, BARRY
b. Sydney, Aug. 27, 1944

| | | |
|---|---|---|
| *Apology of Bony Anderson* | 1978 | Melbourne |
| *Bennelong* | 1988 | Groningen, Neth. |
| *Edward John Eyre* | 1971 | Sydney |
| *Electric Lenin* | 2006 | Lismore, NSW |
| *Fly* | 1984 | Melbourne |
| *Oath of Bad Brown Bill* | 1985 | Melbourne |

COOK, WILL MARION
b. Washington, DC, Jan. 27, 1869; d. New York, July 19, 1944

| | | |
|---|---|---|
| *Abyssinia* (with B. Williams) | 1906 | New York |
| *In Dahomey* | 1903 | New York |

COOKE, ARNOLD A.

b. Gomersal, nr. Leeds, Eng., Nov, 4, 1906; d. Five Oak Green, Kent, Aug, 13, 2005

| | | |
|---|---|---|
| *Invisible Duke* | 1976* | |
| *Mary Barton* | 1954* | |

COOKE, HENRY

b. Litchfield?, Eng., ca. 1615; d. Hampton Court, Eng., July 13, 1672

| | | |
|---|---|---|
| *Siege of Rhodes* (with Lawes, Locke) | 1656 | London |

COOKE, THOMAS SIMPSON (TOM)

b. Dublin, 1782; d. London, Feb. 26, 1848

| | | |
|---|---|---|
| *Abou Hassan* | 1825 | London |
| *Actors al fresco* (with Blewitt, Horn) | 1823 | London |
| *Amoroso* | 1818 | London |
| *Boy of Santillane* (with Blewitt) | 1827 | London |
| *Challenge, The* | 1834 | London |
| *Child of the Wreck* | 1837 | London |
| *David Rizzio* (with Braham et al.) | 1820 | London |
| *Frederick the Great* | 1814 | London |
| *Gustavus III* | 1833 | London |
| *Jewess, The* | 1835 | London |
| *King's Proxy* | 1815 | London |
| *Lestocq* | 1835 | London |
| *Maid or Wife* (with Livius) | 1821 | London |
| *Oberon* | 1826 | London |
| *Red Mask* | 1834 | London |
| *Selima and Azor* (with Bishop, Walsh) | 1813 | London |
| *Siege of Corinth* | 1836 | London |
| *Sweethearts and Wives* (with Nathan) | 1823 | London |
| *Taming of the Shrew* (with Braham) | 1828 | London |
| *Veteran Soldier* (with Whitaker, Perry) | 1822 | London |
| *White Lady* | 1826 | London |

COOMBS, JOHN

b 1937

| | | |
|---|---|---|
| +*Volpone* | 1957 | London |

COOPER, SETH

| | | |
|---|---|---|
| *Echoes of the Shining Prince* | 1985 | New York |

COPELAND, STEWART

b. Alexandria, VA, July 16, 1952

| | | |
|---|---|---|
| *Cask of Amontillado* | 1993 | Barbados |
| *Holy Blood and Crescent Moon* | 1989 | Cleveland, OH |
| *Horse Opera* | 1994 | BBC Channel 4 |

COPLAND, AARON

b. Brooklyn, NY, Nov. 14, 1900; d. N Tarrytown, NY, Dec. 2, 1990

| | | |
|---|---|---|
| *Second Hurricane* | 1937 | New York |
| *Tender Land* | 1954 | New York |

COPPER, WILLIAM

b. 1953

| | | |
|---|---|---|
| +*Half Bird* | 1993 | Middletown, DE |

COPPOLA, ANTON

b. Ybor City, FL, Mar. 21, 1917

| | | |
|---|---|---|
| +*Sacco and Vanzetti* | 2001 | Tampa Bay, FL |

CORBETT, WILLIAM

bapt. London, July 18, 1680; d. there, March 7, 1748

| | | |
|---|---|---|
| *British Enchanters* | 1706 | London |

CORDER, FREDERICK

b. London, Jan. 26, 1852; d. there, Aug. 20, 1932

| | | |
|---|---|---|
| +*Morte d'Arthur* | 1879 | Brighton |
| *Nordisa* | 1887 | Liverpool |

CORIGLIANO, JOHN

b. New York, Feb. 16, 1938

| | | |
|---|---|---|
| *Ghosts of Versailles* | 1987 | New York |
| *Naked Carmen* (with D. Hess) | 1970* | |

CORRI, DOMENICO

b. Rome, Oct. 4, 1744; d. London, May 22, 1825

| | | |
|---|---|---|
| *Travellers, The* | 1806 | London |

CORRI, PHILIP ANTONY. *See* CLIFTON, ARTHUR.

COTEL, MORRIS (MOSHE)

b. Baltimore, MD, Feb. 20, 1943; d. Oct. 24, 2008, New York

| | | |
|---|---|---|
| *Deronda* | 1989* | |
| *Dreyfus* | 1985 | Brooklyn, NY |
| *Jest of Hahalaba* | 1961* | |

COULTHARD, JEAN

b. Vancouver, Feb. 10, 1908; d. there, Mar. 9, 2000

| | | |
|---|---|---|
| +*Return of the Native* (lib. with E. Baxter) | 1993 | Vancouver |

COWARD, NOËL

b. Teddington, Middlesex, Eng., Dec. 16, 1899; d. Port Maria, Jamaica, Mar. 25, 1973

| | | |
|---|---|---|
| +*Bitter-Sweet* | 1929 | London |

COWELL, HENRY

b. Menlo Park, CA, Mar. 11, 1897; d. Shady, NY, Dec. 10, 1965

| | | |
|---|---|---|
| *Building of Bamba* | 1917 | Halcyon, CA |
| *Commission, The* | 1954* | |
| | 1992 | Woodstock, NY |
| *O'Higgins of Chile* | 1949* | |

COWEN, FREDERIC[K] HYMEN

b. Kingston, Jamaica, Jan. 29, 1852; d. London, Oct. 6, 1935

| | | |
|---|---|---|
| *Garibaldi* | 1860 | London |
| *Harold* | 1895 | London |
| *One Too Many* | 1874 | London |
| *Pauline* | 1876 | London |
| *Signa* | 1893 | Milan |
| *Thorgrim* | 1890 | London |

COWIE, EDWARD

b. Birmingham, Eng., Aug. 17, 1943

| | | |
|---|---|---|
| +*Commedia* | 1979 | Kassel, Ger. |

CRATON, JOHN

b. Anniston, AL, 1953

| | | |
|---|---|---|
| +*Curious Affair* (lib. with J. Guion III) | 2004* | |
| +*Inanna* | 2007 | Modesto, CA |
| +*Parliament of Fowls* | 2007* | |

CRAWFORD, GATES

| | | |
|---|---|---|
| +*Joseph! Joseph!* | 2004 | Salt Lake City |

CRAWFORD, JOHN C.
b. Philadelphia, Jan. 19, 1931

| | | |
|---|---|---|
| +*Don Cristóbal* | 1970 | Wellesley, MA |

CRAWLEY, CLIFFORD
b. Dagenham, London, Jan. 29. 1929

| | | |
|---|---|---|
| *Angel Square* | 1996 | Ottawa |
| *Barnardo Boy* | 1982 | Kingston, ON |
| *Creation, The* | 1978 | Kingston, ON |
| *Slaughter of the Innocents* | 1974 | Leicester, Eng. |

CRESSWELL, LYELL
b. Wellington, NZ, Oct. 13, 1944

| | | |
|---|---|---|
| *Good Angel, Bad Angel* | 2005 | Edinburgh |

CROFTON, W. M. WILLIAM MERVYN)
b. 1879

| | | |
|---|---|---|
| +*Deirdre of the Sorrows* | 1925* | |

CROSSE, GORDON
b. Bury, Eng., Dec. 1, 1937

| | | |
|---|---|---|
| *Grace of Todd* | 1969 | Aldeburgh |
| *Holly from the Bongs* | 1974 | Manchester |
| *Potter Thompson* | 1975 | London |
| +*Purgatory* | 1966 | Cheltenham, Eng. |
| *Story of Vasco* | 1974 | London |
| *Wheel of the World* | 1972 | Aldeburgh |

CROWELL, JANE
b. 1921

| | | |
|---|---|---|
| *Bell Witch of Tennessee* | 1985 | Stony Brook, NY |

CROZIER, DANIEL

| | | |
|---|---|---|
| *Reunion, The* | 1989 | Baltimore |
| *With Blood, with Ink* | 1993 | Baltimore |

CRUFT, ADRIAN
b. Mitcham, London, Feb. 10, 1921; d. Hill Head, Hampshire, Feb. 20, 1987

| | | |
|---|---|---|
| *Dr. Syn* | 1983 | Kent |
| *Eatanswill Election* | 1981 | Kent |

CUGLEY, IAN
b. Melbourne, June 22, 1945; d. Nov. 4, 2010, Ramsgate, Eng.

| | | |
|---|---|---|
| +*Sea Change* | 1973* | |

CUMMING, RICHARD
b. Shanghai, China, June 9, 1928

| | | |
|---|---|---|
| *Picnic, The* | 1979 | Central City, CO |

CUMMINGS, CONRAD
b. San Francisco, Feb. 10, 1948

| | | |
|---|---|---|
| +*Eros and Psyche* | 1983 | Oberlin, OH |
| +*Golden Gate* | 2006 | New York |
| *Photo-Op* | 1990 | New York |
| *Tonkin* | 1993 | Wilmington, DE |

CUOMO, DOUGLAS J.

| | | |
|---|---|---|
| *Winter's Journey* | 2009 | Miami |

CURRENT, BRIAN
b. Toronto, May 4, 1972

| | | |
|---|---|---|
| *Airline Icarus* | 2006 | Toronto |
| *Inventory* | 2006 | Toronto |

CURRIE, RUSSELL W.
b. North Arlington, NJ, Apr. 3, 1954

| | | |
|---|---|---|
| *Caliban* | 1992 | New York |
| *Cask of Amontillado* | 1982 | New York |
| *Dream within a Dream* | 1984 | Bronx, NY |
| *Ligeia* | 1987 | Riverdale, NJ |
| *Rimshot* | 1990 | New York |

DAIKEN, MELANIE (RUTH)
b. London, July 27, 1945

| | | |
|---|---|---|
| *Mayakovsky and the Sun* | 1971 | Edinburgh |

DAMASE, JEAN-MICHEL
b. Bordeaux, France, Jan. 27, 1928

| | | |
|---|---|---|
| *Ochelata's Wedding* | 2000 | Bartlesville, OK |

DAMROSCH, WALTER
b. Breslau [Wrocław], Jan. 30, 1862; d. New York, Dec. 22, 1950

| | | |
|---|---|---|
| *Cyrano* | 1913 | New York |
| *Dove of Peace* | 1912 | Philadelphia |
| *Man without a Country* | 1937 | New York |
| *Opera Cloak* | 1942 | New York |
| *Scarlet Letter* | 1896 | Boston |

DANIEL, OMAR
b. Toronto, 1960

| | | |
|---|---|---|
| *Shadow, The* | 2009 | Toronto |

DANIELPOUR, RICHARD
b. New York, Jan. 28, 1956

| | | |
|---|---|---|
| *Margaret Garner* | 2005 | Detroit, MI |

DANIELS, M[ELVIN] L.

| | | |
|---|---|---|
| *Lazarus* | 1989 | Abilene, TX |

DANKWORTH, JOHN
b. London, Sept. 20, 1927; d. there, Feb. 6, 2010

| | | |
|---|---|---|
| *Sweeney Agonistes* | 1965 | London |

DARLEY, FRANCIS T[HOMAS] S[ULLY]
b. Philadelphia, 18??

| | | |
|---|---|---|
| *Fortunio* | 1883 | Philadelphia |

DAUGHERTY, MICHAEL
b. Cedar Rapids, IA, Apr. 28, 1954

| | | |
|---|---|---|
| *Jackie O* | 1997 | Houston |

DAVIDSON, CHARLES S.
b. Pittsburgh, 1929

| | | |
|---|---|---|
| *Gimpel the Fool* | 1965* | |

DAVIDSON, TINA
b. Stockholm, Sweden, 1952

| | | |
|---|---|---|
| *Billy and Zelda* | 1998 | Wilmington, DE |
| *Pearl* | 2009 | Raleigh, NC |

DAVIES, JOHN
fl. 1819–1826

| | | |
|---|---|---|
| *Forest Rose* | 1825 | New York |

DAVIES, PETER MAXWELL
b. Manchester, Eng., Sept. 8, 1934

| | | |
|---|---|---|
| +*Blind Man's Buff* | 1972 | London |
| +*Cinderella* | 1980 | Kirkwall, Scot. |

| | | |
|---|---|---|
| *Doctor of Myddfai* | 1996 | Kirkwall, Scot. |
| *Eight Songs for a Mad King* | 1969 | London |
| +*Jongleur de Notre Dame* | 1978 | Kirkwall, Scot. |
| +*Lighthouse, The* | 1980 | Edinburgh |
| +*Martyrdom of St. Magnus* | 1977 | Kirkwall, Scot. |
| +*Medium, The* | 1981 | Kirkwall, Scot. |
| *Miss Donnithorne's Maggot* | 1974 | Adelaide |
| *Mr. Emmet Takes a Walk* | 2000 | Kirkwell, Scot. |
| +*No. 11 Bus* | 1984 | London |
| +*Notre Dame des Fleurs* | 1973 | London |
| +*Rainbow, The* | 1981 | Kirkwall, Scot. |
| +*Resurrection* | 1988 | Darmstadt |
| +*Taverner* | 1972 | London |
| *Two Fiddlers* | 1978 | Kirkwall, Scot. |

**DAVIS, ALLAN**
b. Watertown, NY, Aug. 29, 1922

| | | |
|---|---|---|
| +*Departure, The* | 1975 | Montevallo, AL |
| +*Ordeal of Osbert* | 1951 | Plymouth, MA |
| +*Otherwise Engaged* | 1958 | New York |
| +*Sailing of the Nancy Belle* | 1948* | Syracuse, NY |
| | 1955 | Duxbury, MA |

**DAVIS, ANTHONY**
b. Paterson, NJ, Feb. 20, 1951

| | | |
|---|---|---|
| *Amistad* | 1997 | Chicago |
| *Lilith* | 2009 | San Diego |
| *Revolution of Forms* (with D. Prieto) | 2010 | New York |
| *Tania* | 1992 | Philadelphia |
| *Under the Double Moon* | 1989 | St. Louis |
| *Wakonda's Dream* | 2007 | Omaha, NB |
| *X* | 1985 | Philadelphia |

**DAVIS, CARL**
b. Brooklyn, NY, Oct. 28, 1936

| | | |
|---|---|---|
| *Arrangement, The* | 1965 | London, BBC |
| *Orpheus in the Underground* | 1977 | London, BBC2 |

**DAVIS, DON**
b. 1957

| | | |
|---|---|---|
| *Río de sangre* | 2010 | Milwaukee |

**DAVIS, JOHN**
b. Birmingham, Eng., Oct. 22, 1867; d. Estoril, Portugal, Nov. 20, 1942

| | | |
|---|---|---|
| *Zaporogues* | 1895 | Birmingham, Eng. |

**DAVIS, JOHN S.**
b. Evanston, IL, Oct. 1, 1935; d. 2009

| | | |
|---|---|---|
| +*Pardoner's Tale* | 1967 | Tucson, AR |

**DAVIS, KATHERINE**
b. St. Joseph, MO, June 25, 1892; d. Littleton, MA, Apr. 20, 1980

| | | |
|---|---|---|
| +*Unmusical Impresario* (lib. with Kent) | 1955 | Duxbury, MA |

**DAVIS, MARY**
b. Boulder, CO

| | | |
|---|---|---|
| *Columbine* | 1973 | Boulder, CO |

**DAVIS, NATHAN**
b. Kansas City, KS, Feb. 15, 1937

| | | |
|---|---|---|
| +*Just Above My Head* | 1985* | |
| (lib. with U. Davis) | 2004 | Pittsburgh |

**DAVY, JOHN**
b. Upton Hellions, Eng., Dec. 23, 1763; d. London, Feb. 22, 1824

| | | |
|---|---|---|
| *Caffres, The* | 1802 | London |
| *Pennyworth of Wit* | 1796 | London |
| *Rob Roy MacGregor* | 1818 | London |
| *Spanish Dollars* | 1805 | London |
| *What a Blunder!* | 1800 | London |
| *Woman's Will* | 1820 | London |

**DAWE, JONATHAN**
b. Boston, Feb. 17, 1965

| | | |
|---|---|---|
| *Armide* | 2009 | New York |
| *Cracked Orlando* | 2010 | New York |

**DAWES, WILLIAM**

| | | |
|---|---|---|
| *Court Masque* | 1833 | London |

**DEANE, RAYMOND**
b. Tuam, County Galway, Jan. 27, 1953

| | | |
|---|---|---|
| +*Poet and His Double* | 1991 | Dublin |
| +*Wall of Cloud* | 1999 | Longford, Ire. |

**DE KENESSEY, STEFANIA MARIA**
b. Budapest, 1956

| | | |
|---|---|---|
| *Bonfire of the Vanities* | 2006 | New York |
| *Monster Bed* | 1990 | New York |
| *Other Wise Man* | 1996 | New York |

**De KOVEN [de KOVEN], REGINALD**
b. Middletown, CT, Apr. 3, 1859; d. Chicago, Jan. 16, 1920

| | | |
|---|---|---|
| *Algerian, The* | 1893 | Philadelphia |
| *Begum, The* | 1887 | New York |
| *Canterbury Pilgrims* | 1917 | New York |
| *Don Quixote* | 1889 | Boston |
| *Fencing Master* | 1892 | New York |
| *Foxy Quiller* | 1900 | New York |
| *Girls of Holland* | 1907 | New York |
| *Golden Butterfly* | 1908 | New York |
| *Highwayman, The* | 1897 | New York |
| *Knickerbockers, The* | 1893 | New York |
| *Maid Marian* | 1902 | New York |
| *Mandarin, The* | 1896 | New York |
| *Paris Doll* | 1897 | Hartford |
| *Red Feather* | 1903 | New York |
| *Rip Van Winkle* | 1920 | Chicago |
| *Robin Hood* | 1891 | New York |
| *Rob Roy* | 1894 | New York |
| *Tzigane* | 1895 | New York |
| *Wedding Trip* | 1911 | New York |

**DE LARA, ISIDORE [ISIDORE COHEN]**
b. London, Aug. 9, 1858; d. Paris, Sept. 2, 1935

| | | |
|---|---|---|
| *Amy Robsart* | 1893 | London |
| *Light of Asia* | 1892 | London |
| *Minna* | 1886 | London |
| *Royal Word* | 1883 | London |

### DELIUS, FREDERICK
b. Bradford, Yorkshire, Jan. 19, 1862; d. Grez-sur-Loing, France, June 10, 1934

| | | |
|---|---|---|
| +*Fennimore and Gerda* | 1910* | |
| | 1919 | Frankfurt |
| +*Irmelin* | 1890–92* | |
| | 1953 | Oxford |
| +*Koanga* (lib. with C. F. Keary) | 1895–97* | |
| | 1899 | London |
| +*Magic Fountain* | 1893–95* | |
| | 1977 | London |
| +*Village Romeo and Juliet* | 1907 | Berlin |

### DELLAIRA, MICHAEL
b. Schenectady, NY

| | | |
|---|---|---|
| *Chéri* | 2002 | New York |
| +*Maud* | 1977 | New York |
| *Secret Agent* | 2008 | New York |

### DELLO JOIO, NORMAN
b. New York, Jan. 24, 1913; d. East Hampton, NY, July 24, 2008

| | | |
|---|---|---|
| *Blood Moon* | 1961 | San Francisco |
| *Nativity* | 1987 | Midland, MI |
| *Ruby, The* | 1955 | Bloomington, IN |
| *Trial at Rouen* | 1956 | New York |
| *Triumph of Joan* | 1950 | Bronxville, NY |

### DEL TREDICI, DAVID
b. Cloverdale, CA, Mar. 16, 1937

| | | |
|---|---|---|
| +*Dum Dee Tweedle* | 1995* | |
| | 2002 | New York |
| *Final Alice* | 1976 | Chicago |

### DEMBO, ROYCE
b. Troy, NY, 1933

| | | |
|---|---|---|
| *Audience, The* | 1982 | New York |

### DENCH, CHRIS
b. London, June 10, 1953

| | | |
|---|---|---|
| *We* | 2010 | Melbourne |

### DENNISON, SAM
b. Geary City, OK, Sept. 26, 1926; d. Oklahoma City, May 2004

| | | |
|---|---|---|
| *Rappaccini's Daughter* | 1984 | Philadelphia |

### DENZER, RALPH

| | | |
|---|---|---|
| *Doctor Faustus* | 2002 | New York |

### DE PUE, WALLACE EARL
b. Columbus, OH, Oct. 1, 1932

| | | |
|---|---|---|
| +*Dr. Jekyll and Mr. Hyde* | 1974 | Bowling Green, OH |
| +*True Story of the Three Little Pigs* | 1986 | Bowling Green, OH |

### DEUTSCH, HERBERT ARNOLD
b. Baldwin, NY, Feb. 9, 1932

| | | |
|---|---|---|
| *Dorian* | 1995 | Garden City, NY |

### DEVAL, HARRY

| | | |
|---|---|---|
| +*Rival Clans* | 1847 | Newcastle u. Tyne |

### DIAMOND, DAVID
b. Rochester, NY, July 19, 1915; d. there, June 3, 2005

| | | |
|---|---|---|
| *Noblest Game* | 1975* | |
| | 1999 | New York |

### DIAMOND, STUART
b. New York, Jan. 15, 1960

| | | |
|---|---|---|
| +*Master of the Astral Plain* | 1982 | Brooklyn, NY |

### DIBDIN, CHARLES
b. Southampton, bapt Mar. 15, 1745; d. London, July 25, 1814

| | | |
|---|---|---|
| *Amelia* | 1771 | London |
| +*Annette and Lubin* | 1778 | London |
| +*Benevolent Tar* | 1785 | London |
| *Blackamoor, The* | 1776 | London |
| *Brickdust Man* | 1772 | London |
| +*Broken Gold* | 1806 | London |
| *Captive, The* | 1769 | London |
| +*Chelsea Pensioner* | 1779 | London |
| *Christmas Tale* | 1773 | London |
| +*Cobler, The* | 1774 | London |
| *Damon and Phillida* | 1768 | London |
| *Deserter, The* | 1773 | London |
| *Ephesian Matron* | 1769 | London |
| +*Graces, The* | 1782 | London |
| *Grenadier, The* | 1773 | London |
| +*Hannah Hewitt* | 1798 | London |
| +*Harvest-Home* | 1787 | London |
| *Institution of the Garter* | 1771 | London |
| +*Islanders, The* | 1780 | London |
| *Jubilee, The* | 1769 | London |
| +*Jupiter and Alcmena* | 1781 | London |
| +*Ladle, The* | 1773 | London |
| +*Liberty Hall* | 1785 | London |
| +*Life, Death, of Tom Thumb* | 1785 | London |
| *Lionel and Clarissa* | 1768 | London |
| +*Long Odds* | 1783 | London |
| *Love in the City* | 1767 | London |
| +*Marriage Act* | 1781 | London |
| *Match for a Widow* | 1788 | London |
| *Metamorphoses, The* | 1776 | London |
| +*Mischance, The* | 1773 | London |
| *Old Woman of Eighty* | 1777 | London |
| *Padlock, The* | 1768 | London |
| *Palace of Mirth* | 1772 | London |
| *Plymouth in an Uproar* | 1779 | London |
| +*Poor Vulcan* | 1778 | London |
| +*Quaker, The* | 1775 | London |
| *Recruiting Sergeant* | 1770 | London |
| *Romp, The* | 1771 | Dublin |
| +*Rose and Colin* | 1778 | London |
| *Round Robin* | 1811 | London |
| +*Seraglio, The* | 1776 | London |
| +*Shepherdess of the Alps* | 1780 | London |
| +*Shepherd's Artifice* | 1764 | London |
| *Sultan, The* | 1775 | London |
| +*Touchstone, The* | 1779 | London |
| *Trip to Portsmouth* | 1773 | London |

| | | |
|---|---|---|
| *Two Misers* | 1775 | London |
| *Waterman, The* | 1774 | London |
| +*Wedding Ring* | 1773 | London |
| +*Wives Revenged* | 1778 | London |
| *Yo, Yea* (Dibdin et al.) | 1777 | London |

**DI CHIERA, DAVID**
b. McKeesport, PA, Apr. 8, 1935

| | | |
|---|---|---|
| *Rumpelstiltskin* (with K. Di Chiera) | 1977 | Detroit |

**Di CHIERA, KAREN VANDERKLOOT**

| | | |
|---|---|---|
| *Rumpelstiltskin* (with D. Di Chiera) | 1997 | Detroit |

**DICKINSON, PETER**
b. Lytham St. Annes, Lancashire, Eng., Nov. 15, 1934

| | | |
|---|---|---|
| *Judas Tree* | 1965 | London |

**DICKMAN, STEPHEN**
b. Chicago, Mar. 2, 1943

| | | |
|---|---|---|
| +*Gilgamesh* | 2002 | New York |
| *Real Magic in New York* | 1971 | New York |
| *Tibetan Dreams* | 1990 | New York |

**Di DOMENICA, ROBERT**
b. New York, Mar. 4, 1927

| | | |
|---|---|---|
| +*Balcony, The* | 1975 | Boston |
| *Scarlet Letter* | 1986* | |
| | 1988 | Boston |
| trilogy: | | |
| +*Beatrice Cenci* | 1993* | |
| +*Cenci, The* | 1995* | |
| +*Francesco Cenci* | 1996* | |

**DiGIACOMO, FRANK**

| | | |
|---|---|---|
| *Beauty and the Beast* | 1974 | Syracuse |
| +*Dybbuk, The* | 1978 | Syracuse |
| +*Journey to Bethlehem* (with E. P. Edmon) | 1977 | Baldwinsville, NY |

**DiJULIO, MAX**
b. Philadelphia, Oct. 10, 1919; d. Denver, Jan. 28, 2005

| | | |
|---|---|---|
| *Baby Doe* | 1952 | Denver |

**DINSMORE, WILLIAM**
b. New York, 1903; d. Martha's Vineyard, MA, June 17, 1976

| | | |
|---|---|---|
| *Thorwald* | 1940 | New York |

**DODGSON, STEPHEN (CUTHBERT VIVIAN)**
b. London, Mar. 17, 1924

| | | |
|---|---|---|
| *Margaret Catchpole* | 1979 | Hadleigh, Suffolk, Eng. |

**DOELLNER, ROBERT**
b. Manchester, CT, Mar. 25, 1899

| | | |
|---|---|---|
| *Escape from Liberty* | 1948 | Hartford |

**DOOLITTLE, QUENTEN**
b. Elmira, NY, May 21, 1925

| | | |
|---|---|---|
| *Boiler Room Suite* | 1989 | Banff, AB |
| +*Charlie the Chicken* | 1975 | Toronto |
| *Leviathan Hook* | 1998 | Toronto |
| *Silver City* | 1983 | Banff, AB |

**DORAN, MATT**
b. Covington, KY, Sept, 1, 1921

| | | |
|---|---|---|
| +*Committee, The* (lib. with Lawrence) | 1958 | New York |
| *Fee First* | 1973 | Los Angeles |
| *Marriage Counselor* | 1977 | Los Angeles |

**DORFF, DANIEL**
b. New Rochelle, NY, Mar. 7, 1956

| | | |
|---|---|---|
| *Stone Soup* | 1983 | Philadelphia |

**DORMAN, JOSEPH**
d 1754

| | | |
|---|---|---|
| *Female Rake* | 1736 | London |

**DOUGHERTY, CELIUS**
b. Glenwood, MN, May 27, 1902; d. Effort, PA, Dec. 22, 1986

| | | |
|---|---|---|
| +*Many Moons* | 1962 | Poughkeepsie, NY |

**DOUGLAS, CLIVE**
b. Rushworth, Victoria, Austral., July 27, 1903; d. Melbourne, Apr. 29, 1977

| | | |
|---|---|---|
| +*Eleanor* | 1943 | Brisbane, Austral |

**DOVE, JONATHAN**
b. London, July 18, 1959

| | | |
|---|---|---|
| *Adventures of Pinocchio* | 2007 | Leeds |
| *Enchanted Pig* | 2006 | London |
| *Flight* | 1998 | London |
| *Greed* | 1993 | London |
| *Man on the Moon* | 2006 | Channel 4 (UK) |
| *Palace in the Sky* | 2000 | London |
| *Pig* | 1992 | London |
| *Siren Song* | 1994 | London |
| *Swanhunter* | 2009 | Leeds |
| *Tobias and the Angel* | 1999 | Christchurch |
| *When She Died* | 2002 | BBC |

**DOWDELL, LINDA**

| | | |
|---|---|---|
| *Norma, The* | 1991 | New York |
| *Tree, The* | 2006 | Los Angeles |

**DOYLE, ROGER**
b. Dublin, July 17, 1949

| | | |
|---|---|---|
| *Love of Don Perlimplin* | 1984 | Dublin |

**DRATTELL, DEBORAH**
b. Brooklyn, NY, 1956

| | | |
|---|---|---|
| *Best Friends* | 2002 | New York |
| *Festival of Regrets* | 1999 | Cooperstown, NY |
| *Lilith* | 1997* | |
| | 1998 | Cooperstown, NY |
| *Marina* | 2003 | New York |
| *Nicholas and Alexandra* | 2003 | Los Angeles |

**DRESHER, PAUL**
b. Los Angeles, Jan. 8, 1951

| | | |
|---|---|---|
| *Awed Behavior* | 1993 | San Francisco |
| *Pioneer* | 1990 | Charleston |
| *Power Failure* | 1989 | IA City, IA |
| *Slow Fire* | 1985 | Los Angeles |
| *Tyrant, The* | 2005 | Seattle |
| *Way of How* | 1980 | Seattle |

## DREYFUS, GEORGE (GEORG)
b. Wuppertal, Ger., July 22, 1928

| | | |
|---|---|---|
| *Garni Sands* | 1965* | |
| | 1972 | Sydney |
| *Gilt-Edged Kid* | 1976 | Melbourne |
| *Lamentable Reign of Charles the Last* | 1976 | Adelaide |
| *Takeover, The* | 1969 | Canberra |

## DROBNY, CHRISTOPHER

| | | |
|---|---|---|
| *Lucy's Lapses* | 1987 | New York |

## DROGIN, BARRY J.
b. May 2, 1960

| | | |
|---|---|---|
| *Love and Idols* | 1986* | |

## DROSSIN, JULIUS
b. PA, 1918; d. 2007

| | | |
|---|---|---|
| *Spinoza* | 1981 | New Orleans |

## DRUMMOND, JOHN
b. Lancaster, Eng., 1944

| | | |
|---|---|---|
| *Beleaguered City* | 2002 | Wellington, NZ |
| +*Birds, The* | 1986 | Dunedin, NZ |
| *Bridge to Somewhere* | 2000 | Dunedin, NZ |
| *Impersonating Maurice* | 2004 | Wellington, NZ |
| +*Larnach* | 2007 | Dunedin, NZ |
| *Marriage a la Mode* | 2004 | Wellington, NZ |
| *Mr. Polly* | 2000 | Dunedin, NZ |
| *Plague upon Eyam* | 1983 | Dunedin, NZ |
| *Stars in Orion* | 1999 | Dunedin, NZ |

## DRURY, ROBERT
fl 1732–1735

| | | |
|---|---|---|
| *Fancy'd Queen* | 1733 | London |

## DRYSDALE, LEARMONT
b. Edinburgh, Oct. 3, 1866; d. there, June 18, 1909

| | | |
|---|---|---|
| *Fionn and Terra* | 1909* | |
| *Red Spider* | 1898 | Lowestoft, Eng. |

## DUBUGNON, RICHARD
b. Lausanne, Switz., 1986

| | | |
|---|---|---|
| +*Proposal, The* | 2000 | London |

## DUCKWORTH, WILLIAM
b. Morgantown, NC, Jan. 13, 1943; d. W New York, NJ, Sept. 13, 2012

| | | |
|---|---|---|
| *iOrpheus* (with N. Farrell) | 2007 | Brisbane, Austral. |

## DUDLEY, GRAHAME
b. Sydney, Aug. 4, 1942

| | | |
|---|---|---|
| *Snow Queen* (orch D. Morgan) | 1985 | Adelaide |

## DUFFY, JOHN
b. New York, June 23, 1928

| | | |
|---|---|---|
| *Black Water* | 1997 | Philadelphia |
| *Eve of Adam* | 1955 | Interlaken, MA |
| *Muhammad Ali* | 2000 | New York |

## DUKE, JOHN
b. Cumberland, MD, July 30, 1869; d. Northampton, MA, Oct. 26, 1984

| | | |
|---|---|---|
| +*Captain Lovelock* | 1953 | Hudson Falls, NY |
| *Sire de Maledroit* | 1958 | Schroon Lake, NY |

## DUKE, VERNON [VLADIMIR DUKELSKY]
b. Parfianovka, Russia, Oct. 1903; d. Santa Monica, CA, Jan. 16, 1969

| | | |
|---|---|---|
| *Cabin in the Sky* | 1940 | New York |
| +*Mistress into Maid* (trans. Golubeff) | 1958 | Santa Barbara, CA |
| *Zenda* | 1963 | San Francisco |

## DUNHILL, THOMAS
b. London, Feb. 1, 1877; d. Scunthorpe, Lincolnshire, Mar. 13, 1946

| | | |
|---|---|---|
| +*Enchanted Garden* | 1928 | London |
| *Happy Families* | 1933 | London |
| *Tantivy Towers* | 1931 | London |

## DUNLOP, ISOBEL
b. Edinburgh, Mar. 4, 1901; d. there, May 12, 1975

| | | |
|---|---|---|
| *Rab the Rhymer* (with H. Oppenheim) | 1953 | Aberdeen, Scot |

## DUSAPIN, PASCAL
b. Nancy, France, May 29, 1955

| | | |
|---|---|---|
| +*Faustus, the last Night* | 2006 | Berlin |

## DUSSEK, JOHN (JAN LADISLAV)
b. Tschaslau, Bohemia, Feb. 12, 1760; d. St. Germain-en-Laye, France, Mar. 20, 1812

| | | |
|---|---|---|
| *Captive of Spilburg* (with Kelly) | 1798 | London |

## DUTTON, DANIEL
b. Somerset, KY, 1959

| | | |
|---|---|---|
| +*Stone Man* | 1990 | Louisville, KY |

## DVORKIN, JUDITH
b. New York, 1930

| | | |
|---|---|---|
| +*Blue Star* | 1983 | New York |
| +*Crescent Eyebrow* | 1956 | New York |
| +*Emperor's New Clothes* | 1989 | New York |
| +*Red-Headed League* | 1991* | |
| +*Three Musketeers* | 1992 | New York |
| +*What's in a Name* | 1985 | Binghamton, NY |

## EAKIN, CHARLES G.
b. Pittsburgh, Feb. 24, 1927

| | | |
|---|---|---|
| +*Box, The* | 1968 | New York |

## EARLS, PAUL
b. Springfield, MO, June 9, 1934; d. 1999

| | | |
|---|---|---|
| *Death of King Philip* | 1976 | Brookline, MA |
| *Grimm Duo* | 1976 | Boston |
| *Icarus* | 1982 | Linz, Austria |

## EARNEST, JOHN DAVID
b. TX, 1940

| | | |
|---|---|---|
| *Desperate Waltz* | 1992 | New York |
| *Howard* | 1987 | New York |
| *Legend of Sleepy Hollow* | 1997 | Norfolk, VA |
| *Theory of Everything* | 2007 | New York |

## EASDALE, BRIAN
b. Manchester, Eng., Aug. 10, 1909; d. London, Oct. 30, 1995

| | | |
|---|---|---|
| *Corn King* | 1935* | |
| | 1950 | London |
| *Sleeping Children* | 1951 | Cheltenham, Eng. |

EASTMAN, DONNA KELLY
  b. 1945
    +*Mirror, The*                    1973*
                                      1998    Bloomington, IN
    *Sir Gawain and the Green Knight* 2000    Greensboro, NC
EASTON, MICHAEL
  b. Stevenage, Hertfordshire, Eng., 1954; d. London, Feb. 5, 2004
    *Beauty and the Beast*            1989    Melbourne
    *Cinderella*                      1989*
    *Little Redinka*                  1991    Melbourne
    *Obelisk, The*                    1984*
    +*Selfish Giant*                  1994*
    +*Snow Queen*                     1986    Melbourne
EASTWOOD, THOMAS
  b. Hawley, Hampshire, Eng., Mar. 12, 1922; d. Oct. 25, 1999
    *Christopher Sly*                 1960    London
    *Rebel, The*                      1969    BBC
EATON, JOHN
  b. Bryn Mawr, PA, Mar. 30, 1935
    *Antigone*                        1999    Chicago
    *Cry of Clytaemnestra*            1980    Bloomington, IN
    *Curious Case of Benjamin Button* 2010    New York
    *Danton and Robespierre*          1978    Bloomington, IN
    +*Don Quixote*                    1996    Chicago
    *Golk*                            1996    Chicago
    *Heracles*                        1972    Bloomington, IN
    *. . . inasmuch*                  2002    New York
    *King Lear*                       2004*
    *Let's Get This Show*             1993    Chicago
    *Lion and Androcles*              1974    Indianapolis
    *Ma Barker*                       1957*
    *Myshkin*                         1973    PBS
    +*Peer Gynt*                      1992    New York
    *Reverend Jim Jones*              1989*
    *Tempest, The*                    1985    Santa Fe, NM
    *Travelling with Gulliver*        1997    Boston
ECCLES, JOHN
  b. London? ca. 1668; d. Hampton Wick, Jan. 12, 1735
    *Acis and Galatea*                1701    London
    *British Enchanters*              1706    London
    *Judgment of Paris*               1701    London
    *Loves of Mars and Venus*         1696    London
      (with Finger)
    *Macbeth*                         1696    London
    *Rape of Europa*                  1694    London
    *Rinaldo and Armida*              1698    London
    *Semele*                          ca. 1706*
ECKERT, RINDE
  b. Mankato, MN, Sept. 20, 1951
    +*And God Created*                2000    New York
    +*Highway Ulysses*                2003    Cambridge, MA
    +*Orpheus X*                      2006    Cambridge, MA

EDLIN, PAUL MAX
  b. 1963
    +*Fisherman, The*                 1989    London
EDWARDS, JULIAN (D. H. BARNARD)
  b. Manchester, Eng., Dec. 11, 1855; d. Yonkers, NY, Sept. 5, 1910
    *Brian Boru*                      1896    New York
    *Dolly Varden*                    1901    London
    *Friend Fritz*                    1893    New York
    *Goddess of Truth*                1896    New York
    *Jupiter*                         1892    New York
    *King Rene's Daughter*            1893    New York
    *Madeline*                        1894    New York
    *Patriot, The*                    1907    Boston
    *Victorian*                       1883    London
    *Wedding Day*                     1897    New York
EDWARDS, LEO
  b. Cincinnati, Jan. 31, 1937
    *Harriet Tubman*                  1986    New York
EDWARDS, ROSS
  b. Sydney, Dec. 23, 1943
    *Christina's World*               1983    Sydney
EFFINGER, CECIL
  b. Colorado Springs, July 22, 1914; d. Boulder, CO, Dec. 22, 1990
    *Cyrano de Bergerac*              1968    Boulder, CO
    *Pandora's Box*                   1962*
EGOYAN [YEGHOYAN], EVE
  b. Cairo, ca. 1962
    *Artaud's Cane* (with Krucker, M. White) 1994  Toronto
EICHBERG, JULIUS
  b. Düsseldorf, June 13, 1824; d. Boston, Jan. 19, 1893
    *Doctor of Alcantara*             1862    Boston
    *Two Cadis*                       1868    Boston
EITZEN, LeROY VICTOR
  b. 1920
    *Aria da capo*                    1960*
EL-DABH, HALIM
  b. Cairo, Mar. 4, 1921
    *Blue Sky Transmission*           2002    Cleveland
    +*Birds, The*                     1988*
    +*Black Epic*                     1968*
    +*Drink of Eternity*              1981    Washington
    +*Eye of Horus*                   1967    Boston
    +*Opera Flies*                    1971    Washington
    +*Ptahmose and the Magic Spell*, trilogy:
      *Aton, the Ankh, and the World* 1972    Washington
      *Osiris Ritual*                 1972    Washington
      *Twelve Hours Trip*             1972–73*
ELGAR, EDWARD
  b. Broadheath, Eng., June 2, 1857; d. Worcester, Feb. 23, 1934
    *Spanish Lady*                    1929–33*
                                      1986    London

**ELKUS, JONATHAN**
b. San Francisco, Aug. 8, 1931

| | | |
|---|---|---|
| *Helen in Egypt* | 1970 | Milwaukee |
| *Mandarin, The* | 1967 | New York |
| *Medea* | 1970 | Milwaukee |
| *Outcasts of Poker Flats* | 1959* | |
| +*Tom Sawyer* | 1953 | San Francisco |

**ELLINGTON, DUKE (EDWARD)**
b. Washington, DC, Apr. 29, 1899; d. New York, May 24, 1974

| | | |
|---|---|---|
| *Queenie Pie* (lib. with McGettigan) | 1974* | |
| | 1986 | Philadelphia |

**ELLIOTT, LIONEL.** *See* WILLIAMS, JOSEPH BENJAMIN.

**ELLSTEIN, ABRAHAM**
b. New York, July 9, 1907; d. there, Mar. 22, 1963

| | | |
|---|---|---|
| +*Golem, The* | 1962 | New York |
| *Thief and the Hangman* | 1959 | Athens, OH |

**ELMORE, ROBERT**
b. Ramapatnam, India, Jan. 2, 1913; d. Ardmore, PA, Sept. 22, 1985

| | | |
|---|---|---|
| *It Began at Breakfast* | 1941 | Philadelphia |

**EMILE, ANDERS**
b. Arendal, Norway, 1893; d. Minneapolis, June 5, 1976

| | | |
|---|---|---|
| *King Harald* | 1948 | New York |
| *Life That Is Free* | 1946 | New York |

**ENENBACH, FREDRIC**
b. Des Moines, IA, Dec. 1, 1945

| | | |
|---|---|---|
| *Crimson Bird* | 1979 | Crawfordsville, IA |

**ENG, RANDALL**

| | | |
|---|---|---|
| *Florida* | 2002 | New York |
| *Henry's Wife* | 2009 | New York |

**ENGEL, LEHMAN**
b. Jackson, MS, Sept. 14, 1910; d. New York, Aug. 29, 1982

| | | |
|---|---|---|
| *Brother Joe* | 1953 | Cleveland |
| *Malady of Love* | 1954 | New York |
| +*Pierrot of the Minute* | 1929 | Cincinnati |
| *Soldier, The* | 1956 | New York |

**EÖTVÖS, PETER**
b. Szekelyudvarhely, Hung, Jan. 2, 1944

| | | |
|---|---|---|
| *Angels in America* | 2004 | Paris |

**EPSTEIN, MARTI**
b. Denver, Nov. 25, 1959

| | | |
|---|---|---|
| +*Rumpelstiltskin* | 2009 | Boston |

**EPSTEIN, SOLOMON**
b. Savannah, GA, 1939

| | | |
|---|---|---|
| +*Moby Dick* | 1989* | |
| +*Wild Boy* | 1986 | Philadelphia |

**ESTACIO, JOHN**
b. 1966

| | | |
|---|---|---|
| *Filumena* | 2003 | Calgary |
| *Frobisher* | 2007 | Calgary |

**EWART, FLORENCE MAUD**
b. London, Nov. 1864; d. Melbourne, Nov. 8, 1949

| | | |
|---|---|---|
| +*Courtship of Miles Standish* | 1931 | Melbourne |
| +*Ekkehard* | 1923 | Melbourne |

**EYERLY, SCOTT**
b. Lake Forest, IL, 1958

| | | |
|---|---|---|
| +*House of the Seven Gables* | 2000 | New York |
| +*On Blue Mountain* | 1986 | New York |

**FARBERMAN, HAROLD**
b. New York, Nov. 2, 1929

| | | |
|---|---|---|
| *Diamond Street* | 2009 | Hudson, NY |
| *Losers, The* | 1971 | New York |
| *Medea* | 1961* | |
| *Song of Eddie* | 2004 | Annandale-on-Hudson, NY |

**FARMER, JOHN**
b. Nottingham, Eng., Aug. 16, 1836; d. Oxford, July 17, 1901

| | | |
|---|---|---|
| *Cinderella* | 1883 | Harrow, Eng. |

**FARQUHAR, DAVID**
b. Cambridge, NZ, Apr. 5, 1928; d. Wellington, NZ, Mar. 8, 2007

| | | |
|---|---|---|
| +*Enchanted Island* | 1997* | |
| | 2005 | Wellington |
| +*Shadow, The* (lib. with E. Hill) | 1970* | |
| | 1988 | Wellington |
| +*Unicorn for Christmas* | 1962 | Wellington |

**FARRELL, NORA**

| | | |
|---|---|---|
| *iOrpheus* (with W. Duckworth) | 2007 | Brisbane, Austral. |

**FAX, MARK OAKLAND**
b. West Baltimore, June 15, 1911; d. Washington, DC, Jan. 2, 1974

| | | |
|---|---|---|
| *Christmas Miracle* | 1968 | Washington |
| *Till Victory Is Won* | 1967 | Bermuda |

**FEDELLI, GIUSEPPE (SAGGIONE)**
fl. 1680–1733

| | | |
|---|---|---|
| *Temple of Love* | 1706 | London |

**FEIGIN, JOEL**
b. New York, 1951

| | | |
|---|---|---|
| +*Ferryman, The* | 1997 | New York |
| +*Mysteries of Eleusis* (lib. with Manrique) | 1986 | Ithaca, NY |
| +*Twelfth Night* | 2005 | Durham, NC |

**FELDMAN, JAMES**
b. Rochester, NY, 1940; d. Berea, OH, Nov. 22, 2008

| | | |
|---|---|---|
| *Intruder, The* | 1984 | Berea, OH |

**FELDMAN, MORTON**
b. New York, Jan. 12, 1926; d. Buffalo, NY, Sept. 3, 1987

| | | |
|---|---|---|
| *Neither* | 1977 | Rome |

**FELSENFELD, DANIEL**
b. 1970

| | | |
|---|---|---|
| +*Bloody Chamber* | 2010 | Berkeley, CA |
| *Last of Manhattan* | 2004 | New York |
| *Sumner and All It Brings* | 2004 | New York |

**FENNIMORE, JOSEPH**
b. New York, Apr. 16, 1940; d. Mar. 20, 2000, Bennington, VT

| | | |
|---|---|---|
| +*Apache Dance* | 1975 | New York |
| +*Don't Call Me by My Right Name* | 1975 | New York |

**FERGUSON, SEAN**
  b. Fort Vermilion, Alberta, Canada, 1962
  *Two Graces*                         2004    Toronto
**FERRIS, WILLIAM**
  b. Chicago, Feb. 26, 1937; d. there, May 16, 2000
  *Diva, The*                          1979*
                                       1987    Chicago
  *Little Moon of Alban*               1974*
**FIDDES, ROSS**
  b. Austral., 1944
  *Proposal, The*                      1986    Sydney
**FINE, ELAINE**
  b. Boston
  +*Sister Beatrice*                   2004*
  +*Snow Queen*                        2002*
**FINE, VIVIAN**
  b. Chicago, Sept. 28, 1913; d. Bennington, VT, Mar. 20, 2000
  *Guide to Life Expectancy of a Rose*  1956    New York
  *Memoirs of Uliana Rooney*           1997    Philadelphia
  *Women in the Garden*                1978    San Francisco
**FINGER, GOTTFRIED**
  b. Olomouc? Moravia, ca. 1660; d. Mannheim, buried Aug. 31, 1730
  *Judgment of Paris*                  1701    London
  *Loves of Mars and Venus* (with Eccles)  1696    London
  *Rival Queens* (with D. Purcell)     1701    London
  *Secular Masque* (with D. Purcell)   1700    London
  *Virgin Prophetess*                  1701    London
**FINK, HAROLD**
  d Aug. 2, 1999
  *Goodman Brown*                      1968    Painesville, OH
**FINK, MYRON**
  b. Chicago, Apr. 19, 1932
  *Animalopera*                        2004    New York
  *Boor, The*                          1955    St. Louis
  *Chinchilla*                         1986    Binghamton, NY
  *Conquistador, The*                  1997    San Diego
  *Edith Wharton*                      2003    San Diego
  *Island of Tomorrow*                 1986    New York
  *Jeremiah*                           1962    Binghamton, NY
  *Judith and Holofernes*              1978    Purchase, NY
  *Susanna and the Elders*             1956    Vienna
**FINK, ROBERT MARTIN [BOB]**
  b. New York, Dec. 29, 1935
  *Lysistrata & the War*               1967    Detroit
**FINNEY, ROSS LEE**
  b. Wells, MN, Dec. 23, 1906; d. Carmel, CA, Feb. 4, 1997
  +*Computer Marriage*                 1989*
  +*Nun's Priest's Tale*               1965    Hanover, NH
  +*Weep Torn Land*                    1984*
**FINNISSY, MICHAEL**
  b. London, Mar. 17, 1946
  +*Thérèse Raquin*                    1993    London
  +*Undivine Comedy*                   1988    Paris

**FIRSOVA, ELENA**
  b. Leningrad (now St. Petersburg), Mar. 21, 1950
  +*Nightingale and the Rose*          1994    London
**FIRST, DAVID**
  b. Philadelphia, 1953
  *Manhattan Book of the Dead*         1995    New York
**FISHER, JOHN ABRAHAM**
  b. Dunstable/London, 1744; d. Dublin/London, May/June 1806
  *Court of Alexander*                 1770    London
  *Golden Pippen*                      1773    London
  *Love Finds the Way*                 1777    London
    (with T. Arne, Sacchini)
**FISHER, TRUMAN REX**
  b. 1929
  +*Lysistrata*                        1957*
**FITTS, CHARLES**
  b. GA, 1953
  *Amonontillado*                      2010*
**FITZWILLIAM, EDWARD**
  b. Deal, Kent, Aug. 1, 1824; d. London, Jan. 20, 1857
  +*Love's Alarms*                     1853    London
  *Queen of a Day*                     1841    London
**FLAGELLO, NICOLAS**
  b. New York, Mar. 15, 1928; d. New Rochelle, NY, Mar. 16, 1994
  *Judgment of St. Francis*            1966    New York
  +*Pied Piper*                        1970    New York
  +*Sisters, The*                      1961    New York
**FLANAGAN, THOMAS J.**
  b. New Haven, Nov. 30, 1927
  *I Rise in Flame*                    1980    New York
  *Statues on a Lawn*                  1983    New York
**FLANAGAN, WILLIAM**
  b. Detroit, Aug. 14, 1923; d. New York, Aug. 31, 1969
  *Bartleby*                           1961    New York
**FLECKNOE, RICHARD**
  d London? ca. 1676
  +*Ariadne Deserted by Theseus*       ca. 1654*
  +*Marriage of Oceanus and*           ca. 1659*
    *Brittania*
**FLETCHER, GRANT**
  b. Hartsburg, IL, Oct. 25, 1913; d. Tempe, AR May 4, 2002
  *Carrion Crow*                       1953    Bloomington, IL
  *Sack of Calabasas*                  1964    Phoenix, AR
**FLORIO, CARYL [WILLIAM JAMES ROBJOHN]**
  b. Tavistock, Devon, Eng., Nov. 3, 1843; d. Morganton, NC, Nov. 21, 1920
  *Uncle Tom's Cabin*                  1882    Philadelphia
  *Undine*                             ca. 1920    Philadelphia
**FLORIO, CHARLES H.**
  b. Eng., ca. 1768; d. Moscow, 1819
  *Egyptian Festival*                  1800    London
  *Outlaws, The*                       1798    London

FLOYD, CARLISLE
b. Latta, SC, June 11, 1926

| | | |
|---|---|---|
| +*Bilby Doll* | 1976 | Houston |
| +*Cold Sassy Tree* | 2000 | Houston |
| +*Flower and Hawk* | 1972 | Jacksonville, FL |
| +*Fugitives* | 1951 | Tallahassee, FL |
| +*Markheim* | 1966 | New Orleans |
| +*Of Mice and Men* | 1970 | Seattle |
| +*Passion of Jonathan Wade* | 1962 | New York |
| +*Slow Dusk* | 1949 | Syracuse, NY |
| +*Sojourner and Mollie Sinclair* | 1963 | Raleigh, NC |
| +*Susannah* | 1955 | Tallahassee, FL |
| +*Willie Stark* | 1981 | Houston |
| +*Wuthering Heights* | 1958 | Santa Fe, NM |

FORBES, HENRY
b. London, 1804; d. there Nov. 24, 1859

| | | |
|---|---|---|
| *Fairy Oak* | 1845 | London |

FORD, ERNEST
b. Warminster, Wiltshire, Eng., Feb. 17, 1858; d. London, June 2, 1919

| | | |
|---|---|---|
| *Jane Annie* | 1893 | London |
| *Joan* | 1890 | London |
| *Wedding Eve* (with Toulmouche, "Yvolde") | 1892 | London |

FORE, BURDETTE
b. Lodi, CA

| | | |
|---|---|---|
| *Aria da capo* | 1951 | Stockton, CA |

FORREST, HAMILTON
b. Chicago, Jan. 8, 1901 ; d. London, Dec. 26, 1963

| | | |
|---|---|---|
| +*Daelia* | 1954 | Interlochen, MI |
| +*Don Fortunato* | 1952 | Interlochen, MI |
| +*Matinee Idyll* | 1954 | Interlochen, MI |

FORSTER, ARNOLD (WILFRED ALLEN)
b. Sheffield, Eng., Dec. 6, 1896; d. London, Sept. 30, 1963

| | | |
|---|---|---|
| *Lord Bateman* | 1958 | London |

FOSS, LUKAS
b. Berlin, Ger., Aug. 15, 1922; d. New York, Feb. 1, 2009

| | | |
|---|---|---|
| *Griffelkin* | 1955 | NBC |
| *Introductions and Good-Byes* | 1960 | New York |
| *Jumping Frog of Calaveras Country* | 1950 | Bloomington, IN |

FOX, ERIKA
b. Vienna, Oct. 3, 1936

| | | |
|---|---|---|
| *Bet, The* | 1990 | London |
| *Dancer Hotoke* | 1991 | London |

FOX, MALCOLM
b. Windsor, Eng., Oct. 13, 1946; d. Adelaide, Nov. 17, 1997

| | | |
|---|---|---|
| *Iron Man* | 1987 | Adelaide |
| *Sid the Serpent* | 1977 | Adelaide |
| *Silence Tree* | 1989 | Perth, Austral. |
| *Zoggy* | 1987 | Melbourne |

FRAGALE, FRANK D.
b. Sciara, Italy 1894; d. 1955

| | | |
|---|---|---|
| *Dr. Jekyll and Mr. Hyde* | 1953 | Berkeley, CA |

FRANCE, SANDRA
b. 1968

| | | |
|---|---|---|
| *Playing with Fire* | 2010 | Melbourne |

FRANCHETTI, ALDO
b. Mantua, Italy, 1883; d. Hollywood, CA, Feb. 13, 1948

| | | |
|---|---|---|
| +*Namiko-San* | 1925 | Chicago |

FRANCHETTI, ARNOLD
b. Lucca, Italy, 1909; d. Cromwell, CT, Mar. 7, 1993

| | | |
|---|---|---|
| *Anachronism* | 1956 | Hartford |
| *Dowser, The* | 1956* | |
| +*Dracula* | 1979* | |
| *Game of Cards* | 1955 | Hartford |
| +*Lion, The* | 1950 | New London, CT |
| *Married Men Go to Hell* | 1975* | |
| *Maypole* | 1952 | Westport, CT |
| *Notturno in La* | 1966 | Hartford |
| *Prelude and Fugue* | 1959 | Hartford |
| *Princess, The* | 1952 | Hartford |
| *Soap Opera* | 1973 | Hartford |
| *Suncatcher* | 1973 | Hartford |

FRANCIS, WILLIAM
b. ca. 1756; d. 1826

| | | |
|---|---|---|
| *Lady of the Lake* | 1811 | Edinburgh |

FRANKEL, ARI
b. Tel Aviv

| | | |
|---|---|---|
| +*To Scratch an Angel* | 2001 | New York |

FRANKLIN, CARY JOHN

| | | |
|---|---|---|
| *Enchantment of Dreams* | 2004 | Bethesda, MD |
| *Loss of Eden* | 2002 | St. Louis |

FRAZIER, JEFFERSON TODD
b. 1969

| | | |
|---|---|---|
| *Breath of Life* | 2007 | Houston |

FREED, ISADORE
b. Brest-Litovsk, Russia, Mar. 26, 1900; d. Rockville Centre, NY, Nov. 10, 1960

| | | |
|---|---|---|
| *Princess and the Vagabond* | 1948 | Hartford |

FREEDMAN, HARRY (HENRYK FRYDMANN)
b. Łódź, Pol, Apr. 5, 1922; d. Toronto, Sept. 16, 2005

| | | |
|---|---|---|
| *Abracadabra* | 1979 | Courtenay, BC |

FREEMAN, HARRY LAWRENCE
b. Cleveland, Oct. 9, 1869; d. New York, Mar. 21, 1954

| | | |
|---|---|---|
| +*African Kraal* | 1903 | Chicago |
| +*Athalia* | 1916* | |
| +*Ephelia* | 1893 | Denver |
| +*Flapper, The* | 1929* | |
| +*Leah Kleschna* | 1930* | |
| +*Martyr, The* | 1893 | Denver |
| +*Nada* | 1900 | Cleveland |
| +*Octoroon, The* | 1904* | |
| | 1931 | CBS radio |
| +*Plantation, The* | 1914* | |
| +*Prophecy, The* | 1912 | New York |

| | | |
|---|---|---|
| +*Tryst, The* | 1911 | New York |
| *Uzziah* | 1931* | |
| +*Valdo* | 1906 | Cleveland |
| +*Vendetta, The* | 1923 | New York |
| +*Voodoo* | 1928 | New York |
| +*Zululand*, triology: | 1934–47* | |
| *Allah* | 1947* | |
| *Nada and the Lily* | 1944* | |
| *Zulu King* | 1934* | |

**FREER, ELEANOR EVEREST**
b. Philadelphia, May 14, 1864; d. Chicago, Dec. 13, 1942

| | | |
|---|---|---|
| *Brownings Go to Italy* | 1938 | Chicago |
| *Chilkoot Maiden* | 1927 | Skagway, Ala. |
| +*Christmas Tale* | 1929 | Houston |
| *Frithiof* | 1929 | Chicago |
| +*Joan of Arc* | 1929 | Chicago |
| +*Legend of Spain* | 1931 | Milwaukee |
| *Legend of the Piper* | 1925 | South Bend, IN |
| +*Little Women* | 1934 | Chicago |
| +*Masque of Pandora* | 1935 | Chicago |
| *Massimilliano* | 1926 | Lincoln, NE |
| +*Preciosa* | 1928* | |

**FRIML, RUDOLF**
b. Prague, Dec. 2, 1879; d. Los Angeles, Nov. 12, 1972

| | | |
|---|---|---|
| *Rose-Marie* (with H. Stothart) | 1924 | Los Angeles |

**FRY, WILLIAM**
b. Philadelphia, Aug. 19, 1813; d. Santa Cruz, VI, Dec. 21, 1864

| | | |
|---|---|---|
| *Leonora* | 1845 | Philadelphia |
| *Notre-Dame of Paris* | 1864 | Philadelphia |

**FUCHS, PETER PAUL**
b. Vienna, Oct. 30, 1916; d. Greensboro, NC, Mar. 26, 2007

| | | |
|---|---|---|
| *Heretic, The* | 1978* | |
| *Serenade at Noon* | 1965 | Baton Rouge, LA |
| +*White Agony* | 1989 | Berlin |

**FULLAM, VICTORIA**

| | | |
|---|---|---|
| +*Mermaid, The* | 1986 | Minneapolis |

**FULLER-HALL, SARAH**
b. NC

| | | |
|---|---|---|
| *Ransom of Red Chief* | 1982 | Boone, NC |

**FUNK, ERIC D.**
b. Deer Lodge, MT, 1949

| | | |
|---|---|---|
| *Pamelia* | 1989 | Billingsley, MT |

**FUSSELL, CHARLES**
b. Winston-Salem, NC, Feb. 14, 1938

| | | |
|---|---|---|
| *Astronaut's Tale* | 1998 | Boston |
| +*Julian* | 1972 | Winston-Salem, NC |

**GABRIEL, VIRGINIA (MARY ANN)**
b. Banstead, Surrey, Eng., Feb. 7, 1825; d. London, Aug. 7, 1877

| | | |
|---|---|---|
| *Follies of a Night* | ca. 1870 | London |

**GABURO, KENNETH**
b. Somerville, NJ, July 5, 1926; d. IA City, IA, Jan. 26, 1993

| | | |
|---|---|---|
| *Snow Queen* | 1952 | Lake Charles, LA |
| +*Widow, The* | 1961 | Saratoga Springs, NY |

**GAL, YOAV**
b. Israel, 19??

| | | |
|---|---|---|
| +*Dwarf, The* | 2003 | Brooklyn, N.Y |
| *Mao Zedong* | 1999 | New York. |
| +*Venus in Furs* | 2004 | New York |

**GALLIARD, JOHN**
b. Ceile, Ger., ca. 1687; d. London, 1749

| | | |
|---|---|---|
| *Calypso and Telemachus* | 1712 | London |
| *Circe* | 1719 | London |
| *Decius and Paulina* | 1718 | London |
| *Happy Captive* | 1741 | London |
| *Pan and Syrinx* | 1718 | London |

**GALLOWAY, JAMES "SANTA FE"**
b. Pekin, IL, Aug. 20, 1938; d. Albuquerque, NM, Aug. 30, 2003

| | | |
|---|---|---|
| +*Mirage* | 2003 | Albuquerque, NM |
| +*Pastoral* | 1988 | Albuquerque, NM |
| +*Rococo Confessional* | 1999 | Albuquerque, NM |
| +*Solid House* | 1998 | Albuquerque, NM |

**GARDNER, JOHN LINTON**
b. Manchester, Eng., Mar. 2, 1917; d. Dec. 12, 2011

| | | |
|---|---|---|
| *Bel and the Dragon* | 1973 | London |
| *Moon and Sixpence* | 1957 | London |
| *Tobermory* | 1977 | London |
| *Visitors, The* | 1972 | Aldeburgh |

**GARDNER, KAY**
b. Freeport, NY, Feb. 8, 1941; d. 2002

| | | |
|---|---|---|
| *Ladies Voices* | 1981* | |

**GARFEIN, HERSHEL**

| | | |
|---|---|---|
| +*Rosencrantz and Guildenstern* | 2006 | New York |

**GARWOOD, MARGARET**
b. Haddonfield, NJ, Mar. 22, 1927

| | | |
|---|---|---|
| +*Joringel* | 1987 | Roxborough, PA |
| +*Nightingale and the Rose* | 1973 | Chester, PA |
| +*Rappaccini's Daughter* | 1980 | Philadelphia |
| +*Scarlet Letter* | 2010 | Phiadelphia |
| *Trojan Women* | 1967 | Chester, PA |

**GARZA, EDWARD CAMERON**
b. San Antonio, TX, 1939

| | | |
|---|---|---|
| *Blue Angel* | 1973 | Tucson, AZ |
| +*Marriage Proposal* | 1984 | Brooklyn, NY |

**GASPARINI, FRANCESCO**
b. Camaiore, near Lucca, Italy, Mar. 5, 1668; d. Rome, Mar. 22, 1727

| | | |
|---|---|---|
| *Love's Triumph* | 1708 | London |
| (with G. Gasparini, C. F. Cesarini) | | |

**GASPARINI, GIOVANNI (d 1755)**

| | | |
|---|---|---|
| *Love's Triumph* | 1708 | London |
| (with F. Gasparini, C. F. Cesarini) | | |

GASTINEL, M

*Robert the Devil* (with Kettenus)      1868      London

GATES, CRAWFORD M.

b. UT, 1921

| | | |
|---|---|---|
| *Joseph! Joseph!* | 2004 | Salt Lake City |
| *Promised Valley* | 1947 | Salt Lake City |

GATTY, NICHOLAS

b. Bradfield, Eng., Sept. 13, 1874; d. London, Nov. 10, 1946

| | | |
|---|---|---|
| *Duke or Devil* | 1909 | Manchester |
| *Greysteel* | 1906 | Sheffield, Eng. |
| *King Alfred and the Cakes* | 1930 | London |
| *Macbeth* | 1920* | |
| +*Prince Ferelon* | 1919 | London |
| *Tempest, The* | 1920 | London |

GAUGHAN, JACK

| | | |
|---|---|---|
| *Abelard and Heloise* | 1980 | New York |

GEBUHR, ANNE K.

b. Des Moines, IA?

| | | |
|---|---|---|
| *Bonhoeffer* | 2000 | Houston |

GEORGE, GRAHAM

b. Norwich, Eng., Apr. 11, 1912; d. Kingston, ON, Dec. 9, 1993

| | | |
|---|---|---|
| *Evangeline* | 1948 | Kingston, ON |
| +*King for Corsica* | 1981 | Kingston, ON |

GERHARD, ROBERTO

b. Valls, Catalonia, Sept. 25, 1896; d. Cambridge, Eng., Jan. 5, 1970

| | | |
|---|---|---|
| +*Duenna, The* | 1951 | Wiesbaden, Ger |

GERMAN, EDWARD

b. Whitchurch, Shropshire, Feb. 17, 1862; d. London, Nov. 11, 1936

| | | |
|---|---|---|
| *Fallen Fairies* | 1909 | London |
| *Merrie England* | 1902 | London |
| *Tom Jones* | 1907 | London |

GERRISH-JONES, ABBIE

b. Vallejo, CA, Sept. 10, 1863; d. Seattle, WA, 1929

| | | |
|---|---|---|
| *Priscilla* | 1887* | |
| *Snow Queen* | 1918 | San Francisco |

GERSHWIN, GEORGE

b. Brooklyn, NY, Sept. 26, 1898; d. Hollywood, CA, July 11, 1937

| | | |
|---|---|---|
| *Blue Monday* | 1922 | New York |
| *Porgy and Bess* | 1935 | New York |

GESSNER, JOHN

| | | |
|---|---|---|
| *Faust Counter Faust* | 1971 | Minneapolis |

GIANNINI, VITTORIO

b. Philadelphia, Oct. 19, 1903; d. New York, Nov. 28, 1966

| | | |
|---|---|---|
| *Beauty and the Beast* | 1938 | CBS Radio |
| *Blennerhasset* | 1939 | CBS Radio |
| +*Harvest, The* | 1961 | Chicago |
| *Lucidia* | 1934 | Munich |
| *Rehearsal Cali* | 1962 | New York |
| *Scarlet Letter* | 1938 | Hamburg |
| *Servant of Two Masters* | 1967 | New York |
| +*Taming of the Shrew* | 1953 | Cincinnati |

GIBBONS, CHRISTOPHER

b. Westminster, Eng., bapt. Aug. 22, 1615; d. there, Oct. 20, 1676

| | | |
|---|---|---|
| *Cupid and Death* (with M. Locke) | 1653 | London |

GIBBS, CECIL ARMSTRONG

b. Great Bradow, nr. Chelmsford, Eng., Aug. 10, 1889; d. Chelmsford, May 12, 1960

| | | |
|---|---|---|
| *Blue Peter* | 1923 | London |
| *Midsummer Madness* | 1924 | London |

GIBSON, JON

| | | |
|---|---|---|
| *Violet Fire* | 2006 | Brooklyn, NY |

GIDEON, MIRIAM

b. Greeley, CO, Oct. 23, 1906; d. New York, June 18, 1996

| | | |
|---|---|---|
| *Fortunato* | 1958* | |

GIFFORD, HELEN

b. Hawthorn, Austral., Sept. 5, 1935

| | | |
|---|---|---|
| *Iphigenia in Exile* | 1985* | |
| | 1990 | Melbourne, ABC radio |
| +*Regarding Faustus* | 1983* | |
| | 1988 | Melbourne |

GILBERT, ANTHONY

b. London, July 26, 1934

| | | |
|---|---|---|
| +*Chakravaka-Bird* | 1982 | London, BBC |
| *Scene Machine* | 1971 | Kassel |

GILBERT, HENRY F.

b. Somerville, MA Sept. 26, 1868; d. Cambridge, MA, May 19, 1928

| | | |
|---|---|---|
| *Fantasy in Delft* | 1919* | |
| *Uncle Remus* | 1905–7* | |

GILBERT, PATRICIA

| | | |
|---|---|---|
| +*Question of Love* | 1985 | London |

GILBERT, PIA

b. Kippenheim, Ger., June 1, 1921

| | | |
|---|---|---|
| +*Dialects* | 1994 | Bonn |

GILFERT, CHARLES

b. Prague?, 1787; d. New York, July 30, 1829

| | | |
|---|---|---|
| *Spanish Patriots* | 1809 | New York |
| *Virgin of the Sun* | 1823 | Philadelphia |

GILLIS, DON

b. Cameron, MO, June 17, 1912; d. Columbia, SC, Jan. 10, 1978

| | | |
|---|---|---|
| +*Gift of the Magi* | 1965 | Ft. Worth, TX |
| +*Legend of Star Valley Junction* | 1969 | New York |
| +*Libretto, The* | 1961 | Norman, OK |
| +*Nazarene, The* | 1970 | Ridgecrest, NC |
| +*Pep Rally* | 1957 | Interlochen, MI |

GIORDANI, TOMMASO

b. Naples, ca. 1730; d. Dublin, Feb. 1806

| | | |
|---|---|---|
| *Calypso* | 1785 | Dublin |
| *Cottage Festival* | 1796 | Dublin |
| *Distressed Knight* | 1791 | Dublin |
| *Don Fulminone* | 1765 | Dublin |
| *Enchanter, The* | 1765 | Dublin |
| *Enchantress, The* | 1783 | Dublin |

| | | |
|---|---|---|
| *Gibraltar* | 1783 | Dublin |
| *Happy Disguise* | 1784 | Dublin |
| *Haunted Castle* | 1783 | Dublin |
| *Love in Disguise* | 1766 | Dublin |
| *Maid of the Mill* | 1765 | Dublin |
| *Phillis at Court* | 1767 | Dublin |
| *Ward of the Castle* | 1793 | London |

GLANVILLE-HICKS, PEGGY
b. Melbourne, Dec. 29, 1912; d. Sydney, June 15, 1990

| | | |
|---|---|---|
| +*Glittering Gate* | 1959 | New York |
| *Nausicaa* | 1961 | Athens |
| *Sappho* | 1963* | |
| +*Transposed Heads* | 1954 | Louisville, KY |

GLASGOW, SCOTT
b. Fairport, NY

| | | |
|---|---|---|
| *Prince of Venosa* | 1998* | |

GLASS, PHILIP
b. Baltimore, Jan. 31, 1937

| | | |
|---|---|---|
| +*Akhnaten* | 1984 | Stuttgart |
| *Appomattox* | 2007 | San Francisco |
| *CIVIL warS, Act V* | 1984 | Rome |
| *Einstein on the Beach* | 1976 | Avignon |
| *Fall of the House of Usher* | 1988 | Louisville, KY |
| +*Galileo, Galilei* (with A. Weinstein, M. Zimmerman) | 2002 | Chicago |
| *Hydrogen Jukebox* | 1990 | Charleston, SC |
| *In the Penal Colony* | 2000 | Seattle |
| *Juniper Tree* (with R. Moran) | 1985 | Cambridge, MA |
| *Madrigal Opera* | 1980 | Amsterdam |
| *Making of the Representative* | 1988 | Houston |
| *Marriages between Zones 3, 4, and 5* | 1995 | New York |
| *Monsters of Grace* | 1998 | Los Angeles |
| *1000 Airplanes* | 1988 | Vienna |
| +*Photographer, The* (lib. with Malasch) | 1982 | Amsterdam |
| +*Satyagraha* (text with De Jong) | 1981 | Rotterdam |
| *Sound of a Voice* | 2003 | Cambridge, MA |
| *Voyage, The* | 1992 | New York |
| *Waiting for the Barbarians* | 2005 | Erfurt, Ger. |

GLEASON, FREDERICK G.
b. Middletown, CT, Dec. 18, 1848; d. Chicago, Dec. 6, 1903

| | | |
|---|---|---|
| *Montezuma* | 1885* | |
| +*Otho Visconti* | 1907 | Chicago |

GLICKMAN, GENE
b. 1934

| | | |
|---|---|---|
| *Bread & Roses* (with M. Shen) | 2000 | New York |

GLOVER, JOHN WILLIAM
b. Dublin, June 19, 1815; d. there, Dec. 18, 1899

| | | |
|---|---|---|
| *Deserted Village* | 1880 | London |

GLOVER, (WILLIAM) HOWARD
b. London, June 6, 1819; d. New York, Oct. 28, 1875

| | | |
|---|---|---|
| +*Ruy Blas* | 1861 | London |

GOEHR, ALEXANDER
b. Berlin, Aug. 10, 1932

| | | |
|---|---|---|
| *Arden Must Die* | 1967 | Hamburg |
| +*Behold the Sun* | 1985 | Duisburg, Ger. |
| +*Kantan and Damask Drum* (lib. with S. Koto) | 1999 | Dortmund, Ger. |
| *Naboth's Vineyard* | 1968 | London |
| *Shadowplay* | 1970 | London |
| +*Sonata about Jerusalem* | 1971 | Jerusalem |
| *Triptych* | 1990 | Aldeburgh |

GOLDENTHAL, ELLIOT
b. Brooklyn, NY, May 2, 1954

| | | |
|---|---|---|
| *Grendel* | 2006 | Los Angeles |

GOLDMAN, EDWARD MERRILL
b. Manchester, CT, July 2, 1917

| | | |
|---|---|---|
| +*David* | 1967* | |
| +*Macbeth* | 1961* | |
| +*Rocket, The* | 1960* | |

GOLDSCHMIDT, BERTHOLD
b. Hamburg, Jan. 18, 1903; d. London, Oct. 17, 1996

| | | |
|---|---|---|
| *Beatrice Cenci* | 1952 | BBC |

GOLDSCHNEIDER, GARY
b. Philadelphia, May 22, 1939

| | | |
|---|---|---|
| +*Call Me Ishmael* | 2004 | Amsterdam |

GOLDSTAUB, PAUL
b. 1947

| | | |
|---|---|---|
| *Marriage Proposal* | 1978 | Mankato, MN |
| +*Rocket, The* | 1960* | |
| *Trojan Women* | 1986 | St. Paul, MN |

GOLDSTEIN, LEE
b. Woodbury, NJ, 1963; d. Chicago, Jan. 12, 1990

| | | |
|---|---|---|
| *Fan, The* | 1989 | Chicago |

GOODMAN [GUTTMANN], ALFRED
b. Berlin, Mar. 1, 1920; d. there Aug. 15, 1999

| | | |
|---|---|---|
| *Audition, The* | 1954 | Athens, OH |
| *Lady and the Maid* | 1981* | |

GOODMAN, JOHN

| | | |
|---|---|---|
| *Garden of Flowers* | 1987 | Boston |

GOOSSENS, EUGENE
b. London, May 26, 1893; d. Hillingdon, Middlesex, June 13, 1962

| | | |
|---|---|---|
| *Don Juan de Mañara* | 1937 | London |
| *Judith* | 1929 | London |

GORDON, MICHAEL
b. Miami, FL, July 20, 1956

| | | |
|---|---|---|
| *Acquanetta* | 2010 | New York |
| *Carbon Copy Building* (with Lang, Wolfe) | 1999 | Turin, Italy |
| *Chaos* | 1998 | New York |
| *Van Gogh Video Opera* | 1991 | New York |
| *What to Wear* | 2006 | Los Angeles |

GORDON, PETER
b. New York, June 20, 1951

| | | |
|---|---|---|
| *Birth of the Poet* | 1985 | Brooklyn, NY |
| *Strange Life of Ivan Osokin* | 1994 | New York |

GORDON, PHILIP
b. US, 19??

| | | |
|---|---|---|
| *Shoe of Nably* | 1957* | |
| *Tale from Chaucer* | 1959* | |
| | 1966 | Trenton, NJ |

GORDON, RICHARD

| | | |
|---|---|---|
| *Jane Heir* (with Norquist) | 1989 | New York |

GORDON, RICKY IAN
b. Long Island, NY, 1956

| | | |
|---|---|---|
| +*Autumn Valentine* | 1992 | Omaha |
| *Grapes of Wrath* | 2007 | Indianapolis |
| *Morning Star* | 2002 | Chicago |
| *Tibetan Book of the Dead* | 1996 | Houston |

GOTHAM, NIC
b. nr. Southampton, Eng., 1959

| | | |
|---|---|---|
| *Nigredo Hotel* | 1992 | Stratford, ON |

GOTTLIEB, JACK
b. New Rochelle, NY, Oct. 12, 1930; d. New York, Feb. 23, 2011

| | | |
|---|---|---|
| +*Death of a Ghost* | 1988 | New York |
| +*Listener's Guide* (lib. with E. Field) | 2009* | |
| +*Movie Opera* | 1986 | New York |
| *Tea Party* | 1957 | Athens, OH |

GOUGEON, DENNIS
b. Granby QC, Nov. 16, 1951

| | | |
|---|---|---|
| *Expensive Embarrassment* | 1989 | Toronto |

GOUGH, ORLANDO
b. 1953, Eng.

| | | |
|---|---|---|
| +*Critical Mass* | 2007 | London |
| *Empress, The* | 1994 | BBC Channel 4 |
| *Finnish Prisoner* | 2007 | Lewes, Eng. |
| *Hotel* | 1997 | London |
| *Mathematics of a Kiss* (with Lunn) | 1989 | London |
| *Ring, Lamp, Thing* | 2010 | London |

GOULD, ELIZABETH
b. 1904; d. 1995

| | | |
|---|---|---|
| *Ray and the Gospel Singer* | 1967 | Toledo, OH |

GRABOWSKY, PAUL
b. Lae, Papua, New Guinea, Sept. 27, 1958

| | | |
|---|---|---|
| *Love in the Age of Therapy* | 2003 | Sydney |
| *Mercenary, The* | 1999* | |

GRABU, LOUIS
b. Catalonia; d. after 1693

| | | |
|---|---|---|
| *Albion and Albanius* | 1685 | London |

GRAHAM, JACK [HARRY JEROME]
b. Mishawaka, IN, Sept. 14, 1896

| | | |
|---|---|---|
| *Lord Byron* | 1926 | South Bend, IN |

GRAHAM [DU BOIS], SHIRLEY
b. Indianapolis, IN, Nov. 11, 1896; d. Beijing, Mar. 27, 1977

| | | |
|---|---|---|
| +*Tom-Tom* | 1932 | Cleveland |

GRANGER, MILTON
b. NJ, 1948

| | | |
|---|---|---|
| +*Bluebeard's Waiting Room* | 2007 | Atlanta |
| +*Great Man's Widow* | 1986 | Roanoke, VA |
| +*Proposal, The* | 1988 | Roanoke, VA |
| +*Spark Plugs* | 1986 | Roanoke, VA |
| +*Talk Opera* | 1999 | New York |
| +*Test Tube* | 1993* | |
| +*Uncharted Waters* | 1998 | New York |

GRANT, JULIAN
b. London, 1960

| | | |
|---|---|---|
| *Anger* | 1993 | London |
| *Family Affair* | 1993 | London |
| *Heroes Don't Dance* | 1998 | Cambridge |
| *Jump into My Sack* | 1996 | London |
| *Odd Numbers* | 2002 | London |
| *Odysseus Unwound* | 2006 | London |
| *Out of Season* | 1991 | London |
| *Platform 10* (*Shorts*, with R. Leach) | 1999 | Battersea, London |
| *Proposal, The* | 1987* | |
| *Queen of Sheba's Legs* | 1991 | London |
| *Shadowtracks* | 2007 | London |
| *Skin Drum* | 1989 | Albuquerque, NM |
| *Uninvited, The* | 1997 | London |
| *Very Private Beach* | 2004 | London |

GRANT, ROBIN
b. Bilston, West Midlands, Eng., 1955

| | | |
|---|---|---|
| *Dee* | 2005 | Birmingham |
| +*I Am . . . in Search* | 1994 | London |

GRANTHAM, DONALD
b. Duncan, OK, Nov. 9, 1947

| | | |
|---|---|---|
| *Boor, The* | 1989 | Austin, TX |

GRAVES, WILLIAM
b. 1916

| | | |
|---|---|---|
| *Juggler, The* | 1959 | Washington, DC |

GRAY, VANESSA

| | | |
|---|---|---|
| *Thirty Minute Don Giovanni* (with T. Lole) | 1999 | Leeds |

GREENBAUM, MATTHEW
b. New York, 1950

| | | |
|---|---|---|
| +*Floating Island* | 2000 | Philadelphia |
| *Ovidiana* | 1997 | Philadelphia |

GREENE, MAURICE
b. London, Aug. 12, 1696; d. there, Dec. 1, 1755

| | | |
|---|---|---|
| *Florimel* (*Love's Revenge*) | 1734 | Winchester, Eng. |
| *Judgment of Hercules* | bef. 1740 | London |
| *Phoebe* | 1747* | |
| | 1755 | London |

GREENHUT, BARRY

| | | |
|---|---|---|
| +*Body of Crime* (lib. with Skipitares) | 1996 | New York |
| +*Body of Crime II* (lib. with Skipitares) | 1999 | New York |
| +*Harlot's Progress* | 1998 | New York |

GREENLEAF, ROBERT
  b. 1949
    Under the Arbor                      1992    Birmingham, AL
GRIBBIN, DEIRDRE
  b. Belfast, 1967
    Hey Persephone!                      1998    London
GRIESBACH, JOHN HENRY
  b. Windsor, June 20, 1798; d. London, Jan. 9, 1875
    Belshazzar's Feast (as Daniel)       1834*
                                         1854    London
    Windsor Castle                       1838    London
GRIFFITH, JENNIFER
    +Dream President                     2004    New York
GRIFFITHS, PAUL
  b. Bridgend, Glamorgan, Nov. 24, 1947
    +Jewel Box (arr. of Mozart)          1991    Nottingham, Eng.
    +Small Jewel Box (arr. of Mozart)    1995    New York
GRIFFITHS, WENDY
    +Quiet American                      1998    New York
GRIGSBY, BEVERLY
  b. Chicago, Jan. 11, 1928
    Mask of Eleanor                      1986    Atlanta
GROSS, ERIC
  b. Vienna, Sept. 16, 1926
    Amorous Judge                        1965    Sydney
GROSS, ROBERT
  b. Colorado Springs, CO, Mar. 23, 1914; d. Los Angeles, Nov. 6, 1983
    +Project 1521                        1974    Los Angeles
GROSSMITH, GEORGE
  b. London, Dec. 9, 1847; d. Folkestone, Mar. 1, 1912
    Haste to the Wedding                 1892    London
GRUENBERG, LOUIS
  b. nr. Brest-Litovsk, Aug. 3, 1884; d. Beverly Hills, CA, June 10, 1964
    +Antony and Cleopatra                1955*
    +Delicate King                       1955*
    +Dumb Wife                           1923*
    Emperor Jones                        1933    New York
    Green Mansions                       1937    CBS
    Helena's Husband                     1938*
    Jack and the Beanstalk               1931    New York
    Miracle of Flanders                  1954*
    +One Night of Cleopatra              1954*
    Volpone                              1948–58
GUNDRY, INGLIS
  b. London, May 8, 1905; d, there, Apr. 13, 2000
    +Avon                                1949    London
    +Galileo                             1992*
    +Logan Rock                          1956    Porthcurno, Eng.
    +Partisans, The                      1946    London
    +Prince of Coxcombs                  1965    London
    +Prisoner Paul                       1970    London
    +Return of Odysseus                  1940    London

    +Three Wise Men                      1967    Kings Langley,
                                                 Hertfordshire, Eng.
    +Tinners of Cornwall                 1953    London
    +Will of Her Own                     1973*
                                         1985    London
GUSTAFSON, DWIGHT
  b. Seattle, WA, Apr. 20, 1930
    Hunted, The                          1960    Greenville, SC
    Jailer, The                          1954    Greenville, SC
    Simeon                               2008    Greenville, SC
GYRING, ELIZABETH
  b. Vienna, 1909; d. New York, 1970
    +Night at Sea                        1954*
HADDOCK, JOHN
  b. Austral.
    Madeline Lee (with Campbell)         2004    Sydney
HADLEY, HENRY
  b. Somerville, MA, Dec. 20, 1871; d. New York, Sept. 7, 1937
    Atonement of Pan                     1912    Philadelphia
    Azora                                1917    Chicago
    Bianca                               1918    New York
    Cleopatra's Night                    1920    New York
    Legend of Hani                       1933    Monte Rio, CA
    Nancy Brown                          1903    New York
    Night in Old Paris                   1924    New York
    Safié                                1909    Mainz, Ger
    Semper virens                        1923    Monte Rio, CA
HAGAR, DONALD
    Inspiration                          2002    New York
HAGEMAN, RICHARD
  b. Leeuwarden, Neth., July 9, 1882; d. Beverly Hills, CA, Mar. 6, 1966
    Caponsacchi                          1937    New York
    Crucible, The                        1943    Los Angeles
HAGEMANN, PHILIP
  b. Mt. Vernon, IN, Dec. 21, 1932
    Androcles and the Lion               2001    New York
    Aspern Papers                        1980    Bloomington, IN
    +Dark and Stormy Night               1997    Dallas
    King Who Saved Himself               1987    Chico, CA
    +Music Cure                          1984*
                                         1998    Cedar Rapids, IA
    +Nightingale and Rose                2003    Wichita, KS
    +Paris and Oenone (lib. with S. Gail) 1999   New York
    +Roman Fever                         2003    New York
    +Ruth                                1990*
                                         2003    Carbondale, IL
    +Shaw Sings!                         2008    New York
        Dark Lady of the Sonnets
        Passion, Poison and Petrification
HAGEN, DARON
  b. Milwaukee, Nov. 4, 1961
    Amelia                               2010    Seattle
    Antient Concert                      2005    Princeton, NJ

| | | |
|---|---|---|
| *Bandanna* | 1997* | |
| | 1999 | Austin, TX |
| *Broken Pieces* | 2005 | Los Angeles |
| +*Elephant's Child* | 1994* | |
| +*Sandbox* | 1985 | Houston |
| *Shining Brow* | 1992 | Madison, WI |
| +*Songs of Madness and Sorrow* | 1997 | Tacoma, WA |
| *Vera of Las Vegas* | 1996 | Las Vegas |

**HAILSTORK, ADOLPHUS**
b. Rochester, NY, Apr. 17, 1941

| | | |
|---|---|---|
| *Joshua's Boots* | 1999 | St. Louis |
| *Paul Laurence Dunbar* | 1995 | Dayton OH |
| *Rise for Freedom* | 2007 | Cincinnati |

**HALAHAN, GUY**
b. 1917; d. 1983

| | | |
|---|---|---|
| +*Elanda and Eclipse* | 1957 | London |
| *Spur of the Moment* | 1959 | BBC |

**HALPERN, MARTIN**
b. Bronx, NY, Oct. 3, 1929

| | | |
|---|---|---|
| +*Boy from Deerfield* | 2000 | New York |
| +*Constancy* | 2007 | Brooklyn, NY |
| +*Death of Oedipus* | 2009 | New York |
| +*Death of Peer Gynt* | 2010* | |
| +*Dwarf Trees* | 2008 | Brooklyn, NY |
| +*Lock of Hair* | 2010* | |
| | 2011 | New York |
| +*Purgatory* | 2009 | New York |
| +*Satin Cloak* | 2001 | New York |

**HALPERN, SIDNEY**

| | | |
|---|---|---|
| +*Macbeth* | 1965 | New York |
| +*Monkey's Paw* | 1965 | New York |

**HAMER, JANICE**

| | | |
|---|---|---|
| *Lost Childhood* | 2001 | New York |

**HAMILTON, IAIN**
b. Glasgow, June 6, 1922; d. London, July 21, 2000

| | | |
|---|---|---|
| +*Agamemnon* | 1987* | |
| +*Anna Karenina* | 1982 | London |
| +*Catiline Conspiracy* | 1974 | Stirling, Scot |
| +*Lancelot* | 1985 | Arundel Castle, W Sussex, Eng. |
| +*London's Fair* | 1992* | |
| +*On the Eve* | 1996* | |
| +*Pharsalia* | 1969 | Edinburgh |
| +*Raleigh's Dream* | 1984 | Durham, NC |
| +*Royal Hunt of the Sun* | 1977 | London |
| +*Tamburlaine* | 1977 | BBC |
| +*Tragedy of Macbeth* | 1994* | |

**HAMM, CHARLES**
b. Charlottesville, VA, Apr. 21, 1925; d. Lebanon, NH, Oct. 16, 2011

| | | |
|---|---|---|
| +*Box, The* | 1961 | New Orleans |
| +*Cask of Amontillado* | 1953 | Cincinnati |
| +*Monkey's Paw* | 1952 | Cincinnati |

| | | |
|---|---|---|
| +*Salesgirl, The* | 1955 | Bristol, VA |
| +*Scent of Sarsaparilla* | 1959 | San Francisco |
| +*Secret Life of Walter Mitty* | 1953 | Athens, OH |

**HAMMOND, TOM**

| | | |
|---|---|---|
| +*Rapunzel* | 1953 | Colchester, Eng. |

**HAND, COLIN**
b. N. Lincolnshire, Eng., 1929

| | | |
|---|---|---|
| *King of the Golden River* | 1969* | |

**HANDEL, GEORGE FRIDERIC**
b. Halle, Ger., Feb. 23, 1685; d. London, Apr. 14, 1759

| | | |
|---|---|---|
| *Acis and Galatea* | 1718 | Cannons |
| *Alceste* | 1749* | |
| *Hercules* | 1745 | London |
| *Semele* | 1744 | London |

**HANNAN, PETER**
b. Montreal, Mar. 19, 1953

| | | |
|---|---|---|
| *Diana Cantata* | 2003 | Vancouver |
| *Gang, The* | 1997 | Vancouver |
| +*One Hundred Twenty Songs* | 2002 | Vancouver |

**HANNAY, ROGER**
b. Plattsburgh, NY, Sept. 22, 1930; d. New York, 2006

| | | |
|---|---|---|
| *Fortune of Saint Macabre* | 1964 | Moorhead, MN |
| +*Journey of Edith Wharton* | 1988 | Chapel Hill, NC |
| +*Scenes from a Literary Life* | 1990* | |
| *Two Tickets to Omaha* | 1960 | Moorhead, MN |

**HANSON, HOWARD**
b. Wahoo, NE, Oct. 28, 1896; d. Rochester, NY, Feb. 26, 1981

| | | |
|---|---|---|
| *Merry Mount* | 1933 | Ann Arbor, MI |

**HANSON, WILLIAM F.**
b. Vernal, UT, Oct. 23, 1887; d. 1969

| | | |
|---|---|---|
| +*Bleeding Heart of Timpanogas* | 1939 | Provo, UT |
| *Sun Dance* | 1913 | Vernal, UT |
| +*Täm-Män'-Näcŭp'* | 1928 | Provo, UT |

**HARBISON, JOHN**
b. Orange, NJ, Dec. 20, 1938

| | | |
|---|---|---|
| +*Full Moon in March* | 1979 | Boston |
| +*Great Gatsby* | 1999 | New York |
| *Winter's Tale* | 1979 | San Francisco |

**HARDY, JOHN**
b. Wales, 1957

| | | |
|---|---|---|
| *Flowers* | 1994 | Cardiff |
| *Roswell Incident* | 1997 | Bury St. Edmunds, Eng. |

**HARLE, JOHN**
b. Newcastle upon Tyne, Sept. 20, 1956

| | | |
|---|---|---|
| *Angel Magick* | 1998 | London |
| *Ballad of Jamie Allan* | 2005 | Gateshead, Eng. |

**HARLING, WILLIAM FRANKE**
b. London, Jan. 18, 1887; d. Sierra Madre, CA, Nov. 22, 1958

| | | |
|---|---|---|
| *Deep River* | 1926 | New York |
| *Light from St. Agnes* | 1925 | Chicago |

HARNICK, SHELDON
b. Chicago, Apr. 30, 1924
+*Frustration*                          1968      Washington
HARPER, EDWARD
b. Taunton, Eng., Mar. 17, 1941; d. Apr. 12, 2009
+*Fanny Robin*                          1975      Edinburgh
+*Hedda Gabler*                         1985      Glasgow
*Mellstock Quire*                       1988      Edinburgh
HARPER, WILLIAM
b. 1949
*El Greco*                              1993      New York
*Snow Leopard*                          1989      St. Paul, MN
HARRIS, MATTHEW
b. 1956
+*Tess of the D'Urbervilles*            2000      New York
HARRIS, ROSS TALBOT
b. Amberley, North Canterbury, NZ, Aug. 1, 1945
*Clockmaker, The*                       1979*
*Tanz der Schwäne*                      1993      Wellington
*Waituhi*                               1984      Chirstchurch, NZ
HARRISON, LOU
b. Portland, OR, May 14, 1917; d. Indianapolis, IN, Feb. 2, 2003
*Rapunzel*                              1959      New York
*Young Caesar*                          1971      Aptos, CA
HARRISS, CHARLES
b. London, Dec. 16–17 (midnight) 1862; d. Ottawa, July 31, 1929
*Torquil*                               1900      Toronto
HARROWAY, JOHN
b. 1810; d. 1857
*Arcadia*                               1841      London
HART, FREDERIC
b. Aberdeen, WA, Sept. 5, 1894
*Farewell Supper*                       1984      Brooklyn, NY
*Poison*                                1984      Brooklyn, NY
HART, FRITZ B.
b. Greenwich, Eng., Feb. 11, 1874; d. Honolulu, July 9, 1949
+*Deirdre in Exile*                     1926      Melbourne
*Deirdre of the Sorrows*                1916*
+*Esther*                               1923*
+*Even unto Bethlehem*                  1943      Honolulu
*Fantastics, The*                       1919      Melbourne
*Forced Marriage*                       1928*
+*Isolt of the White Hands*             1933*
+*King, The*                            1921*
*Land of Heart's Desire*                1914*
*Malvolio*                              1919      Melbourne
*Nativity, The*                         1931*
+*Pierrette*                            1914      Sydney
*Riders to the Sea*                     1915*
+*Ruth and Naomi*                       1917      Melbourne
+*St. Francis of Assisi*                1937*
*St. George and the Dragon*             1930      Melbourne

+*Swineherd and the Princess*           1944*
*Travelling Man*                        1920*
+*Vengeance of Faery*                   1947*
*Woman Who Laughed at Faery*            1924      Melbourne
HARTKE, STEPHEN
b. Orange, NJ, July 6, 1952
*Greater Good*                          2006      Cooperstown, NY
HARVEY, EVA NOEL
b. South Africa?, 1900; d. 1984
*Esther*                                1975      Johannesburg
HARVEY, JONATHAN
b. Sutton Coldfield, Warwickshire, Eng., May 3, 1939
+*Inquest of Love*                      1993      London
*Passion and Resurrection*              1981      Winchester, Eng.
*Wagner Dream*                          2007      Luxembourg City
HASKINS, ROBERT JAMES
b. 1937
*Bell Tower*                            1976*
*Legend of Sleepy Hollow*               1976*
HATTON, JOHN LIPTROT
b. Liverpool, Oct. 12, 1809; d. Margate, Sept. 20, 1886
*Pasqual Bruno*                         1844      Vienna
*Queen of the Thames*                   1842      London
*Rose, The*                             1864      London
HAUBIEL, CHARLES TROWBRIDGE (PRATT)
b. Delta, OH, Jan. 30, 1892; d. Los Angeles, Aug. 26, 1978
*Sunday Costs Five Pesos*               1950      Charlotte, NC
HAUFRECHT, HERBERT
b. New York, 1909; d. Albany, NY, June 23, 1998
+*Boney Quillen*                        1951      Chichester, NY
+*Pot of Broth*                         1965*
HAUGEN, LINDA TUTAS
b. Kenosha, WI
*Pocahontas*                            2007      Norfolk, VA
HAWES, WILLIAM
b. London, June 21, 1785; d. there, Feb. 18, 1846
*Broken Promises*                       1825      London
*Climbing Boy*                          1832      London
*Freebooters, The*                      1827      London
*Gay Deceivers* (with M. Kelly)         1804      London
*Not for Me*                            1828      London
*Oracle, The*                           1826      London
*Robber's Bride*                        1829      London
*Rob Roy MacGregor*                     1818      London
*Tit for Tat*                           1828      London
HAWKINS, JOHN
b. 1949
*Echoes*                                1991      London
HAWKINS, MICAH
b. Head of the Harbor, nr. Stony Brook, NY, Jan. 1, 1777; d. New York, July 29, 1825
*Saw-Mill*                              1824      New York

## HAYES, PHILIP
b. Oxford, bapt. Apr. 17, 1738; d. London, Mar. 19, 1797
| | | |
|---|---|---|
| *Telemachus* | 1763 | Oxford |

## HAYES, WILLIAM
b. Gloucester, Eng., bapt. Jan. 26, 1708; d. Oxford, July 27, 1777
| | | |
|---|---|---|
| *Circe* | 1742* | |
| | 1749 | Aston, Eng. |
| *Peleus and Thetis* | ca. 1749 | |

## HAYM, NICOLA FRANCESCO
b. Rome, July 6, 1678; d. London, Aug. 11, 1729
| | | |
|---|---|---|
| *Pyrrus and Demetrius* | 1708 | London |

## HAYS, SORREL (DORIS ERNESTINE)
b. Memphis, Aug. 6, 1941
| | | |
|---|---|---|
| + *Bee Opera* (lib. with Duhamel et al.) | 2003 | New York |
| +*Glass Woman* (lib. with Ordway, Rhodes) | 1989 | New York |
| +*Mapping Venus* | 1998* | |
| *Our Giraffe* | 2008 | New York |
| *TOOWHOPERA* | 2009 | Rome, GA |

## HEAD, MICHAEL
b. Eastbourne, Eng., Jan. 28, 1900; d. Cape Town, Aug. 24, 1976
| | | |
|---|---|---|
| *After the Wedding* | 1972 | London |
| *Day Return* | 1970 | London |
| *Key Money* | 1970 | London |

## HEALEY, DEREK
b. Wargrave, Eng., May 2, 1936
| | | |
|---|---|---|
| +*Mr. Punch* | 1969* | |
| *Seabird Island* | 1977 | Guelph, ON |

## HECKER, ZEKE (ROBERT)
b. Newark, NJ, 1947
| | | |
|---|---|---|
| +*Forest, The* | 2005 | New York |
| *Kafka Quintet* | 1994* | |
| +*Mushrooms* | 1978 | Brattleboro, VT |
| +*Pericles* | 1981 | Brattleboro, VT |

## HECKSCHER, CELESTE DE LONGPRE
b. Philadelphia, Feb. 23, 1860; d. there, Feb. 18, 1928
| | | |
|---|---|---|
| +*Rose of Destiny* | 1918 | Philadelphia |

## HEGGIE, JAKE
b. West Palm Beach, FL, Mar. 31, 1961
| | | |
|---|---|---|
| *Again* | 2000 | New York |
| *At the Statue of Venus* | 2005 | Denver |
| *Dead Man Walking* | 2000 | San Francisco |
| *End of the Affair* | 2004 | Houston |
| *For a Look or a Touch* | 2007 | Seattle |
| *Last Acts (Three Decembers)* | 2008 | Houston |
| *Moby-Dick* | 2010 | Dallas |
| *To Hell and Back* | 2006 | San Francisco |

## HEIDEN, BERNHARD
b. Frankfurt, Aug. 24, 1910; d. Bloomington, IN, Apr. 30, 2000
| | | |
|---|---|---|
| *Darkened City* | 1963 | Bloomington, IN |

## HEINRICH, ANTHONY PHILIP
b. Schönbüchel, Bohemia, Mar. 11, 1781; d. New York, May 3, 1861
| | | |
|---|---|---|
| *Child of the Mountain* | 1821 | Philadelphia |
| *Minstrel, The* | 1835* | |

## HELLERMANN, WILLIAM
b. Milwaukee, July 15, 1939
| | | |
|---|---|---|
| *Three Sisters Who Are Not Sisters* | 1983 | New York |

## HELLUM, MARK
| | | |
|---|---|---|
| +*Departure, The* | 1985 | Houston |

## HENDERSON, ALVA
b. San Luis, Obispo, CA, Apr. 8, 1940
| | | |
|---|---|---|
| +*Last Leaf* | 1979 | Saratoga, CA |
| *Last of the Mohicans* | 1976 | Wilmington, DE |
| +*Medea* | 1972 | San Diego, CA |
| *Swans, The* | 1986* | |
| *West of Washington Square* | 1988 | San Jose, CA |

## HENDERSON, MOYA
b. Quirindi, NSW, Aug. 2, 1941
| | | |
|---|---|---|
| +*Lindy* (lib. with J. Rodriguez) | 2002 | Sydney |

## HENNESSEY, MARTIN
b. 1953
| | | |
|---|---|---|
| *Good Friar* | 2010 | New York |
| *Letter to E. 11th St.* | 2004 | New York |

## HENZE, HANS WERNER
b. Gütersloh, Ger., July 1, 1926; d. Dresden, Oct. 27, 2012
| | | |
|---|---|---|
| *Bassarids, The* | 1966 | Salzburg |
| *Cimarrón, El* | 1970 | Aldeburgh |
| *Cubana, La* | 1974 | New York |
| *Elegy for Young Lovers* | 1961 | Schwetzingen |
| *English Cat* | 1983 | Schwetzingen |
| *Moralities* | 1968 | Cincinnati |
| *We Come to the River* | 1976 | London |

## HERBERT, VICTOR
b. Dublin, Feb. 1, 1859; d. New York, May 26, 1924
| | | |
|---|---|---|
| *Ameer, The* | 1899 | Scranton, PA |
| *Cyrano de Bergerac* | 1899 | Montreal |
| *Fortune Teller* | 1898 | Toronto |
| *Idols' Eye* | 1897 | Troy, NY |
| *Madeleine* | 1914 | New York |
| *Natoma* | 1911 | Philadelphia |
| *Naughty Marietta* | 1910 | Syracuse |
| *Viceroy, The* | 1900 | San Francisco |
| *Wizard of the Nile* | 1895 | New York |

## HERMAN, MARTIN
b. 1953
| | | |
|---|---|---|
| *Scarlet Letter* | 1992 | Berkeley, CA |

## HERRMANN, BERNARD
b. New York, June 29, 1911; d. Los Angeles, Dec. 24, 1975
| | | |
|---|---|---|
| *Child Is Born* | 1955 | CBS |
| *Christmas Carol* | 1954 | CBS |
| *Wuthering Heights* | 1943* | |
| | 1982 | Portland, OR |

## HESS, DAVID ALEXANDER
b. New York, Sept. 19, 1936; d. Tiburon, CA, Oct. 8, 2011
| | | |
|---|---|---|
| *Naked Carmen* (with J. Corigliano) | 1970* | |

**HEWITT, JAMES**

b. Dartmoor?, June 4, 1770; d. Boston, Aug. 2, 1827

| | | |
|---|---|---|
| *Cottagers, The* | 1801 | New York |
| *Don Raphael* | 1804 | New York |
| *Flash in the Pan* | 1798 | New York |
| *Honey Moon* (with Kelly) | 1805 | London |
| *Snow Storm* | 1823 | Atlanta, GA |
| *Spanish Castle* | 1800 | New York |
| *Tammany* | 1794 | New York |
| *Wild Goose Chase* | 1800 | New York |

**HEWITT, JOHN HILL**

b. New York, July 12, 1801; d. Baltimore, MD, Oct. 7, 1890

| | | |
|---|---|---|
| *Vivandiere, The* | 1863 | Augusta, GA |

**HEWITT, MARK**

| | | |
|---|---|---|
| *Lamentations of Doctor Faustus* | 1994 | London |

**HEWITT, THOMAS J.**

b. 1880

| | | |
|---|---|---|
| *Don Quixote* | 1909 | London |

**HILL, ALFRED**

b. Melbourne, Nov. 16, 1870; d. Sydney, Oct. 30, 1960

| | | |
|---|---|---|
| *Auster* | 1922 | Sydney |
| *Don Quixote* | 1904 | Sydney |
| *Giovanni* | 1914 | Sydney |
| *Lady Dolly* | 1900 | Sydney |
| *Moorish Maid* | 1905 | Auckland, NZ |
| *Rajah of Shivapore* | 1917 | Sydney |
| *Ship of Heaven* | 1923 | Sydney |
| *Tapu* | 1903 | Wellington |
| +*Teora* | 1928 | Sydney |
| *Whipping Boy* | 1896 | Wellington |

**HILL, JACKSON**

b. 1941

| | | |
|---|---|---|
| +*Locust Valley Lovesong* | 1993* | |

**HINDEMITH, PAUL**

b. Hanau, Ger., Nov. 16, 1895; d. Frankfurt, Ger., Dec. 28, 1963

| | | |
|---|---|---|
| +*Long Christmas Dinner* | 1961 | Mannheim, Ger. |

**HINES, JEROME**

b. Hollywood, CA, Nov. 8, 1921; d. New York, Feb. 4, 2003

| | | |
|---|---|---|
| *I Am the Way* | 1959 | South Orange, NJ |

**HINKLEY-TURNER, ANNA ELIZABETH**

| | | |
|---|---|---|
| *Lucifer's Choice* | 1994* | |

**HIVELY, WELLS**

b. 1902; d. 1969

| | | |
|---|---|---|
| +*Junípero Serra* | 1953 | Palma de Mallorca |
| *River, The* | 1938* | |

**HO, FRED WEI-HAN**

b. Palo Alto, CA, Aug. 10, 1957

| | | |
|---|---|---|
| +*Chinaman's Chance* (lib. with G. Lim, addit music by Li) | 1989 | Brooklyn, NY |
| *Night Vision* | 2000 | New York |
| *Warrior Sisters* | 2000 | New York |

**HODDINOTT, ALUN**

b. Bargoed, Wales, Aug. 11, 1929; d. Mar. 12, 2008, Swansea, Wales

| | | |
|---|---|---|
| *Beach of Falesá* | 1974 | Cardiff |
| *Magician, The* | 1976 | Welsh radio |
| *Rajah's Diamond* | 1979 | London |
| *Tower* | 1999 | Swansea |
| *Trumpet Major* | 1981 | Manchester |
| *What the Old Man Does* | 1977 | Fishguard, Wales |

**HODKINSON, SYDNEY**

b. Winnipeg, Jan. 17, 1934

| | | |
|---|---|---|
| *Catsman* | 1985 | Houston |
| *St. Carmen of the Main* | 1988 | Guelph, ON |
| *Swinish Cult* | 1975* | |

**HOFFMAN, STAN**

| | | |
|---|---|---|
| *Twilight Voices* | 1999 | Seattle |

**HOFMEYR, HENDRIK**

b. Cape Town, Nov. 20, 1957

| | | |
|---|---|---|
| +*Fall of the House of Usher* | 1988 | Cape Town |
| +*Land of Heart's Desire* | 1981* | |

**HOGG, BENNETT**

| | | |
|---|---|---|
| *Beyond Men and Dreams* | 1991 | London |

**HOIBY, LEE**

b. Madison, WI, Feb. 17, 1926; d. Bronx, NY, Mar. 28, 2011

| | | |
|---|---|---|
| *Beatrice* | 1959 | NBC-TV |
| *Bon Appétit!* | 1989 | Washington |
| *Italian Lesson* | 1982 | Newport, RI |
| *Natalia Petrovna* | 1964 | New York |
| *Scarf, The* | 1958 | Spoleto, Italy |
| *Something New for the Zoo* | 1982 | Cheverley, MD |
| *Summer and Smoke* | 1971 | St. Paul, MN |
| *Tempest, The* | 1986 | Indianola, IA |
| *This Is the Rill* | 1994 | New York |

**HOLBROOKE, JOSEPH**

b. Croydon, Eng., July 5, 1878; d. London, Aug. 5, 1958

| | | |
|---|---|---|
| *Cauldron of Annwn*, trilogy: | | |
|     *Bronwen* | 1929 | Huddersfield |
|     *Children of Don* | 1912 | London |
|     *Dylan* | 1914 | London |
| *Enchanter, The* | 1915 | Chicago |
| *Pierrot and Pierrette* | 1909 | London |

**HOLLIER, DONALD**

b. Sydney, May 7, 1934

| | | |
|---|---|---|
| +*Beggar's Bloody Op'ra* | 1989 | Melbourne |
| +*Heiress, The* | 1988 | Melbourne |
| +*Knights of the Love Knives* | 1981* | |
| +*Myra Breckinridge* | 1998* | |

**HOLLINGSWORTH, STANLEY**

b. Berkeley, CA, Aug. 27, 1924

| | | |
|---|---|---|
| *Grand Bretèche* | 1957 | New York |
| *Harrison Loved His Umbrella* | 1981 | Charleston, SC |
| +*Mother, The* | 1954 | Philadelphia |
| +*Selfish Giant* | 1981 | Charleston, SC |

**HOLLISTER, DAVID M.**
b. 1929

| | | |
|---|---|---|
| *Change of Hearts* | 1985 | New York |

**HOLLOWAY, ROBIN**
b. Leamington Spa, Eng., Oct. 19, 1943

| | | |
|---|---|---|
| *Boys and Girls* | 1995* | |
| +*Clarissa* | 1990 | London |

**HOLMAN, DEREK**
b. Redruth, Cornwall, May 16, 1931

| | | |
|---|---|---|
| *Dr. Canon's Cure* | 1982 | Toronto |

**HOLST, GUSTAV**
b. Cheltenham, Eng., Sept. 21, 1874; d. London, May 25, 1934

| | | |
|---|---|---|
| +*At the Boar's Head* | 1925 | Manchester |
| *Idea, The* | ca. 1898* | |
| *Lansdown Castle* | 1893 | Cheltenham, Eng. |
| *Magic Mirror* | 1896* | |
| +*Perfect Fool* | 1923 | London |
| *Revoke, The* | 1895* | |
| +*Sāvitri* | 1916 | London |
| +*Sita* | 1899–1906* | |
| *Wandering Scholar* | 1934 | Liverpool |
| *Youth's Choice* | 1902* | |

**HOLST, IMOGEN**
b. Richmond, Surrey, Apr. 12. 1907; d. Aldeburgh, Mar. 9. 1984

| | | |
|---|---|---|
| +*Benedict and Beatrice* | 1951 | Devon |

**HOLT, SIMON**
b. Bolton, Lancashire, Eng., Feb. 21, 1958

| | | |
|---|---|---|
| *Nightingale's to Blame* | 1998 | Huddersfield, Eng. |
| +*Who Put Bella in the Wych Elm?* | 2003 | Aldeburgh |

**HOOK, JAMES**
b. Norwich, Eng., June 1746; d. Boulogne, 1827

| | | |
|---|---|---|
| *Apollo and Daphne* | 1773 | London |
| *Catch Him Who Can* | 1806 | London |
| *Cupid's Revenge* | 1772 | London |
| *Diamond Cut Diamond* | 1797 | London |
| *Dido and Aeneas* | 1771 | London |
| *Dilettante, Il* | 1772 | London |
| *Divorce, The* | 1771 | London |
| *Double Disguise* | 1784 | London |
| *Fair Peruvian* | 1786 | London |
| *Fortress, The* | 1807 | London |
| *Invisible Girl* | 1806 | London |
| *Jack of Newbury* | 1795 | London |
| *Killing No Murder* | 1809 | London |
| *Lady of the Manor* | 1778 | London |
| *Music Mad* | 1807 | London |
| *Poll Booth* | 1784 | London |
| *Queen of the May* | 1787 | London |
| *Safe and Sound* | 1809 | London |
| *Sharp and Flat* | 1813 | London |
| *Soldier's Return* | 1805 | London |
| *Tekeli* | 1806 | London |

| | | |
|---|---|---|
| *Too Civil by Half* | 1782 | London |
| *Triumph of Beauty* | 1786 | London |
| *Wilmore Castle* | 1800 | London |
| *Word to Wives* | 1785 | London |

**HOPKINS, ANTONY**
b. London, Mar. 21, 1921

| | | |
|---|---|---|
| +*Dr. Musikus* | 1969 | London |
| *Hands across the Sky* | 1959 | Cheltenham, Eng. |
| +*Lady Rohesia* | 1948 | London |
| *Man from Tuscany* | 1951 | Canterbury, Eng. |
| *Rich Man, Poor Man* | 1969 | Stroud, Eng. |
| *Scena* | 1953 | London, BBC |
| *Ten O'Clock Call* | 1956 | Cheltenham, Eng. |
| *Three's Company* | 1953 | Crewe, Eng. |
| *Time for Growing* | 1967 | Norwich, Eng. |

**HORN, CHARLES EDWARD**
b. London, June 21, 1786; d. Boston, Oct. 21, 1849

| | | |
|---|---|---|
| *Actors al fresco* (with Blewitt, Cooke) | 1823 | London |
| *Ahmed al Ramel* | 1840 | New York |
| +*Annette* | 1822 | Dublin |
| *Bee-Hive* | 1811 | London |
| *Boarding House* | 1811 | London |
| *Dead Fetch* | 1826 | London |
| *Devil's Bridge* (with Braham, Corri) | 1812 | London |
| *Dido* | 1829 | New York |
| *Dirce* | 1821 | London |
| *Election, The* | 1817 | London |
| *Elphi Bey* (with Attwood, Smart) | 1817 | London |
| *Honest Frauds* | 1830 | London |
| *Justice* | 1820 | London |
| *Lalla Rookh* | 1818 | Dublin |
| *Love Spell* | 1831 | London |
| *Magic Flute* | 1833 | New York |
| *Maid of Saxony* | 1842 | New York |
| *Merry Wives of Windsor* | 1824 | London |
| *M.P.* (with T. Moore) | 1811 | London |
| *Narensky* (with Braham, Reeve) | 1814 | London |
| *Ninth Statue* | 1814 | London |
| *Pay to My Order* | 1827 | London |
| *Persian Hunters* (with G. Perry) | 1817 | London |
| *Peveril of the Peak* | 1826 | London |
| *Philandering* (with Braham) | 1824 | London |
| *Quartette, The* | 1829 | New York |
| *Rich and Poor* | 1812 | London |
| *Shepherd of Derwent Vale* | 1825 | London |
| *Tricks upon Travellers* (with Reeve) | 1810 | London |
| *Wedding Present* | 1825 | London |
| *Wizard, The* | 1817 | London |
| *Woodman's Hut* | 1814 | London |

**HORNE, DAVID**
b. Tillicoultry, Scot, Dec. 12, 1970

| | | |
|---|---|---|
| *Friend of the People* | 1999 | Glasgow |

| | | |
|---|---|---|
| *Jason Field* | 1993 | London |
| *Travellers* | 1998 | London |

**HORNE, LANCE**
b. Sheridan, WY, 1977

| | | |
|---|---|---|
| *Three Lost Chords* | 2008 | New York |

**HOROVITZ, JOSEPH**
b. Vienna, May 26, 1926

| | | |
|---|---|---|
| *Dumb Wife* | 1953 | Lowestoft, Eng. |
| *Gentleman's Island* | 1958 | London |

**HORTON, AUSTIN ASADATA DAFORA**
b. Freetown, Sierra Leone, Aug. 4, 1890; d. New York, Mar. 4, 1965

| | | |
|---|---|---|
| *Kykunkor* | 1934 | New York |

**HOUSELEY, HENRY**
b. Sutton in Ashfield, Nottinghamshire, Eng., Sept. 20, 1852; d. Denver, Mar. 13, 1925

| | | |
|---|---|---|
| +*Pygmalion* | 1912 | Denver |

**HOUSTON, MARK**
b. Jacksonville, TX, Dec. 5, 1946; d. Oklahoma City, OK, Feb. 28, 1995

| | | |
|---|---|---|
| *Hazel Kirke* | 1987 | Glens Falls, NY |

**HOVEY, SERGE**
b. New York, Mar. 10, 1920; d. Los Angeles, May 3, 1989

| | | |
|---|---|---|
| +*Dreams in Spades* | 1949 | Philadelphia |

**HOVHANESS, ALAN [CHAMAKJIAN]**
b. Somerville, MA, Mar. 8, 1911; d. Seattle, June 21, 2000

| | | |
|---|---|---|
| +*Blue Flame* | 1959 | San Antonio, TX |
| +*Burning House* | 1964 | Gatlinburg, TN |
| +*Frog Man* | 1987* | |
| +*Lady of Light* | 1974 | MT |
| +*Leper King* | 1969 | Chicago |
| +*Pericles* | 1975* | |
| | 1979 | Shippensburg, PA |
| +*Pilate* | 1966 | Los Angeles |
| +*Spirit of the Avalanche* | 1963 | Tokyo |
| +*Tale of the Sun Goddess* | 1978 | Salinas, CA |
| +*Travellers* | 1967 | San Francisco |
| +*Wind Drum* | 1964 | Gatlinburg, TN |

**HOWARD, BRIAN**
b. Sydney, Jan. 3, 1941

| | | |
|---|---|---|
| *Inner Voices* | 1985 | London |
| *Metamorphosis* | 1983 | Melbourne |
| *Whitsunday* | 1988 | Sydney |
| +*Wide Sargasso Sea* | 1997 | Sydney |

**HOWARD, GEORGE**
b. 1820; d. 1887

| | | |
|---|---|---|
| *Uncle Tom's Cabin* | 1852 | Troy, NY |

**HOWLAND, WILLIAM LEGRAND**
b. Asbury Park, NJ, 1873; d. Long Island, NY, July 26, 1915

| | | |
|---|---|---|
| +*Sarrona* | 1903 | Bruges, Belg. |

**HUEHNS, COLIN**
b. London, 1966

| | | |
|---|---|---|
| *Solid Assets* | 1993 | London |

**HUGHES, ARWEL**
b. Rhosllanerchrugog, Wales, Aug. 25, 1909; d. Cardiff, Sept. 23, 1988

| | | |
|---|---|---|
| *Menna* | 1953 | Cardiff |

**HUGHES, CURTIS**
b. 1974

| | | |
|---|---|---|
| *Deirdre of the Sorrows* | 1997 | Oberlin, OH |
| *Say It Ain't So Joe* | 2009 | Boston |

**HUGO, JOHN ADAM**
b. Bridgeport, CT, Jan. 5, 1874; d. there, Dec. 29, 1945

| | | |
|---|---|---|
| *Temple Dancer* | 1919 | New York |

**HULLAH, JOHN**
b. Berlin, Ger., Sept. 6, 1855; d. there, Apr. 24, 1928

| | | |
|---|---|---|
| *Barbers of Bassora* | 1837 | London |
| *Outpost, The* | 1838 | London |
| *Village Coquettes* | 1836 | London |

**HUMEL, GERALD**
b. Cleveland, OH, Nov. 7, 1931

| | | |
|---|---|---|
| *Proposal, The* | 1958 | Winfield, Kan. |
| *Triangle, The* | 1958 | Oberlin, OH |

**HUMPHREYS, HENRY RAUSCHER (SIGURD)**
b. Vienna, Nov. 27, 1909; d. 1990

| | | |
|---|---|---|
| +*Mayerling* | 1957 | Cincinnati, OH |

**HUNKINS, EUSEBIA SIMPSON**
b. Troy, OH, June 20, 1902; d. Sept. 9, 1980

| | | |
|---|---|---|
| *Magic Laurel Tree* | 1974 | Cleveland |
| +*Smoky Mountain* | 1954 | Monmouth, IL |
| +*Young Lincoln I* | 1959 | Galesburg, IL |
| +*Young Lincoln II* | 1960* | |

**HURD, MICHAEL**
b. Gloucester, Eng., Dec. 19, 1928; d. Petersfield, Hampshire, Aug. 8, 2006

| | | |
|---|---|---|
| +*Aspern Papers* | 1995 | Pt. Fairy, Victoria |
| +*Little Billy* | 1964 | Stroud, Eng. |
| +*Mr. Punch* | 1970 | Gothenburg |
| +*Night of the Wedding* | 1998 | Pt. Fairy, Victoria |
| +*Widow of Ephesus* | 1971 | Stroud, Eng. |

**IMBRIE, ANDREW**
b. New York, Apr. 6, 1921

| | | |
|---|---|---|
| *Angle of Repose* | 1976 | San Francisco |

**INNERARITY, MEMRIE**
b. 1945

| | | |
|---|---|---|
| +*Moonlight Sonata* | 1988 | New York |
| *Phaedra* | 1999 | New York |

**ISAACS, GREGORY SULLIVAN**

| | | |
|---|---|---|
| +*Death of Tintagiles* | 1973 | Indianola, IN |
| +*Henry Faust* | 1993 | Forest Park, IL |

**ITO, GENJI**
b. 1948; d. New York, Apr. 23, 2001

| | | |
|---|---|---|
| *Ghosts* | 1993 | New York |

IVES, SIMON
b. bapt. Ware, Hertfordshire, July 20, 1600; d. London, July 1, 1662
*Triumph of Peace* (with Lawes, Mell)   1634   London

JACKSON, WILLIAM
b. Exeter, Eng., May 29, 1730; d. there, July 5, 1803
*Lord of the Manor*   1780   London
*+Lycidas*   1767   London
*+Metamorphosis*   1783   London

JACOBI, FREDERICK
b. San Francisco, May 4, 1891; d. New York, Oct. 24, 1952
*Prodigal Son*   1944   Palo Alto, CA

JACOBI, GEORGE
b. Berlin, Ger., Feb. 13, 1840; d. London, Sept. 13, 1906
*Don Quixote*   1894   London

JAFFE, ALLAN
*Mary Shelley*   1996   New York

JANAS, MARK
*+Bagatelle*   1985   Houston

JARRETT, JACK
b. 1934
*+Cinderella*   1956   Gainesville, FL
*Cyrano de Bergerac*   1972   Greensboro, NC

JENKINS, KARL
b. Penclawdd, Wales, Feb. 17, 1944
*Eloise*   1997   London

JENKINS, LEROY
b. Chicago, Mar. 11, 1932; d. Brooklyn, NY, Feb. 24, 2007
*Fresh Faust*   1994   Boston
*Mother of Three Sons*   1990   Munich
*Three Willies*   1996   Philadelphia

JEX, DAVID N.
*Purple Gang*   1991   Toledo, OH

JOHN, ALAN
b. May 7, 1958, Sydney
*+Eighth Wonder* (lib. with D Watkins)   1995   Adelaide
*Frankie*   1987   Sydney
*Through the Looking Glass*   2008   Melbourne

JOHNSON, DEAN
*Intrusions*   1982   New York

JOHNSON, DEAN X.
b. Atlanta, July 22, 1955; d. New York, Jan. 4, 1998
*Song of Martina*   1995   New York

JOHNSON, JAMES [JIMMIE] P.
b. New Brunswick, NJ, Feb. 1, 1894; d. Jamaica, NY, Nov. 17, 1955
*+Dreamy Kid*   ca. 1943*
   2006   Ann Arbor, MI
*Organizer, De*   1940   New York

JOHNSON, JENNY OLIVIA
*+Endings, The*   2007   New York
*+Leaving Santa Monica*   2006   New York

JOHNSON, LOCKREM
b. Davenport, IA, Mar. 15, 1924; d. Seattle, WA, Mar. 5, 1977
*+Letter to Emily*   1951   Seattle, WA

JOHNSON, ROBERT
*Macbeth* (with Locke)   1673   London

JOHNSON, SAMUEL
b. 1691; d. 1773
*+Hurlothrumbo*   1729   London

JOHNSON, TOM
b. Greeley, CO, Nov. 18, 1939
*Five Shaggy-Dog Operas*   1978   New York
*+Four Note Opera*   1972   New York
*+Masque of the Clouds*   1975   New York
*Sopranos Only*   1984   Paris
*+Trigonometry*   1997   Hamburg

JOHNSTON, BEN (JAMIN BURWELL Jr).
b. Macon, GA, Mar. 15, 1926
*Carmilla*   1970   New York
*Gertrude*   1956   Urbana, IL

JOHNSTON, FERGUS
b. Dublin, May 21, 1959
*Bitter Fruit*   1992   Dublin

JONES, DANIEL
b. Pembroke, Wales, Dec. 7, 1912; d. Swansea, Eng., Apr. 23, 1993
*Knife, The*   1963   London

JONES, DARNEL
*+Transcendent Voices*   2000   New York

JONES, ELFYN
b. Wales, 1944
*Nightjar*   1999   Battersea, London

JONES, GEORGE THADDEUS
b. 1917
*Break of Day*   1961   WABC-TV
*Cage, The*   1959   Washington

JONES, JEREMY PAYTON
*Menaced Assassin*   1989   London

JONES, JONATHAN
*Enchanted Horse*   1844   New York

JONES, KELSEY
b. South Norwalk, CT, June 17, 1922; d. Montreal, Oct. 10, 2004
*Sam Slick*   1967   Halifax

JONES, RICHARD
b. l. 17th cent.; d. London, Jan. 20, 1744
*Mock Doctor* (with Carey, Seedo)   1732   London

JONES, SIDNEY
b. London, June 17, 1861; d. there, Jan. 29, 1946
*Geisha, The*   1896   London
*King of Cadonia*   1908   London
*My Lady Molly*   1903   London
*San Toy*   1899   London
*See-See* (with F. Tours)   1906   London

JOPLIN, SCOTT
b. prob. nr. Marshall, TX, Nov. 24, 1868; d. New York, Apr. 1, 1917

| | | |
|---|---|---|
| +*Guest of Honor* | 1903 | St. Louis |
| +*Treemonisha* | 1915 | New York |

JOPLING, ORLANDO
b. Eng.

| | | |
|---|---|---|
| *Flying Fox* (after J. Strauss) | 1998 | London |

JORDAN, JULES
b. Willimantic, CT, Nov. 10, 1850; d. Providence, RI, Mar. 5, 1927

| | | |
|---|---|---|
| +*Rip Van Winkle* | 1897 | Providence, RI |

JOSEPHS, WILFRED
b. Newcastle upon Tyne, July 24, 1927; d. London, Nov. 18, 1997

| | | |
|---|---|---|
| +*Alice in Wonderland* | 1988 | Harrogate, Eng. |
| *Appointment, The* | 1966 | BBC |
| *Pathelin* | 1963* | |
| | 1990 | Norrland, Swed. |
| *Prisoner, The* | 1973 | London |
| *Rebecca* | 1983 | Leeds |
| +*Through the Looking Glass* | 1978 | Harrogate, Eng. |

JOUBERT, JOHN
b. Cape Town, South Africa, Mar. 20, 1927

| | | |
|---|---|---|
| *Antigone* | 1954 | London, BBC |
| *In the Drought* | 1956 | Johannesburg |
| *Jane Eyre* | 1998* | |
| *Prisoner, The* | 1973 | Barnet, Eng. |
| *Quarry, The* | 1965 | London |
| *Silas Marner* | 1961 | Cape Town |
| *Under Western Eyes* | 1969 | London |
| *Wayfarers, The* | 1984 | Huntingdon, Eng. |

KAGEN, SERGIUS
b. St. Petersburg, Aug. 22, 1909; d. New York, Mar. 1, 1964

| | | |
|---|---|---|
| *Hamlet* | 1962 | Baltimore |

KALMANOFF, MARTIN
b. Brooklyn, NY, May 24, 1920

| | | |
|---|---|---|
| +*Aesop* | 1969 | Lake Pemigewasset, NH |
| *Audition, The* (lib. with S. Spaeth) | 1968 | Pittsburgh |
| *Bald Prima Donna* | 1963 | New York |
| *Brandy Is My True Love's Name* | 1953 | New York |
| *Canterville Ghost* | 1967 | New York |
| +*Christopher Columbus* | 1976* | |
| +*Delinquents, The* | 1955 | Philadelphia |
| *Empty Bottle* | 1966 | New York |
| *Fit for a King* | 1949 | New York |
| *Give Me Liberty* | 1975 | New York |
| *Godiva* | 1953 | New York |
| +*Great Stone Face* | 1968 | Muncie, IN |
| *Half Magic in King Arthur's Court* | 1963 | Walding River, NY |
| *Harmfulness of Tobacco* | 1979 | New York |
| +*Hipopera* | 1977 | Boise, ID |
| *Insect Comedy* | 1977* | |
| | 1993 | New York |
| +*King David* | 1969 | New York |

| | | |
|---|---|---|
| *Legends Three* | 1969 | New York |
| +*Lizzie Strotter* | 1958 | Des Moines, IA |
| *Magic Beanstalk* | 1976 | Monticello, NY |
| +*Magic Land of Opera* | 1972 | New York |
| *Mr. Scrooge* | 1966 | New York |
| *Noah and the Stowaway* | 1951 | New York |
| +*Opera, Opera* | 1956 | New York |
| +*Photograph—1920* | 1971 | Lake Placid, NY |
| +*Quiet Game of Cribble* | 1954 | New York |
| *Ralph and the Stalking Bear* | 1979 | Monticello, NY |
| +*Smart Aleck and the Talking Wire* | 1976 | New York |
| +*Victory at Masada* | 1968 | Detroit |
| +*Videomania* | 1965 | Granville, OH |
| *You'll Never Get It Off the Ground* | 1980* | |
| *Young Tom Edison* | 1963 | New York |

KAM, DENNIS
b. 1942

| | | |
|---|---|---|
| *Opera 101* | 2009 | Miami, FL |

KANDER, SUSAN
b. Kansas City, MO

| | | |
|---|---|---|
| +*One False Move* | 2005 | Kansas City, MO |
| *She Never Lost a Passenger* | 1997 | Kansas City, MO |
| +*Somebody's Children* | 2002 | Kansas City, MO |

KANITZ, ERNEST
b. Vienna, Apr. 9, 1894; d. Menlo Park, CA, Apr. 7, 1978

| | | |
|---|---|---|
| *Kumana* | 1953* | |
| *Lucky Dollar* | 1958 | Los Angeles |
| *Perpetual* | 1961 | Los Angeles |
| *Room No. 12* | 1958 | Los Angeles |
| *Royal Auction* | 1958 | Los Angeles |
| *Visions of Midnight* | 1964 | Los Angeles |

KAPILOW, ROBERT
b. Dec. 22, 1952

| | | |
|---|---|---|
| *Many Moons* | 1997 | Princeton, NJ |

KARCHIN, LOUIS
b. Philadelphia, Sept. 8, 1951

| | | |
|---|---|---|
| *Romulus* | 2007 | New York |

KASSERN, TADEUSZ
b. Lemberg (now Lwów), Mar. 19, 1904; d. New York, May 2, 1957

| | | |
|---|---|---|
| *Sun-Up* | 1954 | New York |

KASTLE, LEONARD
b. New York, Feb. 11, 1929; d. Westerlo, NY, May 18, 2011

| | | |
|---|---|---|
| +*Calling of Mother Ann* | 1985 | Albany, NY |
| *Deseret* | 1961 | New York |
| +*Journey of Mother Ann* | 1987 | Postdam |
| +*Pariahs* | 1966* | |
| | 1985 | Albany |
| +*Professor Lookalike* | 1988 | Albany |
| +*Swing, The* | 1956 | NBC |

KATS-CHERNIN, ELENA
b. Tashkent, Uzbekistan, Nov. 4, 1957

| | | |
|---|---|---|
| *Iphis* | 1997 | Sydney |

| | | |
|---|---|---|
| *Matricide* | 1998 | Melbourne |
| *Undertow* | 2004 | Adelaide |

KAUFMAN, W. G.

| | | |
|---|---|---|
| *Don Quixote* | 1903 | New York |

KAUFMANN, WALTER

b. Karlsbad, Ger., Apr. 1, 1907; d. Bloomington, IN, Sept. 9, 1984

| | | |
|---|---|---|
| *Christmas Slippers* | 1955 | Winnipeg |
| +*George from Paradise* | 1958* | |
| (lib. with F. Kaufmann) | | |
| *Golden Touch* | 1954 | Winnipeg |
| +*Hoosier Tale* | 1966 | Bloomington, IN |
| *Little Match Girl* | 1953 | Winnipeg |
| +*Parfait for Irene* | 1952 | Bloomington, IN |
| *Research, The* | 1953 | Tallahassee, FL |
| *Rip Van Winkle* | 1959 | Bloomington, IN |
| +*Scarlet Letter* | 1961 | Bloomington, IN |
| +*Sganarelle* | 1958 | Vancouver |
| +*Three Wishes* | 1942 | Bombay |

KAY, DON HENRY

b. Smithton, Tasmania, Austral., Jan. 23, 1933

| | | |
|---|---|---|
| *Golden Krane* | 1985* | |

KAY, NORMAN

b. Bolton, Lancashire, Eng., Jan. 5, 1929; d. Esher, Surrey, Eng., May 12, 2001

| | | |
|---|---|---|
| *Christmas Carol* | 1978 | Wales, HTV |
| *Rose Affair* | 1968 | London, BBC |

KAY, ULYSSES

b. Tucson, AR, Jan. 7, 1917; d. Englewood, NJ, May 20, 1995

| | | |
|---|---|---|
| +*Boor, The* | 1968 | Lexington, KY |
| *Capitoline Venus* | 1971 | Quincy, IL |
| *Frederick Douglass* | 1991 | Newark, NJ |
| *Jubilee* | 1976 | Jackson, MS |
| *Juggler of Our Lady* | 1962 | New Orleans, LA |

KEANE, DAVID ROGER

b. Akron, OH, Nov. 15, 1943

| | | |
|---|---|---|
| *Devil's Constructs* | 1978 | Napanee, ON |
| *Harlequins* | 1986 | Toronto |
| *Lumina* | 1988 | Toronto |

KECHLEY, GERALD

b. Seattle, WA, Mar. 18, 1919

| | | |
|---|---|---|
| *Beckoning Fair One* | 1954 | Seattle, WA |
| *Golden Lion* | 1959 | Seattle, WA |

KELLEY, EDGAR STILLMAN

b. Sparta, WI, Apr. 14, 1857; d. New York, Nov. 12, 1944

| | | |
|---|---|---|
| *Puritania* | 1892 | Boston |

KELLY, BRYAN

b. Oxford, Jan. 30, 1934

| | | |
|---|---|---|
| *Herod, Do Your Worst* | 1968* | |

KELLY, MICHAEL

b. Dublin, Dec. 25, 1762; d. Margate, Oct. 9, 1826

| | | |
|---|---|---|
| *Benyowsky* | 1826 | London |
| *Blue-Beard* | 1798 | London |
| *Captive of Spilburg* | 1798 | London |
| *Feudal Times* | 1799 | London |
| *Forty Thieves* | 1806 | London |
| *Foundling of the Forest* | 1809 | London |
| *Friend in Need* | 1797 | London |
| *Gipsey Prince* | 1801 | London |
| *Hero of the North* | 1803 | London |
| *Honey Moon* (with J. Hewitt) | 1805 | London, New York |
| *House to Be Sold* | 1802 | London |
| *Hunter of the Alps* | 1804 | London |
| *Illusion, The* | 1813 | London |
| *Lady and the Devil* | 1820 | London |
| *Love Laughs at Locksmiths* | 1803 | London |
| *Of Age Tomorrow* | 1800 | London |
| *Peasant Boy* | 1811 | London |
| *Pizzaro* | 1799 | London |
| *Royal Oak* | 1811 | London |
| *Unknown Guest* | 1815 | London |
| *Wood Daemon* | 1807 | London |
| *Young Hussar* | 1807 | London |
| *Youth, Love, and Folly* | 1805 | London |

KELLY, ROBERT

b. Clarksburg, WV, Sept. 26, 1916

| | | |
|---|---|---|
| +*Tod's Gal* | 1951 | |
| | 1971 | Norfolk, VA |
| +*White Gods* (lib. with C. Israel) | 1966 | Urbana, IL |

KERN, JEROME

b. New York, Jan. 27, 1885; d. there, Nov. 11, 1945

| | | |
|---|---|---|
| *Show Boat* | 1927 | Washington |

KERRY, GORDON

b. Melbourne, Jan. 21, 1961

| | | |
|---|---|---|
| *Medea* | 1993 | Melbourne |

KESSELMAN, LEE

b. Milwaukee, 1951

| | | |
|---|---|---|
| *Bremen Town Musicians* | 1988 | Madison, WI |
| *Emperor's New Clothes* | 1988* | |
| | 1999 | Chicago |

KESSELMAN, WENDY

| | | |
|---|---|---|
| +*Juniper Tree* | 1982 | Lenox, MA |

KETTENUS, Mr.

| | | |
|---|---|---|
| *Robert the Devil* (with Gastinel) | 1868 | London |

KIESERLING, RICHARD

| | | |
|---|---|---|
| *Fairies' Revelry* | 1924* | |

KIEVMAN, CARSON

b. Dec. 27, 1949, Los Angeles

| | | |
|---|---|---|
| *California Mystery Park* | 1993 | New York |
| *Hamlet* | 1990 | New York |
| *Intelligent Systems* | 1984 | Baden-Baden, Ger. |
| *Ladies Voices* | 1973–74* | |
| *Wake Up! It's Time to Go to Bed* | 1978 | Lenox, MA |

KILPATRICK, JACK

b. Stillwater, OK, Sept. 23, 1915; d. Muskogee, OK, Feb. 22, 1967

| | | |
|---|---|---|
| +*Blessed Wilderness* | 1959 | Dallas |
| *Golden Crucible* | 1959 | Pittsburgh |
| +*Unto These Hills* | 1950 | Cherokee, NC |

**KIMPER, PAULA M.**
b. 1956

| | | |
|---|---|---|
| +*Bridge of San Luis Rey* | 2003 | New York |
| +*Captivation of Eunice Williams* | 2004 | Deerfield, MA |
| (devel. with L. McInerney | | |
| *Patience and Sarah* | 1996 | New York |

**KING, JOHN**
b. Nov. 28, 1953

| | | |
|---|---|---|
| +*Dice Thrown* | 2005 | Valencia, CA |

**KING, MATTHEW PETER**
b. London, ca. 1773; d. there, Jan. 1823

| | | |
|---|---|---|
| *Americans, The* (with J. Braham) | 1811 | London |
| *Benyowsky* (with T. Cooke et al.) | 1826 | London |
| *False Alarms* | 1807 | London |
| *Matrimony* | 1804 | London |
| *Oh, This Love* | 1810 | London |
| *One O'Clock* (with M. Kelly) | 1811 | London |
| *Plots, The* | 1810 | London |
| *Too Many Cooks* | 1805 | London |
| *Turn Out!* | 1812 | London |
| *Up All Night* | 1809 | London |
| *Weathercock, The* | 1805 | London |

**KIRCHNER, LEON**
b. Brooklyn, NY, Jan. 24, 1919; d. New York, Sept. 17, 2009

| | | |
|---|---|---|
| +*Lily* | 1977 | New York |

**KIRKPATRICK, HOWARD**
b. Tiskilwa, IL, Feb. 26, 1873

| | | |
|---|---|---|
| +*Olaf* | 1912 | Lincoln, NE |

**KIRSCHNER, BOB**

| | | |
|---|---|---|
| *Bohemians, The* | 1990 | New York |

**KIRSHNER, ANDY**

| | | |
|---|---|---|
| +*Watchtower, The* | 1991 | New York |

**KIRTLEY, DAVID**
b. KY, 1954

| | | |
|---|---|---|
| *In the Father's Garden* | 2007 | New York |

**KITZKE, JEROME P.**
b. Milwaukee, WI, Feb. 5, 1955

| | | |
|---|---|---|
| *Thousand Names* | 1981 | Milwaukee, WI |

**KLEINSINGER, GEORGE**
b. San Bernardino, CA, Feb. 13, 1914; d. New York, July 28, 1982

| | | |
|---|---|---|
| *archy and mehitabel* | 1954 | New York |
| *Tree That Found Christmas* | 1955 | New York |

**KNEHANS, DOUGLAS**
b. St. Louis, MO, 1957

| | | |
|---|---|---|
| +*Ascension of Robert Flau* | 1990 | Sydney |

**KNOLLER, JACOB**
b. Ger.? 1887

| | | |
|---|---|---|
| +*Esther* | ca. 1941* | |
| | 1950 | New York |

**KNOPF, PAUL**

| | | |
|---|---|---|
| *Letter from an Astrologer* | 1976 | New York |
| +*Signals* | 1997 | New York |

**KNOWLTON, E. BRUCE**
b. Hillsboro, WI, June 25, 1895; d. 1941

| | | |
|---|---|---|
| +*Monk of Toledo* | 1926 | Portland, OR |

**KNUSSEN, OLIVER**
b. Glasgow, June 12, 1952

| | | |
|---|---|---|
| +*Higglety Pigglety Pop!* | 1984 | Glyndebourne |
| (lib. with Sendak) | | |
| *Where the Wild Things Are* | 1980 | Brussels |

**KOEHNE, GRAEME**
b. Adelaide, Austral., Aug. 3, 1956

| | | |
|---|---|---|
| *Love Burns* | 1992 | Adelaide |

**KOHS, ELLIS B.**
b. Chicago, May 12, 1916; d. Los Angeles, May 17, 2000

| | | |
|---|---|---|
| +*America* | 1970 | Los Angeles |
| +*Rhinoceros* | 1973* | |

**KONDOROSSY, LESLIE**
b. Pressburg [now Bratislava], June 25, 1915; d. Cleveland, OH, Apr. 22, 1989

| | | |
|---|---|---|
| *Fox, The* | 1961 | Cleveland, OH |
| *Kalamona* | 1971 | Cleveland, OH |
| *Midnight Duel* | 1955 | Cleveland, OH |
| +*Mystic Fortress* | 1955 | Cleveland, OH |
| *Nathan the Wise* | 1964 | Cleveland, OH |
| +*Night in the Puszta* | 1953 | Cleveland, OH |
| *Poorest Suitor* | 1967 | Cleveland, OH |
| *Pumpkin, The* | 1954 | Cleveland, OH |
| *Ruth and Naomi* | 1974 | Cleveland, OH |
| *Shizuka's Dance* | 1969 | Cleveland, OH |
| +*String Quartet* | 1955 | Cleveland, OH |
| +*Two Imposters* | 1955 | Cleveland |
| *Unexpected Visitor* | 1956 | Cleveland, OH |
| *Voice, The* | 1954 | Cleveland, OH |

**KOSTECK, GREGORY**
b. Plainfield, NJ, Sept. 2, 1937; d. Sarasota, FL, Dec. 27, 1991

| | | |
|---|---|---|
| *Maurya* | 1968 | Greenville, NC |
| *Stronger, The* | 1969 | Greenville, NC |

**KOUTZEN, BORIS**
b. Uman, near Kiev, Apr. 1, 1901; d. Mount Kisco, NY, Dec. 10, 1966

| | | |
|---|---|---|
| +*Fatal Oath* | 1955 | New York |
| *You Never Know* | 1962* | |

**KOWALSKI, HENRI**
b. Paris, 1841; d. Bordeaux, France, July 8, 1916

| | | |
|---|---|---|
| *Moustique* | 1883 | Brussels |
| *Vercingetorix* | 1881 | Sydney |

**KRAFT, LEO**
b. New York, July 24, 1922

| | | |
|---|---|---|
| *Caliph's Clock* | 1951 | New York |

**KRAFT, WILLIAM**
b. Chicago, IL, Sept. 6, 1923

| | | |
|---|---|---|
| *Red Azalea* | 2003 | Santa Barbara, CA |

KRANE, SHERMAN
| *Giant's Garden* | 1960 | Norfolk, VA |

KRAUSAS, VERONIKA
b. Sydney, 1963
| *Mortal Thoughts of Lady Macbeth* | 2008 | New York |

KRENEK, ERNST
b. Vienna, Aug. 23, 1900; d. Palm Springs, CA, Dec. 23, 1991
| +*Bell Tower* | 1957 | Urbana, IL |
| +*Dark Waters* | 1951 | Los Angeles |
| *Tarquin* | 1941 | Poughkeepsie, NY |
| +*What Price Confidence?* | 1945* | |
| | 1962 | Saarbrücken, Ger. |

KREUTZ, ARTHUR
b. La Crosse, WI, July 25, 1906; d. Oxford, MI, Mar. 11, 1991
| *Acres of Sky* | 1951 | Fayetteville, AR |
| *Sourwood Mountain* | 1959 | Oxford, MS |
| *University Greys* | 1954 | Clinton, MS |

KROLL, FREDERIC
b. 1945
| *Scarlet Letter* | 1965* | |

KRUCKER, FIDES
b. Canada
| *Artaud's Cane* (with Egoyan, M. White) | 1994 | Toronto |

KUBIK, GAIL
b. South Coffeyville, OK, Sept. 5, 1914; d. Covina, CA, July 20, 1984
| +*Boston Baked Beans* | 1952 | New York |
| *Mirror for the Sky* | 1939 | Eugene, OR |

KULESHA, GARY
b. Canada, 1960
| *Red Emma* | 1995 | Toronto |

KUPFERMAN, MEYER
b. New York, July 3, 1926; d. Rhinebeck, NY, Dec, 3, 2003
| *Curious Fern* | 1957 | New York |
| +*Doctor Faustus* | 1953 | Bronxville, NY |
| +*Draagenfut Girl* | 1958 | Bronxville, NY |
| *In a Garden* | 1949 | New York |
| *Judgment, The* | 1966* | |
| +*Prometheus Condemned* | 1978 | New York |
| +*Proscenium* | 1991 | New York |
| *Voices for a Mirror* | 1957 | New York |

KURKA, ROBERT
b. Cicero, IL, Dec. 22, 1921; d. New York, Dec. 12, 1957
| *Good Soldier Schweik* | 1958 | New York |

KUSKIN, CHARLES
| *Floating* | 1999 | New York |

LA BARBARA, JOAN
b. Philadelphia, June 8, 1947
| *Events in the Elsewhere* | 1990 | Santa Fe |
| *Misfortune of the Immortals* (with Subotnick) | 1992 | Chester, PA |

LaCHIUSA, MICHAEL JOHN
b. 1962
| +*Lovers and Friends* (orch. B. Vieth) | 2001 | Chicago |

LACKMAN, SUSAN COHN
b. 1948
| +*Lisa Stratos* | 1981* | |

LACY, MICHAEL ROPHINO
b. Bilbao, Spain, July 19, 1795; d. London, Sept. 20, 1867
| *Casket, The* | 1829 | London |
| +*Cinderella* (lib. with G. Pons) | 1830 | London |
| *Coiners, The* | 1833 | London |
| +*Fiend-Father* | 1821 | London |
| +*Fra Diavolo* | 1831 | London |
| *Israelites in Egypt* | 1833 | London |
| *Love in Wrinkles* | 1828 | London |
| +*Maid of Judah* | 1829 | London |
| *Turkish Loves* | 1827 | London |

LADERMAN, EZRA
b. Brooklyn, NY, June 29, 1924
| *And David Wept* | 1980 | New York |
| *Galileo Galilei* | 1979 | New York |
| *Goodbye to the Clown* | 1960 | New York |
| *Hunting of the Snark* | 1961 | New York |
| *Jacob and the Indians* | 1957 | Woodstock, NY |
| *Marilyn* | 1993 | New York |
| *Questions of Abraham* | 1973 | CBS |
| *Sarah* | 1958 | New York |
| *Shadows among Us* | 1967* | |
| | 1979 | Philadelphia |

LAITMAN, LORI
b. 1955
| *Come to Me in Dreams* | 2004 | Cleveland |
| *Scarlet Letter* | 2009 | Conway, AR |

LA MONTAINE, JOHN
b. Chicago, Mar. 17, 1920
| +*Be Glad Then America* | 1976 | University Park, PA |
| +*Erode the Greate* | 1969 | Washington |
| +*Magi, The* | 1967 | Washington |
| +*Novellis, Novellis* | 1961 | Washington |
| +*Shepardes Playe* | 1967 | Washington |

LAMPE, JOHN FREDERICK
b. Brunswick, ca. 1703; d. Edinburgh, July 25, 1751
| *Amelia* | 1732 | London |
| *Britannia* | 1732 | London |
| *Dione* | 1733 | London |
| *Dragon of Wantley* | 1737 | London |
| *Margery* | 1738 | London |
| *Orpheus and Eurydice* | 1740 | London |
| +*Pyramus and Thisbe* | 1745 | London |
| *Queen of Spain* | 1744 | London |
| *Sham Conjuror* | 1741 | London |

**LANG, DAVID**
b. Los Angeles, 1957

| | | |
|---|---|---|
| *Carbon Copy Building* | 1999 | New York |
| (with M. Gordon, J. Wolfe) | | |
| *Difficulty of Crossing a Field* | 2002 | San Francisco |
| *Modern Painters* | 1995 | Santa Fe,   NM |

**LARSEN, LIBBY [ELIZABETH BROWN]**
b. Wilmington, DE, Dec. 24, 1950

| | | |
|---|---|---|
| +*Barnum's Bird* (lib. with Carpenter) | 2000 | Minneapolis |
| *Christina Romana* | 1988 | Minneapolis |
| *Clair de Lune* | 1985 | Little Rock, AR |
| +*Dreaming Blue* (lib comp et al.) | 2002 | Salt Lake City, UT |
| *Emperor's New Clothes* | 1979 | Minneapolis, MN |
| +*Eric Hermannson's Soul* | 1998 | Omaha, NE |
| *Every Man Jack* | 2006 | Sonoma, CA |
| +*Frankenstein* | 1990 | St. Paul, MN |
| *Mrs. Dalloway* | 1993 | Cleveland |
| *Picnic* | 2009 | Greensboro, NC |
| *Silver Fox* | 1979 | St. Paul, MN |
| +*Some Pig* | 1973 | Minneapolis |
| *Tumbledown Dick* | 1980 | Minneapolis |
| *Wrinkle in Time* | 1992 | Wilmington, DE |

**LARSON, JONATHAN**
b. White Plains, NY, Feb. 4, 1960; d. New York, Jan. 25, 1996

| | | |
|---|---|---|
| +*Rent* (lib. with L. Thomson) | 1996 | New York |

**LASTOVICKA, CHRIS**
b. Houston, TX, 1973

| | | |
|---|---|---|
| *Crossing the Horizon* | 2007 | New York |

**LATHAM, WILLIAM**
b. Shreveport, LA, Jan. 4, 1917

| | | |
|---|---|---|
| *Orpheus in Pecan Springs* | 1980 | Denton, TX |

**LAUFER, BEATRICE**
b. New York, Apr. 27, 1923

| | | |
|---|---|---|
| *Ile* | 1957 | New York |

**LAURENT, HENRI R.**
fl 1848–1867

| | | |
|---|---|---|
| *Azael* | 1851 | London |
| *Quentin Durward* | 1848 | London |

**LAUTEN, ELODIE**
b. Paris, Oct. 20, 1950

| | | |
|---|---|---|
| +*Death of Don Juan* | 1987 | Boston |
| *OrfReo* | 2004 | New York |
| *Waking in New York* | 1999 | New York |

**LAVALLÉE, CALIXA**
b. Ste. Théodosie de Verchères, Quebec, Dec. 28, 1842; d. Boston, Jan. 21, 1891

| | | |
|---|---|---|
| *Widow, The* | 1882 | Springfield, IL |

**LAVENU, LOUIS HENRY**
b London, 1818; d Sydney, Aug. 1, 1859

| | | |
|---|---|---|
| *Loretta* | 1846 | London |

**LA VIOLETTE, WESLEY**
b. St. James, MN, Jan. 4, 1894; d. Escondido, CA, July 29, 1978

| | | |
|---|---|---|
| +*Enlightened One* | 1955* | |
| +*Shylock* | 1930 | Chicago |

**LAVRY, MARC**
b. Riga, Dec. 22, 1903; d. Haifa, Israel, Mar. 24, 1967

| | | |
|---|---|---|
| +*Tamar and Judah* | 1958* | |
| | 1970 | New York |

**LAWES, HENRY**
b. Dinton, Wiltshire, Eng., Jan. 5, 1596; d. London, Oct. 21, 1662

| | | |
|---|---|---|
| *Comus* | 1634 | Ludlow |
| *Siege of Rhodes* | 1656 | London |
| (with H. Cooke, M. Locke) | | |
| *Triumphs of the Prince d'Amour* | 1636 | London |
| (with W. Lawes) | | |

**LAWES, WILLIAM**
b. Salisbury, Eng., bapt. May 1, 1602; d. Chester, Eng., Sept. 24, 1645

| | | |
|---|---|---|
| *Britannia triumphans* | 1638 | London |
| *Triumph of Peace* (with Ives, Mell) | 1634 | London |
| *Triumphs of the Prince d'Amour* | 1636 | London |
| (with H. Lawes) | | |

**LEACH, RACHEL**
b. 1973

| | | |
|---|---|---|
| *Shorts* (instr interludes) | 1999 | London |

**LEAVITT, BURTON E.**
b. 1871; d. 1912

| | | |
|---|---|---|
| *Charter Oak* | ca. 1885 | |
| *Frogs of Windham* | ca. 1891* | |

**LeBARON, ANNE**
b. May 30, 1953, Baton Rouge, LA

| | | |
|---|---|---|
| *Crescent City* | 2006 | New York |
| +*Croak* (lib. with Jacobson) | 1997 | Washington |
| *E. & O. Line* | 1996 | Annandale, VA |
| *Pope Joan* | 2000 | Pittsburgh |
| *Wet* | 2005 | Los Angeles |

**LEE, DAI-KEONG**
b. Honolulu, Sept. 2, 1915

| | | |
|---|---|---|
| +*Ballad of Kitty* | 1979* | |
| *Jenny Lind* | 1981* | |
| *Open the Gates* | 1951 | New York |
| *Phineas and the Nightingale* | 1952* | |
| *Poet's Dilemma* | 1940 | New York |
| *Speakeasy* | 1957 | New York |
| *Two Knickerbocker Tales* | 1957* | |

**LEE, GEORGE ALEXANDER**
b. London, 1802; d. there, Oct. 8, 1851

| | | |
|---|---|---|
| *Afrancesado* | 1837 | London |
| *Devil's Brother* | 1831 | London |
| *Dragon, The* | 1834 | London |
| *Fairy Lake* | 1839 | London |
| *Invincibles, The* | 1828 | London |
| *Magic Horn* | 1846 | London |
| *Malvina* | 1826 | London |
| *Nothing Superfluous* | 1829 | London |

| | | |
|---|---|---|
| *Nymph of the Grotto* | 1829 | London |
| *Sublime and the Beautiful* | 1828 | London |

**LEE, THOMAS OBOE**
b. Peking (Beijing), Sept. 5, 1945

| | | |
|---|---|---|
| *Photograph, 1920* | 1978* | |

**LEES, BENJAMIN**
b. Harbin, China, Jan. 8, 1924; d. Glen Cove, NY, May 25, 2010

| | | |
|---|---|---|
| *Gilded Cage* | 1964 | New York |
| +*Medea in Corinth* | 1971 | London |
| +*Oracle, The* | 1955* | |

**LeFANU, NICOLA**
b. Wickham Bishops, Essex, Eng., Apr. 28, 1947

| | | |
|---|---|---|
| *Blood Wedding* | 1992 | London |
| +*Dawnpath* | 1997 | London |
| +*Green Children* (lib. with Holland) | 1990 | London |
| *Story of Mary O'Neill* | 1989 | London, BBC |
| *Wildman, The* | 1995 | Aldeburgh |

**LE GENDRE, DOMINIQUE**
b. Trinidad

| | | |
|---|---|---|
| +*Bird of Night* (text with P. Bentley) | 2006 | London |
| +*Burial at Thebes* | 2008 | London |

**LEGG, JAMES**
b. Levittown, NY, 1962; d. New York, Nov. 20, 2000

| | | |
|---|---|---|
| *All My Sons* | 2001 | New York (posth) |
| *Bellarocca* | 1997* | |
| *Informer, The* | 1985 | Houston |
| +*Power of Xingu* | 1998 | Chapel Hill, NC |
| *Wife of Bath's Tale* | 1986 | Aspen, CO |

**LEGINSKA [LIGGINS], ETHEL**
b. Hull, Eng., Apr. 13, 1886; d. Los Angeles, Feb. 26, 1970

| | | |
|---|---|---|
| *Gale* | 1935 | Chicago |
| *Rose and the Ring* | 1932* | |
| | 1957 | Los Angeles |

**LEHMANN, LIZA [ELIZABETH]**
b. London, July 11, 1862; d. Pinner, Eng., Sept. 19, 1918

| | | |
|---|---|---|
| +*Everyman* | 1915 | London |

**LEHRMAN, LEONARD J.**
b. Ft. Riley, Kans., Aug. 20, 1949

| | | |
|---|---|---|
| +*Birthday of the Bank* (lib. with Shatzky) | 1988 | Glens Falls, NY |
| +*Family Man* | 1984 | New York |
| +*Hannah* (lib. with O. Odinov) | 1980 | Mannheim-Seckenheim, Ger. |
| +*Karla* | 1974 | Ithaca, NY |
| +*New World* | 1991 | New York |
| +*Sima* | 1976 | Ithaca, NY |
| +*Suppose a Wedding* | 1996 | Commack, NY |
| *Wooing, The* | 2003 | Queens, NY |

**LEICHTLING, ALAN**
b. 1947

| | | |
|---|---|---|
| *Tempest, The* | 1973* | |
| *White Butterfly* | 1971 | New York |

**LEIGH, WALTER**
b. Wimbledon, London, June 22, 1905; d. nr. Tobruk, Libya, June 12, 1942

| | | |
|---|---|---|
| *Jolly Roger* | 1933 | Manchester |
| *Pride of the Regiment* | 1931 | Midhurst, Eng. |

**LEIGHTON, KENNETH**
b. Wakefield, Yorkshire, Oct. 2, 1929; d. Edinburgh, Aug. 24, 1988

| | | |
|---|---|---|
| *Columba* | 1981 | Glasgow |

**LENEL, LUDWIG**
b. Strasbourg, Alsace, 1914; d. Allentown, PA, 2000

| | | |
|---|---|---|
| *Young Goodman Brown* | 1963 | Allentown, PA |

**LÉON, TANYA**
b. Havana, May 14, 1943

| | | |
|---|---|---|
| +*Scourge of Hyacinths* (with Soyinka) | 1994* | |
| | 1999 | Geneva |

**LEONI, FRANCO**
b. Milan, Oct. 24, 1864; d. London, Feb. 8, 1949

| | | |
|---|---|---|
| *Ib and Little Christina* | 1901 | London |

**LEPAGE, ROBERT**
b. 1957

| | | |
|---|---|---|
| *Letters, Riddles* (with M. Nyman) | 1991 | London, BBC |

**LEPENDORF, JEFFREY**
b. Philadelphia, 1962

| | | |
|---|---|---|
| *American Lit* | 1997 | New York |
| +*Say It with Flowers* | 1996 | New York |

**LEPS, WASSILI**
b. St. Petersburg, Russia, May 12, 1870; d. Toronto, Dec. 22, 1942

| | | |
|---|---|---|
| *Hoshi-San* | 1909 | Philadelphia |

**LESLIE, HENRY**
b. London, June 18, 1822; d. nr. Oswestry, Wales, Feb. 4, 1896

| | | |
|---|---|---|
| *Ida* | 1865 | London |
| *Romance, The* | 1860 | London |

**LESSNER, GEORGE**
b. Budapest, 1905; d. New Rochelle, NY, May 12, 1997

| | | |
|---|---|---|
| *Nightingale and the Rose* | 1942 | NBC radio |

**LESTER, WILLIAM**
b. 1889; d. 1956

| | | |
|---|---|---|
| +*Everyman* | 1927 | Chicago |

**LEVERIDGE, RICHARD**
b. London?, ca. 1670; d. London, Mar. 22, 1758

| | | |
|---|---|---|
| *Macbeth* | 1702 | London |
| +*Pyramus and Thisbe* | 1716 | London |

**LEVI, PAUL ALAN**
b. 1941

| | | |
|---|---|---|
| *Thanksgiving* | 1977 | New York |

**LEVIN, GREGORY**
b. Washington, DC, Mar. 8, 1943

| | | |
|---|---|---|
| +*Electric Gospel* | 1980 | Toronto |
| *Ghost Dance* | 1985 | Toronto |
| +*Rebel and Empire* (lib. with D. Levin) | 1976* | |

**LEVISTER, ALONZO**
b. Nov. 1, 1925, Greenwich, CT

| | | |
|---|---|---|
| *Blues in the Subway* | 1958 | New York |
| *Happy Hypocrite* | 1958 | New York |

**LEVOWITZ, ADAM B.**
b. Nov. 15, 1968

| | | |
|---|---|---|
| +*Brave Little Tailor* | 2003 | Houston, TX |
| *Strands* | 1997* | |
| +*Tell-Tale Heart* | 1999* | |
| +*Three Princes* | 1995 | New York |

**LEVY, MARVIN DAVID**
b. Passaic, NJ, Aug. 2, 1932

| | | |
|---|---|---|
| +*Escorial, The* (lib. with L. Abel) | 1958 | New York |
| *Mourning Becomes Electra* | 1967 | New York |
| *Sotoba Komachi* | 1957 | New York |
| *Tower, The* | 1957 | Santa Fe, NM |

**LEWIN, FRANK**
b. 1925

| | | |
|---|---|---|
| +*Burning Bright* | 1993 | New Haven |

**LI, GUANG MING**

| | | |
|---|---|---|
| *Chinaman's Chance* | 1990 | Brooklyn, NY |
| (F. Ho, addit music) | | |

**LIEBERMANN, LOWELL**
b. Feb. 22, 1961, New York

| | | |
|---|---|---|
| *Miss Lonelyhearts* | 2006 | New York |
| +*Picture of Dorian Gray* | 1996 | Monte Carlo |

**LIEBERMANN, ROLF**
b. Zurich, Sept. 14, 1910; d. there, Jan. 2, 1999

| | | |
|---|---|---|
| *School for Wives* | 1955 | Louisville, KY |

**LIEBERSON, KENNETH**

| | | |
|---|---|---|
| +*Birdbath* | 1982 | New York |

**LIEBERSON, PETER**
b. New York, Oct. 25, 1946; d. Apr. 23, 2011, Tel Aviv, Israel

| | | |
|---|---|---|
| *Ashoka's Dream* | 1997 | Santa Fe, NM |
| *King Gesar* | 1992 | Munich |

**LINDSEY, EDWIN S.**
b. 1897

| | | |
|---|---|---|
| *Elizabeth and Leicester* | 1936 | Chattanooga, TN |

**LINLEY, GEORGE**
b. Leeds, Eng., 1798; d. London, Sept. 10, 1865

| | | |
|---|---|---|
| *Law versus Love* | 1862 | London |
| +*Toy-Maker* | 1861 | London |

**LINLEY, THOMAS, Jr.**
b. Bath, Eng., May 5, 1756; d. Grimsthorpe, Lincolnshire, Aug. 5, 1778

| | | |
|---|---|---|
| *Cadi of Bagdad* | 1778 | London |
| *Duenna, The* (with Linley Sr.) | 1775 | London |

**LINLEY, THOMAS, Sr.**
b. Badminton, Eng., Jan. 17, 1733; d. London, Nov. 19, 1795

| | | |
|---|---|---|
| *Camp, The* | 1778 | London |
| *Carnival of Venice* | 1781 | London |
| *Duenna, The* (with Linley Jr.) | 1775 | London |
| *Gentle Shepherd* | 1781 | London |
| *Love in the East* | 1788 | London |
| *Richard Coeur de Lion* | 1786 | London |

| | | |
|---|---|---|
| *Royal Merchant* | 1767 | London |
| *Selima and Azor* | 1776 | London |
| +*Spanish Rivals* | 1784 | London |
| *Strangers at Home* | 1785 | London |
| *Zoraida* | 1779 | London |

**LINLEY, WILLIAM**
b. Bath, Eng., Feb. 1772; d. London, May 6, 1835

| | | |
|---|---|---|
| +*Honey Moon* | 1797 | London |
| +*Pavilion, The* | 1799 | London |

**LIOTTA, ANDREW**

| | | |
|---|---|---|
| *Romeo and Juliet* | 1969 | New York |

**LIPTAK, DANIEL**
b. Pittsburgh, PA, 1949

| | | |
|---|---|---|
| *Moon Singer* | 1998 | Brevard, NC |

**LIST, KURT**
b. Vienna, June 21, 1913; d. Milan, Nov. 16, 1970

| | | |
|---|---|---|
| +*Wise and Foolish* | 1951 | New York |

**LITTLE, DAVID T.**
b. 1978

| | | |
|---|---|---|
| *Dog Days* | 2009 | New York |
| +*Soldier Songs* | 2008 | New York |

**LIVINGSTON, JULIAN**
b. Spencer, IN, Aug. 25, 1932

| | | |
|---|---|---|
| +*Twist of Treason* | 1977 | Lincroft, NJ |

**LIVIUS, BARHAM**
d. 1865

| | | |
|---|---|---|
| *Benyowsky* (with Cooke et al) | 1826 | London |
| *Maid or Wife* (with Cooke) | 1821 | London |

**LLOYD, ALAN**

| | | |
|---|---|---|
| *Letter for Queen Victoria* | 1974 | Spoleto, Italy |

**LLOYD, GEORGE**
b. St. Ives, Cornwall, June 28, 1913; d. London, July 3, 1998

| | | |
|---|---|---|
| *Iernin* | 1934 | Penzance, Eng. |
| *John Socman* | 1951 | Bristol |
| *Serf, The* | 1938 | London |

**LLOYD, TIMOTHY CAMERON**

| | | |
|---|---|---|
| *Conjur Moon* | 1979 | Houston, TX |

**LLOYD WEBBER, ANDREW**
b. London, Mar. 22, 1948

| | | |
|---|---|---|
| *Evita* | 1978 | London |
| *Jesus Christ Superstar* | 1971 | New York |
| +*Phantom of the Opera* | 1986 | London |
| (lib. with Stilgoe) | | |
| *Tell Me on a Sunday* | 1980 | London |

**LOCKE, MATTHEW**
b. Devon, Eng., ca. 1622; d. London, Aug. 1677

| | | |
|---|---|---|
| *Macbeth* (with R. Johnson) | 1673 | London |
| *Orpheus and Euridice* | 1673 | London |
| *Psyche* | 1675 | London |
| *Siege of Rhodes* | 1656 | London |
| (with H. Cooke, H. Lawes) | | |
| *Tempest, The* (with Banister et al.) | 1674 | London |

LOCKLAIR, DAN
b. Charlotte, NC, Aug. 7, 1949

| | | |
|---|---|---|
| *Good Tidings from the Holy Beast* | 1978 | Lincoln, NE |

LOCKWOOD, NORMAND
b. New York, Mar. 19, 1906; d. Denver, CO, Mar. 9, 2002

| | | |
|---|---|---|
| *Early Dawn* | 1961 | Denver |
| *Hanging Judge* | 1964 | Denver |
| *Requiem for a Rich Young Man* | 1964 | Denver |
| *Scarecrow* | 1945 | New York |
| *Wizards of Balizar* | 1962 | Denver |

LODER, EDWARD
b. Bath, Eng., 1813; d. London, Apr. 5, 1865

| | | |
|---|---|---|
| *Covenanters, The* | 1835 | London |
| *Deer Stalkers* | 1841 | London |
| *Dice of Death* | 1835 | London |
| *Foresters, The* | 1838 | London |
| *Francis the First* | 1838 | London |
| *Heart of Midlothian* | 1849 | London |
| *Marie* | 1849 | London |
| *Night Dancers* | 1846 | London |
| *Nourjahad* | 1834 | London |
| *Raymond and Agnes* | 1855 | Manchester |
| *Robin Goodfellow* | 1848 | London |

LOEFFLER, ALFRED
d Oct. 26, 2003

| | | |
|---|---|---|
| +*Love's Labour's Lost* | 1999* | |

LOESSER, FRANK
b. New York, June 29, 1910; d. there, July 26, 1969

| | | |
|---|---|---|
| +*Most Happy Fella* | 1956 | New York |

LOLE, TIM

| | | |
|---|---|---|
| *Thirty Minute Don Giovanni* (with V. Gray) | 1999 | Leeds |

LONDON, EDWIN
b. Philadelphia, Mar. 16, 1929

| | | |
|---|---|---|
| *Death of Lincoln* | 1976* | |
| | 1988 | Cleveland, OH |

LOOMIS, CLARENCE
b. Sioux City, SD, Dec. 13, 1889; d. Aptos, CA, July 3, 1965

| | | |
|---|---|---|
| *Fall of the House of Usher* | 1941 | Indianapolis |
| *Yolanda of Cyprus* | 1929 | London, ON |

LOUIE, ALEXINA
b. Vancouver, July 30, 1949

| | | |
|---|---|---|
| *Burnt Toast* | 2006 | CBC-TV |
| *Scarlet Princess* | 2002 | Toronto |

LOVER, SAMUEL
b. Dublin, Feb. 24, 1797; d. St. Helier, Jersey, July 6, 1868

| | | |
|---|---|---|
| +*Paddy Whack* | 1841 | London |

LOW, JAMES

| | | |
|---|---|---|
| *Moby Dick* | 1955 | Idylwild, CA |

LOWENSTEIN, MARC
b. 1946

| | | |
|---|---|---|
| +*Fisher King* | 2007 | New York |

LUBIN, ERNEST
b. New York, May 2, 1916

| | | |
|---|---|---|
| *Pardoner's Tale* | 1966 | Denver |

LUCERO, CARLA
b. Los Angeles

| | | |
|---|---|---|
| +*Wuornos* | 2001 | San Francisco |

LUENGEN, RAMONA
b. Vancouver, 1960

| | | |
|---|---|---|
| *Naomi's Road* | 2005 | Vancouver |

LUENING, OTTO
b. Milwaukee, WI, June 15, 1900; d. New York, Sept. 2, 1996

| | | |
|---|---|---|
| +*Evangeline* | 1948 | New York |

LUKE, RAY
b. Fort Worth, TX, May 30, 1926

| | | |
|---|---|---|
| *Medea* | 1979 | Boston |

LUNN, JOHN
b. Glasgow, May 13, 1956

| | | |
|---|---|---|
| *Mathematics of a Kiss* (with Gough) | 1989 | London |
| *Misper* | 1997 | Glyndebourne |
| *Tangier Tattoo* | 2005 | Glyndebourne |
| *Zoë* | 2000 | Glyndebourne |

LUTYENS, ELISABETH
b. London, July 9, 1906; d. there, Apr. 14, 1983

| | | |
|---|---|---|
| *Infidelio* | 1973 | London |
| +*Isis and Osiris* | 1976 | London |
| +*Like a Window* | 1977 | London |
| +*Linnet from the Leaf* | 1979 | London |
| *Numbered, The* | 1965–67* | |
| +*One and the Same* | 1976 | York, Eng. |
| *Pit, The* | 1947 | London |
| +*Time Off?* | 1972 | London |

LUTZ, MEYER
b. Münnerstadt, Ger., 1822; d. London, Jan. 31, 1903

| | | |
|---|---|---|
| *Felix* | 1865 | London |
| *Mephistopheles* | 1855 | Surrey |
| *Zaida* | 1859 | Liverpool |

LYBBERT, DONALD
b. Cresco, IA, Feb. 19, 1923; d. Norwalk, CT, July 26, 1981

| | | |
|---|---|---|
| *Scarlet Letter* | 1964–67* | |

LYFORD, RALPH
b. Worcester, MA, Feb. 22, 1882; d. Cincinnati, OH, Sept. 3, 1927

| | | |
|---|---|---|
| *Castle Agrazant* | 1926 | Cincinnati |

MAAZEL, LORIN
b. Neuilly-sur-Seine, France, Mar. 6, 1930

| | | |
|---|---|---|
| *1984* | 2005 | London |

MacALPIN, COLIN

| | | |
|---|---|---|
| *Cross and the Crescent* | 1903 | London |

MacBRIDE, DAVID
b. Oakland, CA, Oct. 3, 1951

| | | |
|---|---|---|
| *Pond in a Bowl* | 1983 | New York |
| *Vision & Prayer* | 1995 | New York |

MacCRAE, STUART
  b. Inverness, Scot., 1976
  *Assassin Tree*                      2006     Edinburgh
MacCUNN, HAMISH
  b. Greenock, Scot, Mar. 22, 1868; d. London, Aug. 2, 1916
  *Diarmid*                            1897     London
  *Jeanie Deans*                       1894     Edinburgh
  *Masque of War and Peace*            1900     London
  *Pageant of Darkness and Light*      1908*
MACFARREN, GEORGE A.
  b. London, Mar. 2, 1813; d. there, Oct. 31, 1887
  *Adventure of Don Quixote*           1846     London
  *Devil's Opera*                      1838     London
  *Genevieve*                          1834     London
  *Helvellyn*                          1864     London
  *Jessy Lea*                          1863     London
  *King Charles II*                    1849     London
  *Robin Hood*                         1860     London
  *She Stoops to Conquer*              1864     London
  *Sleeper Awakened*                   1850     London
  *Soldier's Legacy*                   1864     London
MACHOVER, TOD
  b. New York, Nov. 24, 1953
  *Brain Opera*                        1996     New York
  *Death and the Powers*               2010     Monte Carlo
  *Resurrection*                       1999     Houston
  *Skellig*                            2008     Newcastle u Tyne
  +*VALIS*                             1987     Paris
MacINTYRE, DAVID
  b. Yorkton, Saskatchewan, 1952
  *Architect, The*                     1994     Vancouver
  *Humulus the Mute*                   1979     Vancouver
MacKENZIE, ALEXANDER
  b. Edinburgh, Aug. 22, 1847; d. London, Apr. 28, 1935
  *Colomba*                            1883     London
  *Cricket on the Hearth*              1914     London
  *Eve of St. John*                    1924     Liverpool
  *Guillem*                            1886     London
  *His Majesty*                        1897     London
MACKEY, STEVEN
  b. Frankfurt, Ger., Feb. 14, 1956
  *Ravenshead*                         1998     New York
MACLEAN, ALICK
  b. Eton, Eng., July 20, 1872; d. London, May 18, 1936
  *Crichton*                           1892*
  *King's Price*                       1904     London
  *Petruccio*                          1895     London
  *Quentin Durward*                    1893     London
MacMILLAN, JAMES
  b. Kilwinning, Scot, Jul. 16, 1959
  +*Inés de Castro*                    1996     Edinburgh
  *Sacrifice, The*                     2007     Cardiff

MACONCHY, ELIZABETH
  b. Broxbourne, Hertfordshire, Eng., Mar. 19, 1907; d. Norwich, Eng.,
    Nov. 11, 1994
  +*Birds, The*                        1968     London
  *Departure, The*                     1962     London
  *Jesse Tree*                         1970     Dorchester, Eng.
  +*Johnny and the Mohawks*            1970     London
  *King of the Golden River*           1975     Oxford
  *Sofa, The*                          1959     London
  +*Three Strangers*                   1968     London
MacSEMS, WILLIAM
  b. New York, 1930
  *Infidel*                            2006*
  *Outcasts of Poker Flat*             1972*
MAGANINI, QUINTO
  b. Fairfield, CA, Nov. 30, 1897; d. Greenwich, CT, Mar. 10, 1974
  *Argonauts, The*                     ca. 1937*
                                       1942     WOR radio
MAGNEY, RUTH TAYLOR
  +*Gift of the Magi*                  1964     Minneapolis
MAGRILL, SAMUEL
  +*Circe's Palace*                    2001     Edmond, OK
  +*Gorgon's Head*                     1998     Edmond, OK
    (lib. with Creed, Osterhaus)
  +*Paradise of Children*              1998     Edmond, OK
  +*Showdown on Two Street*            2000     Edmond, OK
MAILMAN, MARTIN
  b. New York, June 30, 1932
  +*Hunted, The*                       1959     Rochester, NY
MALLETT, CHARLES
  *Governess, The*                     1954     London
MANDEL, JULIE
  *I Wish, I Wish*                     2006     Westerville, OH
MANDELBAUM, JOEL
  b. New York, Oct. 12, 1932
  +*Dybbuk, The*                       1972     New York
  *Village, The*                       1995     Queens, NY
MANN, LESLIE
  b. Edmonton, Aug. 13, 1923, d Balmoral, MN, Dec. 7, 1977
  +*Donkey's Tale*                     1971*
MANN, ROBERT W.
  b. Sandwich, IL, Sept. 11, 1925; d. Rome, Mar. 15, 2010
  +*Little Prince*                     1951*
  +*Scarlet Letter*                    1958*
MANNING, EDWARD
  +*Rip Van Winkle*                    1932     New York
MANNO, ROBERT
  b. Bryn Mawr, PA, 1944
  *Dylan and Caitlin*                  2008     New York

MANSCHINGER, KURT. *See* ASHLEY, VERNON.

MARAIS, JOSEF
b. Sir Lowry Pass, South Africa, Nov. 17, 1905; d. Los Angeles, Apr. 27, 1978

| | | |
|---|---|---|
| *African Heartbeat* | 1953 | Idyllwild, CA |
| *Tony Beaver* | 1953 | Idyllwild, CA |

MARCH, KEVIN
b. Austral?

| | | |
|---|---|---|
| *Leading Lady* | 2004 | New York |
| +*Razing Hypatia* | 2010 | Melbourne |
| *War Prayer* | 1996* | |
| *www.love* | 2001 | New York |

MAREK, ROBERT
b. 1915; d. 1995

| | | |
|---|---|---|
| *Arabesque* | 1967 | Vermillion, SD |

MARETZEK, MAX
b. Brünn [Brno], June 28, 1821; d. Staten Island, NY, May 14, 1897

| | | |
|---|---|---|
| *Sleepy Hollow* | 1879 | New York |

MARKORDT, J.

| | | |
|---|---|---|
| *Tom Thumb* | 1780 | London |

MARSHALL, PAUL

| | | |
|---|---|---|
| +*Mink Stockings* | 1961 | Columbus, OH |

MARSHALL-HALL, GEORGE W. K.
b. London, Mar. 28, 1862; d. Melbourne, July 18, 1915

| | | |
|---|---|---|
| *Alcestis* | 1898 | Melbourne |
| *Harold* | 1888 | London |
| +*Romeo and Juliet* | 1912 | Melbourne |
| *Stella* | 1914 | Melbourne |

MARTÍN, JORGE
b. Santiago de Cuba, Mar. 21, 1959

| | | |
|---|---|---|
| *Beast and Superbeast* | 1996 | Bethesda, MD |
| +*Before Night Falls* (lib. with D. Koch) | 2006 | New York |
| +*Henry and Clara* | 2001 | New York |
| +*Puss in Boots* (lib. with A. Joffe) | 1992 | New York |

MARTIN, VERNON
b. Guthrie, OK, Dec. 15, 1924

| | | |
|---|---|---|
| *Ladies' Voices* | 1956 | Norman, OK |

MARTINEZ, JOSÉ "PEPE"
b. Tecalitlán, Jalisco, Mexico, June 27, 1941

| | | |
|---|---|---|
| *To Cross the Face of the Moon* | 2010 | Houston |

MARTÍNEZ, ODALINE de la
b. Matanzas, Cuba, Oct. 31, 1949

| | | |
|---|---|---|
| *Sister Aimée* | 1984 | New Orleans |

MARTINŮ, BOHUSLAV
b. Polička, Bohemia, Dec. 8, 1890; d. Liestal, Switz., Aug. 28, 1959

| | | |
|---|---|---|
| +*Greek Passion* | 1961 | Zurich |
| +*Marriage, The* | 1953 | NBC |

MARVIN, MEL

| | | |
|---|---|---|
| *Guest from the Future* | 2004 | Purchase, NY |

MASLAND, WILLIAM
b. 1954

| | | |
|---|---|---|
| *Happy Hypocrite* | 1978* | |

MASON, BENEDICT
b. 1954

| | | |
|---|---|---|
| *ChaplinOperas* | 1988* | |
| | 1992 | Strasbourg |
| *Playing Away* | 1994 | Munich |

MASON, CHARLES NORMAN
b. Salt Lake City, UT, Jan. 10, 1955

| | | |
|---|---|---|
| *Daphne at Sea* | 2000 | Birmingham, AL |

MASON, DEBORAH

| | | |
|---|---|---|
| +*Rape of the Lock* | 2002 | New York |

MASON, WILTON ELMAN
b. 1916; d. 1976

| | | |
|---|---|---|
| +*Kingdom Come* | 1953 | Boone, NC |

MATHEWS, PAUL
b. Baltimore, MD

| | | |
|---|---|---|
| +*Chatter and Static* | 1995 | Baltimore, MD |

MATHIAS, WILLIAM
b. Whitland, Carmarthenshire, Wales, Nov. 1, 1934; d. Menai Bridge, Gwynedd, Wales, July 29, 1992

| | | |
|---|---|---|
| *Servants, The* | 1980 | Cardiff |

MATSHIKIZA, TODD THOZAMILE
b. South Africa, 1921; d. London?, 1968

| | | |
|---|---|---|
| *King Kong* | 1959 | Durban, South Africa |

MAURY, LOWNDES
b. Butte, MT, July 7, 1911; d. Encino, CA, Dec. 11, 1975

| | | |
|---|---|---|
| *Celebration, The* | 1955* | |

MAW, NICHOLAS
b. Grantham, Eng., Nov. 5, 1935; d. Washington, DC, May 12, 2009

| | | |
|---|---|---|
| *One Man Show* | 1964 | London |
| *Rising of the Moon* | 1970 | Glyndebourne |
| +*Sophie's Choice* | 2002 | London |

MAXWELL DAVIES, PETER. *See* DAVIES, PETER MAXWELL.

MAYER, CHARLES

| | | |
|---|---|---|
| *Conspiracy of Pontiac* | 1887 | Detroit. MI |

MAYER, WILLIAM
b. New York, Nov. 18, 1925

| | | |
|---|---|---|
| *Brief Candle* | 1967 | New York |
| +*Death in the Family* | 1983 | Minneapolis |
| +*One Christmas Long Ago* | 1962 | Muncie, IN |

MAZZINGHI, JOSEPH
b. London, Dec. 25, 1765; d. Downside, nr. Bath, Eng., Jan. 15, 1844

| | | |
|---|---|---|
| *Exile, The* | 1809 | London |
| *Free Knights* | 1810 | London |
| *Magician No Conjuror* | 1792 | London |
| *Wife of Two Husbands* | 1803 | London |

MAZZOLI, MISSY
b. 1980

| | | |
|---|---|---|
| *Song from the Uproar* | 2009 | Brooklyn, NY |

McANDREW, IAN
b. Vancouver, 1958

| | | |
|---|---|---|
| +*Benjamin Brown* | 1999* | |
| *Cassandra* | 2003 | Toronto |

McCABE, JOHN
b. Huyton, Eng., Apr. 21, 1939

| | | |
|---|---|---|
| *Lion, the Witch* | 1969 | Manchester |
| *Play of Mother Courage* | 1974 | Middlesbrough, Eng. |

McCLURE, LEE

| | | |
|---|---|---|
| *Mother and Child* | 1990 | New York |

McCOY, WILLIAM J.
b. Crestline, OH, Mar. 15, 1848; d. Oakland, CA, Oct. 15, 1926

| | | |
|---|---|---|
| +*Egypt* | 1921 | Berkeley, CA |

McCRAY, CHARLES B.

| | | |
|---|---|---|
| *Annunciation, The* | 1966 | New York |
| +*Trista* | 1966 | New York |

McDERMOTT, VINCENT
b. Atlantic City, NJ, Sept. 5, 1933

| | | |
|---|---|---|
| +*King of Bali* (lib. with K. Foley) | 1990 | Portland, OR |
| *Mata Hari* | 1995 | Dallas, TX |

McFARLAND, RON
b. Marin County, CA

| | | |
|---|---|---|
| *Audition of Molly Bloom* | 2004 | Kentfield, CA |
| *Donner Party* | 1979 | Chico, CA |
| *Song of Pegasus* | 1985 | Murphys, CA |
| *Tamsin Donner* | 1992 | Squaw Valley, CA |

McGUIRE, JANINE

| | | |
|---|---|---|
| *Wake Her Up* | 2004 | New York |

McINTYRE, DAVID L.
b. Edmonton, ON, 1950

| | | |
|---|---|---|
| *Humulus the Mute* | 1979 | Victoria, BC |

McINTYRE, PAUL
b. Peterborough, ON, 1931

| | | |
|---|---|---|
| +*Death of the Hired Man* | 1966* | |
| | 1979 | Toronto |
| +*Macbeth* | 2005* | |
| *This Is Not True* | 1966* | |

McKAY, DAVIS PHARES

| | | |
|---|---|---|
| *As I Lay Dying* | 1991 | Oxford, MS |

McKAY, JUSTIN
b. Narromine, NSW

| | | |
|---|---|---|
| +*Alice in Wonderland* | 2008 | Chico, CA |
| +*Salon, The* | 2009 | Chico, CA |

McKAY, NEIL
b. Ashcroft, BC, 1924

| | | |
|---|---|---|
| +*Kahalaopuna* | 1995 | Honolulu |
| +*La'ie'ikawai* | 1995 | Honolulu |
| *Ring around Harlequin* | 1965* | |

McPEEK, BEN
b. Trail, BC. Aug. 28, 1934; d. Toronto, Jan. 14, 1981

| | | |
|---|---|---|
| *Bargain, The* | 1966 | CBC Montreal |

McQUEEN, IAN
b. Glasgow, 1954

| | | |
|---|---|---|
| *East and West* | 1995 | London |
| +*Hollow Hill* (text with E. Salzman) | 2005 | Buxton |
| *Line of Terror* | 1993 | London |
| *Picasso: Out of the Blue* | 1997 | |

MEACHEM, MARGARET
b. Brooklyn, NY, Jan. 1, 1922

| | | |
|---|---|---|
| +*Alice in Wonderland* | 1982* | |

MEALE, RICHARD
b. Sydney, Aug. 23, 1932; d. there, 23 Nov. 2009

| | | |
|---|---|---|
| *Mer de Glace* | 1991 | Sydney |
| *Voss* | 1986 | Adelaide |

MECHEM, KIRKE
b. Wichita, KS, Aug. 16, 1925

| | | |
|---|---|---|
| +*John Brown* | 1989* | |
| | 2003 | San Francisco |
| *Pride and Prejudice* | 2006 | Winston-Salem, NC |
| +*Rivals, The (Newport Rivals)* | 2003 | San Francisco |
| *Tartuffe* | 1980 | San Francisco |

MECKLER, DAVID

| | | |
|---|---|---|
| +*Apollo 14* | 2002 | New York |

MEIER, MARGARET SHELTON
b. 1936

| | | |
|---|---|---|
| +*On the Edges of Calm* | 1988* | |

MELL, DAVIS
b. Wilton, nr. Salisbury, Eng., Nov. 15, 1604; d. London, Apr. 4, 1662

| | | |
|---|---|---|
| *Triumph of Peace* (with Lawes, Ives) | 1634 | London |

MELLERS, WILFRED
b. Leamington, Warwickshire, Eng., Apr. 26, 1914; d. Scrayingham, North Yorkshire, Eng., May 16, 2008

| | | |
|---|---|---|
| *Borderline, The* | 1959 | London |
| *Tragicall Historie of Christopher Marlowe* | 1950–52* | |

MELLON, ALFRED
b. 1820; d. 1867

| | | |
|---|---|---|
| *Victorine* | 1859 | London |

MENNINI, LOUIS
b. Erie, PA, Nov. 18, 1920; d. 2000

| | | |
|---|---|---|
| +*Rope, The* | 1955 | Lenox, MA |
| *Well, The* | 1951 | Rochester, NY |

MENOTTI, GIAN CARLO
b. Cadegliano, Italy, July 7, 1911; d. Monte Carlo, Feb. 1, 2007

| | | |
|---|---|---|
| +*Amahl and the Night Visitors* | 1951 | New York, NBC |
| +*Amelia Goes to the Ball* | 1937 | Philadelphia |
| +*Boy Who Grew Too Fast* | 1982 | Wilmington, DE |
| +*Bride from Pluto* | 1982 | Washington |
| +*Chip and His Dog* | 1979 | Guelph, ON |
| +*Consul, The* | 1950 | Philadelphia |
| +*Egg, The* | 1976 | Washington |
| *Goya* | 1986 | Washington |
| +*Help, Help, the Globolinks!* | 1968 | Hamburg |

| | | |
|---|---|---|
| +Hero, The | 1976 | Philadelphia |
| +Island God | 1942 | New York |
| +Labyrinth, The | 1963 | NBC |
| +Last Savage | 1963 | Paris |
| +Loca, La | 1979 | San Diego |
| +Maria Golovin | 1958 | Brussels |
| +Martin's Lie | 1964 | Bath, Eng. |
| +Medium, The | 1946 | New York |
| +Most Important Man | 1971 | New York |
| +Old Maid and the Thief | 1939 | NBC radio |
| +Saint of Bleecker Street | 1954 | New York |
| +Singing Child | 1993 | Charleston, SC |
| +Tamu-Tamu | 1973 | Chicago |
| +Telephone, The | 1947 | New York |
| +Trial of the Gipsy | 1978 | New York |
| +Unicorn and the Manticore | 1956 | Washington |
| +Wedding, The | 1988 | Seoul |

**METCALF, JOHN**
b. Swansea, Wales, Aug. 13, 1946

| | | |
|---|---|---|
| Chair in Love | 2005 | Swansea |
| +Crossing, The | 1984 | Cardiff |
| Journey, The | 1981 | Cardiff |
| Kafka's Chimp | 1996 | Banff, AB |
| Tornrak | 1990 | Cardiff |

**MEYEROWITZ, JAN**
b. Breslau [Wrocław, Pol], Apr. 23, 1913; d. Colmar, France, Dec. 15, 1998

| | | |
|---|---|---|
| +Bad Boys in School | 1953 | Lenox, MA |
| Barrier, The | 1950 | New York |
| Eastward in Eden | 1951 | Detroit, MI |
| Esther | 1957 | Urbana, IL |
| Godfather Death | 1961 | New York |
| Port Town | 1960 | Lenox, MA |
| Simoon | 1949 | Lenox, MA |

**MEYERS, ARI BENJAMIN**
b. New York, 1972

| | | |
|---|---|---|
| +Defendants Rosenberg | 1996 | Baltimore. MD |

**MEYERS, EMERSON**
b. 1910

| | | |
|---|---|---|
| Dolcedo | 1959 | Washington, DC |

**MICHAEL, SARAH**

| | | |
|---|---|---|
| +Arachne | 2000 | San Francisco |
| +Sealwoman, The | 1994 | Benicia CA |

**MIDDLETON, ROBERT**
b. Diamond, OH, Nov. 18, 1920

| | | |
|---|---|---|
| Command Performance | 1961 | Poughkeepsie, NY |
| +Life Goes to a Party | 1947 | Lenox, MA |

**MIKI, MINORU**
b. Tokushima, Shikoku, Japan, Mar. 16, 1930; d. Dec. 8, 2011

| | | |
|---|---|---|
| Actor's Revenge | 1979 | London |
| Jōruri | 1985 | St. Louis |
| Tale of Genji | 2000 | St. Louis |

**MILANO, ROBERTO**
b. Brooklyn, NY, Nov. 18, 1936

| | | |
|---|---|---|
| Hired Hand | 1959 | New York |

**MILES, PHILIP NAPIER**
b. Shirehampton, Gloucestershire, Eng., Jan. 21, 1865; d. King's Weston, Gloucestershire, July 19, 1935

| | | |
|---|---|---|
| +Markheim | 1923 | London |
| Westward Ho! | 1913 | London |

**MILLARD, HARRISON**
b. 1830; d. 1890

| | | |
|---|---|---|
| Uncle Tom's Cabin | 1883 | New York |

**MILLER, ROBERT**

| | | |
|---|---|---|
| Cat in the Box | 1993 | New York |

**MILLS, JONATHAN**
b. Sydney, Mar. 21, 1963

| | | |
|---|---|---|
| Eternity Man | 2003 | London |
| Ghost Wife | 1999 | Sydney |

**MILLS, RICHARD**
b. Toowoomba, Queensland, Austral., Nov. 14, 1949

| | | |
|---|---|---|
| Love of the Nightingale | 2007 | Perth, Austral. |
| Summer of the Seventeenth Doll | 1996 | Melbourne |

**MOBBS, KENNETH**
b. Eng., 1935

| | | |
|---|---|---|
| Engaged (after Sullivan) | 1962 | Bristol, Eng. |

**MOERK, ALICE ANN**
b. 1936

| | | |
|---|---|---|
| +Alianor | 1998 | Fairmont, WVA |
| +Flatwoods Monster | 2001* | |
| Unicorn Weeps | 1996* | |
| Wise Woman | 2000 | Fairmont, WVA |

**MOHAUPT, RICHARD**
b. Breslau [Wrocław, Pol], Sept. 14, 1904; d. Reichenau, Austria, July 3, 1957

| | | |
|---|---|---|
| Double Trouble | 1954 | Louisville, KY |

**MOLLICONE, HENRY**
b. Providence, RI, Mar. 20, 1946

| | | |
|---|---|---|
| Coyote Tales | 1998 | Kansas City, MO |
| Dream Child | 1975* | |
| Emperor Norton | 1981 | San Francisco |
| Face on the Barroom Floor | 1978 | Central City, CO |
| Gabriel's Daughter | 2003 | Central City, CO |
| Hotel Eden | 1989 | San Jose, CA |
| Mask of Evil | 1982 | Minneapolis, MN |
| Starbird | 1979 | Houston, TX |
| Young Goodman Brown | 1968 | Saratoga Spr, NY |

**MONK, MEREDITH**
b. Lima, Peru (to American parents), Nov. 20, 1942

| | | |
|---|---|---|
| +Alas | 1991 | New York |
| +Education of the Girlchild | 1973 | New York |
| +Games, The (lib. with Ping Chong) | 1983 | W. Berlin |
| Politics of Quiet | 1996 | Copenhagen |
| +Quarry | 1976 | New York |

MONTGOMERY, BONNIE
  b. AR

| *Billy Blythe* | 2010 | Little Rock, AR |
|---|---|---|

MONTGOMERY, BRUCE
  b. Philadelphia, June 20, 1927; d. 2008

| *John Barleycorn* | 1962* | |
|---|---|---|

MOONIE, W(ILLIAM) B(EATTON)
  b. Stobo, Peeblesshire, Scot., May 29, 1883; d. Edinburgh, Dec. 8, 1961

| *Weird of Colbar* | 1937 | Glasgow |
|---|---|---|

MOORE, ANTHONY

| *Camera* | 1994 | BBC |
|---|---|---|

MOORE, CARMAN
  b. Lorain, OH, Oct. 8, 1936

| *Gethsemane Park* | 1999 | San Francisco |
|---|---|---|
| +*Last Chance Planet* | 1994 | Dayton, OH |
| *Masque of Saxophone's Voice* | 1981* | |
| | 1987 | New York |
| *Sophie Songs* | 1993* | |

MOORE, DOROTHY RUDD
  b. New Castle, DE, June 4, 1940

| *Frederick Douglass* | 1985 | New York |
|---|---|---|

MOORE, DOUGLAS
  b. Cutchogue, NY, Aug. 10, 1893; d. Greenport, NY, July 25, 1969

| *Ballad of Baby Doe* | 1956 | Central City, CO |
|---|---|---|
| *Carry Nation* | 1966 | Lawrence, KS |
| *Devil and Daniel Webster* | 1939 | New York |
| *Emperor's New Clothes* | 1949 | New York |
| *Gallantry* | 1958 | New York |
| *Giants in the Earth* | 1951 | New York |
| *Headless Horseman* | 1937 | Bronxville, NY |
| *White Wings* | 1949 | Hartford |
| *Wings of the Dove* | 1961 | New York |

MOORE, HOMER
  b. nr. Chautauqua, NY, Apr. 29, 1863; d. CA, May 1952

| +*Columbus* | 1903 | St. Louis |
|---|---|---|
| +*Louis XIV* | 1917 | St. Louis |
| +*Puritans, The* | 1902 | St. Louis |

MOORE, MARY CARR
  b. Memphis, Aug. 6, 1873; d. Inglewood, CA, Jan. 9, 1957

| *David Rizzio* | 1932 | Los Angeles |
|---|---|---|
| *Flaming Arrow* | 1922 | San Francisco |
| *Légende Provençale* | 1929–39* | |
| *Leper, The* | 1912* | |
| *Narcissa* | 1912 | Seattle |
| *Rubios, Los* | 1931 | Los Angeles |

MOORE, THOMAS
  b. Dublin, May 28, 1779; d. Sloperton Cottage, nr. Devizes, Feb. 25, 1852

| *M.P.* (with Horn) | 1811 | London |
|---|---|---|

MOOREHEAD, JOHN
  b. Ireland, ca. 1760; d. nr. Deal, Mar. 1804

| +*Birds of a Feather* (with J. Calcott) | 1796 | London |
|---|---|---|
| *Bondocani, Il* (with T. Attwood) | 1800 | London |
| *Cabinet, The* (with Moorehead et al.) | 1802 | London |
| *Family, The* (with Braham, Reeve) | 1802 | London |
| *Family Quarrels* (with Reed) | 1802 | London |
| *Naval Pillar* (with Moorehead et al.) | 1799 | London |
| *Old Fools* | 1800 | London |
| *Speed the Plough* | 1802 | London |

MOPPER, IRVING
  b. Savannah, GA, Dec. 1, 1914

| *Door, The* | 1956 | Newark, NJ |
|---|---|---|
| *Nero's Mother* | 1961 | New York |
| *Red Rose and the Briar* | 1951 | Syracuse, NY |

MORAN, JOHN
  b. Lincoln, NE, 1965

| +*Every Day Newt Burman* | 1993 | New York |
|---|---|---|
| *Jack Benny* | 1989 | New York |
| +*Manson Family* | 1990 | New York |
| *Mathew in the School of Life* | 1994 | New York |

MORAN, ROBERT
  b. Denver, CO, Jan. 8, 1937

| *Desert of Roses* | 1992 | Houston |
|---|---|---|
| *Divertissement No. 3* | 1971 | London |
| *Dracula Diary* | 1994 | Houston, TX |
| *From the Towers of the Moon* | 1992 | St. Paul, MN |
| *Juniper Tree* (with P. Glass) | 1985 | Houston |
| *Let's Build a Nut House* | 1969 | San Jose, CA |
| *Mathew in the School of Life* | 1994 | New York |
| +*Metamenagerie* | 1974 | Berlin |
| *Night Passage* | 1995 | Seattle, WA |
| *Remember Him to Me* | 1996* | |

MORAVEC, PAUL
  b. Buffalo, NY, Nov. 2, 1957

| *Letter, The* | 2009 | Santa Fe |
|---|---|---|

MORE, MARGARET

| *Mermaid, The* | 1951 | Birmingham, Eng. |
|---|---|---|

MORGENSTERN, SAM
  d New York, Dec. 22, 1989

| *Big Black Box* | 1968 | New York |
|---|---|---|
| *Haircut* | 1969 | New York |

MORGULAS, JERROLD
  b. New York, Apr. 5, 1934

| + *Anna and Dedo* | 2005 | Moscow |
|---|---|---|
| +*Calamity, A* | 2008 | Moscow |
| +*Demon, The* | 2009 | Moscow |
| +*Dybbuk, The* | 1999 | New York |
| +*Gentleman Friend* | 2008 | Moscow |
| *Maskerad* | 2010 | Moscow |

MORI, FRANK
  b. London, Mar. 21, 1820; d. Chaumont, France, Aug. 2, 1873

| *River-Sprite* | 1865 | London |
|---|---|---|

MOROSS, JEROME
b. Brooklyn, Aug. 1, 1913; d. Miami, July 25, 1983

| | | |
|---|---|---|
| *Gentlemen, Be Seated!* | 1963 | New York |
| *Golden Apple* | 1954 | New York |
| *Sorry, Wrong Number* | 1980 | Lake George, NY |

MORRILL, KAM
b. Portland, OR

| | | |
|---|---|---|
| +*Bambi* | 1997 | Seattle, WA |
| +*Perlimplín* | 1989 | Philadelphia |

MORRIS, RICHARD

| | | |
|---|---|---|
| *Agamemnon* | 1969 | Oxford |

MORROW, CHARLIE
b. Newark, NJ, 1942

| | | |
|---|---|---|
| *Light Opera* | 1983 | New York |

MOSS, LAWRENCE K.
b. Los Angeles, Nov. 18, 1927

| | | |
|---|---|---|
| *Brute, The* | 1961 | New Haven, CT |
| +*Queen and the Rebels* | 1965* | |

MOSS, M.

| | | |
|---|---|---|
| *Love's Dream* | 1821 | London |

MOSTEL, RAPHAEL

| | | |
|---|---|---|
| +*Travels of Babar* (lib. with Brunhoff) | 2000 | New York |

MULDOWNEY, DOMINIC
b. Southampton, Eng., July 19, 1952

| | | |
|---|---|---|
| *Voluptuous Tango* | 1996 | BBC |

MULLER, GERALD FRANK

| | | |
|---|---|---|
| *Chronicles* | 1977 | Rockville, MD |
| +*Mary Surratt* | 1989 | Ft Washington, MD |

MURDOCH, ELAINE
b. Java, 1944

| | | |
|---|---|---|
| *Tamburlaine* | 1971 | Liverpool |

MURRAY, BAIN
b. Evanston, IL, Dec. 26, 1926; d. Jan. 16, 1993

| | | |
|---|---|---|
| *Legend, The* | 1987 | Cleveland |
| *Mary Stuart* | 1991 | Cleveland |

MURRAY, JEREMIAH

| | | |
|---|---|---|
| +*Beauty and the Beast* | 1974 | New York |
| +*Marriage Proposal* | 1973 | New York |

MURRAY, MICHAEL
b. 1964

| | | |
|---|---|---|
| +*In the Penal Colony* | 1992* | |

MUSGRAVE, FRANK
b. 1834; d. 1888

| | | |
|---|---|---|
| *Caliph of Bagdad* | 1858 | London |
| *Windsor Castle* | 1865 | London |

MUSGRAVE, THEA
b. Barnton, Midlothian, Scot., May 27, 1928

| | | |
|---|---|---|
| *Abbot of Drimock* | 1962 | London |
| +*Christmas Carol* | 1979 | Norfolk, VA |
| *Decision, The* | 1967 | London |
| *Harriet, a Woman Called Moses* | 1985 | Norfolk, VA |
| +*Marko the Miser* | 1963 | Farnham, Eng. |
| *Mary, Queen of Scots* | 1977 | Edinburgh |
| +*Mocking Bird* | 2002 | Boston |
| +*Occurrence at Owl Creek Bridge* | 1982 | London, BBC |
| +*Simón Bolívar* | 1995 | Norfolk, VA |
| *Voice of Ariadne* | 1974 | Aldeburgh |

MUSTO, JOHN
b. Brooklyn, NY, 1954

| | | |
|---|---|---|
| *Bastaniello* | 2008 | New York |
| *Inspector from Rome* | 2010 | Vienna, VA |
| *Later the Same Evening* | 2007 | College Park, MD |
| *Pope Joan* | 1999 | New York |
| *Volpone* | 2004 | Vienna, VA |

MYERS, JEFF

| | | |
|---|---|---|
| *Hunger Art* | 2008 | New York |

NABOKOV, NICOLAS
b. Lubcha, nr. Minsk, Apr. 17, 1903; d. New York, Apr. 6, 1978

| | | |
|---|---|---|
| +*Holy Devil* (lib. with S. Spender) | 1958 | Louisville, KY |
| *Love's Labour's Lost* | 1973 | Brussels |

NAGEL, CHARLES
b. Eng., 1806; d. Liverpool, New South Wales, Austral., 1870

| | | |
|---|---|---|
| +*Mock Catalani* | 1842 | Sydney |

NAKANO, KOJI
b. Japan, Aug. 1974

| | | |
|---|---|---|
| *Brush* | 2004 | Toronto |

NARES, JAMES
b. Stanwell, Middlesex, bapt Apr. 19, 1715; d. London, Feb. 10, 1783

| | | |
|---|---|---|
| *Royal Pastoral* | 1767 | Windsor Castle |

NATHAN, ISAAC
b. Canterbury, Eng., 1790; d. Sydney, Jan. 15, 1864

| | | |
|---|---|---|
| *Alcaid, The* | 1824 | London |
| *Don John of Austria* | 1847 | Sydney |
| *Illustrious Stranger* | 1827 | London |
| *Merry Freaks* | 1843 | Sydney |
| *Sweethearts and Wives* (with Cooke et al.) | 1823 | London |
| *Triboulet* | 1840 | London |

NAYLOR, EDWARD
b. Cambridge, Eng., Nov. 22, 1907; d. Keswick, Cumbria, Eng., May 20, 1986

| | | |
|---|---|---|
| *Angelus, The* | 1909 | London |

NEIL, WILLIAM
b. 1954

| | | |
|---|---|---|
| +*Guilt of Lillian Sloan* | 1986 | Chicago |

NELHYBEL, VACLAV
b. Polanka nad Odrou, Czech., Sept. 24, 1919; d. Scranton, PA, Mar. 22, 1996

| | | |
|---|---|---|
| *Everyman* | 1974 | Memphis, TN |
| *Legend, A* | 1954* | |
| +*Station, The* | 1979 | Lowell, MA |

**NELSON, ROBERT**
b. Phoenix, AR, Sept. 14, 1941

| | | |
|---|---|---|
| *Demon Lover* | 1986 | Dallas |
| *Man Who Corrupted Hadleyville* | 1986* | |
| *Room with a View* | 1993 | Houston |
| *Tickets Please* | 1985 | Houston |

**NELSON, RON (RONALD)**
b. Joliet, IL, Dec. 14, 1929

| | | |
|---|---|---|
| +*Birthday of the Infanta* | 1956 | Rochester, NY |

**NEUENDORF, ADOLF**
b. Hamburg, June 13, 1843; d. New York, Dec. 4, 1897

| | | |
|---|---|---|
| *Don Quixote* | 1881 | New York |

**NEUWIRTH, OLGA**
b. Graz, Austria, Aug. 4, 1968

| | | |
|---|---|---|
| +*Lost Highway* (lib. with E. Jelinek) | 2003 | Graz |

**NEVIN, ARTHUR**
b. Edgeworth, PA, Apr. 27, 1871; d. Sewickley, PA, July 10, 1943

| | | |
|---|---|---|
| *Daughter of the Forest* | 1918 | Chicago |
| *Economites* | 1899 | Sewickley, PA |
| *Poia* | 1907 | Pittsburgh |

**NEWBERN, KENNETH**

| | | |
|---|---|---|
| *Armor of Life* | 1957 | New York |

**NIBLOCK, JAMES**
b. Scappoose, OR, Nov. 1, 1917

| | | |
|---|---|---|
| *Last Leaf* | 2006 | Twin Lake, MI |
| *Ruth* | 2001 | Twin Lake, MI |
| *Ruth and Naomi* | 2009 | Twin Lake, MI |

**NICHOLLS, FREDERICK C.**
b. 1871

| | | |
|---|---|---|
| *Prodigal Son* | 1896 | Liverpool? |

**NIELSEN, ERIK**
b. VT, 1950

| | | |
|---|---|---|
| *Fleeting Animal* | 2000 | Montpelier, VT |

**NIXON, ROGER**
b. Tulare, CA, Aug. 8, 1921

| | | |
|---|---|---|
| *Bride Comes to Yellow Sky* | 1968 | Charleston, IL |

**NOBLE, HAROLD**
b. Blackpool, Lancashire, June 3, 1903; d. Watford, Hertfordshire, Oct. 26, 1998

| | | |
|---|---|---|
| *Lake of Menteith* | 1967 | London |

**NORQUIST, JANET**

| | | |
|---|---|---|
| *Jane Heir* (with R. Gordon) | 1989 | New York |

**NOWAK, (AUGUSTUS) LIONEL**
b. Cleveland, OH, Sept. 25, 1911; d Bennington, VT, Dec 4, 1995

| | | |
|---|---|---|
| +*Clarkstown Witch* | 1959 | Piermont, NY |

**NOYES-GREENE, EDITH**
b. Cambridge, MA, Mar. 26, 1875

| | | |
|---|---|---|
| *Osseo* | 1917 | Brookline, MA |

**NYMAN, MICHAEL**
b. London, Mar. 23, 1944

| | | |
|---|---|---|
| *Facing Goya* | 2000 | Santiago de Compostela, Spain |

| | | |
|---|---|---|
| *Kiss, The* | 1984 | London |
| *Letters, Riddles* (with R. Lepage) | 1991 | London, BBC |
| *Love Counts* | 2005 | Munch |
| *Man Who Mistook His Wife* | 1986 | London |
| *Noises, Sounds* | 1994 | Tokyo |

**O'CONNELL, KEVIN**
b. Derry, N Ireland, Dec. 22, 1958

| | | |
|---|---|---|
| *Fire King* | 1995 | Derry |
| *My Love* | 1997 | Belfast |
| *Sensational!* | 1992 | Dublin |

**OLENICK, ELMER**

| | | |
|---|---|---|
| +*Diet, The* | 1979* | |

**OLIVER, DES**

| | | |
|---|---|---|
| *Miss Treat (Shorts)* | 1999 | Battersea, London |

**OLIVER, HAROLD**
b. Easton, MD, Sept. 15, 1942

| | | |
|---|---|---|
| *King of Cats* | 1976* | |

**OLIVER, JOHN**
b. Vancouver, Sept. 21, 1959

| | | |
|---|---|---|
| *Alternate Visions* | 2007 | Montreal |
| *Guacamayo's Old Song and Dance* | 1991 | Toronto |

**OLIVER, STEPHEN**
b. Chester, Eng., Mar. 10, 1950; d. London, Apr. 29, 1992

| | | |
|---|---|---|
| +*All the Tea in China* | 1969 | Oxford |
| +*Bad Times* | 1975 | London |
| +*Ba-Ta-Clan* | 1988* | |
| +*Beauty and the Beast* | 1985 | London |
| *Britannia Preserv'd* | 1984 | Hampton Court |
| +*Cinderella* | 1991* | |
| +*Dissolute Punished*, tetralogy | 1972 | Edinburgh |
|    *Blind, The* | | |
|    *Dialogue between Jupiter and Cupid* | | |
|    *Dissoluto punito* | | |
|    *Fall of Miss Moss* | | |
| *Donkey, The* | 1973 | Stirling |
| +*Duchess of Malfi* | 1971 | Oxford |
| *Enchanted Shirt* | 1970* | |
| +*Exposition of a Picture* | 1986 | London |
| +*Furcoat for Summer* | 1973* | |
| +*Garden, The* | 1977 | Batignano, Italy |
| +*Girl and the Unicorn* | 1978 | London |
| +*Great McPorridge Disaster* | 1976 | Bath |
| +*Man of Feeling* | 1980 | London |
| +*Mario and the Magician* | 1989 | Milwaukee |
| +*Past Tense:* | | |
|    *Come and Go* | | |
|    *Old Times* | 1974 | Huddersfield |
| +*Perseverance* | 1975 | Liverpool |
| *Phoenix Too Frequent* | 1970 | Oxford |
| +*Ring, The* | 1984 | Manchester |
| +*Sasha* | 1983 | Banff, AB |

| | | |
|---|---|---|
| +*Slippery Soules* | 1969 | Oxford |
| +*Stable Home* | 1977 | Canada |
| +*Sufficient Beauty* | 1974 | Oxford |
| +*Tables Meet* | 1990 | London |
| +*Three Instant Operas* | 1973 | London |
|    *Old Haunts* | | |
|    *Paid Off* | | |
|    *Time Flies* | | |
|    *Three Wise Monkeys* | 1971* | |
| +*Timon of Athens* | 1991 | London |
| +*Tom Jones* | 1976 | Newcastle u Tyne |
| +*Waiter's Revenge* | 1976 | Nottingham |
| +*Waiting* | 1987 | Buxton |

OLIVEROS, PAULINE
b. Houston, May 30, 1932

| | | |
|---|---|---|
| *Lunar Opera* | 2000 | New York |

O'NEAL, BARRY
b. New York, June 9, 1942

| | | |
|---|---|---|
| *Dr. Jekyll and Mr. Hyde* | 1980* | |
| | 2009 | New York |

OPPENHEIM, HANS

| | | |
|---|---|---|
| *Rab the Rhymer* (with I. Dunlop) | 1953 | Aberdeen |

O'REGAN, TARIK
b. London, 1978

| | | |
|---|---|---|
| *Heart of Darkness* | 2006 | Brooklyn, NY |

ORR, BUXTON
b. Glasgow, Apr. 18, 1924; d. Hereford, Dec. 27, 1997

| | | |
|---|---|---|
| *Wager, The* | 1962 | London |

ORR, ROBIN [ROBERT KEMSLEY]
b. Brechin, Angus, Scot., June 2, 1909; d. Cambridge, Eng., Apr. 9, 2006

| | | |
|---|---|---|
| *Full Circle* | 1968 | Perth, Scot. |
| *Hermiston* | 1975 | Edinburgh |
| +*On the Razzle* | 1988 | Glasgow |

OSBORNE, NIGEL
b. Manchester, Eng., June 23, 1948

| | | |
|---|---|---|
| *Electrification of the Soviet Union* | 1987 | Glyndebourne |
| *Hells' Angels* | 1986 | London |
| *Sarajevo* | 1994 | London |
| *Terrible Mouth* | 1992 | London |

OSBORNE, WILLIAM
b. 1951

| | | |
|---|---|---|
| *Alice through the Looking Glass* | 1985 | Jerusalem |
| +*Swineherd, The* | 1980* | |

OVERTON, HALL
b. Bangor, MI, Feb. 23, 1920; d. New York, Nov. 24, 1972

| | | |
|---|---|---|
| *Enchanted Pear Tree* | 1950 | New York |
| +*Huckleberry Finn* | 1971 | New York |
| *Pietro's Petard* | 1963 | New York |

OWEN, RICHARD (Sr.)
b. Dec. 11, 1922, New York

| | | |
|---|---|---|
| +*Abigail Adams* | 1987 | New York |

| | | |
|---|---|---|
| *Death of the Virgin* | 1981 | New York |
| +*Dismissed with Prejudice* | 1956 | New York |
| +*Fisherman Called Peter* | 1965 | Carmel, NY |
| +*Mary Dyer* | 1976 | Suffern, NY |
|   *Moment of War* | 1958* | |
| | 1964 | Buenos Aires |
| +*Rain* | 2003 | New York |
| +*Sadie Thompson* | 1997 | New York |
| +*Tom Sawyer* | 1989 | New York |

PACE, ROBERTO
b. 1949

| | | |
|---|---|---|
| *Cat Lover* | 2000 | Annandale-on-Hudson, NY |

PACKER, CHARLES
b. 1810; d. 1883

| | | |
|---|---|---|
| *Sadak and Kalasrade* | 1835 | London |

PAINE, JOHN KNOWLES
b. Portland, ME, Jan. 9, 1939; d. Cambridge, MA, Apr. 25, 1906

| | | |
|---|---|---|
| +*Azara* | 1883–98* | |
| | 1903 | Boston |

PAINTAL, PRITI
b. New Delhi, Feb. 2, 1960

| | | |
|---|---|---|
| *Biko* | 1992 | Birmingham |
| *Gulliver in Lilliput* | 1995* | |
| *Survival Song* | 1989 | London |

PANNELL, RAYMOND
b. London, ON, Jan. 25, 1935

| | | |
|---|---|---|
| *Luck of Ginger Coffey* | 1967 | Toronto |

PARKE, WILLIAM THOMAS
b. London, Feb. 15, 1761; d. there, Aug. 26, 1847

| | | |
|---|---|---|
| *Nina* (with W. Shield) | 1787 | London |

PARKER, ALICE
b. Boston, Dec. 16, 1925

| | | |
|---|---|---|
| +*Family Reunion* | 1975 | Norman, OK |
| +*Martyr's Mirror* | 1971 | Lansdale, PA |
| +*Ponder Heart* | 1982 | Jackson, MS |
| +*Singer's Glen* | 1978 | Lancaster, PA |

PARKER, HORATIO
b. Auburndale, MA, Sept. 15, 1863; d. Cedarhurst, NY, Dec. 18, 1919

| | | |
|---|---|---|
| *Fairyland* | 1915 | Los Angeles |
| *Mona* | 1912 | New York |

PARROTT, IAN
b. London, March 5, 1916

| | | |
|---|---|---|
| *Black Ram* | 1957 | BBC Wales |

PARRY, JOHN
b. Denbigh, Wales, Feb. 18, 1776; d. London, Apr. 8, 1851

| | | |
|---|---|---|
| *Ivanhoe* | 1820 | London |
| *Oberon's Oath* | 1816 | London |

PARRY, JOSEPH
b. Merthyr Tydfil, Wales, May 21, 1841; d. Penarth, Feb. 17, 1903

| | | |
|---|---|---|
| *Maid of Cefn Ydfa* | 1902 | Cardiff |
| *Sylvia* | 1895 | Cardiff |

PARTCH, HARRY
b. Oakland, CA, June 24, 1901; d. San Diego, Sept. 3, 1974

| | | |
|---|---|---|
| +*Oedipus* | 1952 | Oakland, CA |
| (rev version) | 1954 | Sausalito, CA |
| *Revelation in the Courthouse Park* | 1962 | Urbana, IL |

PASATIERI, THOMAS
b. New York, Oct. 20, 1945

| | | |
|---|---|---|
| *Before Breakfast* | 1980 | New York |
| +*Black Widow* | 1972 | Seattle |
| *Calvary* | 1971 | Seattle |
| +*Divina, La* | 1966 | New York |
| *Family Room* | 2009* | |
| | 2011 | Princeton, NJ |
| *Flowers of Ice* | 1964* | |
| *Frau Margot* | 2006 | New York |
| *God Bless Us Every One!* | 2010 | New York |
| +*Goose Girl* | 1981 | Fort Worth, TX |
| +*Hotel Casablanca* | 2007 | San Francisco |
| *Ines de Castro* | 1976 | Baltimore |
| +*Maria Elena* | 1983 | Tucson, AR |
| +*Padrevia* | 1967 | Brooklyn, NY |
| *Penitentes, The* | 1974 | Aspen, CO |
| *Seagull, The* | 1974 | Houston, TX |
| +*Signor Deluso* | 1974 | Greenway, VA |
| *Three Sisters* | 1986 | Columbus, OH |
| *Trial of Mary Lincoln* | 1972 | NET |
| +*Trysting Place* | 1964* | |
| *Washington Square* | 1976 | Detroit |
| *Women, The* | 1965 | Aspen, CO |

PASCAL, FLORIAN. *See* WILLIAMS, JOSEPH BENJAMIN.

PASQUALI, NICOLO
d. 1757

| | | |
|---|---|---|
| *Temple of Peace* | 1749 | Dublin |
| *Triumphs of Hibernia* | 1748 | Dublin |

PATACCHI, VAL (VALFRIDO)
b. ca. 1920; d. Honolulu, July 3, 1996

| | | |
|---|---|---|
| *Bandit, The* | 1958 | Columbia, MO |
| *Secret, The* | 1955 | Columbia, MO |

PATTERSON, FRANKLIN PEALE
b. Philadelphia, Jan. 5, 1871; d. New Rochelle, NY, July 6, 1966

| | | |
|---|---|---|
| +*Beggar's Love* | 1929 | New York |
| +*Echo, The* | 1926 | Portland, OR |
| +*Mountain Blood* | 1926* | |

PAULUS, STEPHEN
b. Summit, NJ, Aug. 24, 1949

| | | |
|---|---|---|
| *Harmoonia* | 1991 | Muscatine, IA |
| *Heloise and Abelard* | 2002 | New York |
| +*Hester Prynne at Death* | 2004 | New York |
| (lib. with T. Quinn) | | |
| *Postman Always Rings Twice* | 1982 | St Louis |
| *Star Gatherer* | 2006 | St Paul, MN |
| *Summer* | 1999 | Pittsfield, MA |

| | | |
|---|---|---|
| *Three Hermits* | 1997 | St. Paul |
| *Village Singer* | 1979 | St. Louis |
| *Woman at Otowi Crossing* | 1995 | St. Louis |
| *Woodlanders, The* | 1895 | St. Louis |

PAXTON, GLENN
b. 1921

| | | |
|---|---|---|
| *Adventures of Friar Tuck* | 1983 | Saratoga Springs, NY |
| *Monticello* | 2000 | Los Angeles |

PAYNTER, JOHN
b. S London, July 17, 1931; d. July 1, 2010

| | | |
|---|---|---|
| *Voyage of the St. Brendan* | 1979 | Norwich, Eng. |

PEARSON, KATE
b. York, Eng., 1971

| | | |
|---|---|---|
| *Absolute Zero and Rising* | 1999 | Leeds, Eng. |
| *Pied Piper* | 2005 | Hull, Eng. |

PEASLEE, RICHARD
b. 1930

| | | |
|---|---|---|
| *Sir Gawain and the Green Knight* | 2001 | New York |

PELISSIER, VICTOR
b. Paris?, ca. 1740–50; d. ?, New Jersey, ca. 1820

| | | |
|---|---|---|
| *Ariadne Abandoned by Theseus* | 1797 | New York |
| *Bridal Ring* (with H. Condell) | 1810 | London |
| *Edwin and Angelina* | 1796 | New York |
| *Fourth of July* | 1799 | New York |
| *Merry Gardner* | 1801 | New York |
| *Sterne's Maria* | 1799 | New York |
| *Voice of Nature* | 1802 | New York |

PENBERTHY, JAMES
b. Melbourne, May 3, 1917; d. New South Wales, Mar. 29, 1999

| | | |
|---|---|---|
| *Creation of the World* | 1990* | |
| *Dalgerie* | 1959 | Perth, Austral. |
| +*Earth Mother* | 1959* | |
| +*Henry Lawson* | 1989* | |
| +*Miracle, The* | 1964 | Perth, Austral. |
| +*Ophelia* | 1965 | Tasmania, Austral. |
| *Stations* | 1975* | |

PENDERECKI, KRZYSZTOF
b. Dębica, Pol., Nov. 23, 1933

| | | |
|---|---|---|
| *Paradise Lost* | 1978 | Chicago |

PENHORWOOD, EDWIN
b. 1939

| | | |
|---|---|---|
| *Too Many Sopranos* | 2000 | Cedar Rapids, IA |

PENSON, WILLIAM

| | | |
|---|---|---|
| *Gran Uile* | 1832 | Dublin |

PENTLAND, BARBARA
b. Winnipeg, Jan. 2, 1912; d. Vancouver, Feb. 5, 2000

| | | |
|---|---|---|
| *Lake, The* | 1954 | Vancouver |

PEPUSCH, JOHN (JOHANN CHRISTOPH)
b. Berlin, 1667; d. London, July 20, 1752

| | | |
|---|---|---|
| *Apollo and Daphne* | 1716 | London |
| *Beggar's Opera* | 1728 | London |

| | | |
|---|---|---|
| *Death of Dido* | 1716 | London |
| *Myrtillo* | 1715 | London |
| *Orestes* | 1731 | London |
| *Prophetess, The* | 1724 | London |
| *Thomyris* | 1707 | London |
| *Venus and Adonis* | 1715 | London |
| *Wedding, The* | 1729 | London |

**PERERA, RONALD**
b. Boston, Dec. 25, 1941

| | | |
|---|---|---|
| *Araboolies* | 2002 | New York |
| *S.* | 1995 | Northampton, MA |
| *Yellow Wallpaper* | 1989 | Northampton, MA |

**PERL, PAUL**

| | | |
|---|---|---|
| *Judgment Day* | 1951 | New York |

**PERRY, GEORGE FREDERICK**
b. Norwich, 1793; d. London, Mar. 4, 1862

| | | |
|---|---|---|
| *Family Jars* | 1822 | London |
| *Morning, Noon, and Night* | 1822 | London |
| *Sweethearts and Wives* (with Nathan et al.) | 1823 | London |
| *Veteran Soldier* (with Whitaker, Cooke) | 1822 | London |

**PERRY, JULIA**
b. Lexington, KY, Mar. 25, 1924; d. Akron, OH, Apr. 24, 1979

| | | |
|---|---|---|
| +*Cask of Amontillado* (lib. with V. Card) | 1954 | New York |
| +*Selfish Giant* | 1964* | |

**PERSICHETTI, VINCENT**
b. Philadelphia, June 6, 1915; d. there, Aug. 13, 1987

| | | |
|---|---|---|
| +*Sibyl, The* | 1985 | Philadelphia |

**PETERS, RANDOLPH**
b. Winnipeg, Dec. 28, 1959

| | | |
|---|---|---|
| *Golden Ass* | 1999 | Toronto |
| *Inanna's Journey* | 2004 | Toronto |
| *Nosferatu* | 1993 | Toronto |

**PETERSON, HANNIBAL [MARVIN CHARLES]**
b. Smithville, TX, Nov. 11, 1948

| | | |
|---|---|---|
| *Diary of an African-American* | 1991 | New York |

**PHILLIPS, BURRILL**
b. Omaha, Neb., Nov. 9, 1907; d. Berkeley, CA, June 22, 1988

| | | |
|---|---|---|
| *Don't We All?* | 1949 | Rochester, NY |

**PHILLIPS, EDWARD**
fl 1730–1740

| | | |
|---|---|---|
| *Chamber-Maid* | 1730 | London |

**PHILLIPS, MONTAGUE**
b. London, Nov. 13, 1885; d. Esher, Eng., Jan. 4, 1969

| | | |
|---|---|---|
| *Rebel Maid* | 1921 | London |

**PHILLIPS, ROY**

| | | |
|---|---|---|
| *Trevallion* (orch. C. Brill) | 1956 | London |

**PHILPOT, STEPHEN ROWLAND**
b. 1870; d. 1950

| | | |
|---|---|---|
| *Dante and Beatrice* | 1889 | London |

**PICCINNI, NICCOLÒ**
b. Bari, Italy, 1728; d. Passy, 1800

| | | |
|---|---|---|
| *Amelia* | 1768 | London |

**PICKER, TOBIAS**
b. New York, July 18, 1954

| | | |
|---|---|---|
| *American Tragedy* | 2005 | New York |
| *Emmeline* | 1996 | Santa Fe |
| *Fantastic Mr. Fox* | 1998 | Los Angeles |
| *Thérèse Raquin* | 2001 | Dallas |

**PICKETT, LENNY**
b. Las Cruces, NM, Apr. 10, 1954

| | | |
|---|---|---|
| *Welfare* | 1992 | Philadelphia |

**PIKET, FREDERICK**
b. Constantinople, Jan. 6, 1903; d. Long Island City, NY, Feb. 28, 1974

| | | |
|---|---|---|
| *Isaac Levi* | 1956 | White Plains, NY |
| *Satan's Trap* | 1950 | New York |
| *Trilby* | 1967 | New York |

**PINKHAM, DANIEL**
b. Lynn, MA, June 5, 1923; d. Natick, MA, Dec. 18, 2006

| | | |
|---|---|---|
| +*Cask of Amontillado* | 2003 | Boston |
| *Garden of Artemis* | 1948 | Cambridge, MA |
| +*Garden Party* | 1977 | Boston |

**PITTMAN, EVELYN LARUE**
b. McAlester, OK, Jan. 6, 1910

| | | |
|---|---|---|
| +*Esther and Cousin Mordecai* | 1957 | Paris |

**PLISKA, GREG**

| | | |
|---|---|---|
| *Secret Garden* | 1991 | Philadelphia |

**PLOWMAN, LYNNE**
b. Wales

| | | |
|---|---|---|
| *Gwyneth and the Green Knight* | 2002 | Brecon, Wales |

**POKRASS, SAMUEL D.**

| | | |
|---|---|---|
| *Cyrano de Bergerac* | 1932* | |

**POLGAR, TIBOR**
b. Budapest, March 11, 1907; d. Toronto, Aug, 26, 1993

| | | |
|---|---|---|
| *Glove, The* | 1975 | New Liskeard, ON |
| *Troublemaker, The* | 1968* | |

**PORTMAN, RACHEL [MARY BERKELEY]**
b. Haslemere, Surrey, Eng., Dec, 11, 1960

| | | |
|---|---|---|
| *Little Prince* | 2003 | Houston |

**POTTER, A. J. [ARCHIBALD JAMES]**
b. Belfast, Sept. 22, 1918; d. Greystones, County Wicklow, July 5, 1980

| | | |
|---|---|---|
| *Patrick* | 1965 | RTÉ TV, Dublin |
| +*Wedding, The* | 1981 | Dublin |

**POTTER, STEVE**

| | | |
|---|---|---|
| +*Officers, The* | 2008 | New York |

**POÙHE, FRANK JOSEPH**
b. 1939

| | | |
|---|---|---|
| *Pantomime* | 1969 | New York |

**PRATT, SILAS GAMALIEL**
b. Addison, VT, Aug. 4, 1846; d. Pittsburgh, Oct. 30, 1916

| | | |
|---|---|---|
| +*Antonio* | 1874 | Chicago |

| | | |
|---|---|---|
| +*Lucille* | 1887 | Chicago |
| +*Triumph of Columbus* | 1892 | New York |
| *Zenobia* | 1882 | New York |

PRELLEUR, PETER
b. 1705?; d. 1741

| | | |
|---|---|---|
| *Baucis and Philemon* | 1740 | London |

PRESCOTT, JOHN
b. 1959

| | | |
|---|---|---|
| *Reluctant Dragon* | 1999 | Springfield, MO |

PRESTINI, PAOLA
b. 1975

| | | |
|---|---|---|
| *Oceanic Verses* | 2009 | New York |

PREVIN, ANDRÉ
b. Berlin, Apr. 6, 1929

| | | |
|---|---|---|
| *Brief Encounter* | 2009 | Houston |
| *Streetcar Named Desire* | 1998 | San Francisco |

PRIETO, DAFNIS
b. Santa Clara, Cuba, 1974

| | | |
|---|---|---|
| *Revolution of Forms* (with A. Davis) | 2010 | New York |

PRIOLO, CHRISTOPHER E.
b. 1949

| | | |
|---|---|---|
| +*Aria da capo* | 1984* | |

PROTO, FRANK
b. Brooklyn, NY, July 18, 1941

| | | |
|---|---|---|
| *Shadowboxer* | 2010 | College Park, MD |

PROVENZANO, ALDO
b. Philadelphia, May 3, 1930

| | | |
|---|---|---|
| *Cask of Amontillado* | 1968 | Rochester, NY |

PURCELL, DANIEL
b. London, ca. 1660; d. there, Dec. 12, 1717

| | | |
|---|---|---|
| *Brutus of Alba* (with Playford, Scott) | 1696 | London |
| *Grove, The* | 1700 | London |
| *Island Princess* (with Leveridge, Clark) | 1699 | London |
| *Judgment of Paris* | 1701 | London |
| *Rival Queens* (with G. Finger) | 1701 | London |
| *Secular Masque* (with G. Finger) | 1700 | London |
| *World in the Moon* (with J. Clarke) | 1697 | London |

PURCELL, HENRY
b. London, 1658/1659; d. there, Nov. 21, 1695

| | | |
|---|---|---|
| *Dido and Aeneas* | 1689 | London |
| *Dioclesian* | 1690 | London |
| *Fairy Queen* | 1692 | London |
| *Indian Queen* | 1695 | London |
| *King Arthur* | 1691 | London |

PURSER, JOHN
b. Glasgow, 1942

| | | |
|---|---|---|
| *Bell, The* | 1972 | BBC Scotland |
| *Undertaker, The* | 1969 | Edinburgh |

PUTSCHÉ, THOMAS
b. Scarsdale, NY, June 29, 1929

| | | |
|---|---|---|
| +*Cat and the Moon* | 1960 | Hartford |

QUILTER, ROGER
b. 1877; d. 1953

| | | |
|---|---|---|
| *Julia* | 1936 | London |

QUINCY, GEORGE
b. OK, 1937

| | | |
|---|---|---|
| *Home and the River* | 1997 | Long Island |
| *Mummy, The* | 2004 | New York |

RAMINSH, IMANT
b. Ventspils, Latvia, 1943

| | | |
|---|---|---|
| *Nightingale, The* | 2005 | Washington |

RAMSIER, PAUL
b. Louisville, KY, 1937

| | | |
|---|---|---|
| *Man on a Bearskin Rug* | 1969 | Aberdeen, SD |

RAN, SHULAMITH
b. Tel Aviv, Oct. 21, 1949

| | | |
|---|---|---|
| *Between Two Worlds* | 1997 | Chicago |

RANDS, BERNARD
b. Sheffield, Eng., Mar. 2, 1934

| | | |
|---|---|---|
| *Belladonna* | 1999 | Aspen, CO |

RANKL, KARL
b. Gaaden, Austria, Oct. 1, 1898; d. Salzburg, Sept. 6, 1968

| | | |
|---|---|---|
| *Deirdre of the Sorrows* | 1951* | |

RAPCHAK, LAWRENCE
b. Hammond, IN, May 7, 1951

| | | |
|---|---|---|
| *Lifework of Juan Diaz* | 1990 | Chicago |

RAPHLING, SAM
b. Fort Worth, TX, Mar. 19, 1910; d. New York, Jan. 8, 1988

| | | |
|---|---|---|
| +*Cowboy and the Fiddler* | 1085 | Houston |
| *Dr. Heidegger's Experiment* | 1956 | New York |
| *Liar, Liar* | 1972* | |
| +*Mrs. Bullfrog* | 1980 | New York |
| +*President Lincoln* | 1976* | |
| *Tin Pan Alley* | 1954 | New York |

RASCH, TORSTEN
b. Dresden, Aug. 1, 1965

| | | |
|---|---|---|
| *Duchess of Malfi* | 2010 | London |

RATCLIFF, CARY
b. Rochester, NY

| | | |
|---|---|---|
| +*Eleni* (lib. with R. Koch) | 2008 | New York |

RAUM, ELIZABETH
b. Berlin, NH, Jan. 13, 1945

| | | |
|---|---|---|
| +*Final Bid* | 1981 | Regina, SK |
| +*Garden of Alice* | 1985 | Regina, SK |

RAYBOULD, CLARENCE
b. Birmingham, Eng., June 28, 1886; d. Bideford, Mar. 27, 1972

| | | |
|---|---|---|
| *Sumida River* | 1916 | Glastonbury, Eng. |

REA, ALAN
b. 1933

| | | |
|---|---|---|
| *Falstaff in and out of Love* | 1982 | Fresno, CA |
| *Fête at Coqueville* | 1976 | Fresno, CA |
| *Old Pipes and the Dryad* | 1980 | Fresno, CA |

REA, JOHN
b. Toronto, Jan. 14, 1944

| | | |
|---|---|---|
| *Prisoner's Play* | 1973 | Toronto |

READ, GARDNER
b. 1913; d. 2005

| | | |
|---|---|---|
| *Villon* | 1967* | |
| | 1981 | New Orleans |

REAM, MARC

| | | |
|---|---|---|
| *RareArea* | 1985 | Brussels |

REDDING, JOSEPH DEIGHN
b. Sacramento, CA, Sept. 13, 1859; d. San Francisco, Nov. 21, 1932

| | | |
|---|---|---|
| *Land of Happiness* | 1917 | Monte Rio, CA |

REED, H(ERBERT) OWEN
b. Odessa, MO, June 17, 1910

| | | |
|---|---|---|
| *Butterfly Girl* | 1985 | Brooklyn, NY |
| +*Earth-Trapped* | 1962 | East Lansing, MI |
| *Living Solid Face* | 1962 | East Lansing, MI |
| *Peter Homan's Dream* | 1955 | East Lansing, MI |

REED, LOU (LEWIS)
b. Brooklyn, NY, Mar. 2, 1947

| | | |
|---|---|---|
| *Time Rocker* | 1996 | Hamburg |

REED, NANCY BINNS
b. Palo Alto, CA, Dec. 11, 1924; d. Burke, VA, Feb. 26, 2000

| | | |
|---|---|---|
| +*Ali Baba Opera* | 1989 | Arlington, VA |
| +*Blue Opera* | 1989* | |
| | 1997 | Annandale, VA |

REED, THOMAS GERMAN
b. Bristol, June 27, 1817; d. Upper East Sheen, Mar. 21, 1888

| | | |
|---|---|---|
| *Ancient Britons* | 1875 | London |
| *Drama at Home* | 1844 | London |
| *Eyes and No Eyes* | 1875 | London |
| *Golden Fleece* | 1845 | London |
| *He's Coming* | 1874 | London |
| *Indian Puzzle* | 1876 | London |
| *Matched and Mated* | 1876 | London |
| *Mildred's Well* | 1873 | London |
| *Night's Surprise* | 1877 | London |
| *No. 204* | 1877 | London |
| *Our Island Home* | 1870 | London |
| *Sensation Novel* | 1871 | London |
| *Spanish Bond* | 1875 | London |
| *Three Tenants* | 1874 | London |
| *Who's the Composer?* | 1845 | London |
| *Wicked Duke* | 1876 | London |
| *Wonderful Water Cure* | 1846 | London |

REEVE, GEORGE W.
b. London, ca. 1790

| | | |
|---|---|---|
| *Frozen Lake* | 1824 | London |

REEVE, WILLIAM
b. London, 1757; d. there, June 22, 1815

| | | |
|---|---|---|
| *Apparition, The* | 1794 | London |
| *Bannian Day* | 1796 | London |
| *Bantry Bay* | 1797 | London |
| *Blind Girl* (with J. Mazzinghi) | 1801 | London |
| *British Fortitude* (with H. R. Bishop) | 1794 | London |
| *Brother and Sister* | 1815 | London |
| *Caravan, The* | 1803 | London |
| *Chains of the Heart* (with J. Mazzinghi) | 1801 | London |
| *Charity Boy* | 1796 | London |
| *Council of Ten* | 1811 | London |
| *David Rizzio* (with Braham et al.) | 1820 | London |
| *Embarkation, The* | 1799 | London |
| *Family Quarrels* (with J. Moorehead) | 1802 | London |
| *Hero and Leander* | 1787 | London |
| *Jamie and Anna* | ca. 1801* | |
| *Kais* (with J. Braham) | 1808 | London |
| *Magic Minstrel* | 1808 | London |
| *Out of Place* (with J. Braham) | 1805 | London |
| *Paul and Virginia* (with J. Mazzinghi) | 1800 | London |
| *Purse, The* | 1794 | London |
| *Raft, The* | 1798 | London |
| *Ramah Droog* (with J. Mazzinghi) | 1798 | London |
| *Sicilian Romance* | 1794 | London |
| *Thirty Thousand* (with Davy, Braham) | 1804 | London |
| *Thomas and Susan* | 1787 | London |
| *Turnpike Gate* (with J. Mazzinghi) | 1799 | London |
| *Up to Town* (with Condell et al.) | 1811 | London |
| *White Plume* | 1806 | London |
| *Who's to Have Her?* (with J. Whitaker) | 1813 | London |

REICH, STEVE
b. New York, Oct. 3, 1936

| | | |
|---|---|---|
| *Cave, The* (video by B. Korot) | 1993 | Vienna |
| *Three Tales* (video by B. Korot) | 2002 | Vienna |
| *Bikini* | 2002 | Vienna |
| *Dolly* | 2002 | Vienna |
| *Hindenburg* | 1997 | Bonn |

REID, BOB

| | | |
|---|---|---|
| *Africa Is Calling Me* | 1974 | Paris |

REID, MIKE

| | | |
|---|---|---|
| *Different Fields* | 1996 | New York |

REIF, PAUL
b. Prague, Mar. 23, 1910; d. New York, July 7, 1978

| | | |
|---|---|---|
| +*Curse of Mauvais-Air* | 1974 | New York |
| *Mad Hamlet* | 1962* | |
| *Portrait in Brownstone* | 1966 | New York |

REINAGLE, ALEXANDER
b. Portsmouth, Eng., bapt. Apr. 23, 1756; d. Baltimore, Sept. 21, 1809

| | | |
|---|---|---|
| *Columbus* | 1797 | Philadelphia |
| *Savoyard, The* | 1795 | Philadelphia |

REISE, JAY
b. New York, Feb. 9, 1950

| | | |
|---|---|---|
| +*Rasputin* | 1988 | New York |

REMSON, MICHAEL
b. New York, 1962

| | | |
|---|---|---|
| *Last Leaf* | 2000 | New York |
| +*Mary Surratt* | 2005 | Houston |
| +*Sibanda!* | 2003 | Houston |

REYNOLDS, ALBERT
b. 1884

| | | |
|---|---|---|
| *Derby Day* | 1932 | London |
| +*Fountain of Youth* | 1931* | |
| *Policeman's Serenade* | 1926 | London |

RICE, EDWARD EVERETT
b. Brighton, MA, Dec. 21, 1848; d. New York, Nov. 16, 1924

| | | |
|---|---|---|
| *Evangeline* | 1874 | New York |

RICHARDS, SCOTT DAVENPORT

| | | |
|---|---|---|
| +*Charlie Crosses the Nation* | 2008 | New York |
| +*Star across the Ocean* | 2010 | New York |

RICHARDSON, ABIGAIL
b. Oxford, Eng., 1976

| | | |
|---|---|---|
| +*Illusion, The* | 2000* | |
| *Mother Everest* | 2004 | Toronto |
| *Sanctuary Song* | 2007 | Toronto |
| *Seven Stories* | 2002* | |

RIDOUT, ALAN
b. West Wickham, Eng., Dec. 9, 1934; d. Caen, France, Mar. 19, 1996

| | | |
|---|---|---|
| *Angelo* | 1971 | Canterbury |
| *Boy from the Catacombs* | 1965 | Canterbury |
| *Cat, The* | 1971 | Canterbury |
| *Children's Crusade 1939* | 1968 | Canterbury |
| *Creation, The* | 1973 | Ely, Eng. |
| *Gift, The* | 1971 | Canterbury |
| *Greek Kalends* | 1956 | Tunbridge Wells, Eng. |
| *Pardoner's Tale* | 1971 | Canterbury |
| *Phaeton* | 1975 | London, BBC |
| *Rescue, The* | 1963 | Hastings |
| +*Vision, The* | 1974 | Manchester, Eng. |
| *Wenceslas* | 1978 | Bournemouth |
| *White Doe* | 1987 | Ripon, Eng. |

RIDOUT, GODFREY
b. Toronto, May 6, 1918; d. there, Nov. 24, 1984

| | | |
|---|---|---|
| *Lost Child* | 1976 | CBC |

RIES, FERDINAND
b. Bonn, bapt Nov. 28, 1784; d. Frankfurt, Jan. 13, 1838

| | | |
|---|---|---|
| *Sorceress, The* | 1831 | London |

RIETI, VITTORIO
b. Alexandria, Egypt, Jan. 28, 1898; d. Feb. 19, 1994, New York

| | | |
|---|---|---|
| *Clock, The* | 1960* | |
| | 1981 | New York |
| +*Don Perlimplin* | 1952 | Urbana, IL |
| *Maryam the Harlot* | 1966* | |
| *Pet Shop* | 1958 | New York |

RILEY, DENNIS
b. Los Angeles, May 28, 1943; d. New York, May 5, 1999

| | | |
|---|---|---|
| *Cats' Corner* | 1983* | |

| | | |
|---|---|---|
| +*Rappaccini's Daughter* (lib. with J. Pazillo) | 1984* | |

RIMMER, JOHN
b. Auckland, NZ, Feb. 5, 1939

| | | |
|---|---|---|
| *Galileo* | 1999 | Auckland |

RITCHIE, ANTHONY
b. Christchurch, NZ, Sept. 18, 1960

| | | |
|---|---|---|
| *Eagle Has Landed* | 1997 | Wellington |
| *God Boy* | 2004 | Dunedin, NZ |
| *Quartet* | 2004 | Wellington |
| *Trapeze Artist* | 2000 | Dunedin, NZ |

RIVERS, JOSEPH
b. 1931

| | | |
|---|---|---|
| *Prairie Dreams* | 2003 | Tulsa, OK |

RIVERS, SAM
b. El Reno, OK, Sept. 25, 1930

| | | |
|---|---|---|
| *Solomon and Sheba* | 1973 | New York |

RIVINGTON, HILL

| | | |
|---|---|---|
| *Mr. Bellamy Comes Home* | 1950 | London |

ROBERTS, EDWIN

| | | |
|---|---|---|
| *Hunting of the Snark* | 1971 | New York |

ROBINSON, EARL
b. Seattle, WA, July 2, 1910; d. there, July 20, 1991

| | | |
|---|---|---|
| *Sandhog* | 1954 | New York |

ROCHBERG, GEORGE
b. Paterson, NJ, July 5, 1918; d. Bryn Mawr, PA, May 29, 2005

| | | |
|---|---|---|
| +*Confidence Man* | 1982 | Santa Fe, NM |

ROCKWELL, JEFFREY

| | | |
|---|---|---|
| *Rip Van Winkle* | 1989 | San Diego |

RODGERS, LOU
b. 1936

| | | |
|---|---|---|
| +*Afterhours* | 2003 | New York |
| +*Antigone* | 1977 | New York |
| +*Miyako* | 1982 | New York |
| +*Nights of Annabel Lee* | 1996 | New York |
| *Specialist, The* | 1978 | New York |

RODRÍGUEZ, ROBERT XAVIER
b. San Antonio, TX, June 28, 1946

| | | |
|---|---|---|
| *Curandera, La* | 2006 | Denver |
| *Diable amoureux* | 1979 | Dallas |
| *Frida* | 1991 | Philadelphia |
| *Last Night of Don Juan* | 2000 | San Antonio |
| +*Monkey See* | 1987 | Dallas |
| *Old Majestic* | 1988 | San Antonio |
| *Ransom of Red Chief* | 1986 | Mesquite, TX |
| *Suor Isabella* | 1982 | Dallas |
| +*Tango* | 1986 | Dallas |

RODWELL, GEORGE
b. London, Nov. 15, 1800; d. there, Jan. 22, 1852

| | | |
|---|---|---|
| *Black Vulture* | 1830 | London |
| *Bottle Imp* | 1828 | London |
| *Bronze Horse* | 1835 | London |

| | | |
|---|---|---|
| *Cornish Miners* | 1827 | London |
| *Devil's Elixir* | 1829 | London |
| *Don Quixote* | 1840 | London |
| *Earthquake* | 1828 | London |
| *Evil Eye* | 1831 | London |
| *Flying Dutchman* | 1827 | London |
| *Jack Sheppard* | 1839 | London |
| *Last Days of Pompeii* | 1834 | London |
| *Lord of the Isles* | 1834 | London |
| *Mason of Buda* | 1828 | London |
| +*My Own Lover* | 1832 | London |
| *New Don Juan!* | 1828 | London |
| *Paul Clifford* (with J. Blewitt) | 1835 | London |
| *Phantom Ship* | 1827 | London |
| *Quasimodo* | 1836 | London |
| +*Seven Maids of Munich* | 1846 | London |
| *Sexton of Cologne* | 1836 | London |
| *Skeleton Lover* | 1830 | London |
| *Spirit of the Bell* | 1835 | London |
| *Spring Lock* | 1829 | London |
| +*Teddy the Tiler* | 1830 | London |
| +*Thalaba the Destroyer* | 1836 | London |
| *Waverley* | 1824 | London |

**RODWIN, DAVID**
b. New Rochelle, NY, Oct. 22, 1970

| | | |
|---|---|---|
| +*Ecstatic Journey* | 1995 | Aspen, CO |
| + *Virtual Motion* | 1998 | Los Angeles |

**ROE, BETTY**
b. London, July 30, 1930

| | | |
|---|---|---|
| *Brunel* | 2006 | Swindon, Wiltshire |
| *Canterbury Morning* | 1986 | Oakham, Eng. |
| *Flight of Pilgrims* | 1993 | Norlands |
| *Gaslight* | 1983 | London |
| *Lunch at the Cooked Goose* | 2000 | Glasgow |
| *Welcome to Purgatory* | 2003 | Edinburgh |

**ROGERS, AMELIA**
b. 1954

| | | |
|---|---|---|
| *Fortitude* | 1990 | Boston |

**ROGERS, BERNARD**
b. New York, Feb. 4, 1893; d. Rochester, NY, May 24, 1968

| | | |
|---|---|---|
| *Marriage of Aude* | 1931 | New York |
| +*Nightingale, The* | 1955 | New York |
| *Veil, The* | 1950 | Bloomington, IN |
| *Warrior, The* | 1947 | New York |

**ROLFE, JAMES**
b. Toronto, 1961

| | | |
|---|---|---|
| *Aeneas and Dido* | 2007 | Toronto |
| *Beatrice Chancy* | 1998 | Toronto |
| *Elijah's Kite* | 2006 | New York |
| *Enid and the Swans* | 2005 | Toronto |
| *Rosa* | 2004 | Toronto |
| *Swoon* | 2006 | Toronto |

**ROMBERG, SIGMUND**
b. Nagykanizsa, Hung,, July 29, 1887; d. New York, Nov. 9, 1951

| | | |
|---|---|---|
| *Student Prince* | 1924 | New York |

**ROMER, FRANK (FRANCIS)**
b. London, Aug. 5, 1810; d. Malvern, July 1, 1889

| | | |
|---|---|---|
| *Fridolin* | 1840 | London |
| *Pacha's Bridal* | 1836 | London |
| *Rob of the Fens* | 1838 | London |

**ROMERO, MANLY**
b. San Francisco, 1966

| | | |
|---|---|---|
| +*Dreaming of Wonderland* | 2001 | New York |

**ROOKE (O'ROURKE), WILLIAM MICHAEL**
b. Dublin, Sept. 29, 1794; d. London, Oct. 14, 1847

| | | |
|---|---|---|
| *Amilie* | 1818* | |
| | 1837 | London |
| *Henrique* | 1839 | London |
| *Pirate, The* | 1822 | London |

**ROOSEVELT, WILLARD**
b. Madrid, Jan. 16, 1918

| | | |
|---|---|---|
| *And the Walls* | 1976 | New York |

**ROOT, GEORGE F.**
b. Sheffield, MA, Aug. 30, 1820; d. Bailey's Island, ME, Aug. 6, 1895

| | | |
|---|---|---|
| *Belshazzar's Feast* | ca. 1853 | |
| *Flower Queen* | 1853 | New York |
| +*Haymakers, The* | 1860 | Chicago |
| *Pilgrim Fathers* | ca. 1854* | |

**ROOTHAM, CYRIL**
b. Bristol, Eng., Oct. 5, 1875; d. Cambridge, Eng., Mar. 18, 1938

| | | |
|---|---|---|
| *Two Sisters* | 1922 | Cambridge |

**ROREM, NED**
b. Richmond, IN, Oct. 23, 1923

| | | |
|---|---|---|
| *Anniversary, The* | ca. 1961* | |
| *Bertha* | 1973 | New York |
| *Cain and Abel* | ca. 1946* | |
| *Childhood Miracle* | 1955 | New York |
| *Fables* | 1971 | Martin, TN |
| *Hearing* | 1977 | New York |
| *Last Day* | 1967 | New York |
| *Our Town* | 2006 | Bloomington, IN |
| +*Robbers, The* | 1958 | New York |
| *Three Sisters Who Are Not Sisters* | 1971 | Philadelphia |

**ROUSE, MIKEL [MICHAEL JOSEPH]**
b. St. Louis, Jan. 26, 1957

| | | |
|---|---|---|
| +*Dennis Cleveland* | 1996 | New York |
| +*Failing Kansas* | 1995 | New York |

**ROY, KLAUS GEORGE**
b. Vienna, Jan. 24, 1924

| | | |
|---|---|---|
| +*Sterlingman* | 1957 | Boston |

**RÔZE, RAYMOND**
b. London, 1875; d. there, Mar. 31, 1920

| | | |
|---|---|---|
| +*Joan of Arc* | 1913 | London |

RUBINSTEIN, BERYL
b. Athens, GA, Oct. 26, 1908; d. Cleveland, Dec. 22, 1952

| | | |
|---|---|---|
| *Sleeping Beauty* | 1938 | New York |

RUDENSTEIN, ROGER

| | | |
|---|---|---|
| +*Faustus Part One* | 1986 | New York |
| +*Grace* | 2004 | Boston |
| +*Jesus of Nazareth* | 1988 | New York |
| +*Ulysses* | 1999 | Portsmouth, NH |

RUDERS, POUL
b. Ringsted, Denmark, Mar. 27, 1949

| | | |
|---|---|---|
| *Handmaid's Tale* | 2000 | Copenhagen |
| *Kafka's Trial* | 2005 | Copenhagen |

RUEHR, ELENA
b. MI, 1963

| | | |
|---|---|---|
| +*Toussaint before the Spirits*<br>(with Bell, Spires) | 2003 | Boston |

RUFFIN, GARY/HANK RUFFIN

| | | |
|---|---|---|
| *Survival of St. Joan* | 1971 | New York |

RUGER, MORRIS HUTCHINS
b. Superior, WI, Dec. 2, 1902; d. 1974

| | | |
|---|---|---|
| *Fall of the House of Usher* | 1953 | Los Angeles |
| *Gettysburg* | 1938 | Los Angeles |

RUGGLES, CARL
b. Marion, MA, Mar. 11, 1876; d. Bennington, Vt., Oct. 24, 1971

| | | |
|---|---|---|
| *Sunken Bell* | 1927* | |

RUSH, GEORGE
fl. London, ca. 1760–1780

| | | |
|---|---|---|
| *Capricious Lovers* | 1764 | London |
| *Royal Shepherd* | 1764 | London |

RUSSELL, ROBERT
b. 1933

| | | |
|---|---|---|
| *So How Does Your Garden Grow* | 1966 | New York |

RUSSO, WILLIAM
b. Chicago, June 25, 1928; d.there, Jan. 11, 2003

| | | |
|---|---|---|
| *Aesop's Fables* | 1972 | New York |
| *Cabaret Opera* | 1970 | New York |
| *Isabella's Fortune* | 1974 | New York |
| *Island, The* | 1963 | BBC |
| *John Hooten* | 1967 | London |
| *Land of Milk and Honey* | 1967 | Chicago |
| *Pedrolino's Revenge* | 1974 | New York |
| *Shepherds' Christmas* | 1979 | Chicago |

RUTTER, JOHN
b. London, Sept. 24, 1945

| | | |
|---|---|---|
| *Bang!* | 1975 | London |
| *Wind in the Willows* | 1997 | Wilmington, DE |

SACCHINI, ANTONIO M. G.
b. Florence, June 14, 1730; d. Paris, Oct. 6, 1786

| | | |
|---|---|---|
| *Love Finds the Way*<br>(with T. Arne, Fisher) | 1777 | London |

SACCO, PETER
b. Albion, NY, Oct. 25, 1928; d. Aug. 12, 2000

| | | |
|---|---|---|
| +*Mr. Vinegar* (lib. with M. A. Sacco) | 1967 | Redding, PA |

SAHL, MICHAEL
b. Boston, Sept. 2, 1934

| | | |
|---|---|---|
| +*Boxes* | 1981–82 | New York radio |
| +*Civilization & Its Discontents* | 1977 | New York |
| +*Conjurer, The* | 1974 | New York |
| *Dream Beach* | 1988 | New York |
| +*Noah* | 1978 | Brooklyn, NY |
| +*Passion of Simple Simon* | 1979 | New York |
| +*Stauf* | 1976 | New York |
| (all but *Dream Beach* with E. Salzman) | | |

SAINTE CROIX, JUDITH
b. St. Paul, MN

| | | |
|---|---|---|
| +*Secret Circuit* | 1982 | Brooklyn, NY |
| +*Vine of the Soul* (lib. with D. Carulli) | 2001 | Blacksburg, VA |

SALZMAN, ERIC
b. New York, Sept. 8, 1933

| | | |
|---|---|---|
| +*Civilization & Its Discontents* | 1977 | New York |
| +*Conjurer, The* | 1974 | New York |
| +*Noah* | 1978 | Brooklyn, NY |
| +*Passion of Simple Simon* | 1979 | New York |
| +*Stauf* | 1976 | New York |
| *True Last Words* | 1997 | Amsterdam |
| (all but *True Last Words* with M. Sahl) | | |

SAMINSKY, LAZARE
b. Vale-Hotzulovo, nr. Odessa, Nov. 8, 1882; d. Port Chester, NY,
June 30, 1959

| | | |
|---|---|---|
| +*Gagliarda of a Merry Plague* | 1925 | New York |
| +*Julian, the Apostate Caesar* | 1933–38* | |
| +*Vision of Ariel* | 1915* | |
| | 1954 | Chicago |

SANDOW, GREGORY
b. New York, June 3, 1943

| | | |
|---|---|---|
| +*Christmas Carol* | 1977 | Norfolk, VA |
| *Fall of the House of Usher* | 1979 | New York |
| *Frankenstein* | 1980 | Glens Falls, NY |
| *Richest Girl in the World* | 1975 | New York |

SARGON, SIMON
b. Bombay (Mumbai), India, 1938

| | | |
|---|---|---|
| +*Saul* | 1991 | Dallas |
| +*Singing Violin* (lib. with S. Gall) | 1995 | Dallas |
| +*Story of Rapunzel* | 2006 | Dallas |
| +*Thirst* | 1972 | Jerusalem |

SAUNDERS, MAX
b. 1903

| | | |
|---|---|---|
| *Little Beggars* | 1958 | London, BBC |

SAWER, DAVID
b. Stockport, Eng., Sept. 14, 1961

| | | |
|---|---|---|
| +*From Morning to Midnight* | 2001 | London |
| *Panic, The* | 1991 | London |

SAWYER, ERIC

| | | |
|---|---|---|
| *Our American Cousin* | 2008 | Northampton, MA |

SAXON, ROBERT

b. London, Oct. 8, 1953

| | | |
|---|---|---|
| *Caritas* | 1991 | Wakefield, Eng. |

SAYLOR, BRUCE

b. Philadelphia, Apr. 24, 1946

| | | |
|---|---|---|
| *My Kinsman, Major Molineux* | 1976 | Pittsburgh |
| *Orpheus Descending* | 1994 | Chicago |

SCARIM, NICHOLAS

| | | |
|---|---|---|
| *Sumidagawa* | 1979 | New London, CT |

SCHAFER, R. MURRAY

b. Sarnia, ON, July 18, 1933

| | | |
|---|---|---|
| +*Beauty and the Beast* | 1981 | Montreal |
| +*Children's Crusade* | 2009 | Toronto |
| +*Loving/Toi* | 1966 | Montreal, CBC |
| +*Patria, cycle* | | |
| *Patria, Prologue* | 1981 | Heart Lake, ON |
| *Patria, no. 1* | 1974 | Toronto |
| *Patria, no. 2* | 1972 | Stratford, ON |
| *Patria, no. 3* | 1987 | Peterborough, ON |
| *Patria, no. 4* | 1989 | Liège |
| *Patria, no. 5* | 1992 | Toronto |
| *Patria, no 6* | 1983 | Toronto |
| *Patria, no. 7* | 2007* | |
| *Patria, no. 8* | 2001 | Pontypool, ON |
| *Patria, no. 9* | 1994 | Peterboro, ON |
| *Patria, no. 10* | 1997* | |
| | 2005 | Haliburton Forest, ON |
| *Patria, Epilogue* | yearly | |

SCHAT, PETER

b. Utrecht, Holland, June 5, 1935; d. Amsterdam, Feb. 3, 2003

| | | |
|---|---|---|
| *Houdini* | 1979 | Aspen, CO |

SCHELLE, MICHAEL

b. Philadelphia, 1950

| | | |
|---|---|---|
| +*Great Soap Opera* | 1988* | |

SCHICKELE, PETER ("P. D Q. BACH")

b. Ames, IA, July 17, 1935

| | | |
|---|---|---|
| +*Abduction of Figaro* | 1984 | Minneapolis |
| +*Hansel & Gretel & Ted & Alice* | 1972 | Dallas |
| +*Little Nightmare Music* | 1982 | New York |
| +*Oedipus Tex* | 1988 | Minneapolis |
| +*Prelude to Einstein on the Fritz* | 1989 | New York |
| +*Stoned Guest* | 1975 | Ogden, UT |

SCHIFF, DAVID

b. Bronx, NY, Aug. 30, 1945

| | | |
|---|---|---|
| +*Gimpel the Fool* | 1985 | New York |

SCHMIDT, KARL

b. Schwerin, Ger., Sept. 24, 1864; d. 1951

| | | |
|---|---|---|
| *Lady of the Lake* | 1931 | Chicago |

SCHMITZ, ALAN

b. ND, 1950

| | | |
|---|---|---|
| +*Julius Caesar* | 1978 | New Brunswick, NJ |
| *Martin Luther King* | 1992 | Anchorage, AL |
| *Triumph of Love* | 2008 | Cedar Falls, IA |

SCHNAUBER. TOM

b. Los Angeles, 1969

| | | |
|---|---|---|
| *With Such Friends* | 2007 | New York |

SCHOENFIELD, PAUL

b. Detroit, Jan. 24, 1947

| | | |
|---|---|---|
| *Merchant and the Pauper* | 1999 | St. Louis |

SCHONTHAL, RUTH

b. Hamburg, June 27, 1924; d. Scarsdale, NY, July 10, 2006

| | | |
|---|---|---|
| *Courtship of Camilla* | 1980* | |
| *Jocasta* | 1996 | New York |
| *Princess Maleen* | 1989 | White Plains, NY |

SCHREIER, DAN MOSES

| | | |
|---|---|---|
| *Shoulder, The* | 1998 | New York |

SCHUBERT, PETER

New York, Apr. 1, 1946

| | | |
|---|---|---|
| *Bus to Stockport* (with E. Valinsky) | 1986 | New York |
| *Perpetual* | 1983 | New York |

SCHULLER, GUNTHER

b. New York, Nov. 22, 1925

| | | |
|---|---|---|
| *Fisherman and His Wife* | 1970 | Boston |
| +*Visitation, The* | 1966 | Hamburg |

SCHUMAN, WILLIAM

b. New York, Aug. 4, 1910; d. there, Feb. 16, 1992

| | | |
|---|---|---|
| *Mighty Casey* | 1951 | Hartford |
| *Question of Taste* | 1989 | Cooperstown, NY |

SCHURMANN, GERARD

b. Kertosono, Dutch East Indies [now Indonesia], Jan. 19, 1924

| | | |
|---|---|---|
| +*Piers Plowman* | 1980 | Gloucester, Eng. |

SCHWARTZ, PAUL

b. Vienna, July 27, 1907; d. 1999

| | | |
|---|---|---|
| +*Experiment, The* | 1956 | Gambier, OH |

SCHWARTZ, STEPHEN

b. Mar. 6, 1948

| | | |
|---|---|---|
| +*Séance on a Wet Afternoon* | 2009 | Santa Barbara, CA |

SCOTT, CYRIL

b. Oxton, Eng., Sept. 27, 1879; d. Eastbourne, Dec. 31, 1970

| | | |
|---|---|---|
| +*Alchemist, The* | 1925 | Essen, Ger |
| +*Maureen O'Mara* | 1946* | |

SCOTT, TOM (THOMAS JEFFERSON)

b. Campbellsburg, KY, May 28, 1912; d. New York, Aug. 12, 1961

| | | |
|---|---|---|
| *Fisherman, The* | 1956* | |

SCRUTON, ROGER

b. Buslingthorpe, Lincolnshire, Feb. 27, 1944

| | | |
|---|---|---|
| +*Minister, The* | 1996 | Oxford |
| +*Violet* | 2005 | London |

SCULTHORPE, PETER
  b. Launceston, Tasmania, Apr. 29, 1929

| | | |
|---|---|---|
| *Quiros* | 1982 | ABC |
| +*Rites of Passage* | 1974 | Sydney |

SEARELLE, LUSCOMBE
  b. Devon, Eng., 1853; d. 1907

| | | |
|---|---|---|
| *Wreck of the Pinafore* | 1882 | London |

SEARLE, HUMPHREY
  b. Oxford, Aug. 26, 1915; d. London, May 12, 1982

| | | |
|---|---|---|
| +*Diary of a Madman* | 1958 | Berlin |
| +*Hamlet* | 1968 | Hamburg |
| +*Photo of the Colonel* | 1964 | London, BBC |

SEDGWICK, ALFRED B.
  b. Kennington, Surrey, Eng., ca. 1817; d. New York, ca. 1880

| | | |
|---|---|---|
| *Africanus Blue Beard* | 1874 | Gloucester, MA |
| +*Circumstances Alter Cases* | 1876 | New York? |
| *Estranged* | 1876 | New York? |
| *Gambrinus* | 1876 | Jackson, MI |
| *Leap Year* | 1875 | New York |
| *My Walking Photograph* | 1876 | Chicago? |
| +*Queerest Courtship* | 1875 | Chicago? |
| +*Single Married Man* | 1883 | New York? |
| +*Sold Again and Got the Money* | 1876 | New York? |
| +*Twin Sisters* | 1876 | New York? |

SEEDO, MR.
  b. ca. 1700; d. Potsdam, ca. 1754

| | | |
|---|---|---|
| *Lottery, The* | 1732 | London |
| *Mock Doctor* (with Carey, Jones) | 1732 | London |
| *Venus, Cupid* | 1733 | London |

SELETSKY, HAROLD
  b. Brooklyn, NY, 1927

| | | |
|---|---|---|
| *Song of Insanity* | 1987 | New York |

SELLECK, JOHANNA
  b. Melbourne, 1959

| | | |
|---|---|---|
| *Quickening, The* | 1998 | Pt Fairy, Victoria |

SELWYN, DAVID
  b. Bristol, Eng., Nov. 21, 1951

| | | |
|---|---|---|
| +*Rocking Stone* | 1979 | Bristol, Eng. |

SENATOR, RONALD
  b. London, Apr. 17, 1926

| | | |
|---|---|---|
| *Insect Play* | 1981* | |
| *Wolf of Gubbio* | 1980 | London |

SESSIONS, ROGER
  b. Brooklyn, NY, Dec. 28, 1896; d. Princeton, NJ, Mar. 16, 1985

| | | |
|---|---|---|
| *Emperor's New Clothes* | 1984* | |
| *Fall of the House of Usher* | 1925* | |
| *Lancelot and Elaine* | 1910* | |
| *Montezuma* | 1964 | Berlin (West) |
| *Trial of Lucullus* | 1947 | Berkeley, CA |

SEYMOUR, JOHN LAURENCE
  b. Los Angeles, Jan. 18, 1893; d. San Francisco, Feb. 1, 1986

| | | |
|---|---|---|
| *In the Pasha's Garden* | 1935 | New York |

| | | |
|---|---|---|
| *Ramona* | 1970 | Provo, UT |
| +*Two Gentlemen of Verona* (lib. with H. C. Tracy) | 1937* | |

SHADLE, CHARLES
  b. 1960

| | | |
|---|---|---|
| *Friends and Dinosaurs* | 1989 | Needham, MA |
| *Last Goodbye* | 2008 | Boston |
| *Question of Love* | 2006 | Boston |

SHAFFER, JEANNE ELLISON
  b. 1925

| | | |
|---|---|---|
| +*Ghost of Susan B. Anthony* | 1987 | Tuscaloosa, AL |

SHAPIRO, DAVID

| | | |
|---|---|---|
| *April Witch* | 1995 | Baltimore |

SHARMAN, RODNEY
  b. Biggar, SK, May 24, 1958

| | | |
|---|---|---|
| *Elsewhereless* | 1998 | Toronto |

SHATIN (ALLEN), JUDITH
  b. Boston, Nov. 21, 1949

| | | |
|---|---|---|
| +*Coal* | 1994 | Shepherdstown, WVA |
| *Follies and Fancies* | 1987 | New York |
| *Job* | 1980* | |

SHAUGHNESSY, ROBERT

| | | |
|---|---|---|
| *Enchanted Garden* | 1972* | |

SHAW, FRANCIS RICHARD
  b. Maidenhead, Berkshire, Eng., June 23, 1942

| | | |
|---|---|---|
| *Selfish Giant* | 1973* | |

SHAW, GEOFFREY
  b. London, 1879; d. there, Apr. 14, 1943

| | | |
|---|---|---|
| *All at Sea* (posth.) | 1952 | London |

SHAW, MARTIN
  b. London, Mar. 9, 1875; d. Southwold, Oct. 24, 1958

| | | |
|---|---|---|
| *Master Valiant* | 1936 | London |
| *Mr. Pepys* | 1926 | London |
| *Thorn of Avalon* | 1931 | London |
| *Waterloo Leave* | 1928 | Norwich, Eng. |

SHAW, THOMAS
  b. ca. 1760; d. ca. 1830

| | | |
|---|---|---|
| *Island of St. Marguerite* | 1789 | London |

SHAWN, ALLEN
  b. 1948

| | | |
|---|---|---|
| *Ant and the Grasshopper* | 1999 | Bellevue, WA |
| *Music Teacher* | 2006 | New York |

SHEFFER, JONATHAN B.
  b. New York, 1953

| | | |
|---|---|---|
| +*Blood on the Dining Room Floor* | 2000 | New York |
| *Camera obscura* | 1980 | New London, CT |
| *Mistake, The* | 1981 | Denver, CO |

SHELDON, ROBERT
  b. 1938

| | | |
|---|---|---|
| *Fifth for Bridge* | 1961 | San Francisco |

SHELLEY, HARRY ROWE
b. New Haven, June 2, 1858; d. Short Beach, CT, Sept. 12, 1947

| | | |
|---|---|---|
| *Old Black Joe* | 1911 | New York |
| +*Romeo and Juliet* | 1901* | |

SHEN, MIKE

| | | |
|---|---|---|
| +*Bread & Roses* (lib. with Glickman) | 2000 | New York |

SHENG, BRIGHT
b. Shanghai, Dec. 6, 1955

| | | |
|---|---|---|
| *Madame Mao* | 2003 | Santa Fe |
| *Silver River* | 1997 | Santa Fe |
| *Song of Majnun* | 1992 | Chicago |

SHEPHERD, STUART
b. Toronto, 1947

| | | |
|---|---|---|
| +*Hood of the Woods* | 1985 | Rochester, NY |

SHERE, CHARLES EVERETT
b. Berkeley, CA, Aug. 20, 1935

| | | |
|---|---|---|
| *Bride Stripped Bare* | 1984 | Oakland, CA |
| *I Like It to Be a Play* | 1989 | San Francisco |
| *Ladies Voices* | 1987 | Berkeley, CA |
| *What Happened* | 1991* | |

SHERMAN, KIM D.
b. Elgin, IL, Aug. 6, 1954

| | | |
|---|---|---|
| *Three Visitations* | 1996 | Minneapolis |
| *Lamentations* | | |
| *Long Island Dreamer* | 1987 | Minneapolis |
| *Red Tide* | 1989 | Minneapolis |

SHIELD, WILLIAM
b. Swalwell, nr. Newcastle upon Tyne, Mar. 5, 1748; d. London, Jan. 25, 1829

| | | |
|---|---|---|
| *Abroad and at Home* | 1796 | London |
| *Arrived at Portsmouth* | 1794 | London |
| *Campaign, The* | 1785 | Dublin |
| *Choleric Fathers* | 1785 | London |
| *Cobler of Castlebury* | 1778 | London |
| *Crisis, The* | 1778 | London |
| *Crusade, The* | 1790 | London |
| *Czar, The* | 1790 | London |
| *Farmer, The* | 1787 | London |
| *Flitch of Bacon* | 1778 | London |
| *Fontainbleau* | 1784 | London |
| *Hartford Bridge* | 1792 | London |
| *Highland Reel* | 1788 | London |
| *Irish Mimic* | 1795 | London |
| *Italian Villagers* | 1797 | London |
| *Lad of the Hills* | 1796 | London |
| *Lock and Key* | 1796 | London |
| *Love and War* (or comp. J. O'Keefe) | 1787 | London |
| *Love in a Camp* | 1786 | London |
| *Marian* | 1788 | London |
| *Midnight Wanderers* | 1793 | London |
| *Mysteries of the Castle* | 1795 | London |
| *Netly Abbey* (with W. T. Parke) | 1794 | London |
| *Nina* | 1787 | London |

| | | |
|---|---|---|
| *Noble Peasant* | 1784 | London |
| *Nunnery, The* | 1785 | London |
| *Poor Soldier* | 1783 | London |
| *Prophet, The* | 1788 | London |
| *Richard Coeur de Lion* | 1786 | London |
| *Rival Soldiers* | 1797 | London |
| *Robin Hood* | 1784 | London |
| *Rosina* | 1782 | London |
| *Shamrock, The* | 1777 | Dublin |
| *Siege of Gibraltar* | 1780 | London |
| *Sprigs of Laurel* | 1793 | London |
| *To Arms!* | 1793 | London |
| *Travellers in Switzerland* | 1794 | London |
| *Two Faces under a Hood* | 1807 | London |
| *Wicklow Mountains* | 1796 | London |
| *Woodman, The* | 1791 | London |

SHIELDS, ALICE
b. New York, Feb. 18, 1943

| | | |
|---|---|---|
| +*Apocalypse* | 1993 | New York |
| *Criseyde* | 2008 | New York |
| *Mass for the Dead* | 1993 | New York |
| +*Odyssey 1* | 1968* | |
| +*Odyssey 2* | 1975 | Glens Falls, NY |
| +*Odyssey 3* | 1975* | |
| +*Shaman* (with Barrett) | 1978* | |
| | 1987 | New York |
| +*Wraecca* | 1989 | New York |

SHIFLETT, MELISSA

| | | |
|---|---|---|
| *Dora* | 1999 | New York |
| +*My Undying Love* | 2008 | Boston |
| *Without Colors* | 1989 | Minneapolis |

SHORE, HOWARD
b. Toronto, Oct. 18, 1946

| | | |
|---|---|---|
| *Fly, The* | 2008 | Paris |

SIEGEL, NORMAN

| | | |
|---|---|---|
| *Who Stole the American Crown Jewels?* | 1971 | New York |

SIEGMEISTER, ELIE
b. New York, Jan. 15, 1909; d. Manhasset, NY, Mar. 10, 1991

| | | |
|---|---|---|
| *Angel Levine* | 1985 | New York |
| *Darling Corie* | 1954 | Hempstead, NY |
| *Lady of the Lake* | 1985 | New York |
| *Marquesa of O* | 1982* | |
| *Mermaid in Lock No. 7* | 1958 | Pittsburgh |
| *Miranda* | 1956 | Hartford |
| *Night of the Moonspell* | 1976 | Shreveport, LA |
| *Plough and the Stars* | 1963 | St. Louis |

SIERRA, ROBERTO
b. Vega Baja, Puerto Rico, Oct. 9, 1953

| | | |
|---|---|---|
| *Terra Incognita* | 1997 | New York |

SILSBEE, ANN
b. Cambridge, MA, Aug. 21, 1930

| | | |
|---|---|---|
| *Nightingale's Apprentice* | 1984 | Ithaca, NY |

SILVER, SHEILA
 b. Seattle, WA, Oct. 3, 1946

| | | |
|---|---|---|
| +Thief of Love | 1985 | New York |
| Wooden Sword | 2010 | New York |

SILVERMAN, ADAM
 b. New York, 1973

| | | |
|---|---|---|
| Korczak's Orphans | 2003 | Lebanon, NH |

SILVERMAN, FAYE-ELLEN
 b. New York, Oct. 2, 1947

| | | |
|---|---|---|
| +Miracle of Nemirov | 1974* | |

SILVERMAN, STANLEY J.
 b. New York, July 5, 1938

| | | |
|---|---|---|
| Africanus Instructus | 1986 | New York |
| Columbine String Quartet Tonight! | 1981 | Lenox, MA |
| Dr. Selavy's Magic Theatre | 1972 | Stockbridge, MA |
| Elephant Steps (P. Smiley, electronics) | 1968 | Lenox, MA |
| Hotel for Criminals | 1974 | Lenox, MA |
| Madame Adare | 1980 | New York |
| Up from Paradise | 1974 | Ann Arbor, MI |

SIMON, CARLY
 b. New York, June 25, 1945

| | | |
|---|---|---|
| +Romulus Hunt (lib. with J. Brackman) | 1993 | New York |

SIROTA, ROBERT

| | | |
|---|---|---|
| Bontshe the Silent | 1982 | Cambridge, MA |

SIRULNIKOFF, JACK
 b. Winnipeg, Dec. 11, 1931

| | | |
|---|---|---|
| This Evening | 1960 | Bennington, VT |

SISCO, DAVID
 b. 1975

| | | |
|---|---|---|
| Catbird Seat | 1999 | Boston |
| +Sopranos! (lib. with Phillips) | 2002 | New York |

SISKIND, PAUL A.
 b. 1962

| | | |
|---|---|---|
| +In Mighty Silence | 1992 | |
| Sailor-Boy and the Falcon | 2006 | Potsdam, NY |

SITSKY, LARRY
 b. Tientsin [now Tianjin], China, Sept. 10, 1934

| | | |
|---|---|---|
| De Profundis | 1982 | Canberra |
| Fall of the House of Usher | 1965 | Hobart, Austral |
| Fiery Tales | 1976 | Adelaide |
| Golem, The | 1980* | |
| | 1993 | Sydney |
| Lenz | 1974 | Sydney |
| Three Scenes | 1991 | Canberra |
| Voices in Limbo | 1977* | |
| | 1981 | ABC |

SIX, HERBERT
 b. 1909

| | | |
|---|---|---|
| All Cats Turn Gray | 1971 | New York |
| Without Memorial Banners | 1966 | Kansas City, MO |

SKILLING, ROBERT P.

| | | |
|---|---|---|
| David | 1951 | New York |

SKILTON, CHARLES SANFORD
 b. Northampton, MA, Aug. 16, 1868; d. Lawrence, KS, Mar. 12, 1941

| | | |
|---|---|---|
| Sun-Bride | 1930 | NBC radio |

SLATES, PHILIP
 b. Canton, OH, Sept. 24, 1924; d. Indianapolis, Dec. 2, 1966

| | | |
|---|---|---|
| +Bargain, The | 1956 | Athens, OH |
| +Candle, The | 1956 | Athens, OH |

SLAUGHTER, WALTER
 b. London, Feb. 17, 1860; d. there, Mar. 2, 1908

| | | |
|---|---|---|
| Alice in Wonderland | 1886 | London |
| Marjorie | 1890 | London |

SLEEPER, THOMAS
 b. Wagoner, OK, Feb. 16, 1956

| | | |
|---|---|---|
| +Aceldama | 2003 | Miami |
| Sisters Antipodes | 2000 | Miami |

SLOBIN, MARK
 b. Detroit, Mar. 15, 1943

| | | |
|---|---|---|
| +David's Violin (arr. of Mogulesco) | 1976 | Middletown, CT |
| Shloyme Gorgl (arr.) | 1978 | Middletown, CT |

SMALLEY, ROGER
 b. Swinton, Manchester, Eng., July 26, 1943

| | | |
|---|---|---|
| William Derrincourt | 1977 | Perth, Austral. |

SMART, HENRY
 b. London, Oct. 26, 1838; d. there, July 6, 1879

| | | |
|---|---|---|
| Berta | 1854 | London |

SMILEY, PRIL
 b. Mohonk Lake, NY, Mar. 19, 1943

| | | |
|---|---|---|
| Elephant Steps (electronics, for S. Silverman) | 1968 | Lenox, MA |

SMITH, CHARLES
 b. 1786; d. 1856

| | | |
|---|---|---|
| Hit or Miss! | 1810 | London |

SMITH, DAVID STANLEY
 b. Toledo, OH, July 6, 1877; d. New Haven, Dec. 17, 1949

| | | |
|---|---|---|
| Merry Mount | 1912–13* | |

SMITH, DOUGLAS

| | | |
|---|---|---|
| Judith | 1982 | Cincinnati, OH |

SMITH, GREGG
 b. Cincinnati, Aug. 21, 1931

| | | |
|---|---|---|
| Aesop's Fables | 1985 | De Kalb, IL |
| Rip Van Winkle | 1991 | Syracuse |

SMITH, HALE
 b. Cleveland, OH, June 29, 1925; d. Freeport, NY, Nov. 24, 2009

| | | |
|---|---|---|
| Blood Wedding | 1953 | Cleveland. OH |

SMITH, JOHN CHRISTOPHER (JOHANN CHRISTOPH SCHMIDT)
 b. Ansbach, Ger., 1712; d. Bath, Eng., Oct. 3, 1795

| | | |
|---|---|---|
| Enchanter, The | 1760 | London |

| | | |
|---|---|---|
| *Fairies, The* | 1755 | London |
| *Rosalinda* | 1740 | London |
| *Seasons, The* | 1740* | |
| *Tempest, The* | 1756 | London |
| *Teraminta* | 1732 | London |
| *Ulysses* | 1733 | London |

**SMITH, JULIA**
b. Denton, TX, Jan. 25, 1911; d. New York, Apr. 27, 1989

| | | |
|---|---|---|
| *Cockcrow* | 1954 | Austin, TX |
| *Cynthia Parker* | 1939 | Denton, TX |
| *Daisy* | 1973 | Miami |
| *Gooseherd and the Goblin* | 1947 | New York |
| *Shepherdess and the Chimneysweep* | 1966 | Fort Worth, TX |
| *Stranger of Manzano* | 1947 | Dallas |

**SMITH, LARRY ALAN**
b. Canton, OH, Oct. 4, 1955

| | | |
|---|---|---|
| *Aria da capo* | 1980 | Chicago |

**SMITH, LELAND**
b. Oakland, CA, Aug. 6, 1925

| | | |
|---|---|---|
| *Santa Claus* | 1955 | Chicago |

**SMITH, RUSSELL**
b. Tuscaloosa, AL, Apr. 23, 1927

| | | |
|---|---|---|
| *Unicorn in the Garden* | 1957 | Hartford |

**SMITH BRINDLE, REGINALD**
b. Bamber Bridge, Lancashire, Eng., Jan. 5, 1917; d. Caterham, Surrey, Sept. 9, 2003

| | | |
|---|---|---|
| +*Death of Antigone* | 1971 | Oxford |

**SMOLANOFF, MICHAEL**
b. New York, May 11, 1942

| | | |
|---|---|---|
| *Vercingetorix* | 1973* | |

**SMYTH, ETHEL**
b. Marylebone, London, Apr. 22, 1858; d. Woking, Surrey, May 8, 1944

| | | |
|---|---|---|
| +*Boatswain's Mate* | 1916 | London |
| +*Entente Cordiale* | 1925 | London |
| +*Fête Galante* | 1923 | Birmingham |
| +*Forest, The* | 1902 | Berlin |
| *Wreckers, The* | 1906 | Leipzig |

**SOKOLOFF, NOEL**
b. 1923; d. 1998

| | | |
|---|---|---|
| *Franklin's Tale* | 1961 | Baton Rouge, LA |
| *Pardoner's Tale* | 1961* | |

**SOKOLOVIC, ANA**
b. 1968

| | | |
|---|---|---|
| *Midnight Court Opera* | 2005 | Toronto |

**SOLDIER, DAVID**

| | | |
|---|---|---|
| *Naked Revolution* | 1997 | New York |

**SOLOMON, EDWARD**
b. London, July 25, 1855; d. there, Jan. 22, 1895

| | | |
|---|---|---|
| *Lord Bateman* | 1882 | London |
| *Nautch Girl* | 1891 | London |
| *Vicar of Bray* | 1882 | London |

**SOLURI, PATRICK**
b. 1975

| | | |
|---|---|---|
| +*Figaro's Last Hangover* | 2009 | New York |
| *Inferno* | 1999 | New York |
| *Inferno of Dante* | 2003 | New York |

**SOMERS, HARRY**
b. Toronto, Sept. 11, 1925; d. Rosedale, ON, Mar. 9, 1999

| | | |
|---|---|---|
| *Death of Enkidu* | 1977 | Toronto |
| *Fool, The* | 1956 | Toronto |
| *Louis Riel* | 1967 | Toronto |
| *Mario and the Magician* | 1992 | Toronto |
| *Serinette* | 1990 | Sharon, ON |

**SOMERVILLE, REGINALD**
b. 1867

| | | |
|---|---|---|
| +*David Garrick* | 1920 | London |
| +*Mountaineers, The* (lib. with Eden) | 1909 | London |
| '*Prentice Pillar* | 1897 | London |

**SONDHEIM, STEPHEN**
b. New York, Mar. 22, 1930

| | | |
|---|---|---|
| +*Sweeney Todd* | 1979 | New York |

**SONENBERG, DANIEL**

| | | |
|---|---|---|
| +*Summer King* (with D. Nester) | 2005 | Brooklyn, NY |

**SOUSA, JOHN PHILIP**
b. Washington, DC, Nov. 6, 1854; d. Reading, PA, Mar. 6, 1932

| | | |
|---|---|---|
| +*Bride Elect* | 1897 | New Haven |
| *Capitan, El* | 1896 | Boston |
| *Charlatan, The* | 1898 | Montreal |
| *Désirée* | 1884 | Washington |
| *Free Lance* | 1905 | Philadelphia |
| *Merry Monarch* | 1890 | New York |
| *Smugglers, The* | 1882 | Philadelphia |

**SPEKTOR, MIRA J.**
b. 1928

| | | |
|---|---|---|
| *Lady of the Castle* | 1982 | New York |
| *Passion of Lizzie Borden* | 1986 | Buffalo, NY |

**SPELMAN, TIMOTHY (MATHER)**
b. Brooklyn, NY, Jan. 21, 1891; d. Florence, Aug. 21, 1970

| | | |
|---|---|---|
| +*Courtship of Miles Standish* | 1941* | |
| +*Lizzie Hexam* | 1929* | |
| *Magnifica, La* | 1920* | |
| *Sea Rovers* | 1928* | |
| +*Sunken City* | 1930* | |

**SPENSER, WILLARD**
b. Cooperstown, NY, 1852

| | | |
|---|---|---|
| *Little Tycoon* | 1885 | Philadelphia |

**SPIVACK, LARRY**

| | | |
|---|---|---|
| *Cathedral, The* | 1986 | New York |

**SPRATLAN, LEWIS**
b. Miami, Sept. 5, 1940

| | | |
|---|---|---|
| *Earthrise* | 2003 | San Francisco |
| *Life Is a Dream* | 1978* | |
| | 2000 | Amherst, MA |

STAHL, RICHARD
b. 1860; d. New York, 1899

| | | |
|---|---|---|
| *Salem Witch* | 1883 | Boston? |
| *Sea King* | 1889 | New York |

STANFORD, CHARLES VILLIERS
b. Dublin, Sept. 30, 1852; d. London, Mar. 29, 1924

| | | |
|---|---|---|
| *Canterbury Pilgrims* | 1884 | London |
| *Critic, The* | 1916 | London |
| *Much Ado about Nothing* | 1901 | London |
| *Savonarola* | 1884 | Hamburg |
| *Shamus O'Brien* | 1896 | London |
| *Travelling Companion* | 1919* | |
| | 1925 | Liverpool |
| *Veiled Prophet of Khorassan* | 1881 | Hanover, Ger. |

STANHOPE, DAVID
b. Sutton Coldfield, Eng., Dec. 19, 1952

| | | |
|---|---|---|
| +*Un-Dead, The* | 2010 | Melbourne |

STANLEY, JOHN
b. London, Jan. 17, 1712; d. there, May 19, 1786

| | | |
|---|---|---|
| *Arcadia* | 1761 | London |
| *Tears and Triumphs of Parnassus* | 1760 | London |

STANSBURY, GEORGE FREDERICK
b. 1800; d. 1845

| | | |
|---|---|---|
| *Postillion of Longjumeau* | 1837 | London |

STARER, ROBERT
b. Vienna, Jan. 8, 1924; d. New York, Apr. 22, 2001

| | | |
|---|---|---|
| *Anna Marguerita's Will* | 1981 | New York |
| *Apollonia* | 1979 | St. Paul, MN |
| *Intruder, The* | 1956 | New York |
| *Last Lover* | 1975 | Katonah, NY |
| *Mystic Trumpeter* | 1983 | Brooklyn, NY |
| +*Pantagleize* | 1973 | Brooklyn, NY |

STEADMAN, ROBERT FREDERICK
b. Chiswick, London

| | | |
|---|---|---|
| *Sredni Vashtar* | 1988* | |

STEARNS, THEODORE
b. Berea, OH, June 10, 1880; d. Los Angeles, Nov. 1, 1935

| | | |
|---|---|---|
| +*Snowbird, The* | 1923 | Chicago |

STEIBELT, DANIEL
b. Berlin, Oct. 22, 1765; d. St. Petersburg, ca. Oct. 1823

| | | |
|---|---|---|
| *Albert and Adelaide* (with T. Attwood) 1798 | | London |

STEIN, LEON
b. Chicago, Sept. 18, 1910; d. May 9, 2002

| | | |
|---|---|---|
| *Deirdre* | 1957 | Chicago |
| *Fisherman's Wife* | 1955 | St. Joseph, MI |

STEPLETON, JAMES
b. 1941

| | | |
|---|---|---|
| *Awakening, The* | 2003 | New York |
| +*Meanwhile, Back at the Seraglio* | 1997* | |
| *Prodigal Son* | 1983 | New York |

STERN, MAX
b. Valley Stream, NY, Mar. 31, 1947

| | | |
|---|---|---|
| +*Messer Marco Polo* | 1999* | |
| | 2006 | New York |
| *Philosophy Lesson* | 1967* | |

STERNAU, CYNTHIA
b. 1956

| | | |
|---|---|---|
| +*Star Lovers* | 2002* | |
| +*Story of the Bird Feng* | 1997* | |
| +*Tale of Cupid & Psyche* | 2000* | |
| *Way of Humankind*, trilogy | | |
| +*Age of Gold* | 1999* | |
| +*Fall of Atlantis* | 1999* | |
| +*Myth of Er* | 1995* | |
| *World Out of Time*, trilogy | | |
| +*Challenge, The* | 1996* | |
| +*Council of the Dead* | 1996* | |
| +*Solon the Dreamer* | 1996* | |

STEVENS, NOEL SCOTT

| | | |
|---|---|---|
| *Enchanted Canary* | 1961 | Bemidji, MN |

STEVENSON, JOHN
b. Dublin, Nov. 1761; d. Kells, County Meath, Sept. 14, 1833

| | | |
|---|---|---|
| *Bedouins, The* | 1801 | Dublin |
| *Benyowsky* | 1826 | London |
| *Cavern, The* | 1825 | Dublin |
| *Contract, The* | 1782 | Dublin |
| *Love in a Blaze* (with P. Cogan) | 1799 | Dublin |
| *Spanish Patriots* | 1812 | London |

STEWART, FRANK GRAHAM
b. La Junta, CO, Dec. 12, 1920

| | | |
|---|---|---|
| *To Let the Captive Go* | 1974 | New York |

STEWART, HUMPHREY JOHN
b. London, May 22, 1856; d. San Diego, CA, Dec. 28, 1932

| | | |
|---|---|---|
| *Hound of Heaven* | 1924 | San Francisco |
| *King Hal* | 1906* | |
| | 1911 | San Francisco |

STILL, WILLIAM GRANT
b. Woodville, MS, May 11, 1895; d. Los Angeles, Dec. 3, 1978

| | | |
|---|---|---|
| *Bayou Legend* | 1941* | |
| | 1974 | Jackson, MS |
| *Blue Steel* | 1934* | |
| *Costaso* | 1949* | |
| | 1989 | Flagstaff, AR |
| *Highway 1, U.S.A.* | 1963 | Miami |
| *Minette Fontaine* | 1984 | Baton Rouge, LA |
| *Mota* | 1951* | |
| *Pillar, The* | 1955* | |
| *Troubled Island* | 1938* | |
| | 1949 | New York |

STINSON, SCOTT
b. 1961

| | | |
|---|---|---|
| +*Lamentations of Ophelia* | 2009 | Miami |

## STODDARD, MARLA

| | | |
|---|---|---|
| +*Hansel and Gretel* | 1986 | Arcata, CA |

## STOESSEL, ALBERT
b. St. Louis, MO, Oct. 11, 1894; d. New York, May 12, 1943

| | | |
|---|---|---|
| *Garrick* | 1937 | New York |

## STOKER, RICHARD
b. Castleford, Yorkshire, Nov. 8, 1938

| | | |
|---|---|---|
| *Birthday of the Infanta* | 1963 | London |
| +*Chinese Canticle* | 1991 | London |
| *Johnson Preserv'd* | 1967 | London |
| +*Make Me a Willow Cabin* | 1973 | London |
| *Thérèse Raquin* | 1975* | |

## STOKES, ERIC
b. Haddon Heights, NJ, July 14, 1930; d. Minneapolis, MN, Mar. 16, 1999

| | | |
|---|---|---|
| *Apollonia's Circus* | 1994 | Minneapolis, MN |
| *Further Voyages* | 1995* | |
| +*HAPP* | 1977 | Minneapolis, MN |
| *Horspfal* | 1969 | Minneapolis, MN |
| *Jealous Cellist* | 1979 | Minneapolis, MN |
| *We're Not Robots* | 1986 | Minneapolis, MN |

## STORACE, STEPHEN
b. London, Apr. 4, 1762; d. there, Mar. 15/16, 1796

| | | |
|---|---|---|
| *Algonah* (with Kelly) | 1802 | London |
| *Cave of Trophonius* | 1791 | London |
| *Cherokee, The* | 1794 | London |
| *Dido* | 1792 | London |
| *Doctor and the Apothecary* | 1788 | London |
| *Glorious First of June* | 1794 | London |
| *Haunted Tower* | 1789 | London |
| *Iron Chest* | 1796 | London |
| *Lodoiska* | 1794 | London |
| *Mahmoud* | 1796 | London |
| *My Grandmother* | 1793 | London |
| *No Song, No Supper* | 1790 | London |
| *Pirates, The* | 1792 | London |
| *Poor Old Drury!!!* | 1791 | London |
| *Prize, The* | 1793 | London |
| *Siege of Belgrade* | 1791 | London |
| *Three and the Deuce* | 1795 | London |

## STOTHART, HERBERT
b. 1885; d. 1949

| | | |
|---|---|---|
| *Rose-Marie* (with R. Friml) | 1924 | Los Angeles |

## STRASSBURG, ROBERT
b. New York, Aug. 30, 1915; d. Oct. 25, 2003

| | | |
|---|---|---|
| *Chelm* | 1956 | White Plains, NY |

## STRAVINSKY, IGOR
b. Oranienbaum, nr. St. Petersburg, June 17, 1882; d. New York, Apr. 6, 1971

| | | |
|---|---|---|
| *Flood, The* | 1962 | CBS |
| *Rake's Progress* | 1951 | Venice |

## STRICKLAND, DAVID

| | | |
|---|---|---|
| *Phoenix Park* | 2002 | New York |

## STRILKO, ANTHONY
b. New York, 1931

| | | |
|---|---|---|
| *Last Puppet* | 1963 | New York |

## STRINGER, ALAN

| | | |
|---|---|---|
| +*Circle of Love* | 2004 | Albuquerque, NM |
| +*Coyote's Music* | 1994 | Albuquerque, NM |
| +*Divertissement* | 1997 | New York |
| +*Miraculous Staircase* | 1996 | Albuquerque, NM |
| +*Roman Fever* | 1996 | New York |
| +*Sunny Morning* (with J. Benbow) | 1998 | Albuquerque, NM |
| +*Three Stories* | 2007 | Albuquerque, NM |

## STROUSE, CHARLES
b. New York, June 7, 1928

| | | |
|---|---|---|
| +*Family, The* | 1967 | New York |
| +*Nightingale* | 1982 | Vienna, VA |

## STUART, PAUL
b. Omaha, NE, 1956

| | | |
|---|---|---|
| *Kill Bear Comes Home* | 1996 | Rochester, NY |
| *Little Thieves of Bethlehem* | 1997 | Rochester, NY |

## SUBOTNICK, MORTON
b. Los Angeles, Apr. 14, 1933

| | | |
|---|---|---|
| *Intimate Immensity* | 1997 | New York |
| *Jacob's Room* | 1987 | St. Paul, MN |
| *Misfortune of the Immortals* (with J. La Barbara) | 1992 | Chester, PA |

## SULLIVAN, ARTHUR S.
b. London, May 13, 1842; d. there, Nov. 22, 1900

| | | |
|---|---|---|
| *Beauty Stone* | 1898 | London |
| *Chieftain, The* | 1894 | London |
| *Contrabandista* | 1867 | London |
| *Cox and Box* | 1867 | London |
| *Emerald Isle* (compl. E. German) | 1901 | London |
| *Gondoliers, The* | 1889 | London |
| *Grand Duke* | 1896 | London |
| *Haddon Hall* | 1892 | London |
| *H.M.S. Pinafore* | 1878 | London |
| *Iolanthe* | 1882 | London |
| *Ivanhoe* | 1891 | London |
| *Mikado, The* | 1885 | London |
| *Patience* | 1881 | London |
| *Pirates of Penzance* | 1879 | New York |
| *Princess Ida* | 1884 | London |
| *Rose of Persia* | 1899 | London |
| *Ruddigore* | 1887 | London |
| *Sapphire Necklace* | 1867 | London |
| *Sorcerer, The* | 1877 | London |
| *Thespis* | 1871 | London |
| *Trial by Jury* | 1875 | London |
| *Utopia Limited* | 1893 | London |
| *Yeomen of the Guard* | 1888 | London |
| *Zoo, The* | 1875 | London |

SULLIVAN, TIMOTHY
b. Ottawa, ON, Dec. 16, 1954

| | | |
|---|---|---|
| +*Dream Play* | 1988 | Toronto |
| *Florence: The Lady with the Lamp* | 1992 | Elowa, ON |
| +*Imaginary Couple* | 1990 | New York |
| *Josephine* | 2001 | New York |
| +*Tomorrow, Tomorrow* | 1987 | New York |

SUPRYNOWICZ, CLARK

| | | |
|---|---|---|
| *Caliban Dreams* | 2001 | San Francisco |
| *Chrysalis* | 2006 | Berkeley |

SUSA, CONRAD
b. Springdale, PA, Apr. 26, 1935

| | | |
|---|---|---|
| +*Black River* (lib. with R. Street) | 1975 | St. Paul, MN |
| *Dangerous Liaisons* | 1994 | San Francisco |
| +*Love of Don Perlimplin* | 1984 | Purchase, NY |
| *Transformations* | 1973 | Minneapolis, MN |
| +*Wise Women* (lib. with P. Littell) | 1994 | Dallas, TX |

SUSKIND, PAUL

| | | |
|---|---|---|
| *Sailor-Boy and the Falcon* | 2006 | Potsdam, NY |

SUTHERLAND, MARGARET
b. Adelaide, Austral., Nov. 20, 1897; d. Melbourne, Aug. 12, 1984

| | | |
|---|---|---|
| *Young Kabbarli* | 1965 | Hobart, Austral |

SVANE, RANDALL
b. Pittsburgh, PA, 1955

| | | |
|---|---|---|
| *Scarlet Letter* | 1995* | |

SWADOS, ELIZABETH
b. Buffalo, NY, Feb. 5, 1951

| | | |
|---|---|---|
| +*Esther* (lib. with E. Wiesel) | 1988 | New York |
| *Pied Piper* | 1989 | Orlando, FL |

SWENSSON, EVELYN
b. DE?

| | | |
|---|---|---|
| +*From the Mixed-Up Files* | 2002 | Wilmington, DE |
| *Jungle Book* | 1996 | Wilmington, DE |
| +*Redwall* | 1998 | Wilmington, DE |

SWIFT, RICHARD
b. Middlepoint, OH, Sept. 24, 1927; d. Swados, CA, Nov. 8, 2003

| | | |
|---|---|---|
| *Trial of Tender O'Shea* | 1964* | |

SWISHER, GLORIA WILSON
b. 1935

| | | |
|---|---|---|
| *Legend of Poker Alice* | 2010 | Shoreline, WA |

TAHOURDIN, PETER
b. Bramdean, Hampshire, Eng., Aug, 27, 1928

| | | |
|---|---|---|
| +*Heloise and Abelard* | 1993 | Perth, Austral. |
| *Inside Information* | 1959 | London |
| +*Tempest, The* | 2000* | |

TALBOT, HOWARD (MUNKITTRICK)
b. Yonkers, NY, Mar. 9, 1865; d. Reigate, Eng., Sept. 12, 1928

| | | |
|---|---|---|
| *White Chrysanthemum* | 1906 | London |

TALMA, LOUISE
b. Arcachon, France, Oct. 31, 1906; d. Macdowell Colony, VT, Aug. 13, 1996

| | | |
|---|---|---|
| *Alcestiad, The* | 1962 | Frankfurt |
| +*Have You Heard* | 1981 | New York |

TAMKIN, DAVID
b. Aug. 28, 1906, Chernigov, Ukraine; d. Los Angeles, June 21, 1975

| | | |
|---|---|---|
| +*Dybbuk, The* | 1951 | New York |

TAN DUN
b. Simao, Hunan Province, China, Aug. 18, 1957

| | | |
|---|---|---|
| +*First Emperor* (lib. with Ha Jin) | 2006 | New York |
| +*Gate, The* | 1999 | Tokyo |
| *Marco Polo* | 1996 | Munich |
| *Peony Pavilion* | 1998 | Vienna |
| +*Tea* (lib. with Xu Ying, trans. Liao) | 2003 | Tokyo |

TANENBAUM, ELIAS
b. Brooklyn, NY, 1923

| | | |
|---|---|---|
| +*Imposition, The* (with M. Laudor) | 1994* | |

TANNER, JERRÉ E[UGENE]
b. Lock Haven, PA, Jan. 5, 1939

| | | |
|---|---|---|
| *Kona Coffee Cantata* | 1986* | |
| *Naupaka Floret* | 1992* | |
| *Pupu-kani-oe* | 1980* | |

TATE, PHYLLIS
b. Gerrards Cross, Buckinghamshire, Eng., Apr. 6, 1911; d. London, May 27, 1987

| | | |
|---|---|---|
| *Dark Pilgrimage* | 1962 | London, BBC |
| *Lodger, The* | 1960 | London |
| *Twice in a Blue Moon* | 1969 | Farnham, Eng. |
| *What D'Ye Call It* | 1966 | Cheltenham, Eng. |

TATE, ROBERT

| | | |
|---|---|---|
| *Closed Case* | 1998 | Albuquerque, NM |

TAUB, BRUCE
b. New York, Feb. 6, 1948

| | | |
|---|---|---|
| +*Passion, Poison* | 1976 | New York |
| *Waltz on a Merry-Go-Round* | 1979* | |

TAVERNER, JOHN
b. London, Jan. 28, 1944

| | | |
|---|---|---|
| *Cappemakers, The* | 1964 | Sussex, Eng. |
| *Gentle Spirit* | 1977 | Bath, Eng. |
| *Mary of Egypt* | 1992 | Aldeburgh |
| *Thérèse* | 1979 | London |

TAYLOR, CLIFFORD
b. Avalon, PA, Oct. 23, 1923; d. Abington, PA, Sept. 19, 1987

| | | |
|---|---|---|
| *Freak Show* | 1975* | |

TAYLOR, (JOSEPH) DEEMS
b. New York, Dec. 22, 1885; d. there, July 3, 1966

| | | |
|---|---|---|
| +*Dragon, The* | 1958 | New York |
| *King's Henchman* | 1927 | New York |
| +*Peter Ibbetson* | 1931 | New York |
| +*Ramuntcho* | 1942 | Philadelphia |

TAYLOR, RAYNER
b. London, 1747; d. Philadelphia, Aug. 17, 1825

| | | |
|---|---|---|
| *Aethiop, The* | 1814 | Philadelphia |
| *Buxom Joan* | 1778 | London |

| | | |
|---|---|---|
| *Capocchio and Dorinna* | 1793 | Annapolis, MD |
| *Gray Mare's the Best Horse* (arr.) | 1731 | London |
| *Pizzaro* | 1800* | |
| *Rose of Aragon* | 1822 | New York |

**TAYLOR, RICHARD**

| | | |
|---|---|---|
| *Warchild* | 1997 | London |

**TAYLOR, STEPHEN ANDREW**
b. IL, 1965

| | | |
|---|---|---|
| *Paradise Lost* | 2006 | New York |

**TCHEREPNIN, ALEXANDER**
b. St. Petersburg, Jan. 21, 1899; d. Paris, Sept. 29, 1977

| | | |
|---|---|---|
| *Nymph and the Farmer* | 1952 | Aspen, CO |

**TELGMANN, OSCAR F.**
b. Mengeringhausen, Ger., ca. 1855; d. Toronto, Mar. 30, 1946

| | | |
|---|---|---|
| *Leo, the Royal Cadet* | 1889 | Kingston, ON |

**TENDUCCI, FERDINANDO**
b. Siena, Italy, ca. 1735; d. Genoa, Jan. 25, 1790

| | | |
|---|---|---|
| *Revenge of Athridates* | 1766 | Dublin |

**THEOFANIDIS, CHRISTOPHER**
b. Dallas, Dec. 18, 1967

| | | |
|---|---|---|
| *Cows of Apollo* | 2001 | New York |
| *Refuge, The* | 2007 | Houston |
| *Thirteen Clocks* | 2003 | Houston |

**THOMAS, ARTHUR GORING**
b. Ratton Park, Sussex, Eng., Nov. 20, 1850; d. London, Mar. 20, 1892

| | | |
|---|---|---|
| *Esmeralda* | 1883 | London |
| *Golden Web* (compl. S. P. Waddington) | 1893 | Liverpool |
| *Light of the Harem* | 1897 | London |
| *Nadeshda* | 1885 | London |

**THOMAS, AUGUSTA READ**
b. Glen Cove, NY, Apr. 24, 1964

| | | |
|---|---|---|
| *Ligeia* | 1994 | Baltimore |
| *Psychles* | 1987 | Chicago |

**THOMAS, EDWARD**
b. Chisholm, MN, Oct. 1, 1924

| | | |
|---|---|---|
| *Desire under the Elms* | 1978 | New London, CT |

**THOMAS, KAREN P.**
b. 1957

| | | |
|---|---|---|
| *Coyote's Tail* | 1991 | Seattle, WA |

**THOMAS, RICHARD**
b. 1964

| | | |
|---|---|---|
| +*Jerry Springer* | 2003 | London |

**THOMPSON, RANDALL**
b. New York, Apr. 21, 1899; d. Boston, July 9, 1984

| | | |
|---|---|---|
| *Nativity according to St. Luke* | 1961 | Cambridge, MA |
| +*Solomon and Balkis* | 1942 | Cambridge, MA |

**THOMPSON, RICHARD**
b. Aberdeen, Scot

| | | |
|---|---|---|
| *Mask in the Mirror* | 2009* | |
| | 2011 | New York |

**THOMS, HOLLIS**
b. 1948

| | | |
|---|---|---|
| *Moustache, The* | 2009 | Annapolis, MD |
| *Rime of the Ancient Mariner* | 2010 | Annapolis, MD |
| *Socrates* | 2007 | Annapolis, MD |

**THOMSON, JOHN**
b. Sprouston, Roxburgh, Scot., Oct. 28, 1805; d. Edinburgh, May 6, 1841

| | | |
|---|---|---|
| *Hermann* | 1834 | London |
| *Shadow on the Wall* | 1835 | London |

**THOMSON, VIRGIL**
b. Kansas City, MO, Nov. 25, 1896; d. New York, Sept. 30, 1989

| | | |
|---|---|---|
| *Four Saints in Three Acts* | 1933 | Ann Arbor, MI |
| *Lord Byron* | 1972 | New York |
| *Mother of Us All* | 1947 | New York |

**THORNE, FRANCIS**
b. Bay Shore, NY, June 23, 1922

| | | |
|---|---|---|
| *Mario and the Magician* | 1994 | Brooklyn, NY |

**THORNE, T[HOMAS] PEARSALL**

| | | |
|---|---|---|
| *Maid of Plymouth* | 1893 | New York |

**TINSLEY, STERLING**

| | | |
|---|---|---|
| *Flight of Eagles* | 1985 | Houston |

**TIPPETT, MICHAEL**
b. London, Jan. 2, 1905; d. there, Jan. 8, 1998

| | | |
|---|---|---|
| +*Ice Break* | 1977 | London |
| +*King Priam* | 1962 | London |
| +*Knot Garden* | 1970 | London |
| +*Midsummer Marriage* | 1955 | London |
| +*New Year* | 1989 | Houston |
| +*Robin Hood* | 1934 | Boosbeck, Eng. |
| (text with Ayerst, Pennyman) | | |

**TITUS, HIRAM**
b. Minneapolis, MN, Jan. 28, 1947

| | | |
|---|---|---|
| *Rosina* | 1980 | Minneapolis, MN |

**TOCH, ERNST**
b. Vienna, Dec. 7, 1887; d. Santa Monica, Oct. 1, 1964

| | | |
|---|---|---|
| +*Edgar and Emily* | 1965 | New York |
| *Princess and the Pea* | 1954 | Lenox, MA |

**TODD, WILL**
b. County Durham, Eng., Jan. 14, 1970

| | | |
|---|---|---|
| *Blackened Man* | 2002 | London |
| *Screams of Kitty Genovese* | 2001 | Boston |
| *Whirlwind* | 2006 | London |

**TONNING, GERARD**
b. Stavanger, Norway, May 25, 1860; d. New York, June 10, 1940

| | | |
|---|---|---|
| *All in a Garden Fair* | 1913 | Seattle, WA |
| *Blue Wing* | 1917 | Seattle, WA |

**TOOVEY, ANDREW**
b. London, Feb. 21, 1962

| | | |
|---|---|---|
| *Juniper Tree* | 1993 | Broomhill, Kent |
| +*Ubu* (lib. with M. Finnissy) | 1992 | Cardiff |

TORKE, MICHAEL
  b. Milwaukee, WI, Sept. 22, 1961
  *Directions, The*                    1986    Iraklion, Crete
  *King of Hearts*                     1996    Aspen, CO
  *Strawberry Fields*                  1999    Cooperstown, NY
TOULMOUCHE, FRÉDÉRIC
  b. Nantes, France, Aug. 3, 1850; d. Paris, Feb. 20, 1909
  *Wedding Eve* (with E. Ford)         1892    London
TOVEY, SIR DONALD
  b. Elton, Eng., July 17, 1875; d. Edinburgh, July 10, 1940
  *Bride of Dionysus*                  1929    Edinburgh
TOWNSEND, DOUGLAS
  b. New York, Nov. 8, 1921
  *Lima Beans*                         1956    New York
TOWNSEND, JILL
  +*Promise, The*                      1997    London
TOWNSHEND, PETE(R) [DENNIS BLANDFORD]
  b. Chiswick, Eng., May 19, 1945
  *Tommy*                              1968    New York
TRACY, GEORGE LOWELL
  b. 1855; d. 1921
  *Uncle Tom's Cabin*                  1886    Manchester, NH
TRANCHELL, PETER
  b. Cuddalore, India, July 14, 1922; d. Bishops Waltham, Sept. 14, 1993
  +*Mayor of Casterbridge*             1951    Cambridge, Eng.
TRAVIS, ROY
  b. New York, June 24, 1922
  +*Passion of Oedipus*                1968    Los Angeles
TREFOUSSE (TRÉFOUSSE), ROGER
  b. New York, Oct. 21, 1951
  *Blue Margaritas*                    1989    Washington
  *Départ Malgache*                    2000*
                                       2003    New York
  +*Found Objects*                     1991    New York
  *Monkey Opera*                       1982    Brooklyn, NY
TRIMBLE, JOAN
  b. Enniskillen, N. Ire, June 18, 1915; d. there, Aug. 6, 2000
  *Blind Raftery*                      1957    London, BBC
TRIMBLE, LESTER
  b. Bangor, WI, Aug. 28, 1920; d. New York, Dec. 31, 1986
  *Boccaccio's Nightingale*            1962*
TRINKLEY, BRUCE
  b. 1945
  *Ever Since Eden*, trilogy           1997    University Park, PA
     *Cleo*                            1999    University Park, PA
     *Eve's Odds*                      1999    University Park, PA
     *Golden Apple*                    1999    University Park, PA
     *York*                            2002    University Park, PA
TRUAX, BARRY
  b. Chatham, ON, May 10, 1947
  *Powers of Two*                      2006    Vancouver

TRYTHALL, GILBERT
  b. 1930
  +*Music Lesson*                      1960*
TUCKER, CURTIS
  *Stranger's Tale*                    2005    Middletown, OH
TULLY, JAMES H.
  b. 1814; d. 1868
  *Bluebeard Repaired*                 1866    London
TURNAGE, MARK-ANTHONY
  b. Essex, Eng., June 10, 1960
  *Country of the Blind*               1997    Aldeburgh
  +*Greek*                             1988    Munich
  *Silver Tassie*                      2000    London
  *Twice through the Heart*            1997    Aldeburgh
TURNER, ROBERT
  b. Montreal, June 6, 1920
  *Brideship, The*                     1967    Vancouver
  *Vile Shadows*                       1983*
                                       2004    CBC
TURNER, TOM
  *Four-Thousand Dollars*              1969    IA City
TUROK, PAUL
  b. New York, Dec. 3, 1929
  *Richard III*                        1975    Philadelphia
  *Scene: Domestic*                    1955*
                                       1973    Aspen, CO
TURRIN, JOSEPH
  b 1947
  *Scarecrow, The*                     1976*
                                       2006    Austin, TX
UNDERHILL, OWEN
  b. Regina, SK, Jan. 26, 1954
  *Star Catalogues*                    1994    Vancouver
UYEDA, LESLIE
  b. Montreal, 1953
  *Game Misconduct*                    2000    Vancouver
VALENTI, MICHAEL
  b. 1942
  +*Beau Nash*                         2003    New York
VALINSKY, ERIC
  b. 1952
  *Bus to Stockport* (with P. Schubert)  1986  New York
  *Freshwater*                         1984    New York
VALITSKY, KEN
  *Embrace the Monster*                1993    New York
VAN DE VATE, NANCY
  b. Plainfield, NJ, Dec. 30, 1930
  +*All Quiet on the Western Front*    1998*
                                       2003    New York

| | | |
|---|---|---|
| +*Death of the Hired Man* | 1995* | |
| | 1999 | Vienna |
| +*Hamlet* | 2010 | Vienna |
| +*In the Shadow of the Glen* | 1994* | |
| | 1999 | Boston |
| + *Where the Cross Is Made* | 2005 | Normal, IL |

**VAN ETTEN, JANE**
b. St. Paul, MN, ca. 1875

| | | |
|---|---|---|
| *Guido Ferranti* | 1914 | Chicago |

**VAN GROVE, ISAAC**
b. Philadelphia, Sept. 5, 1892; d. 1979

| | | |
|---|---|---|
| *Music Lover* | 1926 | Cincinnati |
| +*Other Wise Man* | 1959 | Bentonville, AR |
| *Shining Chalice* | 1964 | Eureka Spr, AR |

**VAN RIHJN, JACQUES**

| | | |
|---|---|---|
| *Venus* | 1997 | London |

**VAUGHAN WILLIAMS, RALPH**
b. Down Ampney, Gloucestershire, Eng., Oct. 12, 1872; d. London, Aug. 26, 1958

| | | |
|---|---|---|
| *Hugh the Drover* | 1924 | London |
| +*Pilgrim's Progress* | 1951 | London |
| *Poisoned Kiss* | 1936 | Cambridge, Eng. |
| *Riders to the Sea* | 1937 | London |
| +*Shepherds of the Delectable Mountains* | 1922 | London |
| +*Sir John in Love* | 1929 | London |

**VEHAR, PERSIS ANNE PARSHALL**
b. Buffalo, NY, 1937

| | | |
|---|---|---|
| *Eleanor Roosevelt* | 2009 | Lake George, NY |
| *George Sand . . . and Chopin?* | 2005 | Clarksville, TN |

**VERNON, ASHLEY [KURT MANSCHINGER]**
b. Zeil-Wieselburg, Austria, July 25, 1902; d. New York, Feb. 23, 1968

| | | |
|---|---|---|
| *Barber of New York* | 1953 | New York |
| *Cupid and Psyche* | 1956 | Woodstock, NY |
| *Grand Slam* | 1955 | Stamford, CT |
| *Triumph of Punch* | 1969 | Brooklyn, NY |

**VERNON, JOSEPH**
b. Coventry?, bapt. ca. April 12, 1737; d. London, March 19, 1782

| | | |
|---|---|---|
| *Linco's Travels* (with M. Arne) | 1767 | London |

**VERRALL, JOHN**
b. Britt, IA, June 17, 1908; d. Laurelhurst, WA, April 15, 2001

| | | |
|---|---|---|
| *Cowherd and the Sky Maiden* | 1952 | Seattle |
| *Three Blind Mice* | 1955 | Seattle |
| *Wedding Knell* | 1955 | Seattle |

**VICTORY, GERARD**
b. Dublin, Dec. 24, 1921; d. there, Mar. 14, 1995

| | | |
|---|---|---|
| +*Chatterton* | 1971 | Paris, ORTF |
| +*Circe 1991* | 1972 | Dublin, RTE |
| *Eloise and Abelard* | 1973 | Dublin, RTE |
| +*Evening for Three* | 1976 | Dublin, RTE |
| *Magic Trumpet* | 1974 | Dublin, RTE |
| +*Music Hath Mischief* | 1967 | Dublin |

| | | |
|---|---|---|
| *Once upon a Moon* | 1950 | Dublin |
| +*Rendezvous* | 1989 | Dublin |

**VIÑAO, EZEQUIEL**
b. Argentina, 1960

| | | |
|---|---|---|
| *Merlin* | 1999 | Paris |

**VINATIERI, FELIX (FELICE VILLIET)**
b. Turin, Italy, 1834; d. Yankton, SD, Dec. 9, 1891

| | | |
|---|---|---|
| +*American Volunteer* | 1891* | |
| | 1961 | Yanktor, SD |

**VINCENT, JOHN**
b. Birmingham, Ala., May 17, 1902; d. Santa Monica, CA, Jan. 21, 1977

| | | |
|---|---|---|
| *Primal Void* | 1973 | Vienna |

**VIR, PARAM**
b. Delhi, India, Feb. 6, 1952

| | | |
|---|---|---|
| *Broken Strings* | 1992 | Amsterdam |
| *Ion* | 2000 | Aldeburgh |
| *Snatched by the Gods* | 1991 | Amsterdam |

**VOLANS, KEVIN**
b. Pietermaritzburg, South Africa, July 26, 1949

| | | |
|---|---|---|
| *Man with Footsoles of Wind* | 1993 | London |

**VORES, ANDY**
b. Cardiff, Wales, 1956

| | | |
|---|---|---|
| +*Freshwater* | 1994 | Boston |
| +*No Exit* | 2009 | Boston |

**WADE, JAMES**
b. Granite, IL, Jan. 5, 1930

| | | |
|---|---|---|
| +*Martyred, The* | 1970 | Seoul |

**WADE, JOSEPH AUGUSTINE**
b. Dublin, ca. 1801; d. London, July 15, 1845

| | | |
|---|---|---|
| +*Two Houses of Grenada* | 1826 | London |

**WADSWORTH, STEPHEN**
b. Mt. Kisco, NY, Apr. 3, 1953

| | | |
|---|---|---|
| +*Telephone Show* | 1989 | Milwaukee |

**WAITS, TOM**
b. Pomona, CA, Dec. 7, 1949

| | | |
|---|---|---|
| *Alice* | 1992 | Hamburg |
| *Black Rider* | 1990 | Hamburg |

**WALDEN, STANLEY**
b. 1932

| | | |
|---|---|---|
| +*Kafka: Letter to My Father* | 2000 | New York |

**WALDMAN, MARA**

| | | |
|---|---|---|
| +*Love in the Office* | 2002 | New York |

**WALKER, JAMES**
b. 1929; d. 2002

| | | |
|---|---|---|
| *Proposal, The* | 1974* | |

**WALKER, RAYMOND**
b. Dec. 10, 1910

| | | |
|---|---|---|
| *Cinderella in Salerno* | 1976* | |

**WALLACE, STEWART**
b. 1960

| | | |
|---|---|---|
| *Bonesetter's Daughter* | 2008 | San Francisco |
| *Harvey Milk* | 1995 | Houston |
| *Hopper's Wife* | 1997 | Long Beach, CA |
| *Kabbalah, The* | 1989 | Brooklyn, NY |
| *Soap Opera* | 1985 | Houston |
| *Where's Dick?* | 1987 | Omaha, NE |

WALLACE, VINCENT
b. Waterford, Ire., Mar. 11, 1812; d. Château de Haget, Vieuzos, Hautes-Pyrénées, Oct. 12, 1865

| | | |
|---|---|---|
| *Amber Witch* | 1861 | London |
| *Desert Flower* | 1863 | London |
| *Love's Triumph* | 1862 | London |
| *Lurline* | 1860 | London |
| *Maritana* | 1845 | London |
| *Matilda of Hungary* | 1847 | London |

WALLACH, JOELLE
b. New York, June 29, 1946

| | | |
|---|---|---|
| *King's Twelve Moons* | 1989 | New York |

WALLERSTEIN, FERDINAND

| | | |
|---|---|---|
| *Viandière, La* | 1867 | Liverpool |

WALTON, WILLIAM
b. Oldham, Mar. 29, 1902; d. Ischia, Mar. 8, 1983

| | | |
|---|---|---|
| +*Bear, The* | 1967 | Aldeburgh |
| *Troilus and Cressida* | 1954 | London |

WANG JIE
b. Shanghai, 1980

| | | |
|---|---|---|
| +*Nannan* | 2007 | New York |

WARD, DAVID
b. 1941

| | | |
|---|---|---|
| *Death of Ferdia* | 1976 | BBC 3 Radio |
| *Full Moon in March* | 1981 | BBC 3 Radio |
| *Jack's Engagement* | 1987 | Lerwick, Scot. |
| *Snow Queen* | 1984 | BBC 3 Radio |

WARD, ROBERT
b. Cleveland, OH, Sept. 13, 1917

| | | |
|---|---|---|
| *Abelard and Heloise* | 1982 | Charlotte, NC |
| *Claudia Legare* | 1978 | Minneapolis |
| *Crucible, The* | 1961 | New York |
| *He Who Gets Slapped* | 1956 | New York |
| *Lady from Colorado* | 1964 | Central City, CO |
| *Lady Kate* | 1994 | Wooster, OH |
| +*Minutes till Midnight* | 1982 | Miami |
| *Roman Fever* | 1993 | Durham, NC |

WARE, HARRIET
b. Aug. 27, 1877, Waupun, WI; d. New York, Feb. 9, 1962

| | | |
|---|---|---|
| *Undine* | 1923 | Baltimore |

WARE, WILLIAM HENRY

| | | |
|---|---|---|
| *Aladdin* (with H. Condell) | 1813 | London |
| *Mother Goose* | 1806 | London |

WARGO, RICHARD
b. 1957

| | | |
|---|---|---|
| +*Ballymore* | 1999 | Milwaukee |

| | | |
|---|---|---|
| +*Chekhov Trilogy* | 1990 | Chautauqua, NY |
| +*Music Shop* | 1985 | St. Paul, MN |
| +*Seduction of a Lady* | 1985 | Glens Falls, NY |
| +*Sharon's Grave* | 2006 | Brooklyn, NY |
| +*Visit to the Country* | 1990 | Chautauqua, NY |

WARNER, CAPTAIN

| | | |
|---|---|---|
| *Armorer, The* | 1793 | London |

WARNER, HARRY WALDO
b. Northampton, Eng., Jan. 4, 1874; d. London, June 1, 1945

| | | |
|---|---|---|
| *Royal Vagrants* | 1899 | London |

WARREN, BETSY
b. Boston, 19??

| | | |
|---|---|---|
| *Gift of the Magi* | 1985 | New Orleans |
| *Rose and the Ring* | 1980* | |
| +*Seventeen* | 1989* | |
| +*Thomas Shelby* | 1993* | |

WARREN, RAYMOND
b. Weston-Super-Mare, Eng., Nov. 7, 1928

| | | |
|---|---|---|
| *Finn and the Black Hag* | 1959 | Belfast |
| *Graduation Ode* | 1963 | Belfast |
| +*In the Beginning* | 1982 | Clifton, Eng. |
| +*Lady of Ephesus* | 1959 | Belfast |
| +*Let My People Go* | 1972 | Liverpool |
| *St. Patrick* | 1979 | Liverpool |

WARREN, RICHARD HENRY
b. Albany, NY, Sept. 17, 1859; d. South Chatham, MA, Dec. 3, 1933

| | | |
|---|---|---|
| *Phyllis* | 1900 | New York |

WARWICK, MARY CAROL
b. 1939

| | | |
|---|---|---|
| *Cinderella in Spain* | 1998 | Houston |
| *Emperor's New Clothes* | 2001 | Houston |
| +*Lealista* | 1985* | |
| *Princess and the Pea* | 2005 | Houston |

WATERS, EMORY
b. Petersburg, VA

| | | |
|---|---|---|
| *Brave Jack* | 1993 | Minneapolis |
| *Edge of Glory* | 2000 | Petersburg, VA |

WATKINS, RODERICK
b. 1963

| | | |
|---|---|---|
| *Juniper Tree* | 1997 | Munich |

WEAVER, HERMAN BRENT
b. central CA, 1958

| | | |
|---|---|---|
| +*Aria da capo* | 1991* | |

WEBB, JOHN
b. 1969

| | | |
|---|---|---|
| *Phone Call* | 2002 | London |
| *Waiting for Jack* | 2002 | London |

WEBER, CARL MARIA von
b. Eutin, Ger., Nov. 18?, 1786; d. London, June 5, 1826

| | | |
|---|---|---|
| *Oberon* | 1826 | London |

## WEILL, KURT
b. Dessau, Ger., Mar. 2, 1900; d. New York, Apr. 3, 1950

| | | |
|---|---|---|
| Down in the Valley | 1948 | Bloomington, IN |
| Eternal Road | 1937 | New York |
| Kingdom for a Cow | 1935 | London |
| Lady in the Dark | 1941 | Boston |
| Lost in the Stars | 1949 | New York |
| Love Life | 1948 | New York |
| Street Scene | 1946 | Philadelphia |

## WEINER, LAWRENCE
b. Cleveland, June 22, 1932; d. 2009

| | | |
|---|---|---|
| Chipita Rodríguez | 1982 | Corpus Christi, TX |

## WEINER, LAZAR
b. Cherkassy, nr. Kiev, Oct. 27, 1897; d. New York, Jan. 10, 1982

| | | |
|---|---|---|
| Golem, The | 1957 | White Plains, NY |

## WEIR, JUDITH
b. Aberdeen, Scot, May 11, 1954

| | | |
|---|---|---|
| Armida | 2005 | Channel 4 |
| +Black Spider | 1985 | Canterbury, Eng. |
| +Blond Eckbert | 1994 | Santa Fe, NM |
| +Consolations of Scholarship | 1985 | Durham, Eng. |
| +Heaven Ablaze in His Breast | 1989 | Basildon, Eng. |
| +King Harald's Saga | 1979 | Dumfries, Scot. |
| +Night at the Chinese Opera | 1987 | Cheltenham, Eng. |
| +Scipio's Dream (lib. with M. Williams) | 1991 | BBC 2 |
| +Vanishing Bridegroom | 1990 | Glasgow |

## WEISBERG, STEVE

| | | |
|---|---|---|
| Guest of Honor: Scott Joplin | 1989 | New York |

## WEISENSEL, NEIL
b. Vancouver?

| | | |
|---|---|---|
| Bachelor Farmers | 1993 | Winnipeg |
| City Workers | 1992 | Winnipeg |
| Gisela in Her Bathtub | 1991 | Ottawa |
| Master's Stroke | 2001 | Winnipeg |
| Merry Christmas | 1997 | Vancouver |

## WEISER, MARK LANZ
b. Allentown, PA, 1969

| | | |
|---|---|---|
| Purgatory | 1990 | Baltimore |
| Where Angels Fear to Tread | 1999 | Baltimore |

## WEISGALL, HUGO
b. Eibenschütz [Ivançice], Bohemia, Oct. 13, 1912; d. New York, Mar. 11, 1997

| | | |
|---|---|---|
| Athaliah | 1964 | New York |
| Esther | 1993 | New York |
| Gardens of Adonis | 1959* | |
| | 1992 | Omaha, NE |
| Jenny | 1976 | New York |
| +Lillith | 1934* | |
| Night | 1932* | |
| Nine Rivers from Jordan | 1968 | New York |
| Purgatory | 1961 | Washington |
| Six Characters | 1959 | New York |

| | | |
|---|---|---|
| Stronger, The | 1952 | Lutherville, MD/ Westport, CT |
| Tenor, The | 1952 | Baltimore |
| Will You Marry Me? | 1989 | New York |

## WEISMAN, STEFAN
b. 1970

| | | |
|---|---|---|
| Darkling | 2006 | New York |
| Fade | 2008 | London |

## WELCHER, DAN
b. Rochester, NY, Mar. 2, 1948

| | | |
|---|---|---|
| Della's Gift | 1987 | Austin, TX |
| Holy Night | 2005 | Austin, TX |

## WELDON, JOHN
b. Chichester, Jan. 19, 1676; d. London, May 7, 1736

| | | |
|---|---|---|
| Judgment of Paris | 1701 | London |
| Tempest, The | ca. 1712 | London |

## WELLESZ, EGON
b. Vienna, Oct. 21, 1885; d. Oxford, Eng., Nov. 9, 1974

| | | |
|---|---|---|
| Incognita | 1951 | Oxford |

## WELLS, KENNETH
b. Culver City, CA, 1949

| | | |
|---|---|---|
| +First Lady (lib. with G. Patterson et al.) | 2010 | Los Angeles |

## WELNER, GEORGE

| | | |
|---|---|---|
| +Amiable Beast | 1961 | New York |

## WELSCH, JAMES

| | | |
|---|---|---|
| Helen Retires (after Antheil) | 2005 | Deland, FL |

## WELSH, THOMAS
b. ca. 1780; d. Brighton, Eng., Jan. 24/31, 1848

| | | |
|---|---|---|
| For England, Ho! (with H. R. Bishop) | 1813 | London |
| Selima and Azor (with Bishop, T. Cooke) | 1813 | London |
| Up to Town (with W. Reeve et al.) | 1811 | London |

## WERDER, FELIX
b. Berlin, Feb. 24, 1922; d. Kew, Austral., May 3, 2012

| | | |
|---|---|---|
| Affair, The | 1974 | Sydney |
| +Agamemnon | 1967 | ABC |
| Bellyful | 1975* | |
| +Conversion, The | 1973* | |
| +Director, The | 1980 | Melbourne |
| General, The | 1966* | |
| Kisses for a Quid | 1961 | Melbourne |
| Medea | 1985 | Melbourne |
| Private, The | 1969 | ABC |
| Vicious Square | 1971* | |

## WESTBROOK, KATE
b. Guildford, Eng., Sept, 18, 1939

| | | |
|---|---|---|
| Good Friday 1663 (with M. Westbrook) | 1995 | Channel 4, London |

## WESTBROOK, MIKE
b. High Wycombe, Buckinghamshire, Eng., Mar. 21, 1936

| | | |
|---|---|---|
| Coming through Slaughter | 1994 | London |
| Good Friday 1663 (with K. Westbrook) | 1995 | Channel 4, London |

**WESTERGAARD, PETER**
b. Champaign, IL, May 28, 1931

| | | |
|---|---|---|
| +*Alice in Wonderland* | 2006 | New York |
| +*Charivari* | 1953 | Cambridge, MA |
| +*Moby Dick* | 2004 | Princeton, NJ |
| +*Mr. and Mrs. Discobbolos* | 1966 | New York |
| +*Tempest, The* | 1994 | Lawrenceville, NJ |

**WHEELER, SCOTT**
b. Washington DC, Feb, 24, 1952

| | | |
|---|---|---|
| *Construction of Boston* | 1989 | Boston |
| *Democracy* | 1998 | Boston |
| *Gold Standard* | 2000 | New York |

**WHELEN, CHRISTOPHER**
b. London, Apr. 17, 1927

| | | |
|---|---|---|
| *Cancelling Dark* | 1965 | London, BBC |
| +*Findings* | 1972 | London, BBC |
| +*Incident at Owl Creek* | 1969 | London, BBC |
| *Some Place of Darkness* | 1967 | London, BBC |

**WHITAKER (WHITTAKER), JOHN**
b. 1776; d. 1847

| | | |
|---|---|---|
| *Rake's Progress* | 1826 | London |
| *Sweethearts and Wives* (with Nathan et al.) | 1823 | London |
| *Up to Town* (with Reeve et al.) | 1811 | London |
| *Veteran Soldier* (with Cooke, Perry) | 1822 | London |

**WHITE, CLARENCE CAMERON**
b. Clarksville, TN, Aug., 10, 1880; d. New York, June 30, 1960

| | | |
|---|---|---|
| *Ouanga* | 1932 | Chicago |

**WHITE, CLAUDE**

| | | |
|---|---|---|
| *Love, Death, and High Notes* | 1988 | St. Louis |
| +*Miraculous Phonograph Record* (lib. with J. Randich) | 1997 | Dallas |

**WHITE, FRANCES**
b. 1960

| | | |
|---|---|---|
| +*Letter, The* | 1984 | Brooklyn, NY |
| *She Lost Her Voice* | 2004 | New York |

**WHITE, JOHN**
b. Berlin, Apr. 5, 1936

| | | |
|---|---|---|
| *Orpheus* | 1976 | London |
| *Stanley and the Monkey King* | 1975 | London |

**WHITE, MICHAEL**
b. Chicago, Mar. 6, 1931

| | | |
|---|---|---|
| *Artaud's Cane* (with Egoyan, Krucker) | 1994 | Toronto |
| *Metamorphosis* | 1968 | Philadelphia |

**WHITEHEAD, GILLIAN KARAWE**
b. Whangarei, NZ, Apr. 23, 1941

| | | |
|---|---|---|
| *Alice* | 2003 | Auckland |
| *Art of Pizza* | 1995* | |
| *Bride of Fortune* | 1991 | Perth, Austral. |
| *Eleanor of Aquitaine* | 1967 | Sydney |
| *King of the Other Country* | 1984 | Sydney |
| *Outrageous Fortune* | 1998 | Dunedin, NZ |

| | | |
|---|---|---|
| *Pirate Moon* | 1986 | Auckland |
| *Tristan and Iseult* | 1978 | Auckland |

**WHITMAN, THOMAS**
b. 1960

| | | |
|---|---|---|
| *Black Swan* | 1998 | Swarthmore, PA |

**WHITON, PETER**

| | | |
|---|---|---|
| *Bottle Imp* | 1958 | Wilton, CT |

**WIDDOES, LAWRENCE**
b. Wilmington, DL, 1932

| | | |
|---|---|---|
| *How to Make Love* | 1994 | New York |

**WIEGOLD, PETER**
b. Ilford, Essex, Aug. 29, 1949

| | | |
|---|---|---|
| +*Last Tango on the North Circular* | 1989 | London |

**WIENS, RAINER**

| | | |
|---|---|---|
| *Down Here on Earth* | 1998 | Toronto |

**WIGGLESWORTH, FRANK**
b. Boston, Mar. 3, 1918; d. New York, Mar. 19, 1996

| | | |
|---|---|---|
| +*Police Log* | 1984 | New York |
| *Willowdale Handcar* | 1969 | New York |

**WILDER, ALEC**
b. Rochester, NY, Feb. 16, 1907; d. Gainesville, FL, Dec. 24, 1980

| | | |
|---|---|---|
| *Cumberland Fair* | 1953 | Montclair, NJ |
| *Impossible Forest* | 1958 | Westport, CT |
| *Long Way* | 1955 | Nyack, NY |
| *Lowland Sea* | 1952 | Montclair, NJ |
| *Miss Chicken Little* | 1953 | Suffern, NY |
| *Opening, The* | 1969 | Boston |
| *Sunday Excursion* | 1953 | New York |
| *Truth about Windmills* | 1973 | Rochester, NY |

**WILDING-WHITE, RAYMOND**
b. Caterham, Surrey, Eng., Oct. 9, 1922; d. Kewaunee, WI, Aug. 24, 2001

| | | |
|---|---|---|
| *Selfish Giant* | 1952* | |
| | 1955 | Cleveland |
| +*Yerma* | 1962* | |

**WILLAN, HEALEY**
b. Balham, London, Oct. 12, 1880; d. Toronto, Feb. 16, 1968

| | | |
|---|---|---|
| *Deirdre* | 1946 | CBC radio |
| *Order of Good Cheer* | 1928 | Quebec |
| *Transit through Fire* | 1942 | CBC radio |

**WILLIAMS, BURT (EGBERT)**
b. Antigua, prob. Nov. 12, 1874; d. 1922

| | | |
|---|---|---|
| *Abyssinia* (with Cook) | 1906 | New York |

**WILLIAMS, D. M.**

| | | |
|---|---|---|
| *Florence Nightingale* | 1943 | New York |

**WILLIAMS, GRACE**
b. Barry, Glamorganshire, Wales, Feb. 19, 1906; d. there, Feb. 10, 1977

| | | |
|---|---|---|
| +*Parlour, The* | 1966 | Cardiff |

**WILLIAMS, JACK ERIC**
b. Mar. 28, 1944; d. Jan. 28, 1994

| | | |
|---|---|---|
| *Mrs. Farmer's Daughter* | 1983 | Purchase, NY |

## WILLIAMS, JOSEPH BENJAMIN |aka FLORIAN PASCAL/ LIONEL ELLIOTT|
b. London, 1847; d. 1923

| | | |
|---|---|---|
| *Cymbia* | 1883 | London |
| *No Cards* | 1869 | London |

## WILLIAMS, JULIUS P.
b. Bronx, NY, 1954

| | | |
|---|---|---|
| *Guinevere* | 1989 | Aspen, CO |

## WILLIAMSON, MALCOLM
b. Sydney, Nov. 21, 1931; d. Cambridge, Mar. 2, 2003

| | | |
|---|---|---|
| *Dunstan and the Devil* | 1967 | Cookham |
| *English Eccentrics* | 1964 | Aldeburgh |
| +*Genesis* | 1973 | London |
| +*Growing Castle* | 1968 | Dynevor Castle, Wales |
| +*Happy Prince* | 1965 | Farnham, Eng. |
| *Julius Caesar Jones* | 1966 | London |
| *Lucky-Peter's Journey* | 1968 | Dynevor Castle, Wales |
| *Moonrakers, The* | 1967 | Brighton, Eng. |
| *Our Man in Havana* | 1963 | Aldeburgh |
| +*Red Sea* | 1972 | Dartington College, Eng. |
| +*Snow Wolf* | 1968 | Brighton, Eng. |
| *Stone Wall* | 1971 | London |
| *Violins of St. Jacques* | 1966 | London |

## WILLIS, SHARON
b. 1949

| | | |
|---|---|---|
| +*Great Divide* | 2005 | Atlanta |
| +*LaRoche* | 2003 | Atlanta |
| +*Opera Singer* | 2000 | Atlanta |
| +*Seduction of King Solomon* | 2007 | Atlanta |

## WILSON, CHARLES M.
b. Toronto, May 8, 1931

| | | |
|---|---|---|
| *Héloïse and Abelard* | 1973 | Toronto |
| +*Kamouraska* | 1979 | Toronto |
| *Phrases from Orpheus* | 1971 | Guelph, ON |
| *Psycho Red* | 1978 | Guelph, ON |
| *Selfish Giant* | 1973 | Toronto |
| *Strolling Clerk* | ca. 1952* | |
| *Summoning of Everyman* | 1973 | Halifax |

## WILSON, JAMES
b. London, Sept. 27, 1922; d. Loughlinstown, Dublin, Aug. 6, 2005

| | | |
|---|---|---|
| +*Fand* | 1975 | Kilkenny |
| *Grinning at the Devil* | 1989 | Copenhagen |
| *Hunting of the Snark* | 1965 | Dublin |
| +*King of the Golden River* | 1992* | |
| +*Letters to Theo* | 1984 | Dublin |
| *Passionate Man* | 1995 | Dublin |
| *Pied Piper* | 1969 | Wexford |
| *Táin, The* | 1972 | Dublin |
| *Twelfth Night* | 1969 | Wexford |
| +*Virata* | 1999* | |

## WILSON, JANIS DUNSON

| | | |
|---|---|---|
| *Wedding, The* | 2003 | Santa Rosa, CA |

## WILSON, RICHARD
b. Cleveland, May 15, 1941

| | | |
|---|---|---|
| +*Aethelred the Unready* | 2001 | New York |

## WILSON, THOMAS
b. Trinidad, CO, Oct. 10, 1927; d. Glasgow, June 12, 2001

| | | |
|---|---|---|
| *Charcoal Burner* | 1969 | BBC, Scot |
| *Confessions of a Justified Sinner* | 1976 | York |

## WILSON-DICKSON, ANDREW
b. 1946

| | | |
|---|---|---|
| *Errors* | 1980 | Leicester, Eng. |
| *Sir Gawain* | 1977 | Leicester, Eng. |

## WINSLOW, RICHARD
b. 1918

| | | |
|---|---|---|
| *Dr. Faustus Lights the Lights* | 1967* | |
| *Sweeney Agonistes* | 1952 | Middletown, CT |

## WISHART, PETER
b. Crowborough, Eng., June 25, 1921; d. Bath, Aug. 14, 1984

| | | |
|---|---|---|
| *Captive, The* | 1960 | Birmingham |
| *Clandestine Marriage* | 1971 | Cambridge |
| *Clytemnestra* | 1974 | London |
| *Lady of the Inn* | 1983 | Reading, Eng. |
| *Two in the Bush* | 1959 | Birmingham |

## WOLD, ERLING
b. San Francisco, Jan. 30, 1958

| | | |
|---|---|---|
| +*Little Girls Dreams of Taking the Veil* (lib. with C. Harryman) | 1995 | San Francisco |
| *Mordake* | 2008 | San Francisco |
| +*Queer* (lib. with J. Morace) | 2001 | San Francisco |
| *Sub Pontio Pilato* | 2003 | San Francisco |

## WOLF, ANTON
b. 1914; d. 1989

| | | |
|---|---|---|
| *François Villon* | 1984 | Buffalo, NY |
| *Madame Jumel* | 1976 | Buffalo, NY |

## WOLFE, JACQUES
b. Botoşani, Romania, Apr. 29, 1896; d. Bradenton, FL, June 22, 1973

| | | |
|---|---|---|
| *Mississippi Legend* | 1951 | New York |

## WOLFE, JULIA
b. Philadelphia, Dec. 18, 1958

| | | |
|---|---|---|
| *Carbon Copy Building* (with M. Gordon, D Lang) | 1999 | New York |

## WOLFE, NEIL

| | | |
|---|---|---|
| *Birth/Day* | 1993 | Dallas |

## WOLOSOFF, BRUCE
b. 1955

| | | |
|---|---|---|
| *Madimi* | 2007 | New York |

## WOOD, CHARLES
b. Armagh, Ire, June 15, 1866; d. Cambridge, Eng., July 12, 1926

| | | |
|---|---|---|
| *Family Papers* | 1924 | London |
| *Scene from Pickwick* | 1922 | London |

WOOD, JOSEPH
b. Pittsburgh, May 12, 1915

| | | |
|---|---|---|
| *Mother, The* | 1942 | New York |

WOOLF, JULIA
b. 1831; d. West Hempstead, Nov. 20, 1893

| | | |
|---|---|---|
| *Carina* | 1888 | London |

WOOLLEN, RUSSELL
b. Hartford, CT, Jan. 7, 1923; d. Charlottesville, VA, Mar. 16, 1994

| | | |
|---|---|---|
| *Decorator, The* | 1959 | Washington |

WOOLRICH, JOHN
b. Cirencester, Eng., Jan. 3, 1954

| | | |
|---|---|---|
| *Bitter Fruit* | 2000 | Birmingham |
| *In the House of Crossed Desires* | 1996 | Cheltenham, Eng. |
| *Judgement of Paris* | 1991 | London |

WUORINEN, CHARLES
b. New York, June 9, 1938

| | | |
|---|---|---|
| *Haroun* | 2000 | New York |
| *Politics of Harmony* | 1968 | New York |
| *W. of Babylon* | 1975 | New York |

WYKES, ROBERT
b. Aliquippa, PA, May 19, 1926

| | | |
|---|---|---|
| +*Prankster, The* | 1952 | Bowling Green, OH |

YANNATOS, JAMES
b. New York, Mar. 13, 1929; d. Cambridge, MA, Oct. 19, 2011

| | | |
|---|---|---|
| +*Rocket's Red Blare* | 1971 | Cambridge, MA |
| *Silence Bottle* | 1994* | |

YARMOLINSKY, BEN
b. Washington, DC, July 5, 1955

| | | |
|---|---|---|
| +*Blanche* | 1989 | New York |
| *Blind Witness News* | 1990 | New York |
| *Subject, The* | 1991 | New York |

YATES, WILLIAM
d. 1769

| | | |
|---|---|---|
| *Choice of Apollo* | 1765 | London |

YAVELOW, CHRISTOPHER
b. Cambridge, MA, June 15, 1950

| | | |
|---|---|---|
| *Countdown* | 1987 | Boston |
| +*Passion of Vincent Van Gogh* | 1984 | Dallas |

YORK-NORRIS, CATHERINE
b. Dover, NH

| | | |
|---|---|---|
| +*King Lear* | 1994 | Dover, NH |

YOUNG, DOUGLAS
b. London, July 18, 1947

| | |
|---|---|
| +*Tailor of Gloucester* | 1991* |
| (lib. with J. M. Phillips) | |

YOUNG, WEBSTER A.
b. Oyster Bay, LI, 1951

| | |
|---|---|
| +*As You Like It* | 2002* |
| +*Madrid* | 1997* |
| +*Stocks, Bonds, and Doggerel* | 2000* |

| | | |
|---|---|---|
| +*Sun Also Rises* | 2000 | Pt Washington, NY |
| +*Wrong Party* | 1994* | |

ZADOR, EUGENE
b. Bátaszék, Hung., Nov. 5, 1894; d. Hollywood, CA, Apr. 4, 1977

| | | |
|---|---|---|
| +*Inspector General* | 1928* | |
| | 1971 | Torrance, CA |
| *Magic Chair* | 1966 | Baton Rouge, LA |
| *Scarlet Mill* | 1968 | Brooklyn, NY |
| *Virgin and the Fawn* | 1964 | Los Angeles |
| *Yehu* | 1974 | Los Angeles |

ZAIMONT, JUDITH LANG
b. Memphis, TN, Nov. 8, 1945

| | | |
|---|---|---|
| *Goldilocks* | 1986 | Chappaqua, NY |

ZARR, GEORGE

| | | |
|---|---|---|
| +*Who's on Faust?* | 1995 | New York |

ZIEMBA, PAUL

| | | |
|---|---|---|
| +*Dracula, the Opera* | 2000 | Buffalo |

ZIMBALIST, EFREM
b. Rostov-on-the-Don, Apr. 21, 1889; d. Reno, NV, Feb. 22, 1985

| | | |
|---|---|---|
| *Landara* | 1956 | Philadelphia |

ZITO, VINCENT

| | | |
|---|---|---|
| +*Sganarelle* | 1972 | Bronx, NY |

## Adaptations and Arrangements

ADAM, ADOLPHE CHARLES (1803–1856)
**La reine d'un jour** (1839, Paris)

| | | | |
|---|---|---|---|
| *Queen of a Day* | Fitzwilliam, E. | 1841 | London |

ANTHEIL, GEORGE (1900–1959)
**Helen Retires** (1934, New York)

| | | | |
|---|---|---|---|
| *Helen Retires* | Welsch, J. | 2005 | Deland, FL |

ARNE, THOMAS AUGUSTINE (1710–1778)
**Cymon** (1767, London)

| | | | |
|---|---|---|---|
| *Cymon* | Bishop, H. R. | 1815 | London |

AUBER, D.-F.-E. (1782–1871)
**Cheval de bronze** (1835, Paris)

| | | | |
|---|---|---|---|
| *Bronze Horse* | Rodwell, G. | 1835 | London |

**Enfant prodigue, L'** (1850, Paris)

| | | | |
|---|---|---|---|
| *Azael* | Laurent, H. | 1850 | London |

**Fra Diavolo** (1830, Paris)

| | | | |
|---|---|---|---|
| *Devil's Brother* | Lee, A. | 1831 | London |

**Gustave III** (1833, Paris)

| | | | |
|---|---|---|---|
| *Gustavus III* | Cooke, T. S. | 1833 | London |

**Lestocq** (1834, Paris)

| | | | |
|---|---|---|---|
| *Lestocq* | Cooke, T. S. | 1835 | London |

**Maçon, Le** (1825, Paris)

| | | | |
|---|---|---|---|
| *Mason of Buda* | Rodwell, G. | 1828 | London |

**Muette de Portici, La** (1828, Paris)

| | | | |
|---|---|---|---|
| *Masaniello* | Cooke, T. S. | 1829 | London |

**Philtre, Le** (1831, Paris)

| | | | |
|---|---|---|---|
| *Love Charm* | Bishop, H. R. | 1831 | London |

*Serment, Le* (1832, Paris)
Coiners, The | Lacy, M. R. | 1833 | London

BELLINI, VINCENZO (1801–1835)
*Sonnambula, La* (1831, Milan)
Sonnambula, La | Bishop, H. R. | 1833 | London

BISHOP, HENRY ROWLEY (1786–1855)
*Aethiop, The* (1812, London)
Aethiop, The | Taylor, R. | 1814 | Philadelphia

BIZET, GEORGES (1838–1875)
*Carmen* (1875, Paris)
Carmen Jones | Bennett, R. | 1947 | New York
José's Carmen | Ashman, M. | 1984 | London
Naked Carmen | Corigliano/Hess | 1970*

BOIELDIEU, FRANÇOIS ADRIEN (1775–1834)
*Dame blanche, La* (1825, Paris)
White Lady | Cooke, T. S. | 1826 | London
*Deux nuits, Les* (1829, Paris)
Night before the Wedding | Bishop, H. R. | 1829 | London
*Jean de Paris* (1812, Paris)
John of Paris | Bishop, H. R. | 1814 | London

CARAFA, MICHELE (1787–1872)
*Prison d'Edimbourg, La* (1833, Paris)
Heart of Midlothian | Loder, E. | 1849 | London

DALAYRAC, NICOLAS-MARIE (1753–1809)
*Adolphe et Clara* (1799, Paris)
Matrimony | Hewitt, J. | 1804 | London
*Camille* (Paris, 1791)
Captive of Spilburg | Dussek/Kelly | 1798 | London

DEBUSSY, CLAUDE (1862–1918)
*Pelléas et Mélisande* (1902, Paris)
Frustration | Harnick, S. | 1973 | Washington

DITTERSDORF, CARL DITTERS von (1739–1799)
*Doktor und Apotheker* (1786, Vienna)
Doctor and Apothecary | Storace, S. | 1788 | London

DONIZETTI, GAETANO (1797–1848)
*Fille du régiment, La* (1840, Paris)
Vivandiere, The | Hewitt, J. | 1863 | Augusta, GA
Vivandière, La | Wallerstein, F. | 1867 | Liverpool

FÉTIS, FRANÇOIS-JOSEPH (1784–1871)
*Vieille , La* (1826, Paris)
Love in Wrinkles | Lacy, M. R. | 1826 | London

FRANCESCHINI, G. B (1662/63–1732)
*Arsinoe* (1676, Bologna)
Arsinoe | Clayton, T. | 1705 | London

GALUPPI, BALDASSARE (1706–1785)
*Filosofo di campagna, Il* (1754, Venice)
Wedding Ring | Dibdin, C. | 1773 | London

GAVEAUX, PIERRE (1761–1825)
*Petit matelot, Le* (1786, Paris)
Veteran Tar | Arnold, S. | 1801 | London

GRÉTRY, A.-E.-M. (1741–1813)
*Deux avares, Les* (1770, Fontainebleau)
Two Misers | Dibdin, C. | 1775 | London
*Evénements imprévus, Les* (1799, Versailles)
Gay Deceivers | Kelly, M. | 1804 | London

GRISAR, ALBERT (1808–1869)
*Eau merveilleuse, L'* (1839, Paris)
Wonderful Water Cure | Reed T. | 1846 | London

HALÉVY, FROMENTAL (1799–1862)
*Juive, La* (1835, Paris)
Jewess, The | Cooke, T. S. | 1835 | London

HÉROLD, FERDINAND (1791–1833)
*Pré aux clercs, Le* (1832, Paris)
Court Masque | Dawes, W. | 1833 | London

LECOCQ, CHARLES (1832–1918)
*Giroflé Giroflá* (1874, Brussels)
Twin Sisters | Sedgwick, A. | 1876 | New York?

LULLY, JEAN-BAPTISTE (1632–1687)
*Armide* (1656, Paris)
Armide | Dawe, J. | 2009 | New York

MARLIANI, MARCO AURELIO (1805–1849)
*Bravo, Il* (1834, Paris)
Red Mask | Cooke, T. S. | 1834 | London

MARSCHNER, HEINRICH (1796–1861)
*Des Falkners Braut* (1832, Leipzig)
Rob of the Fens | Romer, F. | 1838 | London

MEYERBEER, GIACOMO (1791–1864)
*Robert le diable* (1831, Paris)
Demon, The | Bishop, H. R. | 1832 | London
Fiend-Father | Lacy, M. R. | 1832 | London
Robert the Devil | pastiche | 1868 | London

MOGULESCO, SIGMUND (1858–1914)
*Dovid's fiedele* (1897, New York)
David's Violin | Slobin, M. (arr.) | 1976 | Middletown, CT

MOZART, WOLFGANG AMADEUS (1756–1791)
**various**
Jewel Box | Griffiths, P. | 1991 | New York
Letters, Riddles | Nyman/Lepage | 1991 | BBC
Small Jewel Box | Griffiths, P. | 1995 | New York
*Così fan tutte* (1790, Vienna)
Tit for Tat | Hawes, W. | 1828 | London
*Don Giovanni* (1787, Prague)
Bread & Roses | Glickman/Shen | 2000 | New York
Giovanni in London | anonymous | 1817 | London
Libertine, The | Bishop, H. R. | 1817 | London
Thirty Minute Don Giovanni | Lole/Gray | 1999 | Leeds
*Idomeneo* (1781, Munich)
Casket, The | Lacy, M. R. | 1829 | London

*Nozze di Figaro, Le* (1786, Vienna)

| *Marriage of Figaro* | Bishop, H. R. | 1819 | London |
|---|---|---|---|

*Sogno di Scipione, Il* (1772, Salzburg)

| *Scipio's Dream* | Weir, J. | 1991* | |
|---|---|---|---|

OFFENBACH, JACQUES (1819–1880)

**Ba-Ta-Clan** (1855, Paris)

| *Ba-Ta-Clan* | Oliver, S. | 1988* | |
|---|---|---|---|

PEPUSCH, JOHN (1667–1752)

**Beggar's Opera** (1728, London)

| *Bow-Street Opera* | anonymous | 1773 | London |
|---|---|---|---|

PUCCINI, GIACOMO (1858–1924)

**Bohème, La** (1896, Turin)

| *Bohemians, The* | Kirschner, B. | 1990 | New York |
|---|---|---|---|
| *Rent* | Larson, J. | 1996 | New York |

**Gianni Schicchi** (1918, New York)

| *Buoso's Ghost* | Ching, M. | 1997 | Memphis |
|---|---|---|---|

PURCELL, HENRY (1659–1695)

**Dido and Aeneas**

| *After Dido* | anonymous | 2009 | London |
|---|---|---|---|

RIES, FERDINAND (1784–1838)

**Raüberbraut, Die** (1828, Frankfurt)

| *Robber's Bride* | Hawes, W. | 1892 | London |
|---|---|---|---|

ROSSINI, GIOACHINO (1792–1868)

**Barbiere di Siviglia, Il** (1816, Rome)

| *Barber of Seville* | Bishop, H. R. | 1818 | London |
|---|---|---|---|

**Cenerentola, La** (1817, Rome)

| *Cinderella* | Lacy/Pons | 1830 | London |
|---|---|---|---|

**Gazza ladra, La** (1817, Milan)

| *Magpie or the Maid?* | Bishop, H. R. | 1815 | London |
|---|---|---|---|
| *Ninetta* | Bishop, H. R. | 1830 | London |

**Guillaume Tell** (1829, Paris)

| *Guillaume Tell* | Bishop, H. R. | 1838 | London |
|---|---|---|---|
| *Hofer* | Bishop, H. R. | 1830 | London |

**Siège de Corinthe, Le** (1826, Paris)

| *Siege of Corinth* | Cooke, T. S. | 1836 | London |
|---|---|---|---|

**Tancredi** (1813, Venice)

| *Native Land* | Bishop, H. R. | 1824 | London |
|---|---|---|---|

**Turco in Italia, Il** (1814, Milan)

| *Turkish Lovers* | Lacy, M. R. | 1827 | London |
|---|---|---|---|

SPOHR, LUDWIG (1784–1859)

**Alchemist, Der** (1830, Kassel)

| *Alchemyst, Der* | Bishop, H. R. | 1832 | London |
|---|---|---|---|

STORACE, STEPHEN (1762–1796)

**Pirates, The** (1792, London)

| *Isadore de Merida* | Cooke, T. S. | 1827 | London |
|---|---|---|---|

STRAUSS, JOHANN II (1825–1899)

**Fledermaus, Die** (1974, Vienna)

| *Flying Fox* | Jopling, O., arr. | 1998 | London |
|---|---|---|---|

SULLIVAN, ARTHUR S. (1842–1900)

**various**

| *Engaged* | Rowell/Mobbs | 1962 | Bristol, Eng. |
|---|---|---|---|

*Contrabandista, The* (1867, London)

| *Smugglers, The* | Sousa, J. P. | 1882 | Philadelphia |
|---|---|---|---|

VERDI, GIUSEPPE (1813–1901)

**Trovatore, Il** (1853, Rome)

| *Estranged* | Sedgwick, A. | 1876 | New York? |
|---|---|---|---|

WEBER, CARL MARIA VON (1786–1826)

**Abu Hassan** (1811, Munich)

| *Abou Hassan* | Cooke, T. S. | 1825 | London |
|---|---|---|---|

**Freischütz, Der** (1821, Berlin)

| *Black Rider* | Waits, T. | 1990 | Hamburg |
|---|---|---|---|
| *Freischütz, Der* | parody | 1824 | Edinburgh |
| *Freischütz, Der* | Bishop, H. R. | 1824 | London |

WEIL, KURT (1900–1950)

**Dreigroschenoper, Die** (1928, Berlin)

| *Threepenny Opera* | Blitzstein, M. (arr.) | 1954 | New York |
|---|---|---|---|

**Happy End** (1929, Berlin)

| *Happy End* | M. Feingold (arr.) | 1972 | New Haven |
|---|---|---|---|

**Silbersee, Der** (1933, Leipzig)

| *Silverlake* | Symonette, L. (arr.) | 1980 | New York |
|---|---|---|---|

WINTER, PETER VON (1754–1825)

**Unterbrochene Opferfest, Das** (1796, Vienna)

| *Oracle, The* | Hawes, W. | 1826 | London |
|---|---|---|---|

# Appendix 2: Librettists

Entries include dates of librettist (where known), short title, composer, and year of premiere; * = year of composition (no performance information available); ** anon. composer/ballad opera. For composers who wrote their own librettos, see Appendix 1. See pp. 690–92 for adaptations and arrangements.

**AARONS, LEROY**

| | | |
|---|---|---|
| *Monticello* | Paxton, G. | 2000 |

**ABARBANEL, JONATHAN**

| | | |
|---|---|---|
| *Pedrolino's Revenge* | Russo, W. | 1974 |

**ABBOTT, DELMAS W.**

| | | |
|---|---|---|
| *Sagegrass* | Atwell, S. J. | 1986 |

**A'BECKETT, GILBERT A. (1811–1856)**

| | | |
|---|---|---|
| *Agnes Sorel* | A'Beckett, M. | 1835 |
| *Ancient Britons* | Reed, T. | 1875 |
| *Canterbury Pilgrims* | Stanford, C. | 1884 |
| *Castle of Aymon* | Balfe, M. | 1844 |
| *Geraldine* | Balfe, M. | 1843 |
| *Indian Puzzle* | Reed, T. | 1876 |
| *Postillion of Longjumeau* | Stansbury, G. | 1837 |
| *Savonarola* | Stanford, C. | 1884 |
| *Signa* | Cowen, F. | 1893 |
| *Spanish Bond* | Reed, T. | 1875 |
| *Three Tenants* | Reed, T. | 1874 |

**ABEL, LIONEL (1911–2001)**

| | | |
|---|---|---|
| *Escorial, The* (with comp.) | Levy, M. | 1958 |

**ABRASHKIN, RAYMOND (1911–1960)**

| | | |
|---|---|---|
| *Emperor's New Clothes* | Moore, D. | 1949 |

**ACKER, KATHY (1948–1997)**

| | | |
|---|---|---|
| *Birth of the Poet* | Gordon, P. | 1985 |

**ADAMS, ARTHUR (1872–1936)**

| | | |
|---|---|---|
| *Tapu* | Hill, A. | 1903 |
| *Whipping Boy* | Hill, A. | 1896 |

**ADAMS, RICHARD (b. 1920)**

| | | |
|---|---|---|
| *Sredni Vashtar* | Cassels-Brown, A. | 1983* |
| *Sredni Vashtar* | Steadman, R. | 1988* |

**ADAMS, ROBERT K.**

| | | |
|---|---|---|
| *Give Me Liberty* | Kalmanoff, M. | 1975 |
| *Young Tom Edison* | Kalmanoff, | 1963 |

**ADCOCK, FLEUR (b. 1934)**

| | | |
|---|---|---|
| *Eleanor of Aquitaine* | Whitehead, G. | 1967 |
| *King of the Other Country* | Whitehead, G. | 1984 |

**ADDISON, JOSEPH (1672–1719)**

| | | |
|---|---|---|
| *Rosamond* | Arne, T. A. | 1733 |
| *Rosamond* | Arnold, S. | 1767 |
| *Rosamond* | Clayton, T. | 1707 |

**ADELSON, LENNY (1924–1972)**

| | | |
|---|---|---|
| *Zenda* (lyrics, with Kuller, Charnin) | Duke, V. | 1963 |

**ADLER, JOYCE SPARER (1916–1999)**

| | | |
|---|---|---|
| *Moby Dick* (with comp.) | Solomon, E. | 1989* |

**AIKEN, GEORGE L. (1830–1876)**

| | | |
|---|---|---|
| *Uncle Tom's Cabin* | Howard, G. | 1852 |

**AITKEN, LAURA TAPIA**

| | | |
|---|---|---|
| *Felipe* | Aitken, H. | 1981* |

**ALAN, CHARLES (1908?–1975)**

| | | |
|---|---|---|
| *Eternal Road* (with L. Lewisohn) | Weill, K. | 1937 |

**ALBANO, MICHAEL PATRICK**

| | | |
|---|---|---|
| *Enchantment of Dreams* | Franklin, C. | 2004 |
| *Loss of Eden* | Franklin, C. | 2002 |

**ALBERY, JAMES (1838–1889)**

| | | |
|---|---|---|
| *Oriana* | Clay, F. | 1873 |

**ALDRICH, ELIZABETH (b. 1947)**

| | | |
|---|---|---|
| *Echoes of the Shining Prince* | Cooper, S. | 1985 |

**ALENIER, KARREN LALONDE**

| | | |
|---|---|---|
| *Gertrude Stein* | Banfield, W. | 2005 |

**ALEXIS, ANDRÉ (b. 1957)**

| | | |
|---|---|---|
| *Aeneas and Dido* | Rolfe, J. | 2007 |

**ALISON, JANE (b. 1961)**

| | | |
|---|---|---|
| *Sisters Antipodes* | Sleeper, T. | 2009 |

**ALLAN, LEWIS [ABEL MEEROPOL] (1903–1986)**

| | | |
|---|---|---|
| *Darling Corie* | Siegmeister, E. | 1954 |
| *Good Soldier Schweik* | Kurka, R. | 1958 |
| *Insect Comedy* | Kalmanoff, M. | 1977 |
| *Malady of Love* | Engel, L. | 1954 |
| *Soldier, The* | Engel, L. | 1956 |

**ALLEN, CHRISTOPHER**

| | | |
|---|---|---|
| *Dream Healer* (rev. D. Mowatt) | Burritt, L. | 2008 |

**ALLEN, JO HARVEY**

| | | |
|---|---|---|
| *Slow Fire* (with R. Eckert, J. Allen) | Dresher, P. | 1985 |

**ALLEN, Mr. (fl. 1764–1798)**

| | | |
|---|---|---|
| *Hymen* | Arne, M. | 1764 |

**ALLEN, TERRY**

| | | |
|---|---|---|
| *Slow Fire* (with R. Eckert, J. Allen) | Dresher, P. | 1985 |

**ALLINGHAM, JOHN TILL (fl. 1799–1810)**

| | | |
|---|---|---|
| *Transformation* | Condell, H. | 1810 |
| *Weathercock, The* | King, M. | 1805 |
| *Who Wins?* | Condell, H. | 1808 |

**ALMOND, DAVID (b. 1951)**

| | | |
|---|---|---|
| *Skellig* | Machover, T. | 2008 |

**ALVER, JONATHAN**

| | | |
|---|---|---|
| *Picasso: Out of the Blue* | McQueen, I. | 1997 |

**AMABILE, NARDO**

| | | |
|---|---|---|
| *Lucifer's Choice* | Hinkle-Turner, A. E. | 1993* |

**ANDERSON, DAVID**

| | | |
|---|---|---|
| *Lion and Androcles* (with comp., Walter) | Eaton, J. | 1974 |

**ANDERSON, MAXWELL (1888–1959)**

| | | |
|---|---|---|
| *Christmas Carol* | Hermann, B. | 1954 |
| *Lost in the Stars* | Weill, K. | 1949 |

ANDERSON, NATHALIE (b. 1948)

| | | |
|---|---|---|
| *Black Swan* | Whitman, T. | 1998 |

ANDERSON, ROD (b. 1935)

| | | |
|---|---|---|
| *Mario and the Magician* | Somers, H. | 1992 |

ANDERSON, ROBERT G.

| | | |
|---|---|---|
| *François Villon* | Baron, M. | 1940 |

ANDERSON, TIMOTHY J.

| | | |
|---|---|---|
| *Expensive Embarrassment* | Gougeon, D. | 1989 |

ANDRE, MICHAEL

| | | |
|---|---|---|
| *OrfReo* | Lauten, E. | 2004 |

ANDREWS, MILES PETER (d. 1814)

| | | |
|---|---|---|
| *Belphegor* | Barthelemon, F. | 1778 |
| *Election, The* | Barthelemon, F. | 1774 |
| *Fire and Water!* | Arnold, S. | 1780 |
| *Mysteries of the Castle* (poss. with F. Reynolds) | Shield, W. | 1795 |
| *Summer Amusement* (with W. A. Miles) | Arnold, S. | 1779 |

ANTHEIL, BOSKI (d. 1978)

| | | |
|---|---|---|
| *Flight* (with G. Antheil) | Antheil, G. | 1930* |

ARCHIBALD, WILLIAM (1917–1970)

| | | |
|---|---|---|
| *Far Harbour* | Bergersen, B. | 1948 |

ARGYLL, JOHN, DUKE of (1845–1914)

| | | |
|---|---|---|
| *Diarmid* | MacCunn, H. | 1897 |
| *Fionn and Terra* | Drysdale, L. | 1909 |

ARKELL, REGINALD (1882–1959)

| | | |
|---|---|---|
| *Kingdom for a Cow* (with D. Carter) | Weill, K. | 1935 |

ARLUCK, ELLIOT (b. 1916)

| | | |
|---|---|---|
| *Audition, The* | Goodman, A. | 1954 |
| *Lady and the Maid* | Goodman, A. | 1981* |

ARMITAGE, SIMON (b. 1963)

| | | |
|---|---|---|
| *Assassin Tree* | MacCrae, S. | 2006 |

ARMSTRONG, RICHARD

| | | |
|---|---|---|
| *House of Words* (with comp.) | Bouchard, L. | 2003 |

ARMSTRONG, W[ILLIAM] H[ENRY]

| | | |
|---|---|---|
| *Pay to My Order* (with J. R. Planché) | Horn, C. E. | 1827 |

ARNOLD, BRUCE (b. 1936)

| | | |
|---|---|---|
| *Passionate Man* | Wilson, J. | 1995 |

ARNOLD, SAMUEL JAMES (1774–1852)

| | | |
|---|---|---|
| *Americans, The* | Braham/King | 1811 |
| *Auld Robin Gray* | Arnold, S. | 1794 |
| *Baron Kinkverkankotsdorsprakingatchdern* | Arnold, S. | 1781 |
| *Broken Promises* | Hawes, W. | 1825 |
| *Devil's Bridge* | Horn, C. H. | 1812 |
| *Election, The* | Horn, C. H. | 1817 |
| *Frederick the Great* | Cooke, T. S. | 1814 |
| *Free and Easy* | Addison, J. | 1816 |
| *Hovel, The* | Arnold, S. | 1797 |
| *Illusion, The* | Kelly, M. | 1813 |
| *Irish Legacy* | Arnold, S. | 1797 |
| *King's Proxy* | Cooke, T. | 1815 |
| *Maniac, The* | Bishop, H. R. | 1810 |

| | | |
|---|---|---|
| *My Aunt* | Addison, J. | 1815 |
| *Nourjahad* | Loder, E. | 1834 |
| *Plots, The* | King, M. | 1810 |
| *Russian Imposter* (with H. Siddons) | Addison, J. | 1809 |
| *Shipwreck, The* | Arnold, S. | 1796 |
| *Tit for Tat* | Hawes, W. | 1828 |
| *Unknown Guest* | Kelly, M. | 1815 |
| *Up All Night* | King, M. | 1809 |
| *Veteran Tar* | Arnold, S. | 1801 |
| *Wizard, The* | Horn, C. E. | 1817 |

ARONSON, BILLY

| | | |
|---|---|---|
| *Monster Bed* | de Kenessey, S. | 1990 |

ARRABAL, FERNANDO

| | | |
|---|---|---|
| *Automobile Graveyard* | Ceely, R. | 1995 |

ARSIS, NICHOLAS GIARDINI

| | | |
|---|---|---|
| *Gift of the Magi* | Conte, D. | 1998 |

ARTHUR, JOHN (1708?–1772)

| | | |
|---|---|---|
| *Lucky Discovery* | ** | 1737 |

ARTMAN, DEBORAH

| | | |
|---|---|---|
| *Acquanetta* | Gordon, M. | 2010 |

ARVEY, VERNA (1910–1987)

| | | |
|---|---|---|
| *Bayou Legend* | Still, W. G. | 1941 |
| *Costaso* | Still, W. G. | 1949* |
| *Highway 1, U.S.A.* | Still, W. G. | 1963 |
| *Minette Fontaine* | Still, W. G. | 1984 |
| *Mota* | Still, W. G. | 1951* |
| *Pillar, The* | Still, W. G. | 1955* |

ASHBROOK, WILLIAM (1922–2009)

| | | |
|---|---|---|
| *Bandit, The* | Patacchi, V. | 1958 |
| *Secret, The* | Patacchi, V. | 1955 |

ASTON, ANTHONY (fl. 1682–1747)

| | | |
|---|---|---|
| *Fool's Opera* | ** | 1731 |

ASTON, WALTER, Baron (1660–1748)

| | | |
|---|---|---|
| *Restauration of King Charles II* | ** | 1732 |

ATHERTON, DEBORAH

| | | |
|---|---|---|
| *Mary Shelley* | Jaffe, A. | 1996 |
| *Under the Double Moon* | Davis, A. | 1989 |

ATKINSON, JOSEPH (1743–1818)

| | | |
|---|---|---|
| *Love in a Blaze* | Stevenson, J. | 1799 |
| *Match for a Widow* | Dibdin, C. | 1788 |

ATKINSON, MICHAEL

| | | |
|---|---|---|
| *Selfish Giant* (with comp.) | Easton, M. | 1994 |

ATTWOOD, MARGARET (b. 1939)

| | | |
|---|---|---|
| *Inanna's Journey* | Peters, R. | 2004 |

AUDEN, W. H. (1907–1973)

| | | |
|---|---|---|
| *Bassarids, The* (with C. Kallman) | Henze, H. W. | 1966 |
| *Elegy for Young Lovers* (with C. Kallman) | Henze, H. W. | 1961 |
| *Love's Labour's Lost* (with C. Kallman) | Nabokov, N. | 1973 |
| *Moralities* | Henze, H. W. | 1968 |
| *Paul Bunyan* | Britten, B. | 1941 |
| *Rake's Progress* | Stravinsky, I. | 1951 |

AUDI, PIERRE (b. 1957)

| | | |
|---|---|---|
| Golem (with comp.) | Casken, J. | 1989 |

AULICINO, ARMAND

| | | |
|---|---|---|
| Judgment of St. Francis | Flagello, N. | 1966 |

AUSTIN, SYDNEY

| | | |
|---|---|---|
| Amorous Judge (with L. McGlashan) | Gross, E. | 1965 |

AYERST, DAVID

| | | |
|---|---|---|
| Robin Hood (with comp., Pennyman) | Tippett, M. | 1934 |

AYRES, JAMES (fl. 1742)

| | | |
|---|---|---|
| Queen of Spain | Lampe, J. F. | 1744 |
| Sancho at Court | ** | 1742 |

AZRAEL, MARY (b. 1943)

| | | |
|---|---|---|
| Lost Childhood | Hamer, J. | 2001 |

BAER, ATRA

| | | |
|---|---|---|
| Brandy Is My True Love's Name | Kalmanoff, M. | 1953 |
| Empty Bottle | Kalmanoff, M. | 1966 |
| Fit for a King | Kalmanoff, M. | 1949 |
| Godiva | Kalmanoff, M. | 1953 |
| Noah and the Stowaway | Kalmanoff, M. | 1951 |

BAGG, TERRY

| | | |
|---|---|---|
| Death of Baldur | Bedford, D. | 1980 |
| Fridiof's Saga | Bedford, D. | 1981 |
| Ragnarok, The | Bedford, D. | 1982 |

BAILEY, ANNE HOWARD

| | | |
|---|---|---|
| Deseret | Kastle, L. | 1961 |
| Penitentes, The | Pasatieri, T. | 1974 |
| Rachel | Coe, K. | 1989 |
| Trial of Mary Lincoln | Pasatieri, T. | 1972 |

BAKER, HOWARD

| | | |
|---|---|---|
| Terrible Mouth | Osborne, N. | 1992 |

BAKER, MARY ELIZABETH

| | | |
|---|---|---|
| Grant, Warden of the Plains (with comp.) | Adaskin, M. | 1967 |

BAKER, ROBERT (fl. 1737)

| | | |
|---|---|---|
| Mad House | ** | 1737 |

BALIS, ANDREA

| | | |
|---|---|---|
| Lady of the Castle | Spektor, M. | 1982 |

BALK, H. WESLEY (1933–2003)

| | | |
|---|---|---|
| Faust Counter Faust | Gessner, J. | 1971 |

BALL, WILLIAM (1801–1878)

| | | |
|---|---|---|
| Belshazzar's Feast | Griesbach, J. | 1834* |

BALL, WILLIAM G. (1931–1992)

| | | |
|---|---|---|
| Natalia Petrovna | Hoiby, L. | 1964 |

BALODIS, JANIS

| | | |
|---|---|---|
| Electric Lenin | Conyngham, B. | 2006 |
| Mercenary, The | Grabowsky, P. | 1999* |

BAMBERGER, DAVID

| | | |
|---|---|---|
| Cask of Amontillado | Copeland, S. | 1993* |
| Come to Me in Dreams | Laitman, L. | 2004 |

BANDER, ROBERT GENE

| | | |
|---|---|---|
| Outcasts of Poker Flats | Elkus, J. | 1959* |

BANKES-JONES, BILL

| | | |
|---|---|---|
| Flying Fox | Jopling, O. | 1998 |
| Has It Happened Yet? | Bruce, D. | 2002 |

BANKS, RUSSELL

| | | |
|---|---|---|
| Harmony | Carl, R. | 2006 |

BARBER, BENJAMIN

| | | |
|---|---|---|
| Home and the River | Quincy, G. | 1997 |

BARBER, BRITT

| | | |
|---|---|---|
| Billy Blythe | Montgomery, B. | 2010 |

BARER, MARSHALL (1923–1998)

| | | |
|---|---|---|
| Impossible Forest | Wilder, A. | 1958 |

BARETTI, JOSEPHINE

| | | |
|---|---|---|
| All Fools' Day | Carey, C. | 1921 |

BARING-GOULD, SABINE (1834–1924)

| | | |
|---|---|---|
| Red Spider | Drysdale, L. | 1898 |

BARKER, JAMES NELSON (1784–1858)

| | | |
|---|---|---|
| Indian Princess | Bray, J. | 1808 |

BARKS, COLEMAN

| | | |
|---|---|---|
| Monsters of Grace | Glass, P. | 1998 |

BARLOW, PATRICK

| | | |
|---|---|---|
| Judgement of Paris | Woolrich, J. | 1991 |

BARNARD, FRANCIS

| | | |
|---|---|---|
| Farewell Supper | Hart, F. | 1984 |

BARNES, DUSTINE

| | | |
|---|---|---|
| We | Dench, C. | 1910 |

BARNET, R[OBERT] A[YRES] (1850?–1933)

| | | |
|---|---|---|
| Tabasco | Chadwick, G. W. | 1894 |

BARNETT, C[HARLES] Z[ACHARY]

| | | |
|---|---|---|
| Fair Rosamond | Barnett, J. | 1837 |
| Farinelli | Barnett, J. | 1839 |

BARNETT, IAN

| | | |
|---|---|---|
| Gawain and Ragnall | Blackford, R. | 1983 |
| Lost Domain | Carpenter, G. | 1984 |

BARNETT, JOSEPHINE

| | | |
|---|---|---|
| Inner Voices | Barnett, D. | 1972 |

BARON, BARCLAY

| | | |
|---|---|---|
| Master Valiant | Shaw, M. | 1936 |
| Thorn of Avalon | Shaw, M. | 1931 |

BARON, JEFF

| | | |
|---|---|---|
| Song of Martina | Johnson, D. | 1995 |

BARON-WILSON, MARGARET (1797–1846)

| | | |
|---|---|---|
| Genevieve | Macfarren, G. | 1834 |

BAROSS, JAN

| | | |
|---|---|---|
| Mata Hari | McDermott, V. | 1995 |

BARR, ISABEL HARRISS

| | | |
|---|---|---|
| Jericho Road | Aria, P. | 1969 |

BARRAS, CHARLES M. (1826–1873)

| | | |
|---|---|---|
| Black Crook | ** | 1866 |

BARRATT, CAROL

| | | |
|---|---|---|
| Eloise | Jenkins, K. | 1997 |

BARRETT, WILLIAM A. (1836–1891)
| | | |
|---|---|---|
| *Moro* | Balfe, M. | 1882 |

BARRIE, JAMES M. (1860–1937)
| | | |
|---|---|---|
| *Jane Annie* (with Doyle) | Ford, E. | 1893 |

BARRON, ANDREW SAUL
| | | |
|---|---|---|
| *Psychles* | Thomas, A. R. | 1987 |

BARRY, NATHANIEL
| | | |
|---|---|---|
| *Campaign, The* (with R. Jephson) | Shield, W. | 1784 |

BARSON, ROBIN
| | | |
|---|---|---|
| *Orpheus* | White, J. | 1976 |
| *Stanley and the Monkey King* | White, J. | 1975 |

BARTON, ANDREW [pseud., prob. THOMAS FORREST] (1747–1825)
| | | |
|---|---|---|
| *Disappointment, The* | ** | 1767 |

BARTON, GEORGE EDWARD
| | | |
|---|---|---|
| *Pipe of Desire* | Converse, F. | 1906 |

BARTON, HAL
| | | |
|---|---|---|
| *Love in Transit* | Arnell, R. | 1958 |

BASINSKI, ANNE
| | | |
|---|---|---|
| *Poia* (rev. version, 2005) | Nevins, A. | 1907 |

BASSMAN, GEORGE (1914–1997)
| | | |
|---|---|---|
| *Blue Monday* (with B. De Sylva) | Gershwin, G. | 1922 |

BATE, HENRY (HENRY BATE DUDLEY) (1745–1824)
| | | |
|---|---|---|
| *Blackamoor, The* | Dibdin, C. | 1776 |
| *Flitch of Bacon* | Shield, W. | 1778 |
| *Rival Candidates* | Carter, T. | 1775 |
| *Travellers in Switzerland* | Shield, W. | 1794 |
| *Woodman, The* | Shield, W. | 1791 |

BATES, LAURA
| | | |
|---|---|---|
| *King Lear* | Eaton, J. | 2004* |

BATES, WILLIAM (d. 1813?)
| | | |
|---|---|---|
| *Jovial Crew* | ** | 1760 |

BATHURST, SHEILA
| | | |
|---|---|---|
| *Blind Beggar's Daughter* (with comp.) | Bush, G. | 1954 |

BAX, CLIFFORD (1886–1962)
| | | |
|---|---|---|
| *Midsummer Madness* | Gibbs, C. A. | 1924 |
| *Mr. Pepys* | Shaw, M. | 1926 |
| *Prelude and Fugue* | Franchetti, A. | 1959 |
| *Waterloo Leave* | Shaw, M. | 1928 |

BAXTER, EDNA
| | | |
|---|---|---|
| *Return of the Native* (with comp.) | Coulthard, J. | 1979* |

BAYLEY, THOMAS HAYNES (1797–1839)
| | | |
|---|---|---|
| *Alchymist, The* (with E. Fitzball) | Bishop, H. R. | |

BEACH, LAZARUS (1760–1816)
| | | |
|---|---|---|
| *Jonathan Postfree* | ** | 1807 |

BEATTIE, WILLIAM B.
| | | |
|---|---|---|
| *Don Quixote* | Hill, A. | 1904* |

BEATTY-KINGSTON, WILLIAM (1837–1900)
| | | |
|---|---|---|
| *Irmengarda* | Bach, L. E. | 1892 |
| *Light of Asia* | Bach, L. E. | 1892 |

BEAUMONT, WILLIAM
| | | |
|---|---|---|
| *Cinderella in Salerno* | Walker, R. | 1976* |

BEAZLEY, SAMUEL (1786–1851)
| | | |
|---|---|---|
| *Boarding House* | Horn, C. E. | 1811 |
| *Ivanhoe* | Parry, J. | 1820 |
| *Love's Dream* | Moss, M. | 1821 |
| *My Uncle* | Addison, J. | 1817 |
| *Philandering* | Horn, C. E. | 1824 |
| *Sonnambula, La* | Bishop, H. R. | 1833 |
| *White Lady* | Cooke, T. S. | 1826 |

BECKETT, SAMUEL (1906–1997)
| | | |
|---|---|---|
| *Neither* | Feldman, M. | 1977 |

BEEMAN, MAX
| | | |
|---|---|---|
| *Helen Retires* | Welsch, J. | 2005 |

BEISWENGER, ANNA J.
| | | |
|---|---|---|
| *Pied Piper of Hamelin* | Clokey, J. W. | 1920 |

BELL, BRIAN
| | | |
|---|---|---|
| *Quiros* | Sculthorpe, P. | 1982 |

BELL, H. IDRIS (1879–1967)
| | | |
|---|---|---|
| *Black Ram* | Parrott, I. | 1957 |

BELL, HILARY
| | | |
|---|---|---|
| *Mrs. President* | Bond, V. | 2000 |

BELL, MADISON SMARTT (b. 1957)
| | | |
|---|---|---|
| *Toussaint before the Spirits* (with comp., Spires) | Ruehr, E. | 2003 |

BELLA, NICHOLAS
| | | |
|---|---|---|
| *Nightingale and the Rose* | Lessner, G. | 1942 |

BELLAMY, DANIEL (d. 1788)
| | | |
|---|---|---|
| *Royal Pastoral* | Nares, J. | 1767 |

BELLIN, MARTINE
| | | |
|---|---|---|
| *Ovidiana* | Greenbaum, M. | 1997 |

BELLLINGHAM, HENRY
| | | |
|---|---|---|
| *Bluebeard Repaired* | Tully, J. H. | 1866 |

BELL-RANSKE, JUTTA
| | | |
|---|---|---|
| *Temple Dancer* | Hugo, J. A. | 1919 |

BENBOW, JERRY
| | | |
|---|---|---|
| *Sunny Morning* (with comp.) | Stringer, A. | 1998 |

BENEDICT, MICHAEL
| | | |
|---|---|---|
| *Humulus the Mute* | MacIntyre, D. | 1979 |

BENÉT, STEPHEN VINCENT (1898–1943)
| | | |
|---|---|---|
| *Devil and Daniel Webster* | Moore, D. | 1939 |
| *Headless Horseman* | Moore, D. | 1937 |

BENNETT, ARNOLD (1867–1931)
| | | |
|---|---|---|
| *Don Juan de Mañara* | Goossens, E. | 1937 |
| *Judith* | Goossens, E. | 1929 |
| *Thorgrim* | Cowen, F. | 1890 |

BENNETT, JOSEPH (1831–1911)
| | | |
|---|---|---|
| *Jeanie Deans* | MacCunn, H. | 1894 |
| *Maid of Cefn Ydfa* | Parry, J. | 1902 |

BENNETT-STEPHENSON, CORA
| | | |
|---|---|---|
| *Lover's Knot* | Bucharoff, S. | 1916 |

BENSON, E[DWARD] F[REDERIC] (1867–1940)
| | | |
|---|---|---|
| *Westward Ho!* | Miles, P. N. | 1913 |

**BENSON, EUGENE (b. 1928)**

| | | |
|---|---|---|
| *Héloise and Abelard* | Wilson, C. | 1973 |
| *Psycho Red* | Wilson, C. | 1978 |
| *Summoning of Everyman* | Wilson, C. | 1973 |

**BENSON, Mr. (ROBERT) (1765–1796)**

| | | |
|---|---|---|
| *Britain's Glory* | Arnold, S. | 1794 |
| *Love and Money* | Arnold, S. | 1795 |

**BENTLEY, ERIC (b. 1916)**

| | | |
|---|---|---|
| *Brute, The* | Moss, L. | 1961 |
| *Harmfulness of Tobacco* | Kalmanoff, M. | 1979 |

**BENTLEY, PAUL (b. 1942)**

| | | |
|---|---|---|
| *Bird of Night* (with comp.) | Le Gendre, D. | 2006 |
| *Handmaid's Tale* | Ruders, P. | 2000 |
| *Kafka's Trial* (trans. K. Hoffmann) | Ruders, P. | 2005 |
| *Midnight Court Opera* | Sokolovic, A. | 2005 |

**BENTLEY, RICHARD (1708–1782)**

| | | |
|---|---|---|
| *Prophet, The* | Shield, W. | 1788 |

**BERGER, SIDNEY L.**

| | | |
|---|---|---|
| *Demon Lover* | Nelson, R. | 1986 |
| *Tickets Please* | Nelson, R. | 1985 |

**BERKOFF, STEVEN (b. 1937)**

| | | |
|---|---|---|
| *Metamorphosis* | Howard, B. | 1993 |

**BERNARD, JOHN (1756–1828)**

| | | |
|---|---|---|
| *British Sailor* (?) | Boyton, W. | 1789 |
| *Poor Sailor* | Attwood, T. | 1795 |

**BERNHARD, SANDRA**

| | | |
|---|---|---|
| *Cue 67* | Ching, M. | 1992 |

**BERNIER, ALEXIS**

| | | |
|---|---|---|
| *Henry's Wife* | Eng, R. | 2009 |

**BERNSTEIN, CHARLES (b. 1950)**

| | | |
|---|---|---|
| *Blind Witness News* | Yarmolinsky, B. | 1990 |
| *Lenny Paschen Show* | Yarmolinsky, B. | 1992 |
| *Subject, The* | Yarmolinsky, B. | 1991 |

**BERRONE, LOUIS**

| | | |
|---|---|---|
| *Notturno in La* | Franchetti, A. | 1966 |

**BERTON, MAX (b. 1917)**

| | | |
|---|---|---|
| *Tony Beaver* | Marais, J. | 1953 |

**BETTERTON, THOMAS (1635?–1710)**

| | | |
|---|---|---|
| *Dioclesian* (with Dryden) | Purcell, H. | 1690 |
| *Prophetess, The* | Pepusch, J. | 1724 |

**BICKERSTAFFE, ISAAC (1735–1812)**

| | | |
|---|---|---|
| *Brickdust Man* | Dibdin, C. | 1772 |
| *Captive, The* | Dibdin, C., et al. | 1769 |
| *Daphne and Amintor* | Arnold, S. | 1765 |
| *Ephesian Matron* | Dibdin, C. | 1769 |
| *Jubilee, The* | Dibdin, C. | 1769 |
| *Lionel and Clarissa* | Dibdin, C. | 1768 |
| *Love in a Village* | Arne, T. A. | 1762 |
| *Love in the City* | Dibdin, C. | 1767 |
| *Maid of the Mill* | Arnold, S. | 1765 |
| *Maid of the Mill* | Giordani, T. | 1765 |
| *Maid of the Mill* | Bishop, H. R. | 1814 |
| *Padlock, The* | Dibdin, C. | 1768 |
| *Recruiting Sergeant* | Dibdin, C. | 1770 |
| *Royal Garland* | Arnold, S. | 1768 |
| *Sultan, The* | Dibdin, C. | 1775 |
| *Thomas and Sally* (Bickerstaffe et al.) | Arne, T. A. | 1760 |

**BILLINGS, JAMES (b. 1932)**

| | | |
|---|---|---|
| *Ballad of the Bremen Band* | Arlan, D. | 1977 |
| *Daughter of the Double Duke of Dingle* | Arlan, D. | 1978 |
| *Meanwhile, Back at Cinderella's* | Arlan, D. | 1976 |
| *Reluctant Dragon* | Prescott, J. | 1999 |

**BILLINGSLEY, MILO W. (b. 1890)**

| | | |
|---|---|---|
| *Hopitu* | Albright, L. | 1955 |

**BINGHAM, A.**

| | | |
|---|---|---|
| *Sophie Songs* | Moore, C. | 1993* |

**BIRCH, CYRIL**

| | | |
|---|---|---|
| *Peony Pavilion* | Tan Dun | 1998 |

**BIRCH, JOHN YOULIN**

| | | |
|---|---|---|
| *Moorish Maid* | Hill, A. | 1905 |

**BIRCH, SAMUEL (1757–1841)**

| | | |
|---|---|---|
| *Adopted Child* | Attwood, T. | 1795 |
| *Albert and Adelaide* | Attwood, T. | 1798 |
| *Fast Asleep* | Attwood, T. | 1797 |
| *Mariners, The* | Attwood, T. | 1793 |
| *Packet Boat* | Attwood, T. | 1794 |
| *Smugglers, The* | Attwood, T. | 1796 |

**BIRD, THOMAS**

| | | |
|---|---|---|
| *Tonkin* (with R. Jones) | Cummings, C. | 1993 |

**BIRKIN, KENNETH**

| | | |
|---|---|---|
| *Jane Eyre* | Joubert, J. | 1998* |

**BIRTWHISTLE, JOHN (b. 1946)**

| | | |
|---|---|---|
| *Plumber's Gift* | Blake, D. | 1989 |

**BISBEE, NOAH**

| | | |
|---|---|---|
| *Blockheads, The* | ** | 1782 |

**BISSO, JAMES**

| | | |
|---|---|---|
| *Sub Pontio Pilato* | Wold, E. | 2003 |

**BLACK, DON**

| | | |
|---|---|---|
| *Tell Me on a Sunday* | Lloyd Webber | 1980 |

**BLACKBURN, THOMAS (1916–1977)**

| | | |
|---|---|---|
| *Judas Tree* | Dickinson, P. | 1965 |

**BLAKESLEE, FLORENCE H.**

| | | |
|---|---|---|
| *Legend of Wiwaste* (with comp..) | Blakeslee, S. | 1924 |

**BLANCHARD, EDWARD (1820–1889)**

| | | |
|---|---|---|
| *Arcadia* | Harroway, J. | 1841 |
| *Carina* (with C. Bridgman) | Woolf, J. | 1888 |

**BLASER, ROBIN**

| | | |
|---|---|---|
| *Last Supper* | Birtwistle, H. | 2000 |

**BLECHER, HILARY**

| | | |
|---|---|---|
| *Frida* (with M. Cruz) | Rodríguez, R. | 1991 |
| *Many Moons* | Kapilow, R. | 1997 |

**BLITZSTEIN, MARC (1905–1964)**

| | | |
|---|---|---|
| *Threepenny Opera* | Weill-Blitzstein | 1954 |

BLOOM, HARRY
 *King Kong*       Matshikiza, T.  1959
BOADEN, JAMES (1762–1839)
 *Cambro-Britons*      Arnold, S.   1798
 *Ozmyn and Daraxa*    Attwood, T.   1793
BOBGAN, ROBERT
 *Blue Sky Transmission*   El-Dabn, H.   2002
BOERLAGE, FRANS
 *Diable amoureux*     Rodríguez, R.  1978*
BOESING, MARTHA (b. ca. 1936)
 *Wanderer, The*      Boesing, P.   1970
BOLAN, ROBYN
 *Beyond Men and Dreams*  Hogg, B.    1991
BOLT, CAROL (1941–2000)
 *Red Emma*       Kulesha, G.   1995
BOND, EDWARD
 *English Cat*       Henze, H. W.  1983
BONNARD, ROBERT
 *Fortune of St. Macabre*   Hanay, R.    1964
BONNIN, GERTRUDE (ZITKALA-SA) (1876–1938)
 *Sun Dance*       Hanson, W. F.  1913
BOOTH, BARTON (1681–1733)
 *Death of Dido*      Pepusch, J.   1716
 *Dido and Aeneas*     Arne, T. A.   1734
BORGESE, GIUSEPPE ANTONIO (1882–1952)
 *Montezuma*       Sessions, R.   1964
BOTSFORD, KEITH (b. 1928)
 *Bacchae*        Antoniou, T.  1992
BOTTOMLEY, GORDON (1874–1948)
 *Crier by Night*      Bainton, E. L.  1919*
BOUCICAULT, DION [DIONYSIUS LARDNER] (1820?–1890)
 *Lily of Killarney* (with J. Oxenford) Benedict, J.   1862
BOURJAILY, VANCE (1922–2010)
 *Four-Thousand Dollars*   Turner, T.    1969
BOURNE, C. H.
 *Thais and Talmane*    Campbell, C. M. 1921
BOWMAN, JOHN S. (b. 1931)
 *Emperor Norton*     Mollicone, H.  1981
 *Face on the Barroom Floor*  Mollicone, H.  1978
BOYD, ELIZABETH (fl. 1730–1744)
 *Don Sancho*       **      1739
BRACKMAN, JACOB
 *Romulus Hunt* (with comp..)  Simon, C.    1993
BRADFORD, JOSEPH (1843–1886)
 *Out of Bondage*      **      1876
BRADFORD, ROARK (1896–1948)
 *Mississippi Legend*    Wolfe, J.    1951
BRADY, LEO (b. 1917)
 *Break of Day*      Jones, G. T.   1961
 *Cage, The*       Jones, G. T.   1959

BRAHMS, CARYL (1901–1982)
 *Little Beggars* (with N. Sherrin) Saunders, M.  1958
 *Mañana* (with G. Foa)   Benjamin, A.  1956
BRANN, EVA T. H.
 *Socrates*       Thoms, H.   2007
BRENTON, HOWARD (b. 1942)
 *Playing Away*     Mason, B.    1994
BREVAL, JOHN (1680?–1738)
 *Rape of Helen*      **      1737
BREWER, GEORGE (b. 1766)
 *Bannian Day*      Arnold, S.   1796
 *How to Be Happy*    Arnold, S.   1794
BREWSTER, HENRY (1850–1908)
 *Forest, The* (with comp..)  Smyth, E.    1902
BREWSTER, TOWNSEND (b. 1924)
 *Tower, The*      Levy, M. D.   1957
BRIDGEMAN, JOHN VIPON (1819–1889)
 *Armourer of Nantes*    Balfe, M.    1863
 *Puritan's Daughter*    Balfe, M.    1861
BRIDGES, PENELOPE
 *Luyala*        Banfield, W.   2002
BRIDGES, THOMAS (fl. 1759–1775)
 *Dido and Aeneas*     Hook, J.    1771
BRIDGMAN, CUNNINGHAM
 *Carina* (with E. Blanchard)  Woolf, J.    1888
BROADHURST, GEORGE (1866–1952)
 *Nancy Brown* (with F. Ranken) Hadley, H.   1903
BROCK, DAVID
 *Chicken or Beef?*     Chen, J.    2008
BROCK, SAM HOUSTON
 *Sotoba Komachi*     Levy, M. D.   1957
BROOKE, FRANCES (1724?–1789)
 *Marian*        Shield, W.    1788
 *Rosina*        Shield, W.    1782
BROOKFIELD, CHARLES H. (1857–1913)
 *See-See* (with A. Ross)   Jones, S.    1906
BROUGH, WILLIAM (1826–1870)
 *Caliph of Bagdad*     Musgrave, F.   1858
BROUGHAM, JOHN (1810–1890)
 *Blanche de Nevers*    Balfe, M.    1863
BROUGHTON, THOMAS (1704–1774)
 *Hercules*        Handel, G. F.  1745
BROVSKY, LINDA
 *Love, Death, and High Notes* White, C.    1988
BROWN, CHARLES ARMITAGE (1786–1842)
 *Narensky*       Braham et al.  1814
BROWN, DIANE
 *Bohemians, The* (with L. Olesker) Kirschner, B.  1990
BROWNE, EMANUEL
 *David Rizzio*      Moore, M.    1932

**BROWNE, MARGERY**

| | | |
|---|---|---|
| *Lady Dolly* | Hill, A. | 1900 |

**BROWNE, MICHAEL DENNIS**

| | | |
|---|---|---|
| *Harmoonia* | Paulus, S. | 1991 |
| *Three Hermits* | Paulus, S. | 1997 |
| *Village Singer* | Paulus, S. | 1979 |

**BROWNELL, MARK**

| | | |
|---|---|---|
| *Ice Time* | Chan Ka Nin | 2004 |
| *Iron Road* | Chan Ka Nin | 2001 |
| *Weaving Maiden* | Chan Ka Nin | 2006 |

**BRUCKER, ROGER**

| | | |
|---|---|---|
| *Proposal, The* | Humel, G. | 1958 |
| *Triangle, The* | Humel, G. | 1958 |

**BRUNELLE, PHILIP (b. 1943)**

| | | |
|---|---|---|
| *Newest Opera* | Balk, H. W. | 1974 |

**BRUNHOFF, LAURENT de (b. 1931)**

| | | |
|---|---|---|
| *Travels of Babar* (with comp.) | Mostel, R. | 2000 |

**BRUNYATE, ROGER**

| | | |
|---|---|---|
| *Alien Corn* | Benjamin, T. | 2005 |
| *April Witch* | Shapiro, D. | 1995 |
| *Reunion, The* | Crozier, D. | 1989 |
| *Roman Fever* | Ward, R. | 1993 |
| *Where Angels Fear to Tread* | Weiser, M. | 1999 |

**BRYDEN, BILL (b. 1942)**

| | | |
|---|---|---|
| *Hermiston* | Orr, R. | 1975 |

**BUCKLER, JANE**

| | | |
|---|---|---|
| *Pied Piper* | Person, K. | 2005 |

**BUCKLEY, REGINALD R. (b. 1882)**

| | | |
|---|---|---|
| *Birth of Arthur* | Boughton, R. | 1909 |
| *Immortal Hour* | Boughton, R. | 1914 |
| *Round Table* (with comp..) | Boughton, R. | 1916 |

**BUCKSTONE, JOHN BALDWIN (1802–1879)**

| | | |
|---|---|---|
| *Dead Fetch* | Horn, C. E. | 1826 |
| *Demon, The* (with E. Fitzball) | Bishop, H. R. | 1832 |
| *Don Quixote* | Rodwell, G. | 1833 |
| *Jack Sheppard* | Rodwell, G. | 1839 |
| *Last Days of Pompeii* | Rodwell, G. | 1834 |
| *New Don Juan* | Rodwell, G. | 1828 |
| *Queen of a Day* | Fitzwilliam, E. | 1851 |
| *Rural Felicity* | Bishop, H. R. | 1834 |

**BUDBILL, DAVID (b. 1940)**

| | | |
|---|---|---|
| *Fleeting Animal* | Nielsen, E. | 2000 |

**BULLARD, MARY R.**

| | | |
|---|---|---|
| *Zabette* | Bryant, C. | 1999 |

**BUNN, ALFRED (1796–1860)**

| | | |
|---|---|---|
| *Bohemian Girl* | Balfe, M. | 1843 |
| *Bondman, The* | Balfe, M. | 1846 |
| *Brides of Venice* | Benedict, J. | 1844 |
| *Crusaders, The* | Benedict, J. | 1846 |
| *Daughter of St. Mark* | Balfe, M. | 1844 |
| *Devil's in It* | Balfe, M. | 1852 |
| *Enchantress, The* | Balfe, M. | 1845 |
| *Guillaume Tell* | Bishop, H. R. | 1838 |
| *Loretta* | Lavenu, L. | 1846 |
| *Maid of Artois* | Balfe, M. | 1836 |
| *Matilda of Hungary* | Wallace, V. | 1847 |
| *Sicilian Bride* | Balfe, M. | 1852 |

**BURCH, THAYER**

| | | |
|---|---|---|
| *Mummy, The* | Quincy, G. | 2004 |

**BURGES, JAMES BLAND (1752–1824)**

| | | |
|---|---|---|
| *Tricks upon Travellers* | Horn, C. E. | 1810 |

**BURGOYNE, JOHN (Gen.) (1722–1792)**

| | | |
|---|---|---|
| *Lord of the Manor* | Jackson, W. | 1780 |
| *Maid of the Oaks* | Barthelemon, F. | 1774 |
| *Richard Coeur de Lion* | Linley, T. | 1786 |

**BURKE, DAVID**

| | | |
|---|---|---|
| *Simeon* | Gustafson, D. | 2008 |

**BURNAND, F. C. (FRANCIS COWLEY) (1836–1917)**

| | | |
|---|---|---|
| *Chieftain, The* | Sullivan, A. S. | 1894 |
| *Contrabandista, The* | Sullivan, A. S. | 1867 |
| *Cox and Box* | Sullivan, A. S. | 1867 |
| *He's Coming* | Reed, T. G. | 1874 |
| *His Majesty* | Mackenzie, A. | 1897 |
| *Matched and Mated* | Reed, T. G. | 1876 |
| *Mildred's Well* | Reed, T. G. | 1873 |
| *No. 204* | Reed, T. G. | 1877 |
| *One Too Many* | Cowen, F. | 1874 |

**BURNS, JOHN**

| | | |
|---|---|---|
| *Inspiration* | Hagar, D. | 2002 |

**BURROUGHS, WILLIAM (1914–1997)**

| | | |
|---|---|---|
| *Black Rider* | Waits, T. | 1990 |

**BURROWS, DUDLEY**

| | | |
|---|---|---|
| *Leper, The* | Moore, M. | 1912* |

**BURTON, HAL (b. 1908)**

| | | |
|---|---|---|
| *Love in Transit* | Arnell, R. | 1958 |

**BURTON, IAN**

| | | |
|---|---|---|
| *Duchess of Malfi* | Rasch, T. | 2010 |

**BUSH, NANCY (1907–1991)**

| | | |
|---|---|---|
| *After the Wedding* | Head, M. | 1972 |
| *Day Return* | Head, M. | 1970 |
| *Ferryman's Daughter* | Bush, A. | 1964 |
| *Key Money* | Head, M. | 1970 |
| *Men of Blackmoor* | Bush, A. | 1956 |
| *Sugar Reapers* | Bush, A. | 1966 |

**BUTLER, CHARLES**

| | | |
|---|---|---|
| *Siren's Song* | Butler, M. | 1986 |

**BUTLER, HENRY (1919–1998)**

| | | |
|---|---|---|
| *Mourning Becomes Electra* | Levy, M. D. | 1967 |
| *Picnic, The* | Cumming, R. | 1979 |
| *Portrait in Brownstone* | Reif, P. | 1966 |
| *Tight-Rope* | Biscardi, C. | 1986 |

**BUTLIN, RON**

| | | |
|---|---|---|
| *Good Angel, Bad Angel* | Cresswell, L. | 2005 |

**BYERS, GEORGE (b. 1949)**

| | | |
|---|---|---|
| *Three Wise Women* | Moerk, A. | 2000 |
| *Unicorn Weeps* | Moerk, A. | 1996* |

**BYRNE, JACQUES**
| | | |
|---|---|---|
| *Legend, The* | Breil, J. C. | 1919 |

**CAHALAN, JAMES**
| | | |
|---|---|---|
| *Magic Beanstalk* | Kalmanoff, M. | 1976 |

**CAIRD, JOHN**
| | | |
|---|---|---|
| *Brief Encounter* | Previn, A. | 2009 |

**CALANDRA, DENIS**
| | | |
|---|---|---|
| *Bitter Tears* | Barry, G. | 2005 |

**CALHOUN, MATTHEW**
| | | |
|---|---|---|
| *Statues on a Lawn* | Flanagan, T. J. | 1983 |

**CALIENDO, RICHARD**
| | | |
|---|---|---|
| *Romeo and Juliet* | Liotta, A. | 1969 |

**CALLAN, HARRIET**
| | | |
|---|---|---|
| *Giovanni, the Sculptor* | Hill, A. | 1914 |

**CAMERON, MELISSA**
| | | |
|---|---|---|
| *Guacamayo's Old Song* | Oliver, J. | 1991 |

**CAMERON, GEORGE FREDERICK (1854–1885)**
| | | |
|---|---|---|
| *Leo, the Royal Cadet* | Telgmann, O. F. | 1889 |

**CAMPBELL, ALISTAIR**
| | | |
|---|---|---|
| *Uninvited, The* | Grant, J. | 1997 |

**CAMPBELL, KAREN**
| | | |
|---|---|---|
| *Inspector from Rome* | Musto, J. | 2010 |
| *Rappaccini's Daughter* | Dennison, S. | 1984 |

**CAMPBELL, MARK**
| | | |
|---|---|---|
| *Bastianello* | Musto, J. | 2008 |
| *Inspector from Rome, An* | Musto, J. | 2010 |
| *Later the Same Evening* | Musto, J. | 2007 |
| *Letter to E. 11th St.* | Pace, R. | 2006 |
| *Lucrezia* | Bolcom, W. | 2008 |
| *Three Lost Chords* | Horne, L. | 2008 |
| *Volpone* | Musto, J. | 2004 |

**CAMPBELL, MICHAEL**
| | | |
|---|---|---|
| *Madeline Lee* (with comp.) | Haddock, J. | 2004 |

**CANN, PETER**
| | | |
|---|---|---|
| *Dee* | Grant, R | 2005 |

**CAPASSO, MICHAEL**
| | | |
|---|---|---|
| *God Bless Us, Every One!* (with B. Van Horn) | Pasatieri, T. | 2010 |

**CAPOBIANCO, TITO (b. 1931)**
| | | |
|---|---|---|
| *Zapata* (with Roepke) | Balada, L. | 1985 |

**CARCACHE, MARIAN MOTLEY (b. 1954)**
| | | |
|---|---|---|
| *Under the Arbor* | Greenleaf, R. | 1992 |

**CARD, VIRGINIA (b. 1918)**
| | | |
|---|---|---|
| *Cask of Amontillado* (with comp..) | Perry, J. | 1954 |

**CARDELLI, GIOVANNI, trans.**
| | | |
|---|---|---|
| *Nymph and the Farmer* | Tcherepnin, A. | 1952 |

**CAREY, GEORGE SAVILLE (1743–1807)**
| | | |
|---|---|---|
| *Cottagers, The* | Shield, W. | 1766 |
| *Magic Girdle* | Barthelemon, F. | 1770 |
| *Noble Pedlar* | Barthelemon, F. | 1770 |

**CAREY, HENRY (1687–1743)**
| | | |
|---|---|---|
| *Amelia* | Lampe, J. F. | 1732 |
| *Dragon of Wantley* | Lampe, J. F. | 1737 |
| *Margery* | Lampe, J. F. | 1738 |
| *Teraminta* | Smith, J. C. | 1732 |
| *Teraminta* | Stanley, J. | 1754 |

**CARPENTER, BRIDGET**
| | | |
|---|---|---|
| *Barnum's Bird* (with comp..) | Larsen, L. | 2000 |

**CARR, CALEB (b. 1955)**
| | | |
|---|---|---|
| *Merlin* | Viñao, E. | 1999 |

**CARR, J. COMYNS (1849–1916)**
| | | |
|---|---|---|
| *Beauty Stone* (lyrics) | Sullivan, A. S. | 1898 |

**CARR, SARAH PRATT (b. 1850)**
| | | |
|---|---|---|
| *Flaming Arrow* | Moore, M. | 1922 |
| *Narcissa* | Moore, M. | 1912 |

**CARR, SCOTT**
| | | |
|---|---|---|
| *Scene Changes* | Boswell, W. | 1984 |

**CARRIÈRE, JEAN-CLAUDE**
| | | |
|---|---|---|
| *Wagner Dream* | Harvey, J. | 2007 |

**CARRILLO, LEO**
| | | |
|---|---|---|
| *Chipita Rodríguez* (with J. Wilson) | Weiner, L. | 1982 |

**CARROLL, JOANNE**
| | | |
|---|---|---|
| *New Lands* | de Bromhead, J. | 1993 |

**CARTER, DESMOND**
| | | |
|---|---|---|
| *Kingdom for a Cow* (with R. Arkell) | Weill, K. | 1935 |

**CARTER, SIMON**
| | | |
|---|---|---|
| *Proposal, The* (with E. Fen) | Walker, J. | 1974 |

**CARULLI, DIANA**
| | | |
|---|---|---|
| *Vine of the Soul* | Sainte Croix, J. | 2001 |

**CARUS, HELENA**
| | | |
|---|---|---|
| *Drumlin Legend* | Bacon, E. | 1949 |

**CASEY, MAIE**
| | | |
|---|---|---|
| *Young Kabbarli* | Sutherland, M. | 1965 |

**CASSADAY, JAMES LEWIS**
| | | |
|---|---|---|
| *Lord Byron* (with N. Engels) | Graham, J. | 1926 |

**CAVANAUGH, MICHAEL**
| | | |
|---|---|---|
| *Bachelor Farmers* | Weisensel, N. | 1993 |
| *City Workers* | Weisensel, N. | 1992 |
| *Gisela in Her Bathtub* | Weisensel, N. | 1991 |
| *Master's Stroke* | Weisensel, N. | 2001 |
| *Merry Christmas* | Weisensel, N. | 1997 |

**CAVANDER, KENNETH**
| | | |
|---|---|---|
| *Shadowplay* | Goehr, A. | 1970 |
| *Sir Gawain* | Peaslee, R. | 2001 |

**CAVE, JUDYTH WALKER**
| | | |
|---|---|---|
| *Pandora's Box* | Cave, M. | 1971 |

**CHAI, CAMYAR**
| | | |
|---|---|---|
| *Elijah's Kite* | Rolfe, J, | 2006 |
| *Rosa* | Rolfe, J. | 2004 |

**CHAN, MARJORIE**
| | | |
|---|---|---|
| *Sanctuary Song* | Richardson, P. | 2007 |

CHAPPELL, WILLIAM EVELYN (b. 1908)

| | | |
|---|---|---|
| *Violins of St. Jacques* (with comp.) | Williamson, M. | 1966 |

CHAPPLE, GEOFF

| | | |
|---|---|---|
| *Alley* (with comp.) | Body, J. | 1998 |

CHARNESKY, J. JASON

| | | |
|---|---|---|
| *Ever Since Eden,* trilogy | Trinkley, B. | 1997 |
| *Cleo* | Trinkley, B. | 1999 |
| *Eve's Odds* | Trinkley, B. | 1999 |
| *Golden Apple* | Trinkley, B. | 1999 |
| *York* | Trinkley, B. | 2002 |

CHARNIN, MARTIN

| | | |
|---|---|---|
| *Zenda* (lyrics, with Kuller, Adelson) | Duke, V. | 1963 |

CHATTERTON, ANNA

| | | |
|---|---|---|
| *Swoon* | Rolfe, J. | 2006 |

CHATTERTON, THOMAS (1752–1770)

| | | |
|---|---|---|
| *Revenge, The* | Arnold, S. | 1770 |

CHENAULT, JOHN

| | | |
|---|---|---|
| *Shadowboxer* | Proto, F. | 2010 |

CHERRY, ANDREW (1763–1824)

| | | |
|---|---|---|
| *Spanish Dollars* | Davy, J. | 1805 |
| *Travellers, The* | Corri, D. | 1806 |

CHESSON, NORA (1871–1906)

| | | |
|---|---|---|
| *Muirgheis* (trans. T. O'Donoghue) | Butler, O'B. | 1903 |

CHETWOOD, WILLIAM R. (d. 1766)

| | | |
|---|---|---|
| *Generous Free-Mason* | ** | 1730 |
| *Lover's Opera* | ** | 1729 |

CHILD, CHRISTINE

| | | |
|---|---|---|
| *Purple Gang* | Jex, D. | 1991 |

CHILD, HAROLD (1869–1945)

| | | |
|---|---|---|
| *Hugh the Drover* | Vaughan Williams, R. | 1924 |

CHONG, PING

| | | |
|---|---|---|
| *Games, The* (with comp.) | Monk, M. | 1983 |

CHORLEY, HENRY FOTHERGILL (1808–1872)

| | | |
|---|---|---|
| *Amber Witch* | Wallace, V. | 1861 |
| *Sapphire Necklace* | Sullivan, A. S. | 1867 |

CHORNEY, ALEXANDER

| | | |
|---|---|---|
| *Royal Auction* (with S. Shrager) | Kanitz, E | 1958 |

CHRISTOPHER, TRAY

| | | |
|---|---|---|
| *Howard* | Earnest, J. D. | 1987 |

CHURCHILL, CARYL

| | | |
|---|---|---|
| *Hotel* | Gough, O. | 1997 |
| *Ring, Lamp, Thing* | Gough, O. | 2010 |

CHURCHILL, JORDAN

| | | |
|---|---|---|
| *Oedipus* (rev) | Partch, H. | 1954 |

CIARDI, JOHN (1916–1986)

| | | |
|---|---|---|
| *Inferno of Dante* | Soluri, P. | 2003 |

CIBBER, COLLEY (1671–1757)

| | | |
|---|---|---|
| *Damon and Phillida* | ** | 1729 |
| *Love in a Riddle* | ** | 1729 |
| *Myrtillo* | Pepusch, J. | 1715 |
| *Temple of Dullness* | Arne, T. A. | 1745 |
| *Venus and Adonis* | Pepusch, J. | 1715 |

CIBBER, THEOPHILUS (1703–1758)

| | | |
|---|---|---|
| *Patie and Peggy* | ** | 1730 |

CICOUX, HÉLÈNE (B. 1937)

| | | |
|---|---|---|
| *Jocasta* (trans. J. G. Miller) | Schonthal, H. | 1996 |

CLAFLIN, DOROTHEA

| | | |
|---|---|---|
| *Hester Prynne* | Claflin, A. | 1934 |
| *Uncle Tom's Cabin* | Claflin, A. | 1964 |

CLARK, BARRETT HARPER (1890–1953)

| | | |
|---|---|---|
| *Christmas Tale* | Freer, E. E. | 1929 |

CLARK, WILLY

| | | |
|---|---|---|
| *Legend of Poker Alice* | Swisher, G. | 2010 |

CLARKE, GEORGE ELLIOTT

| | | |
|---|---|---|
| *Beatrice Chancy* | Rolfe, J. | 1996 |

CLARKE, HENRY SAVILE (1841–1893)

| | | |
|---|---|---|
| *Alice in Wonderland* | Slaughter, W. | 1906 |

CLARKE, MARCUS

| | | |
|---|---|---|
| *Moustique* | Kowalski, H. | 1889 |

CLARKE, ROGER

| | | |
|---|---|---|
| *Man with Footsoles* | Volans, K. | 1993 |

CLAY, C.

| | | |
|---|---|---|
| *On the March* (with Yardley, Stephenson) | Clay, F. | 1896 |

CLIFFE, CEDRIC

| | | |
|---|---|---|
| *Blind Raftery* | Trimble, J. | 1957 |
| *Devil Take Her* (lyrics) | Benjamin, A. | 1931 |
| *Prima Donna* | Benjamin, A. | 1949 |
| *Tale of Two Cities* | Benjamin, A. | 1957 |
| *Tartuffe* | Benjamin, A. | 1964 |
| *Under Western Eyes* | Joubert, J. | 1969 |

CLIFTON, LEWIS

| | | |
|---|---|---|
| *Marjorie* (with J. Dilley) | Slaughter, W. | 1890 |

CLINTON-BADDELEY, VICTOR C. (1900–1970)

| | | |
|---|---|---|
| *Jolly Roger* (with S. Mackenzie) | Leigh, W. | 1933 |
| *Pride of the Regiment* | Leigh, W. | 1931 |
| *What D'Ye Call It* | Tate, P. | 1966 |

CLIVE, KITTY (CATHERINE) (1711–1785)

| | | |
|---|---|---|
| *Rehearsal, The* | Boyce, W. | 1750 |

COATES, GEORGE

| | | |
|---|---|---|
| *RareArea* | Ream, M. | 1985 |
| *Way of How* | Dresher, P. | 1980 |

COBB, JAMES (1756–1818)

| | | |
|---|---|---|
| *Algonah* | Storace, S. | 1802 |
| *Catherine* | Burghers, Lord | 1830 |
| *Cherokee* | Storace, S. | 1794 |
| *Doctor and the Apothecary* | Storace, S. | 1788 |
| *Glorious First of June* (Cobb et al.) | Storace, S. | 1794 |
| *Haunted Tower* | Storace, S. | 1789 |
| *House to Be Sold* | Kelly, M. | 1802 |
| *Love in the East* | Linley, T., Sr. | 1788 |

| | | |
|---|---|---|
| *Paul and Virginia* | Reeve, W. | 1800 |
| *Pirates, The* | Storace, S. | 1792 |
| *Poor Old Drury!!!* | Storace, S. | 1791 |
| *Ramah Droog* | Reeve, W. | 1798 |
| *Siege of Belgrade* | Storace, S. | 1791 |
| *Strangers at Home* | Linley, T., Sr. | 1785 |
| *Wife of Two Husbands* | Mazzinghi, J. | 1803 |

**CODE, H[ENRY] B[RERETON]**

| | | |
|---|---|---|
| *Spanish Patriots* | Stevenson, J. | 1812 |

**COFFEY, CHARLES (d. 1745)**

| | | |
|---|---|---|
| *Beggar's Wedding* | ** | 1729 |
| *Boarding School* | ** | 1733 |
| *Devil to Pay* (with J. Mottley) | ** | 1731 |
| *Devil upon Two Sticks* | ** | 1729 |
| *Female Parson* | ** | 1730 |
| *Merry Cobler* | ** | 1735 |

**COGGAN, FORREST W.**

| | | |
|---|---|---|
| *Butterfly Girl* | Reed, H. O. | 1985 |
| *Living Solid Face* | Reed, H. O. | 1962 |

**COHEN, DAVID STEVEN (b. 1943)**

| | | |
|---|---|---|
| *Lilith* | Drattell, D. | 1997* |

**COLLARD, ALAN**

| | | |
|---|---|---|
| *Devil Take Her* (with J. C. Gordon) | Benjamin, A. | 1931 |

**COLLIER, CONSTANCE (1878–1955)**

| | | |
|---|---|---|
| *Peter Ibbetson* (with comp.) | Taylor, D. | 1931 |

**COLLIER, GEORGE (1738–1795)**

| | | |
|---|---|---|
| *Selima and Azor* | Linley, T., Sr. | 1776 |

**COLLS, P. H.**

| | | |
|---|---|---|
| *Mistakes of a Day* | Callcott, J. W. | 1787 |

**COLMAN, GEORGE, Jr. (1762–1836)**

| | | |
|---|---|---|
| *Battle of Hexham* | Arnold, S. | 1789 |
| *Blue-Beard* | Kelly, M. | 1798 |
| *Feudal Times* | Kelly, M. | 1799 |
| *Forty Thieves* | Kelly, M. | 1806 |
| *Inkle and Yarico* | Arnold, S. | 1787 |
| *Iron Chest* | Storace, S. | 1796 |
| *Law of Java* | Bishop, H. R. | 1822 |
| *Love Laughs at Locksmiths* | Kelly, M. | 1803 |
| *Mountaineers, The* | Arnold, S. | 1793 |
| *Review, The* | Arnold, S. | 1800 |
| *Surrender of Calais* | Arnold, S. | 1791 |
| *Turk and No Turk* | Arnold, S. | 1785 |
| *Two to One* | Arnold, S. | 1784 |

**COLMAN, GEORGE, Sr. (1732–1794)**

| | | |
|---|---|---|
| *Achilles in Petticoats* | Arne, T. A. | 1773 |
| *Caractacus* | Arne, T. A. | 1776 |
| *Elfrida* | Arne, T. A. | 1772 |
| *Fairy Prince* | Arne, T. A. | 1771 |
| *Fairy Tale* | Arne, M. | 1777 |
| *Gay Deceivers* | Hawes, W. | 1804 |
| *Midsummer Night's Dream* (with Garrick) | Burney, C. | 1763 |
| *Portrait, The* | Arnold, S. | 1770 |

| | | |
|---|---|---|
| *Sheep-Shearing* | Arnold, S. | 1877 |
| *Spanish Barber* | Arnold, S. | 1777 |
| *Ut Pictora Poesis!* | Arnold, S. | 1789 |

**COLVIN, IAN DUNCAN (1877–1938)**

| | | |
|---|---|---|
| *Leper's Flute* | Bryson, E. | 1926 |

**COMMONS, JEREMY**

| | | |
|---|---|---|
| *Beleaguered City* | Drummond, J. | 2002 |
| *Daughters of the Late Colonel* | Buchanan, D. | 1999 |
| *God Boy* | Ritchie, A. | 2004 |
| *Impersonating Maurice* | Drummond, J. | 2004 |
| *It Began with a Pony* | Buchanan, D. | 2003 |
| *Marriage a la Mode* | Drummond, J. | 2004 |
| *Miss Brill* | Buchanan, D. | 1999 |
| *Mr. Polly at the Potwell Inn* | Drummond, J. | 2000 |
| *Pictures* (with comp.) | Bootham, I. | 2002* |

**CONE, TOM (b. 1948)**

| | | |
|---|---|---|
| *Architect, The* | MacIntyre, D. | 1994 |
| *Game Misconduct* | Uyeda, L. | 2000 |
| *Gang, The* | Hannan, P. | 1997 |

**CONGDON, CONSTANCE**

| | | |
|---|---|---|
| *Earthrise* | Spratlan, L. | 2003 |
| *S.* | Perera, R. | 1995 |
| *Strange Life of Ivan Osokin* | Gordon, P. | 1994 |
| *Yellow Wallpaper* | Perera, R. | 1989 |

**CONGREVE, WILLIAM (1670–1729)**

| | | |
|---|---|---|
| *Judgment of Paris* | Arne, T. A. | 1742 |
| *Judgment of Paris* | Eccles, J. et al. | 1701 |
| *Semele* | Eccles, J. | ca. 1706* |
| *Semele* | Handel, G. F. | 1744 |

**CONNOR, TONY (b. 1938)**

| | | |
|---|---|---|
| *Americana* | Bruce, N. | 1980 |

**CONWAY, JAMES**

| | | |
|---|---|---|
| *My Love* | O'Connell, K. | 1997 |

**COOK, C[HARLES] E[MERSON]**

| | | |
|---|---|---|
| *Red Feather* | De Koven, R. | 1903 |

**COOK, WENDY**

| | | |
|---|---|---|
| *Warchild, The* | Taylor, R. | 1997 |

**COOKE, THOMAS (1703–1756)**

| | | |
|---|---|---|
| *Love and Revenge* | ** | 1729 |
| *Penelope* | ** | 1728 |

**COOPER, GEORGE (1840–1927)**

| | | |
|---|---|---|
| *Uncle Tom's Cabin* | Millard, H. | 1883 |

**COOPER, JAMIE LEE**

| | | |
|---|---|---|
| *Soyazhe* | Anderson, G. | 1979 |

**COPE, HENRY C.**

| | | |
|---|---|---|
| *Fairy Oak* (with E. Fitzball) | Forbes, H. | 1845 |

**COPLAND, MURRAY**

| | | |
|---|---|---|
| *Apology of Bony Anderson* | Conyngham, B. | 1978 |
| *Bennelong* | Conyngham, B. | 1988 |
| *Fly* | Conyngham, B. | 1984 |
| *Oath of Bad Brown Bill* | Conyngham, B. | 1985 |

**CORCORAN, ROBERT**

| | | |
|---|---|---|
| *Mad Hamlet* | Reif, P. | 1962* |

**CORDER, FREDERICK (1852–1932)**

| | | |
|---|---|---|
| *Golden Web* (with B. C. Stephenson) | Thomas, A. G. | 1893 |
| *Nordisa* | Corder, F. | 1887 |

**CORSARI, GARY**

| | | |
|---|---|---|
| *Reverend Everyman* | Brotons, S. | 1990 |

**CORSARO, FRANK (b. 1924)**

| | | |
|---|---|---|
| *Before Breakfast* | Pasatieri, T. | 1980 |
| *Frau Margot* | Pasatieri, T. | 2006 |
| *Heloise and Abelard* | Paulus, F. | 2002 |
| *Rasputin* (with comp.) | Reise, J. | 1988 |

**CORWIN, NORMAN (b. 1910)**

| | | |
|---|---|---|
| *Blennerhasset* (with P. Roll) | Giannini, V. | 1939 |

**COTE, DAVID**

| | | |
|---|---|---|
| *Fade* | Weisman, S. | 2008 |

**COTTERELL, CONSTANCE**

| | | |
|---|---|---|
| *Christmas Rose* (with M. Kemp-Welch) | Bridge, F. | 1931 |

**COULTER, JOHN (1888–1980)**

| | | |
|---|---|---|
| *Deirdre of the Sorrows* | Willan, H. | 1946 |
| *Transit through Fire* | Willan, H. | 1942 |

**COWAN, DAVID**

| | | |
|---|---|---|
| *Wheel of the World* | Crosse, G. | 1972 |

**COWEN, ROSALIND (b. ca. 1843)**

| | | |
|---|---|---|
| *Garibaldi* | Cowen, F. | 1860 |

**COX, DAVID (b. 1933)**

| | | |
|---|---|---|
| *Abigail and the Bushranger* | Beath, B. | 1974 |

**COXE, LOUIS OSBORNE (1918–1993)**

| | | |
|---|---|---|
| *Combat Zone* | Arnell, R. | 1969 |

**CRAFT, ROBERT (b. 1923)**

| | | |
|---|---|---|
| *Flood, The* | Stravinsky, I. | 1962 |

**CRAVEN, ELIZABETH (Lady) (1750–1828)**

| | | |
|---|---|---|
| *Arcadian Pastoral* | Beckford, W. | 1782 |
| *Silver Tankard* | Arnold, S. | 1781 |

**CRAVENS, JUNIOUS**

| | | |
|---|---|---|
| *Legend of Hani* | Hadley, H. | 1933 |

**CREAGH, PATRICK**

| | | |
|---|---|---|
| *Cry of Clytaemnestra* | Eaton, J. | 1980 |
| *Danton and Robespierre* | Eaton, J. | 1978 |
| *Myshkin* | Eaton, J. | 1973 |

**CREED, KAY**

| | | |
|---|---|---|
| *Gorgon's Head* (with comp., Osterhaus) | Magrill, S. | 1998 |
| *Paradise of Children* (with Osterhaus) | Magrill, S. | 1998 |

**CRIMP, MARTIN**

| | | |
|---|---|---|
| *Into the Little Hill* | Benjamin, G. | 2006 |

**CROCKER, CHARLES TEMPLETON**

| | | |
|---|---|---|
| *Land of Happiness* | Redding, J. | 1917 |

**CROFFUT, WILLIAM AUGUSTUS (1835–1915)**

| | | |
|---|---|---|
| *Deseret* | Buck, D. | 1880 |

**CROMER, WEST [A. LAW]**

| | | |
|---|---|---|
| *Night's Surprise* | Reed, T. G. | 1877 |

**CROSBY, FANNY (1820–1915)**

| | | |
|---|---|---|
| *Flower Queen* | Root, G. F. | 1852 |
| *Pilgrim Fathers* | Root, G. F. | ca. 1854* |

**CROSS, BEVERLEY (1931–1998)**

| | | |
|---|---|---|
| *All the King's Men* | Bennett, R. R. | 1969 |
| *Mines of Sulphur* | Bennett, R. R. | 1965 |
| *Rising of the Moon* | Maw, N. | 1970 |
| *Victory* | Bennett, R. R. | 1970 |

**CROSS, JAMES C. (d. 1810)**

| | | |
|---|---|---|
| *Apparition, The* | Reeve, W. | 1794 |
| *British Fortitude* | Reeve, W. | 1794 |
| *Charity Boy* | Reeve, W. | 1796 |
| *Purse, The* | Reeve, W. | 1794 |
| *Raft, The* | Reeve, W. | 1798 |

**CROSSLEY-HOLLAND, KEVIN**

| | | |
|---|---|---|
| *Green Children* (with comp.) | LeFanu, N. | 1990 |
| *Wildman* | LeFanu, N. | 1995 |

**CROWTHERS, MALCOLM**

| | | |
|---|---|---|
| *Tristan and Iseult* (with M. Hill) | Whitehead, G. | 1978 |

**CROZIER, ERIC (1914–1994)**

| | | |
|---|---|---|
| *Albert Herring* | Britten, B. | 1947 |
| *Billy Budd* (with E. M. Forster) | Britten, B. | 1951 |
| *Little Sweep* | Britten, B. | 1949 |
| *Rab the Rhymer* | Dunlop/Oppenheim | 1953 |
| *Ruth* | Berkeley, L. | 1956 |

**CUDDY, MELBA**

| | | |
|---|---|---|
| *Harlequins* | Keane, D. | 1986 |
| *Lumina* | Keane. D. | 1988 |

**CUMBERLAND, RICHARD (1732–1811)**

| | | |
|---|---|---|
| *Amelia* | Dibdin et al. | 1771 |
| *Amelia* | Piccinni et al. | 1768 |
| *Armorer, The* | Warner, Capt. | 1793 |
| *Calypso* | Butler, T. H. | 1779 |
| *Eros and Psyche* | Cummings, C. | 1983 |
| *Summer's Tale* | Arnold, S. | 1765 |

**CUMMINGS, E [DWARD] E[STLIN] (1894–1962)**

| | | |
|---|---|---|
| *Santa Claus* | Smith, L. | 1955 |

**CUNNINGHAM, A. C.**

| | | |
|---|---|---|
| *Lansdown Castle* | Holst, G. | 1893 |

**CURLEY, TOM F.**

| | | |
|---|---|---|
| *Scarlet Letter* | Herman, M. | 1992 |

**CURREY, CLAUDINE**

| | | |
|---|---|---|
| *Mermaid, The* | More, M. | 1951 |

**CURRIE, JOHN**

| | | |
|---|---|---|
| *Confessions of a Justified Sinner* | Wilson, T. | 1976 |

**DALTON, JOHN (1709–1763)**

| | | |
|---|---|---|
| *Comus* | Arne, T. A. | 1738 |
| *Comus* | Bishop, H. R. | 1815 |

**DANCE, CHARLES (1794–1863)**

| | | |
|---|---|---|
| *Magic Horn* | Lee, G. A. | 1846 |
| *Nautch Girl* | Solomon, E. | 1891 |

**DARION, JOE (1911–2001)**

| | | |
|---|---|---|
| *And David Wept* | Laderman, E. | 1971 |
| *archy and mehitabel* (with M. Brooks) | Kleinsinger, G. | 1954 |

| | | |
|---|---|---|
| *Galileo Galilei* | Laderman, E. | 1979 |
| *Questions of Abraham* | Laderman, E. | 1973 |
| *Tree That Found Christmas* | Kleinsinger, G. | 1955 |

**DAVENANT, CHARLES (1656–1714)**

| | | |
|---|---|---|
| *Circe* | Bannister, J. | 1677 |

**DAVENANT, WILLIAM (1606–1668)**

| | | |
|---|---|---|
| *Britannia triumphans* | Lawes, W. | 1638 |
| *Circe* | Galliard, J. E. | 1719 |
| *Macbeth* | Eccles, J. | 1696 |
| *Macbeth* | Leveridge, R. | 1702 |
| *Macbeth* | Locke/Johnson | 1673 |
| *Siege of Rhodes* | Lawes, H. | 1656 |
| *Tempest, The* | Arne, T. A. | 1746 |
| *Tempest, The* (with Dryden, Shadwell) | Weldon, J. | ca. 1712 |
| *Triumphs of the Prince* | Lawes, H./W. Lawes | 1636 |

**DAVIDSON, DONALD**

| | | |
|---|---|---|
| *Singin' Billy* | Bryan, C. | 1952 |

**DAVIDSON, EVA**

| | | |
|---|---|---|
| *Billy and Zelda* | Davidson, T. | 1998 |
| *Pearl* | Davidson, T. | 2009 |

**DAVIES, ROBERTSON (1913–1995)**

| | | |
|---|---|---|
| *Dr. Canon's Cure* | Holman, D. | 1982 |
| *Golden Ass* | Peters, R. | 1999 |

**DAVIS, THULANI (b. 1948)**

| | | |
|---|---|---|
| *Amistad* | Davis, A. | 1997 |
| *E. & O. Line* | LeBaron, A. | 1996 |

**DAVIS, URSULA (b. 1938)**

| | | |
|---|---|---|
| *Just Above My Head* (with comp.) | Davis, N. | 1985* |

**DAWSON-SCOTT, CATHERINE A. (1865–1934)**

| | | |
|---|---|---|
| *Gale* (with Lowry) | Leginska, E. | 1935 |

**DEAL, DENNIS**

| | | |
|---|---|---|
| *Henry David Thoreau* (with Wyss, Evans) | Cionek, E. | 2003 |
| *SPACE* | Cionek, E. | 1991 |

**DEAN, NANCY (b. 1930)**

| | | |
|---|---|---|
| *Criseyde* | Shields, A. | 2008 |

**DEANE, VINCENT**

| | | |
|---|---|---|
| *Intelligence Park* | Barry, G. | 1990 |

**De ANGELIS, APRIL (b. 1960)**

| | | |
|---|---|---|
| *Flight* | Dove, J. | 1998 |
| *Greed* | Dove, J. | 1993 |
| *Pig* | Dove, J. | 1992 |

**DEAR, NICK**

| | | |
|---|---|---|
| *Family Affair* | Grant, J. | 1993 |
| *Palace in the Sky* | Dove, J. | 2000 |
| *Siren Song* | Dove, J. | 1994 |

**DEBNEY, PATRICIA (b. 1964)**

| | | |
|---|---|---|
| *Juniper Tree* | Watkins, R. | 1997 |

**DeCLUE, DENISE**

| | | |
|---|---|---|
| *Pay Off* | Russo, W. | 1984 |

**De GRESAC, FRED**

| | | |
|---|---|---|
| *Wedding Trip* (with H. B. Smith) | De Koven, R. | 1911 |

**DEHN, PAUL (1912–1976)**

| | | |
|---|---|---|
| *Bear, The* (with comp.) | Walton, W. | 1967 |
| *Castaway* | Berkeley, L. | 1967 |
| *Dinner Engagement* | Berkeley, L. | 1954 |

**De JAFFA, KATHLEEN**

| | | |
|---|---|---|
| *Emperor Jones* | Gruenberg, L. | 1933 |

**DeJONG, CONSTANCE (b. 1950)**

| | | |
|---|---|---|
| *Satyagraha* (with comp.) | Glass, P. | 1981 |

**DELAMERE, MARGARET**

| | | |
|---|---|---|
| *All at Sea* (with comp.) | Shaw, G. | 1952 |

**DELL'OSO, ANNA MARIA**

| | | |
|---|---|---|
| *Art of Pizza* | Whitehead, G. | 1995* |
| *Bride of Fortune* | Whitehead, G. | 1991 |
| *Pirate Moon* | Whitehead, G. | 1986 |

**DeLYNN, JANE**

| | | |
|---|---|---|
| *Monkey Opera* | Trefousse, R. | 1982 |

**DEMARIA, ROBERT**

| | | |
|---|---|---|
| *Pietro's Petard* | Overton, H. | 1963 |

**DEMETER, DIANE SIMKIN**

| | | |
|---|---|---|
| *Moon Singer* | Liptak, D. | 1998 |

**DENBY, EDWIN (1903–1983)**

| | | |
|---|---|---|
| *Second Hurricane* | Copland, A. | 1937 |

**DENNEY, REUEL (1913–1995**

| | | |
|---|---|---|
| *Noelani* | Barati, G. | 1971 |

**DENNIS, JOHN (1657–1734)**

| | | |
|---|---|---|
| *Rinaldo and Armida* | Eccles, J. | 1698 |

**DÉNOMMÉ-WELCH, SPY**

| | | |
|---|---|---|
| *River by the Residential Schoolhouse* | Chen, J. | 2008 |

**DENT, JOHN (fl. 1782–1795)**

| | | |
|---|---|---|
| *Too Civil by Half* | Hook, J. | 1782 |

**DERVIN, LEE**

| | | |
|---|---|---|
| *Swinish Cult* | Hodkinson, S. | 1975* |

**DE SYLVA, BUDDY [BUDDY GARD] (1896–1950)**

| | | |
|---|---|---|
| *Blue Monday* (with G. Bassman) | Gershwin, G. | 1922 |

**DEVERELL, REX**

| | | |
|---|---|---|
| *Leviathan Hook* | Doolittle, Q. | 1998 |

**DEVIN, LEE (b. 1938)**

| | | |
|---|---|---|
| *St. Carmen of the Main* | Hodkinson, S. | 1988 |

**DIAMOND, ALEXIS**

| | | |
|---|---|---|
| *Enid and the Swans* | Rolfe, J. | 2005 |
| *Two Graces* | Ferguson, S. | 2004 |

**DIAMOND, MARC**

| | | |
|---|---|---|
| *Star Catalogues* | Underhill, O. | 1994 |

**DIANA, B. A.**

| | | |
|---|---|---|
| *Phone Call* | Webb, J. | 2002 |

**DIBBERN, DANIEL**

| | | |
|---|---|---|
| *Ransom of Red Chief* | Rodríguez, R. | 1986 |
| *Suor Isabella* | Rodríguez, R. | 1982 |

**DIBDIN, CHARLES (1745–1814)**

| | | |
|---|---|---|
| *Gipsies, The* | Arnold, S. | 1778 |

| | | |
|---|---|---|
| *None So Blind* | Arnold, S. | 1782 |
| *Old Fools* | Moorehead, J. | 1800 |
| *Pennyworth of Wit* | Davy, J. | 1796 |

**DIBDIN, CHARLES, Jr. (1768–1833)**

| | | |
|---|---|---|
| *Council of Ten* | Reeve, W. | 1811 |
| *Farmer's Wife* | Bishop, H. R. | 1814 |
| *Magic Minstrel* | Reeve, W. | 1808 |
| *Poor Vulcan* | Bishop, H. R. | 1813 |
| *Rake's Progress* | Whitaker, J. | 1826 |
| *Round Robin* | Dibdin, C. | 1811 |

**DIBDIN, THOMAS (1771–1841)**

| | | |
|---|---|---|
| *Bondoncani, Il* | Attwood, T. | 1800 |
| *Cabinet, The* | Reeve, W., et al. | 1802 |
| *Covenanters, The* | Loder, E. J. | 1835 |
| *Family Quarrels* | Reeve, W. | 1802 |
| *Hermione* | Attwood, T. | 1800 |
| *Morning, Noon* | Perry, G. | 1822 |
| *Mother Goose* | Ware, W. H. | 1806 |
| *Mouth of the Nile* | Attwood, T. | 1798 |
| *Naval Pillar* | Moorehead, J. | 1799 |
| *Of Age Tomorrow* | Kelly, M. | 1800 |
| *St. David's Day* | Attwood, T. | 1800 |
| *Thirty Thousand* | Reeve, W. | 1804 |
| *True Friends* | Attwood, T. | 1800 |
| *Two Faces under a Hood* | Shield, W. | 1807 |
| *Up to Town* | Reeve, W. et al. | 1811 |
| *White Plume* | Reeves, W. | 1806 |
| *Zuma* | Bishop/Braham | 1818 |

**DICKENS, CHARLES (1812–1870)**

| | | |
|---|---|---|
| *Village Coquettes* | Hullah, J. | 1836 |

**DICKINSON, PATRIC (1914–1994)**

| | | |
|---|---|---|
| *Creation* | Ridout, A. | 1973 |
| *Phaeton* | Ridout, A. | 1975 |
| *Scena* | Hopkins, A. | 1953 |
| *Wenceslas* | Ridout, A. | 1978 |

**Di DOMENICA, ROBERT (b. 1927)**

| | | |
|---|---|---|
| *Rappaccini's Daughter* | Bender, E. | 1992 |

**DILLEY, JOSEPH J. (b. 1838)**

| | | |
|---|---|---|
| *Marjorie* (with L. Clifton) | Slaughter, W. | 1890 |

**DIMOND, WILLIAM (fl. 1800–1830)**

| | | |
|---|---|---|
| *Abou Hassan* | Cooke, T. S. | 1825 |
| *Aethiop, The* | Bishop, H. R. | 1812 |
| *Brother and Sister* | Reeve, W. | 1815 |
| *December and May* | Bishop, H. R. | 1818 |
| *Englishmen in India* | Bishop, H. R. | 1827 |
| *Foundling of the Forest* | Kelly, M. | 1809 |
| *Haroun Alraschid* | Bishop, H. R. | 1813 |
| *Hero of the North* | Kelly, M. | 1803 |
| *Hunter of the Alps* | Kelly, M. | 1804 |
| *Lady and the Devil* | Kelly, M. | 1820 |
| *Native Land* | Bishop, H. R. | 1824 |
| *Nymph of the Grotto* | Lee, G. A. | 1829 |
| *Peasant Boy* | Kelly, M. | 1811 |
| *Pirate, The* | Rooke, W. M. | 1822 |

| | | |
|---|---|---|
| *Sea-Side Story* | Attwood, T. | 1801 |
| *Young Hussar* | Kelly, M. | 1807 |
| *Youth, Love* | Kelly, M. | 1805 |

**Di NOVELLI, DONNA**

| | | |
|---|---|---|
| *Oceanic Verses* | Prestini, P. | 2009 |

**DISCH, THOMAS M. (b. 1940)**

| | | |
|---|---|---|
| *Fall of the House of Usher* | Sandow, G. | 1979 |
| *Frankenstein* | Sandow, G. | 1980 |

**DODD, LEE WILSON (1879–1933)**

| | | |
|---|---|---|
| *Merrymount* | Smith, D. S. | 1913* |

**DODSLEY, ROBERT (1703–1764)**

| | | |
|---|---|---|
| *Blind Beggar* | Arne, T. A. | 1741 |
| *Triumph of Peace* | Arne, T. A. | 1748 |

**DODSON, GERALD (1884–1966)**

| | | |
|---|---|---|
| *Rebel Maid* (with A. Thompson) | Phillips, M. | 1921 |

**DODSON, OWEN (1914–1983)**

| | | |
|---|---|---|
| *Christmas Miracle* | Fax, M. | 1958 |
| *Till Victory Is Won* | Fax, M. | 1967 |

**DONAHUE, JOHN**

| | | |
|---|---|---|
| *Postcard from Morocco* | Argento, D. | 1971 |

**DONNELLY, DOROTHY**

| | | |
|---|---|---|
| *Student Prince* | Romberg, S. | 1924 |

**DORMAN, JOSEPH (d. 1754)**

| | | |
|---|---|---|
| *Female Rake* | ** | 1736 |

**DORR, DONALD**

| | | |
|---|---|---|
| *Frederick Douglass* | Kay, U. | 1991 |
| *Jubilee* | Kay, U. | 1976 |

**DOUGLAS, STUART**

| | | |
|---|---|---|
| *Land of Milk and Honey* | Russo, W. | 1967 |

**DOYLE, ARTHUR CONAN (1859–1930)**

| | | |
|---|---|---|
| *Jane Annie* (with Barrie) | Ford, E. | 1893 |

**DRAPER, EVELYN MANACHER**

| | | |
|---|---|---|
| *Game of Chance* | Barab, S. | 1957 |

**DRAYTON, HENRI (1822–1872)**

| | | |
|---|---|---|
| *Mephistopheles* | Lutz, M. | 1855 |

**DRURY, ROBERT (fl. 1732–1735)**

| | | |
|---|---|---|
| *Devil of a Duke* | ** | 1732 |
| *Fancy'd Queen* | ** | 1733 |
| *Mad Captain* | ** | 1733 |
| *Rival Milliners* | ** | 1736 |

**DRURY, WILLIAM PRICE (b. 1861)**

| | | |
|---|---|---|
| *Samuel Pepys* (with R. Pryce) | Coates, A. | 1929 |

**DRYDEN, JOHN (1631–1700)**

| | | |
|---|---|---|
| *Albion and Albanius* | Grabu, L. | 1685 |
| *Indian Queen* (with R. Howard) | Purcell, H. | 1695 |
| *Secular Masque* | Purcell, D.-G. Finger | 1700 |
| *Tempest, The* | Arne, T. A. | 1746 |

**DU, YR HWRRD**

| | | |
|---|---|---|
| *Black Ram* (with Parry-Williams) | Parrott, I. | 1957 |

**DUBOIS (DU BOIS), (Lady) DOROTHY (1728–1774)**

| | | |
|---|---|---|
| *Divorce, The* | Hook, J. | 1772 |
| *Magnet, The* | Arnold, S. | 1771 |

DUCKWORTH, COLIN
| Beauty and the Beast | Easton, M. | 1989 |
| Cinderella | Easton, M. | 1989 |

DUDLEY, HENRY BATE. *See* BATE, HENRY.

DUFFIELD, BRAINERD
| Moby Dick | Low, J. | 1955 |

DUHAMEL, DENISE
| Bee Opera (lib with comp. et al.) | Hays, S. | 2003 |

DUKE, DOROTHY
| Sire de Maletroit | Duke, J. | 1958 |

DUMONT, FRANK
| Africanus Blue Beard | Sedgwick, A. B. | 1874 |
| Gambrinus | Sedgwick, A. B. | 1876 |

DUNBAR, PAUL L. (1872–1906)
| In Dahomey (with J. A. Shipp) | Cook, W. M. | 1903 |

DUNCAN, HARRY
| Last Puppet | Strilko, A. | 1963 |
| Scarf, The | Hoiby, L. | 1958 |

DUNCAN, JEFF
| With Such Friends | Schnauber, T. | 2007 |

DUNCAN, RONALD F.
| Christopher Sly | Eastwood, T. | 1960 |
| Rape of Lucretia | Britten, B. | 1946 |
| Rebel, The | Eastwood, T. | 1969 |

DUNLAP, WILLIAM (1766–1839)
| Alberto Albertini | Bray, J. | 1811 |
| Darby's Return | ** | 1789 |
| Spanish Castle | Hewitt, J. | 1800 |
| Sterne's Maria | Pelissier, V. | 1799 |
| Virgin of the Sun | Gilfert, C. | 1823 |
| Virgin of the Sun | Pelissier, V. | 1800 |
| Voice of Nature | Pelissier, V. | 1802 |

DUNN, GEOFFREY (1903–1981)
| Dunstan and the Devil | Williamson, M. | 1967 |
| English Eccentrics | Williamson, M. | 1964 |
| Julius Caesar Jones | Williamson, M. | 1966 |

DUNTON-DOWNER, LESLIE
| Belladonna | Rands, B. | 1999 |
| Ligeia | Thomas, A. R. | 1994 |

DUNWELL, BEN (b. 1969)
| Blackened Man | Todd, W. | 2002 |
| Whirlwind | Todd, W. | 2006 |

DURACK, MARY (1913–1994)
| Dalgerie | Penberthy, J. | 1959 |

D'URFEY, THOMAS (1653–1723)
| Wonders in the Sun | ** | 1706 |

DURRELL, LAWRENCE (1912–1991)
| Sappho | Glanville-Hicks | 1963 |

DVORKIN, JUDITH (b. 1930)
| Capitoline Venus | Kay, U. | 1971 |

DYNE, MICHAEL (1918–1989)
| Venus in Africa | Antheil, G. | 1957 |

EAGER, EDWARD (1911–1965)
| Barbara Allen | Broekman, D. | 1954 |
| Gentlemen, Be Seated! (with comp.) | Moross, J. | 1963 |
| Half Magic in King Arthur's Court | Kalmanoff, M. | 1963 |
| Miranda and the Dark Young Man | Siegmeister, E. | 1956 |

EASTGATE, NIGEL (1930–2001)
| Bridge to Somewhere | Drummond, J. | 2000 |

EATON, ESTELA
| Curious Case of Benjamin Button | Eaton, J. | 2010 |
| . . . inasuch | Eaton, J. | 2002 |
| Travelling with Gulliver | Eaton, J. | 1997 |

EBERHART, NELLE RICHMOND (1871–1944)
| Garden of Mystery | Cadman, C. W. | 1925 |
| Land of the Misty Water | Cadman, C. W. | 1912* |
| Shanewis | Cadman, C. W. | 1918 |
| Willow Tree | Cadman, C. W. | 1932 |

ECKERT, RINDE (b. 1951)
| Awed Behavior | Dresher, P. | 1993 |
| Pioneer | Dresher, P. | 1990 |
| Power Failure | Dresher, P. | 1989 |
| Ravenshead | Mackey, S. | 1998 |
| Slow Fire (with T. Allen, J. Allen) | Dresher, P. | 1985 |

EDEN, GUY
| Mountaineers, The (with comp.) | Somerville, R. | 1909 |
| 'Prentice Pillar | Somerville, R. | 1897 |

EDMANDS, BENJAMIN FRANKLIN (1807–1874)
| Belshazzar's Feast | Root, G. F. | ca. 1853* |

EDMON, EMUL P.
| Beauty and the Beast | Di Giacomo, F. | 1974 |

EDMONDS, FRED
| Don Quixote | Hewitt, T. J. | 1909 |

EDWARDS, ANNA MARIA
| Enchantress, The | Giordani, T. | 1783 |

EDWARDS, DIC (b. 1948)
| Juniper Tree | Toovey, A. | 1993 |

EDWARDS, GWYNNE
| Dylan and Caitlin | Manno, R. | 2008 |

EDWARDS, HENRY SUTHERLAND (1828–1906)
| Minna | de Lara, I. | 1886 |
| Rose | Hatton, J. L. | 1864 |

EGLIN, E[UGENE] H[ERMANN] (b. 1942)
| Scarlet Letter | Di Domenica, R. | 1986* |

EGOYAN, ATOM (b. 1960)
| Elsewhereless | Sharman, R. | 1998 |

EHN, ERIK
| Phrenic Crush | Lielawa, L. | 1997 |
| Vireo | Lielawa, L. | 1995* |

EISMAN, PAUL
| Strands | Levowitz, A. | 1997 |

ELDER, MARCIA

| | | |
|---|---|---|
| *Robert and Hall* | Brooks, R. | 2004 |

ELGUERA, AMALIA

| | | |
|---|---|---|
| *Voice of Ariadne* | Musgrave, T. | 1974 |

ELIOT, SAMUEL A., Jr. (b. 1893)

| | | |
|---|---|---|
| *Fall of the House of Usher* | Sessions, R. | 1925* |
| *Sganarelle* | Archer, V. | 1974 |

ELIOT, T[HOMAS] S[TEARNS] (1888–1965)

| | | |
|---|---|---|
| *Sweeney Agonistes* | Dankworth, J. | 1965 |

ELLIOT, ALICE

| | | |
|---|---|---|
| *Magic Fishbone* (with Mark, Raab) | Chapin, T. | 1988 |

ELLIS, THOMAS EVELYN (b. 1880)

| | | |
|---|---|---|
| *Cauldron of Annwn* (trilogy): | | |
| *Bronwen* | Holbrooke, J. | 1920 |
| *Children of Don* | Holbrooke, J. | 1912 |
| *Dylan* | Holbrooke, J. | 1914 |

ELM, ROBERT

| | | |
|---|---|---|
| *Merry Benedicts* | Arnold, M. | 1896 |

ELMSLIE, KENWARD (b. 1929)

| | | |
|---|---|---|
| *Lizzie Borden* | Beeson, J. | 1965 |
| *Miss Julie* | Rorem, N. | 1965 |
| *Seagull, The* | Pasatieri, T. | 1974 |
| *Sweet Bye and Bye* | Beeson, J. | 1957 |
| *Three Sisters* | Pasatieri, T. | 1986 |

ELWARD, JAMES

| | | |
|---|---|---|
| *Man on a Bearskin Rug* | Ramsier, P. | 1969 |

ENG, ALVIN

| | | |
|---|---|---|
| *Mao Zedong* | Gal, Y. | 1999 |

ENGELS, NORBERT (b. 1903)

| | | |
|---|---|---|
| *Lord Byron* (with J. L. Cassaday) | Graham, J. | 1926 |

ENGLAND, MARTHA

| | | |
|---|---|---|
| *Maletroit Door* | Barab, S. | 1960 |

ENGLE, PAUL (1908–1991)

| | | |
|---|---|---|
| *Golden Child* | Bezanson, P. | 1959 |

ENGVICK, WILLIAM

| | | |
|---|---|---|
| *Ellen* | Wilder, A. | 1955* |
| *Long Way* | Wilder, A. | 1955 |
| *Miss Chicken Little* | Wilder, A. | 1953 |

ENOS, JOSEPH

| | | |
|---|---|---|
| *Celebration, The* | Maury, L. | 1955* |

ENRIGHT, NICK

| | | |
|---|---|---|
| *Snow Queen* | Dudley, G. | 1985 |

ERDMAN, HARLEY (b. 1962)

| | | |
|---|---|---|
| *Captivation of Eunice Williams* | Kimper, P. | 2004 |

ERICH, W.

| | | |
|---|---|---|
| *Dr. Jekyll and Mr. Hyde* | Fragale F. D. | 1953 |

ERSKINE, JOHN (1879–1951)

| | | |
|---|---|---|
| *Helen Retires* | Antheil, G. | 1934 |
| *Jack and the Beanstalk* | Gruenberg, L. | 1931 |
| *Sleeping Beauty* | Bernstein, B. | 1938 |

ESRIS, ELIZABETH

| | | |
|---|---|---|
| *Elegy for a Prince* | Cervetti, S. | 2007 |

ESSLIN, MARTIN (1918–2002(

| | | |
|---|---|---|
| *Beatrice Cenci* | Goldschmidt, B. | 1952 |

ESTCOURT, RICHARD (1668–1712)

| | | |
|---|---|---|
| *Prunella* | Clayton, T. | 1708 |

EVANS, ALBERT

| | | |
|---|---|---|
| *Henry David Thoreau* (with Wyss, Deal) | Cionek, E. | 2003 |

EVERETT, HORACE [ERIK JOHNS/HORACE EUGENE JOHNSTON] (1927–2001)

| | | |
|---|---|---|
| *Tea Party* | Gottlieb, J. | 1957 |
| *Tender Land* | Copland, A. | 1954 |

EVERETT, LEOLYN LOUISE (SPELMAN) (1888–1971)

| | | |
|---|---|---|
| *Magnifica, La* | Spelman, T. | 1920* |

EWART, GAVIN

| | | |
|---|---|---|
| *Boys and Girls* | Holloway, R. | 1995* |
| *Tobermory* | Gardner, J. | 1977 |

EYRE, EDMUND JOHN (1787–1816)

| | | |
|---|---|---|
| *Caffres, The* | Davy, J. | 1802 |
| *Lady of the Lake* | Francis, W. | 1811 |
| *Vintagers, The* | Bishop, H. R. | 1809 |

FABIAN, R.

| | | |
|---|---|---|
| *Trick for Trick* | ** | 1735 |

FAINLIGHT, RUTH (b. 1931)

| | | |
|---|---|---|
| *Dancer Hotoke* | Fox, E. | 1991 |
| *European Stories* | Álvarez, G. | 1993 |

FAIRCLOUGH, MARY

| | | |
|---|---|---|
| *John Barleycorn* | Montgomery, B. | 1962 |

FALCONER, EDMUND (1814–1879)

| | | |
|---|---|---|
| *Deserted Village* | Glover, S. | 1880 |
| *Rose of Castille* (with A. G. Harris) | Balfe, M. | 1857 |
| *Satanella* (with Harris) | Balfe, M. | 1860 |
| *Victorine* | Mellon, A. | 1859 |

FALLON, KATHLEEN MARY

| | | |
|---|---|---|
| *Matricide* | Kats-Chernin, E. | 1998 |

FANDEL, JOHN (b. 1925)

| | | |
|---|---|---|
| *Mother, The* (with comp.) | Hollingsworth, S. | 1954 |

FANSTONE, DAVID

| | | |
|---|---|---|
| *Devil's Constructs* | Keane, D. | 1978 |

FARJEON, ELEANOR (1881–1965)

| | | |
|---|---|---|
| *Eve of St. John* | Mackenzie, A. | 1924 |

FARLEY, CHARLES (1771–1859)

| | | |
|---|---|---|
| *Aladdin* | Condell–Ware | 1813 |
| *Battle of Bothwell Brigg* | Bishop, H. R. | 1820 |

FARNIE, HENRY B. (1836–1889)

| | | |
|---|---|---|
| *Bride of Song* | Benedict, J. | 1864 |
| *Nell Gwynne* | Cellier, A. | 1878 |
| *Sleeping Queen* | Balfe, M. | 1864 |

FARQUHAR, MARION

| | | |
|---|---|---|
| *Poison* | Hart, F. | 1984 |
| *Princess and the Pea* | Toch, E. | 1954 |

| | | |
|---|---|---|
| **FASULES, NANCY** | | |
| *Hit and Run* (lyrics) | Abels, M. | 2001 |
| **FAUSSET, MARJORIE MINES** | | |
| *Two Sisters* | Rootham, C. | 1922 |
| **FAWCETT, JOHN (1768–1837)** | | |
| *Barber of Seville* (with D. Terry) | Bishop, H. R. | 1818 |
| *Fairies' Revels* | Arnold, S. | 1802 |
| *Marriage of Figaro* | Bishop, H. R. | 1819 |
| *Secret Mine* | Bishop/Condell | 1813 |
| **FAWKES, RICHARD (b. 1944)** | | |
| *Biko* | Paintal, P. | 1992 |
| *Survival Song* | Paintal, P. | 1989 |
| **FEATHER, LORRAINE** | | |
| *Bonfire of the Vanities* | de Kenessey, S. | 2006 |
| **FEE, DOROTHY** | | |
| *Taming of the Shrew* (with comp.) | Giannini, V. | 1953 |
| **FEILDE, MATTHEW (d. 1796)** | | |
| *Vertumnus and Pomona* | Arne, M. | 1782 |
| **FEIN, JUDITH (b. 1941)** | | |
| *Hotel Eden* | Mollicone, H. | 1989 |
| **FEINGOLD, MICHAEL** | | |
| *Happy End* | Weill-Feingold. | 1972 |
| **FEINSTEIN, ELAINE (b. 1930)** | | |
| *Bet, The* | Fox, E. | 1990 |
| **FEIST, MILTON** | | |
| *Brief Candle* | Mayer, W. | 1967 |
| **FELLOWS, DOUGLAS M.** | | |
| *Escape from Liberty* | Doellner, R. | 1947 |
| **FEN, ELIZABETH** | | |
| *Proposal, The* (with S. Carter) | Walker, J. | 1974 |
| **FENTON, JAMES (b. 1949)** | | |
| *Haroun* | Wuorinen, C. | 2000 |
| **FERGUSON, ETHEL O.** | | |
| *Fall of the House of Usher* | Loomis, C. | 1941 |
| **FERRARIO, SARAH BROWN (b. 1974)** | | |
| *Agamemnon* | Simpson, A. | 2003 |
| **FFINCH, MICHAEL (b. 1934)** | | |
| *Selfish Giant* | Shaw, F. | 1973 |
| **FIELD, BARBARA (b. 1933)** | | |
| *Rosina* | Titus, H. | 1980 |
| **FIELD, EDWARD** | | |
| *Listener's Guide* | Gottlieb, J. | 2009* |
| **FIELDING, HENRY (1707–1754)** | | |
| *Author's Farce* | ** | 1730 |
| *Don Quixote in England* | ** | 1734 |
| *Eurydice* | ** | 1743? |
| *Fathers, The* | ** | 1778 |
| *Gray Mare's the Best Horse* | Taylor, A. (arr) | 1731 |
| *Grub-Street Opera* | ** | 1731 |
| *Intriguing Chambermaid* | ** | 1734 |
| *Lottery, The* | Seedo, Mr. | 1732 |
| *Miss Lucy in Town* | Arne, T. A. | 1742 |

| | | |
|---|---|---|
| *Mock Doctor* | Carey et al. | 1732 |
| *Old Man Taught Wisdom* | ** | 1735 |
| *Tumble-Down Dick* | ** | 1736 |
| *Welsh Opera* | ** | 1731 |
| **FINCH, ANNIE (b. 1956)** | | |
| *Marina* | Drattell, D. | 2003 |
| **FINE, MORTON (1916–1991)** | | |
| *Hunted, The* (with D. Friedkin) | Mailman, M. | 1959 |
| **FINK, BONNIE** | | |
| *Boor, The* | Fink, M. | 1955 |
| **FINLETTER, GRETCHEN DAMROSCH (d. 1969)** | | |
| *Opera Cloak* | Damrosch, W. | 1942 |
| **FINN, H[ENRY] J[AMES] (1787–1840)** | | |
| *Ahmed al Ramel* | Horn, C. E. | 1840 |
| **FINNISSY, MICHAEL (b. 1946)** | | |
| *Ubu* (with comp.) | Toovey, A. | 1992 |
| **FISKE, MINNIE MADDERN (1865–1932)** | | |
| *Light from St. Agnes* | Harling, W. F. | 1925 |
| **FITTZ, VIRGINIA** | | |
| *Blue Angel* | Garza, E. | 1973 |
| **FITZBALL, EDWARD (1792–1873)** | | |
| *Adelaide* | *Bishop, H. R.* | *1830* |
| *Alchymist, The* (with T. H. Bayly) | Bishop, H. R. | 1832 |
| *Berta* | Smart, H. | 1854 |
| *Black Vulture* | Rodwell, G. | 1830 |
| *Bottle of Champagne* | Bishop, H. R. | 1832 |
| *Bronze Horse* | Rodwell, G. | 1835 |
| *Demon, The* (with J. B. Buckstone) | Bishop, H. R. | 1832 |
| *Devil's Elixir* | Rodwell, G. | 1829 |
| *Diadesté* | Balfe, M. | 1838 |
| *Earthquake, The* | Rodwell, G. | 1828 |
| *Fairy Oak* (with Cope) | Forbes, H. | 1845 |
| *Flying Dutchman* | Rodwell, G. | 1827 |
| *Joan of Arc* | Balfe, M. | 1837 |
| *Keolanthe* | Balfe, M. | 1841 |
| *Lord of the Isles* | Rodwell, G. | 1834 |
| *Lurline* | Wallace, V. | 1860 |
| *Magic Fan* | Bishop, H. R. | 1832 |
| *Maid of Honour* | Balfe, M. | 1847 |
| *Maritana* | Wallace, V. | 1845 |
| *Night Before the Wedding* | Bishop, H. R. | 1829 |
| *Ninetta* | Bishop, H. R. | 1830 |
| *Pasqual Bruno* | Hatton, J. L. | 1844 |
| *Paul Clifford* | Rodwell, G. | 1835 |
| *Quasimodo* | Rodwell, G. | 1836 |
| *Queen of the Thames* | Hatton, J. L. | 1842 |
| *Raymond and Agnes* | Loder, E. J. | 1855 |
| *Robber's Bride* | Hawes, W. | 1829 |
| *Sedan Chair* | Bishop, H. R. | 1832 |
| *Sexton of Cologne* | Rodwell, G. | 1836 |
| *She Stoops to Conquer* | Macfarren, G. | 1864 |
| *Siege of Rochelle* | Balfe, M. | 1835 |
| *Skeleton Lover* | Rodwell, G. | 1830 |
| *Soldier's Widow* | Barnett, J. | 1833 |

| | | |
|---|---|---|
| *Sorceress, The* | Ries, F. | 1831 |
| *Thalaba* | Rodwell, G. | 1836 |
| *Under the Oak* | Bishop, H. R. | 1830 |
| *Waverly* | Rodwell, G. | 1824 |

**FLAIG, ELEANOR (1902–1954)**

| | | |
|---|---|---|
| *Légende Provençale* | Moore, M. | 1935* |

**FLANDERS, MICHAEL**

| | | |
|---|---|---|
| *Three's Company* | Hopkins, A. | 1953 |

**FLASTER, KARL (1905–1965)**

| | | |
|---|---|---|
| *Harvest, The* (with comp.) | Giannini, V. | 1961 |
| *Lucedia* (with G. M. Sala) | Giannini, V. | 1934 |
| *Scarlet Letter* | Giannini, V. | 1938 |

**FLETCHER, LUCILLE (1912–2000)**

| | | |
|---|---|---|
| *Wuthering Heights* | Herrmann, B. | 1943* |

**FLETCHER, RONALD**

| | | |
|---|---|---|
| *Margaret Catchpole* | Dodgson, S. | 1979 |

**FLOWERS, CHARLES**

| | | |
|---|---|---|
| *Our Giraffe* | Hays, S. | 2008 |

**FLOWERS, PAT**

| | | |
|---|---|---|
| *First Christmas* | Antill, J. H. | 1969 |

**FOGARTY, BRIAN**

| | | |
|---|---|---|
| *Mozart in Manhattan* | Biales, A. | 2005 |

**FOGLIA, LEONARD**

| | | |
|---|---|---|
| *End of the Affair* (rev. version) | Heggie, J, | 2005 |
| *To Cross the Face of the Moon* | Martinez, J. | 2010 |

**FOLEY, BRENDAN**

| | | |
|---|---|---|
| *Maria Concepcion* | Arteaga, E. | 2004* |

**FOLEY, KATHY**

| | | |
|---|---|---|
| *King of Bali* | McDermott, V. | 1990 |

**FONSESCA, FERNANDO**

| | | |
|---|---|---|
| *Leo* | Ching, M. | 1985 |

**FORD, CHARLES HENRI (1913 [1908]–2002)**

| | | |
|---|---|---|
| *Denmark Vesey* | Bowles, P. | 1937 |

**FOREMAN, RICHARD (b. 1937)**

| | | |
|---|---|---|
| *Africanus Instructus* | Silverman, S. | 1986 |
| *Dr. Selavy's Magic Theatre* (with Hendry) | Silverman, S. | 1972 |
| *Elephant Steps* | Silverman, S. | 1968 |
| *Hotel for Criminals* | Silverman, S. | 1974 |
| *Madame Adare* | Silverman, S. | 1980 |
| *Real Magic in New York* | Dickman, S. | 1971 |
| *What to Wear* | Gordon, M. | 2006 |
| *Young Goodman Brown* | Johnston, P. | 1995 |

**FORNÉS, MARÍA IRENE (b. 1930)**

| | | |
|---|---|---|
| *Balseros* | Ashley, R. | 1997 |
| *Terra Incognita* | Sierra, R. | 1997 |

**FORREST, EBENEZER**

| | | |
|---|---|---|
| *Momus Turn'd Fabulist* | ** | 1729 |

**FORREST, LEON**

| | | |
|---|---|---|
| *Soldier Boy, Soldier* | Anderson, T. | 1982 |

**FORREST, THEODOSIUS (1728–1784)**

| | | |
|---|---|---|
| *Weathercock, The* | Arnold, S. | 1775 |

**FORSTER, E. M. (1879–1970)**

| | | |
|---|---|---|
| *Billy Budd* (with E. Crozier) | Britten, B. | 1951 |

**FORSYTHE, BRUCE**

| | | |
|---|---|---|
| *Blue Steel* | Still, W. G. | 1934* |

**FORTUNE, JAN (1892–1979)**

| | | |
|---|---|---|
| *Cynthia Parker* | Smith, J. | 1939 |

**FOX, IAN**

| | | |
|---|---|---|
| *Táin, The* | Wilson, J. | 1972 |

**FOX, SUSAN (b. 1943)**

| | | |
|---|---|---|
| *Village, The* | Mandelbaum, J. | 1995 |

**FRAM, MICHAEL**

| | | |
|---|---|---|
| *Fool, The* | Somers, H. | 1956 |

**FRANCHETTI, MARIE**

| | | |
|---|---|---|
| *Maypole, The* | Franchetti, A. | 1952 |

**FRANKLIN, ANDREW (d. 1845)**

| | | |
|---|---|---|
| *Egyptian Festival* | Florio, C. | 1800 |
| *Embarkation, The* | Reeve, W. | 1799 |
| *Outlaws, The* | Florio, C. | 1798 |

**FRANKLIN, DAVID**

| | | |
|---|---|---|
| *Dark Pilgrimage* | Tate, P. | 1962 |
| *Lodger, The* | Tate, P. | 1960 |

**FREEDMAN, MELVIN**

| | | |
|---|---|---|
| *Wife of Bath's Tale* (with comp.) | Legg, J. | 1986 |

**FREEMAN, DAVID (b. 1945)**

| | | |
|---|---|---|
| *Hell's Angels* | Osborne, N. | 1986 |

**FREEMAN, EVERETT**

| | | |
|---|---|---|
| *Zenda* | Duke, V. | 1963 |

**FREEMAN, PAUL**

| | | |
|---|---|---|
| *Judgment, The* | Kupferman, M. | 1966 |

**FREIER, RECHA**

| | | |
|---|---|---|
| *Sonata about Jerusalem* (with comp.) | Goehr, A. | 1971 |

**FRIED, BARBARA**

| | | |
|---|---|---|
| *Losers, The* | Farberman, H. | 1971 |

**FRIED, MICHAEL**

| | | |
|---|---|---|
| *Heracles* | Eaton, J. | 1972 |

**FRIEDKIN, DAVID**

| | | |
|---|---|---|
| *Hunted, The* (with M. Fine) | Mailman, M. | 1959 |

**FRIEDMAN, SONYA (b. 1932)**

| | | |
|---|---|---|
| *Memoirs of Uliana Rooney* | Fine, V. | 1994 |

**FRIEDMAN, STEVE**

| | | |
|---|---|---|
| *Bread & Roses Opera* | Glickman-Chen | 2000 |

**FROST, TOM**

| | | |
|---|---|---|
| *Capitan, El* (with C. Klein) | Sousa, J. P. | 1896 |

**FRY, CHRISTOPHER (1907–2005)**

| | | |
|---|---|---|
| *Paradise Lost* | Penderecki, K. | 1978 |
| *Phoenix Too Frequent* | Oliver, S. | 1970 |

**FRY, JOSEPH REESE (1811–1865)**

| | | |
|---|---|---|
| *Leonora* | Fry, W. | 1845 |
| *Notre-Dame of Paris* | Fry, W. | 1864 |

**FULLER, JOHN (b. 1937)**

| | | |
|---|---|---|
| *Herod, Do Your Worst* | Kelly, B. | 1968 |

FYLEMAN, ROSE (1877–1957)
| | | |
|---|---|---|
| *Happy Families* | Dunhill, T. | 1931 |

GAIL, SALLY M.
| | | |
|---|---|---|
| *Paris and Oenone* | Hagemann, P. | 1999 |

GALATI, FRANK
| | | |
|---|---|---|
| *Guilt of Lillian Sloan* (with comp.) | Neil, W. | 1986 |

GALE, KATE
| | | |
|---|---|---|
| *Paradise Lost* | Taylor, S. | 2006 |
| *Río de sangre* (transl. A. Partnoy) | Davis, D. | 2010 |

GALL, SALLY M. (b. 1956)
| | | |
|---|---|---|
| *Dalmatia and Dalmatio* | Clark, S. | 2002 |
| *Daphne at Sea* | Mason, C. | 2000 |
| *Kill Bear Comes Home* | Stuart, P. | 1996 |
| *Little Thieves of Bethlehem* | Stuart, P. | 1997 |
| *Singing Violin* (with comp.) | Sargon, S. | 1995 |

GALLOWAY, SALLY
| | | |
|---|---|---|
| *Monster* | Beamish, S. | 2002 |

GARDNER, DOROTHY
| | | |
|---|---|---|
| *Eastward in Eden* | Meyerowitz, J. | 1951 |

GARDNER, JOHN (1933–1982)
| | | |
|---|---|---|
| *Frankenstein* | Baber, Joseph | 1976 |
| *Rumpelstiltskin* | Baber, J. | 1978 |
| *Samson and the Witch* | Baber, J. | 1995 |

GARFEIN, HERSCHEL
| | | |
|---|---|---|
| *Elmer Gantry* | Aldridge, R. | 1992 |

GARNER, ALAN (b. 1934)
| | | |
|---|---|---|
| *Belly Bag* | Ball, M. | 1992 |
| *Holly from the Bongs* | Crosse, G. | 1974 |
| *Potter Thompson* | Crosse, G. | 1975 |

GARRETT, NANCY FALES
| | | |
|---|---|---|
| *Dora* | Shiflett, M. | 1999 |

GARRICK, DAVID (1717–1779)
| | | |
|---|---|---|
| *Christmas Tale* | Dibdin, C. | 1773 |
| *Cymon* | Arne, M. | 1767 |
| *Cymon* | Bishop, H. R. | 1815 |
| *Enchanter, The* | Giordani, T. | 1765 |
| *Enchanter, The* | Smith, J. C. | 1760 |
| *Fairies, The* | Smith, J. C. | 1755 |
| *Florizel and Perdita* | Boyce, W. | 1756 |
| *Grenadier, The* | Dibdin, C. | 1773 |
| *Institution of the Garter* | Dibdin, C. | 1771 |
| *Lethe* | Arne, T. A. | 1749 |
| *Lilliput* | Arnold, S. | 1777 |
| *Linco's Travels* | Arne, M. | 1767 |
| *May Day* | Arne, T. A. | 1775 |
| *Midsummer Night's Dream* (with Colman) | Burney, C. | 1763 |
| *Orpheus* | Barthelemon, F. | 1767 |
| *Quentin Durward* | Laurent, H. R. | 1848 |
| *Tempest, The* | Boyce, W. | 1757 |
| *Tempest, The* | Smith, J. C. | 1756 |
| *Theatrical Candidates* | Bates, W. | 1775 |

GARZA, JULIA
| | | |
|---|---|---|
| *Frieze of Life* | Applebaum, E. | 1983 |

GASS, KEN
| | | |
|---|---|---|
| *Voice for a Future Nightingale* | Chen, J. | 2008 |

GATAKER, THOMAS (fl. 1730)
| | | |
|---|---|---|
| *Jealous Clown* | ** | 1730 |

GATTY, IVOR
| | | |
|---|---|---|
| *Duke or Devil* | Gatty, N. | 1909 |

GATTY, REGINALD (RENÉ)
| | | |
|---|---|---|
| *Greysteel* | Gatty, N. | 1906 |
| *King Alfred* | Gatty, N. | 1930 |
| *Tempest, The* | Gatty, N. | 1920 |

GAWN, C.
| | | |
|---|---|---|
| *Gulliver in Lilliput* | Paintal, P. | 1995* |

GAY, JOHN (1685–1732)
| | | |
|---|---|---|
| *Achilles* | ** | 1733 |
| *Acis and Galatea* | Handel, G. F. | 1718 |
| *Beggar's Opera* | Pepusch, J. | 1728 |
| *Pincushion, The* | Arne, T. A. | 1756 |
| *Polly* | ** | 1729 |

GAYLER, CHARLES (1821–1897)
| | | |
|---|---|---|
| *Sleepy Hollow* | Maretzek, M. | 1879 |

GEIB, BILL
| | | |
|---|---|---|
| *Legend, A* | Nelhybel, V. | 1954* |

GENTLEMAN, FRANCIS (1728–1784)
| | | |
|---|---|---|
| *Cupid's Revenge* | Hook, J. | 1772 |

GEOGHEGAN, EDWARD (b. ca. 1812)
| | | |
|---|---|---|
| *Currency Lass* | ** | 1844 |

GERDINE, ELAINE
| | | |
|---|---|---|
| *Chicken Little* | Benjamin, T. | 1985 |

GERSHWIN, IRA (1896–1983)
| | | |
|---|---|---|
| *Lady in the Dark* (with M. Hart) | Weill, K. | 1941 |
| *Porgy and Bess* (with D. Heyward) | Gershwin, G. | 1935 |

GERSUNY, CARL
| | | |
|---|---|---|
| *Diet, The* (with comp.) | Olenick, E. | 1979* |

GETLEIN, DOROTHY WOOLLEN, and GETLEIN, FRANK
| | | |
|---|---|---|
| *Decorator, The* | Woollen, R. | 1959 |

GIBBON, JOHN MURRAY (1875–1952)
| | | |
|---|---|---|
| *Order of Good Cheer* | Willan, H. | 1928 |

GIBSON, WILLIAM (1914–2008)
| | | |
|---|---|---|
| *Nativity* | Dello Joio, N. | 1987 |
| *Ruby, The* (as William Mass) | Dello Joio, N. | 1955 |

GIKOW, LOUISE
| | | |
|---|---|---|
| *Marita* | Adolphe, B. | 1995 |

GILBERT, ILSA
| | | |
|---|---|---|
| *Bundle Man* | Coid, M. | 1993 |
| *First Word* | Cameron, K. | 1996 |
| *Phoenix Park* | Strickland, D. | 2002 |

GILBERT, WILLIAM S. (1836–1911)
| | | |
|---|---|---|
| *Ages Ago* | Clay, F. | 1869 |
| *Dulcamara* | ** | 1866 |

| | | |
|---|---|---|
| *Eyes and No Eyes* | Pascal, F. | 1875 |
| *Fallen Fairies* | German, E. | 1909 |
| *Gentleman in Black* | Clay, F. | 1870 |
| *Gondoliers, The* | Sullivan, A. S. | 1889 |
| *Grand Duke* | Sullivan, A. S. | 1896 |
| *Haste to the Wedding* | Grossmith, G. | 1892 |
| *His Excellency* | Carr, F. O. | 1894 |
| *H.M.S. Pinafore* | Sullivan, A. S. | 1878 |
| *Iolanthe* | Sullivan, A. S. | 1882 |
| *Mikado, The* | Sullivan, A. S. | 1885 |
| *Mountebanks, The* | Cellier, A. | 1892 |
| *No Cards* | "Elliott, L." | 1869 |
| *Our Island Home* | Reed, T. | 1870 |
| *Patience* | Sullivan, A. S. | 1881 |
| *Pirates of Penzance* | Sullivan, A. S. | 1879 |
| *Princess Ida* | Sullivan, A. S. | 1884 |
| *Princess Toto* | Clay, F. | 1876 |
| *Robert the Devil* | "Kettenus" | 1868 |
| *Ruddigore* | Sullivan, A. S. | 1887 |
| *Sensation Novel* | Reed, T. G. | 1871 |
| *Sorcerer, The* | Sullivan, A. S. | 1877 |
| *Thespis* | Sullivan, A. S. | 1871 |
| *Trial by Jury* | Sullivan, A. S. | 1875 |
| *Utopia Limited* | Sullivan, A. S. | 1893 |
| *Vicar of Bray* | Solomon, E. | 1882 |
| *Vivandière, La* | Wallerstein, F. | 1867 |
| *Yeomen of the Guard* | Sullivan, A. S. | 1888 |

**GILLIAT, SIDNEY (1908–1994)**

| | | |
|---|---|---|
| *Open Window* | Arnold, M. | 1956 |
| *Our Man in Havana* | Williamson, M. | 1963 |

**GINSBERG, ALLEN (1926–1997)**

| | | |
|---|---|---|
| *Hydrogen Jukebox* | Glass, P. | 1990 |

**GIRDLESTONE, MARGARET**

| | | |
|---|---|---|
| *Enchanted Shirt* | Oliver, S. | 1970* |

**GLASS, RICHARD**

| | | |
|---|---|---|
| *Ruth and Naomi* (with S. Hall) | Kondorossy, L. | 1974 |

**GLICKMAN, GARY (b. 1959)**

| | | |
|---|---|---|
| *Tibetan Dreams* | Dickman, S. | 1990 |

**GLOBUS, SEPTIMUS (GROVE, D.)**

| | | |
|---|---|---|
| *Freischütz, Der* | ** | 1824 |

**GODDARD, DAVID**

| | | |
|---|---|---|
| *Donna, La* | Brumby, C. | 1988 |
| *Proposal, The* | Fiddes, R. | 1986 |

**GODFREY, PAUL**

| | | |
|---|---|---|
| *Panic, The* | Sawyer, D. | 1991 |

**GODWIN, GAIL**

| | | |
|---|---|---|
| *Anna Marguerita's Will* | Starer, R. | 1981 |
| *Apollonia* | Starer, R. | 1979 |
| *Last Lover* | Starer, R. | 1975 |

**GOETHE, ANN**

| | | |
|---|---|---|
| *Travels* | Bond, V. | 1995 |

**GOLD, ARTHUR**

| | | |
|---|---|---|
| *Ma Barker* | Eaton, J. | 1957 |

**GOLDBERG, MILTON**

| | | |
|---|---|---|
| *Metamorphosis* | White, M. | 1968 |

**GOLDBERG, MOSES (b. 1940)**

| | | |
|---|---|---|
| *Gulliver* | Bond, V. | 1988 |

**GOLDMAN, RICHARD FRANKO (1910–1980)**

| | | |
|---|---|---|
| *Athaliah* | Weisgall, H. | 1964 |
| *Mandarin, The* | Elkus, J. | 1967 |

**GOLDSMITH, M.**

| | | |
|---|---|---|
| *Angelina* | Bishop, H. R. | 1804 |

**GOLDSTEIN, MERVYN**

| | | |
|---|---|---|
| *Desperate Waltz* | Earnest, J. D. | 1992 |
| *Legend of Sleepy Hollow* | Earnest, J. D. | 1997 |

**GOLDSWORTHY, PETER (b. 1951)**

| | | |
|---|---|---|
| *Batavia* | Mills, R. | 2001 |
| *Summer of the Seventeenth Doll* | Mills, R. | 1996 |

**GOLUBEFF, GREGORY, trans.**

| | | |
|---|---|---|
| *Mistress into Maid* | Duke, V. | 1958 |

**GONZALES, DAVID**

| | | |
|---|---|---|
| *Rise for Freedom* | Hailstork, A. | 2007 |

**GONZALEZ-RISSO, KICO (b. 1954)**

| | | |
|---|---|---|
| *Brush* | Nakano, K. | 2004 |

**GOODALL, WILLIAM (fl. 1740)**

| | | |
|---|---|---|
| *False Guardians Outwitted* | ** | 1740 |

**GOODBY, JOHN**

| | | |
|---|---|---|
| *Fire King* | O'Connell, K. | 1995 |

**GOODMAN, ALICE (b. 1958)**

| | | |
|---|---|---|
| *Death of Klinghoffer* | Adams, J. | 1991 |
| *Nixon in China* | Adams, J. | 1987 |

**GOODMAN, PAUL**

| | | |
|---|---|---|
| *Cain and Abel* | Rorem, N. | ca. 1946* |

**GOODRICH, ARTHUR (1878–1941)**

| | | |
|---|---|---|
| *Caponsacchi* | Hageman, R. | 1937 |

**GOODWIN, JOHN CHEEVER (1850–1912)**

| | | |
|---|---|---|
| *Evangeline* | Rice, E. E. | 1874 |
| *Merry Monarch* (with W. Morse) | Sousa, J. P. | 1890 |

**GORDON, D.**

| | | |
|---|---|---|
| *Creation, The* | Crawford. C. | 1978 |

**GORDON, MEL**

| | | |
|---|---|---|
| *False Messiah* | Adolphe, B. | 1983 |
| *Mikhoels the Wise* | Adolphe, B. | 1982 |

**GOREY, EDWARD (1925–2000)**

| | | |
|---|---|---|
| *Willowdale Handcar* | Wigglesworth, F. | 1969 |

**GOTTLIEB, MARVIN**

| | | |
|---|---|---|
| *Binding of Isaac* | Chlarson, L. | 1998 |

**GRACE, BONNIE**

| | | |
|---|---|---|
| *Mrs. Dalloway* | Larsen, L. | 1993 |

**GRAHAM, COLIN (1931–2007)**

| | | |
|---|---|---|
| *Anna Karenina* | Carlson, D. | 2007 |
| *Golden Vanity* | Britten, B. | 1967 |
| *Jōruri* | Miki, M. | 1985 |
| *Madame Mao* | Sheng, B. | 2003 |
| *Penny for a Song* | Bennett, R. R. | 1967 |

| | | |
|---|---|---|
| *Postman Always Rings Twice* | Paulus, S. | 1982 |
| *Tale of Genji* | Miki, M. | 2000 |

GRANT, DAVID

| | | |
|---|---|---|
| *Bang!* | Rutter, J. | 1975 |
| *Wind in the Willows* | Rutter, J. | 1997 |

GRANVILLE, GEORGE (BARON GEORGE GRANVILLE LANSDOWNE) (1667–1735)

| | | |
|---|---|---|
| *British Enchanters* | Corbett, W. | 1706 |
| *Peleus and Thetis* | Boyce, W. | ca. 1740 |
| *Peleus and Thetis* | Hayes, W. | ca. 1749 |

GRAVES, ROBERT (1895–1985)

| | | |
|---|---|---|
| *Nausicaa* | Glanville-Hicks, P. | 1961 |

GRAY, JACK

| | | |
|---|---|---|
| *Girl from Nogami* | Blyton, C. | 1978 |

GRAY, TYNDALL

| | | |
|---|---|---|
| *Beggar's Love* (with comp.) | Patterson, F. | 1929 |

GRECKI, BARBARA

| | | |
|---|---|---|
| *Broken Pieces* | Hagen, D. | 2005 |

GREEN, WALTER

| | | |
|---|---|---|
| *Wrinkle in Time* | Larsen, L. | 1992 |

GREENAWAY, PETER

| | | |
|---|---|---|
| *Rosa, a Horse Opera* | Andriessen, L. | 1994 |
| *Writing to Vermeer* | Andriessen, L. | 199 |

GREENBANK, HARRY (1866–1899)

| | | |
|---|---|---|
| *Geisha, The* (with O. Hall) | Jones, S. | 1896 |
| *San Toy* (with Ross, Morton) | Jones, S. | 1899 |

GREENBANK, PERCY (1878–1968)

| | | |
|---|---|---|
| *My Lady Molly* (with Jessop, Taylor) | Jones, S. | 1903 |

GREENBERG, ALVIN

| | | |
|---|---|---|
| *Apollonia's Circus* | Stokes, E. | 1994 |
| *Further Voyages of the Santa Maria* | Stokes, E. | 1995* |
| *Horspfal* | Stokes, E. | 1969 |
| *Jealous Cellist* | Stokes, E. | 1979 |

GREENE, ANN T.

| | | |
|---|---|---|
| *Cat Lover* | Pace, R. | 2000 |
| *Mother of Three Sons* | Jenkins, L. | 1990 |
| *Warrior Sisters* | Ho, F. | 2000 |

GREENE, CLAY M. (1850–1933)

| | | |
|---|---|---|
| *Maid of Plymouth* | Thorne, T. P. | 1893 |
| *Old Black Joe* | Shelley, H. R. | 1911 |

GREENFIELD, JEROME

| | | |
|---|---|---|
| *Whirligig* | Brisman, H. | 1977 |

GREENWOOD, ORMEROD

| | | |
|---|---|---|
| *Visitors, The* | Gardner, J. | 1972 |

GREGORY, KEVIN

| | | |
|---|---|---|
| *Again* | Heggie, J. | 2000 |

GRENNAN, EAMON

| | | |
|---|---|---|
| *Bee Opera* (lib with comp. et al.) | Hays, S. | 2003 |

GRESS, ELSA (1919–1988)

| | | |
|---|---|---|
| *Grinning at the Devil* | Wilson, J. | 1989 |

GRIFFITH, [LLEWELYN] WYN (1890–1977)

| | | |
|---|---|---|
| *Menna* | Hughes, A. | 1953 |

GRIFFITHS, PAUL (b. 1947)

| | | |
|---|---|---|
| *Marco Polo* | Tan Dun | 1996 |
| *What Next?* | Carter, E. | 1999 |

GROBE, NANCY

| | | |
|---|---|---|
| *Gift of the Magi* | Brown, R. | 1985 |

GROGAN, WALTER E.

| | | |
|---|---|---|
| *Pierrot and Pierrette* | Holbrooke, J. | 1909 |

GROLNIC, SIDNEY

| | | |
|---|---|---|
| *Buxtehude's Daughter* | Binder, J, | 1989* |
| *Gift, The* | Binder, J. | 1997* |

GRUNDY, CECIL REGINALD (1870–1944)

| | | |
|---|---|---|
| *Gainsborough* | Coates, A. | 1941 |

GRUNDY, SYDNEY (1848–1914)

| | | |
|---|---|---|
| *Haddon Hall* | Sullivan, A. S. | 1892 |

GUBERNAT, SUSAN (b. 1949)

| | | |
|---|---|---|
| *Korczak's Orphans* | Silverman, A. | 2003 |

GUILLERMOPRIETO, ALMA (b. 1949)

| | | |
|---|---|---|
| *Revolution of Forms* (with C. Koppelman) | Davis, Prieto | 2010 |

GUINESS, BRYAN (b. 1905)

| | | |
|---|---|---|
| *Petrified Princess* | Arnell, R. | 1959 |

GUINN III, J. F.

| | | |
|---|---|---|
| *Curious Affair* (with comp.) | Craton, J. | 2004* |

GUITERMAN, ARTHUR (1871–1943)

| | | |
|---|---|---|
| *Man without a Country* | Damrosch, W. | 1937 |

GUNDERSON, KEITH

| | | |
|---|---|---|
| *We're Not Robots* | Stokes, E. | 1986 |

GUNN, GENNI (b. 1949)

| | | |
|---|---|---|
| *Alternate Visions* | Oliver, J. | 2007 |

GURNEY, A. R. (b. 1930)

| | | |
|---|---|---|
| *Strawberry Fields* | Torke, M. | 1999 |

GURY, JEREMY

| | | |
|---|---|---|
| *Mighty Casey* | Schuman, W. | 1951 |

GUTHRIE, TYRONE (1900–1971)

| | | |
|---|---|---|
| *Sleeping Children* | Easdale, B. | 1951 |

HAINES, JOHN THOMAS (1799?–1843)

| | | |
|---|---|---|
| *Amilie* | Rooke, W. M. | 1818 |
| *Henrique* | Rooke, W. M. | 1839 |
| *Queen of a Day* | Fitzwilliam, E. | 1841 |

HA JIN (b. 1956)

| | | |
|---|---|---|
| *First Emperor* (with comp.) | Tan Dim | 2006 |

HALE, PAUL V.

| | | |
|---|---|---|
| *François Villon* | Wolf, A. | 1984 |

HALL, MICHAEL

| | | |
|---|---|---|
| *Infidel* | MacSems, W. | 2006* |
| *Madimi* | Wolosoff, B. | 2007 |

HALL, OAKLEY M. (1920–2008)

| | | |
|---|---|---|
| *Angle of Repose* | Imbrie, A. | 1976 |

**HALL, OWEN [JIMMY DAVIS] (1853–1907)**

| | | |
|---|---|---|
| *Geisha, The* (with H. Greenback) | Jones, S. | 1896 |

**HALL, SHAWN [ELIZABETH DAVIS]**

| | | |
|---|---|---|
| *Kalamona* (with comp.) | Kondorossy, L. | 1971 |
| *Midnight Duel* | Kondorossy, L. | 1955 |
| *Nathan the Wise* | Kondorossy, L. | 1964 |
| *Poorest Suitor* | Kondorossy, L. | 1967 |
| *Pumpkin, The* (with comp.) | Kondorossy, L. | 1954 |
| *Ruth and Naomi* (with R. Glass) | Kondorossy, L. | 1974 |
| *Shizuka's Dance* | Kondorossy, L. | 1969 |
| *Unexpected Visitor* | Kondorossy, L. | 1956 |
| (with Kemeny, comp.) | | |
| *Voice, The* (with S. N. Linek) | Kondorossy, L. | 1954 |

**HAMBLETON, RONALD (b. 1917)**

| | | |
|---|---|---|
| *Luck of Ginger Coffey* | Pannell, R. | 1967 |

**HAMILTON, HENRY (1853–1918)**

| | | |
|---|---|---|
| *Duchess of Dantzic* | Caryll, I. | 1903 |

**HAMILTON, RALPH**

| | | |
|---|---|---|
| *David Rizzio* | Braham, J., et al. | 1820 |
| *Elphi Bey* | Attwood, T. | 1817 |

**HAMILTON, ROBIN**

| | | |
|---|---|---|
| *Rose Garden* | Boyd, A. | 1972 |

**HAMILTON, W. H.**

| | | |
|---|---|---|
| *Enterprise, The* | Clifton, A. | 1822 |

**HAMMERSTEIN II, OSCAR (1895–1960)**

| | | |
|---|---|---|
| *Carmen Jones* | Bizet-Bennett | 1943 |
| *Rose-Marie* (with O. Harbach) | Friml/Stothart | 1924 |
| *Show Boat* | Kern, J. | 1927 |

**HAMMOOD, EMILY E.**

| | | |
|---|---|---|
| *Magic Laurel Tree* | Hunkins, E. S. | 1974 |

**HAMPL, PATRICIA (b. 1946)**

| | | |
|---|---|---|
| *Clair de Lune* | Larsen, L. | 1985 |

**HAMPTON, CHRISTOPHER (b. 1946)**

| | | |
|---|---|---|
| *Appomattox* | Glass, P. | 2007 |
| *Waiting for the Barbarians* | Glass, P. | 2005 |

**HARBACH, OTTO (1873–1963)**

| | | |
|---|---|---|
| *Rose-Marie* (with O. Hammerstein) | Friml/Stothart | 1924 |

**HARDIE, VICTORIA**

| | | |
|---|---|---|
| *Facing Goya* | Nyman, M. | 2000 |

**HARDING, BERTITA**

| | | |
|---|---|---|
| *Daisy* | Smith, J. | 1973 |

**HARNICK, SHELDON (b. 1924)**

| | | |
|---|---|---|
| *Captain Jinks* | Beeson, J. | 1975 |
| *Coyote Tales* | Mollicone, H. | 1998 |
| *Cyrano* | Beeson, J. | 1994 |
| *Dr. Heidegger's Fountain of Youth* | Beeson, J. | 1978 |

**HARRIGAN, NED (EDWARD) (1844–1911)**

| | | |
|---|---|---|
| *Mulligan Guard Ball* | Braham, D. | 1879 |
| *Reilly and the 400* | Braham, D. | 1891 |

**HARRINGTON, LAURA**

| | | |
|---|---|---|
| *Angel Face* | Ames, R. | 1987 |
| *Hearts on Fire* | Ames, R. | 1995 |
| *Lucy's Lapses* | Drobny, C. | 1987 |
| *Resurrection* (with B. Murray) | Machover, T. | 1999 |

**HARRIS, ANNE**

| | | |
|---|---|---|
| *Echoes* | Hawkins, J. | 1991 |

**HARRIS, AUGUSTUS GLOSSOP (1825–1873)**

| | | |
|---|---|---|
| *Amy Robsart* (with Weatherly) | de Lara, I. | 1893 |
| *Desert Flower* (with T. J. Williams) | Wallace, V. | 1863 |
| *Lady of Longford* | Bach, L. E. | 1896 |
| (with F. E. Weatherly) | | |
| *Rose of Castille* (with E. Falconer) | Balfe, M. | 1857 |
| *Satanella* (with E. Falconer) | Balfe, M. | 1860 |

**HARRIS, DAVID**

| | | |
|---|---|---|
| *Lake of Menteith* | Noble, H. | 1967 |

**HARRIS, JAMES (d. 1780)**

| | | |
|---|---|---|
| *Menalcas* | Bach, J. C. | 1764 |

**HARRIS, MARGARET BURNS**

| | | |
|---|---|---|
| *Christmas Carol* | Coleman, E. | 1962 |

**HARRISON, C.**

| | | |
|---|---|---|
| *Light of the Harem* | Thomas, A. G. | 1879 |

**HARRISON, JAY**

| | | |
|---|---|---|
| *Last Day* | Rorem, N. | 1967 |

**HARRISON, TONY (b. 1937)**

| | | |
|---|---|---|
| *Bow Down* | Birtwistle, H. | 1977 |

**HARRYMAN, CARLA**

| | | |
|---|---|---|
| *Little Girl Dreams of Taking* | Wold, E. | 1995 |
| *the Veil* | | |

**HARSENT, DAVID (b. 1942)**

| | | |
|---|---|---|
| *Gawain* | Birtwistle, H. | 1991 |
| *Minotaur, The* | Birtwistle, H. | 2008 |
| *When She Died* | Dove, J. | 2002 |

**HART, CHARLES (b. 1961)**

| | | |
|---|---|---|
| *Jason Field* | Horne, D. | 1993 |
| *Phantom of the Opera* (lyrics) | Lloyd Webber | 1986 |

**HART, FRITZ B. (1874–1949)**

| | | |
|---|---|---|
| *Idea, The* | Holst, G. | ca. 1898* |
| *Magic Mirror* | Holst, G. | 1896 |
| *Revoke, The* | Holst, G. | 1895 |

**HART, MOSS (1904–1961)**

| | | |
|---|---|---|
| *Lady in the Dark* (with I. Gershwin) | Weill, K. | 1941 |

**HART, RICHARD H. (b. 1908)**

| | | |
|---|---|---|
| *Stronger, The* | Weisgall, H. | 1952 |

**HART, TED**

| | | |
|---|---|---|
| *Franklin's Tale* | Sokoloff, N. | 1961 |
| *Pardoner's Tale* | Lubin, E. | 1966 |
| *Pardoner's Tale* | Sokoloff, N. | 1961 |

**HARTIG, HERBERT (1930–1991)**

| | | |
|---|---|---|
| *Fat Tuesday* | Berkowitz, S. | 1956 |

**HARTLEY, RANDOLPH**

| | | |
|---|---|---|
| *Daughter of the Forest* | Nevin, A. | 1918 |
| *Poia* (rev. A. Basinski, 2005) | Nevin, A. | 1907 |

HARTMAN, JAN
*Abelard and Heloise* — Ward, R. — 1982

HARTWIG, GRETA (1899–1971)
*Barber of New York* — Vernon, A. — 1953
*Cupid and Psyche* — Vernon, A. — 1956
*Grand Slam* — Vernon, A. — 1955
*Triumph of Punch* — Vernon, A. — 1969

HARWOOD, GWEN (1920–1995)
*Creation of the World* — Penberthy, J. — 1990*
*De Profundis* — Sitsky, L. — 1982
*Fall of the House of Usher* — Sitsky, L — 1965
*Fiery Tales* — Sitsky, L. — 1976
*Golden Crane* — Kay, D. H. — 1985*
*Golem, The* — Sitsky, L. — 1980*
*Lenz* — Sitsky, L. — 1974
*Stations* — Penberthy, J. — 1975*
*Three Scenes from Aboriginal Life* — Sitsky, L. — 1991
*Voices in Limbo* — Sitsky, L. — 1977

HASSALL, CHRISTOPHER (1912–1963)
*Man from Tuscany* — Hopkins, A. — 1951
*Tobias and the Angel* — Bliss, A. — 1960
*Troilus and Cressida* — Walton, W. — 1954
*Twice in a Blue Moon* — Tate, P. — 1969

HASTINGS, MICHAEL (1938–2011)
*Love Counts* — Nyman, M. — 2005

HATCH, JAMES VERNON (b. 1928)
*Liar, Liar* — Raphling, S. — 1972*

HATCHETT, WILLIAM (fl. 1730–1741)
*Opera of Operas* (with E. Haywood) — Arne, T. A. — 1733
*Opera of Operas* (with E. Haywood) — Lampe, F. — 1733

HATFIELD, HURD
*Mother, The* — Wood, J. — 1942

HATTEN, ROBERT S.
*Bonhoeffer* — Gebuhr, A. — 2000

HATTON, ANN JULIA (1764–1838)
*Tammany* — Hewitt, J. — 1794

HAUN, EUGENE
*Boor, The* — Bucci, M. — 1949

HAWKES, TERENCE
*Thérèse Raquin* — Stoker, R. — 1975*

HAWKESWORTH, JOHN (1715–1773)
*Edgar and Emmeline* — Arne, M. — 1761

HAWKINS-AMBLER, G. A.
*Brownings Go to Italy* — Freer, E. E. — 1938
*Chilkoot Maiden* — Freer, E. E. — 1927

HAWLEY, EARLELNE
*Jeremiah* — Fink, M. — 1962

HAYS, H. R., trans.
*Trilby* — Sessions, R. — 1947

HAYWOOD, ELIZA (1693–1756)
*Opera of Operas* (with W. Hatchett) — Arne, T. A. — 1733
*Opera of Operas* (with W. Hatchett) — Lampe, F. — 1733

HAZARD, JAMES (b. 1935)
*Thousand Names* — Kitzke, J. — 1981

HAZARD, MARION
*Thorwald* — Dinsmore, W. — 1940

HEALEY, PETER WING
*Jane Heir* — Norquist, Gordon — 1989
*Norma, The* — Dowdell, L. — 1991
*Tree, The* — Dowdell, L. — 2006

HEALY, ROBERT
*Ballad of Kitty the Barkeep* (with comp.) — Lee, D.-K. — 1979
*Phineas and the Nightingale* — Lee, D.-K. — 1952
*Speakeasy* — Lee, D.-K. — 1957
*Two Knickerbocker Tales* — Lee, D.-K. — 1957

HEARTWELL, HENRY
*Castle of Sorrento* — Attwood, T. — 1799
*Reform'd in Time* — Attwood, T. — 1798

HELD, JACK
*Ethan Frome* — Beall, J. — 1997

HELFGOT, DANIEL
*Tale of the Nutcracker* — Bohmler, C. — 1999

HELLMAN, LILLIAN (1905–1984)
*Candide* (with Wilbur) — Bernstein, L. — 1956

HELMICH, BERNARD, trans.
*Kantan and the Damask Drum* — Goehr, A. — 1999

HELWIG, DAVID (b. 1938)
*Barnardo Boy* — Crawley, C. — 1982

HENDERSON, WILLIAM J. (1855–1937)
*Cyrano* — Damrosch, W. — 1913

HENDRY, TOM
*Dr. Selavy's Magic Theatre* (with R. Foreman) — Silverman, S. — 1972

HENRY, JAN
*Haircut* — Morgenstern, S. — 1969

HENSHER, PHILIP
*Powder Her Face* — Adès, T. — 1995

HERBERT, ALAN PATRICK (1890–1971)
*Blue Peter* — Gibbs, C. A. — 1923
*Derby Day* — Reynolds, A. — 1932
*Tantivy Towers* — Dunhill, T. — 1931

HERRON, CAROLIVIA
*Let Freedom Sing* — Adolphe, B. — 2009

HERSEE, HENRY (1820–1896)
*Pauline* — Cowen, F. — 1876
*Royal Word* — de Lara, I. — 1883

HESS, HARVEY
*Kona Coffee Cantata* — Tanner, J. — 1986*
*Naupaka Floret* — Tanner, J. — 1992*
*Pupu-kani-oe* — Tanner, J. — 1980*

HEWETT, DOROTHY
*Christina's World* — Edwards, R. — 1983

| | | |
|---|---|---|
| *Merrie England* | German, E. | 1902 |
| *Rose of Persia* | Sullivan, A. S. | 1899 |

HOOK, JAMES, Jr. (1772?–1828)

| | | |
|---|---|---|
| *Diamond Cut Diamond* | Hook, J. | 1797 |
| *Jack of Newbury* | Hook, J. | 1795 |

HOOK, THEODORE EDWARD (1788–1841)

| | | |
|---|---|---|
| *Catch Him Who Can* | Hook, J. | 1806 |
| *Fortress, The* | Hook, J. | 1807 |
| *Invisible Girl* | Hook, J. | 1806 |
| *Music Mad* | Hook, J. | 1807 |
| *Safe and Sound* | Hook, J. | 1809 |
| *Soldier's Return* | Hook, J. | 1805 |
| *Tekeli* | Hook, J. | 1806 |

HOOKER, BRIAN (1880–1946)

| | | |
|---|---|---|
| *Fairyland* | Parker, H. | 1915 |
| *Mona* | Parker, H. | 1912 |

HOPGOOD, ALAN (b. 1934)

| | | |
|---|---|---|
| *Little Redinka* | Easton, M. | 1991 |

HOPKINS, JOHN

| | | |
|---|---|---|
| *Some Place of Darkness* | Whelen, C. | 1967 |

HOPKINS, PAULINE ELIZABETH (1859–1930)

| | | |
|---|---|---|
| *Peculiar Sam* | ** | 1879 |

HOPPER, GARY C.

| | | |
|---|---|---|
| *Noise, The* | Blank, A. | 1986 |

HOPPWOOD, AUBREY (b. 1863)

| | | |
|---|---|---|
| *Lucky Star* (with A. Ross) | Caryll, I. | 1899 |

HORDYK, MARGARET

| | | |
|---|---|---|
| *Door, The* | Mopper, I. | 1956 |

HORGAN, PAUL

| | | |
|---|---|---|
| *Tree on the Plains* | Bacon, E. | 1942 |

HORNCASTLE (HOOK), HARRIET (d. 1795)

| | | |
|---|---|---|
| *Double Disguise* | Hook, J. | 1784 |
| *Triumph of Beauty* | Hook, J. | 1786 |

HORNSBY, JEREMY

| | | |
|---|---|---|
| *Pied Piper of Hamelin* | Bowers-Broadbent | 1972 |

HORTON, DOUGLAS

| | | |
|---|---|---|
| *Two Executions* | Chesworth, D. | 1994 |

HORWITZ, MURRAY

| | | |
|---|---|---|
| *Great Gatsby* (lyrics) | Harbison, J. | 1999 |

HOUGH, JOHN (fl. 1778)

| | | |
|---|---|---|
| *Second Thought Is Best* | Bates, W. | 1778 |

HOULTON, ROBERT (b. 1739)

| | | |
|---|---|---|
| *Calypso* | Giordani, T. | 1785 |
| *Contract, The* | Stevenson, J. | 1782 |
| *Gibraltar* | Giordani, T. | 1783 |
| *Pharnaces* | ** | 1783 |

HOUSMAN, LAURENCE (1865–1959)

| | | |
|---|---|---|
| *Seraphic Vision* | Boughton, R. | 1924 |

HOUSTON, ROXANNE

| | | |
|---|---|---|
| *Governess, The* | Mallett, C. | 1954 |

HOWARD, ROBERT (1626–1698)

| | | |
|---|---|---|
| *Indian Queen* (with J. Dryden) | Purcell, H. | 1695 |

HOWE, TINA (b. 1937)

| | | |
|---|---|---|
| *Columbine String Quartet Tonight!* | Silverman, S. | 1981 |

HOWLEY, JAMES

| | | |
|---|---|---|
| *Harlot and the Monk* | Bohmler, C. | 1985 |

HUBBARD, ALISON

| | | |
|---|---|---|
| *Cop and the Anthem* | Cohen, S. | 1982 |

HUBSKY, JOHN

| | | |
|---|---|---|
| *To Let the Captive Go* | Stewart, F. | 1974 |

HUEFFER, FRANCIS (1843–1889)

| | | |
|---|---|---|
| *Colomba* | Mackenzie, A. | 1883 |
| *Guillem* | Mackenzie, A. | 1886 |

HUFF, KEITH

| | | |
|---|---|---|
| *Bok Choy Variations* (with Servoss, Simonson) | Chen, E. | 1995 |

HUGHES, DAVID (b. 1930)

| | | |
|---|---|---|
| *Widow of Ephesus* (with comp.) | Hurd, M. | |

HUGHES, GLENN (1894–1964)

| | | |
|---|---|---|
| *Three Blind Mice* | Verrall, J. | 1955 |

HUGHES, JOHN (1677–1720)

| | | |
|---|---|---|
| *Apollo and Daphne* | Hook, J. | 1773 |
| *Apollo and Daphne* | Pepusch, J. | 1716 |
| *Telemachus* | Galliard, J. E. | 1712 |

HUGHES, LANGSTON (1902–1967)

| | | |
|---|---|---|
| *Barrier, The* | Meyerowitz, J. | 1950 |
| *Esther* | Meyerowitz, J. | 1957 |
| *Organizer, De* | Johnson, J. | 1940 |
| *Port Town* | Meyerowitz, J. | 1960 |
| *Street Scene* (with Rice) | Weill, K. | 1946 |
| *Troubled Island* | Still, W. G. | 1938 |

HUGHES, TED (b. 1930)

| | | |
|---|---|---|
| *Story of Vasco* | Crosse, G. | 1974 |

HUGHES, WALLACE TAYLOR

| | | |
|---|---|---|
| *Lady of the Lake* | Schmidt, K. | 1931 |

HUHN, EUGENIE von, trans.

| | | |
|---|---|---|
| *Poia* | Nevin, A. | 1907, 1910 |

HULL, THOMAS (1728–1808)

| | | |
|---|---|---|
| *Fairy Favour* | Bach, J. C. | 1767 |
| *Love Finds the Way* | Arne, T. A., et al. | 1777 |
| *Pharnaces* | Bates, W. | 1765 |
| *Royal Merchant* | Linley Sr, T. | 1767 |
| *Spanish Lady* | ** | 1765 |

HUMPHREYS, SAMUEL (1698–1738)

| | | |
|---|---|---|
| *Ulysses* | Smith, J. C. | 1733 |

HUNT, JOHN CLINTON (b. 1925)

| | | |
|---|---|---|
| *Ethan Frome* | Allanbrook, D. | 1952 |

HUPPLER, DUDLEY

| | | |
|---|---|---|
| *Something New* | Hoiby, L. | 1982 |

HURLIN, DAN

| | | |
|---|---|---|
| *Shoulder, The* | Schreier, D. | 1998 |

HURLSTONE, THOMAS (fl. 1792–1794)

| | | |
|---|---|---|
| *Just in Time* | Carter, T. | 1792 |
| *To Arms!* | Shield, W. | 1793 |

**HURST, CYRIL**

| | | |
|---|---|---|
| *Royal Vagrants* | Warner, H. W. | 1899 |

**HWANG, DAVID HENRY (b. 1957)**

| | | |
|---|---|---|
| *Fly, The* | Shore, H. | 2008 |
| *One Thousand Airplanes* | Glass, P. | 1988 |
| *Scarlet Princess* | Louie, A. | 2002 |
| *Silver River* | Sheng, B. | 1997 |
| *Sound of a Voice* | Glass, P. | 2003 |

**IACOVETTI, BETTY**

| | | |
|---|---|---|
| *Fête at Coqueville* | Rea, A. | 1976 |
| *Old Pipes and the Dryad* | Rea, A. | 1980 |

**IHIMAERA, WITI TAME (b. 1944)**

| | | |
|---|---|---|
| *Galileo* | Rimmer, J. | 1999 |
| *Tanz der Schwäne* | Harris, R. | 1993 |
| *Waituhi* | Harris, R. | 1984 |

**IKAM, CATHERINE**

| | | |
|---|---|---|
| *VALIS* (with comp., B. Raymond) | Machover, T. | 1987 |

**IONE**

| | | |
|---|---|---|
| *Lunar Opera* | Oliveros, P. | 2000 |

**IRELAND, KEVIN (b. 1933)**

| | | |
|---|---|---|
| *Full Moon in March* | Ward, D. | 1981 |
| *Jack's Engagement* | Ward, D. | 1987 |
| *Snow Queen* | Ward, D. | 1984 |

**IRWIN, EYLES (1751?–1817)**

| | | |
|---|---|---|
| *Bedouins, The* | Stevenson, J. | 1801 |

**IRWIN, JANET**

| | | |
|---|---|---|
| *Angel Square* | Crawley, C. | 1996 |

**IRWIN, WALLACE (1876–1959)**

| | | |
|---|---|---|
| *Dove of Peace* | Damrosch, W. | 1912 |

**ISDELL, SARAH**

| | | |
|---|---|---|
| *Cavern, The* | Stevenson, J. | 1825 |

**ISRAEL, CHESTER**

| | | |
|---|---|---|
| *White Gods* (with comp.) | Kelly, R. | 1966 |

**ITALLIE, JEAN-CLAUDE VAN (b. 1936)**

| | | |
|---|---|---|
| *Tibetan Book of the Dead* | Gordon, R. | 1996 |

**IVES, DAVID**

| | | |
|---|---|---|
| *Secret Garden* | Pliska, G. | 1991 |

**JACKMAN, ISAAC (fl. 1776–1795)**

| | | |
|---|---|---|
| *Hero and Leander* | Reeve, W. | 1787 |
| *Milesian, The* | Carter, T. | 1777 |

**JACKSON, BARRY (b. 1879)**

| | | |
|---|---|---|
| *Spanish Lady* | Elgar, E. | 1933* |

**JACKSON, CHARLOTTE**

| | | |
|---|---|---|
| *Rat Land* | Beeferman, G. | 2007 |

**JACKSON, GEORGE RUSSELL**

| | | |
|---|---|---|
| *Salem Witch* | Stahl, R. | ca. 1883* |

**JACKSON, HOMER**

| | | |
|---|---|---|
| *Three Willies* | Jenkins, L. | 1996 |

**JACKSON, ISAAC (fl. 1776–1795)**

| | | |
|---|---|---|
| *Hero and Leander* | Reeve, W. | 1787 |

**JACOBS, ARTHUR (b. 1922)**

| | | |
|---|---|---|
| *One Man Show* | Maw, N. | 1964 |

**JACOBS, W[ILLIAM] W[YMARK] (1863–1943)**

| | | |
|---|---|---|
| *Captain's Parrot* | Brent-Smith | ca. 1950 |

**JACOBSON, LESLIE B.**

| | | |
|---|---|---|
| *Croak* | LeBaron, A. | 1997 |

**JAFFE, DAN**

| | | |
|---|---|---|
| *All Cats Turn Gray* | Six, H. | 1971 |
| *Without Memorial Banners* | Six, H. | 1966 |

**JAMES, LEWIS CAIRNS**

| | | |
|---|---|---|
| *Critic, The* | Stanford, C. | 1916 |

**JARRETT, ALBERT**

| | | |
|---|---|---|
| *Sultan of Mocha* | Cellier, A. | 1874 |

**JAYME, WILLIAM NORTH**

| | | |
|---|---|---|
| *Carry Nation* | Moore, D. | 1966 |

**JEANS, RONALD (b. 1887)**

| | | |
|---|---|---|
| *Triple Sec* | Blitzstein, M. | 1929 |

**JELINEK, ELFRIEDE (b. 1946)**

| | | |
|---|---|---|
| *Lost Highway* (with comp.) | Neuwirth, O. | 2003 |

**JELLINEK, GEORGE (1919–2010)**

| | | |
|---|---|---|
| *Magic Chair* | Zador, E. | 1966 |
| *Scarlet Mill* | Zador, E. | 1968 |

**JENNINGS, JOHN (b. 1906)**

| | | |
|---|---|---|
| *Peter Homan's Dream* | Reed, H. O. | 1955 |

**JEPHSON, ROBERT (1736–1803)**

| | | |
|---|---|---|
| *Campaign, The* (with N. Barry) | Shield, W. | 1784 |
| *Love and War* | Shield, W. | 1787 |

**JESSOP, GEORGE HENRY (d. 1915)**

| | | |
|---|---|---|
| *My Lady Molly* | Jones, S. | 1903 |
| (with Greenbank, Taylor) | | |
| *Shamus O'Brien* | Stanford, C. | 1896 |

**JOFFE, ANDREW**

| | | |
|---|---|---|
| *Awakening, The* | Stepleton, J. | 2003 |
| *Beast and Superbeast* | Martín, J. | 1996 |
| *Diamond Street* | Farberman, H. | 2009 |
| *Faust Triumphant* | Anderson, D. | 1995 |
| *Puss in Boots* (with comp.) | Martín, J. | 1992 |
| *Song of Eddie* | Farberman, H. | 2004 |

**JOHNSON, CHARLES (1679–1748)**

| | | |
|---|---|---|
| *Village Opera* | ** | 1729 |

**JOHNSON, CHARLES**

| | | |
|---|---|---|
| *Uncle Remus* | Gilbert, H. | 1907* |

**JOHNSTON, CHRISTINE**

| | | |
|---|---|---|
| *Outrageous Fortune* | Whitehead, G. | 1998 |

**JOHNSTON, DENIS (1901–1984)**

| | | |
|---|---|---|
| *Nine Rivers from Jordan* | Weisgall, H. | 1968 |
| *Six Characters in Search of an Author* | Weisgall, H. | 1959 |

**JOHNSTON, RICHARD**

| | | |
|---|---|---|
| *Nightingale's to Blame* | Holt, S. | 1998 |

**JONAS, GEORGE**

| | | |
|---|---|---|
| *Glove, The* | Polgar, T. | 1975 |

JONES, CHRISTINA (b. 1948)
| | | |
|---|---|---|
| *Heroes Don't Dance* | Grant, J. | 1998 |
| *Odd Numbers* | Grant, J. | 2002 |
| *Platform 10* | Grant, J. | 1999 |
| *Shadowtracks* | Grant, J. | 2007 |

JONES, GLYN (b. 1905)
| | | |
|---|---|---|
| *Beach of Falesá* | Hoddinott, A. | 1974 |

JONES, MAURICE
| | | |
|---|---|---|
| *Belisa* | Biales, A. | 1989 |

JONES, ROBERT T.
| | | |
|---|---|---|
| *Tonkin* (with T. Bird) | Cummings, C. | 1993 |

JONES, ROBIN
| | | |
|---|---|---|
| *Dr. Jekyll and Mr. Hyde* | O'Neal, B. | 1980* |

JONES, ROSABELLE
| | | |
|---|---|---|
| *Sam Slick* | Smith, K. | 1967 |

JONES, WILLIS KNAPP (b. 1895)
| | | |
|---|---|---|
| *Nightingale, The* | Clokey, J. | 1925 |

JORDAN, JUNE (b. 1936)
| | | |
|---|---|---|
| *I Was Looking at the Ceiling* | Adams, J. | 1995 |

JOWETT, BENJAMIN, trans.
| | | |
|---|---|---|
| *Myth of Er* | Sternau, C. | 1995* |

JUDAH, SAMUEL B. H. (ca. 1799–1876)
| | | |
|---|---|---|
| *Rose of Aragon* | Taylor, R. | 1822 |

JULLICH, JEFFREY
| | | |
|---|---|---|
| *American Lit* | Lependorf, J. | 1997 |

JUSTICE, DONALD (1925–2004)
| | | |
|---|---|---|
| *Death of Lincoln* | London, E. | 1988 |

KALLMAN, CHESTER (1921–1975)
| | | |
|---|---|---|
| *Elegy for Young Lovers* (with Auden) | Henze, H. W. | 1961 |
| *Visitors, The* | Chávez, C. | 1957 |

KANDER, SUSAN
| | | |
|---|---|---|
| *Joshua's Boots* | Hailstork, A. | 1999 |

KARSAVINA, JEAN
| | | |
|---|---|---|
| *Jumping Frog* | Foss, L. | 1950 |

KASTENBAUM, ROBERT
| | | |
|---|---|---|
| *Dorian* | Deutsch, H. | 1995 |

KATCHOR, BEN
| | | |
|---|---|---|
| *Carbon Copy Building* | Gordon et al. | 1999 |

KAUFMANN, FREDA (b. 1919)
| | | |
|---|---|---|
| *George from Paradise* (with comp.) | Kaufmann, W. | 1953 |
| *Rip Van Winkle* | Kaufmann, W. | 1959 |

KAY, JACKIE (b. 1961)
| | | |
|---|---|---|
| *Twice through the Heart* | Turnage, M.-A. | 1997 |

KEARNEY, DOUGLAS
| | | |
|---|---|---|
| *Crescent City* | LeBaron, A. | 2006 |
| *Mordake* | Wold, E. | 2008 |

KEARY, CHARLES FRANCIS (1848–1917)
| | | |
|---|---|---|
| *Koanga* (with comp.) | Delius, F. | 1895* |

KEATS, ELINOR
| | | |
|---|---|---|
| *King of Cats* | Oliver. H. | 1976* |

KECHLEY, ELWYN
| | | |
|---|---|---|
| *Golden Lion* | Kechley, G. | 1959 |

KEENE, ANTHONY AND NICHOLAS
| | | |
|---|---|---|
| *Cat in the Box* | Miller, R. | 1993 |

KEENE, CHRISTOPHER (1946–1996)
| | | |
|---|---|---|
| *Cimarrón, El* | Henze, H. W. | 1970 |
| *Duchess of Malfi* | Oliver, S. | 1971 |

KELLAWAY, FRANK (b. 1922)
| | | |
|---|---|---|
| *Garni Sands* | Dreyfus, G. | 1965 |
| *Takeover, The* | Dreyfus, G. | 1969 |

KELLY, JOHN (ca. 1680–1751)
| | | |
|---|---|---|
| *Plot, The* | ** | 1735 |
| *Timon in Love* | ** | 1733 |

KELLY, ROBERT GLYNN
| | | |
|---|---|---|
| *Darkened City* | Heiden, B. | 1963 |

KEMBLE, CHARLES (1775–1854)
| | | |
|---|---|---|
| *Brazen Bust* | Bishop, H. R. | 1813 |

KEMBLE, JOHN PHILIP (1757–1823)
| | | |
|---|---|---|
| *Lodoiska* | Storace, S. | 1794 |

KEMENY, JULIA
| | | |
|---|---|---|
| *Unexpected Visitor* (with Hall, comp.) | Kondorossy, L. | 1956 |

KEMP, EDWARD
| | | |
|---|---|---|
| *Ease* | Beamish, S. | 1993 |

KEMP-WELCH, MARGARET
| | | |
|---|---|---|
| *Christmas Rose* (with C. Cotterell) | Bridge, F. | 1919* |

KENDRICK, WILLIAM
| | | |
|---|---|---|
| *Lady of the Manor* | Hook, J. | 1778 |

KENNEDY-FRASER, MARJORY (1857–1930)
| | | |
|---|---|---|
| *Seal-Woman* | Bantock, G. | 1924 |

KENNEY, JAMES (1780–1849)
| | | |
|---|---|---|
| *Alcaid, The* | Nathan, I. | 1824 |
| *Benyowsky* | King, M. | 1826 |
| *False Alarms* | Addison et al. | 1807 |
| *Illustrious Stranger* (with J. G. Millingen) | Nathan, I. | 1827 |
| *Masaniello* | Cooke/Livius | 1829 |
| *Matrimony* | King, M. | 1804 |
| *Oh, This Love* | King, M. | 1810 |
| *Spirit of the Bell* | Rodwell, G. | 1835 |
| *Sweethearts and Wives* | Nathan, I. | 1823 |
| *Too Many Cooks* | King, M. | 1805 |
| *Turn Out!* | King, M. | 1812 |
| *Wedding Present* | Horn, C. E. | 1825 |

KENNY, MELANIE
| | | |
|---|---|---|
| *Greek Gaze* (with comp.) | Beeferman, G. | 1998 |

KENYON, BERNICE (b. 1897)
| | | |
|---|---|---|
| *Landara* | Zimbalist, E. | 1956 |

KESSLER, JASCHA (b. 1929)
| | | |
|---|---|---|
| *Anniversary, The* | Rorem, N. | ca. 1961* |

KIERNANDER, ADRIAN
| | | |
|---|---|---|
| *Clockmaker, The* | Harris, R. | 1979* |

KINCH, MARTIN
   *Death of Enkidu* — Somers, H. — 1977

KING, ALEXANDER
   *Juggler of Our Lady* — Kay, U. — 1962

KING, THOMAS (1730–1805)
   *Love at First Sight* — ** — 1763

KINOY, ERNEST
   *Goodbye to the Clown* — Laderman, E. — 1960
   *Jacob and the Indians* — Laderman, E. — 1957

KIRBY, MERIE
   *Sanctuary* — Callahan, J. — 2003

KIRKUP, JAMES (b. 1918)
   *Actor's Revenge* — Miki, M. — 1979

KIRTLEY, MARK
   *In the Father's Garden* — Kirtley, D. — 2007

KITSAKOS, STEPHEN
   *Wooden Sword* — Silver, S. — 2010

KLEIN, CHARLES (1867–1915)
   *Capitan, El* (with Frost) — Sousa, J. P. — 1896
   *Charlatan, The* — Sousa, J. P. — 1898
   *Red Feather* — De Koven, R. — 1903

KLIEWER, WARREN (b. 1931)
   *Bird in the Bush* — Bielawa, H. — 1962

KNAPP, HENRY RYDER
   *Hunt the Slipper* — Arnold, S. — 1784

KNIGHT, EDWARD P. (1774–1826)
   *Veteran Soldier* — Cooke, T., et al. — 1822

KNIGHT, JERE
   *Helen in Egypt* — Elkus, J. — 1970

KNIGHT, THOMAS (d. 1820)
   *Turnpike Gate* — Reeve, W. — 1799

KNUTSON, WAYNE
   *Arabesque* — Marek, R. — 1967

KOCH, DOLORES M.
   *Before Night Falls* (with comp.) — Martin, J. — 2006

KOCH, KENNETH (1925–2002)
   *Bertha* — Rorem, N. — 1973
   *Construction of Boston* — Wheeler, S. — 1989
   *Départ Malgache* — Wheeler, S. — 2000*
   *Gold Standard* — Wheeler, S. — 2002

KOCH, ROBERT
   *Eleni* (with comp.) — Ratcliff, C. — 2008

KOESTENBAUM, WAYNE
   *Jackie O* — Daugherty, M. — 1997

KOHN, STEVEN MARK
   *Tale of the Nutcracker* (lyrics) — Bohmler, C — 1999

KOMUNYAKAA, YUSEF
   *Slip Knot* — Anderson, T. J. — 2003
   *Wakonda's Dream* — Davis, A. — 2007

KONDEK, CHARLES
   *Between Two Worlds* — Ran, S. — 1997
   *Borgia Infami* — Blumenfeld, H, — 2005

   *Breakfast Waltzes* — Blumenfeld, H. — 1988
   *Esther* — Weisgall, H. — 1993
   *Fan, The* — Goldstein, L. — 1989
   *Fourscore* — Blumenfeld, H. — 1984
   *Fritzi* — Blumenfeld, H. — 1979
   *Ilbrahim* — Bernstein, D. — 1994
   *Method for Madness* — Bernstein, D. — 1999
   *Seasons in Hell* — Blumenfeld, H. — 1996
   *Tell-Tale Heart* — Bernstein, D. — 1999

KOPPELMAN, CHARLES
   *Revolution of Forms* — Davis/Prieto — 2010
   (with A. Guillermoprieto)

KOPPENHAVER, ALLEN JOHN (b. 1931)
   *Bell Tower* — Haskins, R. — 1976*
   *Legend of Sleepy Hollow* — Haskins, R. — 1976*

KOPS, BERNARD (b. 1926)
   *Appointment, The* — Josephs, W. — 1966

KORIE, MICHAEL
   *Bonesetter's Daughter* — Wallace, S. — 2008
   *Grapes of Wrath* — Gordon, R. I. — 2007
   *Harvey Milk* — Wallace, S. — 1995
   *Hopper's Wife* — Wallace, S. — 1997
   *Kabbalah* — Wallace, S. — 1989
   *Where's Dick* — Wallace, S. — 1987

KORNFELD, ROBERT
   *Dream within a Dream* — Currie, R. — 1984
   *Ligeia* — Currie, R. — 1987

KOSLOFF, DORIS L.
   *Goldilocks* — Zaimont, J. L. — 1986

KRAEMER, TIMOTHY
   *Bel and the Dragon* — Gardner, J. — 1973

KRANE, JUNE
   *Giant's Garden* — Krane, S. — 1960

KRASK, PETER M.
   *Henry and Clara* — Martín, J. — 2001
   *With Blood, with Ink* — Crozier, D. — 1993

KRESH, PAUL
   *Gimpel the Fool* — Davidson, C. — 1965*

KREYMBORG, ALFRED (1883–1966)
   *Lima Beans* — Townshend, D. — 1956
   *Privilege and Privation* — Becker, J. — 1939

KUHN, DAVID
   *Dido and Aeneas* — Beveridge, T. — 1958

KULLER, SID (b. 1910)
   *Zenda* (lyrics, with Adelson, Charnin) — Duke, V. — 1963

LAANES, CARL
   *Cask of Amontillado* — Currie, R. — 1982

LaCHIUSA, MICHAEL JOHN (b. 1962)
   *Desert of Roses* — Moran, R. — 1992
   *From the Towers* — Moran, R. — 1992
   *Tania* — Davis, A. — 1992

LAIDLAW, JACQUELINE
  *Man from Venus*                        Cannon, P.              1966
LAKE, J. (fl. 1880–1899)
  *Vercingetorix*                         Kowalski, H.            1881
LAMB, JEROME
  *Two Tickets to Omaha*                  Hannay, R.              1960
LAMBOURNE, JEFFREY
  *Julia*                                 Quilter, R.             1936
LAN, DAVID (b. 1952)
  *Ion*                                   Vir, P.                 2000
  *Tobias and the Angel*                  Dove, J.                1999
LANCTOT, DENISE
  *Pope Joan*                             Musto, J.               1999
LANG, DANIEL (b. 1935)
  *Minutes till Midnight* (with comp.)    Ward, R.                1982
LANGDON, WILLIAM CHAUNCEY (1871–1947)
  *Judith*                                Chadwick, G.            1901
LANGFORD, ABRAHAM (1711–1774)
  *Lover His Own Rival*                   **                      1736
LARNER, GERALD
  *Lion, the Witch*                       McCabe, J.              1969
LARSON, JACK (b. 1928)
  *Astronaut's Tale*                      Fussell, C.             1998
  *Lord Byron*                            Thomson, V.             1972
LA SHELLE, KIRKE
  *Ameer, The* (with F. Ranken)           Herbert, V.             1899
LATHROP, GEORGE PARSONS (1851–1898)
  *Scarlet Letter*                        Damrosch, W.            1896
LATOUCHE, JOHN (1917–1956)
  *Ballad of Baby Doe*                    Moore, D.               1956
  *Cabin in the Sky* (with L. Root)       Duke, V.                1940
  *Golden Apple*                          Moross, J.              1954
LAUDOR, MICHAEL
  *Imposition, The* (with comp.)          Tanenbaum, E.           1995
LAURENTS, ARTHUR (1918–2011)
  *West Side Story*                       Bernstein, L.           1957
LAURICELLA, E. M.
  *Crossing the Horizon*                  Lastovicka, C.          2007
LAVERY, EMMET (1902–1986)
  *Tarquin*                               Krenek, E.              1941
LAW, ARTHUR (1844–1913)
  *Magic Opal*                            Albéniz, I.             1893
LAWLER, DENNIS
  *Sharp and Flat*                        Hook, J.                1813
LAWRENCE, ROBERT (b. 1912)
  *Veil, The*                             Rogers, B.              1950
LAWRENCE, TRILBY
  *Committee, The* (with comp.)           Doran, M.               1958
LAX, LEAH
  *Refuge, The*                           Theofanidis, C.         2007

LEACH, WILFORD (1929–1988)
  *Carmilla*                              Johnston, B.            1970
  *Gertrude*                              Johnston, B.            1956
LEAVITT, NASON W.
  *Charter Oak*                           Leavitt, B.         ca. 1885*
  *Frogs of Windham*                      Leavitt, B.         ca. 1891*
LEBOWITZ, G.
  *Mr. Scrooge*                           Kalmanoff, M.           1966
LEDIARD, THOMAS (1685–1743)
  *Britannia*                             Lampe, J. F.            1732
LEE, DAVID YOUSUN, trans.
  *Martyred, The*                         Wade, J.                1970
LEE, HENRY (1765–1836)
  *Throw Physic to the Dogs!*             Arnold, S.              1798
LEE, ROBIN
  *Little Mermaid*                        Boyd, A.                1978
LEE, STEWART (b. 1968)
  *Jerry Springer* (with comp.)           Thomas, R.              2003
LeFAIVE, DARLENE
  *Twilight Voices*                       Hoffman, S.             1999
LEHMAN, LEO (1926–2005)
  *Arrangement, The*                      Davis, C.               1965
LEICHT, ALLAN
  *Adventures of Friar Tuck*              Paxton, G.              1983
LEIGH, HENRY S. (1837–1883)
  *Cinderella*                            Farmer, J.              1883
LEITNER, IRVING (b. 1925)
  *Excitement at the Circus*              Blank, A.               1969
LEMON, MARK (1809–1870)
  *Deer Stalkers*                         Loder, E. J.            1841
  *Fridolin*                              Romer, F.               1840
  *Pacha's Bridal*                        Romer, F.               1836
  *Rob of the Fens*                       Romer, F.               1838
LENEL, JANE
  *Young Goodman Brown*                   Lenel, L.               1963
LENNEP, W. VAN
  *Medea*                                 Farberman, H.          1961*
LERNER, ALAN JAY (1918–1986)
  *Love Life*                             Weill, K.               1948
LERT, ERNST (1883–1955)
  *Tenor, The* (with K. Shapiro)          Weisgall, H.            1952
LESSING, DORIS (b. 1919)
  *Making of the Representative*          Glass, P.               1988
  *Marriage between Zones 3, 4, and 5*    Glass, P.               1997
LESTOCQ, W[ILLIAM] (d. 1920)
  *Sultan of Mocha*                       Cellier, A.             1874
LEVI, JONATHAN
  *Guest from the Future*                 Marvin, M.              2004
LEVI, TONI MERGENTIME
  *Thanksgiving*                          Levi, P. A.             1977
LEVIN, DAN
  *Rebel and Empire* (with comp.)         Levin, G.              1976*

LEVINE, RHODA

| | | |
|---|---|---|
| *Harrison Loved His Umbrella* | Hollingsworth, S. | 1981 |
| *Thirteen Clocks* | Chauls, R. | 1983 |

LEVY, CHARLES S. (b. 1919)

| | | |
|---|---|---|
| *Satan's Trap* | Piket, F. | 1960 |

LEVY, DEBORAH

| | | |
|---|---|---|
| *Blood Wedding* | LeFanu, N. | 1992 |

LEWIS, JANET (1899–1998)

| | | |
|---|---|---|
| *Last of the Mohicans* | Henderson, A. | 1976 |
| *Legend, The* | Murray, B. | 1987 |
| *Swans, The* | Henderson, A. | 1986 |
| *Wife of Martin Guerre* | Bergsma, W. | 1956 |

LEWIS, MATTHEW GREGORY (1775–1818)

| | | |
|---|---|---|
| *One O'Clock* | King, M. | 1811 |
| *Rich and Poor* | Horn, C. E. | 1812 |

LEWIS, ROBIN

| | | |
|---|---|---|
| *Tell-Tale Heart* | Álvarez, G. | 1984 |

LEWISOHN, LUDWIG (1882–1955)

| | | |
|---|---|---|
| *Eternal Road* (with C. Alan) | Weill, K. | 1937 |

LEYDEN, JAY

| | | |
|---|---|---|
| *Bartleby* | Aschaffenburg, W. | 1964 |

LIAO, DIANA, trans.

| | | |
|---|---|---|
| *Tea* | Tan Dun | 2003 |

LILLO, GEORGE (1693–1739)

| | | |
|---|---|---|
| *Britannia* | Carey, H. | 1734 |
| *Silvia* | ** | 1731 |

LIM, GENNY

| | | |
|---|---|---|
| *Chinaman's Chance* (with comp.) | Ho, F. | 1990 |

LIND, EDWARD

| | | |
|---|---|---|
| *Freak Show* | Taylor, C. | 1975* |

LINDSAY, MAURICE (1918–2009)

| | | |
|---|---|---|
| *Abbot of Drimock* | Musgrave, T. | 1962 |
| *Decision, The* | Musgrave, T. | 1967 |

LINEBERGER, JAMES

| | | |
|---|---|---|
| *Survival of St. Joan* | Ruffin, G./H. Ruffin | 1971 |

LINEK, STEPHEN N.

| | | |
|---|---|---|
| *Voice, The* (with S. Hall) | Kondorossy, L. | 1954 |

LINES, MARIAN (b. 1933)

| | | |
|---|---|---|
| *Flight of Pilgrims* | Roe, B. | 1993 |
| *Gaslight* | Roe, B. | 1983 |
| *Lunch at the Cooked Goose* | Roe, B. | 2000 |

LINLEY, GEORGE (1798–1865)

| | | |
|---|---|---|
| *Catherine Grey* | Balfe, M. | 1837 |
| *Gipsy's Warning* (with R. B. Peake) | Benedict, J. | 1838 |

LINN, JOHN BLAIR (1777–1804)

| | | |
|---|---|---|
| *Bourville Castle* | Carr, B. | 1797 |

LINNEY, ROMULUS (1930–2011)

| | | |
|---|---|---|
| *Death of King Philip* | Earls, P. | 1976 |
| *Democracy* | Wheeler, S. | 1998 |

LIPSYTE, ROBERT (b. 1938)

| | | |
|---|---|---|
| *Muhammad Ali* | Duffy, J. | 2000 |

LITTELL, PHILIP

| | | |
|---|---|---|
| *Dangerous Liaisons* | Susa, C. | 1994 |
| *Dreamers, The* | Conte, D. | 1996 |
| *Every Man Jack* | Larsen, L. | 2006 |
| *Greater Good* | Hartke, S. | 2006 |
| *Streetcar Named Desire* | Previn, A. | 1998 |

LITTLE, PATRICK

| | | |
|---|---|---|
| *Plague upon Eyam* | Drummond, J. | 1983 |
| *Stars in Orion* | Drummond, J. | 1999 |

LIVESAY, DOROTHY (b. 1909)

| | | |
|---|---|---|
| *Lake, The* | Pentland, B. | 1954 |

LLOYD, DAVID THOMAS

| | | |
|---|---|---|
| *Conjur Moon* | Lloyd, T. C. | 1979 |

LLOYD, JOHN (d. 1790)

| | | |
|---|---|---|
| *Romp, The* | Dibdin, C., et al. | 1771 |

LLOYD, ROBERT (1733–1764)

| | | |
|---|---|---|
| *Arcadia* | Stanley, J. | 1761 |
| *Capricious Lovers* | Rush, G. | 1764 |
| *Phillis at Court* | Giordani, T. | 1767 |
| *Tears and Triumphs of Parnassus* (with A. Murphy) | Stanley, J. | 1760 |

LLOYD, WILLIAM A. C.

| | | |
|---|---|---|
| *Iernin* | Lloyd, G. | 1934 |
| *John Socman* | Lloyd, G. | 1951 |
| *Serf, The* | Lloyd, G. | 1938 |

LOCKE, CHARLES O.

| | | |
|---|---|---|
| *Cyrano de Bergerac* | Pokrass, S. D. | 1932 |

LOCKMAN, JOHN (1698–1771)

| | | |
|---|---|---|
| *Rosalinda* | Smith, J. C. | 1740 |
| *Seasons, The* | Smith, J. C. | 1740 |

LOCKWOOD, DOROTHY

| | | |
|---|---|---|
| *Scarecrow, The* | Lockwood, N. | 1945 |

LOMAX, ELIZABETH

| | | |
|---|---|---|
| *O'Higgins of Chile* | Cowell, H. | 1949* |

LOMBARDO, KATHLEEN

| | | |
|---|---|---|
| *Soap Opera* | Franchetti, A. | 1973 |

LONDON, CHARMIAN

| | | |
|---|---|---|
| *Inside Information* | Tahourdin, P. | 1959 |

LONG, JOHN LUTHER (1861–1927)

| | | |
|---|---|---|
| *Hoshi-San* | Leps, W. | 1909 |

LONSDALE, FREDERICK (1881–1954)

| | | |
|---|---|---|
| *King of Cadonia* | Jones, S. | 1908 |

LOUCHHEIM, KATIE

| | | |
|---|---|---|
| *Noblest Game* | Diamond, D. | 1975* |

LOUISE, DOROTHY

| | | |
|---|---|---|
| *Disappearing Act* | Carbon, J. | 2008* |
| *Out of This World* | Carbon, J. | 2006* |

LOVER, SAMUEL (1797–1968)

| | | |
|---|---|---|
| *Gran Uile* | Penson, W. | 1832 |

LOVOOS, JANICE

| | | |
|---|---|---|
| *Shining Chalice* | Van Grove, I. | 1964 |

LOWELL, JAMES RUSSELL (1819–1891)

| | | |
|---|---|---|
| *Pesceballo, Il* | arr. Child, F. | 1862 |

LOWRY, HENRY DAWSON (1869–1906)

| | | |
|---|---|---|
| *Gale* (with Dawson-Scott) | Leginska, E. | 1935 |

LUCAS, CRAIG

| | | |
|---|---|---|
| *Cousin Lilly* | Busby, G. | 1985* |
| *Orpheus in Love* | Busby, G. | 1992 |
| *Sleepsong* | Busby, G. | 1985 |
| *Viola* | Busby, G. | 1985 |

LUCAS, HENRY

| | | |
|---|---|---|
| *Love in Disguise* | Giordani, T. | 1766 |

LUCE, WILLIAM

| | | |
|---|---|---|
| *Gabriel's Daughter* | Mollicone, H. | 2003 |

LUJÁN, JAMES GRAHAM

| | | |
|---|---|---|
| *Don Perlimplin* (with comp.) | Rieti, V. | 1952 |
| *Love of Don Perlimplin* (with O'Connell) | Doyle, R. | 1984 |

LUKE, LEOFWIN

| | | |
|---|---|---|
| *Catsman* | Hodkinson, S. | 1985 |

LUNCH, LYDIA

| | | |
|---|---|---|
| *Embrace the Monster* | Valitsky, K. | 1993 |

LUNN, JOSEPH (1784–1863)

| | | |
|---|---|---|
| *Family Jars* | Perry, G. | 1822 |
| *Honest Frauds* | Horn, C. E. | 1830 |
| *Shepherd of Derwent Vale* | Horn, C. E. | 1825 |

LYFORD, RALPH (1882–1927)

| | | |
|---|---|---|
| *Mermaid in Lock No. 7* | Siegmeister, E. | 1958 |

LYSAGHT, E.

| | | |
|---|---|---|
| *Robin Hood* (with L. MacNally) | Shield, W. | 1784 |

MABLEY, EDWARD (b. 1906)

| | | |
|---|---|---|
| *Angel Levine* | Siegmeister, E. | 1985 |
| *Lady of the Lake* | Siegmeister, E. | 1985 |
| *Night of the Moonspell* | Siegmeister, E. | 1976 |
| *Plough and the Stars* | Siegmeister, E. | 1963 |
| *Shephardes Play* | La Montaine, J. | 1967 |

MacBETH, GEORGE

| | | |
|---|---|---|
| *Scene Machine* | Gilbert, A. | 1971 |

MACDONALD, ANN-MARIE (b. 1958)

| | | |
|---|---|---|
| *Nigredo Hotel* | Gotham, N. | 1992 |

MacDONALD, CYNTHIA

| | | |
|---|---|---|
| *Rehearsal, The* | Benjamin, T. | 1981 |

MacDONALD, SHARON

| | | |
|---|---|---|
| *Hey Persephone!* | Gribbin, D. | 1998 |

MACDONNELL, JUSTIN

| | | |
|---|---|---|
| *Medea* | Kerry, G. | 1993 |

MACDONOUGH, GLEN (1870–1924)

| | | |
|---|---|---|
| *Algerian, The* | De Koven, R. | 1893 |

MACFARREN, GEORGE, Sr. (1788–1843)

| | | |
|---|---|---|
| *Adventure of Don Quixote* | Macfarren, G., Jr. | 1846 |
| *Auld Robin Gray* | Blewitt, J. | 1828 |
| *Boy of Santillane* | Cooke, T. S. | 1827 |
| *Devil's Opera* | Macfarren, G., Jr. | 1838 |

| | | |
|---|---|---|
| *Lestocq* | Cooke, T. S. | 1835 |
| *Malvina* | Lee, G. A. | 1826 |
| *My Old Woman* | Blewitt, J. | 1829 |
| *Oberon* | Cooke, T. S. | 1826 |
| *Talisman, The* | Blewitt, J. | 1828 |

MACHLIS, JOSEPH (1906–1998)

| | | |
|---|---|---|
| *Caliph's Clock* | Kraft, L. | 1951 |
| *Trial at Rouen* | Dello Joio, N. | 1956 |
| *Triumph of (Saint) Joan* | Dello Joio, N. | 1950 |

MacKAY, CONSTANCE d'ARCY

| | | |
|---|---|---|
| *Cockcrow* | Smith, J. | 1954 |
| *Shepherdess and the Chimneysweep* | Smith, J. | 1966 |

MacKAYE, PERCY W. (b. 1875)

| | | |
|---|---|---|
| *Canterbury Pilgrims* | De Koven, R. | 1917 |
| *Immigrants, The* | Converse, F. | 1912* |
| *Rip Van Winkle* | De Koven, R. | 1920 |

MacKENZIE, ELIZABETH

| | | |
|---|---|---|
| *Incognita* | Wellesz, E. | 1951 |

MACKENZIE, SCOBIE (b. 1906)

| | | |
|---|---|---|
| *Jolly Roger* (with Clinton-Baddeley) | Leigh, W. | 1933 |

MacLENNAN, ROBERT

| | | |
|---|---|---|
| *Friend of the People* | Horne, D. | 1999 |

MacNALLY, LEONARD (1752–1820)

| | | |
|---|---|---|
| *Cottage Festival* | Giordani, T. | 1796 |
| *Critic upon Critic* | ** | ca. 1792 |
| *Richard Coeur de Lion* | Shield, W. | 1786 |
| *Robin Hood* (with E. Lysaght) | Shield, W. | 1784 |
| *Ruling Passion* | Cogan, P. | 1778 |
| *Tristram Shandy* | ** | 1783 |

MACY, JOHN ALBERT (1877–1932)

| | | |
|---|---|---|
| *Sacrifice, The* (with comp.) | Converse, F. | 1911 |

MADDEN, DAVID (b. 1933)

| | | |
|---|---|---|
| *Intimations* | Constantinides, D. | 1982 |

MAGUIRE, MATTHEW

| | | |
|---|---|---|
| *Chaos* | Gordon, M. | 1994 |

MALASCH, ROB

| | | |
|---|---|---|
| *Photographer, The* (with comp.) | Glass, P. | 1982 |

MALET, EDWARD (1837–1908)

| | | |
|---|---|---|
| *Harold* | Cowen, F. | 1895 |

MALFITANO, DAPHNE

| | | |
|---|---|---|
| *Family Room* | Pasatieri, T. | 2009* |

MALLETT, DAVID (1705?–1765)

| | | |
|---|---|---|
| *Alfred* (with Thomson) | Arne, T. A. | 1740 |
| *Britannia* | Arne, T. A. | 1755 |

MALLOCH, DOUGLAS (1877–1938)

| | | |
|---|---|---|
| *Enchanter, The* | Holbrooke, J. | 1915 |

MALOUF, DAVID (b. 1934)

| | | |
|---|---|---|
| *Baa Baa Black Sheep* | Berkeley, M. | 1993 |
| *Jane Eyre* | Berkeley, M. | 2000 |
| *Voss* | Meale, R. | 1982 |

MALOUF, MELISSA

| | | |
|---|---|---|
| *Bellarocca* | Legg, J. | 1997 |

MALTBY, ALFRED (d. 1901)
| | | |
|---|---|---|
| Don Quixote (with H. Paulton) | Clay, F. | 1876 |

MANDEL, EUGENE
| | | |
|---|---|---|
| I Wish, I Wish | Mandel, J. | 2006 |

MANDEL, MEL
| | | |
|---|---|---|
| Cubana, La | Henze, H. W. | 1974 |

MANLOVE, JOHN
| | | |
|---|---|---|
| Christopher Sly | Argento, D. | 1963 |

MANRIQUE, JAIME (b. 1949)
| | | |
|---|---|---|
| Mysteries of Eleusis (with comp.) | Feigin, J. | 1986 |

MARANISS, JAMES (b. 1945)
| | | |
|---|---|---|
| Life Is a Dream | Spratlan, L. | 1978* |

MARCH, LUCILE
| | | |
|---|---|---|
| Necklace, The | Bohrnstedt, W. | 1956 |

MAREN, ROGER
| | | |
|---|---|---|
| Double Trouble | Mohaupt, R. | 1954 |

MARGRAFF, RUTH
| | | |
|---|---|---|
| Night Vision | Ho, B. | 2000 |

MARK, MICHAEL
| | | |
|---|---|---|
| Magic Fishbone (with Elliot, Raab) | Chapin, T. | 1988 |

MARKHAM, EDWIN (1852–1940)
| | | |
|---|---|---|
| Undine | Ware, H. | 1923 |

MARKOE, PETER (1752–1792)
| | | |
|---|---|---|
| Reconciliation, The | ** | 1790 |

MARKS-TARLOW, JEFFREY (b. 1955)
| | | |
|---|---|---|
| Cracked Orlando | Dawe, J. | 2010 |

MAROWITZ, DAVID ZANE
| | | |
|---|---|---|
| Voluptuous Tango | Muldowney, D. | 1996 |

MARQUIS, NITA
| | | |
|---|---|---|
| Rubios, Los | Moore, M. | 1931 |

MARSH, BETTY
| | | |
|---|---|---|
| Christmas Slippers | Kaufmann, W. | 1955 |

MARSH, EDWARD (1912–1991)
| | | |
|---|---|---|
| Pathelin | Josephs, W. | 1963 |
| Rebecca | Josephs, W. | 1983 |

MARSHALL, ALAN (1902–1984)
| | | |
|---|---|---|
| Kisses for a Quid | Werder, F. | 1961 |

MARSHALL, JANE
| | | |
|---|---|---|
| Kumana | Kanitz, E. | 1953 |

MARTIN, HERBERT WOODWARD
| | | |
|---|---|---|
| Paul Laurence Dunbar | Hailstork, A. | 1995 |

MARTIN, ROBERT (fl. 1890)
| | | |
|---|---|---|
| Joan | Ford, E. | 1890 |

MARTIN, THOMAS PHILIP
| | | |
|---|---|---|
| Tartuffe | Mechem, K. | 1980 |

MARTONE, ANTHONY
| | | |
|---|---|---|
| Harriet Tubman | Edwards, L. | 1986 |

MARX, PATRICIA
| | | |
|---|---|---|
| Review | Beck, J. | 2009 |

MARZIALS, T. J. H.
| | | |
|---|---|---|
| Esmeralda (with A. Randegger) | Thomas, A. G. | 1883 |

MASON, DAVID (b. 1954)
| | | |
|---|---|---|
| Scarlet Letter | Laitman, L. | 2009 |

MASON, HAROLD
| | | |
|---|---|---|
| Rapunzel | Brooks, R. | 1971 |

MASON, JOHN HOPE
| | | |
|---|---|---|
| Journey, The | Metcalf, J. | 1981 |

MASON, TIMOTHY
| | | |
|---|---|---|
| Emperor's New Clothes | Larsen, L. | 1979 |

MASS, WILLIAM. See GIBSON, WILLIAM.

MASTEROFF, JOSEPH
| | | |
|---|---|---|
| Desire under the Elms | Thomas, E. | 1978 |

MATHEUS, JOHN FREDERICK (1887–1983)
| | | |
|---|---|---|
| Ouanga | White, C. C. | 1932 |

MAURA, SISTER (b. 1915)
| | | |
|---|---|---|
| Dialogues | Bauman, J. | 1987 |

MAVOR, JAMES
| | | |
|---|---|---|
| Out of Season | Grant, J. | 1991 |

MAXTON, HUGH
| | | |
|---|---|---|
| Words upon the Window Pane | Buckley, J. | 1991 |

MAYER, OLIVER
| | | |
|---|---|---|
| America Tropical | Conte, D. | 2007 |

MAYERS, DANIEL
| | | |
|---|---|---|
| Blake | Adams, H. L. | 1985 |

McCAFFERTY, NELL
| | | |
|---|---|---|
| Bitter Fruit | Johnston, F. | 1992 |

McCLATCHY, J. D. (b. 1945)
| | | |
|---|---|---|
| Emmeline | Picker, T. | 1996 |
| Grendel | Goldenthal, E. | 2006 |
| Mario and the Magician | Thorne, F. | 1994 |
| Miss Lonelyhearts | Liebermann, L. | 2006 |
| 1984 (with T. Meeham) | Maazel, L. | 2005 |
| Our Town | Rorem, N. | 2005 |
| Question of Taste | Schuman, W. | 1989 |
| Secret Agent | Dellaria, M. | 2008 |

McCORD, DAVID (1897–1997)
| | | |
|---|---|---|
| Gift of the Magi | Warren, B. | 1985 |

McCRAE, HUGH (b. 1876)
| | | |
|---|---|---|
| Ship of Heaven | Hill, A. | 1923 |

McDONAGH, DONAGH
| | | |
|---|---|---|
| Patrick | Potter, A. J. | 1965 |

McDONALD, HEATHER (b. 1959)
| | | |
|---|---|---|
| End of the Affair | Heggie, J. | 2004 |

McFALL, GARDNER
| | | |
|---|---|---|
| Amelia | Hagen, D. | 2010 |

McGEE, MOLLY
| | | |
|---|---|---|
| Coyote's Tail | Thomas, K. | 1991 |

McGETTIGAN, BETTY (d. 2009)
| | | |
|---|---|---|
| Queenie Pie (with comp.) | Ellington, D. | 1974* |

McGLASHAN, LEN
| | | |
|---|---|---|
| Amorous Judge (with S. Austin) | Gross, E. | 1965 |

McGRATH, JOHN (b. 1935)
    *Behold the Sun* (with comp.)    Goehr, A.    1985
McGREW, JOHN F. (b. 1942)
    *Quantum Mechanic*    Bilotta, J.    2007
    *Trifles*    Bilotta, J.
McINERNEY, SALLY (b. 1946)
    *Story of Mary O'Neill*    LeFanu, N.    1989
McKINLAN, Mr.
    *Francis the First*    Loder, E. J.    1838
McLARNON, GERARD
    *Gentle Spirit*    Taverner, J.    1977
    *Thérèse*    Taverner, J.    1979
McLELLAN, C[HARLES] M[ORTON] S[TEWART] (1865–1916)
    *Pink Lady*    Caryll, I.    1911
    *Puritania*    Kelley, E. S.    1892
McMURTRIE, H.
    *Child of the Mountain*    Heinrich, A. P.    1821
    *Minstrel, The*    Heinrich, A. P.    1835*
McNAIR, RICK
    *Turtle Wakes*    Bell, A.    2001
McNALLY, LEONARD (1752–1820)
    *Tristram Shandy*    Arne, M.    1783
McNALLY, TERRENCE (b. 1939)
    *At the Statue of Venus*    Heggie, J.    2005
    *Dead Man Walking*    Heggie, J.    2000
    *Food of Love*    Beaser, R.    1999
McNEIL, JANET
    *Finn and the Black Hag*    Warren R.    1959
    *Graduation Ode*    Warren, R.    1963
McPHEE, COLIN (1900–1964)
    *Commission, The*    Cowell, H.    1954
MCPHERSON, ANNE
    *Florence: The Lady with the Lamp*    Sullivan, T.    1992
McQUILKIN, FRANK
    *Stone Soup*    Dorff, D.    1983
    *Vercingetorix*    Smolanoff, M.    1973*
MEDRICK, MARY DUREN
    *Curandera, La*    Rodríguez, R.    2006
    *Monkey See, Monkey Do*    Rodríguez, R.    1987
    (with comp.)
    *Old Majestic*    Rodríguez, R.    1988
MEEHAM, THOMAS (b. 1929)
    *1984* (with J. D. McClatchy)    Maazel, L.    2005
MEEROPOL, ABEL
    *Wooing, The*    Lehrman, L.    2003
MEGROTH, EDWARD J.
    *Goodman Brown*    Fink, H.    1968
MELTZER, C. H.
    *Sunken Bell*    Ruggles, C    1923*
MENDEZ, MOSES (d. 1758)
    *Chaplet, The*    Boyce, W.    1749

    *Double Disappointment*    \*\*    1746
    *Robin Hood*    Burney, C.    1750
    *Shepherd's Lottery*    Boyce, W.    1751
MENDOZA, JOE
    *Dancing Master*    Arnold, M.    1962
    *Spur of the Moment*    Halahan, G.    1959
MENOTTI, GIAN CARLO (1911–2007)
    *Hand of Bridge*    Barber, S.    1959
    *Introductions and Good-Byes*    Foss, L.    1960
    *Vanessa*    Barber, S.    1958
MEREDITH, RICHARD
    *Iphigenia in Exile*    Gifford, H.    1985*
MEREDITH, WILLIAM (1919–2007)
    *Bottle Imp*    Whiton, P.    1958
MERINGTON, MARGUERITE (1857–1951)
    *Daphne*    Bird, A.    1895
MERRY, ROBERT (1755–1798)
    *Magician No Conjuror*    Mazzinghi, J.    1792
MEYERS, JOHN [MYERS] (1906–1988)
    *Sack of Calabasas* (with comp.)    Fletcher, G.    1964
MEZEI, MARI
    *Angels in America*    Eötvös, P.    2004
MICHAELS, STUART
    *Specialist, The*    Rodgers, L.    1978
MIDANI, AKRAM (d. 2001)
    *Town of Greed* (with comp.)    Balada, L.    2000
MIDDLETON, ALASDAIR
    *Adventures of Pinocchio*    Dove, J.    2007
    *Bird in Your Ear*    Bruce. D.    2008
    *Enchanted Pig*    Dove, J.    2006
    *Out of the Ordinary*    Bruce, D.    2007
    *Swanhunter*    Dove, J.    2009
MILES, WILLIAM AUGUSTUS (1753–1817)
    *Artifice, The*    Arne, M.    1780
    *Summer Amusement*    Arnold, S.    1779
    (with M. P. Andrews)
MILLAY, EDNA ST. VINCENT (1892–1950)
    *King's Henchman*    Taylor, D.    1927
MILLER, ARTHUR (1915–2005)
    *View from the Bridge* (with Weinstein)    Bolcom, W.    1999
MILLER, GLEN
    *Audience, The*    Dembo, R.    1981*
MILLER, JAMES (1706–1744)
    *Coffee House*    Carey/Burgess    1738
    *Hospital for Fools*    Arne, T. A.    1739
    *Picture, The*    Arne, T. A.    1745
MILLER, WILLIAM J.
    *Dante and Beatrice*    Philpot, S. R.    1889
MILLIET, PAUL, trans. (b. 1858)
    *Amy Robsart*    de Lara, I.    1893
MILLINGEN, JOHN G. (1782–1862)
    *Bee-Hive, The*    Horn, C. H.    1811

| | | |
|---|---|---|
| *Illustrious Stranger* (with J. Kenney) | Nathan, I. | 1827 |
| *Triboulet* | Nathan, I. | 1840 |

MILLINGTON, FRANCIS
| *Fall of the House of Usher* | Ruger, M. H. | 1953 |

MILLS, ROSWELL GEORGE (1896–1966)
| *Grande Bretèche, La* | Claflin, A. | 1957 |

MILNER, HENRY M.
| *Challenge, The* | Cooke, T. S. | 1834 |

MILNS, WILLIAM (1761–1801)
| *Flash in the Pan* | Hewitt, J. | 1798 |

MILTON, JOHN (1608–1674)
| *Comus* | Lawes, H. | 1634 |

MINGHELLA, ANTHONY
| *Mathematics of a Kiss* | Gough/Lunn | 1989 |

MIRRIAM, LILLIE FULLER
| *Osseo* | Noyes-Greene, E. | 1917 |

MITCHELL, ADRIAN (B. 1932)
| *Houdini* | Schat, P. | 1979 |
| *Ledge, The* | Bennett, R. R. | 1961 |

MITCHELL, JOSEPH (1684–1738)
| *Highland Fair* | ** | 1731 |

MITCHELL, LOFTON (1919–2000)
| *And the Walls* | Roosevelt, W. | 1976 |

MITCHISON, NAOMI (b. 1897)
| *Corn King* | Easdale, B. | 1950 |

MITFORD, MARY RUSSELL (1786–1855)
| *Sadak and Kalasrade* | Packer, C. | 1835 |

MOELLER, PHILIP (1880–195)
| *Helena's Husband* | Gruenberg, L. | 1938 |

MOFFATT, HUGH
| *Corps of Discovery* | Ching, M. | 2003 |
| *King of the Clouds* | Ching, M. | 1996 |
| *Out of the Rain* | Ching, M. | 1998 |

MOHACSI, EUGENE
| *Troublemaker, The* | Polgar, T. | 1968* |

MONACO, RICHARD
| *Politics of Harmony* | Wuorinen, C. | 1968 |

MONSON, WILLIAM
| *Falstaff in and out of Love* | Rea, A. | 1982 |

MONSOUR, SALLY
| *Pandora's Box* | Effinger, C. | 1962 |

MONTAGU, ELIZABETH (b. 1917)
| *School for Wives* | Liebermann, R. | 1955 |

MONTCRIEFF, WILLIAM T. [THOMAS] (1794–1857)
| *Actors al fresco* | Cooke, T. S. | 1823 |
| *Giovanni in London* | ** | 1817 |

MONTEFIORE, JACOB L.
| *Don John of Austria* | Nathan, I. | 1847 |

MONTGOMERY, J. SHERWOOD
| *Rip Van Winkle* | Rockwell, J. | 1989 |

MOODIE, ANDREW
| *Decoherence* | Chen, J. | 2008 |

MOODY, AMANDA
| *Caliban Dreams* | Suprynowicz, C. | 2001 |

MOORE, JONATHAN (b. 1963)
| *East and West* | McQueen, I. | 1995 |
| *Greek* | Turnage, M.-A. | 1988 |
| *Horse Opera* | Copeland, S. | 1994 |

MOORE, MARIANNE (1887–1972)
| *Fables* | Rorem, N. | 1971 |

MOORE, MAVOR (1919–2006)
| *Abracadabra* | Freedman, H. | 1979 |
| *Erewhon* | Applebaum, L. | 2000 |
| *Ghost Dance* | Levin, G. | 1985 |
| *Louis Riel* (with J. Languirand) | Somers, H. | 1967 |

MOORE, THOMAS (1779–1852)
| *Gipsey Prince* | Kelly, M. | 1801 |
| *M.P.* | King, M. P. | 1811 |

MOOREHEAD, JOHN (ca. 1760–1804)
| *Birds of a Feather* | Moorehead/Calcott | 1796 |

MORACE, JOHN
| *Queer* | Wold, E. | 2001 |

MORELAND, DONALD
| *Animalopera* | Fink, M. | 2004 |
| *Chinchilla* | Fink, M. | 1986 |
| *Conquistador, The* | Fink, M. | 1997 |
| *Edith Wharton* | Fink, M. | 2003 |
| *Susanna and the Elders* | Fink, M. | 1956 |

MORGAN, EDWIN (1920–2010)
| *Charcoal Burner* | Wilson, T. | 1969 |
| *Columba* | Leighton, K. | 1981 |

MORGAN, JIM
| *Soap Opera* | Wallace, S. | 1985 |

MORGAN, JOHN
| *Christmas Carol* | Kay, N. | 1978 |
| *Magician, The* | Hoddinott, A. | 1976 |

MORGAN, McNAMARA (d. 1762)
| *Sheep-Shearing* | Arne, T. A. | 1754 |

MORGAN, PETER
| *Sacrapant* | Aston, P. | 1967 |

MORLEY, MALCOLM
| *Trevallion* (with P. Phillips) | Phillips, R. | 1956 |

MORRIS, FRANK
| *Little Match Girl* | Kaufmann, W. | 1953 |

MORRIS, GEORGE POPE (1802–1864)
| *Maid of Saxony* | Horn, C. E. | 1842 |

MORRIS, MARK (b. 1952)
| *Child, Book, and Broomstick* | Burtch, M. | 2000 |
| *Raven King* | Burtch, M. | 1999 |
| *Skin Drum* | Grant, J. | 1987 |

MORRIS, WILLIAM
| *Rapunzel* | Harrison, L. | 1959 |

MORRISON, BLAKE
| *Doctor Ox's Experiment* | Bryars, G. | 1988 |

MORRISON, TONI (b. 1931)
| *Margaret Garner* | Danielpour, R. | 2004 |

MORSE, WOOLSON (1858–1897)
| *Merry Monarch* | Sousa, J. P. | 1890 |
| (with J. C. Goodwin) | | |

MORTON, EDWARD (d. 1922)
| *San Toy* (with Greenbank, Ross) | Jones, S. | 1899 |

MORTON, JOHN MADDISON (1811–1891)
| *Barbers of Bassora* | Hullah, J. | 1837 |
| *Dragon, The* | Lee, G. A. | 1834 |

MORTON, THOMAS (1764–1838)
| *Blind Girl* | Reeve, W. | 1801 |
| *Children in the Wood* | Arnold, S. | 1793 |
| *Columbus* | Reinagle, A. | 1797 |
| *Henri Quatre* | Bishop, H. R. | 1820 |
| *Invincibles, The* | Lee, G. A. | 1828 |
| *Knight of Snowdoun* | Bishop, H. R. | 1811 |
| *Roland for an Oliver* | Bishop, H. R. | 1819 |
| *Slave, The* | Bishop, H. R. | 1816 |
| *Speed the Plough* | Moorehead, J. | 1802 |
| *Sublime and the Beautiful* | Lee, G. A. | 1828 |

MOSS, JEFF (1942–1998)
| *Good Life* | Silverman, S. | 1986 |

MOTTEUX, PETER ANTHONY (1663–1718)
| *Acis and Galatea* | Eccles, J. | 1701 |
| *Arsinoe* | Clayton, T. | 1705 |
| *Island Princess* | Purcell, D. | 1699 |
| *Loves of Mars and Venus* | Eccles, J./Finger, G. | 1696 |
| *Rape of Europa* | Eccles, J. | 1694 |
| *Temple of Love* | Fedelli, G. | 1706 |
| *Thomyris* | Pepusch, J. | 1707 |

MOTTLEY, JOHN (1692–1750)
| *Craftsman, The* | ** | 1728 |

MOUBRAY, GEORGE (fl. 1798)
| *Devil of a Lover* | Attwood, T. | 1798 |

MOULTON, HERBERT
| *Selfish Giant* (with comp.) | Hollingsworth, S. | 1981 |
| *Twelfth Night* | Wilson, J. | 1969 |

MOULTRIE, GEORGE (fl. 1790–1800)
| *False and True* | Arnold, S. | 1798 |

MOYLE, GILBERT
| *Sunset Trail* | Cadman, C. W. | 1922 |

MUDIE, W. G.
| *Economites, The* | Nevin, A. | 1899 |

MULDOON, PAUL (b. 1951)
| *Bandanna* | Hagen, D. | 1999 |
| *Shining Brow* | Hagen, D. | 1992 |
| *Vera of Las Vegas* | Hagen, D. | 1996 |

MÜLLER, HEINER (b. 1929)
| *Forest, The* (with D. Pinckney) | Byrne, D. | 1988 |

MUNDY, DEAN
| *Sisters, The* | Flagello, N. | 1961 |

MURDOCH, IRIS (1919–1999)
| *Servants, The* | Mathias, W. | 1980 |

MURDOCH, JOHN
| *Tamburlaine* | Murdoch, E. | 1971 |

MURPHY, ARTHUR (1727–1805)
| *Tears and Triumphs of Parnassus* | Stanley, J. | 1760 |
| (with Lloyd) | | |

MURRAY, BRAHAM
| *Resurrection* (with L. Harrington) | Machover, T. | 1999 |

MURRAY, GILBERT (1866–1957)
| *Alkestis* | Boughton, R. | 1922 |
| *Hippolytus* | Drysdale, L. | 1905 |

MURRAY-SMITH, JOANNA (b. 1962)
| *Love in the Age of Therapy* | Grabowsky, P. | 2002 |

MURRELL, JOHN (b. 1945)
| *Filumena* | Estacio, J, | 2003 |
| *Frobisher* | Estacio, J. | 2003 |
| *Josephine* | Sullivan, T. | 2001 |

NAGEL, CHARLES (1806–1870)
| *Merry Freaks* | Nathan, I. | 1843 |
| *Mock Catalani* | Nagel, C. | 1842 |

NAKASHIMA, JANE
| *Floating* | Kuskin, C. | 1999 |
| *Phaedra* | Innerarity, M. | 1999 |

NAPIER, HAMPDEN
| *Freebooters, The* | Hawes, W. | 1827 |
| *Not for Me* | Hawes, W. | 1828 |
| *Oracle, The* | Hawes, W. | 1826 |

NARDI, MARCIA (1901–1991)
| *Beatrice* | Hoiby, L. | 1959 |

NAYLOR, HATTIE
| *Odysseus Unwound* | Grant, J. | 2006 |

NELSON, FRANK H.
| *Widow, The* | Lavallée, C. | 1882 |

NELSON, GLEN ALMON (b. 1961)
| *Book of Gold* | Boren, M. | 2005 |
| *Dead, The* | Boren, M. | 1993 |

NESTER, DANIEL
| *Summer King* (with comp.) | Sonenberg, D. | 2005 |

NEVILLE, EDWARD (fl. 1779)
| *Plymouth in an Uproar* | Dibdin, C. | 1779 |

NEWBOLT, HENRY JOHN (1862–1938)
| *Travelling Companion* | Stanford, C. | 1919 |

NEWMAN, MORDECAI
| *Dreyfus* | Cotel, M. | 1985 |

NEWSOM, JEREMY
| *Letters, Riddles* | Nyman, M. | 1991 |

NEWTON, NORMAN (b. 1929)
| *Seabird Island* | Healey, D. | 1977 |
| *Vile Shadows* | Turner, R. | 1983* |

**NIBLOCK, HELEN**

| | | |
|---|---|---|
| *Last Leaf* | Niblock, J. | 2006 |
| *Ruth and Naomi* | Niblock, J. | 2009 |

**NICHOLSON, SIMON**

| | | |
|---|---|---|
| *Doggone* | Carpenter, G. | 1999 |

**NICOLAS, CLAIRE**

| | | |
|---|---|---|
| *Clock, The* | Rieti, V. | 1960 |
| *Maryam the Harlot* | Rieti, V. | 1966* |
| *Pet Shop* | Rieti, V. | 1958 |

**NICOLL, BRUCE (b. 1912)**

| | | |
|---|---|---|
| *Sweetwater Affair* | Beadell, R. | 1961 |

**NIEBOER, ROGER**

| | | |
|---|---|---|
| *Snow Leopard* | Harper, W. | 1989 |

**NIGGLI, JOSEPHINA (1910–1983)**

| | | |
|---|---|---|
| *Sunday Costs Five Pesos* | Haubiel, C. | 1950 |

**NISCEMI, MAITA di**

| | | |
|---|---|---|
| *CIVIL warS* (with R. Wilson) | Glass, P. | 1984 |
| *Naked Revolution* | Soldier, D. | 1997 |

**NIXON, G. DAVID**

| | | |
|---|---|---|
| *Rich Man, Poor Man* | Hopkins, A. | 1969 |

**NOBLE, THOMAS**

| | | |
|---|---|---|
| *Persian Hunters* | Horn, C. E. | 1817 |

**NOLEN, TIMOTHY**

| | | |
|---|---|---|
| *Amarantha* (lib. with comp.) | Ames, R. | 1980 |

**NOLTE, CHARLES (b. 1926)**

| | | |
|---|---|---|
| *Dream of Valentino* | Argento, D. | 1994 |

**NOURSE, HELEN**

| | | |
|---|---|---|
| *Playing with Fire* | France, S. | 2010 |

**NOWRA, LOUIS (b. 1950)**

| | | |
|---|---|---|
| *Inner Voices* | Howard, B. | 1977 |
| *Whitsunday* | Howard, B. | 1988 |

**NYMAN, MICHAEL (b. 1944)**

| | | |
|---|---|---|
| *Down by the Greenwood Side* | Birtwistle, H. | 1969 |

**OAKES, MEREDITH (b. 1946)**

| | | |
|---|---|---|
| *Anger* | Grant, J, | 1993 |
| *Edward John Eyre* | Conyngham, B. | 1971 |
| *Jump into My Sack* | Grant, J. | 1996 |
| *Miss Treat* | Oliver, D. | 1999 |
| *Solid Assets* | Huehns, C. | 1993 |
| *Tempest, The* | Adès, T. | 2004 |
| *Triumph of Beauty and Deceit* | Barry, G. | 1995 |

**OATES, JOYCE (b. 1938)**

| | | |
|---|---|---|
| *Black Water* | Duffy, J. | 1997 |

**O'CONNELL, RICHARD L.**

| | | |
|---|---|---|
| *Love of Don Perlimplin* (with J. G. Lujan) | Doyle, R. | 1984 |

**ODELL, THOMAS (fl. ca. 1730)**

| | | |
|---|---|---|
| *Patron, The* | ** | 1729 |

**ODINGSELLS, GABRIEL (1690–1734)**

| | | |
|---|---|---|
| *Bays's Opera* | ** | 1730 |

**ODINOV, OREL**

| | | |
|---|---|---|
| *Hannah* (with comp.) | Lehrman, L. | 1980 |

**O'DONOGHUE, TADGH, transl.**

| | | |
|---|---|---|
| *Muirgheis* | Butler, O'Brien | 1903 |

**OERKE, ANDREW**

| | | |
|---|---|---|
| *Enchanted Canary* | Stevens, N. | 1961 |

**O'HARA, KANE (1714–1782)**

| | | |
|---|---|---|
| *April Day* | Arnold, S. | 1777 |
| *Golden Pippen* | Fischer, J. A. | 1773 |
| *Midas* | ** | 1762 |
| *Tom Thumb* | Markordt, J. | 1780 |
| *Two Misers* | Dibdin, C. | 1775 |

**OHLSON, E. E.**

| | | |
|---|---|---|
| *Rose and the Ring* | Leginska, E. | 1932* |

**O'HUIGIN, SEAN (b. 1942)**

| | | |
|---|---|---|
| *Dissipation of Purely Sound* | Beecroft, N. | 1988 |

**O'KEEFE, JOHN**

| | | |
|---|---|---|
| *Chrysalis* | Suprynowicz, C. | 2006 |

**O'KEEFFE, JOHN (1747–1833)**

| | | |
|---|---|---|
| *Agreeable Surprise* | Arnold, S. | 1781 |
| *Banditti, The* | Arnold, S. | 1781 |
| *Basket Maker* | Arnold, S. | 1790 |
| *Birth-Day, The* | Arnold, S. | 1783 |
| *Britain's Brave Tars!!* | Attwood, T. | 1797 |
| *Castle of Andalusia* | Arnold, S. | 1782 |
| *Constant Maid* | Carter, T. | 1788 |
| *Czar, The* | Shield, W. | 1790 |
| *Dead Alive* | Arnold, S. | 1781 |
| *Farmer, The* | Shield, W. | 1787 |
| *Fontainbleau* | Shield, W. | 1784 |
| *Gretna Green* (with C. Stuart) | Arnold, S. | 1783 |
| *Highland Reel* | Shield, W. | 1788 |
| *Irish Mimic* | Shield, W. | 1795 |
| *Lad of the Hills* | Shield, W. | 1796 |
| *Love in a Camp* | Shield, W. | 1786 |
| *Peeping Tom* | Arnold, S. | 1784 |
| *Poor Soldier* | Shield, W. | 1783 |
| *Positive Man* | Arnold, S. | 1782 |
| *Rival Soldiers* | Shield, W. | 1797 |
| *Shamrock, The* | Shield, W. | 1777 |
| *Siege of Curzola* | Arnold, S. | 1786 |
| *Son-in-Law* | Arnold, S. | 1779 |
| *Sprigs of Laurel* | Shield, W. | 1793 |
| *Wicklow Mountains* | Shield, W. | 1796 |

**OLDHAM, J. H.**

| | | |
|---|---|---|
| *Greek Kalends* | Ridout, A. | 1956 |

**OLDMIXON, JOHN (1673–1742)**

| | | |
|---|---|---|
| *Grove, The* | Purcell, D. | 1700 |

**OLESKER, LIZZIE**

| | | |
|---|---|---|
| *Bohemians, The* (with D. Brown) | Kirschner, B. | 1990 |

**OLIVE, JOHN (b. 1949)**

| | | |
|---|---|---|
| *Silver Fox* | Larsen, L. | 1979 |

**OLON-SCRYMGEOUR, JOHN**

| | | |
|---|---|---|
| *Boor, The* | Argento, D. | 1957 |
| *Colonel Jonathan the Saint* | Argento, D. | 1961 |

| | | | | | |
|---|---|---|---|---|---|
| *Gardens of Artemis* | Weisgall, H. | 1959* | **PAPP, JOSEPH (1921–1991)** | | |
| *Masque of Angels* | Argento, D. | 1964 | *Twelfth Night* | Amram, D. | 1968 |
| *Miss Havisham's Fire* | Argento, D. | 1979 | **PARIS, MATTHEW (b. 1938)** | | |
| *Miss Havisham's Wedding Night* | Argento, D. | 1981 | *Love and Idols* | Drogin, B. | 1986* |
| *Shoemaker's Holiday* | Argento, D. | 1967 | **PARKER, LOUIS NAPOLEON (1852–1944)** | | |
| *Sicilian Limes* | Argento, D. | 1954 | *Masque of War and Peace* | MacCunn, H. | 1900 |
| **O'NEAL, CHARLES (1904–1996)** | | | **PARRY, MENDELSSOHN** | | |
| *African Heartbeat* | Marais, J. | 1953 | *Sylvia* | Parry, J. | 1895 |
| **OPIE, Mrs. [AMELIA ALDERSON] (1769–1853)** | | | **PARRY-WILLIAMS, T. H. (1887–1975)** | | |
| *Noble Outlaw* | Bishop, H. R. | 1815 | *Black Ram* (with Du, in Welsh) | Parrott, I. | 1957 |
| **ORDWAY, SALLY** | | | **PARTNOY, ALICIA, trans. (b. 1955)** | | |
| *Glass Woman* (with comp., Rhodes) | Hays, S. | 1989 | *Río de sangre* | Davis, D. | 2010 |
| **ORR, J.** | | | **PASCAL, FLORIAN [JOSEPH BENJAMIN WILLIAMS]** | | |
| *Trials of Psyche* | Bruce, N. | 1971 | **(1847–1923)** | | |
| **OSTERHAUS, CARVETH** | | | *No Cards* (with W. S. Gilbert) | "Elliott, L." | 1869 |
| *Gorgon's Head* (with comp., Creed) | Magrill, S. | 1998 | **PATRICK, ROBERT (b. 1937)** | | |
| *Medea* | Luke, R. | 1979 | *Camera Obscura* | Sheffer, R. | 1980 |
| *Paradise of Children* (with Creed) | Magrill, S. | 1998 | *Richest Girl* | Sandow, G. | 1975 |
| **OSWIN, CINDY** | | | **PATTERSON, GAYLE** | | |
| *Better Place* | Butler, M. | 2001 | *First Lady* (comp et al.) | Wells, K. | 2010 |
| **OUELLETTE, MICHAEL** | | | **PAUL, EMILY** | | |
| *Last Goodbye* | Shadle, C. | 2008 | *Wake Her Up* | McGuire, J. | 2004 |
| *Question of Love* | Shadle, C. | 2005 | **PAULTON, HARRY (1842–1917)** | | |
| **OULTON, WALLEY CHAMBERLAIN (1770?–1820?)** | | | *Black Crook* (with J. Paulton) | Clay, F. | 1872 |
| *Happy Disguise* | Giordani, T. | 1784 | *Cymbia* | Pascal, F. | 1883 |
| *Haunted Castle* | Giordani, T. | 1783 | *Don Quixote* (with A. Maltby) | Clay, F. | 1876 |
| *Irish Tar* | Attwood, T. | 1797 | **PAULTON. JOSEPH** | | |
| *Sixty-Third Letter* | Arnold, S. | 1802 | *Black Crook* (with H. Paulton) | Clay, F. | 1872 |
| **OVERMYER, ERIC** | | | **PAYNE, JOHN HOWARD (1791–1852)** | | |
| *Blue Margaritas* | Trefousse, R. | 1989 | *Clari* | Bishop, H. R. | 1823 |
| **OWEN, JOHN** | | | *Fall of Algiers* (or C. E. Walker) | Bishop, H. R. | 1825 |
| *Tower* | Hoddinott, A. | 1999 | *Tyrolese Peasant* | Bishop, H. R. | 1832 |
| **OXENFORD, EDWARD** | | | **PAYNE, ROBERT** | | |
| *Safié* | Hadley, H. | 1909 | *Open the Gates* | Lee, D.-K. | 1951 |
| *Torquil* | Harriss, C. | 1900 | **PAYNTER, ELIZABETH** | | |
| **OXENFORD, JOHN (1812–1877)** | | | *Voyage of St. Brendan* | Paynter, J. | 1979 |
| *Dice of Death* | Loder, E. | 1835 | **PAZILLO, JOSEPH** | | |
| *Felix* | Lutz, M. | 1865 | *Cats' Corner* | Riley, D. | 1983* |
| *Helvellyn* | Macfarren, G. A. | 1864 | *Rappaccini's Daughter* | Riley, D | 1984* |
| *Jessy Lea* | Macfarren, G. A. | 1863 | **PEABODY, JOSEPHINE PRESTON (1874–1922)** | | |
| *Lily of Killarney* | Benedict, J. | 1862 | *Legend of the Piper* | Freer, E. E. | 1925 |
| (with D. Boucicault) | | | **PEAKE, RICHARD BRINSLEY (1792–1847)** | | |
| *Robin Hood* | Macfarren, G. A. | 1860 | *Before Breakfast* | Barnett, J. | 1826 |
| *Sleeper Awakened* | Macfarren, G. A. | 1850 | *Bottle Imp* | Rodwell, G. | 1828 |
| *Soldier's Legacy* | Macfarren, G. A. | 1864 | *Climbing Boy* | Hawes, W. | 1832 |
| **OXENHAM, JOHN (1852–1941)** | | | *Cornish Miners* | Rodwell, G. | 1827 |
| *Pageant of Darkness and Light* | MacCunn, H. | 1908* | *Evil Eye* | Rodwell, G. | 1831 |
| | | | *Gipsy's Warning* (with G. Linley) | Benedict, J. | 1838 |
| **PAIN, NESTA (b. 1905)** | | | *Spring Lock* | Rodwell, G. | 1829 |
| *Time for Growing* | Hopkins, A. | 1967 | **PEARCE, JON (b. 1937)** | | |
| **PANYCH, MORRIS (b. 1952)** | | | *Outcasts of Poker Flat* | Beckler, S. R. | 1960 |
| *Seven Stories* | Richardson, A. | 2002* | **PEARCE, WILLIAM (fl. 1785–1796)** | | |
| | | | *Arrived at Portsmouth* | Shield, W. | 1794 |

| | | |
|---|---|---|
| *Death of Captain Faulknor* | Arnold, S. | 1795 |
| *Hartford Bridge* | Shield, W. | 1792 |
| *Midnight Wanderers* | Shield, W. | 1793 |
| *Netly Abbey* | Shield, W. | 1794 |
| *Nunnery, The* | Shield, W. | 1785 |
| *Windsor Castle* | ** | 1795 |

**PEATTIE, ELIA WILKINSON (1862–1935)**

| | | |
|---|---|---|
| *Massimilliano* | Freer, E. E. | 1926 |

**PEAVEY, LINDA**

| | | |
|---|---|---|
| *Pamelia* (with U. Smith) | Funk, E. | 1989 |

**PENDINO, MARY ANN**

| | | |
|---|---|---|
| *Princess and the Pea* | Warwick, M. C. | 2005 |

**PENICK, DOUGLAS (b. 1944)**

| | | |
|---|---|---|
| *Ashoka's Dream* | Lieberson, P. | 1997 |
| *King Gesar* | Lieberson, P. | 1992 |

**PENNYMAN, RUTH (1893–1983)**

| | | |
|---|---|---|
| *Robin Hood* (with Ayerst, comp.) | Tippett, M. | 1934 |

**PERRY, ALFRED**

| | | |
|---|---|---|
| *Volpone* | Antheil, G. | 1953 |

**PERSONS, WENDE**

| | | |
|---|---|---|
| *Patience and Sarah* | Kimper, P. | 1996 |

**PETERSON, WILLIAM M.**

| | | |
|---|---|---|
| *Enchanted Garden* | Shaughnessy, R. | 1972* |

**PETHERIDGE, LOUISE**

| | | |
|---|---|---|
| *Trapeze Artists* | Ritchie, A. | 2000 |

**PETTIT, THOMAS**

| | | |
|---|---|---|
| *Mortal Thoughts of Lady Macbeth* | Krausas, V. | 2008 |

**PFLANZER, HOWARD**

| | | |
|---|---|---|
| *Dream Beach* | Sahl, M. | 1988 |
| *Guest of Honor: Scott Joplin* | Weisberg, S. | 1989 |

**PHELPS, DORIA A.**

| | | |
|---|---|---|
| *Deirdre of the Sorrows* | Hughes, C. | 1997 |

**PHILLIPS, ALBERTA**

| | | |
|---|---|---|
| *Don't We All?* | Phillips, B. | 1949 |

**PHILLIPS, EDWARD (fl. 1730–1740)**

| | | |
|---|---|---|
| *Britons, Strike Home* | ** | 1739 |
| *Chamber-Maid, The* | ** | 1730 |
| *Livery Rake* | ** | 1733 |
| *Mock Lawyer* | ** | 1733 |

**PHILLIPS, JOHN MICHAEL**

| | | |
|---|---|---|
| *Tailor of Gloucester* (with comp.) | Young, D. | 1991* |

**PHILLIPS, LORENE**

| | | |
|---|---|---|
| *Sopranos!* (with comp.) | Sisco, D. | 2002 |

**PHILLIPS, PHILIP**

| | | |
|---|---|---|
| *Trevallion* (with M. Morley) | Phillips, R. | 1956 |

**PHILLIPS, THOMAS**

| | | |
|---|---|---|
| *Britannia* | Arne, T. A. | 1734 |
| *Rival Captains* | ** | 1736 |

**PHILLIPS, TOM (b. 1937)**

| | | |
|---|---|---|
| *Heart of Darkness* | O'Regan | 2006 |

**PIATIGORSKY, ANTON (b. 1972)**

| | | |
|---|---|---|
| *Airline Icarus* | Current, B. | 2006 |
| *Inventory* | Current, B. | 2006 |

**PICKARD, TOM**

| | | |
|---|---|---|
| *Ballad of Jamie Allan* | Harle, J. | 2005 |

**PICKMAN, HESTER**

| | | |
|---|---|---|
| *Pot of Fat* | Chanler, T. | 1955 |

**PICKTHALL, MARJORIE L. C. (1883–1922)**

| | | |
|---|---|---|
| *Woodcarver's Wife* | Betts, L. | 1960* |

**PIGUENIT, D. G.**

| | | |
|---|---|---|
| *Don Quixote* | Arnold, S. | 1774 |

**PILON, FREDERICK (1750–1788)**

| | | |
|---|---|---|
| *Fair American* | Carter, T. | 1782 |
| *Siege of Gibraltar* | Shield, W. | 1780 |

**PINCKNEY, DARRYL (b. 1935)**

| | | |
|---|---|---|
| *Forest, The* (with H. Müller) | Byrne, D. | 1988 |
| *Time Rocker* | Reed, L. | 1997 |

**PINERO, ARTHUR WING (1855–1934)**

| | | |
|---|---|---|
| *Beauty Stone* | Sullivan, A. S. | 1898 |

**PINSKY, ROBERT**

| | | |
|---|---|---|
| *Death and the Powers* | Machover, T. | 2010 |

**PIPER, MYFANWY (1911–1996)**

| | | |
|---|---|---|
| *Death in Venice* | Britten, B. | 1973 |
| *Owen Wingrave* | Britten, B. | 1971 |
| *Rajah's Diamond* | Hoddinott, A. | 1979 |
| *Trumpet Major* | Hoddinott, A. | 1981 |
| *Turn of the Screw* | Britten, B. | 1954 |

**PIZZATO, MARK (b. 1960)**

| | | |
|---|---|---|
| *Processions* | Callahan, J. | 1996 |

**PLAICE, STEPHEN (b. 1951)**

| | | |
|---|---|---|
| *Finnish Prisoner* | Gough, O. | 2007 |
| *Io Passion* | Birtwistle, H. | 2004 |
| *Misper* | Lunn, J. | 1997 |
| *Tangier Tattoo* | Lunn, J. | 2005 |
| *Zoë* | Lunn, J. | 2000 |

**PLANCHÉ, JAMES ROBINSON (1796–1880)**

| | | |
|---|---|---|
| *Amoroso* | Cooke, T. S. | 1818 |
| *Child of the Wreck* | Cooke, T. S. | 1837 |
| *Cortez* | Bishop, H. R. | 1823 |
| *Court Masque* | Dawes, W. | 1833 |
| *Drama at Home* | Reed, T. G. | 1844 |
| *Follies of a Night* | Gabriel, V. | ca. 1860 |
| *Fortunate Isles* | Bishop, H. R. | 1840 |
| *Frozen Lake* | Reeve, G. W. | 1824 |
| *Golden Fleece* | Reed, T. G. | 1845 |
| *Graciosa and Percinet* | ** | 1845 |
| *Hofer* | Bishop, H. R. | 1830 |
| *Jewess, The* | Cooke, T. | 1835 |
| *Law versus Love* | Linley, G. | 1862 |
| *Lilla* | ** | 1825 |
| *Love Charm* | Bishop, H. R. | 1831 |
| *Love's Triumph* | Wallace, V. | 1862 |
| *Maid Marian* | Bishop, H. R. | 1822 |
| *Mason of Buda* | Rodwell, G. | 1828 |
| *Oberon* | Weber, C. M. | 1826 |
| *Pay to My Order* (with Armstrong) | Horn, C. E. | 1827 |

| | | |
|---|---|---|
| *Red Mask* | Cooke, T. S. | 1834 |
| *Rencontre, The* | Bishop, H. R. | 1827 |
| *Romance of a Day* | Bishop, H. R. | 1831 |
| *Siege of Corinth* | Cooke, T. S. | 1836 |

PLATT, JOHANNA

| | | |
|---|---|---|
| *Angelo* (with N. Platt) | Ridout, A. | 1971 |
| *Cat, The* (with N. Platt) | Ridout, A. | 1971 |
| *Dr. Syn* | Cruft, A. | 1983 |
| *Eatanswill Election* | Cruft, A. | 1981 |
| *Selfish Giant* | Ridout, A. | 1977 |

PLATT, MARTIN

| | | |
|---|---|---|
| *Cio Cio San* | Carroll, B. | 2005 |

PLATT, NORMAN (1920–2004)

| | | |
|---|---|---|
| *Angelo* (with J. Platt) | Ridout, A. | 1971 |
| *Cat, The* (with J. Platt) | Ridout, A. | 1971 |
| *Falcon, The* | Cole, H. | 1968 |
| *Pardoner's Tale* | Ridout, A. | 1971 |

PLAYFAIR, JACK

| | | |
|---|---|---|
| *Dr. Jekyll and Mr. Hyde* | Cannon, P. | 1973 |

PLOMER WILLIAM (1913–1976)

| | | |
|---|---|---|
| *Burning Fiery Furnace* | Britten, B. | 1966 |
| *Curlew River* | Britten, B. | 1964 |
| *Gloriana* | Britten, B. | 1953 |
| *Prodigal Son* | Britten, B. | 1968 |

PLOTKIN, CARY

| | | |
|---|---|---|
| *My Kinsman* | Saylor, B. | 1976 |

PLOTWELL, JOAN (pseud.)

| | | |
|---|---|---|
| *Ragged Uproar* | ** | 1754 |

PLOWDEN, FRANCES (Mrs.) (d. 1827)

| | | |
|---|---|---|
| *Virginia* | Arnold, S. | 1800 |

POCH-GOLDIN, ALEX

| | | |
|---|---|---|
| *Stranger, The* | Daniel, O. | 2009 |

POCOCK, ISAAC (1782–1835)

| | | |
|---|---|---|
| *Antiquary, The* (with D. Terry) | Bishop, H. R. | 1820 |
| *Doom-Kiss, The* | Bishop, H. R. | 1832 |
| *For England, Ho!* | Bishop, H. R. | 1813 |
| *Harry le Roi* | Bishop, H. R. | 1813 |
| *Heir of Vironi* | Bishop, H. R. | 1817 |
| *Hit or Miss!* | Smith, C. | 1810 |
| *Home Sweet Home* | Bishop, H. R. | 1829 |
| *John of Paris* | Bishop, H. R. | 1814 |
| *Libertine, The* | Bishop, H. R. | 1817 |
| *Magpie or Maid* | Bishop, H. R. | 1815 |
| *Miller and His Men* | Bishop, H. R. | 1813 |
| *Montrose* | Bishop, H. R. | 1822 |
| *Peveril of the Peak* | Horn, C. E. | 1826 |
| *Rob Roy MacGregor* | Davy, J. | 1818 |

POGUE, KATE (b. 1940)

| | | |
|---|---|---|
| *Cinderella in Spain* | Warwick, M. C. | 1998 |
| *Emperor's New Clothes* | Warwick, M. C. | 2001 |
| *Flight of Eagles* | Tinsley, S. | 1985 |
| *Man Who Corrupted Hadleyville* | Nelson, R. | 1986* |
| *Mask of Evil* | Mollicone, H. | 1982 |
| *Starbird, The* | Mollicone, H. | 1979 |

POLLOCK, ALICE L.

| | | |
|---|---|---|
| *Cleopatra's Night* | Hadley, H. | 1920 |

POLLON, MICHAEL

| | | |
|---|---|---|
| *Judgment Day* | Berl, P. | 1951 |

PONS, G.

| | | |
|---|---|---|
| *Cinderella* | Lacy, M. R. | 1830 |

POOLE, JOHN (1786?–1872)

| | | |
|---|---|---|
| *Hamlet Travestie* | Bray, J. | 1811 |

PORTAL, ABRAHAM (1726–1809)

| | | |
|---|---|---|
| *Cady of Bagdad* | Linley, T., Jr. | 1778 |

PORTER, ANDREW (b. 1928)

| | | |
|---|---|---|
| *Emperor's New Clothes* | Sessions, R. | 1984* |
| *Song of Majnun* | Sheng, B. | 1992 |
| *Tempest, The* | Eaton, J. | 1985 |

PORTER, DOROTHY FEATHERSTONE (1954–2008)

| | | |
|---|---|---|
| *Eternity Man* | Mills, J. | 2003 |
| *Ghost Wife* | Mills, J. | 1999 |

PORTER, PETER (1929–2010)

| | | |
|---|---|---|
| *Orpheus* | Burgon, G. | 1982 |
| *Wolf of Gubbio* | Senator, R. | 1980 |

PORTER, RUSSELL

| | | |
|---|---|---|
| *Early Dawn* | Lockwood, N. | 1961 |
| *Hanging Judge* | Lockwood, N. | 1964 |

PORTMAN, GORDON

| | | |
|---|---|---|
| *Cassandra* | McAndrew, I. | 2003 |

POTTER, HENRY

| | | |
|---|---|---|
| *Decoy, The* | ** | 1733 |

POTTER, JOHN (fl. 1754–1804)

| | | |
|---|---|---|
| *Choice of Apollo* | Yates, W. | 1765 |

POUNTNEY, DAVID (b. 1947)

| | | |
|---|---|---|
| *Angel Magick* | Harle, J. | 1998 |
| *Doctor of Myddfai* | Davies, P. M. | 1996 |
| *Donkey, The* | Oliver, S. | 1973 |
| *Three Wise Monkeys* | Oliver, S. | 1971* |

POWELL, GEORGE (1658?–1714)

| | | |
|---|---|---|
| *Brutus of Alba* | Purcell, D. | 1696 |
| (prob. librettist, with J. Verbruggen) | | |

POWELL, (Mrs.) H. W.

| | | |
|---|---|---|
| *All in a Garden Fair* | Tonning, G. | 1913 |

POWELL, MARILYN

| | | |
|---|---|---|
| *Nosferatu* | Peters, R. | 1993 |

PRATT, WILLIAM W. (1821–1864)

| | | |
|---|---|---|
| *Ten Nights in a Bar-Room* | ** | 1858 |

PRIDHAM, ROBERT

| | | |
|---|---|---|
| *Scarlet Letter* | Svane, S. | 1995* |

PRIESTLY, JOHN BOYNTON (1894–1984)

| | | |
|---|---|---|
| *Olympians, The* | Bliss, A. | 1949 |

PRUSLIN, STEPHEN

| | | |
|---|---|---|
| *Craig's Progress* | Butler, M. | 1994 |
| *Punch and Judy* | Birtwistle, H. | 1968 |

PRYCE, RICHARD (1864–1942)

| | | |
|---|---|---|
| *Samuel Pepys* (with W. P. Drury) | Coates, A. | 1929 |

PRYCE-JONES, ALAN (1908–2000)

| | | |
|---|---|---|
| *Nelson* | Berkeley, L. | 1954 |

PRYOR, MARY ANNE (b. 1926)

| | | |
|---|---|---|
| *Intruder, The* | Starer, R. | 1956 |

PURSER, J. W. R.

| | | |
|---|---|---|
| *Bell, The* | Purser, J. | 1972 |

QUINN, TERRY (b. 1945)

| | | |
|---|---|---|
| *Hester Prynne at Death* (with comp.) | Paulus, S. | 2004 |

RAAB, VICKI

| | | |
|---|---|---|
| *Magic Fishbone* (with Elliot, Mark) | Chapin, T | 1988 |

RABINOWITZ, ANNA (b. 1933)

| | | |
|---|---|---|
| *Darkling* | Weisman, S. | 2006 |

RACE, GARY

| | | |
|---|---|---|
| *Angels' Voices* | Ain, N. | 1996 |

RADFORD, MAISIE

| | | |
|---|---|---|
| *Morvoren* | Cannon, P. | 1964 |

RADFORD, WINIFRED

| | | |
|---|---|---|
| *Ten O'Clock Call* | Hopkins, A. | 1956 |

RADIC, LEONARD (b. 1935)

| | | |
|---|---|---|
| *Affair, The* | Werder, F. | 1974 |
| *Bellyful* | Werder, F. | 1975 |
| *General, The* | Werder, F. | 1966 |

RADICE, WILLIAM (b. 1951)

| | | |
|---|---|---|
| *Snatched by the Gods* | Vir, P. | 1992 |

RAFFO, HEATHER (b. 1970)

| | | |
|---|---|---|
| *Armide* | Dawe, J. | 2009 |

RAFTER, CAPTAIN

| | | |
|---|---|---|
| *Heart of Midlothian* | ** | 1849 |

RAINE, CRAIG

| | | |
|---|---|---|
| *Electrification of the Soviet Union* | Osborne, N. | 1987 |
| *Sarajevo* | Osborne, N. | 1994 |

RALPH, JAMES (d. 1762)

| | | |
|---|---|---|
| *Fashionable Lady* | ** | 1730 |

RAMSAY, ALLAN (1686–1758)

| | | |
|---|---|---|
| *Gentle Shepherd* | ** | 1729 |

RAMSEY, JAROLD (b. 1937)

| | | |
|---|---|---|
| *Lodge of Shadows* | Adler, S. | 1988 |

RANDAL, JUDITH

| | | |
|---|---|---|
| *Babar the Elephant* (with D. H. Heyward) | Berezowsky, N. | 1953 |

RANDALL, JOHN (fl. 1732)

| | | |
|---|---|---|
| *Disappointment, The* | ** | 1732 |

RANDALL-MILLS, ELIZABETH

| | | |
|---|---|---|
| *Anachronism, The* | Franchetti, A. | 1956 |
| *Dowser, The* | Franchetti, A. | 1956 |
| *Princess, The* | Franchetti, A. | 1952 |

RANDEGGER, ALBERTO (1832–1911)

| | | |
|---|---|---|
| *Esmeralda* (with Marzials) | Thomas, A. G. | 1883 |

RANDICH, JEAN

| | | |
|---|---|---|
| *Miraculous Phonograph Record* (with comp.) | White, C. | 1997 |

RANKEN, FREDERIC

| | | |
|---|---|---|
| *Ameer, The* (with K. La Shelle) | Herbert, V. | 1899 |
| *Nancy Brown* (with G. Broadhurst) | Hadley, H. | 1903 |

RATHKEY, W. A.

| | | |
|---|---|---|
| *Mary Barton* | Cooke, A. | 1954* |

RATNER, CARL J.

| | | |
|---|---|---|
| *Lifework of Juan Diaz* | Rapchak, L. | 1990 |

RAWLENCE, CHRISTOPHER (b. 1945)

| | | |
|---|---|---|
| *King of Hearts* | Torke, M. | 1995 |
| *Man Who Mistook His Wife* | Nyman, M. | 1986 |

RAYMOND, BILL

| | | |
|---|---|---|
| *VALIS* (with C. Ikam, comp.) | Machover, T. | 1987 |

RAYMOND, RICHARD J.

| | | |
|---|---|---|
| *Robert the Devil* | Barnett, J. | 1830 |

REANEY, JAMES (b. 1952)

| | | |
|---|---|---|
| *Crazy to Kill* | Beckwith, J. | 1989 |
| *Night Blooming Cereus* | Beckwith, J. | 1959 |
| *Serinette* | Somers, H. | 1990 |
| *Shivaree* | Beckwith, J. | 1982 |
| *Taptoo!* | Beckwith, J. | 1999 |

REARDON, WILLIAM A.

| | | |
|---|---|---|
| *Stranger in Eden* | Bezanson, P. | 1963* |

REAVEY, JEAN

| | | |
|---|---|---|
| *Who Stole the American Crown Jewels?* | Siegel, N. | 1971 |

REDDING, JOSEPH D. (1859–1924)

| | | |
|---|---|---|
| *Atonement of Pan* | Hadley, H. | 1912 |
| *Natoma* | Herbert, V. | 1911 |
| *Semper virens* | Hadley, H. | 1923 |

REDICAN, DAN

| | | |
|---|---|---|
| *Burnt Toast* | Louie, A. | 2006 |

REDLICH, HANS FERDINAND, trans. (1903–1968)

| | | |
|---|---|---|
| *Lucedia* | Giannini, V. | 1934 |

REECE, ROBERT (1838–1891)

| | | |
|---|---|---|
| *Castle Grim* | Allen, G. B. | 1865 |
| *Cattarina* | Clay, F. | 1874 |
| *In Possession* | Clay, F. | 1871 |
| *Wicklow Rose* | Allen G. B. | 1882 |

REED, ISHMAEL (b. 1938)

| | | |
|---|---|---|
| *Gethsemane Park* | Moore, C. | 1999 |

REED, JOSEPH (1723–1787)

| | | |
|---|---|---|
| *Tom Jones* | Arnold, S. | 1769 |

REED, STUART

| | | |
|---|---|---|
| *Cyrano de Bergerac* | Herbert, V. | 1899 |

REESE, H.

| | | |
|---|---|---|
| *Primal Void* (with comp.) | Vincent, J. | 1973 |

REGAN, SYLVIA

| | | |
|---|---|---|
| *Golem, The* (with comp.) | Ellstein, A. | 1962 |

REID, ALASTAIR (b. 1926)

| | | |
|---|---|---|
| *Curious Fern* | Kupferman, M. | 1957 |
| *Gilded Cage* | Lees, B. | 1964 |
| *Griffelkin* | Foss, L. | 1955 |
| *Voices for a Mirror* | Kupferman, M. | 1957 |

REID, HARRY
 *Wedding, The*   Wilson, J.  2003
REID, JOHN (b. 1915)
 *Lost Child*   Ridout, G.  1976
REITER, SEYMOUR
 *Cask of Amontillado*  Provenzano, A. 1968
REITH, GEORGE MURRAY (b. 1863)
 *Weird of Colbar*  Moonie, W. B. 1937
REMSON, MICHAEL (b. 1962)
 *Breath of Life*  Frazier, J.  2008
RENARD, JOSEPH
 *Pizza del destino*  Cohen, S.  1979*
RESTON, JAMES, Jr. (b. 1941)
 *Reverend Jim*  Eaton, J.  1989
REYNOLDS, ANNA
 *Push!*   Bruce, D.  2006
REYNOLDS, FREDERICK (1764–1841)
 *Bridal Ring*  Condell/Pelissier 1812
 *Burgomaster of Saardam* Bishop, H. R. 1818
 *Caravan*   Reeve, W.  1803
 *Comedy of Errors*  Bishop, H. R. 1819
 *Crusade, The*  Shield, W.  1790
 *Don John*   Bishop, H. R. 1821
 *Duke of Savoy*  Bishop, H. R. 1817
 *Exile, The*   Mazzinghi, J. 1809
 *Free Knights*  Mazzinghi, J. 1810
 *Humorous Lieutenant* Bishop, H. R. 1817
 *Illustrious Traveller*  **   1818
 *Merry Wives of Windsor* Horn et al.  1824
 *Midsummer Night's Dream* Bishop, H. R. 1816
 *Taming of the Shrew* Braham/Cooke 1828
 *Virgin of the Sun*  Bishop, H. R. 1812
REYNOLDS, G[EORGE] N[UGENT] (1770–1802)
 *Bantry Bay*   Reeve, W.  1797
REYNOLDS-ANDERSON, J. F.
 *Victorian*   Edwards, J.  1883
RHEIN, EDWARD
 *It Began at Breakfast* (with M. Zara) Elmore, R. 1941
RHODES, NANCY
 *Glass Woman*  Hays, S.  1989
RICE, CALE YOUNG (1872–1942)
 *Yolanda of Cyprus*  Loomis, C.  1929
RICE, ELMER (1892–1967)
 *Street Scene* (with L. Hughes) Weill, K.  1946
RICE, TIM (b. 1944)
 *Evita*   Lloyd Webber 1978
 *Jesus Christ Superstar* Lloyd Webber 1971
RICHARDS, M. C.
 *Chanticleer*  Barab, S.  1956
RICHARDS, Mr.
 *Device, The*  Bates, W.  1777

RICHARDSON, HOWARD
 *Dream Child*  Mollicone, H. 1975
RIDER, SUE
 *Iron Man* (with J. Vilé) Fox, M.  1987
 *Silence Tree*  Fox, M.  1989
 *Zoggy* (with J. Vilé) Fox, M.  1987
RIDLER, ANNE (1912–2001)
 *Departure, The*  Maconchy, E. 1962
 *Jesse Tree*   Maconchy, E. 1970
RIENIETS, ANDREA
 *Undertow*   Kats-Chernin, E. 2004
RILEY, EDWARD (1769–1829)
 *Spanish Patriots*  Gilfert, C.  1809
RILEY, MICHAEL
 *Gwyneth and the Green Knight* Plowman, L. 2002
ROACH, BARRY
 *Once upon a Moon*  Victory, G.  1950
ROBBINS, MARTIN
 *Silence Bottle*  Yannatos, J.  1972*
ROBERTS, DON (b. 1925)
 *Captive, The*  Wishart, P.  1960
 *Clandestine Marriage* Wishart, P.  1971
 *Clytemnestra*  Wishart, P.  1974
 *Lady of the Inn*  Wishart, P.  1983
 *Two in the Bush*  Wishart, P.  1959
ROBERTS, JAMES (fl. 1794)
 *Rule Britannia*  Arnold, S.  1794
ROBERTS, MICHAEL SYMMONS (b. 1963)
 *Sacrifice, The*  MacMillan, J. 2007
ROBERTSON, THOMAS WILLIAM (1829–1871)
 *Constance*   Clay, F.  1865
ROBERTSON, TIM (b. 1944)
 *Lamentable Reign*  Dreyfus, G.  1976
ROBINETTE, JOSEPH
 *Jungle Book*  Swensson, E.  1996
ROBINSON, ARTHUR (1894–1972)
 *Gettysburg*  Ruger, M. H.  1938
ROBINSON, THOMAS P.
 *Fantasy in Delft*  Gilbert, H. F. 1919
RODDA, CHARLES (b. 1891)
 *Marriage of Aude*  Rogers, B.  1931
RODDICK, PAUL (b. 1922)
 *Evangeline* (with D. Warren) George, G. 1948
RODGERS, JAMES W.
 *River of Time*  Baber, J.  2009
RODGERS, LOU (b. 1936)
 *Island of Tomorrow*  Fink, M.  1986
 *Shadows of the City* (lib with comp, A. Samtur) Bo, T. 2010
RODGERS, WILLIAM ROBERT (1909–1969)
 *Pit, The*   Lutyens, E.  1947

RODRIGUEZ, JUDITH
*Lindy* (with comp.) — Henderson, M. — 2002

ROEPKE, GABRIELA
*Tempest, The* — Leichtling, A. — 1973*
*White Butterfly* (trans. A. Patterson) — Leichtling, A. — 1971
*Zapata* (with T. Capobianco) — Balada, L. — 1985

ROGERS, ALEX
*Abyssinia* (with Shipp) — Cook/Williams — 1906

ROGERS, JOHN WILLIAM
*Stranger of Manzano* — Smith, J. — 1947

ROGERS, RONALD
*Flowers of Ice* — Pasatieri, T. — 1964*

ROLL, PHILIP
*Blennerhasset* (with N. Corwin) — Giannini, V. — 1939

ROLT, RICHARD (1725?–1770)
*Almena* — Arne, M. — 1764
*Amintas* (with F. Tenducci) — Arnold, S. — 1769
*Eliza* — Arne, T. A. — 1754
*Royal Shepherd* — Rush, G. — 1764

ROOME, EDWARD (d. 1729)
*Jovial Crew* — ** — 1731

ROOT, LYNN (b. 1905)
*Cabin in the Sky* (with J. Latouche) — Duke, V. — 1940

RORKE, PETER (1928–1998)
*Private, The* — Werder, F. — 1970
*Vicious Square* — Werder, F. — 1971

ROSE, JOHN (b. 1754)
*Caernarvon Castle* — Attwood, T. — 1793
*Fairy Festival* — Attwood, T. — 1797
*Prisoner, The* — Attwood, T. — 1792

ROSE, PHYLLIS (b. 1942)
*Travels of Babar* — Mostel, R. — 2000

ROSEN, ROSLYN
*Fisherman's Wife* — Stein, L. — 1955

ROSENAU, ANITA
*Guinevere* — Williams, J. — 1989

ROSKAM, CLAIR
*Sarah* — Laderman, E. — 1958

ROSS, ADEN
*Dreamkeepers* — Carlson, D. — 1996

ROSS, ADRIAN (1859–1933)
*Lucky Star* (with A. Hoppwood) — Caryll, I. — 1899
*San Toy* (with Morton, Greenbank) — Jones, S. — 1899

ROSS, BUCK
*Room with a View* — Nelson, R. — 1993

ROSS, GEORGE M.
*Boccaccio's Nightingale* — Trimble, L. — 1958

ROSS, MURRAY (b. 1942)
*Last Night of Don Juan* — Rodrîguez, R. — 2000

ROSS, SHERIDAN
*Crichton* — Maclean, A. — 1892*

*King's Prize* — Maclean, A. — 1904
*Quentin Durward* — Maclean, A. — 1893

ROSTEN, NORMAN (1913–1995)
*Marilyn* — Laderman, E. — 1993
*Marquesa of O* — Siegmeister, E. — 1982
*Shadows among Us* — Laderman, E. — 1967

ROUDEBUSH, RICKARD (b. 1948)
*First Lady* (comp. et al.) — Wells, K. — 2010

ROVER, THOMAS DOMINIC (b. 1920)
*Dolcedo* — Meyers, E. — 1959

ROWELL, GEORGE
*Engaged* — Mobbs-Sullivan — 1962

ROYLE, J[OHN] F[ORBES] (1799–1858)
*Gooseherd and the Goblin* — Smith, J. — 1947

RUDALL, NICHOLAS
*Antigone* — Eaton, J. — 1999

RUDKIN, DAVID (b. 1936)
*Broken Strings* — Vir, P. — 1992
*Grace of Todd* — Crosse, G. — 1969
*Inquest of Love* (with comp.) — Harvey, J. — 1993

RUSSELL, SANDRA
*Informer, The* — Legg, J. — 1985

RUSSO, GLORIA
*Follies and Fancies* — Allen, J. S. — 1987

RYAN, ALLISON
*Inferno* — Soluri, P. — 1999

RYAN, LACY (1694?–1760)
*Cobler's Opera* — ** — 1728

RYVES, ELIZABETH (1750–1797)
*Prude, The* — ** — 1765

SACCO, MARIE ALESSI
*Mr. Vinegar* (with comp.) — Sacco, P. — 1967

SALOMON, ROBERT
*Frog-Hopping* — Boswell, W. — 1982

SALT, WALDO (1914–1987)
*Sandhog* — Robinson, E. — 1954

SALZMAN, EVA (b. 1960)
*Hollow Hill* (with comp.) — McQueen, I. — 2005

SAMSON, FREDERIC
*Marko the Miser* (with comp.) — Musgrave, T. — 1963

SAMPSON, JOANNA
*Columbine* — Davis, M. — 1973

SAMTUR, ADAM
*Shadows of the City* (lib with comp, L. Rodgers) — Bo, T. — 2010

SAMUELSEN, ERIC
*Emma* — Boren, M. — 1984

SAND, GEORGE A.
*Trojan Women* — Goldstaub, P. — 1986

SANDERSON, RUTH HOWARD
*Lion, The* (with comp.) — Franchetti, A. — 1950

SARGENT, BARBARA
*Suncatcher, The* — Franchetti, A. — 1973

SAUNDERS, JAMES (b. 1925)
*Barnstable* — Burt, F. — 1969

SAVAGE, ROGER (b. 1941)
*Mellstock Quire* — Harper, E. — 1988

SAVILLE, JOHN FAUCIT [JOHN S. FAUCIT] (1783–1853)
*Justice* — Horne, C. E. — 1820

SAWYER, RUTH (1880–1970)
*Princess and the Vagabond* — Freed, I. — 1948

SCANLON, MARIE C.
*Shoe of Little Noby* — Gordon, P. — 1957
*Tale from Chaucer* — Gordon, P. — 1959

SCANNELL, VERNON
*Cancelling Dark* — Whelen, C. — 1965

SCAWEN, JOHN (fl. 1733–1790)
*New Spain* — Arnold, S. — 1790

SCHEER, GENE (b. 1958)
*American Tragedy* — Picker, T. — 2005
*For a Look or a Touch* — Heggie, J. — 2007
*Last Acts* — Heggie, J. — 2008
*Moby-Dick* — Heggie, J. — 2010
*Star Gatherer* — Paulus, S. — 2006
*Thérèse Raquin* — Picker, T. — 2001
*To Hell and Back* — Heggie, J. — 2006

SCHEVILL, JAMES (1920–2009)
*This Is Not True* — McIntyre, P. — 1966*

SCHILLER, ZOË LUND
*Acres of Sky* — Kreutz, A. — 1951
*Sourwood Mountain* — Kreutz, A. — 1959
*University Greys* — Kreutz, A. — 1954

SCHLESINGER, SARAH MARIE (b. 1941)
*Amazing Adventure* — Adolphe, B. — 1995
*Different Fields* — Reid, M. — 1996
*Epilogue* — Dansicker, M. — 1980*

SCHMIDT, PAUL (b. 1934)
*Alice* — Waits, T. — 1992
*Black Sea Follies* — Silverman, S. — 1986

SCHMIDT, RICHARD P.
*We're Back* — Armour, E. — 1981

SEARS, JOE
*Ochelata's Wedding* (with Williams) — Damase, J.-M. — 2000

SEATON, MAUREEN (b. 1947)
*Bee Opera* (lib with comp. et al.) — Hays, S. — 2003

SEIDEL, MIRIAM
*Violet Fire* — Gibson, J. — 2006

SELBY, CHARLES (1802?–1863)
*Fairy Lake* — Lee, G. A. — 1839

SELIG, PAUL
*Three Visitations* — Sherman, K. D. — 1996

SELLARS, PETER (b. 1957)
*Doctor Atomic* — Adams, J. — 2005

SELWYN, DAVID (b. 1951)
*Rumpelstiltskin* — Bourgeois, D. — 1974
*St. Patrick* — Warren, R. — 1979

SENDAK, MAURICE (1928–20012)
*Higglety Pigglety Pop!* (with comp.) — Knussen, O. — 1984

SERLE, THOMAS JAMES (1798–1889)
*Afrancesado* — Lee, G. A. — 1837
*Foresters, The* — Loder, E. — *1838*
*Shadow on the Wall* — Thomson, J. — 1835

SERVOSS, FIFI
*Bok Choy Variations* (with Huff, Simonson) — Chen, E. — 1995

SETTLE, ELKANAH (1648–1724)
*Fairy Queen* (possib.) — Purcell, H. — 1692
*Lady's Triumph* — ** — 1718
*Orpheus and Euridice* — Locke, M. — 1673
*Virgin Prophetess* — Finger, G. — 1701
*World in the Moon* — Purcell, Clarke — 1697

SEXTON, ANNE (1928–1974)
*Transformations* — Susa, C. — 1973

SHADWELL, THOMAS (1642–1692)
*Psyche* — Locke, M. — 1675
*Tempest, The* (with Dryden) — Arne, T. A. — 1746
*Tempest, The* — Banister, Locke, et al. — 1674
*Tempest, The* (with Davenant, Dryden) — Weldon, J. — 1712

SHAFFER, PETER (b. 1926)
*Dumb Wife* — Horovitz, J. — 1953

SHANKS, EDWARD (1892–1953)
*Fête Galante* (with comp.) — Smyth, E. — 1923

SHAPCOTT, THOMAS (b. 1935)
*Seven Deadly Sins* — Brumby, C. — 1970
*Summer Carol* — Brumby, C. — 1991

SHAPIRO, DAVID (b. 1947)
*Funeral of Jan Palach* — Beckley, C. — 1990

SHAPIRO, KARL (1913–2000)
*Tenor, The* (with Lert) — Weisgall, H. — 1952

SHAPLI, OMAR
*This Evening* — Sirulnikoff, J. — 1960

SHARP, EVELYN (1869–1955)
*Loafer and the Loaf* — Clarke, H. L. — 1956
*Poisoned Kiss* — Vaughan Williams, R. — 1936

SHARP, JOAN
*Lord Bateman* — Forster, A. — 1958

SHATZKY, JOEL (b. 1943)
*Birthday of the Bank* (with comp.) — Lehrman, L. — 1988

SHAW, BARNETT
*Romulus* — Karchin, L. — 2007

SHAW, CLEMENT B.
*Frithiof* — Freer, E. E. — 1929

SHAW, ROBERT B.
*Bontshe the Silent* — Sirota, R. — 1982

| | | |
|---|---|---|
| **SHAW, SEBASTIAN** | | |
| *All at Sea* (with M. Delamere) | Shaw, G. | 1952 |
| **SHAWN, WALLACE** (b. 1943) | | |
| *Music Teacher* | Shawn, A. | 2006 |
| **SHEELEY, NELSON** | | |
| *Stranger's Tale* | Tucker, C. | 2005 |
| **SHEFFER, ISAIAH** | | |
| *More Perfect Union* | Bond, V. | 2004 |
| **SHEPHERD, ESTHER** (b. 1899) | | |
| *Cowherd and the Sky Maiden* | Verrall, J. | 1952 |
| **SHERIDAN, RICHARD BRINSLEY** (1751–1816) | | |
| *Duenna, The* | Linley Jr./Linley Sr. | 1775 |
| *Pizzaro* | Kelly, M. | 1799 |
| **SHERRIN, NEAL** | | |
| *Little Beggars* (with C. Brahms) | Saunders, M. | 1958 |
| **SHIPP, JESSE A.** (1859–1934) | | |
| *Abyssinia* (with A. Rogers) | Cook, W. M. | 1906 |
| *In Dahomey* (with P. L. Dunbar) | Cook, W. M. | 1903 |
| **SHIRLEY, JAMES** (1596–1666) | | |
| *Cupid and Death* | Gibbons, C. | 1653 |
| *Triumph of Peace* | Lawes, W., et al. | 1634 |
| **SHIRLEY, WILLIAM** (fl. 1739–1780) | | |
| *Birth of Hercules* | Arne, T. A. | 1763 |
| **SHIRWEN, SUSAN** | | |
| *Holy Blood and Crescent Moon* | Copeland, S. | 1989 |
| **SHOMER, ENID** | | |
| *Pope Joan* | LeBaron, A. | 2000 |
| **SHOPTAW, JOHN** (b. 1949) | | |
| *Our American Cousin* | Sawyer, E. | 2008 |
| **SHRAGER, SIDNEY** | | |
| *Royal Auction* (with A. Chorney) | Kanitz, E | 1958 |
| **SHULGASSER, MARK** | | |
| *Bon Appétit!* | Hoiby, L. | 1989 |
| *Italian Lesson* | Hoiby, L. | 1982 |
| *Romeo and Juliet* | Hoiby, L. | 2000 |
| *Tempest, The* | Hoiby, L. | 1986 |
| **SHULMAN, DEBORAH** | | |
| *Emperor's New Clothes* (with comp.) | Bachlund, G. | 1994* |
| *Love Charm* | Bachlund, G. | 1994* |
| **SIAO [XIAO] YU** (b. 1894) | | |
| *Nymph and the Farmer* | Tcherepnin, A. | 1952 |
| **SIDDENS, PAUL** | | |
| *Triumph of Love* | Schmitz, A. | 2008 |
| **SIDDONS, HENRY** (1774–1815) | | |
| *Russian Imposter* | Addison, J. | 1809 |
| **SIENA, JAMES** | | |
| *Photo-Op* | Cummings, C. | 1990 |
| **SIGNAIGO, JOHN AUGUSTINE** (1835–1876) | | |
| *Vivandiere, The* | Hewitt, J. H. | 1863 |
| **SIMON, ROBERT A.** (1897–1981) | | |
| *Beauty and the Beast* | Giannini, V. | 1938 |
| *Enchanted Kiss* | Bennett, R. R. | 1945 |
| *Endymion* | Bennett, R. R. | 1927 |
| *Garrick* | Stoessel, A. | 1937 |
| *Maria Malibran* | Bennett, R. R. | 1935 |
| *Rehearsal Call* (with F. Swann) | Giannini, V. | 1962 |
| **SIMONSON, ERICK** | | |
| *Bok Choy Variations* (with Servoss, Huff) | Chen, E. | 1995 |
| **SIMPATICO, DAVID** | | |
| *Screams of Kitty Genovese* | Todd, W. | 2001 |
| **SIMPSON, HELEN** (b. 1957) | | |
| *Good Friday 1663* | Westbrook, M./ Westbrook, K. | 1995 |
| **SIMPSON, JOHN PALGRAVE** (1807–1887) | | |
| *Bianca* | Balfe, M. | 1860 |
| *Ida* | Leslie, H. | 1865 |
| *Letty* | Balfe, M. | 1871 |
| *Romance, The* | Leslie, H. | 1860 |
| **SIMS, G[EORGE] R[OBERT]** (1847–1922) | | |
| *Golden Ring* | Clay, F. | 1883 |
| *Merry Duchess* | Clay, F. | 1883 |
| **SINGER, RON** | | |
| *Rimshot* | Currie, R. | 1990 |
| **SKELTON, GEOFFREY** (b. 1916) | | |
| *Arden Must Die* (with E. Fried) | Goehr, A. | 1967 |
| **SKIPITARES, THEODORA** | | |
| *Body of Crime* (with comp.) | Greenhut, B. | 1996 |
| *Body of Crime II* (with comp.) | Greenhut, B. | 1999 |
| **SKOFIELD, JAMES** | | |
| *Dracula Diary* | Moran, R. | 1994 |
| *Night Passage* | Moran, R. | 1995 |
| **SLATER, MONTAGU** (1902–1956) | | |
| *Peter Grimes* | Britten, B. | 1945 |
| *Yerma* | Aplvor, D. | 1961 |
| **SLOBIN, MARK** (b. 1943) | | |
| *David's Violin* | Mogulesco, S. | 1976 |
| *Shloyme Gorgl* (with J., N. Slobin) | ** | 1978 |
| **SMITH, ALEXANDER McCALL**, trans. | | |
| *Sibanda* | Remson, M. | 2003 |
| **SMITH, CHARLES** (1749?–1824) | | |
| *Day at Rome* | Attwood, T. | 1798 |
| **SMITH, DEXTER** (1842?–1909) | | |
| *Uncle Tom's Cabin* | Tracy, G. | 1886 |
| **SMITH, ELIHU HUBBARD** (1771–1798) | | |
| *Edwin and Angelina* | Pelissier, V. | 1796 |
| **SMITH, GRADY** (b. 1937) | | |
| *Ring around Harlequin* | McKay, N. | 1965* |
| **SMITH, HAROLD WENDELL** (b. 1922) | | |
| *Command Performance* | Middleton, R. | 1961 |
| **SMITH, HARRY BACHE** (1860–1936) | | |
| *Begum, The* | De Koven, R. | 1887 |
| *Cyrano de Bergerac* | Herbert, V. | 1899 |
| *Don Quixote* | De Koven, R. | 1889 |

| | | |
|---|---|---|
| *Fortune Teller* | Herbert, V. | 1898 |
| *Foxy Quiller* | De Koven, R. | 1900 |
| *Free Lance* | Sousa, J. P. | 1905 |
| *Golden Butterfly* | De Koven, R. | 1908 |
| *Highwayman, The* | De Koven, R. | 1897 |
| *Idols' Eye* | Herbert, V. | 1897 |
| *Jupiter* | Edwards, J. | 1892 |
| *Maid Marian* | De Koven, R. | 1902 |
| *Mandarin, The* | De Koven, R. | 1896 |
| *Paris Doll* | De Koven, R. | 1897 |
| *Robin Hood* | De Koven, R. | 1891 |
| *Rob Roy* | De Koven, R. | 1894 |
| *Tzigane* | De Koven, R. | 1895 |
| *Viceroy, The* | Herbert, V. | 1900 |
| *Wedding Trip* (with F. De Gresac) | De Koven, R. | 1911 |

SMITH, MONICA

| | | |
|---|---|---|
| *Play of Mother Courage* | McCabe, J. | 1974 |

SMITH, SYDNEY GOODSIR (1915–1975)

| | | |
|---|---|---|
| *Full Circle* | Orr, R. | 1968 |

SMITH, URSULA

| | | |
|---|---|---|
| *Pamelia* (with L. Peavey) | Funk, E. | 1989 |

SMOLIN, PAULINE

| | | |
|---|---|---|
| *Judith* | Smith, D. | 1982 |

SMOLLETT, TOBIAS (1721–1771)

| | | |
|---|---|---|
| *Alceste* | Handel, G. F. | 1749 |

SMOLOVER, RAYMOND

| | | |
|---|---|---|
| *Chelm* | Strassburg, R. | 1955 |
| *Golem, The* | Weiner, L. | 1957 |
| *Isaac Levy* | Piket, F. | 1956 |

SNELL, GORDON

| | | |
|---|---|---|
| *Gentleman's Island* | Horovitz, J. | 1959 |
| *Hands across the Sky* | Hopkins, A. | 1959 |

SOANE, GEORGE (1790–1860

| | | |
|---|---|---|
| *Aladdin* | Bishop, H. R. | 1826 |
| *Faustus* | Bishop, H. R. | 1825 |
| *Freischütz, Der* | Bishop, H. R. | 1824 |
| *Masaniello* | Bishop, H. R. | 1825 |
| *Night Dancers* | Loder, E. J. | 1846 |

SOKOLSKI, THOM

| | | |
|---|---|---|
| *Artaud's Cane* | Egoyan et al. | 1994 |

SOLANO, BERNARDO

| | | |
|---|---|---|
| *El Greco* | Harper, W. | 1993 |
| *Hit and Run* | Abels, M. | 2001 |

SOMERS, HARRISON

| | | |
|---|---|---|
| *Pantomime* | Poùhe, J. | 1969 |

SORKIN, JOAN ROSS

| | | |
|---|---|---|
| *Strange Fruit* | Carter, C. | 2003 |

SOUTER, DAVID H. (1862–1935)

| | | |
|---|---|---|
| *Rajah of Shivapore* | Hill, A. | 1917 |

SOYINKA, WOLE (AKINWANDE OLUWOLE) (b. 1934)

| | | |
|---|---|---|
| *Scourge of Hyacinths* (with comp.) | León, T. | 1994 |

SPAETH, SIGMUND (1885–1965)

| | | |
|---|---|---|
| *Audition, The* | Kalmanoff, M. | 1968 |

SPEARE, FLORENCE LEWIS (1886–1965)

| | | |
|---|---|---|
| *Uzziah* | Freeman, H. L. | 1931* |

SPENCER, LILIAN WHITE (1987–1953)

| | | |
|---|---|---|
| *Sun Bride* | Skilton, D. | 1930 |

SPENDER, STEPHEN (1909–1995)

| | | |
|---|---|---|
| *Holy Devil* (with comp.) | Nabokov, N. | 1958 |

SPIRES, ELIZABETH

| | | |
|---|---|---|
| *Toussaint before the Spirits* (with comp., Bell) | Ruehr, E. | 2003 |

SQUIRE, ROGER

| | | |
|---|---|---|
| *Madame Jumel* | Wolf, A. | 1976 |

SQUIRE, WILLIAM BARCLAY (1855–1927)

| | | |
|---|---|---|
| *Veiled Prophet* | Stanford, C. | 1881 |

STAHL, IRWIN

| | | |
|---|---|---|
| *Red Rose and the Briar* | Mopper, I. | 1951 |

STALLINGS, LAURENCE

| | | |
|---|---|---|
| *Deep River* | Harling, W. F. | 1926 |

STAMBLER, BERNARD (1910–1994)

| | | |
|---|---|---|
| *Claudia Legare* | Ward, R. | 1978 |
| *Crucible, The* | Ward, R. | 1961 |
| *He Who Gets Slapped* | Ward, R. | 1956 |
| *Ines de Castro* | Pasatieri, T. | 1976 |
| *Lady from Colorado* | Ward, R. | 1964 |
| *Lady Kate* | Ward, R. | 1994 |
| *Scarecrow, The* | Turrin, J. | 1976* |
| *Servant of Two Masters* | Giannini, V. | 1967 |

STAMPFER, JUDITH

| | | |
|---|---|---|
| *Huckleberry Finn* (with comp.) | Overton, H. | 1971 |

STANFORD, ANN

| | | |
|---|---|---|
| *Lucky Dollar* | Kanitz, E. | 1958 |

STANGÉ, STANISLAUS (d. 1917)

| | | |
|---|---|---|
| *Brian Boru* | Edwards, J. | 1896 |
| *Dolly Varden* | Edwards, J. | 1901 |
| *Girls of Holland* | De Koven, R. | 1907 |
| *Goddess of Truth* | Edwards, J. | 1896 |
| *Madeline* | Edwards, J. | 1894 |
| *Patriot, The* | Edwards, J. | 1908 |

STAVIS, BARRIE

| | | |
|---|---|---|
| *Joe Hill* | Bush, A. | 1970 |

STAVITT, DAVID

| | | |
|---|---|---|
| *Welfare* | Pickett, L. | 1992 |

STEARNS, MARGARET B.

| | | |
|---|---|---|
| *Merchant and the Pauper* | Schoenfield, P. | 1999 |

STEEGMULLER, FRANCIS (1906–1994)

| | | |
|---|---|---|
| *Big Black Box* | Morgenstern, S. | 1968 |

STEIN, DONA LUONGO

| | | |
|---|---|---|
| *Sir Gawain and the Green Night* | Eastman, D. | 2000 |

STEIN, ELLIOTT (b. 1928)

| | | |
|---|---|---|
| *Childhood Miracle* | Rorem, N. | 1955 |

STEIN, GERTRUDE (1874–1946)

| | | |
|---|---|---|
| *Bee Opera* (lib with comp. et al.) | Hays, S. | 2003 |
| *Four Saints in Three Acts* | Thomson, V. | 1933 |
| *Mother of Us All* | Thomson, V. | 1947 |
| *Remember Him to Me* | Moran, R. | 1996* |

STEINBERG, ALAN

| | | |
|---|---|---|
| *Sailor-Boy and the Falcon* | Siskind, P. | 2006 |

STEPHENS, HENRY P.

| | | |
|---|---|---|
| *Lord Bateman* | Solomon, E. | 1882 |

STEPHENS, JAMES BRUNTON (1835-1902)

| | | |
|---|---|---|
| *Fayette* | Allen, G. | 1892 |

STEPHENS, NAN BAGBY

| | | |
|---|---|---|
| *Cabildo* | Beach, A. | 1932 |

STEPHENS, PETER JOHN (1912–2002)

| | | |
|---|---|---|
| *Godfather Death* | Meyerowitz, J. | 1961 |
| *Simoon* | Meyerowitz, J. | 1949 |

STEPHENSON, B. C. (BENJAMIN CHARLES) (d. 1906)

| | | |
|---|---|---|
| *Charity Begins at Home* | Cellier, A. | 1872 |
| *Doris* | Cellier, A. | 1889 |
| *Dorothy* | Cellier, A. | 1886 |
| *Golden Web* (with F. Corder) | Thomas, A. G. | 1893 |
| *Masque of Pandora* | Cellier, A. | 1881 |
| *On the March* (with C. Clay, Yardley) | Clay, F. | 1986 |
| *Out of Sight* | Clay, F. | 1860 |

STERN, RICHARD (b. 1928)

| | | |
|---|---|---|
| *Golk* | Eaton, J. | 1996 |

STEVENS, DAVID K. (1860–1946)

| | | |
|---|---|---|
| *Azora* | Hadley, H. | 1917 |
| *Love's Sacrifice* | Chadwick, G. | 1923 |
| *Padrone, The* | Chadwick, G. | 1912* |

STEVENS, GEORGE ALEXANDER (1710–1784)

| | | |
|---|---|---|
| *Court of Alexander* | Fisher, J. A. | 1770 |
| *Trip to Portsmouth* | Dibdin, C. | 1773 |

STEVENSON, JANET

| | | |
|---|---|---|
| *Lysistrata* | Clarke, H. | 1972* |

STEWART, GRANT (1871–1937)

| | | |
|---|---|---|
| *Bianca* | Hadley, H. | 1918 |
| *Madeleine* | Herbert, V. | 1914 |

STILGOE, RICHARD (b. 1943)

| | | |
|---|---|---|
| *Phantom of the Opera* (with comp.) | Lloyd Weber, A. | 1986 |

ST. JOHN, JOHN

| | | |
|---|---|---|
| *Island of St. Marguerite* | Shaw, T. | 1789 |

STOCALS, GARY

| | | |
|---|---|---|
| *Intruder, The* | Feldman, J. | 1984 |

STOKES, RICHARD L. (1882–1957)

| | | |
|---|---|---|
| *Merry Mount* | Hanson, H. | 1933 |
| *Music Robber* | Van Grove, I. | 1926 |

STOLZENBACH, NORMA F. (b. 1904)

| | | |
|---|---|---|
| *In the Name of Culture* | Bimboni, A. | 1949 |

STOPES, MARIE (1880–1958)

| | | |
|---|---|---|
| *Moon Maiden* | Boughton, R. | 1918 |
| *Sumida River* | Raybould, C. | 1916 |

STORR, CATHERINE

| | | |
|---|---|---|
| *Flax into Gold* | Cole, H. | 1966 |

STOW, RANDOLPH (b. 1935)

| | | |
|---|---|---|
| *Eight Songs for a Mad King* | Davies, P. M. | 1969 |
| *Miss Donnithorne's Maggot* | Davies, P. M. | 1974 |

STRAHAN, LYNNE (b. 1938)

| | | |
|---|---|---|
| *Gilt-Edged Kid* | Dreyfus, G. | 1976 |

STRAIGHT, MICHAEL

| | | |
|---|---|---|
| *Death of the Virgin* | Owen, R. | 1981 |

STRASFOGEL, IAN (b. 1940)

| | | |
|---|---|---|
| *Icarus* | Earls, P. | 1982 |

STRAWN, RICHARD

| | | |
|---|---|---|
| *Crimson Bird* | Enenbach, F. | 1979 |

STREET, RICHARD

| | | |
|---|---|---|
| *Black River* (with comp.) | Susa, C. | 1975 |
| *Love of Don Perlimplin* (with comp.) | Susa, C. | 1984 |

ST. ROMAIN, MADELEINE

| | | |
|---|---|---|
| *Juniper Tree* | Boury, R. | `990 |

STUART, CHARLES (fl. 1777–1791)

| | | |
|---|---|---|
| *Cobler of Castlebury* | Shield, W. | 1778 |
| *Gretna Green* (with J. O'Keeffe) | Arnold, S. | 1783 |

STUART, DONALD R.

| | | |
|---|---|---|
| *Earth Mother* (with comp.) | Penberthy, J. | 1959* |

STURGIS, JULIAN R. (1848–1904)

| | | |
|---|---|---|
| *Cricket on the Heart* | Mackenzie, A. | 1914 |
| *Ivanhoe* | Sullivan, A. S. | 1891 |
| *Much Ado about Nothing* | Stanford, C. | 1901 |
| *Nadeshda* | Thomas, A. G. | 1885 |

STURROCK, DONALD

| | | |
|---|---|---|
| *Fantastic Mr. Fox* | Picker, T. | 1998 |
| *Golden Ticket* | Ash, P. | 2010 |

SULLIVAN, ARTHUR S. (1842–1900)

| | | |
|---|---|---|
| *Happy Arcadia* | Clay, F. | 1872 |

SULLIVAN, M. J.

| | | |
|---|---|---|
| *Lalla Rookh* | Horn, C. E. | 1818 |

SUMMERS, OLIVER

| | | |
|---|---|---|
| *Zaida* | Lutz, M. | 1859 |

SUNDGAARD, ARNOLD (1909–2006)

| | | |
|---|---|---|
| *Cumberland Fair* | Wilder, A. | 1953 |
| *Down in the Valley* | Weill, K. | 1948 |
| *Gallantry* | Moore, D. | 1958 |
| *Giants in the Earth* | Moore, D. | 1951 |
| *Lowland Sea* | Wilder, A. | 1952 |
| *Opening, The* | Wilder, A. | 1969 |
| *Promised Valley* | Gates, C. M. | 1947 |
| *Sunday Excursion* | Wilder, A. | 1953 |
| *Truth about Windmills* | Wilder, A. | 1973 |

SUTHERLAND, DONALD (b. 1939)

| | | |
|---|---|---|
| *Cyrano de Bergerac* | Effinger, C. | 1968 |
| *Requiem for a Rich Young Man* | Lockwood, N. | 1964 |

SUTTON, VERN

| | | |
|---|---|---|
| *Christina Romana* | Larsen, L. | 1988 |
| *Tumbledown Dick* | Larsen, L. | 1980 |

SUTRO, ALFRED (1863–1933)
　　Death of Tintagiles　　　　Collingwood, L.　　1950
SVOBODA, TERESE
　　Wet　　　　　　　　　　LeBaron, A.　　　2005
SWAN, JON
　　Aesop's Fables　　　　　　Russo, W.　　　　1972
　　Shepherds' Christmas　　　　Russo, W.　　　　1979
SWANN, FRANCIS
　　Rehearsal Call (with R. A. Simon)　Giannini, V.　　1962
SWENSSON, EVELYN
　　Wind in the Willows　　　　Ritter, J.　　　　1997
SWIFT, BASIL
　　Virgin and the Fawn　　　　Zador, E.　　　　1964
SWIFT, DOROTHY ZACKRISSON (1928–1990)
　　Trial of Tender O'Shea　　　Swift, R.　　　　1964*
SWIFT, EDMUND LENTHAL (1777–1875)
　　Woman's Will　　　　　　Davy, J.　　　　1820
SWINEY, OWEN (ca. 1675–1754)
　　Pyrrus and Demetrius　　　　Haym, N.　　　　1708
SYNGE, J[OHN] M[ILLINGTON] (1871–1909)
　　Riders to the Sea　　　　　Betts, L.　　　　1955*
　　Riders to the Sea　　　　　Vaughan Williams, R.1937

TABER, EDWARD
　　Désirée　　　　　　　　Sousa, J. P.　　　1884
TAN, AMY (b. 1951)
　　Bonesetter's Daughter (with Korie)　Wallace, S.　　2008
TATE, GREG
　　Fresh Faust　　　　　　　Jenkins, L.　　　1994
TATE, NAHUM (1652–1715)
　　Dido and Aeneas　　　　　Purcell, H.　　ca. 1689
TAYLOR, BAYARD (1825–1878)
　　Faust　　　　　　　　　Becker, J. J.　　　1951
TAYLOR, CHARLES H.
　　My Lady Molly　　　　　　Jones, S.　　　　1903
　　　(with Jessop, Greenbank)
TAYLOR, TOM (1817–1880)
　　Court and Cottage　　　　Clay, F.　　　　1862
　　Wittikind and His Brothers　　**　　　　ca. 1852*
TCHKIRIDES, BILL
　　Hunting of the Snark　　　Roberts, E.　　　1971
TEACHOUT, TERRY (b. 1956)
　　Letter, The　　　　　　　Moravec, P.　　　2009
TENDUCCI, FERDINANDO (ca. 1735–1790)
　　Amintas (with R. Rolt)　　　Arnold, S.　　　1769
TENSING, MARY
　　Rise for Freedom　　　　　Hailstork, A.　　2007
TERRY, DANIEL (1782–1829)
　　Antiquary, The (with I. Pocock)　Bishop, H. R.　　1820
　　Barber of Seville (with J. Fawcett)　Bishop, H. R.　　1818
　　Guy Mannering　　　　　Attwood, T.　　　1816
　　Heart of Midlothian　　　　Bishop, H. R.　　1819

TERRY, ELLEN
　　Perpetual　　　　　　　Kanitz, E.　　　1961
　　Perpetual　　　　　　　Schubert, P.　　　1983
TERRY, PATRICK
　　Moon and Sixpence　　　　Gardner, J.　　　1957
THACKERAY, THOMAS JAMES
　　Mountain Sylph　　　　　Barnett, J.　　　1834
THEKLA, MOTHER (b. 1918)
　　Mary of Egypt　　　　　　Taverner, J.　　　1992
THEOBALD, LEWIS (1688–1744)
　　Decius and Paulina　　　　Galliard, J.　　　1718
　　Happy Captive　　　　　Galliard, J.　　　1741
　　Orpheus and Eurydice　　　Lampe, J. F.　　　1740
　　Orestes　　　　　　　　Pepusch, J.　　　1731
　　Pan and Syrinx　　　　　Galliard, J.　　　1718
THOMSON, JAMES (1700–1748)
　　Alfred (with D. Mallett)　　Arne, T. A.　　　1740
THOMSON, LYNN
　　Rent (with comp.)　　　　Larson, J.　　　1996
THOMPSON, A. M.
　　Rebel Maid (with G. Dodson)　Phillips, M.　　1921
　　Tom Jones　　　　　　　German, E.　　　1907
THOMPSON, BENJAMIN (1776–1816)
　　Oberon's Oath　　　　　　Parry, J.　　　1816
THOMPSON, C. PELHAM
　　Nothing Superfluous　　　　Lee, G. A.　　　1829
THOMPSON, FRANCIS (1859–1907)
　　Hound of Heaven　　　　　Stewart, H.　　　1924
THOMPSON, JOHN
　　Enchanted Pear Tree　　　　Overton, H.　　　1950
THOMPSON, MIKI L.
　　Too Many Sopranos　　　　Penhorwood, E.　　2000
THOMPSON, RICHARD
　　Room No. 12　　　　　　Kanitz, E.　　　1958
THORNE, JOAN VAIL
　　Pocahontas　　　　　　　Haugen, L.　　　2007
　　Summer　　　　　　　　Paulus, S.　　　1999
　　Woman at Otowi Crossing　　Paulus, S.　　　1995
THORNELY, WILFRID (1879–1926)
　　Angelus, The　　　　　　Naylor, E.　　　1909
TICKELL, RICHARD (1751–1793)
　　Camp, The　　　　　　　Linley, T., Sr.　　1778
　　Carnival of Venice　　　　Linley, T., Sr.　　1781
　　Gentle Shepherd　　　　　Linley, T., Sr.　　1781
　　Metamorphosis (with comp.)　Jackson, W.　　　1783
TIERNEY, ANNE
　　Triskelion　　　　　　　Bouchard, L.　　　1982
TILL, NICHOLAS (b. 1955)
　　Albergo Empedocle　　　　Barker, P.　　　1990
TOBIN, JOHN (1770–1804)
　　Honey Moon　　　　　　Hewitt/Kelly　　　1805
TOOP, RICHARD
　　Iphis　　　　　　　　　Kats-Chernin, E.　1997

**TRACEY, EDMUND**

| | | |
|---|---|---|
| *Lucky-Peter's Journey* | Williamson, M. | 1968 |

**TRACY, HENRY C.**

| | | |
|---|---|---|
| *In the Pasha's Garden* | Seymour, J. | 1935 |
| *Ramona* | Seymour, J. | 1970 |

**TRAWICK, LEONARD M.**

| | | |
|---|---|---|
| *Mary Stuart* | Murray, B. | 1991 |
| *Spinoza* | Drossin, J. | 1981 |

**TREADWAY, JESSICA (b. 1961)**

| | | |
|---|---|---|
| *Marble Faun* | Bender, E. | 1996* |

**TREMBLAY, LAURENT**

| | | |
|---|---|---|
| *Chair in Love* | Metcalf, J. | 2005 |

**TREVELYAN, ROBERT C.**

| | | |
|---|---|---|
| *Bride of Dionysus* | Tovey, D. | 1929 |
| *Pearl Tree* | Bainton, E. L. | 1944 |

**TRICKETT, RACHEL (1923–1999)**

| | | |
|---|---|---|
| *Antigone* | Joubert, J. | 1954 |
| *Silas Marner* | Joubert, J. | 1961 |

**TROUTMAN, RON**

| | | |
|---|---|---|
| *Birth/Day* | Wolfe, N. | 1993 |

**TRUESDELL, FREDERICK**

| | | |
|---|---|---|
| *Night in Old Paris* | Hadley, H. | 1924 |

**TRUSS, JAN**

| | | |
|---|---|---|
| *Silver City* | Doolittle, Q. | 1983 |

**TUCKER, JAMES**

| | | |
|---|---|---|
| *Bremen Town Musicians* | Kesselman, L. | 1988 |
| *Emperor's New Clothes* | Kesselman, L. | 1988* |
| *Nightingale, The* | Raminsh, I. | 2005 |

**TUNNICLIFFE, STEPHEN**

| | | |
|---|---|---|
| *Prisoner, The* | Joubert, J. | 1973 |

**TURPIN, ALLAN**

| | | |
|---|---|---|
| *Box, The* | Hamm, C. | 1961 |

**TWEG, SUE**

| | | |
|---|---|---|
| *Quickening, The* | Selleck, J. | 1998 |

**TWIST, BEN**

| | | |
|---|---|---|
| *Marrying the Hangman* | Caltabiano, R. | 2000 |

**TYBURN, GENE**

| | | |
|---|---|---|
| *Antony and Cleopatra* | Chiusano, G. | 2004* |

**TYLER, ROYALL (1757–1826)**

| | | |
|---|---|---|
| *May Day in Town* | ** | 1787 |

**UPDIKE, JOHN (1932–2009)**

| | | |
|---|---|---|
| *Fisherman and His Wife* | Schuller, G. | 1970 |

**UPTON, ANDREW**

| | | |
|---|---|---|
| *Through the Looking Glass* | John, A. | 2008 |

**USSACHEVSKY, VLADIMIR (1911–1990)**

| | | |
|---|---|---|
| *Boor, The* (with comp.) | Kay, U. | 1968 |

**VALENCY, MAURICE (1903–1996)**

| | | |
|---|---|---|
| *Feathertop* | Barnes, E. | 1980 |

**VANCE, WILSON J.**

| | | |
|---|---|---|
| *Smugglers, The* | Sousa, J. P. | 1882 |

**VAN HORN, BILL**

| | | |
|---|---|---|
| *God Bless Us Every One!* (with Capasso) | Pasatieri, T. | 2010 |

**VARIAN, JOHN O.**

| | | |
|---|---|---|
| *Building of Bamba* | Cowell, H. | 1917 |

**VASILEVSKI, VALERIA**

| | | |
|---|---|---|
| *She Lost Her Voice* | White, F. | 2004 |
| *True Last Words* | Salzman, E. | 1997 |

**VAUGHAN WILLIAMS, URSULA (1911–2007)**

| | | |
|---|---|---|
| *Canterbury Morning* | Roe, B. | 1986 |
| *David and Bathsheba* | Barlow, D. | 1969 |
| *Insect Play* | Senator, R. | 1981* |
| *Melita* | Camilleri, C. | 1968 |
| *Sofa, The* | Maconchy, E. | 1959 |

**VAVREK, ROYCE**

| | | |
|---|---|---|
| *Dog Days* | Little, D. | 2009 |
| *Hunger Art* | Myers, J. | 2008 |
| *Song from the Uproar* | Mazzoli, M. | 2009 |

**VEHAR, GABRIELLE**

| | | |
|---|---|---|
| *Eleanor Roosevelt* | Vehar, P. | 2010 |
| *George Sand* | Vehar, P. | 2005 |

**VENABLES, CLARE**

| | | |
|---|---|---|
| *Country of the Blind* | Turnage, M.-A. | 1997 |

**VERBRUGGEN, JOHN (fl. 1688–1707?)**

| | | |
|---|---|---|
| *Brutus of Alba* (prob. librettist, with G. Powell) | Purcell, D. | 1696 |

**VERMEL, ANN**

| | | |
|---|---|---|
| *Serenade at Noon* | Fuchs, P. | 1965 |

**VILÉ, JIM**

| | | |
|---|---|---|
| *Iron Man* (with Rider) | Fox, M. | 1987 |
| *Sid the Serpent* (with S. Vilé) | Fox, M. | 1977 |
| *Zoggy* (with S. Rider) | Fox, M. | 1987 |

**VILÉ, SUSAN**

| | | |
|---|---|---|
| *Sid the Serpent* (with J. Vilé) | Fox, M. | 1977 |

**VINCENT, SEAN**

| | | |
|---|---|---|
| *Birthday of the Infanta* | Stoker, R. | 1963 |

**VOADEN, HERMAN (1903–1991)**

| | | |
|---|---|---|
| *Prodigal Son* | Jacobi, F. | 1944 |

**VOLONAKIS, MINOS**

| | | |
|---|---|---|
| *Numbered, The* | Lutyens, E. | 1967* |

**VON HOFFMAN, NICHOLAS**

| | | |
|---|---|---|
| *Nicholas and Alexandra* | Drattell, D. | 2003 |

**VONNEGUT, KURT (1922–2007)**

| | | |
|---|---|---|
| *Fortitude* | Rogers, A. | 1990 |

**VORRASI, JOHN**

| | | |
|---|---|---|
| *Diva, The* | Ferris, W. | 1987 |
| *Little Moon of Alban* | Ferris, W. | 1974* |

**WADSWORTH, MICHAEL**

| | | |
|---|---|---|
| *Passion and Resurrection* | Harvey, J. | 1981 |

**WADSWORTH, STEPHEN (b. 1929)**

| | | |
|---|---|---|
| *Mistake, The* | Sheffer, J. B. | 1981 |
| *Quiet Place* | Bernstein, L. | 1983 |

WAINRIGHT, JONATHAN HOWARD
*Rip Van Winkle*                          Bristow, G. F.        1855
WALDRON, DANIEL GORDON (b. 1925)
*Circus, The*                             Chudacoff, E.         1953
WALDRON, FRANCIS G. (GODOLPHIN) (1744–1818)
*Love and Madness!*                       Arnold, S.            1795
WALKER, C. E.
*Fall of Algiers* (or J. H. Payne)        Bishop, H. R.         1825
WALKER, JOHN STIRLING
*Famous*                                  Conte, D.             2007
WALKER, THOMAS (1698–1744)
*Quaker's Opera*                          **                    1728
WALLACE, PETER
*Other Wise Man*                          de Kenessey, S.       1996
WALTER, EUGENE
*Let's Get This Show on the Road*         Eaton, J.             1993
*Lion and Androcles*                      Eaton, J.             1974
   (with D. Anderson, comp)
WARD, ANTHONY
*Toussaint*                               Blake, D.             1977
WARD, CHARLES (fl. 1806–1833)
*Circassian Bride*                        Bishop, H. R.         1809
WARD, EDWARD (1667–1731)
*Prisoner's Opera* (prob. librettist)     **                    1730
WARD, HENRY
*Happy Lovers*                            **                    1736
WARD, VICTORIA
*Down Here on Earth*                      Wiens, R.             1998
WARNER, EMMA
*God's Liar* (with comp.)                 Casken, J.            2001
WARNER, KEITH
*Scoring a Century*                       Blake, D.             2010
WARNER, MARINA (b. 1946)
*In the House of Crossed Desires*         Woolrich, J.          1996
*Queen of Sheba's Legs*                   Grant, J.             1991
WARREN, DON
*Evangeline* (with P. Roddick)            George, G.            1948
WARREN, ROGER (b. 1943)
*Errors*                                  Wilson-Dickson, A.    1980
WARWICK, MARY CAROL (b. 1939)
*Achilles' Heel*                          Bohmler, C.           1993
*Tale of the Nutcracker* (lyrics)         Bohmler, C.           1999
WASSERSTEIN, WENDY (1950–2006)
*Best Friends,*                           Drattell, D.          2002
*Festival of Regrets*                     Drattell, D.          1999
WATERS, MARY ANN
*Brave Jack*                              Waters, E.            1993
WATKINS, DENNIS
*Eighth Wonder* (with comp.)              John, A.              1995
WATSON, DONALD (1920–2002)
*Bald Prima Donna*                        Kalmanoff, M.         1963

WATT, JILL
*Johnson Preserv'd*                       Stoker, R.            1967
WEATHERLY, FREDERICK EDWARD
*Amy Robsart* (with Harris)               de Lara, I.           1893
*Lady of Langford* (with A. G. Harris)    Bach, L. E.           1896
WEBER, MAX
*Game of Cards*                           Franchetti, A.        1955
WEBNER, THOMAS
*Martin Luther King*                      Schmitz, A.           1992
WEBSTER, PETER
*Thirteen Clocks*                         Theofanidis, C.       2003
WEINSTEIN, ARNOLD (1927–2005)
*Casino Paradise*                         Bolcom, W.            1989
*Dynamite Tonite*                         Bolcom, W.            1963
*Final Ingredient*                        Amram, D.             1965
*Galileo, Galilei*                        Glass, P.             2002
   (with comp. and M. Zimmerman)
*Greatshot*                               Bolcom, W.            1969
*McTeague* (with R. Altman)               Bolcom, W.            1992
*View from the Bridge* (with A. Miller)   Bolcom, W.            1999
*Wedding, A*                              Bolcom, W.            2004
WEISS, GEORGE DAVID
*Queenie Pie*                             Ellington, E.         1986
WELCH, JACK
*Laughter in Jericho*                     Daniels, M.           1989
WELLMAN, MAC
*Difficulty of Crossing a Field*          Lang, D.              2002
WELLS, FRANCES
*Carrion Crow*                            Fletcher, G.          1953
*Without Colors*                          Shiflett, M.          1989
WELLS, MATT B.
*First Lady* (with comp. et al.)          Wells, K.             2010
WERTENBAKER, TIMBERLAKE (b. 1951)
*Love of the Nightingale*                 Mills, R.             2007
WESKER, ARNOLD (b. 1932)
*Caritas*                                 Saxon, R.             1991
WEST, JESSAMYN (1907–1984)
*Mirror for the Sky*                      Kubik, G.             1939
WEST, MORRIS (1916–1999)
*Heretic, The*                            Brumby, C.            1999*
*Heretic, The*                            Fuchs, P. P.          1978*
WEST, RAY B., Jr. (b. 1908)
*Bride Comes to Yellow Sky*               Nixon, R.             1968
WHEELER, HUGH (b. 1912)
*Silverlake*                              Weill, K.             1980
*Sweeney Todd* (with comp.)               Sondheim, S.          1979
WHITE, EDGAR NKOSI (b. 1947)
*Ghosts*                                  Ito, G.               1993
WHITE, PAUL DAVID
*Cathedral, The*                          Spivack, L.           1986
WHITE, R. J.
*Tragicall Historie*                      Mellers, W.           1952*

WHITE, SARAH
 *Benjamin*      Carbon, J.   1987
WHITING, JOHN
 *Sister Aimée*   Martínez, O. de la 1984
WHITSETT, GEORGE (b. 1889)
 *Parabola and Circula* Blitzstein, M.  1929*
WHYTE, RON (1942–1989)
 *Mother and Child*  McClure, L.  1990
WICKS, ALLAN
 *Gift, The*     Ridout, A.   1971
 *White Doe*     Ridout, A.   1987
WIDDOES, C. C.
 *How to Make Love*  Widdoes, L.  1994
WIESEL, ELIE (b. 1928)
 *Esther* (with comp.)  Swados, E.  1988
WILBOR, ELSIE M.
 *Guido Ferranti*   Van Etten, J.  1914
WILBUR, RICHARD (b. 1921)
 *Candide* (with L. Hellman) Bernstein, L.  1956
WILCOX, MICHAEL
 *Tornrak*     Metcalf, J.   1990
WILDER, THORNTON (1897–1975)
 *Alcestiad, The*   Talma, L.   1962
WILKINSON, F. H.
 *Boy from the Catacombs* Ridout, A.   1965
WILEY, HOWARD A.
 *Trojan Women*   Garwood, M.  1967
WILLET, THOMAS (fl. 1778)
 *Buxom Joan*    Taylor, R.   1778
WILLETT, ERNEST NODDALL
 *Prodigal Son*    Nicholls, F.   1896
WILLHEIM, IMANUEL (b. 1926)
 *Married Men Go to Hell* Franchetti, A.  1975
WILLIAMS, ALBERT
 *Isabella's Fortune*  Russo, W.   1974
WILLIAMS, JASON
 *Ochelata's Wedding* (with J. Sears) Damase, J.-M. 2000
WILLIAMS, JOHN A.
 *Vanqui*      Burrs. L.   1999
WILLIAMS, LYNNE
 *Waiting for Jack*   Webb, J.   2002
WILLIAMS, MARGARET
 *Armida*      Weir, J.    2005
 *Scipio's Dream* (with comp.) Weir, J.    1991
WILLIAMS, PAT
 *King Kong* (lyrics)  Matshikiza, T.  1959
WILLIAMS, TENNESSEE (1911–1983)
 *Lord Byron's Love Letter* Banfield, R. de 1955
WILLIAMS, THOMAS JOHN (1824–1874)
 *Desert Flower* (with A. G. Harris) Wallace, V. 1863

WILSON, A. N. (b. 1950)
 *Britannia Preserv'd*  Oliver, S.   1984
 *Travellers*     Horne, D.   1998
WILSON, BRIAN
 *Abelard and Heloise*  Gaughan, J.  1980
WILSON, JAMES
 *Chipita Rodríguez* (with L. Carrillo) Weiner, L. 1982
WILSON, LANFORD (1937–2011)
 *Summer and Smoke*  Hoiby, L.   1971
WILSON, PEARL CLEVELAND (1882–1976)
 *King Harald*    Emile, A.   1948
 *Life That Is Free*   Emile, A.   1946
WILSON, ROBERT (b. 1928)
 *CIVIL warS* (with M. di Niscemi) Glass, P.  1984
 *Einstein on the Beach*  Glass, P.   1976
 *Letter for Queen Victoria* Lloyd, A.   1974
 *Medea*      Bryars, G.   1984
WILSON, ROWLAND HOLT
 *Meal, The*     Archer, V.   1985
WISHENGRAD, MORTON (1913–1963)
 *Thief and the Hangman* Ellstein, A.  1961
WOLCOTT, DEREK
 *Walker*      Anderson, T. J. 1993
WOLCOTT, JOHN [PETER PINDAR] (1738–1819)
 *Nina*       Shield, W.   1787
WOLFE, GEORGE C.
 *Queenie Pie*    Ellington, E.  1986
WONG, GEORGE K.
 *Iron Road*     Chan Ka Nin  2001
WOOD, ADOLPH
 *In the Drought*   Joubert, J.   1956
WOOD, WALLIS
 *Princess Maleen* (with comp.) Schonthal, R.  1989
WOODCOCK, GEORGE
 *Brideship, The*   Turner, R.   1967
WOODRUFF, PAUL (b. 1943)
 *Della's Gift*     Welcher, D.  1987
 *Holy Night*     Welcher, D.  2005
 *Prisoner's Play*   Rea, J.    1973
WOODWARD, MARIA
 *Audition of Molly Bloom* McFarland, R.  1986
 *Donner Party*    McFarland, R.  1979
 *Song of Pegasus*   McFarland, R.  1985
 *Tamsen Donner*   McFarland, R.  1982
WOODWORTH, SAMUEL (1784–1842)
 *Deed of Gift*     **     1822
 *Forest Rose*     Davies, J.   1825
WOOLF, BENJAMIN E.
 *Doctor of Alcantara*  Eichberg, J.  1862
WORSDALE, JAMES (1692–1767)
 *Cure for a Scold*   **     1735
 *Gasconado the Great*  **     1759?

| WRIGHT, HARRIET SABRA | | |
| --- | --- | --- |
| *Birthday of the Infanta* | Boyack, J. | 1957* |

WRIGHT, NICHOLAS (b. 1940)

| *Little Prince* | Portman, R. | 2003 |
| *Man on the Moon* | Dove, J. | 2006 |

WRIGHT, ROBERT

| *Slaughter of the Innocents* | Crawley, C. | 1975 |

WURLITZER, RUDOLPH

| *In the Penal Colony* | Glass, P. | 2000 |

WYN(-HARDY), HELEDD

| *Flowers* | Hardy, J. | 1994 |
| *Roswell Incident* | Hardy, J. | 1997 |

WYSS, PATTI

| *Henry David Thoreau* (with Evans, Deal) | Cionek, E. | 2003 |

XU YING

| *Tea* (with comp., transl Liao) | Tan Dun | 2003 |

YAGED, KIM

| *Leading Lady* | March, K. | 2004 |
| *www.love* | March, K. | 2001 |

YANKOWITZ, SUSAN

| *Deronda* | Cotel, M. | 1989* |

YARDLEY, WILLIAM (1849–1900)

| *On the March* (with C. Clay, Stephenson) | Clay, F. | 1896 |
| *Wedding Eve* | Ford, E., et al. | 1892 |

YARROW, JOSEPH

| *Love at First Sight* | ** | 1742 |

YEZZI, DAVID

| *Firebird Motel* | Conte, D. | 2003 |

YORINKS, ARTHUR

| *Fall of the House of Usher* | Glass, P. | 1988 |
| *Juniper Tree* | Glass, P. | 1985 |

YOUNG, RIDA JOHNSON (1875–1926)

| *Naughty Marietta* | Herbert, V. | 1910 |

ZARA, MARIA

| *It Began at Breakfast* (with Rhein) | Elmore, R. | 1941 |

ZEFFIRELLI, FRANCO (b. 1923)

| *Antony and Cleopatra* | Barber, S. | 1966 |

ZIMMERMAN, MARY

| *Galileo Galile* (with comp., A. Weinstein) | Glass, P. | 2002 |

ZINOVIEFF, PETER

| *Mask of Orpheus* | Birtwistle, H. | 1986 |

## Adaptations and Arrangements

AUDINOT, NICOLAS MÉDARD (1732–1801)

*Tonnelier, Le,* with Quétant (F.-J. Gossec, 1765)

| *Cooper, The* | Arne, T. A. | 1772 |

AUMER, PIERRE (1774–1833)

*Somnambule, La,* with E. Scribe (vaudeville, 1827)

| *Sonnambula, La* | Bishop, H. R. | 1833 |

BAYARD, JEAN-FRANÇOIS

*Fille du régiment, La,* with Saint-Georges (G. Donizetti, 1840)

| *Vivandiere, The* | Hewitt, J. H. | 1863 |

BERRETTONI, ARCANGELO

*Bravo, Il* (M. A. Marliani, 1834)

| *Red Mask* | Cooke, T. S. | 1834 |

BICKERSTAFFE, ISAAC (1733–1808)

*Love in the City* (C. Dibdin et al., 1767)

| *Romp, The* | Dibdin, C. | 1771 |

BRACCIOLI, GRAZIO (1682–1752)

*Orlando furioso* (Vivaldi, 1727)

| *Cracked Orlando* | Dawe, J. | 2010 |

BRECHT, BERTOLT (1898–1956)

*Dreigroschenoper, Die* (K. Weill, 1928)

| *Threepenny Opera* | Weill-Blitzstein | 1954 |

*Happy End,* with E. Hauptmann (K. Weill, 1929)

| *Happy End* | Weill-Feingold | 1972 |

BRUNSWICK, LÉON LÉVY (1805–1859)

*Poupée de Nuremberg, La,* with A. de Leuven (A. Adam, 1852)

| *Toy-Maker* | Linley, G. | 1861 |

*Quatre fils Aymon, Les,* with A. de Leuven (M. Balfe, 1844)

| *Castle of Aymon* | Balfe, M. | 1844 |

BURNAND, F. C. (FRANCIS COWLEY) (1836–1917)

*Contrabandista, The* (A. S. Sullivan, 1867)

| *Smugglers, The* | Sousa, J. P. | 1882 |

COBB, JAMES (1756–1818)

*Pirates, The* (S. Storace, 1792)

| *Isadore de Merida* | Cooke, T. S. | 1827 |

DA PONTE, LORENZO (1749–1838)

*Così fan tutte* (W. A. Mozart, 1790)

| *Tit for Tat* | Hawes, W. | 1828 |

*Don Giovanni* (W. A. Mozart, 1787)

| *Libertine, The* | Bishop, H. R. | 1817 |

*Nozze di Figaro, Le* (W. A. Mozart, 1786)

| *Marriage of Figaro* | Bishop, H. R. | 1819 |

DELAVIGNE, GERMAIN (1782–1871)

*Maçon, Le,* with Scribe (1825)

| *Mason of Buda* | Rodwell, G. | 1828 |

*Muette de Portici, La,* with Scribe (D. F. E. Auber, 1828)

| *Masaniello* | Cooke, Livius | 1829 |

*Somnambule, La,* with Scribe (1819, Paris)

| *Love's Dream* | M. Moss (arr.) | 1821 |

*Vieille, La,* with Scribe (F.-J. Fétis, 1826)

| *Love in Wrinkles* | Lacy, M. R. | 1826 |

DESVERGERS [ARMAND CHAPEAU]

*Yelva,* with Scribe, Villeneuve (vaudeville, 1828)

| *Yelva* | Bishop, H. R. | 1829 |

DIMOND, WILLIAM (fl. 1800–1830)

*Aethiop, The* (H. R. Bishop, 1812)

| *Aethiop, The* | Taylor, R. | 1814 |

DÖRING, GEORG (1789–1833)

*Räuberbraut, Die* (F. Ries, 1828)

| *Robber's Bride* | Hawes, W. | 1829 |

FAVART, CHARLES-SIMON (1710–1792)
**Annette et Lubin,** with M. Favart, Lourdet de Santerre (A. Blaise, 1762)

| | | |
|---|---|---|
| *Annette and Lubin* | Dibdin, C. | 1778 |

**Caprice amoureux, Le** (E. Duni et al., 1755)

| | | |
|---|---|---|
| *Capricious Lovers* | Rush, G. | 1764 |
| *Phoebe at Court* | Arne, T. | 1776 |

**Fête de Saint-Cloud, La** (opéra-comique, 1741)

| | | |
|---|---|---|
| *Contract, The* | Stevenson, J. | 1782 |

FIELDING, HENRY (1707–1754)
**Grub-Street Opera** (\*\*, 1731)

| | | |
|---|---|---|
| *Grub-Street Opera* | Bowles, A. | 1986 |

GAY, JOHN (1695–1732)
**Achilles** (\*\*, 1733)

| | | |
|---|---|---|
| *Achilles in Petticoats* | Arne, T. A. | 1773 |

**Beggar's Opera, The** (J. Pepusch, 1728 )

| | | |
|---|---|---|
| *Bow-Street Opera* | Pepusch, J. | 1773 |
| *Fool's Opera* | \*\* | 1731 |
| *Macheath in the Shades* | \*\* | 1735 |
| *Macheath Turn'd Pyrate* | \*\* | 1737 |
| *Threepenny Opera* | Weill-Blitzstein | 1954 |

GENÉE, RICHARD (1823–1895)
**Fledermaus, Die,** with K. Haffner (J. Strauss II, 1874)

| | | |
|---|---|---|
| *Flying Fox* | Jopling, O., arr. | 1998 |

GHERADINI, GIOVANNI (1778–1861)
**Gazza ladra, La** (G. Rossini, 1817)

| | | |
|---|---|---|
| *Annette* | Horn, C. E. | 1822 |
| *Ninetta* | Bishop, H. R. | 1830 |

GIACOSA, GIUSEPPE (1847–1906)
general

| | | |
|---|---|---|
| *Audition, The* | Kalmanoff, M. | 1968 |

**Bohème, La,** with L. Illica (G. Puccini, 1896)

| | | |
|---|---|---|
| *Bohemians, The* | Kirschner, B. | 1990 |
| *Rent* | Larson, J. | 1996 |

GOLDONI, CARLO (1707–1793)
**Buona figliuola, La** (N. Piccinni, 1760)

| | | |
|---|---|---|
| *Maid of the Vale* | Arne, M. | 1775 |

HAFFNER, KARL (1804–1876)
**Fledermaus, Die,** with R. Genée (J. Strauss II, 1874)

| | | |
|---|---|---|
| *Flying Fox* | Jopling, O., arr. | 1998 |

HALÉVY, LUDOVIC (1833–1908)
**Ba-Ta-Clan** (J. Offenbach, 1855)

| | | |
|---|---|---|
| *Ba-Ta-Clan* | Oliver, S. | 1988* |

**Madame l'archiduc,** with Millaud, Meilhac (J. Offenbach, 1874)

| | | |
|---|---|---|
| *Single Married Man* | Sedgwick, A. | 1883* |

HAUPTMANN, ELISABETH
**Happy End,** with B. Brecht (K. Weill, 1929)

| | | |
|---|---|---|
| *Happy End* | Weill-Feingold | 1972 |

HÈLE, THOMAS D' (1740–1780)
**Evénéments imprévus, Les** (Grétry, 1799)

| | | |
|---|---|---|
| *Gay Deceivers* | Kelly, M. | 1804 |

HIEMER, FRANZ KARL (1768–1822)
**Abu Hassan** (C. M. von Weber, 1811)

| | | |
|---|---|---|
| *Abou Hassan* | Cooke, T. S. | 1825 |

HUBER, FRANZ XAVER (1755–1814)
**Unterbrochene Opferfest, Das** (P. Winter, 1796)

| | | |
|---|---|---|
| *Oracle, The* | Hawes, W. | 1826 |

ILLICA, LUIGI (1857–1919)
various

| | | |
|---|---|---|
| *Audition, The* | Kalmanoff, M. | 1968 |

**Bohème, La,** with G. Giacosa (G. Puccini, 1896)

| | | |
|---|---|---|
| *Bohemians, The* | Kirschner, B. | 1990 |
| *Rent* | Larson, J. | 1996 |

KAISER, GEORG (1878–1945)
**Silbersee, Der** (K. Weill, 1933)

| | | |
|---|---|---|
| *Silverlake* | Weill-Symonette | 1980 |

LATEINER, JOSEPH (1853–1935)
**Dovid's fiedele** (S. Mogulesco, 1897)

| | | |
|---|---|---|
| *David's Violin* | M. Slobin (arr.) | 1976 |

**Shloyme Gorgl** (\*\*, ca. 1890)

| | | |
|---|---|---|
| *Shloyme Gorgl* | M. Slobin (arr.) | 1978 |

KIND, FRIEDRICH (1768–1843)
**Freischütz, Der** (C. M. von Weber, 1821)

| | | |
|---|---|---|
| *Black Rider* | Waits, T. | 1990 |
| *Freischütz, Der* | \*\* | 1824 |

LEUVEN, ADOLPHE DE (1800–1884)
**Jaguarita l'Indienne,** with Vernoy de St.-Georges (F. Halévy, 1855)

| | | |
|---|---|---|
| *Desert Flower* | Wallace, V. | 1863 |

**Postillon de Longjumeau, Le**

| | | |
|---|---|---|
| *Postillion of Longjumeau* | Stansbury, G. | 1837 |

**Poupée de Nuremberg, La** (A. Adam, 1852)

| | | |
|---|---|---|
| *Toy-Maker* | Linley, G. | 1861 |

**Quatre fils Aymon, Les,** with L. L. Brunswick (M. Balfe, 1844)

| | | |
|---|---|---|
| *Castle of Aymon* | Balfe, M. | 1844 |

LIVIUS, BARHAM (d. 1865)
**Schweizerfamilie, Die** (F. Weigl, 1809)

| | | |
|---|---|---|
| *Lilla* | \*\* | 1825 |

MARMONTEL, JEAN-FRANÇOIS (1723–1799)
**Silvain** (1770, Paris)

| | | |
|---|---|---|
| *Maid of the Oaks* | Barthelemon, F. H. | 1774 |

MARSOLLIER, BENOÎT JOSEPH (1750–1817)
**Adolphe et Clara** (N. Dalayrac, 1799)

| | | |
|---|---|---|
| *Matrimony* | Hewitt, J. | 1804 |

**Camille** (N.-M. Dalayrac, 1791)

| | | |
|---|---|---|
| *Captive of Spilburg* | Dussek/Kelly | 1798 |

MEILHAC, HENRI (1831–1897)
**Carmen,** with L. Halévy (G. Bizet, 1875)

| | | |
|---|---|---|
| *Carmen Jones* | Bennett, R. R. | 1947 |
| *José's Carmen* | Ashman, M. | 1984 |

**Madame l'archiduc,** with Millaud, Halévy (J. Offenbach, 1874)

| | | |
|---|---|---|
| *Single Married Man* | Sedgwick, A. | 1883* |

METASTASIO, PIETRO (1698–1782)
**Demofoonte** (A. Caldara, 1733)
*Dirce*                                     Horne, C. E.          1821
**Didone abbandonata** (D. Sarro, 1724)
*Dido*                                      Storace, S.           1792
MILLAUD, ALBERT (1844–1892)
**Madame l'archiduc,** with H. Meilhac, L. Halévy (J. Offenbach, 1874)
*Single Married Man*                        Sedgwick, A.          1883*
MORSELLI, ADRIANO (17th cent.)
**Pirro e Demetrio** (A. Scarlatti, 1694)
*Pyrrus and Demetrius*                      Haym, N.              1708

PIGAULT-LEBRUN, C. A. G.
**Petit matelot, Le** (P. Gaveaux, 1796, Paris)
*Veteran Tar*                               Arnold, S.            1801
PLANARD, F. A. E. DE (1783–1855)
**Pré aux clercs, Le** (F. Hérold, 1832)
*Challenge, The*                            Cooke, T. S.          1834
*Court Masque*                              Dawes, W.             1833
**Prison d'Edimbourg, Le,** with E. Scribe (M. Carafa, 1833)
*Heart of Midlothian*                       Loder, E.             1849

QUÉTANT, ANTOINE-FRANÇOIS (1733–1823)
**Tonnelier, Le,** with Audinot (F.-J. Gossec, 1765)
*Cooper, The*                               Arne, T. A.           1772

ROMANI, FELICE (1788–1865)
**Elisir d'amore, L'** (G. Donizetti, 1832)
*Dulcamara*                                 **                    1866
**Norma** (V. Bellini, 1831)
*Norma, The*                                Dowdell, L.           2006
ROSSI, GAETANO (1774–1855)
**Tancredi** (G. Rossini, 1813)
*Native Land*                               Bishop, H. R.         1824

SAINT-GEORGES, JULES-HENRI VERNOY de (1799–1875)
**Fille du régiment, La,** with Bayard (G. Donizetti, 1840)
*Vivandiere, The*                           Hewitt, J. H.         1863
**Jaguarita l'Indienne,** with de Leuven (F. Halévy, 1855)
*Desert Flower*                             Wallace, V.           1863
SAINT-HILAIRE, AMABLE VILAIN de (b. 1795)
**Diadesté** (J. J. Godefroid, 1836)
*Diadesté*                                  Balfe, M.             1838
SCRIBE, EUGÈNE (1791–1861)
**Cheval de bronze, Le** (D. F. E. Auber, 1835)
*Bronze Horse*                              Rodwell, G.           1835
**Deux nuits, Les** (A. Boieldieu, 1829)
*Night before the Wedding*                  Bishop, H. R.         1829
**Fra Diavolo** (D. F. E. Auber, 1830)
*Devil's Brother*                           Lee, G. A.            1831
**Juive, La** (F. Halévy, 1835)
*Jewess, The*                               Cooke, T. S.          1835
**Maçon, Le,** with G. Delavigne (D. F. E. Auber, 1825, Paris)
*Mason of Buda*                             Rodwell, G.           1828
**Muette de Portici, La,** with Delavigne (D. F. E. Auber, 1828)
*Masaniello*                                Cooke/Livius          1829

**Prison d'Edimbourg, Le,** with Planard (M. Carafa, 1833)
*Heart of Midlothian*                       Loder, E.             1849
**Ours et la pacha, L'** (1821)
*Meanwhile, Back at the Seraglio*           Stepleton, J.         1997*
**Reine d'un jour, La** (Adam, 1839)
*Queen of a Day*                            Fitzwilliam, E.       1841
**Robert le diable** (G. Meyerbeer, 1831)
*Demon, The*                                Bishop, H. R.         1832
*Fiend-Father*                              Lacy, M. R.           1832
*Robert the Devil*                          Barnett, J.           1830
*Robert the Devil*                          "Kettenus"            1868
**Somnambule, La** (1827, with P. Aumer)
*Sonnambula, La*                            Bishop, H. R.         1833
**Somnambule, La** (1819, with G. Delavigne)
*Love's Dream*                              Moss, M. (arr.)       1821
**Vieille, La,** with Delavigne (F.-J. Fétis, 1826)
*Love in Wrinkles*                          Lacy, M. R.           1826
**Yelva,** with Villeneuve, Desvergers (**, 1828)
*Yelva*                                     Bishop, H. R.         1829
SEDAINE, MICHEL-JEAN (1719–1797)
**Femmes vengées, Les** (F. A. D. Philidor, 1775)
*Wives Avenged*                             Dibdin, C.            1778
**Richard Coeur-de-lion** (A. E. M. Grétry, 1784)
*Richard Coeur de Lion*                     Linley, T., Sr.       1786
*Richard Coeur de Lion*                     Shield, W.            1786
**Rose et Colas** (Paris, 1764)
*Rose and Colin*                            Dibdin, C.            1778
STANZANI, TOMASO (fl. 1677–1684)
**Arsinoe** (G. B. Franceschini, 1676 )
*Arsinoe*                                   Clayton, T.           1705
STEPHANIE, GOTTLIEB, Jr. (1741–1800)
**Doktor und Apotheker** (K. D. von Dittersdorf, 1786)
*Doctor and Apothecary*                     Storace, S.           1788
STERBINI, CESARE (1783–1851)
**Barbiere di Siviglia, Il** (G. Rossini, 1816)
*Barber of Seville*                         Bishop, H. R.         1818

THEOBALD, LEWIS (1688–1744)
**Happy Captive, The** (J. Galliard, 1741)
*Temple of Dullness*                        Arne, T. A.           1745

VILLENEUVE, F. V. de (1799–1858)
**Yelva,** with E. Scribe and Desvergers (**, 1828)
*Yelva*                                     Bishop, H. R.         1829

WOHLBRÜCK, J. G. (1770–1822)
**Des Falkners Braut** (H. Marschner, 1832)
*Rob of the Fens*                           Romer, F.             1838
WOLFF, P. A.
**Preciosa** (C. M. von Weber, 1821)
*Preciosa*                                  Hawes, W.             1825

# Appendix 3: Authors and Sources

Opera entries include short title, composer, and year of premiere. * = year of composition (no performance information available); ** = anon. composer/ballad opera. Dates of authors given where known (honorary titles such as "Sir," Dr., and "Countess" are omitted before the author names). See pp. 734–44 for an alphabetical listing of titles of sources.

## Part I: Authors and Anonymous Works

**ADAMS, ABIGAIL (1744–1818)**
**letters**
| | | |
|---|---|---|
| *Abigail Adams* | Owen, R. | 1987 |

**ADAMS, HENRY (1838–1918)**
***Democracy* (1880) and *Esther* (1884)**
| | | |
|---|---|---|
| *Democracy* | Wheeler, S. | 1998 |

**AESCHYLUS (525–456 B.C.)**
***Agamemnon***
| | | |
|---|---|---|
| *Agamemnon* | Brian, H. | 1957* |
| *Agamemnon* | Hamilton, I. | 1967* |
| *Agamemnon* | Morris, R. | 1969 |
| *Agamemnon* | Werder, F. | 1967 |
| *Clytemnestra* | Wishart, P. | 1974 |
| *Cry of Clytaemnestra* | Eaton, J. | 1980 |

**AESOP (legendary, ca. 6th cent. B.C.)**
***Aesop's Fables***
| | | |
|---|---|---|
| *Cat, The* | Ridout, A. | 1971 |
| *Moralities* | Henze, H. W. | 1968 |

**AFANASYEV, ALEXANDER NIKOLAYEVICH (1826–1871)**
**Russian tales**
| | | |
|---|---|---|
| *Marko the Miser* | Musgrave, T. | 1963 |

**AGEE, JAMES (1909–1955)**
***Death in the Family* (1957, posth.)**
| | | |
|---|---|---|
| *Death in the Family* | Mayer, W. | 1983 |

**AINSWORTH, WILLIAM HARRISON (1805–1882)**
***Jack Sheppard* (1839)**
| | | |
|---|---|---|
| *Jack Sheppard* | Rodwell, G. | 1839 |

**AIZMAN, DAVID IAKOVLEVICH (1869–1922)**
***Krasovitsky Couple***
| | | |
|---|---|---|
| *Sima* | Lehrman, L. | 1976 |

**AKUTAGAWA, RYŪNOSUKE (1892–927)**
***Dragon: The Old Potter's Tale* (1919)**
| | | |
|---|---|---|
| *Dragon, The* | Chen, J. | 2010* |

**ALAIN-FOURNIER (HENRI ALBAN-FOURNIER) (1886–1914)**
***Grand Meaulnes, Le* (1913)**
| | | |
|---|---|---|
| *Lost Domain* | Carpenter, G. | 1984 |

**ALBEE, EDWARD (b. 1928)**
***Sandbox, The* (1959)**
| | | |
|---|---|---|
| *Sandbox, The* | Hagen, D. | 1985 |

**ALCOTT, LOUISA MAY (1832–1888)**
***Little Women* (1868)**
| | | |
|---|---|---|
| *Little Women* | Adamo, M. | 1998 |
| *Little Women* | Freer, E. E. | 1934 |

**ALDEN, RAYMOND MACDONALD (1873–1924)**
***Why the Chimes Rang***
| | | |
|---|---|---|
| *One Christmas Long Ago* | Mayer, W. | 1962 |

**ALEICHEM, SHOLEM (1859–1916)**
***Tale of Chelm***
| | | |
|---|---|---|
| *Chelm* | Strassburg, R. | 1955 |
| *Goat in Chelm* | Binder, A. | 1960 |

**ALEXANDER, HARTLEY BURR (1873–1939)**
**plays**
| | | |
|---|---|---|
| *Butterfly Girl* | Reed, H. O. | 1985 |
| *Living Solid Face* | Reed, H. O. | 1962 |
| ***Manito Masks* (1925)** | | |
| *Earth-Trapped* | Reed, H. O. | 1962 |

**ALMOND, DAVID (b. 1951)**
***Skellig* (1998)**
| | | |
|---|---|---|
| *Skellig* | Machover, T. | 2008 |

**ALTMAN, ROBERT (1925–2006)**
***Wedding, A* (1978, with J. Considine)**
| | | |
|---|---|---|
| *Wedding, A* | Bolcom, W. | 2004 |

**ÁLVAREZ QUINTERO, JOAQUÍN (1873–1944), SERAFÍN ÁLVAREZ QUINTERO (1871–1938)**
***Fortunato***
| | | |
|---|---|---|
| *Fortunato* | Gideon, M. | 1958* |
| ***Mañana de sol*** | | |
| *Sunny Morning* | Stringer, A. | 1998 |

**ANDERSEN, HANS CHRISTIAN (1805–1875)**
***Cat and the Mouse in Partnership***
| | | |
|---|---|---|
| *Pot of Fat* | Chandler, T. | 1955 |
| ***Emperor's New Clothes* (1837)** | | |
| *Emperor's New Clothes* | Bachlund, G. | 1994* |
| *Emperor's New Clothes* | Dvorkin, J. | 1989 |
| *Emperor's New Clothes* | Kesselman, L. | 1988* |
| *Emperor's New Clothes* | Larsen, L. | 1979 |
| *Emperor's New Clothes* | Moore, D. | 1949 |
| *Emperor's New Clothes* | Warwick, M. C. | 2001 |
| *Eyes and No Eyes* | Reed, T. G. | 1875 |
| *Fit for a King* | Kalmanoff, M. | 1949 |
| ***Ib and Little Christina* (1855)** | | |
| *Ib and Little Christina* | Leoni, F. | 1901 |
| ***Little Match Girl* (1845)** | | |
| *Little Match Girl* | Bachlund, G. | 1994* |
| *Little Match Girl* | Kaufmann, W. | 1953 |
| ***Little Mermaid* (1836)** | | |
| *Little Mermaid* | Boyd, A. | 1978 |
| *Mermaid, The* | Fullam, V. | 1986 |
| *Mermaid, The* | More, M. | 1951 |
| ***Nightingale, The* (1844)** | | |

| | | |
|---|---|---|
| *Emperor and the Nightingale* | Bingham, S. | 1982 |
| *Nightingale, The* | Clokey, J. | 1925 |
| *Nightingale, The* | Rogers, B. | 1955 |
| *Nightingale* | Strouse, C. | 1982 |
| **Princess and the Pea** (1835) | | |
| *Princess and the Pea* | Toch, E. | 1954 |
| *Princess and the Pea* | Warwick, M. C. | 2005 |
| **Shadow, The** (1847) | | |
| *Shadow, The* | Farquhar, D. | 1970* |
| **Shepherdess and the Chimney Sweep** (1845) | | |
| *Shepherdess and the Chimneysweep* | Smith, J. | 1966 |
| **Snow Queen** (1844) | | |
| *Snow Queen* | Dudley, G. | 1985 |
| *Snow Queen* | Fine, E. | 2002* |
| *Snow Queen* | Gerrish-Jones, A. | 1917 |
| *Snow Queen* | Ward, David | 1984 |
| **Story of a Mother** (1847) | | |
| *Garden of Flowers* | Goodman, J. | 1987 |
| *Mother, The* | Hollingsworth, S. | 1954 |
| *Mother, The* | Wood, J. | 1942 |
| **Swineherd, The** (1841) | | |
| *Swineherd, The* | Osborne, W. | 1980* |
| **Talisman, The** | | |
| *Love Charm* | Bachlund, G. | 1994* |
| **Ugly Duckling** (1844) | | |
| *Enid and the Swans* | Rolfe, J. | 2005 |
| **What the Old Man Does Is Always Right** | | |
| *What the Old Man Does Is Always Right* | Hoddinott, A. | 1977 |
| **Wild Swans** (1838) | | |
| *Wild Swans* | Bingham, S. | 1988 |

ANDERSON, ROBERT G.
**Villon** (1937)

| | | |
|---|---|---|
| *François Villon* | Baron, M. | 1940 |

ANDREYEV, LEONID (1871–1919)
**He Who Gets Slapped** (1922)

| | | |
|---|---|---|
| *He Who Gets Slapped* | Ward, R. | 1956 |

ANOUILH, JEAN (1910–1987)
**Humulus le muet** (with J. Aurench, 1929)

| | | |
|---|---|---|
| *Humulus the Mute* | MacIntyre, D | 1979 |

ANSKY, S. (AN-SKI) [SHLOYME-ZANVL ben AARON
HACOHEN RAPPOPORT] (1863–1920)
**Dybbuk, The (Der dibek)** (1920, post.)

| | | |
|---|---|---|
| *Between Two Worlds* | Ran, S. | 1997 |
| *Dybbuk, The* | DiGiacomo, F. | 1978 |
| *Dybbuk, The* | Mandelbaum, J. | 1972 |
| *Dybbuk, The* | Tamkin, D. | 1951 |

*APOTHICAIRE de MURCIA, L'* (Fr., anon.)

| | | |
|---|---|---|
| *Doctor and the Apothecary* | Storace, S. | 1788 |

APULEIUS, LUCIUS (2nd cent.)
**Golden Ass**

| | | |
|---|---|---|
| *Tale of Psyche & Cupid* | Sternau, C. | 2000* |
| *Trials of Psyche* | Bruce, N. | 1971 |

*ARDEN OF FAVERSHAM* (1592, anon.)

| | | |
|---|---|---|
| *Arden Must Die* | Goehr, A. | 1967 |

ARENAS, REINALDO (1943–1990)
**memoir**

| | | |
|---|---|---|
| *Before Night Falls* | Martín, J. | 2004 |

ARISTOPHANES (ca. 450–ca. 388 B.C.)
**general**

| | | |
|---|---|---|
| *Sweeney Agonistes* | Dankworth, J. | 1965 |
| **Birds, The** | | |
| *Birds, The* | Ahlstrom, D. | 1990 |
| *Birds, The* | Drummond, J. | 1986 |
| *Birds, The* | El-Dabh, H. | 1988* |
| *Birds, The* | Maconchy, E. | 1968 |
| **Lysistrata** | | |
| *Lisa Stratos* | Lackman, S. | 1981* |
| *Lizzie Strotter* | Kalmanoff, M. | 1958 |
| *Lysistrata* | Adamo, M. | 2005 |
| *Lysistrata* | Barthelson, J. | 1981 |
| *Lysistrata* | Clarke, H. | 1972* |
| *Lysistrata* | Fisher, T. | 1957* |
| *Lysistrata & the War* | Fink, R. | 1967 |

ARNOLD, EDWIN (1832–1904)
**Light of Asia** (1879)

| | | |
|---|---|---|
| *Light of Asia* | Lara, I. de | 1892 |

ARRABAL, FERNANDO (b. 1932)
**Cimetière des voitures** (1960)

| | | |
|---|---|---|
| *Automobile Graveyard* | Ceely, R. | 1995 |
| **Deux bourreaux, Les** | | |
| *Two Executioners* | Chesworth, D. | 1994 |

ARTAUD, ANTONIN (1896–1948)
**Cenci, Les** (1935)

| | | |
|---|---|---|
| *Francesco Cenci* | Di Domenica, R. | 1996 |

ARTHUR, TIMOTHY SHAY (1809–1885)
**Ten Nights in a Bar-Room** (1854)

| | | |
|---|---|---|
| *Ten Nights in a Bar-Room* | ** | 1858 |

ASCH, SHOLEM (1880–1957)
**Night** (1916)

| | | |
|---|---|---|
| *Night* | Weisgall, H. | 1932* |

ATWOOD, MARGARET (b. 1939)
**Eating Fire** (1965–1995)

| | | |
|---|---|---|
| *Marrying the Hangman* | Caltabiano, R. | 2000 |
| **Handmaid's Tale** (1985) | | |
| *Handmaid's Tale* | Ruders, P. | 2000 |

AUBIGNEY, T. BADOUIN d'
**Pie voleuse, La** (1815, with Caigniez)

| | | |
|---|---|---|
| *Magpie or the Maid* | Bishop, H. R. | 1815 |
| *Ninetta* | Bishop, H. R. | 1830 |

*AUCASSIN ET NICOLLETE* (13th cent., anon.)

| | | |
|---|---|---|
| *Azara* | Paine, J. K. | 1883* |

AUCHINCLOSS, LOUIS (1917–2010)
**Portrait in Brownstone** (1962)

| | | |
|---|---|---|
| *Portrait in Brownstone* | Reif, P. | 1966 |

BEAUMONT, FRANCIS (1584–1616)
   **Chances, The** (possibly with J. Fletcher)
     *Don John*                  Bishop, H. R.     1821
   **Humorous Lieutenant** (1697, with J. Fletcher)
     *Humorous Lieutenant*       Bishop, H. R.     1817
   **Royal Merchant** (1761, with J. Fletcher)
     *Royal Merchant*         Linley Sr., T., 1767
BECKETT, SAMUEL (1906–1989)
   **general**
     *Past Tense*              Oliver, S.        1974
   **Molloy** (1951)
     *Stiff*                   Chance, F.       1985
   **Neither**
     *Neither*                Feldman, M.     1977
BEERBOHM, MAX (1872–1956)
   **Happy Hypocrite**
     *Happy Hypocrite*       Levister, A.      1958
     *Happy Hypocrite*       Masland, W.     1978*
BEHN, APHRA (1610–1689)
   **poetry**
     *Powers of Two*         Truax, B.        2006
   **Emperor of the Moon** (1688)
     *Emperor of the Moon*    Arne, M.        1777
BELL, MADISON SMARRT (b. 1957)
   **All Souls' Rising** (1995), **Master of the Crossroads** (2000)
     *Toussaint before the Spirits*   Ruehr, E.       2003
BELLOW, SAUL (1915–2005)
   **Henderson the Rain King** (1959)
     *Lily*                   Kirchner, L.     1977
BENÉT, STEPHEN VINCENT (1898–1943)
   **Child Is Born** (1942)
     *Child Is Born*          Herrmann, B.    1955
   **Devil and Daniel Webster** (1937)
     *Devil and Daniel Webster*  Moore, D.       1939
   **Jacob and the Indians** (1938)
     *Jacob and the Indians*   Laderman, E.    1957
   **King of Cats**
     *King of Cats*          Oliver, H.       1976*
BERKOFF, STEVEN (b. 1937)
   **Greek** (1979)
     *Greek*                 Turnage, M.-A.   1988
BERLIOZ, HECTOR (1803–1869)
   **Soirées de l'orchestre, Les** (1852)
     *Euphonia 2344*        Austin, L.       1997*
BERNEY, WILLIAM (b. 1920)
   **Dark of the Moon** (with H. Richardson)
     *Conjur Moon*         Lloyd, T. C.    1979
BERR, GEORGES (1867–1942)
   **Satyr, Le** (with M. Guillemaud)
     *Pink Lady*           Caryll, I.        1911
BETTI, UGO (1892–1953)
   **Regina e gli insorti, La** (1949)
     *Queen and the Rebels*   Moss, L.       1965*

*BHAGHAVAD-GHITA*
     *Satyagraha*          Glass, P.        1981
BHARATCHANDRA (1712–1760)
   **Bengali tales**
     *Thief of Love*         Silver, S.       1985
BIBLE, The, APOCRYPHA
     *Bel and the Dragon*    Gardner, J.      1973
     *Hannah*             Lehrman, L.    1980
     *Judith*              Chadwick, G,   1901
     *Judith*              Goossens, E.   1929
     *Judith*              Smith, D.       1982
     *Judith and Holofernes*  Fink, M.        1978
     *Line of Terror*        McQueen, I.    1993
     *Susanna and the Elders*  Fink, M.        1956
     *Susannah*          Floyd, C.       1955
     *Tobias and the Angel*   Bliss, A.        1960
     *Tobias and the Angel*   Dove, J.        1999
BIBLE, The, NEW TESTAMENT
     *Amahl*              Menotti, G. C.   1951
     *Calvary*            Pasatieri, T.    1971
     *Dialogues*          Bauman, J.     1987
     *Erode the Great*      La Montaine, J.  1969
     *Gethsemane Park*    Moore, C.      1999
     *Jericho Road*        Aria, P.        1969
     *Jesus Christ Superstar*  Lloyd Webber   1971
     *Jesus of Nazareth*    Rudenstein, R.  1988
     *Judas*              Barlow, D.     1974*
     *Judas Tree*         Dickinson, P.   1965
     *Nativity*           Dello Joio, N.  1987
     *Nativity, The*        Hart, F.        1931*
     *Nativity, The*        Thompson, R.  1961
     *Last Supper*        Birtwistle, H.  2000
     *Lazarus*           Daniels, M.    1989
     *Novellis, Novellis*    La Montaine, J.  1961
     *Prodigal Son*        Britten, B.     1968
     *Prodigal Son*        Stepleton, J.   1983
     *Promise, The*        Townshend, J.  1997
     *Wenceslas*         Ridout, A.     1978
     *Yehu*               Zador, E.       1974
BIBLE, The, OLD TESTAMENT
     *Akhnaten*          Glass, P.        1984
     *Belshazzar's Feast*    Griesbach, J.   1835*
     *Belshazzar's Feast*    Root, G.    ca. 1853*
     *Bellyful*           Werder, F.     1975*
     *Binding of Isaac*     Chlarson, L.    1998
     *Burning Fiery Furnace*  Britten, B.     1966
     *Creation*          Ridout, A.     1973
     *David*             Goldman, E.   1967*
     *David and Bathsheba*  Barlow, D.     1969
     *Esther*            Hart, F.        1923
     *Esther*            Harvey, E. N.   1975
     *Esther*            Knoller, J.   ca. 1941
     *Esther*            Swados, E.    1988
     *Esther*            Meyerowitz, J.  1957
     *Esther*            Weisgall, H.   1993

BRADFORD, ROARK (1896–1948)
**John Henry** (1931)
| *Mississippi Legend* | Wolfe, J. | 1951 |

BRAGHT, THIELEMAN J. van (1625–1664)
**Bloody Theater** (1660)
| *Martyr's Mirror* | Parker, A. | 1971 |

BRAHMS, CARYL [DORIS CAROLINE ABRAHAMS]
(1901–1982)
**Under the Juniper Tree**
| *Mañana* | Benjamin, A. | 1956 |

BRAZIER, NICHOLAS (1783–1838)
**Pierre, ou, Le Couvreur** (with Carmouche, 1829)
| *Teddy the Tiler* | Rodwell, G. | 1830 |

BRECHT, BERTOLT (1898–1956)
**Kaukasische Kreidekreis, Der** (1944)
| *Caucasian Chalk Circle* | Chisholm, E. | 1963* |
**Kinderkreuzzug**
| *Children's Crusade 1939* | Ridout, A. | 1968 |
**Spitzel, Der**
| *Informer, The* | Legg, J, | 1985 |
**Verhör des Lukullus, Das** (1940)
| *Trial of Lucullus* | Sessions, R. | 1947 |

BREEN, T. H.
writings
| *Slip Knot* | Anderson, T. J. | 2003 |

BRIDIE, JAMES (OSBORNE HENRY MAVOR) (1888–1951)
**Tobias and the Angel** (1930)
| *Tobias and the Angel* | Dove, J. | 1999 |

BROD, MAX (1884–1968)
**Amerika**
| *America* | Kohs, E. B. | 1970 |

BROME, RICHARD (d. 1652?)
**Jovial Crew** (1641)
| *Jovial Crew* | ** | 1731 |

BRONTË, CHARLOTTE (1816–1855)
**Jane Eyre** (1847)
| *Jane Eyre* | Berkeley, M. | 2000 |
| *Jane Eyre* | Joubert, J. | 1998* |
| *Jane Heir* | Gordon, Norquist | 1989 |

BRONTË, EMILY (1818–1848)
**Wuthering Heights** (1846)
| *Wuthering Heights* | Floyd, C. | 1958 |
| *Wuthering Heights* | Herrmann, B. | 1943* |

BROOKE, HENRY (1703?–1783)
**Gustavus Vasa** (1739)
| *Hero of the North* | Kelly, M. | 1803 |
| *Zorinski* | Arnold, S. | 1795 |

BROOKE, RUPERT (1887–1915)
poems
| *Practice in the Art of Elocution* | Beeson, J. | 1999 |

BROUGHAM, JOHN (1810–1880)
**Duke's Motto**
| *Blanche de Nevers* | Balfe, M. | 1863 |

BROWN, GEORGE MACKAY (1921–1996)
general
| *Two Fiddlers* | Davies, P. M. | 1978 |
**Magnus** (1973)
| *Martyrdom of St. Magnus* | Davies, P. M. | 1977 |

BROWN, JOHN (1800–1859)
speeches and writings
| *John Brown* | Mechem, K. | 1989* |

BROWN, MAUD MORROW (1877–1968)
**University Greys** (1940)
| *University Greys* | Kreutz, A. | 1954 |

BROWNING, ROBERT (1812–1889)
**Pied Piper of Hamelin** (1842)
| *Pied Piper* | Swados, E. | 1989 |
| *Pied Piper of Hamelin* | Clokey, J. W. | 1920 |
| *Pied Piper of Hamelin* | Wilson, J. | 1969 |
**Pippa Passes** (1841)
| *Pippa's Holiday* | Beach, J. P. | 1915 |
**Ring and the Book** (1868–69)
| *Caponsacchi* | Hageman, R. | 1937 |

BRUNHOFF, JEAN de (1899–1937)
**Babar the Elephant** (1932)
| *Travels of Babar* | Mostel, R. | 2000 |

BÜCHNER, GEORG (1813–1837)
**Lenz** (1838)
| *Lenz* | Sitsky, L. | 1974 |
**Leonce und Lena** (1836)
| *Blind Man's Buff* | Davis, P. M. | 1972 |

BUDBILL, DAVID (b. 1940)
**Judevine** (1986)
| *Fleeting Animal* | Nielsen, E. | 2000 |

BUDNITZ, JUDY (b. 1973)
**Dog Days** (1998)
| *Dog Days* | Little, D. | 2009 |

BULGAKOV, M. A. (1891–1940)
**Heart of a Dog** (1925)
| *Murder of Comrad Sharik* | Bergsma, W. | 1973 |

BULLA, CLYDE ROBERT (1914–2007)
**Moon Singer** (1969)
| *Moon Singer* | Liptak, D. | 1998 |

BULWER-LYTTON, EDWARD (1803–1873)
**Eugene Aram** (1832)
| *Eugene Aram* | Bantock, G. | 1892* |
**Lady of Lyons** (1838)
| *Leonora* | Fry, W. | 1845 |
| *Pauline* | Cowen, F. | 1876 |
**Last Days of Pompeii** (1834)
| *Last Days of Pompeii* | Rodwell, G. | 1834 |
**Paul Clifford** (1830)
| *Paul Clifford* | Rodwell, G. | 1835 |

BUNYAN, JOHN (1628–1688)
**Pilgrim's Progress** (1678)
| *Little Women* | Adamo, M. | 1998 |
| *Shepherds of the Delectable Mountains* | Vaughan Williams | 1922 |

BURNETT, FRANCES HODGSON (1849–1924)
*Secret Garden* (1911)
*Secret Garden*                     Pliska, G.         1991
BURNS, OLIVE ANN
*Cold Sassy Tree* (1984)
*Cold Sassy Tree*          Floyd, C.               2000
BURNS, ROBERT (1759–1796)
**poems, correspondence**
*Life and Loves of Robert Burns*   Chisholm, E.       1963*
BURROUGHS, WILLIAM S. (1914–1997)
*Queer* (1953)
*Queer*                    Wold, E.                2001
BUTLER, SAMUEL (1835–1902)
*Erewhon* (1972), *Erewhon Revisited* (1901)
*Erewhon*                  Applebaum, L.           2000
BYRNE, DONN [BRIAN OSWALD DONN-BYRNE] (1889–1928)
*Blind Raftery and His Wife, Hilaria* (1924)
*Blind Raftery*            Trimble, J.             1957
*Messer Marco Polo* (1921)
*Messer Marco Polo*        Stern, M.               1999*
BYRON, (Lord) GEORGE GORDON(1788–1824)
**poems**
*Lord Byron*               Graham, J.              1926
*Don Juan* (1824)
*New Don Juan*             Rodwell, G.             1828

CABLE, GEORGE W. (1844–1925)
*Grandissimes, The* (1880)
*Koanga*                   Delius, F.              1895*
CAGE, JOHN (1912–1992)
*Silence, Year from Monday* (1961, 1967)
*But to Stockport*         Schubert/Valinsky       1986
CAIGNIEZ, LOUIS-CHARLES (1762–1842)
*Jugement de Salomon, Le* (1802)
*Voice of Nature*          Pelessier, V.           1802
*Pie voleuse, La* (1815, with d'Aubigny)
*Magpie or the Maid*       Bishop, H. R.           1815
*Ninetta*                  Bishop, H. R.           1830
CAIN, JAMES M. (1892–1977)
*Postman Always Rings Twice* (1934)
*Postman Always Rings Twice*   Paulus, S.          1982
CALHOUN, MATTHEW
*Statues on a Lawn*
*Statues on a Lawn*        Flanagan, T. J.         1983
CALLAGHAN, MORLEY (1903–1990)
**Christmas tale**
*Lost Child*               Ridout, G.              1976
CALVINO, ITALO (1923–1985)
*Città invisibili, Le* (1972)
*Invisible Cities*         Cerrone, C.             2009
*Cosmicomics* (1965)
*Without Colors*           Shiflett, M.            1989

*Fiabe Italiane* (1956)
*Jump into My Sack*        Grant, J.               1996
*Sotto il sole giaguaro* (1986)
*Tyrant, The*              Dresher, P.             2005
CAMPBELL, JOHN FRANCIS, comp., trans. (1822–1885)
*Popular Tales of the West Highlands* (1890)
*Vanishing Bridegroom*     Weir, J.                1992
CANETTI, ELIAS (1905–1994)
*Befristeten, Die* (1964)
*Numbered, The*            Lutyens, E.             1967*
ČAPEK, JOSEF (1887–1945)
*Insect Life* (1923, with K. Čapek)
*Insect Comedy*            Kalmanoff, M.           1977*
*Insect Play*              Senator, R.             1981*
ČAPEK, KAREL (1890–1938)
*Insect Life* (1923, with J. Čapek)
*Insect Comedy*            Kalmanoff, M.           1977*
*Insect Play*              Senator, R.             1981*
*White Plague* (1937)
*White Agony*              Fuchs, P. P.            1989
CAPELLANUS, ANDREAS [ANDRÉ, LE CHAPELAIN]
(12th cent.)
*De amore et amoris remedio*
*De Amore*                 Barkin, E.              1982
CAPOTE, TRUMAN (1924–1984)
*In Cold Blood* (1969)
*Failing Kansas*           Rouse, M.               1995
*CAPTIVE WILD WOMAN* (film, 1943)
*Acquanetta*               Gordon, M.              2010
CARACHE, MARIAN MOTLEY (b. 1954)
*Under the Arbor*
*Under the Arbor*          Greenleaf, R.           1992
CARAVAGGIO, POLIDORO CALDARA da (ca. 1495–ca. 1543)
*Death of the Virgin* (1606)
*Death of the Virgin*      Owen, R.                1981
CARDWELL, ANN [JEAN MAKINS PAWLEY]
*Crazy to Kill* (1941)
*Crazy to Kill*            Beckwith, J.            1989
CAREY, HENRY (1687–1743)
*Crown's Stratagem* (1730)
*Betty*                    Carey, H.               1732
CARMICHAEL, ALEXANDER, comp. (1832–1912)
*Carmina gadelica*
*Vanishing Bridegroom*     Weir, J.                1990
CARMICHAEL, JOHN
*Grace* (with E. Langois, 1988)
*Grace*                    Rudenstein, R.          2004
CARMOUCHE, PIERRE-FRÉDÉRIC-ADOLPHE (1792–1868)
*Pierre, ou, Le Couvreur* (with Brazier, 1829)
*Teddy the Tiler*          Rodwell, G.             1830
CARROLL, LEWIS [CHARLES DODGSON] (1832–1898)
*Alice's Adventures in Wonderland* (1865)
*Alice*                    Bachlund, G.            2004*

| | | |
|---|---|---|
| *Alice* | Osborne, W. | 1985 |
| *Alice* | Waits, T. | 1992 |
| *Alice in Wonderland* | Chauls, R. | 1976 |
| *Alice in Wonderland* | Chin, U. | 2007 |
| *Alice in Wonderland* | Josephs, W. | 1988 |
| *Alice in Wonderland* | McKay, J. | 2008 |
| *Alice in Wonderland* | Meachem, M. | 1982* |
| *Alice in Wonderland* | Slaughter, W. | 1906* |
| *Alice in Wonderland* | Westergaard, P. | 2006 |
| *Alice Meets the Mock Turtle* | Bingham, S. | 1988 |
| *Dreaming of Wonderland* | Romero, M. | 2001 |
| *Dum Tweedle Dee* | Del Tredici, D. | 1995* |
| *Final Alice* | Del Tredici, D. | 1976 |
| *Garden of Alice* | Raum, E. | 1985 |
| *Scenes in Wonderland* | Barab, S. | 2000 |
| **Alice through the Looking-Glass** (1871) | | |
| *Alice in Wonderland* | Chin, U. | 2007 |
| *Wonderglass* | Botti, S. | 1993 |
| **Hunting of the Snark** (1876) | | |
| *Hunting of the Snark* | Laderman, E. | 1961 |
| *Hunting of the Snark* | Roberts, E. | 1971 |
| *Hunting of the Snark* | Wilson, J. | 1965 |
| **Through the Looking-Glass** (1872) | | |
| *Alice in Wonderland* | McKay, J. | 2008 |
| *Through the Looking Glass* | John, A. | 2008 |
| *Through the Looking Glass* | Josephs, W. | 1978 |

CASANOVA, GIOVANNI GIACOMO (1725–1798)
**Histoire de ma vie, L'**

| | | |
|---|---|---|
| *Casanova's Homecoming* | Argento, D. | 1985 |

CATHER, WILLA (1873–1947)
**Eric Hermannson's Soul** (1900)

| | | |
|---|---|---|
| *Eric Hermannson's Soul* | Larsen, L. | 1998 |

CAVALCANTI, GUIDO (1255–1300)
**poetry**

| | | |
|---|---|---|
| *Powers of Two* | Truax, B. | 2006 |

CAZOTTE, JACQUES (1719–1792)
**Diable amoureux, Le** (1776)

| | | |
|---|---|---|
| *Diable amoureux, Le* | Rodriguez, F. | 1979 |

CENTLIVRE, SUSANNA (1667–1723)
**Bold Stroke for a Wife, A** (1718)

| | | |
|---|---|---|
| *Win Her* | Barnett, J. | 1832 |

CERVANTES, MIGUEL de (1547–1616)
**general**

| | | |
|---|---|---|
| *Happy Captive* | Galliard, J. | 1741 |
| **Cueva de Salamanca, La** | | |
| *Student from Salamanca* | Bach, J. | 1980 |
| **Don Quixote** | | |
| *Adventure of Don Quixote* | Macfarren, G. | 1846 |
| *Don Quixote* | Arnold, S. | 1774 |
| *Don Quixote* | Clay, F. | 1876 |
| *Don Quixote* | De Koven, R. | 1889 |
| *Don Quixote* | Hewitt, T. J. | 1909 |
| *Don Quixote* | Hill, A. | 1904 |

| | | |
|---|---|---|
| *Don Quixote* | Rodwell, G. | 1833 |
| *Don Quixote in England* | ** | 1734 |
| *Mountaineers, The* | Arnold, S. | 1793 |
| **Novelas exemplares** (1613): **Celoso extremeño, El** | | |
| *Felipe* | Aitken, H. | 1981 |
| *Padlock, The* | Dibdin, C. | 1768 |
| **Gitanella, La** (ca. 1614) | | |
| *Bohemian Girl* | Balfe, M. | 1843 |
| *Preciosa* | Hawes, W. | 1825 |

CHAO FAMILY ORPHAN (13th cent. tale)

| | | |
|---|---|---|
| *Night at the Chinese Opera* | Weir, J. | 1987 |

CHASE-RIBOUD, BARBARA
**Egypt's Nights**

| | | |
|---|---|---|
| *Egypt's Nights* | Burrs, L. S. | 2008 |

CHATRIAN, ALEXANDRE (1826–1890)
**Ami Fritz** (1846, with E. Erckmann)

| | | |
|---|---|---|
| *Friend Fritz* | Edwards, J. | 1893 |

CHATWIN, BRUCE (1940–1989)
**Songlines, The** (1987)

| | | |
|---|---|---|
| *Man with Footsoles* | Volans, K. | 1993 |

CHAUCER, GEOFFREY (d. 1400)
**Canterbury Tales** (ca. 1387–1400)
**general**

| | | |
|---|---|---|
| *Canterbury Tale* | Roe, B. | 1986 |
| *Fiery Tales* | Sitsky, L. | 1976 |
| **Cock and the Fox** | | |
| *Tales from Chaucer* | Gordon, P. | 1959* |
| **Franklin's Tale** | | |
| *Franklin's Tale* | Sokoloff, N. | 1961 |
| **Nun's Priest's Tale** | | |
| *Chanticleer* | Barab, S. | 1956* |
| *Chanticleer* | Barthelson, J. | 1967 |
| *Nun's Priest's Tale* | Finney, R. L. | 1965 |
| *Tale from Chaucer* | Gordon, P. | 1959* |
| *Wheel of the World* | Crosse, G. | 1972 |
| **Pardoner's Tale** | | |
| *Pardoner's Tale* | Chisholm, E. | 1961 |
| *Pardoner's Tale* | Davis, J. S. | 1967 |
| *Pardoner's Tale* | Lubin, E. | 1966 |
| *Pardoner's Tale* | Rorem, N. | 1958 |
| *Pardoner's Tale* | Ridout, A. | 1970 |
| *Wayfarers, The* | Joubert, J. | 1984 |
| **Parlement of Foules** | | |
| *Parliament of Fowls* | Craton, J. | 2007* |
| **Troilus and Criseyde** | | |
| *Criseyde* | Shields, A. | 2008 |
| *Troilus and Cressida* | Walton, W. | 1954 |
| **Wife of Bath's Tale** | | |
| *Wife of Bath's Tale* | Legg, J. | 1986 |
| *Woman's Will* | Davy, J. | 1820 |

CHEKHOV, ANTON (1860–1904)
**Bear, The (The Boor)** (1888)

| | | |
|---|---|---|
| *Bear, The* | Walton, W. | 1967 |

*Elfrida*
| *Elfrida* | Arne, T. A. | 1772 |

COLVIN, IAN DUNCAN (1877–1938)
   **Leper's Flute** (1920)
| *Leper's Flute* | Bryson, E. | 1926 |

CONGEAU, EMILY
   **Princess Mona**
| *Auster* | Hill, A. | 1922 |

CONGREVE, WILLIAM (1670–1729)
   **Incognita** (1691)
| *Incognita* | Wellesz, E. | 1951 |
   **Love for Love** (1695)
| *Buxom Joan* | Taylor, R. | 1778 |

CONLEY, ROBERT J. (b. 1940)
   **Mountain Windsong**
| *Mountain Windsong* | Chlarson, L. | 1995 |

CONRAD, JOSEPH (1857–1924)
   **Heart of Darkness** (1899)
| *Heart of Darkness* | O'Regan, T. | 2006 |
   **Under Western Eyes** (1911)
| *Under Western Eyes* | Joubert, J. | 1969 |
   **Victory** (1915)
| *Victory* | Bennett, R. R. | 1970 |

CONSIDINE, JOHN (b. 1935)
   **Wedding, A** (with R. Altman)
| *Wedding, A* | Bolcom, W. | 2004 |

COOPER, JAMES FENNIMORE (1789–1851)
   **Last of the Mohicans** (1826)
| *Last of the Mohicans* | Henderson, A. | 1976 |

COPPÉE, FRANÇOIS (1842–1908)
   **Pour la couronne** (1895)
| *Cross and the Crescent* | MacAlpin, C. | 1903 |

CORNEILLE, PIERRE (1606–1684)
   **Illusion comique, L'** (1636)
| *Illusion, The* | Richardson, A. | 2000* |

*CORONATION STREET*, TV series (beg. 1960)
| *Ring, The* | Oliver, S. | 1984 |

*CORPUS CHRISTI PLAYS* (medieval)
| *Shephardes Play* | La Montaine, J. | 1967 |

CORSARO, FRANK (b. 1924)
   **Lyric Suite** (1996)
| *Frau Margot* | Pasatieri, T. | 2006 |

COSTA, SEBASTIAN
   **memoirs**
| *King for Corsica* | George, G. | 1981 |

COSTIGAN, JAMES (1926–2007)
   **Little Moon of Alban** (1958)
| *Little Moon of Alban* | Ferris, W. | 1974* |

COTTIN, SOPHIE (1770–1807)
   **Elisabeth, ou, Les éxilés de Sibérie** (1806)
| *Exile, The* | Mazzinghi, J. | 1808 |

*COVENTRY NATIVITY PLAY*
| *Bethlehelm* | Boughton, R. | 1915 |

COX, LOUISE
   **Olaf**
| *Olaf* | Kirkpatrick, H. | 1912 |

CRANE, STEPHEN (1871–1900)
   **Bride Comes to Yellow Sky** (1898)
| *Bride Comes to Yellow Sky* | Nixon, R. | 1968 |
| *Showdown on Two Street* | Magrill, S. | 2000 |

CRAVEN, LADY (ELIZABETH, 1750–1828)
   **Tale for Christmas**
| *Baron Kinkverkanksdors- prakingatchdern* | Arnold, S. | 1781 |

CRÉBILLON, C. P. J. de (1707–1777)
   **Sofa, Le**
| *Sofa, The* | Maconchy, E. | 1959 |

CROCKER, CHARLES TEMPLETON
   **Land of Happiness** (1917)
| *Fay-Yen-Fah* | Redding, J. | 1925 |

CRONENBURG, DAVID (b. 1943)
   **Fly, The** (1986)
| *Fly, The* | Shore, H. | 2008 |

CROSS, IAN (b. 1925)
   **God Boy** (1957)
| *God Boy* | Ritchie, A. | 2004 |

CROY, HOMER (1883–1965)
   **Lady from Colorado** (1957)
| *Lady from Colorado* | Ward, R. | 1964 |
| *Lady Kate* | Ward, R. | 1994 |

CROZIER, ERIC (1914–1994)
   **Rab the Rhymer** (1953)
| *Rab the Rhymer* | Dunlop/Oppenheim | 1953 |

CUMBERLAND, RICHARD (1732–1811)
   **Summer's Tale** (1765)
| *Amelia* | Dibdin, C., et al. | 1771 |
| *Amelia* | Piccinni et al. | 1768 |

CUMMINGS, E. E. (1894–1962)
   **general**
| *America, I Love You* | Ahlstrom, D. | 1981 |
| *Cabaret Opera* | Russo, W. | 1970 |
   **Santa Claus** (1946)
| *Santa Claus* | Smith, L. | 1955 |

CUSACK, DYMPHNA (1902–1981)
   **Shallow Cups** (1934)
| *Quickening, The* | Selleck, J. | 1998 |

DAHL, ROALD (1916–1990)
   **Charlie and the Chocolate Factory** (1964)
| *Golden Ticket* | Ash, P. | 2010 |
   **Fantastic Mr. Fox** (1970)
| *Fantastic Mr. Fox* | Picker, T. | 1998 |
   **Soldier, The**
| *Soldier, The* | Engel, L. | 1956 |

DOGGET, THOMAS (d. 1721)
**Hob, or, The Country Wake** (1696)
*Flora*                                      **                     1729
DONNE, JOHN (1572–1631)
**poems**
*Doctor Atomic*                      Adams, J.              2005
DOOLITTLE, HILDA (1886–1961)
**Helen in Egypt** (1954)
*Helen in Egypt*                     Elkus, J.              1970
DORVIGNY, L. F. A. (1742–1812)
**plays**
*None So Blind*                      Arnold, S.             1782
DOSTOYEVSKY, FEODOR MIKHAILOVICH (1821–1881)
**Gentle Creature** (1876)
*Gentle Spirit*                      Taverner, J.           1977
**Idiot, The** (1869)
*Myshkin*                            Eaton, J.              1973
DOWSON, ERNEST (1867–1900)
**Pierrot of the Minute** (1897)
*Pierrot of the Minute*              Engel, L.              1929
DOYLE, ARTHUR CONAN, Sir (1859–1930)
**general**
*Out of This World*                  Caron, J.              2006*
**Red-Headed League**
*Red-Headed League*                  Dvorkin, J.            1992
DOYLE, BRIAN (b. 1935)
**Angel Square** (1987)
*Angel Square*                       Crawley, C.            1996
DRAPER, RUTH (1884–1956)
**Italian Lesson**
*Italian Lesson*                     Hoiby, L.              1982
DREISER, THEODORE (1871–1945)
**American Tragedy** (1925)
*American Tragedy*                    Picker, T.             2005
**St. Columba and the Stream**
*Sandhog*                            Robinson, E.           1954
DRINKWATER, JOHN (1882–1937)
**X=0**
*Equation, The*                      Bush, G.               1968
DRYDEN, JOHN (1631–1700)
**Amphitryon** (1690)
*Jupiter and Alcmena*                Dibdin, C.             1781
**Cymon and Iphigenia**
*Cymon*                              Arne, M.               1767
**Indian Emperor** (1665)
*Indian Queen*                       Purcell, H.            1695
**Secular Masque** (1700)
*Secular Masque*                     Boyce, W.              1749
*Secular Masque*                     Purcell, D.            1700
DUCHAMP, MARCEL (1887–1968)
**Mariée mise à nu**
*Bride Stripped Bare*                Shere, C.              1981

DUMANOIR, M. (PHILLIPE) (1805–1865)
**Don César de Bazan** (1844, with A. d'Ennery)
*Maritania*                          Wallace, V.            1845
DUMAS, ALEXANDRE, fils (1824–1895)
**general**
*Delicate King*                      Gruenberg, L.          1955
DUMAS, ALEXANDRE, père (1802–1870)
**Pasqual Bruno** (1838)
*Pasqual Bruno*                      Hatton, J. L.          1844
**Romulus** (1854)
*Romulus*                            Karchin, L.            2007
Du MAURIER, DAPHNE (1907–1989)
**Rebecca** (1938)
*Rebecca*                            Josephs, W.            1983
Du MAURIER, GEORGE (1834–1896)
**Trilby**
*Trilby*                             Piket, F.              1967
DUNCAN, ISADORA (1877–1927)
**writings**
*Woman in the Garden*                Fine, V.               1978
DUNSANY, LORD (1878–1957)
**Glittering Gate** (1923)
*Glittering Gate*                    Glanville-Hicks, P.    1959
**Jest of Hahalabra** (1928)
*Jest of Hahalabra*                  Cotel, M.              1961
**Night at an Inn**
*Ruby, The*                          Dello Joio, N.         1955
DURACK, MARY (1913–1994)
**Keep Him My Country**
*Dalgerie*                           Penberthy, J.          1959
DURAN, LEO (b. 1883)
**Daymio, The** (1921)
*Namiko-San*                         Franchetti, A.         1925
D'URFEY, THOMAS (1653–1723)
**Love for Money** (1629)
*Boarding School*                    **                     1733
DWIGHT, H. G. (1875–1959)
**Stamboul Nights** (1916)
*In the Pasha's Garden*              Seymour, J.            1935

EBERHARD, ISABELLE
**journals** (1923)
*Song from the Uproar*               Mazzoli, M.            2009
EDDA, PROSE EDDA
*Ragnarok*                           Bedford, D.            1982
*Snow Queen*                         Fine, E.               2002*
EDGEWORTH, MARIA (1767–1849)
**Prussian Vase**
*Maid of Saxony*                     Horn, C. E.            1842
**Will, The**
*Thirty Thousand*                    Reeve, W., et al.      1804
EGOYAN, ATOM (b. 1960)
**Elsewhereless**
*Elsewhereless*                      Sharman, R.            1998

*EGYPTIAN BOOK OF THE DEAD*
 *Odyssey 1*   Shields, A.  1968*
 *Odyssey 2*   Shields, A.  1975
ELGUERA, AMALIA
 **Earl of Moray**
 *Mary, Queen of Scots* Musgrave, T. 1977
ELIOT, GEORGE (1819–1880)
 **Silas Marner** (1861)
 *Silas Marner*  Joubert, J.  1961
ELIOT, T[HOMAS] S[TEARNS] (1888–1965)
 **general**
 *Black Roses*  Chisholm, E.  1954
 **Sweeney Agonistes** (1932)
 *Sweeney Agonistes* Dankworth, J. 1965
 *Sweeney Agonistes* Winslow, R.  1952
ELMAN, LOIS
 **plays**
 *Lillith*   Weisgall, H.  1934*
EMANUEL, JAMES A.
 **poems**
 *Dreaming Blue*  Larsen, L.  2002
ENNERY, ADOLPHE d' (1811–1899)
 **Don César de Bazan** (1844, with M. Dumanoir)
 *Maritania*  Wallace, V.  1845
ENRIGHT, ELIZABETH (1909–1968)
 **Moment of Rain, The**
 *Tale for a Deaf Ear* Bucci, M.  1957
EPIMENIDES (6th century B.C.)
 *Solon the Dreamer* Sternau, C.  1996*
ERCKMANN, EMILE (1822–1899)
 **Ami Fritz,** with P.-A. Chatrian (1846)
 *Friend Fritz*  Edwards, J.  1893
ERNST, MAX (1901–1976)
 **Rêve d'une petite fille** (1930)
 *Little Girl Dreams* Wold, E.  1995
ERSKINE, JOHN (1879–1951)
 **Private Life of Helen of Troy** (1925)
 *Helen Retires*  Antheil, G.  1934
EURIPIDES (ca. 484–ca. 406 B.C.)
 **Alkestis** (438 B.C.)
 *Alceste*   Handel, G. F. 1749*
 *Alcestiad, The*  Talma, L.  1962
 *Alkestis*   Boughton, R.  1922
 **Antigone**
 *Death of Antigone* Smith Brindle, R. 1971
 **Bacchae, The**
 *Bacchae, The*  Antoniou, T.  1992
 *Bacchae, The*  Buller, J.  1992
 *Bassarids, The*  Henze, H. W.  1966
 *Revelation in the Courthouse Park* Partch, H. 1962
 **Hippolytus**
 *Hippolytus*  Drysdale, L.  1905

*Ion*
 *Ion*   Vir, P.  2000
 **Iphigenia in Tauris**
 *Iphigenia in Exile* Gifford, H.  1985*
 **Medea**
 *Medea*   Bryars, G.  1982
 *Medea*   Elkus, J.  1970
 *Medea*   Henderson, A.  1972
 *Medea*   Werder, F.  1985
 **Trojan Women**
 *Sarajevo*   Osborne, N.  1958
 *Trojan Women*  Garwood, M.  1967
EVANS, GEORGE EYRE (1857–1939)
 **Lampeter, House of Peterwell**
 *Black Ram*  Parrott, I.  1957
*EVERYMAN* (ca. 1500)
 *Everyman*  Lester, W.  1927
 *Everyman*  Lehmann, L.  1915
 *Reverend Everyman* Brotons, S.  1990
 *Summoning of Everyman* Wilson, C.  1973
EYRE, EDWARD JOHN (1815–1901)
 **Journals of Expeditions of Discovery** (1845)
 *Edward John Eyre* Conyngham, B.  1971
FAINLIGHT, RUTH (b. 1931)
 **European Story**
 *European Story*  Álvarez, G.  1993
FARBER, NORMA
 **poems**
 *Garden Party*  Pinkham, D.  1977
FASSBINDER, RAINER WERNER (1945–1982)
 **Bitteren Tränen der Petra von Kant, Die**
 *Bitter Tears of Petra von Kant* Barry, G. 2005
FAUST legend
 *Bargain, The*  McPeek, B.  1966
FAVART, CHARLES (1710–1792)
 **Bohémienne, La**
 *Gipsies, The*  Arnold, S.  1778
FÉNELON de la MOTHE (1651–1715)
 **Télémaque** (1699)
 *Calypso and Telemachus* Galliard, J. E. 1712
FERBER, EDNA (1887–1968)
 **Show Boat** (1926)
 *Show Boat*  Kern, J.  1927
FERMOR, PATRICK LEIGH (b. 1915)
 **Violins of Saint-Jacques** (1953)
 *Violins of St. Jacques* Williamson, M. 1966
FERRIER, PAUL (1843–1920)
 **Troisième lune, La** (with P. Ferrier)
 *See-See*   Jones/Tours  1906
FÉVAL, PAUL (1817–1887)
 **Bossu, Le** (1858)
 *Blanche de Nevers* Balfe, M.  1863

**FEYDEAU, GEORGES (1862–1921)**
  *Puce à l'oreille, La* (1907)
    *Hotel Casablanca*      Pasatieri, T.      2007
**FIELDING, HENRY (1707–1754)**
  *Don Quixote in England*
    *Sot, The*      Arne, T. A.      1775
    *Squire Badger*      Arne, T. A.      1772
  *Tom Jones* (1749)
    *Tom Jones*      Arnold/Arne      1769
    *Tom Jones*      German, E.      1907
    *Tom Jones*      Oliver, S.      1976
  *Tragedy of Tragedies* (1730)
    *Life, Death, of Tom Thumb*      Dibdin, C.      1785
    *Opera of Operas*      Arne, T. A.      1733
    *Tom Thumb*      Markordt, J.      1780
  *Tumble-down Dick* (1736)
    *Tumbledown Dick*      Larsen, L.      1980
  *Wedding Day*
    *Wedding Day*      Barthelemon, F.      1773
**FINCH, ANNE (1661–1720)**
  **poetry**
    *Powers of Two*      Truax, B.      2006
**FINDLAY, TIMOTHY**
  *Pilgrim* (1999)
    *Dream Healer*      Burritt, L.      2008
**FINDLER, GERALD**
  *Legends of the Lake Counties* (1967)
    *Will of Her Own*      Gundry, I.      1973*
  *Fisher King* (1991)
    *Fisher King*      Lowenstein, M.      2007
**FINE, MORTON (1916–1991)**
  *Hunted, The* (with D. Friedkin)
    *Hunted, The*      Mailman, M.      1959
**FITCH, CLYDE (1865–1909)**
  *Captain Jinks* (1902)
    *Captain Jinks*      Beeson, J.      1975
**FITZGERALD, DUDLEY FITTS-ROBERT, trans.**
  *Antigone* (Sophocles)
    *Antigone*      Constantinides, D.      1993
**FITZGERALD, F. SCOTT (1896–1940)**
  *Great Gatsby*
    *Great Gatsby*      Harbison, J.      1999
  *Tales of the Jazz Age* (1922)
    *Curious Case of Benjamin Button*      Eaton, J.      2010
**FLAUBERT, GUSTAVE (1821–1880)**
  *Bouvard et Pécuchet* (1881)
    *Bouvard and Pécuchet*      Aplvor, D.      1974*
  *Julian l'Hospitalier* (1877)
    *Julian*      Fussell, C.      1972
**FLECKER, JAMES ELROY (1884–1915)**
  *Don Juan*
    *Juan*      Alwyn, W.      1971*

**FLETCHER, JOHN (1579–1625)**
  *Chances, The* (possibly with F. Beaumont)
    *Don John*      Bishop, H. R.      1821
  *Humorous Lieutenant* (1697, with F. Beaumont)
    *Humorous Lieutenant*      Bishop, H. R.      1817
  *Island Princess* (1687)
    *Island Princess*      Purcell, D.      1698
  *Pilgrim, The*
    *Noble Outlaw*      Bishop, H. R.      1815
  *Prophetess, The* (with P. Massinger)
    *Dioclesian*      Purcell, H.      1690
  *Royal Merchant* (1761, with Beaumont)
    *Royal Merchant*      Linley, T., Sr.      1767
  *Two Noble Kinsmen* (1612–13, prob. with Shakespeare)
    *Love and Madness*      Arnold, S.      1795
**FLETCHER, LUCILLE (1912–2000)**
  *Sorry, Wrong Number* (1943)
    *Sorry, Wrong Number*      Beeson, J.      1999
    *Sorry, Wrong Number*      Moross, J.      1980
**FONTENELLE, BERNARD LE BOVIER de (1657–1757)**
  *Endymion*
    *Endymion*      Bennett, R. R.      1927*
**FORBES, BRYAN (b. 1926)**
  *Séance on a Wet Afternoon* (1964)
    *Séance on a Wet Afternoon*      Schwartz, S.      2009
**FORBES, ESTHER (1891–1967)**
  *Mirror for Witches, A* (1928)
    *Bilby's Doll*      Floyd, C.      1976
**FORNÉS, MARÍA IRENE (b. 1930)**
  *Terra Incognita* (1992)
    *Terra Incognita*      Sierra, R.      1997
**FORSCHER, J.**
  **general**
    *Christopher Columbus*      Kalmanoff, M.      1976
**FORSTER, E[DWARD] M[ORGAN] (1879–1970)**
  *Albergo Empedocle*
    *Albergo Empedocle*      Barker, P.      1990
  *Obelisk, The*
    *Obelisk, The*      Eaton, M.      1984
  *Room with a View*
    *Room with a View*      Nelson, R.      1993
  *Where Angels Fear to Tread* (1905)
    *Where Angels Fear to Tread*      Weiser, M.      1999
**FORSYTH, JAMES (1913–2005)**
  *Other Heart*
    *Villon*      Read, G.      1967*
**FOUQUÉ, FRIEDRICH de la MOTTE (1777–1843)**
  *Undine* (1811)
    *Ondine*      Barab, S.      1995
    *Undine*      Ware, H.      1923
**FRANCE, ANATOLE (1844–1924)**
  *Celui qui épousa une femme muette* (1908)
    *Dumb Wife*      Gruenberg, L.      1923*
    *Thais and Talmaae*      Campbell, C..      1921

**FRAZER, JAMES GEORGE (1854–1941)**
**Golden Bough** (1922)
Assassin Tree | MacCrae, S. | 2006
**FREEMAN, MARY WILKINS (1852–1930)**
**Village Singer**
Village Singer | Paulus, S. | 1979
**FREUD, SIGMUND (1856–1939)**
**Fragment of an Analysis** (1905)
Dora | Shiflett, M. | 1999
**FRIEDKIN, DAVID**
**Hunted**, The (with M. Fine)
Hunted, The | Mailman, M. | 1959
**FRIEDMAN, STEVE**
**Bread and Roses**
Bread & Roses | Glickman/Chen | 2000
**FRIEL, BRIAN (b. 1929)**
**Lovers** (1967)
Ballymore | Wargo, R. | 1999
**FROST, ROBERT (1874–1963)**
**Death of the Hired Man** (1905)
Death of the Hired Man | McIntyre, P. | 1966*
Death of the Hired Man | Van de Vate, N. | 1999
**FRY, CHRISTOPHER (1907–2005)**
**Phoenix Too Frequent** (1946)
Phoenix Too Frequent | Oliver, S. | 1970
**FUZELIER, LOUIS (1672–1752)**
**Momus fabuliste ou, Les nôces de Vulcain** (with Le Grand, 1720)
Momus Turn'd Fabulist | ** | 1729

**GAGE, NICHOLAS (b. 1939)**
**Eleni** (1983)
Eleni | Ratcliff, C. | 2008
Jacob's Room | Subotnick, M. | 1993
**GALEANO, EDUARDO (b. 1940)**
**Book of Embraces** (1991)
House of Words | Bouchard, L. | 2003
**GALILEO, GALILEI (1564–1642)**
**letters**
Galileo Galilei | Glass, P. | 2002
**GALLARDO, EDWARD F. (b. 1949)**
**Waltz on a Merry-Go-Round**
Waltz on a Merry-Go-Round | Taub, B. | 1979*
**GALLOWAY, JAMES "SANTA FE" (1938–2003)**
**Mirage** (1981)
Mirage | Galloway, J. | 2003
**GARCÍA LORCA, FEDERICO (1898–1936)**
**Amor de Don Perlimplín con Belisa en su jardín** (1931)
Belisa | Biales, A. | 1989
Don Perlimplin | Rieti, V. | 1952
Love of Don Perlimplin | Doyle, R. | 1984
Love of Don Perlimplin | Susa, C. | 1984
Nightingale's to Blame | Holt, S. | 1998
Perlimplín | Morrill, K. | 1989

*Asi que pasen cinco anos*
Wind Remains | Bowles, P. | 1943
**Bodas de sangre** (1933)
Blood Wedding | LeFanu, N. | 1992
Blood Wedding | Smith, H. | 1953
**Retablillo de Don Cristóbal**
Don Cristóbal | Crawford, J. | 1970
**Yerma** (1934)
Yerma | Aplvor, D. | 1961
Yerma | Bowles, P. | 1958
Yerma | Wilding-White | 1962*
**GARDNER, DOROTHY (b. 1926)**
**Eastward in Eden** (1947)
Eastward in Eden | Meyerowitz, J. | 1951
**GARDNER, EARLE STANLEY (1889–1970)**
**Case of the Substitute Face**
Night at Sea | Gyring, E. | 1954*
**GARDNER, JOHN (1933–1982)**
**Grendel** (1971)
Grendel | Goldenthal, E. | 2006
**GARRICK, DAVID (1717–1779)**
**general**
Garrick | Stoessel, A. | 1937
Jubilee | Dibdin, C. | 1769
**Catherine and Petruccio** (1756)
Taming of the Shrew | Braham/Cooke | 1828
**Clandestine Marriage, The,** with Colman Sr. (1766)
Clandestine Marriage | Wishart, P. | 1971
**GARRO, ELENA (1920–1998)**
**Hogar sólido, Un** (1958)
Solid House | Galloway, J. | 1998
**GASKELL, ELIZABETH CLEGHORN (1810–1865)**
**Mary Barton** (1848)
Mary Barton | Cooke, A. | 1954*
**GAUTIER, THÉOPHILE (1811–1872)**
**Nuit de Cléopâtre, Une**
Cleopatra's Night | Hadley, H. | 1920
One Night of Cleopatra | Gruenberg, L. | 1954
*GAWAIN* (late 14th cent.)
Gawain | Birtwistle, H. | 1991
**GAY, JOHN (1695–1732)**
**What D'Ye Call It** (ca. 1715)
What D'Ye Call It | Tate, P. | 1966
**GENET, JEAN (1910–1986)**
**Balcon, Le** (1956)
Balcony, The | Di Domenica, R. | 1975
**GENLIS, STÉPHANIE FÉLICITÉ, Comtesse de (1746–1830)**
**Adèle et Théodore**
Captive of Spilburg | Dussek/Kelly | 1798
**Siège de La Rochelle, La**
Siege of Rochelle | Balfe, M. | 1835
**Zuma, ou, La découverte du quinquina**
Zuma | Bishop/Braham | 1818

GEORGE, W. L.
**Shadows**
*Impersonating Maurice*         Drummond, J.      2004
GESSNER, SALOMON (1730–1788)
**Erast** (1775)
*Reconciliation, The*              **            1790*
GHELDERODE, MICHEL de (1898–1962)
**Escuriale** (1928)
*Escorial, The*                 Levy, M.         1958
*Pantagleize*                   Starer, R.       1973
GIBSON, WILLIAM (b. 1914)
**Father of the Child**
*Father of the Child*           Barab, S.        1985
GIFFORD, BARRY (b. 1946)
**Lost Highway** (with D. Lynch, 1997)
*Lost Highway*                  Neuwirth, O.     2003
GILBERT, WILLIAM S. (1836–1911)
**Engaged!** (1877)
*Engaged*                       Rowell/Mobbs     1962
**Etiquette** (1869)
*Gentleman's Island*            Horovitz, J.     1958
**Tom Cobb** (1875)
*Perfect Plan*                  Barab, S.        2004
GILBERT-LECOMTE, ROGER (1907–1943)
**Odyssey of Ulysses the Palimped**
*Odyssey 1*                     Shields, A.      1968*
*Odyssey 2*                     Shields, A.      1975
*GILGAMESH, EPIC OF* (ca. 2000 B.C., Babylonian)
*Death of Enkidu*               Somers, H.       1977
*Forest, The*                   Byrne, D.        1988
*Gilgamesh*                     Dickman, S.      2002
GILHAM, GEOFF
**Crossing, The**
*Crossing, The*                 Metcalf, J.      1984
GILMAN, CHARLOTTE PERKINS (1860–1935)
**Yellow Wallpaper** (1986)
*Yellow Wallpaper*              Perera, R.       1989
GILROY, FRANK D. (b. 1925)
**Far Rockaway** (1965)
*Hero, The*                     Bucci, M.        1965
GINSBERG, ALLEN (1926–1997)
**poems**
*Waking in New York*            Lauten, E.       1999
GIRAUDOUX, JEAN (1882–1944)
**Judith** (1931)
*Judith and Holofernes*         Fink, M.         1978
**Ondine** (1939)
*Ondine*                        Barab, S.        1995
GLASPELL, SUSAN (1876–1948)
**Trifles** (1916)
*Trifles*                       Bilotta, G.      2010
GODWIN, FRANCIS (BISHOP) (1562–1633)
**Man in the Moon, The**
*Wonders in the Sun*              **            1706

GODWIN, WILLIAM (1756–1836)
**Things as They Are, or, The Adventures of Caleb Williams**
(1794)
*Iron Chest*                    Storace, S.      1796
GOETHE, JOHANN WOLFGANG VON (1749–1832)
**Faust** (1832)
*Faust*                         Becker, J. J.    1951
*Faust Counter Faust*           Gessner, J.      1971
*Faustus*                       Bishop, H. R.    1825
*Faustus Part 1*                Rudenstein, R.   1986
*Henry Faust*                   Isaacs, G.       1993
*Lamentations of Doctor Faustus* Hewitt, M.      1994
*Mephistopheles*                Lutz, M.         1855
**Prometheus** (1774)
*Prometheus Condemned*          Kupferman M.     1978
GOGOL, NIKOLAI VASIL'EVICH (1809–1852)
**Diary of a Madman** (1835)
*Diary of a Madman*             Searle, H.       1958
**Inspector General** (1836)
*Inspector from Ro.ne*          Musto, J.        2010
*Inspector General*             Zador, E.        1928
**Marriage** (1842)
*Marriage, The*                 Martinů, B.      1953
**Tale of How Ivan Ivanovich Quarreled with Ivan Nikiforovich**
*With Such Friends*             Schnauber, T.    2007
GOLDBERG, LEA (1911–1970)
**Lady of the Castle** (1955)
*Lady of the Castle*            Spektor, M.      1982
*GOLDEN BULL, THE*
*Cabinet, The*                  Reeve et al.     1802
GOLDONI, CARLO (1707–1793)
**Locandiera, La** (1753)
*Bianca*                        Hadley, H.       1918
**Servitore di due padroni** (1753)
*Servant of Two Masters*        Giannini, V.     1967
**Ventaglio, Il**
*Fan, The*                      Goldstein, L.    1989
GOLDMANN, EMMA (1869–1940)
**Living My Life** (1931)
*Emma*                          Fine, E.         2005*
GOLDSMITH, OLIVER (1730–1774)
**Deserted Village** (1770)
*Deserted Village*              Glover, J.       1880
**Edwin and Angelina** (1764)
*Edwin and Angelina*            Pelissier, V.    1796
**She Stoops to Conquer** (1773)
*She Stoops to Conquer*         Aplvor, D.       1947*
*She Stoops to Conquer*         Macfarren, G.    1864
**Vicar of Wakefield** (1766)
*Robin Hood*                    Shield, W.       1784
GOODMAN, PAUL (1911–1972)
**Jonah**
*Jonah*                         Beeson, J.       1950*

GORDON, MARY (b. 1949)
**Pearl** (2005)

| | | |
|---|---|---|
| *Pearl* | Davidson, T. | 2009 |

GOTTHELF, JEREMIAS (1797–1854)
**Schwarze Spinne, Die** (1842)

| | | |
|---|---|---|
| *Black Spider* | Weir, J. | 1985 |

GRAHAM, GEORGE (1728?–1767)
**Telemachus** (1763)

| | | |
|---|---|---|
| *Telemachus* | Bishop, H. R. | 1815 |
| *Telemachus* | Hayes, P. | 1763 |

GRAHAME, KENNETH (1859–1932)
**Wind in the Willows** (1908)

| | | |
|---|---|---|
| *Wind in the Willows* | Rutter, J. | 1981* |

GRANVILLE, GEORGE [LANDSDOWNE, GEORGE GRANVILLE, BARON] (1667–1735)
**Poems** (1712)

| | | |
|---|---|---|
| *Peleus and Thetis* | Boyce, W. | ca. 1740 |
| *Peleus and Thetis* | Hayes, W. | ca. 1749 |
| *Positive Man* | Arne/Arnold | 1782 |

GRAVES, ROBERT (1895–1985)
**Homer's Daughter** (1955)

| | | |
|---|---|---|
| *Nausicaa* | Glanville-Hicks | 1961 |

GRAVES, RUSSELL
**"E"**

| | | |
|---|---|---|
| *Journey of Edith Wharton* | Hannay, R. | 1988 |
| *Scenes from a Literary Life* | Hannay, R. | 1990* |

GRAY, JACK
**Girl from Nogami**

| | | |
|---|---|---|
| *Girl from Nogami* | Blyton, C. | 1978 |

GREENE, GRAHAM (1904–1991)
**End of the Affair** (1951)

| | | |
|---|---|---|
| *End of the Affair* | Heggie, J. | 2004 |

**Our Man in Havana** (1958)

| | | |
|---|---|---|
| *Our Man in Havana* | Williamson, M. | 1963 |

**Quiet American** (1955)

| | | |
|---|---|---|
| *Quiet American* | Griffiths, W. | 1998 |

GREGORY, ISABELLA AUGUSTA (1852–1932)
**Dragon, The**

| | | |
|---|---|---|
| *Dragon, The* | Taylor, D. | 1958 |

**Spreading the News** (1904)

| | | |
|---|---|---|
| *Bubbles* | Bath, H. | 1923 |

**Travelling Man** (1909)

| | | |
|---|---|---|
| *Travelling Man* | Hart, F. | 1920* |

GRÉSAC, FRED de
**Troisesiéme lune, La** (with P. Ferrier)

| | | |
|---|---|---|
| *See-See* | Jones/Tours | 1906 |

GRIFFITHS, JANE MONTGOMERY
**Razing Hypatia**

| | | |
|---|---|---|
| *Razing Hypatia* | March, K. | 2010 |

GRIMM, JACOB LUDWIG CARL (1785–1863)/GRIMM, WILHELM CARL (1786–1859)
**fairy tales, various**

| | | |
|---|---|---|
| *Transformations* | Susa, C. | 1973 |
| *Wise and Foolish* | List, K. | 1951 |

**Brementown Musicians**

| | | |
|---|---|---|
| *Ballad of the Bremen Band* | Arlen, D. | 1977 |
| *Bremen Town Musicians* | Kesselman, L. | 1988 |
| *Grimm Duo* | Earls, P. | 1976 |
| *Musicians of Bremen* | Balkin, A. | 1972 |

**Maid Maleen**

| | | |
|---|---|---|
| *Princess Maleen* | Schonthal, R. | 1989 |

**Fisherman and His Wife**

| | | |
|---|---|---|
| *Fisherman and His Wife* | Bingham, S. | 1987 |
| *Fisherman and His Wife* | Schuller, G. | 1970 |
| *Fisherman's Wife* | Stein, L. | 1955 |

**Golden Bird**

| | | |
|---|---|---|
| *Golden Bird* | Russo, W. | 1984* |

**Goose Girl, The**

| | | |
|---|---|---|
| *Goose Girl* | Pasatieri, T. | 1981 |

**Hansel and Gretel**

| | | |
|---|---|---|
| *Hansel and Gretel* | Bruce, N. | 1997 |
| *Hansel & Gretel* | Schickele, P. | 1972 |
| *Hansel and Gretel* | Stoddard, M. | 1986 |

**Jorinda and Joringel**

| | | |
|---|---|---|
| *Joringel* | Garwood, M. | 1987 |

**Juniper Tree**

| | | |
|---|---|---|
| *Juniper Tree* | Boury, R. | 1990 |
| *Juniper Tree* | Glass, P. | 1985 |
| *Juniper Tree* | Kesselman, W. | 1982 |
| *Juniper Tree* | Toovey, A. | 1993 |
| *Juniper Tree* | Watkins, R. | 1997 |

**Little Red Riding Hood**

| | | |
|---|---|---|
| *Little Redinka* | Eaton, M. | 1991 |
| *Little Red Riding Hood* | A'Becket, M. | 1842 |

**Rapunzel**

| | | |
|---|---|---|
| *Rapunzel* | Brooks, R. | 1971 |
| *Rapunzel* | Hammond, T. | 1953 |
| *Rapunzel* | Harrison, L. | 1959 |

**Rumpelstiltskin**

| | | |
|---|---|---|
| *Rumpelstiltskin* | Baber, J. | 1977 |
| *Rumpelstiltskin* | Bourgeois, D. | 1974* |
| *Rumpelstiltskin* | Di Chiera, D., K. | 1977 |

**Willow-Wren and the Bear**

| | | |
|---|---|---|
| *Forest, The* | Hecker, Z. | 2005 |

GRIMMELSHAUSEN, J. J. C. von (1622–1676)
**Trutz Simplex** (1669)

| | | |
|---|---|---|
| *Play of Mother Courage* | McCabe, J. | 1974* |

GUERDON, DAVID (pseud.)
**Buanderie, La**

| | | |
|---|---|---|
| *Dream Child* | Mollicone, H. | 1975 |

**GUTTIL JATTAK** (Buddhist tale)

| | | |
|---|---|---|
| *Broken Strings* | Vir, P. | 1992 |

HAGGARD, H. RIDER (1856–1925)
**general**

| | | |
|---|---|---|
| *Zululand, trilogy* | Freeman, H. L. | 1934–47* |

*Nada the Lily* (1892)

| | | |
|---|---|---|
| *Nada and the Lily* | Freeman, H. L. | 1944* |

*HAGOROMO* (Noh play)

| | | |
|---|---|---|
| *Moon Maiden* | Boughton, R. | 1918 |

HALE, EDWARD EVERETT (1822–1909)

**Man without a Country** (1863)

| | | |
|---|---|---|
| *Man without a Country* | Damrosch, W. | 1937 |

HALPERN, MARTIN (b. 1929)

**Tameem** (1996)

| | | |
|---|---|---|
| *Satin Cloak* | Halpern, M. | 2001 |

HAMILTON, PATRICK (1904–1962)

**Gas Light** (1938)

| | | |
|---|---|---|
| *Gaslight* | Roe, B. | 1983 |

HARDY, THOMAS (1840–1928)

**Darkling Thrush** (1901)

| | | |
|---|---|---|
| *Darkling* | Weisman, S. | 2006 |

**Mayor of Casterbridge** (1874)

| | | |
|---|---|---|
| *Mayor of Casterbridge* | Tranchell, P. | 1951 |

**Ruined Maid** (1866)

| | | |
|---|---|---|
| *Ruined Maid* | Barab, S. | 1981 |

**Tess of the D'Urbervilles** (1891)

| | | |
|---|---|---|
| *Tess of the D'Urbervilles* | Harris, M. | 2000 |

**Three Strangers**

| | | |
|---|---|---|
| *Three Strangers* | Maconchy, E. | 1968 |

**Trumpet Major** (1879)

| | | |
|---|---|---|
| *Trumpet Major* | Hoddinott, A. | 1981 |

**Under the Greenwood Tree** (1872)

| | | |
|---|---|---|
| *Mellstock Quire* | Harper, E. | 1988 |

**Woodlanders, The** (1887)

| | | |
|---|---|---|
| *Woodlanders, The* | Paulus, S. | 1985 |

HARRIS, ED (1943–2006)

**Flowers of the Dead Red Sea** (1991)

| | | |
|---|---|---|
| *Flowers* | Hardy, J. | 1994 |

HARRIS, JOEL CHANDLER (1848–1908)

**Uncle Remus** (1880)

| | | |
|---|---|---|
| *Uncle Remus* | Johnson, C. | 1907* |

HARTE, BRETT (1836–1902)

**Outcasts of Poker Flat** (1869)

| | | |
|---|---|---|
| *Outcasts of Poker Flat* | Adler, S. | 1962 |
| *Outcasts of Poker Flat* | Beckler, S. R. | 1960 |
| *Outcasts of Poker Flats* | Elkus, J. | 1959* |
| *Outcasts of Poker Flat* | MacSems, W. | 1972* |

HAŠEK, JAROSLAV (1883–1923)

**Good Soldier Schweik** (1930)

| | | |
|---|---|---|
| *Good Soldier Schweik* | Kurka, R. | 1958 |

HAUPTMANN, GERHARD (1862–1946)

**Versunkene Glocke, Die** (1896)

| | | |
|---|---|---|
| *Sunken Bell* | Ruggles, C. | 1923* |

HAVIS, ALLAN (b. 1951)

**Lilith** (1990)

| | | |
|---|---|---|
| *Lilith* | Davis, A. | 2009 |

HAWTHORNE, NATHANIEL (1804–1864)

general

| | | |
|---|---|---|
| *American Lit* | Lependorf, J. | 1997 |
| *Wedding Knell* | Verrall, J. | 1955 |

**Dr. Heidegger's Experiment** (1837)

| | | |
|---|---|---|
| *Dr. Heidegger's Experiment* | Raphling, S. | 1956 |
| *Dr. Heidegger's Fountain of Youth* | Beeson, J. | 1978 |
| *Experiment, The* | Schwartz, P. | 1956 |

**Feathertop** (1846)

| | | |
|---|---|---|
| *Clarkstown Witch* | Nowak, L. | 1959 |
| *Feathertop* | Barnes, E. | 1980 |
| *Feathertop* | Barthelson, J. | 1968 |
| *Scarecrow, The* | Lockwood, N. | 1945 |
| *Scarecrow, The* | Turrin, J. | 1976* |

**Gentle Boy**

| | | |
|---|---|---|
| *Ilbrahim* | Bernstein, D. | 1994 |

**Great Stone Face** (1851)

| | | |
|---|---|---|
| *Great Stone Face* | Kalmanoff, M. | 1968 |

**House of the Seven Gables**

| | | |
|---|---|---|
| *House of the Seven Gables* | Eyerly, S. | 2000 |

**Marble Faun** (1860)

| | | |
|---|---|---|
| *Marble Faun* | Bender, E. | 1996* |

**Maypole of Merry Mount** (1836)

| | | |
|---|---|---|
| *Merry Mount* | Hanson, H. | 1933 |
| *Merry Mount* | Smith, D. S. | 1913* |

**Mrs. Bullfrog** (1837)

| | | |
|---|---|---|
| *Mrs. Bullfrog* | Raphling, S. | 1980 |

**My Kinsman, Major Molineux**

| | | |
|---|---|---|
| *Boy from Deerfield* | Halpern, M. | 2000 |
| *My Kinsman* | Saylor, B. | 1976 |

**Rappaccini's Daughter** (1844)

| | | |
|---|---|---|
| *Garden of Mystery* | Cadman, C. W. | 1925 |
| *Poisoned Kiss* | Vaughan Williams, R. | 1936 |
| *Rappaccini's Daughter* | Bender, E. | 199? |
| *Rappaccini's Daughter* | Dennison, S. | 1984 |
| *Rappaccini's Daughter* | Garwood, M. | 1980 |
| *Rappaccini's Daughter* | Riley, D. | 1984* |

**Scarlet Letter** (1850)

| | | |
|---|---|---|
| *Hester Prynne* | Claflin, A. | 1934 |
| *Hester Prynne at Death* | Paulus, S. | 2004 |
| *Scarlet Letter* | Damrosch, W. | 1896 |
| *Scarlet Letter* | Di Domenica, R. | 1972* |
| *Scarlet Letter* | Garwood, M. | 2010 |
| *Scarlet Letter* | Giannini, V. | 1938 |
| *Scarlet Letter* | Herman, M. | 1992 |
| *Scarlet Letter* | Kaufmann, W. | 1961 |
| *Scarlet Letter* | Kroll, F. | 1965* |
| *Scarlet Letter* | Laitman, L. | 2009 |
| *Scarlett Letter* | Lybbert, D. | 1967* |
| *Scarlet Letter* | Mann, R. W. | 1970* |
| *Scarlet Letter* | Svane, R. | 1995* |

**Snow Image** (1852)

| | | |
|---|---|---|
| *Childhood Miracle* | Rorem, N. | 1955 |

**Tanglewood Tales for Boys and Girls** (1853)

| | | |
|---|---|---|
| *Circe's Palace* | Magrill, S. | 2001 |

| | | |
|---|---|---|
| ***Wedding Knell*** | | |
| *Wedding Knell* | Verrall, J. | 1955 |
| ***Wonder Book for Girls and Boys*** (1852) | | |
| *Gorgon's Head* | Magrill, S. | 1998 |
| *Paradise of Children* | Magrill, S. | 1998 |
| ***Young Goodman Brown*** (1835) | | |
| *Goodman Brown* | Fink, H. | 1968 |
| *Young Goodman Brown* | Lenel, L. | 1963 |

**HEANEY, SEAMUS (b. 1939)**

| | | |
|---|---|---|
| ***Burial at Thebes*** (2004, after *Antigone* of Sophocles) | | |
| *Burial at Thebes* | Le Gendre, D. | 2008 |

**HÉBERT, ANNE (1916–2000)**

| | | |
|---|---|---|
| ***Kamouraska*** (1973) | | |
| *Kamouraska* | Wilson, C. | 1979 |

**HELLMAN, LILLIAN (1905–1984)**

| | | |
|---|---|---|
| ***Little Foxes*** (1939) | | |
| *Regina* | Blitzstein, M. | 1949 |

**HEMINGWAY, ERNEST (1900–1961)**

| | | |
|---|---|---|
| **general** | | |
| *Madrid* | Young, W. | 1997* |
| ***Fifth Column*** (1938) | | |
| *Lealista* | Warwick, M. C. | 1985* |
| ***Sun Also Rises*** (1926) | | |
| *Sun Also Rises* | Young, W. | 2000 |

**HENRICI, CHRISTIAN FRIEDRICH (1700–1764)**

| | | |
|---|---|---|
| ***Coffee Cantata*** | | |
| *Kona Coffee Cantata* | Tanner, J. | 1986* |

**HENRY, O. [WILLIAM SYDNEY PORTER] (1862–1910)**

| | | |
|---|---|---|
| **general** | | |
| *Cop and the Anthem* | Cohen, S. | 1982 |
| ***Enchanted Kiss*** | | |
| *Enchanted Kiss* | Bennett, R. R. | 1945 |
| ***Gift of the Magi*** (1906) | | |
| *Della's Gift* | Welcher, D. | 1987 |
| *Enchanted Kiss* | Bennett, R. R. | 1945 |
| *Gift of the Magi* | Bingham, S. | 1984 |
| *Gift of the Magi* | Brown, R. | 1985 |
| *Gift of the Magi* | Conte, D. | 1998 |
| *Gift of the Magi* | Gillis, D. | 1965 |
| *Gift of the Magi* | Magney, R. T. | 1964 |
| ***Last Leaf*** (1907) | | |
| *Last Leaf* | Bingham, S. | 1984 |
| *Last Leaf* | Henderson, A. | 1979 |
| *Last Leaf* | Niblock, J. | 2006 |
| *Last Leaf* | Remson, M. | 2000 |
| *West of Washington Square* | Henderson, A. | 1988 |
| ***Ransom of Red Chief*** (1910) | | |
| *Ransom of Red Chief* | Fuller-Hall, S. | 1982 |
| *Ransom of Red Chief* | Rodríguez, R. | 1986* |
| ***Room across the Hall*** | | |
| *West of Washington Square* | Henderson, A. | 1988 |
| ***Whirligig of Life*** (1910) | | |
| *Whirligig* | Brisman, H. | 1977 |

**HENSON, JOSIAH (1789–1883)**

| | | |
|---|---|---|
| ***Father Henson's Story of His Life*** (1858) | | |
| *Transcendent Voices* | Jones, D. | 2000 |

**HERGESHEIMER, JOSEPH (1880–1954)**

| | | |
|---|---|---|
| ***Mountain Blood*** (1915) | | |
| *Mountain Blood* | Patterson, F. | 1926* |

**HERTZ, HENRIK (1798–1870)**

| | | |
|---|---|---|
| ***Kong Renes Datter*** (1845) | | |
| *King Rene's Daughter* | Edwards, J. | 1893 |

**HEYWOOD, THOMAS (ca. 1570–1641)**

| | | |
|---|---|---|
| **general** | | |
| *Dialogue between Jupiter and Cupid* | Oliver, S. | 1972 |

**HILL, SUSAN (b. 1942)**

| | | |
|---|---|---|
| ***Albatross, The*** | | |
| *Albatross, The* | Burrell, D. | 1997 |

**HOADLY, JOHN (1711–1776)**

| | | |
|---|---|---|
| ***Love's Revenge*** | | |
| *Cupid's Revenge* | Hook, J. | 1772 |

**HOFFMANN, E. T. A. (1776–1822)**

| | | |
|---|---|---|
| ***Elixiere des Teufels, Die*** (1815) | | |
| *Devil's Elixir* | Rodwell, G. H. | 1829 |
| ***Sandmann, Der*** (1816) | | |
| *Heaven Ablaze* | Weir, J. | 1989 |
| *Sandman, The* | Cabaniss, T. | 2002 |
| ***Nussknacker und Mausekönig, Der*** (1816) | | |
| *Tale of the Nutcracker* | Bohmler, C. | 1999 |

**HOFMANNSTHAL, HUGO von (1874–1929)**

| | | |
|---|---|---|
| ***Jedermann*** (1911) | | |
| *Everyman* | Brotons, S. | 1970 |

**HOGARTH, WILLIAM (1697–1764)**

| | | |
|---|---|---|
| ***Enraged Musician*** (1741) | | |
| *Ut Pictora Poesis* | Arnold, S. | 1789 |
| ***Harlot's Progress*** (1732) | | |
| *Harlot's Progress* | Greenhut, B. | 1998 |
| ***Rake's Progress*** (1735) | | |
| *Rake's Progress* | Stravinsky, I. | 1953 |

**HOGG, JAMES (1770–1835)**

| | | |
|---|---|---|
| ***Private Memoirs and Confessions of a Justified Sinner*** (1824) | | |
| *Confessions of a Justified Sinner* | Wilson, T. | 1976 |

**HOLBERG, LUDVIG (1684–1754)**

| | | |
|---|---|---|
| ***Changed Bridegroom*** | | |
| *Captain Lovelock* | Duke, J. | 1953 |

**HÖLDERLIN, FRIEDRICH (1770–1843)**

| | | |
|---|---|---|
| **general** | | |
| *Undivine Comedy* | Finnissy, M. | 1988 |

**HOMER (9th–8th cent. B.C.)**

| | | |
|---|---|---|
| ***Hymn to Demeter*** | | |
| *Mysteries of Eleusis* | Feigin, J. | 1986 |
| ***Iliad, The*** | | |
| *Cassandra* | McAndrew, J. | 2003 |
| *Golden Apple* | Moross, J. | 1954 |
| ***Odyssey, The*** | | |
| *Castaway* | Berkeley, L. | 1967 |

| | | |
|---|---|---|
| *Circe's Palace* | Magrill, S. | 2001 |
| *Golden Apple* | Moross, J. | 1954 |
| *Odysseus Unwound* | Grant, J. | 2006 |
| *Odyssey 3* | Shields, A. | 1975 |
| *Return of Odysseus* | Bedford, B. | 1988 |
| *Return of Odysseus* | Gundry, I. | 1940 |
| *Ulysses* | Smith, J. C. | 1733 |

**HOOD, THOMAS (1799–1845)**
**Dream of Eugene Aram**

| | | |
|---|---|---|
| *Eugene Aram* | Bantock, G. | 1892* |

**HOPPER, EDWARD (1882–1967)**
**paintings**

| | | |
|---|---|---|
| *Later the Same Evening* | Musto, J. | 2007 |

**HOUSMAN, LAURENCE (1865–1959)**
**Seraphic Vision (1922)**

| | | |
|---|---|---|
| *Seraphic Vision* | Boughton, R. | 1924 |

**HOWARD, SIDNEY (1891–1939)**
**They Knew What They Wanted (1924)**

| | | |
|---|---|---|
| *Most Happy Fella* | Loesser, F. | 1956 |

**HOYLE-POGLE, FRANCES P.**
**Standard American Speaker (1901)**

| | | |
|---|---|---|
| *Practice in the Art of Elocution* | Beeson, J. | 1999 |

**HUDSON, WILLIAM HENRY (1841–1922)**
**Green Mansions (1904)**

| | | |
|---|---|---|
| *Green Mansions* | Gruenberg, L. | 1937 |

**HUGHES, GLENN (1894–1964)**
**Red Carnations (1925)**

| | | |
|---|---|---|
| *Red Carnations* | Baksa, R. | 1974 |

**HUGHES, LANGSTON (1905–1967)**
**Mother & Child (1966)**

| | | |
|---|---|---|
| *Meetin', The* | Baskin-Watson, P. | 1997 |

**Mulatto (1935)**

| | | |
|---|---|---|
| *Barrier, The* | Meyerowitz, J. | 1950 |

**Soul Gone Home (1937)**

| | | |
|---|---|---|
| *Soul Gone Home* | Banfield, W. | 2001 |

**HUGHES, TED (1930–1988)**
**Iron Man (1968)**

| | | |
|---|---|---|
| *Iron Man* | Fox, M. | 1987 |

**HUGO, VICTOR (1802–1885)**
**Marie Tudor (1833)**

| | | |
|---|---|---|
| *Armourer of Nantes* | Balfe, M. | 1863 |

**Notre-Dame de Paris (1831)**

| | | |
|---|---|---|
| *Esmerelda* | Thomas, A. G. | 1883 |
| *Notre-Dame of Paris* | Fry, W. | 1864 |
| *Quasimodo* | Rodwell, G. | 1836 |

**On ne badine pas avec l'amour (1834)**

| | | |
|---|---|---|
| *No Trifling with Love* | Burton, S. | 1970* |

**Ruy Blas (1838)**

| | | |
|---|---|---|
| *Ruy Blas* | Glover, W. H. | 1861 |

**HUNTER, KERMIT**
**Unto These Hills (1950)**

| | | |
|---|---|---|
| *Unto These Hills* | Kilpatrick, J. | 1950 |

**HUON DE BORDEAUX (16th cent.)**

| | | |
|---|---|---|
| *Oberon* | Weber | 1826 |

**HUPTON, ROBERT**
**Consider the Lilies**

| | | |
|---|---|---|
| *Letter to Emily* | Johnson, L. | 1951 |

**HURD, THACHER (b. 1949)**
**Mama Don't Allow (1984)**

| | | |
|---|---|---|
| *Muskrat Lullaby* | Barnes, E. | 1989 |

**HUXLEY, ALDOUS (1894–1963)**
**Devils of Loudun (1952)**

| | | |
|---|---|---|
| *Devil Builds a Chapel* | Casey, P. | 2010 |

**HWANG, DAVID HENRY (b. 1957)**
**Sound of a Voice (1983)**

| | | |
|---|---|---|
| *Sound of a Voice* | Glass, P. | 2003 |

**IBSEN, HENRIK (1828–1906)**
**Hedda Gabler (1890)**

| | | |
|---|---|---|
| *Claudia Legare* | Ward, R. | 1978 |
| *Hedda Gabler* | Harper, E. | 1985 |

**Peer Gynt (1867)**

| | | |
|---|---|---|
| *Death of Peer Gynt* | Halpern, M. | 2005* |
| *Peer Gynt* | Eaton, J. | 1992 |

**I CHING (Book of Changes, Chinese)**

| | | |
|---|---|---|
| *Hood of the Woods* | Shepherd, S. | 1988 |
| *Journey, The* | Metcalf, J. | 1981 |
| *Wanderer, The* | Boesing, P. | 1970 |

**IHIMAERA, WITI TAME (b. 1944)**
**Whanau**

| | | |
|---|---|---|
| *Waituhi* | Harris, R. | 1984 |

**INGE, WILLIAM (1913–1973)**
**Picnic (1953)**

| | | |
|---|---|---|
| *Picnic* | Larsen, L. | 2009 |

**INGRISCH, LOTTE (b. 1930)**
**general**

| | | |
|---|---|---|
| *Evening for Three* | Victory, G. | 1976 |

**IONESCO, EUGÈNE (1912–1997)**
**Cantatrice chauve, La (1948)**

| | | |
|---|---|---|
| *Bald Prima Donna* | Kalmanoff, M. | 1963 |

**Jacques, ou, La soumission (1953)**

| | | |
|---|---|---|
| *Jack and Roberta* | Cain, T. | 1981 |
| *Price of Eggs* | Cain, T. | 1982 |

**Leçon, La (1951)**

| | | |
|---|---|---|
| *Lesson, The* | Cain, T. | 1979 |

**Rhinocéros (1959)**

| | | |
|---|---|---|
| *Rhinoceros* | Kohs, E. | 1973* |

**Tueur sans gages (1958)**

| | | |
|---|---|---|
| *Photo of the Colonel* | Searle, H. | 1964 |

**IRVING, WASHINGTON (1783–1859)**
**Alhambra (1832)**

| | | |
|---|---|---|
| *Ahmed al Ramel* | Horn, C. E. | 1840 |

**Legend of Sleepy Hollow (1820)**

| | | |
|---|---|---|
| *Headless Horseman* | Moore, D. | 1937 |
| *Legend of Sleepy Hollow* | Haskins, R. | 1976* |
| *Sleepy Hollow* | Maretzek, M. | 1879 |

*Rip Van Winkle* (1819)

| | | |
|---|---|---|
| *Rip Van Winkle* | Bristow, G. F. | 1855 |
| *Rip Van Winkle* | De Koven, R. | 1920 |
| *Rip Van Winkle* | Jordan, J. | 1897 |
| *Rip Van Winkle* | Manning, E. | 1932 |
| *Rip Van Winkle* | Rockwell, R. W. | 1989 |
| *Rip Van Winkle* | Smith, G. | 1991 |

**Student of Salamanca**

| | | |
|---|---|---|
| *Alchymist, The* | Bishop, H. R. | 1832 |

JACKSON, HELEN HUNT (1830–1885)

**Ramona** (1884)

| | | |
|---|---|---|
| *Ramona* | Seymour, J. | 1970 |

JACOB, JOSEPH (1854–1916)

**Celtic Fairy Tales** (1892)

| | | |
|---|---|---|
| *Jack's Engagement* | Ward, D. | 1987 |

JACOBS, WILLIAM WYMARK (1863–1943)

**Captains All** (1905)

| | | |
|---|---|---|
| *Boatswain's Mate* | Smyth, E. | 1916 |

**Grey Parrot**

| | | |
|---|---|---|
| *Captain's Parrot* | Brent-Smith, A. | 1947 |

**Monkey's Paw** (1902)

| | | |
|---|---|---|
| *Monkey's Paw* | Alexander, W. | 1972 |
| *Monkey's Paw* | Halpern, S. | 1965 |
| *Monkey's Paw* | Hamm, C. | 1952 |

JACOBSEN, JENS PETER (1847–1885)

**Niels Lyhne** (1880)

| | | |
|---|---|---|
| *Fennimore and Gerda* | Delius, F. | 1919 |

JACQUES, BRIAN

**Redwall**

| | | |
|---|---|---|
| *Redwall* | Swensson, E. | 1998 |

JAMES, C. L. R. (b. 1901)

**Black Jacobins**

| | | |
|---|---|---|
| *Toussaint* | Blake, D. | 1977 |

JAMES, HENRY (1843–1916)

**Aspern Paper** (1888)

| | | |
|---|---|---|
| *Aspern Papers* | Argento, D. | 1988 |
| *Aspern Papers* | Hurd, M. | 1995 |

**Last of the Valerii** (1874)

| | | |
|---|---|---|
| *Voice of Ariadne* | Musgrave, T. | 1974 |

**Owen Wingrave** (1892)

| | | |
|---|---|---|
| *Owen Wingrave* | Britten, B. | 1971 |

**Turn of the Screw** (1898)

| | | |
|---|---|---|
| *Turn of the Screw* | Britten, B. | 1954 |

**Washington Square** (1881)

| | | |
|---|---|---|
| *Heiress, The* | Hollier, D. | 1988 |
| *Washington Square* | Pasatieri, T. | 1976 |

**Wings of the Dove** (1902)

| | | |
|---|---|---|
| *Wings of the Dove* | Moore, D. | 1961 |

JARRY, ALFRED (1873–1907)

**Ubu roi** (1896)

| | | |
|---|---|---|
| *Ubu* | Toovey, A. | 1992 |
| *Ubu Roi* | Aplvor, D. | 1967* |

JEFFERIES, RICHARD (1848–1887)

**Story of My Heart**

| | | |
|---|---|---|
| *Vision, A* | Ridout, A. | 1974 |

JEFFERS, ROBINSON (1872–1962)

**Medea** (1946)

| | | |
|---|---|---|
| *Medea in Corinth* | Lees, B. | 1971 |

JEFFERSON, JOSEPH (1829–1905)

**Rip Van Winkle** (with D. Boucicault, 1895)

| | | |
|---|---|---|
| *Rip Van Winkle* | Rockwell, J. | 1989 |

JEVON, THOMAS (1652–1688)

**Devil of a Wife** (1686, possib. with T. Shadwell)

| | | |
|---|---|---|
| *Devil to Pay* | ** | 1731 |

JOHNSON, CHARLES (1679–1748)

**Country Lasses** (1715)

| | | |
|---|---|---|
| *Lady of the Manor* | Hook, J. | 1778 |

JONES, ELIZABETH INGLIS

**Peacocks in Paradise** (1950)

| | | |
|---|---|---|
| *Black Ram* | Parrott, I. | 1957 |

JONSON, BEN (1573–1637)

**Alchemist, The** (1612)

| | | |
|---|---|---|
| *Alchemist, The* | Scott, C. | 1925 |

**Catiline Conspiracy** (1611)

| | | |
|---|---|---|
| *Catiline Conspiracy* | Hamilton, I. | 1974 |

**Devil Is an Ass** (1616)

| | | |
|---|---|---|
| *Spanish Lady* | Elgar, E. | 1933* |

**Oberon, the Fairy Prince** (1611)

| | | |
|---|---|---|
| *Fairy Prince* | Arne, T. A. | 1771 |

**Volpone** (1606)

| | | |
|---|---|---|
| *Volpone* | Antheil, G. | 1953 |
| *Volpone* | Burt, F. | 1960 |
| *Volpone* | Coombs, J. | 1957 |
| *Volpone* | Gruenberg | 1958* |

JOYCE, JAMES (1882–1941)

**Dead, The** (1914)

| | | |
|---|---|---|
| *Dead, The* | Boren, M. | 1993 |

**Ulysses** (1922)

| | | |
|---|---|---|
| *Audition of Molly Bloom* | McFarland, R. | 1986 |
| *Molly Manybloom* | Bond, V. | 1991 |
| *Ulysses* | Rudenstein, R. | 1999 |

KAFKA, FRANZ (1883–1924)

**general**

| | | |
|---|---|---|
| *Kafka: Leter to My Father* | Walden, S. | 2000 |
| *Kafka Quintet* | Hecker, Z. | 1994* |
| *Three Lost Chords* | Horne, L. | 2008 |
| *Visitation, The* | Schuller, G. | 1967 |

**Amerika** (*Der Verschollene,* pub. 1927)

| | | |
|---|---|---|
| *America* | Kohs, E. B. | 1970 |

**Hungerkünstler, Ein** (1924)

| | | |
|---|---|---|
| *Hunger Art* | Myers, J. | 2008 |

**In der Strafkolonie** (1919)

| | | |
|---|---|---|
| *In the Penal Colony* | Glass, P. | 2000 |
| *In the Penal Colony* | Murray, M. | 1992* |

*Prozess, Der* (pub. 1925)

| | | |
|---|---|---|
| *Kafka's Trial* | Ruders, P. | 2005 |
| *Stanley and the Monkey King* | White, J. | 1975 |

*Verwandlung, Die* (1915)

| | | |
|---|---|---|
| *Metamorphosis* | Howard, B. | 1983 |
| *Metamorphosis* | White, M. | 1968 |

KAGUYAHME LEGEND

| | | |
|---|---|---|
| *From the Towers of the Moon* | Moran, R. | 1992 |

*KALEVALA, THE* (19th cent.)

**First Lemminkäinen Cycle**

| | | |
|---|---|---|
| *Swanhunter* | Dove, J. | 2009 |

KAISER, GEORG (1878–1945)

**Von morgens bis mitternachts** (1912)

| | | |
|---|---|---|
| *From Morning to Midnight* | Sawyer, D. | 2001 |

KARINTHY, FERENC (1921–1992)

**tales**

| | | |
|---|---|---|
| *Magic Chair* | Zador, E. | 1966 |

KAZANTZAKIS, NIKOS (1883–1957)

**Christ Recrucified** (1951)

| | | |
|---|---|---|
| *Greek Passion* | Martin°u, B. | 1961 |

KEANE, JOHN (1928–2002)

**Sharon's Grave** (1960)

| | | |
|---|---|---|
| *Sharon's Grave* | Wargo, R. | 2006 |

KEATS, JOHN (1795–1821)

**Endymion** (1817)

| | | |
|---|---|---|
| *Endymion* | Antill, J. H. | 1953 |

KEITHLEY, GEORGE (b. 1935)

**Donner Party** (1972)

| | | |
|---|---|---|
| *Donner Party* | McFarland, R. | 1979 |
| *Tamsen Donner* | McFarland, R. | 1982 |

KELLER, GOTTFRIED (1819–1890)

**Leute von Seldwyla, Die** (pts. 1 and 2, 1856, 1874): **Romeo und Julia auf dem Dorfe**

| | | |
|---|---|---|
| *Satan's Trap* | Piket, F. | 1960 |
| *Village Romeo and Juiliet* | Delius, F. | 1907 |

KELLY, JAMES PATRICK

**Faith**

| | | |
|---|---|---|
| *Faith: DWF, 235* | Ching, M. | 1999 |

KEMENY, JULIA

**tales**

| | | |
|---|---|---|
| *Unexpected Visitor* | Kondorossy, L. | 1956 |

KENNEDY-FRASER, MARJORY (1857–1930)

**Songs of the Hebrides** (1909–21)

| | | |
|---|---|---|
| *Seal-Woman* | Bantock, G. | 1924 |

KEPLER, JOHANNES (1571–1631)

**Somnium** (1611)

| | | |
|---|---|---|
| *Star Catalogues* | Underhill, O, | 1994 |

KIM, RICHARD E. (b. 1932)

**Martyred, The** (1964)

| | | |
|---|---|---|
| *Martyred, The* | Wade, J. | 1970 |

KIM KI-PAL (b. 1937)

**Martyred, The**

| | | |
|---|---|---|
| *Martyred, The* | Wade, J. | 1970 |

*KING KONG* (1933)

| | | |
|---|---|---|
| *Second Mrs. Kong* | Birtwistle, H. | 1994 |

KINGSLY, CHARLES (1819–1875)

**Westward Ho!** (1855)

| | | |
|---|---|---|
| *Westward Ho!* | Miles. P. N. | 1913 |

KIPLING, RUDYARD (1865–1936)

general

| | | |
|---|---|---|
| *Elephant's Child* | Hagen, D. | 1994* |

**Jungle Book** (1894)

| | | |
|---|---|---|
| *Baa Baa Black Sheep* | Berkeley, M. | 1993 |

**Just So Stories** (1902)

| | | |
|---|---|---|
| *Solomon and Balkis* | Thompson, R. | 1942 |

KLEIST, HEINRICH von (1777–1811)

**Marquise von O, Die** (1808)

| | | |
|---|---|---|
| *Marquesa of O* | Siegmeister, E. | 1982 |

**Zerbrochene Krug, Der** (1811)

| | | |
|---|---|---|
| *Amorous Judge* | Gross, E. | 1965 |

KOCH, KENNETH (1925–2002)

**poems**

| | | |
|---|---|---|
| *Hearing* | Rorem, N. | 1977 |

**Bertha** (1959)

| | | |
|---|---|---|
| *Bertha* | Rorem, N. | 1973 |

**Change of Hearts** (1973)

| | | |
|---|---|---|
| *Change of Hearts* | Hollister, D. | 1985 |

**Construction of Boston** (1962)

| | | |
|---|---|---|
| *Construction of Boston* | Wheeler, S. | 1989 |

**Gold Standard** (1966)

KOGAWA, JOY (b. 1935)

**Obasan** (1981)

| | | |
|---|---|---|
| *Naomi's Road* | Luengen, R. | 2005 |

KONIGSBURG. E. L. [ELAINE LOBL] (b. 1930)

**From the Mixed-Up Files** (1967)

| | | |
|---|---|---|
| *From the Mixed-Up Files* | Swensson, E. | 2002 |

KOTZEBUE, AUGUST von (1761–1819)

**Graf Benjowski** (1795)

| | | |
|---|---|---|
| *Benyowksy* | King, M. et al. | 1826 |

**Spanier von Peru, Die** (1797)

| | | |
|---|---|---|
| *Virgin of the Sun* | Bishop, H. R. | 1812 |
| *Virgin of the Sun* | Gilfert, C. | 1823 |
| *Virgin of the Sun* | Pelissier, V. | 1800 |

**Wildfang, Der**

| | | |
|---|---|---|
| *Of Age Tomorrow* | Kelly, M. | 1800 |

KRAFT, BARBARA (b. 1939)

**biography** (unpub.)

| | | |
|---|---|---|
| *Anaïs* | Hurley, S. | 2010 |

KRASINSKI, ZYGMUNT (1812–1859)

**Nie-boska komedia** (1835)

| | | |
|---|---|---|
| *Undivine Comedy* | Finnissy, M. | 1988 |

KREYMBORG, ALFRED (1883–1966)

**Lima Beans** (1925)

| | | |
|---|---|---|
| *Lima Beans* | Townsend, D. | 1956 |

KUSHNER, TONY (b. 1956)

**Angels in America** (1991)

| | | |
|---|---|---|
| *Angels in America* | Eötvös, P. | 2004 |

LESSING, GOTTHOLD EPHRAIM (1729–1781)
**Nathan der Weise** (1779)
*Nathan the Wise*                Kondorossy, L.         1964
LESY, MICHAEL (b. 1945)
**Wisconsin Death Trip** (1973)
*Black River*                    Susa, C.               1975
LEVINE, RHODA
**Harrison Loved His Umbrella**
*Harrison Loved His Umbrella*    Hollingsworth, S.      1981
LEVY, JONATHAN (b. 1935)
**Charlie the Chicken**
*Charlie the Chicken*            Doolittle, Q.          1975
LEWIN, MANFRED (b. 1905)
**diary**
*For a Look or a Touch*          Heggie, J.             2007
LEWIS, C. S. (1898–1963)
**Lion, the Witch, and the Wardrobe** (1950)
*Lion, the Witch, and the Wardrobe*  McCabe, J.         1990
LEWIS, JANET (1899–1998)
**Invasion, The** (1932)
*Legend, The*                    Murray, B.             1987
**Wife of Martin Guerre** (1941)
*Wife of Martin Guerre*          Bergsma, W.            1956
LEWIS, MATTHEW G. (1775–1818)
**East Indian** (1800)
*Rich and Poor*                  Horn, C. E.            1812
**Monk, The** (1796)
*Raymond and Agnes*              Loder, E. J.           1855
**Rugantino, or, The Bravo of Venice**
*Bianca*                         Balfe, M.              1860
LEYA, LEON
**Portrait vivant, Le** (1842, with Mélesville)
*Love's Triumph*                 Wallace, V.            1862
LIADOV, ANTOL C. (1855–1914)
**Soeur Béatrice**
*Beatrice*                       Hoiby, L.              1959
LINNEY, ROMULUS (1930–2011)
**Death of King Philip**
*Death of King Philip*           Earls, P.              1976
LONG, JOHN LUTHER (1861–1927)
**Madame Butterfly** (1898)
*Cio Cio San*                    Carroll, B.            2005
LONGFELLOW, HENRY WADSWORTH (1807–1882)
**poems**
*Practice in the Art of Elocution*  Beeson, J.          1999
**Courtship of Miles Standish** (1858)
*Courtship of Miles Standish*    Ewart, F.              1931
*Courtship of Miles Standish*    Spelman, T.            1941
**Evangeline** (1847)
*Evangeline*                     George, G.             1948
*Evangeline*                     Luening, O.            1948
*Evangeline*                     Rice, E. E.            1874

**Masque of Pandora** (1875)
*Masque of Pandora*              Cellier, A.            1881
*Masque of Pandora*              Freer, E. E.           1933
**Spanish Student** (1842)
*Preciosa*                       Freer, E. E.           1928*
*Spanish Student*                Bath, H.               1904
*Victorian*                      Edwards, J.            1883
LOOMIS, JOHN
**Revolution of Forms**
*Revolution of Forms*            Davis-Prieto           2010
LOOVIS, JANICE
**Shining Chalice**
*Shining Chalice*                Van Grove, I.          1964
LOTI, PIERRE (L. M. J. VIAUD, 1850–1923)
**Madame Chrysathème** (1887)
*Geisha, The*                    Jones, S.              1896
**Ramuntcho** (1897)
*Ramuntcho*                      Taylor, D.             1942
LOVOOS, JANICE
**Shining Chalice**
*Shining Chalice*                Van Grove, I.          1964
LOWELL, ROBERT
**My Kinsman, Major Molineux** (1964)
*Boy from Deerfield*             Halpern, M.            2000
LOWNDES BELLOC, MARIE (1868–1947)
**Lodger, The** (1913)
*Lodger, The*                    Tate, P.               1960
LUCAN [MARCUS ANNAEUS LUCANUS] (39–65 AD)
**Pharsalia**
*Pharsalia*                      Hamilton, I.           1969
LUCE, CLARE BOOTHE (1903–1987)
**Women, The** (1936)
*Best Friends*                   Drattell, D.           2002
LU WEI
**Legend of the Bloody Zheng**
*First Emperor*                  Tan Dun                2006
LYNCH, DAVID
**Lost Highway** (with B. Gifford, 1997)
*Lost Highway*                   Neuwirth, O.           2003

**MABINOGION, THE** (medieval Welsh)
*Cauldron of Annwn*, triology
  *Bronwen*             Holbrooke, J.          1929
  *Children of Don*     Holbrooke, J.          1912
  *Dylan*               Holbrooke, J.          1914
*Sacrifice, The*                 MacMillan, J.          2007
MacCALLUM, CATHER
**Rococo Confessional**
*Rococo Confessional*            Galloway, J.           1999
MacDONALD, GEORGE (1824–1905)
**Phantastes** (1858)
*Magic Mirror*                   Holst, G.              1896

MACDONALD, SHARON
**Winter Guest**
*Hey Persephone!* Gribbin, D. 1998
MacDONOUGH, GLEN (1870–1924)
**Night in Old Paris, A**
*Night in Old Paris* Hadley, H. 1924
MACHIAVELLI, NICCOLÒ (1469–1527)
**Belfagor arcidiavolo** (1515)
*Married Men Go to Hell* Franchetti, A. 1975
**Mandragola, La** (1518)
*Lucrezia* Bolcom, W. 2008
MacKAY, CONSTANCE D'ARCY
**Beau of Bath** (1915)
*Beau Nash* Valenti, M. 2003
MACKAYE, PERCY (1875–1956)
**Scarecrow, The** (1917)
*Scarecrow, The* Lockwood, N. 1945
*Scarecrow, The* Turrin, J. 1976*
MacKAYE, STEELE (1842–1894)
**Hazel Kirke** (1880)
*Hazel Kirke* Houston, M. 1987
MACLEISH, ARCHIBALD (1892–1982)
**Fall of the City** (1937)
*Fall of the City* Cohn, J. 1955
MacLEOD, FIONA [WILLIAM SHARP] (1855–1905)
**Immortal Hour** (1908), poems
*Immortal Hour* Boughton, R. 1914
MACPHERSON, JAMES (1736–1796)
**Poems of Ossian: Son of Fingal** (1765)
*Oithona* Barthelemon, F. 1768
MADDEN, DAVID (b. 1933)
**Fugue for Two Voices** (1968)
*Intimations* Constantinides, D. 1982
MAETERLINCK, MAURICE (1862–1949)
**Aveugles, Les** (1890)
*Blind, The* Oliver, S. 1972
**Intruse, L'** (1891)
*Intruder, The* Feldman, J. 1984
**Mort de Tintagiles, La** (1894)
*Death of Tintagiles* Collingwood, L. 1950
*Death of Tintagiles* Isaacs, G. 1973
**Soeur Beatrice**
*Sister Beatrice* Fine, E. 2004
*MAHABHARATA* (ancient Indian)
*Sāvitri* Holst, G. 1916
MAHADEVI (b. 1946)
**poems**, trans. A. K. Ramanujan, D. Ingalls
*Chakravaka-Bird* Gilbert, A. 1982
MALAMUD, BERNARD (1914–1986)
**Angel Levine**
*Angel Levine* Siegmeister, E. 1985
**German Refugee** (1963)
*German Refugee* Cabaniss, T. 2008
**Idiots First** (1963)
*Idiots First* Blitzstein, M. 1976
**Lady of the Lake**
*Lady of the Lake* Siegmeister, E. 1985
**Magic Barrel** (1958)
*Magic Barrel* Blitzstein, M. 1964*
**Notes from a Lady at a Dinner Party**
*Karla* Lehrman, L. 1974
**Suppose a Wedding**
*Suppose a Wedding* Lehrman, L. 1996
MALLARMÉ, STEPHANE (1842–1898)
**Coup de dés jamais n'abolira le hasard, Un**
*Dice Thrown* King, J. 2010
MALORY, THOMAS (ca. 1405–1471)
**Morte d'Arthur, Le**
*Morte d'Arthur* Corder, F. 1879
MANN, THOMAS (1875–1955)
**memoirs**
*King for Corsica* George, G. 1981
**Betrogene, Die**
*Black Swan* Whitman, T. 1998
**Mario und der Zauberer** (1929)
*Mario and the Magician* Oliver, S. 1988
*Mario and the Magician* Somers, H. 1992
*Mario and the Magician* Thorne, F. 1994
**Tod in Venedig, Der** (1912)
*California Fictions* Bates. M. 2006
*Death in Venice* Britten, B. 1973
**Vertauschten Köpfe, Die** (1940)
*Transposed Heads* Glanville-Hicks, P. 1954
MANSFIELD, KATHERINE (1888–1923)
short stories
*Daughters of the Late Colonel* Buchanan, D. 1999
*Fall of Miss Moss* Oliver, S. 1972
*Marriage a la Mode* Drummond, J. 2004
*Miss Brill* Buchanan, D. 1999
*Pictures* Bootham, I, 2002*
*Poison* Hart, F. 1984
MARGUERITE de NAVARRE (1492–1549)
**Heptameron**
*Summer Night* Clutsam, G. 1910
MARIE de FRANCE (13th cent.)
**Lai le Freine**
*Crimson Bird* Enenbach, F. 1979
MARINO, GIOVAMBATTISTA (1569–1625)
**poetry**
*Powers of Two* Truax, B. 2006
MARLOWE, CHRISTOPHER (1564–1593)
**Tamburlaine the Great** (ca. 1587)
*Tamburlaine* Hamilton, I. 1977
**Tragicall History of Doctor Faustus** (1604)
*Doctor Faustus* Menzer, R. 1994
*Faustus Part One* Rudenstein, R. 1996

| | | |
|---|---|---|
| *Faustus, the Last Night* | Dusapin, P. | 2006 |
| *Regarding Faustus* | Gifford, H. | 1983* |

**MARMONTEL, JEAN FRANÇOIS (1723–1799)**
  **Contes moraux (1768):**
    **Bergère des Alpes, La**

| | | |
|---|---|---|
| *Shepherdess of the Alps* | Dibdin, C. | 1780 |

    **Soliman II**

| | | |
|---|---|---|
| *Sultan, The* | Dibdin, C. | 1775 |

    **Incas, Les (1777)**

| | | |
|---|---|---|
| *Columbus* | Reinagle, A. | 1797 |

    **Laurette**

| | | |
|---|---|---|
| *Clari* | Bishop, H. R. | 1823 |

**MARSH, NGAIO (EDITH) (1895–1982)**
  **Wyvern and Unicorn (1955)**

| | | |
|---|---|---|
| *Unicorn for Christmas* | Farquhar, D. | 1962 |

**MARTÍ, JOSÉ (1853–1895)**
  **Niña, La**

| | | |
|---|---|---|
| *Child, The* | Bernardo, J. R. | 1974 |

**MASON, WILLIAM (1725–1797)**
  **Caractacus (1759)**

| | | |
|---|---|---|
| *Caractacus* | Arne, T. A. | 1776 |

**MASSEY, CAL**
  **Leo Spat**

| | | |
|---|---|---|
| *Leo* | Ching, M. | 1985 |

**MASSINGER, PHILIP (1583–1640)**
  **Prophetess, The (with J. Fletcher)**

| | | |
|---|---|---|
| *Dioclesian* | Purcell, H. | 1690 |

**MATTIUZZI, ANTONIO [ANTONIO COLLALTO] (1717?–1778)**
  **Trois jumeaux vénitiens (1774)**

| | | |
|---|---|---|
| *Three and the Deuce* | Storace, S. | 1795 |

**MAUGHAM, W. SOMERSET (1874–1965)**
  **Alien Corn (1931)**

| | | |
|---|---|---|
| *Alien Corn* | Benjamin, T. | 2005 |

  **Moon and Sixpence (1919)**

| | | |
|---|---|---|
| *Moon and Sixpence* | Gardner, J. | 1957 |

  **Rain (1921)**

| | | |
|---|---|---|
| *Rain* | Owen, R. | 2003 |
| *Sadie Thompson* | Owen, R. | 1997 |

**MAUPASSANT, GUY de (1850–1893)**
  **Boule de suif**

| | | |
|---|---|---|
| *Greater Good* | Hartke, S. | 2006 |

  **Bout de ficelle, Un**

| | | |
|---|---|---|
| *Piece of String* | Barab, S. | 1985 |

  **En famille (1861)**

| | | |
|---|---|---|
| *Parlour, The* | Williams, G. | 1966 |

  **Rosier de Madonne Husson, Le (1828)**

| | | |
|---|---|---|
| *Albert Herring* | Britten, B. | 1947 |

  **Signe, Le**

| | | |
|---|---|---|
| *The Gift* | Binder, J. | 1997* |

**MAXWELL-SCOTT, MARY MONICA (1852–1920)**
  **Tragedy of Fotheringay**

| | | |
|---|---|---|
| *To Let the Captive Go* | Stewart, F. | 1974 |

**MAY, THOMAS (1595–1650)**
  **Death of Rosamond**

| | | |
|---|---|---|
| *Rosamond* | Arne, T. A. | 1740 |
| *Rosamond* | Arnold, S. | 1767 |
| *Rosamond* | Clayton, T. | 1707 |

**MAYAKOVSKY, VLADIMIR (1893–1930)**
  **general**

| | | |
|---|---|---|
| *Mayakovsky and the Sun* | Daiken, M. | 1971 |

**McCLINTOCK, WALTER (1870–1949)**
  **Old North Trail**

| | | |
|---|---|---|
| *Poia* | Nevin, A. | 1909 |

**McGAHERN, JOHN (b. 1934)**
  **short stories**

| | | |
|---|---|---|
| *My Love* | O'Connell, K. | 1997 |

**McLELLAN, CHARLES (1865–1916)**
  **Leah Kleschna (1920)**

| | | |
|---|---|---|
| *Leah Kleschna* | Freeman, H. L. | 1930 |

**McQUEEN, CILLA (b. 1949)**
  **writings**

| | | |
|---|---|---|
| *Trapeze Artists* | Ritchie, A. | 2000 |

**McSHANE, MICHAEL**
  **Séance on a Wet Afternoon (1961)**

| | | |
|---|---|---|
| *Séance on a Wet Afternoon* | Schwartz, S. | 2009 |

**MEADE, MARION**
  **Stealing Heaven (1979)**

| | | |
|---|---|---|
| *Heloise and Abelard* | Paulus, S. | 2002 |

**MEINHOLD, WILHELM (1797–1851)**
  **Maria Schweidler (1843)**

| | | |
|---|---|---|
| *Amber Witch* | Wallace, V. | 1861 |

**MÉLÉSVILLE [A.-H.-J. DUVEYRIER] (1787–1865)**
  **Chevalier de Saint-Georges, Le (1840)**

| | | |
|---|---|---|
| *Bondman, The* | Balfe, M. | 1846 |

  **Portrait vivant, Le (1842, with L. Leya)**

| | | |
|---|---|---|
| *Love's Triumph* | Wallace, V. | 1862 |

**MELFI, LEONARD (1935–2001)**
  **Birdbath (1968)**

| | | |
|---|---|---|
| *Birdbath* | Lieberson, K. | 1982 |

**MELVILLE, HERMAN (1819–1891)**
  **letters**

| | | |
|---|---|---|
| *American Lit* | Lependorf, J. | 1997 |

  **Bartleby the Scrivener (1853)**

| | | |
|---|---|---|
| *Bartleby* | Aschaffenburg | 1964 |
| *Bartleby* | Flanagan, W. | 1961 |

  **Bell Tower (1856)**

| | | |
|---|---|---|
| *Bell Tower* | Haskins, R. | 1976* |
| *Bell Tower* | Krenek, E. | 1957 |

  **Billy Budd (1891, pub. 1924)**

| | | |
|---|---|---|
| *Billy Budd* | Britten, B. | 1951 |

  **Chola Widow (1856)**

| | | |
|---|---|---|
| *Widow, The* | Gaburo, K. | 1961 |

  **Confidence Man**

| | | |
|---|---|---|
| *Confidence Man* | Rochberg, G. | 1982 |

*Moby-Dick* (1851)

| | | |
|---|---|---|
| *And God Created Great Whales* | Eckert, R. | 2000 |
| *Call Me Ishmael* | Goldschneider, G. | 2004 |
| *Moby Dick* | Brooks, R. | 1987* |
| *Moby Dick* | Epstein, S. | 1989* |
| *Moby-Dick* | Heggie, J. | 2010 |
| *Moby Dick* | Low, J. | 1955 |
| *Moby Dick* | Westergaard, P. | 2004 |

MÉRIMÉE, PROSPER (1803–1870)

*Colomba* (1841)

| | | |
|---|---|---|
| *Colomba* | Mackenzie, A. | 1883 |

MERRIMAN, BRIAN (1749–1805)

**Ceirt an mhean oiche** (1780)

| | | |
|---|---|---|
| *Midnight Court* | Chisholm E. | 1961* |
| *Midnight Court Opera* | Sokolovic, A. | 2005 |

MEYER-FÖRSTER, WILHELM (1862–1934)

*Alt-Heidelberg* (1902)

| | | |
|---|---|---|
| *Student Prince* | Romberg, S. | 1924 |

**Midrash, The**

| | | |
|---|---|---|
| *Lilith* | Drattel, D. | 1997* |

MIKAMI, OTOKICHI (1891–1944)

**Yokinojo Henge**

| | | |
|---|---|---|
| *Actor's Revenge* | Miki, M. | 1979 |

MIKSZATH, KALMAN (1847–1910)

**stories**

| | | |
|---|---|---|
| *Fox, The* | Kondorossy, L. | 1961 |

MILLAY, EDNA ST. VINCENT (1892–1950)

*Aria da Capo* (1920)

| | | |
|---|---|---|
| *Aria da capo* | Axelrod, L.. | 1997* |
| *Aria da capo* | Baksa, R. | 1968 |
| *Aria da capo* | Blank, A. | 1960* |
| *Aria da capo* | Bouck, M. | 1974* |
| *Aria da capo* | Burnham, C. | 1955 |
| *Aria da capo* | Eitzen, L. V. | 1960* |
| *Aria da capo* | Fore, B. | 1951 |
| *Aria da capo* | Priolo, C. | 1984* |
| *Aria da capo* | Smith, L. | 1980 |
| *Aria da capo* | Weaver, H. B. | 1991 |

MILLER, ARTHUR (1915–2005)

*All My Sons* (1947)

| | | |
|---|---|---|
| *All My Sons* | Legg, J. | 2001 |

*Creation of the World* (1973)

| | | |
|---|---|---|
| *Up from Paradise* | Silverman, S. | 1983 |

*Crucible, The* (1953)

| | | |
|---|---|---|
| *Crucible, The* | Ward, R. | 1961 |

**View from the Bridge**

| | | |
|---|---|---|
| *View from the Bridge* | Bolcom, A. | 1999 |
| *View from the Bridge* | Morris, H. | 1981 |

MILLER, ISABEL (b. 1924)

*Place for Us* (1969)

| | | |
|---|---|---|
| *Patience and Sarah* | Kimper, P. | 1996 |

MILNE, A. A. (1882–1956)

**Ugly Duckling**

| | | |
|---|---|---|
| *Courtship of Camilla* | Schonthal, R. | 1980* |

MILNER, HENRY M.

*Masaniello* (1824)

| | | |
|---|---|---|
| *Masaniello* | Bishop, H. R. | 1825 |

MILTON, JOHN (1608–1674)

*Comus* (1634)

| | | |
|---|---|---|
| *Comus* | Arne, T. A. | 1738 |
| *Comus* | Bishop, H. R. | 1815 |

*Paradise Lost* (1667)

| | | |
|---|---|---|
| *In the Beginning* | Warren, R. | 1982 |
| *Paradise Lost* | Penderecki, K. | 1978 |

MITCHISON, NAOMI (1897–1999)

**Corn King and the Spring Queen**

| | | |
|---|---|---|
| *Corn King* | Easdale, B. | 1950 |

MOELLER, PHILIP (1880–1958)

**Helena's Husband** (1915)

| | | |
|---|---|---|
| *Helena's Husband* | Gruenberg, L. | 1938* |

MOLIÈRE [JEAN-BAPTISTE POQUELIN] (1622–1673)

**general**

| | | |
|---|---|---|
| *Imaginary Couple* | Sullivan, T. | 1990 |
| *Philosophy Lesson* | Stern, M. | 1967* |

*Amphitryon* (1668)

| | | |
|---|---|---|
| *Amphitryon 4* | Blumenthal, H. | 1962* |

*Ecole des femmes, Les* (1662)

| | | |
|---|---|---|
| *School for Wives* | Liebermann, R. | 1955 |

*George Dandin* (1668)

| | | |
|---|---|---|
| *Metamorphoses, The* | Dibdin, C. | 1776 |

*Mariage forcé, Le* (1664)

| | | |
|---|---|---|
| *Forced Marriage* | Hart, F. | 1928 |

*Médecin malgré lui, Le*

| | | |
|---|---|---|
| *Dr. Love* | Bell, W. H. | 1930 |
| *Mock Doctor* | Carey et al. | 1732 |

*Précieuses ridicules, Les* (1659)

| | | |
|---|---|---|
| *If the Cap Fits* | Bush, G. | 1956 |

*Sganarelle, ou, Le cocu imaginaire* (1660)

| | | |
|---|---|---|
| *Picture, The* | Arne, T. A. | 1745 |
| *Sganarelle* | Archer, V. | 1974 |
| *Sganarelle* | Kaufmann, W. | 1958 |
| *Sganarelle* | Zito, V. | 1972 |
| *Signor Deluso* | Pasatieri, T. | 1974 |

*Sicilien, Le* (1667)

| | | |
|---|---|---|
| *Metamorphoses* | Dibdin, C. | 1776 |

*Tartuffe* (1664)

| | | |
|---|---|---|
| *Tartuffe* | Benjamin, A. | 1964 |
| *Tartuffe* | Mechem, K. | 1980 |

MOLNÁR, FERENC [FERENC NEUMANN] (1878–1952)

**Witch, The**

| | | |
|---|---|---|
| *Breakfast Waltzes* | Blumenfeld, H. | 1991* |
| *Fritzi* | Blumenfeld, H. | 1979* |

**Vörös Malum**

| | | |
|---|---|---|
| *Scarlet Mill* | Zador, E. | 1968 |

MONCRIEFF, W. T. (1794–1857)

**Rochester, or, King Charles the Second's Merry Days** (1818)

| | | |
|---|---|---|
| *Nell Gwynne* | Cellier, A. | 1878 |

MONTAGU, Lady MARY WORTLEY (1689–1762)
  poetry
    *Powers of Two*                    Truax, B.           2006
MONTEJO, ESTEBAN (1860–1973)
  **Autobiography of a Runaway Slave**
    *Cimarrón, El*                     Henze, H. W.        1970
MONTIGNY, LOUVIGNY de (1876–1955)
  **Ordre du bon temps, L'**
    *Order of Good Cheer*              Willan, H.          1928
MOORE, BRIAN (b. 1921)
  **Luck of Ginger Coffey**
    *Luck of Ginger Coffey*           Pannell, R.         1967
MOORE, THOMAS (1779–1852)
  general
    *Light of the Harem*               Thomas, A. G.       1879
  **Lallah Rookh** (1817)
    *Lallah Rookh*                     Horn, C. E.         1818
    *Veiled Prophet of Khorassan*      Sanford, C.         1881
  **Ring, The**
    *Fairies' Revels*                  Arnold, S.          1802
MORAVIA, ALBERTO [ALBERTO PINCHERLE] (1907–1990)
  **Beatrice Cenci** (1958)
    *Beatrice Cenci*                   Di Domenica, R.     1993
MOREAU, EMILE (1852–1922)
  **Madame Sans-Gêne** (with V. Sardou)
    *Duchess of Dantzic*               Caryll, I.          1903
MORELL, CHARLES, SIR [JAMES KENNETH RIDLEY]
(1736–1765)
  **Tales of the Genii** (1797)
    *Sadak and Kalasrade*              Packer, C.          1835
MORGENSTERN, CHRISTIAN (1871–1914)
  **Egon und Emilie** (pub. 1928)
    *Edgar and Emily*                  Toch, E.            1965
MORLEY, CHRISTOPHER (1890–1957)
  **Tree That Didn't Get Trimmed** (1942)
    *Tree That Found Christmas*        Kleinsinger, G.     1955
MORLEY, JAMES
  **Pastoral**
    *Pastoral*                         Galloway, J.        1988
MORRISON, TONI (b. 1931)
  **Beloved** (1987)
    *Margaret Garner*                  Danielpour, R.      2004
*MORTE D'ARTHUR, LE* (1470)
    *Lancelot*                         Hamilton, I.        1985
MORTON, JOHN MADISON (1811–1891)
  **Box and Cox** (1848)
    *Cox and Box*                      Sullivan, A. S.     1867
  **Our Wife** (1856)
    *Désirée*                          Sousa, J. P.        1884
MORTON, THOMAS (1764?–1838)
  **Columbus** (1792)
    *Columbus*                         Reinagle, A.        1797

MOSEL, TAD (1922– 2008)
  **All the Way Home** (1961)
    *Death in the Family*              Mayer, W.           1983
MOSENTHAL, SALOMON (1821–1877)
  **Sonnenwendhof, Der**
    *Helvellyn*                        Macfarren, G.       1864
MOSS, ANDREW
  papers
    *Phrenic Crush*                    Bielawa, L.         1997
MOSS, CARLETON (1909–1997)
  story
    *Blue Steel*                       Grant, W. S.        1934*
MOTOKYIYO, ZEAMI (ca. 1363–ca. 1443)
  **Atsumori**
    *Greenleaf*                        Buchanan, D.        1985*
    *Kantan and the Damask Drum*       Goehr, A.           1999
      (adapt Y. Mishima)
MOTOMASA, JŪRO (1395–1432)
  **Sumidagawa**
    *Curlew River*                     Britten, B.         1964
    *Sumidagawa*                       Scarem, N.          1979
    *Sumida River*                     Raybould, C.        1916
MOTTEUX, PETER ANTHONY
  **Loves of Mars and Venus** (1695)
    *Loves of Mars and Venus*          Dibdin, C.          1778
MUNCH, EDVARD (1864–1944)
  **Frieze of Life** cycle (1893)
    *Frieze of Life*                   Applebaum, E.       1983

MUNRO, H. H. *See* SAKI.

MURDOCH, IRIS (1919–1999)
  **Servants and the Snow**
    *Servants, The*                    Matthias, W.        1980
MURGER, HENRY (HENRI) (1822–1861)
  **Scènes de la vie de bohème** (1847–49)
    *Bohemians, The*                   Kirschner, B.       1990
    *Rent*                             Larson, J.          1996
MURPHY, ARTHUR (1727–1805)
  **School for Guardians** (1767)
    *Love Finds the Way*               Arne, T., et al.    1777
MURRELL, JOHN (b. 1945)
  **Power in the Blood** (1975)
    *Electric Gospel*                  Levin, G.           1980
MUSSET, ALFRED de (1810–1857)
  **Notre-Dame**
    *Notre-Dame of Paris*              Fry, W.             1864

NACHMAN, RABBI [of BRATSLAV] (1772–1811)
  tale (1809)
    *Merchant and the Pauper*          Schoenfield, P.     1999
NAGGLI, JOSEPHINA (b. 1910)
  **Sunday Costs Five Pesos** (1937)
    *Sunday Costs Five Pesos*          Haubiel, C.         1950

PAIN, BARRY (1864–1928)
**Friendships and Enmities**
It Began with a Pony — Buchanan, D. — 2003

PANIZZA, OSKAR (1853–1921)
**Liebeskonzil, Das** (1894)
Hell's Angels — Osborne, N. — 1986

PANJI CYCLES (Java, Bali)
King of Bali — McDermott, V. — 1990

PANYCH, MORRIS (b. 1952)
**Seven Stories** (1990)
Seven Stories — Richardson, A. — 2002*

PARIS, MATTHEW (b. 1938)
**All in Good Time**
Love and Idols — Drogin, B. — 1986*

PARKER, DOROTHY (1893–1967)
**Autumn Valentine**
Autumn Valentine — Gordon, R. I. — 1992

PARKMAN, FRANCIS (1823–1893)
**Conspiracy of Pontiac** (1870)
Conspiracy of Pontiac — Mayer, C. — 1887

PASTERNAK, BORIS (1890–1960)
**Last Summer; Spectorsky** (1931)
Electrification of the Soviet Union — Osborne, N. — 1987

PÁSZTOR, BÉLA (1908–1945)
**Pumpkin, The**
Pumpkin, The — Kondorossy, L. — 1954

PATON, ALAN (1903–1988)
**Cry the Beloved Country** (1948)
Lost in the Stars — Weill, K. — 1949

PATRAT, JOSEPH (1732–1801)
**Heureuse erreur, L'** (1783)
Brother and Sister — Bishop, H. R. — 1815
Match for a Widow — Dibdin, C. — 1788

PAYNE, JOHN HOWARD (1791–1852)
**Charles the Second** (1824)
King Charles II — Macfarren, G. — 1849

PEABODY, JOSEPHINE PRESTON (1874–1922)
**Piper, The** (1921)
Legend of the Piper — Freer, E. E. — 1925

PEACOCK, THOMAS L. (1785–1866)
**Maid Marian** (1822)
Maid Marian — Bishop, H. R. — 1822
**Nightmare Abbey** (1818)
Nightmare Abbey — Allanbrook, D. — 1960*

PEELE, GEORGE (1556–1596)
**Old Wives' Tale** (1595)
Sacrapant — Aston, P. — 1967*

PERETZ, ISAAC LEIB (1852–1915)
**If Not Higher**
Miracle of Nemirov — Silverman, F.-E. — 1974*

**Bontshe Shvayg**
Bontshe the Silent — Sirota, R. — 1982

PERRAULT, CHARLES (1628–1703)
**Contes de ma mère l'Oye** (1697)
**Barbe bleue**
Blue-Beard — Kelly, M. — 1798
**Belle au bois dormant, La**
Sleeping Beauty — Rubinstein, B. — 1938
**Cendrillon**
Cinderella — Lacy, M. R. — 1830

PETRONIUS, GAIUS (d. A.D. 66)
**Satyricon, The**
Ephesian Matron — Dibdin, C. — 1769

PHILIPS, KATHERINE (1631–1664)
**poetry**
Powers of Two — Truax, B. — 2006

PHILPOTT, TOM
**Glory Denied**
Glory Denied — Cipullo, T. — 2004

PIGAULT-LEBRUN (1753–1835)
**Rivaux d'eux mêmes, Les**
Bee-Hive, The — Horn, C. E. — 1811

PIRANDELLO, LUIGI (1867–1936)
**Six Characters in Search of an Author** (1921)
Six Characters in Search of an Author — Weisgall, H. — 1959

PITT, CHARLES DIBDIN (1818/1819–1866)
**String of Pearls** (1847)
Sweeney Todd — Blyton, C. — 1980*
Sweeney Todd — Sondheim, S. — 1979

PIXÉRÉCOURT, R. C. G. de (1773–1844)
**Femme à deux maris, La**
Wife of Two Husbands — Mazzinghi, J. — 1803
**Fortresse du Danube, La** (1805)
Fortress, The — Hook, J. — 1807
**Pèlerin blanc, Le**
Wandering Boys — Bishop, H. R. — 1814
**Tékéli, ou, Le siège de Montgatz** (1803)
Tekeli — Hook, J. — 1806

PLANCHÉ, JAMES ROBINSON (1796–1880)
**Fortunio** (1843)
Fortunio — Darley, F. — 1883

PLATH, SYLVIA (1932–1963)
**selections**
After Dido — Purcell (arr.) — 2009

PLATO (ca. 428–348 B.C.)
**general**
Jacob's Room — Subotnick, M. — 1993
**Gorgias**
Council of the Dead — Sternau, C. — 1996*
**Republic, The**
Myth of Er — Sternau, C. — 1995*
Shadowplay — Goehr, A. — 1970

RHYS, JEAN (1890–1979)
  *Wide Sargasso Sea* (1966)
  *Wide Sargasso Sea*                 Howard, B.           1997
RICE, CALE YOUNG (1872–1943)
  *Yolanda of Cyprus*
  *Yolanda of Cyprus*                 Loomis, C.           1929
RICE, ELMER (1892–1967)
  *Street Scene* (1929)
  *Street Scene*                      Weill, K.            1946
RICHARDSON, HOWARD
  *Dark of the Moon* (with W. Berney)
  *Conjur Moon*                       Lloyd, T. C.         1979
RICHARDSON, SAMUEL (1689–1761)
  *Clarissa Harlowe* (1747–48)
  *Clarissa*                          Holloway, R.         1990
  *Pamela* (1740)
  *Maid of the Mill*                  Arnold, S.           1765
  *Maid of the Mill*                  Bishop, H. R.        1814
  *Maid of the Mill*                  Giordani, T.         1765
  *Maid of the Vale*                  Arne, M.             1775
RILEY, J. W.
  **poems**
  *Practice in the Art of Elocution*  Beeson, J.           1999
RILKE, RAINER MARIA (1875–1926)
  **poetry**
  *Powers of Two*                     Truax, B.            2006
RIMBAUD, ARTHUR (1854–1891)
  **general**
  *Seasons of Hell*                   Blumenfeld, H.       1996
ROBERTS, EUGENE L. (1880–1953)
  *Story of Utahna and Red Eagle/Indian Legend of Timpanogas*
  *Bleeding Heart of Timpanogas*      Hanson, W. F.        1928
ROBERTSON, T. W. (1829–1871)
  *David Garrick* (1800)
  *David Garrick*                     Somerville, R.       1920
  *Garrick*                           Stoessel, R.         1937
ROBINETTE, JOSEPH
  *Jungle Book*
  *Jungle Book*                       Swensson, E.         1996
*ROBIN HOOD BALLAD*
  *Robin Hood*                        Ashton, W.           1730
  *Robin Hood*                        Burney, C.           1750
  *Robin Hood*                        De Koven, R.         1891
  *Robin Hood*                        Hewitt, J.           1800
  *Robin Hood*                        Macfarren, G.        1860
  *Robin Hood*                        Shield, W.           1784
  *Robin Hood*                        Tippett, M.          1934*
ROBINSON, EDWIN ARLINGTON (1869–1935)
  *Tristram* (1927)
  *Isolt of the White Hands*          Hart, F.             1933
ROCHE, JAMES JEFFREY (1847–1908)
  **writings**
  *By Gemini*                         Baylor, H.           1949

ROEPKE, GABRIELA (b. 1920)
  *Mariposa blanca, Una* (1957)
  *White Butterfly*                   Leichtling, A.       1971
RÖLVAAG, OLE E. (1876–1931)
  *Giants in the Earth* (1927)
  *Giants in the Earth*               Moore, D.            1951
ROSE, REGINALD (b. 1920)
  *Final Ingredient* (1959)
  *Final Ingredient*                  Amram, D.            1965
ROSSETTI, CHRISTINA GEORGINA (1830–1894)
  **poems**
  *Nightingale and the Rose*          Firsova, E.          1994
  *Goblin Market* (1893)
  *Gift, The*                         Ridout, A.           1971
ROSSNER, JUDITH (1935–2005)
  *Emmeline* (1980)
  *Emmeline*                          Picker, T.           1996
ROSTAND, EDMOND (1868–1918)
  **general**
  *Fantastics, The*                   Hart, F.             1918
  *Cyrano de Bergerac* (1897)
  *Cyrano*                            Beeson, J.           1994
  *Cyrano*                            Damrosch, W.         1913
  *Cyrano de Bergerac*                Effinger, C.         1968
  *Cyrano de Bergerac*                Herbert, V.          1899
  *Cyrano de Bergerac*                Jarrett, J.          1972
  *Cyrano de Bergerac*                Pokrass, S. D.       1932
  *Dernière Nuit de Don Juan, La*
  *Last Night of Don Juan*            Rodríguez, R.        2000
  *Trois Mousquetaires, Les* (1844)
  *Three Musketeers*                  Dvorkin, J.          1991
ROSTEN, NORMAN (1914–1995)
  *Marilyn: The Untold Story*
  *Marilyn*                           Laderman, E.         1993
ROUSSEAU, JEAN-JACQUES (1712–1778)
  *Café, Le*
  *Coffee House*                      Carey/Burgess        1738
  *Devin du village, Le* (1752)
  *Cunning Man*                       Burney, C.           1766
  *Curandera, La*                     Rodríguez, R.        2006
  *Magic Girdle*                      Barthelemon, F.      1770
RUMI (JALAL AL-DIN RUMI, MAULANA) (1207–1273)
  **poetry**
  *Monsters of Grace*                 Glass, P.            1998
  *Powers of Two*                     Truax, B.            2006
RUSHDIE, SALMAN (b. 1947)
  *Haroun and the Sea of Stories* (1990)
  *Haroun and the Sea of Stories*     Wuorinen, C.         2000
RUSKIN, JOHN (1819–1900)
  *King of the Golden River* (1851)
  *King of the Golden River*          Hand, C.             1969
  *King of the Golden River*          Maconchy, E.         1975
  *King of the Golden River*          Wilson, J.           1992*

RUTHENBURG, GRACE
**Hans Bulow's Last Puppet** (1930)
*Last Puppet* — Strilko, A. — 1963
RYERSON, FLORENCE (1892–1965)
**All on a Summer's Day** (1928, with C. Clements)
*Game of Chance* — Barab, S. — 1957

SACHER-MASOCH, LEOPOLD von (1836–1905)
**Venus im Pelz** (1870)
*Venus in Furs* — Gal, Y. — 2004
SACHS, HANS (1494–1576)
**Fahrende Schüler im Paradies, Der** (1550)
*George from Paradise* — Kaufmann, W. — 1958*
*Strolling Clerk from Paradise* — Wilson, C. — ca. 1952
SACKS, OLIVER (b. 1933)
**Man Who Mistook His Wife for a Hat** (1985)
*Man Who Mistook His Wife for a Hat* — Nyman, M. — 1986
SADE, MARQUIS DE (1705–1778)
**general**
*Undivine Comedy* — Finnissy, M. — 1988
SAINT-EXUPÉRY, ANTOINE DE (1900–1944)
**Petit Prince, Le** (1943)
*Little Prince* — Mann, R. W. — 1951*
*Little Prince* — Portman, R. — 2003
SAINT-FOIX [GERMAIN-FRANÇOIS POULLAIN] (1698–1776)
**Isle sauvage, L'** (1760)
*Islanders, The* — Dibdin, C. — 1780
**Oracle, L'**
*Daphne and Amintor* — Arnold, S. — 1765
SAKI [H. H. MUNRO] (1870–1916)
**Background, The**
*One Man Show* — Maw, N. — 1964
**Baker's Dozen**
*Fortune's Favorites* — Barab, S. — 1982
**Beasts and Superbeasts** (1914)
*Beast and Superbeast* — Martín, J. — 1996
*Sredni Vashtar* — Cassels-Brown, A. — 1983*
*Sredni Vasthar* — Steadman, R. — 1988*
**Open Window**
*Open Window* — Arnold, M. — 1956
**Tobermory**
*Tobermory* — Gardner, J. — 1977
SALTEN, FELIX [SIEGMUND SALZMANN] (1869–1945)
**Bambi, A Life in the Woods** (1923)
*Bambi* — Morrill, K. — 1997
SALZMAN, EVA (b. 1960)
**Hollow Hill**
*Hollow Hill* — McQueen, I. — 2005
SAMUEL BEN YAHYA BEN AL MAGHRIBI (12th cent.)
**Chronicle**
*Sonata about Jerusalem* — Goehr, A. — 1971
SANDBURG, CARL (1878–1967)
**Abe Lincoln Grows Up** (1928)
*Young Lincoln I* — Hunkins, E. — 1959

SANGE, GARY
**Maud**
*Maud* — Dellaria, M. — 1977
SARDOU, VICTORIEN (1831–1908)
**Madame Sans-Gêne** (1893. with E. Moreau)
*Duchess of Dantzic* — Caryll, I. — 1903
SAROYAN, WILLIAM (1908–1981)
**general**
*Opera, Opera* — Kalmanoff, M. — 1956
**short stories**
*Shala Fears for the Poor* — Braxton, A. — 1996
**Hello Out There** (1941)
*Hello Out There* — Beeson, J. — 1954
*Hello Out There* — Colilla, R. — 1990*
**Miraculous Phonograph Record** (1921)
*Miraculous Phonograph Record* — White, C. — 1997
**My Heart's in the Highlands** (1939)
*My Heart's in the Highlands* — Ahlstrom, D. — 1955*
*My Heart's in the Highlands* — Beeson, J. — 1970
SARTRE, JEAN-PAUL (1905–1980)
**No Exit** (1944)
*Closed Case* — Tate, R. — 1998
*No Exit* — Vores, A. — 2008
SAUNDERS, JAMES (b. 1925)
**Barnstable** (1961)
*Barnstable* — Burt, F. — 1969
SCHEFFEL, JOSEPH VIKTOR von (1826–1886)
**Ekkehard** (1857)
*Ekkehard* — Ewart, F. — 1923
SCHEHADÉ, GEORGES (b. 1910)
**Histoire de Vasco, L'** (1956)
*Story of Vasco* — Crosse, G. — 1974
SCHILLER, FRIEDRICH (1759–1805)
**Handschuh, Der** (1797)
*Glove, The* — Polgar, T. — 1975
**Räuber, Die** (1782)
*Red Cross Knights* — Attwood, T. — 1799
**Wilhelm Tell** (1804)
*Archers, The* — Carr, B. — 1796
*Helvetic Liberty* — ** — 1792
SCHNITZLER, ARTHUR (1862–1931)
**Anatol** (1893)
*Farewell Supper* — Hart, F. — 1984
**Empfindsame, Der** (1895)
*Man of Feeling* — Oliver, S. — 1980
SCHWARTZ, HOWARD (b. 1945)
**Gabriel's Palace** (1993)
*Rabbi Nachman's Chair* — Bingham, S. — 1995
SCHWARZ, YEVGENY (1896–1958)
**Dragon, The** (1943)
*Dragon, The* — Biales, A. — 1996
SCOTT, (Sir) WALTER (1771–1832)
**general**

| | | |
|---|---|---|
| *Lord of the Isles* | Rodwell, G. | 1834 |
| *White Plume* | Reeve, W. | 1806 |
| **Antiquary, The** (1826) | | |
| *Antiquary, The* | Bishop, H. R. | 1820 |
| **Black Dwarf** (1817) | | |
| *Wizard, The* | Horn, C. E. | 1817 |
| **Guy Mannering** (1815) | | |
| *Guy Mannering* | Attwood, T. | 1816 |
| *White Lady* | Cooke, T. S. | 1826 |
| **Heart of Midlothian** (1818) | | |
| *Heart of Midlothian* | Bishop, H. R. | 1819 |
| *Heart of Midlothian* | ** | 1849 |
| *Jeanie Deans* | MacCunn, H. | 1894 |
| **Ivanhoe** (1819) | | |
| *Ivanhoe* | Parry, J. | 1820 |
| *Ivanhoe* | Sullivan, A. S. | 1891 |
| **Kenilworth** (1821) | | |
| *Amy Robsart* | Lara, I. de | 1893 |
| **Lady of the Lake** (1810) | | |
| *Knight of Snowdoun* | Bishop, H. R. | 1811 |
| *Lady of the Lake* | Francis, W. | 1811 |
| *Lady of the Lake* | Schmidt, K. | 1931* |
| **Legend of Montrose** (1820) | | |
| *Montrose* | Bishop, H. R. | 1822 |
| **Monastery, The** | | |
| *White Lady* | Cooke, T. S. | 1826 |
| **Old Morality** (1817) | | |
| *Battle of Bothwell Brigg* | Bishop, H. R. | 1820 |
| **Pirate, The** (1821) | | |
| *Pirate, The* | Rooke, W. | 1822 |
| **Quentin Durward** (1823) | | |
| *King's Prize* | Maclean, A. | 1904 |
| *Quentin Durward* | Laurent, H. R. | 1848 |
| *Quentin Durward* | Maclean, A. | 1893* |
| **Rob Roy** (1811) | | |
| *Rob Roy* | De Koven, R. | 1894 |
| *Rob Roy Macgregor* | Davy, J. | 1818 |
| **Talisman, The** (1825) | | |
| *Talisman, The* | Bishop, H. R. | 1825 |
| **Waverley** (1814) | | |
| *Waverley* | Rodwell, G. | 1824 |

SCRIBE, EUGÈNE (1791–1861)

| | | |
|---|---|---|
| **Ours et la pacha, L'** (1821) | | |
| *Meanwhile, Back at the Seraglio* | Stepleton, J. | 1997* |
| **Premières amours, Les** | | |
| *Casket, The* | Lacy, M. | 1829 |

SEAFARER, THE (Anglo-Saxon poem)

| | | |
|---|---|---|
| *Wraeca* | Shields, A. | 1989 |

SECOND SHEPHERDS' PLAY

| | | |
|---|---|---|
| *Shepherds' Christmas* | Russo, W. | 1979 |

SEI SHONAGON (b. ca. 967)

| | | |
|---|---|---|
| **Pillow Book** (ca. 1002) | | |
| *Pillow Book* | Barry, G. | 1980 |

SELZER, RICHARD (b. 1928)

| | | |
|---|---|---|
| **Black Swan Revisited** | | |
| *Black Swan* | Whitman, T. | 1998 |

SENECA THE YOUNGER (4 B.C.–A.D. 65)

| | | |
|---|---|---|
| **Hercules Oetaeus** | | |
| *Heracles* | Eaton, J. | 1972 |
| **Medea** | | |
| *Medea* | Kerry, G. | 1994 |

SETH, VIKRAM (b. 1952)

| | | |
|---|---|---|
| **Golden Gate** (1986) | | |
| *Golden Gate* | Cummings, C. | 2006 |

SEXTON, ANNE (1928–1974)

| | | |
|---|---|---|
| **selections** | | |
| *After Dido* | ** | 2009 |

SHADWELL, CHARLES (d. 1726)

| | | |
|---|---|---|
| **Fair Quaker of Deal** | | |
| *Quaker, The* | Dibdin, C. | 1775 |

SHAFFER, PETER (b. 1926)

| | | |
|---|---|---|
| **Amadeus** (1980) | | |
| *Little Nightmare Music* | Schickele, P. | 1982 |
| **Royal Hunt of the Sun** (1965) | | |
| *Royal Hunt of the Sun* | Hamilton, I. | 1977 |

SHAKESEPARE, WILLIAM (1564–1616)

| | | |
|---|---|---|
| **general** | | |
| *Hood of the Woods* | Shepherd, S. | 1988 |
| **Anthony and Cleopatra** (1607) | | |
| *Antony and Cleopatra* | Barber, S. | 1966 |
| *Antony and Cleopatra* | Chiusano, G. | 2004* |
| *Antony and Cleopatra* | Gruenberg, L. | 1955* |
| **As You Like It** (1599–1600) | | |
| *As You Like It* | Young, W. | 2002* |
| **Comedy of Errors** (1592–93) | | |
| *Comedy of Errors* | Bishop, H. R. | 1819 |
| *Errors* | Wilson-Dickson | 1980 |
| **Hamlet** (1600–1601) | | |
| *Hamlet* | Kagen, S. | 1962 |
| *Hamlet* | Kievman, C. | 1990 |
| *Hamlet* | Searle, H. | 1968 |
| *Hamlet* | Van de Vate, N. | 2010 |
| *Hamlet Travestie* | Bray, J. | 1811 |
| *Lamentations of Ophelia* | Stimson, S. | 2009 |
| *Rosencrantz and Guildenstern Are Dead* | | |
| Garfein, H. | | 2006 |
| **Henry IV** (ca. 1597) | | |
| *At the Boar's Head* | Holst, G. | 1925 |
| **Henry V** (1599) | | |
| *Agincourt* | Boughton, R. | 1924 |
| **Julius Caesar** (1599) | | |
| *Julius Caesar* | Schmitz, A. | 1978 |
| **King Lear** | | |
| *King Lear* | Eaton, J. | 2004* |
| *King Lear* | York-Norris, C. | 1994 |
| **Love's Labour's Lost** (1594–95) | | |

| | | | | | | |
|---|---|---|---|---|---|---|
| *Love's Labour's Lost* | Bush, G. | 1988 | *Christopher Sly* | Eastwood, T. | 1960 |
| *Love's Labour's Lost* | Loeffler, A. | 1999* | *Cure for a Scold* | ** | 1735 |
| *Love's Labour's Lost* | Nabokov, N. | 1973 | *Petruccio* | Maclean, A. | 1895 |
| **Macbeth** (1605–6) | | | *Taming of the Shrew* | Braham/Cooke | 1828 |
| *Macbeth* | Collingwood, A. | 1934 | *Taming of the Shrew* | Clapp, P. | 1948* |
| *Macbeth* | Eccles, J. | 1696 | *Taming of the Shrew* | Giannini, V. | 1953 |
| *Macbeth* | Gatty, N. | 1920* | **Tempest, The** (1611–12) | | |
| *Macbeth* | Goldman, E. | 1961* | *Caliban* | Currie, R. | 1992 |
| *Macbeth* | Halpern, S. | 1965 | *Caliban Dreams* | Suprynowicz, C. | 2001 |
| *Macbeth* | Leveridge, R. | 1702 | *Enchanted Island* | Farquhar, D. | 1997* |
| *Macbeth* | Locke/Johnson | 1673 | *Noises, Sounds* | Nyman, M. | 1991 |
| *Macbeth* | McIntyre, P. | 2005* | *Tempest, The* | Adès, T. | 2004 |
| *Mortal Thoughts of Lady Macbeth* | Krausas, V. | 2004 | *Tempest, The* | Arne, T. A. | 1746 |
| *Three, Two, One, Bang!* | Chen, J. | 2008 | *Tempest, The* | Banister, Locke, et al. | 1674 |
| *Tragedy of Macbeth* | Hamilton, I. | 1994* | *Tempest, The* | Boyce, W. | 1757 |
| **Merchant of Venice** (1596) | | | *Tempest, The* | Eaton, J. | 1985 |
| *Merchant of Venice* | Beecham, A. | 1922 | *Tempest, The* | Gatty, N. | 1920 |
| *Shylock* | La Violette, W. | 1930 | *Tempest, The* | Hoiby, L. | 1986 |
| **Merry Wives of Windsor** (1600–161) | | | *Tempest, The* | Leichtling, A. | 1973* |
| *Falstaff in and out of Love* | Rea, A. | 1982 | *Tempest, The* | Smith, J. C. | 1756 |
| *Merry Wives of Windsor* | Horn et al. | 1824 | *Tempest, The* | Tahourdin, P. | 2000* |
| *Sir John in Love* | Vaughan Williams | 1929 | *Tempest, The* | Weldon, J. | 1712 |
| **Midsummer Night's Dream** (1596) | | | *Tempest, The* | Westergaard, P. | 1994 |
| *Fairies, The* | Smith, J. C. | 1755 | **Timon of Athens** (1607–8) | | |
| *Fairy Queen* | Purcell, H. | 1692 | *Timon of Athens* | Oliver, S. | 1991 |
| *Midsummer Night's Dream* | Bishop, H. R. | 1816 | **Twelfth Night** (1599–1600) | | |
| *Midsummer Night's Dream* | Britten, B. | 1960 | *Make Me a Willow Cabin* | Stoker, R. | 1973 |
| *Midsummer Night's Dream* | Burney, C. | 1763 | *Malvolio* | Hart, F. | 1919 |
| *Pyramus and Thisbe* | Bruce, N. | 1965 | *Twelfth Night* | Amram, D. | 1968 |
| *Pyramus and Thisbe* | Converly R. | 1982 | *Twelfth Night* | Feigen, J. | 2005 |
| **Much Ado about Nothing** (1598–99) | | | *Twelfth Night* | Wilson, J. | 1969 |
| *Benedict and Beatrice* | Holst, I. | 1951 | **Two Gentlemen of Verona** (1594–95) | | |
| *Much Ado about Nothing* | Stanford, C. | 1901 | *Two Gentlemen of Verona* | Seymour, J. | 1935* |
| *Sir John in Love* | Vaughan Williams | 1929 | **Two Noble Kinsmen** (1612–13, prob. with Fletcher) | | |
| **Othello** (1604) | | | *Love and Madness* | Arnold, S. | 1795 |
| *John Hooten* | Russo, W. | 1963 | **Venus and Adonis** (1593) | | |
| *Telaio: Desdemona* | Botti, S. | 1995 | *Garden of Adonis* | Weisgall, H. | 1959 |
| **Pericles** (1608–9) | | | **Winter's Tale** (1610–11) | | |
| *Night of the Moonspell* | Siegmeister, E. | 1976 | *Florizel and Perdita* | Boyce, W. | 1756 |
| *Pericles* | Hecker, Z. | 1980* | *Sheep Shearing* | Arnold, S. | 1777 |
| *Pericles* | Hovhaness, A. | 1975 | *Winter's Tale* | Harbison, J. | 1979 |
| **Rape of Lucrece** (1594) | | | SHAW, GEORGE BERNARD (1856–1950) | | |
| *Rape of Lucretia* | Britten, B. | 1946 | **Admirable Bashville** | | |
| **Richard III** (1592–93) | | | *Admirable Bashville* | Berry, W. | 1954* |
| *Richard III* | Turok, P. | 1975 | **Androcles and the Lion** | | |
| **Romeo and Juliet** (1594–95) | | | *Androcles and the Lion* | Hagemann, P. | 2001 |
| *Romeo and Juliet* | Barkworth, J. | 1916 | **Devil's Disciple** | | |
| *Romeo and Juliet* | Hoiby, L. | 1999 | *Devil's Disciple* | Barthelson, J. | 1977 |
| *Romeo and Juliet* | Liotta, A. | 1969 | *Passion, Passion* | Taub, B. | 1976 |
| *Romeo and Juliet* | Marshall-Hall | 1912 | **Music Cure** (1913) | | |
| *Romeo and Juliet* | Shelley, J. | 1901* | *Music Cure* | Hagemann, P. | 1984* |
| *West Side Story* | Bernstein, L. | 1957 | **Passion, Poison, and Petrifaction** | | |
| **Taming of the Shrew** (1593–94) | | | *Passion, Poison, and Petrifaction* | Taub. B. | 1976 |
| *Christopher Sly* | Argento, D. | 1963 | | | |

SHEFFER, JONATHAN B. (b. 1935)
  **Camera Obscura** (1969)

| | | |
|---|---|---|
| Camera Obscura | Dhrggrt, J. | 1980 |

SHELLEY, MARY (1797–1851)
  **general**

| | | |
|---|---|---|
| Awed Behavior | Dresher, P. | 1993 |
| Monster | Beamish, S. | 2002 |

  **Frankenstein** (1818)

| | | |
|---|---|---|
| Frankenstein | Baber, J. | 1976 |
| Frankenstein | Blyton, C. | 1987 |
| Frankenstein | Larsen, L. | 1990 |
| Frankenstein | Sandow, G. | 1980 |

SHELLEY, PERCY BYSSHE (1792–1822)
  **Cenci, The** (1819)

| | | |
|---|---|---|
| Beatrice Cenci | Di Domenica, R. | 1993* |
| Beatrice Chancy | Rolfe, J. | 1996 |
| Cenci, The | Brian, H. | 1952* |
| Cenci, The | Coke, R. S. | 1959 |
| Cenci, The | Di Domenica, R. | 1995* |
| Francesco Cenci | Di Domenica, R. | 1996* |

SHERIDAN, ELIZABETH ANN (1754–1792)
  **History of Nourjahad**

| | | |
|---|---|---|
| Illusion, The | Kelly, M. | 1813 |

SHERIDAN, RICHARD BRINSLEY (1751–1816)
  **Arabian Night's Entertainment**

| | | |
|---|---|---|
| Forty Thieves | Kelly, M. | 1806 |

  **Critic, The** (1779)

| | | |
|---|---|---|
| Critic, The | Stanford, C. | 1916 |

  **Duenna, The** (1775)

| | | |
|---|---|---|
| Duenna, The | Gerhard, R. | 1951 |

  **Rivals, The** (1775)

| | | |
|---|---|---|
| Rivals, The | Mechem, K. | 2003 |

SHIKIBU, LADY MURASAKI (ca. 973–ca. 1025)
  **Tale of Genji** (ca. 1000)

| | | |
|---|---|---|
| Echoes of the Shining Prince | Cooper, S. | 1985 |
| Tale of Genji | Miki, M. | 2000 |

SHOLOKHOV, MIKHAIL ALEKSANDROVICH (1905–1984)
  **short stories** (1925)

| | | |
|---|---|---|
| Family Man | Lehrman, L. | 1984 |

SIAO YU
  **short stories**

| | | |
|---|---|---|
| Farmer and the Faun | Tcherepnin, A. | 1952 |

SIMMONS, RACHEL (b. 1974)
  **Odd Girl Out** (2002)

| | | |
|---|---|---|
| One False Move | Kander, S. | 2003 |

SIMON, NEIL (b. 1927)
  **Good Doctor** (1973)

| | | |
|---|---|---|
| Seduction of a Lady | Wargo, R. | 1985 |

SINGER, ISAAC BASHEVIS (1902–1991)
  **Gimpel the Fool** (1953)

| | | |
|---|---|---|
| Gimpel the Fool | Davidson, C. | 1965* |
| Gimpel the Fool | Schiff, D. | 1985 |

SIQUEIROS, DAVID ALFARO (1896–1974)
  **América Tropical, La** (1932)

| | | |
|---|---|---|
| America Tropical | Conte, D. | 2007 |

SITWELL, EDITH (1887–1964)
  **English Eccentrics** (1933)

| | | |
|---|---|---|
| English Eccentrics | Williamson, M. | 1964 |

SMITH, EVELYN E.
  **Floyd and the Eumenides**

| | | |
|---|---|---|
| I Can't Stand Wagner | Barab, S. | 1986 |

SMITH, LILLIAN (1897–1966)
  **Strange Fruit** (1944)

| | | |
|---|---|---|
| Strange Fruit | Carter, C. | 2003 |

SOKOLOSKI, THOM
  **Nosferatu**

| | | |
|---|---|---|
| Nosferatu | Peters, R. | 1993 |

SOPHOCLES (ca. 496–406 B.C.)
  **Agamemnon**

| | | |
|---|---|---|
| Cassandra | McAndrew, J. | 2003 |

  **Antigone**

| | | |
|---|---|---|
| Antigone | Constantinides, D. | 1993 |
| Antigone | Eaton, J. | 1999 |
| Antigone | Joubert, J. | 1954 |
| Antigone | Rodgers, L. | 1977 |
| Antigone | Smith Brindle, R. | 1971 |
| Burial at Thebes | Le Gendre, D. | 2008 |

  **Oedipus at Colonus**

| | | |
|---|---|---|
| Death of Oedipus | Halpern, M. | 2009 |

  **Oedipus Rex**

| | | |
|---|---|---|
| Oedipus | Partch, H. | 1952 |
| Oedipus Tex | Schickele, P. | 1988 |

  **Women of Trachis (Trachimiae)**

| | | |
|---|---|---|
| Heracles | Eaton, J. | 1972 |
| Hercules | Handel, G. F. | 1745 |

SOTOBA KOMACHI (Noh play)

| | | |
|---|---|---|
| Jenny | Weisgall, H. | 1976 |
| Sotoba Komachi | Levy, M. | 1957 |

SOUTHERN ARANDA POEMS (Australian Aboriginal)

| | | |
|---|---|---|
| Rites of Passage | Sculthorpe, P. | 1974 |

SOUTHEY, ROBERT (1774–1843)
  **Joan of Arc** (1796)

| | | |
|---|---|---|
| Joan of Arc | Balfe, M. | 1837 |

  **Thalaba the Destroyer** (1801)

| | | |
|---|---|---|
| Thalaba the Destroyer | Rodwell, G. | 1836 |

SOYINA, WOLE (b. 1934)
  **Scourge of Hyacinths** (1991)

| | | |
|---|---|---|
| Scourge of Hyacinths | León, T. | 1994 |

SPARK, MURIEL (1918–2006)
  **stories**

| | | |
|---|---|---|
| Three Lost Chords | Horne, L. | 2008 |

SPEED, SCOTT
  **Best**

| | | |
|---|---|---|
| Rimshot | Currie, R. | 1990 |

SSU-MA CH'IEN (ca. 145–ca. 90 B.C.)
  **Records of the Historian**
  Chinese Canticle                    Stoker, R.          1991
STAVIS, BARRIE (b. 1905)
  **Man Who Never Died** (1954)
  Joe Hill                            Bush, A.            1970
STEELE, RICHARD (1672–1729)
  **essay**
  Inkle and Yariko                    Arnold, S.          1787
STEELE, WILBUR D. (1886–1970)
  **How Beautiful with Shoes**
  Amarantha                           Ames, R.            1980
STEGNER, WALLACE (b. 1909)
  **Angle of Repose** (1971)
  Angle of Repose                     Imbrie, A.          1976
STEIN, GETRUDE (1874–1946)
  **Blood on the Dining Room Floor**
  Blood on the Dining Room Floor      Sheffer, J.         1999
  **First Reader** (1946)
  In a Garden                         Kupferman, M.       1949
  Woman in the Garden                 Fine, V.            1978
  **Three Plays**
  Doctor Faustus                      Ahlstrom, D.        1982
  Doctor Faustus                      Kupferman, M.       1953
  Dr. Faustus                         Hagemann, P.        1967*
  I Like It to be a Play              Shere, C.           1989
  Ladies Voices                       Gardner, K.         1981*
  Ladies Voices                       Kievman, C.         1974*
  Ladies' Voices                      Martin, V.          1956
  Ladies Voices                       Shere, C.           1987
  What Happened                       Shere, C.           1991*
  **List, A** (1923)
  Mapping Venue                       Hays, S.            1998*
  **Say It with Flowers** (1931)
  Say It with Flowers                 Lependorf, J.       1996
  **Three Sisters Who Are Not Sisters** (1946)
  Three Sisters Who Are Not Sisters   Ahlstrom, D.        1953
  Three Sisters Who Are Not Sisters   Hellerman, W.       1983
  Three Sisters Who Are Not Sisters   Rorem, N.           1971
STEINBECK, JOHN (1902–1968)
  **Burning Bright** (1950)
  Burning Bright                      Lewin, F.           1993
  **Grapes of Wrath**
  Grapes of Wrath                     Gordon, R. I.       2007
  **Of Mice and Men** (1937)
  Of Mice and Men                     Floyd, C.           1970
STEPHEN, JAMES (1882–1950)
  **Isle of Youth**
  Feast of Samhain                    Chisholm, E.        1941
STERN, RICHARD (b. 1928)
  **Golk** (1960)
  Golk                                Eaton, J.           1996

STERNE, LAURENCE (1713–1768)
  **Sentimental Journey** (1768)
  Sterne's Maria                      Pelissier, V.       1799
  **Tristram Shandy** (1759–67)
  Tristram Shandy                     McNally, L.         1783
STEVENS, WALLACE (1879–1955)
  **Bowl, Cat, and Broomstick** (1917)
  Bowl, Cat, and Broomstick           Boury, R.           1989
STEVENSON, ROBERT LOUIS (1850–1894)
  **Beach of Falesá** (1897)
  Beach of Falesá                     Hoddinott, A.       1974
  **Bottle Imp** (1891)
  Bottle Imp                          Whiton, P.          1958
  **Markheim** (1884)
  Markheim                            Floyd, C.           1966
  Good Angel, Bad Angel               Cresswell, L.       2005
  Markheim                            Miles, P. N.        1923
  **Rajah's Diamond** (1878)
  Rajah's Diamond                     Hill, A.            1979
  **Sire de Malétroit's Door** (1877)
  Door, The                           Mopper, I.          1956
  Maletroit Door                      Barab, S.           1959
  Mouse Trap                          Bell, W. H.         1928*
  Sire de Maletroit                   Duke, J.            1958
  **Strange Case Dr. Jekyll and Mr. Hyde** (1886)
  Dr. Jekyll and Mr. Hyde             Cannon, P.          1973
  Dr. Jekyll and Mr. Hyde             De Pue, W.          1974
  Dr. Jekyll and Mr. Hyde             Fragale, F. D.      1953
  Dr. Jekyll and Mr. Hyde             O'Neal, B.          1980*
  **Weir of Hermiston** (1896)
  Hermiston                           Orr, R.             1975
ST. GEORGE AND THE DRAGON (mummers' play)
  St. George and the Dragon           Hart, F.            1931
STOCKTON, FRANK R. (1834–1902)
  **Old Pipes and the Dryad**
  Old Pipes and the Dryad             Rea, A.             1980
STOKER, BRAM (1847–1912)
  **Dracula** (1897)
  Dracula                             Blyton, C.          1983
  Dracula                             Franchetti, A.      1979
  Dracula                             Ziemba, P.          2000
  Un-Dead, The                        Stanhope, D.        2010
STOPPARD, TOM (b. 1937)
  **On the Razzle** (1981)
  On the Razzle                       Orr, R.             1988
  **Rosencrantz and Guildenstern Are Dead** (1966)
  Rosencrantz and Guildenstern Are Dead  Garfein, H.      2006
STOWE, HARRIET BEECHER (1811–1896)
  **Uncle Tom's Cabin** (1852)
  Thomas Shelby                       Warren, B.          1993*
  Transcendent Voices                 Jones, D.           2000
  Uncle Tom's Cabin                   Florio, C.          1882
  Uncle Tom's Cabin                   Grossmith, L.       1928*
  Uncle Tom's Cabin                   Howard, G.          1852

| | | |
|---|---|---|
| *Uncle Tom's Cabin* | Millard, H. | 1883 |
| *Uncle Tom's Cabin* | Tracy, G. | 1866 |

**STRACHEY, LYTTON (1880–1932)**
**Elizabeth and Essex** (1928)

| | | |
|---|---|---|
| *Gloriana* | Britten, B. | 1953 |

**STRASSBURG, GOTTFRIED von (d. ca. 1210)**
**Tristan**

| | | |
|---|---|---|
| *Tristan and Iseult* | Cohen, J. | 1988 |

**STRINDBERG, AUGUST (1849–1912)**
**Dream Play** (1902)

| | | |
|---|---|---|
| *Dream Play* | Sullivan, T. | 1988 |
| *Growing Castle* | Williamson, M. | 1968 |

**Lucky Peter's Travels** (1882)

| | | |
|---|---|---|
| *Lucky-Peter's Journey* | Williamson, M. | 1968 |

**Miss Julie** (1888)

| | | |
|---|---|---|
| *Miss Julie* | Alwyn, W. | 1983 |
| *Miss Julie* | Rorem, N. | 1965 |

**Simoon** (1905)

| | | |
|---|---|---|
| *Simoon* | Chisholm, E. | 1954 |
| *Simoon* | Meyerowitz, J. | 1950 |

**Stronger, The** (1869)

| | | |
|---|---|---|
| *Stronger, The* | Kosteck, G. | 1969 |
| *Stronger, The* | Weisgall, H. | 1952 |

**STYRON, WILLIAM (1925–2006)**
**Sophie's Choice** (1979)

| | | |
|---|---|---|
| *Sophie's Choice* | Maw, N, | 2002 |

**SUEZKINT [SÜSSKIND] von TRIMBERG (13th cent.)**
**poems**

| | | |
|---|---|---|
| *In Mighty Silence* | Siskind, P. | 1992* |

**SUTRO, ALFRED (1863–1933)**
**Marriage Has Been Arranged** (1904)

| | | |
|---|---|---|
| *Will You Marry Me?* | Weisgall, H. | 1989 |

**SWANN, FRANCIS**
**Out of the Frying Pan** (1941)

| | | |
|---|---|---|
| *Rehearsal Call* | Giannini, V. | 1962 |

**SWIFT, JONATHAN (1667–1745)**
**Gulliver's Travels** (1726)

| | | |
|---|---|---|
| *Floating Island* | Greenbaum, M. | 2000 |
| *Gulliver* | Bond, V. | 1988 |
| *Gulliver in Lilliput* | Paintal, P. | 1995* |
| *Lilliput* | Arnold, S. | 1777 |
| *Travels* | Bond, V. | 1995 |

**SWOPE, SAM**
**Araboolies of Liberty Street** (1989)

| | | |
|---|---|---|
| *Araboolies of Liberty Street* | Perera, R. | 2002 |

**SYLVIUS, AENEAS [POPE PIUS II] (1405–1464)**
**works**

| | | |
|---|---|---|
| *Lion and Androcles* | Eaton, J. | 1974 |

**SYNGE, J[OHN] M[ILLINGTON] (1871–1909)**
**Deirdre of the Sorrows** (1909, unfin.)

| | | |
|---|---|---|
| *Deirdre of the Sorrows* | Becker, J. | 1945 |
| *Deirdre of the Sorrows* | Crofton, W. | 1925* |
| *Deirdre of the Sorrows* | Hart, F. | 1916 |
| *Deirdre of the Sorrows* | Rankl, K. | 1951 |

**In the Shadow of the Glen** (1902)

| | | |
|---|---|---|
| *In the Shadow of the Glen* | Van de Vate, N. | 1994* |

**Riders to the Sea** (1904)

| | | |
|---|---|---|
| *Maurya* | Kosteck, G. | 1968 |
| *Riders to the Sea* | Betts, L. | 1955* |
| *Riders to the Sea* | Hart, F. | 1915* |
| *Riders to the Sea* | Vaughan Williams, R | 1937 |

**TAGORE, RABINDRANATH (1861–1941)**
**poems**

| | | |
|---|---|---|
| *Snatched by the Gods* | Vir, P. | 1992 |

**TAÍN, THE** (early Irish literature)

| | | |
|---|---|---|
| *Death of Ferdia* | Ward, D. | 1976 |

**TALE OF THE HEIKE** (12th-century Japan)

| | | |
|---|---|---|
| *Greenleaf* | Buchanan, D. | 1985* |

**TAN, AMY (b. 1952)**
**Bonesetter's Daughter** (2001)

| | | |
|---|---|---|
| *Bonesetter's Daughter* | Wallace, S. | 2008 |

**TANG XIANZU (1550–1616)**
**Peony Pavilion** (1598)

| | | |
|---|---|---|
| *Peony Pavilion* | Tan Dun | 1998 |

**TARKINGTON, BOOTH (1869–1946)**
**Seventeen** (1916)

| | | |
|---|---|---|
| *Seventeen* | Warren, B. | 1989* |

**TARUHITO, KAMO**
**Mount Kagu**

| | | |
|---|---|---|
| *Greenleaf* | Buchanan, D. | 1985* |

**TASSO, TORQUATO (1544–1595)**
**Gerusalemme liberata** (1580–81)

| | | |
|---|---|---|
| *Armida* | Weir, J. | 2005 |
| *Rinaldo and Armida* | Eccles, J. | 1698 |

**TATE, NAHUM (1652–1715)**
**Duke and No Duke**

| | | |
|---|---|---|
| *Devil of a Duke* | ** | 1732 |

**TATI, JACQUES (1907–1982)**
**Traffic** (1970)

| | | |
|---|---|---|
| *What Next?* | Carter. E. | 1999 |

**TAYLOR, KEN**
**Decision, The**

| | | |
|---|---|---|
| *Decision, The* | Musgrave, T. | 1967 |

**TEGNÉR, ESAIAS (1782–1846)**
**Frithiofs Saga** (1825)

| | | |
|---|---|---|
| *Frithiof* | Freer, E. E. | 1929 |

**TELLER, EDWARD (1908–2003)**
**memoirs**

| | | |
|---|---|---|
| *Doctor Atomic* | Adams, J. | 2005 |

**TENNYSON, ARTHUR LORD (1809–1892)**
**general**

| | | |
|---|---|---|
| *Powers of Two* | Truax, B. | 2006 |

**Lancelot and Elaine**

| | | |
|---|---|---|
| *Lancelot and Elaine* | Sessions, R. | 1910* |

**Princess, The: A Medley** (1847)

| | | |
|---|---|---|
| *Princess Ida* | Sulivan, W. S. | 1884 |

THACKERAY, WILLIAM M. (1811–1863)
  ***Little Billy***
    Little Billy                        Hurd, M.              1964
  ***Rose and the Ring*** (1855)
    Rose and the Ring                   Leginska, E.          1957
    Rose and the Ring                   Warren, B.            1980*
THIBOUST, LAMBERT (1826–1867)
  ***Je dîne chez ma mère*** (1867, with A. Decourcelle)
    Madeleine                           Herbert, V.           1914
*THIEF OF LOVE* (Bengali tale)
    Thief of Love                       Silver, S.            1986*
THOMAS, DYLAN (1914–1953)
  ***Vision and Prayer*** (1945)
    Vision and Prayer                   Macbride, D.          1995
THORNDIKE, RUSSELL (1885–1972)
  ***Dr. Syn*** (1916)
    Dr. Syn                             Cruft, A.             1981*
*THOUSAND AND ONE NIGHTS (ARABIAN NIGHTS)*
    Aladdin                             Bishop, H. R.         1826
    Ali Baba Opera                      Reed, N.              1989
    Bondocani, Il                       Attwood/Moorehead     1800
    Cadi of Bagdad                      Linley Jr., T.        1778
    Caliph of Bagdad                    Musgrave, F.          1867
    Enchanter, The                      Jones, J.             1844
    Forty Thieves                       Kelly, M.             1806
    Mahmoud                             Storace, S.           1796
    Mischance, The                      Dibdin, C.            1773
    Ninth Statue                        Horn, C. E.           1814
    Ring, Lamp, Thing                   Gough, O.             2010
    Sleeper Awakened                    Macfarren, G.         1850
    Troublemaker, The                   Polgar, T.            1968*
THURBER, JAMES (1894–1961)
  ***Catbird Seat*** (1942)
    Catbird Seat                        Sisco, D.             1999
  ***Fables for Our Time*** (1940)
    Unicorn in the Garden               Smith, R.             1957
  ***Many Moons*** (1943)
    Many Moons                          Dougherty, C.         1962
    Many Moons                          Kapilow, R.           1997
  ***Thirteen Clocks*** (1950)
    Thirteen Clocks                     Chauls, R.            1983
    Thirteen Clocks                     Theofanidis, C.       2003
TIECK, LUDWIG (1773–1853)
  ***Blonde Eckbert, Der*** (1797)
    Blond Eckbert                       Weir, J.              1994
  ***Gestiefelte Kater, Der***
    Puss in Boots                       Martín, J.            1992
TOKLAS, ALICE B. (1877–1967)
  ***Cookbook***
    Blood on the Dining Room Floor      Sheffer, J.           1999
TOLSTOY, LEO (1828–1910)
  ***Anna Karenina*** (1876)
    Anna Karenina                       Carlson, D.           2007
    Anna Karenina                       Hamilton, I.          1982

  ***Father Serius*** (1898)
    God's Liar                          Casken, J.            2001
  ***Resurrection*** (1899)
    Resurrection                        Machover, T.          1999
  ***Three Hermits***l
    Three Hermits                       Paulus, S.            1997
  ***Too Dear!***
    Prisoner, The                       Joubert, J.           1973
TOURTE, FRANCIS
  ***Voilà Madame Angot*** (1875)
    Circumstances Alter Cases           Sedgwick, A. B.       1876
*TREE TO SING* (trans. Alexander McCall Smith)
    Sibanda!                            Remson, M.            2003
*TRISTAN AND ISEULT* (medieval cycle)
    Tristan and Iseult                  Cohen, J.             1988
TSIANINA REDFEATHER (b. 1892)
  **general**
    Shanewis                            Cadman, C. W.         1918
TURGENEV, IVAN SERGEYEVICH (1818–1883)
  ***Month in the Country*** (1850)
    Natalia Petrovna                    Hoiby, L.             1964
  ***On the Eve***
    On the Eve                          Hamilton, I.          1996*
  ***Song of Triumphant Love***
    Triumph of Love                     Schmitz, A.           2008
TUWHARE, HONE (1922–2008)
  **writings**
    Trapeze Artists                     Ritchie, A.           2000
TWAIN, MARK [SAMUEL LANGHORNE CLEMENS]
(1835–1910)
  ***Celebrated Jumping Frog of Calaveras County*** (1865)
    Jumping Frog of Calaveras County    Foss, L.              1950
  ***Huckleberry Finn*** (1884)
    Huckleberry Finn                    Overton, H.           1971
  ***Tom Sawyer*** (1876)
    Tom Sawyer                          Elkus, J.             1953
    Tom Sawyer                          Owen, R.              1989
  ***War Prayer*** (posth. 1916)
    War Prayer                          March, K.             1996*
*TWA SISTERS O'BINNORIE* (ballad)
    Bow Down                            Birtwistle, H.        1977
    Two Sisters                         Rootham, C.           1922

ULTRA VIOLET (ISABELLE COLLIN DUFRESNE) (b. 1935)
  ***Famous for Fifteen Minutes*** (1990)
    Famous                              Conte, D.             2007

UNAMUNO, MIGUEL DE (1864–1936)
  ***Dos madres***
    Black Widow                         Pasatieri, T.         1972
UPDIKE, JOHN (1932–2009)
  ***S.*** (1988)
    S.                                  Perera, R.            1995

VALMIKI
   *Ramayana* (ca. 500 B.C.)
    *Sita*                  Holst, G.        1906*
VANBRUGH, JOHN (1664–1726)
   *Relapse, The* (1696)
    *Prince of Coxcombs*      Gundry, I.      1965
VAN DER VELDE, C. F.
   *Arwed Gyllenstjerna* (1822)
    *Sorceress, The*        Ries, F.       1831
VAN DYKE, HENRY (1852–1933)
   *Other Wise Man* (1896)
    *Other Wise Man*     de Kenessey, S.   1996
    *Other Wise Man*     Van Grove, I.    1959
VAN GOGH, VINCENT (1853–1890)
   **letters**
    *Letters to Theo*      Wilson, J.     1984
    *Like a Window*      Lutyens, E.    1977
    *Passion of Vincent Van Gogh*  Yavelow, C.    1984
VERNE, JULES (1828–1905)
   *Fantaisie du Docteur Ox, Une* (1872)
    *Dr. Ox's Experiment*   Bryars, G.    1997
VIAN, BORIS (1920–1959)
   *Bâtisseurs d'empire, Les* (1957)
    *Noise, The*         Blank, A.     1986
VIDAL, GORE (1925–2012)
   *Myra Breckinridge* (1968)
    *Myra Breckinridge*   Hollier, D.    1998*
VIRGIL (70 B.C.–19 B.C.)
   *Aeneid*
    *Cassandra*       McAndrew, J.   2003
    *Death of Dido*      Pepusch, J.    1716
    *Last of Manhattan*   Felsenfeld, D.  2004
VOLTAIRE [F. M. AROUET] (1694–1778)
   *Anecdote sur l'homme au masque de fer* (1764)
    *Island of St. Marguerite*  Shaw, T.     1789
   *Candide* (1759)
    *Candide*         Bernstein, L.   1956

WADDELL, HELEN (1889–1965)
   *Wandering Scholars* (1928)
    *Wandering Scholar*   Holst, G.     1934
WADSWORTH, STEPHEN (b. 1929)
   **short story**
    *Amelia*         Hagen, D.     2010
WADSWORTH, WILLIAM (1821–1893)
   *White Doe of Rylstone*
    *White Doe*       Ridout, A.    1987
WAKEFIELD MASTER (fl. 1400)
   *Wakefield Mystery Plays*
    *Glory Coach*      Barnard, F.   1982
WALKER, MARGARET (1915–1998)
   *Jubilee* (1966)
    *Jubilee*         Kay, U.      1976

WALKER, GEORGE (1772–1847)
   *Don Raphael* (1803)
    *Don Raphael*      Hewitt, J.    1804
WALPOLE, HORACE (1717–1797)
   **memoirs**
    *King for Corsica*    George, G.   1981
   *Castle of Otranto* (1764)
    *Sicilian Romance*   Reeve, W.    1794
WANDERER, THE (Anglo-Saxon poem)
    *Wraecca*        Shields, A.    1989
WARREN, MERCY (Mrs.) (1728–1814)
   *Blockheads, The*
    *Blockheads, The*    **         1782?
WARREN, ROBERT PENN (1905–1989)
   *All the King's Men* (1946)
    *Willie Stark*      Floyd, C.     1981
   *Ballad of Billie Potts, The*
    *Land between the Rivers*  Buskirk, C.   1956
WATERS, FRANK (1902–1995)
   *Woman at Otowi Crossing* (1966)
    *Woman at Otowi Crossing*  Paulus, S.   1995
WEBSTER, BENJAMIN (1797–1882)
   *Paul Clifford, the Highwayman of 1770* (1832)
    *Paul Clifford*     Rodwell, G.   1835
WEBSTER, JOHN (ca. 1580–1625)
   *Duchess of Malfi* (ca. 1613)
    *Duchess of Malfi*   Burton, S. D.  1978
    *Duchess of Malfi*   Oliver, S.    1971
WEDEKIND, FRANK (1864–1918)
   **general**
    *Conversion, The*   Werder, F.    1973
   *Kaiserin von Neufundland* (1902)
    *Empress, The*     Gough, O.    1994
   *Kammersänger, Der* (1899)
    *Tenor, The*      Weisgall, H.   1952
WELLS, H. G. (1866–1946)
   *Country of the Blind* (1911)
    *Country of the Blind*  Turnage, M.-A.  1997
   *History of Mr. Polly*
    *Mr. Polly at the Potwell Inn*  Drummon, J.  2000
   *Time Machine* (1895)
    *Time Rocker*     Reed, L.     1997
WERFEL, FRANZ (1890–1945)
   *Weg der Verheissung, Der* (1935)
    *Eternal Road*     Weill, K.    1937
WESKER, ARNOLD (b. 1932)
   *Caritas* (1981)
    *Caritas*         Saxon, R.    1991
WEST, GILBERT (1703–1756)
   *Institution of the Order of the Garter*
    *Institution of the Garter*  Dibdin, C.   1771

WEST, MORRIS (1916–1999)
**Heretic, The** (1969)

| | | |
|---|---|---|
| Heretic, The | Fuchs, P. P. | 1978* |

WEST, NATHANIEL [NATHAN von WALLENSTEIN WEINSTEIN] (1903–1940)
**Miss Lonelyhearts** (1933)

| | | |
|---|---|---|
| Miss Lonelyhearts | Liebermann, L. | 2006 |

WHARTON, EDITH (1862–1937)
**Ethan Frome** (1911)

| | | |
|---|---|---|
| Ethan Frome | Allanbrook, D. | 1952 |
| Ethan Frome | Beall, J. | 1997 |

**Roman Fever**

| | | |
|---|---|---|
| Roman Fever | Hagemann, P. | 2003 |
| Roman Fever | Stringer, A. | 1996 |
| Roman Fever | Ward, R. | 1993 |

**Summer** (1917)

| | | |
|---|---|---|
| Summer | Paulus, S. | 1999 |

**Xingu** (1916)

| | | |
|---|---|---|
| Power of Xingu | Legg, J. | 1998 |

WHITE, E[LWYN] B[ROOKS] (1899–1985))
**Charlotte's Web** (1952)

| | | |
|---|---|---|
| Some Pig | Larsen, L. | 1973 |

WHITE, PATRICK (1912–1990)
**Voss** (1957)

| | | |
|---|---|---|
| Voss | Meale, R. | 1982 |

WHITING, JOHN ROBERT (1917–1963)
**Penny for a Song** (1951)

| | | |
|---|---|---|
| Penny for a Song | Bennett, R. R. | 1967 |

WHITMAN, RUTH ((1922–1999)
**Passion of Lizzie Borden** (1973)

| | | |
|---|---|---|
| Passion of Lizzie Borden | Spektor, M. | 1986 |

WHITMAN, WALT (1819–1892)
**poetry**

| | | |
|---|---|---|
| Powers of Two | Truax, B. | 2006 |

**Mystic Trumpeter** (1872)

| | | |
|---|---|---|
| Mystic Trumpeter | Starer, R. | 1983 |

WIELAND, CHRISTOPH MARTIN (1733–1813)
**Oberon** (1780)

| | | |
|---|---|---|
| Oberon | Cooke, T. S. | 1826 |
| Oberon | Weber, C. M. v. | 1826 |

WIESEL, ELIE (b. 1928)
**Night** (1958)

| | | |
|---|---|---|
| Jacob's Room | Subotnick, M. | 1987 |

WILDE, OSCAR (1854–1900)
**Birthday of the Infanta** (1889)

| | | |
|---|---|---|
| Birthday of the Infanta | Boyack, J. | 1957* |
| Birthday of the Infanta | Nelson, R. | 1956 |
| Birthday of the Infanta | Stoker, R. | 1963 |

**Canterville Ghost** (1887)

| | | |
|---|---|---|
| Canterville Ghost | Kalmanoff, M. | 1967 |
| Death of a Ghost | Gottlieb, J. | 1988 |

**De Profundis** (1905)

| | | |
|---|---|---|
| De Profundis | Sitsky, L. | 1982 |

**Duchess of Padua** (1891)

| | | |
|---|---|---|
| Guido Ferranti | Van Etten, J. | 1914 |

**Fisherman and His Soul**

| | | |
|---|---|---|
| Fisherman, The | Edlin, P. | 1989 |
| Fisherman, The | Scott, T. | 1954* |

**Happy Prince** (1888)

| | | |
|---|---|---|
| Elegy for a Prince | Cervvetti, S. | 2007 |
| Happy Prince | Williamson, M. | 1965 |

**Lord Arthur Savile's Crime** (1891)

| | | |
|---|---|---|
| Lord Arthur Savile's Crime | Bush, G. | 1972 |

**Nightingale and the Rose** (1888)

| | | |
|---|---|---|
| Nightingale and the Rose | Firsova, E. | 1994 |
| Nightingale and the Rose | Garwood, M. | 1973 |
| Nightingale and the Rose | Hagemann, P. | 2003 |
| Nightingale and the Rose | Lessner, G. | 1942 |

**Picture of Dorian Gray** (1891)

| | | |
|---|---|---|
| Dorian | Deutsch, H. A. | 1995 |
| Picture of Dorian Gray | Liebermann, L. | 1996 |

**Selfish Giant** (1888)

| | | |
|---|---|---|
| Giant's Garden | Krane, S. | 1960 |
| Selfish Giant | Barlow, D. | 1974* |
| Selfish Giant | Burtch, M. | 1969 |
| Selfish Giant | Easton, M. | 1994* |
| Selfish Giant | Hollingsworth, S. | 1981 |
| Selfish Giant | Perry, J. | 1964* |
| Selfish Giant | Ridout, A. | 1977 |
| Selfish Giant | Shaw, F. | 1973* |
| Selfish Giant | Wilding-White | 1955 |
| Selfish Giant | Wilson, C. | 1973 |

WILDER, THORNTON (1897–1975)
**Bridge of San Luis Rey** (1927)

| | | |
|---|---|---|
| Bride of San Luis Ray | Kimper, P. | 2003 |

**Life in the Sun** (1955)

| | | |
|---|---|---|
| Alcestiad, The | Talma, L. | 1962 |

**Long Christmas Dinner** (1931)

| | | |
|---|---|---|
| Long Christmas Dinner | Hindemith, P. | 1961 |

**Our Town** (1838)

| | | |
|---|---|---|
| Our Town | Rorem, N. | 2006 |

WILLIAMS, TENNESSEE (1911–1983)
**I Rise in Flame, Cried the Phoenix** (1951)

| | | |
|---|---|---|
| I Rise in Flame | Flanagan, T. J. | 1980 |

**Streetcar Named Desire** (1947)

| | | |
|---|---|---|
| Streetcar Named Desire | Previn, A. | 1998 |

**Summer and Smoke** (1948)

| | | |
|---|---|---|
| Summer and Smoke | Hoiby, L. | 1971 |

WILLIS, JEANNE
**Monster Bed**

| | | |
|---|---|---|
| Monster Bed | de Kenessey, S. | 1990 |

WILSON, CHARLES MORROW (1905–1977)
**Acres of Sky** (1930)

| | | |
|---|---|---|
| Acres of Sky | Kreutz, A. | 1951 |

WILSON, JOHN MACKAY (1804–1835)
**Tales of the Borders** (1834–40)

| | | |
|---|---|---|
| Abbot of Drimock | Musgrave, T. | 1962 |

WILSON, LANFORD (1937–2011)
**This Is the Rill Speaking** (1965)

| This Is the Rill Speaking | Hoiby, L. | 1994 |

WISEMAN, FREDERICK (b. 1930)
**Welfare** (1975)

| Welfare | Pickett, L. | 1992 |

WODEHOUSE, P. G. (1881–1975)
**Mr. Mulliner Speaking** (1929)

| Ordeal of Osbert | Davis, A. | 1951 |

WOLFE, THOMAS (b. 1938)
**Bonfire of the Vanities** (1987)

| Bonfire of the Vanities | de Kenessey, S. | 2006 |

WOOLF, VIRGINIA (1882–1941)
**writings**

| Woman in the Garden | Fine, V. | 1978 |

**Freshwater** (1923)

| Freshwater | Vores, A. | 1994 |

**Jacob's Room** (1922)

| Jacob's Room | Subotnick, M. | 1993 |

**Mrs. Dalloway** (1925)

| Mrs. Dalloway | Larsen, L. | 1995 |

WORDSWORTH, WILLIAM (1770–1850)
**White Doe of Rylstone** (1805)

| White Doe | Ridout, A. | 1987 |

WYCHERLY, WILLIAM (1610?–1716)
**Gentleman Dancing Master** (1673)

| Dancing Master | Arnold, M. | 1962 |

YAMAGUCHI, TOHR
**Golden Crane**

| Golden Crane | Kay, D. H. | 1985* |

YEATS, WILLIAM BUTLER (1865–1939)
**Cat and the Moon**

| Cat and the Moon | Putsché, T. | 1960 |

**Calvary**

| Calvary | Pasatieri, T. | 1971 |

**Death of Cuchulain** (1892)

| Death of Cuchulain | Brettingham Smith, J. | 1973* |

**Deirdre** (1907)

| Deirdre | Stein, L. | 1957 |

**King Oedipus** (1934, after Sophocles)

| Oedipus | Partch, H. | 1952 |

**Land of Heart's Desire** (1904)

| Land of Heart's Desire | Hart, F. | 1914 |
| Land of Heart's Desire | Hofmeyr, H. | 1981* |

**Full Moon in March** (1935)

| Full Moon in March | Harbison, J. | 1979 |
| Full Moon in March | Ward, D. | 1981 |

**Pot of Broth** (1929)

| Pot of Broth | Haufrecht, H. | 1965* |

**Purgatory** (1938)

| Purgatory | Crosse, G. | 1966 |
| Purgatory | Halpern, M. | 2009 |
| Purgatory | Weiser, M. | 1990 |

**Words upon the Window Pane** (1930)

| Words upon the Window Pane | Buckley, J. | 1991 |

YORK MYSTERY PLAYS (early 14th cent.)

| Cappemakers, The | Taverner, J. | 1964 |

ZAMYATIN, YEVGENY IVANOVICH (1884–1937)
**We** (1921)

| We | Dench, C. | 2010 |

ZIEGENHAGEN, JOHN
**Red Soliloquy**

| Dreaming Blue | Larsen, L. | 2002 |

ZILAHY, LAJOS (1891–1974)
**Szűz és a gödölye**

| Virgin and the Fawn | Zador, E. | 1964 |

ZINN, HOWARD (1922–2010)
**Emma: A Play about Emma Goldman, American Anarchist** (2002)

| Emma | Fine, E. | 2005* |

ZOLA, ÉMILE (1840–1902)
**Fête à Coqueville, La** (1883)

| Fête at Coqueville | Rea, A. | 1976 |

**Thérèse Raquin** (1867)

| Thérèse Raquin | Finnissy, M. | 1993 |
| Thérèse Raquin | Picker, T. | 2001 |
| Thérèse Raquin | Stoker, R. | 1975* |

ZORRILLA y MORAL, JOSÉ (1817–1893)
**Don Juan Tenorio** (1844)

| Last Night of Don Juan | Rodríguez, R. | 2000 |

ZWEIG, STEFAN (1881–1942)
**Augen des ewigen Bruders, Die** (1925)

| Virata | Wilson, J. | 1999 |

## Part II: Titles Cited in Part I

*Abe Lincoln Grows Up* (C. Sandburg)
*Abschiedssouper* (A. Schnitzler)
*Acres of Sky* (C. M. Wilson)
*Adèle et Théodore* (S. F. Genlis)
*Admirable Bashville* (G. B. Shaw)
*Adoration of the Magi* (H. Bosch)
*Advice to Husbands* (C. S. Lancaster)
*Agamemnon* (Aeschylus)
*Albergo Empedocle* (E. M. Forster)
*Alchemist, The* (B. Jonson)
*Alhambra* (W. Irving)
*Alice's Adventures in Wonderland* (L. Carroll)
*Alkestis* (Euripides)
*All in Good Time* (M. Paris)
*All on a Summer's Day* (Ryerson/Clements)
*All Souls' Rising* (M. Bell)
*All the King's Men* (R. P. Warren)
*All the Way Home* (T. Mosel)
*Alt-Heidelberg* (W. Meyer-Förster)

*Amadeus* (P. Shaffer)
*American Tropical, La* (D. Siqueiros)
*Amerika* (*Der Verschollene*, F. Kafka)
*Ami Fritz* (Erckmann-Chatrian)
*Amor de Don Perlimplín con Belisa en su jardín* (F. García Lorca)
*Amphitryon* (J. Dryden)
*Amphitryon* (Molière)
*Anatol* (A. Schnitzler)
*Anecdote sur l'homme au masque de fer* (Voltaire)
*Angel Levine* (B. *Malamud)*
*Angels in America* (T. *Kushner)*
*Angle of Repose* (W. Stegner)
*Anna Karenina* (L. Tolstoy)
*Anthony and Cleopatra* (W. Shakespeare)
*Antigone* (Sophocles)
*Antiquary, The* (W. Scott)
*Apothicaire de Murcia, L'*
*Arabian Night's Entertainment* (R. B. Sheridan)
*Araboolies of Liberty Street* (S. Swope)
*Arden of Faversham*
*Aria da Capo* (St. Vincent Millay)
*Artists and Admirers* (A. N. Ostrovsky)
*Arwed Gyllenstjerna* (C. F. van der Velde)
*Asi que pasen cinco anos* (García Lorca)
*Athalie* (J. Racine)
*Atsumori* (Z. Motokiyo)
*Auberon* (H. de Bordeaux)
*Aucassin et Nicollete*
*Augen des ewigen Bruders, Die* (S. Zweig)
*Autobiography of a Runaway Slave* (E. Montejo)
*Autumn Valentine* (D. Parker)
*Aveugles, Les* (M. Maeterlinck)
*Awakening, The* (K. Chopin)

*Bacchae, The* (Euripides)
*Background, The* (Saki)
*Baghavad-Ghita*
*Baker's Dozen* (Saki)
*Balcon, Le* (J. Genet)
*Ballad of Billie Potts* (R. P. Warren)
*Ballad of the Cruel Mother*
*Barbier de Seville, Le* (Beaumarchais)
*Barnaby Rudge* (C. Dickens)
*Barnstable* (J. Saunders)
*Bartleby the Scrivener* (H. Melville)
*Bâtisseurs d'empire, Les* (B. Vian)
*Beach of Falesá* (R. L. Stevenson)
*Bear, The* (A. Chekhov)
*Beasts and Superbeasts* (Saki)
*Beatrice Cenci* (A. Moravia)
*Before Breakfast* (E. O'Neill)
*Befristeten, Die* (E. Canetti)
*Belfagor arcidiavolo* (Machiavelli)
*Belle Belle* (M.-C. d'Aulnoy)

*Belle et la bête, La* (Leprince de Beaumont)
*Bell Tower* (Melville)
*Beloved* (T. Morrison)
*Belsazer* (H. Heine)
*Bergere des Alpes, La* (J. F. Marmontel)
*Bertha* (K. Koch)
*Best* (S. Speed)
*Betrogene, Die* (T. Mann)
*Betrothed* (A. Chekhov)
Bible, The
*Biche au bois, La* (T. Cogniard)
*Billy Budd* (H. Melville)
*Birds, The* (Aristophanes)
*Birds of America* (J. J. Audubon)
*Birthday of the Infanta* (O. Wilde)
*Bitteren Tränen der Petra von Kant* (R. Fassbinger)
*Black Dwarf* (W. Scott)
*Black Grave and Green Grave* (M. Lavin)
*Black Jacobins* (James)
*Black Swan Revisited* (R. Selzer)
*Black Water* (J. Oates)
*Blake, or, The Huts of America* (M. Delany)
*Bleeding Heart* (E. L. Roberts)
*Blind Raftery and His Wife, Hilaria* (D. Byrne)
*Blonde Eckbert, Der* (L. Tieck)
*Blood on the Dining Room Floor* (G. Stein)
*Bloody Theatre* (T. van Braght)
*Bodas de sangre* (F. García Lorca)
*Bohémienne, La* (C. Favart)
*Boiler Room Suite* (R. Deverell)
*Bold Stroke for a Wife* (S. Centlivre)
*Bonfire of the Vanities* (T. Wolfe)
*Bontshe Shvayg* (I. Peretz)
*Book of Embraces* (E. Galeano)
*Book of Leinster*
*Bossu, Le* (P. Féval)
*Bottle Imp* (R. L. Stevenson)
*Boule de suif* (G. de Maupassant)
*Bout de ficelle, Un* (G. de Maupassant)
*Bouvard et Pécuchet* ( G. Flaubert)
*Bowl, Cat, and Broomstick* (W. Stevens)
*Box, The* (A. Chekhov)
*Box and Cox* (J. M. Morton)
*Brementown Musicians* (Brothers Grimm)
*Bride Comes to Yellow Sky* (S. Crane)
*Bridge of San Luis Rey* (T. Wilder)
*Buanderie, La* (D. Guerdon)
*Burial at Thebes* (S. Heaney)
*Burning Bright* (J. Steinbeck)

*Café, Le* (J.-J. Rousseau)
*Calvary* (W. B. Yeats)
*Canción de Rachel, La* (M. Barnet)
*Candide* (Voltaire)

*Cantatrice chauve, La* (E. Ionesco)
*Canterbury Tales* (G. Chaucer)
*Canterville Ghost* (O. Wilde)
*Captain Jinks* (C. Fitch)
*Captains All* (W. W. Jacobs)
*Caractacus* (W. Mason)
*Caritas* (A. Wesker)
*Carrion Crow* (J. J. Niles)
*Case of the Substitute Face* (E. S. Gardner)
*Cask of Amontillado* (E. A. Poe)
*Castle of Otranto* (H. Walpole)
*Cat and the Moon* (W. B. Yeats)
*Catherine and Petruccio* (D. Garrick)
*Catherine Paar* (M. Baring)
*Catiline Conspiracy* (B. Jonson)
*Cat Who Went to Heaven* (E. Coatsworth)
*Ceirt an mhean oiche* (B. Merriman)
*Celebrated Jumping Frog of Calaveras County* (M. Twain)
*Celoso extremeño, El* (Cervantes)
*Celui qui épousa une femme muette* (A. France)
*Cenci, Les* (A. Artaud)
*Cenci, The* (P. B. Shelley)
*Chances, The* (Fletcher/Beaumont?)
*Changed Bridegroom* (L. Holberg)
*Chao Family Orphan*
*Chapeau de paille d'Italie, Un* (Labiche)
*Charles the Second* (J. H. Payne)
*Charlie and the Chocolate Factory* (R. Dahl)
*Charlot* (J. P. Lockroy et al.)
*Charlotte's Web* (E. B. White)
*Chatterton* (A. de Vigny)
*Chevalier de Saint-Georges, Le* (Mélésville)
*Chicken Little*
*Chola Widow* (H. Melville)
*Chosen Vessel* (B. Baynton)
*Christmas Carol* (C. Dickens)
*Christ Recrucified* (N. Kazantzakis)
*Cimitières des voitures* (F. Arrabal)
*Cinderella* (G. Basile)
*Città invisibili, Le* (I. Calvino)
*Clandestine Marriage* (Garrick/Colman Sr.)
*Clarissa Harlowe* (S. Richardson)
*Cock and the Fox* (see *Canterbury Tales*)
*Cold Sassy Tree* (O. Burns)
*Colleen Bawn* (D. Boucicault)
*Colomba* (P. Mérimée)
*Columbus* (T. Morton)
*Comedy of Errors* (W. Shakespeare)
*Comus* (J. Milton)
*Confidence Man* (H. Melville)
*Consider the Lilies* (R. Hupton)
*Consolation of Philosophy* (Boethius)
*Construction of Boston* (K. Koch)
*Contes de ma mère l'Oye* (C. Perrault)

*Corn King and the Spring Queen* (N. Mitchison)
*Coronation Street*
*Corpus Christi Plays*
*Country Lasses* (C. Johnson)
*Country of the Blind* (H. G. Wells)
*Country-Wake* (T. Dogget)
*Coup de dés jamais n'abolira le hasard, Un* (S. Mallarmé)
*Courtship of Miles Standish* (H. W. Longfellow)
*Crazy to Kill* (A. Cardwell)
*Creation of the World* (A. Miller)
*Cricket on the Hearth* (C. Dickens)
*Critic, The* (R. Sheridan)
*Cross and the Crescent* (J. Davidson)
*Crossing, The* (G. Gilham)
*Crown's Stratagem* (H. Carey)
*Crucible, The* (A. Miller)
*Cry the Beloved Country* (A. Paton)
*Cueva de Salamanca, La* (Cervantes)
*Cymon and Iphigenia* (J. Dryden)
*Cyrano de Bergerac* (E. Rostand)

*Darkling Thrush* (T. Hardy)
*Dark of the Moon* (H. Richardson)
*David Garrick* (T. W. Robertson)
*Daymio, The* (L. Duran)
*Dead, The* (J. Joyce)
*Death of Cuchulain* (W. B. Yeats)
*Death of Rosamond* (T. May)
*Death of the Virgin* (Caravaggio)
*Decameron, The* (G. Boccaccio)
*Decision, The* (K. Taylor)
*Deirdre* (W. B. Yeats)
*Deirdre of the Sorrows* (J. M. Synge)
*Democracy* (H. Adams)
*Demon* (M. Lermontov)
*De Profundis* (O. Wilde)
*Dernière Nuit de Don Juan, La* (E. Rostand)
*Deserted Village* (O. Goldsmith)
*Desire under the Elms* (E. O'Neill)
*Devil and Daniel Webster* (S. V. Benét)
*Devil Is an Ass* (B. Jonson)
*Devil of a Wife* (T. Jevon)
*Devil's Disciple* (G. B. Shaw)
*Devils of Loudun* (A. Huxley)
*Devil to Pay* (C. Coffey)
*Devin du village, Le* (J.-J. Rousseau)
*Diable amoureux, Le* ( J. de Cazotte)
*Diary of a Madman* (N. Gogol)
*Divine Comedy* (Dante)
*Don César de Bazan* (D. Ennery)
*Don Juan* (Byron)
*Don Juan* (J. A. Flecker)
*Don Juan Tenorio* (J. Zorrilla)
*Donner Party* (G. Keithley)
*Don Quixote* (Cervantes)

*Don Quixote in England* (H. Fielding)
*Don Raphael* (G. Walker)
*Don't Call Me by My Right Name* (J. Purdy)
*Dos madres* (M. de Unamuno)
*Dracula* (B. Stoker)
*Dragon, The* (Lady Gregory)
*Dragon, The* (Y. Schwarz)
*Dragon: The Old Potter's Tale* (A. Ryūnosuke)
*Dream of Eugene Aram* (T. Hood)
*Dream Play* (A. Strindberg)
*Dr. Heidegger's Experiment* (N. Hawthorne)
*Dr. Syn* (R. Thorndike)
*Duchess of Malfi* (J. Webster)
*Duchess of Padua* (O. Wilde)
*Duenna, The* (R. B. Sheridan)
*Duke and No Duke, A* (N. Tate)
*Duke's Motto* (J. Brougham)
*Dybbuk, The* (S. Ansky)

*"E"* (R. Graves)
*Earl of Moray* (A. Elguera)
*East Indian* (M. G. Lewis)
*Eastward in Eden* (D. Gardner)
*Eating Fire* (M. Atwood)
*Egon und Emilie* (C. Morgenstern)
*Egypt's Nights* (B. Chase-Riboud)
*Einem Jux will er sich machen* (J. Nestroy)
*Ekkehard* (J. V. von Scheffel)
*Eleanor: Her Secret Journey* (R. Lerman)
*Election, The* (J. Baillie)
*Eleni* (N. Gage)
*Elfrida* (G. Colman Sr.)
*Elisabeth, ou, Les Exilés de Sibérie* (S. Cottin)
*Elixiere des Teufels, Die* (E. T. A. Hoffmann)
*Elizabeth and Essex* (L. Strachey)
*Elsewhereless* (A. Egoyan)
*Emma* (H. Zinn)
*Emmeline* (J. Rossner)
*Emperor Jones* (E. O'Neill)
*Emperor of the Moon* (A. Behn)
*Emperor's New Clothes* (H. C. Andersen)
*Empfindsame, Der* (A. Schnitzler)
*Enchanted Kiss* (O. Henry)
*Endymion* (Fontenelle)
*Endymion* (J. Keats)
*En famille* (G. de Maupassant)
*Engaged!* (W. S. Gilbert)
*English Eccentrics* (E. Sitwell)
*Enraged Musician* (W. Hogarth)
*Erast* (S. Gessner)
*Erewhon* (S. Bulter)
*Erewhon Revisited* (S. Butler)
*Eric Hermannson's Soul* (W. Cather)
*Escurial, The* (Ghelderode)

*Esther* (H. Adams)
*Ethan Frome* (E. Wharton)
*Etiquette* (W. S. Gilbert)
*Eugene Aram* (E. Bulwer-Lytton)
*European Story* (R. Failight)
*Evangeline* (H. W. Longfellow)
*Everyman*

*Fables* (J. de La Fontaine)
*Fables for Our Time* (J. Thurber)
*Face upon the Floor* (H. A. D'Arcy)
*Fahrenheit 451* (R. Bradbury)
*Fair Quaker of Deal* (C. Shadwell)
*Faith* (J. P. Kelly)
*Fall of the City* (A. MacLeish)
*Fall of the House of Usher* (E. A. Poe)
*Famous for Fifteen Minutes* (Ultra Violet)
*Fantaisie du Docteur Ox, Une* (J. Verne)
*Fantastic Mr. Fox* (R. Dahl)
*Fantôme de l'Opéra, Le* (Leroux)
*Far from the Madding Crowd* (T. Hardy)
*Far Rockaway* (F. D. Gilroy)
*Father Henson's Story of His Life* (J. Henson)
*Father of the Child* (W. Gibson)
*Father Sergius* (L. Tolstoy)
*Faust* (Goethe)
*Feathertop* (N. Hawthorne)
*Femme à deux maris, La* (Pixérécourt)
*Femme Muette* (F. Rabelais)
*Fête à Coqueville, La* (E. Zola)
*Fiabe Italiane* (I. Calvino)
*Fifth Column* (E. Hemingway)
*Fire on the Wind* (A. Coburn)
*First Lemminkäinen Cycle* (see *The Kalevala*)
*Fisherman and His Soul* (O. Wilde)
*Fisherman and His Wife* (Brothers Grimm)
*Floyd and the Eumenides* (E. E. Smith)
*Fly, The* (D. Cronenberg)
*Forgot* (A. Chekhov)
*For the Crown* (J. Davidson)
*Fortresse du Danube, La* (Pixérecourt)
*Fortunato* (S., J. Álvarez Quintero)
*Fortunio* (J. R. Planché)
*Fragment of an Analysis* (S. Freud)
*Frankenstein* (M. Shelley)
*Franklin's Tale* (see *Canterbury Tales*)
*Friendships and Enmities* (B. Pain)
*Frieze of Life* (E. Munch)
*Frithiofs Saga* (E. Tegnér)
*From the Mixed-Up Files* (E. G. Konigsberg)
*Fugue for Two Voices* (D. Madden)
*Full Moon in March* (W. B. Yeats)

*Gabriel's Palace* (H. Schwartz)
*Gas Light* (P. Hamilton)

*Gawain*
*Gentle Boy* (N. Hawthorne)
*Gentle Creature* (F. Dostoyevsky)
*Gentleman Dancing* Master (W. Wycherly)
*Gentleman Friend* (A. Chekhov)
*George Dandin* (Molière)
*German Refugee* (Malamud)
*Gerusalemme liberata* (Tasso)
*Gestiefelte Kater, Der* (L. Tieck)
*Giants in the Earth* (O. E. Rölvaag)
*Gift of the Magi* (O. Henry)
*Gilgamesh, Epic of*
*Gimpel the Fool* (I. Singer)
*Gisli, the Soursop* (trans. G. W. Dasent)
*Gitanella, La* (M. Cervantes)
*Goblin Market* (C. Rossetti)
*God Boy* (I. Cross)
*Golden Ass* (L. Apuleius)
*Golden Bird* (Brothers Grimm)
*Golden Bough* (J. Frazer)
*Golden Crane* (T. Yamaguchi)
*Golden Gate* (V. Seth)
*Golk* (R. Stern)
*Good Soldier Schweik* (J. Hašek)
*Goose Girl* (Brothers Grimm)
*Gorgias* (Plato)
*Goylem* (H. Leivick)
*Grace* (E. Langois/J. Carmichael
*Gracieuse et Percinet* (M.-C. d'Aulnoy)
*Grande Bretèche, La* (H. Balzac)
*Grandissimes, The* (G. W. Cable)
*Great Expectations* (C. Dickens)
*Great Gatsby* (S. Fitzgerald)
*Great Stone Face* (N. Hawthorne)
*Greek* (S. Berkoff)
*Grendel* (J. Gardner)
*Grey Parrot* (W. W. Jacobs)
*Gulliver's Travels* (J. Swift)
*Gustavus Vasa* (H. Brooke)
*Guttil Jattak* (Buddhist tale)
*Guy Mannering* (W. Scott)

*Haircut, The* (R. Lardner)
*Hamlet* (W. Shakespeare)
*Handschuh, Der* (F. Schiller)
*Hänsel und Gretel* (Brothers Grimm)
*Happy Hypocrite* (M. Beerbohm)
*Happy Prince* (O. Wilde)
*Hard Times* (C. Dickens)
*Harlot's Progress* (W. Hogarth)
*Haroun and the Sea of Stories* (S. Rushdie)
*Harrison Loved His Umbrella* (R. Levine)
*Haunting, The* (C. A. Dawson-Scott)
*Haus der Temperamente, Das* ( J. Nestroy)

*Hazel Kirke* (S. MacKaye)
*Heart of a Dog* (M. Bulgakov)
*Heart of Darkness* (J. Conrad)
*Heart of Midlothian* (W. Scott)
*Hedda Gabler* (H. Ibsen)
*Helena's Husband* (P. Moeller)
*Helen in Egypt* (H. Doolittle)
*Hello Out There* (W. Saroyan)
*Henderson the Rain King* (S. Bellow)
*Henry V* (W. Shakesepare)
*Hercules Oetaeus* (Seneca)
*Heretic, The* (M. West)
*Heureuse erreur, L'* (J. Patrat)
*Hippolytus* (Euripides)
*Histoire de Gil Blas de Santillane* (Le Sage)
*Histoire de ma vie, L'* (J. Casanova)
*Histoire de Vasco, L'* (G. Schehadé)
*History of Mr. Polly* (H. G. Wells)
*History of Nourjahad* (Mrs. Sheridan)
*History of the Conquest of Mexico* (W. H. Prescott)
*Hogar sólido, Un* (E. Garro)
*Hollow Hill* (E. Salzman)
*Homer's Daughter* (R. Graves)
*House of Peterwell* (H. Jones)
*House of the Seven Gables* (N. Hawthorne)
*How Beautiful with Shoes* (W. D. Steele)
*Huckleberry Finn* (M. Twain)
*Humulus le muet* (Anouilh/Aurenche)
*Hunted, The* (M. Fine/D. Friedkin)
*Hunting of the Snark* (L. Carroll)
*Huon de Bordeaux*
*Hymn to Demeter* (Homer)

*Ib* (H. C. Andersen)
*I Ching*
*Idiot, The* (F. Dostoyevsky)
*If Not Higher* (I. L. Peretz)
*Ile* (E. O'Neill)
*Iliad, The* (Homer)
*Illusion, The* (T. Kusher)
*Illusion comique, L'* (P. Corneille)
*Immortal Hour* (F. Macleod)
*Incas, Les* (J. F. Marmontel)
*Incognita* (W. Congreve)
*In Cold Blood* (T. Capote)
*In der Strafkolonie* (F. Kafka)
*Indian Emperor* (J. Dryden)
*Inés de Castro* (J. Clifford)
*Ingoldsby Legends* (R. H. Barham)
*Insect Life* (K. Čapek/J. Čapek)
*Inspector General* (N. Gogol)
*In the Pasha's Garden* (H. G. Dwight)
*In the Shadow of the Glen* (Synge)
*Intruse, L'* (M. Maeterlinck)

*Invasion, The* (J. Lewis)
*Ion* (Euripides)
*Iphigenia in Tauris* (Euripides)
*I Rise in Flame, Cried the Phoenix* (T. Williams)
*Iron Man* (T. Hughes)
*Island God* (G. S. Mumford)
*Island Princess* (J. Fletcher)
*Italian Lesson* (R. Draper)
*Ivanhoe* (W. Scott)

*Jacob's Room* (W. Woolf)
*Jacques, ou, La soumission* (E. Ionesco)
*Jane Eyre* (C. Brontë)
*Jedermann* (H. von Hofmannsthal)
*Je dîne chez ma mère* (Decourcelle/Thiboust)
*Jest of Hahalabra* (Lord Dusaney)
*Jésus-Christ en Flandrel* (H. de Balzac)
*Joan of Arc* (J. Bastien-Lepage)
*Joan of Arc* (R. Southey)
*John Henry* (B. Roark)
*Jorinda and Joringel* (Brothers Grimm)
*Journals of Expeditions of Discovery* (E. J. Eyre)
*Jovial Crew* (R. Brome)
*Jubilee* (A. Chekhov)
*Jubilee* (M. Walker)
*Judevine* (D. Budbill)
*Jugement de Salomon, Le* (L.-C. Caignez)
*Julian* (G. Flaubert)
*Julius Caesar* (W. Shakespeare)
*Jungle Book* (R. Kipling)
*Just Above My Head* (J. Baldwin)
*Just So Stories* (R. Kipling)

*Kaguyahme legend*
*Kammersänger, Der* (F. Wedekind)
*Kamouraska* (A. Hébert)
*Keep Him My Country* (M. Durack)
*Kenilworth* (W. Scott)
*Kinderkreuzzug* (B. Brecht)
*King and the Miller of Mansfield* (R. Dodsley)
*King Kong*
*King Oedipus* (W. B. Yeats)
*King of Cats* (S. V. Benét)
*King of the Golden River* (J. Ruskin)
*King Who Saved Himself* (J. Ciardi)
*Kong Renes Datter* (H. Hertz)
*Krasovitsky Couple* (D. Aizman)

*Lady of Lyons* (E. Bulwer-Lytton)
*Lady of the Castle* (L. Goldberg)
*Lady of the Lake* (W. Scott)
*Lai le Freine* (Marie de France)
*Lallah Rookh* (T. Moore)
*Lampeter* (H. Bell)
*Lancelot and Elaine* (A. Tennyson)
*Land of Happiness* (C. T. Crocker)

*Language of the Birds*
*Last Days of Pompei* (E. Bulwer-Lytton)
*Last Leaf* (O. Henry)
*Last of the Mohicans* (J. F. Cooper)
*Last of the Valerii* (H. James)
*Last Summer* (B. Pasternak)
*Laurette* (J.-F. Marmontel)
*Layla and Majnun* (G. Nizami)
*Leah Kleschna* (C. McLellan)
*Leçon, La* (Ionesco)
*Legend of Montrose* (W. Scott)
*Legend of Sleepy Hollow* (W. Irving)
*Legend of the Bloody Zheng* (Lu Wei)
*Legends of the Lake* (G. Findler)
*Lenz* (G. Büchner)
*Leonce und Lena* (G. Büchner)
*Leo Spat* (C. Massey)
*Leper's Flute* (I. D. Colvin)
*Leute von Seldwyla, Die* (G. Keller)
*Liaisons dangereuses, Les* (P. C. de Laclos)
*Life in the Sun* (T. Wilder)
*Lilith* (A. Havis)
*Lima Beans* (A. Kreymborg)
*Lion, the Witch, and the Wardrobe* (C. S. Lewis)
*List, A* (G. Stein)
*Little Billy* (W. Thackeray)
*Little Foxes* (L. Hellman)
*Little Match Girl* (H. C. Andersen)
*Little Mermaid* (H. C. Andersen)
*Little Moon of Alban* (J. Costigan)
*Little Red Riding Hood* (Brothers Grimm)
*Little Women* (L. M. Alcott)
*Living My Life* (E. Goldman)
*Locandiera, La* (C. Goldoni)
*Lodger, The* (Mrs. Belloc Lowndes)
*Long Christmas Dinner* (T. Wilder)
*Lost Highway* (Gifford-Lynch)
*Love for Love* (W. Congreve)
*Love for Money* (T. D'Urfey)
*Lovers* (B. Friel)
*Love's Labour's Lost* (W. Shakespeare)
*Loves of Mars and Venus* (P. A. Motteux)
*Love's Revenge* (J. Hoadly)
*Luck of Ginger Coffey* (B. Moore)
*Lucky Peter's Travels* (A. Strindberg)
*Lyric Suite* (F. Corsaro)
*Lysistrata* (Aristophanes)

*Mabinogion, The*
*Macbeth* (W. Shakespeare)
*Madame Butterfly* (J. Long)
*Madame Chrysathème* (P. Loti)
*Madame Sans-Gêne* (V. Sardou)
*Magic Barrel* (B. Malamud)

*Magic Fishbone* (Dickens)
*Mahabharata*
*Maid Maleen* (Brothers Grimm)
*Maid Marian* (T. L. Peacock)
*Maison de compagne, La* (Dancourt)
*Making of the Representative for Planet 8* (D. Lessing)
*Mama Don't Allow* (T. Hurd)
*Mañana de sol* (J., S. Quintero)
*Mandragola, La* (Machiavelli)
*Man in the Moon* (F. Godwin)
*Manito Masks* (H. Alexander)
*Man Who Never Died* (B. Stavis)
*Man without a Country* (E. E. Hale)
*Many Moons* (J. Thurber)
*Maria Concepcion* (K. Porter)
*Mariage forcé, Le* ( Molière)
*Maria Schweidler* (W. Meinhold)
*Marie Tudor* (V. Hugo)
*Marilyn: The Untold Story* (N. Rosten)
*Mario und der Zauberer* (T. Mann)
*Mariposa blanca, Una* (G. Roepke)
*Markheim* (R. L. Stevenson)
*Marquise von O, Die* (H. von Keist)
*Marriage a la Mode* (K. Mansfield)
*Marriage Has Been Arranged* (A. Sutro)
*Marriages between Zones 3, 4, and 5* (D. Lessing)
*Martin Chuzzlewit* (C. Dickens)
*Mary Barton* (E. Gaskell)
*Masaniello* (H. M. Milner)
*Maskarad* (M. Lermontov)
*Masque of Pandora* (Longfellow)
*Masque of the Red Death* (E. A. Poe)
*Master of the Crossroads* (M. Bell)
*Maud* (G. Sange)
*Mayor of Casterbridge* (T. Hardy)
*Maypole of Merry Mount* (N. Hawthorne)
*McTeague* (F. Norris)
*Medea* (Euripides)
*Medea* (Seneca)
*Médecin malgré lui, Le* (Molière)
*Mejnoun and Leila* (I. Disraeli)
*Menaechmi* (Plautus)
*Merchant of Venice* (W. Shakespeare)
*Mère coupable, La* (Beaumarchais)
*Merry Wives of Windsor* (W. Shakespeare)
*Messer Marco Polo* (D. Byrne)
*Metamorphoses* (Ovid)
*Midrash, The*
*Midsummer Night's Dream* (W. Shakespeare)
*Miraculous Phonograph Record* (W. Saroyan)
*Mirage* (J. Galloway)
*Mirror for Witches* (E. Forbes)
*Misfortune, A* (A. Chekhov)
*Miss Hargreaves* (F. Baker)

*Miss Julie* (A. Strindberg)
*Miss Lonelyhearts* (N. West)
*Mixture of Frailties* (R. Robertson)
*Moby-Dick* (H. Melville)
*Mocking Bird* (A. Bierce)
*Molloy* (S. Beckett)
*Moment of Rain* (E. Enright)
*Momus fabuliste* (Fuzelier/Le Grand)
*Monastery, The* (Scott)
*Monk, The* (M. G. Lewis)
*Monkey's Paw* (W. W. Jacobs)
*Monster Bed* (J. Willis)
*Month in the Country* (I. S. Turgenev)
*Moon and Sixpence* (S. Maugham)
*Moonlit Road* (A. Bierce)
*Morning Star* (S. Regan)
*Mort de Tintagiles, La* (M. Maeterlinck)
*Morte d'Arthur, Le*
*Mountain Blood* (J. Hergesheimer)
*Mountain Windsong* (R. Conley)
*Mount Kagu* (K. Taruhito)
*Mourning Becomes Electra* (E. O'Neill)
*Mr. and Mrs. Discobbolos* (E. Lear)
*Mr. Mulliner Speaking* (P. G. Wodehouse)
*Mrs. Bullfrog* (N. Hawthorne)
*Mrs. Dalloway* (V. Woolf)
*Much Ado about Nothing* (W. Shakespeare)
*Mulatto, The* (L. Hughes)
*My Heart's in the Highlands* (W. Saroyan)
*My Kinsman, Major Molineux* (Hawthorne, Lowell)
*Myra Breckinridge* (G. Vidal)
*Mysteries of Eudolpho* (A. Radcliffe)
*Mystic Trumpeter* (W. Whitman)
*Nada the Lily* (H. R. Haggard)
*Naomi's Road* (J. Kogawa)
*Narcotic, The* (J. Powell)
*Nathan der Weise* (G. E. Lessing)
*Neither* (S. Beckett)
*Nie-boska komedia* (Z. Krasinski)
*Niels Lyhne* (J. P. Jacobsen)
*Night* (S. Asch)
*Night* (E. Wiesel)
*Night at an Inn* (Lord Dusany)
*Nightingale, The* (H. C. Andersen)
*Nightingale and the Rose* (O.Wilde)
*Night in Old Paris* (G. McDonough)
*Nightmare Abbey* (T. Peacock)
*Niña, La* (J. Martí)
*Nineteen Eighty-Four* (G. Orwell)
*No Exit* (J.-P. Sartre)
*Nosferatu* (T. Sokoloski)
*Notes from a Lady* (B. Malamud)
*Notre-Dame de Paris* (V. Hugo)
*Novelas exemplares* (M. Cervantes)

*Nuit de Cléopâtre, Une* (T. Gautier)
*Nussknacker und Mausekönig, Der* (E. T. A. Hoffmann)
*Nut-Brown Maid* (M. Prior)

*Oath of Bad Brown Bill* (S. Axelson)
*Obasan* (J. Kogawa)
*Obelisk, The* (E. M. Forster)
*Oberon* (C. M. Wieland)
*Oberon, the Fairy Prince* (B. Jonson)
*Occurence at Owl Creek Bridge* (A. Bierce)
*Octoroon, The* (M. E. Braddon)
*Odd Girl Out* (R. Simmons)
*Odyssey, The (Homer)*
*Odyssey of Ulysses the Palimped* (R. Gilbert-Lecomte)
*Oedipus at Colonus* (Sophocles)
*Oedipus Rex* (Sophocles)
*Of Mice and Men* (J. Steinbeck)
*Olaf* (L. Cox)
*Old Morality* (W. Scott)
*Old North Trail* (W. McClintock)
*Old Wives' Tale* (G. Peele)
*O mandarim* (Eça de Queiroz)
*Ondine* (J. Giraudoux)
*1001 Nights* (see *Thousand and One Nights*)
*On ne badine pas avec l'amour* (V. Hugo)
*On the Eve* (I. Turgenev)
*On the Harmfulness of Smoking Tobacco* (A. Chekhov)
*On the Razzle* (T. Stoppard)
*Open Window* (Saki)
*Oracle, L'* (Saint-Foix)
*Ordre du bon temps, L'* (L. de Montigny)
*Othello* (W. Shakespeare)
*Other Heart* (J. Forsyth)
*Other Wise Man* (H. van Dyke)
*Our Man in Havana* (G. Greene)
*Ours et la pacha, L'* (E. Scribe)
*Our Town* (T. Wilder)
*Our Wife* (J. M. Morton)
*Outcasts of Poker Flat* (B. Harte)
*Out of Africa* (I. Dinesen)
*Out of the Frying Pan* (F. Swann)
*Owen Wingrave* (H. James)

*Pamela* (S. Richardson)
*Paradise Lost* (U. Le Guin)
*Paradise Lost* (J. Milton)
*Pardoner's Tale* (see *Canterbury Tales*)
*Parlement of Foules* (G. Chaucer)
*Pasqual Bruno* (A. Dumas)
*Passion of Lizzie Borden* (R. Whitman)
*Passion, Poison, and Petrifaction* (G. B. Shaw)
*Pastoral* (J. Morley)
*Paul Clifford* (E. Bulwer-Lytton)
*Paul Clifford, the Highwayman of 1770* (B. Webster)
*Peacock in Paradise* (E. Jones)

*Péché Véniel, Le* (H. Balzac)
*Peer Gynt* (H. Ibsen)
*Peines de coeur* (H. Balzac)
*Pelerin blanc, Le* (Pixérecourt)
*Penny for a Song* (J. Whiting)
*Peony Pavilion* (Tang Xianzu)
*Pericles* (W. Shakespeare)
*Petit Prince, Le* (Saint-Exupéry)
*Phantastes* (G. Macdonald)
*Pharsalia* (Lucan)
*Phoenix Too Frequent* (C. Fry)
*Pickwick Papers* (C. Dickens)
*Picnic* (W. Inge)
*Picture of Dorian Gray* (O. Wilde)
*Pied Piper of Hamelin* (R. Browning)
*Pierre, ou, Le Couvreur* (Brazier/Carmouche)
*Pierrot of the Minute* (E. Dowson)
*Piers Plowman* (W. Langland)
*Pie voleuse, La* (D'Aubigny/Caigniez)
*Pilgrim* (T. Findlay)
*Pilgrim, The* (Fletcher)
*Pilgrim's Progress* (J. Bunyan)
*Pillow Book* (Sei Shonagon)
*Piper, The* (J. P. Peabody)
*Pippa Passes* (R. Browning)
*Pirate, The* (W. Scott)
*Place for Us* (I. Miller)
*Plough and the Stars* (S. O'Casey)
*Poems of Ossian* (J. Macpherson)
*Poison* (K. Mansfield)
*Popular Tales of the West Highlands* (J. F. Campbell)
*Portrait in Brownstone* (L. Auchincloss)
*Portrait vivant, Le* (Mélesville/Laya)
*Postman Always Rings Twice* (J. Cain)
*Pot of Broth* (Yeats)
*Pour la couronne* (F. Coppée)
*Précieuses ridicules, Les* (Molière)
*Prelude and Fugue* (C. Bas)
*Premières amours, Les* (M. Lacy)
*Pride and Prejudice* (Austen)
*Princess, The* (Tennyson)
*Princess and the Pea* (H. C. Andersen)
*Princess Mona* (E. Congeau)
*Private Life of Helen of Troy* (J. Erskine)
*Private Memoirs and Confessions of a Justified Sinner* (J. Hogg)
*Prometheus* (Goethe)
*Prometheus Bound* (R. Lowell)
*Prophetess, The* (J. Fletcher/P. Massinger)
*Proposal, The* (A. Chekhov)
*Prozess, Der* (F. Kafka)
*Prussian Vase* (M. Edgeworth)
*Puce à l'oreille, La* (G. Feydeau)
*Puissance du néant, La* (A. David-Neel)
*Pumpkin, The* (B. Pásztor)

*Queer* (W. Burroughs)
*Quentin Durward* (W. Scott)
*Quiet American* (G. Greene)

*Rab the Rhymer* (E. Crozier)
*Rain* (S. Maugham)
*Rajah's Diamond* (R. L. Stevenson)
*Ramayana* (Valmiki)
*Ramona* (H. Jackson)
*Ramuntcho* (P. Loti)
*Ransom of Red Chief* (O. Henry)
*Rape of Lucrece* (W. Shakespeare)
*Rape of the Lock* (A. Pope)
*Rappaccini's Daughter* (N. Hawthorne)
*Rapunzel* (Brothers Grimm)
*Räuber, Die* (F. Schiller)
*Rebecca* (D. du Maurier)
*Recollections* (P. T. Barnum)
*Records of the Historian* (S. Chien)
*Red Carnations* (G. Hughes)
*Red Emma* (C. Bolt)
*Red-Headed League* (A. C. Doyle)
*Red Soliloquy* (J. Ziegenhagen)
*Red Spider* (S. Baring-Gould)
*Regina e gli insorti, La* (U. Betti)
*Reine de Chypre, La* (J. H. Vernoy de Saint-Georges)
*Relapse, The* (J. Vanbrugh)
*Rendezvous, The* (M. Renard)
*Republic, The* (Plato)
*Resurrection* (L. Tolstoy)
*Retablillo de Don Cristóbal* (F. García Lorca)
*Retour imprévu, Le* (J.-F. Regnard)
*Rêve d'une petite fille* (M. Ernst)
*Revolution of Forms* (J. Loomis)
*Rhinocéros* (E. Ionesco)
*Richard III* (W. Shakespeare)
*Riders to the Sea* (J. M. Synge)
*Rime of the Ancient Mariner* (S. T. Coleridge)
*Ring, The* (T. Moore)
*Ring and the Book* (R. Browning)
*Rip Van Winkle* (Boucicault/Jefferson)
*Rip Van Winkle* (W. Irving)
*Rivals, The* (R. Sheridan)
*Rivaux d'eux mêmes, Les* (Pigault-Lebrun)
*Robin Hood*
*Rob Roy* (W. Scott)
*Rochester* (Moncrieff)
*Rocket, The* (R. Bradbury)
*Rococo Confessional* (C. MacCallum)
*Roman Fever* (E. Wharton)
*Romeo and Juliet* (W. Shakespeare)
*Romulus* (Dumas père)
*Room across the Hall* (O. Henry)
*Room with a View* (E. M. Forster)

*Rope, The* (E. O'Neill)
*Rose Affair* (A. Owen)
*Rose and the Ring* (W. P. Thackeray)
*Rosencrantz and Guildenstern Are Dead* (T. Stoppard)
*Rosier de Madonne Husson, Le* (G. de Maupassant)
*Royal Hunt of the Sun* (P. Shaffer)
*Royal Merchant* (Beaumont/ Fletcher)
*Rugantino* (M. Lewis)
*Ruined Maid* (T. Hardy)
*Ruy Blas* (V. Hugo)

*S.* (J. Updike)
*Sailor-Boy's Tale* (I. Dinesen)
*Sainte-Carmen de la Main* (M. Tremblay)
*Sandbox, The* (E. Albee)
*Sandmann, Der* (E. T. A. Hoffmann)
*Santa Claus* (E. E. Cummings)
*Satyricon* (Petronius)
*Sauny the Scot* (J. Lacy)
*Say It with Flowers* (G. Stein)
*Scarecrow, The* (P. MacKaye)
*Scarlet Letter* (N. Hawthorne)
*Scènes de la vie de bohème* (H. Murger)
*Scent of Sarsaparilla* (R. Bradbury)
*Schlimmen Buben in der Schule, Die* ( J. Nestroy)
*School for Guardians* (A. Murphy)
*Schwarze Spinne, Die* (J. Gotthelf)
*Scourge of Hyacinths* (W. Soyinka)
*Seagull, The* (A. Chekhov)
*Séance on a Wet Afternoon* (B. Forbes)
*Séance on a Wet Afternoon* (M. McShane)
*Secret Garden* (F. J. Burnett)
*Secular Masque* (J. Dryden)
*Selfish Giant* (O. Wilde)
*Sentimental Journey* (L. Sterne)
*Seraphic Vision* (L. Housman)
*Servants and the Snow* (I. Murdoch)
*Servitore di due padroni* (C. Goldoni)
*Seven Stories* (M. Panych)
*Sganarelle* (Molière)
*Shadow, The* (H. C. Andersen)
*Shadows* (W. L. George)
*Shallow Cups* (D. Cusack)
*Sharon's Grave* (J. Keane)
*She Gallants* (J. O'Keeffe)
*She Stoops to Conquer* (O. Goldsmith)
*Shining Chalice* (J. Lovoos)
*Shoemaker's Holiday* (T. Dekker)
*Show Boat* (E. Ferber)
*Sicilian Romance* (A. W. Radcliffe)
*Sicilien, Le* (Molière)
*Siège de La Rochelle, La* (Madame de Genlis)
*Signa* (Ouida)
*Silas Marner* (G. Eliot)

*Silver Queen* (C. Bancroft)
*Simoon* (A. Strindberg)
*Sire de Malétroit's Door* (R. L. Stevenson)
*Six Characters in Search of an Author* (L. Pirandllo)
*Skellig* (D. Almond)
*Snow Image* (N. Hawthorne)
*Snow Queen* (H. C. Andersen)
*Soeur Béatrice* (A. C. Liadov)
*Sofa, Le* (Crébillon)
*Soirées de l'orchestre, Les* (H. Berlioz)
*Soliman II* (J. F. Marmontel)
*Somnium* (J. Kepler)
*Songlines, The* (B. Chatwin)
*Song of Roland*
*Song of Triumphant Love* (A. Turgenev)
*Songs of a Sentimental Bloke* (C. J. Dennis)
*Sonnenwendhof, Der* (S. Mosenthal)
*Sophie's Choice* (W. Styron)
*Sorry, Wrong Number* (L. Fletcher)
*Sotoba Komachi*
*Sotto il sole giaguaro* (I. Calvino)
*Sound of a Voice* (D. H. Hwang)
*Southern Aranda* poems
*Spanish Student* (W. W. Longfellow)
*Spectorsky* (B. Pasternak)
*Spreading the News* (Lady Gregory)
*Stamboul Nights* (H. G. Dwight)
*Standard American Speaker* (F. Hoyle-Pogle)
*St. Columba and the Stream* (T. Dreiser)
*Stealing Heaven* (M. Meade)
*St. George and the Dragon*
*Story of a Mother* (H. C. Andersen)
*Story of My Heart* (R. Jefferies)
*Story of the Other Wise Man* (H. Van Dyke)
*Strange Case of Dr. Jekyll and Mr. Hyde* (R. L. Stevenson)
*Strange Fruit* (L. Smith)
*Strange Life of Ivan Osokin* (P. D. Ouspensky)
*String of Pearls* (G. D. Pitt)
*Stronger, The* (Strindberg)
*Student of Salamanca* (W. Irving)
*Sumida-gawa* (J. Montomasa)
*Summer* (E. Wharton)
*Summer and Smoke* (T. Williams)
*Summer of the Seventeenth Doll* (R. Lawler)
*Summer's Tale* (R. Cumberland)
*Sun Also Rises* (E. Hemingway)
*Sunday Costs Five Pesos* (J. Niggli)
*Superhuman Life of Gesar of Ling* (A. Neels)
*Suppose a Wedding* (B. Malamud)
*Sweeney Agonistes* (T. S. Eliott)
*Sweeney Todd* (C. Bond)ii
*Swineherd, The* (H. C. Andersen)
*System of Doctor Tarr* (E. A. Poe)
*Szüz és a gödölye* (L. Zilahy)

*Tailor of Gloucester* (B. Potter)
*Tale for Christmas* (Lady Craven)
*Tale of Chelm* (S. Aleichem)
*Tale of Genji* (M. Shikib)
*Tale of How Ivan Ivanovich Quarreled with Ivan Nikiforovich* (Gogol)
*Tale of the Heike*
*Tale of Two Cities* (C. Dickens)
*Tales of Soldiers and Civilians* (A. Bierce)
*Tales of the Border* (J. M. Wilson)
*Tales of the Genii* (C. Morell)
*Tales of the Late Ivan Petrovich Belkin* (A. S. Pushkin)
*Talisman, The* (H. C. Andersen)
*Talisman, The* (W. Scott)
*Tamburlaine the Great* (C. Marlowe)
*Tameem* (M. Halpern)
*Taming of the Shrew* (W. Shakespeare)
*Tanglewood Tales* (N. Hawthorne)
*Tartuffe* (Molière)
*Tekeli* (Pixérecourt)
*Telemachus* (G. Graham)
*Télémaque* (Fénelon)
*Tell-Tale Heart* (E. A. Poe)
*Tempest, The* (W. Shakespeare)
*Ten Nights in a Bar-Room* (T. S. Arthur)
*Terra Incognita* (M. Fornés)
*Tess of the D'Urbervilles* (T. Hardy)
*Thais* (A. France)
*Thérèse Raquin* (E. Zola)
*They Knew What They Wanted* (S. Howard)
*Thief of Love* (Bengali tale)
*Thimon le misanthrope* (L. F. Delisle)
*Things as They Are* (W. Godwin)
*Thirst* (E. O'Neil)
*Thirteen Clocks* (J. Thurber)
*This Is the Rill Speaking* (L. Wilson)
*Thousand and One Nights (Arabian Nights)*
*Three Bears Cottage* (J. Collier)
*Three Hermits* (L. Tolstoy)
*Three Sisters* (A. Chekhov)
*Three Sisters Who Are Not Sisters* (G. Stein)
*Three Strangers* (T. Hardy)
*Through the Looking Glass* (L. Carroll)
*Tickets, Please* (D. H. Lawrence)
*Time Machine* (H. G. Wells)
*Timon of Athens* (W. Shakespeare)
*Tobermory* (Saki)
*Tobias and the Angel* (J. Bridie)
*Tod in Venedig, Der* (T. Mann)
*Tom Cobb* (W. S. Gilbert)
*Tom Jones* (H. Fielding)
*Tom Sawyer* (M. Twain)
*Tom Thumb* (H. Fielding)
*Tonnelier, Le* (A. F. Quétant)
*Too Dear!* (L. Tolstoy)

*Trachimiae* (Sophocles)
*Traffic* (J. Tati)
*Tragedy of Fotheringay* (Maxwell-Scott)
*Tragedy of Tragedies* (H. Fielding)
*Tragicall History of Doctor Faustus* (C. Marlowe)
*Travelling Companions* (H. James)
*Travelling Man* (Lady Gregory)
*Tree That Didn't Get Trimmed* (C. Morley)
*Trilby* (G. du Maurier)
*Tristan* (G. von Strassburg)
*Tristan and Iseult* (medieval)
*Tristram* (E. A. Robinson)
*Tristram Shandy* (L. Sterne)
*Troilus and Criseyde* (G. Chaucer)
*Troisième lune, La* (F. de Grésac/P. Ferrier)
*Trois jumeaux vénitiens, Les* (A. Mattiuzzi)
*Trois Mousquetaires, Les* (E. Rostand)
*Trumpet Major* (T. Hardy)
*Trutz Simplex* (Grimmelshausen)
*Tueur sans gages* (E. Ionesco)
*Tumble-down Dick* (H. Fielding)
*Turn of the Screw* (H. James)
*Twa Sisters o'Binnorie* (ballad)
*Twelfth Night* (W. Shakespeare)
*Two Gentlemen of Verona* (W. Shakespeare)
*Two Noble Kings* (Shakespeare/Fletcher)

*Ubu roi* (A. Jarry)
*Ugly Duckling* (A. A. Milne)
*Ulysses* (J. Joyce)
*Uncle Remus* (J. H. Harris)
*Uncle Tom's Cabin* (H. B. Stowe)
*Under the Arbor* (M. M. Carcache)
*Under the Greenwood Tree* (T. Hardy)
*Under the Juniper Tree* (C. Brahms)
*Undine* (de La Motte Fouqué)
*University Greys* (M. Brown)
*Unto These Hills* (K. Hunter)

*VALIS* (P. Dick)
*Venus im Pelz* (L. von Sacher-Masoch)
*Verwandlung, Die* (F. Kafka)
*View from the Bridge* (A. Miller)
*Vile Shadows* (N. Newton)
*Villon* (R. Anderson)
*Vision and Prayer* (D. Thomas)
*Visit to the Country* (A. Chekhov)
*Voilà Madame Angot* (F. Tourte)
*Volpone* (B. Jonson)
*Von morgen bis mitternachts* (G. Kaiser)
*Vörös Malum* (F. Molnár)
*Voss* (P. White)

*Waiting for the Barbarians* (J. M. Coetzee)
*Wakefield Mystery Plays* (Wakefield Master)
*Waltz on a Merry-Go-Round* (E. Gallardo)

*Wandering Scholars* (H. Waddell)
*Washington Square* (H. James)
*Waverley* (W. Scott)
*We* (Y. Zamyatin)
*Wedding, A* (Altman-Considine)
*Wedding Knell* (N. Hawthorne)
*Weg der Verheissung, Der* (F. Werfel)
*Weir of Hermiston* (R. L.Stevenson)
*Westward Ho!* (C. Kingsley)
*Whanau* (W. Ihrmaera)
*What D'Ye Call It* (J. Gay)
*Where Angels Fear to Tread* (E. M. Forster)
*Where the Cross Is Made* (E. O'Neill)
*White Doe of Rylstone* (W. Wordsworth)
*White Plague* (K. Čapek)
*White Wings* (P. Barry)
*Why the Chimes Rang* (R. M. Alden)
*Wife of Martin Guerre* (J. Lewis)
*Wildfang, Die* (A. von Kotzebue)
*Wild Swans* (H. C. Andersen)
*Wilhelm Tell* (F. Schiller)
*Will, The* (M . Edgeworth)
*Wind in the Willows* (K. Grahame)
*Wings of the Dove* (H. James)
*Winter Guest* (S. Macdonald)
*Winter's Tale* (W. Shakespeare)
*Wisconsin Death Trip* (M. Lesy)
*Witch, The* (A. Chekhov)
*Witch, The* (F. Molnár)
*Woman at Ottowi Crossing* (F. Waters)
*Woman on the Wall* (Rabbi Newman)
*Women of Trachis* (Sophocles)
*Wonder Book* (N. Hawthorne)
*Woodlanders, The* (T. Hardy)
*Wuthering Heights* (E. Brontë)

*X=0* (J. Drinkwater)
*Xingu* (E. Wharton)

*Yellow Wallpaper* (C. P. Gilman)
*Yerma* (F. García Lorca)
*Yokinojo Henge* (O. Mikami)
*Yolanda of Cyprus* (C. Y. Rice)
*York Mystery Plays* (ca. 14th cent.)
*Young Goodman Brown* (N. Hawthorne)

*Zerbrochene Krug, Der* (H. von Kleist)
*Zuma* (S. F. Genlis)

# Appendix 4: Chronology

Dates given are of premiere; * = year of composition where year of premiere unknown or at later date (given in parentheses); ? = month/city of premiere unknown; ** = ballad opera/anon. composer. Hyphenated composer names = adaptations.

| DATE | TITLE | CITY | COMPOSER |
|------|-------|------|----------|
| **1634** | | | |
| Feb. 3 | Triumph of Peace | London | Lawes, W. |
| Sept. 29 | Comus | Ludlow | Lawes, H. |
| **1636** | | | |
| Feb. 24 | Triumphs of the Prince d'Amour | London | Lawes, H./W. |
| **1638** | | | |
| Jan. 7 | Britannia triumphans | London | Lawes, W. |
| **1653** | | | |
| Mar. 26 | Cupid and Death | London | Gibbons, C. |
| **1654** | | | |
| * (ca.) | Ariadne Deserted by Theseus | -- | Flecknoe, R. |
| **1656** | | | |
| Sept. | Siege of Rhodes | London | Lawes, H. |
| **1659** | | | |
| * (ca.) | Marriage of Oceanus | -- | Flecknoe, R. |
| **1673** | | | |
| July 3? | Orpheus and Euridice | London | Locke, M. |
| **1674** | | | |
| Apr. 30? | Tempest, The | London | Banister et al. |
| **1675** | | | |
| Feb. 18? | Macbeth | London | Locke, M. |
| Feb. 27 | Psyche | London | Locke, M. |
| **1683** | | | |
| (ca.) | Venus and Adonis | London | Blow, J. |
| **1685** | | | |
| June 3 | Albion and Albanius | London | Grabu, L. |
| **1689** | | | |
| ca. Dec. | Dido and Aeneas | London | Purcell, H. |
| **1690** | | | |
| June | Dioclesian | London | Purcell, H. |
| **1691** | | | |
| May | King Arthur | London | Purcell, H. |
| **1692** | | | |
| May 2 | Fairy Queen | London | Purcell, H. |
| **1694** | | | |
| Oct. | Rape of Europa | London | Eccles, J. |
| **1695** | | | |
| autumn | Indian Queen | London | Purcell, H. |

| DATE | TITLE | CITY | COMPOSER |
|------|-------|------|----------|
| **1696** | | | |
| Oct. | Brutus of Alba | London | Purcell, D. |
| Nov. | Loves of Mars and Venus | London | Eccles, J. |
| ? | Macbeth | London | Eccles, J. |
| **1697** | | | |
| June | World in the Moon | London | Purcell, D. |
| **1698** | | | |
| Nov. | Rinaldo and Armida | London | Eccles, J. |
| **1699** | | | |
| Jan. | Island Princess | London | Purcell, D. |
| **1700** | | | |
| Feb. 19 | Grove, The | London | Purcell, D. |
| Mar. 25 | Secular Masque | London | Purcell, D.-Finger, G. |
| **1701** | | | |
| Feb. | Rival Queens | London | Finger, G. |
| Mar. 21 | Judgment of Paris | London | Eccles, J. |
| Mar. 28 | Judgment of Paris | London | Finger, G. |
| Apr. 11 | Judgment of Paris | London | Purcell, D. |
| May? | Acis and Galatea | London | Eccles, J. |
| May 2 | Virgin Prophetess | London | Finger, G. |
| May 6 | Judgment of Paris | London | Weldon, J. |
| **1702** | | | |
| Nov. 21 | Macbeth | London | Leveridge, R. |
| **1705** | | | |
| Jan. 16 | Arsinoe | London | Clayton, T. |
| **1706** | | | |
| Feb. 21 | British Enchanters | London | Corbett/Eccles |
| Mar. 7 | Temple of Love | London | Fedelli, G. |
| Apr. 5 | Wonders in the Sun | London | ** |
| * | Semele | Oxford (1964) | Eccles, J. |
| **1707** | | | |
| Mar. 4 | Rosamond | London | Clayton, T. |
| Apr. 1 | Thomyris | London | Pepusch, J. |
| **1708** | | | |
| Feb. 12 | Prunella | London | Clayton, T. |
| Feb. 26 | Love's Triumph | London | Cesarini et al. |
| Dec. 14 | Pyrrus and Demetrius | London | Haym, N. |
| **1712?** | | | |
| Jan. 7 | Tempest, The | London | Weldon, J. |

| Date | Title | City | Composer |
|---|---|---|---|
| **1712** | | | |
| May 14 | **Calypso and Telemachus** | London | Galliard, J. |
| **1715** | | | |
| Mar. 12 | **Venus and Adonis** | London | Pepusch, J. |
| Nov. 5 | **Myrtillo** | London | Pepusch, J. |
| **1716** | | | |
| Jan. 12 | **Apollo and Daphne** | London | Pepusch, J. |
| Apr. 11 | **Pyramus and Thisbe** | London | Leveridge, R. |
| Apr. 17 | **Death of Dido** | London | Pepusch, J. |
| **1718** | | | |
| Jan. 14 | **Pan and Syrinx** | London | Galliard, J. |
| Mar. 22 | **Decius and Paulina** | London | Galliard, J. |
| Mar. 22 | **Lady's Triumph** | London | ** |
| summer | **Acis and Galatea** | Cannons | Handel, G. F. |
| **1719** | | | |
| Apr. 11 | **Circe** | London | Galliard, J. |
| **1724** | | | |
| Nov. 28 | **Prophetess. The** | London | Pepusch, J. |
| **1728** | | | |
| Jan. 29 | **Beggar's Opera** | London | Pepusch, J. |
| Apr. 26 | **Cobler's Opera** | London | ** |
| May 8 | **Penelope** | London | ** |
| Sept. 24 | **Quaker's Opera** | London | ** |
| Oct. 15 | **Craftsman, The** | London | ** |
| * | **Polly** | London (1777) | ** |
| **1729** | | | |
| Jan. 7 | **Love in a Riddle** | London | ** |
| Jan. 29 | **Gentle Shepherd** | Edinburgh | ** |
| Feb. 6 | **Village Opera** | London | ** |
| Mar. 13 | **Beggar's Wedding** | Dublin | ** |
| Mar. 29 | **Hurlothrumbo** | London | Johnson, S. |
| Apr. 16 | **Devil upon Two Sticks** | London | ** |
| Apr. 18 | **Flora** | London | ** |
| May 6 | **Wedding, The** | London | Pepusch, J. |
| May 7 | **Patron, The** | London | ** |
| May 14 | **Lover's Opera** | London | ** |
| June 20 | **Contrivances, The** | London | Carey, H. |
| Aug. 16 | **Damon and Phillida** | London | ** |
| Dec. 3 | **Momus Turn'd Fabulist** | London | ** |
| ? | **Love and Revenge** | London? | ** |
| **1730** | | | |
| Feb. 10 | **Chamber-Maid** | London | ** |
| Mar. 11 | **Metamorphosis of the Beggar's Opera** | London | ** |
| Mar. 30 | **Author's Farce** | London | ** |
| Mar. 30 | **Bays's Opera** | London | ** |
| Apr. 2 | **Fashionable Lady** | London | ** |
| Apr. 27 | **Female Parson** | London | Coffey, C. |
| May 1 | **Patie and Peggy** | London | ** |
| summer | **Prisoner's Opera** | London | ** |
| Aug. 20 | **Generous Free-Mason** | London | ** |
| Aug. 22 | **Robin Hood** | London | ** |
| Dec. 16 | **Jealous Clown** | London | ** |
| **1731** | | | |
| Feb. 8 | **Jovial Crew** | London | ** |
| Mar. ? | **Fool's Opera** | Oxford | ** |
| Mar. 20 | **Highland Fair** | London | ** |
| Apr. 3 | **Orestes** | London | Pepusch, J. |
| Apr. 22 | **Welsh Opera** | London | ** |
| May 4 | **Judgment of Paris** | London | ** |
| July | **Gray Mare's the Best Horse** | London | Taylor, R. (arr). |
| Aug. 6 | **Devil to Pay** | London | ** |
| Nov. 10 | **Silvia** | London | ** |
| ? | **Grub-Street Opera** | London | ** |
| **1732** | | | |
| Jan. 1 | **Lottery** | London | Seedo, Mr. |
| Mar. 13 | **Amelia** | London | Lampe, J. F. |
| Mar. 20 | **Sequel to Flora** | London | Carey et al. |
| June 26 | **Mock Doctor** | London | ** |
| Aug. 17 | **Devil of a Duke** | London | ** |
| Nov. 16 | **Britannia** | London | Lampe, J. F. |
| Nov. 20 | **Teraminta** | London | Smith, J. C. |
| Dec. 1 | **Betty** | London | Carey, H. (arr) |
| ? | **Disappointment, The** | London | ** |
| ? | **Restauration of King Charles II** | London | ** |
| **1733** | | | |
| Jan. 29 | **Boarding School** | London | ** |
| Feb. 5 | **Decoy, The** | London | ** |
| Feb. 10 | **Achilles** | London | ** |
| Feb. 23 | **Dione** | London | Lampe, F. |
| Mar. 5 | **Mad Captain** | London | ** |
| Mar. 7 | **Rosamond** | London | Arne, T. A. |
| Apr. 16 | **Ulysses** | London | Smith, J. C. |
| Apr. 27 | **Mock Lawyer** | London | ** |
| May 5 | **Livery Rake** | London | ** |
| May 21 | **Venus, Cupid** | London | Seedo, Mr. |
| May 31 | **Opera of Operas** | London | Lampe, J. F. |
| summer? | **Oxford Act** | Oxford | ** |
| Aug. 14 | **Fancy'd Queen** | London | ** |
| Nov. 7 | **Opera of Operas** | London | Arne, T. A. |
| Nov. 24 | **Happy Nuptials** | London | Carey, H. |
| Dec. 5 | **Timon in Love** | London | ** |
| **1734** | | | |
| Jan. 12 | **Dido and Aeneas** | London | Arne, T. A. |
| Feb. 22 | **Chrononhotonthologos** | London | Carey, H. |
| Feb? | **Britannia** | London | Carey, H. |
| Mar. 21 | **Britannia** | London | Arne, T. A. |
| Apr. 5 | **Don Quixote in England** | London | ** |
| ? | **Florimel/Love's Revenge** | Winchester | Greene, M. |

| DATE | TITLE | CITY | COMPOSER | DATE | TITLE | CITY | COMPOSER |
|------|-------|------|----------|------|-------|------|----------|
| ? | Intriguing Chambermaid | London | ** | **1743** | | | |
| ? | Whim, The | London | ** | * | Eurydice | -- | ** |
| **1735** | | | | **1744** | | | |
| Jan. 6 | Old Man Taught Wisdom | London | ** | Jan. 19 | Queen of Spain | London | Lampe, J. F. |
| Jan. 22 | Plot, The | London | ** | Feb. 10 | Semele | London | Handel, G. F. |
| Feb. 25 | Cure for a Scold | London | ** | **1745** | | | |
| May 6 | Merry Cobler | London | ** | Jan. 5 | Hercules | London | Handel, G. F. |
| May 10 | Trick for Trick | London | ** | Jan. 17 | Temple of Dullness | London | Arne, T. A. |
| July 15 | Honest Yorkshireman | London | Carey, H. | Jan. 25 | Pyramus and Thisbe | London | Lampe, F. |
| ? | Macheath in the Shades | London | ** | Feb. 11 | Picture, The | London | Arne, T. A. |
| **1736** | | | | Apr. 15 | King Pepin's Campaign | London | Arne, T. A. |
| Feb. 10 | Lover His Own Rival | London | ** | **1746** | | | |
| Apr. | Tumble-Down Dick | London | ** | Jan. | Tempest, The | London | Arne, T. A. |
| Apr. 26 | Female Rake | London | ** | Mar. 18 | Double Disappointment | London | ** |
| May 26 | Rival Captains | London | ** | **1747** | | | |
| ? | Happy Lovers | London | ** | Apr. 29 | Peleus and Thetis | London | Boyce, W. |
| **1737** | | | | * | Phoebe | London (1755) | Greene, M. |
| May 16 | Dragon of Wantley | London | Lampe, J. F. | **1748** | | | |
| May 30 | Macheath Turn'd Pyrate | London | ** | Feb. 21 | Triumph of Peace | London | Arne, T. A. |
| ? | Lucky Discovery | London | ** | Nov. 4 | Triumphs of Hibernia | Dublin | Pasquali, N. |
| ? | Mad House | London | ** | **1749** | | | |
| ? | Rape of Helen | London | ** | Jan. 18 | Lethe | London | Arne, T. A. |
| **1738** | | | | Feb. 9 | Temple of Peace | London | Pasquali, N. |
| Jan. 26 | Coffee-House | London | Carey/Burgess | Mar. 31 | Henry and Emma | London | Arne, T. A. |
| Mar. 4 | Comus | London | Arne, T. A. | July | Secular Masque | London | Boyce, W. |
| Dec. 9 | Margery | London | Lampe, J. F. | Dec. 2 | Chaplet, The | London | Boyce, W. |
| **1739** | | | | * | Alceste | -- | Handel, G. F. |
| Nov. 15 | Hospital for Fools | London | Arne, T. A. | * | Peleus and Thetis | -- | Hayes, W. |
| Dec. 1 | Nancy | London | Carey, H. | **1750** | | | |
| Dec. 31 | Britons, Strike Home | London | ** | Feb. 15 | Don Saverio | London | Arne, T. A. |
| ? | Don Sancho | London | ** | Mar. 1 | Rehearsal, The | London | Boyce, W. |
| **1740** | | | | Dec. 13 | Robin Hood | London | Burney, C. |
| Jan. 4 | Rosalinda | London | Smith, J. C. | **1751** | | | |
| Feb. 12 | Orpheus and Eurydice | London | Lampe, J. F. | Nov. 19 | Shepherd's Lottery | London | Boyce, W. |
| Apr. 7 | Baucis and Philemon | London | Prelleur, P. | **1754** | | | |
| Aug. 1 | Alfred | London | Arne, T. A. | Mar. 25 | Sheep Shearing | London | Arne, T. A. |
| ? | False Guardians Outwitted | London | ** | May 29 | Eliza | London | Arne, T. A. |
| ? | Judgment of Hercules | London | Greene, M. | ? | Ragged Uproar | London | ** |
| * | Seasons, The | -- | Smith, J. C. | * | Teraminta | BBC (1950s) | Stanley, J. |
| **1741** | | | | **1755** | | | |
| Apr. 3 | Blind Beggar | London | Arne, T. A. | Feb. 3 | Fairies, The | London | Smith, J. C. |
| Apr. 16 | Happy Captive | London | Galliard, J. | May 9 | Britannia | London | Arne, T. A. |
| Apr. 18 | Sham Conjuror | London | Lampe, F. | **1756** | | | |
| **1742** | | | | Jan. 21 | Florizel and Perdita | London | Boyce, W. |
| Mar. 12 | Judgment of Paris | London | Arne, T. A. | Feb. 11 | Tempest, The | London | Smith, J. C. |
| May 6 | Miss Lucy in Town | London | Arne, T. A. | Mar. 17 | Pincushion, The | Dublin | Arne, T. A. |
| ? | Love at First Sight | London | ** | | | | |
| ? | Sancho at Court | London | ** | | | | |
| * | Circe | -- | Hayes, W. | | | | |

| DATE | TITLE | CITY | COMPOSER | DATE | TITLE | CITY | COMPOSER |
|---|---|---|---|---|---|---|---|
| **1757** | | | | **1767** | | | |
| Oct. 20 | Tempest, The | London | Boyce, W. | Jan. 2 | Cymon | London | Arne, M. |
| **1759?** | | | | Jan. 31 | Fairy Favour | London | Bach, J. C. |
| ? | Gasconado the Great | London | ** | Feb. 21 | Love in the City | London | Dibdin, C. |
| **1760** | | | | Feb. 25 | Phillis at Court | Dublin | Giordani, T. |
| Feb. 14 | Jovial Crew | London | ** | Mar. 6 | Linco's Travels | London | Arne/Vernon |
| Nov. 17 | Tears and Triumphs of Parnassus | London | Stanley, J. | Apr. 20 | Disappointment, The | Philadelphia | Barton, A. |
| | | | | Apr. 21 | Rosamond | London | Arnold, S. |
| Nov. 28 | Thomas and Sally | London | Arne, T. A. | Oct. 23 | Orpheus | London | Barthelemon, J. H. |
| Dec. 13 | Enchanter, The | London | Smith, J. C. | | | | |
| **1761** | | | | Nov. 4 | Lycidas | London | Jackson, W. |
| Jan. 31 | Edgar and Emmeline | London | Arne, M. | Dec. 14 | Royal Merchant | London | Linley Sr. |
| Oct. 26 | Arcadia | London | Stanley, J. | ? | Royal Pastoral | Windsor Castle | Nares, J. |
| **1762** | | | | **1768** | | | |
| Jan. 22 | Midas | Dublin | ** | Feb. 25 | Lionel and Clarissa | London | Dibdin, C. |
| Feb. 2 | Artaxerxes | London | Arne, T. A. | Mar. 3 | Oithona | London | Barthelemon, F. H. |
| Dec. 8 | Love in a Village | London | Arne, T. A. | | | | |
| **1763** | | | | Aug. 16 | Damon and Phillida | London | ** |
| May 10 | Telemachus | Oxford | Hayes, P. | Oct. 3 | Padlock, The | London | Dibdin, C. |
| Oct. 17 | Love at First Sight | London | ** | Oct. 10 | Royal Garland | London | Arnold. S. |
| Nov. 23 | Midsummer Night's Dream | London | Burney, C. | Dec. 21 | Damon and Phillida | London | Dibdin, C. |
| * | Birth of Hercules | -- | Arne, T. A. | ? | Amelia | London | Piccinni et al. |
| **1764** | | | | **1769** | | | |
| Jan. 20 | Arcadian Nuptials | London | Arne, T. A. | Jan. 14 | Tom Jones | London | Arnold, S. |
| Jan. 23 | Hymen | London | Arne, M. | May 12 | Ephesian Matron | London | Dibdin, C. |
| Feb. 24 | Royal Shepherd | London | Rush, G. | June 21 | Captive, The | London | Dibdin et al. |
| May 21 | Shepherd's Artifice | London | Dibdin, C. | Oct. 14 | Jubilee | London | Dibdin, C. |
| Aug. | Menalcas | Salisbury | Bach, J. C. | Dec. 15 | Amintas | London | Arnold et al. |
| Nov. 2 | Almena | London | Arne/ Battishill | **1770** | | | |
| | | | | Jan. 5 | Court of Alexander | London | Fisher, J. A. |
| Nov. 28 | Capricious Lovers | London | Rush, G. | Apr. 25 | Flora | London | Bates, W. |
| Dec. 12 | Guardian Outwitted | London | Arne, T. A. | May 7 | Ladies' Frolick | London | Bates, W. |
| **1765** | | | | June 16 | Servant Mistress | London | Arnold, S. |
| Jan. 7 | Don Fulminone | Dublin | Giordani, T. | July 17 | Magic Girdle | London | Barthelemon, F. H. |
| Jan. 17 | The Enchantress | Dublin | Giordani, T. | | | | |
| Jan. 31 | Maid of the Mill | London | Arnold, S. | July 20 | Recruiting Sergeant | London | Dibdin, C. |
| Feb. 15 | Pharnaces | London | Bates, W. | Aug. 21 | Noble Pedlar | London | Barthelemon, F. H. |
| Mar. 11 | Choice of Apollo | London | Yates, W. | | | | |
| Mar. 26 | Maid of the Mill | London | Giordani, T. | Aug. 28 | Madman, The | London | Arnold, S. |
| May 2 | Spanish Lady | London | ** | Nov. 22 | Portrait, The | London | Arnold, S. |
| Oct. 8 | Daphne and Amintor | London | Arnold, S. | ? | Revenge, The | London | Arnold, S. |
| Dec. 6 | Summer's Tale | London | Arnold, S. | **1771** | | | |
| ? | Prude, The | London | ** | Jan. 23 | Romp, The | Dublin | Dibdin, C. |
| **1766** | | | | June 27 | Magnet, The | London | Arnold, S. |
| Apr. 24 | Love in Disguise | Dublin | Giordani, T. | July 24 | Dido and Aeneas | London | Hook, J. |
| Nov. 21 | Cunning Man | London | Burney, C. | Oct. 28 | Institution of the Garter | London | Dibdin, C. |
| Dec. 12 | Revenge of Athridates | Dublin | Tenducci, F. | Nov. 12 | Fairy Prince | London | Arne, T. A. |
| ? | Cottagers, The | London | ** | Dec. 14 | Amelia | London | Dibdin, C. |
| | | | | ? | Divorce, The | London | Hook, J. |
| | | | | ? | Portrait, The | Dublin | Barthelemon, F. H. |

| Date | Title | City | Composer | Date | Title | City | Composer |
|------|-------|------|----------|------|-------|------|----------|
| **1772** | | | | **1777** | | | |
| Mar. 16 | Squire Badger | London | Arne, T. A. | Mar. 20 | Milesian, The | London | Carter, T. |
| June 10 | Cooper, The | London | Arne, T. A. | Mar. 22 | Emperor of the Moon | London | Arne, M. |
| July 27 | Cupid's Revenge | London | Hook, J. | Apr. 15 | Shamrock, The | Dublin | Shield, W. |
| Aug. 28 | Dilettante, Il | London | Hook, J. | May 5 | Device, The | London | Bates, W. |
| Nov. 21 | Elfrida | London | Arne, T. A. | May 15 | Lilliput | London | Arnold, S. |
| Dec. 2 | Rose, The | London | Arne, T. A. | July 18 | Fairy Tale | London | Arne, M. |
| ? | Brickdust Man | London | Dibdin, C. | July 18 | Sheep Shearing | London | Arnold, S. |
| ? | Palace of Mirth | London | Dibdin, C. | Aug. 18 | Yo, Yea | London | Dibdin, C. |
| | | | | Aug. 22 | April Day | London | Arnold, S. |
| **1773** | | | | Aug. 30 | Spanish Barber | London | Arnold, S. |
| Feb. 1 | Wedding Ring | London | Dibdin, C. | Nov. 18 | Love Finds the Way | London | Arne et al. |
| Feb. 6 | Golden Pippen | London | Fischer, J. A. | ? | Old Woman of Eighty | London | Dibdin, C. |
| Apr. 14 | Ladle, The | London | Dibdin, C. | | | | |
| Apr. 19 | Grenadier, The | London | Dibdin, C. | **1778** | | | |
| July 12 | Mischance, The | London | Dibdin, C. | Feb. 4 | Poor Vulcan | London | Dibdin, C. |
| July 15 | Wedding Day | London | Barthelemon | Feb. 19 | Cadi of Bagdad | London | Linley Jr. |
| Aug. 11 | Trip to Portsmouth | London | Dibdin, C. | Feb. 24 | Ruling Passion | Dublin | Cogan, P. |
| Aug. 21 | Zingara, La | London | Barthelemon, F. H. | Mar. 16 | Belphegor | London | Barthelemon, F. H. |
| Sept. 27 | Apollo and Daphne | London | Hook, J. | Mar. 30 | Second Thought Is Best | London | Bates, W. |
| Nov. 2 | Deserter, The | London | Dibdin, C. | May 1 | Crisis, The | London | Shield, W. |
| Dec. 16 | Achilles in Petticoats | London | Arne, T. A. | June 25 | Buxom Joan | London | Taylor, R. |
| Dec. 27 | Christmas Tale | London | Dibdin, C. | Aug. 3 | Gipsies, The | London | Arnold, S. |
| ? | Bow-Street Opera | London | Pepusch, J. | Aug. 17 | Cobler of Castlebury | London | Shield, W. |
| | | | | Aug. 17 | Flitch of Bacon | London | Shield, W. |
| **1774** | | | | Sept. 18 | Rose and Colin | London | Dibdin, C. |
| June 30 | Don Quixote | London | Arnold, S. | Sept. 18 | Wives Revenged | London | Dibdin, C. |
| Aug. 8 | Waterman, The | London | Dibdin, C. | Oct. 2 | Annette and Lubin | London | Dibdin, C. |
| Oct. 19 | Election, The | London | Barthelemon, F. H. | Oct. 15 | Camp, The | London | Linley Sr. |
| Nov. 5 | Maid of the Oaks | London | Barthelemon, F. H. | Nov. 23 | Lady of the Manor | London | Hook, J. |
| Dec. 9 | Cobler, The | London | Dibdin, C. | Nov. 30 | Fathers, The | London | ** |
| | | | | | | | |
| **1775** | | | | **1779** | | | |
| Jan. 21 | Two Misers | London | Dibdin, C. | Apr. | Calypso | Dublin | Butler, T. H. |
| Feb. 1 | Rival Candidates | London | Carter, T. | May 6 | Chelsea Pensioner | London | Dibdin, C. |
| Feb. 15 | Maid of the Vale | London | Arne, M. | July 1 | Summer Amusement | London | Arnold, S. |
| Feb. 16 | Sot, The | London | Arne, T. A. | Aug. 14 | Son-in-Law | London | Arnold, S. |
| May 3 | Quaker, The | London | Dibdin, C. | Oct. 20 | Plymouth in an Uproar | London | Dibdin, C. |
| Sept. 23 | Theatrical Candidates | London | Bates, W. | Nov. 12 | William and Nancy | London | Baumgarten, K. |
| Oct. 17 | Weathercock, The | London | Arnold, S. | Dec. 13 | Zoraida | London | Linley, T. |
| Oct. 28 | May Day | London | Arne, T. A. | ? | Touchstone, The | London | Dibdin, C. |
| Nov. 21 | Duenna, The | London | Linley Jr., Sr. | | | | |
| Dec. 12 | Sultan, The | London | Dibdin, C. | **1780** | | | |
| | | | | Jan. 18 | Shepherdess of the Alps | London | Dibdin, C. |
| **1776** | | | | Feb. 2 | Widow of Delphi | London | Butler, T. |
| Feb. 1 | Blackamoor, The | London | Dibdin, C. | Apr. 14 | Artifice, The | London | Arne, M. |
| Aug. 26 | Metamorphoses | London | Dibdin, C. | Apr. 25 | Siege of Gibraltar | London | Shield, W. |
| Nov. 14 | Seraglio, The | London | Dibdin, C. | July 8 | Fire and Water! | London | Arnold, S. |
| Dec. 5 | Selima and Azor | London | Linley Sr. | Aug. 12 | Wedding Night | London | Arnold, S. |
| Dec. 7 | Caractacus | London | Arne, T. A. | Oct. 3 | Tom Thumb | London | Markordt, J. |
| ? | Phoebe at Court | London | Arne, T. A. | Nov. 25 | Islanders, The | London | Dibdin, C. |
| | | | | Dec. 27 | Lord of the Manor | London | Jackson, W. |

| DATE | TITLE | CITY | COMPOSER | DATE | TITLE | CITY | COMPOSER |
|------|-------|------|----------|------|-------|------|----------|
| Mar. 31 | Raft, The | London | Reeve, W. | May 12 | Sea-Side Story | London | Attwood, T. |
| May 7 | Hannah Hewitt | London | Dibdin, C. | July 24 | Gipsey Prince | London | Kelly, M. |
| May 23 | Reform'd in Time | London | Attwood, T. | Oct. 14 | Escapes, The | London | Attwood, T. |
| July 8 | Throw Physic to the Dogs! | London | Arnold, S. | Dec. 9 | Chains of the Heart | London | Reeve, W. |
| July 21 | Cambro-Britons | London | Arnold, S. | * | Jamie and Anna | -- | Reeve, W. |
| Aug. 11 | False and True | London | Arnold, S. | **1802** | | | |
| Oct. 17 | Day at Rome | London | Attwood, T. | Feb. 9 | Cabinet, The | London | Reeve et al. |
| Oct. 25 | Mouth of the Nile | London | Attwood, T. | Apr. 30 | Algonah | London | Storace, S. |
| Nov. 12 | Ramah Droog | London | Reeve, W. | June 2 | Caffres, The | London | Davy, J. |
| Nov. 14 | Captive of Spilburg | London | Dussek, J. | July 18 | Sixty-Third Letter | London | Arnold, S. |
| Dec. 11 | Albert and Adelaide | London | Attwood/ Steibelt | July 31 | Voice of Nature | London | Pelissier, V. |
| | | | | Aug. 14 | Fairies' Revels | London | Arnold, S. |
| ? | Flash in the Pan | New York | Hewitt, J. | Nov. 17 | House to Be Sold | London | Kelly, M. |
| **1799** | | | | Dec. 18 | Family Quarrels | London | Reeve, W. |
| Jan. 14 | Sterne's Maria | New York | Pelissier, V. | **1803** | | | |
| Jan. 19 | Feudal Times | London | Kelly, M. | Feb. 19 | Hero of the North | London | Kelly, M. |
| Apr. 2 | Old Cloathsman | London | Attwood, T. | July 25 | Love Laughs at Locksmiths | London | Kelly, M. |
| Apr. 29 | Pizzaro | London | Kelly, M. | Nov. 1 | Wife of Two Husbands | London | Mazzinghi, J. |
| May 29 | Love in a Blaze | Dublin | Stevenson, J. | Dec. 5 | Caravan, The | London | Reeve, W. |
| July 4 | Fourth of July | New York | Pelissier, V. | Dec. 14 | English Fleet in 1342 | London | Braham, J. |
| July 13 | Castle of Sorrento | London | Attwood, T. | **1804** | | | |
| Aug. 21 | Red Cross Knights | London | Attwood, T. | Mar. 8 | Paragraph, The | London | Braham, J. |
| Oct. 3 | Embarkation, The | London | Reeve, W. | July 4 | Hunter of the Alps | London | Kelly, M. |
| Oct. 7 | Naval Pillar | London | Moorehead | Aug. 22 | Gay Deceivers | London | Hawes, W. |
| Nov. 14 | Turnpike Gate | London | Reeve, W. | Aug. 30 | Angelina | London | Bishop, H. R. |
| Nov. 16 | Pavilion, The | London | Linley, W. | Nov. 20 | Matrimony | London | King, M. |
| ? | Bird Catcher | London | Cleve, V. de | Dec. 10 | Thirty Thousand | London | Reeve, W. |
| **1800** | | | | ? | Don Raphael | New York | Hewitt, J. |
| Feb. 1 | Of Age Tomorrow | London | Kelly, M. | **1805** | | | |
| Feb. 8 | Speed the Plough | London | Moorehead, J. | Jan. 31 | Honey Moon | London | Hewitt, J., Kelly, M. |
| Feb. 19 | True Friends | London | Attwood, T. | Feb. 12 | Too Many Cooks | London | King, M. |
| Mar. 11 | Egyptian Festival | London | Florio, C. | Feb. 28 | Out of Place | London | Reeve, W. |
| Mar. 12 | Virgin of the Sun | New York | Pelissier, V. | Apr. 23 | Soldier's Return | London | Hook, J. |
| Mar. 25 | St. David's Day | London | Attwood, T. | May 9 | Spanish Dollars! | London | Davy, J. |
| Apr. 5 | Hermione | London | Attwood, T. | May 24 | Youth, Love | London | Kelly, M. |
| Apr. 14 | Old Fools | London | Moorehead, J. | Nov. 18 | Weathercock, The | London | King, M. |
| May 1 | Paul and Virginia | London | Reeve, W. | **1806** | | | |
| Aug. 14 | What a Blunder | London | Davy, J. | Jan. 22 | Travellers, The | London | Corri, D. |
| Sept. 1 | Review, The | London | Arnold, S. | Feb. 8 | Broken Gold | London | Dibdin, C. |
| Oct. 1 | Wilmore Castle | London | Hook, J. | Feb. 24 | Tars from Tripoli | New York | Hewitt, J. |
| Oct. 30 | Virginia | London | Arnold, S. | Apr. 8 | Forty Thieves | London | Kelly, M. |
| Nov. 15 | Bondocani, Il | London | Attwood/ Moorehead | Apr. 10 | White Plume | London | Reeve, W. |
| | | | | Apr. 28 | Invisible Girl | London | Hook, J. |
| Dec. 5 | Spanish Castle | New York | Hewitt, J. | June 12 | Catch Him Who Can | London | Hook, J. |
| ? | Wild Goose Chase | New York | Hewitt, J. | Nov. 24 | Tekeli | London | Hook, J. |
| **1801** | | | | Dec. 26 | Mother Goose | London | Ware, W. H. |
| Jan. 29 | Veteran Tar | London | Arnold, S. | **1807** | | | |
| Feb. 3 | Merry Gardner | New York | Pelissier, V. | Jan. 12 | False Alarms | London | Addison et al. |
| Apr. 22 | Blind Girl | London | Reeve, W. | | | | |
| May 1 | Bedouins, The | Dublin | Stevenson, J. | | | | |
| May 6 | Cottagers, The | New York | Hewitt, J. | | | | |

| Date | Title | City | Composer | Date | Title | City | Composer |
|---|---|---|---|---|---|---|---|
| Mar. 12 | **Young Hussar** | London | Kelly, M. | Sept. 22 | **Spanish Patriots** | London | Stevenson, J. |
| Apr. 1 | **Wood Daemon** | London | Kelly, M. | Oct. 6 | **Aethiop, The** | London | Bishop, H. R. |
| July 16 | **Fortress, The** | London | Hook, J. | **1813** | | | |
| Aug. 27 | **Music Mad** | London | Hook, J. | Jan. 11 | **Haroun Alraschid** | London | Bishop, H. R. |
| Nov. 17 | **Two Faces under a Hood** | London | Shield, W. | Feb. 3 | **Poor Vulcan** | London | Bishop, H. R. |
| ? | **Jonathan Postfree** | New York | ** | May 29 | **Brazen Bust** | London | Bishop, H. R. |
| **1808** | | | | July 2 | **Harry le Roi** | London | Bishop, H. R. |
| Feb. 11 | **Kais** | London | Reeve, W. | Aug. 4 | **Sharp and Flat** | London | Hook, J. |
| Feb. 25 | **Who Wins?** | London | Condell, H. | Oct. 21 | **Miller and His Men** | London | Bishop, H. R. |
| Apr. 6 | **Indian Princess** | Philadelphia | Bray, J. | Nov. 22 | **Who's to Have Her?** | London | Reeve, W. |
| Whitsun | **Magic Minstrel** | London | Reeve, W. | Dec. 15 | **For England, Ho!** | London | Bishop, H. R. |
| **1809** | | | | ? | **Aladdin** | London | Condell, H. Ware, W. |
| Jan. 4 | **Spanish Patriots** | New York | Gilfert, C. | ? | **Illusion, The** | London | Kelly, M. |
| Feb. 23 | **Circassian Bride** | London | Bishop, H. R. | ? | **Secret Mine** | London | Bishop, H. R. |
| June 26 | **Up All Night** | London | King, M. | **1814** | | | |
| July 22 | **Russian Imposter** | London | Addison, J. | Jan. 11 | **Narensky** | London | Horn, C. E. |
| Aug. 1 | **Vintagers, The** | London | Bishop, H. R. | Feb. 1 | **Farmer's Wife** | London | Bishop et al. |
| Aug. 21 | **Killing No Murder** | London | Hook, J. | Feb. 24 | **Wandering Boys** | London | Bishop, H. R. |
| ? | **Exile, The** | London | Mazzinghi, J. | Apr. 12 | **Woodman's Hut** | London | Horn, C. E. |
| ? | **Foundling of the Forest** | London | Kelly, M. | Aug. 4 | **Frederick the Great** | London | Cooke, T. |
| ? | **Safe and Sound** | London | Hook, J. | Oct. 18 | **Maid of the Mill** | London | Bishop, H. R. |
| **1810** | | | | Nov. 12 | **John of Paris** | London | Bishop, H. R. |
| Feb. 8 | **Free Knights** | London | Mazzinghi, J. | Nov. 29 | **Ninth Statue** | London | Horn, C. E. |
| Feb. 26 | **Hit or Miss!** | London | Smith, C. | ? | **Aethiop, The** | Philadelphia | Taylor, R. |
| Mar. 13 | **Maniac, The** | London | Bishop, H. R. | **1815** | | | |
| June 12 | **Oh, This Love** | London | King, M. | Feb. 1 | **Brother and Sister** | London | Reeve, W. |
| July 9 | **Tricks upon Travellers** | London | Horn, C. E. | Mar. 29 | **Unknown Guest** | London | Kelly, M. |
| Sept. 3 | **Plots, The** | London | King, M. | Apr. 7 | **Noble Outlaw** | London | Bishop, H. R. |
| Oct. 18 | **Bridal Ring** | London | Condell, H., Pelissier, V. | Apr. 28 | **Comus** | London | Bishop, H. R. |
| | | | | June 7 | **Telemachus** | London | Bishop, H. R. |
| ? | **Transformation** | London | Condell, H. | Aug. 1 | **My Aunt** | London | Addison, J. |
| **1811** | | | | Aug. 15 | **King's Proxy** | London | Cooke, T. S. |
| Jan. 15 | **Lady of the Lake** | Edinburgh | Francis, W. | Sept. 15 | **Magpie or the Maid** | London | Bishop, H. R. |
| Jan. 19 | **Bee-Hive** | London | Horn, C. E. | Nov. 20 | **Cymon** | London | Bishop/Arne |
| Jan. 24 | **Hamlet Travestie** | London | Bray, J. | **1816** | | | |
| Jan. 28 | **Alberto Albertini** | New York | Bray, J. | Jan. 17 | **Midsummer Night's Dream** | London | Bishop, H. R. |
| Feb. 5 | **Knight of Snowdoun** | London | Bishop, H. R. | Mar. 12 | **Guy Mannering** | London | Attwood/Bishop |
| Apr. 27 | **Americans, The** | London | Braham/King | Apr. 16 | **Who Wants a Wife?** | London | Bishop, H. R. |
| June 3 | **Council of Ten** | London | Reeve, W. | May 21 | **Oberon's Oath** | London | Parry, J. |
| June 10 | **Royal Oak** | London | Kelly, M. | Sept. 16 | **Free and Easy** | London | Addison, J. |
| June 21 | **Round Robin** | London | Dibdin, C. | Nov. 12 | **Slave, The** | London | Bishop, H. R. |
| Aug. 1 | **One O'Clock** | London | King, Kelly | **1817** | | | |
| Aug. 26 | **Boarding House** | London | Horn, C. E. | Jan. 18 | **Humorous Lieutenant** | London | Bishop, H. R. |
| Sept. 9 | **M.P.** | London | King, M. P. | Feb. 27 | **Heir of Vironi** | London | Bishop, H. R. |
| Nov. 6 | **Up to Town** | London | Reeve et al. | Apr. 17 | **Elphi Bey** | London | Attwood et al. |
| ? | **Peasant Boy** | London | Kelly, M. | May 20 | **Libertine, The** | London | Bishop, H. R. |
| **1812** | | | | June 7 | **Election, The** | London | Horn, C. |
| Jan. 31 | **Virgin of the Sun** | London | Bishop, H. R. | June 23 | **My Uncle** | London | Addison, J. |
| Mar. 7 | **Turn Out!** | London | King, M. P. | | | | |
| May 6 | **Devil's Bridge** | London | Horn, C. E. | | | | |
| July 22 | **Rich and Poor** | London | Horn, C. E. | | | | |

| Date | Title | City | Composer | Date | Title | City | Composer |
|------|-------|------|----------|------|-------|------|----------|
| July 26 | Wizard, The | London | Horn, C. E. | Nov. 5 | Cortez | London | Bishop, H. R. |
| Aug. 13 | Persian Hunters | London | Horn, C. E. | ? | Actors al fresco | London | Blewitt et al. |
| Sept. 29 | Duke of Savoy | London | Bishop, H. R. | ? | Snow Storm | Atlanta | Hewitt, J. |
| **1818** | | | | ? | Virgin of the Sun | Philadelphia | Gilfert, C. |
| Feb. 3 | Illustrious Traveller | London | ** | **1824** | | | |
| Feb. 21 | Zuma | London | Bishop/Braham | Jan. 13 | Philandering | London | Horn, C. E. |
| Mar. 12 | Rob Roy Macgregor | London | Davy, J. | Jan. 29 | Saw-Mill | New York | Hawkins, M. |
| Mar. 13 | Barber of Seville | London | Bishop, H. R. | Feb. 10 | Native Land | London | Bishop, H. R. |
| Apr. 21 | Amoroso | London | Cooke, T. S. | Feb. 20 | Merry Wives of Windsor | London | Horn et al. |
| May 16 | December and May | London | Bishop, H. R. | Mar. 1 | Waverly | London | Rodwell, G. |
| Sept. 23 | Burgomaster of Saardam | London | Bishop, H. R. | Aug. 10 | Alcaid, The | London | Nathan, I. |
| ? | Lalla Rookh | Dublin | Horn, C. E. | Nov. 10 | Freischütz, Der | London | Bishop, H. R. |
| * | Amilie | London (1837) | Rooke, W. | Nov. 26 | Frozen Lake | London | Reeve, G. |
| **1819** | | | | ? | Freischütz, Der | -- | ** |
| Mar. 6 | Marriage of Figaro | London | Bishop, H. R. | **1825** | | | |
| Apr. 17 | Heart of Midlothian | London | Bishop, H. R. | Jan. 19 | Fall of Algiers | London | Bishop, H. R. |
| Apr. 29 | Roland for an Oliver | London | Bishop, H. R. | Feb. 12 | Shepherd of Derwent Vale | London | Horn, C. E. |
| Dec. 11 | Comedy of Errors | ? | Bishop, H. R. | Feb. 17 | Masaniello | London | Bishop, H. R. |
| **1820** | | | | Apr. 4 | Abou Hassan | London | Cooke, T. S. |
| Jan. 25 | Antiquary, The | London | Bishop, H. R. | Apr. 22 | Cavern, The | London | Stevenson, J. |
| Mar. 2 | Ivanhoe | London | Parry, J. | Apr. 28 | Preciosa | London Hawes | Weber- |
| Apr. 23 | Henri Quatre | London | Bishop, H. R. | May 16 | Faustus | London | Bishop, H. R. |
| June 17 | David Rizzio | London | Braham et al. | July 6 | Broken Promises | London | Hawes, W. |
| July 20 | Woman's Will | London | Davy, J. | Oct. 7 | Forest Rose | New York | Davies, J. |
| May 3 | Lady and the Devil | London | Kelly, M. | Oct. 21 | Lilla | London | ** |
| May 22 | Battle of Bothwell Brigg | London | Bishop, H. R. | Oct. 28 | Wedding Present | London | Horn, C. E. |
| Nov. 28 | Justice | London | Horne, C. | * | Talisman, The | -- | Bishop, H. R. |
| **1821** | | | | **1826** | | | |
| Feb. 10 | Child of the Mountain | Philadelphia | Heinrich, A. | Jan. 28 | Malvina | London | Lee, G. A. |
| Feb. 20 | Don John | London | Bishop, H. R. | Mar. 16 | Benyowsky | London | King, M. |
| June 2 | Dirce | London | Horne, C. | Mar. 27 | Oberon | London | Cooke, T. |
| July 5 | Love's Dream | London | Moss, M. | Apr. 12 | Oberon | London | Weber |
| ? | Maid or Wife | London | Livius/Cooke | Apr. 29 | Aladdin | London | Bishop, H. R. |
| **1822** | | | | May 29 | Knights of the Cross | London | Bishop, H. R. |
| Jan. 15 | Pirate, The | London | Rooke, W. | July 10 | Rake's Progress | London | Whitaker, J. |
| Feb. 14 | Montrose | London | Bishop, H. R. | July 25 | Dead Fetch | London | Horn, C. E. |
| Feb. 23 | Veteran Soldier | London | Cooke, T. S. | Aug. 7 | Oracle, The | London | Winter-Hawes |
| May | Enterprise, The | Baltimore | Clifton, A. | Aug. 31 | Before Breakfast | London | Barnett, J. |
| May 11 | Law of Java | London | Bishop | Oct. 9 | White Lady | London | Cooke, T. S. |
| July 6 | Annette | Dublin | Horn, C. E. | Oct. 21 | Peveril of the Peak | London | Horn, C. E. |
| Aug. 26 | Family Jars | London | Perry, G. | Oct. 31 | Two Houses of Grenada | London | Wade, J. |
| Sept. 9 | Morning, Noon | London | Perry, G. | **1827** | | | |
| Dec. 3 | Maid Marian | London | Bishop, H. R. | Jan. 1 | Flying Dutchman | London | Rodwell, G. |
| ? | Deed of Gift | Boston | ** | Jan. 1 | Phantom Ship | London | Rodwell, G. |
| ? | Rose of Aragon | New York | Taylor, R. | Jan. 27 | Englishmen in India | London | Bishop, H. R. |
| **1823** | | | | Apr. 16 | Boy of Santillane | London | Blewitt/Cooke |
| May 8 | Clari | London | Bishop, H. R. | May 1 | Turkish Loves | London | Lacy, M. R. |
| July 7 | Sweethearts and Wives | London | Nathan, I. | July 2 | Cornish Miners | London | Rodwell, G. |
| | | | | July 9 | Pay to My Order | London | Horn, C. E. |

| DATE | TITLE | CITY | COMPOSER | DATE | TITLE | CITY | COMPOSER |
|------|-------|------|----------|------|-------|------|----------|
| July 12 | **Rencontre, The** | London | Bishop, H. R. | Oct. 27 | **Love Spell** | London | Horn, C. E. |
| Aug. 20 | **Freebooters, The** | London | Hawes, W. | Nov. 3 | **Fra Diavolo** | London | Lacy, M. R. |
| Oct. ? | **Illustrious Stranger** | London | Nathan, I. | Nov. 3 | **Love Charm** | London | Bishop, H. R. |
| **1828** | | | | **1832** | | | |
| Feb. 28 | **Invincibles, The** | London | Lee, G. A. | Jan. 11 | **My Own Lover** | London | Rodwell, G. |
| Mar. 17 | **Auld Robin Gray** | Surrey | Blewitt, J. | Feb. 9 | **Grana Uile** | Dublin | Penson, W. |
| Apr. 7 | **Talisman, The** | Surrey | Blewitt, J. | Feb. 20 | **Demon, The** | London | Bishop, H. R. |
| July 7 | **Bottle Imp** | London | Rodwell, G. | Feb. 21 | **Fiend-Father** | London | Lacy, M. R. |
| July 29 | **Tit for Tat** | London | Hawes, W. | Mar. 20 | **Alchymist, The** | London | Bishop, H. R. |
| Aug. 23 | **Not for Me** | London | Hawes, W. | May 8 | **Tyrolese Peasant** | London | Bishop, H. R. |
| Sept. 2 | **Sylvana** | London | Weber-Blewitt | June 18 | **Magic Fan** | London | Bishop, H. R. |
| Oct. 1 | **Mason of Buda** | London | Rodwell, G. | July 27 | **Bottle of Champagne** | London | Bishop, H. R. |
| Dec. 4 | **Love in Wrinkles** | London | Lacy, M. R. | Aug. 27 | **Sedan Chair** | London | Bishop, H. R. |
| Dec. 15 | **Earthquake, The** | London | Rodwell, G. | Oct. 29 | **Doom-Kiss** | London | Bishop, H. R. |
| ? | **New Don Juan!** | London | Rodwell, G. | Dec. 18 | **Win Her** | London | Barnett, J. |
| ? | **Sublime and the Beautiful** | London | Lee, G. A. | ? | **Climbing Boy** | London | Hawes, W. |
| ? | **Taming of the Shrew** | London | Braham, J. | **1833** | | | |
| **1829** | | | | Jan. 7 | **Don Quixote** | London | Rodwell, G. |
| Jan. 14 | **My Old Woman** | London | Blewitt, J. | Feb. 22 | **Israelites in Egypt** | London | Lacy, M. R. |
| Jan. 15 | **Nymph of the Grotto** | London | Lee, G. A. | Mar. 23 | **Coiners, The** | London | Lacy, M. R. |
| Feb. 5 | **Yelva** | London | Bishop, H. R. | Apr. 17 | **Magic Flute** | New York | Horn, C. E. |
| Mar. 7 | **Maid of Judah** | London | Lacy, M. R. | May 1 | **Sonnambula, La** | London | Bishop, H. R. |
| Mar. 10 | **Casket, The** | London | Lacy, M. R. | May 4 | **Soldier's Widow** | London | Barnett, J. |
| Mar. 19 | **Home, Sweet Home** | London | Bishop, H. R. | Sept. 9 | **Court Masque** | London | Dawes, W. |
| Apr. 9 | **Dido** | New York | Horn, C. E. | Nov. 13 | **Gustavus III** | London | Cooke, T. S. |
| Apr. 20 | **Devil's Elixir** | London | Rodwell, G. | **1834** | | | |
| Apr. 29 | **Quartette, The** | New York | Horn, C. E. | Apr. 1 | **Challenge, The** | London | Cooke, T. S. |
| May 4 | **Masaniello** | London | Cooke/Livius | June 9 | **Rural Felicity** | London | Bishop, H. R. |
| June | **Nothing Superfluous** | London | Lee, G. A. | July 21 | **Nourjahad** | London | Loder, E. |
| July 15 | **Robber's Bride** | London | Hawes, W. | Aug. 4 | **Dragon, The** | London | Lee, G. A. |
| Aug. 18 | **Spring Lock** | London | Rodwell, G. | Aug. 25 | **Mountain Sylph** | London | Barnett, J. |
| Oct. 10 | **Night before the Wedding** | London | Bishop, H. R | Oct. 2 | **Hermann** | London | Thomson, J. |
| **1830** | | | | Nov. 3 | **Genevieve** | London | Macfarren |
| Feb. 2 | **Robert the Devil** | London | Barnett, J. | Nov. 15 | **Red Mask** | London | Cooke, T. S. |
| Feb. 4 | **Ninetta** | London | Bishop, H. R. | Nov. 20 | **Lord of the Isles** | London | Rodwell, G. |
| Feb. 8 | **Teddy the Tiler** | London | Rodwell, G. | Dec. 15 | **Last Days of Pompeii** | London | Rodwell, G. |
| Apr. 13 | **Cinderella** | London | Lacy, M. R. | * | **Belshazzar's Feast** | London (1854, as Daniel) | Griesbach, J. |
| May 1 | **Hofer** | London | Bishop, H. R. | | | | |
| June 25 | **Under the Oak** | London | Bishop, H. R. | **1835** | | | |
| July 16 | **Skeleton Lover** | London | Rodwell, G. | Feb. 21 | **Lestocq** | London | Cooke, T. S. |
| July 23 | **Adelaide** | London | Bishop, H. R. | Apr. 20 | **Sadak and Kalasrade** | London | Packer, C. |
| July 29 | **Honest Frauds** | London | Horn, C. E. | Apr. 20 | **Shadow on the Wall** | London | Thomson, J. |
| Oct. 4 | **Black Vulture** | London | Rodwell, G. | June 8 | **Spirit of the Bell** | London | Rodwell, G. |
| Nov. 30 | **Catherine** | London | Burghersh, J. | Aug. 10 | **Covenanters, The** | London | Loder, E. J. |
| **1831** | | | | Sept. 14 | **Dice of Death** | London | Loder, E. J. |
| Feb. 1 | **Devil's Brother** | London | Lee, G. A. | Oct. 28 | **Paul Clifford** | London | Rodwell, G. |
| Feb. 3 | **Romance of a Day** | London | Bishop, H. R. | Oct. 29 | **Siege of Rochelle** | London | Balfe, M. |
| Aug. 4 | **Sorceress, The** | London | Ries, F. | Dec. 14 | **Agnes Sorel** | London | A' Beckett, M. |
| Aug. 18 | **Evil Eye** | London | Rodwell, G. | Dec. 14 | **Bronze Horse** | London | Rodwell, G. |
| | | | | ? | **Jewess, The** | London | Cooke, T. |
| | | | | * | **Minstrel, The** | -- | Heinrich, A. |

| DATE | TITLE | CITY | COMPOSER | DATE | TITLE | CITY | COMPOSER |
|------|-------|------|----------|------|-------|------|----------|
| **1836** | | | | Aug. 14 | **Geraldine** | London | Balfe, M. |
| Feb. 2 | **Quasimodo** | London | Rodwell, G. | Nov. 27 | **Bohemian Girl** | London | Balfe, M. |
| May 26 | **Maid of Artois** | London | Balfe, M. | **1844** | | | |
| June 13 | **Sexton of Cologne** | London | Rodwell, G. | Mar. 2 | **Pasqual Bruno** | Vienna | Hatton, J. L. |
| Sept. 8 | **Pacha's Bridal** | London | Romer, F. | Apr. 8 | **Drama at Home** | London | Reed, T. G. |
| Nov. 8 | **Siege of Corinth** | London | Cooke, T. S. | Apr. 22 | **Brides of Venice** | London | Benedict, J. |
| Dec. 6 | **Village Coquettes** | London | Hullah, J. | May 27 | **Currency Lass** | Sydney | ** |
| ? | **Thalaba** | London | Rodwell, G. | Sept. 30 | **Enchanted Horse** | New York | Jones, J. |
| **1837** | | | | Nov. 20 | **Castle of Aymon** | London | Balfe, M. |
| Feb. 28 | **Fair Rosamond** | London | Barnett, J. | Nov. 27 | **Daughter of St. Mark** | London | Balfe, M. |
| Mar. 13 | **Postillion of Longjumeau** | London | Stansbury, G | **1845** | | | |
| May 27 | **Catherine Grey** | London | Balfe, M. | Mar. 24 | **Golden Fleece** | London | Reed, T. G. |
| Oct. 7 | **Child of the Wreck** | London | Cooke, T. S. | May 14 | **Enchantress, The** | London | Balfe, M. |
| Oct. 19 | **Afrancesado, The** | London | Lee, G. A. | June 4 | **Leonora** | Philadelphia | Fry, W. |
| Nov. 11 | **Barbers of Bassora** | London | Hullah, J. | Oct. 18 | **Fairy Oak** | London | Forbes, H. |
| Nov. 30 | **Joan of Arc** | London | Balfe, M. | Oct. 28 | **Who's the Composer?** | London | Reed, T. G. |
| **1838** | | | | Nov. 15 | **Maritana** | London | Wallace, V. |
| Apr. 19 | **Gipsy's Warning** | London | Benedict, J. | ? | **Graciosa** | London | ** |
| May 17 | **Diadesté** | London | Balfe, M. | **1846** | | | |
| May 17 | **Outpost, The** | London | Hullah, J. | Feb. 3 | **Adventure of Don Quixote** | London | Macfarren, G. |
| July 7 | **Rob of the Fens** | London | Romer, F. | Feb. 26 | **Crusaders, The** | London | Benedict, J. |
| Aug. 13 | **Devil's Opera** | London | Macfarren, G. | July 15 | **Wonderful Water Cure** | London | Reed, T. G. |
| Oct. 19 | **Foresters, The** | London | Loder, E. | Oct. 28 | **Night Dancers** | London | Loder, E. J. |
| Nov. 6 | **Francis the First** | London | Loder, E. J. | Nov. 9 | **Loretta** | London | Lavenu, L. |
| Dec. 3 | **Guillaume Tell** | London | Bishop, H. R. | Dec. 11 | **Bondman, The** | London | Balfe, M. |
| ? | **Windsor Castle** | London | Griesbach, J. | Dec. 19 | **Seven Maids of Munich** | London | Rodwell, G. |
| **1839** | | | | ? | **Magic Horn** | London | Lee, G. A. |
| Feb. 8 | **Farinelli** | London | Barnett, J. | **1847** | | | |
| May 2 | **Henrique** | London | Rooke, W. | Jan. 27 | **Rival Clans** | Newcastle | Deval, H. |
| Oct. 26 | **Fairy Lake** | London | Lee, G. A. | Feb. 22 | **Matilda of Hungary** | London | Wallace, V. |
| Oct. 28 | **Jack Sheppard** | London | Rodwell, G. | May 7 | **Don John of Austria** | Sydney | Nathan, I. |
| **1840** | | | | Dec. 20 | **Maid of Honour** | London | Balfe, M. |
| Feb. 12 | **Fortunate Isles** | London | Bishop, H. R. | **1848** | | | |
| Oct. 12 | **Ahmed al Ramel** | London | Horn, C. E. | Dec. 6 | **Quentin Durward** | London | Laurent, H. |
| Dec. 1 | **Fridolin** | London | Romer, F. | Dec. 6 | **Robin Goodfellow** | London | Loder, E. J. |
| ? | **Triboulet** | London | Nathan, I. | **1849** | | | |
| **1841** | | | | Jan. 18 | **Marie** | London | Loder, E. J. |
| Mar. 9 | **Keolanthe** | London | Balfe, M. | Apr. 18 | **Heart of Midlothian** | London | ** |
| Apr. 12 | **Deer Stalkers** | London | Loder, E. J. | Oct. 27 | **King Charles II** | London | Macfarren, G. |
| Apr. 19 | **Arcadia** | London | Harroway, J. | **1850** | | | |
| Apr. 22 | **Paddy Whack in Italia** | London | Lover, S. | Nov. 15 | **Sleeper Awakened** | London | Macfarren, G. |
| June 14 | **Queen of a Day** | London | Fitzwilliam, E. | **1852** | | | |
| **1842** | | | | Mar. 6 | **Sicilian Bride** | London | Balfe, M. |
| Feb. 25 | **Queen of the Thames** | London | Hatton, J. L. | July 26 | **Devil's in It** | London | Balfe, M. |
| May 4 | **Mock Catalani** | Sydney | Nagel, C. | Sept. 27 | **Uncle Tom's Cabin** | Troy, NY | Howard, G. |
| May 23 | **Maid of Saxony** | New York | Horn, C. E. | * | **Wittikind and His Brothers** | -- | ** |
| Aug. | **Little Red Riding Hood** | London | A'Beckett, M. | **1853** | | | |
| **1843** | | | | Mar. 11 | **Flower Queen** | New York | Root, G. F. |
| May 29 | **Merry Freaks** | Sydney | Nathan, I. | | | | |

| Date | Title | City | Composer |
|------|-------|------|----------|
| Nov. 17 | Love's Alarms | London | Fitzwilliam, E. |
| **1854** | | | |
| May 29 | Berta | London | Smart, H. |
| * | Pilgrim Fathers | -- | Root, G. F. |
| **1855** | | | |
| Apr. 14 | Raymond and Agnes | Man | Loder, E. J. |
| May 16 | Mephistopheles | Surrey | Lutz, M. |
| Sept. 27 | Rip van Winkle | New York | Bristow, G. |
| **1857** | | | |
| Oct. 29 | Rose of Castille | London | Balfe, M. |
| **1858** | | | |
| Aug. 23 | Ten Nights in a Bar-Room | New York | Pratt, W. W. |
| **1859** | | | |
| Feb. 14 | Zaida | Liverpool | Lutz, M. |
| Dec. 19 | Victorine | London | Mellon, A. |
| **1860** | | | |
| Jan. 10 | Haymakers, The | Chicago | Root, G. F. |
| Feb. 2 | Romance | London | Leslie, H. |
| Feb. 4 | Garibaldi | London | Cowen, F. |
| Feb. 23 | Lurline | London | Wallace, V. |
| Feb. ? | Out of Sight | London | Clay, F. |
| Oct. 11 | Robin Hood | London | Macfarren |
| Dec. 6 | Bianca | London | Balfe, M. |
| Dec. 6 | Satanella | London | Balfe, M. |
| ? | Follies of a Night | London | Gabriel, V. |
| * | Belshazzar's Feast | -- | Root, G. F. |
| **1861** | | | |
| Feb. 28 | Amber Witch | London | Wallace, V. |
| Oct. 24 | Ruy Blas | London | Glover, W. |
| Nov. 19 | Toy-Maker | London | Linley, G. |
| Nov. 30 | Puritan's Daughter | London | Balfe, M. |
| **1862** | | | |
| Feb. 8 | Lily of Killarney | London | Benedict, J. |
| Mar. 22 | Court and Cottage | London | Clay, F. |
| Apr. 7 | Doctor of Alcantara | | Eichberg, J. |
| May ? | Pesceballo, Il | Boston | Child, F. J. |
| Nov. 3 | Love's Triumph | London | Wallace, V. |
| Dec. 6 | Law Versus Love | London | Linley, G. |
| **1863** | | | |
| Feb. 12 | Armourer of Nantes | London | Balfe, M. |
| Mar. 3 | Vivandiere, La | Augusta, GA | Hewitt, J. H. |
| Oct. 12 | Desert Flower | London | Wallace, V. |
| Nov. 2 | Jessy Lea | London | Macfarren, G. |
| Nov. 21 | Blanche de Nevers | London | Balfe, M. |
| **1864** | | | |
| Feb. 11 | She Stoops to Conquer | London | Macfarren, G. |
| Feb. 11 | Soldier's Legacy | London | Macfarren, G. |
| May 4 | Notre-Dame of Paris | Philadelphia | Fry, W. |

| Date | Title | City | Composer |
|------|-------|------|----------|
| Sept. 8 | Sleeping Queen | London | Balfe, M. |
| Nov. 3 | Helvellyn | London | Macfarren, G. |
| Nov. 26 | Rose, The | London | Hatton, J. L. |
| Dec. 3 | Bride of Song | London | Benedict, J. |
| **1865** | | | |
| Jan. 23 | Constance | London | Clay, F. |
| Feb. 9 | River-Sprite | London | Mori, F. |
| Oct. 21 | Castle Grim | London | Allen, G. |
| Oct. 23 | Felix | London | Lutz, M. |
| Nov. 15 | Ida | London | Leslie, H. |
| ? | Windsor Castle | London | Musgrave, F. |
| **1866** | | | |
| June 2 | Bluebeard Repaired | London | Tully, J. H. |
| Sept. 12 | Black Crook | New York | ** |
| Dec. 29 | Dulcamara | London | ** |
| **1867** | | | |
| Apr. 13 | Sapphire Necklace | London | Sullivan, A. S. |
| May 11 | Cox and Box | London | Sullivan, A. S. |
| June 15 | Viandière, La | Liverpool | Wallerstein, F. |
| Dec. 18 | Contrabandista, The | London | Sullivan, A. S. |
| Dec. 26 | Caliph of Bagdad | London | Musgrave, F. |
| **1868** | | | |
| Mar. 5 | Two Cadis | Boston | Eichberg, J. |
| **1869** | | | |
| Mar. 29 | No Cards | London | "Elliott, L." |
| Nov. 26 | Ages Ago | London | Clay, F. |
| **1870** | | | |
| May 26 | Gentleman in Black | London | Clay, F. |
| June 20 | Our Island Home | London | Reed, T. |
| * | Antoni | Oxford | Pratt, S. |
| **1871** | | | |
| June 14 | Letty Basket-Maker | London | Balfe, M. |
| June 20 | In Possession | London | Clay, F. |
| Dec. 26 | Thespis | London | Sullivan, A. |
| Dec. 30 | Sensation Novel | London | Reed, T. G. |
| **1872** | | | |
| Feb. 7 | Charity Begins at Home | London | Cellier, A. |
| Oct. 28 | Happy Arcadia | London | Clay, F. |
| Dec. 23 | Black Crook | London | Clay, F. |
| **1873** | | | |
| Feb. 16 | Oriana | London | Clay, F. |
| May 5 | Mildred's Well | London | Reed, T. G. |
| **1874** | | | |
| May 17 | He's Coming | London | Reed, T. G. |
| June 24 | One Too Many | London | Cowen, F. |
| July 27 | Evangeline | New York | Rice, E. E. |
| Aug. 17 | Cattarina | Man | Clay, F. |
| Sept. 11 | Africanus Blue Beard | Gloucester, MA | Sedgwick, A. |

| Date | Title | City | Composer |
|---|---|---|---|
| Oct. 16 | Sultan of Mocha | Manchester | Cellier, A. |
| Dec. 16 | Three Tenants | London | Reed, T. G. |

**1875**

| Date | Title | City | Composer |
|---|---|---|---|
| Jan. 25 | Ancient Britons | London | Reed, T. G. |
| Mar. 25 | Trial by Jury | London | Sullivan, A. S. |
| June 5 | Zoo, The | London | Sullivan, A. S. |
| July 5 | Eyes and No Eyes | London | Reed, T. G. |
| Oct. 4 | Tower of Man | London | Cellier, A. |
| Nov. 1 | Spanish Bond | London | Reed, T. G. |
| ? | Leap Year | New York | Sedgwick, A. |
| ? | Queerest Courtship | Chicago? | Sedgwick, A. |

**1876**

| Date | Title | City | Composer |
|---|---|---|---|
| Feb. 28 | Indian Puzzle | London | Reed, T. G. |
| Mar. 20 | Out of Bondage | Lynn, MA | ** |
| June 9 | Wicked Duke | London | Reed, T. G. |
| June 26 | Princess Toto | Nottingham | Clay, F. |
| July 21 | Gambrinus | Jackson, MI | Sedgwick, A. |
| Sept. 25 | Don Quixote | London | Clay, F. |
| Nov. 6 | Matched and Mated | London | Reed, T. G. |
| Nov. 22 | Pauline | London | Cowen, F. |
| ? | Circumstances Alter Cases | NY? | Sedgwick, A. |
| ? | Estranged | NY? | Sedgwick, A. |
| ? | My Walking Photograph | Chicago? | Sedgwick, A. |
| ? | Sold Again | NY? | Sedgwick, A. |
| ? | Twin Sisters | NY? | Sedgwick, A. |

**1877**

| Date | Title | City | Composer |
|---|---|---|---|
| Feb. 12 | Night's Surprise | London | Reed, T. G. |
| May 7 | No. 204 | London | Reed, T. G. |
| Nov. 17 | Sorcerer, The | London | Sullivan, A. S. |

**1878**

| Date | Title | City | Composer |
|---|---|---|---|
| May 25 | H.M.S. Pinafore | London | Sullivan, A. S. |
| Oct. 16 | Nell Gwynne | Manchester | Cellier, A. |

**1879**

| Date | Title | City | Composer |
|---|---|---|---|
| Jan. 8 | Morte d'Arthur | London | Corder, F. |
| Jan. 13 | Mulligan Guard | New York | Braham, D. |
| Sept. 25 | Sleepy Hollow | New York | Maretzek, M. |
| Nov. 7 | Light of the Harem | London | Thomas, A. G. |
| Dec. 8 | Peculiar Sam | Boston | ** |
| Dec. 31 | Pirates of Penzance | London | Sullivan, A. S. |

**1880**

| Date | Title | City | Composer |
|---|---|---|---|
| Oct. 11 | Deseret | New York | Buck, D. |
| ? | Deserted Village | London | Glover, J. |

**1881**

| Date | Title | City | Composer |
|---|---|---|---|
| Jan. 10 | Masque of Pandora | Boston | Cellier, A. |
| Feb. 6 | Veiled Prophet of Khorassan | Hanover | Stanford, C. |
| Apr. 1 | Vercingetorix | Sydney | Kowalski, H. |
| Apr. 23 | Patience | London | Sullivan, A. S. |

**1882**

| Date | Title | City | Composer |
|---|---|---|---|
| Jan. 22 | Moro | London | Balfe, M. |
| Apr. 1 | Widow, The | Springfield, IL | Lavallée, C. |
| Mar. 25 | Smugglers, The | Philadelphia | Sousa, J. P. |
| May 3 | Wicklow Rose | Manchester | Allen, G. B. |
| May 27 | Wreck of the Pinafore | London | Searelle, L. |
| June 15 | Zenobia | New York | Pratt, S. G. |
| July 22 | Vicar of Bray | London | Solomon, E. |
| Nov. 25 | Iolanthe | London | Sullivan, A. S. |
| ? | Lord Bateman | London | Solomon, E. |
| ? | Uncle Tom's Cabin | Philadelphia | Florio, C. |

**1883**

| Date | Title | City | Composer |
|---|---|---|---|
| Mar. 6 | Victorian | London | Edwards, J. |
| Mar. 21 | Cymbia | London | Pascal, F. |
| Mar. 26 | Esmeralda | London | Thomas, A. |
| Mar. 26 | Fortunio | Philadelphia | Darley, F. |
| Apr. 9 | Colomba | London | Mackenzie |
| Apr. 17 | Royal Word | London | de Lara, I. |
| Apr. 23 | Merry Duchess | London | Clay, F. |
| Dec. | Cinderella | Harrow, Eng | Farmer, J. |
| Dec. 3 | Golden Ring | London | Clay, F. |
| ? | Moustique | Brussels | Kowalski, H. |
| ? | Salem Witch | Boston | Stahl, R. |
| ? | Single Married Man | New York? | Sedgwick, A. |
| ? | Uncle Tom's Cabin | New York | Millard, H. |

**1884**

| Date | Title | City | Composer |
|---|---|---|---|
| Jan. 5 | Princess Ida | London | Sullivan, A. S. |
| Apr. 18 | Savonarola | Hamburg | Stanford, C. |
| Apr. 28 | Pilgrims, The | London | Stanford, C. |
| May 1 | Désirée | Washington | Sousa, J. P. |

**1885**

| Date | Title | City | Composer |
|---|---|---|---|
| Jan. ? | Little Tycoon | Philadelphia | Spenser, W. |
| Mar. 14 | Mikado, The | London | Sullivan, A. S. |
| Apr. 16 | Nadeshda | London | Thomas, A. |
| * (ca.) | Charter Oak | -- | Leavitt, B. |
| * | Montezuma | -- | Gleason, F. |

**1886**

| Date | Title | City | Composer |
|---|---|---|---|
| June 8 | Guillem the Troubadour | London | Mackenzie, A. |
| Sept. 25 | Dorothy | London | Cellier, A. |
| Oct. 23 | Uncle Tom's Cabin | Manchester, NH | Tracy, G. |
| ? | Minna | London | de Lara, I. |

**1887**

| Date | Title | City | Composer |
|---|---|---|---|
| Jan. 22 | Ruddigore | London | Sullivan, A. S. |
| Jan. 26 | Nordisa | Liverpool | Corder, F. |
| Jan. 27 | Conspiracy of Pontiac | Detroit | Mayer, C. |
| Mar. 14 | Lucille | Chicago | Pratt, S. |
| Nov. 21 | Begum, The | New York | De Koven, R. |
| * | Priscilla | -- | Gerrish-Jones. A. |

**1888**

| Date | Title | City | Composer |
|---|---|---|---|
| Sept. 27 | Carina | London | Woolf, J. |
| Oct. 3 | Yeomen of the Guard | London | Sullivan, A. S. |

| DATE | TITLE | CITY | COMPOSER |
|------|-------|------|----------|
| **1889** | | | |
| Apr. 20 | **Doris** | London | Cellier, A. |
| June 23 | **Sea King** | New York | Stahl, R. |
| July 11 | **Leo the Royal Cadet** | Kingston, ON | Telgmann, O. |
| Nov. 18 | **Don Quixote** | Boston | De Koven, R. |
| Nov. 25 | **Dante and Beatrice** | London | Philpot, S. R. |
| Dec. 7 | **Gondoliers, The** | London | Sullivan, A. S. |
| * | **Serâpis** | -- | Buck, D. |
| **1890** | | | |
| Apr. 22 | **Thorgrim** | London | Cowen, F. |
| June 9 | **Joan** | London | Ford, E. |
| June 9 | **Robin Hood** | Chicago | De Koven, R. |
| Aug. 18 | **Merry Monarch** | New York | Sousa, J. P. |
| * | **Irmelin** | Oxford (1953) | Delius, F. |
| **1891** | | | |
| Jan. 15 | **Knight of the Leopard** | London | Balfe, M. |
| Jan. 31 | **Ivanhoe** | London | Sullivan, A. S. |
| June 30 | **Nautch Girl** | London | Solomon, E. |
| Dec. 29 | **Reilly and the 400** | New York | Braham, D. |
| * | **American Volunteer** | Yankton, SD (1981) | Vinatieri, F. |
| * (ca.) | **Frogs of Windham** | Windham, CT (1983) | Leavitt, B. E. |
| **1892** | | | |
| Jan. 4 | **Mountebanks, The** | London | Cellier, A. |
| Apr. 14 | **Jupiter** | New York | Edwards, J. |
| June 6 | **Puritania** | Boston | Kelley, E. S. |
| June 11 | **Light of Asia** | London | de Lara, I. |
| July 12 | **Caedmar** | London | Bantock, G. |
| July 27 | **Haste to the Wedding** | London | Grossmith, L. |
| Sept. 10 | **Wedding Eve** | London | Ford, E. |
| Sept. 24 | **Haddon Hall** | London | Sullivan, A. S. |
| Oct. 10 | **Triumph of Columbus** | New York | Pratt, S. |
| Nov. 14 | **Fencing Master** | New York | De Koven, R. |
| Dec. 8 | **Irmengarda** | London | Bach, L. E. |
| ? | **Fayette** | Brisbane? | Allen, G. B. |
| * | **Crichton** | -- | Maclean, A. |
| * | **Eugene Aram** | -- | Bantock, G. |
| **1893** | | | |
| Jan. 19 | **Magic Opal** | London | Albéniz, I. |
| Jan. 26 | **Friend Fritz** | New York | Edwards, J. |
| Feb. 7 | **Lansdown Castle** | Cheltenham | Holst, G. |
| Feb. 9 | **Ephelia** | Denver | Freeman, H. |
| Feb. 15 | **Golden Web** | Liverpool | Thomas, A. |
| May 3 | **Jane Annie** | London | Ford, E. |
| May 29 | **Knickerbockers** | New York | De Koven, R. |
| July 20 | **Amy Robsart** | London | de Lara, I. |
| Sept. | **Martyr, The** | Denver | Freeman, H. |
| Oct. 7 | **Utopia Limited** | London | Sullivan, A. S. |
| Oct. 26 | **Algerian, The** | Philadelphia | De Koven, R. |

| DATE | TITLE | CITY | COMPOSER |
|------|-------|------|----------|
| Nov. 12 | **Signa** | Milan | Cowen, F. |
| Nov. 22 | **King Rene's Daughter** | New York | Edwards, J. |
| ? | **Quentin Durward** | London | Maclean, A. |
| * | **Magic Fountain** | London (1977) | Delius, F. |
| * | **Maid of Plymouth** | -- | Thorne, T. P. |
| **1894** | | | |
| Jan. 29 | **Tabasco** | Boston | Chadwick, G. |
| July 31 | **Madeline** | New York | Edwards, J. |
| Oct. 29 | **Rob Roy** | New York | De Koven, R. |
| Nov. 15 | **Jeanie Deans** | Edinburgh | MacCunn, H. |
| Dec. 12 | **Chieftain, The** | London | Sullivan, A. S. |
| ? | **His Excellency** | London | Carr, F. O. |
| ? | **Pearl of Iran** | Leipzig | Bantock, G. |
| **1895** | | | |
| Apr. 1 | **Daphne** | New York | Bird, A. |
| May 7 | **Zaporogues, The** | Birmingham | Davis, J. |
| May 16 | **Tzigane** | New York | De Koven, R. |
| June 8 | **Harold** | London | Cowen, F. |
| June 13 | **Woodlanders** | St Louis | Paulus, S. |
| June 29 | **Petruccio** | London | Maclean, A. |
| Aug. 12 | **Sylvia** | Cardiff | Parry, J. |
| Nov. 4 | **Wizard of the Nile** | New York | Herbert, V. |
| * | **Gentleman Joe** | -- | Slaughter, W. |
| * | **Koanga** | London (1899) | Delius, F. |
| * | **Revoke, The** | -- | Holst, G. |
| **1896** | | | |
| Feb. 10 | **Scarlet Letter** | Boston | Damrosch, W. |
| Feb. 26 | **Goddess of Truth** | New York | Edwards, J. |
| Mar. 2 | **Shamus O'Brien** | London | Stanford, C. |
| Mar. 7 | **Grand Duke** | London | Sullivan, A. S. |
| Apr. 13 | **Capitan, El** | Boston | Sousa, J. P. |
| Apr. 20 | **Lady of Longford** | London | Bach, L. E. |
| Apr. 25 | **Geisha, The** | London | Jones, S. |
| May 18 | **On the March** | Sheffield, Eng. | Clay, F. |
| Oct. 19 | **Brian Boru** | New York | Edwards, J. |
| Nov. 2 | **Mandarin, The** | New York | De Koven, R. |
| ? | **French Maid** | London | Slaughter, W. |
| ? | **Merry Benedicts** | Brooklyn, NY | Arnold, M. |
| ? | **Prodigal Son** | Liverpool? | Nicholls, F. |
| ? | **Whipping Boy** | Wellington | Hill, A. |
| * | **Magic Mirror** | -- | Holst, G. |
| **1897** | | | |
| Feb. 20 | **His Majesty** | London | Mackenzie, A. |
| Apr. 8 | **Wedding Day** | New York | Edwards, J. |
| May 25 | **Rip Van Winkle** | Providence, RI | Jordan, J. |
| Sept. 14 | **Paris Doll** | Hartford | De Koven, R. |

| DATE | TITLE | CITY | COMPOSER | DATE | TITLE | CITY | COMPOSER |
|---|---|---|---|---|---|---|---|
| Sept. 20 | Idols' Eye | Troy, NY | Herbert, V. | June 30 | African Kraal | Chicago | Freeman, H. |
| Oct. 23 | Diarmid | London | MacCunn, H. | Aug. 3 | Sarrona | Bruges | Howland, W. |
| Dec. 13 | Highwayman, The | New York | De Koven, R. | Oct. 17 | Duchess of Dantzic | London | Caryll, I. |
| Dec. 27 | Bride Elect | New Haven | Sousa, J. P. | Nov. 9 | Red Feather | New York | De Koven, R. |
| ? | 'Prentice Pillar | London | Somerville, R. | Nov. 22 | Cross and the Crescent | London | MacAlpin, C. |
| | | | | Dec. 7 | Muirgheis | Dublin? | Butler, O'B. |
| **1898** | | | | ? | Columbus | St. Louis | Moore, H. |
| May 28 | Beauty Stone | London | Sullivan, A. S. | ? | Guest of Honor | St. Louis | Joplin, S. |
| July 25 | Red Spider | Lowestoft, Eng | Drysdale, L. | **1904** | | | |
| Aug. 29 | Charlatan | Montreal | Sousa, J. P. | Apr. 29 | King's Prize | London | MacLean, A. |
| Sept. 14 | Fortune Teller | Toronto | Herbert, V. | ? | Spanish Student | London | Bath, H. |
| ? | Zuluki | Cleveland | Freeman, H. | ? | Don Quixote | Sydney | Hill, A. |
| * | Azara (1903, NY) | -- | Paine, J. K. | * | Octoroon, The | -- | Freeman, H. |
| * | Idea, The | -- | Holst, G. | **1905** | | | |
| **1899** | | | | June 26 | Moorish Maid | Auckland | Hill, A. |
| Jan. 7 | Lucky Star | London | Caryll, I. | Dec. | Hippolytus | Glasgow | Drysdale, L. |
| Feb. 2 | Economites | Sewickley, PA | Nevin, A. | ? | Free Lance | Philadelphia | Sousa, J. P. |
| Sept. 11 | Cyrano de Bergerac | Montreal | Herbert, V. | * | Uncle Remus | -- | Gilbert, H. F. |
| Oct. 9 | Ameer, The | Scranton, PA | Herbert, V. | **1906** | | | |
| Oct. 21 | San Toy | London | Jones, S. | Jan. 31 | Pipe of Desire | Boston | Converse, F. |
| Oct. 27 | Royal Vagrants | London | Warner, H. | Feb. 2 | Abyssinia | New York | Cook, W. M. |
| Nov. 29 | Rose of Persia | London | Sullivan, A. S. | Mar. 1 | Greysteel | Sheffield, Eng | Gatty, N. |
| * | Sita | -- | Holst, G. | June 20 | See-See | London | Jones, S. |
| **1900** | | | | Aug. 31 | White Chrysanthemum | London | Talbot, H. |
| Feb. 12 | Viceroy, The | San Francisco | Herbert, V. | Nov. 11 | Wreckers, The | Leipzig | Smyth, E. |
| Feb. 13 | Masque of War and Peace | London | MacCunn, H. | * | Alice in Wonderland | -- | Slaughter, W. |
| Mar. 31 | Lady Dolly | Sydney | Hill, A. | * | King Hal | -- | Stewart, H. |
| May 7 | Phyllis | New York | Warren, R. | **1907** | | | |
| Nov. 5 | Foxy Quiller | New York | De Koven, R. | Jan. 16 | Poia | Pittsburgh | Cadman, C. |
| ? | Nada | Cleveland | Freeman, H. | Feb. 21 | Village Romeo and Juliet | Berlin | Delius, F. |
| **1901** | | | | Apr. 18 | Tom Jones | London | German, E. |
| Apr. 27 | Emerald Isle | London | Sullivan, A. S. | June 4 | Otho Visconti | Chicago | Gleason, F. |
| May 30 | Much Ado about Nothing | London | Stanford, C. | Nov. 18 | Girls of Holland | New York | De Koven, R. |
| Sept. 26 | Judith | Worcester, MA | Chadwick, G. | Sept. 3 | King of Cadonia | London | Lonsdale, F. |
| Nov. 14 | Ib and Little Christina | London | Leoni, F. | Oct. 12 | Golden Butterfly | New York | De Koven, R. |
| ? | Dolly Varden | London | Edwards, J. | Nov. 23 | Patriot, The | New York | Edwards, J. |
| * | Romeo and Juliet | -- | Shelley, H. | * | Pageant of Darkness and Light | -- | MacCunn, H. |
| **1902** | | | | **1909** | | | |
| Jan. 27 | Maid Marian | New York | De Koven, R. | Jan. 27 | Angelus, The | London | Naylor, E. |
| Apr. 2 | Merrie England | London | German, E. | Apr. 4 | Safié | Mainz, Ger | Hadley, H. |
| Apr. 9 | Forest, The | Berlin | Smyth, E. | May 21 | Hoshi-San | Philadelphia | Leps, W. |
| June 12 | Puritans, The | St. Louis | Moore, H. | Sept. 29 | Mountaineers, The | London | Somerville, R. |
| Dec. 15 | Maid of Cefn Ydfa | Cardiff | Parry, J. | Nov. 11 | Pierrot and Pierrette | London | Holbrooke, J. |
| * | Youth's Choice | -- | Holst, G. | Dec. 15 | Fallen Fairies | London | German, E. |
| **1903** | | | | Dec. 16 | Duke or Devil | Manchester | Gatty, N. |
| Feb. 16 | Nancy Brown | New York | Hadley, H. | ? | Don Quixote | London | Hewitt, T. J. |
| Feb. 16 | Tapu | Wellington | Hill, A. | * | Birth of Arthur | Glastonbury (1920) | Boughton, R. |
| Feb. 18 | In Dahomey | New York | Cook, W. M. | * | Fionn and Terra | -- | Drysdale, L. |
| Mar. 14 | My Lady Molly | London | Jones, S. | * | Land of the Misty Water | -- | Cadman, C. |

| Date | Title | City | Composer | Date | Title | City | Composer |
|------|-------|------|----------|------|-------|------|----------|
| **1910** | | | | **1915** | | | |
| July 23 | Summer's Night | London | Clutsam, G. | July 1 | Fairyland | London | Parker, H. |
| Oct. 24 | Naughty Marietta | Syracuse | Herbert, V. | Aug. 11 | Oithona | Glastonbury | Bainton, E. |
| Oct. 27 | Love Laughs at Locksmiths | Portsmouth, ME | Breil, J. C. | Dec. 28 | Bethlehem | Street, Eng | Boughton, R. |
| | | | | Dec. 28 | Everyman | London | Lehmann, L. |
| * | Lancelot and Elaine | -- | Sessions, R. | ? | Enchanter, The | Chicago | Holbrooke, J. |
| **1911** | | | | ? | Pippa's Holiday | Paris | Beach, J. P. |
| Feb. 25 | Natoma | Philadelphia | Herbert, V. | * | Riders to the Sea | -- | Hart, F. |
| Feb. 26 | Old Black Joe | New York | Shelley, H | * | Vision of Ariel | Chicago (1955) | Saminsky, L. |
| Mar. 3 | Sacrifice, The | Boston | Converse, F. | | | | |
| Mar. 13 | Pink Lady | New York | Caryll, I. | **1916** | | | |
| May | Tryst, The | New York | Freeman, H. | Jan. 7 | Romeo and Juliet | Middles-brough, Eng | Barkworth, J. |
| Dec. 25 | Wedding Trip | New York | De Koven, R. | Jan. 14 | Critic, The | London | Stanford, C. |
| * | Treemonisha | New York (1915) | Joplin, S. | Jan. 15 | Lover's Knot | Chicago | Bucharoff, S. |
| | | | | Jan. 28 | Boatswain's Mate | London | Smyth, E. |
| **1912** | | | | Aug. 14 | Round Table | Glastonbury | Boughton, R. |
| Jan. 30 | Pygmalion | Dublin | Houseley, H. | Aug. 15 | Sumida River | Glastonbury | Raybould, C. |
| Mar. 5 | Olaf | London | Kirkpatrick, H. | Dec. 5 | Sāvitri | London | Holst, G. |
| Mar. 14 | Mona | New York | Parker, H. | * | Athalia | -- | Freeman, H. |
| May 4 | Stella | Sydney | Marshall-Hall, G. | * | Deirdre of the Sorrows | -- | Hart, F. |
| Apr. 22 | Narcissa | Seattle | Moore, M. | * | Tigers, The | London (1976) | Brian, H. |
| June 15 | Children of Don | London | Holbrooke, J. | | | | |
| Aug. 10 | Atonement of Pan | Philadelphia | Hadley, H. | **1917** | | | |
| Oct. 15 | Dove of Peace | Philadelphia | Damrosch, W. | Feb. 9 | Snow Queen | San Francisco | Gerrish-Jones, A. |
| Dec. 14 | Romeo and Juliet | London | Marshall-Hall, G. | Feb. 16 | Louis XIV | St. Louis | Moore, H. |
| ? | Prophecy, The | ? | Freeman, H. | Mar. 8 | Canterbury Pilgrims | New York | De Koven, R. |
| * | Immigrants, The | -- | Converse, F. | May 18 | Blue Wing | Seattle | Tonning, G. |
| * | Leper, The | -- | Moore, M. | July 7 | Ruth and Naomi | Melbourne | Hart, F. |
| * | Padrone, The | Waterbury, CT (1995) | Chadwick, G. | Aug. 4 | Land of Happiness | San Francisco | Redding, J. |
| | | | | Aug. 18 | Building of Bamba | Halcyon, CA | Cowell, H. |
| **1913** | | | | Dec. 15 | Rajah of Shivapore | Sydney | Hill, A. |
| Feb. 20 | Sun Dance | Vernal, UT | Hanson, W. | Dec. 26 | Azora | Chicago | Hadley, H. |
| Feb. 27 | Cyrano | New York | Damrosch, W. | ? | Osseo | Brookline, MA | Noyes-Greene, E. |
| Nov. 1 | All in a Garden Fair | Seattle | Tonning, G. | | | | |
| Nov. 1 | Joan of Arc | London | Rôze, R. | **1918** | | | |
| Dec. 4 | Westward Ho! | London | Miles, P. N. | Jan. 5 | Daughter of the Forest | Chicago | Nevin, A. |
| ? | Professor Tattle | New York | Breil, J. C. | Mar. 23 | Shanewis | New York | Cadman, C. |
| * | Merrymount | -- | Smith, D. S. | Apr. 23 | Moon Maiden | Glastonbury | Boughton, R. |
| | | | | May 2 | Rose of Destiny | Philadelphia | Heckscher |
| **1914** | | | | Oct. 15 | Bianca | New York | Hadley, H. |
| Jan. 24 | Madeleine | New York | Herbert, V. | | | | |
| June 6 | Cricket on the Heart | London | Mackenzie, A. | **1919** | | | |
| July 4 | Dylan | London | Holbrooke, J. | Mar. 12 | Legend, The | New York | Breil, J. C. |
| Aug. | Chapel in Lyonesse | Glastonbury | Boughton, R. | Mar. 12 | Temple Dancer | New York | Hugo, J. A. |
| Aug. 3 | Giovanni | Sydney | Hill, A. | Oct. 21 | Fennimore and Gerda | Frankfurt | Delius, F. |
| Aug. 3 | Pierrette | Sydney | Hart, F. | Nov. 27 | Prince Ferelon | London | Gatty, N. |
| Aug. 26 | Immortal Hour | Glastonbury | Boughton, R. | Dec. 5 | Malvolio | Melbourne | Hart, F. |
| Dec. 29 | Guido Ferranti | Chicago | Etten, J. Van | ? | Fantastics, The | Melbourne | Hart, F. |
| * | Land of Heart's Desire | -- | Hart, F. | * | Christmas Rose | London (1931) | Bridge, F. |
| * | Plantation, The | -- | Freeman, H. | * | Crier by Night | BBC (1942) | Bainton, E. |
| | | | | * | Fantasy in Delft | -- | Gilbert, H. |
| | | | | * | Travelling Companion | London (1925) | Stanford, C. |

| DATE | TITLE | CITY | COMPOSER |
|------|-------|------|----------|
| **1920** | | | |
| Jan. 2 | **Rip Van Winkle** | Chicago | De Koven, R. |
| Jan. 31 | **Cleopatra's Night** | New York | Hadley, H. |
| Apr. 17 | **Tempest, The** | London | Gatty, N. |
| May 20 | **Pied Piper of Hamelin** | Miami | Clokey, J. |
| Nov. 9 | **Myth Beautiful** | London | Coates, A. |
| Dec. 9 | **David Garrick** | London | Somerville, R. |
| * | **Macbeth** | -- | Gatty, N. |
| * | **Magnifica, La** | -- | Spelman, T. |
| * | **Travelling Man** | -- | Hart, F. |
| **1921** | | | |
| Mar. 12 | **Rebel Maid** | London | Phillips, M. |
| Aug. 29 | **All Fools' Day** | Glastonbury | Carey, C. |
| Sept. 13 | **Thais and Talmaae** | Manchester | Campbell, C. |
| Sept. 17 | **Egypt** | Berkeley, CA | McCoy, W. |
| * | **King, The** | -- | Hart, F. |
| **1922** | | | |
| Feb. 14 | **Two Sisters** | Cambridge | Rootham, C. |
| Mar. 27 | **Flaming Arrow** | San Francisco | Moore, M. |
| May 23 | **White Bird** | New York | Carter, E. |
| June 16 | **Shepherds of the Delectable Mountains** | London | Vaughan Williams, R. |
| June 19 | **Scene from Pickwick** | London | Wood, C. |
| Aug. 26 | **Alkestis** | Glastonbury | Boughton, R. |
| Aug. 28 | **Blue Monday** | New York | Gershwin, G. |
| Aug. 31 | **Auster** | Sydney | Hill, A. |
| Sept. 18 | **Merchant of Venice** | Brighton | Beecham, A. |
| Dec. 5 | **Sunset Trail** | Denver | Cadman, C. |
| * | **Dumb Wife** | -- | Gruenberg, L. |
| **1923** | | | |
| Jan. 13 | **Snowbird** | Chicago | Stearns, T. |
| Feb. 1 | **Love's Sacrifice** | Chicago | Chadwick, G. |
| Feb. 10 | **Markheim** | London | Miles, P. N. |
| May 14 | **Perfect Fool** | London | Holst, G. |
| May 19 | **Undine** | Baltimore | Ware, H. |
| June 4 | **Fête Galante** | Birmingham | Smyth, E. |
| Nov. 12 | **Vendetta** | New York | Freeman, H. |
| Nov. 23 | **Ekkehard** | London | Ewart, F. |
| Nov. 26 | **Bubbles** | London | Bath, H. |
| Dec. 11 | **Blue Peter** | London | Gibbs, C. A. |
| ? | **Ship of Heaven** | Sydney | Hill, A. |
| * | **Esther** | -- | Hart, F. |
| * | **Fall of the House of Usher** | -- | Claflin, A. |
| * | **Sunken Bell** | -- | Ruggles, C. |
| **1924** | | | |
| Feb. 12 | **Family Papers** | London | Wood, C. |
| Apr. 16 | **Eve of St. John** | London | Mackenzie, A. |
| Apr. 24 | **Hound of Heaven** | San Francisco | Stewart, H. |
| Apr. 25 | **Legend of Wiwaste** | Ontario | Blakeslee, S. |

| DATE | TITLE | CITY | COMPOSER |
|------|-------|------|----------|
| July 3 | **Midsummer Madness** | London | Gibbs, C. A. |
| July 4 | **Hugh the Drover** | London | Vaughan Williams, R. |
| Aug. 20 | **Seraphic Vision** | Glastonbury | Boughton, R. |
| Aug. 21 | **Queen of Cornwall** | Glastonbury | Boughton, R. |
| Aug. 26 | **Agincourt** | Glastonbury | Boughton, R. |
| Sept. 2 | **Rose-Marie** | New York | Friml/Stothart |
| Sept. 27 | **Seal-Woman** | Birmingham | Bantock, G. |
| Dec. 2 | **Student Prince** | New York | Romberg, S. |
| Dec. 14 | **Night in Old Paris** | New York | Hadley, H. |
| * | **Fairies' Revelry** | -- | Kieserling, R. |
| * | **Woman Who Laughed at Faery** | -- | Hart, F. |
| **1925** | | | |
| Feb. 22 | **Gagliarda of a Merry Plague** | New York | Saminsky, L. |
| Feb. 24 | **Legend of the Piper** | S Bend, IN | Freer, E. E. |
| Mar. 20 | **Garden of Mystery** | New York | Cadman, C. |
| Apr. 3 | **At the Boar's Head** | Manchester | Holst, G. |
| May 17 | **Song of David** | New York | Arnstein, I. |
| May 28 | **Alchemist, The** | Essen, Ger | Scott, C. |
| July 22 | **Entente cordiale** | London | Smyth, E. |
| Dec. 11 | **Namiko-San** | Chicago | Franchetti, A. |
| Dec. 12 | **Nightingale, The** | Miami | Clokey, J. |
| Dec. 26 | **Light from St. Agnes** | Chicago | Harling, W |
| * | **Deirdre of the Sorrows** | -- | Crofton, W. |
| * | **Fall of the House of Usher** | -- | Sessions, R. |
| * | **Gay Musketeers** | -- | Baron, M. |
| **1926** | | | |
| Jan. 19 | **Massimilliano** | London | Freer, E. E. |
| Feb. 11 | **Mr. Pepys** | London | Shaw, M. |
| Apr. 10 | **Policeman's Serenade** | London | Reynolds, A. |
| Apr. 29 | **Castle Agrazant** | Cincinnati | Lyford, R. |
| May 10 | **Monk of Toledo** | Portland | Knowlton, E. |
| June 9 | **Echo, The** | Portland | Patterson, F. |
| July 4 | **Music Robber** | Cincinnati | Van Grove, I. |
| Sept. 22 | **Deirdre in Exile** | Melbourne | Hart, F. |
| Oct. 4 | **Deep River** | New York | Harling, W. |
| Oct. 15 | **Leper's Flute** | Glasgow | Bryson, E. |
| Nov. 11 | **Winona** | Portland | Bimboni, A. |
| Dec. 8 | **Witch of Salem** | Chicago | Cadman, C. |
| Dec. 17 | **Lord Byron** | S. Bend, IN | Graham, J. |
| * | **Mountain Blood** | -- | Patterson, F. |
| **1927** | | | |
| Feb. 17 | **King's Henchman** | New York | Taylor, D. |
| Apr. 24 | **Everyman** | Chicago | Lester, W. |
| Nov. 15 | **Show Boat** | Washington | Kern, J. |
| ? | **Chilkoot Maiden** | Skagaway, AK | Freer, E. E. |
| * | **Endymion** | Rochester, NY (1935) | Bennett, R. |
| * | **Pearl Tree** | Sydney (1944) | Bainton, E. |

| Date | Title | City | Composer | Date | Title | City | Composer |
|------|-------|------|----------|------|-------|------|----------|
| **1928** | | | | Sept. 19 | **Pride of the Regiment** | Midhurst, Eng | Leigh, W. |
| Mar. | **Enchanted Garden** | London | Dunhill, T. | Dec. 6 | **Lady of the Lake** | Chicago | Schmidt, K. |
| Mar. 25 | **Teora** | Sydney | Hill, A. | Dec. 8 | **Blonde Donna** | Brooklyn | Carter, E. |
| May | **Witches' Well** | Tacoma, WA | Appleton, A. | Dec. 11 | **Devil Take Her** | London | Benjamin, A. |
| May 3 | **Täm-Män'-Nǎcŭp'** | Provo, UT | Hanson, W. | * | **Cyrano de Bergerac** | -- | Pokrass, S. |
| May 25 | **Order of Good Cheer** | Quebec | Willan, H. | * | **Harpies, The** | New York (1953) | Blitzstein, M. |
| Sept. 10 | **Voodoo** | New York | Freeman, H. | | | | |
| Nov. 12 | **Waterloo Leave** | Norwich, Eng | Shaw, M. | * | **Nativity** | -- | Hart, F. |
| * | **Forced Marriage** | -- | Hart, F. | * | **Night** | -- | Weisgall, H. |
| * | **Mouse Trap** | -- | Bell, W. H. | * | **Uzziah** | -- | Freeman, H. |
| * | **Preciosa** | -- | Freer, E. E. | **1932** | | | |
| * | **Sea Rovers** | -- | Spelman, T. | Feb. 12 | **Rip Van Winkle** | New York | Manning, E. |
| **1929** | | | | Feb. 24 | **Derby Day** | London | Reynolds, A. |
| Feb. 1 | **Bronwen** | Huddersfield | Holbrooke, J. | May 26 | **David Rizzio** | Los Angeles | Moore, M. |
| Mar. 21 | **Sir John in Love** | London | Vaughan Williams, R. | Oct. 3 | **Willow Tree** | NBC | Cadman, C. |
| | | | | Nov. | **Ouanga** | Chicago | White, C. C. |
| Apr. 3 | **Pierrot of the Minute** | Cincinnati | Engel, L. | * | **Cabildo** | Athens, GA (1945) | Beach, A. |
| Apr. 11 | **Frithiof** | Chicago | Freer, E. E. | | | | |
| Apr. 23 | **Bride of Dionysus** | Edinburgh | Tovey, D. | * | **Condemned, The** | -- | Blitzstein, M. |
| May 9 | **Triple Sec** | Philadelphia | Blitzstein, M. | * | **Fountain of Youth** | -- | Reynolds, A. |
| June 25 | **Judith** | London | Goossens, E. | * | **Isolt of the White Hands** | -- | Hart, F. |
| July 18 | **Bitter-Sweet** | London | Coward, N. | * | **Rose and the Ring** | Los Angeles (1957) | Leginska, E. |
| Sept. 25 | **Yolanda of Cyprus** | London, ON | Loomis, C. | | | | |
| Dec. 3 | **Joan of Arc** | Chicago | Freer, E. E. | **1933** | | | |
| Dec. 8 | **Beggar's Love** | New York | Patterson, F. | Jan. 7 | **Emperor Jones** | New York | Gruenberg, L. |
| Dec. 21 | **Samuel Pepys** | Munich | Coates, A. | Feb. 13 | **Jolly Roger** | Manchester | Leigh, W. |
| Dec. 27 | **Christmas Tale** | Houston | Freer, E. E. | May 20 | **Four Saints in Three Acts** | Ann Arbor | Thomson, V. |
| * | **Ever Young** | Bath, Eng (1935) | Boughton, R. | May 20 | **Merry Mount** | Ann Arbor | Hanson, H. |
| | | | | July 3 | **Tom-Tom** | Cleveland | Graham, S. |
| * | **Flapper, The** | -- | Freeman, H. | July 29 | **Legend of Hani** | Monte Rio, CA | Hadley, H. |
| * | **Lizzie Hexam** | -- | Spelman, T. | | | | |
| * | **Parabola and Circula** | -- | Blitzstein, M. | Nov. 1 | **Happy Families** | Guildford, Eng | Dunhill, T. |
| **1930** | | | | | | | |
| Feb. 9 | **Shylock** | Chicago | La Violette | Nov. 23 | **Masque of Pandora** | Chicago | Freer, E. E. |
| April 17 | **Sun-Bride** | NBC radio | Skilton, C. | **1934** | | | |
| May 25 | **Transatlantic** | Frankfurt | Antheil, G. | Jan. 31 | **Wandering Scholar** | Liverpool | Holst, G. |
| Dec. 10 | **King Alfred and the Cakes** | London | Gatty, N. | Feb. 28 | **Helen Retires** | New York | Antheil, G. |
| * | **Flight** | -- | Antheil, G. | Apr. 2 | **Little Women** | Chicago | Freer, E. E. |
| * | **Leah Kleschna** | -- | Freeman, H. | Apr. 12 | **Macbeth** | London | Collingwood, L. |
| * | **Sunken City** | -- | Spelman, T. | | | | |
| **1931** | | | | May 7 | **Kykunkor the Witch** | New York | Horton, A. |
| Jan. 16 | **Tantivy Towers** | London | Dunhill, T. | Sept. 10 | **Lily Maid** | Stroud, Eng | Boughton, R. |
| Feb. 7 | **Peter Ibbetson** | New York | Taylor, D. | Nov. 6 | **Iernin** | Penzance, Eng | Lloyd, G. |
| May | **Courtship of Miles Standish** | Melbourne | Ewart, F. | | | | |
| May 22 | **Marriage of Aude** | New York | Rogers, B. | Dec. 15 | **Hester Prynne** | Hartford | Claflin, A. |
| June 6 | **Thorn of Avalon** | London | Shaw, M. | * | **Blue Steel** | -- | Still, W. G. |
| June 19 | **Legend of Spain** | Milwaukee | Freer, E. E. | * | **Lillith** | -- | Weisgall, H. |
| July 10 | **St. George and the Dragon** | Melbourne | Hart, F. | * | **Robin Hood** | -- | Tippett, M. |
| Nov. 19 | **Jack and the Beanstalk** | New York | Gruenberg, L. | * | **Tom and Lily** | -- | Carter, E. |
| | | | | * | **Zululand**, tetralogy | -- | Freeman, H. |
| Sept. 10 | **Rubios, Los** | Los Angeles | Moore, M. | **1935** | | | |
| | | | | Jan. 24 | **In the Pasha's Garden** | New York | Seymour, J. |

| DATE | TITLE | CITY | COMPOSER | DATE | TITLE | CITY | COMPOSER |
|---|---|---|---|---|---|---|---|
| Apr. 8 | Maria Malibran | New York | Bennett, R. | May 18 | Devil and Daniel Webster | New York | Moore, D. |
| June 28 | Kingdom for a Cow | London | Weill, K. | May 23 | Mirror for the Sky | Eugene, OR | Kubik, G. |
| Oct. 10 | Porgy and Bess | New York | Gershwin, G. | May 25 | Return of Odysseus | London | Gundry, I. |
| Nov. 23 | Gale | Chicago | Leginska, E. | Nov. 22 | Blennerhasset | CBS radio | Giannini, V |
| * | Corn King | London (1950) | Easdale, B. | * | Privilege and Privation | Amsterdam (1982) | Becker, J. |

| 1936 | | | | 1940 | | | |
|---|---|---|---|---|---|---|---|
| Apr. 21 | Elizabeth and Leicester | Chattanooga, TN | Lindsey, E. | Feb. 26 | Jewel Merchants | Baltimore | Cheslock, L. |
| | | | | Mar. 17 | Thorwald | New York | Dinsmore, W. |
| May 12 | Poisoned Kiss | Cambridge | Vaughan Williams | Apr. 12 | Poet's Dilemma | New York | Lee, D.-K. |
| | | | | Apr. 14 | François Villon | New York radio | Baron, M. |
| June | Master Valiant | London | Shaw, M. | May 25 | Return of Odysseus | London | Gundry, I. |
| Nov. 20 | Pickwick | London | Coates, A. | May 32 | Organizer, De | New York | Johnson, J. |
| Dec. 3 | Julia | London | Quilter, R. | Oct. 25 | Cabin in the Sky | New York | Duke, V. |

| 1937 | | | | 1941 | | | |
|---|---|---|---|---|---|---|---|
| Jan. 7 | Eternal Road | New York | Weill, K. | Jan. 5 | No for an Answer | New York | Blitzstein, M. |
| Feb. 4 | Caponsacchi | New York | Hageman, R. | Jan. 11 | Fall of the House of Usher | Indianapolis | Loomis, C. |
| Feb. 24 | Garrick | New York | Stoessel, A. | | | | |
| Mar. 4 | Headless Horseman | Bronxville, NY | Moore, D. | Feb. 18 | It Began at Breakfast | Philadelphia | Elmore, R. |
| Mar. 22 | Weird of Colbar | Glasgow | Moonie, W. B. | Apr. 20 | Gainsborough | Los Angeles | Coates, A. |
| Apr. 1 | Amelia Goes to the Ball | Philadelphia | Menotti, G. C. | May 5 | Paul Bunyan | New York | Britten, B. |
| Apr. 21 | Second Hurricane | New York | Copland, A. | May 13 | Tarquin | Poughkeepsie, NY | Krenek, E. |
| May 12 | Man without a Country | New York | Damrosch, W. | | | | |
| June 16 | Cradle Will Rock | New York | Blitzstein, M. | Dec. 30 | Lady in the Dark | Boston | Weill, K. |
| June 24 | Don Juan de Mañara | London | Goossens, E. | * | Bayou Legend | PBS (1974) | Still, W. G. |
| Oct. 17 | Green Mansions | CBS | Gruenberg, L. | * | Courtship of Miles Standish | -- | Spelman, T. |
| Dec. 1 | Riders to the Sea | London | Vaughan Williams, R. | * | Esther | -- | Knoller, J. |
| ? | Denmark Vesey | New York | Bowles, P. | * | Feast of Samhain | -- | Chisholm, E. |
| * | Argonauts, The | -- | Maganini, Q. | 1942 | | | |
| * | St. Francis of Assisi | -- | Hart, F. | Feb. 7 | Ramuntcho | Philadelphia | Taylor, D. |
| * | Two Gentlemen of Verona | -- | Seymour, J. | Feb. 20 | Island God | New York | Menotti, G. C. |
| 1938 | | | | Mar. 8 | Transit through Fire | CBC radio | Willan, H. |
| Jan. 19 | Sleeping Beauty | New York | Rubinstein, B. | Mar. 29 | Solomon and Balkis | Cambridge, MA | Thompson, R. |
| May 11 | Brownings Go to Italy | Chicago | Freer, E. E. | Apr. 25 | Nightingale and the Rose | NBC radio | Lessner, G. |
| June 2 | Scarlet Letter | Hamburg | Giannini, V. | May 2 | Tree on the Plains | Spartanburg, SC | Bacon, E. |
| Sept. 23 | Gettysburg | Los Angeles | Ruger, M. | | | | |
| Oct. 20 | Serf, The | London | Lloyd, G. | Aug. 11 | Crier by Night | ABC | Bainton, E. |
| Nov. | Daughter of the South | Chicago | Collins, E. | Nov. 3 | Opera Cloak | New York | Damrosch, W. |
| Nov. 24 | Beauty and the Beast | CBS radio | Giannini, V. | Dec. 9 | Mother, The | New York | Wood, J. |
| * | Helena's Husband | -- | Gruenberg, L. | 1943 | | | |
| * | Julian, the Apostate | -- | Saminsky, L. | Jan. 6 | Eleanor | Brisbane | Douglas, C. |
| * | Caesar | | | Feb. 4 | Crucible, The | Los Angeles | Hageman, R. |
| | Légende Provençale | -- | Moore, M. | Mar. 30 | Wind Remains | New York | Bowles, P. |
| * | River, The | -- | Hively, W. | May 3 | Florence Nightingale | New York | Williams, D. |
| * | Troubled Island | New York (1949) | Still, W. G. | Dec. 2 | Carmen Jones | New York | Bizet-Bennett |
| | | | | Dec. 20 | Even unto Bethlehem | Honolulu | Hart, F. |
| 1939 | | | | * | Dreamy Kid | Ann Arbor, MI (2006) | Johnson, J. |
| Feb. 16 | Cynthia Parker | Denton, TX | Smith, J. | | | | |
| Apr. 7 | Bleeding Heart of Timpanogas | Provo, UT | Hanson, W. | * | Galahad | -- | Boughton, R. |
| Apr. 22 | Old Maid and the Thief | NBC radio | Menotti, G. C. | * | She Stoops to Conquer | -- | Aplvor, D. |

| DATE | TITLE | CITY | COMPOSER |
|------|-------|------|----------|
| * | **Wuthering Heights** | Portland, OR (1986) | Herrmann, B. |
| **1944** | | | |
| May 23 | **Gate, The** | New York | Brand, M. |
| Aug. | **Prodigal Son** | Palo Alto, CA | Jacobi, F. |
| * | **Avalon** | -- | Boughton, R. |
| * | **Swineherd and the Princess** | -- | Hart, F. |
| **1945** | | | |
| May 19 | **Scarecrow, The** | New York | Lockwood, N. |
| June 7 | **Peter Grimes** | London | Britten, B. |
| Dec. 30 | **Enchanted Kiss** | New York | Bennett, R. |
| * | **Deirdre of the Sorrows** | Chicago (1957) | Becker, J. |
| * | **What Price Confidence?** | Saarbrücken (1962) | Krenek, E. |
| **1946** | | | |
| Jan. 7 | **Life That Is Free** | New York | Emile, A. |
| Apr. 20 | **Deirdre** | CBC radio | Willan, H. |
| May 8 | **Medium, The** | New York | Menotti, G. C. |
| May 28 | **Partisans, The** | London | Gundry, I. |
| July 12 | **Rape of Lucretia** | Glyndebourne | Britten, B. |
| Dec. 16 | **Street Scene** | Philadelphia | Weill, K. |
| * | **Cain and Abel** | -- | Rorem, N. |
| * | **Maureen O'Mara** | -- | Scott, C. |
| **1947** | | | |
| Jan. 11 | **Warrior, The** | New York | Rogers, B. |
| Feb. 18 | **Telephone, The** | New York | Menotti, G. C. |
| Feb. 22 | **Gooseherd and the Goblin** | New York | Smith, J. |
| Mar. 7 | **Press Gang** | Letchworth | Bush, A. |
| Apr. 9 | **Captain's Parrot** | Stroud, Eng | Brent-Smith, A. |
| Apr. 11 | **Avon** | London | Gundry, I. |
| Apr. 18 | **Trial of Lucullus** | Berkeley, CA | Sessions, R. |
| May 6 | **Stranger of Manzano** | Dallas | Smith, J. |
| May 7 | **Mother of Us All** | New York | Thomson, V. |
| May 18 | **Pit, The** | London | Lutyens, E. |
| June 20 | **Albert Herring** | Glyndebourne | Britten, B. |
| July 21 | **Promised Valley** | Salt Lake City | Gates, C. M. |
| * | **Allah** | -- | Freeman, H. |
| * | **Vengeance of Faery** | -- | Hart, F. |
| **1948** | | | |
| Jan. 7 | **King Harald** | New York | Emile, A. |
| Jan. 22 | **Far Harbour** | New York | Bergersen, B. |
| Mar. 17 | **Lady Rohesia** | London | Hopkins, A. |
| Apr. 1 | **Escape from Liberty** | Hartford | Doellner, R. |
| May 10 | **Evangeline** | New York | Luening, O. |
| May 13 | **Princess and the Vagabond** | Hartford | Freed, I. |
| July 15 | **Down in the Valley** | Bloomington | Weill, K. |
| Aug. 13 | **Life Goes to a Party** | Lenox, MA | Middleton, R. |

| DATE | TITLE | CITY | COMPOSER |
|------|-------|------|----------|
| Oct. 7 | **Love Life** | New York | Weill, K. |
| Aug. 1 | **Sailing of the Nancy Belle** | Syracuse, NY | Davis, A. |
| Dec. 1 | **Evangeline** | Kingston, ON | George, G. |
| ? | **Garden of Artemis** | Cambridge, MA | Pinkham, D. |
| * | **Taming of the Shrew** | -- | Clapp, P. |
| * | **Volpone** | -- | Gruenberg, L. |
| **1949** | | | |
| Jan. 20 | **Lyneia** | Cincinnati | Byrd, W. C. |
| Feb. 9 | **White Wings** | Hartford | Moore, D. |
| Feb. 13 | **Fit for a King** | New York | Kalmanoff, M. |
| Feb. 19 | **Emperor's New Clothes** | New York | Moore, D. |
| Feb. 23 | **Prima Donna** | London | Benjamin, A. |
| Mar. 2 | **By Gemini** | Galesburg, IL | Baylor, H. |
| April 11 | **Avon** | London | Gundry, I. |
| May 4 | **Drumlin Legend** | New York | Bacon, E. |
| May 2 | **Slow Dusk** | Syracuse, NY | Floyd, C. |
| May 9 | **Catherine Parr** | New York | Collins, A. |
| May 9 | **Don't We All?** | Rochester | Burrill, P. |
| May 9 | **In the Name of Culture** | Rochester | Bimboni, A. |
| June 14 | **Let's Make an Opera!/ Little Sweep** | Aldeburgh | Britten, B. |
| summer | **Ordeal of Osbert** | Duxbury, MA | Davis, A. |
| Sept. 29 | **Olympians, The** | London | Bliss, A. |
| Oct. 30 | **Lost in the Stars** | New York | Weill, K. |
| Oct. 31 | **Regina** | New York | Blitzstein, M. |
| Dec. 15 | **Dreams in Spades** | Philadelphia | Hovey, S. |
| Dec. 29 | **Boor, The** | New York | Bucci, M. |
| Dec. 29 | **In a Garden** | New York | Kupferman, M. |
| * | **Costaso** | Flagstaff, AR (1989) | Still, W. S. |
| * | **O'Higgins of Chile** | -- | Cowell, H. |
| **1950** | | | |
| Jan. 18 | **Barrier, The** | New York | Meyerowitz, J. |
| Feb. 7 | **Enchanted Pear Tree** | New York | Overton, H. |
| Feb. 14 | **Age of Chivalry** | Gloucester, Eng | Brent-Smith, A. |
| Mar. 1 | **Consul, The** | Philadelphia | Menotti, G. C. |
| May 4 | **Catherine Parr** | Hopkinton, NH | Barring, M. |
| May 18 | **Jumping Frog** | Bloomington | Foss, L. |
| May 18 | **Veil, The** | Bloomington | Rogers, B. |
| May | **Triumph of (Saint) Joan** | Bronxville, NY | Dello Joio, N. |
| June | **Once upon a Moon** | Dublin | Victory, G. |
| July 1 | **Unto These Hills** | Cherokee, NC | Kilpatrick, J. |
| Aug. 2 | **Simoon** | Lenox, MA | Meyerowitz, J. |
| Oct. 13 | **Mr. Bellamy Comes Home** | London | Rivington, H. |
| Nov. 6 | **Sunday Costs Five Pesos** | Charlotte, NC | Haubiel, C. |
| Nov. 21 | **Corn King** | London | Easdale, B. |
| Dec. 12 | **Asses' Ears** | Los Angeles | Cole, H. |

| DATE | TITLE | CITY | COMPOSER | DATE | TITLE | CITY | COMPOSER |
|---|---|---|---|---|---|---|---|
| Dec. 16 | Lion, The | New London | Franchetti, A. | Mar. 14 | Oedipus | Oakland, CA | Partch, H. |
| * | Jonah | -- | Beeson, J. | Mar. 16 | Princess, The | Hartford | Franchetti, A. |
| **1951** | | | | Mar. 30 | Don Perlimplin | Urbana, IL | Rieti, V. |
| Feb. 18 | Noah and the Stowaway | New York | Kalmanoff, M. | Apr. 23 | Singin' Billy | Nashville, TN | Bryan, C. |
| | | | | May 2 | Monkey's Paw | Cincinnati | Hamm, C. |
| Feb. 22 | Open the Gates | New York | Lee, D.-K. | May 5 | Snow Queen | Lake Charles, LA | Gaburo, K. |
| Mar. 28 | Giants in the Earth | New York | Moore, D. | | | | |
| Mar. 30 | Caliph's Clock | New York | Kraft, L. | May 8 | Lowland Sea | Montclair, NJ | Wilder, A. |
| Apr. 17 | Fugitives, The | Tallahassee | Floyd, C. | May 12 | All at Sea | London | Shaw, G. |
| Apr. 24 | Letter to Emily | Seattle | Johnson, L. | May 16 | Sweeney Agonistes | Middletown, CT | Winslow, R. |
| Apr. 24 | Mississippi Legend | New York | Wolfe, J. | | | | |
| Apr. 26 | Pilgrim's Progress | London | Vaughan Williams, R. | May 24 | Baby Doe | Denver | DiJulio, M. |
| | | | | June 12 | Trouble in Tahiti | Waltham, MA | Bernstein, L. |
| May 2 | Dark Waters | Los Angeles | Krenek, E. | July 6 | Maypole, The | Westport | Franchetti, A. |
| May 3 | David | New York | Skilling, R. | July 17 | Statue for the Mayor | London | Cole, H. |
| May 4 | Mighty Casey | Hartford | Schuman, W. | July 22 | Don Fortunato | Interlochen | Forrest, H. |
| May 5 | Red Rose and the Briar | Hartford | Mopper, I. | Aug. 9 | Stronger, The | Lutherville, MD | Weisgall, H. |
| May 8 | Well, The | Rochester | Mennini, L. | | | | |
| May 15 | John Socman | Bristol | Lloyd, G. | Aug. 13 | Nymph and the Farmer | Aspen | Tcherepnin, A. |
| May 19 | Aria da capo | Stockton, CA | Fore, B. | Oct. 29 | Dark Sonnet | Cape Town | Chisholm, E. |
| May 28 | Judgment Day | New York | Perl, P. | ? | Van Hunks and the Devil | Cape Town | Coates, A. |
| June 27 | Duenna, The | Wiesbaden, Ger. | Gerhard, R. | * | Cenci, The | -- | Brian, H. |
| | | | | * | Ethan Frome | -- | Allanbrook, D. |
| June 2 | Wise and Foolish | New York | List, K. | | | | |
| July 9 | Sleeping Children | Cheltenham | Easdale, B. | * | Phineas and the Nightingale | -- | Lee, D.-K. |
| July 20 | Benedict and Beatrice | Devon | Holst, I. | | | | |
| July 20 | Man from Tuscany | Canterbury | Hopkins, A. | * | Selfish Giant | Cleveland (1955) | Wilding-White, R. |
| July 30 | Mayor of Casterbridge | Cambridge | Tranchell, P. | * | Strolling Clerk from Paradise | -- | Wilson, C. |
| Aug. 18 | Boney Quillen | Chichester, NY | Haufrecht, H. | | | | |
| Sept. 4 | Mermaid, The | Birmingham | More, M. | * | Tragicall Historie of Christopher Marlowe | -- | Mellers, M. |
| Sept. 11 | Rake's Progress | Venice | Stravinsky, I. | | | | |
| Oct. 4 | Dybbuk, The | New York | Tamkin, D. | **1953** | | | |
| Nov. 16 | Acres of Sky | Fayetteville, AR | Kreutz, A. | Jan. 9 | Volpone | Los Angeles | Antheil, G. |
| | | | | Jan. 31 | Taming of the Shrew | Cincinnati | Giannini, V. |
| Nov. 16 | Eastward in Eden | Detroit | Meyerowitz, J. | Feb. 7 | Marriage, The | NBC | Martinů, B. |
| | | | | Feb. 15 | Godiva | New York | Kalmanoff, M. |
| Dec. 1 | Billy Budd | London | Britten, B. | | | | |
| Dec. 5 | Incognita | Oxford | Wellesz, E. | Feb. 21 | Babar the Elephant | New York | Berezowsky, N. |
| Dec. 24 | Amahl and the Night Visitors | NY, NBC | Menotti, G. C. | | | | |
| * | Deirdre of the Sorrows | -- | Rankl, K. | Mar. 1 | Cask of Amontillado | Cincinnati | Hamm, C. |
| * | Faust | -- | Becker, J. J. | Mar. 1 | Open Window | Cincinnati | Ahlstrom, D. |
| * | Little Prince | -- | Mann, R. W. | Mar. 1 | Three Sisters Who Are Not Sisters | Cincinnati | Ahlstrom, D. |
| * | Mota | -- | Still, W. G. | | | | |
| * | Tod's Gal | Norfolk, VA (1971) | Kelly, R. | Mar. 5 | Rapunzel | Colchester | Hammond, T. |
| | | | | Mar. 20 | Carrion Crow | Bloomington | Fletcher, G. |
| **1952** | | | | Mar. 28 | Junípero Serra | Palma de Mallorca, Spain | Hively, W. |
| Jan. 12 | Prankster, The | Bowling Green, OH | Wykes, R. | | | | |
| | | | | Apr. 5 | Doctor Faustus | Bronxville, NY | Kupferman, M. |
| Jan. 17 | Cowherd and the Sky Maiden | Seattle | Verrall, J. | Apr. 15 | Fall of the House of Usher | Los Angeles | Ruger, M. |
| | | | | Apr. 17 | Sunday Excursion | New York | Wilder, A. |
| Feb. 11 | Tenor, The | Baltimore | Weisgall, H. | May 1 | Scena | BBC radio | Hopkins, A. |
| Feb. 21 | Parfait for Irene | Bloomington | Kaufmann, W. | May 13 | Charivari | Cambridge, MA | Westergaard, P. |
| Mar. 9 | Boston Baked Beans | New York | Kubik, G. | | | | |

| DATE | TITLE | CITY | COMPOSER |
|---|---|---|---|
| May 22 | Cumberland Fair | Montclair, NJ | Wilder, A. |
| May 22 | Tom Sawyer | San Francisco | Elkus, J. |
| May 26 | Barber of New York | New York | Vernon, A. |
| May 28 | Brother Joe | Cleveland | Engel, L. |
| June 8 | Gloriana | London | Britten, B. |
| June 17 | Brandy Is My True Love's Name | New York | Kalmanoff, M. |
| June 28 | Night in the Puszta | Cleveland | Kondorossy, L. |
| July 2 | Circus, The | Interlochen, MI | Chudacoff, E. |
| July 3 | Rab the Rhymer | Aberdeen | Dunlop/ Oppenheim |
| July 22 | Endymion | Sydney | Antill, J. H. |
| July 30 | Secret Life of Walter Mitty | Athens, OH | Hamm, C. |
| Aug. 1 | Tony Beaver | Idyllwild, CA | Marais, J. |
| Aug. 17 | Bad Boys in School | Lenox, MA | Meyerowitz, J. |
| Aug. 17 | Kingdom Come | Boone, NC | Mason, W. |
| Aug. 18 | Captain Lovelock | Hudson Falls, NY | Duke, J. |
| Aug. 28 | African Heartbeat | Idyllwild, CA | Marais, J. |
| Aug. 28 | Dr. Jekyll and Mr. Hyde | Berkeley, CA | Fragale, F. |
| Sept. 6 | Wat Tyler | Leipzig | Bush, A. |
| Sept. 25 | Little Match Girl | Winnipeg | Kaufmann, W. |
| Sept. 30 | Tinners of Cornwall | London | Gundry, I. |
| Oct. 8 | Dress, The | New York | Bucci, M. |
| Oct. 21 | Inland Woman | Cape Town | Chisholm, E. |
| Nov. 9 | Menna | Cardiff | Hughes, A. |
| Nov. 10 | Three's Company | Crewe, Eng | Hopkins, A. |
| Nov. 21 | Dumb Wife | London | Horovitz, J. |
| Nov. 24 | Miss Chicken Little | Suffern, NY | Wilder, A. |
| Dec. 8 | Sweet Betsy from Pike | New York | Bucci, M. |
| ? | Blood Wedding | Cleveland | Smith, H. |
| ? | Music Critic | Sydney | Antill, J. H. |
| ? | Research, The | Tallahassee, FL (1953) | Kaufmann, W. |
| * | Kumana | -- | Kanitz, E. |

**1954**

| DATE | TITLE | CITY | COMPOSER |
|---|---|---|---|
| Jan. 21 | Blind Beggar's Daughter | Farnham, Eng | Bush, G. |
| Feb | Smoky Mountain | Monmouth, IL | Hunkins, E. |
| Feb. 18 | Darling Corie | Hempstead, NY | Siegmeister, E. |
| Mar. 3 | Lake, The | Vancouver | Pentland, B. |
| Mar. 10 | Threepenny Opera | New York | Weill-Blitzstein |
| Mar. 11 | Golden Apple | New York | Moross, J. |
| Mar. 15 | University Greys | Clinton, MS | Kreutz, A. |
| spring | Sicilian Limes | Baltimore | Argento, D. |
| Mar. 29 | Mother, The | Philadelphia | Hollingsworth, S. |
| Apr. 1 | Tender Land | New York | Copland, A. |
| Apr. 4 | Transposed Heads | Louisville, KY | Glanville-Hicks, P. |
| Apr. 23 | Charlie's Uncle | Columbus, OH | Ahlstrom, D. |

| DATE | TITLE | CITY | COMPOSER |
|---|---|---|---|
| Apr. 24 | Cockcrow | Austin, TX | Smith, J. |
| May 15 | Pumpkin, The | Cleveland | Kondorossy, L. |
| May 15 | Voice, The | Cleveland | Kondorossy, L. |
| May 20 | Scandal at Mulford Inn | Cincinnati | Byrd, W. C. |
| May 27 | Hello Out There | New York | Beeson, J. |
| May 27 | Malady of Love | New York | Engel, L. |
| June 6 | Tin Pan Alley | New York | Raphling, S. |
| June 8 | Quiet Game of Cribble | New York | Kalmanoff, M. |
| June 17 | Dinner Engagement | Aldeburgh | Berkeley, L. |
| July 6 | Murder in Three Keys | New York | Chisholm, E. |
| July 21 | Antigone | BBC | Joubert, J. |
| July 21 | Daelia | Interlochen | Forrest, H. |
| July 27 | Audition, The | Athens, OH | Goodman, A |
| July 28 | Brothers, The | Denver | Antheil, G. |
| July 27 | Princess and the Pea | Lenox, MA | Toch, E. |
| Aug. 17 | Matinee Idyll | Interlochen | Forrest, H. |
| Sept. 5 | Scent of Sarsaparilla | San Francisco | Hamm, C. |
| Sept. 14 | Turn of the Screw | Venice | Britten, B. |
| Sept. 22 | Nelson | London | Berkeley, L. |
| Oct. 14 | Apollo and Persephone | Chicago | Cockshott, G. |
| Oct. 18 | Governess, The | London | Mallett, C. |
| Oct. 19 | Golden Touch | Winnipeg | Kaufmann, W. |
| Nov. 10 | Sun-Up | New York | Kassern, T. |
| Nov. 20 | Cask of Amontillado | New York | Perry, J. |
| Nov. 23 | Sandhog | New York | Robinson, E. |
| Nov. 30 | Beckoning Fair One | Seattle | Kechley, G. |
| Dec. 3 | Troilus and Cressida | London | Walton, W. |
| Dec. 4 | Double Trouble | Louisville, KY | Mohaupt, R. |
| Dec. 5 | Cancelling Dark | London | Whelen, C. |
| Dec. 6 | archy and mehitabel | New York | Kleinsinger, G. |
| Dec. 23 | Christmas Carol | CBS | Herrmann, B. |
| Dec. 27 | Barbara Allen | New York | Broekman, D. |
| Dec. 27 | Saint of Bleecker Street | New York | Menotti, G. C. |
| * | Admirable Bashville | -- | Berry, W. |
| * | Commission, The | Woodstock, NY (1992) | Cowell, H. |
| * | Legend, A | -- | Nelhybel, V. |
| | Mary Barton | -- | Cooke, A. |
| * | Night at Sea | -- | Gyring, E. |
| * | Miracle of Flanders | -- | Gruenberg, L. |
| * | One Night of Cleopatra | -- | Gruenberg, L. |

**1955**

| DATE | TITLE | CITY | COMPOSER |
|---|---|---|---|
| Jan. 10 | Fisherman's Wife | St. Joseph, MI | Stein, L. |
| Jan. 19 | Lord Byron's Love Letter | New Orleans | Banfield, R. de |
| Jan. 27 | Midsummer Marriage | London | Tippett, M. |
| Feb. 16 | Hopitu | New York | Albright, L. |
| Feb. 24 | Susannah | Tallahassee | Floyd, C. |
| Mar. 1 | Salesgirl, The | Bristol, VA | Hamm, C. |
| Mar. 13 | Pepito's Golden Flower | Pasadena, CA | Caldwell, M. |

| DATE | TITLE | CITY | COMPOSER |
|------|-------|------|----------|
| Mar. 20 | **Game of Cards** | Hartford, CT | Franchetti, A. |
| Mar. 29 | **Midnight Duel** | Cleveland | Kondorossy, L. |
| Apr. 2 | **Wish, The** | Louisville, KY | Antheil, G. |
| Apr. 10 | **Two Imposters** | Cleveland | Kondorossy, L. |
| Apr. 17 | **Aria da capo** | New Orleans | Burnham, C. |
| Apr. 26 | **Delinquents, The** | Philadelphia | Kalmanoff, M. |
| May 8 | **String Quartet** | Cleveland | Kondorossy, L. |
| May 9 | **Pot of Fat** | Cambridge, MA | Chanler, T. |
| May 10 | **Childhood Miracle** | New York | Rorem, N. |
| May 10 | **Nightingale** | New York | Rogers, B. |
| May 13 | **Peter Homan's Dream** | E Lansing, MI | Reed, H. O. |
| May 13 | **Ruby, The** | Bloomington | Dello Joio, N. |
| May 22 | **Three Blind Mice** | Seattle | Verrall, J. |
| May 25 | **Fatal Oath** | New York | Koutzen, B. |
| June 1 | **Eve of Adam** | Interlaken, MA | Duffy, J. |
| June 3 | **Long Way** | Nyack, NY | Wilder, A. |
| June 12 | **Mystic Fortress** | Cleveland | Kondorossy, L. |
| June 25 | **Grand Slam** | Stamford, CT | Vernon, A. |
| July 14 | **Persephone** | London | Cole, H. |
| July 15 | **Unmusical Impresario** | Duxbury, MA | Davis, K. |
| July 29 | **Fall of the City** | Athens, OH | Cohn, J. |
| Aug. 8 | **Rope, The** | Lenox, MA | Mennini, L. |
| Sept. 2 | **Moby Dick** | Idylwild, CA | Low, J. |
| Nov. 6 | **Griffelkin** | New York | Foss, L. |
| Dec. | **Christmas Slippers** | Winnipeg | Kaufmann, W. |
| Dec. 3 | **School for Wives** | Louisville, KY | Liebermann, R. |
| Dec. 5 | **Santa Claus** | Chicago | Smith, L. |
| Dec. 5 | **Secret, The** | Columbia, MO | Patacchi, V. |
| Dec. 5 | **Wedding Knell** | Seattle | Verrall, J. |
| Dec. 17 | **Tree That Was Christmas** | New York | Kleinsinger, G. |
| Dec. 29 | **Boor, The** | St Louis | Fink, M. S. |
| * | **Antony and Cleopatra** | -- | Gruenberg, L. |
| * | **Celebration, The** | -- | Maury, L. |
| * | **Delicate King** | -- | Gruenberg, L. |
| * | **Ellen** | -- | Wilder, A. |
| * | **Enlightened One** | -- | La Violette, W. |
| * | **My Heart's in the Highlands** | -- | Ahlstrom, D. |
| * | **Oracle, The** | -- | Lees, B. |
| * | **Pillar, The** | -- | Still, W. G. |
| * | **Riders to the Sea** | -- | Betts, L. |
| * | **Stormy Interlude** | -- | Brand, M. |

**1956**

| DATE | TITLE | CITY | COMPOSER |
|------|-------|------|----------|
| Jan. 7 | **Lima Beans** | New York | Townsend, D. |
| Jan. 8 | **Crescent Eyebrow** | New York | Dvorkin, J. |

| DATE | TITLE | CITY | COMPOSER |
|------|-------|------|----------|
| Jan. 27 | **Experiment, The** | Gambier, OH | Schwartz, P. |
| Feb. 1 | **Mañana** | BBC | Benjamin, A. |
| Feb. 15 | **Wife of Martin Guerre** | NY | Bergsma, W. |
| Feb. 18 | **Dr. Heidegger's Experiment** | New York | Raphling, S. |
| Feb. 22 | **Opera, Opera** | New York | Kalmanoff, M. |
| Mar. 4 | **Anachronism** | Hartford | Franchetti, A. |
| Mar. 12 | **Necklace, The** | Redlands, CA | Bohrnstedt, W. |
| Mar. 21 | **Trevallion** | London | Phillips, R. |
| Apr. 6 | **Landara** | Philadelphia | Zimbalist, E. |
| Apr. 8 | **Trial at Rouen** | New York | Dello Joio, N. |
| May | **Susanna and the Elders** | Vienna | Fink, M. |
| May 1 | **Loafer and the Loaf** | Los Angeles | Clarke, H. |
| May 1 | **Nitecap** | New Orleans | Burnham, C. |
| May 3 | **Most Happy Fella** | New York | Loesser, F. |
| May 9 | **Miranda** | Hartford | Siegmeister, E. |
| May 14 | **Beyond Belief** | Rochester | Canning, T. |
| May 14 | **Birthday of the Infanta** | Rochester | Nelson, R. |
| May 15 | **Guide to Life Expectancy** | New York | Fine, V. |
| May 17 | **He Who Gets Slapped** | New York | Ward, R. |
| May 18 | **Land between the Rivers** | Bloomington | Buskirk, C. van |
| June 3 | **Ladies Voices** | Norman, OK | Martin, V. |
| June 11 | **Swing, The** | NBC | Kastle, L. |
| July 7 | **Ballad of Baby Doe** | Central City | Moore, D. |
| July 10 | **If the Cap Fits** | Cheltenham | Bush, G. |
| July 11 | **Ten O'Clock Call** | Cheltenham | Hopkins, A. |
| July 26 | **Bargain, The** | Athens, OH | Slates, P. |
| July 26 | **Candle, The** | Athens, OH | Slates, P. M. |
| July 27 | **Cupid and Psyche** | Woodstock, NY | Vernon, A. |
| Aug. 4 | **Chanticleer** | Aspen | Barab, S. |
| Aug. 11 | **Fat Tuesday** | Tamiment, PA | Berkowitz, S. |
| Aug. 15 | **Logan Rock** | Porthcurno, Eng. | Gundry, I. |
| Oct. 2 | **Ruth** | London | Berkeley, L. |
| Oct. 20 | **In the Drought** | Johannesburg | Joubert, J. |
| Oct. 21 | **Unexpected Visitor** | Cleveland | Kondorossy, L. |
| Oct. 21 | **Unicorn and the Manticore** | Washington | Menotti, G. C. |
| Oct. 29 | **Candide** | New York | Bernstein, L. |
| Nov. 2 | **Dismissed with Prejudice** | New York | Owen, R. |
| Nov. 10 | **Hello, World!** | New York | Mayer, W. |
| Nov. 15 | **Fool, The** | Toronto | Somers, H. |
| Nov. 18 | **Men of Blackmoor** | Weimar | Bush, A. |
| Nov. 25 | **Soldier, The** | New York | Engel, L. |
| Dec. 2 | **Door, The** | Newark | Mopper, I. |
| Dec. 4 | **Intruder, The** | New York | Starer, R. |
| Dec. 11 | **Chelm** | White Plains | Strassburg, R. |
| Dec. 11 | **Isaac Levi** | White Plains | Piket, F. |
| Dec. 14 | **Open Window** | BBC | Arnold, M. |
| Dec. 25 | **Child Is Born** | CBS | Herrmann, B. |
| ? | **Cinderella** | Gainesville, FL | Jarrett, J. |

| Date | Title | City | Composer |
|------|-------|------|----------|
| ? | **Gertrude** | Urbana IL | Johnston, B. |
| ? | **Greek Kalends** | Tunbridge Wells, Eng | Ridout, A. |
| * | **Dowser, The** | -- | Franchetti, A. |
| * | **Fisherman, The** | -- | Scott, T. |

**1957**

| Date | Title | City | Composer |
|------|-------|------|----------|
| Jan. 11 | **Game of Chance** | Rock Island, IL | Barab, S. |
| Jan. 13 | **Golem, The** | White Plains | Weiner, L. |
| Feb. 3 | **Grande Bretèche** | NBC | Claflin, A. |
| Feb. 8 | **Speakeasy** | New York | Lee, D.-K. |
| Feb. 10 | **Grande Bretèche** | NBC | Hollings-worth, S. |
| Feb. 25 | **Black Ram** | BBC (Welsh) Aberystwyth, Wales (1966, Eng) | Parrott, I. |
| Feb. 26 | **Armor of Life** | New York | Newbern, K. |
| Mar. 17 | **Bell Tower** | Urbana, IL | Krenek, E. |
| Mar. 17 | **Esther** | Urbana, IL | Meyerowitz, J. |
| Apr. 7 | **Bandit, The** | Columbia, MO | Patacchi, V. |
| Apr. 7 | **Sotoba Komachi** | New York | Levy, M. D |
| Apr. 18 | **Sterlingman** | Boston | Roy, K. G. |
| Apr. 28 | **Ile** | New York | Laufer, B. |
| May 1 | **Unicorn in the Garden** | Hartford | Smith, R. |
| May 2 | **Volpone** | London | Coombs, J. |
| May 6 | **Boor, The** | Rochester | Argento, D. |
| May 8 | **Esther and Cousin Mordecai** | Paris | Pittman, E. |
| May 9 | **Visitors, The** | New York | Chávez, C. |
| May 18 | **Deirdre** | Chicago | Stein, L. |
| May 22 | **Blind Raftery** | BBC | Trimble, J. |
| May 24 | **Moon and Sixpence** | London | Gardner, J. |
| May 24 | **Venus in Africa** | Denver | Antheil, G. |
| June 5 | **Curious Fern** | New York | Kupferman, M. |
| June 5 | **Voices for a Mirror** | NY | Kupferman, M. |
| July 23 | **Tale of Two Cities** | London | Benjamin, A. |
| July 26 | **Jacob and the Indians** | Woodstock, NY | Laderman, E. |
| Aug. 2 | **Tower, The** | San Francisco | Levy, M. D. |
| Aug. 4 | **Tea Party** | Athens, OH | Gottlieb, J. |
| Aug. 5 | **Tale for a Deaf Ear** | Lenox, MA | Bucci, M. |
| Aug. 15 | **Pep Rally** | Interlochen, MI | Gillis, D. |
| Sept. 12 | **Elanda and Eclipse** | London | Halahan, G. |
| Sept. 26 | **West Side Story** | New York | Bernstein, L. |
| Nov. 16 | **Mayerling** | Cincinnati | Humphreys |
| Nov. 22 | **Sweet Bye and Bye** | New York | Beeson, J. |
| * | **Agamemnon** | -- | Brian, H. |
| * | **Lysistrata** | -- | Fisher, T. |
| * | **Ma Barker** | -- | Eaton, J. |
| * | **Shoe of Little Noby** | -- | Gordon, P. |
| * | **Two Knickerbocker Tales** | -- | Lee, D.-K. |

**1958**

| Date | Title | City | Composer |
|------|-------|------|----------|
| Jan. 15 | **Vanessa** | New York | Barber, S. |
| Feb. 6 | **Dragon, The** | New York | Taylor, D. |
| Feb. 14 | **Dido and Aeneas** | Boston | Beveridge, T. |
| Feb. 26 | **Room No. 12** | Los Angeles | Kanitz, E. |
| Feb. 26 | **Royal Auction** | Los Angeles | Kanitz, E. |
| Feb. 27 | **Love in Transit** | London | Arnell, R. |
| Mar. 6 | **Christmas Miracle** | Washington | Fax, M. |
| Mar. 6 | **Lizzie Strotter** | Des Moines | Kalmanoff, M. |
| Mar. 11 | **Lord Bateman** | London | Forster, A. |
| Mar. 15 | **Committee, The** | New York | Doran, M. |
| Mar. 19 | **Gallantry** | New York | Moore, D. |
| Mar. 20 | **Little Beggars** | BBC | Saunders, M. |
| Apr. 10 | **Bottle Imp** | Wilton, CT | Whiton, P. |
| Apr. 14 | **Pet Shop** | New York | Rieti, V. |
| Apr. 14 | **Robbers, The** | New York | Rorem, N. |
| Apr. 18 | **Holy Devil** | Louisville, KY | Nabokov, N. |
| Apr. 23 | **Good Soldier Schweik** | New York | Kurka, R. |
| Apr. 23 | **Otherwise Engaged** | NY | Davis, A. |
| Apr. 29 | **Rajah's Ruby** | New York | Barab, S. |
| May 4 | **Escorial, The** | New York | Levy, M. D. |
| May 8 | **Draagenfut Girl** | Bronxville, NY | Kupferman, M. |
| June 18 | **Noye's Fludde** | Aldeburgh | Britten, B. |
| June 20 | **Scarf, The** | Spoleto, Italy | Hoiby, L. |
| July 13 | **Impossible Forest** | Westport, CT | Wilder, A. |
| July 16 | **Wuthering Heights** | Santa Fe | Floyd, C. |
| July 20 | **Mermaid in Lock No. 7** | Pittsburgh | Siegmeister, E. |
| July 29 | **Yerma** | Denver | Bowles, P. |
| Aug. 15 | **Sire de Maletroit** | Schroon Lake, NY | Duke, J. |
| Aug. 20 | **Maria Golovin** | Brussels | Menotti, G. C. |
| Aug. 28 | **Sganarelle** | Vancouver | Kaufmann, W. |
| Sept. 27 | **Blues in the Subway Happy Hypocrite** | NY | Levister, A. |
| Oct. 3 | **Diary of a Madman** | Berlin | Searle, H. |
| Nov. 14 | **Triangle, The** | Oberlin | Humel, G. |
| Nov. 30 | **Sarah** | New York | Laderman, E. |
| Dec. 12 | **Mistress into Maid** | Santa Barbara | Duke, V. |
| Dec. 14 | **Gentleman's Island** | London | Horovitz, J. |
| ? | **Little Red Riding Hood** | San Francisco | Barab, S. |
| ? | **Lucky Dollar** | Los Angeles | Kanitz, E. |
| ? | **Proposal, The** | Winfield, KS | Humel, G. |
| * | **Earth Mother** | -- | Penberthy, J. |
| * | **Fortunato** | -- | Gideon, M. |
| * | **Moment of War** | Buenos Aires (1964) | Owen, R. |
| * | **Tamar and Judah** | New York (1970) | Lavry, M. |

**1959**

| Date | Title | City | Composer |
|------|-------|------|----------|
| Jan. 8 | **Sourwood Mountain** | Clinton, MS | Kreutz, A. |

| DATE | TITLE | CITY | COMPOSER |
|---|---|---|---|
| Jan. 17 | Thief and the Hangman | Athens, OH | Ellstein, A. |
| Jan. 22 | Dalgerie | Perth, Austral. | Penberthy, J. |
| Feb. 16 | Lady of Ephesus | Belfast | Warren, R. |
| Mar. 4 | Night Blooming Cereus | Toronto | Beckwith, J. |
| Mar. 23 | Hired Hand | New York | Milano, R. |
| Mar. 24 | I Am the Way | Orange, NJ | Hines, J. |
| Apr. 6 | Cage, The / Decorator, The / Dolcedo / Juggler, The | Washington | Jones, G. T. / Woollen, R. / Meyers, E. / Graves, W. |
| Apr. 14 | Hand of Bridge | New York | Barber, S. |
| Apr. 18 | Blessed Wilderness | Dallas | Kilpatrick, J. |
| Apr. 21 | Prelude and Fugue | Hartford | Franchetti, A. |
| Apr. 26 | Six Characters | New York | Weisgall, H. |
| Apr. 27 | Hunted, The | Rochester | Mailman, M. |
| Apr. 28 | Golden Lion | Seattle | Kechley, G. |
| May 5 | Petrified Princess | London | Arnell, R. |
| May 14 | Glittering Gate | New York | Glanville-Hicks, P. |
| May 11 | King Kong | Durban, SA | Matshikiza, T. |
| May 14 | Rapunzel | New York | Harrison, L. |
| June 4 | Borderline, The | London | Mellers, W. |
| June 10 | Inside Information | London | Tahourdin, P. |
| June 17 | Spur of the Moment | BBC | Halahan, G. |
| June 20 | This Evening | Bennington, VT | Sirulnikoff, J. |
| July 8 | Hands across the Sky | Cheltenham | Hopkins, A. |
| July 11 | Clarkstown Witch | Piermont, NY | Novak, L. |
| July 14 | Other Wise Man | Bentonville, AR | Van Grove, I. |
| July 23 | Moon Flowers | Kent, Eng | Arnell, R. |
| July 28 | Golden Child | Iowa City, IA | Bezanson, P. |
| Aug. 9 | Faun in the Forest | Westport, CT | Cockshott, G. |
| Aug. 25 | Rip Van Winkle | Bloomington, IN | Kaufmann, W. |
| Oct. | Young Lincoln I | Galesburg, IL | Hunkins, E |
| Oct. 23 | Beatrice | NBC-TV | Hoiby, L. |
| Nov. 5 | Cenci, The | London | Coke, R. |
| Dec. 11 | Finn and the Black Hag | Belfast | Warren, R. |
| Dec. 13 | Sofa, The | London | Maconchy, E. |
| Dec. 15 | Blue Flame | San Antonio | Hovhaness, A. |
| ? | Golden Crucible | Pittsburgh | Kilpatrick, J. |
| * | Gardens of Adonis | Omaha (1992) | Weisgall, H. |
| * | Outcasts of Poker Flats | -- | Elkus, J. |
| * | Sacco and Vanzetti | Westport, CT (2001, compl. Lehrman) | Blitzstein, M. |
| * | Tale from Chaucer | Trenton, NJ (1966) | Gordon, P. |

**1960**

| DATE | TITLE | CITY | COMPOSER |
|---|---|---|---|
| Jan. 28 | Maletroit Door | New York | Barab, S. |
| Jan. 24 | Christopher Sly | London | Eastwood, T. |
| Mar. 12 | Giant's Garden | Nor | Krane, S. |
| Mar. 20 | Goat in Chelm | New York | Binder, A. |
| May | Valdo | Cleveland | Freeman, H. |
| May 5 | Introductions and Good-Byes | New York | Foss, L. |

| DATE | TITLE | CITY | COMPOSER |
|---|---|---|---|
| May 19 | Tobias and the Angel | BBC | Bliss, A. |
| May 22 | Cat and the Moon | Hartford | Putsché, T. |
| May 22 | Goodbye to the Clown | New York | Laderman, E. |
| May 26 | Hunted, The | Greenville, SC | Gustafson, D. |
| June 2 | Volpone | Stuttgart | Burt, F. |
| June 11 | Midsummer Night's Dream | Aldeburgh | Britten, B. |
| June 29 | Captive, The | Birmingham | Wishart, P. |
| July 16 | Lodger, The | London | Tate, P. |
| July 21 | Two Tickets to Omaha | Moorehead, MN | Hannay, R. |
| Aug. 4 | Port Town | Lenox. MA | Meyerowitz, J. |
| Nov. 26 | Satan's Trap | New York | Piket, F. |
| Oct. 24 | Tunnel, The | London | Cole, H. |
| Dec. 16 | Outcasts of Poker Flat | Stockton, CA | Beckler, S. |
| * | Aria da capo | -- | Blank, A. |
| * | Aria da capo | -- | Eitzen, L. V. |
| * | Clock, The | -- | Rieti, V. |
| * | Music Lesson | -- | Trythall, G. |
| * | Nightmare Abbey | -- | Allanbrook, D. |
| * | Rocket, The | -- | Goldman, E. |
| * | Woodcarver's Wife | -- | Betts, L. |
| * | Young Lincoln II | -- | Hunkins, E. |

**1961**

| DATE | TITLE | CITY | COMPOSER |
|---|---|---|---|
| Jan. 1 | Deseret | NBC | Kastle, L. |
| Jan. 24 | Bartleby | New York | Flanagan, W. |
| Jan. 28 | Fox, The | Cleveland | Kondorossy, L. |
| Feb. 4 | Box, The | New Orleans | Hamm, C. |
| Feb. 8 | Sweetwater Affair | London | Beadell, R. |
| Feb. 12 | Mink Stockings | Columbus, OH | Marshall, P. |
| Feb. 17 | Purgatory | Washington | Weisgall, H. |
| Feb. 22 | Nero's Mother | New York | Mopper, I. |
| Feb. 22 | Sisters, The | New York | Flagello, N. |
| Feb. 26 | Widow, The | Saratoga Springs, NY | Gaburo, K. |
| Mar. 18 | Enchanted Canary | Bemidji, MN | Stevens, N. |
| Mar. 23 | Kisses for a Quid | Melbourne | Werder, F. |
| Mar. 25 | Hunting of the Snark | NY | Laderman, E. |
| Apr. 2 | Break of Day | New York | Jones, G. T. |
| Apr. 26 | Perpetual | Los Angeles | Kanitz, E. |
| May 6 | Scarlet Letter | Bloomington | Kaufmann, W. |
| May 20 | Elegy for Young Lovers | Schwetzingen | Henze, H. W. |
| May 20 | Silas Marner | Capetown | Joubert, J. |
| June 2 | Godfather Death | New York | Meyerowitz, J. |
| June 9 | Greek Passion | Zurich | Martinů, B. |
| July 25 | Amiable Beast | New York | Welner, G. |
| July 29 | Brute, The | New Haven | Moss, L. |
| Aug. 7 | Early Dawn | Denver | Lockwood, N. |
| Aug. 19 | Nausicaa | Athens | Glanville-Hicks, P. |

| DATE | TITLE | CITY | COMPOSER |
|---|---|---|---|
| Sept. 12 | Ledge, The | London | Bennett, R. |
| Sept. 18 | Blood Moon | San Francisco | Dello Joio, N. |
| Oct. 12 | Wings of the Dove | New York | Moore, D. |
| Oct. 26 | Crucible, The | New York | Ward, R. |
| Nov. | Pardoner's Tale | Cape Town | Chisholm, E. |
| Nov. 10 | Franklin's Tale | Baton Rouge | Sokoloff, N. |
| Nov. 11 | Command Performance | Poughkeepsie, NY | Middleton, R. |
| Nov. 25 | Harvest, The | Chicago | Giannini, V. |
| Dec. 1 | Libretto, The | Norma, OK | Gillis, D. |
| Dec. 3 | Fifth for Bridge | San Francisco | Sheldon, R. |
| Dec. 3 | Gift of Song | Pasadena | Caldwell, M. |
| Dec. 10 | No Neutral Ground | Pullman, WA | Brandt, W. |
| Dec. 12 | Nativity, The | Cambridge, MA | Thompson, R. |
| Dec. 17 | Long Christmas Dinner | Mannheim, Ger. | Hindemith, P. |
| Dec. 17 | Yerma | BBC | Aplvor, D. |
| Dec. 24 | Novellis, Novellis | Washington | La Montaine |
| * | Anniversary, The | -- | Rorem, N. |
| * | Canterbury Tales | -- | Chisholm, E. |
| * | Colonel Jonathan the Saint | Denver (1971) | Argento, D. |
| * | Fourth Day | -- | Ahlstrom, D. |
| * | Jest of Hahalaba | -- | Cotel, M. |
| * | Macbeth | -- | Goldman, E. |
| * | Medea | -- | Farberman, H. |
| * | Midnight Court | -- | Chisholm, E. |
| * | Pardoner's Tale | -- | Sokoloff, N. |

**1962**

| DATE | TITLE | CITY | COMPOSER |
|---|---|---|---|
| Feb. 3 | Juggler of Our Lady | New Orleans | Kay, U. |
| Feb. 15 | Rehearsal Call | New York | Giannini, V. |
| Feb. 24 | Earth-Trapped | E Lansing, MI | Reed, H. O. |
| Feb. 24 | Living Solid Face | E Lansing, MI | Reed, H. O. |
| Mar. 1 | Alcestiad, The | Frankfurt | Talma, L. |
| Mar. 1 | Dancing Master | London | Arnold, M. |
| Mar. 22 | Golem, The | New York | Ellstein, A. |
| Mar. 27 | Engaged! | Bristol, Eng | Sullivan-Rowell, Mobbs |
| Apr. 11 | Revelation | Urbana, IL | Partch, H. |
| May 25 | Jeremiah | Binghamton | Fink, M. |
| May 29 | King Priam | London | Tippett, M. |
| June 8 | Outcasts of Poker Flat | Denton, TX | Adler, S. |
| June 14 | Flood, The | CBS TV | Stravinsky, I. |
| July 5 | Dark Pilgrimage | London | Tate, P. |
| July 10 | Bird in the Bush | Los Angeles | Bielawa, H. |
| Aug. 1 | Wizards of Balizar | Denver | Lockwood, N. |
| Oct. 11 | Passion of Jonathan Wade | New York | Floyd, C. |
| Nov. 9 | One Christmas Long Ago | Muncie, IN | Mayer, W. |
| Nov. 11 | Hamlet | Baltimore | Kagen, S. |
| Dec. 3 | Unicorn for Christmas | Wellington | Farquhar, D. |

| DATE | TITLE | CITY | COMPOSER |
|---|---|---|---|
| Dec. 6 | Many Moons | Poughkeepsie | Dougherty, C. |
| Dec. 16 | Departure, The | London | Maconchy, E. |
| Dec. 16 | Wager, The | London | Orr, B. |
| Dec. 19 | Abbot of Drimock | London | Musgrave, T. |
| Dec. 24 | Christmas Carol | London | Coleman, E. |
| ? | Pandora's Box | Boulder, CO | Effinger, C. |
| * | Amphitryon 4 | -- | Blumenfeld, H. |
| * | Boccaccio's Nightingale | -- | Trimble, L. |
| * | John Barleycorn | -- | Montgomery |
| * | Mad Hamlet | -- | Reif, P. |
| * | Pathelin | Norrland, Sweden (1990) | Josephs, W. |
| * | Yerma | -- | Wilding-White, R. |
| * | You Never Know | -- | Koutzen, B. |

**1963**

| DATE | TITLE | CITY | COMPOSER |
|---|---|---|---|
| Feb | Darkened City | Bloomington | Heiden, B. |
| Feb. 15 | Bald Prima Donna | New York | Kalmanoff, M. |
| Feb. 15 | Spirit of the Avalanche | Tokyo | Hovhaness, A. |
| Mar. 3 | Labyrinth, The | NBC TV | Menotti, G. C. |
| Mar. 11 | Highway 1, U.S.A. | Miami | Still, W. G. |
| Apr. | Young Tom Edison | New York | Kalmanoff, M. |
| Apr. 25 | Young Goodman Brown | Allentown, PA | Lenel, L. |
| May | Marko the Miser | Farnham, Eng. | Musgrave, T. |
| May 15 | Plough and the Stars | St. Louis | Siegmeister, E. |
| May 17 | Half Magic | Walding River, NY | Kalmanoff, M. |
| May 31 | Christopher Sly | Minneapolis | Argento, D. |
| June 23 | Pietro's Petard | New York | Overton, H. |
| July 2 | Our Man in Havana | Aldeburgh | Williamson, M. |
| July 10 | Birthday of the Infanta | London | Stoker, R. |
| Aug. 5 | Zenda | San Francisco | Duke, V. |
| Oct. 10 | Gentlemen, Be Seated! | New York | Moross, J. |
| Oct. 22 | Last Savage | Paris | Menotti, G. C. |
| Nov. 20 | Graduation Ode | Belfast | Warren, R. |
| Dec. | Last Puppet | New York | Strilko, A. |
| Dec. 2 | Knife, The | London | Jones, D. |
| Dec. 2 | Sojourner and Mollie Sinclair | Raleigh, NC | Floyd, C. |
| Dec. 21 | Dynamite Tonite | New York | Bolcom, W. |
| ? | Rescue, The | -- | Ridout, A. |
| * | Caucasian Chalk Circle | -- | Chisholm, E. |
| * | Importance of Being Earnest | -- | Chisholm, E. |
| * | Life and Loves of Robert Burns | -- | Chisholm, E. |
| * | Magic Barrel | -- | Blitzstein, M. |
| * | Sappho | -- | Glanville-Hicks, P. |

| Date | Title | City | Composer |
|---|---|---|---|
| * | Scarlet Letter | -- | Lybbert, D. |
| * | Stranger in Eden | -- | Bezanson, P. |
| **1964** | | | |
| Jan. 9 | Masque of Angels | Minneapolis | Argento, D. |
| Feb. 17 | Athaliah | New York | Weisgall, H. |
| Feb. 26 | Visions of Midnight | Los Angeles | Kanitz, E. |
| Mar. 6 | Ferryman's Daughter | Letchworth, Eng. | Bush, A. |
| Mar. 6 | Hanging Judge | Denver | Lockwood, N. |
| Mar. 8 | Photo of the Colonel | London | Searle, H. |
| Mar. 21 | Fortune of Saint Macabre | Moorhead, MN | Hannay, R. |
| Mar. 25 | Little Billy | Stroud, Eng. | Hurd, M. |
| Mar. 28 | Miracle, The | Perth, Austral. | Penberthy, J. |
| Apr. 6 | Sack of Calabasas | Phoenix, AR | Fletcher, G. |
| Apr. 16 | Gift of the Magi | Minneapolis | Magney, R. |
| Apr. 19 | Montezuma | W. Berlin | Sessions, R. |
| May 23 | Wind Drum | Gatlinburg, TN | Hovhaness, A. |
| June 3 | Martin's Lie | Bath | Menotti, G. C. |
| June 11 | English Eccentrics | Aldeburgh | Williamson, M. |
| June 13 | Curlew River | Aldeburgh | Britten, B. |
| June 14 | Cappemakers, The | Charleston Manor, Sussex | Taverner, J. |
| July 3 | Lady from Colorado | Central City, CO | Ward, R. |
| July 15 | Morvoren | London | Cannon, P. |
| July 30 | Shining Chalice | Eureka Springs, AR | Van Grove, I. |
| Aug. 24 | Burning House | Gatlinburg, TN | Hovhaness, A. |
| Oct. 8 | Natalia Petrovna | New York | Hoiby, L. |
| Oct. 24 | Virgin and the Fawn | Los Angeles | Zador, E. |
| Nov. | Gilded Cage | New York | Lees, B. |
| Nov. 12 | Bartleby | Oberlin, OH | Aschaffenburg, W. |
| Nov. 12 | One Man Show | London | Maw, N. |
| Nov. 24 | Requiem for a Rich Young Man | Denver | Lockwood, N. |
| Nov. 30 | Tartuffe | London | Benjamin, A. |
| Dec. 12 | Brideship, The | Vancouver | Turner, R. |
| ? | In Memoriam | Ann Arbor | Ashley, R. |
| ? | Nathan the Wise | Cleveland | Kondorossy, L. |
| ? | Pot of Broth | New York | Haufrecht, H. |
| ? | Uncle Tom's Cabin | New York | Claflin, A. |
| * | Flowers of Ice | -- | Pasatieri, T. |
| * | Idiots First | Ithaca, NY (1974) | Blitzstein, M. |
| * | Selfish Giant | -- | Perry, J. |
| * | Trial of Tender O'Shea | -- | Swift, R. |
| * | Trysting Place | -- | Pasatieri, T. |

| Date | Title | City | Composer |
|---|---|---|---|
| **1965** | | | |
| Jan. 5 | Hunting of the Snark | Denver | Wilson, J. |
| Feb. 3 | Prince of Coxcombs | London | Gundry, I. |
| Feb. 18 | Videomania | Granville, OH | Kalmanoff, M. |
| Feb. 24 | Mines of Sulphur | London | Bennett, R. |
| Mar. 3 | Prince of Coxcombs | London | Gundry, I. |
| Mar. 14 | Fisherman Called Peter | Carmel, NY | Owen, R. |
| Mar. 17 | Patrick | Dublin, RTÉ TV | Potter, A. J. |
| spring | Pyramus and Thisbe | Tuscaloosa, AL | Bruce, N. |
| Mar. 22 | Serenade at Noon | Baton Rouge | Fuchs, P. P. |
| Mar. 25 | Lizzie Borden | New York | Beeson, J. |
| Apr. 2 | Amorous Judge | Sydney | Gross, E. |
| Apr. 4 | Macbeth | New York | Halpern, S. |
| Apr. 4 | Monkey's Paw | New York | Halpern, S. |
| Apr. 11 | Final Ingredient | New York | Amram, D. |
| Apr. 21 | Edgar and Emily | New York | Toch, E. |
| May 15 | Alissa | Geneva | Banfield, R. de |
| May 22 | Happy Prince | Farnham | Williamson, M. |
| May 26 | Quarry, The | Wembley | Joubert, J. |
| May 27 | Judas Tree | London | Dickinson, P. |
| May 30 | Arrangement, The | London | Davis, C. |
| June | Sweeney Agonistes | London | Dankworth, J. |
| July | Ophelia | Tasmania | Penberthy, J. |
| July 4 | Johnson Preserv'd | London | Stoker, R. |
| Aug. | Nun's Priest's Tale | Hanover, NH | Finney, R. |
| Aug. 18 | Fall of the House of Usher | Hobart, Austral | Sitsky, L. |
| Aug. 19 | Young Kabbarli | Hobart, Austral. | Sutherland, M. |
| Aug. 20 | Women, The | Aspen | Pasatieri, T. |
| Sept. 24 | Hero, The | New York | Bucci, M. |
| Nov. 4 | Miss Julie | New York | Rorem, N. |
| Dec. 7 | Gift of the Magi | San Francisco | Gillis, D. |
| ? | Boy from the Catacombs | Canterbury | Ridout, A. |
| * | Gimpel the Fool | -- | Davidson, C. |
| * | Noah | -- | Carlos, W. |
| * | Queen and the Rebels | College Pk., MD (1989) | Moss, L. |
| * | Ring around Harlequin | -- | McKay, N. |
| * | Scarlet Letter | -- | Kroll, F. |
| **1966** | | | |
| Jan. 5 | Julius Caesar Jones | London | Williamson, M. |
| Feb. 3 | Loving/Toi | Toronto | Schafer, R. |
| Mar. 16 | Divina, La | New York | Pasatieri, T. |
| Mar. 18 | Judgment of St. Francis | New York | Flagello, N. |
| Mar. 21 | Mr. and Mrs. Discobbolos | New York | Westergaard, P. |
| Mar. 21 | Without Memorial Banners | Kansas City | Six, H. |

| DATE | TITLE | CITY | COMPOSER | DATE | TITLE | CITY | COMPOSER |
|------|-------|------|----------|------|-------|------|----------|
| Mar. 31 | **Markheim** | New Orleans | Floyd, C. | Mar. 11 | **Canterville Ghost** | New York | Kalmanoff, M. |
| Apr. 3 | **Empty Bottle** | New York | Kalmanoff, M. | Mar. 17 | **Mourning Becomes Electra** | New York | Levy, M. D. |
| Apr. 28 | **Carry Nation** | Lawrence, KS | Moore, D. | spring | **Eye of Horus** | Boston | El-Dabh, E. |
| May 5 | **Parlour, The** | Cardiff | Williams, G. | Apr. | **Virgil's Dream** | Brighton, Eng | Colgrass, M. |
| May 14 | **Magic Chair** | Baton Rouge | Zador, E. | Apr. 14 | **Arabesque** | Vermillion, SD | Marek, R. |
| May 15 | **Portrait in Brownstone** | New York | Reif, P. | Apr. 15 | **Chanticleer** | New York | Barthelson, J. |
| June 9 | **Burning Fiery Furnace** | Aldeburgh | Britten, B. | Apr. 15 | **Family, The** | New York | Strouse, C. |
| June 21 | **Annunciation, The Trista** | New York | McCray, C. | Apr. 15 | **Trilby** | New York | Piket, F. |
| June 26 | **Pilate** | Los Angeles | Hovhaness, A. | Apr. 22 | **Moonrakers** | Brighton, Eng | Williamson, M. |
| July 3 | **White Gods** | Urbana, IL | Kelly, R. | Apr. 22 | **Travellers, The** | San Francisco | Hovhaness, A. |
| July 7 | **Purgatory** | Cheltenham | Crosse, G. | May 12 | **Mr. Vinegar** | Redding, CA | Sacco, P. |
| July 7 | **What D'Ye Call It** | Cheltenham | Tate, P. | May 19 | **Dunstan and the Devil** | Cookham, Austral | Williamson, M. |
| July 30 | **Hoosier Tale** | Bloomington | Kaufmann, W. | May 22 | **Brief Candle** | New York | Mayer, W. |
| Aug. 6 | **Bassarids, The** | Salzburg | Henze, H. W. | May 23 | **Pardoner's Tale** | Tucson | Davis, J. S. |
| Sept. 1 | **Antony and Cleopatra** | New York | Barber, S. | May 24 | **Poorest Suitor** | Cleveland | Kondorossy, L. |
| Oct. 11 | **Visitation, The** | Hamburg | Schuller, G. | May 27 | **Last Day** | New York | Rorem, N. |
| Oct. 20 | **Notturno in La** | Hartford | Franchetti, A. | May 31 | **Grant, Warden of the Plains** | Winnipeg | Adaskin, M. |
| Nov. 19 | **Pardoner's Tale** | Dublin | Lubin, E. | June 1 | **Shoemaker's Holiday** | Minneapolis | Argento, D. |
| Nov. 29 | **Violins of St. Jacques** | London | Williamson, M. | June 3 | **Bear, The** | Aldeburgh | Walton, W. |
| Dec. 3 | **Mr. Scrooge** | New York | Kalmanoff, M. | June 3 | **Castaway** | Aldeburgh | Berkeley, L. |
| Dec. 5 | **Man from Venus** | Waltham Abbey, Essex | Cannon, P. | June 3 | **Golden Vanity** | Aldeburgh | Britten, B. |
| Dec. 11 | **Sugar Reapers** | Leipzig | Bush, A. | June 5 | **Time for Growing** | Norwich, Eng | Hopkins, A. |
| Dec. 28 | **Shepherdess and the Chimneysweep** | Fort Worth, TX | Smith, J. | Aug. 13 | **Lake of Menteith** | BBC | Noble, H. |
| ? | **Appointment, The** | BBC | Josephs, W. | Sept. | **Luck of Ginger Coffey** | Toronto | Pannell, R. |
| ? | **Bargain, The** | CBC, Montreal | McPeek, B. | Sept. 3 | **Ray and the Gospel Singer** | Toledo, OH | Gould, E. |
| ? | **Flax into Gold** | -- | Cole, H. | Sept. 5 | **Sam Slick** | Halifax | Jones, K. |
| * | **Death of the Hired Man** | Toronto (1979) | McIntyre, P. | Sept. 23 | **Louis Riel** | Toronto | Somers, H. |
| * | **General, The** | -- | Werder, F. | Oct. | **Eleanor of Aquitaine** | Sydney | Whitehead, G. |
| * | **Judgment, The** | -- | Kupferman, M. | Oct. 20 | **Music Hath Mischief** | Dublin | Victory, G. |
| * | **Maryam the Harlot** | -- | Rieti, V. | Oct. 26 | **Mandarin, The** | New York | Elkus, J. |
| * | **Pariahs, The** | Albany, NY (1985) | Kastle, L. | Oct. 31 | **Penny for a Song** | London | Bennett, R. |
| * | **So How Does Your Garden Grow** | -- | Russell, R. | Nov. 18 | **Padrevia** | Brooklyn, NY | Pasatieri, T. |
| * | **Philosophy Lesson** | -- | Stern, M. | Nov. 30 | **Decision, The** | London | Musgrave, T. |
| * | **This Is Not True** | -- | McIntyre, P. | Dec. 1 | **Shephardes Playe** | Washington | La Montaine |
| * | **Ubu Roi** | -- | Aplvor, D. | Dec. 12 | **Brideship, The** | Vancouver | Turner, R. |
| | | | | Dec. 20 | **Gentlemen in Waiting** | New York | Booth, T. |
| **1967** | | | | Dec. 27 | **Magi, The** | Washington | La Montaine |
| Jan. 7 | **Three Wise Men** | Kings Langley | Gundry, I. | ? | **Agamemnon** | ABC | Werder, F. |
| Jan. 12 | **John Hooten** | London | Russo, W. | ? | **Lysistrata & the War** | Detroit | Fink, R |
| Jan. 23 | **Some Place of Darkness** | BBC | Whelen, C. | ? | **Till Victory Is Won** | Bermuda | Fax, M. |
| Jan. 29 | **Land of Milk and Honey** | Chicago | Russo, W. | * | **David** | -- | Goldman, E. |
| Mar. 5 | **Arden Must Die** | Hamburg | Goehr, A. | * | **Dr. Faustus** | -- | Hagemann, P. |
| Mar. 9 | **Servant of Two Masters** | New York | Giannini, V. | * | **Jonah** | -- | Cole, H. |
| Mar. 10 | **Orpheus** | Austin, TX | Austin, J. | * | **Numbered, The** | -- | Lutyens, E. |
| | | | | * | **Sacrapant** | -- | Aston, P. |
| | | | | * | **Scarlet Letter** | -- | Lybbert, D. |

| DATE | TITLE | CITY | COMPOSER | DATE | TITLE | CITY | COMPOSER |
|---|---|---|---|---|---|---|---|
| * | Shadows among Us | Philadelphia (1979) | Laderman, E. | Nov. 10 | Victory at Masada | Detroit | Kalmanoff, M. |
| * | Villon | New Orleans (1981) | Read, G. | Nov. 14 | Great Stone Face | Muncie, IN | Kalmanoff, M. |
| | | | | Nov. 28 | Melita | Belfast | Camilleri, C. |
| **1968** | | | | Dec. 19 | Help, Help, the Globolinks! | Hamburg | Menotti, G. C. |
| Jan. 11 | Equation, The | London | Bush, G. | ? | Children's Crusade 1939 | Canterbury | Ridout, A. |
| Jan. 26 | Box, The | New York | Eakin, C. G. | ? | Frustration | Washington | Harnick, S. |
| Jan. 26 | Feathertop | New York | Barthelson, J. | * | Black Epic | -- | El-Dabh, H. |
| Feb. 6 | Aria da capo | New York | Baksa, R. | * | Herod, Do Your Worst | -- | Kelly, B. |
| Feb. 8 | That Morning Thing | Ann Arbor | Ashley, R. | * | Troublemaker, The | -- | Polgar, T. |
| Feb. 13 | Big Black Box | New York | Morgenstern, S. | | | | |
| Feb. 20 | Bride Comes to Yellow Sky | Charleston, IL | Nixon, R. | **1969** | | | |
| Mar. | Lysistrata | New York | Barthelson, J. | Jan. 5 | Pantomime | New York | Poùhe, J. |
| Mar. 1 | Rehearsal, The | New York | Benjamin, T. | Jan. 7 | Legend of Star Valley Junction | New York | Gillis, D. |
| Mar. 5 | Hamlet | Hamburg | Searle, H. | Jan. 7 | Romeo and Juliet | New York | Liotta, A. |
| Mar. 12 | Jericho Road | Philadelphia | Aria, P. | Jan. 25 | Triumph of Punch | Brooklyn, NY | Vernon, A. |
| Apr. 3 | Boor, The | Lexington, KY | Kay, U. | Feb. 15 | Horspfal | Minneapolis | Stokes, E. |
| Apr. 9 | Goodman Brown | Painesville, OH | Fink, H. | Mar. 12 | Jericho Road | Philadelphia | Aria, P. |
| Apr. 10 | Full Circle | Perth, Scot. | Orr, R. | Mar. 16 | Charcoal Burner | BBC, Scot | Wilson, T. |
| Apr. 26 | Cask of Amontillado | Rochester, NY | Provenzano, A. | Mar. 20 | Dr. Musikus | London | Hopkins, A. |
| | | | | spring | Excitement at the Circus | Paterson, NJ | Blank, A. |
| Apr. 30 | Snow Wolf | Brighton | Williamson, M. | Mar. 28 | All the King's Men | Coventry, Eng | Bennett, R. |
| May | Metamorphosis | Philadelphia | White, M. | Apr. 4 | Rebel, The | BBC | Eastwood, T. |
| May 2 | We're Back | New York | Armour, E. | Apr. 13 | Man on a Bearskin Rug | Aberdeen, SD | Ramsier, P. |
| May 18 | Moralities | Cincinnati | Henze, H. W. | Apr. 19 | Let's Build a Nut House | San Jose | Moran, R. |
| May 19 | Rose Affair | London | Kay, N | Apr. 22 | Eight Songs for a Mad King | London | Davies, P. M. |
| June 5 | Birds, The | London | Maconchy, E. | Apr. 22 | Shizuka's Dance | Cleveland | Kondorossy, L. |
| June 5 | Three Strangers | London | Maconchy, E. | Apr. 27 | Combat Zone | Hempstead, NY | Arnell, R. |
| June 8 | Punch and Judy | Aldeburgh | Birtwistle, H. | Apr. 29 | Lion, the Witch | Manchester | McCabe, J. |
| June 10 | Prodigal Son | Aldeburgh | Britten, B. | Apr. 30 | Stronger, The | Greenville, NC | Kosteck, G. |
| July 16 | Naboth's Vineyard | London | Goehr, A. | May 2 | Haircut | New York | Morgenstern, S. |
| July 24 | Cyrano de Bergerac | Boulder, CO | Effinger, C. | | | | |
| Aug. 1 | Twelfth Night | Glens Falls, NY | Amram, D. | May 8 | Down by the Greenwood Side | Brighton, Eng | Birtwistle, H. |
| Aug. 7 | Elephant Steps | Lenox, MA | Silverman, S. | May 12 | Twice in a Blue Moon | Farnham, Eng | Tate, P. |
| Aug. 13 | Growing Castle | Dynevor Castle, Wales | Williamson, M. | May 15 | Greatshot | New Haven | Bolcom, W. |
| | | | | May 19 | Opening, The | Boston | Wilder, A. |
| Aug. 13 | Lucky-Peter's Journey | Dynevor Castle Wales | Williamson, M. | May 26 | Incident at Owl Creek | BBC | Whelen, C. |
| Aug. 21 | Audition, The | Pittsburgh | Kalmanoff, M. | May 29 | Under Western Eyes | London | Joubert, J. |
| | | | | May 29 | Willowdale Handcar | New York | Wigglesworth, F. |
| Aug. 23 | Young Goodman Brown | Saratoga Springs, NY | Mollicone, H. | June 7 | Grace of Todd | Aldeburgh | Crosse, G. |
| Aug. 24 | Maurya | Greenville, NC | Kosteck, G., | July 29 | Four-Thousand Dollars | Iowa City | Turner, T. |
| Aug. 29 | Falcon, The | Bath | Cole, H. | Aug. | Aesop | Pemigewasset, NH | Kalmanoff, M. |
| Oct. 9 | Nine Rivers from Jordan | New York | Weisgall, H. | Aug. 27 | Pharsalia | Edinburgh | Hamilton, I. |
| Oct. 20 | Tommy | New York | Townshend, P. | Sept. 1 | Undertaker, The | Edinburgh | Purser, J. |
| | | | | Oct. 15 | David and Bathsheba | Newcastle | Barlow, D. |
| Oct. 26 | Scarlet Mill | Brooklyn, NY | Zador, E. | Oct. 25 | Pied Piper of Hamelin | Wexford | Wilson, J. |
| Oct. 28 | Politics of Harmony | New York | Wuorinen, C. | Oct. | All the Tea in China | Oxford | Oliver, S. |
| Nov. 8 | Passion of Oedipus | Los Angeles | Travis, R. | Oct. 6 | Takeover, The | Canberra | Dreyfus, G. |

| DATE | TITLE | CITY | COMPOSER |
|------|-------|------|----------|
| Oct. 12 | **King David** | New York | Kalmanoff, M. |
| Oct. 18 | **Rich Man, Poor Man** | Stroud, Eng | Hopkins, A. |
| Nov. 1 | **Twelfth Night** | Wexford | Wilson, J. |
| Nov. 11 | **Legends Three** | New York | Kalmanoff, M. |
| Nov. 25 | **Agamemnon** | Oxford | Morris, R. |
| Nov. 30 | **Barnstable** | Kassel, Ger | Burt, F. |
| Dec. | **Slippery Soules** | Oxford | Oliver, S. |
| Dec. 25 | **First Christmas** | Sydney | Antill, J. H. |
| Dec. 25 | **Selfish Giant** | BBC, Wales | Burtch, M. |
| Dec. 31 | **Erode the Greate** | Washington | La Montaine, J. |
| ? | **Leper King** | Chicago | Hovhaness, A. |
| * | **King of the Golden River** | -- | Hand, C. |
| * | **Mr. Punch** | -- | Healey, D. |
| * | **Private** | -- | Werder, F. |
| * | **Sacrapant the Sorcerer** | -- | Aston, P. |
| * | **Three Mimes** | -- | Cantrick, R. |

**1970**

| DATE | TITLE | CITY | COMPOSER |
|------|-------|------|----------|
| Jan. 22 | **Of Mice and Men** | Seattle | Floyd, C. |
| Mar. 17 | **My Heart's in the Highlands** | NET | Beeson, J. |
| Mar. | **Johnny and the Mohawks** | London | Maconchy, E. |
| Mar. | **Wanderer, The** | Minneapolis | Boesing, P. |
| Apr. | **Day Return** | London | Head, M. |
| Apr. | **Key Money** | London | Head, M. |
| Apr. 3 | **Mr. Punch** | Gothenburg | Hurd, M. |
| Apr. 8 | **Martyred, The** | Seoul | Wade, J. |
| Apr. 13 | **Victory** | London | Bennett, R. |
| Apr. 15 | **Don Cristóbal** | Wellesley, MA | Crawford, J. |
| Apr. 18 | **Pied Piper** | New York | Flagello, N. |
| May 9 | **Fisherman and His Wife** | Boston | Schuller, G. |
| May 19 | **America** | Los Angeles | Kohs, E. B. |
| June | **Phoenix Too Far** | Oxford | Oliver, S. |
| June 22 | **Cimarrón, El** | Aldeburgh | Henze, H. W. |
| July 7 | **Nazarene, The** | Ridgecrest, NC | Gillis, D. |
| July 8 | **Shadowplay** | London | Goehr, A. |
| July 19 | **Rising of the Moon** | Glyndebourne | Maw, N. |
| Sept. 12 | **Seven Deadly Sins** | Brisbane | Brumby, C. |
| Sept. 29 | **Joe Hill** | East Berlin | Bush, A. |
| Oct. 7 | **Jesse Tree** | Dorchester | Maconchy, E. |
| Oct. 16 | **Prisoner Paul** | London | Gundry, I. |
| Nov. 11 | **Ramona** | Provo, UT | Seymour, J. |
| Nov. 12 | **Carmilla** | New York | Johnston, B. |
| Nov. 13 | **Medea** | Milwaukee | Elkus, J. |
| Nov. 30 | **Helen in Egypt** | Milwaukee | Elkus, J. |
| Dec. 2 | **Knot Garden** | London | Tippett, M. |
| ? | **Cabaret Opera** | New York | Russo, W. |
| * | **Enchanted Shirt** | -- | Oliver, S. |
| * | **Fee First** | -- | Doran, M. |
| * | **Joan of Arc** | -- | Burgon, G. |

| DATE | TITLE | CITY | COMPOSER |
|------|-------|------|----------|
| * | **Naked Carmen** | -- | Corigliano/ Hess |
| * | **No Trifling with Love** | -- | Burton, S. |
| * | **Scarlet Letter** | -- | Mann, R. W. |
| * | **Shadow, The** | Wellington (1988) | Farquhar, D. |

**1971**

| DATE | TITLE | CITY | COMPOSER |
|------|-------|------|----------|
| Jan. 10 | **Medea in Corinth** | London | Lees, B. |
| Jan. 22 | **Rapunzel** | Binghamton | Brooks, R. |
| Jan. 28 | **Chatterton** | ORTF, Paris | Victory, G. |
| Jan. 30 | **Faust Counter Faust** | Minneapolis | Gessner, J. |
| Feb. 18 | **White Butterfly** | New York | Leichtling, A. |
| Feb. 28 | **Survival of St. Joan** | New York | Ruffin, H. |
| Mar. | **Journey of Snow White** | New York | Carmines, A. |
| Mar. 12 | **Capitoline Venus** | Quincy, IL | Kay, U. |
| Mar. 12 | **Most Important Man** | New York | Menotti, G. C. |
| Mar. 26 | **Losers, The** | New York | Farberman, H. |
| April | **Death of Antigone** | Oxford | Brindle, R. |
| Apr. 1 | **Pardoner's Tale** | Canterbury | Ridout, A. |
| Apr. 1 | **Scene Machine** | Kassel | Gilbert, A. |
| Apr. 7 | **Calvary** | Seattle | Pasatieri, T. |
| Apr. 11 | **And David Wept** | CBS TV | Laderman, E. |
| Apr. 17 | **Pandora's Box** | Los Angeles | Cave, M. |
| May | **Rocket's Red Blare** | Cambridge, MA | Yannatos, J. |
| May 1 | **Edward John Eyre** | Sydney | Conyngham, B. |
| May 5 | **Opera Flies** | Washington | El-Dabh, H. |
| May 5 | **Who Stole the Crown Jewels?** | New York | Siegel, N. |
| May 10 | **Phrases from Orpheus** | Guelph | Wilson, C. |
| May 16 | **Owen Wingrave** | NET/BBC | Britten, B. |
| May 20 | **Huckleberry Finn** | New York | Overton, H. |
| May 21 | **All Cats Turn Gray** | New York | Six, H. |
| May 21 | **Fables** | Martin, Tenn | Rorem, N. |
| June 8 | **Clandestine Marriage** | London | Wishart, P. |
| June 11 | **Inspector General** | Torrance, CA | Zador, E. |
| June 19 | **Summer and Smoke** | St Paul, MN | Hoiby, L. |
| July 24 | **Three Sisters Who Are Not Sisters** | Philadelphia | Rorem, N. |
| July 27 | **Photograph—1920** | Lake Placid | Kalmanoff, M. |
| July 29 | **Fair Traders** | Somerset, Eng | Cole, H. |
| Aug. 21 | **Young Caesar** | Aptos, CA | Harrison, L. |
| Sept. 1 | **Mayakovsky** | Edinburgh | Daiken, M. |
| Sept. 9 | **Hunting of the Snark** | New York | Roberts, E. |
| Sept. 10 | **Tamburlaine** | Liverpool | Murdoch, E. |
| Sept. 12 | **Kalamona** | Cleveland | Kondorossy, L. |
| Sept. 18 | **Stone Wall** | London | Williamson, M. |
| Oct. | **Vessel** | New York | Monk, M. |
| Oct. 14 | **Postcard from Morocco** | Minneapolis | Argento, D. |
| Oct. 21 | **Jesus Christ Superstar** | New York | Lloyd Webber, A. |

| Date | Title | City | Composer |
|---|---|---|---|
| Oct. 23 | **Widow of Ephesus** | Stroud, Eng | Hurd, M. |
| Oct. 31 | **Divertissement No. 3** | London | Moran, R. |
| Nov. 21 | **Joan** | New York | Carmines, A. |
| Nov. 23 | **Duchess of Malfi** | Oxford | Oliver, S. |
| Dec. 14 | **Angelo** | Canterbury | Ridout, A. |
| ? | **Cat, The** | Berkshire, NY | Ridout, A. |
| ? | **Gift, The** | Canterbury | Ridout, A. |
| ? | **Martyr's Mirror** | Lansdale, PA | Parker, A. |
| ? | **Noelani** | Aptos, CA? | Barati, G. |
| ? | **Real Magic in New York** | New York | Dickman, S. |
| ? | **Sonata about Jerusalem** | Jerusalem | Goehr, A. |
| ? | **Trials of Psyche** | Urbana-Champaign | Bruce, N. |
| * | **Bouvard and Pécuchet** | -- | Aplvor, D. |
| * | **Donkey's Tale** | -- | Mann, L. |
| * | **Juan (The Libertine)** | -- | Alwyn, W. |
| * | **Three Wise Monkeys** | -- | Oliver, S. |
| * | **Vicious Square** | -- | Werder, F. |
| * | **Will of Her Own** | London (1985) | Gundry, I. |

## 1972

| Date | Title | City | Composer |
|---|---|---|---|
| Jan. 28 | **Marriage Machine** | Sydney | Brumby, C. |
| Feb. 14 | **Trial of Mary Lincoln** | NET | Pasatieri, T. |
| Mar. | **Hansel & Gretel & Ted & Alice** | Dallas | Schickele, P. |
| Mar. 1 | **Time Off?** | London | Lutyens, E. |
| Mar. 2 | **Black Widow** | Seattle | Pasatieri, T. |
| Mar. 22 | **Let My People Go** | Liverpool | Warren, R. |
| Apr. 6 | **Happy End** | New Haven | Weill-Feingold |
| Apr. 14 | **Red Sea** | Devon, Eng | Williamson, M. |
| Apr. 15 | **Julian** | Winston-Salem, NC | Fussell, C. |
| Apr. 20 | **Lord Byron** | New York | Thomson, V. |
| Apr. 27 | **Cyrano de Bergerac** | Greensboro, NC | Jarrett, J. |
| May 6 | **Tea Symphony** | Banff, AB | Charpentier, G. |
| May 15 | **Heracles** | Bloomington | Eaton, J. |
| May 16 | **Flower and Hawk** | Jacksonville, FL | Floyd, C. |
| May 16 | **Four Note Opera** | New York | Johnson, T. |
| May 24 | **Dybbuk, The** | New York | Mandelbaum, J. |
| May 29 | **Blind Man's Bluff** | London | Davis, P. M. |
| June 5 | **Wheel of the World** | Aldeburgh | Crosse, G. |
| June 7 | **Visitors, The** | Aldeburgh | Gardner, J. |
| June 22 | **Wrestler, The** | Dallas | Adler, S. |
| June 29 | **Táin, The** | Dublin | Wilson, J. |
| July | **Orpheus II** | Stratford, ON | Charpentier, G. |
| July 4 | **Pied Piper of Hamelin** | London | Bowers-Broadbent, C. |
| July 12 | **Taverner** | London | Davies, P. M. |

| Date | Title | City | Composer |
|---|---|---|---|
| July 16 | **Findings, The** | BBC | Whelen, C. |
| Aug. | **Dissolute Punished** | Edinburgh | Oliver, S. |
| Aug. 12 | **Dr. Selavy's Magic Theatre** | Stockbridge | Silverman, S. |
| Aug. 12 | **Garni Sands** | Sydney | Dreyfus, G. |
| Aug. 17 | **Aesop's Fables** | New York | Russo, W. |
| Aug. 23 | **Patria, no. 2** | Stratford, ON | Schafer, R. |
| Sept. 22 | **Circe 1991** | Dublin, RTÉ | Victory, G. |
| Oct. 25 | **Three Wishes** | Bombay | Kaufmann, W. |
| Nov. 29 | **Medea** | San Diego | Henderson, A. |
| Dec. | **Aton, the Ankh, and the World** | Washington | El-Dabh, H. |
| Dec. | **Osiris Ritual** | Washington | El-Dabh, H. |
| Dec. 5 | **Lord Arthur** | London | Bush, G. |
| Dec. 17 | **Inner Voices** | New York | Barnett, D. |
| Dec. 17 | **Thirst** | Jerusalem | Sargon, S. |
| Dec. 20 | **Sganarelle** | Bronx, NY | Zito, V. |
| Dec. 27 | **Bell, The** | BBC | Purser, J. |
| ? | **After the Wedding** | London | Head, M. |
| ? | **Magic Land of Opera** | New York | Kalmanoff, M. |
| * | **Enchanted Garden** | -- | Shaughnessy |
| * | **Liar, Liar** | -- | Raphling, S. |
| * | **Lysistrata** | Marlboro, VT (1984) | Clarke, H. |
| * | **Outcasts of Poker Flat** | -- | MacSems, W. |
| * | **Rose Garden** | -- | Boyd, A. |
| * | **Twelve Hours Trip** | -- | El-Dabh, H. |

## 1973

| Date | Title | City | Composer |
|---|---|---|---|
| winter | **Education of the Girlchild** | New York | Monk, M. |
| Feb. 1 | **Marriage Proposal** | New York | Murray, J. |
| Feb. 7 | **Love's Labour's Lost** | Brussels | Nabokov, N. |
| Feb. 8 | **Suncatcher, The** | Hartford | Franchetti, A. |
| Feb. 14 | **Make Me a Willow Cabin** | Brussels | Stoker, R. |
| Mar. 11 | **Daisy** | Miami | Smith, J. |
| Mar. 14 | **Prisoner, The** | London | Joubert, J. |
| Mar. 17 | **Notre Dame des Fleurs** | London | Davies, P. M. |
| Apr. 6 | **King's Breakfast** | Atlantic City, NJ | Barthelson, J. |
| Apr. 6 | **Summoning of Everyman** | Halifax | Wilson, C. |
| Apr. 7 | **Pantagleize** | Brooklyn, NY | Starer, R. |
| Apr. 13 | **Blue Angel** | Tucson, AZ | Garza, E. |
| Apr. 17 | **Infidelio** | London | Lutyens, E. |
| Apr. 23 | **Columbine** | Boulder, CO | Davis, M. |
| Apr. 23 | **Genesis** | London | Williamson, M. |
| Apr. 23 | **Myshkin** | PBS | Eaton, J. |
| Apr. 27 | **Fee First** | Los Angeles | Doran, M. |
| May 5 | **Transformations** | Minneapolis | Susa, C. |
| May 12 | **Prisoner's Play** | Toronto | Rea, J. |
| May 14 | **Primal Void** | Vienna | Vincent, J. |
| June 6 | **Some Pig** | Minneapolis | Larsen, L. |
| June 16 | **Death in Venice** | Venice | Britten, B. |
| June 23 | **Solomon and Sheba** | New York | Rivers, S. |

| Date | Title | City | Composer |
|---|---|---|---|
| Aug. 2 | **Scene: Domestic** | Aspen | Turok, P. |
| Sept. 3 | **Héloise and Abelard** | Toronto | Wilson, C. |
| Sept. 5 | **Tamu-Tamu** | Chicago | Menotti, G. C. |
| Sept. 20 | **Donkey, The** | Stirling, Scot | Oliver, S. |
| Sept. 30 | **Questions of Abraham** | CBS-TV | Laderman, E. |
| Oct. 12 | **Truth about Windmills** | Rochester, NY | Wilder, A. |
| Oct. 21 | **Nightingale and the Rose** | Chester, PA | Garwood, M. |
| Nov. 26 | **Bertha** | New York | Rorem, N. |
| Dec. 1 | **Queen Christina** | Oakland, CA | Anderson, B. |
| Dec. 15 | **Bel and the Dragon** | London | Gardner, J. |
| Dec. 21 | **Selfish Giant** | Toronto | Wilson, C. |
| ? | **Antigonae** | Stockholm | Kupferman, M. |
| ? | **Creation** | Ely, Eng | Ridout, A. |
| ? | **Dr. Jekyll and Mr. Hyde** | New York | Cannon, P. |
| ? | **Eloise and Abelard** | Dublin | Victory, G. |
| ? | **Murder of Comrade Sharik** | Seattle | Bergsma, W. |
| ? | **Patria, no. 1** | Toronto | Schafer, R. |
| ? | **Soap Opera** | Hartford | Franchetti, A. |
| ? | **Three Instant Operas** | London | Oliver, S. |
| * | **Conversion, The** | -- | Werder, F. |
| * | **Death of Cuchulain** | Bielefeld (1975) | Brettingham Smith, J. |
| * | **Dr. Jekyll and Mr. Hyde** | New York | Cannon, P. |
| * | **Furcoat for Summer** | -- | Oliver, S. |
| * | **Mirror** | Bloomington (1998) | Eastman, D. |
| * | **Rhinoceros** | -- | Kohs, E. |
| * | **Sea Change** | New York (1989) | Cugley, I. |
| * | **Tempest, The** | -- | Leichtling, A. |
| * | **Will of Her Own** | London (1985) | Gundry, I. |

**1974**

| Date | Title | City | Composer |
|---|---|---|---|
| Jan. 25 | **Magic Trumpet** | Dublin, RTÉ | Victory, G. |
| Feb. 5 | **Sganarelle** | Edmonton, AB | Archer, V. |
| Feb. 13 | **Clytemnestra** | London | Wishart, P. |
| Mar. 4 | **Cubana, La** | New York | Henze, H. W. |
| Mar. 5 | **Seagull, The** | Houston | Pasatieri, T. |
| Mar. 5 | **System, The** | New York | Bach, J. |
| Mar. 5 | **To Let the Captive Go** | New York | Stewart, F. |
| Mar. 9 | **Miss Donnithorne's Maggot** | Adelaide | Davies, P. M. |
| Mar. 13 | **Story of Vasco** | London | Crosse, G. |
| Mar. 14 | **Affair, The** | Sydney | Werder, F. |
| Mar. 14 | **Lenz** | Sydney | Sitsky, L. |
| Mar. 16 | **Catiline Conspiracy** | Stirling, Scot | Hamilton, I. |
| Mar. 26 | **Beach of Falesá** | Cardiff | Hoddinott, A. |
| Apr. 25 | **Dr. Jekyll and Mr. Hyde** | Bowling Green, OH | De Pue, W. |
| Apr. 28 | **Ruth and Naomi** | Cleveland | Kondorossy, L. |
| May | **Newest Opera in the World** | Minneapolis | Balk, W. |

| Date | Title | City | Composer |
|---|---|---|---|
| May 1 | **Lion and Androcles** | Indianapolis | Eaton, J. |
| May 8 | **Beauty and the Beast** | New York | Murray, J. |
| May 9 | **Curse of Mauvais-Air** | New York | Reif, P. |
| May 24 | **Beauty and the Beast** | Syracuse | Di Giacomo, F. |
| May 25 | **Africa Is Calling Me** | Paris | Reid, B. |
| June 5 | **Past Tense** | Huddersfield | Oliver, S. |
| June 11 | **Voice of Ariadne** | Aldeburgh | Musgrave, T. |
| July 12 | **Magic Laurel Tree** | Cleveland | Hunkins, E. |
| July 12 | **Philip Marshall** | Chautauqua, NY | Barab, S. |
| June 15 | **Letter for Queen Victoria** | Spoleto, Italy | Lloyd, A. |
| June 21 | **Duel, The** | Brooklyn, NY | Carmines, A. |
| July 27 | **Signor Deluso** | Greenway, VA | Pasatieri, T. |
| Aug. 1 | **Hotel for Criminals** | Lenox, MA | Silverman, S. |
| Aug. 3 | **Idiots First** | Ithaca, NY | Lehrman, L. |
| Aug. 3 | **Karla** | Ithaca, NY | Lehrman, L. |
| Aug. 3 | **Penitentes, The** | Aspen | Pasatieri, T. |
| Aug. 8 | **Child, The** | Albany, NY | Bernardo, J. |
| Sept. 11 | **Isabella's Fortune** | New York | Russo, W. |
| Sept. 11 | **Pedrolino's Revenge** | New York | Russo, W. |
| Sept. 27 | **Rites of Passage** | Sydney | Sculthorpe, P. |
| Oct. 3 | **Play of Mother Courage** | Middlesbrough, Eng. | McCabe, J. |
| Oct. 17 | **Abigail** | Brisbane | Beath, B. |
| Oct. 17 | **Francis** | Brisbane | Beath, B. |
| Oct. 24 | **Red Carnations** | New York | Baksa, R. |
| Oct. 30 | **Everyman** | Memphis | Nelhybel, V. |
| Nov. 1 | **Project 1521** | Los Angeles | Gross, R. |
| Dec. 9 | **Holly from the Bongs** | Manchester | Crosse, G. |
| Dec. 14 | **Conjurer, The** | New York | Sahl, M. |
| Dec. 17 | **Sufficient Beauty** | Oxford | Oliver, S. |
| Dec. 21 | **Yehu** | Los Angeles | Zador, E. |
| ? | **Lady of Light** | ? MT | Hovhaness, A. |
| ? | **Metamenagerie** | Berlin | Moran, R. |
| ? | **Vision, A** | Manchester | Ridout, A. |
| * | **Aria da capo** | -- | Bouck, M. |
| * | **Judas Iscariot** | -- | Barlow, D. |
| * | **Ladies Voices** | -- | Kievman, C. |
| * | **Miracle of Nemirov** | -- | Silverman, F. |
| * | **Proposal, The** | -- | Walker, J. |
| * | **Rumpelstiltskin** | -- | Bourgeois, D. |

**1975**

| Date | Title | City | Composer |
|---|---|---|---|
| Jan. 2 | **Give Me Liberty** | New York | Kalmanoff, M. |
| Jan. 4 | **Apache Dance** | New York | Fennimore, J. |
| Jan. 9 | **Potter Thompson** | London | Crosse, G. |
| Feb. 5 | **Fanny Robin** | Edinburgh | Harper, E. |
| Feb. 23 | **Glove, The** | New Liskeard, ON | Polgar, T. |
| Mar. 13 | **Nightingale, Inc.** | Urbana, IL | Colgrass, M. |
| Mar. 14 | **Bang!** | London | Rutter, J. |
| Mar. 27 | **Stanley and the Monkey King** | London | White, J. |

| Date | Title | City | Composer | Date | Title | City | Composer |
|------|-------|------|----------|------|-------|------|----------|
| Apr. 24 | Departure, The | Montevallo, AL | Davis, A. | Mar. 23 | Lamentable Reign of Charles | Adelaide | Dreyfus, G. |
| May 6 | Slaughter of the Innocents | Leicester | Crawley, C. | Mar. 26 | Death of King Peter | Brookline, MA | Earls, P. |
| May 9 | Balcony, The | Boston | Di Domenica, R. | Mar. 30 | Ines de Castro | Bloomington | Pasatieri, T |
| June 15 | Waiter's Revenge | Nottingham | Oliver, S. | Apr. 1 | Passion, Poison | New York | Taub, B. |
| June 19 | Charlie the Chicken | Toronto | Doolittle, Q. | Apr. 6 | Orpheus: Eurydice | London | White, J. |
| Aug. | Odyssey 2 | Glens Falls, NY | Shields, A. | Apr. 6 | Tom Jones | Newcastle | Oliver, S. |
| | | | | Apr. 11 | Fête at Coqueville | Fresno, CA | Rea, A. |
| Aug. 2 | Last Lover | Katonah, NY | Starer, R. | Apr. 11 | Gilt-Edged Kid | Melbourne | Dreyfus, G. |
| Aug. 26 | Fand | Kilkenny, Ire. | Wilson, J. | Apr. 22 | Jenny | New York | Weisgall, H. |
| Aug. 27 | Hermiston | Edinburgh | Orr, R. | Apr. 24 | Voyage of Edgar Allan Poe | St. Paul | Argento, D. |
| Sept. 20 | Captain Jinks | Kansas City | Beeson, J. | May 13 | Meanwhile, Back at Cinderella's | New York | Arlen, D. |
| Oct. 1 | Don't Call Me by My Right Name | New York | Fennimore, J. | May 25 | Stauf | New York | Sahl/Salzman |
| Oct. 6 | Black River | St. Paul, MN | Susa, C. | June 1 | Hero, The | Philadelphia | Menotti, G. C. |
| Oct. 10 | Masque of the Clouds | NY | Johnson, T. | June 12 | Last of the Mohicans | Wilmington, DE | Henderson, A. |
| Oct. 29 | King of the Golden River | Oxford | Maconchy, E. | June 12 | Mary Dyer | Suffern, NY | Owen, R. |
| Nov. | Stoned Guest | Ogden, UT | Schickele, P. | June 15 | Confessions of a Justified Sinner | York, Eng | Wilson, T. |
| Nov. 1 | Fables | Washington | Aitken, H. | | | | |
| Dec. 1 | Richest Girl in the World | Washington | Sandow, G. | June 17 | Egg, The | Washington | Menotti, G. C. |
| Dec. 8 | Family Reunion | Norman, OK | Parker, A. | June 21 | One and the Same | York, Eng | Lutyens, E. |
| Dec. 15 | W. of Babylon | New York | Wuorinen, C. | July 12 | We Come to the River | London | Henze, H. W. |
| ? | Esther | Johannesburg | Harvey, E. | July 19 | Evening for Three | Dublin, RTÉ | Victory, G. |
| ? | Perseverance | Liverpool | Oliver, S. | June 21 | One and the Same | York, Eng | Lutyens, E. |
| ? | Phaeton | BBC | Ridout, A. | July 25 | Einstein on the Beach | Avignon | Glass, P. |
| * | American Triptych | Alexandria, VA (1989) | Burton, S. | Apr. 2 | Quarry | New York | Monk, M. |
| | | | | Aug. 6 | Sima | Ithaca, NY | Lehrman, L. |
| * | Bad Times | -- | Oliver, S. | Aug. 28 | My Kinsman | Pittsburgh | Saylor, B. |
| * | Bellyful | -- | Werder, F. | Oct. 1 | Washington Square | Detroit | Pasatieri, T. |
| * | Dream Child | -- | Mollicone, H. | Oct. 7 | Final Alice | Chicago | Del Tredici, D. |
| * | Freak Show | -- | Taylor, C. | | | | |
| * | Married Men Go to Hell | -- | Franchetti, A. | Nov. 6 | Angle of Repose | San Francisco | Imbrie, A. |
| * | Nativity in Threes | -- | Barnard, F. | Nov. 14 | Night of the Moonspell | Shreveport, LA | Siegmeister, E. |
| * | Noblest Game | New York (1999) | Diamond, D. | Nov. 20 | Jubilee | Jackson, MS | Kay, U. |
| * | Pericles | -- | Hovhaness, A. | Nov. 26 | Isis and Osiris | London | Lutyens, E. |
| * | Richard III | Philadelphia (1980) | Turok, P. | Dec. 3 | Madame Jumel | Buffalo | Wolf, A. |
| | | | | Dec. ? | Cat Who Went to Heaven | London | Bush, G. |
| * | Stations | -- | Penberthy, J. | Dec. 22 | Lost Child | CBC | Ridout, G. |
| * | Swinish Cult | -- | Hodkinson, S. | Dec. 31 | Grimm Duo | Boston | Earls, P. |
| **1976** | | | | ? | David's Violin | Middletown, CT | Mogulesco-Slobin |
| Jan. 16 | Alice in Wonderland | Van Nuys, CA | Chauls, R. | | | | |
| Feb. 6 | Be Glad Then America | Univ Park, PA | La Montaine, J. | ? | Death of Ferdia | BBC Radio 3 | Ward, D. |
| | | | | ? | Frankenstein | Lexington, KY | Baber, J. |
| Feb. 11 | Magician, The | Welsh radio | Hoddinott, A. | ? | Magic Beanstalk | Monticello, NY | Kalmanoff, M. |
| Feb. 27 | Bilby Doll | Houston | Floyd, C. | | | | |
| Mar. | Christopher Columbus | New York | Kalmanoff, M. | ? | Music with Roots | Paris | Ashley, R. |
| Mar. 13 | Letter from an Astrologer | New York | Knopf, P. | ? | Smart Aleck and the Talking Wire | New York | Kalmanoff, M. |
| Mar. 14 | Tales of Malamud: | Bloomington | | * | Bell Tower | -- | Haskins, R. |
| | Idiots First | | Blitzstein, M. | * | Cinderella in Salerno | -- | Walker, R. |
| | Karla | | Lehrman, L. | * | Great McPorridge Disaster | -- | Oliver, S. |
| Mar. 16 | And the Walls | New York | Roosevelt, W. | * | Invisible Duke | -- | Cooke, A. |
| Mar. 23 | Fiery Tales | Adelaide | Sitsky, L. | | | | |

| Date | Title | City | Composer |
|---|---|---|---|
| * | King of Cats | -- | Oliver, H. |
| * | Legend of Sleepy Hollow | -- | Haskins, R. |
| * | President Lincoln | -- | Raphling, S. |
| * | Rebel and Empire | -- | Levin, G. |

**1977**

| Date | Title | City | Composer |
|---|---|---|---|
| Feb. 2 | Royal Hunt of the Sun | London | Hamilton, I. |
| Feb. 25 | Inner Voices | London | Howard, B. |
| Mar. 12 | Marriage Counselor | LA | Doran, M. |
| Mar. 14 | Tamburlaine | BBC | Hamilton, I. |
| Mar. 15 | Hearing | New York | Rorem, N. |
| Mar. 25 | Garden Party | Boston | Pinkham, D. |
| Apr. 9 | Hipopera | Boise, ID | Kalmanoff, M. |
| Apr. 14 | Lily | New York | Kirchner, L. |
| Apr. 21 | Maud | New York | Dellaria, M. |
| Apr. 29 | Sun and the Wind | Binghamton | Borroff, E. |
| May | Sid the Serpent | Adelaide | Fox, M. |
| May 6 | Orpheus in the Underground | BBC2 | Davis, C. |
| May 7 | Seabird Island | Guelph | Healey, D. |
| May 13 | Neither | Rome | Feldman, M. |
| May 19 | Civilization & Its Discontents | New York | Sahl, M., Salzman, E. |
| May 19 | Water Bird Talk | Brooklyn, NY | Argento, D. |
| May 25 | Garden Party | Boston | Pinkham, D. |
| June 6 | Gentle Spirit | Bath | Taverner, J. |
| June 18 | Martyrdom of St. Magnus | Kirkwall, Scot. | Davies, P. M. |
| June 25 | Ballad of the Bremen Band | Katonah, NY | Arlen, D. |
| July 4 | Bow Down | London | Birtwistle, H. |
| July 7 | Ice Break | London | Tippett, M. |
| July 27 | Garden, The | Batignano, Italy | Oliver, S. |
| July 27 | What the Old Man Does | Fishguard Festival, Wales | Hoddinott, A. |
| Aug. | William Derrincourt | Perth, Austral. | Smalley, R. |
| Sept. 6 | Mary, Queen of Scots | Edinburgh | Musgrave, T. |
| Sept. 28 | Toussaint | London | Blake, D. |
| Sept. 29 | Dawnpath | London | LeFanu, N. |
| Oct. | Chronicles | Rockville, MD | Muller, G. F. |
| Oct. 1 | Twist of Treason | Lincroft, NJ | Livingston, J. |
| Oct. 11 | HAPP | Minneapolis | Stokes, E. |
| Oct. 25 | Whirligig | Muncie, IN | Brisman, H. |
| Oct. 26 | Tobermory | London | Gardner, J. |
| Oct. 30 | Antigone | New York | Rodgers, L. |
| Nov. 2 | Thanksgiving | New York | Levi, P. |
| Nov. 4 | Devil's Disciple | White Plains | Barthelson, J. |
| Nov. 24 | Like a Window | BBC | Lutyens, E. |
| Dec. 7 | Death of Enkidu | Toronto | Somers, H. |
| Dec. 21 | Christmas Carol | Stratford, CT | Sandow, G. |
| ? | Frankenstein | Lexington, KY | Baber, J. |
| ? | Journey to Bethlehem | Baldwinsville, NY | Di Giacomo, F. |
| ? | Not a Spanish Kiss | New York | Barab, S. |
| ? | Rumpelstiltskin | Detroit | Di Chiera, D., Di Chiera, K. |
| ? | Selfish Giant | Kent, Eng. | Ridout, A. |
| ? | Sir Gawain | Leicester, Eng. | Wilson-Dickson, A. |
| * | Insect Comedy | New York (1993) | Kalmanoff, M. |
| * | Stable Home | -- | Oliver, S. |
| * | Voices in Limbo | Austral radio (1981) | Sitsky, L. |

**1978**

| Date | Title | City | Composer |
|---|---|---|---|
| Feb. 4 | Judith and Holofernes | Purchase, NY | Fink, M. |
| Feb. 10 | Noah | Brooklyn, NY | Sahl, M., Salzman, E. |
| Feb. 12 | Women in the Garden | San Francisco | Fine, V. |
| Mar. 7 | Girl from Nogami | London | Blyton, C. |
| Apr. 1 | Singer's Glen | Lancaster, PA | Parker, A. |
| Apr. 1 | Specialist, The | New York | Rodgers, L. |
| Apr. 7 | Julius Caesar | New Brunswick | Schmitz, A. |
| Apr. 14 | Claudia Legare | Minneapolis | Ward, R. |
| Apr. 21 | Danton and Robespierre | Bloomington | Eaton, J. |
| May | Something's Gonna Happen | Toronto | Colgrass, M. |
| May | Tristan and Iseult | Auckland | Whitehead, G. |
| May 12 | Creation, The | Kingston, ON | Crawley, C. |
| May 16 | Psycho Red | Guelph | Wilson, C. |
| May 19 | Dybbuk, The | Syracuse | DiGiacomo, F. |
| May 24 | Trial of the Gipsy | New York | Menotti, G. C. |
| May 25 | Marriage Proposal | Mankato, MN | Goldstaub, P. |
| June 3 | Toy Shop | New York | Barab, S. |
| June 16 | Two Fiddlers | Kirkwall, Scot. | Davies, P. M. |
| June 17 | Daughter of the Double Duke | Katonah, NY | Arlan, D. |
| June 18 | Jongleur de Notre Dame | Kirkwall, Scot | Davies, P. |
| June 21 | Evita | London | Lloyd Webber |
| June 21 | Perfect Lives | Minneapolis | Ashley, R. |
| Jul. 22 | Face on the Barroom Floor | Central City | Mollicone, H. |
| Aug. 3 | Through the Looking Glass | Harrogate, Eng. | Josephs, W. |
| Aug. 8 | Desire under the Elms | New London, | Thomas, E. |
| Aug. 9 | Wake Up | Lenox, MA | Kievman, C. |
| Aug. 18 | Duchess of Malfi | Oxford | Oliver, S. |
| Sept. 1 | Apology of Bony Anderson | Melbourne | Conyngham, B. |
| Oct. 16 | Devil's Constructs | Napanee, ON | Keane, D. |
| Nov. 19 | Dr. Heidegger's Fountain of Youth | New York | Beeson, J. |
| Nov. 29 | Paradise Lost | Chicago | Penderecki, K. |
| Dec. 9 | Girl and the Unicorn | London | Oliver, S. |
| Dec. 25 | Good Tidings | Lincoln, NE | Locklair, D. |
| Dec. 26 | Rumpelstiltskin | Philadelphia | Barber, J. |
| ? | Christmas Carol | HTV (Wales) | Kay, N. |

| Date | Title | City | Composer |
|---|---|---|---|
| ? | **Prometheus Condemned** | New York | Kupferman, M. |
| ? | **Shloyme Gorgl** | Middletown, CT | Slobin, M. (arr.) |
| ? | **Sir Gawain** | Oxfordshire | Blackford, R. |
| ? | **Tale of the Sun Goddess** | Salinas, CA | Hovhaness, A. |
| ? | **Wenceslas** | Bournemouth | Ridout, A. |
| * | **Five Shaggy-Dog Operas** | -- | Johnson, T. |
| * | **Happy Hypocrite** | -- | Masland, W. |
| * | **Heretic, The** | -- | Fuchs, P. P. |
| * | **Life Is a Dream** | Amherst, MA (2000) | Spratlan, L. |
| * | **Little Mermaid** | -- | Boyd, A. |
| * | **Love and Psyche** | -- | Chlarson, L. |
| * | **Photograph, 1920** | -- | Lee, T. O. |
| * | **Scarecrow, The** | Austin, TX (2006) | Turrin, J. |
| * | **Shaman** | -- | Shields, A. |

**1979**

| Date | Title | City | Composer |
|---|---|---|---|
| Jan. 1 | **Rime of the Ancient Mariner** | London | Bedford, D. |
| Jan. 23 | **Miss Julie** | London | Alwyn, W. |
| Feb. 1 | **Passion of Simple Simon** | New York | Sahl, M., Salzman, E. |
| Feb. 2 | **Jealous Cellist** | Minneapolis | Stokes, E. |
| Feb. 3 | **Fall of the House of Usher** | New York | Sandow, G. |
| Feb. 3 | **Galileo Galilei** | Binghamton | Laderman, E. |
| Mar. 1 | **Sweeney Todd** | New York | Sondheim, S. |
| Mar. 14 | **Humulus the Mute** | Victoria, BC | MacIntyre, D. |
| Mar. 15 | **Rocking Stone** | Bristol, Eng | Selwyn, D. |
| Mar. 22 | **Harmfulness of Tobacco** | New York | Kalmanoff, M. |
| Mar. 22 | **Miss Havisham's Fire** | New York | Argento, D. |
| Mar. 31 | **Faust** | BBC | Brian, H. |
| Apr. 11 | **Diable amoureux** | Dallas | Rodriguez, F. |
| Apr. 19 | **Crimson Bird** | Crawfordsville, IN | Enenbach, F. |
| Apr. 24 | **Saga** | New York | Hamilton, K. |
| Apr. 30 | **Full Moon in March** | Boston | Harbison, J. |
| May 3 | **Medea** | Boston | Luke, R. |
| May 3 | **St. Patrick** | Liverpool | Warren, R. |
| May 5 | **Chip and His Dog** | Guelph | Menotti, G. C. |
| May 11 | **Silver Fox** | St. Paul | Larsen, L. |
| May 17 | **Conjur Moon** | Houston | Lloyd, T. C. |
| May 17 | **Starbird** | Houston | Mollicone, H. |
| May 19 | **King Harald's Saga** | Dumfries, Scot. | Weir, J. |
| May 22 | **Apollonia** | St. Paul | Starer, R. |
| June 3 | **Loca, La** | San Diego | Menotti, G. C. |
| June 8 | **Margaret Catchpole** | Hadleigh, Suffolk | Dodgson, S. |
| June 9 | **Village Singer** | St. Louis | Paulus, S. |
| June 10 | **Commedia** | Kassel, Ger | Cowie, E. |
| June 14 | **Little Stories** | New York | Barab, S. |
| June 17 | **Last Leaf** | Saratoga, CA | Henderson, A. |

| Date | Title | City | Composer |
|---|---|---|---|
| July | **Abracadabra** | Courtenay, BC | Freedman, H. |
| July 8 | **Ralph and the Stalking Bear** | Monticello, NY | Kalmanoff, M. |
| July 27 | **Sumidagawa** | New London | Scarim, N. |
| July 29 | **Picnic, The** | Central City, CO | Cumming, R. |
| | **Soyazhe** | | Anderson, G. |
| Aug. 4 | **Houdini** | Aspen | Schat, P. |
| Aug. 20 | **Winter's Tale** | San Francisco | Harbison, J. |
| Oct. 1 | **Thérèse** | London | Taverner, J. |
| Oct. 5 | **Actor's Revenge** | London | Miki, M. |
| Oct. 13 | **Emperor's New Clothes** | Minneapolis | Larsen, L. |
| Nov. 3 | **Kamouraska** | Toronto | Wilson, C. |
| Nov. 11 | **Linnet, The** | BBC | Lutyens, E. |
| Nov. 14 | **Donner Party** | Chico, CA | McFarland, R. |
| Nov. 24 | **Rajah's Diamond** | London | Hoddinott, A. |
| Dec. | **Shepherds' Christmas** | Chicago | Russo, W. |
| Dec. 7 | **Christmas Carol** | Norfolk, VA | Musgrave, T. |
| Dec. 30 | **Lesson, The** | Riverdale, MD | Cain, T. |
| ? | **Rock Justice** | San Francisco | Balin, M. |
| ? | **Station, The** | Lowell, MA | Nelhybel, V. |
| ? | **Voyage of St. Brendan** | Norwich, Eng | Paynter, J. |
| * | **Ballad of Kitty** | -- | Lee, D.-K. |
| * | **Clockmaker, The** | -- | Harris, R. |
| * | **Diet, The** | - | Olenick, E. |
| * | **Dracula** | -- | Franchetti, A. |
| * | **Fritzi** | -- | Blumenfeld, H. |
| * | **Pizza del destino** | -- | Cohen, S. |
| * | **Return of the Native** | Vancouver (1993) | Coulthard, J. |

**1980**

| Date | Title | City | Composer |
|---|---|---|---|
| Feb. 7 | **I Rise in Flame** | New York | Flanagan, T. |
| Feb. 20 | **Old Pipes and the Dryad** | Fresno, CA | Rea, A. |
| Feb. 24 | **Things That Gain** | London | Barry, G. |
| Feb. 7 | **Feathertop** | New York | Barnes, E. |
| Mar. 1 | **Cry of Clytaemnestra** | Bloomington | Eaton, J. |
| Mar. 20 | **Death of Baldur** | Elgin, Scot | Bedford, D. |
| Mar. 20 | **Silverlake** | New York | Weill-Symonette |
| Apr. | **Americana** | Middletown, CT | Bruce, N. |
| Apr. 26 | **Rosina** | Minneapolis | Titus, H. |
| May 16 | **Tumbledown Dick** | Minneapolis | Larsen, L. |
| May 22 | **Hannah** | Mannheim, Ger | Lehrman, L. |
| May 27 | **Tartuffe** | San Francisco | Mechem, K. |
| June | **Abelard and Heloise** | New York | Gaughan, J. |
| June 7 | **Director, The** | Melbourne | Werder, F. |
| June 11 | **Aria da capo** | Chicago | Smith, L. |
| June 21 | **Cinderella** | Kirkwall, Scot | Davies, P. M. |
| June 25 | **Madrigal Opera** | Amsterdam | Glass, P. |
| July 9 | **Amarantha** | London | Ames, R. |
| July 9 | **Mrs. Bullfrog** | New York | Raphling, S. |

| DATE | TITLE | CITY | COMPOSER |
|------|-------|------|----------|
| July 19 | **Camera Obscura** | New London | Sheffer, J. |
| Aug. 7 | **Frankenstein** | Glens Falls, NY | Sandow, G. |
| Aug. 7 | **Sorry, Wrong Number** | Lake George, NY | Moross, J. |
| Aug. 8 | **Way of How** | Seattle | Dresher, P. |
| Aug. 22 | **Piers Plowman** | Gloucester, Eng. | Schurmann, G. |
| Sept. | **Servants, The** | Cardiff | Mathias, W. |
| Sept. 2 | **Lighthouse, The** | Edinburgh | Davies, P. M. |
| Sept. 5 | **Satyagraha** | Rotterdam | Glass, P. |
| Sept. 18 | **Errors** | Leicester, Eng | Warren, R. |
| Oct. 9 | **Before Breakfast** | New York | Pasatieri, T. |
| Oct. 9 | **Madame Adare** | New York | Silverman, S. |
| Oct. 9 | **Student from Salamanca** | New York | Bach, J. |
| Nov. 17 | **Man of Feeling** | London | Oliver, S. |
| Nov. 23 | **Rappaccini's Daughter** | Philadelphia | Garwood, M. |
| Nov. 28 | **Where the Wild Things Are** | Brussels | Knussen, O. |
| Dec. 4 | **Aspern Papers** | Bloomington | Hagemann, P. |
| Dec. 4 | **Orpheus in Pecan Springs** | Denton, TX | Latham, W. |
| ? | **Electric Gospel** | Toronto | Levin, G. |
| ? | **Sacrifice of Isaac** | New Haven | Bingham, S. |
| ? | **Tell Me on a Sunday** | London | Lloyd Webber |
| ? | **Wolf of Gubbio** | London | Senator, R. |
| * | **Amistad** | -- | Ames, R. |
| * | **Beginning of the Day** | -- | Boyd, A. |
| * | **Courtship of Camilla** | -- | Schonthal, R. |
| * | **Dr. Jekyll and Mr. Hyde** | New York (2009) | O'Neal, B. |
| * | **Epilogue** | -- | Dansicker, M. |
| * | **Golem, The** | -- | Sitsky, L. |
| * | **Job** | -- | Shatin, J. |
| * | **Montezuma's Death** | -- | Chlarson, L. |
| * | **Pericles** | -- | Hecker, Z. |
| * | **Pupu-kani-oe** | Honolulu (1986) | Tanner, J. |
| * | **Rose and the Ring** | -- | Warren, B. |
| * | **Sweeney Todd** | -- | Blyton, C. |
| * | **You'll Never Get It Off the Ground** | -- | Kalmanoff, M. |

## 1981

| DATE | TITLE | CITY | COMPOSER |
|------|-------|------|----------|
| Jan. | **Death of the Virgin** | New York | Owen, R. |
| Jan. | **Spinoza** | New Orleans | Drossin, J. |
| Jan. 1 | **Fridiof's Saga** | Edinburgh | Bedford, D. |
| Jan. 6 | **America, I Love You** | New Orleans | Ahlstrom, D. |
| Jan. 8 | **Have You Heard** | New York | Talma, L. |
| Jan. 16 | **Jack and Roberta** | Riverdale, MD | Cain, T. |
| Jan. 23 | **King for Corsica** | Kingston, ON | George, G. |
| Jan. 30 | **Bride Stripped Bare** | San Francisco | Shere, C. |
| Feb. 6 | **Anna Marguerita's Will** | New York | Starer, R. |
| Feb. 15 | **Goose Girl** | Fort Worth | Pasatieri, T. |
| Feb. 27 | **Final Bid** | Regina, SN | Raum, E. |
| Mar. 1 | **Rehearsal, The** | New York | Benjamin, T. |
| Mar. 21 | **Passion and Resurrection** | Winchester | Harvey, J. |

| DATE | TITLE | CITY | COMPOSER |
|------|-------|------|----------|
| spring | **Drink of Eternity** | Washington | El-Dabh, H. |
| Mar. 27 | **Lysistrata** | New York | Barthelson, J. |
| Apr. 1 | **Beauty and the Beast** | Montreal | Schafer, R. M. |
| Apr. 1 | **Trumpet Major** | Manchester | Hoddinott, A. |
| May 1 | **Miss Havisham's Wedding Night** | Minneapolis | Argento, D. |
| May 1 | **Willie Stark** | Houston | Floyd, C. |
| May 2 | **We're Back** | New York | Armour, E. |
| May 14 | **Emperor Norton** | San Francisco | Mollicone, H. |
| May 24 | **Selfish Giant** | Charleston, SC | Hollingsworth, S. |
| May 27 | **Harrison Loved His Umbrella** | Charleston, SC | Hollingsworth, S. |
| June 3 | **Ruined Maid** | New York | Barab, S. |
| June 8 | **Wedding, The** | Dublin | Potter, A. J. |
| June 12 | **Journey, The** | Cardiff | Metcalf, J. |
| June 20 | **Rainbow, The** | Kirkwall, Scot | Davies, P. M. |
| June 21 | **Medium, The** | Kirkwall, Scot | Davies, P. |
| June 28 | **Lessons, The** | New York | Ashley, R. |
| July | **Eatanswill Election** | -- | Cruft, A. |
| July 2 | **Columbine String Quartet** | Stockbridge | Silverman, S. |
| Aug. 16 | **Mistake, The** | Denver | Sheffer, J. B. |
| Sept. 18 | **Thousand Names to Come** | Milwaukee | Kitzke, J. |
| Sept. 26 | **Patria, Prologue** | Heart Lake, ON | Schafer, R. |
| Nov. 14 | **Pericles, Prince of Tyre** | Brattleboro, VT | Hecker, Z. |
| Dec. 4 | **Full Moon in March** | BBC Radio 3 | Ward, D. |
| ? | **Boxes, The** | New York | Sahl, Salzman |
| * | **Columba** | -- | Leighton, K. |
| * | **Land of Heart's Desire** | -- | Hofmeyr, H. |
| * | **Felipe** | -- | Aitken, H. |
| * | **Insect Play** | -- | Senator, R. |
| * | **Jenny Lind** | -- | Lee, D.-K. |
| * | **Knights of the Long Knives** | -- | Hollier, D. |
| * | **Ladies Voices** | -- | Gardner, K. |
| * | **Lady and the Maid** | -- | Goodman, A. |
| * | **Lisa Stratos** | -- | Lackman, S. |
| * | **Masque of Saxophone's Voice** | New York (1987) | Moore, C. |

## 1982

| DATE | TITLE | CITY | COMPOSER |
|------|-------|------|----------|
| winter | **Ransom of Red Chief** | Boone, NC | Fuller-Hall, S. |
| Jan. | **Chakravaka-Bird** | London | Gilbert, A. |
| Jan. 1 | **Ragnarok, The** | Elgin, Scot | Bedford, D. |
| Jan. 22 | **Tell-Tale Heart** | Boston | Adolphe, B. |
| Jan. 24 | **Price of Eggs** | Riverdale, MD | Cain, T. |
| Feb | **Secret Circuit** | Brooklyn, NY | Sainte Croix, J. |
| Feb. 2 | **Lady of the Castle** | New York | Spektor, M. |
| Feb. 3 | **United States** | Brooklyn, NY | Anderson, L. |
| Feb. 5 | **Frog-Hopping** | Brooklyn, NY | Boswell, W. |
| Feb. 5 | **Implications of Melissa** | Brooklyn, NY | Carlsen, P. |
| Feb. 5 | **Intimations** | Brooklyn, NY | Constantinides, D. |

| Date | Title | City | Composer |
|---|---|---|---|
| Feb. 5 | **Intrusions** | Brooklyn, NY | Johnson, D. |
| Feb. 5 | **Master of the Astral Plain** | Brooklyn, NY | Diamond, S. |
| Feb. 14 | **De Amore** | Oberlin | Barkin, E. |
| Feb. 19 | **Abelard and Heloise** | Charlotte, NC | Ward, R. |
| Mar. 28 | **Glory Coach** | New York | Barnard, F. |
| Apr. 3 | **Cask of Amontillado** | New York | Currie, R. |
| Apr. 3 | **Chipita Rodríguez** | Corpus Christi, TX | Weiner, L. |
| Apr. 3 | **Shivaree** | Toronto | Beckwith, J. |
| Apr. 14 | **Bride from Pluto** | Washington | Menotti, G. C. |
| Apr. 16 | **Nightingale** | Vienna, VA | Strouse, C. |
| Apr. 17 | **Monkey Opera** | Brooklyn, NY | Trefousse, R. |
| Apr. 30 | **Mask of Evil** | Minneapolis | Mollicone, H. |
| May | **Pyramus and Thisbe** | Waterford, CT | Convery, R. |
| May 6 | **Thirteen Clocks** | Waterford, CT | Chauls, R. |
| May 7 | **Anna Karenina** | London | Hamilton, I. |
| May 7 | **Audience, The** | New York | Dembo, R. |
| May 7 | **Miyako** | New York | Rodgers, L. |
| May 7 | **Mr. Lion** | New York | Chlarson, L. |
| May 8 | **Bontshe the Silent** | Cambridge, MA | Sirota, R. |
| May 8 | **Mikhoels the Wise** | New York | Adolphe, B. |
| May 9 | **Barnaby Boy** | Kingston, ON | Crawley, C. |
| May 17 | **Something New for the Zoo** | Cheverly, MD | Hoiby, L. |
| May 30 | **Photographer, The** | Amsterdam | Glass, P. |
| June | **Emperor and the Nightingale** | New Haven | Bingham, S. |
| June 4 | **Minutes till Midnight** | Miami | Ward, R. |
| June 11 | **Cop and the Anthem** | New York | Cohen, S. |
| June 19 | **Fortune's Favorites** | New York | Barab, S. |
| June 19 | **Postman Always Rings Twice** | St. Louis | Paulus, S. |
| July | **Italian Lesson** | Newport, RI | Hoiby, L. |
| July | **Juniper Tree** | Lenox, MA | Kesselman, W. |
| July 1 | **Quiros** | Austral TV | Sculthorpe, P. |
| July 7 | **Suor Isabella** | Dallas | Rodríguez, F. |
| July 17 | **Orpheus** | Wells, Eng | Burgon, G. |
| July 22 | **In the Beginning** | Bristol, Eng | Warren, R. |
| July 31 | **Confidence Man** | Santa Fe | Rochberg, G. |
| Aug. 1 | **Birdbath** | New York | Lieberson, K. |
| Sept. 2 | **Icarus** | Linz, Austria | Earls, P. |
| Sept. 4 | **Judith** | Cincinnati | Smith, D. |
| Sept. 10 | **Ponder Heart** | Jackson, MS | Parker, A. |
| Sept. 14 | **Occurrence at Owl Creek Bridge** | BBC | Musgrave, T. |
| Sept. 24 | **Boy Who Grew Too Fast** | Wilmington, DE | Menotti, G. C. |
| Oct. | **Falstaff in and out of Love** | Fresno, CA | Rea, A. |
| Oct. 1 | **De Profundis** | Canberra | Sitsky, L. |
| Oct. 10 | **Hangman, Hangman!** | Barcelona | Balada, L. |
| Oct. 23 | **Soldier Boy, Soldier** | Bloomington | Anderson, T. |

| Date | Title | City | Composer |
|---|---|---|---|
| Oct. 24 | **William Penn** | Philadelphia | Cascarino, R. |
| Oct. 29 | **Doctor Faustus** | San Francisco | Ahlstrom, D. |
| Nov. | **Atalanta** | Paris | Ashley, R. |
| Dec. 13 | **Triskelion** | New York | Bouchard, L. |
| Dec. 27 | **Little Nightmare Music** | New York | Schickele, P. |
| ? | **Dr. Canon's Cure** | Toronto | Holman, D. |
| ? | **Musicians of Bremen** | New York | Balkin, A. |
| ? | **Voss** | Adelaide | Meale, R. |
| * | **Alchemist of Trenton** | -- | Busch, D. |
| * | **Alice in Wonderland** | -- | Meachem, M. |
| * | **Marquesa of O** | -- | Siegmeister, E. |
| * | **Simple Decision** | -- | Busch, D. |

**1983**

| Date | Title | City | Composer |
|---|---|---|---|
| Jan. 6 | **Gaslight** | London | Roe, B. |
| Jan. 29 | **Frieze of Life** | Newport, Beach, CA | Applebaum, E. |
| Feb. 4 | **Mystic Trumpeter** | Brooklyn, NY | Starer, R. |
| Feb. 12 | **Silver City** | Banff, AB | Doolittle, Q. |
| Feb. 22 | **Stone Soup** | Philadelphia | Dorff, D. |
| Mar. 11 | **Death in the Family** | Minneapolis | Mayer, W. |
| Mar. 23 | **Metamorphoses** | London | Blackford, R. |
| Mar. 24 | **Pond in a Bowl** | New York | Macbride, D. |
| Mar. 24 | **Statues on a Lawn** | New York | Flanagan, T. |
| Apr. 6 | **Maria Elena** | Tucson | Pasatieri, T. |
| Apr. 7 | **Sasha** | Banff, AB | Oliver, S. |
| Apr. 9 | **False Messiah** | New York | Adolphe, B. |
| May 4 | **Patria, no. 6** | Toronto | Schafer, R. |
| May 8 | **Perpetual** | New York | Schubert, P. |
|  | **Prodigal Son** |  | Stepleton, J. |
| May 31 | **Maximillian's Dream** | Washington | Chlarson, L. |
| June 2 | **English Cat** | Schwetzingen, Ger. | Henze, H. W. |
| June 6 | **Light Opera** | New York | Morrow, C. |
| June 17 | **Lady of the Inn** | Reading, Eng | Wishart, P. |
| June 17 | **Quiet Place** | Houston | Bernstein, L. |
| summer | **Up from Paradise** | New York | Silverman, S. |
| July 27 | **Mrs. Farmer's Daughter** | Purchase, NY | Williams, J. |
| Aug. 10 | **Lament of Kamuela** | Hanover, NH | Appleton, J. |
| Aug. 11 | **Adventures of Friar Tuck** | Saratoga Springs, NY | Paxton, G. |
| Aug. 12 | **Miraculous Turnip** | Toronto | Bissell, K. |
| Sept. | **Games, The** | W Berlin | Monk, M. |
| Oct. 1 | **Metamorphosis** | Melbourne | Howard, B. |
| Oct. 15 | **Rebecca** | Leeds | Josephs, W. |
| Nov. 16 | **Eros and Psyche** | Oberlin, OH | Cummings, C. |
| Dec. 5 | **Blue Star** | New York | Dvorkin, J. |
| Dec. 6 | **Gawain and Ragnall** | Birmingham | Blackford, R. |
| ? | **Christina's World** | Sydney | Edwards, R. |
| ? | **Dr. Syn** | Kent | Cruft, A. |
| ? | **Plague upon Eyam** | Dunedin, NZ | Drummond, J. |
| * | **Cats' Corner** | -- | Riley, D. |
| * | **Dracula** | -- | Blyton, C. |

| DATE | TITLE | CITY | COMPOSER |
|------|-------|------|----------|
| * | Magic Bonbons | -- | Blank, A. |
| * | Marie Laveau | -- | Carbon, J. |
| * | Regarding Faustus | Adelaide (1988) | Gifford, H. |
| * | Secret of the Mirror | -- | Busch, D. |
| * | Sredni Vashtar | -- | Cassels-Brown, A. |
| * | Vile Shadows | CBC (2004) | Turner, R. |
| **1984** | | | |
| Jan. 11 | Family Man | New York | Lehrman, L. |
| Jan. 16 | Pay Off | Chicago | Russo, W. |
| Jan. 26 | Emma | Provo, Utah | Boren, M. |
| Jan. 27 | Anne Boleyn | New York | Beck, J. |
| Feb. 3 | Farewell Supper | Brooklyn, NY | Hart, F. |
| | Letter, The | | White, F. |
| | Poison | | Hart, F. |
| | Scene Changes | | Boswell, W. |
| Feb. 10 | Intruder, The | Berea, OH | Feldman, J. |
| Feb. 10 | Police Log | New York | Wigglesworth, F. |
| Mar. 20 | No. 11 Bus | London | Davies, P. M. |
| Mar. 25 | CIVIL warS | Rome | Glass, P. |
| Apr. 4 | Wayfarers, The | Huntingdon, Eng | Joubert, J. |
| Apr. 12 | Sister Aimée | New Orleans | Martínez, O. |
| Apr. 13 | Nightingale's Apprentice | New York | Silsbee, A. |
| Apr. 24 | Abduction of Figaro | Minneapolis | Schickele, P. |
| Apr. 27 | Knee Plays | Minneapolis | Byrne, D. |
| Apr. 29 | Dream within a Dream | Bronx, NY | Currie, R. |
| May 17 | François Villon | Buffalo | Wolf, A. |
| May 18 | Eli W. | New Haven | Bingham, S. |
| May 19 | Bishop's Horse | San Francisco | Ahlstrom, D. |
| May 30 | Britannia Preserv'd | London | Oliver, S. |
| June 3 | Raleigh's Dream | Durham, NC | Hamilton, I. |
| June 5 | King of the Other Country | Sydney | Whitehead, G. |
| July 26 | Beauty and the Beast | Batignano, Italy | Oliver, S. |
| Aug. | Weep Torn Land | Hanover, NH | Finney, R. |
| Aug. 2 | Love of Don Perlimplin | Purchase, NY | Susa, C. |
| Aug. 4 | Snow Queen | BBC | Ward, D. |
| Aug. 24 | Siren's Song | Heraklion, Crete | Butler, M. |
| Aug. 25 | Fly | Melbourne | Conyngham, B. |
| Sept. 20 | Crossing, The | Cardiff | Metcalf, J. |
| Oct. 12 | Akhnaten | Stuttgart | Glass, P. |
| Oct. 13 | Higglety Pigglety Pop! | Glyndebourne | Knussen, O. |
| Oct. 13 | Kiss, The | London | Nyman, M. |
| Oct. 14 | Passion of Vincent Van Gogh | Dallas | Yavelow, C. |
| Oct. 17 | Trio | New York | Ain, N. |
| Oct. 20 | Intelligent Systems | Baden-Baden | Kievman, C. |
| Oct. 23 | Medea | Lyons | Bryars, G. |
| Oct. 24 | Minette Fontaine | Baton Rouge | Still, W. G. |
| Nov. | Woman Who Dared | Rochester | Bokser, Z. |

| DATE | TITLE | CITY | COMPOSER |
|------|-------|------|----------|
| Nov. 5 | Three Sisters Who Are Not Sisters | New York | Hellermann, W. |
| Nov. 22 | José's Carmen | London | Ashman, M. |
| Nov. 26 | Letters to Theo | Dublin | Wilson, J. |
| Dec. 1 | Gift of the Magi | New Haven | Bingham, S. |
| Dec. 1 | Last Leaf | New Haven | Bingham, S. |
| ? | At Last I've Found You | Charlotte, SC | Barab, S. |
| ? | Birth of the Poet | Rotterdam | Gordon, P. |
| ? | Freshwater | New York | Valinsky, E. |
| ? | Love of Don Perlimplin | Dublin | Doyle, R. |
| ? | Rappaccini's Daughter | Philadelphia | Dennison, S. |
| ? | Tell-Tale Heart | London | Álvarez, G. |
| * | Aria da capo | -- | Priolo, C. |
| * | Emperor's New Clothes | -- | Sessions, R. |
| * | Fourscore | -- | Blumenfeld, H. |
| * | Golden Bird | -- | Russo, W. |
| * | Music Cure | Cedar Rapids, IA (1998) | Hagemann, P. |
| * | Obelisk, The | -- | Eaton, M. |
| * | Rappaccini's Daughter | -- | Riley, D. |
| * | Ring, The | -- | Oliver, S. |
| * | Sopranos Only | -- | Johnson, T. |
| * | When Opportunity Knocks | -- | Ashley, R. |
| **1985** | | | |
| Jan. 6 | Oath of Bad Brown Bill | Melbourne | Conyngham, B. |
| Jan. 17 | Dreyfus | Brooklyn, NY | Cotel, M. |
| Jan. 19 | Garden of Alice | Regina, SK | Raum, E. |
| Jan. 27 | Fair Means or Foul | New York | Barab, S. |
| Feb | Harlot and the Monk | Banff, AB | Bohmler, C. |
| Feb. 8 | Butterfly Girl and Mirage Boy | Brooklyn, NY | Reed, H. R. |
| Feb. 22 | Clair de Lune | Little Rock, AR | Larsen, L. |
| Feb. 24 | Sojourner | New York | Capers, V. |
| Mar. 1 | Harriet, a Woman Called Moses | Norfolk, VA | Musgrave, T. |
| Mar. 19 | Alice | Jerusalem | Osborne, W. |
| Apr. 10 | Marriage between Zones | London | Barker, P. |
| Apr. 11 | Aesop's Fables | De Kalb, IL | Smith, G. |
| Apr. 11 | Blake | Oberlin, Ohio | Adams, L. |
| Apr. 12 | Casanova's Homecoming | St. Paul | Argento, D. |
| Apr. 13 | Sibyl, The | Philadelphia | Persichetti, V. |
| Apr. 19 | Behold the Sun | Duisburg, Ger | Goehr, A. |
| Apr. 20 | Gimpel the Fool | New York | Schiff, D. |
| Apr. 26 | Echoes of the Shining Prince | New York | Cooper, S. |
| May 1 | Pillow-Song | London | Barker, P. |
| May 5 | Consolations of Scholarship | Durham, Eng. | Weir, J. |
| May 12 | Out the Window | New York | Barab, S. |
| May 12 | Predators | New York | Barab, S. |

| DATE | TITLE | CITY | COMPOSER | DATE | TITLE | CITY | COMPOSER |
|------|-------|------|----------|------|-------|------|----------|
| May 13 | Snow Queen | Adelaide | Dudley, G. | * | Greenleaf | -- | Buchanan, D. |
| May 23 | Piece of String | Greeley, CO | Barab, S. | * | Iphigenia in Exile | Melbourne (1990) | Gifford, H. |
| May 30 | Jōruri | St. Louis | Miki, M. | | | | |
| June | Thief of Love | New York | Silver, S. | * | Just Above My Head | Pittsburgh (1985) | Davis, N. |
| June 5 | Hedda Gabler | Glastonbury | Harper, E. | | | | |
| June 6 | Bagatelle | Houston | Janas, M. | * | Lealista | -- | Warwick, M. |
| | Catsman | | Hodkinson, S. | **1986** | | | |
| | Chicken Little | | Benjamin, T. | Jan. 4 | Hells' Angels | London | Osborne, N. |
| | Flight of Eagles | | Tinsley, S. | Jan. 5 | Goldilocks | Chappaqua, NY | Zaimont, J. |
| | Informer, The | | Legg, J. | | | | |
| June 7 | Departure, The | | Hellum, M. | Jan. 13 | Sagegrass | New York | Atwell, S. J. |
| | Leo | | Ching, M. | Jan. 14 | Africanus Instructus | New York | Silverman, S. |
| | Miranda | | Brown, A. | Jan. 18 | Chinchilla | Binghamton | Fink. M. |
| | Sandbox, The | | Hagen, D. | Jan. 29 | Tango | Dallas | Rodríguez, F. |
| | Tickets, Please | | Nelson, R. | Feb | Hansel and Gretel | Arcata, CA | Stoddard, M. |
| June 8 | Cowboy and the Fiddler | | Raphling, S. | Feb. 20 | Bus to Stockport | New York | Valinsky, E., Schubert, P. |
| | Sleepsong | | Busby, G. | | | | |
| | Soap Opera | | Wallace, S. | Mar. 13 | Three Sisters | Columbus, OH | Pasatieri, T. |
| | Stiff | | Chance, F. | Apr. | Aesop's Fables | San Francisco | Ahlstrom, D. |
| | Viola | | Busby, G. | Apr. 18 | Good Life | Washington | Silverman, S. |
| June 26 | Trio Sonata | New York | Chlarson, L. | Apr. 26 | Trojan Women | St. Paul | Goldstaub, P. |
| June 28 | Frederick Douglass | New York | Moore, D. R. | Apr. 26 | Noise, The | Richmond, VA | Blank, A. |
| June 28 | Song of Pegasus | Forest Meadows, CA | McFarland, R. | May | Audition of Molly Bloom | Forest Meadows, CA | McFarland, R. |
| July 17 | Change of Hearts | New York | Hollister, D. | May | Mermaid, The | Minneapolis | Fullam, V. |
| July 28 | Tempest, The | Santa Fe | Eaton, J. | May 15 | Cathedral, The | New York | Spivack, L. |
| Aug. 20 | Seduction of a Lady | Glens Falls, NY | Wargo, R. | May 15 | Harlequins | Toronto | Keane, D. |
| | | | | May 15 | Spanish Lady | London | Elgar, E. |
| Aug. 24 | Lancelot | Arundel Castle, Wales | Hamilton, I. | May 21 | Mask of Orpheus | London | Birtwistle, H. |
| | | | | May 30 | Grub Street Opera | New York | Bowles, A. |
| Sept. 17 | Medea | Melbourne | Werder, F. | June 5 | Demon Lover | Dublin | Nelson, R. |
| Sept. 23 | What's in a Name | Binghamton | Dvorkin, J. | June 6 | Guilt of Lillian Sloan | Chicago | Neil, W. |
| Oct. | Music Shop | St Paul | Wargo, R. | June 19 | Island of Tomorrow | New York | Fink, M. |
| Oct. | X | Philadelphia | Davis, A. | June 21 | Tempest, The | Indianola, IA | Hoiby, L. |
| Oct. 5 | Angel Levine | New York | Siegmeister, E. | summer | Wife of Bath's Tale | Aspen | Legg, J. |
| | Lady of the Lake | | | June 24 | Exposition of a Picture | London | Oliver, S. |
| Oct. 7 | Father of the Child | Bayside, NY | Barab, S. | Aug. | Pirate Moon | Auckland, NZ | Whitehead, G. |
| Oct. 19 | Meal, The | Edmonton | Archer, V. | Aug. 5 | Yan Tan Tethera | London | Birtwistle, H. |
| Oct. 23 | Ghost of Susan B. Anthony | Tuscaloosa, AL | Shaffer, J. | Aug. 6 | Black Sea Follies | Stockholm | Silverman, S. |
| | | | | Aug. 6 | Directions, The | Iraklion, Crete | Torke, M. |
| Nov. | Slow Fire | Los Angeles | Dresher, P. | Sept. 13 | Bartolo | Birmingham, AL | Bugg, G. W. |
| Nov. 7 | Question of Love | London | Gilbert, P. | | | | |
| Dec. 4 | Birth of the Poet | Brooklyn, NY | Gordon, P. | Sept. 20 | Queenie Pie | Philadelphia | Ellington, E. |
| Dec. 11 | Juniper Tree | Cambridge, MA | Glass, P. | fall | We're Not Robots | Minneapolis | Stokes, E. |
| ? | Atalanta Strategy | Montreal | Ashley, R. | Oct. | Proposal, The | Sydney | Fiddes, R. |
| ? | Gift of the Magi | New Orleans | Warren, B. | Oct. 5 | Tight-Rope | Madison, WI | Biscardi, C. |
| ? | Only a Miracle | New York | Barab, S. | Oct. 9 | Canterbury Morning | Oakham, Eng | Roe, B. |
| ? | RareArea | Brussels | Ream, M. | Oct. 9 | Phantom of the Opera | London | Lloyd Webber |
| ? | Zapata! | Philadelphia | Balada, L. | Oct. 10 | Ransom of Red Chief | Mesquite, TX | Rodríguez, F. |
| * | Alice in Wonderland | -- | Josephs, W. | Oct. 16 | On Blue Mountain | New York | Eyerly, S. |
| * | Cousin Lillie | -- | Busby, G. | Oct. 27 | Man Who Mistook His Wife | London | Nyman, M. |
| * | Gift of the Magi | -- | Brown, R. | | | | |
| * | Golden Crane | -- | Kay, D. H. | Oct. 29 | Lorenzaccio | Sydney | Brumby, C. |

| Date | Title | City | Composer | Date | Title | City | Composer |
|------|-------|------|----------|------|-------|------|----------|
| Oct. 30 | Ladies Voices | Berkeley, CA | Shere, C. | Oct. 23 | Nixon in China | Houston | Adams, J. |
| Nov. | Great Man's Widow | Roanoke, VA | Granger, M. | Nov. 2 | Jacob's Room | St. Paul, MN | Subotnick, M. |
| Nov. 9 | Harriet Tubman | New York | Edwards, L. | Nov. 7 | Going, The | Cincinnati | Beall, M. |
| Nov. 28 | Goya | Washington | Menotti, G. C. | Nov. 21 | Patria, no. 1 | Toronto | Schafer, R. |
| Dec. 12 | I Can't Stand Wagner | New York | Barab, S. | Dec. | Dialogues | Frostburg, MD | Bauman, J. |
| Dec. 18 | Snow Queen | Melbourne | Easton, M. | Dec. 4 | Nativity | Midland, MI | Dello Joio, N. |
| ? | Birds, The | Dunedin, NZ | Drummond, J. | Dec. 12 | Europeras 1 & 2 | Glyndebourne | Cage, J. |
| | | | | Dec. 14 | Abigail Adams | New York | Owen, R. |
| ? | Mask of Eleanor | Atlanta | Grigsby, B. | ? | Angel Face | Brooklyn, NY | Ames, R. |
| ? | Mysteries of Eleusis | Ithaca, NY | Feigin, J. | ? | Death of Don Juan | Boston | Lauten, E. |
| ? | Wild Boy | Philadelphia | Epstein, S. | ? | Denmark Vesey | Waterford, CT | Cabaniss, T. |
| * | Foreign Experiences | New York (1991) | Ashley, R. | ? | Psychles | Chicago | Thomas, A. |
| | | | | ? | White Doe | Ripon, Eng | Ridout, A. |
| * | Idle Rumor | -- | Busch, D. | ? | Zoggy | Melbourne | Fox, M. |
| * | Improvement | New York (1991) | Ashley, R. | * | Agamemnon | -- | Hamilton, I. |
| | | | | * | Albatross, The | London (1997) | Burrell, D. |
| * | Kona Coffee Cantata | -- | Tanner, J. | * | Fisherman and His Wife | -- | Bingham, S. |
| * | Love and Idols | -- | Drogin, B. | * | Foreign Experiences | New York (1991) | Ashley, R. |
| * | Man Who Corrupted Hadleyville | -- | Nelson, R. | | | | |
| * | Spark Plugs | -- | Granger, M. | * | Frankenstein | -- | Blyton, C. |
| * | Swans, The | -- | Henderson, A. | * | Frog Man | -- | Hovhaness, A. |
| | | | | * | Moby Dick | -- | Brooks, R. |
| **1987** | | | | * | On the Edges of Calm | -- | Meier, M. |
| Feb. 2 | Della's Gift | Austin, TX | Welcher, D. | * | Proposal, The | University Park, MD | Granger, G. |
| Feb. 12 | Countdown | Boston | Yavelow, C. | | | | |
| Feb. 18 | Monkey See | Dallas | Rodríguez, F. | * | Station, The | Haywards Heath, W. Sussex (1992) | Blake, H. |
| Mar. | Howard | New York | Earnest, J. | | | | |
| Mar. 28 | Tomorrow, Tomorrow | New York | Sullivan, T. | **1988** | | | |
| Apr. 4 | King Who Saved Himself | Chico, CA | Hagemann, P. | Jan. 1 | Return of Odysseus | London | Bedford, D. |
| Apr. 5 | Ligeia | Riverdale, NJ | Currie, R. | Jan. 18 | Hood of the Woods | Rochester, NY | Shepherd, S. |
| Apr. 8 | Frankie | Adelaide | John, A. | Feb. | Tristan and Iseult | New York | Cohen, J. |
| Apr. 11 | Iron Man | Adelaide | Fox, M. | Feb. 10 | Mellstock Quire | Edinburgh | Harper, E. |
| Apr. 15 | Skin Drum | Banff, AB | Grant, J. | Feb. 28 | Esther | New York | Swados, E. |
| Apr. 23 | Benjamin | Lancaster, Pa | Carbon, J. | Mar. 13 | Rasputin | New York | Reise, J. |
| May 1 | Garden of Flowers | Boston | Goodman, J. | Mar. 15 | Oedipus Tex | Minneapolis | Schickele, P. |
| May 8 | Legend, The | Cleveland | Murray, B. | Mar. 17 | Gulliver | Louisville, KY | Bond, V. |
| June | Waiting | Buxton | Oliver, S. | Mar. 20 | Dream Beach | New York | Sahl, M. |
| June 13 | Diva, The | Chicago | Ferris, W. | Mar. 28 | Alice Meets the Mock Turtle | New York | Bingham, S. |
| June 14 | Follies and Fancies | New York | Allen, J. S. | | | | |
| June 14 | Song of Insanity | New York | Seletsky, H. | Mar. 30 | Journey of Edith Wharton | Chapel Hill, NC | Hannay, R. |
| July 8 | Night at the Chinese Opera | Cheltenham | Weir, J. | | | | |
| July 30 | Haydn's Head | Cleveland | Baker, L. | Apr. 7 | Moonlight Sonata | New York | Innerarity, M. |
| Aug. 6 | Patria, no. 3 | Peterborough, ON | Schafer, R. | Apr. 21 | Bennelong | Groningen, Neth. | Conyngham, B. |
| Aug. 6 | Jack's Engagement | Lerwick, Shetland Is. | Ward, D. | Apr. 25 | Wild Swans | New Haven | Bingham, S. |
| Aug. 7 | Hazel Kirke | Glens Falls, NY | Houston, M. | May | Undivine Comedy | Paris | Finnissy, M. |
| | | | | May 3 | Lodge of Shadows | Ft Worth, TX | Adler, S. |
| Aug. 20 | Lucy's Lapses | New York | Drobny, C. | May 11 | Dream Play | Toronto | Sullivan, T. |
| Sept. 26 | Where's Dick | Omaha | Wallace, S. | May 11 | Lumina | Toronto | Keane, D. |
| Oct. 5 | Electrification of the Soviet Union | Glyndebourne | Osborne, N. | May 11 | Realitillusion | Toronto | Brégent, M. |
| | | | | May 13 | Christina Romana | Minneapolis | Larsen, L. |
| Oct. 23 | Ghost of Susan B. Anthony | Tuscaloosa, AL | Shaffer, J. | May 19 | St. Carmen of the Main | Guelph | Hodkinson, S. |

| DATE | TITLE | CITY | COMPOSER |
|---|---|---|---|
| May 22 | **Pastoral** | Albuquerque | Galloway, J. |
| May 28 | **Old Majestic** | San Antonio | Rodríguez. F. |
| May 29 | **Fall of the House of Usher** | Louisville, KY | Glass, P. |
| June 1 | **Nell** | London | Bauld, A. |
| June 17 | **Greek** | Munich | Turnage, M. |
| June 27 | **On the Razzle** | Glasgow | Orr, R. |
| July 2 | **Donna, La** | Sydney | Brumby, C. |
| July 8 | **Making of the Representative** | Houston | Glass, P. |
| July 15 | **One Thousand Airplanes** | Vienna | Glass, P. |
| Aug. 3 | **Birthday of the Bank** | Glens Falls, NY | Lehrman, L. |
| Aug. 6 | **Mario and the Magician** | Batignano, Italy | Oliver, S. |
| Sept. 2 | **Whitsunday** | Sydney | Howard, B. |
| Sept. 3 | **Bremen Town Musicians** | Madison, WI | Kesselman, L. |
| Sept. 8 | **Resurrection** | Darmstadt | Davies, P. M. |
| Sept. 16 | **Wedding, The** | Seoul | Menotti, G. C. |
| Sept. 29 | **Snow White** | Oklahoma City | Barab, S. |
| Oct. 1 | **Love, Death** | St. Louis | White, C. |
| Oct. 8 | **Magic Fishbone** | New York | Chapin, T. |
| Oct. 18 | **Forest, The** | W Berlin | Byrne, D. |
| Oct. 21 | **Jesus of Nazareth** | New York | Rudenstein, R. |
| Nov. | **Heiress, The** | Melbourne | Hollier, D. |
| Nov. | **My Brother Called** | Chicago | Ashley, R. |
| Nov. 19 | **Aspern Papers** | Dallas | Argento, D. |
| Nov. 26 | **West of Washington Square** | San Jose | Henderson, A. |
| Nov. 30 | **Breakfast Waltzes** | Chicago | Blumenfeld, H. |
| Dec. 13 | **Death of a Ghost** | New York | Gottlieb, J. |
| ? | **Death of Lincoln** | Cleveland | London, E. |
| ? | **Dissipation of Purely Sound** | Toronto | Beecroft, N. |
| ? | **eL/Aficionado** | Marseilles | Ashley, R. |
| ? | **Fall of the House of Usher** | Pretoria | Hofmeyr, H. |
| ? | **Who Am I?** | New York | Barab, S. |
| * | **Ba-Ta-Clan** | -- | Oliver, S. |
| * | **Birds, The** | -- | El-Dabh, H. |
| * | **Bowl, Cat, Broomstick** | New York (2002) | Boury, R. |
| * | **ChaplinOperas** | Strasbourg (1992) | Mason, B. |
| * | **Emperor's New Clothes** | Chicago (1999) | Kesselman, L. |
| * | **Great Soap Opera** | -- | Schelle, M. |
| * | **Love's Labour's Lost** | -- | Bush, G. |
| * | **Now Eleanor's Idea** | -- | Ashley, R. |
| * | **Sredni Vashtar** | -- | Steadman, R. |

**1989**

| DATE | TITLE | CITY | COMPOSER |
|---|---|---|---|
| Jan. | **Pied Piper** | Orlando, Fla | Swados, E. |
| Jan. 4 | **Story of Mary O'Neill** | London | LeFanu, N. |
| Jan. 27 | **Construction of Boston** | Boston | Wheeler, S. |
| Jan. 29 | **Belisa** | St. Paul, MN | Biales, A. |

| DATE | TITLE | CITY | COMPOSER |
|---|---|---|---|
| Feb | **Boor, The** | Austin, TX | Grantham, D. |
| Feb. 6 | **I Like It to Be a Play** | San Francisco | Shere, C. |
| Feb. 18 | **Perlimplín** | Philadelphia | Morrill, K. |
| Feb. 26 | **Guest of Honor** | New York | Weisberg, S. |
| Feb. 28 | **Grinning at the Devil** | Copenhagen | Wilson, J. |
| Mar. | **Blue Margaritas** | Washington | Trefousse, R. |
| Mar. 8 | **Bon Appétit!** | Washington | Hoiby, L. |
| Mar. 8 | **Will You Marry Me?** | New York | Weisgall, H |
| Mar. 9 | **Patria, no. 4** | Liège | Schafer, R. |
| Mar. 23 | **Without Colors** | Minneapolis | Shiflett, M. |
| spring | **Lazarus** | Abilene, TX | Daniels, M. |
| Apr. 1 | **Bowl, Cat, and Broomstick** | Little Rock, AZ | Boury, R. |
| Apr. 8 | **Casino Paradise** | Philadelphia | Bolcom, W. |
| Apr. 9 | **Chinaman's Chance** | Brooklyn, NY | Ho, F. |
| Apr. 9 | **Rachel** | Knoxville, TN | Coe, K. |
| Apr. 9 | **Tom Sawyer** | New York | Owen, R. |
| Apr. 22 | **Vagabond Queen** | Los Angeles | Barnes, E. |
| Apr. 28 | **Jane Heir** | New York | Healey, P. |
| May 4 | **Power Failure** | Iowa City | Dresher, P. |
| May 11 | **Crazy to Kill** | Guelph | Beckwith, J. |
| May 16 | **Expensive Embarrassment** | Toronto | Gougeon, D. |
| May 17 | **Yellow Wallpaper** | Northampton, MA | Perera, R. |
| May 18 | **Last Tango** | London | Wiegold, P. |
| | **Menaced Assassin** | | Jones, J. P. |
| | **Survival Song** | | Paintal, P. |
| May 20 | **Friends and Dinosaurs** | Needham, MA | Shadle, C. |
| May 20 | **Princess Maleen** | White Plains, NY | Schonthal, R. |
| May 23 | **Fisherman, The** | London | Edlin, P. |
| May 25 | **Plumber's Gift** | London | Blake, D. |
| June | **Blanche** | New York | Yarmolinsky, B. |
| June 7 | **Malinche, La** | London | Wiegold, P. |
| June 8 | **Empty Places** | Charleston, SC | Anderson, L. |
| June 17 | **Fan, The** | Chicago | Goldstein, L. |
| June 24 | **Question of Taste** | Cooperstown, NY | Schuman, W. |
| June 27 | **Wraecca** | New York | Shields, A. |
| June 28 | **Golem** | London | Casken, J. |
| July 15 | **Under the Double Moon** | St. Louis | Davis, A. |
| Aug. | **Computer Marriage** | Hanover, NH | Finney, R. L. |
| Aug. 1 | **Glass Woman** | New York | Hays, S. |
| Aug. 14 | **Boiler Room Suite** | Banff, AB | Doolittle, Q. |
| Aug. 25 | **Pamelia** | Billingsley, MT | Funk, E. |
| Sept. | **Emperor's New Clothes** | New York | Dvorkin, J. |
| Sept. 27 | **Jack Benny** | New York | Moran, J. |
| Oct. 5 | **Heaven Ablaze in His Breast** | Basildon, Essex | Weir, J. |
| Oct. 10 | **Holy Blood and Crescent Moon** | Cleveland | Copeland, S. |

| Date | Title | City | Composer |
|------|-------|------|----------|
| Oct. 14 | Reunion, The | Baltimore | Crozier, D. |
| Oct. 18 | Rip Van Winkle | San Diego | Rockwell, J. |
| Oct. 25 | Telephone Show | Milwaukee | Wadsworth, S. |
| Oct. 27 | New Year | Houston | Tippett, M. |
| Oct. 28 | Mary Surratt | Ft. Washington, MD | Muller, G. |
| Nov. 2 | Rendezvous, The | Dublin | Victory, G. |
| Nov. 6 | Pizza con funghi | New York | Barab, S. |
| Nov. 16 | Kabbalah | Brooklyn, NY | Wallace, S. |
| Nov. 25 | Hotel Eden | San Jose | Mollicone, H. |
| Dec. 1 | VALIS | Paris | Machover, T. |
| ? | Ali Baba Opera | Arlington, VA | Reed, N. |
| ? | Beauty and the Beast | Melbourne | Easton, M. |
| ? | Beggar's Bloody Op'ra | Melbourne | Hollier, D. |
| ? | Guinevere | Aspen, CO | Williams. J. |
| ? | King's Twelve Moons | New York | Wallach, J. |
| ? | Mathematics of a Kiss | London | Gough, Lunn |
| ? | Muskrat Lullaby | Los Angeles | Barnes, E. |
| ? | Prelude to Einstein on the Fritz | New York | Schickele, P. |
| ? | Silence Tree | Perth, Austral. | Fox, M. |
| * | Blue Opera | Annandale, VA (1997) | Reed, N. |
| * | Buxtehude's Daughter | -- | Binder, J. |
| * | Cinderella | -- | Easton, M. |
| * | Deronda | -- | Cotel, M. |
| * | Henry Lawson | -- | Penberthy, J. |
| * | John Brown | San Francisco (2003) | Mechem, K. |
| * | Moby Dick | -- | Epstein, S. |
| * | Reverend Jim | -- | Eaton, J. |
| * | Seventeen | -- | Warren, B. |

**1990**

| Date | Title | City | Composer |
|------|-------|------|----------|
| Feb. 4 | Imaginary Couple | New York | Sullivan, T. |
| Feb. 8 | Fortitude | Boston | Rogers, A. |
| Mar. 31 | Black Rider | Hamburg | Waits, T. |
| Apr. 13 | Hamlet | New York | Kievman, C. |
| Apr. 20 | King of Bali | Portland, OR | McDermott, V. |
| Apr. 21 | Lifework of Juan Diaz | Chicago | Rapchak, L. |
| May | Mother of Three Sons | Munich | Jenkins, L. |
| May 5 | Birds, The | San Francisco | Ahlstrom, D. |
| May 18 | Clarissa | London | Holloway, R. |
| May 19 | Tornrak | Cardiff | Metcalf, J. |
| May 21 | Photo-Op | New York | Cummings, C. |
| May 23 | Mother and Child | New York | McClure, L. |
| May 25 | Frankenstein | St. Paul | Larsen, L. |
| May 26 | Hydrogen Jukebox | Charleston | Glass, P. |
| May 26 | Pioneer | Charleston | Dresher, P. |
| June 1 | Bohemians, The | New York | Kirschner, B. |
| June 10 | Triptych | Aldeburgh | Goehr, A. |

| Date | Title | City | Composer |
|------|-------|------|----------|
| June 14 | Albergo Empedocle | London | Barker, P. |
| June 17 | Europeras 3 & 4 | London | Cage, J. |
| summer | Reverend Everyman | Tallahassee | Brotons, S. |
| July 6 | Intelligence Park | London | Barry, G. |
| July 7 | Serinette | Sharon, ON | Somers, H. |
| July 17 | Manson Family | New York | Moran, J. |
| July 18 | Bet, The | London | Fox, E. |
| July 18 | Green Children | London | LeFanu, N. |
| July 28 | Chekhov Trilogy | Chautauqua, NY | Wargo, R. |
| Aug. 17 | Juniper Tree | Atlanta | Boury, R. |
| Aug. 24 | Events in the Elsewhere | Santa Fe | La Barbara, J. |
| Sept. 15 | Purgatory | Baltimore | Weiser, M. |
| Oct. | Chinaman's Chance | Brooklyn, NY | Ho, F, Li, G. M. |
| Oct. 17 | Vanishing Bridegroom | Glyndebourne | Weir, J. |
| Oct. 20 | Tibetan Dreams | New York | Dickman, S. |
| Oct. 24 | Chinese Canticle | London | Stoker, R. |
| Nov. | Ascension of Robert Flau | Sydney | Knehans, D. |
| Dec. 4 | Monster Bed | New York | de Kenessey, S. |
| Dec. 7 | Blind Witness News | New York | Yarmolinsky, B. |
| Dec. 7 | Funeral of Jan. Palach | New York | Beckley, C. |
| ? | Rimshot New York | | Currie, R. |
| ? | Stone Man | Louisville, KY | Dutton, D. |
| ? | Tables Meet | London | Oliver, S. |
| ? | Visit to the Country | Chautauqua, NY | Wargo, R. |
| * | Creation of the World | -- | Penberthy, J. |
| * | Hello Out There | -- | Colilla, R. |

**1991**

| Date | Title | City | Composer |
|------|-------|------|----------|
| Jan. 6 | Found Objects | New York | Trefousse, R. |
| Feb | SPACE | New York | Cionek, E. |
| Feb. 18 | Bride of Fortune | Perth, Austral. | Whitehead, G. |
| Feb. 19 | Jewel Box | Nottingham | Mozart-Griffiths |
| Feb. 22 | Atlas | New York | Monk, M. |
| Feb. 22 | Secret Garden | Philadelphia | Pliska, G. |
| Feb. 23 | Harmoonia | Muscatine, LA | Paulus, S. |
| Feb. 26 | Guacamayo's Old Song | Toronto | Oliver, J. |
| Mar. 1 | Mary Stuart | Cleveland | Murray, B. |
| Mar. 10 | Molly ManyBloom | Albany, NY | Bond, V. |
| Mar. 19 | Death of Klinghoffer | Brussels | Adams, J. |
| Apr. | Norma, The | New York | Dowdell, L. |
| Apr. 11 | Frida | Philadelphia | Rodríguez, F. |
| Apr. 14 | Frederick Douglass | Newark, NJ | Kay, U. |
| Apr. 18 | Europa 5 | Buffalo, NY | Cage, J. |
| Apr. 19 | Purple Gang | Toledo, OH | Jex, D. |
| May | Saul | Dallas | Sargon, S. |
| May 3 | Rip Van Winkle | Syracuse | Smith, G. |
| May 17 | Timon of Athens | London | Oliver, S. |
| May 30 | Gawain | London | Birtwistle, H. |

| DATE | TITLE | CITY | COMPOSER | DATE | TITLE | CITY | COMPOSER |
|------|-------|------|----------|------|-------|------|----------|
| May 31 | Judgement of Paris | London | Woolrich, J. | Mar. 27 | Wrinkle in Time | Wilmington, DE | Larsen, L. |
| May 31 | Panic, The | London | Sawyer, D. | Apr. 3 | Scarlet Letter | Berkeley, CA | Herman, M. |
| June 1 | Beyond Men and Dreams | London | Hogg, B. | Apr. 4 | Shining Brow | Madison, WI | Hagen, D. |
| June 1 | Dancer Hotoke | London | Fox, E. | Apr. 9 | Song of Majnun | Chicago | Sheng, B. |
| June 1 | Out of Season | London | Grant, J. | Apr. 24 | Pig | London | Dove, J, |
| June 6 | Echoes | London | Hawkins, J. | May 5 | Bacchae, The | London | Buller, J. |
| July | Van Gogh Video | New York | Gordon, M. | May 11 | Broken Strings | Amsterdam | Vir, P. |
| July 24 | Noises, Sounds | Avignon | Nyman, M. | May 11 | Snatched by the Gods | Amsterdam | Vir, P. |
| July 28 | As I Lay Dying | Oxford, MS | McKay, D. | May 19 | Mario and the Magician | Toronto | Somers, H. |
| Aug. 10 | Summer Carol | Canberra | Brumby, C. | May 19 | Nigredo Hotel | Stratford, ON | Gotham, N. |
| Sept. 25 | Fire on the Wind | Brisbane | Brumby, C. | May 20 | King Gesar | Munich | Lieberson, P. |
| Oct. | Three Scenes | Canberra | Sitsky, L. | May 28 | Caliban | New York | Currie, R. |
| Oct. 3 | Mer de Glace | Sydney | Meale, R. | May 28 | Folktale Operas | New Haven | Bingham, S. |
| Oct. 12 | New World | New York | Lehrman, L. | June 4 | Peer Gynt | New York | Eaton, J. |
| Oct. 17 | Poet and His Double | Dublin | Deane, R. | June 10 | Biko | London | Paintal, P. |
| Oct. 17 | Words upon the Window Pane | Dublin | Buckley, J. | June 17 | Tania | Philadelphia | Davis, A. |
| Oct. 31 | Diary of an African-American | New York | Peterson, H. | June 24 | Mary of Egypt | Aldeburgh | Taverner, J. |
| Nov. | Snow Leopard | St Paul, MN | Harper, W. | June 27 | Misfortune of the Immortals | Chester, PA | La Barbara/Subotnick |
| Nov. 2 | Coyote's Tail | Seattle | Thomas, K. | July 10 | Terrible Mouth | London | Osborne, N. |
| Nov. 3 | Proscenium | New York | Kupferman, M. | July 31 | Florence | Elora, ON | Sullivan, T. |
| | | | | Sept. 16 | Autumn Valentine | Omaha | Gordon, R. I. |
| Nov. 10 | Letters, Riddles | BBC | Nyman, M. | Sept. 23 | Ubu | Cardiff | Toovey, A. |
| Nov. 12 | Subject, The | New York | Yarmolinsky, B. | Oct. 12 | Voyage, The | New York | Glass, P. |
| Nov. 21 | Caritas | Wakefield, Eng | Saxon, R. | Oct. 16 | Under the Arbor | Birmingham, AL | Greenleaf, R. |
| Nov. 24 | Scipio's Dream | BBC 2 | Weir, J. | Oct. 22 | Fahrenheit 451 | Sydney | Broadstock, B. |
| Dec. 10 | Queen of Sheba's Legs | London | Grant, J. | Oct. 25 | Desperate Waltz | New York | Earnest, J. |
| Dec. 17 | Watchtower, The | New York | Kirschner, A. | Oct. 26 | Blood Wedding | London | LeFanu, N. |
| Dec. 23 | Ghosts of Versailles | New York | Corigliano, J. | Oct. 28 | Rappaccini's Daughter | Boston | Bender, E. |
| ? | Gisela in Her Bathtub | Ottawa | Weisensel, N. | Nov | Lenny Paschen Show | New York | Yarmolinsky, B. |
| ? | Little Redinka | Melbourne | Easton, M. | Nov. 3 | McTeague | Chicago | Bolcom, W. |
| * | Aria da capo | -- | Weaver, H. B. | Nov. 17 | Bitter Fruit | Dublin | Johnston, F. |
| * | Cinderella | -- | Oliver, S. | Dec. 1 | Puss in Boots | New York | Martín, J. |
| * | Hard Times | -- | Burgon, G. | Dec. 9 | Bacchae | Boston | Antoniou, T. |
| * | Monkey's Paw | -- | Alexander, W. | Dec. 15 | Orpheus in Love | New York | Busby, G. |
| * | Scenes from a Literary Life | -- | Hannay, R. | Dec. 19 | Alice | Hamburg | Waits, T. |
| * | Tailor of Gloucester | -- | Young, D. | ? | City Workers | Winnipeg | Weisensel, N. |
| * | Three Musketeers | -- | Dvorkin, J. | ? | Divertissement | New York | Stringer, A. |
| * | What Happened | -- | Shere, C. | ? | Love Burns | Adelaide | Koehne, G. |
| **1992** | | | | ? | Welfare | New York | Pickett, L. |
| Jan. 24 | Cue 67 | Norfolk, VA | Ching, M. | * | Belly Bag | -- | Ball, M. |
| Feb. 20 | Desert of Roses | Houston | Moran, R. | * | Galileo | -- | Gundry, I. |
| Feb. 27 | Elmer Gantry | Boston | Aldridge, R. | * | In Mighty Silence | -- | Senator, R. |
| Mar. 2 | Place to Call Home | Los Angeles | Barnes, E. | * | In the Penal Colony | -- | Murray, M. |
| Mar. 3 | Patria, no. 5 | Toronto | Schafer, R. | * | King of the Golden River | -- | Wilson, J. |
| Mar. 20 | Martin Luther King | Anchorage, AK | Schmitz, A. | * | London's Fair | -- | Hamilton, I. |
| Mar. 27 | From the Towers of the Moon | St. Paul. MN | Moran, R. | * | Naupaka Floret | -- | Tanner, J. |
| Mar. 27 | White Agony | Greensboro, NC | Fuchs, P. | * | Red-Headed League | -- | Dvorkin, J. |

| Date | Title | City | Composer |
|------|-------|------|----------|
| **1993** | | | |
| Jan. 18 | **King of the Clouds** | Dayton, OH | Ching, M. |
| Feb. 16 | **Ghosts** | New York | Ito, G. |
| Feb. 21 | **Wonderglass** | Brookfield Hills, MI | Botti, S. |
| Feb. 22 | **Achilles Heel** | Houston | Bohmler, C. |
| Feb. 22 | **Romulus Hunt** | New York | Simon, C. |
| Mar. | **Flight of Pilgrims** | London | Roe, B. |
| Mar. 1 | **Heloise and Abelard** | Perth, Austral. | Tahourdin, P. |
| Mar. 5 | **Every Day Newt Burman** | New York | Moran, J. |
| Mar. 17 | **Antigone** | Baton Rouge | Constantinides, D. |
| Mar. 18 | **Bundle Man** | New York | Cold, M. |
| Mar. 24 | **Awed Behavior** | San Francisco | Dresher, P. |
| Apr. 21 | **California Mystery Park** | New York | Kievman, C. |
| Apr. 21 | **Cat in the Box** | New York | Miller, R. |
| Apr. 21 | **Embrace the Monster** | New York | Valitsky, K. |
| May | **European Story** | London | Álvarez, G. |
| May 7 | **With Blood, with Ink** | Baltimore | Crozier, D. |
| May 16 | **Cave, The** | Vienna | Reich, S. |
| May 28 | **Ease** | London | Beamish, S. |
| May 28 | **Jason Field** | London | Horne, D. |
| May 28 | **Solid Assets** | London | Huehns, C. |
| May 31 | **Singing Child** | Charleston, SC | Menotti, G. C. |
| June 5 | **Inquest of Love** | London | Harvey, J. |
| June 9 | **Roman Fever** | Durham, NC | Ward, R. |
| June 13 | **Seven Deadly Sins:** | London | |
| | Anger | | Grant, J. |
| | Aspects of Lust | | Sams, J. |
| | Avarice | | Holloway, R. |
| | Envy | | Roth, A. |
| | Greed | | Dove, J. |
| | Pride | | Matthews, D. |
| | Sloth | | Matthews, C. |
| July | **Family Affair** | London | Grant, J. |
| July | **Mrs. Dalloway** | Cleveland | Larsen, L. |
| July 2 | **Man with Footsoles** | London | Volans, K. |
| July 3 | **Baa Baa Black Sheep** | London | Berkeley, M. |
| July 14 | **Line of Terror** | London | McQueen, I. |
| July 27 | **Juniper Tree** | Broomhill, Kent | Toovey, A. |
| Aug. 10 | **Tanz der Schwäne** | Wellington | Harris, R. |
| Sept. 24 | **El Greco** | New York | Harper, W. |
| Oct. | **Dead, The** | New York | Boren, M. |
| Oct. 6 | **Marilyn** | New York | Laderman, E. |
| Oct. 8 | **Esther** | New York | Weisgall, H. |
| Oct. 15 | **Birth/Day** | Dallas | Wolfe, N. |
| Oct. 17 | **Mass for the Dead** | New York | Shields, A. |
| Nov. 5 | **Room with a View** | Houston | Nelson, R. |
| Nov. 7 | **Brave Jack** | Minneapolis | Waters, E. |
| Nov. 27 | **Tonkin** | Wilmington, DE | Cummings, C. |
| Dec. 8 | **Let's Get This Show** | Chicago | Eaton, J. |
| Dec. 8 | **Nosferatu** | Toronto | Peters, R. |
| ? | **Bachelor Farmers** | Winnipeg | Weisensel, N. |

| Date | Title | City | Composer |
|------|-------|------|----------|
| ? | **Cask of Amontillado** | Barbados | Copeland, S. |
| ? | **Half Bird** | Middletown, DE | Copper, W. |
| ? | **New Lands** | Dublin | de Bromhead, J. |
| * | **Apocalypse** | -- | Shields, A. |
| * | **Beatrice Cenci** | -- | Di Domenica, R. |
| * | **Locust Valley Love Song** | -- | Hill, J. |
| * | **Lucifer's Choice** | -- | Hinkley-Turner, A. E. |
| * | **Sophie Songs** | -- | Moore, C. |
| * | **Test Tube** | Lewisburg, PA (2004) | Granger, M. |
| * | **Thomas Shelby** | -- | Warren, B. |
| * | **Tragedy of Macbeth** | -- | Hamilton, I. |
| **1994** | | | |
| Jan. | **Last Chance Planet** | Dayton, OH | Moore, C. |
| Jan. 13 | **How to Make Love** | New York | Widdoes, L. |
| Jan. 15 | **Dream of Valentino** | Washington | Argento, D. |
| Feb | **Memoirs of Uliana Rooney** | New York | Fine, V. |
| Feb. 6 | **Camera** | BBC | Moore, A. |
| Feb. 13 | **Horse Opera** | BBC | Copeland, S. |
| Jan. 30 | **Empress, The** | BBC | Gough, O. |
| Feb. 20 | **Ligeia** | Baltimore | Thomas, A. G. |
| Mar. | **Fresh Faust** | Boston | Jenkins, L. |
| Mar. 12 | **Mario and the Magician** | Brooklyn, NY | Thorne, F. |
| Mar. 13 | **Three Mimes** | New York | Cantrick, R. |
| Mar. 18 | **Flowers** | Cardiff | Hardy, J. |
| Mar. 18 | **Dracula Diary** | Houston | Moran, R. |
| Apr. | **Strange Life of Ivan Osokin** | New York | Gordon, P. |
| May 1 | **Scourge of Hyacinths** | Munich | León, T. |
| May 13 | **Apollonia's Circus** | Minneapolis | Stokes, E. |
| May 22 | **Dialects** | Bonn | Gilbert, P. |
| June 8 | **Lady Kate** | Wooster, OH | Ward, R. |
| June 11 | **Architect, The** | Vancouver | MacIntyre, D. |
| June 24 | **Craig's Progress** | London | Butler, M. |
| July 8 | **Nightingale and Rose** | London | Firsova, E. |
| July 8 | **Tempest, The** | Lawrenceville, NJ | Westergaard, P. |
| July 15 | **Siren Song** | London | Dove, J. |
| Aug. 14 | **Blond Eckbert** | Santa Fe | Weir, J. |
| Aug. 14 | **Two Executioners** | Melbourne | Chesworth, D. |
| Aug. 23 | **Sarajevo** | London | Osborne, N. |
| Sept. 10 | **Cyrano** | Hagen, Ger. | Beeson, J. |
| Oct. 7 | **Mathew in the School of Life** | New York | Moran, R. |
| Oct. 8 | **Esther** | New York | Weisgall, H. |
| Oct. 16 | **Thérèse Raquin** | London | Finnissy, M. |
| Oct. 17 | **Dangerous Liaisons** | San Francisco | Susa, C. |
| Oct. 21 | **Star Catalogues** | Vancouver | Underhill, O. |
| Oct. 24 | **Ibrahim** | Akron, OH | Bernstein, D. |
| Oct. 24 | **Second Mrs. Kong** | Glyndebourne | Birtwistle, H. |
| Oct. 28 | **Sealwoman** | Benicia, CA | Michael, S. |

| DATE | TITLE | CITY | COMPOSER |
|------|-------|------|----------|
| Nov. 11 | **King Lear** | Dover, NH | York-Norris, C. |
| Nov. 11 | **This Is the Rill Speaking** | New York | Hoiby, L. |
| Nov. 12 | **I Am in Search** | London | Grant, R. |
| Nov. 12 | **Lamentations of Doctor Faustus** | London | Hewitt, M. |
| Nov. 13 | **Coal** | Shepherdstown, WV | Shatin, J. |
| Dec. 1 | **Artaud's Cane** | Toronto | Egoyan et al. |
| Dec. 1 | **Freshwater** | Boston | Vores, A. |
| ? | **American Punchlines** | New York | Barab, S. |
| ? | **Playing Away** | Munich | Mason, B. |
| * | **Chaos** | -- | Gordon, M. |
| * | **Elephant's Child** | -- | Hagen, D. |
| * | **In the Shadow of the Glen** | Boston (1999) | Van de Vate, N. |
| * | **Kafka Quintet** | -- | Hecker, Z. |
| * | **Prelude to a Fable: Emperor's New Clothes Love Charm Little Match Girl** | Pasadena, CA (2001) | Bachlund, G. |
| * | **Selfish Giant** | -- | Easton, M. |
| * | **Wrong Party** | -- | Young, W. |

**1995**

| DATE | TITLE | CITY | COMPOSER |
|------|-------|------|----------|
| Jan. 20 | **Simón Bolívar** | Norfolk, VA | Musgrave, T. |
| Jan. 21 | **Harvey Milk** | Houston | Wallace, S. |
| Jan. 27 | **Amazing Adventure** | New York | Adolphe, B. |
| Jan. 27 | **Marita** | New York | Adolphe, B. |
| Feb. 3 | **Dorian** | Garden City, NY | Deutsch, H. |
| Feb. 3 | **Failing Kansas** | New York | Rouse, M. |
| Feb. 10 | **Paul Laurence Dunbar** | Dayton, OH | Hailstork, A. |
| Feb. 19 | **Rabbi Nachman's Chair** | New Haven | Bingham, S. |
| Feb. 21 | **Automobile Graveyard** | Boston | Ceely, R. |
| Mar. | **Song of Martina** | New York | Johnson, D. X. |
| Mar. 5 | **Triumph of Beauty** | London | Barry, G. |
| Mar. 10 | **Faust Triumphant** | New York | Anderson, D. |
| Mar. 10 | **Who's on Faust?** | New York | Zarr, G. |
| Mar. 12 | **Good Friday 1663** | London | Westbrook, M., K. |
| Mar. 23 | **Village, The** | Queens, NY | Mandelbaum, J. |
| Mar. 24 | **Ondine** | New York | Barab, S. |
| Apr. 2 | **Telaio: Desdemona** | Bloomfield Hills, MI | Botti, S. |
| Apr. 26 | **Outcast, The** | Brooklyn | Ain, N. |
| Apr. 27 | **Manhattan Book of the Dead** | New York | First, D. |
| Apr. 27 | **Night Passage** | Seattle | Moran, R. |
| Apr. 30 | **April Witch** | Baltimore | Shapiro, D. |
| Apr. 30 | **Chatter and Static** | Baltimore | Matthews, P. |
| Apr. 30 | **Singing Violin** | Dallas | Sargon, S. |
| May 3 | **Mata Hari** | Dallas | McDermott, V. |

| DATE | TITLE | CITY | COMPOSER |
|------|-------|------|----------|
| May 11 | **Hearts on Fire** | Minneapolis | Ames, R. |
| May 11 | **I Was Looking** | Berkeley, CA | Adams, J. |
| May 18 | **Travels** | Roanoke, VA | Bond, V. |
| June 1 | **Heavenfields** | Victoria, BC | Buhr, G. |
| June 2 | **Wildman, The** | London | LeFanu, N. |
| June 8 | **Lady Kate** | Wooster, OH | Ward, R. |
| June 10 | **Bok Choy Variations** | St. Paul, MN | Chen, E. |
| June 17 | **Woman at the Otowi Crossing** | St. Louis | Paulus, S. |
| June 21 | **Passionate Man** | Dublin | Wilson, J. |
| June 22 | **Small Jewel Box** | New York | Mozart-Griffiths |
| summer | **Lā'ie'ikawa** | Honolulu | McKay, N. |
| July 5 | **Powder Her Face** | Santa Fe | Adès, T. |
| July 18 | **East and West** | London | McQueen, I. |
| July 29 | **Modern Painters** | Santa Fe | Lang, D. |
| Aug. 15 | **Ecstatic Journey** | Aspen, CO | Rodwin, D. |
| Sept. | **S.** | Northampton, MA | Perera, R. |
| Sept. 23 | **Mountain Windsong** | Tallequah, OK | Chlarson, L. |
| Oct. 2 | **Fire King** | Derry, Ire | O'Connell, K. |
| Oct. 14 | **Aspern Papers** | Port Fairy, Austral | Hurd, M. |
| Oct. 14 | **Eighth Wonder** | Sydney | John, A. |
| Nov. 11 | **Say Cheese** | Queens, NY | Barab, S. |
| Nov. 28 | **Red Emma** | Toronto | Kulesha, G. |
| Dec. 10 | **Vision and a Prayer** | New York | Macbride, D. |
| ? | **Ghost Dance** | Toronto | Levin, G. |
| ? | **Imposition, The** | New York | Tanenbaum, E. |
| ? | **Three Princes** | New York | Levowitz, A. |
| * | **Art of Pizza** | -- | Whitehead, G. |
| * | **Boys and Girls** | -- | Holloway, R. |
| * | **Cenci, The** | -- | Di Domenica, R. |
| * | **Death of the Hired Man** | Vienna (1999) | Van de Vate, N. |
| * | **Dum Tweedle Dee** | New York (2002) | Del Tredici, D. |
| * | **Further Voyages** | -- | Stokes, E. |
| * | **Gulliver in Lilliput** | -- | Paintal, P. |
| * | **Little Girl Dreams** | San Francisco | Wold, E. |
| * | **Myth of Er** | -- | Sternau, C. |
| * | **Scarlet Letter** | -- | Svane, R. |
| * | **Vireo** | -- | Bielawa, L. |

**1996**

| DATE | TITLE | CITY | COMPOSER |
|------|-------|------|----------|
| Jan. 13 | **Dreamkeepers, The** | Salt Lake City | Carlson, D. |
| Feb. 7 | **Different Fields** | New York | Reid, M. |
| Feb. 8 | **Seasons in Hell** | Cincinnati | Blumenfeld, H. |
| Feb. 13 | **Rent** | New York | Larson, J. |
| Feb. 23 | **Dragon, The** | St. Paul, MN | Biales, A. |
| Mar. | **Beast and Superbeast** | Washington | Martín, J. |

| Date | Title | City | Composer | Date | Title | City | Composer |
|---|---|---|---|---|---|---|---|
| Mar. 2 | Jungle Book | Wilmington, DE | Swensson, E. | * | Council of the Dead | -- | Sternau, C. |
| Mar. 8 | First Word | New York | Cameron, K. | * | Francesco Cenci | -- | Di Domenica, R. |
| Mar. 8 | Roman Fever | New York | Stringer, A. | | | | |
| Mar. 8 | Vera of Las Vegas | Las Vegas | Hagen, D. | * | Kona Coffee Cantata | -- | Tanner, J. |
| Mar. 16 | Angels' Voices | Washington | Race, G. | * | Marble Faun | -- | Bender, E. |
| Apr. | Kill Bear Comes Home | Rochester, NY | Stuart, P. | * | On the Eve | -- | Hamilton, I. |
| Apr. 10 | Terra Incognita | New York | Sierra, R. | * | Remember Him to Me | -- | Moran, R. |
| Apr. 19 | Processions | St. Paul, MN | Callahan, J. | * | Solon the Dreamer | -- | Sternau, C. |
| May 1 | Minister, The | Oxford | Scruton, R. | * | Unicorn Weeps | -- | Moerks, A. |
| May 7 | Marco Polo | Munich | Tan Dun | * | War Prayer | -- | March, K. |
| May 8 | Picture of Dorian Gray | Monte Carlo | Liebermann, L. | **1997** | | | |
| May 31 | Tibetan Book of the Dead | Houston | Gordon, R. | Jan. | Dark and Stormy Night | Dallas | Hagemann, P. |
| June | Patience and Sarah | New York | Kimper, P. | Jan. 18 | Many Moons | Princeton | Kapilow, R. |
| June | Time Rocker | Hamburg | Reed, L. | Jan. 27 | Buoso's Ghost | Pittsburgh | Ching, M. |
| June | True Story of the Three Little Pigs | Bowling Green, OH | De Pue, W. | Jan. 31 | Songs of Madness and Sorrow | Tacoma, WA | Hagen, D. |
| June 4 | Jump into My Sack | London | Grant. J. | Feb. 28 | Misper | Glyndebourne | Lunn, J. |
| June 6 | Don Quixote | Chicago | Eaton, J. | Mar. 1 | Conquistador, The | San Diego | Fink, M. |
| June 6 | Golk | Chicago | Eaton, J. | Mar. 8 | Wind in the Willows | Wilmington, DE | Rutter, J. |
| June 7 | Beatrice Chancy | Toronto | Rolfe, J. | | | | |
| June 13 | Three Visitations | Minneapolis | Sherman, K. | Mar. 14 | Jackie O | Houston | Daugherty, M. |
| June 28 | E. & O. Line | Annandale, VA | LeBaron, A. | Mar. 17 | Promise, The | London | Townsend, J. |
| July | Brain Opera | New York | Machover, T. | Apr. | Juniper Tree | Munich | Watkins, R. |
| July 5 | Doctor of Myddfai | Cardiff | Davies, P. M. | Apr. 10 | Croak | Washington | LeBaron, A. |
| July 6 | In the House of Crossed Desires | Cheltenham | Woolrich, J. | Apr. 10 | She Never Lost a Passenger | Kansas City | Kander, S. |
| July 20 | Miraculous Staircase | Albuquerque | Stringer, A. | Apr. 10 | Terra Incognita | New York | Sierra, R. |
| July 27 | Emmeline | Santa Fe | Picker, T. | Apr. 17 | Ever Since Eden, trilogy: Eve's Odds Golden Apple Cleo | Univ Park, PA | Trinkley, B. |
| July 27 | King of Hearts | Aspen | Torke, M. | | | | |
| Aug. | Dreamers, The | Sonoma, CA | Conte, D. | Apr. 19 | Warchild | London | Taylor, R. |
| Aug. 1 | Kafka's Chimp | Banff, AB | Metcalf, J. | Apr. 22 | Hotel | London | Gough, O. |
| Aug. 13 | Mary Shelley | New York | Jaffe, N. | Apr. 24 | Three Hermits | St. Paul, MN | Paulus, S. |
| Aug. 23 | Inés de Castro | Edinburgh | MacMillan, J. | Apr. 27 | Black Water | Philadelphia | Duffy, J. |
| Sept. 2 | Suppose a Wedding | Commack, NY | Lehrman, L. | May | Bambi | Kirkland, WA | Morrill, K. |
| Oct. 10 | Politics of Quiet | Copenhagen | Monk, M. | May 4 | Ovidiana | Philadelphia | Greenbaum, M. |
| Oct. 19 | Summer of the 17th Doll | Melbourne | Mills, R. | | | | |
| Oct. 25 | Jocasta | New York | Schonthal, R. | May 9 | Roswell Incident | Bury St. Edmunds, Eng | Hardy, J. |
| Oct. 25 | Shala Fears for the Poor | New York | Braxton, A. | May 10 | Marriages between Zones | Heidelberg | Glass, P. |
| Nov. | Body of Crime | New York | Greenhut, B. | May 16 | Balseros | Miami Beach | Ashley, R. |
| Nov. | Dennis Cleveland | New York | Rouse, M. | May 16 | Hansel and Gretel | W Hartford, CT | Bruce, N. |
| Nov. | Three Willies | Philadelphia | Jenkins, L. | | | | |
| Nov. 18 | Voluptuous Tango | BBC | Muldowney, D. | May 23 | Eagle Has Landed | Wellington | Ritchie, A. |
| | | | | May 30 | Travelling with Gulliver | Boston | Eaton, J. |
| Dec. 13 | Nights of Annabel Lee | New York | Rodgers, L. | June 10 | Home and the River | New York | Quincy, G. |
| Dec. 13 | Other Wise Man | New York | de Kenessey, S. | June 11 | Gang, The | Vancouver | Hannan, P. |
| | | | | June 13 | Meetin', The | New York | Baskin-Watson, P. |
| Dec. 18 | Angel Square | Ottawa | Crawley, C. | | | | |
| ? | Defendants Rosenberg | Baltimore | Meyers, A. | June 13 | Country of the Blind | Aldeburgh | Turnage, M. |
| ? | Say It with Flowers | -- | Lependorf, J. | June 13 | Twice through the Heart | Aldeburgh | Turnage, M. |
| * | Challenge, The | -- | Sternau, C. | June 14 | Hopper's Wife | Long Beach, CA | Wallace, S. |
| * | Christmas on the Underground | -- | Bourgeois, D. | | | | |

| Date | Title | City | Composer | Date | Title | City | Composer |
|------|-------|------|----------|------|-------|------|----------|
| June 20 | Between Two Worlds | Chicago | Ran, S. | Feb. 12 | Heroes Don't Dance | Cambridge | Grant, J. |
| June 23 | Hindenburg | Berlin | Reich, S. | Feb. 21 | Gorgon's Head | Edmond, OK | Magrill, S. |
| June 25 | Doctor Ox's Experiment | BBC | Bryars, G. | Feb. 27 | Alley | Wellington | Body, J. |
| June 25 | Kahalaopuna | Honolulu | McKay, N. | Feb. 24 | Cinderella in Spain | Houston | Warwick, M. |
| July | Intimate Immensity | New York | Subotnick, M. | Mar. | Alianor | Fairmont, WVA | Moerk, A. |
| July 18 | Uninvited, The | London | Grant, J. | | | | |
| July 26 | Ashoka's Dream | Santa Fe | Lieberson, P. | Mar. | Hansel and Gretel | Hartford | Bruce, N. |
| July 24 | Wide Sargasso Sea | Melbourne | Howard, B. | Mar. 7 | Coyote Tales | Kansas City | Mollicone, H. |
| July 27 | Silver River | Santa Fe | Sheng, B. | Mar. 7 | Redwall | Wilmington, DE | Swensson, E. |
| July 31 | Phrenic Crush | San Francisco | Bielawa, L. | | | | |
| Sept. 8 | Legend of Sleepy Hollow | Norfolk, VA | Gillis D. | Mar. 11 | Woman at the Store | Wellington | Buchanan, D. |
| Sept. 18 | American Lit | New York | Lependorf, J. | Mar. 12 | Down Here on Earth | Toronto | Wiens, R. |
| Oct. 4 | Venus | London | Van Rhijn, J. | Mar. 13 | Little Women | Houston | Adamo, M. |
| Oct. 11 | Naked Revolution | New York | Soldier, D. | Mar. 28 | Greek Gaze | Ann Arbor, MI | Beeferman, G. |
| Nov. | Trigonometry | Hamburg | Johnson, T. | Apr. | Democracy | Boston | Wheeler, S. |
| Nov. 14 | My Love | Belfast | O'Donnell, K. | Apr. | Binding of Isaac | Norwalk, CT | Chlarson, L. |
| Nov. 18 | Ethan Frome | Morgantown, WVA | Beall, J. | Apr. 3 | Fisherman's Dock | St Paul, MN | Banfield, W. |
| | | | | Apr. 14 | Power of Xingu | Chapel Hill, NC | Legg, J. |
| Nov. 20 | Ferryman, The | New York | Feigin, J. | | | | |
| Nov. 20 | Laughter in Jericho | New York | Beck, J. | Apr. 15 | Monsters of Grace | Los Angeles | Glass, P. |
| Nov. 20 | Sadie Thompson | New York | Owen, R. | Apr. 23 | Elsewhereless | Toronto | Sharman, R. |
| Nov. 29 | Amistad | Chicago | Davis, A. | May | Angel Magick | Salisbury, Eng. | Harle, J. |
| Dec. | Miraculous Phonograph Record | Dallas | White, C. | May 12 | Peony Pavilion | London | Tan Dun |
| Dec. | Merry Christmas | Vancouver | Weisensel, N. | May 14 | Harlot's Progress | New York | Greenhut, B. |
| Dec. 3 | Iphis | Sydney | Kats-Chernin, E. | May 17 | Astronaut's Tale | Boston | Fussell, C. |
| | | | | June 1 | Travellers | London | Horne, D. |
| Dec. 6 | Eloise | London | Jenkins, K. | July 1 | Hey Persephone! | London | Gribbin, D. |
| Dec. 7 | Little Thieves | Rochester, NY | Stuart, P. | July 12 | Moon Singer | Brevard, NC | Liptak, D. |
| Dec. 12 | True Last Words | Amsterdam | Salzman, E. | Aug. 6 | Virtual Motion | Los Angeles | Rodwin, D. |
| Dec. 21 | Signals | New York | Knopf, P. | Aug. 25 | Leviathan Hook | Toronto | Doolittle, Q. |
| ? | Picasso: Out of the Blue | London | McQueen, I. | Sept. 11 | Black Swan | Swarthmore, PA | Whitman, T. |
| * | Aria da capo | -- | Axelrod, L. | | | | |
| * | Bellarocca | -- | Legg, J. | Sept. 15 | Pied Piper | Norfolk, VA | Barab, S. |
| * | Council on the Arts | -- | Binder, J. | Sept. 19 | Streetcar Named Desire | San Francisco | Previn, A. |
| * | Enchanted Island | Wellington (2005) | Farquhar, D. | Sept. 25 | Quiet American | New York | Griffiths, W. |
| | | | | Sept. 26 | Flight | Glyndebourne | Dove, J. |
| * | Euphonia 2344 | -- | Austin, L. | Sept. 28 | Outrageous Fortune | Dunedin, NZ | Whitehead, G. |
| * | Gift, The | -- | Binder, J. | Oct. | Quickening, The | Port Fairy, Victoria | Selleck, J. |
| * | Jane Eyre | -- | Joubert, J. | | | | |
| * | Lilith | Cooperstown, NY (1998) | Drattell, D. | Oct. 9 | Night of the Wedding | Port Fairy, Victoria | Hurd, M. |
| * | Madrid | -- | Young, W. | Oct. 10 | Chaos | New York | Gordon, M. |
| * | Meanwhile, Back at the Seraglio | -- | Stepleton, J. | Oct. 10 | Reunion | Wilmington, DE | Ching, M. |
| * | Patria, no. 10 | Haliburton Forest, ON | Schafer, R. | Oct. 30 | Bacchae, The | Cambridge, MA | Harper, W. |
| * | Story of the Bird Feng | -- | Sternau, S. | Nov. 6 | Ravenshead | Philadelphia | Mackey, S. |
| * | Strands | -- | Levowitz, A. | Nov. 11 | Eric Hermannson's Soul | Omaha, NE | Larsen, L. |
| | | | | Nov. 18 | Nightingale's to Blame | Huddersfield, Eng. | Holt, S. |
| **1998** | | | | | | | |
| Jan. | Shoulder, The | New York | Schreier, D. | Nov. 27 | Matricide | Melbourne | Kats-Chernin, E. |
| Jan. 10 | Closed Case | Albuquerque | Fox, R. | | | | |
| | Solid House | | Galloway, J. | Dec. 9 | Fantastic Mr. Fox | Los Angeles | Picker, T. |
| | Sunny Morning | | Stringer, A. | | | | |

| Date | Title | City | Composer |
|---|---|---|---|
| Dec. 11 | **Billy and Zelda** | Washington, DE | Davidson, T. |
| Dec. 12 | **Paradise of Children** | Edmond, OK | Magrill, S. |
| ? | **Gift of the Magi** | San Francisco | Conte, D. |
| ? | **Out of the Rain** | Wilmington, DE | Ching, M. |
| * | **All Quiet on the Western Front** | New York (2003) | Van de Vate, N. |
| * | **De Soto** | Gainesville, FL (2008) | Bailey, C. |
| * | **Myra Breckinridge** | -- | Hollier, D. |
| * | **Prince of Venosa** | -- | Glasgow, S. |

**1999**

| Date | Title | City | Composer |
|---|---|---|---|
| Jan. 10 | **Paris and Oenone** | New York | Hagemann, P. |
| Jan. 11 | **Talk Opera** | New York | Granger, M. |
| Jan. 29 | **Ballymore** | Milwaukee | Wargo, R. |
| Feb. 5 | **Merlin** | Paris | Viñao, E. |
| Feb. 11 | **Mao Zedong** | New York | Gal, Y. |
| Feb. 25 | **Bandanna** | Austin, TX | Hagen, D. |
| Feb. 25 | **Where Angels Fear to Tread** | Baltimore | Weiser, M. |
| Feb. 27 | **Vanqui** | Columbus, OH | Burrs, L. |
| Mar. | **Dybbuk, The** | New York | Morgulas, J. |
| Mar. 1 | **Night Vision** | New York | Ho, F. |
| Mar. 8 | **Romeo and Juliet** | New York | Hoiby, L. |
| Mar. 12 | **Inferno** | New York | Soluri, P. |
| Mar. 13 | **Taptoo!** | Montreal | Beckwith, J. |
| Mar. 28 | **Floating** | New York | Kuskin, C. |
| Apr. | **Dust** | New York | Ashley, R. |
| Apr. 3 | **Daughters of the Late Colonel** **Miss Brill** | Wellington | Buchanan, D. |
| Apr. 15 | **Avow** | New York | Adamo, M. |
| Apr. 15 | **Body of Crime II** | New York | Greenhut, B. |
| Apr. 15 | **Golden Ass** | Toronto | Peters, R. |
| Apr. 16 | **Cleo** | Univ Park, PA | Trinkley, B. |
| Apr. 17 | **Golden Apple** | Univ Park, PA | Trinkley, B. |
| Apr. 18 | **Galileo** | Auckland | Rimmer, J. |
| Apr. 25 | **Resurrection** | Houston | Machover, T. |
| Apr. 29 | **Zabette** | Atlanta | Willis, S. |
| May | **Stars in Orion** | Dunedin, NZ | Drummond, J. |
| May 4 | **Pope Joan** | New York | Musto, J. |
| May 5 | **Blood on the Dining Room Floor** | New York | Sheffer, J. |
| May 5 | **Dora** | New York | Shiflett, M. |
| | **Gethsemane Park** | New York | Moore, C. |
| | **Pope Joan** | New York | Musto, J. |
| | **Welfare** | New York | Pickett, L. |
| May 12 | **Practice in the Art of Elocution** | New York | Beeson, J. |
| May 25 | **Sorry, Wrong Number** | New York | Beeson, J. |
| June 11 | **Joshua's Boots** | St. Louis | Hailstork, J. |

| Date | Title | City | Composer |
|---|---|---|---|
| June 17 | **Merchant and the Pauper** | New York | Schoenfield, P. |
| July 25 | **Central Park** trilogy: **Festival of Regrets** **Food of Love** **Strawberry Fields** | Cooperstown, NY | Drattell, D., Beaser, R. Torke, M., |
| July 7 | **Tobias and the Angel** | Christchurch | Dove, J. |
| July 29 | **Belladonna** | Aspen | Rands, B. |
| Aug. 11 | **Raven King** | Banff, AB | Burtch, M. |
| Aug. 26 | **Shorts:** | Battersea, London | |
| | **Doggone** | | Carpenter, G. |
| | **Miss Treat** | | Oliver, D. |
| | **Nightjar** | | Jones, E. |
| | **Platform 10** | | Grant, J. |
| | **Seven Tons** | | Bruce, D. |
| Aug. 28 | **Summer** | Pittsfield, MA | Paulus, S. |
| Sept. 2 | **Faith** | New York | Ching, M. |
| Sept. 2 | **Ulysses** | Portsmouth, NH | Rudenstein, R. |
| Sept. 9 | **Carbon Copy Building** | Turin | Gordon et al. |
| Sept. 10 | **Twilight Voices** | Seattle | Hoffman, S. |
| Sept. 16 | **What Next?** | Berlin | Carter, E. |
| Sept. 19 | **Kantan and the Damask Drum** | Dortmund, Ger | Goehr, A. |
| Oct. | **Ghost Wife** | Melbourne | Mills, J. |
| Oct. 10 | **View from the Bridge** | Chicago | Bolcom, W. |
| Oct. 13 | **Wall of Cloud** | Longford, Ire | Deane, R. |
| Oct. 16 | **Waking in New York** | New York | Lauten, E. |
| Oct. 26 | **Tower** | Swansea | Hoddinott, A. |
| Nov. | **Reluctant Dragon** | Springfield, MO | Prescott, J. |
| Nov. 6 | **Friend of the People** | Glastonbury | Horne, D. |
| Nov. 6 | **Method for Madness** **Tell-Tale Heart** | Akron, OH | Bernstein, D. |
| Nov. 12 | **Strawberry Fields** | Cooperstown, NY | Torke, M. |
| Nov. 13 | **Coyote's Music** | Albuquerque | Stringer, A. |
| Nov. 13 | **Rococo Confessional** | Albuquerque | Galloway, J. |
| Nov. 13 | **Tale of the Nutcracker** | San Jose, CA | Bohmler, C. |
| Nov. 16 | **Absolute Zero** | Leeds | Pearson, K. |
| Nov. 16 | **Thirty Minute Don Giovanni** | Leeds | Mozart-Lole-Gray |
| Nov. 25 | **Gate, The** | Tokyo | Tan Dun |
| Nov. 27 | **Ant and Grasshopper** | Bellevue, WA | Shawn, A. |
| Dec. 1 | **Writing to Vermeer** | Amsterdam | Andriessen, L. |
| Dec. 9 | **Antigone** | Chicago | Eaton, J. |
| Dec. 20 | **Great Gatsby** | New York | Harbison, J. |
| ? | **Catbird Seat** | Boston | Sisco, D. |
| ? | **Waking in New York** | New York | Lauten, E. |
| * | **Age of Gold** | -- | Sternau, C. |
| * | **Benjamin Brown** | -- | McAndrew, I. |
| * | **Composer's Nightmare** | -- | Martín, J. |
| * | **Fall of Atlantis** | -- | Sternau, C. |
| * | **Heretic, The** | -- | Brumby, C. |
| * | **Love's Labour's Lost** | -- | Loeffler, A. |

| DATE | TITLE | CITY | COMPOSER | DATE | TITLE | CITY | COMPOSER |
|------|-------|------|----------|------|-------|------|----------|
| * | Marco Polo | New York (2006) | Stern, M. | June 10 | Ochelata's Wedding | Bartlesville, OK | Damase, J.-M. |
| * | Mercenary, The | -- | Grabowsky, P. | June 11 | And God Created Great Whales | New York | Eckert, R. |
| * | Scoring a Century | Birmingham (2010) | Blake, D. | June 14 | Travels of Babar | New York | Mostel, R. |
| * | System of Doctor Tarr | -- | Bernstein, D. | June 16 | Too Many Sopranos | Cedar Rapids | Penhorwood, E. |
| * | Tell-Tale Heart | -- | Levowitz, A. | June 18 | Mr. Emmet Takes a Walk | Orkney Is | Davies, P. M. |
| * | Virata | -- | Wilson, J. | June 28 | Kafka: Letter to My Father | New York | Walden, S. |
| **2000** | | | | June 30 | Jane Eyre | Cheltenham | Berkeley, M. |
| Feb. | Gold Standard | New York | Wheeler, S. | July 1 | Showdown on Two Street | Edmond, OK | Magrill, S. |
| Feb | Monster | Glasgow | Beamish, S. | July 15 | Tale of Genji | St. Louis | Miki, M. |
| Feb. 4 | Mr. Polly at the Potwell Inn | Dunedin, NZ | Drummond, J. | July 21 | Cat Lover | Annandale-on-Hudson, NY | Pace, R. |
| Feb. 16 | Silver Tassie | London | Turnage, M. | Aug. | Lunch at the Cooked Goose | Glasgow | Roe, B. |
| Feb. 19 | Erewhon | Ottawa | Applebaum, L. | Aug. 3 | Facing Goya | Santiago de Comp, Spain | Nyman, M. |
| Mar. 1 | Zoë | Glyndebourne | Lunn, J. | Aug. 11 | Game Misconduct | Vancouver | Uyeda, L. |
| Mar. 6 | Handmaid's Tale | Copenhagen | Riders, P. | Aug. 17 | Lunar Opera | New York | Oliveros, P. |
| Mar. 6 | Proposal, A | London | Dubugnon, R. | Aug. 31 | In the Penal Colony | Seattle | Glass, P. |
| Apr. | Arachne | San Francisco | Michael, S. | Sept. 13 | Patria, no. 8 | Ponytail, ON | Schafer, R. |
| Apr. | Wise Woman | Fairmont, WVA | Moerk, A. | Oct. 6 | Bridge to Somewhere | Dunedin, NZ | Drummond, J. |
| Apr. 8 | Scenes in Wonderland | New York | Barab, S. | | Trapeze Artists | Dunedin, NZ | Ritchie, A. |
| Apr. 9 | Sir Gawain | Greensboro, NC | Eastman, D. | Oct. 8 | Dead Man Walking | San Francisco | Heggie, J. |
| Apr. 13 | Daphne at Sea | Birmingham, AL | Mason, C. | Oct. 14 | Pope Joan | Pittsburgh | LeBaron, A. |
| Apr. 14 | Cold Sassy Tree | Houston | Floyd, C. | Oct. 20 | Fleeting Animal | Montpelier, VT | Nielsen, E. |
| Apr. 16 | Floating Island | Philadelphia | Greenbaum, M. | Oct. 21 | Last Supper | Berlin | Birtwistle, H. |
| Apr. 18 | Last Supper | Berlin | Birtwistle, H. | Oct. 22 | Fleeting Animal | Montpelier, VT | Nielsen, E. |
| Apr. 19 | Barnum's Bird | Minneapolis | Larsen, L. | Oct. 27 | Bread & Roses | New York | Glickman, G., Shen, M. |
| Apr. 26 | Monticello | Los Angeles | Paxton, G. | Nov. | Transcendent Voices | New York | Jones, D. |
| Apr. 28 | Dracula, the Opera | Buffalo | Ziemba, P. | Nov. 3 | Palace in the Sky | London | Dove, J. |
| Apr. 28 | Opera Singer | Atlanta | Willis, S. | Nov. 6 | Marrying the Hangman | New York | Caltabiano, R. |
| Apr. 29 | Sun Also Rises | Rockville Centre, NY | Young, W. | Nov. 17 | No Easy Walk to Freedom | Hempstead, NY | Chandler, C. |
| Apr. 30 | Edge of Glory | Petersburg, VA | Waters, V. | Nov. 20 | Warrior Sisters | New York | Ho, F. |
| May 1 | Zoë | Glyndebourne | Lunn, J. | Dec. 2 | Child, Book, Broomstick | Vancouver | Burtch, M. |
| May 2 | Haroun | New York | Wuorinen, C. | Dec. 6 | House of the Seven Gables | New York | Eyerly, S. |
| May 4 | Again | New York | Heggie, J. | * | Illusion, The | -- | Richardson, A. |
| May 8 | Homies & Popz | Los Angeles | Abels, M. | * | Tale of Psyche & Cupid | -- | Sternau, C. |
| May 9 | Don Quixote | New York | Eaton, J. | * | Tempest, The | -- | Tahourdin, P. |
| May 10 | Highway, The | New York | Beck, J. | **2001** | | | |
| May 11 | Last Leaf | New York | Remson, M. | Jan. 27 | Caliban Dreams | San Francisco | Suprynowicz, C. |
| May 11 | Muhammad Ali | New York | Duffy, J. | Feb. 17 | Circe's Palace | Edmond, OK | Margill, S. |
| May 12 | Tess of the D'Urbervilles | New York | Harris, M. | Apr. 13 | Queer | San Francisco | Wold, E. |
| May 19 | Bonhoeffer | Houston | Gebuhr, A. | Apr. 21 | Iron Road | Toronto | Chan Ka Nin |
| May 19 | Last Night of Don Juan | San Antonio | Rodríguez, R. | Apr. 22 | Town of Greed | Pittsburgh | Balada, L. |
| May 21 | Boy from Deerfield | New York | Halpern, M. | | | | |
| May 29 | Bitter Fruit | Birmingham | Woolrich, J. | | | | |
| June | Anniversary Tales | New Haven | Bingham, S. | | | | |
| June 9 | Ion | Aldeburgh | Vir, P. | | | | |

| DATE | TITLE | CITY | COMPOSER |
|------|-------|------|----------|
| Apr. 27 | **From Morning to Midnight** | London | Sawer, D. |
| May | **Lost Childhood** | New York | Hamer, J. |
| May 4 | **Soul Gone Home** | Durham, NC | Banfield, W. |
| May 8 | **Dreaming of Wonderland** | New York | Romero, M. |
| May 9 | **Androcles and the Lion** | New York | Hagemann, P. |
| May 11 | **Batavia** | Melbourne | Mills, R. |
| May 12 | **Sacco and Vanzetti** | New York | Coppola, A. |
| May 13 | **Aethelred** | New York | Wilson, R. |
| May 15 | **Henry and Clara** | New York | Martín, J. |
| May 15 | **To Scratch an Angel** | New York | Frankel, A. |
| May 17 | **All My Sons** | New York | Legg, J. |
| May 17 | **Cows of Apollo** | New York | Theofanidis, C. |
| May 17 | **Hit and Run** | New York | Abel, M. |
| May 17 | **www.love** | New York | March, K. |
| June 15 | **Biddle Boys** | Pittsburgh | Beck, J. |
| June 22 | **Wuornos** | San Francisco | Lucero, C. |
| June 23 | **Satin Cloak** | New York | Halpern, M. |
| July 4 | **Better Place** | London | Butler, M. |
| July 6 | **God's Liar** | London | Casken, J. |
| Aug. | **Jerry Springer** | Edinburgh | Thomas, R. |
| Aug. | **Master's Stroke** | Winnipeg | Weisensel, N. |
| Aug. | **Turtle Wakes** | Calgary | Bell, A. |
| Oct. | **Sir Gawain** | New York | Peaslee, R. |
| Oct. 1 | **Vine of the Soul** | Blacksburg, VA | St. Croix, J. |
| Oct. 25 | **Screams of Kitty Genovese** | Boston | Todd, W. |
| Nov. 30 | **Thérèse Raquin** | Dallas | Picker, T. |
| ? | **Emperor's New Clothes** | Houston | Warwick, M. |
| ? | **Josephine** | New York | Sullivan, T. |
| ? | **Maker of Dreams** | New York | Bortz, Y. |
| * | **Flatwoods Monster** | -- | Moerk, A. |

## 2002

| DATE | TITLE | CITY | COMPOSER |
|------|-------|------|----------|
| Jan. 2 | **Trippin'** | New York | Rodwin, D. |
| Jan. 23 | **Somebody's Children** | Kansas City | Kander, S. |
| Feb. 14 | **Six-Pack:** | London | |
| | **Doorstepping Susannah** | | Grime, H. |
| | **Has It Happened Yet?** | | Bruce, D. |
| | **Jack & Jill** | | Leach, R. |
| | **Odd Numbers** | | Grant, J. |
| | **Phone Call** | | Webb, J. |
| | **Waiting for Jack** | | Webb, J. |
| Feb. 22 | **Uncharted Waters** | New York | Granger, M. |
| Feb. 26 | **Dreaming Blue** | Salt Lake City | Larsen, L. |
| Mar. 2 | **From the Mixed-Up Files** | Wilmington, DE | Swensson, E. |
| Mar. 2 | **One Hundred Twenty Songs** | Vancouver | Hannan, P. |
| Mar. 8 | **One False Move** | Kansas City | Kander, S. |
| Mar. 22 | **Difficulty of Crossing a Field** | San Francisco | Lang, D. |
| Mar. 31 | **Luyala** | Chapel Hill, NC | Banfield, W. |

| DATE | TITLE | CITY | COMPOSER |
|------|-------|------|----------|
| Apr. 2 | **Bowl, Cat, and Broomstick** | Boury, R. | New York |
| Apr. 5 | **Araboolies** | New York | Perera, R. |
| Apr. 16 | **Gwyneth and the Green Knight** | Brecon, Wales | Plowman, L. |
| Apr. 19 | **Doctor Faustus** | New York | Denzer, R. |
| Apr. 23 | **Scarlet Princess** | Toronto | Louie, A. |
| Apr. 24 | **Heloise and Abelard** | New York | Paulus, S. |
| May | **. . . inasmuch** | New York | Eaton, J. |
| May 2 | **Dum Dee Tweedle** | New York | Del Tredici, D. |
| May | **Rape of the Lock** | New York | Mason, D. |
| May 1 | **Lovers and Friends** | New York | LaChiusa, J. |
| May 3 | **Mocking Bird** | Boston | Musgrave, T. |
| May 5 | **Inspiration** | New York | Hagar, D. |
| May 9 | **Apollo 14** | New York | Meckler, D. |
| May 9 | **Mrs. President** | East Hampton, NY | Bond, V. |
| May 12 | **Three Tales** | Vienna | Reich, S. |
| May 19 | **Death of Venus** | Wellington | Bootham, I. |
| May 22 | **Sandman, The** | Brooklyn, NY | Cabaniss, T. |
| May 26 | **Beleaguered City** | Wellington | Drummond, J. |
| June 2 | **Loss of Eden** | St. Louis | Franklin, C. |
| June 14 | **Morning Star** | Chicago | Gordon, R. I. |
| June 20 | **Gilgamesh** | New York | Dickman, S. |
| June 24 | **Galileo Galilei** | Chicago | Glass, P. |
| July | **Chéri** | New York (1 act) New York (2005, compl.) | Yankowitz, S. |
| July 1 | **Love in the Office** | New York | Waldman, M. |
| July 21 | **Dalmatia and Dalmatio** | San Francisco | Clark, S. |
| Aug. 5 | **When She Died** | BBC 4 | Dove, J. |
| Aug. 12 | **Sopranos!** | New York | Sisco, D. |
| Sept. | **Blue Sky Transmission** | Cleveland | El-Dabn, H. |
| Sept. | **Patria, no. 9** | Oak Ridges Moraine, ON | Schafer, R. |
| Sept. 26 | **Blackened Man** | London | Todd, W. |
| Oct. 25 | **Lindy** | Melbourne | Henderson, M. |
| Nov. 2 | **Phoenix Park** | New York | Strickland, D. |
| Dec. 4 | **Best Friends** | New York | Drattell, D. |
| * | **As You Like It** | -- | Young, W. |
| * | **Pictures** | -- | Bootham, I. |
| * | **Seven Stories** | -- | Richardson, A. |
| * | **Snow Queen** | -- | Fine, E. |
| * | **Star Lovers** | -- | Sternau, C. |

## 2003

| DATE | TITLE | CITY | COMPOSER |
|------|-------|------|----------|
| Jan. | **Love in the Age of Therapy** | Sydney | Grabowsky, P. |
| Jan. | **Tea** | Tokyo | Tan Dun |
| Jan. | **Thirteen Clocks** | Houston | Theofanidis, C. |
| Jan. 2 | **Trippin'** | New York | Rodwin, D. |
| Jan. 8 | **Nightingale and the Rose** | Wichita, KS | Hagemann, P. |
| Jan. 17 | **Dwarf, The** | Brooklyn, NY | Gal, Y. |

| Date | Title | City | Composer |
|------|-------|------|----------|
| Jan. 21 | **Sibanda!** | Houston | Remson, M. |
| Feb. 1 | **Filumena** | Calgary | Estacio, J. |
| Feb. 2 | **Rain** | New York | Owen, R. |
| Feb. 4 | **Diana Cantata** | Vancouver | Hannan, P. |
| Feb. 7 | **Red Azalea** | Santa Barbara | Kraft, W. |
| Feb. 14 | **Odd Numbers** | London | Grant, J. |
| Feb. 23 | **Wooing, The** | Queens, NY | Lehrman, L. |
| Mar. 1 | **Highway Ulysses** | Cambridge, MA | Eckert, R. |
| Mar. 16 | **Bridge of San Luis Rey** | New York | Kimper, P. |
| Mar. 22 | **Celestial Excursions** | Berlin | Ashley, R. |
| Mar. 23 | **Corps of Discovery** | New York | Ching, M. |
| Mar. 28 | **Prairie Dreams** | Tulsa, OK | Rivers, J. |
| spring | **House of Words** | New York | Armstrong/ Bouchard |
| Apr. 10 | **Sub Pontio Pilato** | San Francisco | Wold, E. |
| Apr. 25 | **Agamemnon** | Washington | Simpson, A. |
| Apr. 25 | **Molly Brant** | Kingston, ON | Cecconi-Bates, A. |
| Apr. 26 | **Henry David Thoreau** | New York | Cionek, E. |
| Apr. 26 | **Slip Knot** | Evanston, IL | Anderson, T. |
| May | **Awakening, The** | New York | Stepleton, J. |
| May 1 | **Florida** | New York | Eng, R. |
| May 1 | **It Began with a Pony** | Wellington | Buchanan, D. |
| May 4 | **Marina** | New York | Drattell, D. |
| May 5 | **Cassandra** | Toronto | McAndrew, I. |
| May 7 | **Borgia Infami** | New York | Blumenfeld, H. |
| May 7 | **Inferno of Dante** | New York | Soluri, M. |
| May 10 | **Mirage** | Albuquerque | Galloway, J. |
| May 23 | **Korczak's Orphans** | New Lebanon, NH | Silverman, A. |
| May 24 | **Sound of a Voice** | Cambridge, MA | Glass, P. |
| May 31 | **Little Prince** | Houston | Portman, R. |
| June | **Earthrise** | San Francisco | Spratlan, L. |
| June 5 | **Cask of Amontillado** | Boston | Pinkham, D. |
| June 7 | **Toussaint before the Spirits** | Boston | Ruehr, E. |
| June 12 | **Afterhours** | New York | Rodgers, L. |
| July 12 | **Gabriel's Daughter** | Central City, CO | Mollicone, H. |
| June 13 | **Beau Nash** | New York | Valenti, M. |
| June 20 | **Who Put Bella in the Wych Elm?** | Aldeburgh | Holt, S. |
| July | **LaRoche** | Atlanta | Willis, S. |
| July 17 | **Alice** | Auckland | Whitehead, G. |
| July 23 | **Eternity Man** | London | Mills, J. |
| July 26 | **Madame Mao** | Santa Fe | Sheng, B. |
| Aug. 24 | **John Brown** | San Francisco | Mechem, K. |
| Aug. 24 | **Newport Rivals (The Rivals)** | San Francisco | Mechem, K. |
| Sept. 13 | **Nicholas and Alexander** | Los Angeles | Drattell, D. |
| Sept. 21 | **Edith Wharton** | San Diego | Fink, M. |
| Oct. 10 | **Départ Malgache** | New York | Trefousse, R. |

| Date | Title | City | Composer |
|------|-------|------|----------|
| Oct. 24 | **Roman Fever** | New York | Hagemann, P. |
| Oct. 24 | **Wedding, The** | Santa Rosa, CA | Wilson, J. |
| Oct. 31 | **Lost Highway** | Graz | Neuwirth, O. |
| Nov. 7 | **Sanctuary** | St Paul, MN | Callahan, J. |
| Nov. 14 | **Captivation of Eunice Williams** | Amherst, MA | Kimper, P. |
| Nov. 17 | **Firebird Motel** | San Francisco | Conte, D. |
| ? | **Aceldama** | Miami | Sleeper, T. |
| ? | **Brave Little Tailor** | Houston | Levowitz, A. |
| ? | **Powerful Potion of Doctor D** | Springfield, MO | Bird, H. |
| ? | **Welcome to Purgatory** | Edinburgh | Roe, B. |

**2004**

| Date | Title | City | Composer |
|------|-------|------|----------|
| June 18 | **Grace** | Boston | Rudenstein, R. |
| Feb. 10 | **Tempest, The** | London | Adès, T. |
| Feb. 26 | **Perfect Plan** | New York | Barab, S. |
| Feb. 27 | **Undertow** | Adelaide | Kats-Chernin, E. |
| Mar. 3 | **End of the Affair** | Houston | Heggie, J. |
| Mar. 4 | **Venus in Furs** | New York | Gal, Y. |
| Mar. 8 | **Hester Prynne at Death** | New York | Paulus, S. |
| Mar. 10 | **Volpone** | Vienna, VA | Musto, J. |
| Apr. | **Inanna's Journey** | Toronto | Peters, R. |
| Apr. 1 | **Two Graces** | Toronto | Ferguson, S. |
| Apr. 2 | **Animalopera** | New York | Fink, M. |
| Apr. 4 | **Brush** | Toronto | Nakano, K. |
| | **Ice Time** | | Chan Ka Nin |
| | **Rosa** | | Rolfe, J. |
| Apr. 30 | **Joseph! Joseph!** | Salt Lake City | Gates, C. |
| May | **Dream President** | New York | Griffith, J. |
| May 6 | **Impersonating Maurice** | Wellington | Drummond, J. |
| May 11 | **Last of Manhattan** | New York | Felsenfeld, D. |
| Mar. 16 | **Quartet** | Wellington | Ritchie, A. |
| May 16 | **Leading Lady** | New York | March, K. |
| May 22 | **Marriage a la Mode** | Wellington | Drummond, J. |
| May 24 | **More Perfect Union** | New York | Bond, V. |
| May 24 | **Very Private Beach** | London | Grant, J. |
| May 26 | **Margaret Garner** | New York | Danielpour, R. |
| May 26 | **Summer and All It Brings** | New York | Felsenfeld, D. |
| May 30 | **Call Me Ishmael** | Amsterdam | Goldschneider, G. |
| June | **Earthrise** | San Francisco | Spratlan, L. |
| June 1 | **Before Night Falls** | New York | Martín, J. |
| June 3 | **OrfReo** | New York | Lauten, E. |
| June 9 | **Come to Me in Dreams** | Cleveland | Laitman, L. |
| June 11 | **Io Passion** | Aldeburgh | Birtwistle, H. |
| June 12 | **Beau Nash** | New York | Valenti, M. |
| June 16 | **Letter to E. 11th St.** | New York | Hennessy, M. |
| July | **Captivation of E. Williams** | Deerfield, MA | Kimper, P. |
| July 2 | **Song of Eddie** | Annandale-on-Hudson | Farberman, H. |

| Date | Title | City | Composer |
|---|---|---|---|
| July 23 | Guest from the Future | Purchase, NY | Marvin, M. |
| Aug. 15 | Enchantment of Dreams | Washington | Franklin, C. |
| Oct. 1 | God Boy | Dunedin, NZ | Ritchie, A. |
| Oct. 8 | Madeline Lee | Sydney | Haddock, J. |
| Oct. 9 | Robert and Hal | New York | Brooks, R. |
| Oct. 27 | Moby Dick | Princeton, NJ | Westergaard, P. |
| Oct. 29 | She Lost Her Voice | New York | White, F. |
| Nov. 23 | Angels in America | Paris | Eötvös, P. |
| Nov. 12 | Wake Her Up | New York | McGuire, J. |
| Dec. | Breath of Life | Houston | Frazier, J. |
| Dec. 11 | Wedding, A | Chicago | Bolcom, W. |
| ? | Circle of Love | Albuquerque | Stringer, A |
| ? | Glory Denied | New York | Cipullo, Y. |
| ? | OrfReo | New York | Lauten, E. |
| * | Alice | -- | Bachlund, G. |
| * | Antony and Cleopatra | -- | Chiusano, G. |
| * | Curious Affair | -- | Craton, J. |
| * | King Lear | -- | Eaton, J. |
| * | Leading Lady | -- | March, K. |
| * | Maria Concepcion | -- | Arteaga, E. |

**2005**

| Date | Title | City | Composer |
|---|---|---|---|
| Jan. 5 | Nightingale, The | Washington | Raminsh, I. |
| Jan. 18 | Princess and the Pea | Houston | Warwick, M. |
| Feb. 4 | Anna and Dedo | Moscow | Morgulas, J. |
| Feb. 4 | Mozart in Manhattan | St Paul, MN | Biales, A. |
| Feb. 12 | Helen Retires | Deland, FL | Welsch, J. |
| Mar. | Dee | Birmingham | Grant, R. |
| Mar. 1 | Love Counts | Munich | Nyman, M. |
| Mar. 4 | Lysistrata | Houston | Adamo, M. |
| Mar. 9 | Alien Corn | Baltimore | Benjamin, T. |
| Mar. 8 | Broken Pieces | Los Angeles | Hagen, D. |
| Mar. 13 | George Sand | Clarksville, TN | Vehar, P. |
| Mar. 13 | Kafka's Trial | Copenhagen | Pulers, R. |
| Apr. 5 | Araboolies | New York | Perera, R. |
| Apr. 17 | Antient Concert | Princeton, NJ | Hagen, D. |
| Apr. 19 | Summer King | Brooklyn, NY | Sonenberg, D. |
| Apr. 22 | Stranger's Tale | Middletown, OH | Tucker, C. |
| Apr. 23 | Ballad of Jamie Allan | Gateshead, Eng. | Harle, J. |
| Apr. 29 | Holy Night | Austin, TX | Welcher, D. |
| May 5 | Tyrant, The | Seattle | Dresher, P. |
| May 3 | 1984 | London | Maazel, L. |
| May 20 | Broken Pieces | Los Angeles | Hagen, D. |
| May 20 | Good Angel, Bad Angel | Edinburgh | Cresswell, L. |
| May 25 | Mary Surratt | Houston | Remson, M. |
| May 27 | Bitter Tears | Dublin | Barry, G. |
| June 5 | Cask of Amontillado | Boston | Pinkham, D. |
| June 11 | Cio Cio San | Hot Springs, AZ | Carroll, B. |
| June 13 | Midnight Court Opera | Toronto | Sokolovic, A. |
| June 15 | Gertrude Stein | New York | Banfield, W. |

| Date | Title | City | Composer |
|---|---|---|---|
| June 18 | Forest, The | New York | Hecker, Z. |
| July 10 | Hollow Hill | Buxton | McQueen, I. |
| Aug. 25 | Question of Love | Boston | Shadle, C. |
| Sept. 1 | Where the Cross Is Made | Normal, IL | Van de Vate, N. |
| Sept. 10 | At the Statue of Venus | Denver | Heggie, J. |
| Sept. 10 | Waiting for the Barbarians | Erfurt, Ger. | Glass, P. |
| Sept. 16 | Maiden Tower | New York | Chen, J. |
| Sept. 30 | Naomi's Road | Vancouver | Luengen, R. |
| Oct. 1 | Doctor Atomic | San Francisco | Adams, J. |
| Oct. 6 | Twelfth Night | Durham, NC | Feigin, J. |
| Oct. 20 | Chair in Love | Swansea, Wales | Metcalf, J. |
| Oct. 22 | Tangier Tattoo | Glyndebourne | Lunn, J. |
| Oct. 25 | Pied Piper | Hull, Eng | Pearson, K. |
| Nov. 4 | Book of Gold | Provo, UT | Boren, M. |
| Nov. 11 | License to Marry | Erie, PA | Barab, S. |
| Nov. 30 | Violet | London | Scruton, R. |
| Dec. 3 | American Tragedy | New York | Picker, T. |
| Dec. 25 | Armida | Channel 4 | Weir, J. |
| ? | Enid and the Swans | Toronto | Rolfe, J. |
| ? | Great Divide | Atlanta | Willis, S. |
| * | Emma | -- | Fine, E. |
| * | Macbeth | -- | McIntyre, P. |

**2006**

| Date | Title | City | Composer |
|---|---|---|---|
| Jan. 21 | Faustus, the Last Night | Berlin | Dusapin, P. |
| Feb. | Into the Little Hill | Paris | Benjamin, G. |
| Feb. 9 | Burnt Toast | CBC-TV | Louie, A. |
| Feb. 6 | Weaving Maiden | Toronto | Chan Ka Nin |
| Feb. 24 | Our Town | Bloomington | Rorem, N. |
| Feb. 26 | Darkling | New York | Weisman, S. |
| Mar. | Tree, The | Los Angeles | Dowdell, L. |
| Mar. 6 | Music Teacher | New York | Shawn, A. |
| Mar. 12 | Pride and Prejudice | Winston-Salem, NC | Mechem, K. |
| Mar. 26 | Orpheus X | Cambridge, MA | Eckert, R. |
| Apr. 9 | Elijah's Kite | New York | Rolfe, J. |
| Apr. 22 | Chrysalis | Berkeley, CA | Suprynowicz, C. |
| Apr. 26 | Miss Lonelyhearts | New York | Liebermann, L. |
| May 3 | I Wish, I Wish | Westerville, OH | Mandel, J. |
| May 6 | Airline Icarus | Toronto | Current, B. |
| May 6 | Frau Margot | New York | Pasatieri, T. |
| May 6 | Harmony | New York | Carl, R. |
| May 6 | Rosencrantz and Guildenstern | New York | Garfein, H. |
| May 7 | California Fictions | New York | Bates, M. |
| May 7 | Crescent City | New York | LeBaron, A. |
| May 7 | Leaving Santa Monica | New York | Johnson, J. |
| May 7 | Messer Marco Polo | New York | Stern, M. |

| DATE | TITLE | CITY | COMPOSER |
|---|---|---|---|
| May 7 | Paradise Lost | New York | Taylor, S. |
| May 13 | Curandera, La | Denver | Rodríguez, R. |
| June 1 | Grendel | Los Angeles | Goldenthal, E. |
| June 2 | Bonfire of the Vanities | Brooklyn, NY | de Kenessey, S. |
| une 2 | Heart of Darkness | Brooklyn, NY | O'Regan, T. |
|  | Sharon's Grave |  | Wargo, R. |
| June 2 | Powers of Two | Vancouver | Truax, B. |
| June 19 | Alice in Wonderland | New York | Westergaard, P. |
| June 30 | Midnight Court Opera | Toronto | Sokolovic, A. |
| July | Last Leaf | Twin Lake, MI | Niblock, J. |
| July 22 | Greater Good | Cooperstown, NY | Hartke, S. |
| Aug. 25 | Assassin Tree | Edinburgh | MacCrae, S. |
| Sept. 19 | What to Wear | Los Angeles | Gordon, M. |
| Sept. 21 | Edith Wharton | San Diego | Fink, M. |
| Sept. 22 | Golden Gate | Brooklyn, NY | Cummings, C. |
| Oct. | Violet Fire | Brooklyn, NY | Gibson, J. |
| Oct. 10 | Odysseus Unwound | London | Grant, J. |
| Oct. 19 | Bird of Night | London | Le Gendre, D. |
| Oct. 21 | Star Gatherer | St. Paul, MN | Paulus, S. |
| Oct. 26 | Whirlwind | London | Todd, W. |
| Oct. 28 | Before Night Falls | Boston | Martín, J. |
| Oct. 29 | She Lost Her Voice | New York | White, F. |
| Nov. 2 | To Hell and Back | Palo Alto, CA | Heggie, J. |
| Nov. 11 | Every Man Jack | Sonoma, CA | Larsen, L. |
| Nov. 22 | Electric Lenin | Lismore, NSW | Conyngham, B. |
| Dec. | Enchanted Pig | London | Dove, J. |
| Dec. 1 | Wet | Los Angeles | LeBaron, A. |
| Dec. 5 | Swoon | Toronto | Rolfe, J. |
| Dec. 21 | First Emperor | New York | Tan Dun |
| Dec. 26 | Man on the Moon | Channel 4 | Dove, J. |
| ? | Story of Rapunzel | Dallas | Sargon, S. |
| * | Infidel | -- | MacSems, W. |
| * | Out of This World | -- | Carbon, J. |

**2007**

| DATE | TITLE | CITY | COMPOSER |
|---|---|---|---|
| Jan. 17 | Concrete | New York | Ashley, R. |
| Feb. 2 | Madimi | New York | Wolosoff, B. |
| Feb. 10 | Grapes of Wrath | Minneapolis | Gordon, R. I. |
| Feb. 10 | Love of the Nightingale | Perth, Austral. | Mills, R. |
| Feb. 18 | Socrates | Annapolis, MD | Thoms, H. |
| Mar. 7 | Dwarf Trees | Brooklyn, NY | Halpern, M. |
| Mar. 7 | Wakonda's Dream | Omaha NB | Davis, A. |
| Mar. 29 | Breath of Life | Houston | Frazier, J. T. |
| Apr. 25 | Aeneas and Dido | Toronto | Rolfe, J. |
| April 27 | America Tropical | San Francisco | Conte, D. |
| Apr. 28 | Wagner Dream | Luxembourg City | Harvey, J. |

| DATE | TITLE | CITY | COMPOSER |
|---|---|---|---|
| Apr. 28 | Anna Karenina | Miami | Carlson, D. |
| May | Crossing the Horizon | New York | Lastovicka, C. |
| May 1 | Alternate Visions | Montreal | Oliver, J. |
| May 5 | Larnach | Dunedin, NZ | Drummond, J. |
| May 7 | Inventory | Toronto | Current, B. |
| May 12 | Elegy for a Prince | New York | Cervetti, S. |
|  | Endings, The | New York | Johnson, J. O. |
|  | In the Father's Garden | New York | Kirtley, D. |
|  | Rat Land | New York | Beeferman, G. |
| May 13 | Fisher King | New York | Lowenstein, M. |
|  | Nannan | New York | Wang Jie |
|  | With Such Friends | New York |  |
| May 17 | Duel, The | New York | Barab, S. |
| May 19 | Pocahontas | Norfolk, VA | Haugen, L. |
| May 20 | Romulus | New York | Karchin, L. |
| June 2 | Frau Margot | New York | Pasatieri, T. |
| June 3 | Inanna | Modesto, CA | Craton, J. |
| June 15 | Strange Fruit | Chapel Hill, NC | Carter, C. |
| June 17 | Three Stories | Albuquerque | Stringer, A. |
| June 22 | Bluebeard's Waiting Room | Atlanta | Granger, M. |
| June 30 | Alice in Wonderland | Munich | Chin, U. |
| Jul 11 | Finnish Prisoner | Lewes, Eng. | Gough, O. |
| Jul 21 | Critical Mass | London | Gough, O. |
| Aug. 3 | Hotel Casablanca | San Francisco | Pasatieri, C |
| Aug. 15 | Quantum Mechanic | Am Fork, UT | Bilotta, J. |
| Aug. 31 | iOrpheus | Brisbane | Duckworth/Farrell |
| Sept. 7 | Out of the Ordinary | London | Bruce, D. |
| Sept. 7 | Seduction of King Solomon | Atlanta | Willis, S. |
| Sept. 22 | Sacrifice, The | Cardiff | MacMillan, J. |
| Oct. | Constancy | Brooklyn, NY | Halpern, M. |
| Oct. 5 | Appomattox | San Francisco | Glass, P. |
| Oct. 13 | Rise for Freedom | Cincinnati | Hailstork, A. |
| Nov. 10 | Refuge, The | Houston | Theofanidis, C. |
| Nov. 12 | Blind Date: | London |  |
|  | Anger |  | Grant, J. |
|  | Big But |  | Yarde, J. |
|  | Feathered Friend |  | Chadwick, H. |
|  | Houses |  | Mayo, C. |
|  | Nyanyushka |  | Carpenter, G. |
|  | On Such a Day |  | Meredith, A. |
| Nov. 16 | Later the Same Evening | College Park, MD | Musto, J. |
| Dec. | Sanctuary Song | Toronto | Richardson, P. |
| Dec. 15 | Shadowtracks | London | Grant, J. |
| Dec. 21 | Adventures of Pinocchio | Leeds | Dove, J. |
| * | Parliament of Fowls | -- | Craton, J. |
| * | Patria, no. 7 | -- | Schafer, R. |

| DATE | TITLE | CITY | COMPOSER | DATE | TITLE | CITY | COMPOSER |
|------|-------|------|----------|------|-------|------|----------|
| **2008** | | | | **2009** | | | |
| Jan. 7 | **Three Lost Chords** | New York | Horne, L. | Feb. | **Demon, The** | Moscow | Morgulas, J. |
| Jan. 8 | **Hunger Art** | New York | Myers, J. | Feb. 15 | **Moustache, The** | Annapolis, MD | Thoms, H. |
| Jan. 18 | **My Undying Love** | Boston | Shiflett, M. | Mar. 19 | **Let Freedom Sing** | Washington | Adolphe, B. |
| Feb. 26 | **Calamity, A. Gentleman Friend** | Moscow | Morgulas, J. | Apr. | **Salon, The** | Chico, CA | McKay, J. |
| | | | | Apr. 2 | **Picnic** | Greensboro, NC | Larsen, L. |
| Feb. 29 | **Last Acts** | Houston | Heggie, J. | Apr. 15 | **After Dido** | London | Mitchell, K. (arr.) |
| Mar. 8 | **Dream Healer** | Vancouver | Burritt, L. | | | | |
| Mar. 11 | **Bastianello** | New York | Musto, M. | Apr. 29 | **Game of Poker** | New York | Burke, R. |
| Mar. 11 | **Lucrezia** | New York | Bolcom, W. | May 1 | **Brief Encounter** | Houston | Previn, A. |
| Mar. 18 | **Good Friar** | New York | Hennessey, M. | May 2 | **Armide** | New York | Dawe. J. |
| Mar. 22 | **Bird in Your Ear** | Annandale-on-Hudson, NY | Bruce, D. | May 9 | **Dog Days** | New York | Little, D. |
| | | | | May 9 | **Invisible Cities** | New York | Cerrone, C. |
| Apr. 12 | **Alice in Wonderland** | Chico, CA | McKay, J. | May 22 | **Shadow, The** | Toronto | Daniel, O. |
| Apr. 15 | **Minotaur, The** | London | Birtwistle, H. | May 27 | **Rumpelstiltskin** | Boston | Epstein, M. |
| Apr. 17 | **Triumph of Love** | Cedar Falls, IA | Schmitz, A. | May 29 | **Song from the Uproar** | Brooklyn, NY | Mazzoli, M. |
| Apr. 28 | **Criseyde** | New York | Shields, A. | June 7 | **Children's Crusade** | Toronto | Schafer, F. M. |
| Apr. 28 | **No Exit** | Boston | Vores, A. | | | | |
| May | **Officers, The** | New York | Potter, S. | July 11 | **Eleanor Roosevelt** | Lake George, NY | Vehar, P. |
| May | **Through the Looking Glass** | Melbourne | John, A. | | | | |
| | | | | July 25 | **Letter, The** | Santa Fe | Moravec, P. |
| May 9 | **Eleni** | New York | Ratcliff, C. | July 31 | **Ruth and Naomi** | Twin Lake, MI | Niblock, J. |
| May 10 | **Our Giraffe** | New York | Hays, S. | Sept. 10 | **Review** | Houston | Beck, J. |
| May 11 | **Charlie Crosses the Nation** | New York | Richards, S. | Sept. 19 | **Say It Ain't So, Joe** | Boston | Hughes, C. |
| | **Dylan and Caitlin** | New York | Chen, J. | Oct. 1 | **Death of Oedipus Purgatory** | New York | Halpern, M. |
| | **Jeanne** | New York | Chen, J. | | | | |
| | **Mortal Thoughts of Lady Macbeth** | New York | Krausas, V. | Oct. 1 | **Diamond Street** | Hudson, NY | Farberman, H. |
| | **Soldier Songs** | New York | Little, D. | Oct. 1 | **Figaro's Last Hangover** | New York | Soluri, P. |
| May 18 | **Last Goodbye** | Boston | Shadle, C. | Oct. 8 | **River of Time** | Lexington, KY | Baber, J. |
| May 22 | **Mordake** | San Francisco | Wold, E. | | | | |
| June 7 | **Egypt's Nights** | Philadelphia | Burrs, L. S. | Oct. 13 | **Lamentations of Ophelia** | Miami | Stinson, S. |
| June 11 | **Three, Two, One, Bang!** | Carrboro, NC | Chen, J. | | **Opera 101** | | Kam, D. |
| June 20 | **Our American Cousin** | Northampton, MA | Sawyer, E. | | **Sisters Antipodes** | | Sleeper, T. |
| | | | | | **Winter's Journey** | | Cuomo, D. |
| June 30 | **Shaw Sings!** | New York | Hagemann, P. | Nov. 5 | **TOOWHOPERA** | Rome, GA | Hays, S. |
| | **Dark Lady of the Sonnets** | | | Nov. 6 | **Scarlet Letter** | Conway, AK | Laitman, L. |
| | **Passion, Poison, and Petrification** | | | Nov. 13 | **Swanhunter** | Leeds | Dove, J. |
| July 2 | **Fly, The** | Paris | Shore, H. | Sept. 26 | **Séance on a Wet Afternoon** | Santa Barbara | Schwartz, S. |
| Sept. 26–28 | **Chicken or Beef?** | Toronto | Chen, J. | Dec. 4 | **Lilith** | San Diego | Davis, A. |
| | **Decoherence** | | | ? | **Henry's Wife** | New York | Eng, R. |
| | **River by the Residential Schoolhouse** | | | ? | **Oceanic Verses** | New York | Prestini, P. |
| | **Voice for a Future Nightingale** | | | * | **Family Room** | Princeton, NJ (2011) | Pasatieri, T. |
| Sept. 13 | **Bonesetter's Daughter** | San Francisco | Wallace, S. | * | **Listener's Guide** | -- | Gottlieb, J. |
| Oct. 11 | **Burial at Thebes** | London | Le Gendre, D. | * | **Mask in the Mirror** | New York (2011) | Thompson, R. |
| Oct. 22 | **Fade** | London | Weisman, S. | | | | |
| Nov. | **German Refugee** | New York | Cabaniss, T. | **2010** | | | |
| Nov. 24 | **Skellig** | Newcastle, Eng. | Machover, T. | Feb. 11 | **Anaïs** | New York | Hurley, S. |
| | | | | Feb. 14 | **Rime of the Ancient Mariner** | Annapolis, MD | Thoms, H. |
| Dec. 7 | **Song of Rhiannon** | London | Bowden, M. | | | | |
| Dec. 8 | **Simeon** | Greenville, SC | Gustafson, D. | Feb. 18 | **Legend of Poker Alice** | Shoreline, WA | Swisher, G. |
| * | **Disappearing Act** | -- | Carbon, J. | | | | |

| Date | Title | City | Composer | Date | Title | City | Composer |
|------|-------|------|----------|------|-------|------|----------|
| Feb. 19 | **First Lady** | Los Angeles | Wells, K. | Sept. 24 | **Death and the Powers** | Monte Carlo | Machover, T. |
| Mar. 10 | **Volpone** | Vienna, VA | Musto, J. | Oct. 15 | **Cracked Orlando** | New York | Dawe, J. |
| Apr. 10 | **Dice Thrown** | Valencia, CA | King, J. | Oct. 24 | **Tell-Tale Heart** | Rockaway, NJ | Butts, R. |
| Apr. 17 | **Shadowboxer** | College Park, MD | Proto, F. | Nov. | **Wooden Sword** | Storrs, CT | Silver, S. |
| Apr. 26 | **Clara** | New York | Bond, V. | Nov 1 | **Poe Project:** | New York | |
| Apr. 30 | **Moby-Dick** | Dallas | Heggie, J. | | **Buried Alive** | | Myers, J. |
| Apr. 30 | **Star Across the Ocean** | New York | Richards, S. | | **Embedded** | | Soluri, P. |
| May | **Río de Sangre** | Milwaukee | Davis, D. | | **Of the Flesh** | | Gach, J. A. |
| May 1 | **Acquanetta** | New York | Gordon, M. | Nov. 13 | **To Cross the Face of the Moon** | Houston | Martinez, J. |
| May 8 | **Amelia** | Seattle | Hagen, D. | Nov. 19 | **Billy Blythe** | Little Rock, AR | Montgomery, B. |
| May 24 | **Maskarad** | Moscow | Morgulas, J. | | | | |
| June | **Bloody Chamber** | Berkeley, CA | Felsenfeld, D. | Nov. 19 | **Scarlet Letter** | Philadelphia | Garwood, M. |
| June | **Inspector from Rome** | Vienna, VA | Musto, J. | Dec. 16 | **God Bless Us, Every One!** | New York | Pasatieri, T. |
| June | **Shadows of the City** | New York | Bo, T. | * | **Amontillado** | -- | Fitts, C. |
| July 13 | **Duchess of Malfi** | London | Rasch, T. | * | **Death of Peer Gynt** | New York (2011) | Halpern, M. |
| June 13 | **Golden Ticket** | St Louis | Ash, P. | | | | |
| June 15 | **Curious Case of Benjamin Button** | New York | Eaton, J. | * | **Dragon, The** | -- | Chen, J. |
| June 17 | **Trifles** | Berkeley, CA | Bilotta, J. | * | **Lock of Hair** | New York (2011) | Halpern, M. |
| June 18 | **Ring, Lamp, Thing** | London | Gough, O. | | | | |
| Aug. | **Devil Build a Chapel** | Melbourne | Casey, P. | | | | |
| | **Playing with Fire** | | France, H. | | | | |
| | **Razing Hypatia** | | March, K. | | | | |
| | **Un-Dead, The** | | Stanhope, D. | | | | |

# Selective Bibliography

## ANTHOLOGIES AND CATALOGS

### GENERAL

*The Ballad Opera: A Collection of 171 Original Texts of Musical Plays*. Edited by Walter Rubsamen. New York: Garland, 1974. 29 vols.

The British Museum. *Catalogue of Manuscript Music in the British Museum*. Vol. 2: *Secular Vocal Music*. Edited by Augustus Hughes-Hughes. London: Trustees of the British Museum, 1908. xxvi, 961 p. Repr. ed. London: British Museum, 1966.

____. *Catalogue of Printed Music Published between 1487 and 1800 Now in the British Museum*. 2 vols. Edited by William Barclay Squire. London: Trustees of the British Museum, 1912. Reprint Nendeln, Liechtenstein: Kraus Reprint, 1968.

*Catalog of the Opera Collections in the Music Libraries: University of California, Berkeley/University of California, Los Angeles*. Boston: G. K. Hall, 1983. viii, 697 p.

*Eighteenth Century Collections Online*. More than 180,000 titles of books, pamphlets, essays, and broadsides of works published in the United Kingdom and elsewhere, primarily in English, "full-text searchable." Available through participating institutions at http://find.galegroup.com/ecco/.

Fuld, James. *The Book of World-Famous Libretti: The Musical Theater from 1598 to Today*. 4th ed., rev. and enlarged. Foreword by Patrick J. Smith. New York: Pendragon Press, 1994. xxxviii, 363 p.

G. Schirmer and Associated Music Publishers. *Opera & Ballet Catalogue*. Compiled and edited by Margaret Ross Griffel. New York: G. Schirmer/Associated Music Publishers, 1988. viii, 183 p.

*Literature Online*. Fully searchable library of more than 350,000 works of English and American poetry, drama, and prose, 344 full-text literature journals, and other key criticism and reference resources, at http://lion.chadwyck.com/marketing/index.jsp.

*The Mellen Opera Reference Index*. Compiled by Charles H. Parsons. Lewiston, N.Y., and Queenston, Ont.: Edwin Mellen Press, 1986–. Vols. 1–4: *Opera Composers and Their Works* (1986). Vols. 5–6: *Opera Librettists and Their Works* (1987). Vols. 7–8: *Opera Premieres: A Geographical Index* (1989). Vols. 13–14: *Opera Premieres: An Index of Casts* (1992). Vol. 19: *Opera Premiere Reviews and Re-assessments: A Listing* (2002). Vol. 20: *An Opera Videography* (1997). Vol. 21: *Printed Opera Scores in American Libraries* (1998). Vols. 22–25: *Recent International Opera Discography* (2003–5).

Royal College of Music. *Catalogue of Printed Music in the Library of the Royal College of Music*. Edited by William Barclay Squire. London: Royal College of Music, 1909.

368 p. Online: http://hdl.handle.net/2027/uc2.ark:/13960/t9h420s1v.

Sonneck, Oscar George Theodore. *Catalogue of Opera Librettos Printed before 1800*. 3 vols. Washington, D.C.: Library of Congress, 1914. Repr. New York: Burt Franklin, 1967. 1,674 p.

____. *Dramatic Music: Catalogue of Full Scores in the Collection of the Library of Congress*. Washington, D.C.: Library of Congress, 1908. 170 p. 2nd rev. ed., 1917. Repr. of 1908 ed. New York: Da Capo Press, 1969.

Wolff, Barbara Mahrenholz. *Music Manuscripts at Harvard. A Catalogue of Music Manuscripts from the 14th to the 20th Centuries in the Houghton Library at the Eda Kuhn Loeb Music Library*. Cambridge, Mass.: Harvard University Library, 1992. xx, 245 p.

Wood, David A. *Music in Harvard Libraries: A Catalogue of Early Printed Music and Books on Music in the Houghton Library and the Eda Kuhn Loeb Music Library*. Cambridge, Mass.: Harvard University Press, 1980. xiv, 306 p.

### BY COUNTRY

#### England

Bradley, Ian, ed. *The Complete Annotated Gilbert and Sullivan*. New York: Oxford University Press, 1996. 1,197 p. Pbk. 2001.

*A Collection of the Most Esteemed Farces and Entertainments Performed on the British Stage, A*. 6 vols. Edinburgh: C. Elliot, 1786–88.

Hunter, David. *Opera and Song Books Published in England, 1703–1726. A Descriptive Bibliography*. London: Bibliographical Society, 1997; New York: Oxford University Press, 1998. xlix, 521 p.

Inchbald, Elizabeth, comp. *A Collection of Farces and Other Afterpieces*. 7 vols. London: Longman et al., 1809. Repr. ed. Hildesheim and New York: Georg Olms, 1969.

Ledbetter, Steven, and Percy M. Young, eds. *The Operas/W. S. Gilbert, Arthur Sullivan*. 13 vols. projected. Williamstown, Mass.: Broude Brothers. Vol. 1: *Trial by Jury* (1994, ed. Ledbetter). Vol. 3: *H.M.S. Pinafore*, pt. A: music, pt. B: commentary (2003, ed. Young).

*The London Stage: 1660–1800. A Calendar of Plays, Entertainments & Afterpieces with Artists, Box Receipts, and Contemporary Comment*. 5 volumes in 11. Carbondale, Ill.: Southern Illinois University Press, 1960–68. Vol. 1: *1660–1770*, ed. William van Lennap. Vol. 2: *1700–1729*, ed. Emmett L. Avery (2 parts). Vol. 3: *1729–1747*, ed. Arthur W. Scouten (3 parts). Vol. 4: *1747–1776*, ed. G. W. Stone (3 parts). Vol. 5: *1776–1800*, ed. Charles Beecher Hogan (3 parts). *Index*, ed. Ben Ross Schneider. 1979.

MacMillan, Dougald, comp. *Catalogue of the Larpent Plays in the Huntington Library*. San Marino, Calif., 1939. xv, 442 p.

MacMillan, Kyle. "Has American Opera Finally Arrived? Born in the '50s, the U.S. Version Still Searches for Its Voice." *Denver Post* (June 18, 2006): F, 1.

*Modern British Drama*. Vol. 4: *Comedies*. Vol. 5: *Operas and Farces*. London: William Miller, 1811. viii, 668 p.

Stedman, Jane W. *Gilbert before Sullivan: Six Comic Plays*. Chicago: University of Chicago Press, 1967. xii, 270 p. Includes *Ages Ago* and *Happy Arcadia*. With music.

### United States (including Colonial America)

Davidson, Celia Elizabeth. "Operas by Afro-American Composers: A Critical Survey and Analysis of Selected Works." Ph.D. diss., The Catholic University of America, 1980. 526 p. Studies of Harry Lawrence Freeman *(The Martyr, Vendetta, Voodoo);* Scott Joplin *(Treemonisha);* Clarence Cameron White *(Ouanga);* William Grant Still *(Highway 1, U.S.A.);* Mark Fax *(A Christmas Miracle);* Ulysses Kay *(Jubilee)*.

Dennison, Sam, and Martha Furman Schleifer, eds. *Three Centuries of American Music: A Collection of Sacred and Secular Music*. New York: G. K. Hall & Co., 1990. Vol. 5: *The Volunteers* (Reinagle), *The Ethiop* (Taylor), *The Enterprise* (Clifton), and *Robin Hood* (De Koven); Vol. 6: *Iolan (The Pipe of Desire)* (Converse) and *Naughty Marietta* (Herbert).

Graziano, John, general ed. *Recent Researches in American Music*. Madison, Wisc.: A-R Editions. Vols. 3–4: Andrew Barton's *The Disappointment*, ed. Jerold C. Graue and Judith Layng (1976). Vols. 9–10: George F. Root's *The Haymakers*, ed. Dennis R. Martin (1984). Vols. 13–14: Pelissier's *Columbian Melodies*, ed. Karl Kroeger, with music from Pelissier's operas composed between 1794 and 1813 (1984). Vol. 25: Will Marion Cook's *In Dahomey*, ed. Thomas J. Riis (1996).

Hummel, David. *The Collector's Guide to the American Musical Theatre*. Vol. 1: *The Shows*. Vol. 2: *Index*. 2nd printing. Metuchen, N.J.: Scarecrow Press, 1984. *Supplement*. Grawn, Mich.: D. H. Enterprises, 1979–.

Krasker, Tommy, and Robert Kimball. *Catalog of the American Musical: Musicals of Irving Berlin, George & Ira Gershwin, Cole Porter, Richard Rodgers & Lorenz Hart*. Washington, D.C.: National Institute for Opera and Musical Theater, 1988. xv, 442 p.

Root, Deane L., ed. *Nineteenth-Century American Musical Theater*. 16 vols. New York: Garland, 1994.

Rubsamen, Walter, ed. *The Ballad Opera: A Collection of 171 Original Texts of Musical Plays*. New York: Garland, 1974. Vol. 28: *American Ballad Operas*.

Vernon, Grenville, comp. *Yankee Doodle-Doo: A Collection of Songs of the Early American Stage*. New York: Payson & Clarke, [1927]. 165 p.

## BIBLIOGRAPHIES

Grout, Donald. *A Short History of Opera*. 2nd ed. New York: Columbia University Press, 1965, 585–768. 3rd ed., with Hermine Weigel Williams. New York: Columbia University Press, 1988, 731–825 (abridged and updated). 4th ed., 2003, [797]–896.

Marco, Guy A. *Opera: A Research and Information Guide*. New York; London: Garland, 1984. xvii, 373 p. 2nd ed. 2001. xx, 632 p.

Sonneck, Oscar G. T. *A Bibliography of Early Secular American Music*. Rev. and enlarged by William Treat Upton. Washington, D.C.: Library of Congress, Music Division, 1945. xvi, 616 p. Repr. ed. New York: Da Capo, 1964.

Wildbihler, Hubert, and Sonja Völklein. *The Musical: An International Annotated Bibliography/Eine internationale annotierte Bibliographie*. Foreword by Thomas Siedhoff. Munich and New York: Saur, 1986. 320 p.

Wolfe, Richard J. *Secular Music in America 1801–1825. A Bibliography*. Introduction by Carleton Sprague Smith. Vol. 3. New York: New York Public Library, 1964.

## DISCOGRAPHIES

Blyth, Alan. *Opera on CD: The Essential Guide to the Best CD Recordings of 100 Operas*. London: Kyles Cathie, 1992. viii, 183 p. Rev. and updated 3rd ed., 1994.

_____, ed. *Opera on Record*. 3 vols. Discographies compiled by Malcolm Walker. London: Hutchinson, 1979, 1983, 1984. 663, 399, 375 p.

Marco, Guy, ed. *Encyclopedia of Recorded Sound in the United States*. With Frank Andrews. New York: Garland, 1993. xlix, 910 p. 2nd ed., as *Encyclopedia of Recorded Sound*. Edited by Frank Hoffmann and Howard Ferstler. New York: Routledge, 2005. xii, 1,289 p.

*The Mellen Opera Reference Index*. Vols. 22–25: *Recent International Opera Discography*. Compiled by Charles H. Parsons. Lewiston, N.Y., and Queenston, Ont.: Edwin Mellen Press, 2003–5.

Wechsler, Bert. "A Native Harvest." *ON* 53 (Aug. 1988): 30–32, 46.

## DICTIONARIES AND ENCYCLOPEDIAS

Anderson, James. *Bloomsbury Dictionary of Opera and Operetta*. London, 1984. 2nd ed. London: Bloomsbury, 1989. New York: Wing Books, 1993. ix, 691 p.

Ewen, David. *The New Encyclopedia of the Opera*. 3rd ed. New York: Hill and Wang, 1971. 759 p. Includes terms, cities, houses, plots, characters, singers.

Gänzl, Kurt. *The Encyclopedia of the Musical Theatre*. 2nd ed. 3 vols. New York: Schirmer Books, 2001. Includes bibliographical references and discographies.

Hamilton, David. *The Metropolitan Opera Encyclopedia*. New York: Simon & Schuster, 1987. 416 p. Listing by title;

includes operas, performers, terms; two dozen essays on most famous works; brief plots.

*Die Musik in Geschichte und Gegenwart.* Edited by Ludwig Fischer. Kassel, New York: Bärenreiter; Stuttgart: Metzler, 1994–2007. *Sachteil,* vols. 1–9 + *Register; Personenteil,* vols. 1–17 + *Suppl.*

*The New Grove Dictionary of Opera.* Edited by Stanley Sadie. 4 vols. London, New York: Macmillan Press, 1992, 1994 (repr. with corrections). 5,424 p. Covers 1,800 operas. Online version: http://www.grovemusic.com, by subscription.

*The Norton/Grove Dictionary of Women Composers.* Edited by Julie Anne Sadie and Rhian Samuel. New York and London: W. W. Norton, 1994, 1995. xliii, 548 p.

Orrey, Leslie. *The Encyclopedia of Opera.* New York: Scribner's, 1976. 376 p. Listing by title, with operas, performers, terms; very brief plots.

Osborne, Charles. *The Dictionary of the Opera.* New York: Simon & Schuster, 1983. 382 p. Listing by title, with operas, performers, terms; brief plots. Revised and updated edition. New York: Welcome Rain: 2001. 383 p.

*Oxford Music Online, Grove Music Online.* Online resource (since 2001, with updates) offering the full text of *The New Grove Dictionary of Music and Musicians,* 2nd edition (2001), ed. Deane L. Root; and *The New Grove Dictionary of Opera* (see above). Accessible by subscription at www.oxfordmusiconline.com.

Pallay, Steven G., comp. *Cross Index Title Guide to Opera and Operetta.* New York: Greenwood Press, 1989. viii, 214 p.

*Pipers Enzyklopädie des Musiktheaters.* Edited by Carl Dahlhaus. Munich: Piper, 1986–97. Vol. 1: *Abbiatini-Donizetti.* Vol. 2: *Donizetti-Henze.* Vol. 3: *Henze-Massine.* Vol. 4: *Massine-Piccinni.* Vol. 5: *Piccinni-Spontini.* Vol. 6: *Spontini-Zumsteeg.* Vol. 7: *Register.* Detailed coverage of operas, operettas, musicals, ballets, with information on the premiere, plot, and stylistic elements. Online version: http://catalog.hathitrust.org/api/volumes/oclc/15662219.html, by subscription.

Rosenthal, Harold, and John Warrack, eds. *The Concise Oxford Dictionary of Opera.* 2nd ed. London: Oxford University Press, 1979. 561 p. On operas, composers, performers, cities.

*The Simon & Schuster Book of the Opera.* New York: Simon & Schuster, 1978. An English translation of *L'opera: repertorio della lirica dal 1597,* edited by Riccardo Mezzanote. Milan: Arnoldo Monadori Editore, 1977. 511 p. Listings by year, then by title; brief plots.

Stieger, Franz. *Opernlexikon/Opera Catalogue* .... Part 1 (3 vols.): *Titelkatalog.* Part 2 (2 vols.): *Komponisten.* Part 3 (3 vols.): *Librettisten.* Part 4 (2 vols.): *Nachträge.* Tutzing: Hans Schneider, 1975–83. Completed in 1934. Lists some 50,000 theater works.

Towers, John. *Dictionary Catalog of Operas and Operettas Which Have Been Performed on the Public Stage.* 2 vols.

Morgantown, W. Va.: Acme, 1910. 1,045 p. Repr. ed. New York: Da Capo Press, 1967. Lists more than 28,000 works, with name of composer, nationality.

Warrack, John, and Ewan West. *The Concise Oxford Dictionary of Opera.* Oxford and New York: Oxford University Press. xiv, 571 p. Updating and shortening of *The Oxford Dictionary of Opera.* 3rd ed. Oxford, New York: Oxford University Press, 1996. xiv, 571 p.

____. *The Oxford Dictionary of Opera.* Oxford and New York: Oxford University Press, 1992. xviii, 782 p. Listing by title, with operas, performers, cities, brief plots.

Wlaschin, Ken. *Encyclopedia of Opera on Screen: A Guide to More Than 100 Years of Opera Films, Videos, and DVDs.* New Haven: Yale University Press, 2004. xi, 872 p.

## ICONOGRAPHY

Beauvert, Thierry. *Opera Houses of the World.* Photographs by Jacques Moatti and Florian Kleinefenn. New York: Vendome Press, 1996. 277 p.

Eaton, Quaintance. *Opera. A Pictorial Guide.* New York: Abaris Books, 1980. 528 p.

Preston, Stuart. *Farewell to the Old House: The Metropolitan Opera House, 1883–1966.* Garden City, N.Y., Doubleday [ca. 1966]. 68 p. (chiefly illus.).

Robinson, Francis. *Celebration: The Metropolitan Opera.* Picture editor Gerald Fitzgerald. Garden City, N.Y.: Doubleday, 1979. 287 p. (chiefly illus.).

## PERFORMANCE INFORMATION

### GENERAL

Barnes, Jennifer. *Television Opera: The Fall of Opera Commissioned for Television.* Woodbridge, Suffolk: Boydell Press, 2003. x, 124 p. One chapter on Britten.

British Broadcasting Corporation. *BBC Music Library. Choral and Opera Catalogue.* Vol. 1: *Composers.* Vol. 2: *Titles.* London: BBC, 1967.

Central Opera Service. *Central Opera Service Bulletin,* vol. 29, no. 3. New York: Central Opera Service, 1989. iv, 111 p.

____. *Directory of American and Foreign Contemporary Operas and American Opera Premieres 1975–1980.* New York: Central Opera Service, 1980. *Central Opera Service Bulletin,* vol. 22, no. 2. iv, 76 p. Succeeded in part by *Opera America* (see below).

____. *Directory of Contemporary Operas and Music Theater Works and North American Premieres, 1980–1989.* New York: Central Opera Service, 1990. *Central Opera Service Directory/Bulletin,* vol. 30, nos. 2–4. viii, 325 p.

Citron, Stephen. *The Musical: From the Inside Out.* London: R. Hodder & Stoughton, 1991. 256 p. Chicago: Elephant Paperbacks, 1997, 1992.

Eaton, Quaintance. *Opera Production. A Handbook.* Minneapolis: University of Minnesota Press, 1961. ix,

265 p. Repr. New York: Da Capo, 1974. By title. Includes brief plots, major and minor roles, orchestral forces needed, available performance materials.

____. *Opera Production II. A Handbook*. Minneapolis: University of Minnesota Press, 1974. xx, 347 p. Same arrangement as vol. 1.

Loewenberg, Alfred. *Annals of Opera 1597–1940*. 3rd rev. ed. Totowa, N.J.: Rowman and Littlefield, 1978. xxv p., 1,756 columns. Organized by year, with title, composer, librettist, city and date of first performance, significant subsequent performances; four indexes.

*The Musical Woman: An International Perspective*. Edited by Judith Lang Zaimont, Catherine Overhauser, and Jane Gottlieb. 3 vols. I: 1983. II: 1984–1985. III: 1986–1990. Westport, Conn.: Greenwood Press, 1984, 1986, 1991. Extensive listings on first or subsequent performances of the works, including operas, of women composers.

Northouse, Cameron. *Twentieth Century Opera in England and the United States*. Boston: G. K. Hall, 1976. viii, 400 p. Listings include composers, titles, first performances, literary sources.

*Opera America*. Established in 1970 and available online at www.operaamerica.org. Provides information and technical and administrative resources to the opera community. Took over the services of Central Opera Service in 1990.

"Operatic Premières, 1939–1954." In *Opera Annual* 1 (1954–55): 168–78. An update of Loewenberg (see above).

Rich, Maria. *Who's Who in Opera: An International Biographical Directory of Singers, Conductors, Directors, Designers, and Administrators*. New York: Arno Press, 1976. xxi, 684 p.

Summers, W. Franklin. *Operas in One Act. A Production Guide*. Lanham, Md., and London: Scarecrow Press, 1997; 2003 (paper). xiii, 383 p. Similar in format to the Eaton volumes (see above).

Sutcliffe, Tom. *Believing in Opera*. Princeton, N.J.: Princeton University Press, 1996. xv, 464 p. About opera directors after World War II.

## BY COUNTRY

### Australia

Holmes, Robyn, ed. *Through the Opera Glass: A Chronological Register of Operas Performed in South Australia, 1836 to 1988*. Adelaide: Friends of the State Opera of South Australia, 1991. 369 p.

____. *Through the Opera Glass: A Supplement 1989 to 1995*. 369 p. Incorporates additions and corrections to the above. Adelaide: Friends of the State Opera of South Australia, 1997.

### England

Nicoll, Allardyce. *A History of English Drama, 1660–1900*. 6 vols. Cambridge: University Press, 1952–59. Information on plays produced or printed in England.

White, Eric Walter, comp. *A Register of First Performances of English Operas and Semi-Operas: From the 16th Century to 1980*. London: Society for Theatre Research, 1983. vi, 130 p.

### United States

Borroff, Edith. *American Operas: A Checklist*. Edited by J. Bunker Clark. Detroit Studies in Music Bibliography, no. 69. Warren, Mich.: Harmonie Park Press, 1992. xxiv, 334 p. Listings for operas, operettas, music-theater works, some musicals, radio plays.

Central Opera Service. *Directory of American Contemporary Operas*. New York: Central Opera Service, 1967. 79 p.

____. *Directory of Contemporary Operas and Music Theater Works and North American Premieres, 1980–1989*. New York: Central Opera Service, 1990. viii, 325 p.

Drummond, Andrew H. *American Opera Librettos*. Metuchen, N.J.: Scarecrow Press, 1973. v, 277 p.

Hipsher, Edward Ellsworth. *American Opera and Its Composers*. Philadelphia: Theodore Presser, 1927. 478 p. Repr. ed. with new introduction by H. Earle Johnson. New York: Da Capo, 1978. Brief plots and descriptions of numerous (and now forgotten) operas from the later nineteenth and early twentieth century. Includes works by Bimboni, Bristow, Cadman, Chadwick, Converse, Damrosch, De Koven, Freeman, Freer, Hadley, Hanson, Moore, Parker, and Pratt, and the early operas of George Antheil, Louis Gruenberg, Deems Taylor, and Virgil Thomson.

Kornick, Rebecca Hodell. *Recent American Opera: A Production Guide*. New York: Columbia University Press, 1991. xvii, 352 p. A continuation of Eaton's books (see above), with much the same format and including reviews.

Mattfeld, Julius. *Handbook of American Operatic Premieres, 1731–1962*. Detroit Studies in Music Bibliography, no. 5. Detroit: Information Service, 1963. 142 p.

## PLOTS, CHARACTERS

Cross, Milton, and Karl Kohrs. *More Stories of the Great Operas*. Garden City, N.Y.: Doubleday, 1971. 752 p. Rev. and expanded by Karl Kohrs. Garden City, N.Y.: Doubleday, 1980. xi, 802 p. Listing by title.

Ewen, David. *The Book of European Light Opera*. New York: Holt, Rinehart, and Winston, 1962. xiii, 297 p. Repr. ed. Westport, Conn.: Greenwood Press, 1977. Listing by title.

Harewood, Earl of, ed. *The New Kobbé's Complete Opera Book*. New York: G. P. Putnam's Sons, 1976. Rev. as *The Definitive Kobbé's Opera Book*. New York: G. P. Putnam's Sons, 1987. xv, 1,404 p. Detailed plots, some performance information, musical descriptions; listed by nationality and, chronologically, by composer.

____, and Antony Peattie, eds. *The New Kobbé's Opera Book*. New York: Putnam, 1997. xviii, 1,012 p. Rev. ed. of *The Definitive Kobbé's Opera Book*. This edition covers almost 500 works and includes operas by composers such as

Peter Maxwell Davies, Judith Weir, and Dominick Argento. Eleventh ed., with corrections, New York: G. P. Putnam's Sons, 2000. xviii, 1012 p.

Kennedy, Joyce Bourne. *Who's Who in Opera: A Guide to Opera Characters*. Consulting editor Michael Kennedy. Oxford, New York: Oxford University Press, 1998. 457 p. Lists 2,500 operatic characters, with synopses of more than 250 major works.

Lubbock, Mark Hugh. *The Complete Book of Light Opera*. With an American section by David Ewen. London: Putnam, [1962]. xviii, 953 p. About 300 works.

*The Victor Book of Operas*. 13th ed. Rev. by Henry W. Simon. New York: Simon & Schuster, 1968. 475 p. Includes about 120 works.

## VIDEOS

Blyth, Alan. *Opera on Video: The Essential Guide*. London: Kyle Cathie, 1995. x, 246 p.

Gruber, Paul. *The Metropolitan Opera Guide to Opera on Video*. New York: Metropolitan Opera Guild, W. W. Norton, 1997. xvi, 483 p.

Levine, Robert. *Guide to Opera and Dance on Videocassette*. Consumer Reports Books. Mount Vernon, N.Y.: Consumers Union, 1989. vii, 213 p.

*The Mellen Opera Reference Index*. Vol. 20: *An Opera Videography*. Compiled by Charles H. Parsons. Lewiston, N.Y., and Queenston, Ont.: Edwin Mellen Press, 1997. 368 p.

Wlaschin, Ken. *Encyclopedia of Opera on Screen: A Guide to More Than 100 Years of Opera Films, Videos, and DVDs*. New Haven: Yale University Press, 2004. xi, 872 p.

## HISTORY

### GENERAL

Grout, Donald. *A Short History of Opera*. 2nd ed. New York: Columbia University Press, 1965. xviii, 852 p. 3rd ed., with Hermine Weigel Williams. New York: Columbia University Press, 1988. xix, 913 p. 4th ed. New York: Columbia University Press, 2003. xii, 1,030 p.

Huebner, Stephen. *National Traditions in Nineteenth-Century Opera*. Volume 1: *Italy, France, England, and the Americas*. Farnham, Surrey: Highgate, 2010. 566 p.

Moss, Harold. "Popular Music and the Ballad Opera." *JAMS* 26 (1973): 365–82.

Porter, Susan L. "English-American Interaction in American Musical Theater at the Turn of the Nineteenth Century. *AM* 4 (Spring 1986): 6–19.

### BY COUNTRY

#### Australia

Bebbington, Warren, ed. *The Oxford Companion to Australian Music*. Melbourne: Oxford University Press, 1997. xvi, 608 p.

Callaway, Frank, and David Tunley, eds. *Australian Composition in the Twentieth Century*. Melbourne and New York: Oxford University Press, 1978. x, 248 p.

Gyger, Alison. *Opera for the Antipodes: Opera in Australia 1881–1939*. Sydney: Currency Press and Pellinor, 1990. viii, 364 p.

Holmes, Robyn. *Through the Looking Glass: A Chronological Register of Opera Performed in South Australia, 1836 to 1988*. Adelaide: Friends of the State Opera of South Australia, 1991. 369 p.

____. *Through the Opera Glass: A Supplement 1989 to 1995*. Incorporates additions and corrections to the above. Adelaide: Friends of the State Opera of South Australia, 1997.

#### Canada

Domville, Eric. "Canadian Overtures." *Opera Canada* 43 (Winter 2002): 22–24.

____. "Canadian Themes and Variations." *Opera Canada* 44 (Spring 2003): 18–21.

*Encyclopedia of Music in Canada*. Edited by Helmut Kallmann, Gilles Potvin, and Kenneth Winters. 2nd ed. Toronto and Buffalo: University of Toronto Press, 1992. 1,524 p. Online updates (2001–): www.library.ualberta.ca/databases/databaseinfo/index.cfm?ID=3061.

MacMillan, Keith, and John Beckwith, eds. *Contemporary Canadian Composers*. Toronto and New York: Oxford University Press, 1975. xxiv, 248 p.

Schabas, Ezra, and Carl Morey. *Opera Viva: Canadian Opera Company: The First Fifty Years*. Toronto: Dundurn Press, 2000. 312 p.

#### England

Altieri, Joanne. *The Theatre of Praise: The Panegyric Tradition in Seventeenth-Century English Drama*. Newark, Del.: University of Delaware Press, 1986. 240 p.

Biddlecombe, George. *English Opera from 1834 to 1864 with Particular Reference to the Works of Michael Balfe*. New York and London: Garland, 1994. xiii, 351 p.

Burrows, Donald, and Rosemary Dunhill. *Music and Theatre in Handel's World: The Family Papers of James Harris 1732–1780*. Oxford, New York: Oxford University Press, 2002. 1,258 p.

Carr, Bruce. "The First All-Sung English 19th-Century Opera." *MT* 115 (Feb. 1974): 125–26.

Fenner, Theodore. *Opera in London: Views of the Press, 1785–1830*. Carbondale: Southern Illinois University Press, 1994. xvi, 788 p.

Fiske, Roger. *English Theatre Music in the Eighteenth Century*. Oxford: Oxford University Press, 1973. xv, 684 p. 2nd ed. Oxford and New York: Oxford University Press, 1986. xvi, 684 p. Descriptions and analyses of numerous stage works.

Foreman, Lewis. *From Parry to Britten: British Music in Letters 1900–1945*. New York: Amadeus Press, 1988. 232 p. Musical examples.

Gänzl, Kurt. *The British Musical Theatre*. Vol. 1: 1865–1914. Vol. 2: 1915–1984. Basingstoke, Eng.: Macmillan, 1986.

Gibson, Elizabeth. *The Royal Academy of Music 1719–1728: The Institution and Its Directors*. New York: Garland, 1989. 465 p.

Johnstone, H. Diack, and Roger Fiske, eds. *Music in Britain: The Eighteenth Century*. Oxford, UK, Cambridge, Mass.: Blackwell Reference, 1990, pp. 96–158.

Lamb, Andrew. *150 Years of Popular Music Theatre*. New Haven: Yale University Press, 2000. Part II: *Comic Opera and Musical Comedy: Britain and America*, pp. 95–194.

Schmidgall, Gary. *Shakespeare and Opera*. New York: Oxford University Press, 1990. xii, 394 p.

Temperley, Nicholas. "The English Romantic Opera." *Victorian Studies* 9 (1966), 293–301.

____. "Musical Nationalism in English Romantic Opera." *The Lost Chord: Essays on Victorian Music*. Bloomington, Ind.: Indiana University Press, 1989, pp. 143–57.

Troost, Linda V. "The Rise of English Comic Opera 1762–1800." Ph.D. diss., University of Pennsylvania, 1985. v, 262 p.

Walls, Peter. *Music in the English Courtly Masque, 1604–1640*. Oxford: Clarendon Press; New York: Oxford University Press, 1996. xix, 372 p.

White, Eric Walter. *A History of English Opera*. London: Faber, 1983. 472 p.

Winkler, Amanda Eubanks. *O Let Us Howle Some Heavy Note: Music for Witches, the Melancholic, and the Mad on the Seventeenth-Century English Stage*. Bloomington : Indiana University Press, 2006. x, 232 p.

## Ireland

Grimes, Jonathan, ed. *Irish Composers*. 9th ed.: 2001–2 (2001). 10th ed.: 2002–3 (2002). 11th ed.: 2003–4 (2003). 12th ed.: 2004–5 (2004). 14th ed.: 2006 (2006). Dublin: Contemporary Music Centre.

O'Kelly, Eve, ed. *Irish Composers*. Dublin: Contemporary Music Centre, 1993. 32 p. 2nd ed.: 1994–95 (1994). 3rd ed.: 1995–96 (1995). 4th ed.: 1996–97 (1996). 5th ed.: 1997–98 (1997). 6th ed.: 1998–99 (1998). 7th ed.: 2001–2 (2001). 8th ed.: 2000–1 (2000).

## New Zealand

Simpson, Adrienne. *Capital Opera: Wellington's Opera Company, 1982–1999*. [Wellington, N.Z.]: National Opera of Wellington, 2000. 152 p.

____. *Opera's Farthest Frontier: A History of Professional Opera in New Zealand*. Birkenhead, Auckland, N.Z.: Reed, 1996. 288 p.

## Scotland

Oliver, Cordelia. *It Is a Curious Story: The Tale of Scottish Opera, 1962–1987*. Edinburgh: Mainstream Publishing, 1987. 199 p.

Wilson, Conrad. *Scottish Opera—The First Ten Years*. London: Collins, 1972. [8], 168 p.

## United States

Block, Adrienne Fried, and Carol Neuls-Bates, comps. and eds. *Women in American Music. A Bibliography of Music and Literature*. Westport, Conn.: Greenwood Press, 1979. xxxvi, 302 p.

Bordman, Gerald Martin. *American Musical Theatre. A Chronicle*. 2nd ed. New York and Oxford: Oxford University Press, 1992. viii, 206 p. 3rd ed., 2001. xvi, 917 p.

____. *American Operetta: from H.M.S. Pinafore to Sweeney Todd*. New York: Oxford University Press, 1981. ix, 821 p.

Cheatnam, Wallace. *Dialogues on Opera and the African-American Experience*. Lanham, Md.: Scarecrow Press, 1997. xvii, 185 p.

Crawford, John C., and Dorothy L. Crawford. *Expressionism in Twentieth-Century Music*. Bloomington, Ind.: Indiana University Press, 1993. xv, 331 p.

Davis, Ronald L. *The History of Opera in the American West*. Englewood Cliffs, N.J.: Prentice Hall, 1965. xii, 178 p.

Dizikes, John. *Opera in America: A Cultural History*. New Haven: Yale University Press, 1993. xi, 611 p. Through 1977.

Engel, Lehman. *The American Musical Theater*. Rev. ed. New York: Macmillan, 1975. xx, 266 p.

Ewen, David. *New Complete Book of the American Musical Theater*. New York: Holt, Rinehart, and Winston, [1970]. xxv, 800 p.

Green, Stanley. *Broadway Musicals, Show by Show*. 3rd ed. Milwaukee: H. Leonard, 1990. xi, 372 p. 4th ed. Rev. and updated by Kay Green. Milwaukee, Wisc.: H. Leonard Pub. Corp., 1994. xix, 372 p.

Hischak, Thomas S. *The Oxford Companion to the American Musical*. Oxford, New York: Oxford University Press, 2008. xxxiv, 923 p.

____. *Stage It with Music: An Encyclopedic Guide to the American Musical Theatre*. Westport, Conn.: Greenwood Press, 1993. viii, 341 p.

Hummel, David. *The Collector's Guide to the American Musical Theater*. 2 vols. Metuchen, N.J.: Scarecrow Press, 1984. Repr. with additions and corrections.

Layng, Judith. "Black Images in Opera." *OJ* 7 (Winter 1969): 29–32.

Lehrman, Leonard. "What Is Jewish Opera?" *OJ* 29 (June 1, 1996): 56–61.

Ottenberg, June C. *Opera Odyssey: Toward a History of Opera in Nineteenth-Century America*. Westport, Conn.: Greenwood Press, 1994. xi, 203 p.

Porter, Susan L. *With an Air Debonair: Musical Theatre in America, 1785–1815*. Washington, D.C.: Smithsonian Institution Press, 1991. xii, 631 p. Includes "Checklist of Musical Entertainments, 1785–1815," pp. 425–500.

Preston, Katherine. "Between the Cracks: The Performance of English-Language Opera in Late Nineteenth-Century America." *AM* 21 (Fall 2003): 349–74.

____. *Opera on the Road: Traveling Opera Troupes in the United States, 1825–60*. Urbana: University of Illinois Press, 1993. xvii, 479 p.

Rich, Maria. "Opera USA — Perspective: American Opera after the Bicentennial." *OQ* 1 (Autumn 1983): 90–113.

Riis, Thomas L. *More Than Just Minstrel Shows: The Rise of Black Musical Theatre at the Turn of the Century*. Institute for Studies in American Music Monographs, no. 33. Brooklyn, N.Y.: Institute for Studies in American Music, 1992. 62 p.

Root, Deane L. *American Popular Stage Music, 1860–1880*. Ann Arbor, Mich.: UMI Research Press, 1981. x, 284 p.

Rorem, Ned. "In Search of American Opera." *ON* 56 (July 1991): 8–10, 12, 14–17, 44.

Salzman, Eric. "Wither American Music Theater?" *MQ* 65 (Apr. 1979): 230–44; repr. *MQ* 75 (Winter 1991): 235–47.

Salzman, Jack, David Lionel Smith, and Cornel West, eds. *Encyclopedia of African-American Culture and History*. Vol. 4: *Mia–Ryd*. New York: Simon & Schuster/Macmillan, 1996.

Simmons, Walter. *Voices in the Wilderness: Six American Neo-Romantic Composers*. Lanham, Md.: Scarecrow Press, 2004. ix, 419 p. Includes Howard Hanson, Vittorio Giannini, Samuel Barber, and Nicolas Flagello.

Smith, Eric Ledell. *Blacks in Opera: An Encyclopedia of People and Companies, 1873–1993*. Jefferson, N.C.: McFarland, 1995. xi, 236 p.

Sonneck, Oscar G. T. "Early American Operas." *SIMG* 6 (1904–6): 428–95.

____. *Early Concert-Life in America, 1731–1800*. Leipzig: Breitkopf & Härtel, 1907. 338 p. Reprint Mansfield Centre, Conn.: Martino Publishing, 2006.

____. *Early Opera in America*. New York: G. Schirmer; Boston: Boston Music Co., [1963, 1915]. viii, 230 p.

Stempel, Larry. "The Musical Play Expands." *AM* 9 (Winter 1992): 136–69.

Tick, Judith. *American Women Composers before 1870*. Ann Arbor, Mich.: UMI Press, 1983. 302 p.

Virga, Patricia H. *The American Opera to 1790*. Studies in Musicology, no. 61. Ann Arbor, Mich.: UMI Research Press, 1982. xix, 393 p.

Woll, Allen. *Black Musical Theatre: From Coontown to Dreamgirls*. Baton Rouge: Louisiana State University, 1989. xiv, 301 p.

Wynne, Peter. "Return of the Native." *ON* 60 (Jan. 6, 1996): 28–30. On works about Native Americans.

Zietz, Karyl Lynn. *Opera Companies and Houses of the United States: A Comprehensive, Illustrated Reference*. Jefferson, N.C.: McFarland, 1994. xv, 335 p.

### Wales

Fawkes, Richard. *Welsh National Opera*. London: J. MacRae, 1986. x, 368 p.

Leech, Caroline. *Welsh National Opera*. Cardiff: Graffeg, 2006. 192 p.

## CITIES AND FESTIVALS

### Aldeburgh

Bankes, Ariane and Jonathan Reekie, comps. *New Aldeburgh Anthology*. Foreword by Ronald Blythe. Woodbridge, UK; Rochester, N.Y.: Aldeburgh Music/Boydell, 2009. 306 p.

Blythe, Ronald, ed. *Aldeburgh Anthology*. London: Faber, 1972. xiii, 436 p.

### Bloomington, Ind.

Tobias, Marianne Williams. *Opera for All Seasons: 60 Years of Indiana University Opera Theater*. Bloomington: Indiana University Press, 2010. viii, 480 p.

### Boston

Bishop, Cardell. *Boston National Opera Company and Boston Theatre Opera Company*. [Santa Monica, Calif.]: C. Bishop, [1981]. vii, 41 leaves. Includes "Repertoire 1915–1918."

Eaton, Quaintance. *The Boston Opera Company*. New York: Da Capo Press, 1980, 1965. xiv, 338 p.

### Central City, Colorado

Johnson, Charles A. *Opera in the Rockies: The History of the Central City Opera House Association, 1932–1992*. [Central City, Colo.]: The Association, 1992. ix, 123 p.

Young, Allen. *Opera in Central City*. Denver: Spectographics, 1993. 117 p.

### Chicago

Cassidy, Claudia. *Lyric Opera of Chicago*. Foreword by Saul Bellow; recollections by Carol Fox; graphic design by R. D. Scudellari. [Chicago]: The Opera, 1979. 233 p.

Davis, Ronald. *Opera in Chicago*. New York: Appleton-Century, 1966. xi, 393 p.

Lyric Opera of Chicago. *Twenty Years: A Pictorial Souvenir Album to Celebrate the Twentieth Anniversary of the Founding of Lyric Opera in 1954*. With a specially written foreword by Claudia Cassidy. [Chicago, 1974]. 1 vol. (not paginated) of illustrations.

Marsh, Robert C., and Norman Pellegrini. *150 Years of Opera in Chicago*. DeKalb, Ill.: Northern Illinois University Press, 2006. xiv, 316 p.

### Dublin

Walsh, T. J. *Opera in Dublin: 1705–1797: The Social Scene*. Dublin: A. Figgis, 1973. xv, 386 p.

____. *Opera in Dublin: 1798–1820. Frederick Jones and the Crow Street Theatre*. Oxford: Oxford University Press, 1993. xiv, 294 p.

### Edinburgh

Bruce, George. *Festival in the North: The Story of the Edinburgh Festival*. London: Hale, 1975. 253 p.

### Glyndebourne

Higgins, John, ed.. *Glyndebourne: A Celebration*. London: J. Cape, 1984. xii, 172 p.

Hughes, Spike. *Glyndebourne: A History of the Festival Opera Founded in 1934 by Audrey and John Christie*. Devon: Newton Abbott, 1981; North Pomfret, Vt.: David and Charles, 1981. 388 p. Revision of 1965 edition (London, Methuen).

### London

### General

Fenner, Theodore. *Opera in London: Views of the Press, 1785–1830*. Carbondale, Ill.: Southern Illinois University Press, 1994. xvi, 788 p.

Lowerre, *Kathryn. Music and Musicians on the London Stage, 1695–1705*. Farnham, Eng.; Burlington, Vt.: Ashgate, 2009. xvi, 412 p.

### Covent Garden

Chapman, Clive. "'Sir, It Will Not Do!' John Rich and Covent Garden's Early Years." *MT* 123 (1982): 831–35.

Donaldson, Frances Lonsdale. *The Royal Opera House in the Twentieth Century*. London: Weidenfeld and Nicolson, 1988. xvii, 238 p.

Handley, Ellenor, and Martin Kinna. *Royal Opera House Covent Garden: A History*. West Wickham, Eng.: Fourlance Books, 1978. 64 p.

Hume, Robert D. "Covent Garden Theatre in 1732. *MT* 123 (1982): 823–26.

Langley, Leanne. "'Our Thing Called Opera.' Some Covent Garden Productions of the 1820s through Contemporary Eyes." *MT* 123 (1982): 836–38.

Lebrecht, Norman. *Covent Garden: The Untold Story: Dispatches from the English Culture War, 1945–2000*. Boston: Northeastern University Press, 2001. 580 p.

Rosenthal, Harold. *Opera at Covent Garden. A Short History*. London: Gollancz, 1967. 192 p.

____. *Two Centuries of Opera at Covent Garden*. London: Putnam, 1958. xiv, 849 p.

Saint, Andrew. "The Three Covent Gardens." *MT* 123 (1982): 826–31.

Saint, Andrew, et al. *A History of the Royal Opera House, Covent Garden, 1732–1982*. London: The Royal Opera House, 1982. 128 p.

### Drury Lane Theatre

Dobbs, Brian. *Drury Lane: Three Centuries of the Theatre Royal, 1663–1971*. London: Cassell, 1972. xiv, 226 p.

Girdham, Jane. *English Opera in Late Eighteenth-Century London: Stephen Storace at Drury Lane*. New York: Clarendon Press, 1997. xiv, 272 p.

### Haymarket Theatre (King's Theatre)

Burling, William J. *Summer Theatre in London, 1661–1820, and the Rise of the Haymarket Theatre*. Madison, N.J.: Fairleigh Dickinson University Press; London: Associated University Presses, 2000. 326 p.

Woodfield, Ian. *Opera and Drama in Eighteenth-Century London: The King's Theatre, Garrick and the Business of Performance*. Cambridge; New York: Cambridge University Press, 2001. xii, 339 p.

### Montreal

Amtmann, Willy. *Music in Canada 1600–1800*. Cambridge, Ont.: Habitex Books, [1975]. 320 p. Enlarged as *La musique au Québec 1600–1875*. Montreal: Les Editions de l'Homme, 1976. 420 p.

Cooper, Dorith Rachel. "Opera in Montreal and Toronto: A Study of Performance Tradition and Repertoire 1783–1980." Ph.D. diss., University of Toronto, 1983.

### New York

### General

Ahlquist, Karen. *Democracy at the Opera: Music, Theater, and Culture in New York City, 1815–60*. Urbana: University of Illinois Press, 1997. xvii, 248 p.

Green, Stanley. *Broadway Musicals, Show by Show*. Milwaukee, Wisc.: Applause Theatre & Cinema Books, 2011. 7th ed. xxx, 481 p.

Honig, Joel. "Is It Curtains for American Chamber Opera?" *ON* 62 (Aug. 1997): 10–15.

Krehbiel, Henry Edward. *Chapters of Opera: Being Historical and Critical Observations and Records Concerning the Lyric Drama in New York from Its Earliest Days Down to the Present Time*. New York: Holt, 1909. xvii, 435 p. Repr. ed. New York: Da Capo Press, 1980.

Riis, Thomas L. *Just before Jazz: Black Musical Theater in New York, 1890–1915*. Washington, D.C.: Smithsonian Institution Press, 1989. xxiv, 309 p.

Stempel, Larry. *Showtime: A History of the Broadway Musical Theater*. New York; London: W. W. Norton, 2010. xx, 826 p.

Zucker, Stefan. "New York Underground: Opera on a Shoestring," *ON* 53 (Jan. 7, 1989): 20–23.

## Academy of Music

Cone, John Frederick. *First Rival of the Metropolitan Opera*. New York: Columbia University Press, 1983. On the Academy and James Henry Mapleson, 1830–1901. xvi, 257 p.

## Columbia University

Beeson, Jack. "Opera at Columbia University, 1941–1958." *Current Musicology* 70 (2000): 193–211.

Cerf, Steven R. "Pioneers on Morningside Heights." *ON* 56 (July 1991): 22–24.

Griffel, Margaret Ross. "Opera at Columbia: A Shining Legacy." *Current Musicology* 79–80 (2005): 95–133. About campus performances (1941–2004) of many original English-language works, including the premieres of Britten's *Paul Bunyan* and Menotti's *The Medium*.

Sponaugle, Harlie. "Columbia University, the Columbia Opera Workshop and the Efflorescence of American Opera in the 1940s and 1950s." Parts 1–3, Appendix. *US OperaWeb* (Autumn 2002): www.usoperaweb.com/2002/september/columbia.htm.

## Juilliard School

Gottlieb, Jane, Stephen E. Novak, and Taras Pavlovsky, comps. *Guide to the Juilliard School Archives*. New York: The Juilliard School, 1992. 113 p.

## Manhattan Opera Company

Cone, John F. *Oscar Hammerstein's Manhattan Opera Company*. Norman, Okla.: University of Oklahoma Press, 1966. xvi, 399 p.

## Metropolitan Opera

*Annals of the Metropolitan Opera: The Complete Chronicle of Performances and Artists*. Edited by Gerald Fitzgerald. 2 vols. Vol. 1: *Chronology, 1883–1985*. Vol. 2: *Tables, 1883–1985*. New York: Metropolitan Opera Guild, and Boston: G. K. Hall, 1989. xxviii, 1,000 p.; xxvi, 313 p.

Fiedler, Johanna. *Molto Agitato: The Mayhem behind the Music at the Metropolitan Opera*. New York: Nan A. Talese/Doubleday, 2001.

Jackson, Paul. *Saturday Afternoons at the Old Met: The Metropolitan Opera Broadcasts, 1931–1950*. Portland, Oreg.: Amadeus Press, 1992. xvi, 569 p.

____. *Sign-Off for the Old Met: The Metropolitan Opera Broadcasts, 1950–1966*. Portland, Oreg.: Amadeus Press, 1997. xv, 644 p.

Kolodin, Irving. *The Metropolitan Opera, 1883–1966: A Candid History*. 4th ed. New York: A. A. Knopf, 1966. xxi, 762, xlvii p. illus.

Mayer, Martin. *The Met: One Hundred Years of Grand Opera*. Picture editor Gerald Fitzgerald. New York : Simon and Schuster: Metropolitan Opera Guild, 1983. 368 p.

Merkling, Frank, et al. *The Golden Horseshoe: The Life and Times of the Metropolitan Opera House*. Prologue by Eleanor R. Belmont. Epilogue by Anthony A. Bliss. New York: Viking Press, [1965]. 319 p.

Preston, Stuart. *Farewell to the Old House: The Metropolitan Opera House, 1883–1966*. Garden City, N.Y., Doubleday, [1966]. 68 p. (chiefly illus.).

Robinson, Francis. *Celebration: The Metropolitan Opera*. Picture editor Gerald Fitzgerald. Garden City, N.Y.: Doubleday, 1979. 287 p. (chiefly illus.).

## New York City Opera

Cohn, Fred. "The Ballad of NYCO." *ON* 76 (Jan. 2012): 24–29.

Drummond, Andrew H. "The New York City Opera." In *American Opera Librettos*. Metuchen, N.J.: Scarecrow Press, 1973.

McKenna, Harold J., ed. *New York City Opera Sings: Stories and Productions of the New York City Opera, 1944–79*. New York: Richard Rosen Press, 1981. xvii, 404 p.

Sokol, Martin L. *The New York City Opera: An American Adventure*. New York: Macmillan, 1981. xiv, 562 p.

## Philadelphia

Albrecht, Otto E. "Opera in Philadelphia, 1800–1830," *JAMS* 32 (1979): 499–515.

## San Francisco

Bloomfield, Arthur. *Fifty Years of the San Francisco Opera*. San Francisco: San Francisco Book Co., [1972]. xi, 450 p.

____. *The San Francisco Opera, 1922–1978*. Sausalito, Calif.: Comstock Editions, [1978]. 552 p.

Chatfield-Taylor, Joan. *San Francisco Opera: The First Seventy-five Years*. San Francisco: Chronicle Books, 1997. x, 181 p.

## Santa Fe, New Mexico

Scott, Eleanor. *The First Twenty Years of the Santa Fe Opera*. Santa Fe, N.M.: Sunstone Press, 1976. 166 p.

## Sydney

Hubble, Ava. *More Than an Opera House*. Sydney and New York: Lansdowne, 1983. 176 p.

## Tanglewood (Lenox, Mass.)

Pincus, Andrew L. *Scenes from Tanglewood*. Boston: Northeastern University Press, 1989. xii, 287 p.

____. *Tanglewood: The Clash between Tradition and Change*. Boston: Northeastern University Press, 1998. xiv, 210 p.

## Toronto

Cooper, Dorith Rachel. "Opera in Montreal and Toronto: A Study of Performance Tradition and Repertoire 1783–1980." Ph.D. diss., University of Toronto, 1983.

Morey, Carl. "Pre-Confederation Opera in Toronto." *Opera in Canada* 10, no. 3 (1969): 13–15.

Schabas, Ezra, and Carl Morey. *Opera Viva: Canadian Opera Company: The First Fifty Years*. Toronto: Dundurn Press, 2000. 312 p.

## COMPOSERS

(*see also* individual works in A–Z section)

### Adaskin, Murray

Lazarevich, Gordana. *The Musical World of Frances James and Murray Adaskin*. Toronto, Buffalo: University of Toronto Press, 1988. x, 331 p.

### ApIvor, Denis

Wright, David C. F. "Denis ApIvor." *MR* 50 (1989): 53–63.

### Arne, Michael

Parkinson, John A. *An Index to the Vocal Works of Thomas Augustine Arne and Michael Arne*. Detroit: Detroit Information Coordinators, 1972. 82 p.

### Arne, Thomas A.

Adas, Jane. "Arne's Progress: An English Composer in Eighteenth-Century London." Ph.D. diss., Rutgers University, 1993. x, 524 leaves.

Parkinson, John A. *An Index to the Vocal Works of Thomas Augustine Arne and Michael Arne*. Detroit: Detroit Information Coordinators, 1972. 82 p.

### Attwood, Thomas

Moss, D. J. *Thomas Attwood: The Biography of a Radical*. Montreal; Buffalo: McGill-Queen's University Press, 1990. 377 p.

Oldman, C. B. "Attwood's Dramatic Works." *MT* 106 (1966): 23–27.

### Bainton, Edgar

Jones, Michael. "Edgar Bainton: Musical and Spiritual Traveller." *Journal of the British Music Society* 12 (1990): 19–40.

Tunley, David E. "Thoughts on the Music of Edgar Bainton." *Westerly,* no. 2 (1963): 55–57.

### Balfe, Michael

Tyldesley, William. *Michael William Balfe: His Life and His English Operas*. Aldershot, Hants, Eng.; Burlington, Vt.: Ashgate, 2003. xix, 256 p.

Walsh, Basil. *Michael W. Balfe: A Unique Victorian Composer*. Dublin; Portland, Oreg.: Irish Academic Press, 2008. xxiii, 296 p.

### Barber, Samuel

Dickinson, Peter, ed. *Samuel Barber Remembered: A Centenary Tribute*. Rochester, N.Y.: University of Rochester Press, 2010. xv, 196 p.

Felsenfeld, Daniel. *Britten and Barber: Their Lives and Their Music*. Pompton Plains, N.J.: Amadeus Press. 2005. viii, 180 p.

Hennessee, Don A. *Samuel Barber: A Bio-Bibliography*. Westport, Conn.: Greenwood Press, 1985. xii, 404 p.

Heyman, Barbara B. *Samuel Barber. A Thematic Catalogue of the Complete Works*. Oxford University Press, 2012. 608 p.

____. *Samuel Barber: The Composer and His Music*. New York and Oxford: Oxford University Press, 1992. xviii, 586 p.

Simmons, Walter. *Voices in the Wilderness: Six American Neo-Romantic Composers*. Lanham, Md.: Scarecrow Press, 2004. ix, 419 p.

### Beach, Amy

Block, Adrienne Fried. *Amy Beach, Passionate Victorian*. New York: Oxford University Press, 1998. xiii, 409 p.

### Beeson, Jack

Hawkshaw, Susan. "A Master of the American Opera." *Columbia Magazine* (Spring 2002): 45–48.

### Benjamin, Arthur

Boustead, Alan. "Arthur Benjamin and Opera." *Opera* 15 (1964): 709–14.

### Bergsma, William

Shulsky, Abraham. "The Music of William Bergsma." *Juilliard Review* 3 (Spring 1956): 12–26.

### Bernstein, Leonard

Burton, Humphrey. *Leonard Bernstein*. New York: Doubleday, 1994. xiv, 594 p.

Fluegel, Jane, ed. *Bernstein Remembered*. Introduction by Donal Henahan. Preface by Isaac Stern. New York: Carroll & Graf, 1991. 160 p.

Gottlieb, Jack. *Leonard Bernstein: A Complete Catalogue of His Works*. New York: Jalni Publications/Boosey & Hawkes, 1988. 95 p.

Peyser, Joan. *Bernstein: A Biography*. New York: Ballantine Books, 1988. xviii, 461 p. Revised and updated, New York: Billboard Books, 1998. 510 p.

Secrest, Meryle. *Leonard Bernstein: A Life*. New York: A. A. Knopf, 1994. xv, 471 p.

Smith, Helen. *There's a Place for Us: The Musical Theatre Works of Leonard Bernstein*. Farnham, Surrey, Eng.; Burlington, Vt.: Ashgate Press, 2011. xviii, 300 p.

### Bishop, Henry Rowley

Corder, Frederick. "The Works of Sir Henry Rowley Bishop." *MQ* 4 (1918): 78–97.

### Blitzstein, Marc

Gordon, Eric A. *Mark the Music. The Life and Work of Marc Blitzstein*. New York: St. Martin's Press, 1989. xviii, 605 p.

Lehrman, Leonard. *Marc Blitzstein: A Bio-Bibliography*. Westport, Conn.: Praeger, 2006. 645 p.

**Boughton, Rutland**

Hurd, Michael. "Rutland Boughton, 1878–1960." *MT* 119 (1978): 31–33.

____. *Rutland Boughton and the Glastonbury Festivals.* Oxford: Clarendon Press, 1994. xiv, 415 p.

**Boyce, William**

Taylor, Eric. "William Boyce and the Theatre." *MR* 14 (1953): 275–87.

**Brian, Havergal**

Schaarwächter, Jürgen, ed. *HB. Aspects of Havergal Brian.* Edited from the Havergal Brian newsletters. Aldershot and Brookfield, Vt.: Ashgate, 1997. xii, 424 p.

**Bridge, Frank**

Little, Karen R. *Frank Bridge: A Bio-Bibliography.* New York: Greenwood Press, 1991. xii, 263 p.

**Britten, Benjamin**

Brett, Philip, and George E. Haggerty. *Music and Sexuality in Britten: Selected Essays.* Berkeley: University of California Press, 2006. xix, 280 p.

Carpenter, Humphrey. *Benjamin Britten: A Biography.* London: Faber and Faber, 1992. x, 680 p.

Cooke, Mervyn, ed. *The Cambridge Companion to Benjamin Britten.* Cambridge: Cambridge University Press, 1999. xviii, 350 p.

Corse, Sandra. *Opera and the Uses of Language: Mozart, Verdi, and Britten.* Rutherford, N.J.: Fairleigh Dickinson University Press, 1986. 168 p.

Craggs, Stewart R. *Benjamin Britten: A Bio-Bibliography.* Westport, Conn.: Greenwood Press, 2002. x, 300 p.

Elliott, Graham. *Benjamin Britten: The Spiritual Dimension.* Oxford; New York: Oxford University Press, 2006. xiv, 169 p.

Evans, John, Philip Reed, and Paul Wilson, comps. *A Britten Source Book.* Aldeburgh, Suffolk: Britten Estate, 1987. 328 p.

Evans, Peter. *The Music of Benjamin Britten.* London: Clarendon Press; New York: Oxford University Press, 1996. vii, 564 p.

Felsenfeld, Daniel. *Britten and Barber: Their Lives and Their Music.* Pompton Plains, N.J.: Amadeus Press. 2005. viii, 180 p.

Herbert, David, ed. *The Operas of Benjamin Britten. The Complete Librettos.* New York: Columbia University Press, 1979. xxxi, 382 p. Rev. ed. London: Herbert Press, 1989. 384 p.

Howard, Patricia. *The Operas of Benjamin Britten.* London: Praeger, 1969. 236 p.

Kendall, Alan. *Benjamin Britten.* London: Macmillan, 1973. 112 p.

Kennedy, Michael. *Britten.* London: Dent, 1981. xi, 356 p. Rev. ed. Oxford; New York: Oxford University Press, 2001, xi, 359 p.

Mark, Christopher. *Early Benjamin Britten: A Study of Stylistic and Technical Evolution.* New York: Garland, 1995. xi, 350 p.

Matthews, David. *Britten.* London: Haus, 2003. ix, 182 p.

Mitchell, Donald. *Britten and Auden in the Thirties: The Year 1936.* London: Faber, 1981. 176 p.

____. "Britten's 'Dramatic' Legacy." *Opera* 28 (1977): 127–30.

Mitchell, Donald, and John Evans. *Benjamin Britten 1913–1976: Pictures from a Life.* London: Faber, 1978. viii, [192], 16 p.

Oliver, Michael. *Benjamin Britten.* London: Phaidon, 1996. 240 p.

Parsons, Charles H. *A Benjamin Britten Discography.* Lewiston, N.Y.: The Edwin Mellen Press, 1990. 247 p.

White, Eric Walter. *Benjamin Britten: His Life and Operas.* 2nd ed. London: Faber, 1983. 322 p.

Whittall, Arnold. *The Music of Britten and Tippett. Studies in Themes and Techniques.* Cambridge and New York: Cambridge University Press, 1982. vii, 314 p.

**Cadman, Charles Wakefield**

Levy, Beth Ellen. "Frontier Figures: American Music and the Mythology of the American West, 1895–1945." Ph.D. diss., University of California, Berkeley, 2002. 448 p. Discusses *The Land of the Misty Water, Shanewis,* and *The Sunset Trail.*

Ziegel, Aaron Benjamin. "Making America Operatic: Six Composers' Attempts at an American Opera, 1910–1918." Ph.D. diss., University of Illinois, Urbana-Champaign, 2011. Discusses Cadman, Converse, Hadley, Herbert, Moore, and Nevin.

**Cage, John**

Fetterman, William. *John Cage's Theatre Pieces.* Amsterdam: Overseas Publishing Association, 1996. xviii, 282 p.

Kuhn, Laura. "John Cage's *Europeras 1 & 2:* The Musical Means of Revolutions." Ph.D. diss. University of California, Los Angeles, 1992.

Nicholls, David. *John Cage.* Urbana : University of Illinois Press, 2007. 144 p.

Silverman, Kenneth. *Begin Again: A Biography of John Cage.* New York: Alfred A. Knopf, 2010. 483 p.

**Carr, Benjamin**

Siek, Stephen. "Benjamin Carr's Theatrical Career." *AM* 11 (Summer 1993): 158–84.

Sprenkle, Charles Aaron. "The Life and Works of Benjamin Carr (1768–1831)." D.M.A. thesis. Peabody Conservatory of Music, 1970.

**Chadwick, George W.**

Yellin, Victor Fell. *Chadwick: Yankee Composer.* Washington, D.C.: Smithsonian Institution Press, 1990. xvi, 238 p.

### Coates, Albert

Jongh, Santie de. "From St Petersburg to the Cape: Three Autobiographical Texts by Albert Coates." *Fontes Artis Musicae* 54 (July 2007): 320–30.

### Cowell, Henry

Hicks, Michael. *Henry Cowell, Bohemian.* Urbana: University of Illinois Press, 2002. ix, 204 p.

Sachs, Joel. *Henry Cowell: A Man Made of Music.* New York, London: Oxford University Press, 2012. 624 p.

### Delius, Frederick

Klein, John W. "Delius as a Musical Dramatist." *MR* 22 (1961): 294–301.

Redwood, Christopher. *A Delius Companion.* London: J. Calder, 1976. 270 p.

____. "Delius in the Opera House." *MT* 125 (June 1984): 319–21.

### Dibdin, Charles

Fahrner, Robert. *The Theatre Career of Charles Dibdin the Elder (1745–1814).* New York: Lang, 1989. 241 p.

Sear, H. G. "Charles Dibdin: 1745–1814." *ML* 26 (1945): 61–65.

### Elgar, Edward

Anderson, Robert. *Elgar.* London: Dent, 1993. xv, 493 p.

Kennedy, Michael. *The Life of Elgar.* Cambridge; New York: Cambridge University Press, 2004. x, 228.

Kent Christopher. *Edward Elgar: A Guide to Research.* Garland Composer Resource Manuals. New York: Garland, 1993. xvii, 523 p.

Moore, Jerrold Northrop. *Edward Elgar: A Creative Life.* Oxford; New York: Oxford University Press, 1999. xiv, 841 p.

____. *Elgar: Child of Dreams.* London: Faber, 2004. viii, 212.

### Engel, Lehman

Engel, Lehman. *This Bright Day: An Autobiography.* New York: Macmillan, 1974. xiv, 366 p.

### Finney, Ross Lee

Borroff, Edith. *Three American Composers.* Lanham, Md.: University Press of America, 1986. 289 p.

Finney, Ross Lee. *Profile of a Lifetime: A Musical Autobiography.* New York: C. F. Peters, 1992. 247 p.

### Flagello, Nicolas

Simmons, Walter. *Voices in the Wilderness: Six American Neo-Romantic Composers.* Lanham, Md.: Scarecrow Press, 2004. ix, 419 p.

### Gershwin, George

Gilbert, Steven E. *The Music of Gershwin.* Composers of the Twentieth Century. New Haven: Yale University Press, 1995. xi, 255 p.

Hyland, William. *George Gershwin: A New Biography.* Westport, Conn.: Praeger, 2003. xv, 279 p.

Kimball, Robert, and Alfred Simon. *The Gershwins.* New York: Atheneum, 1973. xlii, 292 p.

Jablonski, Edward. *Gershwin.* New York: Doubleday, 1987. xv, 436 p.

Jablonski, Edward, and Lawrence D. Stewart. *The Gershwin Years.* Garden City, N.Y.: Doubleday, 1973. 416 p.

Peyser, Joan. *The Memory of All That: The Life of George Gershwin.* New York: Simon & Schuster, 1993. 319 p.

Pollack, Howard. *George Gershwin: His Life and Work.* Berkeley: University of California Press, 2006. xvii, 884 p.

Rimler, Walter. *George Gershwin: An Intimate Portrait.* Urbana: University of Illinois Press, 2009. 204 p.

Schwartz, Charles. *Gershwin: His Life and Music.* Indianapolis: Bobbs-Merrill, 1973. 428 p.

Starr, Larry. *George Gershwin.* New Haven: Yale University Press, 2011. xviii, 194 p.

### Giannini, Vittorio

Parris, Robert, "Vittorio Giannini and the Romantic Tradition," *Juilliard Review* 4, no. 2 (1957): 32–46.

Simmons, Walter. *Voices in the Wilderness: Six American Neo Romantic Composers.* Lanham, Md.: Scarecrow Press, 2004. ix, 419 p.

Simpson, Anne, and Karl Wonderly Flaster. "A Working Relationship: The Giannini-Flaster Collaboration." *American Music* 6 (Winter 1988): 375–408. Discusses the operas done jointly, including *Lucedia* and *The Scarlet Letter.*

### Glanville-Hicks, Peggy

Hayes, Deborah. *Peggy Glanville-Hicks: A Bio-Bibliography.* New York: Greenwood, 1990. x, 274 p.

Rogers, Victoria. *The Music of Peggy Glanville-Hicks.* Farnham, Eng.; Burlington, Vt.: Ashgate, 2009. xviii, 279 p.

### Glass, Philip

Jones, Robert T., ed. *Music by Philip Glass.* New York: Harper & Row, 1987. 222 p. Concentrates on *Einstein on the Beach, Satyagraha,* and *Akhnaten.*

Kostelanetz, Richard, ed. *Writings on Glass: Essays, Original Writings, Interviews, Criticism.* New York: Schirmer Books, 1997. viii, 368 p.

Maycock, Robert. *Glass: A Portrait.* London: Sanctuary Publishing, 2002. 191 p.

### Gruenberg, Louis

Nisbett, Robert. "Louis Gruenberg: A Forgotten Figure of American Music." *Current Musicology* 18 (1974): 90–95.

____. "Louis Gruenberg: His Life and Works." Ph.D. diss., Ohio State University, 1979.

### Gundry, Inglis

Gundry, Inglis. *Last Boy of the Family: A Musical Memoir.* London: Thames Publishing, 1998. vii, 156 p.

## Hadley, Henry Kimball

Canfield, John. "Henry Kimball Hadley: His Life and Works (1871–1937)." Ed.D., Florida State University. 1960. 385 p.

## Handel, George Frideric

Dean, Winton. *Handel's Operas, 1726–1741.* Woodbridge, Eng.; Rochester, N.Y.: Boydell Press, 2006. xx. 565 p.

Dean, Winton, and J. Merrill Knapp. *Handel's Operas 1704–1726.* Oxford and New York: Clarendon Press, 1987. xx, 751 p.

Harris, Ellen. *Handel and the Pastoral Tradition.* London and New York: Oxford University Press, 1980. xii. 292 p.

____. *The Librettos of Handel's Operas.* Vol. 1, ix–xl. New York: Garland, 1989.

## Hanson, Howard

Simmons, Walter. *Voices in the Wilderness: Six American Neo-Romantic Composers.* Lanham, Md.: Scarecrow Press, 2004. ix, 419 p.

## Henze, Hans Werner

*Hans Werner Henze: Ein Werkverzeichnis 1946–1996.* Mainz and New York: Schott, 1996. 436 p. In German, with parallel English and Italian translations.

Henze, Hans Werner. *Music and Politics: Collected Writings 1953–1981.* Translated by Peter Labanyi. London: Faber, 1982; Ithaca, N.Y.: Cornell University Press, 1982. 286 p.

## Herbert, Victor

Waters, Edward N. *Victor Herbert: A Life in Music.* New York: Macmillan, 1955. xvi, 653 p.

## Herrmann, Bernard

Smith, Steven C. *A Heart at Fire's Center: The Life and Music of Bernard Hermann.* Berkeley, Calif.: University of California Press, 1991. 415 p.

## Hill, Alfred

Thomson, John Mansfield. *A Distant Music: The Life and Times of Alfred Hill, 1870–1960.* Auckland and New York: Oxford University Press, 1980. vii, 239 p.

## Holst, Gustav

Dickinson, A. E. F. *Holst's Music: A Guide.* Edited by Alan Gibbs. London: Thames, 1995. xv, 219 p.

Mitchell, Jon C. *A Comprehensive Biography of Composer Gustav Holst, with Correspondence and Diary Excerpts, including His American Years.* Lewiston, N.Y. : E. Mellen Press, 2001. vii, 698 p.

## Johnson, Tom

Johnson, Tom. "At Home Abroad." *ON* 59 (Oct. 1994): 32–35.

## Joplin, Scott

Argyle, Ray. *Scott Joplin and the Age of Ragtime.* Jefferson, N.C. : McFarland, 2009. x, 221 p.

Haskins, James, and Kathleen Benson. *Scott Joplin.* Garden City, N.Y.: Doubleday, 1978. xiii, 248 p.

## Kalmanoff, Martin

Renard, Ellis. "The Operas of Martin Kalmanoff." *OJ* 7, no. 3 (1974): 14–22.

## Kern, Jerome

Banfield, Stephen. *Jerome Kern.* Foreword by Geoffrey Block. New Haven: Yale University Press, 2006. xii, 375 p.

Bordman, Gerald. *Jerome Kern: His Life and Music.* New York: Oxford University Press, 1980. viii, 438 p.

## Krenek, Ernst

Bailey, O. J. "The Influence of Ernst Krenek on the Musical Culture of the Twin Cities." Ph.D. diss., University of Minnesota, 1980.

Bowles, Garrett H. *Ernst Krenek: A Bio-Bibliography.* New York: Greenwood, 1989. xiv, 428 p.

## Lampe, John Frederick

Martin, Dennis. *The Operas and Operatic Style of John Frederick Lampe.* Detroit: Information Coordinators, 1985. xx, 190 p.

## Loesser, Frank

Loesser, Susan. *A Most Remarkable Fella: Frank Loesser and the Guys and Dolls in His Life: A Portrait by His Daughter.* New York: D. I. Fine, 1993. xvi, 304 p.

Riis, Thomas Laurence. *Frank Loesser.* New Haven: Yale University Press, 2008. xix, 332 p.

## MacDowell, Edward

Beeson, Jack. "Da Ponte, MacDowell, Moore, and Lang: Four Biographical Essays." *Columbia Magazine* (2000): www.columbia.edu/cu/alumni/Magazine/Summer2000/Beeson.html.

Levy, Alan Howard. *Edward MacDowell, an American Master.* Lanham, Md.: Scarecrow Press, 1998. xii, 269 p.

## Menotti, Gian Carlo

Hixon, Donald L. *Gian Carlo Menotti: A Bio-Bibliography.* Westport, Conn.: Greenwood Press, 2000. xii, 339.

Wlaschin, Ken. *Gian Carlo Menotti on Screen: Opera, Dance, and Choral Works on Film, Television, and Video.* Jefferson, N.C. : McFarland, 1999. vi, 186 p.

## Moore, Douglas

Beeson, Jack. "Da Ponte, MacDowell, Moore, and Lang: Four Biographical Essays." *Columbia Magazine* (2000): www.columbia.edu/cu/alumni/Magazine/Summer2000/Beeson.html.

McBride, Jerry L. *Douglas Moore: A Bio-Bibliography.* Middleton, Wisc.: A-R Editions, 2011. 658 p.

## Moore, Mary Carr

Smith, Catherine Parsons. *Mary Carr Moore, American Composer.* Ann Arbor: University of Michigan Press, 1987. xi, 286 p.

**Musgrave, Thea**

Hixon, Donald L. *Thea Musgrave: A Bio-Bibliography.* Westport, Conn.: Greenwood Press, 1984. x, 187 p.

**Parker, Horatio**

Kearns, William K. *Horatio Parker, 1863–1919: His Life, Music, and Ideas.* Metuchen, N.J.: Scarecrow Press, 1990. xvii, 356 p.

**Persichetti, Vincent**

Patterson, Donald L., and Janet L. Patterson. *Vincent Persichetti: A Bio-Bibliography.* New York: Greenwood, 1988. xiv, 336 p.

**Purcell, Henry**

Burden, Michael, ed. *Henry Purcell's Operas: The Complete Texts.* Oxford, New York: Oxford University Press, 2000. xvi, 528 p.

_____. *The Purcell Companion.* London: Faber and Faber, 1994. x, 504 p.

_____. *Purcell Remembered.* London: Faber and Faber, 1995. xxv, 188 p.

Price, Curtis Alexander. *Henry Purcell and the London Stage.* Cambridge and New York: Cambridge University Press, 1984. xiv, 380 p.

Zimmermann, Franklin B. *Henry Purcell 1659–1695: His Life and Times.* London and New York: Macmillan, 1967. xvii, 429 p. 2nd rev. ed. Philadelphia: University of Pennsylvania Press, 1983. xxxvi, 473 p.

_____. *Henry Purcell: A Guide to Research.* New York: Garland, 1989. xi, 333 p.

**Ridout, Alan**

Scott, Robert, ed. *Alan Ridout: The Complete Catalogue.* Ampleforth, Eng.: Emerson Edition, 1997. 61 p.

**Rorem, Ned**

McDonald, Arlys L. *Ned Rorem: A Bio-Bibliography.* New York: Greenwood Press, 1989. 284 p.

O'Connor, Patrick. "Imagination Snared." *ON* 53 (Oct. 1988): 24–26, 70.

**Schafer, R. Murray**

Adams, Stephen. *R. Murray Schafer.* Canadian Composers 4. Toronto: University of Toronto Press, 1983. x, 240 p.

**Schuman, William**

Polisi, Joseph. *American Muse: The Life and Times of William Schuman.* New York: Amadeus Press, 2008. xvii, 595 p.

**Sessions, Roger**

Olmstead, Andrea. *Roger Sessions and His Music.* Ann Arbor: UMI Research Press, 1985. xvii, 218 p.

_____. *Roger Sessions: A Biography.* New York: Routledge, 2008. xvii, 441 p.

Prausnitz, Frederik. *Roger Sessions: How a "Difficult" Composer Got That Way.* Oxford, New York: Oxford University Press, 2002. xi, 348 p.

**Silverman, Stanley**

Hillyer, Dirk M. "Constructing a Model of Consciousness: The Music Theatre of Richard Foreman and Stanley Silverman." Ph.D. dissertation, Tufts University, 1995. 340 p.

**Sitsky, Larry**

Wood, Alison. "Operatic Narratives: Textual Transformations in Gwen Harwood's and Larry Sitsky's *Golem* and *Lenz.*" *Journal of the Association for the Study of Australian Literature* 5 (2006): 178–90.

**Smyth, Ethel**

Smyth, Ethel. *Memoirs.* Abridged and introduced by Ronald Crichton. New York: Viking, 1987. 392 p.

**Somers, Harry**

Cherney, Brian. *Harry Somers.* Toronto and Buffalo: University of Toronto Press, 1975. xii, 185 p.

**Sondheim, Stephen**

Banfield, Stephen. *Sondheim's Broadway Musicals.* Ann Arbor: University of Michigan Press, 1993. xvi, 453 p.

Gottfried, Martin. *Sondheim.* New York: H. N. Abrams, 2000. 207 p. Revised and updated from first version (1993).

Secrest, Meryle. *Stephen Sondheim: A Life.* New York: Knopf, 1998. ix, 461 p.

**Stanford, Charles**

Dibble, Jeremy. *Charles Villiers Stanford: Man and Musician.* Oxford; New York: Oxford University Press, 2002. xvi, 535 p.

Hauger, George. "Stanford's Early Operas." *Opera* 35 (1984): 724–29.

Rodmell, Paul. *Charles Villiers Stanford.* Aldershot: Ashgate, 2002. xx, 495 p.

**Still, William Grant**

Cutsforth-Huber, Bonnie. "Pride and Perseverance: The Operas of William Grant Still." *OJ* 36 (June 2003): 3–23.

Smith, Catherine Parsons. *William Grant Still.* Urbana: University of Illinois Press, 2008. xi, 116 p. Chapter on *Troubled Island.*

_____. *William Grant Still: A Study in Contradictions.* Berkeley, Calif.: University of California Press, 2000. xvi, 368 p.

**Storace, Stephen**

Girdham, Jane Catherine. *English Opera in Late Eighteenth-Century London: Stephen Storace at Drury* Lane. New York: Clarendon Press, 1997. xiv, 272 p.

Graves, Richard. "The Comic Operas of Stephen Storace." *MT* 95 (Oct. 1954): 530–32.

## Sullivan, Arthur S.

Ainger, Michael. *Gilbert and Sullivan: A Dual Biography.* Oxford, New York: Oxford University Press, 2002. xv, 504 p.

Allen, Reginald, ed. *The First Night Gilbert and Sullivan: Containing the Complete Librettos of the Fourteen Operas, Exactly as Presented at Their Premiere Performances; Together with Facsims. of the Firstnight Programmes.* New York, Heritage Press, 1958. 465 p. + 27 facsimiles. Revised centennial edition. London: Chappell, 1975 (without facsimiles). 465 p.

Bradley, Ian C. *Oh Joy! Oh Rapture! The Enduring Phenomenon of Gilbert and Sullivan.* Oxford; New York: Oxford University Press, 2005. xii, 220 p.

Dillard, Philip H. *Sir Arthur Sullivan. A Resource Book.* Lanham, Maryland, and London: Scarecrow Press, 1996. xiii, 428 p.

Eden, David. *Gilbert and Sullivan: The Creative Conflict.* Rutherford, N.J.: Fairleigh Dickinson University Press, 1986. 224 p.

Eden, David, and Meinhard Saremba, eds. *The Cambridge Companion to Gilbert and Sullivan.* Cambridge: Cambridge University Press, 2009. xiv, 274 p.

Jacobs, Arthur. *Arthur Sullivan: A Victorian Musician.* 2nd ed. Aldershot, Eng.: Scolar Press, 1992. xv, 494 p.

Oost, Regina. *Gilbert and Sullivan: Class and the Savoy Tradition, 1875–1896.* Farnham, Eng., Burlington, Vt.: Ashgate, 2009, xii. 168 p.

Smith, Geoffrey. *The Savoy Operas. A New Guide to Gilbert and Sullivan.* London: Robert Hale, 1983. 236 p.

Williams, Carolyn. *Gilbert and Sullivan: Gender, Genre, Parody.* New York: Columbia University Press, 2011.

## Thomson, Virgil

Meckna, Michael. *Virgil Thomson: A Bio-Bibliography.* New York: Greenwood Press, 1986. xiv, 203 p.

Tommasini, Anthony. *Virgil Thomson: Composer on the Aisle.* New York: W. W. Norton, 1997. 605 p.

Wittke, Paul, ed. *Virgil Thomson: Vignettes of His Life and Times.* [New York]: Virgil Thomson Foundation, 1996. v, 106 p.

## Tippett, Michael

Clarke, David. *The Music and Thought of Michael Tippett: Modern Times and Metaphysics.* Cambridge; New York: Cambridge University Press, 2001. xi, 343 p.

_____. *Tippett Studies.* Cambridge : Cambridge University Press, 1999. xv, 232 p.

John, Nicholas, ed. *The Operas of Michael Tippett.* English National Opera Guide, vol. 29. London: J. Calder; New York: Riverrun Press, 1985. 144 p. Includes *The Midsummer Marriage, King Priam, The Knot Garden,* and *The Ice Break.*

Kemp, Ian. *Tippett: The Composer and His Music.* London: Eulenburg; New York: Da Capo, 1984. xiii, 516 p.

Scheppach, Margaret. *Dramatic Parallels in the Operas of Michael Tippett.* Lewiston, N.Y.: Edwin Mellen Press, 1990. viii, 184 p.

Whittall, Arnold. *The Music of Britten and Tippett. Studies in Themes and Techniques.* 2nd ed. Cambridge and New York: Cambridge University Press, 1990. vii, 325 p.

## Vir, Param

Hughes, Bernard. "Magical Theatres: The Music of Param Vir." *Tempo* 58 (Apr. 2004): 2–13.

## Walton, William

Burton, Humphrey. *William Walton: The Romantic Loner: A Centenary Portrait Album.* Oxford: Oxford University Press, 2002. viii, 182 p.

Smith, Carolyn J. *William Walton: A Bio-Bibliography.* New York: Greenwood Press, 1988. x, 246 p.

## Ward, Robert

Benson, Shannon Laura. "The Twentieth-Century Operas of Robert Ward." Ph.D. diss., University of Western Ontario (Canada), 2010. 609 p.

## Weber, Carl Maria von

Henderson, Donald G., and Alice H. Henderson. *Carl Maria von Weber: A Guide to Research.* New York. Garland, 1990. xxii, 385 p.

Jones, Gaynor Gray. "Backgrounds and Themes in the Operas of Carl Maria von Weber." Ph.D. diss., Cornell University, 1972.

Kirby, Percival. "Weber's Operas in London, 1824–6," *MQ* 32 (1946): 333–53.

Warrack, John. *Carl Maria von Weber.* 2nd ed. Cambridge: Cambridge University Press, 1976. 411 p.

## Weill, Kurt

Drew, David. *Kurt Weill—A Handbook.* London and Boston: Faber and Faber, 1987. 480 p.

Hinton, Stephen. *Weill's Musical Theater: Stages of Reform.* Berkeley: University of California Press, 2012. xvi, 569 p.

Hirsch, Foster. *Kurt Weill on Stage: From Berlin to Broadway.* New York: Alfred A. Knopf, 2002. 403 p.

Kowalke, Kim H., ed. *A New Orpheus. Essays on Kurt Weill.* New Haven: Yale University Press, 1986. xvi, 374 p.

Kowalke, Kim H., and Horst Edler, eds. *A Stranger Here Myself: Kurt Weill-Studien.* Wissenschaftlichen Abhandlungen, vol. 8. Hildesheim and New York: Georg Olms, 1993. 384 p. Preface and abstracts in English and German.

Mercado, Mario R., comp. and ed. *Kurt Weill: A Guide to His Works.* 2nd ed. New York: Kurt Weill Foundation for Music, 1994. x, 79 p.

Sanders, Ronald. *The Days Grow Short.* New York: Holt, Rinehart, and Winston, 1980. 469 p.

## Weir, Judith

Morgan, T. "Judith Weir." In *New Music 88,* edited by Michael Finnissy et al. Oxford, New York: Oxford University Press, 1988, pp. 22–50.

## Wilder, Alec

Stone, Desmond. *Alec Wilder in Spite of Himself.* New York: Oxford University Press, 1996. x, 244 p.

## Willan, Healey

Clarke, F. R. C. *Healey Willan: Life and Music.* Toronto: University of Toronto Press, 1983. xii, 300 p.

## Wood, Charles

Copley, I[an] A[lfred]. *The Music of Charles Wood.* London: Thomas, 1978. 215 p.

## LIBRETTISTS, LYRICISTS

### General

Hischak, Thomas S. *Boy Loses Girl: Broadway's Librettists.* Lanham, Md.: Scarecrow Press, 2002. 277 p.

_____. *Word Crazy: Broadway Lyricists from Cohan to Sondheim.* New York: Praeger, 1991. xvii, 241 p.

### Allan, Lewis [Abel Meeropol]

Baker, Nancy Kovaleff. "Abel Meeropol (a.k.a. Lewis Allan): Political Commentator and Social Conscience." *AM* 20 (Spring 2002): 25–79.

### Auden, W. H.

Marx, Robert. "Auden in Opera: The Libretto as Poetic Style." *ON* 62 (Jan. 17, 1998): 8–11.

Mendelson, Edward, ed. *W. H. Auden and Chester Kallman: Libretti and Other Dramatic Writings.* Princeton, N.J.: Princeton University Press, 1993. xxxvi, 758 p.

### Fitzball, Edward

Clifton, Larry Stephen. *The Terrible Fitzball: The Melodramatist of the Macabre.* Bowling Green, Ohio: Bowling Green State University Popular Press, 1993. 191 p.

### Foreman, Richard

Hillyer, Dirk M. "Constructing a Model of Consciousness: The Music Theatre of Richard Foreman and Stanley Silverman." Ph.D. diss., Tufts University, 1995. 340 p.

### Gershwin, Ira

Furia, Philip. *Ira Gershwin: The Art of the Lyricist.* New York: Oxford University Press, 1996. vii, 278 p.

Kimball, Robert, and Alfred Simon. *The Gershwins.* New York: Atheneum, 1973. xlii, 292 p.

### Gilbert, William S.

Ainger, Michael. *Gilbert and Sullivan: A Dual Biography.* Oxford; New York: Oxford University Press, 2002. xv, 504 p.

Bradley, Ian C. *Oh Joy! Oh Rapture! The Enduring Phenomenon of Gilbert and Sullivan.* Oxford; New York: Oxford University Press, 2005. xii, 220 p.

Eden, David, and Meinhard Saremba, eds. *The Cambridge Companion to Gilbert and Sullivan.* Cambridge: Cambridge University Press, 2009. xiv, 274 p.

Longyear, Katherine. "Henry F. Gilbert. His Life and Works." Ph.D. diss., University of Rochester, 1968.

Oost, Regina. *Gilbert and Sullivan: Class and the Savoy Tradition, 1875–1896.* Farnham, Eng., Burlington, Vt.: Ashgate. 2009, xii, 168 p.

Smith, Geoffrey. *The Savoy Operas. A New Guide to Gilbert and Sullivan.* London: Robert Hale, 1983. 236 p.

Stedman, Jane W. *Gilbert before Sullivan. Six Comic Plays by W. S. Gilbert.* Chicago: University of Chicago Press, 1967. xii, 270 p. With analyses.

_____. *W. S. Gilbert. A Classic Victorian and His Theatre.* New York: Oxford University Press, 1996. xviii, 374 p.

Williams, Carolyn. *Gilbert and Sullivan: Gender, Genre, Parody.* New York: Columbia University Press, 2011.

### Hammerstein II, Oscar

Citron, Stephen: *The Wordsmiths: Oscar Hammerstein 2nd and Alan Jay Lerner.* New York: Oxford University Press, 1995. xii, 446 p.

Hammerstein, Oscar Andrew. *The Hammersteins: A Musical Theatre Family.* New York: Black Dog & Leventhal, 2010. 236 p.

### Harwood, Gwen

Trigg, Stephanie. *Gwen Harwood.* Melbourne and New York: Oxford University Press, 1994. viii, 120 p.

Wood, Alison. "Operatic Narratives: Textual Transformations in Gwen Harwood's and Larry Sitsky's *Golem* and *Lenz*." *Journal of the Association for the Study of Australian Literature* 5 (2006): 178–90.

### Kallman, Chester

Mendelson, Edward, ed. *W. H. Auden and Chester Kallman: Libretti and Other Dramatic Writings.* Princeton, N.J.: Princeton University Press, 1993. xxxvi, 758 p.

### Lerner, Alan Jay

Citron, Stephen. *The Wordsmiths: Oscar Hammerstein 2nd and Alan Jay Lerner.* New York: Oxford University Press, 1995. xii, 446 p.

### Malouf, David

Patrick, Annie. "David Malouf the Librettist." In *Provisional Maps: Critical Essays on David Malouf*, edited by Amanda Nettlebeck, 133–48. Perth, Austral.: University of Western Australia, 1994.

### Piper, Myfanwy

Spalding, Frances. *John Piper, Myfanwy Piper: Lives in Art.* Oxford, New York: Oxford University Press, 2009. xxvi, 598 p.

### Smith, Harry Bache

Franceschina, John. *Harry B. Smith: A Biography.* New York, London: Routledge, 2003. 224 p.

# Index of Characters

Each entry includes the character's name, the vocal range (where known), the short title of the opera(s) in which the character appears, and the last name of the composer(s) (or date of premiere/composition, if anonymous). Characters are listed under the names under which they are best known, e.g., "Billy Budd" under "Billy," "Anne Trulove" under "Anne," but "Trulove" [her father] under "Trulove." Titles usually follow names, e.g., "Alfred, King"; "Valmont, Vicomte de." Covers proper names, specific titles, and personifications, e.g., "Anne," "Caliph of Bagdad," "Beauty"; but not generic characters, e.g., "the king"; a = alto; b = bass; bar = baritone; ct = countertenor; dr = dancer; m = mezzo; s = soprano; sp = speaking; sr = singer; st = silent; t = tenor; tr = treble

Aaron, (t) **Victory at Masada** (Kalmanoff)

Aaron Blunder, (b) **Toy Shop** (Barab)

Aaron James, **Different Fields** (Reid)

Ab, **Astronaut's Tale** (Fussell)

Abbess Madre Maria del Pilar, **Bridge of San Luis Rey** (Kimper)

Abbie Cabot, (s) **Desire under the Elms** (Thomas)

Abbot of Drimock, **Abbot of Drimock** (Musgrave)

Abdala, **Thalaba** (Rodwell)

Abdallah, **Il Bondocani** (Attwood/Moorehead); **Caliph of Bagdad** (Musgrave); **The Seraglio** (Dibdin)

Abdul, (bar) **Last Savage** (Menotti)

Abdullah, **Cady of Bagdad** (Linley Jr.); **Holy Blood** (Copeland); **Wizards of Balizar** (Lockwood)

Abel, Mr., **Green Mansions** (Gruenberg)

Abel Conn, **Idols' Eye** (Herbert)

Abel Gudgeon, **Foxy Quiller** (De Koven)

Abelard, Peter, **Abelard and Heloise** (Gaughan); (t) **Abelard and Heloise** (Ward); **Eloise and Abelard** (Victory); bar) **Heloise and Abelard** (Paulus); **Heloise and Abelard** (Tahourdin); **Héloïse and Abelard** (Wilson)

Abigail, **Abigail and the Bushranger** (Beath); (s) **Lizzie Borden** (Beeson); (a) **Puritania** (Kelley)

Abigail Adams, (s) **Abigail Adams** (Owen)

Abigail Williams, (s) **The Crucible** (Ward)

Abimelach Jones, (bar) **Sack of Calabasas** (Fletcher)

Abou Hassan, **Abou Hassan** (Cooke)

Abraham, **Bontshe the Silent** (Sirota); (bar) **Eternal Road** (Weill); **Maiden Tower** (Chen); **Sarah** (Laderman)

Abraham Bentley, (b) **The Rope** (Mennini)

Absalom Kumalo, (sp) **Lost in the Stars** (Weill)

Abudah, **Almena** (Arne/Battishill)

Acacis, **Indian Queen** (H. Purcell)

Acantha, **The Echo** (Patterson)

Accaro, King, **Sarrona** (Howland)

Achilles, **Achilles** (1733); **Achilles Heel** (Bohmler); **Achilles in Petticoats** (Arne); (t) **Helen in Egypt** (Elkus); **Helen Retires** (Antheil); (b) **Inferno of Dante** (Soluri); (t) **King Priam** (Tippett)

Achior, (t) **Judith** (Chadwick); **Judith** (Goossens)

Achlamah, Princess, (s) **The Tower** (Levy)

Achmet, **Sadak and Kalasrade** (Packer)

Acis, **Acis and Galatea** (Eccles); (t) **Acis and Galatea** (Handel)

Acquanetta, (m) **Acquanetta** (Gordon)

Action, **Britannia triumphans** (Lawes)

Ada Lewin, (m) **Karla** (Lehrman)

Adah, **Naughty Marietta** (Herbert)

Adam, **Aceldama** (Sleeper); **Amorous Judge** (Gross); (t) **Eve's Odds** (Trinkley); **Garden Party** (Pinkham); **Hotel Eden** (Mollicone); . . . **inasmuch** (Eaton); **Lilith** (Davis); **Lilith** (Drattell); **Paradise Lost** (Penderecki); (t) **So How Does Your Garden** (Russell)

Adam Brant, (bar) **Mourning Becomes Electra** (Levy)

Adam de Francton, **Caernarvon Castle** (Attwood)

Adams, John, (t) **Abigail Adams** (Owen); (t) **Mother of Us All** (Thomson)

Adams, John Quincy, (bar) **Abigail Adams** (Owen); **Amistad** (Ames); (b) **Amistad** (Davis)

Adcock, Alice, **Alice** (Whitehead)

Addie Bunren, **As I Lay Dying** (McKay)

Adela, **English Fleet** (Braham); **Harold** (Cowen); (s) **Haunted Tower** (Storace)

Adelaide, **Albert and Adelaide** (Attwood, Steibelt); **The Vintagers** (Bishop)

Adèle, (s) **Jane Eyre** (Berkeley)

Adeline, **Battle of Hexham** (Arnold)

Adine, **Faustus** (Bishop)

Admetus, **Alceste** (Handel); **Alcestiad** (Talma); **Alkestis** (Boughton)

Admiral Culpepper, **The Boardinghouse** (Horn)

Admiral of Rhodes, **Siege of Rhodes** (Lawes et al.)

Adolphe, **Daughter of St. Mark** (Balfe)

Adolph Savigny, **Love's Triumph** (Wallace)

Adolphus, **Leap Year** (Sedgwick); **Passion, Poison** (Hagemann)

Adolphus Bastable, (t) **Passion, Poison** (Taub)

Adonis, (t) **Gardens of Adonis** (Weisgall); **Venus** (Van Rhijn); **Venus and Adonis** (Blow); (s) **Venus and Adonis** (Pepusch)

Adrian, **Ida** (Leslie); (b-bar/bar) **Poison** (Hart)

Adrian Hodgepodge, (bar) **Bad Boys** (Meyerowitz)

Adriana, (s) **The Magician** (Hoddinott)

Aeacus (b-bar), **Council of the Dead** (Sternau)

Aegidius, **Godfather Death** (Meyerowitz)

Aegisthus, **Agamemnon** (Brian); (t) **Agamemnon** (Hamilton); (t) **Agamemnon** (Simpson); (ct) **Agamemnon** (Werder); **Clytemnestra** (Wishart)

Aegon, **Damon and Phillida** (1729); **Damon and Phillida** (Dibdin); **Love in a Riddle** (1792)

Aelfrida, (s) **King's Henchmen** (Taylor)

Aeneas (Eneas), **Aeneas and Dido** (Rolfe); **After Dido** (arr. Mitchell); **Death of Dido** (Pepusch); **Dido** (Hook); **Dido** (Storace); **Dido and Aeneas** (Arne); **Dido and Aeneas** (Beveridge); **Dido and Aeneas** (Hook); (t) **Dido and Aeneas** (Purcell); (t) **Golden Apples** (Trinkley)

Aeneas, Mr., (bar) **Happy Hypocrite** (Masland)

Aengus, **Ever Young** (Boughton)

Aeolia, **Mountain Sylph** (Barnett)

Aesop, **Aesop the Fabulist** (Kalmanoff); **Blanche de Nevers** (Balfe); **Lethe** (Arne); **Quantum Mechanic** (Bilotta)

Aethelred, (t) **Aethelred** (Wilson)

Aethelwold, (t) **King's Henchmen** (Taylor)

Aethon, (bar) **Nausicaa** (Glanville-Hicks)

Affenkoff, Baron von, **Golden Butterfly** (De Koven)

African Rain Queen, **Bee Story** (Hays)

Agafia, (a) **Anna Karenina** (Carlson)

Agamemnon, **Agamemnon** (Brian); (b) **Agamemnon** (Hamilton); **Agamemnon** (Morris); (bar) **Agamemnon** (Simpson); (b) **Agamemnon** (Werder); **Cassandra** (McAndrew); **Clytemnestra** (Wishart); **Cry of Clytaemnestra** (Eaton); (bar) **Myth of Er** (Sternau)

Agatha Lawson, **Crazy to Kill** (Beckwith)

Agave, **The Bacchae** (Antoniou); (m) **The Bassarids** (Henze); **Revelation** (Partch)

Agebda Akawasir, Mrs., (s) **Most Important Man** (Menotti)

Agenor, **Royal Shepherd** (Rush)

Agneh, (m) **Julian** (Saminsky)

Agnes, (m) **Caritas** (Saxon); (s) **Free Knights** (Mazzinghi); **Growing Castle** (Williamson); **Joan of Arc** (Balfe); (s) **School for Wives** (Liebermann); **Second Thought Is Best** (Bates)

Agnes, Donna, **Don John of Austria** (Nathan)

Agnes, Lady, (s) **Raymond and Agnes** (Loder)

Agnes, Queen, **Sleeping Queen** (Balfe)

Agnes Sorel, **Agnes Sorel** (A'Beckett)

Agravain, (bar) **Gawain** (Birtwistle)

Agrippina, **Hell's Angels** (Osborne)

Aguabone, Dr., **Chaos** (Gordon)

Ah Chin Honk, (t) **Sack of Calabasas** (Fletcher)

Ahab, Captain, **Call Me Ishmael** (Goldschneider); **Moby Dick** (Heggie); **Moby Dick** (Westergaard)

Ahab, King, **Naboth's Vineyard** (Goehr)

Ahasuerus, (t) **Esther** (Harvey); (b-bar) **Esther** (Meyerowitz)

Ahmed, **Safié** (Hadley)

Ahmet, **Our Giraffe** (Hays)

Ahrat, (t) **S.** (Perera)

Aileen, **Wuornos** (Lucero)

Ainsworth, Lord, **Maid of the Mill** (Arnold)

Aisha, **Angels' Voices** (Ain)

Ajax, **Cassandra** (McAndrew); (b) **Transatlantic** (Antheil)

Akashi, (s) **Tale of Genji** (Miki)

Akhnaten, (ct) **Akhnaten** (Glass)

Akira, **Miyako** (Rodgers)

Akhmatova, Anna, **Guest from the Future** (Marvin)

Al, **City Workers** (Weisensel)

Aladdin, **Aladdin** (Bishop), **Aladdin** (Condell-Ware); **Ring, Lamp, Thing** (Gough)

Alain, (t) **The Door** (Mopper)

Alain de Rouzie, **Merrymount** (Smith)

Alan, (bar) **Yan Tan Tethera** (Birtwistle)

Alan-a-Dale, (a) **Robin Hood** (De Koven); **Robin Hood** (Shields); **Robin Hood** (Tippett)

Alasman, **Safié** (Hadley)

Alastair Frontenac, (t) **The Opening** (Wilder)

Alaster, **Highland Fair** (1731)

Alba, (s) **La Curandera** (Rodríguez)

Albanius, **Albion and Albanius** (Grabu)

Alberquerque, Duchess d', **Ruy Blas** (Glover)

Albert, **Albert and Adelaide** (Attwood, Steibelt); (bar) **Fade** (Weisman); **Letty, the Basket-Maker** (Balfe); **Maid of Saxony** (Horn); **Night Dancers** (Loder); (t) **The Ruby** (Dello Joio); **Who Pays the Reckoning?** (Arnold)

Albert Goody, **Brief Encounter** (Previn)

Albert Herring, (t) **Albert Herring** (Britten)

Albertine, (b) **W. of Babylon** (Wuorinen)

Alberto, (t) **La Cubana** (Henze); (t) **La Curandera** (Rodríguez); (bar) **Fortunato** (Gideon)

Alberto, Count, **Heir of Vironi** (Bishop)

Albina, (s) **Elfrida** (Arne)

Albion, **Albion and Albanius** (Grabu)

Alceste, **Alceste** (Handel)

Alcestis, **The Alcestiad** (Talma); **Alcestis** (Marshall-Hall)

Alcibiades, **Timon of Athens** (Oliver)

Alcina, (s) **Cracked Orlando**

Alcino, (t) **Prima Donna** (Benjamin)

Alcinous, King, (b) **Castaway** (Berkeley)

Alcmena, **Jupiter and Alcmena** (Dibdin)

Alcmene, **Amphitryon 4** (Blumenfeld)

Alcott, Abigail May, (m) **On the Edges of Calm** (Meier)

Alcott, Bronson, **On the Edges of Calm** (Meier)

Alcott, Louisa May (s) **On the Edges of Calm** (Meier)

Alden, John, **Courtship of Miles Standish** (Ewart)

Aldiborontiphoscophornia, **Chrononhotonthologos** (Carey)

Al Donfonso, (bar) **Abduction of Figaro** (Schickele)

Aldrin, Buzz, (bar) **Eagle Has Landed** (Ritchie); (bar) **Man on the Moon** (Dove)

Aldrin, Joan, (s) **Man on the Moon** (Dove)

Alec, **Tess of the D'Urbervilles** (Harris)

Alec Harvey, **Brief Encounter** (Previn)

Alecto, **Gasconado the Great** (1759)

Alethe, **The Earthquake** (Rodwell)

Alex, **Ecstatic Journey** (Rodwin)

Alexander, King, **Royal Shepherd** (Rush)

Alexander, Sir, (t/bar) **Simple Decision** (Busch)

Alexander VI, Pope, **Hell's Angels** (Osborne)

Alexander Marshall, **Joe Hill** (Bush)

Alexander the Great, **Court of Alexander** (Fisher); **Macheath in the Shades** (1735); **Rival Queens** (Finger)

Ambrose, **Apollonia's Circus** (Eric Stokes)

Ambrose Everett, (tr) **Julius Caesar Jones** (Williamson)

Amelia, **Amelia** (Dibdin et al.); (m) **Amelia** (Hagen); **Amelia** (Lampe); (s) **Amelia** (Piccinni et al.); **Amelia Goes to the Ball** (Menotti); **Felix** (Lutz); **Perfect Plan** (Barab); **The Reconciliation** (1790)

Amélie, **Wide Sargasso Sea** (Howard)

Amenophis, **Azael** (Laurent)

America, (m) **The Mistake** (Sheffer)

Americana, **Americana** (Bruce); **The Blockheads** (1782)

Amie, **Jovial Crew** (1731)

Amiel, **Légende Provençale** (Moore)

Amilie, **Amilie** (Rooke)

Aminta, **Black Crook** (Operti)

Amintas, **Amintas** (1769); **The Blockheads** (1782); **Royal Shepherd** (Rush)

Amintor, **Daphne and Amintor** (Arnold)

Amira, **East and West** (McQueen)

Amiranthus, **Cupid's Revenge** (Hook)

Aminta, **The Blockheads** (1782);

Amory, (b-bar) **Miracle of Flanders** (Gruenberg)

Amos, (t) **Golden Lion** (Kechley)

Amparo, **Rosina** (Titus)

Amphitryon, **Amphitryon 4** (Blumenfeld); **Jupiter and Alcmena** (Dibdin)

Amphitrite, **Cinthia and Endimion** (D. Purcell)

Amurath, King (Caliph), **Generous Free-Mason** (1730); **Sadak and Kalasrade** (Packer)

Amy, (s) **Don't We All?** (Phillips); **Song of Insanity** (Seletsky)

Amy Everton, (s) **Shanewis** (Cadman)

Amy March, (s) **Little Women** (Adamo)

Amy Robsart, (s) **Amy Robsart** (de Lara)

Amyas Leigh, **Westward Ho!** (Miles)

Amyntas, **Love in a Riddle** (1729); **Phoebe** (Greene)

Analisa, (s) **Gift of Song** (Caldwell)

Ananda, (m) **Snatched by the Gods** (Vir); (t) **Wagner Dream** (Harvey)

Ananias, (bar) **Burning Fiery Furnace** (Britten)

Anastasia Kavankina, **Gentleman Friend** (Morgulas)

Anatol, (t) **Vanessa** (Barber)

Anaya, Señora, (m) **The Sacrifice** (Converse)

Ancient Mariner, (s/t) **Rime of the Ancient Mariner** (Bedford); **Rime of the Ancient Mariner** (Thoms)

Anderson, Chief, (b-bar) **Hoosier Tale** (Kaufmann)

Anderson, Marian, **Let Freedom Sing** (Adolphe)

Andre (André), **Rat Land** (Beeferman); (bar) **The Specialist** (Rodgers)

Andrea, **Daughter of St. Mark** (Balfe)

Andreas de Caravajal, **The Alcaid** (Nathan)

Andrei, **A Calamity** (Morgulas); (bar) **Three Sisters** (Pasatieri)

Andreozzi, **Sicilian Bride** (Balfe)

Andrew, **Death in the Family** (Mayer); (bar) **Elsewhereless** (Sharman); (t) **Kumana** (Kanitz); **Love and Money** (Arnold)

Andrew Aguecheek, Sir, (t) **Twelfth Night** (Amram)

Andrew List, (t) **Tell-Tale Heart** (Adolphe)

Andrew Martin, Dr. (b) **The Picnic** (Cumming)

Androcles, **Androcles and the Lion** (Hagemann); **Lion and Androcles** (Eaton)

Andy, (b) **Smoky Mountain** (Hunkins); **Travellers** (Horne)

Andy Warhol, **Jackie O** (Daugherty)

Angela, **The Commission** (Cowell)

Angela, Lady, (m) **Patience** (Sullivan)

Angelica, (s) **Cracked Orlando** (Dawe); **Fair Americans** (Carter); **The Shipwreck** (Arnold)

Angelina, **Edwin and Angelina** (Pelissier); **Robin Hood** (Shields)

Angeline, **Midnight Angel** (Carlson)

Angel More, (s) **Mother of Us All** (Thomson)

Angelo, (t) **The Magician** (Hoddinott)

Angel of Bright Future, (s) **Confidence Man** (Rochberg)

Angel of Death, **The Angelus** (Naylor); (b) **Eternal Road** (Weill)

Angel Shunard, **Rent** (Larson)

Anippe, (m) **Tamburlaine** (Hamilton)

Anita, **West Side Story** (Bernstein)

Ann, **Astronaut's Tale** (Fussell); **Fisher King** (Lowenstein); **Inquest of Love** (Harvey); **Maid of Cefn Ydfa** (Parry); (s) **Masque of Angels** (Argento)

Anna, **After Dido** (arr. Mitchell); **Black Swan** (Whitman); (m) **The Boor** (Grantham); (s) **Chaos** (Gordon); **The Charlatan** (Sousa); **Doctor and Apothecary** (Dittersdorf-Storace); (s) **Frobisher** (Estacio); **Helvellyn** (Macfarren); **Holy Devil** (Nabokov); **Inner Voices** (Howard); **Jamie and Anna** (Reeve); **The Mother** (Hollingsworth); **Spanish Lady** (1765); **Tobias and the Angel** (Dove); **Twilight Voices** (Hoffman); **White Lady** (Cooke)

Anna Akhmatova, **Anna and Dedo** (Morgulas); (actress) **Marina** (Drattell)

Anna Arild, (s) **Electrification of the Soviet Union** (Osborne)

Anna Barbauld, **Friend of the People** (Horne)

Annabel, (s) **Robin Hood** (De Koven)

Annabella, (s) **Black Roses** (Chisholm); **Confidence Man** (Rochberg);

Annabella Milbanke, (m) **Lord Byron** (Thomson)

Annabella Penrose, Miss, **No Cards** (Elliott)

Anna Douglass, **Frederick Douglass** (Moore)

Anna Ferris, (s) **The Picnic** (Cumming)

Anna Karenina, (s) **Anna Karenina** (Carlson); (s) **Anna Karenina** (Hamilton); **Platform 10** (Grant)

Anna Maurrant, (s) **Street Scene** (Weill)

Anna Roosevelt Boettiger, (s) **First Lady** (Wells)

Anna Semyonovna, (m) **Natalia Petrovna** (Hoiby)

Anne, **Cue 67** (Ching); **Floating** (Kuskin); (a) **Mother of Us All** (Thomson); (s/m) **The Opening** (Wilder); **River of Time** (Baber); **To Hell and Back** (Heggie)

Anne Boleyn, **Anne Boleyn** (Beck)

Anne Dante, (m) **Zoggy** (Fox)

Ariane, **Patria, no. 9** (Schafer)

Aricia, **Phaedra** (Innerarity)

Ariel, **Caliban Dreams** (Suprynowicz); **Cue 67** (Ching); **Enchanted Island** (Farquhar); (s) **The Mistake** (Sheffer); **The Tempest** (Banister); (m) **The Tempest** (Eaton); **The Tempest** (Gatty); (s) **The Tempest** (Hoiby); **The Tempest** (Smith); **The Tempest** (Westergaard); **Vision of Ariel** (Saminsky)

Ariela Hilbo, (s) **Whirligig** (Brisman)

Ariella, **Girls of Holland** (De Koven)

Arietta, **Opera 101** (Kam)

Arimanes, (b) **Satanella** (Balfe)

Arionelli, Signor, **Son-in-Law** (Arnold)

Aristaeus, (b-bar/mime) **Mask of Orpheus** (Birtwistle)

Aristo, **Cave of Trophonius** (Storace)

Arkady Sergeitch Islaev, (t) **Natalia Petrovna** (Hoiby)

Arlecchino, (t) **Perpetual** (Kanitz)

Arlequin, (bar) **Eyes and No Eyes** (Reed)

Arline, (s) **Bohemian Girl** (Balfe)

Armen Xykl, (b-bar) **Primal Void** (Vincent)

Armida (Armide), **Armida** (Weir); **Armide** (Dawe); **Rinaldo and Armida** (Eccles)

Armstrong, Colonel, **Happy Disguise** (Giordani)

Armstrong, Neil, (bar) **Eagle Has Landed** (Ritchie)

Arnek, Dr., (t) **Most Important Man** (Menotti)

Arnheim, (bar) **Bohemian Girl** (Balfe)

Arnie, (b-bar) **Thanksgiving** (Levi)

Arnold, (b) **English Cat** (Henze)

Arnold, Benedict, **Twist of Treason** (Livingston)

Arnold, George, (t) **Capitoline Venus** (Kay)

Arnold Talbot, **Witch of Salem** (Cadman)

Arnolphe, (bar) **School for Wives** (Liebermann)

Arowhena, **Erewhon** (Applebaum)

Arsinoe, (s) **Arsinoe** (Clayton)

Artaban, **Other Wise Man** (de Kenessey); (t) **Other Wise Man** (Van Grove)

Artabanes, (t) **Artaxerxes** (Arne)

Artaxerxes, **Artaxerxes** (Arne)

Art Banker (a), **Facing Goya** (Nyman)

Artemis, (m/a) **Garden of Artemis** (Pinkham)

Arth, (b) **Mona** (Parker)

Arthur, (b-bar) **Boys and Girls** (Holloway); **Dracula** (Ziemba); **Hazel Kirke** (Houston); (b) **The Lighthouse** (Davies); **Séance on a Wet Afternoon** (Schwartz); **Slip Knot** (Anderson)

Arthur, King, **Birth of Arthur** (Boughton); (t) **Gawain** (Birtwistle); (sp) **King Arthur** (Purcell); **Morte d'Arthur** (Corder); **Opera of Operas** (Arne, Lampe); **Round Table** (Boughton); **Sir Gawain** (Blackford); **Tom Thumb** (Markordt)

Arthur Cecil, **Our Island Home** (Reed)

Arthur Jarvis, (sp) **Lost in the Stars** (Weill)

Arthur Montana, **Just Above My Head** (Davis)

Arthur Romanoff, (bar) **The Audience** (Dembo)

Art Kamen (bar), **Bonesetter's Daughter** (Wallace)

Aruhm, **Satin Cloak** (Halpern)

Arveragus, (b) **Franklin's Tale** (Sokoloff)

Ascanio, Lord, **Massimilliano** (Freer)

Aschenbach, Gustav von, (t) **Death in Venice** (Britten)

Ase, (m) **King's Henchmen** (Taylor)

Ashoka, **Ashoka's Dream** (Lieberson)

Asmoday, **Tobias and the Angel** (Bliss)

Aspasia, **Pharnaces** (1783); **Revenge of Athridates** (Tenducci); **Timon in Love** (1733)

Aspatia, **Almena** (Arne/Battishill)

Aspern, **Aspern Papers** (Argento); **Aspern Papers** (Hurd)

Astolpho, **Capricious Lovers** (Rush)

Astoreth, (s) **Merry Mount** (Hanson)

Astra, **Night Dancers** (Loder)

Astrolabe, (bar) **Heloise and Abelard** (Paulus)

Astron, (m and t/ct) **Ice Break** (Tippett)

Atahuallpa, (bar) **Royal Hunt of the Sun** (Hamilton)

Ataliba, **Virgin of the Sun** (Bishop)

Atalanta, **Atalanta** (Ashley); **Atalanta Strategy** (Ashley)

Atalanta Lillywhite, (s) **Rising of the Moon** (Maw)

Athalia, **Athalia** (Freeman); **Athaliah** (Weisgall)

Athamas, (ct) **Semele** (Handel)

Athelwold, **Elfrida** (Arne); **King's Proxy** (Cooke)

Athena (Athene), **Arachne** (Michael); (m) **The Challenge** (Sternau; **Ion** (Vir); **Zenda** (Duke)

Athridates, **Pharnaces** (Bates)

Atkins, **Covenanters** (Loder)

Atropos, (m) **Myth of Er** (Sternau)

Attall, Captain, **Mad Captain** (1733)

Attic, **Critic upon Critic** (MacNally)

Atys, **Menna** (Hughes)

Auburn, King, (t) **Fairyland** (Parker)

Aude, **Marriage of Aude** (Rogers)

Audrey Ralls, (s) **Purple Gang** (Jex)

Audubon, John James, **Mirror for the Sky** (Kubik)

Augusta, **Brutus of Alba** (D. Purcell et al.); **Just in Time** (Carter); **The Parlour** (Williams)

Augusta Leigh, (s) **Lord Byron** (Thomson)

Augusta Tabor, (m) **Ballad of Baby Doe** (Moore)

Augustin, **Lost Domain** (Carpenter)

Augustin, Don, (bar) **Big Black Box** (Morgenstern)

Augustine St. Clair, **Uncle Tom's Cabin** (Tracy)

Augustus Gloop, (t) **Golden Ticket** (Ash)

Aunt Bea, (s/m) **A Wedding** (Bolcom)

Aunt Cynthia, (s) **Curious Fern** (Kupferman)

Aunt Hannah, **Death in the Family** (Mayer); (m) **Emmeline** (Picker)

Auntie, (m) **Howard** (Earnest); (a) **Peter Grimes** (Britten)

Auntirosa, **Baa Baa Black Sheep** (Berkeley)

Aunt Lou, (m/s) **Highway 1, U.S.A.** (Still)

"Aunt" Lydia, (s) **Handmaid's Tale** (Ruders)

Aunt Maud Lowder, (a) **Wings of the Dove** (Moore)

Aunt Nan, (m) **Miranda** (Siegmeister)

Aunt Sary, (m) **Smoky Mountain** (Hunkins)

Aunt Sue, (m) **Slow Dusk** (Floyd)

Aurelia, **Dioclesian** (Purcell); (a) **Lizzie Strotter** (Kalmanoff); **Love at First Sight** (1742)

Aurelian (t) **Zenobia** (Pratt)

Aurelia Trentoni, (s) **Captain Jinks** (Beeson)

Aurelio di Montalto, **Native Land** (Bishop)

Aurelius, (t) **Franklin's Tale** (Sokoloff)

Aurora, **Tumble-Down Dick** (1736)

Aurora, Donna, **The Pirates** (Storace)

Aurore, (s) **Bayou Legend** (Still)

Austin, Professor, (bar) **The Mummy** (Quincy)

Autonoe, (s) **The Bassarids** (Henze)

Avano, **Osseo** (Noyes-Greene)

Avery, Pastor, **Emmeline** (Picker)

Avis, (s) **The Wreckers** (Smyth)

Avril, **Love Counts** (Nyman)

Axel Heyst, (b-bar) **Victory** (Bennett)

Aye, (b) **Akhnaten** (Glass)

Ayl, **Without Colors** (Shiflett)

Aymar, (bar) **Azara** (Paine)

Ayreneh, (s) **Julian** (Saminsky)

Aza, **Wedding Trip** (De Koven)

Azael, **Azael** (Laurent

Azara, (s) **Azara** (Paine)

Azarias, (b) **Burning Fiery Furnace** (Britten); **Tobias and the Angel** (Bliss)

Azelia, (m) **Troubled Island** (Still)

Azim, **Veiled Prophet** (Stanford)

Azor, **Selima and Azor** (Linley Sr.)

Azora, **Azora** (Hadley)

Azriel (Azrael), Rabbi (Reb), **Between Two Worlds** (Ran); **The Dybbuk** (Morgulas); **The Dybbuk** (Tamkin)

Azul (m), **Dreaming Blue** (Larsen)

B., Mrs., (a) **Boney Quillen** (Haufrecht)

Baba, **Siege of Curzola** (Arnold); *see also* Madame Flora

Babar, **Babar** (Berezowsky); **Travels of Babar** (Mostel)

Baba the Turk, (m) **Rake's Progress** (Stravinsky)

Babette, (m) **English Cat** (Henze)

Babs, (s) **Julius Caesar Jones** (Williamson)

Baby Blue, (s) **Dreaming Blue** (Larsen)

Baby Doe, **Baby Doe** (DiJulio); (s) **Ballad of Baby Doe** (Moore)

Bacchanal, **Comus** (Arne)

Bacchus, **Ariadne Deserted by Theseus** (Flecknoe); **Long Odds** (Dibdin); (t) **The Olympians** (Bliss); **The Revenge** (Arnold)

Bach, Johann Sebastian, **Buxtehude's Daughter**

Backstich, **Boarding School** (1733)

Badger, Mr., **Wind in the Willows** (Rutter)

Badger, 'Squire, **Don Quixote in England** (1734); **The Sot** (Arne); **'Squire Badger** (Arne)

Baggott, Miss, (a) **Little Sweep** (Britten)

Baglione, (bar) **Rape of Lucretia** (Britten)

Bagoas, **Judith** (Goossens)

Bags, **Letter from an Astrologer** (Knopf)

Bailie, **Felix** (Lutz)

Bajazeth, (t) **Tamburlaine** (Hamilton)

Baker, Josephine, **Star across the Ocean** (Richards)

Baldovino, (t) **Voice of Ariadne** (Musgrave)

Baldur, (s/tr) **Death of Baldur** (Bedford)

Baldwin, (t) **Gawain** (Birtwistle)

Baldwin, Roger, **Amistad** (Ames)

Balkis, (m) **Solomon and Balkis** (Thompson)

Ballad, Mr., **Fashionable Lady** (1730); **Miss Lucy in Town** (Arne)

Balstrode, Captain, (bar) **Peter Grimes** (Britten)

Balthazar, **Honey Moon** (Hewitt/Kelly)

Balthazar, King, (b) **Amahl** (Menotti); (b) **Erode the Greate** (La Montaine)

Bamboola, (b) **Pantagleize** (Starer)

Bampton, (b-bar) **Wat Tyler** (Bush)

Bang, Captain, **Our Island Home** (Reed)

Bankhead, Sam, **Summer King** (Sonenberg)

Bannadonna, **Bell Tower** (Krenek)

Banquo, **Three, Two, One** (Chen)

Baptista, (b) **Taming of the Shrew** (Giannini)

Baptiste, **The Vintagers** (Bishop); **Wide Sargasso Sea** (Howard); **Yelva** (Bishop)

Barbara, (s) **Casanova's Homecoming** (Argento); (s) **The Hero** (Menotti); (s) **Iron Chest** (Storace); **Love and Money** (Arnold); **Question of Love** (Gilbert)

Barbara Allen, **Barbara Allen** (Broekman)

Barbara Ansley, **Roman Fever** (Hagemann); **Roman Fever** (Stringer); (m) **Roman Fever** (Ward)

Barbara de la Guerra, (s) **Natoma** (Herbert)

Barbarino, **Noble Pedlar** (Barthelemon)

Barberini, Cardinal, (b) **Galileo Galilei** (Glass); (t) **Galileo Galilei** (Laderman)

Bardolph, (bar) **At the Boar's Head** (Holst); (b) **King Hal** (Stewart)

Barelli, **Aspern Papers** (Argento)

Bark, Mr., **Lucky Discovery** (1737)

Bark, Mrs. **Lucky Discovery** (1737)

Barlow, Dr. Stanley, (bar) **Malady of Love** (Engel)

Barlow, Rev. William, **Vicar of Bray** (Solomon)

Barnacle, Nora, **Antient Concert** (Hagen)

Barney, **Silver Tassie** (Turnage)

Barnum, P. T., (t) **Barnum's Bird** (Larsen)

Ben, (t) **Buxom Joan** (Taylor); (b) **Harriet** (Musgrave); **Plymouth in an Uproar** (Dibdin); (t) **Smoky Mountain** (Hunkins); (bar) **The Telephone** (Menotti)

Ben Alexander, (t) **My Heart's in the Highlands** (Beeson)

Ben Blake, **Cumberland Fair** (Wilder)

Benbow, Justice, (sp) **Flitch of Bacon** (Shield)

Benbow, Major, (b) **Flitch of Bacon** (Shield)

Bendrix, Henry, **End of the Affair** (Heggie)

Benedict, **Benedict and Beatrice** (Holst)

Benjamin Button, **Curious Case of Benjamin Button** (Eaton)

Benjamin Coffin III, **Rent** (Larson)

Benjamin Giddens, (bar) **Regina** (Blitzstein)

Benjie, (t) **Harriet** (Musgrave)

Ben Mainstay, **Silver Tankard** (Arnold)

Bennelong, **Bennelong** (Conyngham)

Bennet, Mr., (b) **Pride and Prejudice** (Mechem)

Bennet, Mrs., (high s) **Pride and Prejudice** (Mechem)

Benno, **East and West** (McQueen)

Ben Palmer, (bar) **Old Majestic** (Rodríguez)

Ben Porter, (bar/b) **Sourwood Mountain** (Kreutz)

Ben Scrooge, (bar) **Christmas Carol** (Musgrave)

Benvolio, (bar) **Romeo and Juliet** (Shelley)

Beowulf, (dr) **Grendel** (Goldenthal)

Beppo, **Africanus Blue Beard** (Sedgwick); **Bianca** (Balfe); **Dulcamara** (1866)

Berel (bar), **Chelm** (Strassburg)

Berengaria, **Knight of the Leopard** (Balfe); **Richard Coeur de Lion** (Shield)

Bérenger, (t) **Photo of the Colonel** (Searle)

Beret, (s) **Giants in the Earth** (Moore)

Berezowski, Count, **Fortune Teller** (Herbert)

Berkman, Alexander, (bar) **Emma** (Fine)

Berlin, Isaiah, **Guest from the Future** (Marvin)

Bernardo, Father, **The Disappointment** (1732)

Bernal, (t) **The Sacrifice** (Converse)

Bernal Diaz del Castillo, (bar, t) **Montezuma** (Sessions)

Bernard, **Twilight Voices** (Hoffman); **Where the Wild Things Are** (Knussen)

Bernard, Abbot, (t) **Abelard and Heloise** (Ward)

Bernardino de Sahagún, **The Conquistador** (Fink)

Bernardo, **West Side Story** (Bernstein)

Beroe, (m) **The Bassarids** (Henze)

Bert, (bar) **The Barrier** (Meyerowitz); **Berta** (Smart); (s) **Black Widow** (Pasatieri)

Bertha, (s) **Bad Boys in School** (Meyerowitz), **The Crusaders** (Benedict); **I Rise in Flame** (Flanagan); **Last Chance Planet** (Moore); **Night Dancers** (Loder)

Bertha, Queen, (m) **Bertha** (Rorem)

Berthe, **Blond Eckbert** (Weir); (s) **Violins of St. Jacques** (Williamson)

Bertie, **David's Violin** (Mogulesco); **Black Roses** (Chisholm)

Bertilak de Hautdesert, (Sir), (bar) **Gawain** (Birtwistle); **Sir Gawain** (Blackford)

Bertilak, Lady, **Sir Gawain** (Blackford)

Bertram, **The Demon** (Bishop); **Robert the Devil** (Meyerbeer-"Kettenus")

Bertram, Henry, **Guy Mannering** (Attwood)

Bertrand, Felix (Lutz)

Bertrand, Father, **The Savoyard** (Reinagle)

Bertrand, Père, **Light from St. Agnes** (Harling)

Bertrand de Valencourt, **Young Hussar** (Kelly)

Bertrande, (s) **Wife of Martin Guerre** (Bergsma)

Bess, **Abbot of Drimock** (Musgrave); **Blind Beggar's Daughter** (Bush); (s) **Oath of Bad Brown Bill** (Conyngham); (s) **Porgy and Bess** (Gershwin)

Bess Rigby, (m) **The Scarecrow** (Lockwood)

Bessie Burgess, (m) **Plough and the Stars** (Siegmeister)

Bessie Throckmorton, (s) **Merrie England** (German)

Bessy, **Blind Beggar of Bethnal Green** (Arne)

Beth, (m) **Elsewhereless** (Sharman); (s) **Room No. 12** (Kanitz)

Beth March, (s) **Little Women** (Adamo)

Betsy, **Master's Stroke** (Weisensel); **Mozart in Manhattan** (Biales); (s) **Sweet Betsy from Pike** (Bucci)

Betsy Ross, (s) **Horspfal** (Stokes)

Betta, (s) **Not a Spanish Kiss** (Barab)

Betterbotham, Mrs., (m) **Chinchilla** (Fink)

Betts, Dr., (bar) **The Veil** (Rogers)

Betty, **Betty** (Carey); **Chamber-Maid** (Phillips); **The Craftsman** (Mottley); **Faith: DWF, 235** (Ching); **Flora** (Hippisley); **Mad Captain** (1733); **Mock Lawyer** (1733); **Village Opera** (1729); **Welsh Opera** (1731)

Betty Blackberry, **The Farmer** (Shield)

Betty Drostepate, **The Decoy** (1733)

Betty Shabazz, (s) **X** (Davis)

Bevil, **The Artifice** (Arne)

Beyla, **David's Violin** (Mogulesco)

Bezano, (t) **He Who Gets Slapped** (Ward)

Bhaer, Professor Friedrich (b-bar), **Little Women** (Adamo)

Bianca, **Bianca** (Balfe); (s) **Bianca** (Hadley); **Garden of Mystery** (Cadman); **Inés de Castro** (MacMillan); (s) **Pantagleize** (Starer); (a) **Rape of Lucretia** (Britten); **Sicilian Bride** (Balfe); (s) **Taming of the Shrew** (Giannini)

Bianca, Queen, **Bride Elect** (Sousa)

Bianca Bianchi, (m) **Voice of Ariadne** (Musgrave)

Biddle, Ed, **Biddle Boys** (Beck)

Biddle, John, **Biddle Boys** (Beck)

Biden, Joe, **Say It Ain't So, Joe** (Hughes)

Bidover, **Expensive Embarrassment** (Gougeon)

Big Bad Wolf, **True Story of the Three Little Pigs** (De Pue)

Big Bully Brett, **Elijah's Kite** (Rolfe)

Biko, **Biko** (Paintal)

Bilby, **Bilby's Doll** (Floyd)

Bonhoeffer, Dietrich, (dram bar) **Bonhoeffer** (Gebuhr)

Boniface Severe (bar), **Curious Affair** (Craton)

Bonifacio, Padre, (b) **Blonde Donna** (Carter)

Bonner, Edward, (b) **Voss** (Meale)

Bonnie, **Ecstatic Journey** (Rodwin)

Bonny Jack, (bar) **Mermaid in Lock No. 7** (Siegmeister)

Bonoro, Doctor, **Zuma** (Bishop)

Bontshe, **Bontshe the Silent** (Sirota)

Bony Anderson, **Apology of Bony Anderson** (Conyngham)

Booth, John Wilkes, (bar) **Death of Lincoln** (London); (bar) **Mary Surratt** (Muller); **The Moustache** (Thoms); **Our American Cousin** (Sawyer)

Booze, **Belphegor** (Barthelemon)

Borans, Stathis, (t) **The Fly** (Shore)

Borden, Andrew, (b-bar) **Lizzie Borden** (Beeson)

Borgia, Cesare, (b-bar) **Hell's Angels** (Osborne)

Boris, **Animalopera** (Fink)

Boris, Prince, **The Charlatan** (Sousa)

Bosola, Daniel de, (bar) **Duchess of Malfi** (Burton); **Duchess of Malfi** (Oliver); (bar) **Duchess of Malfi** (Rasch)

Boswell, **Johnson Preserv'd** (Stoker)

Bothwell, Earl of, (t) **Mary, Queen of Scots** (Musgrave)

Bottom, **Midsummer Night's Dream** (1763); (b-bar) **Midsummer Night's Dream** (Britten)

Botzenheim, Baroness von, (a) **Good Soldier Schweik** (Kurka)

Bouché, Thomas, (b) **Down in the Valley** (Weill)

Bougrelas, **Ubu Roi** (Aplvor)

Boule de Suif, **Greater Good** (Hartke)

Bouncer, (bar) **Cox and Box** (Sullivan)

Bounderby, **Hard Times** (Burgon)

Bouvard, **Bouvard and Pécuchet** (Aplvor)

Bowen, **Different Fields** (Reid)

Bowring, (t) **Grace of Todd** (Crosse)

Bowspirit, **Britons, Strike Home** (1739)

Box, John James, (t) **Cox and Box** (Sullivan)

Boyanna, **Ever Young** (Boughton)

Boy Minor, (t) **Zoggy** (Fox)

Boy Sam, (t) **Difficulty of Crossing a Field** (Lang)

Brack, Judge, **Hedda Gabler** (Harper)

Brack Weaver, (t) **Down in the Valley** (Weill)

Braddock, Bashford, (bar) **Ordeal of Osbert** (Davis)

Bradford, Count, (t) **Secret of the Mirror** (Busch)

Bragadocia, Emperor of, **Free Lance** (Sousa)

Brainkoff, Dr., (t) **The Hero** (Menotti)

Brainly, Mr., **The Cottagers** (1766)

Brainly, Mrs., **The Cottagers** (1766)

Brainworm, **Love and Revenge** (1729)

Brainy Woman, (s) **Acquanetta** (Gordon)

Bramble, (t) **Our Man in Havana** (Williamson)

Brandon, (b) **Long Christmas Dinner** (Hindemith)

Brant, Joseph, (t) **Molly Brant** (Cecconi-Bates)

Brayer, Mr., (t) **The System** (Bach)

Braxton, **Mines of Sulphur** (Bennett)

Brennan, Captain, (b) **Plough and the Stars** (Siegmeister)

Brett Ashley, Lady, **Sun Also Rises** (Young)

Brettschneider, (t) **Good Soldier Schweik** (Kurka)

Brian Boru, **Brian Boru** (Edwards)

Bridal Du, **Peony Pavilion** (Tan Dun)

Bride, **Ever Young** (Boughton)

Bridgenorth, **Peveril of the Peak** (Horn)

Bridget, **Letty, the Basket-Maker** (Balfe); **Love Finds the Way** (Arne et al.)

Bridget Lochmuller, **Mulligan Guard Ball** (Braham)

Bridie, **Midnight Court Opera** (Sokolovic)

Brighella, (bar) **Commedia** (Cowie); **Servant of Two Masters** (Giannini)

Brigid, **Little Moon of Alban** (Ferris)

Briquet, (b-bar) **He Who Gets Slapped** (Ward)

Brissac, **Follies of a Night** (Gabriel)

Britannia, **Britannia** (Arne); **Britannia** (Carey), **Britannia** (Lampe); **Choice of Apollo** (Yates); **Restauration of Charles II** (1732)

British Blunt, Sir, **Guardian Outwitted** (Arne)

Briton, Captain, **Britons, Strike Home** (1739)

Brixcowicz, Mr., (bar) **Bad Boys in School** (Meyerowitz)

Broichan, **Columba** (Leighton)

Brom Van Brunt, **Headless Horseman** (Moore)

Bronislav, (b) **Hunger Art** (Myers)

Bronwen, **Bronwen** (Holbrooke)

Brother Juniper, **Bridge of San Luis Rey** (Kimper)

Brother Shannon, (bar) **Hanging Judge** (Lockwood)

Brother Smiley, (b) **Sweet Bye and Bye** (Beeson)

Brown, **Ages Ago** (Clay)

Brown, Captain, **Guy Mannering** (Attwood)

Brown, David, (t) **The Diva** (Ferris)

Brown, Farmer, (bar) **Boney Quillen** (Haufrecht)

Brown, George, **White Lady** (Cooke)

Brown, Goodman, **Goodman Brown** (Fink); (t/bar) **Young Goodman Brown** (Lenel)

Brown, John, (bar) **The Decision** (Musgrave); (bar) **John Brown** (Mechem)

Brown, Oliver, (t) **John Brown** (Mechem)

Bruce (bar), **Boys and Girls** (Holloway)

Brumpton, Young, **Love Finds the Way** (Arne et al.)

Brundle, Seth, (bar) **The Fly** (Shore)

Bruno, (bar) **Where the Wild Things Are** (Knussen)

Bruno Broast, (bar) **Ballad of the Bremen Band** (Moore)

Brusard, **Deep River** (Harling)

Brutus, **Brutus of Alba** (D. Purcell et al.)

Buchanan, Dr., (b-bar) **Summer and Smoke** (Hoiby)

Cara, **Push!** (Bruce)

Caraboo, Princess, (s) **English Eccentrics** (Williamson)

Caradoc, **Bronwen** (Holbrooke); (t) **Mona** (Parker)

Caravaggio, (bar) **Death of the Virgin** (Owen)

Careful, Timothy, Sir, **Happy Lovers** (1736)

Carina, **Carina** (Woolf)

Cariola, **Duchess of Malfi** (Burton)

Carl, (t) **The Picnic** (Cumming)

Carl Linden, **Bitter-Sweet** (Coward)

Carlo, (t) **Doctor of Alcantara** (Eichberg); (bar) **La Loca** (Menotti); **Twilight Voices** (Hoffman)

Carlo di Cinchona, **Zuma** (Bishop)

Carlos, **Doctor and Apothecary** (Dittersdorf-Storace); **Happy Captive** (Galliard)

Carlos, Brother, **Don John of Austria** (Nathan)

Carlos, Col., **Restauration of King Charles II** (1732)

Carlos, Don, **Loretta** (Lavenu)

Carlos Arachnid, (t) **Civilization** (Sahl/Salzman)

Carlotta, Donna, **Vendetta** (Freeman)

Carmela, (s) **Saint of Bleecker Street** (Menotti)

Carmelita, (s) **The Legend** (Breil)

Carmen, **The Balcony** (Di Domenica); **José's Carmen** (Ashman); **Rose of Castille** (Balfe); **Saint Carmen of the Main** (Hodkinson)

Carmen Capulet, **Figaro's Last Hangover** (Soluri)

Carmen Carmen, (s) **The Audition** (Kalmanoff)

Carmen Ghia, (s) **Stoned Guest** (Schickele)

Carmen Jones, **Carmen Jones** (Bizet-Bennett)

Carmilla, **Carmilla** (Johnston)

Carol, (s) **The Fox** (Kondorossy); **Turtle Wakes** (Bell)

Carol Cutrere, (m) **Orpheus Descending** (Saylor)

Caroline, **Dead Alive** (Arnold); **Jeanie Deans** (MacCunn); **The Prize** (Storace); **Young Hussar** (Kelly)

Caroline, Countess, (a) **Elegy for Young Lovers** (Henze)

Caroline Abbott, **Where Angels Fear to Tread** (Weiser)

Caroline Crabstick, **Family Quarrels** (Reeve et al.)

Caroline Gaines, (s) **Margaret Garner** (Danielpour)

Caroline Hartley, **The Boardinghouse** (Horn)

Caroline Sedley, **False Alarms** (Addison)

Caroline Tibbs, (s) **Edge of Glory** (Waters)

Carré-Lamadon, M. (bar), **Greater Good** (Hartke)

Carré-Lamadon, Mme., (s) **Greater Good** (Hartke)

Carrie, (m) **Last Goodbye** (Shadle)

Carroll, Lewis, (t) **Alice** (Bachlund); (t) **Through the Looking Glass** (John)

Carruthers, Dame, (a) **Yeomen of the Guard** (Sullivan)

Carry Nation, (m) **Carry Nation** (Moore)

Carter, (bar) **Our Man in Havana** (Williamson)

Carter, Hal (bar), **Picnic** (Larsen)

Carter, Tallulah (s), **Hotel Casablanca** (Pasatieri)

Carter, Tim, (t) **The Mummy** (Quincy)

Carter, Tom, (b-bar), **Hotel Casablanca** (Pasatieri)

Carton, Sydney, (bar) **Tale of Two Cities** (Benjamin)

Cartridge, Corporal, **Britain's Glory** (Arnold)

Cartwright, **The Wedding** (Wilson)

Casanova, (bar) **Casanova's Homecoming** (Argento)

Casey, (bar) **Beach of Falesá** (Hoddinott); **Different Fields** (Reid); (actor/dr) **Mighty Casey** (Schuman)

Casey Flood, (bar) **Zoë** (Lunn)

Casgan, **Desert Flower** (Wallace)

Casia, (s) **Golden Lion** (Kechley)

Casilda, (s) **The Gondoliers** (Sullivan); **Ruy Blas** (Glover)

Casimir, King, **Zorinski** (Arnold)

Casimir, Prince, **Amelia** (Lampe)

Cass, Squire, **Silas Marner** (Joubert)

Cassandra, **Agamemnon** (Brian); (s) **Agamemnon** (Hamilton); **Agamemnon** (Werder); **Cassandra** (McAndrew); (s) **Christmas Miracle** (Fax); **Croak** (LeBaron); **Cry of Clytaemnestra** (Eaton); **Final Bid** (Raum); **Virgin Prophetess** (Finger)

Cassandre, (b) **Eyes and No Eyes** (Reed)

Cassie, **Achilles Heel** (Bohmler)

Castro, Don, **Vendetta** (Freeman)

Castro, José, (bar) **Natoma** (Herbert)

Casy, Jim, **Grapes of Wrath** (Gordon)

Caterina, (s) **Boccaccio's Nightingale** (Trimble); **Daughter of St. Mark** (Balfe)

Caterpillar, (bcl), **Alice in Wonderland** (Chin); **Alice in Wonderland** (Westergaard)

Cathbad, (bar), **Deirdre of the Sorrows** (Hughes)

Catherine, **Siege of Belgrade** (Storace)

Catherine Bolnes, (s) **Writing to Vermeer** (Andriessen)

Cathbad, (bar) **Deirdre of the Sorrows** (Hughes)

Catherine, (s) **View from the Bridge** (Bolcom)

Catherine Follett, **Death in the Family** (Mayer)

Catherine the Great, **Bee Story** (Hays)

Catherine Greene, **Eli W.** (Bingham)

Catherine Grey, (s) **Catherine Grey** (Balfe)

Catherine Parr, (s) **King's Breakfast** (Barthelson)

Catherine Sloper, **The Heiress** (Hollier); (s) **Washington Square** (Pasatieri)

Catherine Wright, **Shining Brow** (Hagen)

Cathleen, (s) **Riders to the Sea** (Vaughan Williams)

Cathy, (s) **Last Leaf** (Henderson)

Cathy Earnshaw, (s) **Wuthering Heights** (Floyd); (s) **Wuthering Heights** (Herrmann)

Catilina, **Castle of Andalusia** (Arnold)

Catiline, (bar), **Catiline Conspiracy** (Hamilton)

Cavil, Mr., **The Whim** (1734)

Cavil, Mrs., **The Whim** (1734)

Cawwawkee, **Polly** (1729)

Cazarro, Luiz, Dom, **El Capitan** (Sousa)

Cecil, (t) **Catherine Grey** (Balfe)

Letter (Herman); (b) **Scarlet Letter** (Kaufmann); **Scarlet Letter** (Laitman)

China Aster, (t) **Confidence Man** (Rochberg)

Chinese Woman, (m) **The Letter** (Moravec)

Chino, **West Side Story** (Bernstein)

Chip, (s) **Chip and His Dog** (Menotti); **The Raft** (Reeve)

Chloe, **Happy Arcadia** (Clay); **The Lottery** (Seedo)

Chonita, (s) **The Sacrifice** (Converse)

Choobukov, **The Proposal** (Walker)

Chopin, Frederic, **George Sand** (Vehar)

Chora, (s) **Matricide** (Kats-Chernin)

Choragos, **Antigone** (Constantinides)

Choregos, (bar) **Punch and Judy** (Birtwistle)

Chou En-lai, (bar) **Nixon in China** (Adams)

Chris, (t) **Boys and Girls** (Holloway); (t) **Miracle of Flanders** (Gruenberg)

Christ, (bar) **Calvary** (Pasatieri); (t) **Thérèse** (Taverner)

Christian, (t) **Cyrano** (Beeson); (t) **Cyrano** (Damrosch); **Cyrano** (Herbert)

Christian Berninck, (s) **Behold the Sun** (Goehr)

Christian Delacruz, (bar) **Río de Sangre** (Davis)

Christiano Lovewealth, **False Guardians Outwitted** (1740)

Christina, (s) **Hermiston** (Orr); **Ib and Little Christina** (Leoni); (s) **Voices for a Mirror** (Kupferman)

Christina, Grand Duchess, (s) **Galileo Galilei** (Glass)

Christina, Queen, **Queen Christina** (Anderson); (m) **Christina Romana** (Larsen)

Christine, (s) **Caritas** (Saxon); (m) **Miss Julie** (Rorem)

Christine Mannon, (s) **Mourning Becomes Electra** (Levy)

Christoph Kaufmann, (bar) **Lenz** (Sitsky)

Christopher, Sir, **Canterbury Pilgrims** (Stanford)

Christopher Curry, Sir, **Inkle and Yarico** (Arnold)

Christopher Lynn, (bar) **Nitecap** (Burnham)

Christopher Sly, (b-bar) **Christopher Sly** (Argento); **Christopher Sly** (Eastwood)

Christopher Toxado, Don, **The Alcaid** (Nathan)

Christophine, **Wide Sargasso Sea** (Howard)

Chrononhotonthologos, King, **Chrononhotonthologos** (1734)

Chronos, **Secular Masque** (Boyce)

Chrysalis, (s) **Insect Comedy** (Kalmanoff)

Chrysostom, (t) **Juggler of Our Lady** (Kay)

Chu, **San Toy** (Jones)

Chubukov, (b-bar) **The Proposal** (Fiddes); (b-bar/b) **Marriage Proposal** (Goldstaub)

Chucho, **Lucrezia** (Bolcom)

Churchmouse, Mr., **No Cards** (Elliott)

Cibber, **Coffee-House** (Carey)

Cicely, **Canterbury Pilgrims** (Stanford); **Trip to Portsmouth** (Dibdin); **Veteran Tar** (Arnold)

Cicero, **Catiline Conspiracy** (Hamilton)

Cilla, (s) **Margaret Garner** (Danielpour)

Cimon, **Damon and Phillida** (1729); Damon and Phillida (Dibdin); **Love in a Village** (1729)

Cinderella, **Cinderella** (Davies); **Cinderella** (Easton); **Cinderella** (Farmer); **Cinderella** (Jarrett); **Cinderella** (Lacy); **Cinderella** (Oliver); **Cinderella in Spain** (Warwick)

Cinderella Nabgratz, (m) **Meanwhile, Back at Cinderella's** (Arlan)

Cindy Lou, **Carmen Jones** (Bizet-Bennett)

Cinque, (b-bar) **Amistad** (Davis); **Tania** (Davis)

Cinthia, **Cinthia and Endimion** (D. Purcell)

Cinthio, **Emperor of the Moon** (Arne)

Cio Cio San, **Cio Cio San** (Carroll)

Cipolla, **Mario and the Magician** (Oliver); **Mario and the Magician** (Somers); **Mario and the Magician** (Thorne)

Circe, **Circe** (Galliard); (s) **Circe** (Hayes); **Circe 1991** (Victory); **Circe's Palace** (Magrill); **Orestes** (Pepusch); **Prisoner's Play** (Rea); **Return of Odysseus** (Bedford)

Circula, (s) **Parabola and Circula** (Blitzstein)

Cis Fergeson, **Casino Paradise** (Bolcom)

Cissie, **Ballymore** (Wargo)

Cissy, (a) **Tickets Please** (Nelson)

Clac, **Green Children** (LeFanu)

Claggart, (b) **Billy Budd** (Britten)

Clair, (s) **Clair de Lune** (Larsen)

Claire, (a) **Dark Waters** (Krenek); **Hearts on Fire** (Ames); (s) **Infidel** (MacSems); **Lilith** (Davis)

Claire Clairmont, (s) **Mary Shelley** (Jaffe)

Clara, (s) **America** (Kohs); **Billy and Zelda** (Davidson); **The Disappointment** (1732); (s) **The Duenna** (Linley Jr./Sr.); **Hartford Bridge** (Shield); **Heaven Ablaze in His Breast** (Weir); (lyric s) **Judgment of St. Francis** (Flagello); **Lover's Opera** (1729); **The Magnet** (Arnold); (s) **Porgy and Bess** (Gershwin); (s) **The Sandman** (Cabaniss); (s) **Siege of Rochelle** (Balfe); (s) **Signor Deluso** (Pasatieri)

Clara, Don, **Big Black Box** (Morgenstern)

Clara, Donna, (s) **The Duenna** (Gerhard)

Clara Brown, (m) **Gabriel's Daughter** (Mollicone)

Clara Chase, **No for an Answer** (Blitzstein)

Clara Rathbone, **Henry and Clara** (Martín)

Clara Schumann, **Clara** (Bond)

Clara Stirling, **Hit or Miss!** (Smith)

Clare, John, **I Am in Search** (Grant)

Clarence, (bar) **The Opening** (Wilder)

Clarence Cratwell, **Soldier Boy** (Anderson)

Clarice, **Don Fulminone** (Giordani); **Don Saverio** (Arne); (s) **The Mountaineers** (Somerville); **Savonarola** (Stanford)

Clarice de Noyan, (s) **Minette Fontaine** (Still)

Clarinda, **Robin Hood** (Burney); **The Sot** (Arne); **'Squire Badger** (Arne)

Clarinda Wilmore, **Wilmore Castle** (Hook)

Clarise Willoughby, **Witch of Salem** (Cadman)

Clarissa, (s) **Clarissa** (Holloway); **Lionel and Clarissa** (Dibdin); **Servant of Two Masters** (Giannini)

Clarissa Dalloway, **Mrs. Dalloway** (Larsen)

Clark, William, **Corps of Discovery** (Ching); **York** (Trinkley)

Clarkwell, Mrs., **The Decoy** (1733)

Clatter, (m) **Silence Tree** (Fox)

Clatter, Mrs., **Clandestine Marriage** (Wishart)

Claude Hopper, (bar) **Ballad of the Bremen Band** (Moore)

Claude Melnotte, (bar) **Pauline** (Cowen)

Claudia Kinkaid, **From the Mixed-Up Files** (Swensson)

Claudia Legare Lowndes, (s) **Claudia Legare** (Ward)

Claudine, **Devil's Bridge** (Arnold); **Miller and His Men** (Bishop); **Pink Lady** (Caryll); **The Savoyard** (Reinagle)

Claudio, **Much Ado about Nothing** (Stanford)

Claudius, (t) **Hamlet** (Searle); **The Magnet** (Arnold)

Clay Chandler, (t) **The Hunted** (Mailman)

Clayborn, Thomas, (b) **Edge of Glory** (Waters)

Claypool, Lady, **Restauration of Charles II** (1732)

Clem, (t) **Little Sweep** (Britten)

Clem Harris, (b-bar) **Karla** (Lehrman)

Clementina, **The Prude** (1765)

Clementine, (s) **Boston Baked Beans** (Kubik); **Leap Year** (Sedgwick)

Clemm, Mrs., (m) **Voyage of Edgar Allan Poe** (Argento)

Clemons, Mr., **Fee First** (Doran)

Cleo, **Most Happy Fella** (Loesser)

Cleon, (t) **Tarquin** (Krenek)

Cleopatra, (s) **Antony and Cleopatra** (Barber); **Antony and Cleopatra** (Chiusano); **Antony and Cleopatra** (Gruenberg); (s) **Cleopatra's Night** (Hadley); **Egypt** (McCoy); (s) **Inferno of Dante** (Soluri); **Macheath in the Shades** (1735); **Wizard of the Nile** (Herbert)

Cleora, **Thomyris** (Pepusch)

Cleota, **Voodoo** (Freeman)

Cleremont, **Generous Free-Mason** (1730)

Clerimont, **Female Rake** (1736)

Cleveland, Dennis, **Dennis Cleveland** (Rouse)

Clifford, (t) **House of the Seven Gables** (Eyerly)

Clifton, Captain, **The Slave** (Bishop)

Clinton, Hillary, **Say It Ain't So, Joe**

Clio, (ct-s) **Aethelred** (Wilson); **Crossing the Horizon** (Lastovicka)

Clive, (ct) **Odd Numbers** (Grant)

Clobberton, Captain, **The Covenanters** (Loder)

Clochette, (s) **Eyes and No Eyes** (Reed)

Cloe, **Triumph of Peace** (Arne)

Clorinda, **Cinderella** (Lacy); (s) **Garden of Artemis** (Pinkham)

Clotaldo, (bar) **Life Is a Dream** (Spratlan)

Clothilde, (s) **Bayou Legend** (Still)

Clotho, (m) **Myth of Er** (Sternau)

Clotilda, (a) **Koanga** (Delius)

Clover, **The Mariners** (Attwood)

Clovis Sangrail, (narr) **Beast and Superbeast** (Martín)

Clump, **Brazen Bust** (Bishop)

Cluny, (bar) **Redwall**

Clyde Griffiths, (bar) **American Tragedy** (Picker)

Clym, **Return of the Native** (Coulthard)

Clymante, **Native Land** (Bishop)

Clytemnestra, **Agamemnon** (Brian); (s) **Agamemnon** (Hamilton); (s) **Agamemnon** (Werder); **Cassandra** (McAndrew); **Clytemnestra** (Wishart); **Cry of Clytaemnestra** (Eaton)

Clytoneus, (t) **Nausicaa** (Glanville-Hicks)

Cocardasse, **Blanche de Nevers** (Balfe)

Cocoliche, (t) **Don Cristóbal** (Crawford)

Cogan, Mrs., (m) **Plough and the Stars** (Siegmeister)

Cohenberg, Colonel, (sp) **Siege of Belgrade** (Storace)

Cohn, Robert, **Sun Also Rises** (Young)

Cohn, Roy, **Angels in America** (Eötvös)

Cold Feet, (s) **Kill Bear Comes Home** (Stuart)

Colette, **Cunning Man** (Burney)

Colin, **Arcadian Nuptials** (Arne); **Capricious Lovers** (Rush); (t) **The Cooper** (Arne); **Cunning Man** (Burney); **Happy Arcadia** (Clay); **Phillis at Court** (Giordani); **Phoebe at Court** (Arne); **Plumber's Gift** (Blake); **Rose and Colin** (Dibdin); **Secret Garden** (Pliska); **Shepherd's Lottery** (Boyce); **Tower** (Hoddinott)

Collatinus, (b) **Rape of Lucretia** (Britten)

Colleen, **Phoenix Park** (Strickland)

Collins, Mr., (b-bar) **Pride and Prejudice** (Mechem)

Colomba, **Colomba** (Mackenzie)

Colombina, **Jewel Box** (Mozart-Griffiths); (s) **Perpetual** (Kanitz)

Colombine, **The Portrait** (Barthelemon)

Colonel Bluff, **Intriguing Chambermaid** (1734)

Columba, **Columba** (Leighton)

Columbine, (s) **Aria da capo** (Baksa); (s) **Aria da capo** (Blank); **Aria da capo** (Smith); **Aria da capo** (Weaver); (s) **Commedia** (Cowie); (m) **Eyes and No Eyes** (Reed); **Fête Galante** (Smyth); **Paris Doll** (De Koven); **The Portrait** (Barthelemon); **The Touchstone** (Dibdin)

Columbus, Christopher, **Apollonia's Circus** (Stokes); **Christopher Columbus** (Kalmanoff); **Columbus** (Moore); **Further Voyages** (Stokes); **Pioneer** (Dresher); **Tammany** (Hewitt); (b-bar) **The Voyage** (Glass)

Columbus Hebbelthwaite, **Ages Ago** (Clay)

Comedy, **Theatrical Candidates** (Bates)

Commander, (b) **Handmaid's Tale** (Ruders); **Plumber's Gift** (Blake)

Commendatore, **Thirty Minute Don Giovanni** (Lole-Gray)

Commendatoreador, Il, (b) **Stoned Guest** (Schickele)

Commerce, **Triumph of Peace** (Arne)

Commère, (m) **Four Saints** (Thomson)

Compere (Compère), (b-bar) **Crimson Bird** (Enenbach); (b) **Four Saints** (Thomson)

Compson, Capt. Richard, **Midnight Angel** (Carlson)

Compton, **Agreeable Surprise** (Arnold)

Comus, **Comus** (Arne); **Comus** (Bishop); **Comus** (Lawes)

Conchas, (bar) **Kingdom for a Cow** (Weill)

Concord, **Britannia** (Lampe)

Denmark Vesey, **Denmark Vesey** (Bowles); **Denmark Vesey** (Cabaniss)

Dennis, **Little Moon of Alban** (Ferris); **Monster Bed** (de Kenessey)

Denys, **Grinning at the Devil** (Wilson)

Derek, **Say Cheese** (Barab)

Derek Dude, (bar) **Civilization** (Sahl/Salzman)

Dermott (Dermot), **Poor Soldier** (Shield); **The Shamrock** (Shields)

De Rocher, Mrs., (m) **Dead Man Walking** (Heggie)

DeRopp, Mrs., **Beast and Superbeast** (Martín)

Derrincourt, William, **William Derrincourt** (Smalley)

Desdemona, **Telaio: Desdemona** (Botti)

Deserter, (t) **We Come to the River** (Henze)

Desideria, (m) **Saint of Bleecker Street** (Menotti)

De Soto, Hernando, **De Soto** (Bailey); (t) **Royal Hunt of the Sun** (Hamilton)

Despard Murgatroyd, Sir, (bar) **Ruddigore** (Sullivan)

Dessalines, **Toussaint** (Blake); (bar) **Troubled Island** (Still)

Devilshoof, (b) **Bohemian Girl** (Balfe)

Dewain, **I Was Looking at the Ceiling** (Adams)

Diaghilev, **Madame Adare** (Silverman)

Diana, **Assassin Tree** (MacCrae); **Endymion** (Bennett); **Lionel and Clarissa** (Dibdin); (s) **The Olympians** (Bliss); **Secular Masque** (Boyce); **Thespis** (Sullivan)

Diana Smith, (s) **Nitecap** (Burnham)

Diana Vernon, **Rob Roy Macgregor** (Davy)

Diarmid, **Diarmid** (MacCunn); **Muirgheis** (Butler)

Dick, **Flora** (Hippisley); **St. David's Day** (Attwood)

Dick, Captain, **Naughty Marietta** (Herbert)

Dick Deadeye, (b) **H.M.S. Pinafore** (Sullivan)

Dick Dewy, **Mellstock Quire** (Harper)

Dick Fitzgerald, (t) **The Highwayman** (De Koven)

Dickie, (m) **The Clock** (Rieti)

Dickinson, Edward, (b-bar) **Letter to Emily** (Johnson)

Dickinson, Emily, **Eastward in Eden** (Meyerowitz); (s) **Letter to Emily** (Johnson); **Women in the Garden** (Fine)

Dickson, (t) **King Hal** (Stewart); (t) **The Scarecrow** (Lockwood); **White Lady** (Cooke)

Dicky, **Abroad and at Home** (Shield)

Dicky Doo, (t) **Simple Decision** (Busch)

Dicky Gossip, **My Grandmother** (Storace)

Didier, (b) **Madeleine** (Herbert)

Dido, **Aeneas and Dido** (Rolfe); **After Dido** (arr. Mitchell); **Cleo** (Trinkley); **Dido** (Hook); **Dido** (Horn); **Dido** (Storace); **Dido and Aeneas** (Arne); **Dido and Aeneas** (Beveridge); (s) **Dido and Aeneas** (Purcell); (s) **Golden Apples** (Trinkley); (m) **Inferno of Dante** (Soluri)

Diego, **Bird of Night** (LeGendre); **Junípero Serra** (Hively); **The Padlock** (Dibdin); **Ruy Blas** (Glover); **Triumph of Columbus** (Pratt); **Wonders in the Sun** (1706)

Dilla, **Automobile Graveyard** (Ceely)

Dimitri Nekhlyudov, Prince, **Resurrection** (Machover)

Dimitri Petrovsky, (bar) **Music Shop** (Wargo)

Dimitry, Deputy, **Wives Revenged** (Dibdin)

Dimitry, Mrs., **Wives Revenged** (Dibdin)

Dimmesdale, Arthur, **Hester Prynne** (Claflin); (t) **Scarlet Letter** (Damrosch); **Scarlet Letter** (Di Domenica); **Scarlet Letter** (Garwood); **Scarlet Letter** (Giannini); **Scarlet Letter** (Herman); (t) **Scarlet Letter** (Kaufmann); **Scarlet Letter** (Laitman)

Dimmly, Prince, (t) **Meanwhile, Back at Cinderella's** (Arlan)

Din, Dame, **Belphegor** (Barthelemon)

Dina, **Honey Moon** (Linley)

Dinah, (m) **Trouble in Tahiti** (Bernstein)

Dingle, Mrs., (m/a) **King of Cats** (Oliver)

Dino, (t) **A Wedding** (Bolcom)

Dinzie, **Sharon's Grave** (Wargo)

Diocles (Dioclesian), **Dioclesian** (Purcell)

Diomede, (bar) **Troilus and Cressida** (Walton)

Diomedes, (bar) **Sappho** (Glanville-Hicks)

Dion, **Revelation in the Courthouse** (Partch)

Dione, **Dione** (Lampe)

Dioneo, **The Visitors** (Chávez)

Dionisia, (m) **La Curandera** (Rodríguez)

Dionysos, **Apocalypse** (Shields)

Dionysus, **The Bacchae** (Antoniou); (t) **The Bacchae** (Buller); (t) **The Bassarids** (Henze); (bar) **Death in Venice** (Britten); **Revelation in the Courthouse** (Partch)

Dipsacus, (b) **Poisoned Kiss** (Vaughan Williams)

Dirce, **Dirce** (Horne)

Diron Hachard, (t) **Minette Fontaine** (Still)

Discobbolos, Mr., (t) **Mr. and Mrs. Discobbolos** (Westergaard)

Discobbolos, Mrs., (s) **Mr. and Mrs. Discobbolos** (Westergaard)

Dismas, **Child Is Born** (Herrmann)

Divara, (s) **Behold the Sun** (Goehr)

Djami, (bar) **Man with Footsoles** (Volans)

D. K., (t) **Demon Lover** (Nelson)

Dobbin, **Ballad of the Bremen Band** (Arlan)

Dobe, Lord, (b) **Actor's Revenge** (Miki)

Doc, Mrs., (a) **Quiet Place** (Bernstein)

Doc Stair, (bar) **Haircut** (Morgenstern)

Doctor Higgins, **Where the Cross Is Made** (Van de Vate)

Doctor John, **Marie Laveau** (Carbon)

Doda Malone, (s) **The Clock** (Rieti)

Dodge, (t) **Amelia** (Hagen)

Dodgson, Charles, (t) **Alice** (Bachlund); **Alice** (Waits)

Dodo, **Abracadabra** (Freedman)

Doeg, (bar) **Making of the Representative** (Glass)

Doll, (s) **Vera of Las Vegas** (Hagen)

Dollallolla, Queen, **Opera of Operas** (Arne, Lampe); **Tom Thumb** (Markordt)

Doll Bilby, (s) **Bilby's Doll** (Floyd)

Dolly, **Britain's Glory** (Arnold); **Chamber-Maid** (Phillips); **May-Day** (Arne); **Sultan of Mocha** (Cellier)

Eva, **Desert Flower** (Wallace); **Evita** (Lloyd Webber); **Uncle Tom's Cabin** (Howard); (s) **Picasso** (McQueen)

Evadne, (m) **Troilus and Cressida** (Walton)

Evan, (bar) **The Sacrifice** (MacMillan)

Evander, **Dione** (Lampe)

Evangeline Bellefontaine, **Evangeline** (George); (s) **Evangeline** (Luening); **Evangeline** (Rice)

Evans, Owen, (t) **Guilt of Lillian Sloan** (Neil)

Evarist, Signor, (t) **The Fan** (Goldstein)

Eve, **Aceldama** (Sleeper); **David's Violin** (Mogulesco); (s) **Eve's Odds** (Trinkley); **Garden Party** (Pinkham); **Hotel Eden** (Mollicone); **Lilith** (Davis); **Lilith** (Drattell); **Paradise Lost** (Penderecki); (s) **So How Does Your Garden (Russell)**

Even, **The Architect** (MacIntyre)

Everett, Mr., (bar) **Julius Caesar Jones** (Williamson)

Everett, Mrs., (s) **Julius Caesar Jones** (Williamson)

Evergreen, Miss Dorothy, **Double Disguise** (Hook)

Evergreen, Sir Richard, **Double Disguise** (Hook)

Everton, Mrs., (a) **Shanewis** (Cadman)

Everyman, **Everyman** (Lester); **Everyman** (Lehmann); **Everyman** (Nelhybel); **Reverend Everyman** (Brotons)

Eve St. John, (m) **Lady from Colorado** (Ward); **Lady Kate** (Ward)

Evol, **Lucedia** (Giannini)

Evvy, **Death and the Powers** (Machover)

Export, Mr., **Britons, Strike Home** (1739)

Eyre, Edward John, **Edward John Eyre** (Conyngham)

Faber, (bar) **Knot Garden** (Tippett)

Fabiani, Fabio, **Armourer of Nantes** (Balfe)

Fabio, **Choleric Fathers** (Shield); **The Islanders** (Dibdin); **Marriage Act** (Dibdin); **Triumph of Love** (Schmitz)

Fabricio, (bar) **Bianca** (Hadley)

Fabricio, Don, **Choleric Fathers** (Shield

Fabulina, **The Pirates** (Storace)

Fairfax, (t) **Man without a Country** (Damrosch)

Fairfax, Colonel, (t) **Yeomen of the Guard** (Sullivan)

Fairfax, John, **Dolly Varden** (Edwards)

Fairfax, John, Colonel, **Reform'd in Time** (Attwood)

Fairfax, Reginald, Lieutenant, **The Geisha** (Jones)

Fairles, Sir John, **Blackened Man** (Todd)

Fairlop, **The Woodman** (Shield)

Fairlove, **The Sot** (Arne)

Fairly, Lawyer, **The Farmer** (Shield)

Fairy Frank, **The Shamrock** (Shields)

Fairy Godmother, **Child, Book, Broomstick** (Burtch)

Fairy Grandmarina, **Magic Fishbone** (Chapin)

Faith, **Faith: DWF, 235** (Ching)

Faith Brown, **Goodman Brown** (Fink); (s) **Young Goodman Brown** (Lenel)

Falcon, Lord, **The Patron** (1729)

Falstaff, (b) **At the Boar's Head** (Holst); **Falstaff in and out of Love** (Rea); (bar) **Sir John in Love** (Vaughan Williams)

Fa Mu Lan, **Warrior Sisters** (Ho)

Fan Braxton, **God Bless Us** (Pasatieri)

Fancy Day, **Mellstock Quire** (Harper)

Fanny, **Before Breakfast** (Barnett); (s) **The Cooper** (Arne); **Killing No Murder** (Hook); **The Raft** (Reeve)

Fanny Holland, Miss, **Our Island Home** (Reed)

Fanny Robin, (s) **Fanny Robin** (Harper)

Fan-Tan, **The Mandarin** (De Koven)

Fantomas, (bar) **Hotel for Criminals** (Silverman)

Farfrae, **Mayor of Casterbridge** (Tranchell)

Farinelli, **Farinelli** (Barnett); **Queen of Spain** (Lampe)

Farmer John, (t) **Child, Book, Broomstick** (Burtch)

Farolles, Rev. Mr., **Daughters of the Late Colonel** (Buchanan)

Farquhar, Peyton, (bar) **Occurrence at Owl Creek** (Musgrave)

Farrell, Dr. James, **Leviathan Hook** (Doolittle)

Fashion, Lord, **Female Rake** (1736)

Fastodio, **Americana** (Bruce)

Fat, (b) **Second Hurricane** (Copland)

Fate, **Rose of Destiny** (Heckscher)

Father Christmas, **Down by the Greenwood Side** (Birtwistle)

Father Corman, **Lost Child** (Ridout)

Father Dominique, **Britons, Strike Home** (1739)

Father Luke, **The Shamrock** (Shields)

Father O'Flynn, **Shamus O'Brien** (Stanford)

Father Sergius (b-bar), **God's Liar** (Casken)

Fatima, **Africanus Blue Beard** (Sedgwick); **Blue-Beard** (Kelly); (s) **Oberon** (Weber); **Selima and Azor** (Linley Sr.); **Veiled Prophet** (Stanford)

Fatime, **Abou Hassan** (Cooke); **Cady of Bagdad** (Linley Jr.); **The Captive** (Dibdin et al.)

Faulkland, **The Oracle** (Winter-Hawes)

Faulknor, Captain Robert, **Death of Captain Faulknor** (Arnold)

Fauna, **Earthrise** (Spratlan)

Faust, **Faust** (Becker); **Faust Counter Faust** (Gessner); **Faust Triumphant** (Anderson); **Faustus Part One** (Rudenstein); **Faustus** (Bishop); **Fresh Faust** (Jenkins); **Lamentations of Doctor Faustus** (Hewitt); **Mephistopheles** (Lutz); **Who's on Faust?** (Zarr)

Fausto, Don, (b) **Big Black Box** (Morgenstern)

Faustus, (b-bar) **Faustus** (Dusapin); **Faustus** (Rudenstein)

Favell, Jack, **Rebecca**

Fawcett, Col. Percy, **Heroes Don't Dance** (Grant)

Fay, (s) **Ray and the Gospel Singer** (Gould)

Fay Doyle, (m) **Miss Lonelyhearts** (Liebermann)

Fay-Yen-Fah, **Land of Happiness** (Redding)

FDR, **Eleanor Roosevelt** (Vehar)

Feathertop, **Feathertop** (Barnes); (t) **Feathertop** (Barthelson)

Federico, (bar) **La Cubana** (Henze)

Fedora, **Yelva** (Bishop)

Florestine, (s) **Ghosts of Versailles** (Corigliano)

Floretta, **The Cabinet** (Reeve et al.); **Honey Moon** (Linley)

Floreville, **Count, Bondman** (Balfe)

Florian, **Devil's Bridge** (Arnold); **Notre-Dame of Paris** (Fry); **Young Hussar** (Kelly)

Florian, Prince, **Free Lance** (Sousa)

Florida, **Florida** (Eng)

Florimel, (s) **Florimel** (Greene); **Positive Man** (Arnold)

Florimore, **Noble Pedlar** (Barthelemon)

Florina, **The Birth-Day** (Arnold)

Florinda, **Loretta** (Lavenu)

Florindo, (bar) **Prima Donna** (Benjamin); **Servant of Two Masters** (Giannini)

Florizel, **Florizel and Perdita** (Boyce); **Sheep-Shearing** (Arne); **Sheep- Shearing** (Arnold); (t) **Winter's Tale** (Harbison)

Flummery, Counsellor, **The Farmer** (Shield)

Flourish, Sir Simon, **Abroad and at Home** (Shield)

Flourish, Young, **Abroad and at Home** (Shield)

Flute, **Midsummer Night's Dream** (1763); (t) **Midsummer Night's Dream** (Britten)

Fluther Good, (b-bar) **Plough and the Stars** (Siegmeister)

Flynn, Peter, (t) **Plough and the Stars** (Siegmeister)

Foible, Mrs., **Fashionable Lady** (1730)

Folial, (t) **The Escorial** (Levy)

Folinsbee, (bar) **The Argonauts** (Maganini)

Fong, **Bok Choy Variations** (Chen)

Fopling, **Jonathan Postfree** (1807)

Forage, **Turn Out!** (King)

Ford, (b) **Sir John in Love** (Vaughan Williams)

Ford, Betty, **Tania** (Davis)

Ford, Mrs., (m) **Sir John in Love** (Vaughan Williams)

Foreman, Larry, **Cradle Will Rock** (Blitzstein)

Foremast, **Britons, Strike Home** (1739)

Forest, (bar) **Masque of Clouds** (Johnson)

Formaggio, Count, **Pizza con Funghi** (Barab)

Fortespada, **Bianca** (Balfe)

Fortún, (t) **Junípero Serra** (Hively)

Fortunato, (t) **Casket of Amontillado** (Currie); **Cask of Amontillado** (Pinkham); (bar) **Fortunato** (Gideon)

Fortunato, Don, **Don Fortunato** (Forrest)

Fortune, **Scipio's Dream** (Weir)

Fortunio, **Fencing Master** (De Koven); (s) **Fortunio** (Darley)

Fotis, **Golden Ass** (Peters); (b-bar) **Greek Passion** (Martinů)

Fox, Mr., (bar) **Chanticleer** (Barab); (t) **Chanticleer** (Barthelson)

Fox, Mrs., **Chanticleer** (Barab); (a) **Chanticleer** (Barthelson)

Foxglove, **Family Quarrels** (Reeve et al.)

Foxy Quiller, **Foxy Quiller** (De Koven); (bar) **The Highwayman** (De Koven)

Fractioso, **Mysteries of the Castle** (Shield)

Frade, **The Dybbuk** (Tamkin)

Frances, (s) **Spanish Lady** (Elgar)

Frances, Countess, (m) **Gloriana** (Britten)

Francesca, **Fencing Master** (De Koven); **Inferno of Dante** (Soluri)

Francine, **Trio** (Ain)

Francis, **The Angelus** (Naylor); **Francis** (Beath); (t) **Judgment of St. Francis** (Flagello); (bar) **Jump into My Sack** (Grant)

Francis I, **Francis the First** (Loder)

Francis Osbaldistone, **Rob Roy** (Davy)

Francisca, **Monk of Toledo** (Knowlton)

Francisca, Donna, **The Alcaid** (Nathan)

Francisco, (bar) **Simón Bolívar** (Musgrave)

Francisco, Don, (b) **Natoma** (Herbert)

Francisco de Matos, Doña, **The Conquistador** (Fink)

François, **Lost Domain** (Carpenter); (t) **Madeleine** (Herbert); (t) **Quiet Place** (Bernstein)

Frank, (b-bar) **The Mistake** (Sheffer); (bar) **Scene Machine** (Gilbert); **The Tree** (Dowdell)

Frank Chambers, (bar) **Postman Always Rings Twice** (Paulus)

Frank Duryea, **Twin Sisters** (Sedgwick)

Frankenstein, **Birth/Day** (Wolfe); **Frankenstein** (Baber); **Frankenstein** (Blyton); **Frankenstein** (Larsen); **Frankenstein** (Sandow)

Frankenstein, Victor, (t) **Frankenstein** (Larsen)

Frankie, **Birdbath** (Lieberson)

Frank Innes, (t) **Hermiston** (Orr)

Franklin, Benjamin, **Americana** (Bruce); **Benjamin** (Carbon)

Frank Maurrant, (b-bar) **Street Scene** (Weill)

Frank Montague, **Vile Shadows** (Turner)

Frank Troy, Sergeant, (t) **Fanny Robin** (Harper)

Frank Wildblood, **World in the Moon** (Purcell/ Clarke)

Frantz Wolf, (t) **Romulus** (Karchin)

Franz, **Golden Butterfly** (De Koven)

Franz, Dr., **Girls of Holland** (De Koven)

Frau K, **Dora** (Shiflett)

Fred, **Again** (Heggie); **The Bargain** (McPeek); **Christmas Carol** (Musgrave); **Desperate Waltz** (Earnest); **Festival of Regrets** (Drattell); **God Bless Us** (Pasatieri); (t) **Have You Heard** (Talma); (actor) **Lost Highway** (Neuwirth); (boy s) **Tale of the Nutcracker** (Bohmler); (t) **"You Never Know"** (Koutzen)

Fred Burger, (t) **Sandhog** (Robinson)

Fred Jesson, **Brief Encounter** (Previn)

Frederic, (t) **Pirates of Penzance** (Sullivan)

Frederica, **Maid of Saxony** (Horn)

Frederick (Frederic), **Amelia** (Dibdin et al.); **Amelia** (Piccinni et al.); **The Blackamoor** (Dibdin); **Fire and Water!** (Arnold); **No Song, No Supper** (Storace); **The Seraglio** (Dibdin)

Frederick, Don, **Don John** (Bishop)

Frederick II, **Maid of Saxony** (Horn)

Freehold, Sir John, **Britons, Strike Home** (1739)

Freeman (Colin), **Chamber-Maid** (Phillips); **Village Opera** (1729)

Freeman, Captain, **Britain's Glory** (Arnold)

Freud, Anna, **Dora** (Shiflett)

Freud, Sigmund, **Dora** (Shiflett)

Freya, **Diarmid** (MacCunn)

Freyde, **Between Two Worlds** (Ran)

Friar Lawrence, (st) **Romeo and Juliet** (Shelley)

Friar Tuck, (bar) **Adventures of Friar Tuck** (Paxton); **Maid Marian** (Bishop); (b) **Robin Hood** (De Koven); **Robin Hood** (Tippett)

Friberg, Count Frederick, **Miller and His Men** (Bishop)

Fricka, (s) **Death of Baldur** (Bedford)

Frida Kahlo, **Frida** (Rodríguez)

Fridolin, **Night Dancers** (Loder)

Frieda, **I Rise in Flame** (Flanagan)

Friederike Brion, (m) **Lenz** (Sitsky)

Friendly, **Flora** (Hippisley); **Jealous Clown** (1730)

Friendly, Sir George, **Female Rake** (1736)

Friponi, Count, **Travellers in Switzerland** (Shield)

Frisk, Mrs., **The Decoy** (1733)

Frisketta, **Cupid's Revenge** (Hook)

Frithiof, **Frithiof** (Freer)

Fritz, **Friend Fritz** (Edwards); **Man of Feeling** (Oliver); (bar) **The Mountaineers** (Somerville)

Fritzi, (t) **Breakfast Waltzes** (Blumenfeld); **Wedding Trip** (De Koven)

Frizaletta, **Tom Thumb** (Markordt)

Frobisher, Marin (bar), **Frobisher** (Estacio)

Frollo, **Esmeralda** (Thomas); **Notre-Dame of Paris** (Fry); **Quasimodo** (Rodwell)

Front, **The Savoyard** (Reinagle)

Fry, Detective, **Crazy to Kill** (Beckwith)

Fulbert, (t) **Abelard and Heloise** (Ward); **Abelard and Heloise** (Gaughan); (t) **Heloise and Abelard** (Paulus)

Fulminone, Don, **Don Fulminone** (Giordani)

Funk, Joseph, **Singer's Glen** (Parker)

Furies, **I Can't Stand Wagner** (Barab)

Furlong, (bar/b) **Grace of Todd** (Crosse)

Furrow, **May-Day** (Arne)

Furst, Walter, **The Archers** (Carr)

Fustian, **Tumble-Down Dick** (1736)

Fyodor Kropotkin, (b) **Chinchilla** (Fink); (t) **Three Sisters** (Pasatieri)

Gabby Martin, **Chatter and Static** (Mathews)

Gabi, **Bitter Tears of Petra von Kant** (Barry)

Gabriel, **Angel Face** (Ames); **The Dead** (Boren); (t) **Erode the Greate** (La Montaine); **Evangeline** (Rice); **Father of the Child** (Barab); **Garden Party** (Pinkham); **Paradise Lost** (Penderecki); **The Promise** (Townsend); (t) **Taverner** (Davies); (st) **Too Many Sopranos** (Penhorwood)

Gabriel, Padre, (t) **Casanova's Homecoming** (Argento); **Danton and Robespierre** (Eaton); (b) **The Sacrifice** (Converse)

Gabriel Lajeunesse, **Evangeline** (George); (t) **Evangeline** (Luening)

Gabrielle, **Vile Shadows** (Turner)

Gad Beck, (actor) **For a Look or a Touch** (Heggie)

Gaga, Lady, **Enchanted Canary** (Stevens)

Gainlove, **Cure for a Scold** (1735); **The Rose** (Arne)

Gainsborough, Thomas, **Gainsborough's Duchess** (Coates)

Galahad, **Galahad** (Boughton)

Galatea, **Acis and Galatea** (Eccles); (s) **Acis and Galatea** (Handel); **Britannia triumphans** (Lawes)

Galeazzo Visconti, **Fencing Master** (De Koven)

Galileo, **Galileo** (Gundry); **Galileo** (Rimmer); (bar, t) **Galileo Galilei** (Glass); (b-bar) **Galileo Galilei** (Laderman); **Time for Growing** (Hopkins)

Gallanthus, (bar) **Poisoned Kiss** (Vaughan Williams)

Gallup, Donald, (bar) **Mother of Us All** (Thomson)

Galuchet, Father, (t) **Beach of Falesá** (Hoddinott)

Galuppi, Sam, **Patria, no. 3** (Schafer)

Galzetto, **The Earthquake** (Rodwell)

Gambia, **The Slave** (Bishop)

Gambogi, La, (m) **Happy Hypocrite** (Masland)

Gambrinus, **Gambrinus** (Sedgwick)

Gamma, King, (bar) **Princess Ida** (Sullivan)

Gandhi, (t) **Satyagraha** (Glass)

Ganges, **Cinthia and Endimion** (Purcell)

Gantry, Allan, **Young Lincoln II** (Hunkins)

Gantry, Elmer, (bar) **Elmer Gantry** (Aldridge)

Gao Jianli, (t) **First Emperor** (Tan Dun)

Garcia, **The Islanders** (Dibdin); **Marriage Act** (Dibdin); **Rosalinda** (Smith)

Garcias, Don, **New Spain** (Arnold); **Trick for Trick** (1735)

Gardiner, **Faith: DWF, 235** (Ching)

Gardinier, Edward, (t) **Rip Van Winkle** (Bristow)

Gardner, Ava, **Hopper's Wife** (Wallace)

Garibaldi, (t) **CIVIL warS** (Glass); **Garibaldi** (Cowen)

Garrett, Mr. (Thomas), (b) **Harriet** (Musgrave); (bar) **She Never Lost a Passenger** (Kander)

Garrick, David, **David Garrick** (Somerville); **Garrick** (Simon)

Garsie, (a) **Azara** (Paine)

Garvey, Marcus, (bar) **Till Victory Is Won** (Fax)

Gascoigne, Mrs., (b) **The Experiment** (Schwartz)

Gasconado, **Gasconado the Great** (1759)

Gaspara Stampa, **Telaio: Desdemona** (Botti)

Gathe Geezle, (bar) **Carrion Crow** (Fletcher)

Gathergold, (t) **Great Stone Face** (Kalmanoff)

Gatsby, Jay, (t) **Great Gatsby** (Harbison)

Gatz, Harry, (bar) **Great Gatsby** (Harbison)

Gaul, **Oithona** (Barthelemon)

Gavin, **Phoenix Park** (Strickland)

Gawain, (bar) **Gawain** (Birtwistle); **Gawain and Ragnall** (Blackford); (t) **Gwyneth and the Green Knight** (Plowman); **Sir Gawain** (Blackford); **Sir Gawain** (Eastman); **Sir Gawain** (Wilson-Dickson)

Gaxulta, (bar) **Under the Double Moon** (Davis)

Gay Brook, (tr) **Little Sweep** (Britten)

Gayford, **Love at First Sight** (1742)

Gayland, Lady, **False Alarms** (Addison)

Gayland, Sir Damon, **False Alarms** (Addison)

Gayle, (s) **Ice Break** (Tippett)

Gaylord Ravenal, **Show Boat** (Kern)

Gaylove, **False Guardians Outwitted** (1740)

Gaylove, Miss, **False Guardians Outwitted** (1740)

Gaynor, **Menna** (Hughes)

Gaywood, **Coffee-House** (Carey)

Geills, **Abbot of Drimock** (Musgrave)

General Biante, **Queen and the Rebels** (Moss)

General Wilmore, **Wilmore Castle** (Hook)

General Worry, **Rival Candidates** (Carter)

Genevieve, **Genevieve** (Macfarren); (m) **Long Christmas Dinner** (Hindemith)

Genius, **Britannia** (Arne)

Genji, Prince, **Echoes of the Shining Prince** (Cooper); (bar), **Tale of Genji** (Miki)

Gentooba, **Love in a Blaze** (Stevenson-Cogan)

Geodesa, (b-bar) **Parabola and Circula** (Blitzstein)

Geoffrey, **Canterbury Pilgrims** (Stanford); **Dorothy** (Cellier)

Geoffrey, King, **Three Princes** (Levowitz)

Geoffrey of Lisiac, (bar) **Castle Agrazant** (Lyford)

George, **Female Rake** (1736); (t) **George from Paradise** (Kaufmann); **Heroes Don't Dance** (Grant); (bar) **Jenny** (Weisgall); (b-bar) **Of Mice and Men** (Floyd); **Passion, Poison** (Hagemann); (bar) **Room No. 12** (Kanitz); (bar) **Smoky Mountain** (Hunkins)

George Gibbs, (t) **Our Town** (Rorem)

George Insight, Sir, **Reform'd in Time** (Attwood)

George III, (t) **Be Glad Then America** (La Montaine)

Georgette, **Rose** (Hatton); (a) **School for Wives** (Liebermann)

Geppetto, **Adventures of Pinocchio** (Dove)

Gerald, (bar) **The Opening** (Wilder)

Geraldine, **Geraldine** (Balfe); (s) **Hand of Bridge** (Barber)

Geraldine Polo, **Farinelli** (Barnett)

Gerard, **Dancing Master** (Arnold)

Gerardo, (t) **The Tenor** (Weisgall)

Geraud, (b-bar) **The Departure** (Davis)

Gerda, (s) **Fennimore and Gerda** (Delius); **Snow Queen** (Fine); **Snow Queen** (Gaburo)

Gerin, (t) **Ouanga** (White)

Germain, **Castle of Sorrento** (Attwood)

Geronio, **Turkish Lovers** (Lacy)

Géronte, **Sganarelle** (Kaufmann)

Gerry, **Cue 67** (Ching); **Luck of Ginger Coffey** (Pannell)

Gertrude, (s), **Fade** (Weisman); (m) **Hamlet** (Searle); **Mapping Venus** (Hays)

Gertrude S. (Stein), **Blood on the Dining Room Floor** (Sheffer); **Gertrude** (Johnston); (m) **Gertrude Stein** (Banfield);(s) **Mother of Us All** (Thomson); (t) **Picasso** (McQueen); **We're Back** (Armour); **Women in the Garden** (Fine)

Gesar, King, **King Gesar** (Lieberson)

Gesler, **The Archers** (Carr)

Ghiva, (m) **Lurline** (Wallace)

Ghost, (m) **Last Supper** (Birtwistle)

Giacinta, **Don Fulminone** (Giordani)

Giacomina, (m) **Boccaccio's Nightingale** (Trimble)

Giafer, **Nothing Superfluous** (Lee)

Gianetta, **The Alcaid** (Nathan)

Gianni Schicchi, **Buoso's Ghost** (Ching)

Gibson, Josh, **Summer King** (Sonenberg)

Gideon, **The Outcast** (Ain)

Giglio, Prince, **Rose and the Ring** (Leginska)

Gilbert, Sir Ralph, **Love at First Sight** (1763)

Gilbert, Young, **Love at First Sight** (1763)

Gilbert Griffiths, (t) **American Tragedy** (Picker)

Gilda, **Talk Opera** (Granger)

Gilead Merton, (b) **The Scarecrow** (Lockwood)

Giles, **Maid of the Mill** (Arnold)

Giles Winterbourne, (bar) **The Woodlanders** (Paulus)

Gilgamesh, **The Forest** (Byrne); **Gilgamesh** (Dickman)

Gillian, **The Quaker** (Dibdin)

Gillian, Dame, **Don John** (Bishop)

Gil Perez, **Marriage Act** (Dibdin)

Gil Polo, Don, **Farinelli** (Barnett)

Gimpel, **Gimpel the Fool** (Davidson); **Gimpel the Fool** (Schiff)

Ginger, (s) **Bartleby** (Aschaffenburg)

Ginger Coffey, **Luck of Ginger Coffey** (Pannell)

Ginny, **Tod's Gal** (Kelly)

Gino Carella, **Where Angels Fear to Tread** (Weiser)

Ginsburg, Allen, **Waking in New York** (Lauten)

Ginzberg, (bar) **Idiots First** (Blitzstein)

Gioachino, **Day at Rome** (Attwood)

Giovanni, **Bell Tower** (Krenek); **Garden of Mystery** (Cadman); **Giovanni, the Sculptor** (Hill); **Giovanni in London** (1827); (t) **Rape of Lucretia** (Britten)

Giovanni, Don, **The Libertine** (Mozart-Bishop)

Gisela (s), **Gisela in Her Bathtub** (Weisensel)

Giselle, **Night Dancers** (Loder)

Gismonda, (s) **Padrevia** (Pasatieri)

Gitele, **Shloyme Gorgl** (Lateiner)

Gittel, **Between Two Worlds** (Ran); **The Dybbuk** (Tamkin)

Giulietta, (s) **Casanova's Homecoming** (Argento)

Giuseppe, **The Immigrants** (Converse)

Giuseppe Palmieri, (bar) **The Gondoliers** (Sullivan)

Giuseppo, **Native Land** (Bishop)

Gladys, (s) **Requiem for a Rich Young Man** (Lockwood)

Glanville, **Harvest-Home** (Dibdin)

Glaud, **Gentle Shepherd** (1729)

Glavis, (t) **Pauline** (Cowen)

Glee, Sir Holly, **The Patron** (1729)

Gloom, (bar) **Mona** (Parker)

Gloomy Domingo, (t/bar) **Curious Fern** (Kupferman)

Gloria, **Saint Carmen of the Main** (Hodkinson); (m) **VALIS** (Machover); (s) **What Price Confidence** (Krenek)

Gluck, **King of the Golden River** (Hand)

Glumdalca, **Tom Thumb** (Markordt)

Gobbler, **Chanticleer** (Barab); (b) **Chanticleer** (Barthelson)

Gobineau, Mr., (bar) **The Medium** (Menotti)

Gobineau, Mrs., (s) **The Medium** (Menotti)

God, **Garden Party** (Pinkham); **Leviathan Hook** (Doolittle); (b-bar) **So How Does Your Garden** (Russell)

Goddess of Dullness, **Temple of Dullness** (Arne)

Goddess of the Waters, (m) **Amistad** (Davis)

Goddess Weaver, **Silver River** (Sheng)

God the Father, (ct) **Taverner** (Davies)

Godthefather, **Noah** (Sahl/Salzman)

Goewin, (bar, s) **Children of Don** (Holbrooke)

Gogol, **The Charlatan** (Sousa)

Goldberg, Abe, (bar) **Nine Rivers** (Weisgall)

Goldbury, Mr., **Utopia Limited** (Sullivan)

Golden Bells, **Marco Polo** (Stern)

Golden Buffalo, **Silver River** (Sheng)

Goldilocks, **Goldilocks** (Zaimont)

Golem, (b-bar) **The Golem** (Casken); (bar) **The Golem** (Ellstein); **The Golem** (Sitsky)

Golfredo de la Barca, General (b) **La Curandera** (Rodríguez)

Golk, Sidney, (bar) **Golk** (Eaton)

Golux, **Thirteen Clocks** (Theofanidis)

Gomez, Don, **Ruy Blas** (Glover)

Gomez, Dr., **White Agony** (Fuchs)

Gondibert, **Battle of Hexham** (Arnold)

Gontran, (t) **Azara** (Paine)

Gonzagues, Prince de, **Blanche de Nevers** (Balfe)

Gonzagues, Princess de, **Blanche de Nevers** (Balfe)

Gonzago, Count Vasquez de, **The Chieftain** (Sullivan)

Gonzales, **Wonders in the Sun** (1706)

Gonzalo (Don), (t) **Student from Salamanca** (Bach); **Sunny Morning** (Stringer)

Goodall, **Intriguing Chambermaid** (1734)

Good Deeds, **Everyman** (Lester)

Good Fairy, **Lucky-Peter** (Williamson)

Goodwill, **Miss Lucy in Town** (Arne)

Goody Fidget, **Rose and Colin** (Dibdin)

Goody Price, **Merrymount** (Smith)

Goody Scratch, **Welsh Opera** (1731)

Gookin, Judge, (b) **Feathertop** (Barthelson)

Goosequill, **Rival Milliners** (1736)

Gorenslat, **Fatal Oath** (Koutzen)

Gorgibus, (b-bar) **Signor Deluso** (Pasatieri)

Goro (sp), **Cio Cio San** (Carroll)

Govannion, (b) **Children of Don** (Holbrooke); **Dylan** (Holbrooke)

Governess, (s) **Turn of the Screw** (Britten)

Governor, **Chelsea Pensioner** (Dibdin)

Gower Lackland, Sir, (t) **Merry Mount** (Hanson)

Goya, (bar) **Facing Goya** (Nyman); **Goya** (Menotti); **Terrible Mouth** (Osborne)

Gozanes, (b) **Teraminta** (Stanley)

Grace, (s), **Beyond Men and Dreams** (Hogg); **Fleeting Animal** (Nielsen); **Midnight Court Opera** (Sokolovic); **Single Married Man** (Sedgwick); **Summer King** (Sonenberg)

Grace Ansley, **Roman Fever** (Hagemann); (m) **Roman Fever** (Ward)

Grace Kumalo, (sp) **Lost in the Stars** (Weill)

Grace Melbury, (s) **The Woodlanders** (Paulus)

Grace O'Malley, **Two Graces** (Ferguson)

Grace Poole, **Wide Sargasso Sea** (Howard)

Gracieuse, (s) **Ramuntcho** (Taylor)

Graciosa, **Graciosa and Percinet** (1845)

Gradgrind, **Hard Times** (Burgon)

Graeme, Donald, **The Covenanters** (Loder)

Graeme, Malcolm, (t) **Lady of the Lake** (Schmidt)

Grahame, (t) **Lake of Menteith** (Noble)

Grammer Oliver, (a) **The Woodlanders** (Paulus)

Grand Chateau, Marquis de, **The Cabinet** (Reeve et al.)

Grandpa Jones, **The Harvest** (Giannini)

Grandpa Moss, (b) **Tender Land** (Copland)

Grange, **Follies and Fancies** (Allen)

Grange, Mr., (t) **If the Cap Fits** (Bush)

Grania, **Diarmid** (MacCunn)

Granma Joad, **Grapes of Wrath** (Gordon)

Grant, **Grant, Warden of the Plains** (Adaskin)

Grant, Julia, (s) **Appomattox** (Glass); **Democracy** (Wheeler)

Grant, Ulysses S., (bar) **Appomattox** (Glass); **Democracy** (Wheeler); (bar) **Mother of Us All** (Thomson)

Grasshopper, (bar) **Ant and the Grasshopper** (Shawn)

Gray, Mr., (t) **Gentleman's Island** (Horovitz)

Green, Dr., (b-bar) **The System** (Bach)

Green, Malcolm, **Knight of Snowdoun** (Bishop)

Green, Mrs., (s) **Down by the Greenwood Side** (Birtwistle)

Greene, (t) **Arden Must Die** (Goehr)

Greenhorn, **Moby Dick** (Heggie)

Green Knight, (b) **Gwyneth and the Green Knight** (Plowman); **Sir Gawain** (Blackford); **Sir Gawain** (Eastman)

Gregg, Dr., (bar) **Gallantry** (Moore)

Gregor, (t) **Metamorphosis** (Beversdorf); **Metamorphosis** (White)

Gregorio, **The Alcaid** (Nathan)

Gregory, **Rose and Colin** (Dibdin); **Turn Out!** (King)

Gregory Greybeard, Sir, **Cupid's Revenge** (Hook)

Gremio, (t) **Taming of the Shrew** (Giannini)

Grendel (b), **Grendel** (Goldenthal)

Greppo, **Africanus Blue Beard** (Sedgwick)

Greta, **Festival of Regrets** (Drattell); **Snow Queen** (Ward)

Greta Bloch, **Kafka's Trial** (Ruders)

Gretchen, **Gambrinus** (Sedgwick); **Rumpelstiltskin** (Epstein)

Grete, (s) **Metamorphosis** (Beversdorf); **Metamorphosis** (White)

Gretel, **Hansel and Gretel** (Bruce); **Hansel and Gretel** (Stoddard); **Hansel & Gretel & Ted & Alice** (Schickele)

Greville, Captain, (t) **Flitch of Bacon** (Shield)

Grey, Lord, (b) **Catherine Grey** (Balfe)

Grideline, (a) **Rosamond** (Clayton)

Griffelkin, (s) **Griffelkin** (Foss)

Grigoris, (b-bar) **Greek Passion** (Martinů)

Grimbald, (bar) **King Arthur** (Purcell); **Restauration of Charles II** (1732)

Grimes, Peter, (t) **Peter Grimes** (Britten)

Grindoff (Wolf), **Miller and His Men** (Bishop)

Gripanck, **Africanus Blue Beard** (Sedgwick)

Gripes, **Two Cadis** (Dibdin)

Gripewell, **Gasconado the Great** (1759)

Griselda, **Free Lance** (Sousa)

Grist, **Benevolent Tar** (Dibdin)

Griswold, (bar) **Voyage of Edgar Allan Poe** (Argento)

Grizzle, Lord, **Tom Thumb** (Markordt)

Grog, **Positive Man** (Arnold)

Grose, Mrs., (s) **Turn of the Screw** (Britten)

Gross, **Pardoner's Tale** (Ridout)

Grosvenor, (bar) **Patience** (Sullivan)

Grosz, George, **Crossing** (Metcalf)

Groveby, Sir, **Maid of the Oaks** (Barthelemon)

Groves, Gen. Leslie, (b) **Doctor Atomic** (Adams)

Grub, **Magician No Conjurer** (Mazzinghi)

Gruber, Mama, (m) **Gift of Song** (Caldwell)

Gruber, Papa, (bar) **Gift of Song** (Caldwell)

Grumble, **Cinderella** (Davies)

Gryphon, (b) **Alice in Wonderland** (Chauls)

Guardian Angel, (s) **Eve's Odds** (Trinkley)

Guatama, Prince, **Light of Asia** (de Lara)

Gubbins, (t) **Dragon of Wantley** (Lampe); **Margery** (Lampe)

Gudule, **Notre-Dame of Paris** (Fry)

Guiche, Count de, (b cantante) **Cyrano** (Beeson)

Guido, **Bride Elect** (Sousa); **Caponsacchi** (Hageman)

Guido Ferranti, **Guido Ferranti** (Van Etten)

Guildenstern, **Rosencrantz and Guildenstern** (Garfein)

Guillem de Cabestanh, **Guillem the Troubadour** (Mackenzie)

Guimard, **Simoon** (Chisholm)

Guinevere (Guenevere), (Queen), (s) **Gawain** (Birtwistle); **Guinevere** (Williams); **Round Table** (Boughton); **Sir Gawain** (Blackford)

Guiscardo, (t) **Padrevia** (Pasatieri)

Gulliver (Gull), **Gulliver** (Bond); **Lilliput** (Arnold); **Travelling with Gulliver** (Eaton); **Travels** (Bond)

Gulnare, **Englishmen in India** (Bishop); **Nothing Superfluous** (Lee)

Gun Rod, **Mountain Windsong** (Chlarson)

Gunter, Hal, **Acres of Sky** (Kreutz)

Gus, (bar) **Ray and the Gospel Singer** (Gould)

Gustavus III, **Gustavus III** (Cooke)

Gustavus Vasa, **Hero of the North** (Kelly)

Guy, **Green Children** (LeFanu)

Guy of Gisbourne, **Maid Marian** (De Koven); (t) **Robin Hood** (De Koven)

Guzman, **Trick for Trick** (1735)

Guzman, Don, **Westward Ho!** (Miles)

Gwang Gung, **Chinaman's Chance** (Ho)

Gwawl, **Song of Rhiannon** (Bowden)

Gwen, **The Journey** (Metcalf); (a) **Kumana** (Kanitz); (st) **The Sacrifice** (MacMillan); (a) **Second Hurricane** (Copland)

Gwern, **Bronwen** (Holbrooke)

Gwinneth, **St. David's Day** (Attwood)

Gwydion, **Dylan** (Holbrooke)

Gwyn, **Menna** (Hughes)

Gwyneth, (s) **Gwyneth and the Green Knight** (Plowman)

Gyp, (bar) **Second Hurricane** (Copland)

Habbacuc, **Bel and the Dragon** (Gardner)

Hackum, Captain, **Fashionable Lady** (1730)

Hadassah, **Shloyme Gorgl** (Lateiner)

Hades, (b) **Orpheus** (Burgon)

Hadrian, **Hadrian** (Wells)

Haemon, **Antigone** (Joubert); (bar) **La Divina** (Pasatieri)

Hager, **Sarah** (Laderman)

Hagga, **Thirteen Clocks** (Theofanidis)

Haggith, **Judith** (Goossens)

Haimon, **Antigone** (Constantinides); **Antigone** (Eaton)

Haines, Lord, (bar) **Simple Decision** (Busch)

Hainessa, **Oxford Act** (1733)

Hal, **Wet** (LeBaron)

Hal, King, (bar) **King Hal** (Stewart)

Hal, Prince, (t) **At the Boar's Head** (Holst)

Hal Carter, (bar) **Picnic** (Larsen)

Hal Montana, **Just Above My Head** (Davis)

Hal (Harold) Newbury, (bar) **Robert and Hal** (Brooks)

Hale, Reverend John, (b) **The Crucible** (Ward)

Hal o'Chepe, **Canterbury Pilgrims** (Stanford)

Haman, (bar) **Esther** (Harvey); (bar) **Esther** (Knoller); (bar) **Esther** (Meyerowitz); **Esther** (Weisgall)

Hamid, (t) **Infidel** (MacSems)

Hamilton, Alexander, **Madame Jumel** (Wolf)

Hamilton, Sir William, (bar) **Nelson** (Berkeley)

(Russo); (s) **Lady of the Lake** (Siegmeister); **The Portrait** (Arnold); **The Portrait** (Barthelemon); **Quentin Durward** (Laurent); **Sicilian Romance** (Reeve)

Isabella, Queen, **Triumph of Columbus** (Pratt); (m) **The Voyage** (Glass)

Isabella Beecher, (s) **Mrs. President** (Bond)

Isabella Linton, (s) **Wuthering Heights** (Floyd); (m) **Wuthering Heights** (Herrmann)

Isabella Wardour, **The Antiquary** (Bishop)

Isabelle, (s) **Face on the Barroom Floor** (Mollicone)

Isabelle Eberhardt, (m) **Song from the Uproar** (Mazzoli)

Isabelle Rimbaud, (s) **Man With Footsoles** (Volans)

Isabetta, (s) **Fourth Day** (Ahlstrom)

Isadora Duncan, **Gertrude** (Johnston)

Isaiah, (bar) **Orpheus in Pecan Springs** (Latham)

Iseult, **The Crusaders** (Benedict); **Queen of Cornwall** (Boughton); **Tristan and Iseult** (Cohen); **Tristan and Iseult** (Whitehead)

Ishmael, **Call Me Ishmael** (Goldschneider); **Moby Dick** (Westergaard)

Ishtar, (m) **Loving/Toi** (Schafer)

Isidore, **Isidore de Merida** (Braham)

Isis, **Lovers and Friends** (LaChiusa); (col s), **The Mummy** (Quincy)

Isleman, (t) **Seal-Woman** (Bantock)

Ismad, (t) **Wizards of Balizar** (Lockwood)

Ismaël, **The Crusaders** (Benedict)

Ismena, **The Sultan** (Dibdin)

Ismene, **Antigone** (Constantinides); **Antigone** (Eaton)

Isolde, **Perfect Lives** (Ashley)

Isoline, **Maid of Artois** (Balfe)

Isolt, **Isolt of the White Hands** (Hart)

Itard, Dr. Jean-Marc, (bar) **Wild Boy** (Epstein)

Ithuriel, **Britannia** (Carey)

Itsele, **David's Violin** (Mogulesco)

Itys, (tr) **Love of the Nightingale** (Mills)

Itzak, (t) **Idiots First** (Blitzstein)

Ivan, **Bird in Your Ear** (Bruce); **Firebird Motel** (Conte); **Inner Voices** (Howard); **Menna** (Hughes); (bar) **Pastoral** (Galloway); **Sailor-Boy and the Falcon** (Siskind)

Ivanhoe, **Ivanhoe** (Parry); (t) **Ivanhoe** (Sullivan); **Maid of Judah** (Lacy)

Ivan Ivanovich, **With Such Friends** (Schnauber)

Ivan Nikiforovich, **With Such Friends** (Schnauber)

Ivan Stepanovich, (t) **Music Shop** (Wargo)

Ivan the Terrible, **Flight** (Antheil)

Ives, Charles, **Harmony** (Carl)

Ivona, (s) **Hunger Art** (Myers)

Jabar, **Ali Baba Opera** (Reeve)

Jabe Torrance, (b-bar) **Orpheus Descending** (Saylor)

Jabez, **The Alcaid** (Nathan)

Jabez Bookstaver, (bar) **Sold Again** (Sedgwick)

Jabez Stone, (b) **Devil and Daniel Webster** (Moore)

Jacinta, **World in the Moon** (Purcell, Clarke)

Jack, **Brave Jack** (Waters); **Fisher King** (Lowenstein); **Heroes Don't Dance** (Grant); **Jack and Roberta** (Cain); **Jack and the Beanstalk** (Gruenberg); **Jack of Newbury** (Hook); (t) **Midsummer Marriage** (Tippett); **Sharon's Grave** (Wargo); **Something's Gonna Happen** (Colgrass); **Waiting for Jack** (Webb)

Jack Absolute, (bar) **The Rivals** (Mechem)

Jack Average, **The Cherokee** (Storace)

Jack Benny, (actor) **Jack Benny** (Moran)

Jack Burden, **Willie Stark** (Floyd)

Jack Churly, **Friend in Need** (Kelly)

Jack Finney, (mime) **Down by the Greenwood Side** (Birtwistle)

Jack Hammer, (t) **Sold Again** (Sedgwick)

Jackie O, **Jackie O** (Daugherty)

Jack Junk, **Mouth of the Nile** (Attwood)

Jack Ketch, (bar) **Punch and Judy** (Birtwistle)

Jack London (bar), **Every Man Jack** (Larsen)

Jack Point, (bar) **Yeomen of the Guard** (Sullivan)

Jack Potter, **Bride Comes to Yellow Sky** (Nixon)

Jack Keefem, **Silver Tankard** (Arnold)

Jack Scarlett, **Bachelor Farmers** (Weisensel)

Jack Sheppard, **Jack Sheppard** (Rodwell); **Quaker's Opera** (1728)

Jackson, Andrew, **Rachel** (Coe)

Jack Spaniard, (bar) **Lady from Colorado** (Ward); **Lady Kate** (Ward)

Jack Taste, **Don Sancho** (1739)

Jack Turner, (bar) **Woman at the Otowi Crossing** (Paulus)

Jacob, **Jacob and the Indians** (Laderman); (t/bar) **Victory at Masada** (Kalmanoff); **The Wrestler** (Adler)

Jacob, Senator, (b) **America** (Kohs)

Jacob Bila, **Bachelor Farmers** (Weisensel)

Jacob Buzzard, **Climbing Boy** (Hawes)

Jacob Vredenburgh, **Barber of New York** (Vernon)

Jacobs, Max, (t) **Picasso** (McQueen)

Jacqueline, (m/s) **Sterlingman** (Roy)

Jacques, **Rose** (Hatton); **The Savoyard** (Reinagle)

Jade Emperor, **Silver River** (Sheng)

Jake, (bar) **Porgy and Bess** (Gershwin)

Jake Barnes, **Sun Also Rises** (Young)

Jake Weiss, **Bachelor Farmers** (Weisensel)

Jakob Lenz, (t) **Lenz** (Sitsky)

Jakobus Rey, **In the Drought** (Joubert)

James, **Female Rake** (1736); **Gethsemane Park** (Moore); **Perfect Plan** (Barab); **Plumber's Gift** (Blake); **Sasha** (Oliver)

James V, **Knight of Snowdoun** (Bishop); (t) **Lady of the Lake** (Schmidt)

James, Mrs., (s) **Edge of Glory** (Waters)

James Bell, **Passion of Jonathan Wade** (Harvey)

James Dee, Captain, (t) **Deseret** (Kastle)

James Dillingham Young, (bar) **Gift of the Magi** (Magney)

James Fergus, **Pamelia** (Funk)

Jessamy, **Lionel and Clarissa** (Dibdin)

Jessel, Miss, (s) **Turn of the Screw** (Britten)

Jessica, **Festival of Regrets** (Drattell); **The Tree** (Dowdell)

Jessie, **Mountain Sylph** (Barnett); **Silver Tassie** (Turnage)

Jessie Tibbs, **Edge of Glory** (Waters)

Jessy Lea, **Jessy Lea** (Macfarren)

Jesus (Christ), (t) **Hell's Angels** (Osborne); **I Am the Way** (Hines); **Jesus Christ** (Lloyd Webber); **Jesus of Nazareth** (Rudenstein); (bar) **Last Supper** (Birtwistle); (bar) **Passion and Resurrection** (Harvey); **The Promise** (Townsend)

Jezebel, **Don Quixote in England** (1734); **Naboth's Vineyard** (Goehr)

Jian Ching I, II, (m, s), **Madame Mao** (Sheng)

Jill Goodheart, (s) **Civilization** (Sahl/Salzman)

Jim, (bar) **Glittering Gate** (Glanville-Hicks); (t) **Mr. Polly at the Potwell Inn** (Drummond); **Music Teacher** (Shawn); (t) **Oath of Bad Brown Bill** (Conyngham)

Jim Kendall, (bar) **Haircut** (Morgenstern)

Jim Kenyon, **Rose-Marie** (Friml/Stothart)

Jimmy, **Say Cheese** (Barab)

Jimmy Sullivan, **God Boy** (Ritchie)

Jim Smiley, (t) **Jumping Frog** (Foss)

Jim Young, (bar) **Della's Gift** (Welcher); **Gift of the Magi** (Conte)

Jinks, Captain Jonathan, (t) **Captain Jinks** (Beeson)

Ji-Saburo, **Hoshi-San** (Leps)

J. J. Fergeson, **Casino Paradise** (Bolcom)

Joan, Buxom, (s) **Buxom Joan** (Taylor)

Joan, Pope, **Pope Joan** (LeBaron); **Pope Joan** (Musto)

Jo Ann, (s) **New Year** (Tippett)

Joanna Enfield, (s) **Dr. Jekyll and Mr. Hyde** (O'Neal)

Joanne, (s) **Secret of the Mirror** (Busch)

Joanne Jefferson, **Rent** (Larson)

Joan of Arc, **Joan of Arc** (Balfe); **Joan of Arc** (Burgon); **Joan of Arc** (Freer); **Time for Growing** (Hopkins); **Trial at Rouen** (Dello Joio); **Triumph of (Saint) Joan** (Dello Joio)

Joash, (bar) **The Tower** (Levy)

Jobling, Will, **Blackened Man** (Todd)

Jobson, **Devil to Pay** (1731); **Merry Cobler** (1735)

Jobson, Nell, **Devil to Pay** (1731)

Job Spokewoppen, **Hofer** (Rossini-Bishop)

Jocasta, (s, actor, dancer) **Jocasta** (Schonthal); (s) **Oedipus** (Partch); **Passion of Oedipus** (Travis)

Jocelyn, **Night before the Wedding** (Bishop)

Joe, **Ballymore** (Wargo); **The Bee-Hive** (Horn); (t) **Blue Monday** (Gershwin); **Brazen Bust** (Bishop); **Carmen Jones** (Bizet-Bennett); **Dark Waters** (Krenek); **Flowers** (Hardy); (t) **The Ledge** (Bennett); (t) **Lucky Dollar** (Kanitz); **Most Happy Fella** (Loesser); **Black Roses** (Chisholm); (bar) **One-Man Show** (Maw); (bar) **Room No. 12** (Kanitz); **Show Boat** (Kern); (b) **Till Victory Is Won** (Fox)

Joe, Uncle, (bar) **The Fox** (Kondorossy)

Joe Curious, **Don Sancho** (1739)

Joe Hill, **Joe Hill** (Bush)

Joe Info, Jr., Mrs., (s) **Videomania** (Kalmanoff)

Joe Info, Sr., (b-bar) **Videomania** (Kalmanoff)

Joe Kyriakos, **No for an Answer** (Blitzstein)

Joe Pitt, **Angels in America** (Eötvös)

Joe Rimshot, **Rimshot** (Currie)

Joe Saul, **Burning Bright** (Lewin)

Joe Shady, (b) **Second Mrs. Kong** (Birtwistle)

Joe Sikes, (b-bar/bar) **No Neutral Ground** (Brandt)

Joe Smith, **Silver City** (Doolittle)

Joey, **British Fortitude** (Reeve)

Johanna, (s) **Sweeney Todd** (Sondheim)

John, **Before Breakfast** (Barnett); **Brickdust Man** (Dibdin); (bar) **Face on the Barroom Floor** (Mollicone); **Gethsemane Park** (Moore); **Golden Gate** (Cummings); (b) **Golden Lion** (Kechley); (b-bar) **Hugh the Drover** (Vaughan Williams); **Inquest of Love** (Harvey); **John of Paris** (Bishop); (tr) **Julius Caesar Jones** (Williamson); (t) **Masque of Angels** (Argento); **Miraculous Turnip** (Bissell); (b-bar) **Miss Julie** (Rorem); **Orpheus X** (Eckert); (t) **Passion and Resurrection** (Harvey); (b-bar) **Prodigal Son** (Jacobi); **The Proposal** (Granger); **Travelling Companion** (Stanford); **Welsh Opera** (1731); **Yellow Wallpaper** (Perera)

John, Duke of Argyle, **Jeanie Deans** (MacCunn)

John, Prince, **Maid Marian** (Bishop)

John Barleycorn, **John Barleycorn** (Montgomery)

John Brooke, (bar) **Little Women** (Adamo)

John Buchanan, (bar) **Summer and Smoke** (Hoiby)

John Bull, Sir, **Fontainbleau** (Shield)

John Bunting, **The Lodger** (Tate)

John Clitheroe, (bar) **Plough and the Stars** (Siegmeister)

John Harvard, (b) **Boston Baked Beans** (Kubik)

John Henry, **Mississippi Legend** (Wolfe)

John Loveday, **Trumpet Major** (Hoddinott)

John Maddox, **Village Coquettes** (Hullah)

Johnnie, (t/bar) **The Pumpkin** (Kondorossy)

Johnny, (t) **Hangman, Hangman!** (Balada); **Johnny and the Mohawks** (Maconchy); (boy s) **My Heart's in the Highlands** (Beeson); (boy s) **Ransom of Red Chief** (Rodríguez); (bar) **Shadows of the City** (Bo); **Tin Pan Alley** (Raphling)

Johnny Adams, (boy s) **Abigail Adams** (Owen)

Johnny Dee, (bar) **Lowland Sea** (Wilder)

Johnny O'Sullivan, (t) **Sandhog** (Robinson)

Johnny Reb, **Gentlemen, Be Seated!** (Moross)

John Peerybingle, **Cricket on the Hearth** (Mackenzie)

John Rolfe, (b-bar) **Pocahontas** (Haugen)

John Seal, **Bachelor Farmers** (Weisensel)

John Smith, (t) **Pocahontas** (Haugen)

Johnson, Andrew, (t) **Mother of Us All** (Thomson)

Johnson, Sir William, (bar) **Molly Brant** (Cecconi-Bates)

John Sorel, (bar) **The Consul** (Menotti)

John South, (t) **The Woodlanders** (Paulus)

Johnstone, John, **The Legend** (Murray)

John the Baptist, **Fisherman Called Peter** (Owen); **The Promise** (Townsend)

John Thomas, (bar/t) **Tickets Please** (Nelson)

John Triptolemus (t), **Finnish Prisoner** (Gough)

Johor, (b) **Making of the Representative** (Glass)

Joker, **The Losers** (Farberman)

Joking Jesus, (bar) **Taverner** (Davies)

Joll, Colonel, **Waiting for the Barbarians** (Glass)

Jo March, (m) **Little Women** (Adamo); **Little Women** (Freer)

Jonah, (b) **Boy from Deerfield** (Halpern); **Jonah** (Beeson); **Jonah** (Cole)

Jonathan, (t) **Boys and Girls** (Holloway); **The Commission** (Cowell); (t) **Philip Marshall** (Barab); (b) **Saul** (Sargon); **Silvia** (Lillo); (t) **Sterlingman** (Roy)

Jonathan Gilourin, (t) **Colonial Jonathan** (Argento)

Jonathan Postfree, **Jonathan Postfree** (1807)

Jones, (bar) **No Neutral Ground** (Brandt); **Victory** (Bennett)

Jones, Brutus, (bar) **Emperor Jones** (Gruenberg)

Jones, Carter, (bar) **The Visitation** (Schuller)

Jones, Dr. Jasper, **Fisherman's Dock** (Banfield)

Jones, Gregory, (bar) **The Affair** (Werder)

Jones, Jim, **Reverend Jim** (Eaton)

Jones, Leslie, (bar) **Kingdom for a Cow** (Weill)

Jones, Paul, (bar) **Dove of Peace** (Damrosch)

Jones, Quincy, **Star across the Ocean** (Richards)

Jones, Sissieretta (Matilda Sissieretta Joyner Jones), (s) **Edge of Glory** (Waters); **Opera Singer** (Willis)

Jonson, Ben, **Johnson Preserv'd** (Stoker); **Macheath in the Shades** (1735)

Jonson, Henry, (bar), **Aspern Papers** (Hagemann)

Jordan Baker, (m) **Great Gatsby** (Harbison)

Jorge Manuel, **El Greco** (Harper)

Jorinda, **Joringel** (Garwood)

Joringel, **Joringel** (Garwood)

José, Don, **José's Carmen** (Bizet-Ashman); (bar) **Maritana** (Wallace)

José Antonio Páez, (b) **Simón Bolívar** (Musgrave)

José Martinez, Don, (b) **Koanga** (Delius)

Joseph, **Bethlehem** (Boughton); (st) **Erode the Greate** (La Montaine); (bar) **Eternal Road** (Weill); **Father of the Child** (Barab); (bar) **Good Tidings** (Locklair); **Little Thieves** (Stuart); **Pearl** (Davidson); **Simeon** (Gustafson)

Joseph de Rocher (bar), **Dead Man Walking** (Heggie)

Josephine, (s) **H.M.S. Pinafore** (Sullivan); **Hofer** (Rossini-Bishop); **Josephine** (Sullivan); (m) **Violins of St. Jacques** (Williamson); **Wreck of the Pinafore** (Searelle)

Josephine Pinner, **Daughters of the Late Colonel** (Buchanan)

Joseph K., **Kafka's Trial** (Ruders)

Josh, **Inquest of Love** (Harvey); (t) **Song of Eddie** (Farberman)

Joshua, (b) **And the Walls** (Roosevelt); (bar) **Joshua's Boots** (Hailstork)

Josiah, (bar) **Harriet** (Musgrave)

Josiah Creach, (t) **Markheim** (Floyd)

Josie, (s) **Last Leaf** (Niblock)

Jove, Dr., **Stauf** (Sahl)

Jovian, (t) **Julian** (Saminsky)

Jowler, Colonel, (bar) **Rising of the Moon** (Maw)

Joy, (s) **Araboolies of Liberty Street** (Perera)

Joyce, Howard, (bar) **The Letter** (Moravec)

Joyce, James, **Antient Concert** (Hagen)

Joyce, Jane, **Antient Concert** (Hagen)

Juan, **The Alcaid** (Nathan); (bar) **Black Widow** (Pasatieri); (t) **Kingdom for a Cow** (Weill)

Juan, Don, **Castle of Andalusia** (Arnold)

Juan Bautista Alvarado, (bar) **Natoma** (Herbert)

Juan de Mañara, Don, (t) **Don Juan de Mañara** (Goossens)

Juana la Loca, Queen, (s) **La Loca** (Menotti)

Juanita, (lyr s) **Kingdom for a Cow** (Weill)

Juanita Mendoza, (m) **Dove of Peace** (Damrosch)

Juanito, Don, **Loretta** (Lavenu)

Juan Manual de Rosa, **Rosa** (Andriessen)

Juba, **The Prize** (Storace)

Judah, **Tamar and Judah** (Lavry)

Judas (Iscariot), **Automobile Graveyard** (Ceely); (t) **Calvary** (Pasatieri); **Jesus Christ** (Lloyd Webber); **Judas Iscariot** (Barlow); **Judas Tree** (Dickinson); (t) **Last Supper** (Birtwistle); (b) **Passion and Resurrection** (Harvey)

Judd, **Voss** (Meale)

Judex, (b) **Hotel for Criminals** (Silverman)

Judith, (m) **Judith** (Chadwick); **Judith** (Goossens); **Judith and Holofernes** (Fink); **Line of Terror** (McQueen)

Judson, Mrs., (m) **Question of Taste** (Schuman)

Judy, **Baa Baa Black Sheep** (Berkeley); (m) **Punch and Judy** (Birtwistle)

Julek, **Lost Childhood** (Hamer)

Jules, **Deep River** (Harling); (bar) **Game of Poker** (Burke); **Maid of Artois** (Balfe)

Julia, **The Commission** (Cowell); **Guy Mannering** (Attwood); **Mysteries of the Castle** (Shield); **1984** (Maazel); **Travellers in Switzerland** (Shield); (s) **Zenobia** (Pratt)

Julian, **The Ferryman** (Feigin); **Quartet** (Ritchie)

Juliana, **Day at Rome** (Attwood)

Julia Oddfish, **The Blackamoor** (Dibdin)

Julie, **Firebird Motel** (Conte); (s) **Miracle of Flanders** (Gruenberg); (s) **Miss Julie** (Rorem)

Julie, Miss, (s) **Miss Julie** (Alwyn)

Julie Corinne, **The Bondman** (Balfe)

Julie Gregg, (s) **Haircut** (Morgenstern)

Julie La Verne, **Show Boat** (Kern)

Julien, **Victorine** (Mellon)

Juliet, (s) **The Gate** (Tan Dun); **Romeo and Juliet** (Barkworth); **Romeo and Juliet** (Liotta); **Romeo and Juliet** (Marshall-Hall); (s) **Romeo and Juliet** (Shelley)

Juliet Brook, (s) **Little Sweep** (Britten)

Julietta, **The Marquesa** (Siegmeister)

Luis de Carvajal, Don, **The Conquistador** (Fink)

Luiz, (t) **The Gondoliers** (Sullivan)

Luka, (b) **The Bear** (Walton); (t) **The Boor** (Kay); (t) **The Boor** (Grantham); (t) **The Brute** (Moss)

Lukash, Lt., (bar) **Good Soldier Schweik** (Kurka)

Luke, (t) **Ice Break** (Tippett); **The Promise** (Townsend)

Luke, Father, **Love in a Camp** (Shield); **Poor Soldier** (Shield)

Luke Bentley, (bar) **The Rope** (Mennini)

Lula Belle, **Tod's Gal** (Kelly)

Luling Liu Young, (m) **Bonesetter's Daughter** (Wallace)

Lulu, (s) **Elmer Gantry** (Aldridge); (m) **Jumping Frog** (Foss)

Lumei, **Nannan** (Wang Jie)

Lure, Miss, **Female Parson** (Coffey)

Lusignan, **Daughter of St. Mark** (Balfe)

Lustra Chancy, (s) **Beatrice Chancy** (Rolfe)

Lutece, **Three Visitations** (Sherman)

Luther Dane, **Tight-Rope** (Biscardi)

Luxemburg, Rosa, **Realitillusion** (Brégent)

Luyala, **Luyala** (Banfield)

Lycidas, **Happy Arcadia** (Clay)

Lycomedes, **Achilles** (1733)

Lyd, **Dylan** (Holbrooke)

Lydia, **Colomba** (Mackenzie); **Fisher King** (Lowenstein); **Forest Rose** (Daniels); **The Seraglio** (Dibdin)

Lydia Bennet, (s) **Pride and Prejudice** (Mechem)

Lydia Larkspur, (s) **The Rivals** (Mechem)

Lyman Ward, **Angle of Repose** (Imbrie)

Lynn, (m) **Love, Death** (White)

Lyonnel, **Maid of Honour** (Balfe)

Lysander, **Fairy Queen** (Purcell); (t) **Midsummer Night's Dream** (Britten)

Lysia/Lysistrata, (s) **Lysistrata** (Adamo)

Lysistrata, (s) **Lysistrata** (Barthelson)

**M, One Thousand Airplanes** (Glass)

Maardokai, (b) **Esther** (Knoller); (m) **Curious Fern** (Kupferman); (s) **Pirates of Penzance** (Sullivan)

Mabel Flourish, **Love in a Camp** (Shield)

Mabel Petherick, (s) **Ordeal of Osbert** (Davis)

Macbeth, **Macbeth** (Collingwood); **Macbeth** (Eccles); **Macbeth** (Goldman); **Macbeth** (Halpern); **Macbeth** (Leveridge); **Macbeth** (Locke et al.); **Three, Two, One** (Chen)

Macbeth, Lady, **Macbeth** (Locke/Johnson); **Mortal Thoughts of Lady Macbeth** (Krausas)

MacCooper, (bar) **Midnight Duel** (Kondorossy)

Maccus, (bar) **Beggar's Opera** (Pepusch); (b) **King's Henchmen** (Taylor); **Macheath in the Shades** (1735); **Polly** (1729)

Macdonald, Sir John, **Louis Riel** (Somers)

MacDougald, Dougald (b-bar), **Sojourner and Mollie Sinclair** (Floyd)

MacGregor, Jasper, (b-bar) **My Heart's in the Highlands** (Beeson)

Macheath/Mack, **Little Beggars** (Saunders); (t) **Threepenny Opera** (Weill-Blitzstein)

Mac Rusty, **Day at Rome** (Attwood)

Mac Subtle, Sir, **Critic upon Critic** (MacNally)

Madame, **Unmusical Impresario** (Davis)

Madame Adare, **Madame Adare** (Silverman)

Madame Altina, (s) **La Divina** (Pasatieri)

Madame Angôt, **Circumstances Alter Cases** (Sedgwick)

Madame Bardac, **Blood Moon** (Dello Joio)

Madame Bardeau, (m) **The Olympians** (Bliss)

Madame Chauvenet, (m) **The System** (Bach)

Madame Defarge, (s) **Tale of Two Cities** (Benjamin)

Madame d'Urfé, (a) **Casanova's Homecoming** (Argento)

Madame Euterpova, (s) **Help, Help** (Menotti)

Madame Fifi, (m) **Old Majestic** (Rodríguez)

Madame Flora (Baba), (a) **The Medium** (Menotti)

Madame Grabski, (s) **Lizzie Strotter** (Kalmanoff)

Madame Jumel, **Madame Jumel** (Wolf)

Madame Larole, **Young Hussar** (Kelly)

Madame Pompous, (s) **Too Many Sopranos** (Penhorwood)

Madame Queen, **Under the Arbor** (Greenleaf)

Madame Raquin, **Thérèse Raquin** (Picker)

Madame Rimbaud, (s) **Man With Footsoles** (Volans)

Madame Sganarelle, (s) **Sganarelle** (Archer)

Madame X, **What to Wear** (Gordon)

Madam Peep, (m) **Oedipus Tex** (Schickele)

Mad bird, (s) **Spirit of the Avalanche** (Hovhaness)

Maddy, **Push!** (Bruce)

Madeleine, (s) **Blennerhasset** (Giannini); (s) **If the Cap Fits** (Bush); (s) **The Olympians** (Bliss)

Madeleine Fleury, (s) **Madeleine** (Herbert)

Madeline, **The Architect** (MacIntyre); (s) **Face on the Barroom Floor** (Mollicone); **Madeline** (Edwards)

Madeline Mitchell, (m) **Last Acts** (Heggie)

Madeline Usher, **Dream within a Dream** (Currie); **Fall of the House of Usher** (Glass); (s) **Fall of the House of Usher** (Sitsky)

Madelon, **Joan of Arc** (Balfe)

Madge, **Gentle Shepherd** (1729); **Heart of Midlothian** (Bishop)

Madge Wildfire, **Heart of Midlothian** (Loder); **Jeanie Deans** (MacCunn)

Mad Hatter, (bar), **Alice** (Bachlund); (bar) **Alice in Wonderland** (Chin)

Madge Owens, (s) **Picnic** (Larsen)

Madimi, **Madimi** (Wolosoff)

Mad Margaret, (m) **Ruddigore** (Sullivan)

Madonna Pica, (s) **Judgment of St. Francis** (Flagello)

Mae, **Grapes of Wrath** (Gordon); **Hearts on Fire** (Ames); (s) **Room No. 12** (Kanitz)

Mafairy, **Africanus Blue Beard** (Sedgwick)

Mag, **Ballymore** (Wargo)

Magdalena, (s) **The Sacrifice** (Converse)

Magdalene Forensic, (s/m) **Bird in the Bush** (Bielawa)

Magda Sorel, (s) **The Consul** (Menotti)

Magdelon, **Follies and Fancies** (Allen)

Magenta, **Arachne** (Michael)

Maggie, **Abbot of Drimock** (Musgrave); (m) **The Fox** (Kondorossy)

Maggie Dempster, (m) **One-Man Show** (Maw)

Maggie Hargrave, (m) **Fly** (Conyngham)

Maggy, **Highland Fair** (1731)

Magi, the, **Gift of the Magi** (Conte)

Magistrate of Athens, (bar) **Lysistrata** (Barthelson)

Magnolia, **Show Boat** (Kern)

Magnus, **Martyrdom of St. Magnus** (Davies)

Magnus, Count, **Matilda of Hungary** (Wallace)

Magnus Taylor, (bar) **Primal Void** (Vincent)

Mago, **Devil of a Duke** (1732)

Magua, (bar) **Last of the Mohicans** (Henderson)

Maguire, (bar) **Emmeline** (Picker)

Magus, **Children's Crusade** (Schafer)

Mahadevi, Princess, **Chakravaka-Bird** (Gilbert)

Mahana, **Kahalaopuna, Princess of Manoa** (McKay)

Maharajah of Rajaputana, (b) **Last Savage** (Menotti)

Maharal, (bar), **The Golem** (Casken); (bar) **The Golem** (Ellstein)

Maharani of Rajaputana, (a) **Last Savage** (Menotti)

Mahler, **Marco Polo** (Tan Dun)

Mahler, Alma, (female voice) **Memoirs of Uliana Rooney** (Fine)

Mahler, Gustav, (bar) **Memoirs of Uliana Rooney** (Fine)

Mahmoud, **Il Bondocani** (Attwood/Moorehead); **Caliph of Bagdad** (Musgrave); **Fall of Algiers** (Bishop); (sp) **Mahmoud** (Storace)

Mahmoud, Sultan, **Rose of Persia** (Sullivan)

Mahomet II, **Siege of Corinth** (Rossini-Cooke)

Mahud Khan, **Safié** (Hadley)

Maia, **Cows of Apollo** (Theofanidis)

Maid Marian, **Adventures of Friar Tuck** (Paxton); **Maid Marian** (Bishop); (s) **Robin Hood** (De Koven); **Robin Hood** (Macfarren); **Robin Hood** (Shield); **Robin** Hood (Tippett)

Maire, **Muirgheis** (Butler)

Maitland, Mr., **The Covenanters** (Loder)

Maitra, (bar) **Snatched by the Gods** (Vir)

Maive, (a) **Immortal Hour** (Boughton)

Majnun, **Song of Majnun** (Sheng)

Ma Joad, **Grapes of Wrath** (Gordon)

Major, (b) **Zoggy** (Fox)

Makart, Lea, (s) **Alien Corn** (Benjamin)

Makepile, Farmer, **The Borderline** (Mellers)

Makesafe, **Transformation** (Condell)

Maki, (boy's voice) **Wizards of Balizar** (Lockwood)

Mal, (t) **The Sacrifice** (MacMillan)

Malaprop, Mrs., (m) **The Rivals** (Mechem)

Malcolm X, (bar) **X** (Davis)

Male chorus, (t) **Rape of Lucretia** (Britten)

Maleen, Princess, **Princess Maleen** (Schonthal)

Malek, (bar) **Azara** (Paine)

Malespina, Count, **Bianca** (Balfe)

Malinche, (s) **Montezuma** (Sessions)

Malinoff, General, **Something New** (Hoiby)

Malkyn, **The Wayfarers** (Joubert)

Malooko, **The Cherokee** (Storace)

Malvina, **Malvina** (Lee)

Malvolio, **Malvolio** (Hart); (bar) **Twelfth Night** (Amram)

Mamah, **Shining Brow** (Hagen)

Ma Moss, (a) **Tender Land** (Copland)

Manana, **Tammany** (Hewitt)

Manawydan, **Song of Rhiannon** (Bowden)

Mancini, Count, (t) **He Who Gets Slapped** (Ward)

Mandane, (s) **Artaxerxes** (Arne); **Nourjahad** (Loder)

Mandela, Nelson, **No Easy Walk to Freedom** (Carter)

Mandela, Winnie, **No Easy Walk to Freedom** (Carter)

Mando, **Voodoo** (Freeman)

Manette, Dr., (t) **Tale of Two Cities** (Benjamin)

Manfred, **Sicilian Romance** (Reeve)

Manfred Geyer, **Lost Childhood** (Hamer)

Manfred Lewin, (bar) **For a Look or a Touch** (Heggie)

Mangus, (bar) **Knot Garden** (Tippett)

Manheim, (bar) **The Patriot** (Edwards)

Mani, **Angels' Voices** (Ain)

Manikin, **The Cabinet** (Reeve et al.)

Manischevitz, Fanny, **Angel Levine** (Siegmeister)

Manischevitz, Nathan, **Angel Levine** (Siegmeister)

Manly, **Cure for a Scold** (1735); **Lady of the Manor** (Hook); (t) **Spanish Lady** (Elgar)

Mannering, Guy, **Guy Mannering** (Attwood)

Manners, John, **Haddon Hall** (Sullivan)

Manningham, Jack, **Gaslight** (Roe)

Mannon, General Ezra, (b-bar) **Mourning Becomes Electra** (Levy)

Manolios, (t) **Greek Passion** (Martinů)

Manuel, (t) **Big Black Box** (Morgenstern); **The Egg** (Menotti); **Rose of Castille** (Balfe)

Manuela, **Miraculous Staircase** (Stringer)

Manuela, Doña, (m) **La Loca** (Menotti)

Manuela Sáenz, (s) **Simón Bolívar** (Musgrave)

Manus, (b) **Immortal Hour** (Boughton)

Manus, King, **The Dragon** (Taylor)

Man Who Chose a Tyranny, (t) **Myth of Er** (Sternau)

Man-with-No-Boat, **Mother of Three Sons** (Jenkins)

Man with Red Eyes, (b) **Wrinkle in Time** (Larsen)

Manworth, Capt., **Lady's Triumph** (Settle)

Manz, (bar) **Village Romeo and Juliet** (Delius)

Mao Tse-tung (Zedong), (bar) **Madame Mao** (Sheng); **Mao Zedong** (Gal); (t) **Nixon in China** (Adams)

Mapelson, Colonel, (b cantante) **Captain Jinks** (Beeson)

Mara, **Scarlett Mill** (Zador)

Maraquita, **Idols' Eye** (Herbert)

Marc, **Florida** (Eng)

Marcel, (bar) **Violins of St. Jacques** (Williamson)

Marcella, **The Rehearsal** (Boyce)

March, Alma, (s) **Little Women** (Adamo)

March, Gideon, (bar) **Little Women** (Adamo)

March Hare (ct), **Alice in Wonderland** (Chin)

Marchioness of Calatrava, **The Caravan** (Reeve)

Marcia, (st) **The Opening** (Wilder)

Marco, (bar) **View from the Bridge** (Bolcom); (bar) **View from the Bridge** (Morris)

Marcolfa, **Nightingale's to Blame** (Holt)

Marco Palmieri, (t) **The Gondoliers** (Sullivan)

Marco Polo, **Invisible Cities** (Cerrone); **Marco Polo** (Tan Dun); **Messer Marco Polo** (Stern)

Marco Valerio, (bar) **Voice of Ariadne** (Musgrave)

Marcus, **The Equation** (Bush)

Marcus Hale, (t) **Somebody's Children** (Kander)

Marcus Schouler, (bar) **McTeague** (Bolcom)

Marcus Whitman, (t) **Narcissa** (Moore)

Margaret, **The Deserter** (Dibdin); (m) **The Duenna** (Linley Jr./Sr.); **King Pepin's Campaign** (Arne); (s) **Night of the Moonspell** (Siegmeister)

Margaret, Duchess of Argyll, **Powder Her Face** (Adès)

Margaret, Lady, **White Plume** (Reeve)

Margaret, Queen, **Battle of Hexham** (Arnold)

Margaret Elliott, **Eric Hermannson's Soul** (Larsen)

Margaret Garner, (m) **Margaret Garner** (Danielpour)

Margaret Leval, **Midnight Angel** (Carlson)

Margaret Meadows, (s) **University Greys** (Kreutz)

Margaretta, **The Alcaid** (Nathan); **Glorious First of June** (Storace); **No Song, No Supper** (Storace)

Margarita, **Stauf** (Sahl)

Margery, (Dame), **The Armorer** (1793); **Canterbury Pilgrims** (Stanford); (s) **Dragon of Wantley** (Lampe); **Jealous Clown** (1730); **Margery** (Lampe); **Veteran Tar** (Arnold); **The Wedding** (Pepusch); **Welsh Opera** (1731)

Margery Wilmore, Miss, **Wilmore Castle** (Hook)

Marghanza, Princess, (m) **El Capitan** (Sousa)

Margherita, **Bride Elect** (Sousa)

Margherita, Lady, **Massimilliano** (Freer)

Margie, **The Fox** (Kondorossy)

Margo, (m) **Miracle of Flanders** (Gruenberg)

Margot, (s) **Fête at Coqueville** (Rea)

Margot, Frau (s), **Frau Margot** (Pasatieri)

Margret, (s) **Lizzie Borden** (Beeson)

Marguerita, (s) **Junípero Serra** (Hively)

Marguerite, **Louis Riel** (Somers); **Mephistopheles** (Lutz); (s) **Story of Vasco** (Crosse)

Maria, (s) **The Argonauts** (Maganini); **Devil upon Two Sticks** (Coffey); **Empty Bottle** (Kalmanoff); **Generous Free-Mason** (1730); (s) **Good Tidings** (Locklair); **The Immigrants** (Converse); (s) **Inspector General** (Zador); **Maid of the Oaks** (Barthelemon); **Maria Elena** (Pasatieri); (s) **Maria Golovin** (Menotti); (s) **Monkey's Paw** (Hamm); **Pearl** (Davidson); (a) **Porgy and Bess** (Gershwin); **Sterne's Maria** (Pelissier); (m) **Twelfth Night** (Amram); **Vendetta** (Freeman); **West Side Story** (Bernstein)

Maria Callas Epstein, (a) **The Audition** (Kalmanoff)

Maria Celeste, (s) **Galileo Galilei** (Glass)

Maria Ledger, **Jonathan Postfree** (1807)

Maria Luisa, Queen, **Goya** (Menotti)

Maria Macapa, **McTeague** (Bolcom)

Maria Malibran, **Maria Malibran** (Bennett)

Marian, **Plumber's Gift** (Blake); (a) **Thanksgiving** (Levi)

Mariana, **Cortez** (Bishop); **Leonora** (Fry); (s) **Student from Salamanca** (Bach); **The Whim** (1734)

Mariane, (s) **Tartuffe** (Benjamin); (s) **Tartuffe** (Mechem)

Marianna, (s) **The Sacrifice** (Converse)

Mariano Vallejo, General, **The Dreamers** (Conte)

Marian Ramsay, **Turn Out!** (King)

Maria Tebaldi O'Rourke, (s) **The Audition** (Kalmanoff)

Maria Thins, (m) **Writing to Vermeer** (Andriessen)

Maria von Wedemeyer, (s) **Bonhoeffer** (Gebuhr)

Marie, **Armourer of Nantes** (Balfe); **Hofer** (Rossini-Bishop); **The Losers** (Farberman); (s) **On the Razzle** (Orr); **Tale of the Nutcracker** (Bohmler)

Marie Antoinette, (s) **Ghosts of Versailles** (Corigliano)

Marie Curie, **Chaos** (Gordon)

Marie Laveau, **Marie Laveau** (Carbon); (a) **Minette Fontaine** (Still)

Marietta, **Naughty Marietta** (Herbert)

Marie Violet, **Monk of Toledo** (Knowlton)

Marigny, Contesse de, **Phaedra** (Innerarity)

Marigold, Princess, (s) **Golden Touch** (Kaufmann)

Marigold Sandys, Lady, (s) **Merry Mount** (Hanson)

Marilyn Monroe, **Marilyn** (Laderman)

Marina, (s) **Blonde Donna** (Carter)

Marina, Dona, **Robin Hood** (1730); **The Servants** (Mathias)

Marina Tsvetaeva, (s) **Marina** (Drattell)

Marinus, (t) **Blonde Donna** (Carter)

Mario, **Mario and the Magician** (Oliver); **Mario and the Magician** (Somers); **Mario and the Magician** (Thorne)

Marion, (s) **The Patriot** (Edwards); (s) **Twin Sisters** (Sedgwick)

Marion Hacket, (m) **Christopher Sly** (Argento)

Marisa, **Henry's Wife** (Eng)

Maritana, (s) **Maritana** (Wallace)

Marius, (bar) **Apollonia** (Starer); (bar) **Tarquin** (Krenek)

Mark, **The Harvest** (Giannini); (t) **In the Father's Garden** (Kirtley); (t) **Midsummer Marriage** (Tippett); (t) **The Wreckers** (Smyth)

Mark, King, **Queen of Cornwall** (Boughton)

Mark Antony, (bar) **Cleopatra's Night** (Hadley)

Mark Cohen, **Rent** (Larson)

Markheim, (b-bar) **Good Angel, Bad Angel** (Cresswell); (b-bar) **Markheim** (Floyd); **Markheim** (Miles)

Mark McGregor, **Los Rubios** (Moore)

Marko, **Marko the Miser** (Musgrave)

Marley, Ghost of, **Christmas Carol** (Coleman); **Christmas Carol** (Hermann)

Marlinspike, **Benevolent Tar** (Dibdin)

Marlow, **Heart of Darkness** (O'Regan)

Marlowe, Christopher, **Tragicall Historie** (Mellers)

Marmaduke Pointdextre, Sir, (b-bar) **The Sorcerer** (Sullivan)

Marquis, **Maid of Artois** (Balfe)

Marquis de Champlain, **Basket-Maker** (Arnold)

Marquis Imari (bar), **The Geisha** (Jones)

Marquis of Calatrava, **The Caravan** (Reeve)

Marquise de Babylon, (s) **W. of Babylon** (Wuorinen)

Marret, **Robin Hood** (Tippett)

Marrotte, **Follies and Fancies** (Allen)

Mars, **Birth of Hercules** (Arne); **Britannia** (Arne); **Britannia** (Lampe); **Momus** (1729); (b-bar) **The Olympians** (Bliss); **Thespis** (Sullivan); (t/b) **Venus and Adonis** (Pepusch)

Marshal, **White Agony** (Fuchs)

Marshall, William, (t) **Regina** (Blitzstein)

Mars Plaisir, **Toussaint** (Blake)

Marta, (m) **The Legend** (Breil)

Marta, Doña, (m) **Black Widow** (Pasatieri)

Martel, **The Crusaders** (Benedict)

Martha, (s) **The Audience** (Dembo); **Christmas Carol** (Musgrave); **The Clock** (Rieti); **Gethsemane** Park (Moore); (s) **Romulus** (Karchin); **The Sisters** (Flagello); (s) **Voice of Ariadne** (Musgrave)

Martha Barber, (s) **John Brown** (Mechem)

Marti, (bar) **Village Romeo and Juliet** (Delius)

Martial, (bar) **Gardens of Adonis** (Weisgall)

Martin, **The Arrangement** (Davis); **Haunted Tower** (Storace); (bar) **Juggler of Our Lady** (Kay); **Maid of Artois** (Balfe); **Martin's Lie** (Menotti); (t) **Tender Land** (Copland); **Who Pays the Reckoning?** (Arnold)

Martin, Mr., (b-bar) **Bald Prima Donna** (Kalmanoff)

Martin, Mrs., (a) **Bald Prima Donna** (Kalmanoff)

Martina, **Song of Martina** (Johnson)

Martin Chuzzlewit, **Family Papers** (Wood)

Martin Guerre, **Wife of Martin Guerre** (Bergsma)

Martinetti, Filippo, **Voluptuous Tango** (Muldowney)

Martini, Signor, (bar) **Opera Cloak** (Damrosch)

Martin Ruiz, (b-bar) **Royal Hunt of the Sun** (Hamilton)

Marty South, (m-s) **The Woodlanders** (Paulus)

Marva Trotter, **Shadowboxer** (Proto)

Marvin, (bar) **Sunday Excursion** (Wilder)

Marvin Heeno, **Dream of Valentino** (Argento)

Maryam, **Maryam the Harlot** (Rieti)

Marx, Eleanor, **Ease** (Beamish)

Mary, **Amber Witch** (Wallace); (a) **And the Walls** (Roosevelt); (s) **Bald Prima Donna** (Kalmanoff); **Bethlehem** (Boughton); **Black Roses** (Chisholm); **Cabildo** (Beach); **Early Dawn** (Lockwood); (s) **Erode the Greate** (La Montaine); **Father of the Child** (Barab); (s) **Highway 1, U.S.A.** (Still); (s) **Hugh the Drover** (Vaughan Williams); **Little Thieves** (Stuart); **Lord Byron** (Graham); (s) **Mary of Egypt** (Taverner); **Mary Stuart** (Murray); **Open the Gates** (Lee); **The Promise** (Townsend); **Queerest Courtship** (Sedgwick); (sp) **The Rope** (Mennini); **Sancho at Court** (1742); **Secret Garden** (Pliska); (m) **Shining Chalice** (Grove); **Signals** (Knopf); **Simeon** (Gustafson); **Sprigs of Laurel** (Shield); **Trio** (Ain); **Turnpike Gate** (Reeve-Mazzinghi); **Who Pays the Reckoning?** (Arnold); **York** (Trinkley); (s) **"You Never Know"** (Koutzen)

Mary, Duchess, (s) **Peter Ibbetson** (Taylor)

Mary, Queen (Stuart), (s) **David Rizzio** (Moore); (s) **Mary, Queen of Scots** (Musgrave); **To Let the Captive Go** (Stewart); (m) **Welcome to Purgatory** (Roe)

Mary(-)Ann, **Love Finds the Way** (Arne et al.); **Love in a Blaze** (Stevenson-Cogan)

Maryanna, (s) **The Sisters** (Flagello)

Mary Barton, **Mary Baron** (Cooke)

Mary Dyer, (s) **Mary Dyer** (Owen)

Mary Follett, **Death in the Family** (Mayer)

Mary Hamilton, **The Covenanters** (Loder)

Mary Magdalene, **Gethsemane Park** (Moore); **Jesus Christ** (Lloyd Webber); **Open the Gates** (Lee); (s) **Passion and Resurrection** (Harvey); **The Promise** (Townsend)

Mary Morgan, **Ten Nights in a Bar-Room** (1858)

Mary Phillips, (s) **Capitoline Venus** (Kay)

Mary Rutledge, (s) **Man without a Country** (Damrosch)

Mary Shelley, (m) **Mary Shelley** (Jaffe); **Monster** (Beamish)

Mary Stone, (m/s) **Devil and Daniel Webster** (Moore)

Mary Surratt, (s) **Mary Surratt** (Muller); **Mary Surratt** (Remson)

Mary Weber, **Joe Hill** (Bush)

Masaniello, **Masaniello** (Auber-Cooke, Barham)

Masetto, **Thirty Minute Don Giovanni** (Lole-Gray)

Masha, (s) **Music Shop** (Wargo); (s) **The Seagull** (Pasatieri); (s) **Three Sisters** (Pasatieri)

Mason, **Maiden Tower** (Chen); (b) **Tell-Tale Heart** (Adolphe)

Massey, Colonel, **All the King's Men** (Bennett)

Massimilliano, **Massimilliano** (Freer)

Mata Hari, **Mata Hari** (McDermott)

Match girl, **Elegy for a Prince** (Cervetti)

Mateo Visconti, **Bianca** (Balfe)

Math, (bar) **Children of Don** (Holbrooke)

Mathematician, **Charivari** (Westergaard)

Mathew, **Mathew in the School of Life** (Moran)

Mathilda Malone, (a) **The Clock** (Rieti)

Matholoc, **Bronwen** (Holbrooke)

Matilaha, (m) **Junípero Serra** (Hively)

Matilda, **Matilda of Hungary** (Wallace); **Richard Coeur de Lion** (Linley Sr.); **Robin Hood** (1730); **Second Thought Is Best** (Bates)

Mercutio, (b) **Romeo and Juliet** (Shelley)

Mercy, **Down Here on Earth** (Wiens)

Meriamum, Queen, (m) **The Martyr** (Freeman)

Meriel, **Jovial Crew** (1731)

Merit, **Fashionable Lady** (1730); **The Patron** (1729)

Merlin, **Britannia triumphans** (Lawes); **Caernarvon Castle** (Attwood); (bar) **Cymon** (Arne); **Merlin** (Viñao); (t) **New Year** (Tippett); **Round Table** (Boughton); **Tom Thumb** (Markordt)

Merret, Count de, **Fatal Oath** (Koutzen)

Merret, Countess de, **Fatal Oath** (Koutzen)

Merriman, **Midnight Court Opera** (Sokolovic)

Merrill, Paul, (t) **Natoma** (Herbert)

Merry, (s) **Mighty Casey** (Schuman)

Merteuil, Marquise de, (m) **Dangerous Liaisons** (Susa)

Merville, **Love in a Blaze** (Stevenson/Cogan)

Meryll, Leonard, (t) **Yeomen of the Guard** (Sullivan)

Meryll, Sergeant, (b-bar) **Yeomen of the Guard** (Sullivan)

Mesholem, **Shloyme Gorgl** (Lateiner)

Mesrour, **Il Bondocani** (Attwood/Moorehead); **Caliph of Bagdad** (Musgrave)

Messer Facio, **Summer's Night** (Clutsam)

Messer Niccolo, **Summer's Night** (Clutsam)

Messias, **Paradise Lost** (Penderecki)

Metatron, (bar) **Masque of Angels** (Argento)

Meyerhof, Cardinal, **Leviathan Hook** (Doolittle)

Mica, **Romulus Hunt** (Simon)

Micah, (t) **Slow Dusk** (Floyd); **Thief and Hangman** (Ellstein)

Micuccio, **Sicilian Limes** (Argento)

Michael, **Berta** (Smart); **Cue 67** (Ching); **For England, Ho!** (Bishop); **Frobisher** (Estacio); **In the Shadow of the Glen** (Van de Vate); (t) **Opera Cloak** (Damrosch); **Paradise Lost** (Penderecki); **The Rescue** (Ridout); (bar) **Royal Auction** (Kanitz); (t) **Skellig** (Machover); (b) **Taverner** (Davies); **Vile Shadows** (Turner)

Michael Chamberlain, (t) **Lindy** (Henderson)

Michel, (bar) **Better Place** (Butler); (t) **Ouanga** (White)

Michele, **Bianca** (Balfe); (t) **Saint of Bleecker Street** (Menotti)

Michel Kerouac, **Light from St. Agnes** (Harling)

Michigo, **Girl from Nogami** (Blyton)

Mick, (bar) **Oath of Bad Brown Bill** (Conyngham)

Midas, King, **Asses' Ears** (Cole); **Midas** (1762)

Midir, **Immortal Hour** (Boughton)

Miguel de Denia, (t) **La Loca** (Menotti)

Miguel de Estete, (t) **Royal Hunt of the Sun** (Hamilton)

Miguel Domingo, (bar) **Scourge of Hyacinths** (León)

Mihail Mihailovitch, (b-bar) **Natalia Petrovna** (Hoiby)

Mike, (bar) **Grace** (Rudenstein); **I Was Looking at the Ceiling** (Adams); **Virtual Motion** (Rodwin)

Mike Murphy, **Shamus O'Brien** (Stanford)

Mike Teavee, (ct) **Golden Ticket** (Ash)

Mila, **Palace in the Sky** (Dove)

Mildred, **Have You Heard** (Talma); (m) **Thanksgiving** (Levi)

Mildred Murphy, (m) **The Hero** (Menotti)

Miles, (boy s) **Turn of the Screw** (Britten)

Miles Bradford, (t) **The Knickerbockers** (De Koven)

Miles Dunster, (bar) **Wings of the Dove** (Moore)

Millais, John Everett, **Modern Painters** (Lang)

Millichip, (b) **Grace of Todd** (Crosse)

Millie Owens, (s) **Picnic** (Larsen)

Milly, (s) **Our Man in Havana** (Williamson)

Milly Theale, (s) **Wings of the Dove** (Moore)

Milo, **Three Visitations** (Sherman)

Milos, (ct) **Hunger Art** (Myers)

Milton, **Paradise Lost** (Penderecki)

Mimi, **The Bohemians** (Kirschner)

Mimi Márquez, **Rent** (Larson)

Mimosa San, O, (s) **The Geisha** (Jones)

Mina, (s) **Skellig** (Machover); **Yelva** (Bishop)

Mina Murray, **Dracula** (Ziemba)

Minerva, **License to Marry** (Barab)

Minette, (s) **English Cat** (Henze); **Our Giraffe** (Hays)

Minette Fontaine, (s) **Minette Fontaine** (Still)

Mingle, **The Bee-Hive** (Horn)

Mingle, Mrs., **The Bee-Hive** (Horn)

Minshen, **Nannan** (Wang Jie)

Minos, (b) **Council of the Dead** (Sternau); (low male voice) **Inferno of Dante** (Soluri); (b-bar) **Sappho** (Glanville-Hicks)

Minto, Lord, (b-bar) **Nelson** (Berkeley)

Minutezza, Princess, **Bride Elect** (Sousa)

Mira, **Better Sort** (1789)

Miranda, (s) **Blake** (Adams); **Dancing Master** (Arnold); (s) **Death and the Powers** (Machover); **Maiden Tower** (Chen); (s) **Miranda** (Siegmeister); **The Tempest** (Banister); (s) **The Tempest** (Eaton); **The Tempest** (Gatty); **The Tempest** (Smith); **The Tempest** (Westergaard)

Miriam, (s) **Christmas Rose** (Bridge); **Early Dawn** (Lockwood); **Elijah's Kite** (Rolfe); (s) **Eternal Road** (Weill); (s) **The Golem** (Casken); **Marble Faun** (Bender); (s) **The Scarf** (Hoiby)

Mirovich, **Inner Voices** (Howard)

Mirror, **Journey of Snow White** (Carmines); **Snow White** (Barab)

Mirvan, **Zuma** (Bishop)

Misael, (t) **Burning Fiery Furnace** (Britten)

Misfortune, **Rose of Destiny** (Heckscher)

Misha, **Mata Hari** (McDermott); (t) **Visit to the Country** (Wargo)

Miss Bingley, (m) **Pride and Prejudice** (Mechem)

Miss Blandford, **Speed the Plow** (Moorehead)

Miss Brill, **Miss Brill** (Buchanan)

Miss Charm-Strange, (m) **Quantum Mechanic** (Bilotta)

Miss Di Clackit, **The Woodman** (Shield)

Miss Donnithorne, (a) **Miss Donnithorne's Maggot** (Maxwell Davies)

Miss Freeman, **Plymouth in an Uproar** (Dibdin)

Miss Hatchard, (s) **Summer** (Paulus)

Miss Lonelyhearts, (t) **Miss Lonelyhearts** (Liebermann)

Miss Titmouse, (s) **Too Many Sopranos** (Penhorwood)

Miss Top-Bottom, (s) **Quantum Mechanic** (Bilotta)

Miss Up-Down, (s) **Quantum Mechanic** (Bilotta)

Mister Banjo, **Gentlemen, Be Seated!** (Moross)

Mister Bones, **Gentlemen, Be Seated!** (Moross)

Mister Interlocutor, **Gentlemen, Be Seated!** (Moross)

Mister Tambo, **Gentlemen, Be Seated!** (Moross)

Mistress Hibbons, **Scarlet Letter** (Laitman)

Mistress MacMotherly, **Ages Ago** (Clay)

Mitch, **Streetcar Named Desire** (Previn)

Mitchell, Dr., **Yellow Wallpaper** (Perera)

Mittenhofer, Gregor, (bar) **Elegy for Young Lovers** (Henze)

Mittelstaedt, **All Quiet on the Western Front** (Van de Vate)

Mitty, Walter, **Secret Life of Walter Mitty** (Hamm)

Mizen, **The Mariners** (Attwood)

Mizra, **Almena** (Arne-Battishill); **Generous Free-Mason** (1730)

Mocanna, **Veiled Prophet** (Stanford)

Mocenigo, **Daughter of St. Mark** (Balfe)

Mock, **Flowers** (Hardy)

Mock Turtle, (t) **Alice in Wonderland** (Chauls); **Alice Meets the Mock Turtle** (Bingham)

Modely, Mr., **Fashionable Lady** (1730)

Modesty, (s) **Loving/Toi** (Schafer)

Modigliani, Amadeo, **Anna and Dedo** (Morgulas)

Modish, **Happy Lovers** (1736)

Modish, Squire, **Lucky Discovery** (1737)

Mohammed, **Almena** (Arne-Battishill)

Moira, **Weird of Colbar** (Moonie)

Moishe, (t) **Where the Wild Things Are** (Knussen)

Moksada, (s) **Snatched by the Gods** (Vir)

Mole, Mr., **Wind in the Willows** (Rutter)

Molineux, Major, (bar) **My Kinsman** (Saylor)

Moll, **Brickdust Man** (Dibdin); **Cradle Will Rock** (Blitzstein)

Moll Hackabout, **Harlot's Progress** (Greenhut)

Moll Plackett, **The Disappointment** (Barton)

Mollie Sinclair (m), **Sojourner and Mollie Sinclair** (Floyd)

Mollser, (s) **Plough and the Stars** (Siegmeister)

Molly, **Boarding School** (1733); **Welsh Opera** (1731)

Molly Bloom, **Audition of Molly Bloom** (McFarland); (s) **Molly ManyBloom** (Bond); **Ulysses** (Rudenstein)

Molly Brant, (s) **Molly Brant** (Cecconi-Bates)

Molly Maybush, **The Farmer** (Shield)

Molly Mistress, (m) **Ballad of the Bremen Band** (Arlan)

Molly Seamore (m), **The Geisha** (Jones)

Molly Wheedle, **Rival Milliners** (1736)

Momoolie Araboolie, (m) **Araboolies of Liberty Street** (Perera)

Mompesson, William, (bar) **Plague upon Eyam** (Drummond)

Momus, **Momus** (1729)

Mona, (m) **Mona** (Parker); **Swoon** (Rolfe)

Monica, **Helvellyn** (Macfarren); (s) **The Medium** (Menotti)

Monisha, (m) **Treemonisha** (Joplin)

Monk, General, **Restauration of Charles II** (1732)

Monongahela Sal, (a) **Mermaid in Lock No. 7** (Siegmeister)

Monsieur Le Truffle, **The Whim** (1734)

Montag, **Fahrenheit 451** (Broadstock)

Montalban, (b) **Siege of Rochelle** (Balfe)

Montalban, Count, **Honey Moon** (Hewitt/Kelly)

Montalto, **Bianca** (Balfe); **Leonora** (Fry)

Montalvan, **Spanish Castle** (Hewitt)

Monteblanco, (a) **Dinner Engagement** (Berkeley)

Montenegro, Prince of, **The Algerian** (De Koven)

Montereale, **Bianca** (Balfe)

Montezuma, **Azora** (Hadley); **Indian Queen** (Purcell); **Montezuma** (Gleason); (t) **Montezuma** (Sessions); (t) **Montezuma's Death** (Chlarson)

Montfleury, (t) **Cyrano** (Damrosch)

Montoni, Count, **Mysteries of the Castle** (Shield)

Montresor, (b-bar/t) **Casket of Amontillado** (Currie); **Cask of Amontillado** (Pinkham)

Montval, **The Vintagers** (Bishop)

Moody, Jasper, Sir, **Generous Free-Mason** (1730)

Moody, Mr., **Lover's Opera** (1729)

Moon, Lord Cecil, (t) **Lady from Colorado** (Ward); **Lady Kate** (Ward)

Moon Goddess, **From the Towers** (Moran)

Moon Maiden, **Moon Maiden** (Boughton)

Moore, (t) **Dragon of Wantley** (Lampe); **Margery** (Lampe)

Moore, Alice Ruth, **Mask in the Mirror** (Thompson)

Moore, Thomas, (bar) **Lord Byron** (Thomson)

Mopsa, (s) **Fairy Queen** (Purcell)

Mopsus, **Damon and Phillida** (1729); **Damon and Phillida** (Dibdin); **Love in a Riddle** (1729)

Morano, **Polly** (1729)

Morat, **Happy Captive** (Galliard)

Mordake, Edward, (t), **Mordake** (Wold)

Mordaunt, **Climbing Boy** (Hawes)

Mordecai, (bar), **Esther** (Harvey); (t) **Esther** (Meyerowitz); **Esther** (Weisgall); **Esther and Cousin Mordecai** (Pittman)

Mordeen Saul, **Burning Bright** (Lewin)

Moremi, **Vanqui** (Burrs)

Morgan, Colonel, (b) **Man without a Country** (Damrosch)

Morgan, Joe, **Ten Nights in a Bar-Room** (1858)

Morgan le Fay, (s) **Gawain** (Birtwistle); (m) **Gwyneth and the Green Knight** (Plowman)

Morgianna, **Ali Baba Opera** (Reed)

Morley, **Second Thought Is Best** (Bates)

Morlière, Viscount, **The Bondman** (Balfe)

Moro, **Moro** (Balfe)

Moroc, **The Enchanter** (Smith)

Morrington, **Speed the Plow** (Moorehead)

Morris, Major, (bar) **Monkey's Paw** (Alexander)

Morris, T. Chester, (t) **Appomattox** (Glass)

Morris Townsend, **The Heiress** (Hollier); (bar) **Washington Square** (Pasatieri)

Morton, Thomas, (bar) **Merry Mount** (Hanson); **Merrymount** (Smith)

Mosca, **Volpone** (Antheil); (t) **Volpone** (Musto)

Moscone, George, (b) **Harvey Milk** (Wallace)

Moseley, Winston, **Screams of Kitty Genovese** (Todd)

Moses, (bar) **Eternal Road** (Weill); (bar) **Let My People Go** (Warren); **Reverend Richard**, (b) **Beatrice Chancy** (Rolfe)

Mosher, Mr., **Emmeline** (Picker)

Mother Ann, **Journey of Mother Ann** (Kastle)

Mother Bayard, (a) **Long Christmas Dinner** (Hindemith)

Mother Courage, **Play of Mother Courage** (McCabe)

Mother Magdalene, **Miraculous Staircase** (Stringer)

Mother Nature, (s) **Cupid and Death** (Gibbons/Locke)

Mother Rainey, (m) **Sweet Bye and Bye** (Beeson)

Mother Rigby, (m) **Feathertop** (Barthelson); (m) **The Scarecrow** (Turrin)

Mother Shipton, (a) **Outcasts of Poker Flat** (Beckler)

Mother Superior, (a) **Lake of Menteith** (Noble)

Mother Theresa, (m) **The Proposal** (Granger)

Mouchel, (bar) **Fête at Coqueville** (Rea)

Mougali, (a) **Ouanga** (White)

Mountararat, Earl, (bar) **Iolanthe** (Sullivan)

Mowdrey, Lieutenant, **Flying Dutchman** (Rodwell)

Mowgli, **Jungle Book** (Swensson)

Moyse, **Toussaint before the Spirits** (Ruehr)

Mozart, Leopold, (b) **Letters, Riddles** (Nyman)

Mozart, Wolfgang Amadeus, (ct) **Letters, Riddles** (Nyman); (st) **Little Nightmare Music** (Schickele); **Mozart in Manhattan** (Biales); **Music Robber** (Van Grove)

Mr. Fox, (bar) **Fantastic Mr. Fox** (Pasatieri)

Mr. Hale, (bar) **Trifles** (Bilotta)

Mr. Machine, **Tumble-Down Dick** (1736)

Mr. Mister, **Cradle Will Rock** (Blitzstein)

Mr. Slum, **Land of Milk and Honey** (Russo)

Mr. Toppit, **The Paragraph** (Braham)

Mrs. Toppit, **The Paragraph** (Braham)

Mr. Vermilion, **Wives Revenged** (Dibdin)

Mr. Wonomi, **Angels' Voices** (Ain)

Mrs. Ansley, **Roman Fever** (Stringer)

Mrs. Ballinger, **Power of Xingu** (Legg)

Mrs. Basil Frankweiler, **From the Mixed-Up Files** (Swensson)

Mrs. D'Urberville, **Tess of the D'Urbervilles** (Harris)

Mrs. Fox, (m) **Fantastic Mr. Fox** (Pasatieri)

Mrs. Hale, (m) **Trifles** (Bilotta)

Mrs. Highman, **Intriguing Chambermaid** (1734)

Mrs. Ledger, Jonathan Postfree (1807)

Mrs. Ned, **Family Papers** (Wood)

Mrs. Peters, (s) **Trifles** (Bilotta)

Mrs. Ramsay, **Turn Out!** (King)

Mrs. Schroedinger, (s) **Quantum Mechanic** (Bilotta)

Mrs. Slade, **Roman Fever** (Stringer)

Mrs. Van Hopper, **Rebecca** (Josephs)

Mrs. Vermilion, **Wives Revenged** (Dibdin)

Mrs. Watchet, **Killing No Murder** (Hook)

Mrs. Wright, (s) **Trifles** (Bilotta)

Mtalba, Princess, (s) **Lily** (Kirchner)

Muffin, (s) **A Wedding** (Bolcom)

Mugette, **Deep River** (Harling)

Muhammad Ali, **Muhammad Ali** (Duffy)

Muir, Thomas, **Friend of the People** (Horne)

Muirgheis, **Muirgheis** (Butler)

Muli Alouf Hali Hassan, **The Seraglio** (Dibdin)

Muller, Mrs., (s) **Good Soldier Schweik** (Kurka)

Mulligrub, Mrs., **Love and Revenge** (1729)

Mummy of Prince Takarmo, (t) **The Mummy** (Quincy)

Mungo, **The Padlock** (Dibdin)

Munpa, (t) **Tibetan Dreams** (Dickman)

Muoma, **Luyala** (Banfield)

Murasaki, Lady, **Things That Gain** (Barry)

Murgatroyd, Major, (bar) **Patience** (Sullivan)

Muriel, **Lady of Longford** (Bach)

Murphy, David, (bar) **The Hero** (Menotti)

Murray, Lord, (bar) **David Rizzio** (Moore)

Murry, Dr., (t) **Wrinkle in Time** (Larsen)

Murtagh Mulrooney, **William and Nanny** (Baumgarten)

Murteza, **Egyptian Festival** (Florio)

Murville, **Castle of Sorrento** (Attwood)

Muse for America, (m) **Be Glad Then America** (La Montaine)

Musette, **Fortune Teller** (Herbert)

Music, **Choice of Apollo** (Yates)

Musikus, Dr., **Dr. Musikus** (Hopkins)

Musil, **Broken Strings** (Vir)

Musset, Alfred de, **Flight of Eagles** (Tinsley)

Mustapha, **Siege of Rhodes** (Lawes et al.)

Mustapha Muley Bey, **Egyptian Festival** (Florio)

Muybridge, Eadweard, **The Photographer** (Glass)

Muzio, **Triumph of Love** (Schmitz)

Myles na Coppaleen, (t) **Lily of Killarney** (Benedict)

Mylo, (t) **The Picnic** (Cumming)

Mynherr van Groot, **Love's Triumph** (Wallace)

Myra Foster, **Séance on a Wet Afternoon** (Schwartz)

Obadiah, **Sonata about Jerusalem** (Goehr); **Tristram Shandy** (1783)

Oberlin, (b) **Lenz** (Sitsky)

Oberon, **Fairy Queen** (Purcell); **Midsummer Night's Dream** (1763); (ct) **Midsummer Night's Dream** (Britten); **Oberon** (Cooke); (t) **Oberon** (Weber); **Oberon's Oath** (Parry)

O'Blunder, Phelim, **Double Disappointment** (1746)

O'Bowling, **The Raft** (Reeve)

O'Brien, (t) **1984** (Maazel)

O'Cloghorty, **May Day** (Arne)

Oconeechee, **Mountain Windsong** (Chlarson)

Octave, Don, (t) **Stoned Guest** (Schickele)

Octavian, **Egypt** (McCoy); **The Mountaineers** (Arnold)

Octavian von Herren-Hosen, **Dark and Stormy Night** (Hagemann)

Octavie, **Deep River** (Harling)

Octavius Caesar, (t) **Antony and Cleopatra** (Barber)

O'Curragh, **Zorinski** (Arnold)

O'Daub, **The Camp** (Linley Sr.)

Odin, (bar) **Death of Baldur** (Bedford)

Odo, (m) **Azara** (Paine)

O'Donnell, **Il Paddy Whack in Italia** (Lover)

Odysseus, (bar) **Castaway** (Berkeley); (b-bar) **Odysseus 1, 2, 3** (Shields); (bar) **Odysseus Unwound** (Grant); **Return of Odysseus** (Bedford); (b-bar) **Myth of Er** (Sternau); **Return of Odysseus** (Gundry); **Siren's Song** (Butler)

Oedipus, **Death of Oedipus** (Halpern); (bar, actor) **Jocasta** (Schonthal); (b) **Oedipus** (Partch); **Passion of Oedipus** (Travis)

Oedipus Tex, (bar) **Oedipus Tex** (Schickele)

Oenone, **Paris and Oenone** (Hagemann); **Phaedra** (Innerarity)

Ofelia, (s) **La Cubana** (Henze)

Officer, (b-bar), **In the Penal Colony** (Glass)

Offred, **Handmaid's Tale** (Ruders)

Ogleby, Lord, **Clandestine Marriage** (Wishart)

Ohiya, **Sun Dance** (Hanson)

Oithona, **Oithona** (Bainton); **Oithona** (Barthelemon)

O-ko-mo-bo, **Flaming Arrow** (Moore)

Olaf, **Olaf** (Kirkpatrick)

Old Adam Goodheart, (b) **Ruddigore** (Sullivan)

Old Benson, **Village Coquettes** (Hullah)

Old Blood and Thunder, (b) **Great Stone Face** (Kalmanoff)

Oldboy, Colonel, **Lionel and Clarissa** (Dibdin)

Oldbuck, Jonathan, **The Antiquary** (Bishop)

Oldcastle, **Love Finds the Way** (Arne et al.)

Older Woman, **Flight** (Dove)

Old Fisherman, **Moon Maiden** (Boughton)

Old Henrik, **Ib and Little Christina** (Leoni)

Old Herdy, **Jonathan Postfree** (1807)

Old Insight, **Reform'd in Time** (Attwood)

Old Ledger, **Jonathan Postfree** (1807)

Old Man, **Astronaut's Tale** (Fussell)

Old Martin, (bar) **The Cooper** (Arne)

Old Maythorn, **Turnpike Gate** (Reeve-Mazzinghi)

Old Morality, **Battle of Bothwell Brigg** (Bishop)

Old Phaeton, **Tumble-Down Dick** (1736)

Old Rachel, (sp) **La Cubana** (Henze)

Oldrents, **Jovial Crew** (1731)

Old Rosemary, **Silver Tankard** (Arnold)

Old Shaver, **The Blockheads** (1782)

Old Stony Phiz, (bar) **Great Stone Face** (Kalmanoff)

Old Townly, **St. David's** Day (Attwood)

O'Leary, Capt., **British Fortitude** (Reeve)

Olga, (m) **Three Sisters** (Pasatieri)

Olim, (bar) **Silverlake** (Weill-Symonette)

Olimpia, (s) **Prima Donna** (Benjamin)

Olin Blitch, (b-bar) **Susannah** (Floyd)

Olindo, **Love's Triumph** (1708)

Olive, **Summer of the Seventeenth Doll** (Mills)

Oliver Bailey, (t) **Nitecap** (Burnham)

Oliver Stark, (b) **The Diva** (Ferris)

Olivia, **And God Created Whales** (Eckert); (a) **Requiem for a Rich Young Man** (Lockwood); **Spanish Castle** (Hewitt); (s) **Twelfth Night** (Amram)

Olmedo de la Merced, Fray, (t) **Montezuma** (Sessions)

Olof, **Thorgrim** (Cowen)

Oluf, King, **Lucky Star** (Caryll)

Olmutz, **Love in a Camp** (Shield)

Olympia, **Heaven Ablaze in His Breast** (Weir)

Olympion, (t) **Ice Break** (Tippett)

Olympus, **Midas** (1762)

Omar, **Abou Hassan** (Cooke); **Cady of Bagdad** (Linley Jr.); **Death of Klinghoffer** (Adams)

Ometh, (ct) **The Golem** (Casken)

Omy Caldwell, **Acres of Sky** (Kreutz)

Onassis, Aristotle, **Jackie O** (Daugherty)

Ondine, **Ondine** (Barab)

One Boy, **Land of Milk and Honey** (Russo)

O'Neil, Captain, **Abroad and at Home** (Shield)

Onita, (s) **Big Black Box** (Morgenstern)

Ophelia, (s) **Hamlet** (Searle); (s) **Lamentations of Ophelia** (Stinson); (s) **Ophelia** (Penberthy)

Oppenheimer, J. Robert, (bar) **Doctor Atomic** (Adams)

Oppenheimer, Kitty, (m) **Doctor Atomic** (Adams)

Oracle, (t) **The Minotaur** (Birtwistle)

Oracle of Apollo, (t) **Tale of Psyche & Cupid** (Sternau)

Orasmin, **Fall of Algiers** (Bishop)

Orazia, **Indian Queen** (Purcell)

Orbit, Sir George, **Honey Moon** (Linley)

Orchis, **Confidence Man** (Rochberg); **The Earthquake** (Rodwell)

Ordgar, (b) **King's Henchmen** (Taylor)

Orestes, **Orestes** (Pepusch)

Pantalone, (b) **Commedia** (Cowie); **Jewel Box** (Mozart-Griffiths); **Servant of Two Masters** (Giannini)

Pantaloon, (bar) **He Who Gets Slapped** (Ward); **The Portrait** (Arnold); **The Portrait** (Barthelemon)

Pantomime, **Bays's Opera** (1730); **Theatrical Candidates** (Bates)

Paolo, **Artaud's Cane** (Egoyan et al.)

Papagallo, King, **Bride Elect** (Sousa)

Papageno, **Small Jewel Box** (Mozart-Griffiths)

Papa Gonzales, (sp) **Summer and Smoke** (Hoiby)

Papaloi, (bar) **Ouanga** (White)

Papillon, **Duchess of Dantzic** (Caryll)

Parabola, (bar) **Parabola and Circula** (Blitzstein)

Paracelsus, Mrs., (s) **Doctor of Alcantara** (Eichberg)

Paramount, King, **Utopia Limited** (Sullivan)

Parchment, **The Disappointment** (Barton)

Paris, **Golden Apple** (Moross); **Golden Pippen** (Fischer); **Helen Retires** (Antheil); (bar) **Inferno of Dante** (Soluri); **Judgment of Paris** (Congreve settings); (s, t) **King Priam** (Tippett); **Paris and Oenone** (Hagemann); (st) **Romeo and Juliet** (Shelley); **Virgin Prophetess** (Finger)

Park, Captain, (t) **The Martyred** (Wade)

Parke, (t) **Man without a Country** (Damrosch)

Parker, James P., **Rise for Freedom** (Hailstork)

Parker, Mr., **Blood Moon** (Dello Joio)

Parkis, **End of the Affair** (Heggie)

Parlaine, **Palace in the Sky** (Dove)

Parris, Reverend Samuel, (t) **The Crucible** (Ward)

Parry, **Fisher King** (Lowenstein)

Parthenia, **Dione** (Lampe)

Parthenope, **Florence** (Sullivan); (s) **Telemachus** (Hayes)

Parthy Ann, **Show Boat** (Kern)

Partlet, Mrs., (a) **The Sorcerer** (Sullivan)

Pasagma, (s) **Tibetan Dreams** (Dickman)

Pascal, **Henry's Wife** (Eng)

Pascoe, (b-bar) **The Wreckers** (Smyth)

Pasiphaë, **Icarus** (Earls)

Pasquali, Nicolo, **Apollo and Daphne** (Hook)

Pasqualita, (m) **Doctor Atomic** (Adams)

Pasquil, **The Prisoner** (Attwood)

Pasternak, Boris, (bar) **Electrification of the Soviet Union** (Osborne); (actor) **Marina** (Drattell)

Pastora, **The Chaplet** (Boyce); **Love in a Riddle** (1729)

Pat, **The Shamrock** (Shields)

Patchett, Mrs., **Ferryman's Daughter** (Bush)

Pathelin, **Pathelin** (Josephs)

Patie, **Gentle Shepherd** (1729); **Patie and Peggy** (1730)

Patience, (s) **Patience** (Sullivan); **Patience and Sarah** (Kimper)

Patience Crabstick, Lady, **Family Quarrels** (Reeve et al.)

Pat Murphy, **Emerald Isle** (Sullivan)

Pat Nixon, (s) **Nixon in China** (Adams)

Patricho, **Carina** (Woolf)

Patrick, **British Fortitude** (Reeve); **Deserted Village** (Glover); **Love in a Camp** (Shield); **Poor Soldier** (Shield); **The Wedding** (Wilson)

Patroclus, (bar) **King Priam** (Tippett)

Patsy, **Love Counts** (Nyman)

Patsy Jefferson, **Monticello** (Paxton)

Patty, **Maid of the Mill** (Arnold); **Tania** (Davis)

Paul, (bar) **Amelia** (Hagen); (t) **Haircut** (Morgenstern); **Paul and Virginia** (Reeve); (t) **The Sisters** (Flagello); (t) **Toy Shop** (Barab); **Witches' Well** (Appleton)

Paul V, Pope, **Galileo Galilei** (Laderman)

Paula, (s) **Love, Death** (White)

Paul Baumer, **All Quiet on the Western Front** (Van de Vate)

Paul Chase, **No for an Answer** (Blitzstein)

Paulina, **Decius and Paulina** (Galliard)

Pauline, **Toussaint** (Blake); (s) **Toy Shop** (Barab)

Pauline Deschapelles, **Pauline** (Cowen)

Pauline L'Allemand, **Black River** (Susa)

Paullinus, (b-bar) **Julian** (Saminsky)

Pauloff, Stephen, (t) **The Legend** (Breil)

Pavayoykyasi, **Coyote Tales** (Mollicone)

Payne, Mr., (sr) **Improvement** (Ashley)

P. D. Q. Bach, (st) **Little Nightmare Music** (Schickele)

Peace, **Britannia** (Lampe); **Triumph of Peace** (Arne)

Peachum, (s) **Beggar's Opera** (Pepusch); (b-bar) **Threepenny Opera** (Weill-Blitzstein)

Peachum, Mrs., (b) **Beggar's Opera** (Pepusch); (a) **Threepenny Opera** (Weill-Blitzstein)

Peader Minogue, **Sharon's Grave** (Wargo)

Pearce, Mother, **Love and Revenge** (1729)

Pearl, **Pearl** (Davidson); (s) **Second Mrs. Kong** (Birtwistle)

Peartree, **The Wedding** (Pepusch)

Pecadillo, (t) **Abduction of Figaro** (Schickele)

Pecksniff, **Family Papers** (Wood)

Pecos Bill, **Tony Beaver** (Marais)

Pécuchet, **Bouvard and Pécuchet** (Aplvor)

Peculiar Sam, **Peculiar Sam** (1879)

Pedant, **Oxford Act** (1733)

Pedrillo, **Adventure of Don Quixote** (Macfarren); **Castle of Andalusia** (Arnold)

Pedro, **Choleric Fathers** (Shield); **Cinderella** (Lacy); **Inés de Castro** (MacMillan); **Ines de Castro** (Pasatieri)

Pedro, Don, (bar) **Black Widow** (Pasatieri); **The Disappointment** (1732); **Rose of Castille** (Balfe)

Pedro, Lady, **The Disappointment** (1732)

Pedro de Alvarado, (t) **Montezuma** (Sessions)

Pedro de Mendoza, Don, **The Prude** (1765)

Pedrolino, **Pedrolino's Revenge** (Russo)

Pedrosa, **The Alcaid** (Nathan)

Peer Gynt, **Death of Peer Gynt** (Halpern)

Peg, (s) **Beggar's Love** (Patterson); **Cure for a Scold** (1735)

Pegasus, **Song of Pegasus** (McFarland)

Peggy, **Brazen Bust** (Bishop); **Britain's Glory** (Arnold); **Gentle Shepherd** (1729); (s) **Goodbye to the Clown** (Laderman); **Lord of the Manor** (Jackson); **Magician No Conjurer** (Mazzinghi); **Turn Out!** (King); **Turnpike Gate** (Reeve-Mazzinghi)

Peggy Lure, **The Patron** (1729)

Pegleg, **Black Rider** (Waits)

Peg Welfleet, **Cobler's Opera** (1728)

Pelagia, (m) **Last Lover** (Starer)

Pelegrin, (t) **New Year** (Tippett)

Peleus, **Peleus and Thetis** (Boyce); (t) **Peleus and Thetis** (Hayes)

Pelléas, **Frustration** (Debussy-Harnick)

Pelsaert, Francisco, **Batavia** (Mills)

Pembrook, Earl of, **Robin Hood** (1730)

Penance, **The Rescue** (Ridout)

Penelope, (s) **Gloriana** (Britten); **Golden Apple** (Moross); (m) **Odysseus Unwound** (Grant); **Penelope** (1728); **Quartet** (Ritchie); **Return of Odysseus** (Bedford); **Return of Odysseus** (Gundry); **Ulysses** (Smith)

Penelope Newkirk, Miss, (m) **Help, Help** (Menotti)

Penn, William, **William Penn** (Cascarino)

Pennypacker, **Drumlin Legend** (Bacon)

Pennythorne, Mrs., **No Cards** (Elliott)

Pentheus, (t) **The Bacchae** (Buller); (bar) **The Bassarids** (Henze); **Revelation in the Courthouse Park** (Partch)

Penultimate Plenipotentiary, (bar) **Fair Means or Foul** (Barab)

Peony, (s) **Childhood Miracle** (Rorem)

Pepe, **Before Night Falls** (Martín)

Pepin of France, King, **King Pepin's Campaign** (Arne)

Pepito, **Pepito's Golden Flower** (Caldwell)

Peppercoal, Captain, **Flying Dutchman** (Rodwell)

Peppercorn Crabstick, Sir, **Family Quarrels** (Reeve/Mazzinghi)

Peralta, Father, (b) **Natoma** (Herbert)

Percinet, **Graciosa and Percinet** (1845)

Perdita, **Florizel and Perdita** (Boyce); **Sheep-Shearing** (Arne); **Sheep-Shearing** (Arnold); (s) **Winter's Tale** (Harbison)

Perdito, (t) **Monkey's Paw** (Hamm)

Peregrine Forester, **Hartford Bridge** (Shield)

Perez, **Tammany** (Hewitt)

Perez, Don, **The Divorce** (Hook)

Perfect Fool, (sp) **Perfect Fool** (Holst)

Per Hansa, (bar) **Giants in the Earth** (Moore)

Pericles, **Pericles** (Hovhaness); **Pericles, Prince of Tyre** (Hecker)

Perkins, Lt., (t) **Passion of Jonathan Wade** (Harvey)

Perks, Mrs., (s) **Mr. Polly at the Potwell Inn** (Drummond)

Perlimplin (Perlimplín), Don, **Belisa** (Biales); **Don Perlimplin** (Rieti); **Love of Don Perlimplin** (Doyle); **Love of Don Perlimplin** (Susa); **Nightingale's to Blame** (Holt); **Perlimplín** (Morrill)

Perón, Juan, **Evita** (Lloyd Webber)

Persephone, **Apollo and Persephone** (Cockshott); **Hey Persephone!** (Gribbin); **Mysteries of Eleusis** (Feigin); **Orpheus X** (Eckert); **Persephone** (Cole)

Perseus, **Gorgon's Head** (Magrill)

Persicaria, Empress, (a) **Poisoned Kiss** (Vaughan Williams)

Pertelote, (s) **Chanticleer** (Barab); (s) **Chanticleer** (Barthelson)

Peshofki, Captain, **The Charlatan** (Sousa)

Peter, (bar) **Beggar's Love** (Patterson); **Burgomaster of Saardam** (Bishop); **The Forest** (Smyth); **Gethsemane Park** (Moore); (high bar) **Lost Highway** (Neuwirth); **Love and Money** (Arnold); **Love Finds the Way** (Arne); **Lucky-Peter's Journey** (Williamson); **Mason of Buda** (Rodwell); **Miraculous Turnip** (Bissell); (b) **Passion and Resurrection** (Harvey); (t) **Romeo and Juliet** (Shelley); **Sleeping Beauty** (Rubinstein); **Spanish Rivals** (Linley Sr.); **To Hell and Back** (Heggie)

Peter I, **Burgomaster of Saardam** (Bishop); **The Czar** (Shield)

Peter Adolphus Grigg, **The Chieftain** (Sullivan)

Peter Flounder, **Bird Catcher** (Cleve)

Peter Ibbetson, (t) **Peter Ibbetson** (Taylor)

Peter Jack, **The Servants** (Mathias)

Peterkee Vedder, (s) **Rip Van Winkle** (De Koven)

Peter Niles, (bar) **Mourning Becomes Electra** (Levy)

Peter Panick, **Magician No Conjurer** (Mazzinghi)

Peter Popper, **Queerest Courtship** (Sedgwick)

Peter Schlafer, (t) **Little Nightmare Music** (Schickele)

Peter Semyonych, (t) **Seduction of a Lady** (Wargo)

Peter Severe (t), **Curious Affair** (Craton)

Peter Simonson, **Resurrection** (Machover)

Peter the Venerable, (b) **Abelard and Heloise** (Ward)

Peter Turph, (t) **Christopher Sly** (Argento)

Peter Walsh, **Mrs. Dalloway** (Larsen)

Petherick, Sir, (b) **Ordeal of Osbert** (Davis)

Petra von Kant, **Bitter Tears of Petra von Kant** (Barry)

Petruccio, **Petruccio** (Maclean)

Petruchio, (bar) **Taming of the Shrew** (Giannini)

Petunia Jackson, **Cabin in the Sky** (Duke)

Peveril, Julian, **Peveril of the Peak** (Horn)

Peyrolles, **Blanche de Nevers** (Balfe)

Phaedra, **Phaedra** (Innerarity)

Phaon, (t) **Sappho** (Glanville-Hicks)

Pharnaces, **Pharnaces** (1783); **Pharnaces** (Bates)

Phebe, **Beggar's Wedding** (1729)

Pheby, (m) **Twice in a Blue Moon** (Tate)

Phelim, **The Shamrock** (Shields)

Phemius, (t) **Nausicaa** (Glanville-Hicks)

Pheraules (b-bar) **Council of the Dead** (Sternau)

Pherecydes (bar), **Council of the Dead** (Sternau)

Phil, (t) **Dark Waters** (Krenek); **Golden Gate** (Cummings)

Philander, **Pharsalia** (Hamilton)

Philautus, **Love in a Riddle** (1729)

Priam, **Cassandra** (McAndrew); (b-bar) **King Priam** (Tippett)

Priest of the Island, **Love in a Blaze** (Stevenson-Cogan)

Priestess of the Island, **Love in a Blaze** (Stevenson-Cogan)

Primrose, **Circe's Children** (Magrill)

Prince, (actor) **Dog Days** (Little); **Elegy for a Prince** (Cervetti); (s), **Happy Prince** (Williamson); **Vanqui** (Burrs)

Prince Anthony, **Three Princes** (Levowitz)

Prince Bishop, (bar) **Behold the Sun** (Goehr)

Prince Charming, (bar) **The Opening** (Wilder)

Prince Daniel, **Three Princes** (Levowitz)

Prince of Arragon, **The Birth-Day** (Arnold)

Prince of Persia, **Enchanted Horse** (Jones)

Prince of Provence, **Felix** (Lutz)

Prince of the Island, **Love in a Blaze** (Stevenson-Cogan)

Prince Peter, **Three Princes** (Levowitz)

Princess, **Patria, Epilogue** (Schafer)

Princess Betsy, (m) **Anna Karenina** (Carlson)

Princess Flavia, **Zenda** (Duke)

Princess Lan, **Tea** (Tan Dun)

Princess of Monte Carlo, **Grand Duke** (Sullivan)

Prince Zorn, **Thirteen Clocks** (Chauls); **Thirteen Clocks** (Theofanidis)

Prince Zvezdich, **Maskarad** (Morgulas)

Pringle, Carrie, (actor) **Wagner Dream** (Harvey)

Prior Walter, **Angels in America** (Eötvös)

Priscilla, (m) **The Knickerbockers** (De Koven); **Time Rocker** (Reed)

Priscilla Mullins, **Courtship of Miles Standish** (Ewart)

Prism, (t) **Parabola and Circula** (Blitzstein)

Procne, (s) **Love of the Nightingale** (Mills)

Procopius, Dr., **Time Rocker** (Reed)

Proctor, Jane, **Annie** (Ford)

Proctor, John, (bar) **The Crucible** (Ward)

Proctor, Nurse, **Boy Who Grew Too Fast** (Menotti)

Prometheus, **Peleus and Thetis** (Boyce); (b) **Peleus and Thetis** (Hayes); **Prometheus Condemned** (Kupferman)

Propertius, **Birth of the Poet** (Gordon)

Proserpine, **Eurydice** (Fielding); **Orpheus and Euridice** (Locke)

Prospero, **Cue 67** (Ching); **The Tempest** (Banister); (bar) **The Tempest** (Eaton); (b-bar) **The Tempest** (Hoiby); **The Tempest** (Smith); **The Tempest** (Westergaard)

Proteus, **Calypso and Telemachus** (Galliard)

Prudence Strawberry, Miss, **Climbing Boy** (Hawes)

Prunella, **Prunella** (Clayton)

Pryderi, **Song of Rhiannon** (Bowden)

Psyche, **Cinthia and Endimion** (Purcell); (s) **Eros and Psyche** (Cummings); **Psyche** (Locke); (s) **Tale of Psyche & Cupid** (Sternau)

Psyche, Lady, (s) **Princess Ida** (Sullivan)

Ptarmigan, **Wizard of the Nile** (Herbert)

Puck, **Fairy Favour** (Bach); **Fairy Queen** (Purcell); (sp, acrobat) **Midsummer Night's Dream** (1763); **Midsummer Night's Dream** (Britten); (m) **Oberon** (Weber)

Puff, **The Critic** (Stanford); **King Pepin's Campaign** (Arne)

Puff, Lord, (t) **English Cat** (Henze)

Pumpolino, Baron, **Cinderella** (Lacy)

Punch, **Gasconado the Great** (1759); (bar) **Punch and Judy** (Birtwistle); **Triumph of Punch** (Vernon)

Punch Mowgli, **Baa Baa Black Sheep** (Berkeley)

Punka, Rajah, **Nautch Girl** (Solomon)

Putnam, Thomas, (bar) **The Crucible** (Ward)

Pwyll, **Song of Rhiannon** (Bowden)

Pyefleet, **Cobler's Opera** (1728)

Pyramus, **Pyramus and Thisbe** (Bruce); **Pyramus and Thisbe** (Lampe); **Pyramus and Thisbe** (Leveridge)

Pyrrus, **Pyrrus and Demetrius** (Haym)

Pythia, **Ion** (Vir)

Qfwiq, **Without Colors** (Shiflett)

Qin Shi Huang, (t) **First Emperor** (Tan Dun)

Quadrant, **The Disappointment** (Barton)

Quaint, **Devil upon Two Sticks** (Coffey)

Qualla, **Mountain Windsong** (Chlarson)

Quantum Mechanic, (t) **Quantum Mechanic** (Bilotta)

Quasimodo, **Esmeralda** (Thomas); **Notre-Dame of Paris** (Fry); **Quasimodo** (Rodwell)

Quatermaine, Lady Sybil, **Dream Healer** (Burritt)

Queen Ameer, **Seduction of King Solomon** (Willis)

Queenie, **Queenie Pie** (Ellington); (s) **Second Hurricane** (Copland)

Queen of Hearts, (b/b-bar), **Alice** (Bachlund); (m) **Alice in Wonderland** (Chauls); (s), **Alice in Wonderland** (Chin)

Queen of Sheba, **Queen of Sheba's Legs** (Grant)

Queen of the Ashante, **Warrior Sisters** (Ho)

Queen of the Blues, **Bee Story** (Hays)

Queen of the Mardi Grass, (m) **Night of the Moonspell** (Siegmeister)

Queequeg, **Moby Dick** (Heggie)

Quentin Durward, **King's Prize** (Maclean); **Quentin Durward** (Laurent); **Quentin Durward** (Maclean)

Quexada, Don, **Don John of Austria** (Nathan)

Quibble Quibus, Sir, **Female Parson** (Coffey)

Quibus, Lady, **Female Parson** (Coffey)

Quickly, Mrs., (m/a) **Sir John in Love** (Vaughan Williams)

Quince, **Midsummer Night's Dream** (1763); (b) **Midsummer Night's Dream** (Britten)

Quint, Peter, (t) **Turn of the Screw** (Britten)

Quintus, (t) **Mona** (Parker)

Quiroga, Archbishop, **El Greco** (Harper)

Quiteria, **Adventure of Don Quixote** (Macfarren)

Quixote, Don, **Adventure of Don Quixote** (Macfarren); **Don Quixote** (Arnold); **Don Quixote** (De Koven); **Don Quixote** (Hewitt); **Don Quixote** (Rodwell); **Don Quixote in England** (1734)

Reed, Thomas German, **Our Island Home** (Reed)

Reede, (b) **Arden Must Die** (Goehr)

Reeve, (bar) **Man without a Country** (Damrosch)

Refugee, **Flight** (Dove)

Reg, (b-bar) **Oath of Bad Brown Bill** (Conyngham)

Regan, (s) **New Year** (Tippett)

Reggie, **Music Cure** (Hagemann)

Regina Giddens, (s) **Regina** (Blitzstein)

Reginald, (bar) **X** (Davis)

Reginald, Sir, (t) **The Affair** (Werder); **Ballad of the Bremen Band** (Arlan); **White Chrysanthemum** (Talbot)

Reginald Warren, **White Bird** (Carter)

Regnard, Baron, (b-bar) **He Who Gets Slapped** (Ward)

Rei, (b) **The Martyr** (Freeman)

Reinaldo, **Before Night Falls** (Martín)

Remus, (t) **Treemonisha** (Joplin)

Renaud, **Armide** (Dawes); **Joan of Arc** (Balfe)

Renée, (s) **Lost Highway** (Neuwirth)

Renfield, **Dracula** (Ziemba)

Resa, **Caernarvon Castle** (Attwood)

Reuben, **Azael** (Laurent); (m) **Christmas Rose** (Bridge)

Reuben Ranzo, **Cumberland Fair** (Wilder)

Reuben Waterford, **Dr. Heidegger's Fountain** (Beeson)

Reuel, (t) **The Scarf** (Hoiby); (b-bar) **The Tower** (Levy)

Reiza, (s) **Oberon** (Weber)

Rezio, **Sancho at Court** (1742)

Rhadamanthys, (t) **Council of the Dead** (Sternau)

Rheba, (s/m) **Hanging Judge** (Lockwood)

Rhiannon, **Song of Rhiannon** (Bowden)

Rhineberg, (bar) **Lurline** (Wallace)

Rhodope, **Orpheus** (Barthelemon)

Ribalda, Donna, (m) **Stoned Guest** (Schickele)

Ribaldi, **Heir of Vironi** (Bishop)

Ricciardo, (t) **Boccaccio's Nightingale** (Trimble)

Riccio, David, (b-bar) **Mary, Queen of Scots** (Musgrave); *see also* Rizzio, David

Richard, **Alternate Visions** (Oliver); **Brazen Bust** (Bishop); (bar) **Clair de Lune** (Larsen); (bar) **Fortune's Favorites** (Barab); (t) **John Socman** (Lloyd); (t) **What Price Confidence** (Krenek); **Wide Sargasso Sea** (Howard)

Richard II, (t) **Wat Tyler** (Bush)

Richard III, **Richard III** (Turok)

Richard, King, **Adventures of Friar Tuck** (Paxton); **Canterbury Pilgrims** (De Koven); (b) **Ivanhoe** (Sullivan); **Knight of the Leopard** (Balfe); **Richard Coeur de Lion** (Linley Sr.); **Richard Coeur de Lion** (Shield); **Zenda** (Duke)

Richard Dauntless, (t) **Ruddigore** (Sullivan)

Richard Malone, (bar) **The Clock** (Rieti)

Richard of Agrazant, (t) **Castle Agrazant** (Lyford)

Richard Talbot, (t) **The Scarecrow** (Lockwood)

Richard Taverner, (bar) **Taverner** (Davies)

Rick, **I Was Looking at the Ceiling** (Adams); **Marilyn** (Laderman)

Rick Driscoll, (t) **Letter to E. 11th St.** (Hennessey)

Rickett, Mr., **False Guardians Outwitted** (1740)

Ricky, **Again** (Heggie)

Ridgdumfunnidos, **Chrononhotonthologos** (Carey)

Rigoletto, **Talk Opera** (Granger)

Riel, **Louis Riel** (Somers)

Riff, **West Side Story** (Bernstein)

Rima, **Green Mansions** (Gruenberg)

Rimbaud, Arthur, (t, tr) **Man with Footsoles** (Volans); **Seasons in Hell** (Blumenfeld); (t) **Thérèse** (Taverner)

Rinaldo, **Armida** (Weir); **Rinaldo and Armida** (Eccles)

Rinaldo, Count, (b-bar) **Prima Donna** (Benjamin)

Rinuccio, **Buoso's Ghost** (Ching)

Rip Van Winkle, (b) **Rip Van Winkle** (Bristow); (bar) **Rip Van Winkle** (De Koven); **Rip Van Winkle** (Jordan); **Rip Van Winkle** (Kaufmann); **Rip Van Winkle** (Manning); **Rip Van Winkle** (Rockwell)

Rip Van Winkle Jr., (t) **Rip Van Winkle** (Bristow)

Rit, (m) **Harriet** (Musgrave)

River, **Mother of Three Sons** (Jenkins)

Rivera, Diego, **Frida** (Rodríguez)

River Lethe, (bar) **Myth of Er** (Sternau)

Rivers, **Day at Rome** (Attwood); **The Raft** (Reeve)

Rizzio, **David Rizzio** (Braham); (t) **David Rizzio** (Moore); *see also* Riccio, David

Roberta Alden, (s) **American Tragedy** (Picker)

Robbins, (t) **Porgy and Bess** (Gershwin)

Robert, **Final Bid** (Raum); (t) **Haunted Tower** (Storace); (t) **King Hal** (Stewart); (t) **Prodigal Son** (Jacobi); (bar) **The Soldier** (Engel); **Turtle Wakes** (Bell); **Vile Shadows** (Turner)

Roberta, **Jack and Roberta** (Cain)

Robert Baden-Powell, Sir, (bar) **Daisy** (Smith)

Robert Bruce, **Lord of the Isles** (Rodwell)

Robert Dudley, (t) **Amy Robsart** (de Lara); **Kenilworth** (Klein)

Robert Garner, (bar) **Margaret Garner** (Danielpour)

Robert Hart Jr., (t) **Robert and Hal** (Brooks)

Robert Hart Sr., (b-bar) **Robert and Hal** (Brooks)

Robert Lonle, (t) **Caritas** (Saxon)

Robert Maythorn, **Turnpike Gate** (Reeve-Mazzinghi)

Robert of Artois, **English Fleet** (Braham)

Robert (Duke) of Normandy, **Fiend-Father** (Meyerbeer-Lacy); **Robert the Devil** (Barnett); **Robert the Devil** (Meyerbeer-"Kettenus")

Robeson, Paul, **Star across the Ocean** (Richards)

Robespierre, (b-bar) **Danton and Robespierre** (Eaton)

Robin, **The Contrivances** (Carey); **Glorious First of June** (Storace); (t) **My Kinsman** (Saylor); (t) **Night of the Moonspell** (Siegmeister); **Robin Hood** (Burney); **The Waterman** (Dibdin); **Welsh Opera** (1731)

Robin Gray, **Auld Robin Gray** (Arnold); **Auld Robin Gray** (Blewitt)

Robin Hood, (t) **Adventures of Friar Tuck** (Paxton); **Maid Marian** (Bishop); **Maid Marian** (De Koven); **Robin Hood** (1730); (t) **Robin Hood** (De Koven); **Robin Hood** (Macfarren); **Robin Hood** (Shield); **Robin Hood** (Tippett)

Robin Oakapple, (bar) **Ruddigore** (Sullivan)

Robin Redhead, **To Arms!** (Shield)

Robin Snare, **Bird Catcher** (Cleve)

Robinson, (t) **America** (Kohs)

Rob Roy, **Rob Roy** (De Koven); **Rob Roy Macgregor** (Davy)

Robson, Mrs., **My Walking Photograph** (Sedgwick)

Robson, Richard, **My Walking Photograph** (Sedgwick)

Rocca Marina, Count, (t) **The Fan** (Goldstein)

Rochester, Mr., (b-bar) **Jane Eyre** (Berkeley); **Wide Sargasso Sea** (Howard)

Rochester, Mrs., (a) **Jane Eyre** (Berkeley)

Rockalda, **Flying Dutchman** (Rodwell)

Rockwardine, Admiral, **Fall of Algiers** (Bishop)

Roddie, (t/s) **Christmas Miracle** (Fax)

Roderic de Froila, **Red Cross Knights** (Attwood)

Roderic Murgatroyd, Sir, (b) **Ruddigore** (Sullivan)

Roderick, (bar) **Long Christmas Dinner** (Hindemith)

Roderick Dhu, **Knight of Snowdoun** (Bishop); (bar) **Lady of the Lake** (Schmidt)

Roderick Usher, **Dream within a Dream** (Currie); **Fall of the House of Usher** (Glass); (bar) **Fall of the House of Usher** (Sitsky)

Rodolfo, **Sicilian Bride** (Balfe)

Rodolpho, **Amelia** (Lampe)

Rodríguez, (bar) **Simón Bolívar** (Musgrave)

Roger, **Gentle Shepherd** (1729); (b) **Kumana** (Kanitz); **Patie and Peggy** (1730)

Roger Davis, **Rent** (Larson)

Roger Doremus, (t) **Summer and Smoke** (Hoiby)

Rogier, (t) **Diable amoureux** (Nelson)

Rohesia, Lady, (s) **Lady Rohesia** (Hopkins)

Rokujo, (s) **Tale of Genji** (Miki)

Roland, Count, **Free Knights** (Mazzinghi)

Roland, Countess, **Free Knights** (Mazzinghi)

Roland, Lord, **Gasconado the Great** (1759)

Rolando, **Honey Moon** (Hewitt/Kelly)

Rolf, (b-bar) **Irmelin** (Delius)

Rolla, **Virgin of the Sun** (Bishop)

Romanoff, **The Exile** (Mazzinghi)

Romeo, **City Workers** (Weisensel); **Romeo and Juliet** (Barkworth); **Romeo and Juliet** (Liotta); **Romeo and Juliet** (Marshall-Hall); (t) **Romeo and Juliet** (Shelley)

Romilayu, (t) **Lily** (Kirchner)

Romney, Captain, **My Lady Molly** (Jones)

Romulus, **Romulus Hunt** (Simon)

Ronald, **Lord of the Isles** (Rodwell)

Ronnie, (bar) **The Opening** (Wilder)

Roo, **Summer of the Seventeenth Doll** (Mills)

Rosa, **Ages Ago** (Clay); **The Caravan** (Reeve); **Fontainbleau** (Shield); **Red Cross Knights** (Attwood); **Rosa** (Andriessen)

Rosabel, **The Alcaid** (Nathan)

Rosabella, **Most Happy Fella** (Loesser)

Rosa Gonzales, (m) **Summer and Smoke** (Hoiby)

Rosalba, Princess, **Rose and the Ring** (Leginska)

Rosalie, **Black Swan** (Whitman); **Climbing Boy** (Hawes); **Fatal Oath** (Koutzen)

Rosalie Smith, (s) **Kumana** (Kanitz)

Rosalind, **Mines of Sulphur** (Bennett)

Rosalinda, **Rosalinda** (Smith)

Rosalinda Ross, (s) **The Audition** (Goodman)

Rosalvina, Countess, **Devil's Bridge** (Arnold)

Rosa Martini, (s) **Opera Cloak** (Damrosch)

Rosambert, Countess de, **Robert the Devil** (Barnett)

Rosamond, **The Armorer** (1793); **Beau Nash** (Valenti); **Fair Rosamond** (Barnett); (h s) **Fairyland** (Parker); **Rosamond** (Arne); **Rosamond** (Arnold); (s) **Rosamond** (Clayton)

Rosamund, Maid, **Eleanor** (Douglas)

Rosaura, (s) **Life Is a Dream** (Spratlan)

Röschen, **The Forest** (Smyth)

Rose, **At the Statue of Venus** (Heggie); **Double Disguise** (Hook); **Marilyn** (Laderman); **Night before the Wedding** (Bishop); **Rose and Colin** (Dibdin); **Rose Garden** (Boyd); (s) **Shoemaker's Holiday** (Argento); **Village Coquettes** (Hullah); (s) **What Next?** (Carter)

Rosei, (t) **Kantan and the Damask Drum** (Goehr)

Rosella, **Chamber-Maid** (Phillips); **Village Opera** (1729)

Rosellen, (s) **Philip Marshall** (Barab)

Rose-Marie, **Rose-Marie** (Friml/Stothart)

Rosemary, **Desperate Waltz** (Earnest); (m) **The Pumpkin** (Kondorossy)

Rose Maurrant, (s) **Street Scene** (Weill)

Rose Maybud, (s) **Ruddigore** (Sullivan)

Rosemonde, Mme. de, (s) **Dangerous Liaisons** (Susa)

Rosenberg, Count, (b) **Siege of Rochelle** (Balfe)

Rosenberg, Ethel, **Angels in America** (Eötvös); (s) **Defendants Rosenberg** (Meyers)

Rosenberg, Julius, (t) **Defendants Rosenberg** (Meyers)

Rosencrantz, **Rosencrantz and Guildenstern** (Garfein)

Rose Parrowe, (m) **Taverner** (Davies)

Rosetta, **Love in a Village** (Arne)

Rosey, **Tin Pan Alley** (Raphling)

Roshana, (sp) **Oberon** (Weber)

Rosie, **Bride from Pluto** (Menotti)

Rosie Pippin, Lady, **Emerald Isle** (Sullivan)

Rosina, **Castle of Sorrento** (Attwood); (s) **Ghosts of Versailles** (Corigliano); **Rosina** (Shield); **Rosina** (Titus); **Spanish Barber** (Arnold)

Rosine, **Signor Deluso** (Pasatieri)

Rosita, (s) **Don Cristóbal and Rosita** (Crawford)

Ross, **The Covenanters** (Loder)

Rossmann, Karl, (t) **America** (Kohs)

Rough, Inspector, **Gaslight** (Roe)

Rouvières, Baron des, (b-bar) **Diable amoureux** (Nelson)

Rovewell, **The Contrivances** (Carey); **Love and Revenge** (1729)

Rowan, (s) **Little Sweep** (Britten)

Rowena, **Ligeia** (Thomas)

Rowena, Lady, (s) **Ivanhoe** (Sullivan)

Rowland, Mrs., **Dark Sonnet** (Chisholm)

Rowland Lacy, (t) **Shoemaker's Holiday** (Argento)

Roxalana, **The Sultan** (Dibdin)

Roxana, **Rival Queens** (Finger)

Roxane, (s) **Cyrano** (Beeson); (s) **Cyrano** (Damrosch); **Cyrano de Bergerac** (Herbert)

Roxborough, John, **Shadowboxer** (Proto)

Roy, (bar) **Demon Lover** (Nelson); **Swoon** (Rolfe)

Rozanne, **Légende Provençale** (Moore)

Ruby Bates, **Ghosts** (Ito)

Ruby Herter, **Amarantha** (Ames)

Rucello, **Savonarola** (Stanford)

Rucker Lattimore, (b-bar) **Cold Sassy Tree** (Floyd)

Rudiger, Count, **Amber Witch** (Wallace)

Rudolf, **Black Crook** (Operti)

Rudolph, **The Forest** (Smyth); **Grand Duke** (Sullivan); **Ida** (Leslie); **Sylvana** (Weber-Blewitt)

Rudolph, Count, (t) **Lurline** (Wallace)

Rudolpho, (t) **View from the Bridge** (Bolcom); (t) **View from the Bridge** (Morris)

Rudy Rolando, **The Bohemians** (Kirschner)

Rufus Follett, **Death in the Family** (Mayer)

Ruggio, (b) **Bianca** (Hadley)

Ruins, (t) **Soyazhe** (Anderson)

Rumpelstiltskin, **Rumpelstiltskin** (Baber); **Rumpelstiltskin** (Bourgeois); **Rumpelstiltskin** (Di Chiera); **Rumpelstiltskin** (Epstein)

Rupee, **Positive Man** (Arnold)

Rupert, **Haddon Hall** (Sullivan); **Love in a Camp** (Shield); (t) **Satanella** (Balfe)

Rupert Padgourney, **Bachelor Farmers** (Weisensel)

Ruskin, **Modern Painters** (Lang)

Russell, Lillian, (s) **Mother of Us All** (Thomson)

Rust, **Quaker's Opera** (1728)

Rustichello, **Marco Polo** (Tan Dun)

Ruta, **The Outcast** (Ain)

Ruth, (m) **Eternal Road** (Weill); (a) **Pirates of Penzance** (Sullivan); (m) **Prodigal Son** (Jacobi); (m) **Ruddigore** (Sullivan); (s) **Ruth** (Berkeley); **Ruth** (Hagemann); **Ruth and Naomi** (Hart); **Ruth and Naomi** (Kondorossy); **Ruth and Naomi** (Niblock); (s) **Song of David** (Arnstein); **Trippin'** (Rodwin)

Ruth Austin, (s) **The Mummy** (Quincy)

Ruth Seal, **Bachelor Farmers** (Weisensel)

Ruth Young Kamen, (s) **Bonesetter's Daughter** (Wallace)

Ruthven, Lord, (b) **David Rizzio** (Moore)

Ruthven Murgatroyd, (bar) **Ruddigore** (Sullivan)

Ruy Blas, **Ruy Blas** (Glover)

Ruy Gomes, Don, **Don John of Austria** (Nathan)

S, Dr., **Man Who Mistook His Wife** (Nyman)

Sabrina, (s) **Colonial Jonathan** (Argento); **Comus** (Arne)

Sacagawea, **Corps of Discovery** (Ching)

Sacco, **Sacco and Vanzetti** (Blitzstein)

Sacramento Sadie, (m) **The Argonauts** (Maganini)

Sacrapant, **Sacrapant** (Aston)

Sadak, **Sadak and Kalasrade** (Packer)

Sadie, (s) **Slow Dusk** (Floyd)

Sadie Burke, **Willie Stark** (Floyd)

Sadie Thompson, **Sadie Thompson** (Owen)

Safié, **Safié** (Hadley)

Saïda, **Beauty Stone** (Sullivan)

Sai-Jen, (s) **Story of the Bird Feng** (Sternau)

Saint Phalle, Niki de, **Construction of Boston** (Wheeler)

Saladin, Sultan, **Nathan the Wise** (Kondorossy)

Salamander, (t) **Pipe of Desire** (Converse)

Sali, (tr, t) **Village Romeo and Juliet** (Delius)

Salieri, Antonio, (bar) **Little Nightmare Music** (Schickele)

Sallust (de Bazan), Don, **Rose of Castille** (Balfe); **Ruy Blas** (Glover)

Sally, **Barber of New York** (Vernon); (s) **The Barrier** (Meyerowitz); **Englishmen in India** (Bishop); (a) **Hand of Bridge** (Barber); **The Purse** (Reeve); (s) **Royal Auction** (Kanitz); **Silver Tankard** (Arnold); **Thomas and Sally** (Arne)

Sally Hemings, **Monticello** (Paxton)

Sally Herdy, **Jonathan Postfree** (1807)

Salome, (s) **Hell's Angels** (Osborne)

Salt Woman, (s) **Nine Rivers from Jordan** (Weisgall)

Salvador, Don, **Choleric Fathers** (Shield)

Salviati, **Bianca** (Balfe)

Sam, (bar) **Blue Monday** (Gershwin); **Double Disguise** (Hook); **The Harvest** (Giannini); (tr) **Little Sweep** (Britten); (b) **Quiet Place** (Bernstein); **Ransom of Red Chief** (Rodríguez); **Stranger's Tale** (Tucker); (t) **Thanksgiving** (Levi); (b-bar) **Trouble in Tahiti** (Bernstein)

Samantha, (s) **Chronicles** (Muller)

Sam Cooper, (b-bar) **Love Life** (Weill)

Sam Double, **Single Married Man** (Sedgwick)

Sam Kaplan, (t) **Street Scene** (Weill)

Sammy, **Black Roses** (Chisholm)

Sammy May, (b) **Old Majestic** (Rodríguez)

Sammy Sapling, **Magician No Conjurer** (Mazzinghi)

Sam Polk, (t) **Susannah** (Floyd)

Sampson Harvey, **The Covenanters** (Loder)

Samson, **Samson and the Witch** (Baber); **The Warrior** (Rogers)

Samuel, **The Jewess** (Halévy-Cooke); (bar) **Pirates of Penzance** (Sullivan); (t) **Three Sisters Who Are Not Sisters** (Rorem)

Selima, **Il Bondocani** (Attwood/ Moorehead); **Cady of Bagdad** (Linley Jr.); **Selima and Azor** (Linley Sr.)

Selina Sugarcane, Lady, **Family Quarrels** (Reeve et al.)

Sellem, (t) **Rake's Progress** (Stravinsky)

Selvay, Dr., **Dr. Selvay's Magic Theatre** (Silverman)

Semele, **Semele** (Eccles); **Semele** (Handel)

Semibreve, Mr., **Pyramus and Thisbe** (Lampe)

Semira, (s) **Artaxerxes** (Arne)

Semiramis, (s) **Inferno of Dante** (Soluri)

Sententious, Mr., **Better Sort** (1789)

Sententious, Mrs., **Better Sort** (1789)

Septimus, (t) **Mrs. Dalloway** (Larsen)

Seraphina, **The Birth-Day** (Arnold)

Seraskier Mahamed, (t) **Siege of Belgrade** (Storace)

Serena, (s) **Porgy and Bess** (Gershwin)

Serena Joy, **Handmaid's Tale** (Ruders)

Sergeant Jack, **Highland Reel** (Shield)

Sergeant Peterman, **Desert Flower** (Wallace)

Sergei, **The Prisoner** (Joubert)

Serpilla, **Servant Mistress** (Arnold)

Sesto, (bar) **The Magician** (Hoddinott)

Seth, **Enchantment of Dreams** (Franklin)

Seven Nemeses, (bar) **Death in Venice** (Britten)

Severeid, Eric, **Gertrude Stein** (Banfield)

Severin, (t) **Silverlake** (Weill-Symonette); (t) **Venus in Furs** (Gal)

Sganarelle, **Forced Marriage** (Hart); (bar) **Sganarelle** (Archer); **Sganarelle** (Kaufmann)

Shaban, (b) **In the Pasha's Garden** (Seymour)

Shabbethai Zevi, **False Messiah** (Adolphe)

Shadow of Euripides, (sp) **The Bacchae** (Buller)

Shakebag, (t) **Arden Must Die** (Goehr)

Shakespeare, **Marco Polo** (Tan Dun); **Dark Lady of the Sonnets** (Hagemann)

Shakti, **Apocalypse** (Shields)

Shakur, Assata, **Warrior Sisters** (Ho)

Shala, **Shala Fears for the Poor** (Braxton)

Shaman, (t) **Seabird Island** (Healey)

Shamanka, **Patria, no. 8** (Schafer)

Shameless, **Love and Revenge** (1729)

Shamus O'Brien, **Shamus O'Brien** (Stanford)

Shanewis, (m) **Shanewis** (Cadman)

Sharah, (s) **Yehu** (Zador)

Shard, (bar) **Grace of Todd** (Crosse)

Sharik, (t) **Murder of Comrade Sharik** (Bergsma)

Sharkey, (bar) **Sandhog** (Robinson)

Sharon, **How to Make Love** (Widdoes)

Sharon Falconer, (m) **Elmer Gantry** (Aldridge)

Shaun Ferris, (bar) **The Picnic** (Cumming)

Shawntel, **Jerry Springer** (Thomas)

Shayne, Lord, **Bitter-Sweet** (Coward)

Sheba, **Della's Gift** (Welcher); **Solomon and Sheba** (Rivers)

Sheela Cavanaugh, (a) **Sandhog** (Robinson)

Sheherezada, **Marco Polo** (Tan Dun)

Sheila Meloy, **Witch of Salem** (Cadman)

Shelley, Percy, **Mary Shelley** (Jaffe)

Shelly Ward, **Angle of Repose** (Imbrie)

Shem, **Noah** (Sahl/Salzman)

Shepard, Alan, **Apollo 14** (Meckler)

Sherasmin, (bar) **Oberon** (Weber)

Sheriff of Nottingham, **Adventures of Friar Tuck** (Paxton); **Maid Marian** (De Koven); (bar) **Robin Hood** (De Koven)

Sheriff Peters, **Trifles** (Bilotta)

Sherrin, **Mines of Sulphur** (Bennett)

Shifra, **Shloyme Gorgl** (Lateiner)

Shii No Shosho, (male dr) **Sotoba Komachi** (Levy)

Shin, Reverend, (bar) **The Martyred** (Wade)

Shinken, Madam ap, **Welsh Opera** (1731)

Shinken, Squire ap, **Welsh Opera** (1731)

Shirah, (s) **The Martyr** (Freeman)

Shirley, (s) **Out of Season** (Grant); (s) **The Pumpkin** (Kondorossy)

Shirley Fisher, (m/a) **Karla** (Lehrman)

Shiunin, **Land of Happiness** (Redding)

Shiva, **Apocalypse** (Shield)

Shloyme Gorgl, **Shloyme Gorgl** (Lateiner)

Shojo, (b) **Jōruri** (Miki)

Shonagon, (m) **Tale of Genji** (Miki)

Shostakovich, Dmitri, **Black Sea Follies** (Silverman)

Shridaman, (t) **Transposed Heads** (Glanville-Hicks)

Shrike, (bar) **Miss Lonelyhearts** (Liebermann)

Shrike, Mary, (s) **Miss Lonelyhearts** (Liebermann)

Shrink, Dr., **Boy Who Grew Too Fast** (Menotti)

Shylock, **Shylock** (La Violette)

Shylock Homestead, **In Dahomey** (Cook)

Sian, (s) **The Sacrifice** (MacMillan)

Sibyl, (s) **Lord Arthur Savile's Crime** (Bush)

Sibyl Vane, **Picture of Dorian Gray** (Liebermann)

Sid, **Sid the Serpent** (Fox)

Sidney, Lord, **Travellers in Switzerland** (Shield)

Sidney Hodkins, (bar) **The Audition** (Goodman)

Sidney, Philip, (ct) **Angel Magick** (Harle)

Sidonie von Grasenabb, **Bitter Tears of Petra von Kant** (Barry)

Siegmund, (bar) **The Sandman** (Cabaniss)

Sieh King King, **Warrior Sisters** (Ho)

Sifrid, **Edwin and Angelina** (Pelissier)

Sigmund Lump, **Free Lance** (Sousa)

Signor Deluso, (bar) **Signor Deluso** (Pasatieri)

Signor Rafael, **Lady and the Devil** (Kelly)

Silas, **Silas Marner** (Joubert)

Silas Gapteeth, (tr) **Julius Caesar Jones** (Williamson)

Silence, (s), **Silence Tree** (Fox)

Silent Wings, (a) **Pilate** (Hovhaness)

Silenus, **Fairy Prince** (Arne)

Sillimon, **Thespis** (Sullivan)

Silva, **Maria Elena** (Pasatieri)

Silverside, Lord, **Triple Sec** (Blitzstein)

Silvia, **Philander and Silvia** (Carr); **Silvia** (Lillo)

Silvio, **Empty Bottle** (Kalmanoff); **Servant of Two Masters** (Giannini)

Sima, **Sima** (Lehrman)

Simeon, **Simeon** (Gustafson)

Simkin, **The Deserter** (Dibdin)

Simon, **The Cottagers** (1766); **The Equation** (Bush); **Fisherman Called Peter** (Owen); **Lucky Discovery** (1737); **Naughty Marietta** (Herbert); **The Reconciliation** (1790); **Sailor-Boy and the Falcon** (Siskind); (bar) **Shining Chalice** (Van Grove); **Turn Out!** (King); (b) **Yehu** (Zador)

Simond, **The Savoyard** (Reinagle)

Simon Eyre, (bar) **Shoemaker's Holiday** (Argento)

Simon Perez, (t) **Koanga** (Delius)

Simon Price, (t) **Demon Lover** (Nelson)

Simple Simon, **Passion of Simple Simon** (Sahl)

Simpson, **Trip to Portsmouth** (Dibdin)

Sims, Jane **Annie** (Ford)

Sin, **Paradise Lost** (Penderecki)

Sinclair, **Sprigs of Laurel** (Shield)

Sindarina, (s) **Zenobia** (Pratt)

Singbe, **Amistad** (Ames)

Singing Sue, (s) **The Argonauts** (Maganini)

Sinister Woman, **Girl and the Unicorn** (Oliver)

Sinon, **Humorous Lieutenant** (Bishop)

Siqueiros, **America Tropical** (Conte)

Sir Abel Handy, **Speed the Plow** (Moorehead)

Sir Antony (Anthony) Withers, **Amelia** (Dibdin et al.); **Amelia** (Piccinni et al.)

Sir Edward, **Turnpike Gate** (Reeve-Mazzinghi)

Sirena, **Sicilian Bride** (Balfe)

Sir Harry Muff, **Rival Candidates** (Carter)

Sir Jeoffry Wisepate, **Happy Disguise** (Giordani)

Sir John Freeman, **Silvia** (Lillo)

Sir Nicholas Wiseacre, **Village Opera** (1729)

Sirocco, **Lucky Star** (Caryll); **Merry Monarch** (Sousa)

Sir Oliver Oddfish, **The Blackamoor** (Dibdin)

Sir Philip Blandford, **Speed the Plow** (Moorehead)

Sir Roger Ramble, **Turk and No Turk** (Arnold)

Sir Simon Simple, **Turk and No Turk** (Arnold)

Sir Thomas Loveland, **Don Quixote in England** (1734); **The Sot** (Arne); **'Squire Badger** (Arne)

Sir William Freeman, **Village Opera** (1729)

Siskadee, (a) **Narcissa** (Moore)

Sister Aimée, **Sister Aimée** (Martínez)

Sister Angela, **God Boy** (Ritchie)

Sister Angelica, (s) **Three Hermits** (Paulus)

Sister Ficcanaso, (s) **Suor Isabella** (Rodríguez)

Sister Gladys, (s) **Sweet Bye and Bye** (Beeson)

Sister Isabella, (s) **Suor Isabella** (Rodríguez)

Sister Miriam, (s) **Three Hermits** (Paulus)

Sister Rees, (s) **Sweet Bye and Bye** (Beeson)

Sister Rose Ora Easter, (s) **Sweet Bye and Bye** (Beeson)

Sister Sgridaretta, (m) **Suor Isabella** (Rodríguez)

Sita, (s) **Transposed Heads** (Glanville-Hicks)

Sitting Bull, Chief, **Ghost Dance** (Levin)

Siward, (t) **Better Place** (Butler)

Skellig, (bar) **Skellig** (Machover)

Skipjack, **Pennyworth of Wit** (Davy)

Skobeloff, **The Charlatan** (Sousa)

Skosvodmonit, Mrs., **Boy Who Grew Too Fast** (Menotti)

Sleep, (b) **Fairy Queen** (Purcell)

Sleeping Beauty, **Sleeping Beauty** (Rubinstein)

Sleeping Hero, **Potter Thompson** (Crosse)

Slender, (t) **Sir John in Love** (Vaughan Williams)

Slim, (t) **Cop and the Anthem** (Cohen); (bar) **Of Mice and Men** (Floyd); (t) **Paul Bunyan** (Britten)

Slim Parr, (bar) **Sack of Calabasas** (Fletcher)

Sloane, (bar) **Dreamkeepers** (Carlson)

Sloper, Dr., (b-bar) **Washington Square** (Pasatieri)

Sly, (t) **Faustus** (Dusapin)

Sly, John, **Blind Beggar of Bethnal Green** (Arne)

Slyfox, Mr., **Circumstances Alter Cases** (Sedgwick)

Smart, **Turnpike Gate** (Reeve-Mazzinghi)

Smeraldina, **Servant of Two Masters** (Giannini)

Smiley, Mrs., (m) **Bad Boys in School** (Meyerowitz)

Smirnov, Grigory Stepanovitch, (bar) **The Bear** (Walton); (bar) **The Boor** (Grantham); (bar) **The Boor** (Kay); (bar) **The Brute** (Moss)

Smith, **Music Teacher** (Shawn)

Smith, Bessie, (s) **Till Victory Is Won** (Fox)

Smith, John, **Indian Princess** (Bray)

Smith, Joseph, **Book of Gold** (Boren); **Joseph! Joseph!** (Crawford)

Smith, Mr., (t) **Bald Prima Donna** (Kalmanoff)

Smith, Mrs., (s) **Bald Prima Donna** (Kalmanoff)

Smithurst, Reverend John, **Florence** (Sullivan)

Smitty, **Port Town** (Meyerowitz)

Smooth, Mr., **Fashionable Lady** (1730)

Smutta, **Flying Dutchman** (Rodwell)

Snake, (bar) **Eve's Odds** (Trinkley)

Snakepeace, Parson, **Good Friday 1663** (Westbrook)

Snarlygob, **Midnight Court Opera** (Sokolovic)

Snatchem, Joe, **Bird Catcher** (Cleve)

Sulnier, Count, **Maid of Artois** (Balfe)

Sun, (t) **Masque of Clouds** (Johnson)

Sundar, (t) **Thief of Love** (Silver)

Sunniva, **Sailor-Boy and the Falcon** (Siskind)

Superstition, **Britannia** (Carey)

Supplejack, Charles, **Family Quarrels** (Reeve et al.)

Supplejack, Mrs., **Family Quarrels** (Reeve et al.)

Supplejack, Squire, **Family Quarrels** (Reeve et al.)

Susan, **Britain's Glory** (Arnold); **Devil upon Two Sticks** (Coffey); (s) **Dinner Engagement** (Berkeley); **Family Quarrels** (Reeve et al.); **Glorious First of June** (Storace); (s) **Letter to E. 11th St.** (Hennessey); **The Mariners** (Attwood); (s) **Opera Cloak** (Damrosch); **Pennyworth of Wit** (Davy); (m) **Thanksgiving** (Levi); **Thomas and Susan** (Reeve); **To Arms!** (Shield); **Turtle Wakes** (Bell)

Susan Cooper, (s) **Love Life** (Weill)

Susanna, (s) **Ghosts of Versailles** (Corigliano); (s/m) **Simple Decision** (Busch)

Susannah, **Tristram Shandy** (1783)

Susannah Polk, (s) **Susannah** (Floyd)

Susanna Susannadanna, (m) **Abduction of Figaro** (Schickele)

Susan Rowley, (s) **Robert and Hal** (Brooks)

Susan Whyley, (m) **Julius Caesar Jones** (Williamson)

Susie, (a) **Last Leaf** (Niblock); (m) **Quiet Place** (Bernstein)

Sussmayer, Franz, **Music Robber** (Van Grove)

Suzanne, **Alternate Visions** (Oliver); (m) **Better Place** (Butler); **Toussaint** (Blake)

Suzel, **Friend Fritz** (Edwards)

Suzuki, (m) **Cio Cio San** (Carroll)

Swallow, **Elegy for a Prince** (Cervetti); (s) **Happy Prince** (Williamson); (b) **Peter Grimes** (Britten)

Sweeney, Pat, (t) **The Rope** (Mennini)

Sweeney Agonistes, **Sweeney Agonistes** (Winslow)

Sweeney Todd, (bar) **Sweeney Todd** (Sondheim)

Sweet, Mrs., (m) **Opera Cloak** (Damrosch)

Sweetheart, (s) **Hangman, Hangman!** (Balada)

Sweetissa, **Welsh Opera** (1731)

Swift, Jonathan, **Words upon the Window Pane** (Buckley)

Swindle Scribble, **Critic upon Critic** (MacNally)

Switzerkase, **Gambrinus** (Sedgwick)

Swivel, Commodore, **The Czar** (Shield)

Sybil, (s) **John Socman** (Lloyd); **White Chrysanthemum** (Talbot)

Sycorax, **The Tempest** (Banister)

Sydney, **Sanctuary Song** (Richardson)

Sykes, Brabazon, **Merry Duchess** (Clay)

Sylphid Queen, **Mountain Sylph** (Barnett)

Sylphinia, (s) **Only a Miracle** (Barab)

Sylvana, **Sylvana** (Weber-Blewitt)

Sylvester, (bar) **Three Sisters Who Are Not Sisters** (Rorem)

Sylvia, (s) **Cymon** (Arne); (s) **The Dress** (Bucci); **Female Rake** (1736); **Plumber's Gift** (Blake); **Shepherd's Artifice** (Dibdin)

Sylvio, **The Enchantress** (Balfe); **Phoebe** (Greene)

Symon, **Gentle Shepherd** (1729)

Synnelet, **Maid of Artois** (Balfe)

Syrena, **Wuornos** (Lucero)

Syrinx, **Pan and Syrinx** (Galliard)

Syvert, (t) **Giants in the Earth** (Moore)

Tabele, **David's Violin** (Mogulesco)

Tabitha, (m) **The Tower** (Levy)

Taché, Bishop, **Louis Riel** (Somers)

Tacit, Lady, **Positive Man** (Arnold)

Tackleton, **Cricket on the Hearth** (Mackenzie)

Taco, (t) **Vera of Las Vegas** (Hagen)

Tadzio, (dr) **Death in Venice** (Britten)

Taffy, (m) **The Departure** (Davis)

Tailbush, Lady, (m) **Spanish Lady** (Elgar)

Ta-Khai, (t) **Story of the Bird Feng** (Sternau)

Talia, **Enchantment of Dreams** (Franklin)

Talisman, **Magician No Conjurer** (Mazzinghi)

Talisman, Miss, **Magician No Conjurer** (Mazzinghi)

Tallulah Carter, (s) **Hotel Casablanca** (Pasatieri)

Talmaae, **Thais and Talmaae** (Campbell)

Talum, (b) **Magic Fountain** (Delius)

Tamar, **Tamar and Judah** (Lavry)

Tamara, **The Demon** (Morgulas)

Tamburlaine, (bar) **Tamburlaine** (Hamilton); **Tamburlaine** (Murdoch)

Tameem, **Satin Cloak** (Halpern)

Taminent, Chief, **William Penn** (Cascarino)

Tamino, **Small Jewel Box** (Mozart-Griffiths)

Tamiris, **Pharnaces** (Bates)

Täm-män', (s) **Täm-Män'-Näcŭp'** (Hanson)

Tammany, **Tammany** (Hewitt)

Tamsen Donner, **Donner Party** (McFarland); **Tamsen Donner** (McFarland)

Tamsin, **Return of the Native** (Coulthard)

Tancred, **Englishmen in India** (Bishop); **Holy Blood** (Copeland); (b-bar) **Padrevia** (Pasatieri)

Tancredi, **Native Land** (Bishop)

Tania, **Grinning at the Devil** (Wilson); **Tania** (Davis); (s) **Visit to the Country** (Wargo)

Tannhäuser, Dr., **Grand Duke** (Sullivan)

Tap, **Killing No Murder** (Hook)

Tarj, (bar) **Under the Double Moon** (Davis)

Tarnish, **Boarding School** (1733)

Tarquinius, (bar) **Rape of Lucretia** (Britten)

Tartuffe, (bar) **Tartuffe** (Benjamin); **Tartuffe** (Mechem)

Täv-a-moŭ-i-scie, (t) **Täm-Män'-Näcŭp'** (Hanson)

Taverner, (t) **Taverner** (Davies)

Tawdry, **Miss Lucy in Town** (Arne)

Veronica Quaife, (m) **The Fly** (Shore)

Veronus, (bar) **Last Lover** (Starer)

Vershinin, (bar) **Three Sisters** (Pasatieri)

Vertumnus, **Vertumnus and Pomona** (Arne)

Vi, (s) **Blue Monday** (Gershwin)

Vicki, (s) **The Dress** (Bucci)

Vicki, Queen, **Magic Fishbone** (Chapin)

Victor, **Before Night Falls** (Martín); **Burning Bright** (Lewin); (t) **Frankenstein** (Larsen)

Victor I, (actor/mime) **Wild Boy** (Epstein)

Victor II, (dr) **Wild Boy** (Epstein)

Victoria, **Castle of Andalusia** (Arnold)

Victoria, Queen, **Freshwater** (Vores)

Victorian, **Victorian** (Edwards)

Victorine, **Victorine** (Mellon)

Victorio, Don, (t) **Fortunato** (Gideon)

Victory, **Britannia** (Lampe)

Vidya, (s) **Thief of Love** (Silver)

Villars, **Match for a Widow** (Dibdin); **Night before the Wedding** (Bishop)

Villon, François, **François Villon** (Baron); **François Villon** (Wolf); **Villon** (Read)

Vincent, **Yelva** (Bishop)

Vincente de Valverde, Fray, (b) **Royal Hunt of the Sun** (Hamilton)

Vincenzo, **Empty Bottle** (Kalmanoff); **Good Friar** (Hennessey)

Vindicta, Princess, (m) **Fortunio** (Darley)

Vinessa, **Oxford Act** (1733)

Vinnie, **Marilyn** (Laderman)

Viola, **Strangers at Home** (Linley Sr.); (m) **Twelfth Night** (Amram)

Violante, **The Divorce** (Hook)

Violentina, **Magic Girdle** (Barthelemon)

Violet, (m) **Childhood Miracle** (Rorem); **Little Tycoon** (Spenser)

Violet, Colonel, **Monk of Toledo** (Knowlton)

Violet Beauregard, (col s) **Golden Ticket** (Ash)

Violet Gordon-Woodhouse, (s) **Violet** (Scruton)

Violetta, **Absolute Zero** (Pearson)

Virata, **Virata** (Wilson)

Virgil, (bar) **Golden Apple** (Trinkley); **Inferno** (Soluri); **Inferno of Dante** (Soluri): **Virgil's Dream** (Colgrass)

Virgil T., (bar) **Mother of Us All** (Thomson)

Virginia, **Paul and Virginia** (Reeve)

Virginia Clemm, **Ligeia** (Thomas); **Nights of Annabel Lee** (Rodgers)

Virginia Creeper, **Difficulties of Crossing a Field** (Lang)

Virginia Woolf, **Women in the Garden** (Fine)

Virgin Mary, (m) **Taverner** (Davies)

Virtue, (s) **Circe** (Hayes); **Judgment of Hercules** (Greene)

Virtuosa, **Temple of Dullness** (Arne)

Visitor, (t) **In the Penal Colony** (Glass)

Vivian, (m) **What Price Confidence** (Krenek)

Vivian Smith, (s) **Puritania** (Kelley)

Vladimir, **Inner Voices** (Howard); (t) **Three Sisters** (Pasatieri)

Voice in the Box, **Paradise of Children** (Magrill)

Voice of God, (bar) **Eternal Road** (Weill); (sp) **Noye's Fludde** (Britten)

Volante, **Honey Moon** (Hewitt/Kelly)

Volhek, **Eloise** (Jenkins)

Volpone, **Volpone** (Antheil); **Volpone** (Burt); **Volpone** (Coombs); **Volpone** (Gruenberg); (b-bar) **Volpone** (Musto)

Voltore, (bar) **Volpone** (Musto)

Voluptua, **Pizza con Funghi** (Barab)

Voodooiene, (a) **The Departure** (Davis)

Voodoo Queen, **Deep River** (Harling)

Vorchiekleff, General, **Something New** (Hoiby)

Voss, (bar) **Voss** (Meale)

Vreli, (girl s, s) **Village Romeo and Juliet** (Delius)

Vronsky, Alexei, (bar), **Anna Karenina** (Carlson); (t) **Anna Karenina** (Hamilton)

Vulcan, **Bitter Fruit** (Woolrich); **Poor Vulcan** (Dibdin

Vyry, (m) **Jubilee** (Kay)

Wabashaw, **Winona** (Bimboni)

Wade, (bar) **Monkey's Paw** (Alexander)

Wade, Adam, (t) **Dreamkeepers** (Carlson)

Wade, John, (t) **Monkey's Paw** (Alexander)

Wade, Jonathan, (bar) **Passion of Jonathan Wade** (Harvey)

Wade, Mrs., (s) **Monkey's Paw** (Alexander)

Wadsworth, Reverend, **Eastward in Eden** (Meyerowitz)

Wagner, **Faustus** (Bishop)

Wagner, Richard, (actor) **Wagner Dream** (Harvey)

Waguli, **Mountain Windsong** (Chlarson)

Walford, John, (t) **Charcoal Burner** (Wilson)

Walker, David, **Walker** (Anderson)

Walsegg, Count Johann von, **Music Robber** (Van Grove)

Walter, **Caernarvon Castle** (Attwood); **Maid of Honour** (Balfe); (t) **The Mistake** (Sheffer); **Spark Plugs** (Granger)

Walter, Sir, **Dead Alive** (Arnold); **The Woodman** (Shield)

Walter Harmond, (t) **The Audition** (Goodman)

Walther, **Blond Eckbert** (Weir )

Walton (bar), **Frankenstein** (Larsen)

Walworth, (b-bar) **Wat Tyler** (Bush)

Wampum, **The Tryst** (Freeman)

Wanda, **Game of Poker** (Burke); (s) **Venus in Furs** (Gal)

Wang, General, (b) **First Emperor** (Tan Dun)

Wapanacki, (b) **Magic Fountain** (Delius)

Warble, **Boarding School** (1733)

Wardlaw, Lucas, (t) **Passion of Jonathan Wade** (Harvey)

Wardour, Sir Arthur, **The Antiquary** (Bishop)

Wardwell, John, **White Bird** (Carter)

Warner, (b) **Catherine Grey** (Balfe); (b) **John Socman** (Lloyd)

# Index of Names

The index includes names of singers, conductors (excluding composers conducting or otherwise performing in their own work), producers, composers (of other English settings), directors, choreographers, and arrangers, listed in the A–Z section of this volume (for premieres, arrangements, and revivals), followed by the short title(s) of the work(s) in which they have appeared; the name of the composer (or date of premiere) is included where there is more than one setting of the title. First names are given where known. Names of composers of works on similar subjects and names of performers in noteworthy works on the same stories are also included.

Benedict, Lew, **Gambrinus**

Beni, Gimi, **Grande Brèteche** (Hollingsworth); **Martin's Lie**

Beni, James, **In a Garden**; **Riders to the Sea** (Vaughan Williams)

Benichou, Pascal, **Manhattan Book**

Benjamin, Peter, **Resurrection** (Davies)

Bennet, G., **Robert the Devil** (Barnett)

Bennet, Mrs., **Miss Lucy in Town**; **The Picture**

Bennet, W., **Climbing Boy**

Bennett, Edward, **The Martyr**

Bennett, Larry, **Acis and Galatea** (Handel)

Bennett, Mark, **Happy End**

Bennett, Michael, **Ion**

Bennett, Mr. W., **Before Breakfast** (Barnett)

Bennigsen, Lillian, **Elegy for Young Lovers**

Benoliel, Ross, **Passion, Poison** (Hagemann)

Bensley, Mr., **Cymon**; **Elfrida**; **Enchanted Wood**

Benson, Mr. (Robert), **Britain's Glory**; **Caernarvon Castle**; **Who Pays the Reckoning?**

Benson, Sally, **Seventeen**

Bentham, George, **The Sorcerer**

Bentley, Mr., **Felix**

Bentley, Jo-Anne, **Cassandra**

Bentley, Julia, **Antigone** (Eaton); **Song of Majnun**

Benton, Kimberly, **Twelfth Night** (Feigin)

Berberian, Ara, **And David Wept**; **Curlew River**; **Lily**; **My Heart's in the Highlands** (Beeson); **Sarah**

Beresford, Bruce, **Cold Sassy Tree**

Berg, Chris, **Harlot's Progress**

Berg, Maria, **Holy Blood**

Berg, Miriam, **Enchanted Kiss**

Bergan, Lindsey, **Judgment of St. Francis**

Bergen, Nella, **Bride Elect**; **The Charlatan**; **Free Lance**

Berger, David, **Stone Man**

Berger, Hedwig, **The Sacrifice**

Bergeson, Scott, **Casanova's Homecoming**; **Griffelkin**; **Vanishing Bridegroom**

Bergey, Carol, **The Tower**

Bergman, Yaacov, **Beau Nash**

Bergmann, Anna, **Bonfire of the Vanities**

Beriza, Marguerita, Louis XIV

Berkeley, Edward, **Belladonna**; **King of Hearts**; **Our Town**; **Powder Her Face**

Berkeley-Squire, Richard, **Thomas and Sally** (Arne)

Berkolds, Paul, **Wet**

Berl, Paul, **The Box**; **Cat and the Moon**; **Sunday Costs Five Pesos**; **To Let the Captive Go**

Berlioz, Hector, **Dido and Aeneas** (Beveridge)

Bernard, Annabelle, **Montezuma**

Bernard, Emma, **Critical Mass**

Bernard, Miss, **The Gondoliers**

Bernas, Richard, **Golem** (Casken); **Thérèse Raquin** (Picker)

Berneche, Alicia, **Ballymore**; **Galileo Galilei** (Glass)

Berner, Matthew, **Antient Concert**

Bernstein, Leonard, **Cradle Will Rock**; **The Dybbuk** (DiGiacomo); **Frau Margot**; **Peter Grimes**; **Second Hurricane**; **Threepenny Opera**; **Wind Remains**

Bernstein, Malcolm, **The Rope**

Bernstein, Richard, **American Tragedy**; **View from the Bridge** (Bolcom)

Berrardo, F., **The Disappointment** (1732)

Berriman, Mrs., **Orestes**

Berry, Kayce, **Edge of Glory**

Berry, Miss, **Long Odds**

Berry, Mr., **Bays's Opera**; **Blind Beggar of Bethnal Green**; **Boarding School**; **Britons, Strike Home**; **Trick for Trick**

Berry, Noreen, **The Decision**; **King Priam**; **Martin's Lie**; **The Parlour**

Berry, Stafford, Jr., **Luyala**

Berry, Walter, **School for Wives**

Bertelson, Harold, **Cask of Amontillado** (Perry)

Berthald, Barron, **Rob Roy** (De Koven); **Scarlet Letter** (Damrosch)

Bertini, Gary, **Europeras 1 & 2**

Bertram, Helen, **The Viceroy**

Bertrandt, Max, **And the Walls**

Bertsche, Samuel, **The Lion**

Besch, Anthony, **Abbot of Drimock**; **Inner Voices**; **Menna**; **Tale of Two Cities**

Best, Michael, **Mines of Sulphur**

Besuner, Pearl, **Emperor Jones**; **Jack and the Beanstalk**

Betterton, Thomas, **King Arthur**

Bettina, Judith, **W. of Babylon**

Bettis, Valerie, **The Soldier**

Bevan, Benjamin, **Call Me Ishmael**

Bevan, Lyall, **De Profundis**

Bevan, Lucy, **Hotel**

Bevan, Stanley, **Our Man in Havana**

Bevis, Andrew, **Jerry Springer**

Beymer, Richard, **West Side Story**

Bhise, Swati, **Mass for the Dead**

Bianchart, Roman, **The Sacrifice**

Bianchi, Francesco, **Acis and Galatea** (Handel)

Bibalo, Antonio, **Miss Julie** (Alwyn)

Bible, Frances, **The Crucible** (Ward); **The Dybbuk**; **Voice of Ariadne**

Bibo, Franz, **Wise and Foolish**

Bickley, Susan, **After Dido**; **Bitter Tears of Petra von Kant**; **Last Supper**; **The Station** (Blake); **Writing to Vermeer**

Biddle, Marvel, **Helen Retires**

Bidlack, Andrew, **Hotel Casablanca**

Bidleman, Tracy, **Kafka** (Walden); **Summer**

Bielawa, Lisa, **Shala Fears for the Poor**

Billings, James, **Command Performance; Madame Adare; Tale for a Deaf Ear**

Billington, F., **The Mikado**

Billington, Mrs. (Elizabeth), **Algonah; The Czar; Fair Peruvian; Fontainbleau; Magician No Conjurer; Marian; The Prophet; Richard Coeur de Lion** (Shield)

Bincks (Binks), Miss, **Mock Lawyer; Rape of Helen**

Binder, Peter, **The Tower; Transposed Heads**

Binotto, Paul, **Civilization**

Birch, Patricia, **The Losers**

Birnbaum, Nathan, **Scarlett Letter** (Damrosch)

Birney, Mr., Jr., **Fashionable Lady**

Birt, Mr., **Adventure of Don Quixote**

Bisch, Jordan, **Amelia** (Hagen)

Bischoff, Herr, **Poia**

Bishop, Adelaide, **Devil and Daniel Webster; Grande Brèteche; Griffelkin; Six Characters; The Stronger**

Bishop, Anna, **Loretta**

Bishop, Carol, **Lunch at the Cooked Goose**

Bishop, Elizabeth, **Handmaid's Tale**

Bishop, Henry Rowley, **Sadak and Kalasrade; The Tempest** (Westergaard); **Twelfth Night; Two Gentlemen of Verona**

Bishop, Margaret, **Funeral of Jan Palach; Photo-Op**

Bishop, Ronald, **Survival of St. Joan**

Bispham, David, **Atonement of Pan; The Forest** (Smyth); **Harold** (Cowen); **Much Ado about Nothing**

Bixler, Rebecca Rodd, **Sopranos!**

Björnson, Maria, **Phantom of the Opera**

Black, Frank, **Nightingale and the Rose** (Lessner)

Black, Patricia, **Blind Raftery**

Black, Randall, **Antigone** (Constantinides)

Black, Robert, **Blind Witness News; Funeral of Jan Palach**

Black, William, **Beauty and the Beast** (Di Giacomo)

Blackburn, Harold, **Mines of Sulphur; Story of Vasco**

Blackett, Joy, **Lily; Sāvitri**

Blackham, Joyce, **Mines of Sulphur;**

Blackstone, **Tsianina Redfeather; Legend of Wiwaste**

Blackwood, Easley, **Gulliver**

Blake, Mr., **King Pepin's Campaign**

Blakeslee, Carolyn, **Mother of Us All**

Blakey, Evelyn, **Letter from an Astrologer**

Blanchard, Jonathan, **Seduction of King Solomon**

Blanchard, Mr. J(ames), **The Cabinet; The Czar; Dice of Death; Drama at Home; Free Knights; Magician No Conjurer; The Sultan**

Blanchard, Mrs., **Love in a Blaze**

Bland, James, **Before Breakfast** (Barnett); **The Covenanters; Love's Dream**

Bland, Mr. (Charles), **Britain's Glory; The Mariners** (Attwood); **Oberon** (Weber); **Sadak and Kalsarade**

Bland, Mrs. (Maria Theresa), **Blue-Beard; Britain's Glory; Caernarvon Castle; Cambro-Britons; The Cherokee; Egyptian Festival; The Embarkation; Honey Moon** (Linley); **Lady and the Devil; The Pavilion; The Pirates; The Prize; Red Cross Knights; Siege of Belgrade; Soldier's Return; Who Pays the Reckoning?; Young Hussar; Zorinski**

Blankenheim, Toni, **Arden Must Die; Hamlet**

Blant, Josef, **Thorwald**

Blanton, Jim, **Aria da capo** (Smith)

Blastock, Mr., **Rival Milliners**

Blatchley, John, **The Ledge; Our Man in Havana**

Blau, Herbert, **Jacob's Room**

Bleckmann, Theo, **Carbon Copy Building; Politics of Quiet; True Last Words**

Bledsoe, Jules, **Deep River; Show Boat; Tom-Tom**

Blegen, Judith, **Help, Help**

Blevins, Timothy Robert, **Scourge of Hyacinths; Sir Gawain** (Peaslee)

Blewitt, Jonathan, **Paul Clifford**

Blier, Steven, **Bastianello; Lucrezia**

Blight, David, **Letters, Riddles**

Blinn, Holbrook, **Duchess of Dantzic; Ib and Little Christina**

Bliss, Arthur, **Beggar's Opera; Sāvitri**

Bliss, Helena, **Troubled Island**

Bloch, Ernest, **Macbeth** (McIntyre)

Bloch, Henry, **The Commission**

Block, John, **The Marriage**

Block, Vivienne, **Second Hurricane**

Blum, Mark, **Music Teacher**

Blum, Suzanne, **Philip Marshall**

Blunt, Arthur, **Cox and Box**

Blyth, Peta, **The Proposal** (Fiddes)

Blyth, Stephanie, **Sailor-Boy and the Falcon**

Bo, Thomas Carlo, **The Duel** (Barab); **Robert and Hal**

Boardman, Arthur, **Hester Prynne**

Boardman, Susan, **Cleo; Golden Apple**

Boatner, Adelaide, **Ouanga**

Boatwright, McHenry, **Ouanga**

Bobick, James, **Dog Days; Elmer Gantry; Lysistrata** (Adamo); **Soldier Songs**

Bobrov, Roman, **Maskarad**

Bock, Jerry, **Canterville Ghost**

Bodanzky, Artur, **Canterbury Pilgrims** (De Koven)

Boddeke, Saskia, **Writing to Vermeer**

Boden, Miss, **Before Breakfast** (Barnett); **Zuma**

Boduin, Cavin, **Manhattan Book**

Boehler, Matt, **Bastianello; Lucrezia; Maiden Tower**

Boese, Ursula, **Help, Help**

Boesing, Jennifer Palmer, **Wuornos**

Boesmans, Philippe, **Winter's Tale**

Bogarde, Carol, **Trial of Mary Lincoln**

Boyd, Thomas, **Ordeal of Osbert**

Boykin, Phillip, **Porgy and Bess**

Boylan, Orla, **Love of the Nightingale**

Brabbins, Martyn, **From Morning to Midnight; Wagner Dream**

Bracco, Donato, **Turn of the Screw**

Bracegirdle, Michael, **The Crucible** (Ward)

Bracegirdle, Mr., **King Arthur**

Bracegirdle, Mrs. (Anne), **Temple of Love**

Bracey, Henry, **Princess Ida**

Bracht, Roland, **English Cat**

Bracken, Eddie, **archy and mehitabel**

Brackett, Kevin, **The Dreamers**

Bradel, Jean, **Rappaccini's Daughter** (Garwood)

Braden, John, **Journey of Snow White**

Bradford, Carmen, **Queenie Pie**

Bradley, Kristen, **Hood of the Woods**

Bradshaw, Richard, **Ashoka's Dream; Every Man Jack; Golden Ass; Guacamayo's Old Song; Nosferatu; The Tempest** (Eaton)

Brady, Judy, **Ghosts**

Braham, Charles, **Heart of Midlothian** (Carafa-Loder)

Braham, Hamilton, **Raymond and Agnes**

Braham, Miss (Leonora), **Iolanthe; The Mikado; Night's Surprise; No. 204; Patience; Princess Ida; Princess Toto; Ruddigore; Sultan of Mocha**

Braham, Mr. (John), **The Cabinet; Chains of the Heart; Family Quarrels; Love in Wrinkles; Mahmoud; Narensky; Oberon** (Weber); **The Paragraph; Village Coquettes; Zuma**

Brainerd, Joan, **Ordeal of Osbert**

Braitman, Sylvie, **The Dreamers**

Brajovic, Ana Zorana, **Violet Fire**

Bramwell, Raymond, **Jeanie Deans**

Brand, John E., **Dorothy**

Brand, Oscar, **Lima Beans**

Brandham, Miss Rosina, **Beauty Stone; The Chieftain; Emerald Isle; The Gondoliers; Grand Duke; Haddon Hall; Jane Annie; The Mikado; Pirates of Penzance; Princess Ida; Rose of Persia; Ruddigore; Utopia Limited; Yeomen of the Guard**

Brandon, Michael, **Jerry Springer**

Brandstetter, John, **Beauty and the Beast** (Oliver); **Claudia Legare; Feathertop** (Barnes); **Jōruri; Vanishing Bridegroom**

Brandt, Barbara, **Claudia Legare; Death in the Family; Postcard from Morocco; Punch and Judy; Voyage of Edgar Allan Poe; The Wanderer**

Brandt, Roxanne, **Turn of the Screw**

Brannigan, Owen, **Midsummer Night's Dream** (Britten); **Moon and Sixpence; Noye's Fludde; Our Man in Havana; Peter Grimes**

Braslau, Sophie, **Shanewis**

Brassard, Andre, **Orpheus II**

Braswell, John, **Carmilla**

Bratcher, James, **Closed Case; Mirage; Rococo Confessional; Solid House; Sunny Morning**

Bratfield, Alan, **Elanda and Eclipse**

Brathwaite, Maureen, **Call Me Ishmael**

Braun, Mel, **Master's Stroke**

Braun, Victor, **Hamlet; We Come to the River; Wuthering Heights** (Herrmann)

Braunfels, Victor, **The Birds** (Ahlstrom)

Braunstein, Ronald, **Beggar's Opera**

Braxton, Anthony, **Shala Fears for the Poor**

Bray, John, **Hamlet Travestie; Transformation**

Breardsworth, Craig, **Beleaguered City**

Breckenridge, Marnie, **Dog Days**

Brecknock, John, **Story of Vasco**

Bredach, Sheila, **Pet Shop**

Bredemann, Dan, **The Golem** (Weiner)

Bredin, Henrietta, **Seven Deadly Sins**

Breen, Karen, **Ghost Wife**

Breese, Timothy, **Making of the Representative**

Brehm, Ellen, **Dark Sonnet**

Breisach, Paul, **Rape of Lucretia**

Brema, Marie, **Much Ado about Nothing**

Bremert, Ingeborg, **Elegy for Young Lovers**

Bremmer, Rory, **Silverlake**

Brenner, Anderson, **Bowl, Cat, and Broomstick**

Brenner, Janis, **Politics of Quiet**

Brent, Bix, **archy and mehitabel**

Brent, Charlotte, **Artaxerxes; Guardian Out-witted; Jovial Crew** (Bates); **Love in a Village; Maid of the Mill** (Arnold); **Summer's Tale**

Brentano, Felix, **The Barrier; Hello Out There; Malady of Love; Sweeney Agonistes**

Bressler, Charles, **The Bassarids; Yellow Wallpaper**

Bret, Mr., **The Metamorphoses** (Dibdin)

Brett, Jonathan, **I Am in Search**

Brett, Miss, **Il Bondocani; Spanish Castle**

Brett, Mr., **Flitch of Bacon; The Shamrock**

Brett-Crowther, Monica, **Odysseus Unwound**

Brewer, Daniel, **Greek Passion**

Brewster-Jones, Hooper, **Deirdre of the Sorrows** (Rankl)

Brian, Havergal, **Faustus Part One**

Brice, Carol, **Gentlemen, Be Seated!; Ouanga; Porgy and Bess**

Bridge, Frank, **Christmas Rose**

Bridgwater, Mr., **Beggar's Wedding; Devil of a Duke; Timon in Love**

Brieger, Nicholas, **What Next?**

Briggle, Gary, **Barnum's Bird; Death in the Family; Mrs. Dalloway**

Briggs, Conor, **Resurrection** (Davies)

Brightman, Sarah, **Phantom of the Opera**

Brill, Charles, **Trevallion**

Brindal, Mr., **Nothing Superfluous** (Lee)

Brinton, Mr., **Leonora**

Bristol, Brenda Box, **Birth/Day**

Clarke, Jocelyn, **Antigone** (Eaton)

Clarkson, Stanley, **Crier by Night**; **Nelson**

Clary, Miss, **Thespis**

Clatworthy, Ara, **Curlew River**

Clatworthy, David, **Prodigal Son** (Britten)

Claycomb, Laura, **Grendel**

Clayton, Beth, **Doctor Atomic**

Clayton, Kristin, **At the Statue of Venus**; **Last Acts**

Cleamons, Duke, **Letter from an Astrologer**

Clegg, Edith, **Everyman** (Lehmann)

Clegg, Peter, **Blue Margaritas**

Clemmons, François, **Hangman, Hangman!**

Clendining, Mrs., **The Armorer**; **Hartford Bridge**; **Midnight Wanderers**; **Travellers in Switzerland**

Cleveland, Mark-Andrew, **Freshwater** (Vores)

Cleveland, Mr., **The Archers**

Clifton, Frederick, **Pirates of Penzance**; **The Sorcerer**

Clifton, John, **The Conjurer**

Cline, Charles, **Massimilliano**

Clive, Mr. Franklin, **Sylvia**

Clive, Mrs. (Catherine), **Alfred**; **Blind Beggar of Bethnal Green**; **Britons, Strike Home**; **The Chaplet**; **Coffee-House**; **Comus**; **Cupid and Death**; **Devil to Pay**; **Don Saverio**; **Intriguing Chambermaid**; **Judgment of Paris** (Arne); **King Pepin's Campaign**; **The Lottery**; **Merry Cobler**; **Miss Lucy in Town**; **The Rehearsal** (Boyce); **Rosamond** (Arne); **Shepherd's Lottery**; **Timon in Love**; *see also* Raftor, Miss

Clough, Mr., **Midsummer Night's Dream** (1763)

Cluthier, André, **The Architect**

Coates, Albert, **The Serf**

Coates, Edith, **Candide**; **The Olympians**; **The Parlour**; **Peter Grimes**

Coates, John, **Much Ado about Nothing**; **The Wreckers**

Coats, Jacqueline, **Beleaguered City**; **Death of Venus**

Coburn, Sarah, **Anna Karenina** (Carlson)

Coccia, Carlo, **Mary Stuart**

Cockrun, James, **Billy Budd**

Cocteau, Jean, **Beauty and the Beast** (Easton)

Coerne, Louis, **Zenobia**

Coffey, Denise, **Boy Who Grew Too Fast**

Coffin, Hayden, **Dorothy**; **The Geisha**; **The Mountebanks**; **Tom Jones** (German)

Cogan, Suzanne, **The Box**

Coghill, Harry, **Royal Hunt**; **Story of Vasco**

Coghill, Joy, **Midsummer Night's Dream** (Britten)

Cohan, Richard, **Scarlet Letter** (Herman)

Cohen, Brad, **Flight** (Dove)

Cohen, Fred, **Memoirs of Uliana Rooney**

Cohen, Frederic, **Peter Grimes**; **Rehearsal Call**; **Sweet Bye and Bye**; **Wife of Martin Guerre**

Cohn, Charlotte, **Anaïs**; **Madimi**

Coid, Marshall, **Alice in Wonderland** (Westergaard); **OrfReo**

Coker, Laura A., **Little Women** (Adamo)

Coini, Jacques, **Naughty Marietta**

Cokorinos, Philip, **Marilyn**

Colaneri, Joseph, **Esther** (Weisgall)

Colantti, Stephen, **Idiots First**

Colbert, Helen, **Porgy and Bess**

Cole, Allen, **The Gang**

Cole, Casey, **The Mummy**

Cole, Dorothy, **Blood Moon**

Cole, Joanna, **Lindy**

Cole, John, **The Birds** (Maconchy); **Three Strangers** (Maconchy)

Cole, Kelley, **Poia**

Cole, Nora, **And God Created Great Whales**; **Highway Ulysses**

Cole, Vinson, **Bohemian Girl**

Cole, William, **Singing Child**

Coleman, Basil, **Gloriana**; **Rajah's Diamond**; **Turn of the Screw**

Coleman, Leo, **The Medium**

Coleman, Mrs. Edward, **Siege of Rhodes**

Coleman, Warren, **Porgy and Bess**

Coleman-Wright, Peter, **End of the Affair**; **Inquest of Love**; **Plumber's Gift**

Coleridge-Taylor, Samuel, **Endymion** (Bennett)

College, Charles, **Carina**

Collett, Miss, **Selima and Azor**

Collet, Mr., **Fashionable Lady**

Colletta, Kathleen, **Sopranos!**

Collier, Frederic(k), **Hugh the Drover**; **Perfect Fool**

Collier, Marie, **King Priam**; **Mourning Becomes Electra**

Collingwood, Lawrance, **Travelling Companion**

Collins, Angelene, **Hopitu**

Collins, Anne, **Inés de Castro** (MacMillan)

Collins, Elizabeth, **Apollonia's Circus**

Collins, Mr., **Double Disappointment**; **Honey Moon** (Hewitt/Kelly); **The Picture**

Collis, David, **Royal Hunt**

Collis, Mrs., **Sheep-Shearing** (Arnold)

Colman, Philip, **Shadowtracks**; **Song of Rhiannon**

Colnot, Cliff, **Antigone** (Eaton); **Twice through the Heart**

Comboy, Ian, **Martyrdom of St. Magnus**

Comeaux, Elisabeth, **Frankenstein** (Larsen); **From the Towers of the Moon**; **Oedipus Tex**; **Tale of Genji**; **Tender Land**

Comerford, Rebecca, **Sopranos!**

Comlish, Michael, **Darkling**

Commendador, Elena, **How to Make Love**

Comparone, Elaine, **OrfReo**

Compson, Christy, **Three Princes**

Condell, H. A., **The Barrier**

Condrashoff, Marion, **Abracadabra**

Ferrante, John, **Abduction of Figaro**

Ferraro, Dolores, **William Penn**

Ferrero, Lorenzo, **Marilyn**

Ferriero, Maria, **Transposed Heads**

Ferrier, Kathleen, **Rape of Lucretia**

Feuillade, Louis, **Hotel for Criminals**

Feveisky, Michael, **Guido Ferranti**

Fiacco, Michael, **Confidence Man**

Fiasconaro, Gregorio, **Silas Marner**

Fiddes, Ross, **Abelard and Heloise** (Ward)

Field, Helen, **The Cenci** (Brian); **Greek Passion**; **Handmaid's Tale**; **Inés de Castro** (MacMillan); **Inquest of Love**; **New Year**

Field, Jonathan, **Moon Singer**

Field, Jonathon, **Lost Highway**

Field, Leah, **Florence**

Field, Lucille, **Bad Boys in School**

Field, Rebecca, **Greek Passion**

Field-Hyde, Margaret, **Poisoned Kiss**; **Riders to the Sea** (Vaughan Williams)

Fielding, David, **Ease**; **Jason Field**

Fielding, Mr., **Beggar's Wedding**; **Highland Fair**; **Love and Revenge** (1729)

Fields, Branch, III, **Pocahontas**

Fields, Debra, **Wrinkle in Time**

Fieldsend, David, **Clandestine Marriage**

Filion, Robert, **Angel Square**

Finch, Robert, **Closed Case**; **Coyote's Music**; **Rococo Confessional**

Finckel, Chris, **Things That Gain**

Fink, Richard Paul, **Doctor Atomic, Great Gatsby**

Finke, Martin, **English Cat**

Finley, Gerald, **Doctor Atomic**; **Fantastic Mr. Fox**; **Silver Tassie**

Finney, John, **Cask of Amontillado**; **Garden Party**

Finucane, John, **Poet and His Double**

Fiore, John, **Madame Mao** (Sheng)

Firestone, Adria, **The Conquistador**; **Tight-Rope**

Firmager, Ronald, **The Cenci** (Coke)

Firmin, Richard, **The Box**

Firth, Colin, **Pride and Prejudice**

Fische, Scott, **The Chieftain**; **Utopia Limited**

Fischer, Abigail, **Alice in Wonderland** (Westergaard); **Song from the Uproar**

Fischer, Aileen, **Lucky-Peter's Journey**

Fischer, Beth, **Floating**

Fischer, Gisela, **Triumph of Joan**

Fischer, Hanne, **Handmaid's Tale**

Fischer, Karl, **Lucedia**

Fischer, Robert, **Holy Devil**; **School for Wives**

Fischer-Dieskau, Dietrich, **Elegy for Young Lovers**

Fiser, Lee, **The Veil**

Fisher, Bernice, **The Sacrifice**

Fisher, Grace, **The Sacrifice**

Fisher, Harry, **Mulligan Guard Ball**; **Reilly and the 400**

Fisher, Sylvia, **Owen Wingrave**

Fiske, Katherine, **Poia**

Fiske, Roger, **Ephesian Matron**; **Peleus and Thetis**

Fissell, April, **Power of Xingu**

Fitch, Bernard, **The Golem** (Weiner)

Fitch, Doug, **What Next?**

Fitch, Isabel, **Jeanie Deans**

Fitzgerald, Will, **Maid Marian** (De Koven)

Fitziu, Anna, **Azora**

Fitzjames, Miss, **The Crusaders**

Fitzpatrick, Thomas, **Chanticleer** (Barab)

Fitzwater, Leslie, **Ballymore**

Fitzwilliam, Mrs., **Flying Dutchman**

Flagello, Ezio, **Antony and Cleopatra** (Barber); **Command Performance**; **Final Ingredient**; **I Am the Way**

Flanigan, Lauren, **Antony and Cleopatra** (Barber); **Bohemian Girl**; **Esther** (Weisgall); **Family Room**; **Festival of Regrets**; **Food of Love**; **Frau Margot**; **Lizzie Borden**; **Marina**; **Peter Ibbetson**; **Vanishing Bridegroom**; **Séance on a Wet Afternoon**; **A Wedding**; **Where's Dick**

Fleming, Anthony le, **Ephesian Matron**; **Peleus and Thetis**

Fleming, Renée, **Dangerous Liaisons**; **Ghosts of Versailles**; **Streetcar Named Desire**; **Susannah**

Fleming, Ruth, **Malady of Love**

Flemming, Claude, **The Mountaineers** (Somerville)

Fletcher, Allen, **The Crucible** (Ward); **Passion of Jonathan Wade**

Fletcher, Robert, **Servant of Two Masters** (Giannini)

Flight, Paul, **S.**

Flint, Mark, **Postman Always Rings Twice**

"Flintstone, Trauma" (Joe Wicht), **Queer**

Flusser, Beth, **Buxom Joan**

Floyd, Julia, **The Proposal** (Granger)

Flynn, Peter, **Romulus**

Fogarty, Melissa, **Fisher King**

Foggin, Myers, **The Lodger**

Foglia, Leonard, **Best Friends**; **End of the Affair**; **Moby Dick** (Heggie)

Foldi, Andrew, **Blood Moon**; **Midsummer Night's Dream** (Britten)

Foley, Peter, **Highway Ulysses**

Follett, Mrs., **Reform'd in Time**

Fonesca, F., **Two Gentlemen of Verona**

Fontenelle, Miss (Louisa), **Basket-Maker**; **New Spain**

Foote, Barrington, **Canterbury Pilgrims** (Stanford)

Forakis, Gia, **Song from the Uproar**

Forbes, Amy D., **Song of Martina**

Ford, Bruce Edwin, **Abduction of Figaro**

Friedemann, Rainer, **Cyrano** (Beeson)

Friedlander, Claudia, **Chatter and Static**

Friedman, Maria, **Voluptuous Tango**

Friedman, Stephanie, **Death of Klinghoffer**

Friedsell, Louis, **David's Violin**

Friend, Lionel, **Mary of Egypt**; **Plumber's Gift**; **Scoring a Century**; **The Tigers**

Friend, Mr., **Bianca** (Balfe)

Friendship, Elizabeth, **The Parlour**

Fries, Kathlyn, **Music Shop**

Frisch, Richard, **Angel Levine**; **Final Ingredient**; **W. of Babylon**

Frothingham, George B., **Robin Hood** (De Koven)

Frühbeck de Burgos, Rafael, **Goya**

Fry, Betsey, **Mountain Sylph**

Fry, William, **Leonora**

Fryatt, John, **Mines of Sulphur**; **Penny for a Song**; **Rising of the Moon**; **Story of Vasco**

Frye, David, **Funeral of Jan Palach**

Frye, Rosalie Barker, **David Rizzio**

Fuchs, Elissa Minet, **White Agony**

Fuchs, Olivia, **Pied Piper** (Pearson)

Fuchs, Peter Paul, **The Departure** (Davis); **Franklin's Tale**; **Plough and the Stars**

Fuerstner, Fiona, **Burning House**

Fulljames, John, **Tobias and the Angel** (Dove)

Fulmer, David, **Cracked Orlando**

Fulu, Qui, **Alley**

Funk, Andrew, **Galileo Galilei** (Glass)

Funk, Ian, **City Workers**

Furlong, Peter, **Thérèse Raquin** (Picker)

Furman, Richard, **Eve's Odds**; **Stranger's Tale**

Furnival, Mr., **Welsh Opera**

Furnival, Mrs., **Welsh Opera**

Furst, Janos, **David and Bathsheba**

Fusaro, Peter, **From the Towers of the Moon**

Futral, Elizabeth, **Blond Eckbert**; **Brief Encounter**; **First Emperor**; **Six Characters**; **Streetcar Named Desire**

Fyson, Leslie, **Incognita**

Gaal, Mark, **The Proposal** (Fiddes)

Gabrieli, Lena, **Hello Out There**

Gadski, Johanna, **Scarlet Letter** (Damrosch)

Gagnon, David, **John Brown**

Gailey, Pamela, **Countdown**

Gain, Sally June, **Palace in the Sky**

Gaines, Daphne, **Night Vision**

Gainey, Andrew, **Tender Land**

Gal, Yoav, **Eternal Road**

Galanter, Michael Lynn, **Simón Bolívar**

Galati, Frank, **View from the Bridge** (Bolcom)

Galbraith, Robert, **Quiet Place**

Gale, Carol, **The Woodlanders**

Gale, David, **The Empress**

Gale, Elizabeth, **Christmas Carol** (Kay); **The Magician**

Gale, Rhona, **Molly Brant**

Galer, Elliot, **Felix**

Galia, Maria, **Temple of Love**

Galjour, Warren, **Malady of Love**; **The Soldier**

Gall, Ferenz, **The Bear** (Walton)

Gall, Jeffrey, **Taverner**

Gallacher, Andrew, **Where the Wild Things Are**

Gallia, Maria, **Rosamond**

Galliard, John, **Apollo and Daphne** (Hook)

Gallott, Mr., **The Earthquake**

Gallup, Michael, **Wuthering Heights** (Herrmann)

Galterio, Louis, **Beauty and the Beast** (Murray); **Insect Comedy**

Galton, Blanche, **Felix**

Galton, Susan, **Felix**

Galuppi, Baldassare, **Artaxerxes**

Galvin, Eugene, **Mary Surratt**

Galyon, Jeremy, **Appomattox**

Gamberoni, Kathryn, **English Cat**; **Fennimore and Gerda**; **Marilyn**

Gamley, Douglas, **Beggar's Opera**

Gammon, Newton, **Judgment Day**

Gamper, David, **Lunar Opera**

Gantvoort, Carl, **The Sacrifice**

Garber, Herbert, **Open the Gates**

Garber, Victor, **Sweeney Todd**

Garcia, José, **The Outcast**

Garcia, Robert, **Silas Marner**

Garcia-Nuthmann, Andre, **Circle of Love**

Garden, Mary, **Native Land**

Gardner, Edward, **Riders to the Sea**

Gardner, Jake, **Chinchilla**; **Mary, Queen of Scots**; **Occurrence at Owl Creek** (Musgrave); **Under the Double Moon**

Gardner, Jill, **Greater Good**

Gardner, Mr., **Choleric Fathers**; **Turnpike Gate**

Gardner, Robert, **Before Night Falls**

Garfalo, Robert, **Agamemnon**

Garman, Brian, **Elegy for a Prince**

Garrad, Don, **Curlew River**; **Regina**; **Willie Stark**

Garrett, Eric, **Tartuffe** (Benjamin)

Garrett, Lesley, **The Journey**; **Thomas and Sally** (Arne)

Garrett, Matthew, **Secret Agent**; **What Next?**

Garrett, Nicholas, **Kantan and the Damask Drum**

Garrial, Petra, **Barber of New York**

Garrick, Mr. (David), **Britannia**

Garrick, Mrs., **The Alcaid**

Garrison, Joe, **Holy Blood**

Giradina, Gary, **Shepherds' Christmas**

Girschner, Karl Friedrich Johann, **Undine**

Giubilei, Mr., **Diadesté**; **Farinelli**

Giuseppe, Enrico di, **Rehearsal Call**

Giustinelli, Mr., **Almena**; **Pharnaces** (Bates)

Givens, Hughes, **From the Towers of the Moon**

Gizzi, Elena, **Kill Bear Comes Home**; **Little Thieves**

Gladen, Kendall, **Appomattox**

Glaser, Carola, **Found Objects**

Glaser, Lulu, **Cyrano de Bergerac** (Herbert); **Dolly Varden**

Glass, Philip, **Computer Marriage**; **Beauty and the Beast** (Easton); **Orpheus** (Burgon)

Glasser, Alan, **The Mermaid** (Fullam); **Sicilian Limes**

Glassman, Allan, **Dreyfus**; **Frau Margot**; **Karla**; **Life Is a Dream**; **Sacco and Vanzetti** (Coppola)

Glassman, Robert, **Nightingale and the Rose** (Hagemann)

Glauser, Elisabeth, **English Cat**

Glenn, Thomas, **Doctor Atomic**

Glenville, Mr., **Happy Disguise**

Glinka, Mikhael, **Hartford Bridge**

Glover, Andre Solomon, **Summer King**

Glover, Jane, **Where the Wild Things Are**

Glover, Miss M., **Black Vulture**

Glover, Mrs., **The Alcaid**; **Royal Oak**; **The Sultan**

Glover, Stephen, **Beauty and the Beast** (Giannini)

Gluck, Christoph Willibald, **Alcestis**; **Artaxerxes**; **Hartford Bridge**

Glynn, Carlin, **Chéri**

Glynne, Howell, **The Olympians**

Goberman, Max, **Devil and Daniel Webster**

Gobrud, Irene, **Anna Margarita's Will**

Goddard, James, **Azora, Daughter of the Forest**

Goddin, Heather, **Lord Bateman**

Godefroid, Félix, **Diadesté**

Godfrey, Louis, **Sumida River**

Godfrey, Victor, **Burning Fiery Furnace**; **King Priam**

Godwin, James, **Every Day Newt Burman**

Goedicke (Gedike), Alexander, **Macbeth** (McIntyre)

Goehr, Alexander, **Ariadne** (1654)

Goerz, Thomas, **Erewhon**

Goetz, Hermann, **Taming of the Shrew** (Giannini)

Goff, Lewin, **Carry Nation**

Gohl, Matthias, **Romulus Hunt**

Golan, Jeanne, **Glory Denied**

Gold, Andrew, **The Borderline**

Goldbourne, Jeneice, **Summer King**

Golden, Emily, **Blond Eckbert**; **McTeague**

Golden, Grace, **Fencing Master**

Goldfaden, Abraham, **David's Violin**; **Shloyme Gorgl**

Goldie, Elliot, **Call Me Ishmael**

Goldmark, Karl, **Cricket on the Hearth**; **Winter's Tale**

Golovsky, Boris, **Albert Herring**; **Eastward in Eden**; **Griffelkin**; **Life Goes to a Party**; **The Rope**; **Tale for a Deaf Ear**

Goldray, Martin, **Hydrogen Jukebox**

Goldschmidt, Berthold, **The Cenci** (Coke); **Threepenny Opera**

Goldschmidt, Nicholas, **Headless Horseman**

Goldstein, Amy, **Insect Comedy**

Goldstein, Gila, **The Dwarf**

Goldstein, Jonathan, **Ghosts**

Goldstein, Stanley, **The Dragon**

Goldstein, Steven, **Bundle Man**; **Eric Hermannson's Soul**; **Orpheus in Love**

Golembiski, Deborah, **Visit to the Country**

Gomez, Jill, **Knot Garden**; **Miss Julie** (Alwyn); **Powder Her Face**; **Voice of Ariadne**

Gomez, Ricardo, **Mata Hari**

Gondek, Juliana, **Harvey Milk**; **Hopper's Wife**

Gonzalez, Ching, **Atlas**; **Politics of Quiet**

Gonzalez, Jose J., **In the Penal Colony** (Glass)

Gonzalez, Susan, **Game of Poker**

Gonzalez, Valerie, **Guacamayo's Old Song**

Good, Christopher, **Angel Magick**

Good, Michael, **Doctor Faustus** (Ahlstrom)

Goodall, Mrs., **Battle of Hexham**; **New Spain**

Goodall, Reginald, **Peter Grimes**

Goodbar, Carolyn, **Mayerling**

Goodchild, Chloe, **Mary of Egypt**

Goodell, John, **Deirdre of the Sorrows** (Hughes)

Goodey, Tom, **Ever Young**; **Markheim** (Napier)

Goodman, George, **Tin Pan Alley**

Goodrich, Wallace, **Pipe of Desire**; **The Sacrifice**

Goossens, (Sir) Eugene, **Beggar's Opera**; **The Cenci** (Coke); **The Critic**; **Perfect Fool**

Gordon, David, **Alice in Wonderland** (Westergaard)

Gordon, Edith, **Babar, the Elephant**; **Isaac Levi**

Gordon, E. Taylor, **Vendetta**

Gordon, Harriet, **Berta**

Gordon, Haskell, **Land of Milk and Honey**

Gordon, Jeanne, **Cleopatra's Night**

Gordon, Richard, **Mrs. President**

Gore, Leigh Gibbs, **Desire under the Elms**; **Lord Byron** (Thomson)

Gori, Aurelius, **Queen and the Rebels**

Goring, Marius, **Metamorphoses** (Blackford)

Gormley, Clare, **Eighth Wonder**; **The Outcast**; **Wide Sargasso Sea**

Gort, Cristian, **Alternate Visions**

Gosling, Stephen, **Terra Incognita**

Gosman [Brueggergosman], Measha, **Beatrice Chancy**

Goss, Robert, **Barbara Allen**; **The Barrier**; **Triumph of Joan**

Gottlieb, Peter, **Rising of the Moon**

Griffiths, Hugh, **Beggar's Opera**

Griffiths, Paul, **Judgement of Paris** (Woolrich)

Grigg, Jessica, **Summer**

Grimaldi, Mr., **Bird Catcher**

Grimes, Tammy, **Cradle Will Rock**

Grimsley, Greer, **Ashoka's Dream; Romulus Hunt**

Grimson, Brian, **Hunting of the Snark** (Wilson)

Grindley, Lawrence, **Jane Annie; Utopia Limited**

Grist, Augustus, **Tom-Tom**

Griswold, Putnam, **Cyrano** (Damrosch); **Mona; Much Ado about Nothing; Poia**

Groban, Benjamin, **Music Robber**

Grodd, Uwe, **Galileo**

Grodecki, Debra, **Danton and Robespierre**

Grodikaite, Liora, **Bird of Night**

Groenendaal, Cris, **Adventures of Friar Tuck; Sweeney Todd**

Gromov, Igor, **A Calamity; Gentleman Friend**

Gronlund, Carolyn, **Roman Fever** (Hagemann)

Grooms, Luke, **Passion, Poison** (Hagemann)

Grooters, Robert, **Mother of Us All**

Gross, Arye, **Silver River**

Gross, Robert, **Bald Prima Donna; Padrevia**

Gross, Stephen, **Strange Fruit**

Grossman, Henry, **Marriage Proposal**

Grossman, Herbert, **Golden Child; The Labyrinth; Triumph of Joan**

Grossmith, George, **Haste to the Wedding; His Majesty; Iolanthe; The Mikado; Patience; Pirates of Penzance; Princess Ida; Ruddigore; The Sorcerer; Yeomen of the Guard**

Grove, Alexander, **Out of the Ordinary**

Grove, Jill, **Tibetan Book of the Dead**

Grove, Mr., **Gay Deceivers; Killing No Crime; Love's Dream**

Groves, Glenys, **Lilly Maid**

Groves, Paul, **First Emperor**

Grundheber, Franz, **Help, Help**

Grunebaum, Hermann, **Sāvitri**

Guahardo, Christian, **Thirteen Clocks**

Guan, Jamie, **Silver River**

Guardia, Aliana de la, **Rumpelstiltskin** (Epstein); **Say It Ain't So, Joe**

Guarino, Robert, **Letter to E. 11th St.**

Guarino, Robin, **Again; Avow; Camera Obscura**

Guay, Heide, **Dracula** (Ziemba)

Gueden, Hilde, **Rake's Progress** (Stravinsky)

Guéret, Éthel, **Alternate Visions**

Guerin, Mrs., **Don John of Austria**

Guggenheim, Stephen, **Simón Bolívar**

Guhr, Glenn, **Twilight Voices**

Guise, T. S., **El Capitan**

Gulick, James T., **Gambrinus**

Gunderson, Margaret S., **Giants in the Earth**

Gunn, Nathan, **Amelia** (Hagen); **American Tragedy; Brief Encounter; Man on the Moon**

Gunton, Bob, **Evita; Happy End**

Gunzman, Suzanna, **Blind Witness News**

Gurney, John, **Devil and Daniel Webster; Immortal Hour; Man without a Country**

Gurney, Robert, **John Brown; The Rivals**

Gustafson, Laverne, **Fit for a King**

Gustafson, Nancy, **Love of Don Perlimplin; Nicholas and Alexandra; 1984**

Gustafson, William, **King's Henchmen**

Guth, Otto, **Sunday Costs Five Pesos**

Guthrie, Thomas, **I Am in Search**

Guthrie, Tyrone, **Beggar's Opera; Candide**

Gutknecht, Carol, **Casanova's Homecoming; Madame Adare**

Gutman, Irving, **Wuthering Heights** (Floyd)

Gutstein, Ernst, **The Alcestiad**

Guttry, Paul, **Astronaut's Tale**

Guyse, Sheila, **Lost in the Stars**

Guzmán, Suzanna, **Fantastic Mr. Fox; Four Saints in Three Acts**

Gwinn, Deborah, **Little Girl Dreams**

Gwynne, Julia, **Patience; Pirates of Penzance**

Gwynne, Robert, **Entente Cordiale**

Gyrowetz, Adalbert, **Agnes Sorel; Aladdin** (Bishop)

Haas, Amelia, **The Lion**

Haas, Betsabé, **Bird of Night**

Habunek, Vlado, **Nine Rivers from Jordan**

Hacker, Alan, **Io Passion; Vanishing Bridegroom**

Hackett, Charles, **Witch of Salem**

Hadani, Gail, **The Outcast**

Haddock, Marcus, **Tight-Rope**

Hadley, Jerry, **The Conquistador; Great Gatsby; Rake's Progress** (Stravinsky); **Susannah; A Wedding**

Hagegård, Håkan, **Ghosts of Versailles**

Hageman, Carol, **Lady Kate**

Hagemann, Philip, **Roman Fever**

Hagen, Daron, **Daughter of the South**

Hagen, Donna, **Vera of Las Vegas**

Hagen, Matthew, **Robert and Hal**

Hager, Gita, **Medea** (Henderson)

Haggart, Margaret, **Fly**

Hagopian, Sara, **Boy Who Grew Too Fast**

Haigh, Henry. **Bride of Song**

Haijing Fu, **First Emperor; Tea**

Haines, J. T., **Raymond and Agnes**

Hains, Mr., **Berta**

Hairston, Jeff, **Romulus Hunt**

Hal, Johnny van, **Kafka's Trial**

Livingstone, Laureen, **Inner Voices**; **Rosina** (Shield)

Lixenberg, Lore, **Jerry Springer**

Ljungberg, Göta, **Judith** (Goossens); **Merry Mount**

Llewellyn, Redvers, **Wat Tyler**

Lloyd, David, **Albert Herring**; **Black Widow**; **Fête Galante**

Lloyd, Gareth, **Flowers**; **Roswell Incident**

Lloyd, Lisbeth, **Abduction of Figaro**; **The Woodlanders**

Lloyd, Margaret, **Cold Sassy Tree**; **Ecstatic Journey**; **Little Women** (Adamo); **Strawberry Fields**

Lloyd, Phyllida, **Handmaid's Tale**

Lloyd, Robert, **Tower**

Lloyd, Trevor Anthony, **Black Ram**

Lloyd-Jones, David, **Christmas Carol** (Kay); **Rebecca**; **Royal Hunt**

Lloyd-Schanzer, Whitfield, **Philip Marshall**

Loader, Linden, **Marriage a la Mode**; **Quartet**; **Tanz der Schwäne**

Lochner, Susan, **Game of Poker**

Lock, Randolph, **Corps of Discovery**

Locke, Matthew, **Siege of Rhodes**

Loeb, Jaemi B., **Pope Joan** (Le Baron)

Loehle, Peter, **My Heart's in the Highlands** (Beeson)

Loesser, Frank, **Happy End**

Loessin, Edgar, **Sojourner and Mollie Sinclair**

Loew, Albie, **Silas Marner**

Lofton, Michael, **Mary Shelley**; **Summer**

Loftus, Jean, **Galileo Galilei**, **Women in the Garden**

Lohse, Katharina, **The Forest** (Smyth)

Lohse, Otto, **The Forest** (Smyth)

Lole, Timothy, **Biko**

Lomon, Ruth, **Many Moons** (Kapilow)

London, George, **Last Savage**

London, Jeanne, **Caliph's Clock**

Long, Aubrey, **Gethsemane Park**

Long, Avon, **Gentlemen, Be Seated!**

Long, Charles, **Ant and the Grasshopper**; **Twilight Voices**

Long, Lawrence, **Criseyde**

Long, Shorty, **Most Happy Fella**

Long, Timothy, **Binding of Isaac**; **Mountain Windsong**; **Shadowboxer**

Longmire, James, **Hangman, Hangman!**; **Town of Greed**

Lopez, Elena, **Love of Don Perlimplin** (Doyle)

Lopez, Sandra, **Aceldama**

Loquasto, Santo, **Washington Square**

Lora, Antonio, **Grande Bretèche** (Claflin)

Lord, Matthew, **Tonkin**

Loren, Nicholas, **Travels**

Lorenz, Max, **The Alcestiad**

Loring, Estelle, **Cradle Will Rock**

Loring, Eugene, **Carmen Jones**

Loring, Francis, **Spur of the Moment**

Lortzing, Albert, **The Czar**; **Burgomaster of Saardam**; **Undine**

LoSchiavo, Joseph, **Love in a Village**

Lott, Felicity, **Clytemnestra**

Loud, David, **Porgy and Bess**

Loughran, James, **Our Man in Havana**

Louise, Merle, **Sweeney Todd**

Louther, William, **Dawnpath**

Louvrier, Lucie, **Scoring a Century**

Love, Fred, **Stone Man**

Love, Mr., **Midsummer Night's Dream** (1763)

Love, Mrs., **Beggar's Opera**; **The Deserter**

Lovegrove, Mr., **The Bee-Hive**

Lovell, John, **The Dragon**

Lovett, Julia, **The Decision**; **Full Moon in March** (Harbison); **Philip Marshall**; **Purgatory** (Crosse); **Some Place of Darkness**; **Tale of Two Cities**

Lovett, Leon, **Lake of Menteith**

Lowder, Mr., **Female Rake**

Lowe, Mr. (Thomas), **Blind Beggar of Bethnal Green**; **Double Disappointment**; **The Enchanter**; **Jovial Crew** (Bates); **Judgment of Paris** (Arne); **King Pepin's Campaign**; **Miss Lucy in Town**; **The Picture**

Lowell, Robert, **Prometheus Condemned**

Lowenstein, Marc, **Crescent City**; **Dice Thrown**; **Scarlet Letter** (Herman); **Wet**; **What to Wear**

Lowrie, Jeanette, **Free Lance**

Lowry, Melvin, **Paradise Lost**

Lubman, Bradley, **Hindenburg**; **Three Tales**

Luca, Gwen de, **Rosina** (Shield)

Lucas, James, **Sganarelle** (Kaufmann)

Lucas, Jonathan, **Golden Apple**

Lucas, Sam, **Peculiar Sam**

Ludgin, Chester, **Angle of Repose**; **The Crucible** (Ward); **Giants in the Earth**; **Lady from Colorado**; **Quiet Place**; **Wuthering Heights** (Herrmann)

Ludlam, Charles, **English Cat**

Ludwig, Christa, **School for Wives**

Ludwig, Hanna, **Holy Devil**

Ludwig, Leopold, **Blood Moon**

Ludwig, William, **Canterbury Pilgrims** (Stanford)

Lundy, Nancy Allen, **Tea**

Luening, Otto, **Acres of Sky**; **Drumlin Legend**; **The Medium**; **Mother of Us All**

Luka, Milo, **Snow Bird**

Lully, Jean-Baptiste, **Acis and Galatea** (Handel); **Alcestis**; **Rinaldo and Armida**

Lumet, Sidney, **Eternal Road**

Lumpkin, William, **Before Night Falls**; **Flight** (Dove)

Lumsden, Norman, **The Bear** (Walton); **Little Sweep**; **Midsummer Night's Dream** (Britten)

Lund, Art, **Most Happy Fella**

Magelssen, Ralph, **Wise and Foolish**

Mager, Stephen, **Joshua's Boots**

Magill, Nelson, **Far Harbour; Solomon and Balkis**

Mahler, Albert, **Triple Sec**

Mahon, John, **Lionel and Clarissa; The Touchstone**

Mahowald, Joseph, **Different Fields**

Main, Alexander, **In a Garden**

Maine, Olive, **Legend of the Piper**

Maitland, Mr., **The Covenanters; Lord of the Isles**

Maitland, Robert, **The Critic; Village Romeo and Juliet**

Maizel, Yefim, **Tale of the Nutcracker**

Major, Leon, **Adventures of Friar Tuck; Bastianello; Later the Same Evening; Louis Riel; Lucrezia; Ochelata's Wedding; Shadowboxer; Volpone** (Musto)

Makepeace, Jonathan, **What Next?**

Makis, Julie, **Second Hurricane**

Maksymiuk, Jerzy, **Jack's Engagement**

Malas, Spiro, **Merchant and the Pauper; Nausicaa; Taming of the Shrew** (Giannini)

Malbin, Elaine, **Tobias and the Angel** (Bliss); **Trial at Rouen**

Malde, Melissa, **Eros and Psyche**

Maldjian, Ani, **Wet**

Maler, Steven, **Angels in America**

Malfitano, Catherine, **Bilby's Doll; Family Room; McTeague; Saint of Bleecker Street; View from the Bridge** (Bolcom); **Washington Square; A Wedding**

Malibran, Maria, **Maid of Artois; La Sonnambula**

Malina, Judith, **Curious Fern; Voices for a Mirror**

Malipiero, Gian Francesco, **Antony and Cleopatra** (Chiusano); **Prodigal Son** (Stepleton)

Maliponte, Adriana, **Last Savage**

Malis, David, **Love of Don Perlimplin**

Mallette, Patrick, **Alternate Visions**

Mallin, Francesca, **Orpheus** (White)

Malloné, Caroline Joanna, **Gift of the Magi** (Conte)

Mallory, Louise, **Vendetta**

Malone, Kirby, **Chatter and Static**

Mamoulian, Rouben, **Lost in the Stars; Porgy and Bess**

Manager, Richetta, **New Year**

Manahan, George, **All Quiet on the Western Front; Blond Eckbert; Borgia Infami; Dum Tweedle Dee; Emmeline; Frau Margot; Haroun; Korczak's Orphans; Letter to E. 11th St.; Lizzie Borden; Lysistrata** (Adamo); **Margaret Garner; Modern Painters; Séance on a Wet Afternoon**

Mancinelli, **Much Ado about Nothing**

Mancini, Rochelle, **The Dybbuk** (Morgulas)

Mandac, Evelyn, **The Bassarids; Black Widow; Ines de Castro** (Pasatieri); **Mines of Sulphur**

Mandat, Eric, **Don Quixote** (Eaton)

Mandel, Robert, **Bartleby** (Flanagan)

Mandell, Douglas, **Dalmatia and Dalmatio**

Mandikian, Arda, **Incognita; Turn of the Screw**

Mangan, Buddy, **Second Hurricane**

Mangin, Noel, **Help, Help; Taverner**

Manguem, Thomas, **W. of Babylon**

Maniaci, Michael, **Belladonna**

Manina, Signora (Maria), **Calypso and Telemachus;** *see also* Seedo, Mrs.

Mann, Joseph, **Song of David**

Mann, Laura, **Vine of the Soul**

Mann, Miss, **Boarding School**

Mann, Theodore, **Jewel Box**

Manners, Charles, **Iolanthe**

Manning, Florence, **Peter Grimes**

Manning, Jane, **Dawnpath; Death of Ferdia**

Manning, Peter, **Burial at Thebes**

Manso, Anne, **Democracy**

Manson, Anne, **The Albatross; Craig's Progress; Our Town**

Mansoori, Alex, **Our Town**

Mansouri, Lofti, **Black Widow**

Mantel, Sarah, **The Box**

Manton, Raymond, **Midsummer Night's Dream** (Britten)

Manton, Stephen, **Dumb Wife** (Horovitz); **Gentleman's Island; Ten O'Clock Call; Three's Company**

Manvers, Mr., **Berta; Maid of Saxony**

Manzari, Robert J., **Tamu-Tamu**

Mara, Mme., **Egyptian Festival**

Maran, George, **Midsummer Night's Dream** (Britten)

Marandola, Tom, **Lost Domain**

Marathe, Mukund, **Triskelion**

Marbá, Antoni Ros, **The Duenna** (Gerhard)

Marcell, Carolyn, **Ruined Maid**

March, Frederic, **Christmas Carol** (Herrmann)

Marchese, Joseph, **This Is the Rill Speaking**

Marchetti, Filippo, **Ruy Blas**

Marcinco, Kerri, **Criseyde**

Marcks, Doug, **The Shoulder**

Margeram, Mrs., **The Sultan**

Margison, Richard, **1984**

Margulis, John, **Birdbath**

Marheinek, Regina, **English Cat**

Maria, Mark Hernandez, **America Tropical**

Mariana, Michele, **Marita**

Marika, Denise, **Orpheus X**

Mark, Peter, **Christmas Carol** (Musgrave); **Harriet; Mary, Queen of Scots; Simón Bolívar**

Marken, Maria, **Trifles**

Marken, Nathaniel, **Trifles**

Markham, Pauline **La Vivandière**

Marks, Dana, **Highway Ulysses**

Mattaliano, Christopher, **Esther** (Weisgall); **The Tempest** (Westergaard)

Matters, Arnold, **Gloriana**; **Nelson**; **Pilgrim's Progress**; **Travelling Companion**

Mattfeld, Maria, **Cyrano** (Damrosch)

Matthen, Paul, **Pot of Fat**

Mattheson-Bruce, **Clarissa**

Mat[t]hews, Charles, **Circassian Bride**

Matthews, Edward (Eddie), **Four Saints in Three Acts**; **Porgy and Bess**

Matthews, Emma, **Batavia**; **Love of the Nightingale**

Matthews, F., **Climbing Boy**; **Love's Dream**

Matthews, Frank, **Dulcamara**

Matthews, Inez, **Lost in the Stars**

Matthews, Miss, **Guy Mannering**

Matthews, Mr. C, **Drama at Home**; **Hit or Miss!**

Matthews, Sally, **Alice in Wonderland** (Chin)

Matthews, T., **The Crusaders**

Matthews, Tamara, **Black Swan**

Mattinely, James, **The Lion**

Mattocks, Master, **Robin Hood** (Burney)

Mattocks, Mr. (George), **Amelia** (Piccinni et al.); **Artaxerxes**; **Castle of Andalusia**; **Chelsea Pensioner**; **Don't We All?**; **The Duenna** (Linley); **Elfrida** (Arne); **Fairy Prince**; **Guardian Outwitted**; **The Islanders**; **Jovial Crew** (Bates); **Lionel and Clarissa**; **Love Finds the Way**; **Love in a Village**; **Maid of the Mill** (Arnold); **Marriage Act**; **Spanish Lady** (1765); **Nancy**; **Rosamond** (Arnold); **Thomas and Sally** (Arne); **Plymouth in an Uproar**; **Poor Vulcan**; **Wives Revenged**

Mattocks, Mrs. (Isabella), **Amelia** (Piccinni et al.); **The Apparition**; **The Cabinet**; **The Duenna** (Linley); **Family Quarrels**; **The Farmer**; **Fontainbleau**; **Nancy**; **Spanish Lady** (1765); **Travellers in Switzerland**; **Wives Revenged**; *see also* Hallam, Miss

Mature, Victor, **Lady in the Dark**

Matuté, Marco, **Phaedra**

Matveyeva, Olga, **A Calamity**

Matzke, Calvin, **Cat and the Moon**

Mauceri, John, **Candide**; **Lady in the Dark**; **Quiet Place**; **Regina**

Maultsby, Nancy, **Tea**

Maunder, Dennis, **Clandestine Marriage**

Maunder, Stuart, **Lindy**

Maurer, Louis, **Not for Me**

Maxfield, William, **American Lit**

Maxner, Jodi, **Binding of Isaac**

Maxwell, Donald, **Angel Magick**; **Angels in America**; **Nightingale's to Blame**

Maxwell, Paul, **Paul Bunyan**

May, Alice, **The Sorcerer**

May, Huw, **The Parlour**

Mayall, Rik, **Horse Opera**

Mayfield, Julian, **Lost in the Stars**

Maynor, Kevin, **Frederick Douglass** (Kay); **Harriet**; **Soldier Boy**

Mayo, Christopher, **Blind Date**

Mayo, Conrad, **Amelia Goes to the Ball**

Mayo, Eleanor, **King Rene's Daughter**

Mayoss, Miss, **Lord of the Isles**

Mayr, Johann Simon, **Alfred the Great**; **Bianca** (Hadley); **Lodoiska**; **Medea in Corinth**

Maze, David, **Cue 67**

Mazer, Andrew, **Coyote's Music**

Mazerole, Dion, **Turtle Wakes**

Mazor, Marya, **Jocasta**

Mazzagatti, Pacien, **The Crucible** (Ward)

McAdams, Ryan, **Cracked Orlando**; **Maiden Tower**

McAfee, Patricia, **Europera 3**

McAlister, Barbara, **Mountain Windsong**

McAlister, David, **Full Moon in March** (Ward)

McAlpine, William, **Martin's Lie**

McBride, Michele, **Casanova's Homecoming**; **Clair de Lune**

McCann, Chris, **Body of Crime II**

McCarry, Patricia, **Music Hath Mischief**

McCarthy, Michael, **Gwyneth and the Green Knight**; **In the House of Crossed Desires**; **Ion**; **Roswell Incident**

McCauley, Barry, **Taming of the Shrew** (Giannini)

McCauley, Lois, **Judgment Day**

McChesney, Ernest, **Six Characters**

McClendon, Rose, **Deep River**

McClennan, James, **Elijah's Kite**

McClernan, Leonora, **Bowl, Cat, and Broomstick**

McClinton, David, **Birth/Day**

McCloskey, John, **Wedding Trip**

McCloud, Andy, **Diary of an African-American**

McCluny, Marjory, **Deseret**

McClure, Deirdre, **Little Girl Dreams**; **Queer**

McClure, Theron, **Mink Stockings**

McCollum, Jeffrey, **Antigone** (Eaton); **. . . inasmuch**

McCollum, John, **Natalia Petrovna**, **The Scarf**

McCollum, Sadie, **The Intruder** (Starer)

McConnell, Michael, **Mrs. Dalloway**

McConochy, Millicent, **The Ruby**

McCord, Nancy, **Devil and Daniel Webster**

McCormack, John, **Native Land**

McCormick, Austin, **Cracked Orlando**

McCormick, Douglas, **Maiden Tower**

McCormick, Marianne, **archy and mehitabel**

McCormick, Marie, **Massimilliano**

McCormick, Mary, **Snow Bird**

McCoy, Patrick, **Edge of Glory**

McCrae, Donna, **Pastoral**; **Rococo Confessional**

McCrae, Hilton, **King of Hearts**

Walker, Mr., **Flora** (1729); **Judgment of Paris** (1731); **Momus; Silvia**

Walker, Nancy, **Goat in Chelm**

Walker, Norman, **Pilgrim's Progress**

Walker, Penelope, **Tornrak**

Walker, Raymond, **The Libertine**

Walker, Sandra, **Voice of Ariadne**

Walker, Sarah, **The Bacchae; Toussaint**

Walker, Suzanne, **Lunch at the Cooked Goose; Welcome to Purgatory**

Walker, Tamara, **Strange Life of Ivan Osokin**

Walker, Thomas, **Beggar's Opera**

Walker, William, **Different Fields**

Wall, Joan, **Pet Shop**

Wall, Stephen, **Twilight Voices**

Wallace, Ian, **Rajah's Diamond**

Wallace, J. E., **Wandering Scholar**

Wallace, Jennifer, **First Lady**

Wallace, Suzanne Elder, **Arachne**

Wallach, Eli, **Travels of Babar**

Wallenstein, Alfred, **Rake's Progress** (Stravinsky)

Waller, Helen, **Turn of the Screw**

Waller, Juanita, **Bayou Legend**

Wallerstein, Lothar, **Island God**

Wallis, Bertram, **King of Cadonia**

Wallis, Miss, **Mysteries of the Castle; Windsor Castle**

Wallprecht, Klaus, **Facing Goya**

Walls, Peter, **Enchanted Island** (Farquhar); **Tanz der Schwäne**

Wallworth, Mr., **Bianca** (Balfe)

Walmsley-Clark, **Down by the Greenwood Side; Gawain; Penelope**

Walpole, Miss, **The Camp**

Walsh, Jack, **Abduction of Figaro**

Walsh, Kelly, **Nannan**

Walsh, Master Thomas, **Adopted Child**

Walsh, Michael, **Three Princes**

Walsh, Philip, **Miss Brill; Woman at the Store**

Walson, Chester, **Triumph of Joan**

Walters, Jess, **Saint of Bleecker Street**

Walters, Jesteena, **Blue Monday**

Walters, Mark, **Corps of Discovery**

Walton, Gavin, **Man from Venus**

Waltz, Mr. (Gustav[us]), **Britannia; Dione; King Pepin's Campaign; Queen of Spain; Temple of Dullness**

Waltzinger, Bertha, **The Mandarin** (De Koven)

Wamsley, Alice M., **Gift of Song**

Wanamaker, Sam, **Ice Break; King Priam**

Warburton, Ernest, **Three Strangers** (Maconchy)

Warchoff, Milton, **Paul Bunyan**

Ward, Candyce, **Miraculous Staircase**

Ward, Cecilia, **Gallantry; Lord Byron's Love Letter**

Ward, David, **All at Sea; Nelson**

Ward, Joseph, **Christopher Sly** (Eastwood); **Midsummer Night's Dream** (Britten)

Ward, Leslie Churchill, **Beast and Superbeast**

Ward, Matthew, **We're Back**

Ward, Mr., **Happy Lovers** (1736)

Ward, Pat, **The Box**

Ward, Perry, **Music Shop; Tonkin**

Ward, Trisha, **Macbeth** (McIntyre)

Ware, Clifton, **Summer and Smoke**

Ware, Mr., **Lucky Discovery**

Warfield, Sandra, **Greek Passion**

Warfield, William, **Porgy and Bess; Regina; Snow White**

Warford, Frederick, **Narcissa**

Warner, Keith, **God's Liar; Whirlwind**

Warner, Leo, **After Dido**

Warnery, Edmond, **Rip Van Winkle** (De Koven)

Warnock, Isobel, **The Parlour**

Warrell, Mr., **The Savoyard** (Reinagle)

Warren, Elton J., **Carmen Jones**

Warren, Leonard, **Island God**

Warren, Michael, **The Losers**

Warren, Miss, **Cobler's Opera**

Warren, Mr., **The Savoyard** (Reinagle)

Warren, Paulyn, **The Harpies**

Warren, W., **Berta**

Warshawski, Benjamin, **Inferno**

Warshawsky, Mark M., **David's Violin**

Warwell, Mr., **The Disappointment**

Warwick, Giulia, **The Sorcerer**

Washington, Daniel, **Biko; Blue Monday**

Watanabe, Kotaro, **Cio Cio San**

Watanabe, Scott, **Bok Choy Variations**

Waterhouse, Mr., **Basket-Maker; New Spain**

Waters, Ethel, **Cabin in the Sky**

Waters, Miss, **Turnpike Gate**

Waters, Susannah, **Again; Finnish Prisoner**

Wathen, Mr., **Love and Money**

Watkins, Amelia, **Korczak's Orphans**

Watkins, Dana, **Kafka** (Walden)

Watkins, Julius, **All Cats Turn Gray**

Watkins, Toney, **Letter from an Astrologer**

Watling, Tabitha, **Jane Eyre** (Berkeley)

Watson, Alistair, **Mr. Polly at the Potwell Inn**

Watson, Bobby, **The Meetin'**

Watson, Catherine, **Freshwater** (Vores)

Watson, Chester, **Good Soldier Schweik; Trial at Rouen**

## About the Author

Margaret Ross Griffel is senior editor at Columbia University's Office of Publications. She has done editorial work for Schirmer Books, Oxford University Press, Novello, the American Bach Society, Macmillan, and Random House. Before coming to Columbia, she was the editor and compiler of various catalogues for G. Schirmer/Associated Music; the consulting editor for the *Schirmer History of Music;* and the music production editor for Garland Publishing.

Dr. Griffel earned a Ph.D. degree in historical musicology from Columbia University and is the author of a companion volume to the present work, *Operas in German* (Greenwood, 1990), also under revision. She also has a master's degree in European and American history from Boston University.